Brings you up-to-date on dozens of significant changes to Ohio juvenile statutes, rules and case law…

Ohio Juvenile Law, 3rd Edition
By William A. Kurtz and Paul C. Giannelli

If you want a complete understanding of Ohio juvenile law as it stands today, you'll want *Ohio Juvenile Law, 3rd Edition* in your office and in the courtroom.

In one convenient volume, two expert authors analyze dozens of significant recent changes to statutes and juvenile rules. They also analyze hundreds of judicial decisions from the Ohio state courts, other states' courts, and the federal courts.

Ohio Juvenile Law, 3rd Edition, covers every important aspect of the juvenile courts' criminal and custody jurisdiction over children—including constitutional rights, confidentiality of proceedings, juvenile victims of abuse, neglect and dependency, and juvenile traffic offenders. To order your copy, call today: **1-800-328-9352**.

CALL TOLL-FREE: 1-800-328-9352.

Ohio's complete legal resource

West products available through Banks-Baldwin in Ohio and Kentucky.   © 1995 Banks-Baldwin Law Publishing Company 6-9234-2/9-95 594503

1-191-613-9

United States School Laws and Rules

Edited by Michael I. Levin

The first compilation of federal laws
and rules governing every aspect of education

Intended for superintendents and other administrators, teachers and their representatives, school board members, and attorneys, *United States School Laws and Rules* presents the full text of federal statutes and rules in an accessible, user-friendly format. It is the only publication that combines education law materials from the United States Code and the Code of Federal Regulations in a single, convenient volume.

All materials are authoritative and completely up-to-date

A User's Guide offers hints for effective use; a Federal Reference Table points you to additional statutory law and agency regulations; and a comprehensive Subject Index speeds your access to every pertinent part of the law.

Materials selected with the help of an Editorial Advisory Board of prominent school attorneys and administrators

Among the materials included are:

▶ General Education Provisions Act
▶ Individuals with Disabilities Education Act
▶ Carl D. Perkins Vocational Education Act
▶ Elementary and Secondary Education Act
▶ Americans with Disabilities Act
▶ Much more!

Call 1-800-328-9352 for additional information.

West. An American company serving the legal world.

© 1995 West Publishing 6-9234-2/9-95 594503
1-191-613-9

OHIO SCHOOL LAW

Baldwin's
OHIO HANDBOOK SERIES

by
Jonathan F. Buchter,
Susan C. Hastings,
Timothy J. Sheeran &
Gregory W. Stype
Squire, Sanders & Dempsey

1995-96

Banks-Baldwin Law Publishing Company
A West Publishing Affiliated Company

This book is sold with the understanding that the publisher is not engaged in furnishing any legal or other professional advice. Although prepared by professionals, this book should not be used as a substitute for professional services in specific situations. If legal advice or other expert assistance is required, the services of a specialist should be sought. Non-attorneys are cautioned against using these materials on behalf of others or engaging in conduct which might be considered the unauthorized practice of law.

For information, please call or write:

Banks-Baldwin Law Publishing Company
6111 Oak Tree Boulevard
P.O. Box 318063
Cleveland, Ohio 44131
800/362-4500

WEST'S COMMITMENT TO THE ENVIRONMENT
In 1906, West Publishing Company began recycling materials left over from the production of books. This began a tradition of efficient and responsible use of resources. Today, 100% of our legal bound volumes are printed on acid-free, recycled paper consisting of 50% new paper pulp and 50% paper that has undergone a de-inking process. We also use vegetable-based inks to print all of our books. West recycles nearly 22,650,000 pounds of scrap paper annually—the equivalent of 187,500 trees. Since the 1960s, West has devised ways to capture and recycle waste inks, solvents, oils, and vapors created in the printing process. We also recycle plastics of all kinds, wood, glass, corrugated cardboard, and batteries, and have eliminated the use of polystyrene book packaging. We at West are proud of the longevity and the scope of our commitment to the environment.

West pocket parts and advance sheets are printed on recyclable paper and can be collected and recycled with the newspapers. Staples do not have to be removed. Bound volumes can be recycled after removing the cover.

Copyright 1987, 1988, 1989, 1990, 1991, 1992, 1993, 1994 by Banks-Baldwin Law Publishing Company.

Copyright 1995 by Banks-Baldwin Law Publishing Company, A West Publishing Affiliated Company. All rights reserved. This publication contains the results of proprietary research. No part of this book may be reproduced or transmitted in any form or by any means, electronic or mechanical, including photocopying, recording, or by any information storage and retrieval system, without prior permission in writing from the publisher.

ISBN 0-8322-0625-3

Foreword

The 1995-96 Edition marks the ninth year of publication of "the portable Red Book" as part of Banks-Baldwin's Ohio Handbook Series. This year, prior edition authors Jonathan F. Buchter and Timothy J. Sheeran, of Squire, Sanders & Dempsey, are joined by their colleagues, Susan C. Hastings and Gregory W. Stype. Our mutual goal is to give educators, attorneys, and interested members of the general public convenient access to expert commentary in a format geared to their everyday practical needs. In terms of quality and timeliness, we believe the 1995-96 Edition surpasses this goal.

During the past year, the laws governing education have been significantly changed by the Ohio General Assembly, the United States Congress, and a host of courts. In response, we have intensified our efforts to provide subscribers with a comprehensive and up-to-date treatise on all important aspects of the subject. This 1995-96 Edition reflects the most current and thorough analysis available anywhere, and we hope that even the most difficult issues have been explained clearly and completely.

Accordingly, this edition provides *complete* coverage of recent state and federal legislation, new federal and Ohio case law, and important court decisions from other states affecting Ohio—through November 1, 1995, and including:

- Comprehensive changes made by 1995 House Bill 117, the state budget bill, and 1995 Senate Bill 162, on state government reorganization (throughout the authors' Text)

- New holdings from the Supreme Court of Ohio on nonrenewal of teachers' limited contracts (T Ch 9) and school administrators' contracts (T Ch 7)

- Updates to Ohio's ethics law (T Ch 45) and sunshine law (T 5.12)

- New SERB rulings on collective bargaining issues (T Ch 18)

- Revised regulations adopted by the U.S. Secretary of Labor under the Family and Medical Leave Act (T 17.16)

- Teacher evaluation (*Thomas v Newark City School Dist Bd of Ed*, T 9.13)

- Constitutionality of two-year statute of limitations on suit against school district (*Adamsky v Buckeye Local School Dist*, T 46.05), and

- Constitutionality of random drug-screening program for athletes (*Veronia School Dist 47J v Acton*, T 47.01).

The portable Red Book also features unreported Ohio appellate decisions, which are extremely important for a thorough understanding of school law in Ohio. For example, the 1995-96 Edition includes coverage of:

- *State ex rel Wilson v Lucas County Office of Ed*, employment by county board of education (now called educational service center governing board) in determining teacher's eligibility for continuing contract (T 4.03)

- *Bolding v Dublin Local School Dist*, school board liability (T 46.02), and

- *Springfield Local School Dist Bd of Ed v Ohio Assn of Public School Employees, Local 530*, application of Sunshine Law to board discussions of subcontracting issues (T 5.12).

We again thank our authors for their exemplary work and the law firm of Squire, Sanders & Dempsey for its continuing interest in and involvement with the publication. We also acknowledge with appreciation the contributions of our editorial and production staffs—particularly Deborah Burns, Tom Gilmartin, Kathy O'Dell, Kelly Weissfeld, and Patrice Yarham—in preparing this edition for publication.

As always, we encourage our subscribers' comments and suggestions for further improvements to *Ohio School Law*.

The Publisher

Cleveland, Ohio
December, 1995

Table of Contents

TEXT

		Page
	Text Outline	1

Chapter

INTRODUCTION—GOVERNANCE

1	Historical Perspective	57
2	Ohio's School System: An Overview	62
3	State Administration of Elementary and Secondary Education	70
4	School Districts	82
5	Boards of Education	100

PERSONNEL

6	Treasurer of the Board of Education, Business Manager, Legal Counsel	123
7	School Administrators	133
8	Teachers: Certification and Appointment	146
9	Teachers: Contracts and Tenure	154
10	Teachers: Compensation, Fringe Benefits, and Leave	189
11	Teachers: Retirement	210
12	Nonteaching Personnel: Introduction	225
13	Nonteaching Personnel: Compensation, Fringe Benefits, and Leave	247
14	Nonteaching Personnel: Retirement	252
15	Unemployment Compensation	258
16	Workers' Compensation, Occupational Safety and Health	264
17	Equal Employment Opportunity, Family and Medical Leave	276
18	Collective Bargaining	311

Chapter		Page

PUPILS

19	Pupils: Desegregation and Nondiscrimination	363
20	Pupils: Compulsory Education and School Attendance	375
21	Pupils: Health and Safety	389
22	Transportation of Pupils	400
23	Pupils: Tuition and Fees	415
24	Care and Protection of Pupils, Offenses Against Minors	427
25	Conduct and Discipline of Pupils	442

PROGRAMS

26	Curriculum and Educational Programs	463
27	Vocational Education and Programs	479
28	Education for Children with Disabilities	487
29	Administration of Programs for the Retarded and Developmentally Disabled	511
30	Physical Education, Athletics, and Recreation	526
31	Schools, Parents, and Community Affairs	536
32	Religion and the Public Schools	539

TEXTBOOKS—LIBRARIES—SUPPLIES—SERVICES—PROPERTY

33	Textbooks	547
34	Libraries	552
35	School Supplies and Food Service	560
36	Acquiring and Disposing of Property	563
37	Construction and Repair of School Buildings	570
38	Management and Use of School Property	579

FINANCES—RECORDS

39	Sources of Revenue	584
40	Tax Budget, Tax Levies, and Appropriations	596
41	Borrowing Money	607
42	Deposits and Investments	632
43	Financial Transactions and Accounting	643
44	Records of Employees and Pupils	656

Chapter		Page
	PUBLIC DUTY—SEARCH AND SEIZURE—LIABILITY	
45	Ethics Requirements and Education Personnel	672
46	Liability of Schools, Officers, and Employees	682
47	Search and Seizure	704
	NONPUBLIC SCHOOL SYSTEM	
48	Private and Parochial Schools	708

APPENDICES

		Page
A	Table of Cases	727
B	Table of Laws and Rules	805
C	Calendar for School District Officials	837

INDEX

	Page
Index	845

ABBREVIATIONS

A(2d)	Atlantic Reporter, Second Series
Abs	Ohio Law Abstract
ADA	Americans with Disabilities Act
ADEA	Age Discrimination in Employment Act
ADM	Average daily membership
AFSCME	American Federation of State, County and Municipal Employees
AHERA	Asbestos Hazard Emergency Response Act of 1986
Ala	Alabama Reports
ALR2d	American Law Reports Annotated, Second Series
ALR3d	American Law Reports Annotated, Third Series
ALR4th	American Law Reports Annotated, Fourth Series
Am	Amendment
Am Jur 2d	American Jurisprudence, Second Series
Annot	Annotation
App	Court of Appeals
App	Ohio Appellate Reports
App(2d)	Ohio Appellate Reports, Second Series
App(3d)	Ohio Appellate Reports, Third Series
Ariz	Arizona Reports
Art	Article
Assn	Association
Auth	Authority
BAT	Breath alcohol technician
Bd of Ed	Board of Education
BEA	Bilingual Education Act of 1974
BTA	Board of Tax Appeals
Bull	Weekly Law Bulletin
Cal	California Reports
Cal(2d)	California Reports, Second Series
Cal App(2d)	California Appellate Reports, Second Series
Cal App(3d)	California Appellate Reports, Third Series
Cal Rptr	California Reporter
CB	Cumulative Bulletin (federal)
CC	Ohio Circuit Court Reports
CC(NS)	Ohio Circuit Court Reports, New Series
CD	Ohio Circuit Decisions
CDL	Commercial driver's license
CETA	Comprehensive Employment and Training Act Amendments of 1978
CFR	Code of Federal Regulations
Ch	Chapter
Cir	Circuit Court
CJS	Corpus Juris Secundum
Cleve St L Rev	Cleveland State Law Review
COBRA	Consolidated Omnibus Budget Reconciliation Act
Comm	Commission
Commrs	Commissioners

Cong	Congress
Conn L Rev	Connecticut Law Review
Corp	Corporation
CP	Common Pleas Court
Ct App	Court of Appeals
D	Ohio Decisions
DC	District Court
DD	Developmental disabilities
Del	Delaware Reports
Dept	Department
Dist	District
Doc	Docket
EBT	Evidential breath testing
Ed	Education
ED	Eastern District
EEOC	Equal Employment Opportunity Commission
eff.	Effective
EHA	Education for All Handicapped Children Act
EHLR	Education for the Handicapped Law Report
EMR	Educable mentally retarded
ERISA	Employee Retirement Income Security Act
ESY	Extended school year
Ethics Op	Ethics Commission Opinions (Ohio)
EPA	Environmental Protection Agency
F(2d)	Federal Reporter, Second Series
F(3d)	Federal Reporter, Third Series
FAPE	Free appropriate public education
FCC	Federal Communications Commission
Fed Reg	Federal Register
Fla	Florida
Fla St U L Rev	Florida State University Law Review
FLSA	Fair Labor Standards Act
FMLA	Family and Medical Leave Act
FSupp	Federal Supplement
GC	General Code (Ohio)
GFOA	Government Finance Officers Association
H	House Bill
Haw	Hawaii Reports
HCPA	Handicapped Children's Protection Act
HEW	Department of Health, Education and Welfare
HMO	Health Maintenance Organization
Hts	Heights
IBEW	International Brotherhood of Electrical Workers
IDELR	Individuals with Disabilities Education Law Report
IEP	Individualized education program
Ill App(3d)	Illinois Appellate Court Reports, Third Series
Ind	Indiana Reports
Inf OAG	Informal Opinions of the Ohio Attorney General
Intl	International
Iowa L Rev	Iowa Law Review
IQ	Intelligence quotient
IRC	Internal Revenue Code

J Law & Ed	Journal of Law and Education
Juv Ct	Juvenile Court
Kan	Kansas Reports
La App	Louisiana Courts of Appeal Reports
LC	Limited Circulation (Ohio Attorney General Opinions)
LEd	Supreme Court Reports, Lawyers' Edition
LEd(2d)	Supreme Court Reports, Lawyers' Edition, Second Series
LRRM	Labor Relations Reference Manual
Mass	Massachusetts Reports
MBE	Minority business enterprise
Md	Maryland Reports
MFOA	Municipal Finance Officers Association
Mich	Michigan Reports
Minn	Minnesota Reports
Misc	Ohio Miscellaneous Reports
Misc(2d)	Ohio Miscellaneous Reports, Second Series
Mont	Montana Reports
MR/DD	Mental retardation and developmental disabilities
MRO	Medical review officer
Mt.	Mount
Muni	Municipal Court
NAACP	National Association for the Advancement of Colored People
Natl	National
NC App	North Carolina Court of Appeals Reports
ND	Northern District
NE	Northeastern Reporter
NE(2d)	Northeastern Reporter, Second Series
NEA	National Education Association
Neb	Nebraska Reports
Neb L Rev	Nebraska Law Review
Nev	Nevada
NFSHSA	National Federation of State High School Associations
NH	New Hampshire
NJ	New Jersey Reports
NLRB	National Labor Relations Board
NM	New Mexico Reports
NP	Nisi Prius Reports (Ohio)
NP(NS)	Nisi Prius Reports, New Series (Ohio)
NW(2d)	Northwestern Reporter, Second Series
NY(2d)	New York Reports, Second Series
NY Misc(2d)	New York Miscellaneous Reports, Second Series
NYS(2d)	New York Supplement, Second Series
OAC	Ohio Administrative Code
OAG	Ohio Opinions of the Attorney General
OAPSE	Ohio Association of Public School Employees
OBR	Ohio Bar Reports
O Const	Ohio Constitution
OCRC	Ohio Civil Rights Commission
ODOT	Ohio Department of Transportation
OEA	Ohio Education Association
OEC	Ohio Ethics Commission
Ohio St L J	Ohio State Law Journal

OHSAA	Ohio High School Athletic Association
OJur 2d	Ohio Jurisprudence, Second Series
OJur 3d	Ohio Jurisprudence, Third Series
Okla	Oklahoma Reports
OO(2d)	Ohio Opinions, Second Series
OO(3d)	Ohio Opinions, Third Series
Op	Opinion
OPER	Ohio Public Employee Reporter
Or App	Oregon Reports, Court of Appeals
Ore	Oregon
OS	Ohio State Reports
OS(2d)	Ohio State Reports, Second Series
OS(3d)	Ohio State Reports, Third Series
OSEP	Office of special education and policy
OWE	Occupational work experience
P	Pacific Reporter
P(2d)	Pacific Reporter, Second Series
PERRAC	Public Employment Risk Reduction Advisory Commission
PERS	Public Employees Retirement System
PHSA	Public Health Service Act
Pub L	Public Law (federal)
RC	Revised Code (Ohio)
Rev Rul	Revenue Ruling (federal)
RI	Rhode Island
Rptr	Reporter
S	Senate Bill
SAP	Substance abuse professional
SAWW	Statewide average weekly wage
SC	South Carolina Reports
SCt	Supreme Court Reporter (United States)
SD	Southern District
SE(2d)	Southeastern Reporter, Second Series
SERB	State Employment Relations Board
SERS	School Employees Retirement System
Sess	Session
So(2d)	Southern Reporter, Second Series
Stat	Statutes
STRS	State Teachers Retirement System
SW(2d)	South Western Reporter, Second Series
Syllabi	Bureau of Inspection and Supervision of Public Offices opinion
Tenn	Tennessee Reports
Tex	Texas Reports
Twp	Township
UGESP	Uniform Guidelines on Employee Selection Procedures
UMKC L Rev	University of Missouri—Kansas City Law Review
US	United States Reports
USC	United States Code
USCA	United States Code, Annotated
US Code Cong & Admin News	United States Code Congressional and Administrative News
US Const	United States Constitution

USLW	United States Law Week
v	Versus
Va	Virginia Reports
VEBA	Voluntary Employees' Beneficiary Association
Vol	Volume
Wash	Washington Reports
WD	Western District
Wis(2d)	Wisconsin Reports, Second Series
WL	Westlaw
WLB	Weekly Law Bulletin
WVa	West Virginia Reports

TEXT

Text Outline

INTRODUCTION—GOVERNANCE

Chapter 1
Historical Perspective

1.01 The new republic and the idea of universal education
1.02 Northwest Territory and school lands
1.03 First schools in Ohio
1.04 Ohio Constitution of 1802
1.05 Inadequacy of school lands income and advent of school taxes
1.06 Early education for the handicapped
1.07 Horace Mann and the common school movement
1.08 Common school movement in Ohio
1.09 Ohio Constitution of 1851
1.10 Secondary education and completion of the public school framework

Chapter 2
Ohio's School System: An Overview

2.01 Introduction

OHIO'S SCHOOLS
2.02 Public schools and pupils
2.03 Nonpublic schools and pupils
2.04 School personnel
2.05 Curriculums and special programs

FUNDING THE SCHOOL SYSTEM
2.06 Cost of education
2.07 Sources of revenue

GOVERNING THE SCHOOLS
2.08 Role of school districts and boards of education
2.09 Roles of the state board of education and superintendent of public instruction
2.10 Interaction between Ohio and other states

EDUCATION AND THE FEDERAL GOVERNMENT

2.11 Role of the federal government
    (A) In general
    (B) Goals 2000: Educate America Act

2.12 Federal aid

2.13 Conditions of federal aid, nondiscrimination

SCHOOL LAW AND ITS SOURCES

2.14 Constitutional mandates

2.15 Statutes

2.16 Court decisions
    (A) State courts
    (B) Federal courts

2.17 Attorney general opinions

Chapter 3
State Administration of Elementary and Secondary Education

3.01 Introduction

3.02 State board of education
    (A) Members and qualifications
    (B) Oath of office, term, compensation
    (C) Board members as public officials
    (D) Business of board, vacancies

3.03 Powers and duties of state board of education
    (A) Policy-making and administration
    (B) Prescribing standards
    (C) Organizing and reorganizing school districts
    (D) Evaluation of district and building education performance
        (1) Significance of educational excellence
        (2) Significance of educational deficiency
    (E) Innovative education pilot programs
    (F) Statewide education management information system
    (G) Other powers and duties

3.04 Department of education
    (A) Department as administrative unit
    (B) Headquarters
    (C) Chief administrative officer
    (D) Education data management unit

3.05 Superintendent of public instruction: appointment and qualifications

3.06 Duties of superintendent of public instruction

3.07 Other personnel of department of education
    (A) Assistant superintendents and division heads
    (B) Employees

Chapter 4
School Districts

4.01 Introduction

4.02 School districts and boundaries of other political subdivisions

CLASSIFICATION OF SCHOOL DISTRICTS

4.03 Classification of school districts
- (A) City school district
- (B) Educational service center
- (C) New educational service centers
- (D) Local school district
- (E) Joint vocational school district
- (F) Exempted village school district
- (G) Cooperative education school district

CREATION AND REORGANIZATION OF SCHOOL DISTRICTS

4.04 Authority to create or reorganize school districts

4.05 General factors in creating or reorganizing school districts
- (A) Efficiency of school system: maintenance of kindergarten through grade twelve
- (B) Geography: contiguous territory, neighborhood schools
- (C) Demography: population shifts
- (D) Finances: transfer of territory because of eroded tax base

4.06 Reclassification of school districts without transfer of territory
- (A) Change from city school district to local school district when city reduced to village
- (B) Change from exempted village school district to local school district
- (C) Change from local or exempted village school district to city school district
- (D) Change to city school district on incorporation as municipality

REORGANIZATIONS INVOLVING TRANSFERS OF TERRITORY

4.07 Transfer of territory, in general
- (A) Types of transfers, initiation and approval
- (B) Agreements among school districts as to boundaries
- (C) Requirement of acceptance by transferee board

4.08 Transfers of school district territory following municipal annexation

4.09 Territorial transfers initiated by state board of education
- (A) Study of possible consolidation or transfer: scope
- (B) Proposed reorganization
- (C) Election
- (D) Dissolution on failure to meet standards

4.10 Transfers of territory from local school districts
- (A) Initiating proposals, governing board resolution, voter petition
- (B) Procedure on proposals, referendum
- (C) Effect of consolidation, challenge

4.11 Transfers from city and exempted village school districts
- (A) Proposal to transfer territory, hearing

(B) Approval of state board, completion of transfer

DIVISION OF ASSETS AND LIABILITIES ON REORGANIZATION; GOVERNANCE

4.12 Allocation of state funds, minimum guarantee
4.13 Fair division of assets and liabilities
4.14 Effect of reorganization on tax levies
    (A) In general
    (B) Annexation
4.15 Board of education in reorganized district
    (A) Abolition of board or membership on board
    (B) Board of new local district
    (C) Board of new city district
    (D) Duties of educational service center governing board as to dissolved local school district board

Chapter 5
Boards of Education

5.01 Introduction

COMPOSITION OF BOARDS OF EDUCATION; MEMBERS

5.02 Composition of board of education
    (A) Local and exempted village school districts, and educational service centers
    (B) Boards of city school districts
        (1) Referendum to determine composition of city school district board
        (2) Subdistricts of city school district
5.03 Members of board of education
    (A) Nomination and election
    (B) Term, oath of office
    (C) Filling vacancies
5.04 Compensation and expenses of board members
    (A) Compensation and retirement
    (B) Reimbursement for expenses
5.05 Removal from office

POWERS OF BOARD OF EDUCATION

5.06 General powers of board of education
    (A) Statutory origin of powers
    (B) Construing powers of board
    (C) Board discretion in exercising powers
5.07 Capacity to sue and be sued
5.08 Rule-making and regulatory power
    (A) Management of schools
    (B) Regulations affecting pupils and teachers
    (C) Open enrollment policies

5.08　Rule-making and regulatory power—*continued*
  (D) Enrollment of students from adjacent districts
  (E) Administrative due process

5.09　Miscellaneous powers
  (A) Employing consultants
  (B) Contracting for mechanical, clerical, or record-keeping services
  (C) Operating preschool programs
  (D) Cooperation with other agencies
  (E) Membership in associations
  (F) Training new board members and personnel
  (G) Disseminating information
  (H) Criminal background checks
  (I) Agreements with educational service center governing boards for services
  (J) Agreements with educational service center governing boards for supplies and equipment
  (K) Teacher education loan programs
  (L) Latchkey programs
  (M) Healthcheck programs
  (N) Community service education programs
  (O) Policy on parental involvement
  (P) Assessing skills of students with visual disabilities
  (Q) Tuition credit scholarship programs
  (R) Career planning
  (S) School savings banks
  (T) Other powers

5.10　Authority of probate court or educational service center governing board to exercise powers of defaulting board of education

MEETINGS AND PROCEDURES

5.11　Board meetings in general
  (A) Organizational meeting
  (B) Regular and special meetings
  (C) Quorum
  (D) Minutes

5.12　Open meetings: the sunshine law
  (A) In general
  (B) Executive sessions
  (C) Notice to interested persons
  (D) Consequences of violation

5.13　Board action, resolutions
  (A) In general, roll call
  (B) Vote required for passage
  (C) Dispensing with resolutions in certain cases

PERSONNEL

Chapter 6
Treasurer of the Board of Education, Business Manager, Legal Counsel

6.01 Introduction

TREASURER OF THE BOARD OF EDUCATION

6.02 Election or appointment of treasurer, qualifications
    (A) In general, incompatible offices, joint employment
    (B) Licensure, continuing education
    (C) Term
    (D) Bond

6.03 Removal from office, nonrenewal of contract, resignation
    (A) In general
    (B) Appointment of substitute to make reports

6.04 Absence or incapacity, temporary treasurer

6.05 Compensation

6.06 Duties of treasurer as board secretary

6.07 Duties of treasurer as fiscal officer
    (A) In general
    (B) Accounts
    (C) Certifying availability of money
        (1) Fiscal officer certificate
        (2) Treasurer, superintendent, and board president certificate
    (D) Certifying accuracy of reports needed to calculate state funding

6.08 Miscellaneous duties of treasurer
    (A) Payment of teachers' salaries
    (B) Receiving and recording bids
    (C) Reporting school district boundary changes
    (D) Executing conveyances

6.09 Duties of treasurer at end of term: audit

BUSINESS MANAGER

6.10 Business manager, qualifications

6.11 Election or appointment, term, salary, bond

6.12 Suspension or removal, vacancy, resignation

6.13 Powers and duties of business manager

LEGAL COUNSEL

6.14 Legal adviser: county prosecutor, city law director, house counsel
    (A) In general
    (B) Duties of statutory legal advisers
    (C) Compensation of statutory legal counsel

6.15 Legal adviser: outside counsel
    (A) In general, authority to employ private counsel
    (B) Services

Chapter 7
School Administrators

7.01　Introduction

SUPERINTENDENT OF SCHOOLS

7.02　Superintendent of schools as chief executive

7.03　Qualifications of superintendent
　　　(A)　Statutory requirement that candidate possess certificate
　　　(B)　Requirements for obtaining certificate
　　　　　　(1)　Provisional certificate, renewal
　　　　　　(2)　Professional certificate, renewal
　　　　　　(3)　Permanent certificate

7.04　Appointment of superintendent, term
　　　(A)　In general, time of appointment, term
　　　(B)　Reemployment and nonrenewal
　　　(C)　Employment of local school district superintendent
　　　(D)　Superintendent of joint vocational school district
　　　(E)　Vacancy

7.05　Superintendent's contract, compensation
　　　(A)　Contract, termination
　　　(B)　Compensation, expenses

7.06　Duties of superintendent
　　　(A)　In general
　　　(B)　Assignment of personnel
　　　　　　(1)　Teachers and administrators
　　　　　　(2)　Nonteaching personnel
　　　(C)　Assignment of pupils

7.07　Temporary superintendent

7.08　Educational service center superintendent's offices and equipment

OTHER SCHOOL ADMINISTRATORS

7.09　Assistant superintendents, principals, and other administrators
　　　(A)　In general, authority to hire
　　　(B)　Assistant superintendents
　　　(C)　Principals and assistant principals

7.10　Employment of administrators

7.11　Administrators' contracts
　　　(A)　In general
　　　(B)　Reemployment and nonrenewal

7.12　Supervisors and special teachers in educational service centers

7.13　Teacher employed as administrator, tenure

7.14　Evaluation of school administrators
　　　(A)　Evaluation of superintendent
　　　(B)　Evaluation of other administrators

Chapter 8
Teachers: Certification and Appointment

8.01 Introduction

8.02 Meaning of "teacher"
    (A) Administrators
    (B) Tutors, guidance counselors, school nurses
    (C) Substitute teachers, educational aides

8.03 Qualifications and certification in general
    (A) Certification generally mandatory
    (B) Adopting standards for teacher training and certification
    (C) Interstate certification

8.04 Grades of certificates
    (A) Temporary certificate
    (B) One-year vocational certificate
    (C) Provisional certificate
    (D) Professional certificate
        (1) Tenure
        (2) Duty of teacher to apply for certificate
    (E) Permanent certificate
    (F) Internship certificate

8.05 Types of certification

8.06 Education and experience requirements, renewing and upgrading certificates

8.07 Revocation or suspension of certificate
    (A) In general
    (B) Conflict of interest
    (C) Suspension for breach of contract
    (D) Reinstatement

8.08 Nomination and appointment

8.09 Reemployment of teachers

Chapter 9
Teachers: Contracts and Tenure

INTRODUCTION

9.01 Requirement for contract, contents
    (A) Necessity for written contract
    (B) Terms of contract

9.02 Types of contracts: continuing, limited, extended limited, and supplemental

9.03 Contract employing relative of board member

CONTINUING CONTRACTS AND TENURED TEACHERS

9.04 Continuing contracts and tenure

9.05 Eligibility for continuing contract: introduction
   (A) In general
   (B) Burden on teacher to give notice of eligibility
9.06 Eligibility for continuing contract: certificate requirement
   (A) Professional, permanent, or life certificate
   (B) Time of issuance of certificate, filing
9.07 Eligibility for continuing contract: teaching requirement
   (A) Who are "teachers"
       (1) Statutory definition, teachers per se
       (2) Administrators
       (3) Other certificated persons
   (B) Teaching not limited to certificated areas
9.08 Eligibility for continuing contract: service requirement
   (A) Service in district
   (B) Tenure acquired elsewhere
   (C) Time served, school year, teaching days
   (D) Service as substitute teacher
   (E) Interrupted service
9.09 Employment options where teacher is eligible for continuing service status
   (A) Impact of 1988 House Bill 330
   (B) When continuing contract mandatory
   (C) Extended limited contract for professional improvement
   (D) Nonrenewal followed by reemployment
   (E) Waiver of continuing contract status

LIMITED CONTRACTS AND NONTENURED TEACHERS
9.10 Employment options where teacher is not eligible for continuing service status
   (A) When limited contract required
   (B) Duration, automatic reemployment, nonrenewal after evaluation and notice
   (C) Reemployment despite superintendent's nonrenewal recommendation
   (D) Waiver of right to automatic renewal
9.11 Notice of nonrenewal, timeliness, form
   (A) Time of notice, actual receipt required, method of service
   (B) Evasion of service
   (C) Form of notice
   (D) Burden of proof
9.12 Nonrenewal and reemployment as means to change contract terms
9.13 Statutory evaluation and due process requirements
   (A) Mandatory evaluation procedures
   (B) Right to written statement of circumstances
   (C) Right to hearing
9.14 Supplemental contracts
   (A) In general
   (B) Reemployment under supplemental contract
   (C) Athletics

9.15 Substitute teacher contracts
    (A) In general
    (B) Compensation, fringe benefits
    (C) Nonrenewal, reemployment, conversion to regular contract
    (D) Tenure
    (E) Regular teacher acting as substitute

9.16 Exchange teachers

SUSPENSION AND TERMINATION OF CONTRACTS

9.17 Resignation

9.18 Retirement

9.19 Layoff
    (A) Reduction in force
    (B) Continuing contracts, seniority
    (C) Reduction by nonrenewal
    (D) Reduction by termination for cause
    (E) Layoff procedure
    (F) Recall after layoff
    (G) Reducing teacher from full-time to part-time status

9.20 Disciplinary suspension

9.21 Termination for cause, in general
    (A) Gross inefficiency
    (B) Immorality
    (C) Willful and persistent violations of board regulations
    (D) "Other good and just cause"
    (E) Constitutionally protected conduct
    (F) Protection of whistleblowers

9.22 Termination for cause, procedure
    (A) Written charges, temporary suspension
    (B) Demand for hearing, scheduling hearing
    (C) Hearing by board or referee
    (D) Rules of procedure, privacy, record of proceedings
    (E) Referee's report
    (F) Decision by board

9.23 Appeal of termination
    (A) Perfecting appeal to common pleas court
    (B) Scope of review
    (C) Waiver of defects

9.24 Nonrenewal of teacher limited (or extended limited) contract

9.25 Teacher termination

Chapter 10
Teachers: Compensation, Fringe Benefits, and Leave

COMPENSATION

10.01 Teachers' salaries in general
- (A) Salary as mandatory contract provision, annual salary notice
- (B) Salary decreases
- (C) Salary increases, bonuses

10.02 Pay scales
- (A) State minimum salary schedule
- (B) Salary schedule adopted by school board
- (C) Board discretion as to salaries, restrictions
- (D) Failure to adopt schedule or to pay at least minimum

10.03 Service credit for salary purposes
- (A) Years of service
- (B) Years of teaching service
- (C) Teaching service in Ohio or elsewhere
- (D) Military service

10.04 Service credit established by school board
- (A) Minimum service credit
- (B) Service credits exceeding statutory minimum
- (C) Credit for partial service, excluding leave time
- (D) Failure to establish local service requirements

10.05 Training credit for salary purposes
- (A) In general
- (B) Duty of teacher to inform board of completed training

10.06 Preconditions to payment of salary

10.07 Underpayment and overpayment of salary
- (A) Recovery of underpayment, statute of limitations, laches, waiver
- (B) Recovery of overpayment, statute of limitations

10.08 Payroll deductions
- (A) In general
- (B) Union dues checkoff, fair share fees
  - (1) Dues checkoff
  - (2) Agency shop fees checkoff

FRINGE BENEFITS, PAID DAYS, AND INSURANCE

10.09 Paid days, continuing education, lunch period
- (A) Emergency school closings
- (B) Jury duty
- (C) Continuing education, professional days
- (D) Lunch period

10.10 Group insurance
- (A) In general
- (B) Classification of employees for insurance purposes
- (C) Deductible feature
- (D) Self-insurance, trust funds

10.11 Board payment for continuing insurance coverage during illness or pending separation

10.12 Payment for continuing health insurance coverage by terminated employees
- (A) Federal law
  - (1) Introduction, applicability
  - (2) Coverage provided
  - (3) Notice requirements
  - (4) Payment for coverage
  - (5) Termination of coverage
  - (6) Penalties
  - (7) Conversion Option
- (B) Coverage provided under Ohio law
  - (1) Eligible employees
  - (2) Obtaining continuing coverage

SICK LEAVE

10.13 Accumulating sick leave
- (A) Annual entitlement, monthly accumulation, rate
- (B) Part-time employees, substitute teachers
- (C) Maximum accumulation, transfer of sick leave credit
- (D) Uniform application of sick leave policy

10.14 Adopting state standards on sick leave, caveat

10.15 Advance of unearned sick leave

10.16 Use of sick leave

10.17 Severance pay on basis of accumulated sick leave
- (A) In general, payment on retirement, amount payable
- (B) Adoption of liberalized severance pay plan

10.18 Enforced leave for certain illnesses

LEAVES OF ABSENCE

10.19 Requested leave
- (A) In general, return to service after leave
- (B) Leave with partial pay for professional growth

10.20 Unrequested disability leave
- (A) In general, hearing
- (B) Pregnancy and child care

10.21 Miscellaneous leaves of absence
- (A) Military leave: active duty, reserve training
- (B) Assault leave, injury in line of duty
- (C) Personal leave
- (D) Family and Medical Leave Act

Chapter 11
Teachers: Retirement

INTRODUCTION

11.01 State teachers retirement system (STRS)

11.02 State teachers retirement board
    (A) In general, composition
    (B) Conflict of interest
    (C) Powers and duties

11.03 Funds and investments
    (A) Sources and purposes of separate funds
    (B) Investments

MEMBERS OF SYSTEM

11.04 Membership in STRS
    (A) Persons required to be members
    (B) Exclusion from membership

11.05 STRS membership and teachers' contracts

11.06 Certifying teachers' names and payroll reports to STRS

CONTRIBUTIONS TO SYSTEM

11.07 Mandatory contributions by members
    (A) Contribution rate, payroll deduction
    (B) Contributions while on disability leave

11.08 Voluntary contributions by members
    (A) Contributions while on leave of absence
    (B) Extra deposits to increase annuity income

11.09 Mandatory contributions by employers

11.10 Additional contributions by employers
    (A) Fringe benefit pickup
    (B) Pickup through salary reduction

11.11 Withdrawal of contributions from STRS

SERVICE CREDIT

11.12 Importance of service credit, accumulation
    (A) In general
    (B) Combining credits from other public employees retirement systems

11.13 Purchasing service credit
    (A) In general
    (B) Redeposit of withdrawn contributions
    (C) Contributions by part-time personnel
    (D) Payroll deduction plans

11.14 Military service credit
    (A) Military service credit acquired without purchase
    (B) Purchasing service credit

11.15 Prior service credit, certificate

DISABILITY COVERAGE
11.16 Entitlement to disability benefit
    (A) Who is eligible
    (B) Relationship to accrued sick leave

11.17 Termination of disability benefit

SERVICE RETIREMENT
11.18 Eligibility for service retirement
    (A) In general
    (B) Mandatory retirement

11.19 Amount of retirement benefits
    (A) Payment options
    (B) Computation
    (C) Final average salary

11.20 Health benefits for retirees

11.21 Early retirement incentive plans
    (A) In general
    (B) Eligibility
    (C) Purchase of additional service credit
    (D) Checklist for establishing plan

11.22 Employment of retired teachers

11.23 Optional compensation deferral plans

SURVIVORS' BENEFITS
11.24 Death before retirement
    (A) Lump sum payment
    (B) Monthly benefits
    (C) Termination of monthly payments

11.25 Death after retirement

11.26 Lump sum burial payment

Chapter 12
Nonteaching Personnel: Introduction

12.01 Authority to hire nonteaching employees

CIVIL SERVICE AND NON-CIVIL SERVICE EMPLOYEES
12.02 Civil service and non-civil service employees
    (A) School districts covered by civil service: effect of coverage and noncoverage
    (B) Effect of new school district or transfer of territory
    (C) Variations arising from city charter or collective bargaining agreement

12.03 Civil service commission, sharing cost of administration
    (A) Commission in single- and multi-city school districts
    (B) School district's share of costs

12.04 Classified and unclassified civil service
    (A) School personnel in the unclassified civil service
        (1) Administrative and professional personnel, library staff
        (2) Clerical and administrative support personnel
        (3) Unskilled labor
    (B) Tenure

APPOINTMENT OF EMPLOYEES

12.05 Appointment of classified civil service employees
    (A) Competitive classified civil service
        (1) Examination
        (2) Eligibility list
        (3) Effect of rank on list
    (B) Classified unskilled labor positions

12.06 Appointing authority for civil service positions

12.07 Probationary period for civil service employees
    (A) In general, probationary period
    (B) Permanent employee status

12.08 Hiring independent contractors in lieu of civil service personnel

12.09 Appointment of non-civil service employees
    (A) Introduction, limited and continuing contracts for regular employees
    (B) Who are considered regular employees
    (C) Wages and hours
    (D) Right to express contract
    (E) Indeterminate contracts
    (F) Reemployment
    (G) Supplemental contracts not authorized

12.10 Employment of noncertificated persons to direct extracurricular activity
    (A) Introduction, preconditions to hiring noncertificated person
    (B) What constitutes pupil-activity program
    (C) General qualifications
    (D) Additional qualifications for coaches
    (E) Compensation

PROMOTION AND TRANSFER

12.11 Promotion

12.12 Transfer

LAYOFF

12.13 Layoff or job elimination: non-civil service employees

12.14 Layoff or job elimination: civil service employees
    (A) In general
    (B) Reasons for layoff
    (C) Layoff procedure
    (D) Bumping rights
    (E) Appeal

DEMOTION, REDUCTION, SUSPENSION, TERMINATION, AND RESIGNATION

- 12.15 Demotion, reduction, and suspension
  - (A) Demotion or suspension, appeal
  - (B) Pay reduction, appeal
- 12.16 Termination: non-civil service employees
  - (A) Introduction, grounds for termination
  - (B) Notice of termination, due process
  - (C) Hearing, evidence, board action
- 12.17 Termination: civil service employees
  - (A) Introduction, grounds for termination
  - (B) Notice to employee, removal order
  - (C) Appeal to civil service commission
  - (D) Appeal to common pleas court
- 12.18 Resignation

EDUCATIONAL AIDES
- 12.19 Employment of educational aides

Chapter 13
Nonteaching Personnel: Compensation, Fringe Benefits, and Leave

COMPENSATION
- 13.01 Pay scales and job classifications
  - (A) In general
  - (B) Notice of job classification and pay scale
  - (C) Duty of civil service commission
- 13.02 Work week: overtime and compensatory time
  - (A) In general
  - (B) Overtime or compensatory time
- 13.03 Holiday pay
  - (A) In general
  - (B) Overtime and compensatory time
- 13.04 Vacation pay
  - (A) Allowable vacation time
  - (B) Using accrued vacation before full amount earned
  - (C) Effect of contract provision
- 13.05 Other paid days
  - (A) Emergency school closings
  - (B) Jury duty
  - (C) Professional days
- 13.06 Payroll deductions

INSURANCE AND LEAVE
- 13.07 Insurance
- 13.08 Sick leave
  - (A) In general
  - (B) Use of sick leave

13.09 Severance pay on basis of accumulated sick leave

13.10 Personal and other leaves of absence
    (A) Personal leave
    (B) Other leaves of absence

Chapter 14
Nonteaching Personnel: Retirement

INTRODUCTION

14.01 School employees retirement system (SERS)

14.02 School employees retirement board
    (A) In general, composition
    (B) Conflict of interest
    (C) Powers and duties

14.03 Sources and purposes of separate funds

MEMBERS OF SYSTEM

14.04 Membership in SERS

CONTRIBUTIONS TO SYSTEM

14.05 Mandatory contributions by members

14.06 Voluntary contributions by members
    (A) Contributions while on leave
    (B) Extra deposits to increase annuity income

14.07 Mandatory contributions by employers

14.08 Additional contributions by employers
    (A) Fringe benefit pickups
    (B) Pickup through salary reduction

SERVICE CREDIT

14.09 Service credit: definition

14.10 Purchasing service credit
    (A) In general
    (B) Redeposit of withdrawn contributions
    (C) Payroll deduction plans

BENEFITS

14.11 Disability coverage

14.12 Service retirement

14.13 Early retirement incentive plans

14.14 Employment of retired members

14.15 Optional compensation deferral plans

14.16 Survivor benefits

Chapter 15
Unemployment Compensation

15.01 School participation in unemployment compensation system
15.02 Eligibility for unemployment compensation benefits
    (A) Unemployment
    (B) Actively seeking suitable work
    (C) Minimum employment prior to separation
    (D) Disqualifications
15.03 Benefits
15.04 Student eligibility for unemployment compensation
15.05 Work gap between school terms not considered unemployment
    (A) In general
    (B) Reasonable assurance of work in succeeding term
    (C) Employee with two jobs
15.06 Unemployment arising from labor dispute
15.07 Voluntary resignation
15.08 Suspension or discharge for cause
    (A) Grounds for discipline or discharge
    (B) Standard of proof, procedure and effect of determinations

Chapter 16
Workers' Compensation, Occupational Safety and Health

16.01 Introduction
16.02 Employees covered by workers' compensation
16.03 Compensable injuries
    (A) In general
    (B) Injury arising out of employment
    (C) Injury in course of employment
    (D) Exclusions
16.04 Compensable occupational diseases
16.05 Compensation and benefits
    (A) In general
    (B) Temporary total disability
    (C) Wage loss
    (D) Permanent partial disability
    (E) Impairment of earning capacity
    (F) Permanent total disability
    (G) Funeral expenses, payment to dependents
    (H) Additional awards for violation of specific safety requirements
16.06 Filing claims
16.07 Disputed claims
    (A) Administrative appeals
    (B) Appeals to common pleas court

16.08 Employer immunity from suit, exception for intentional torts

16.09 Occupational safety and health
- (A) In general
- (B) Good faith refusals to work under dangerous conditions
- (C) Retaliation prohibited
- (D) Information
- (E) No-fault inspection

Chapter 17
Equal Employment Opportunity, Family and Medical Leave

17.01 Introduction

KEY ANTIDISCRIMINATION LAWS

17.02 The Thirteenth and Fourteenth Amendments, federal Civil Rights Acts of 1866 and 1871
- (A) In general
- (B) Application
  - (1) Disparate treatment, intent
  - (2) Punitive damages, attorney fees

17.03 Title VII, federal Civil Rights Act of 1964
- (A) Race, color, religion, sex, or national origin
- (B) Exceptions
- (C) "Disparate treatment" and "disparate impact"
- (D) Enforcement by Equal Employment Opportunity Commission (EEOC)
- (E) Actions, remedies
- (F) Proof of discrimination
  - (1) Disparate treatment cases
  - (2) Disparate impact cases
  - (3) Pattern or practice cases
  - (4) Statistical evidence
- (G) Pursuing state and federal remedies

17.04 Ohio Fair Employment Practices Act
- (A) Race, color, religion, sex, national origin, handicap, age, or ancestry
- (B) Parallels between Ohio and federal law
- (C) Enforcement by Ohio Civil Rights Commission (OCRC)
- (D) Remedies
- (E) Appeals, standards of review

17.05 Antidiscrimination requirements for contractors dealing with schools
- (A) Mandatory contract provisions
- (B) Affirmative action by contractors

PARTICULAR APPLICATIONS

17.06 Age discrimination
- (A) Alternative procedures
- (B) Proof of discrimination

17.06 Age discrimination—*continued*
    (C) Retirement
        (1) Mandatory retirement prohibited
        (2) Discriminatory mortality tables

17.07 Hiring and promotion practices
    (A) In general: disparate impact
    (B) Uniform Guidelines on Employee Selection

17.08 Equal pay
    (A) In general
    (B) Actions, statutes of limitations
    (C) "Equal pay for equal work" and "comparable worth"

17.09 Pregnancy
    (A) In general
    (B) Treatment as other temporary disability
    (C) Commencement and duration of maternity leave

17.10 Nonrenewal of contract for discriminatory purpose

17.11 Sexual harassment

17.12 Retaliatory discharge

17.13 Discrimination against the handicapped
    (A) Ohio and pre-ADA federal standards
    (B) Americans with Disabilities Act of 1990

17.14 National origin discrimination

17.15 Religious discrimination

FAMILY AND MEDICAL LEAVE
17.16 Family and Medical Leave Act of 1993

RECORDS
17.17 Notices, record-keeping, and reports

AFFIRMATIVE ACTION
17.18 Affirmative action and reverse discrimination

WAIVERS
17.19 Waiver of claims not prohibited

17.20 Table of laws affecting equal employment opportunity

Chapter 18
Collective Bargaining

INTRODUCTION
18.01 Historical background
    (A) Ferguson Act
    (B) Early denial of collective bargaining rights
    (C) Recognition of unions
    (D) Public Employees' Collective Bargaining Act

18.02 State Employment Relations Board (SERB)

COVERAGE
18.03 Public employers

18.04 Employee organizations and bargaining rights
    (A) In general
    (B) Bargaining with excluded employees

18.05 Excluded employees: management level
    (A) In general
    (B) Educational supervisors
    (C) Other managerial employees

18.06 Excluded employees: confidential employees

18.07 Excluded employees: casual and seasonal workers

18.08 Professional and nonprofessional employees in same bargaining unit

EMPLOYEE RIGHTS
18.09 Employee rights in general

18.10 Collective bargaining

BARGAINING UNIT
18.11 Statutory guidelines for determining bargaining unit
    (A) Authority of SERB
    (B) Factors used in determining unit

18.12 Teacher bargaining units

18.13 Nonteaching employee bargaining units

CERTIFICATION OF BARGAINING REPRESENTATIVE
18.14 Recognition of exclusive bargaining representative

18.15 Representation elections
    (A) Petition for election
    (B) Consent election agreement
    (C) Election to settle representation question, results
    (D) Challenge to election
    (E) Service of notice of certification
    (F) Appealability of SERB orders

18.16 Voluntary recognition
    (A) In general
    (B) Procedure
    (C) Rival employee organization, objection, election

18.17 Challenges to incumbent representative
    (A) In general, when challenge may be made
    (B) Election petition by rival organization
    (C) Union affiliation votes

18.18 Decertification

COLLECTIVE BARGAINING AGREEMENTS
18.19 Requirements for contract
    (A) In general
    (B) Peer review plan

18.20 Supremacy of contract over certain laws

18.21 Agency shop
- (A) "Fair share" union dues for nonmembers
- (B) Rebates and exemptions
- (C) Constitutional issues arising from agency shop

18.22 Grievance procedure and arbitration
- (A) In general
- (B) Arbitration and unfair labor practice proceedings

18.23 Expiration of contracts

UNFAIR LABOR PRACTICES

18.24 Unfair labor practices by employer
- (A) In general
- (B) Interference and coercion
- (C) Refusal to bargain, unilateral action at point of ultimate impasse
- (D) Direct dealing
- (E) Employer domination of union
- (F) Discrimination
- (G) Failure to process grievances

18.25 Unfair labor practices by union
- (A) In general
- (B) Restraint and coercion
- (C) Refusal to bargain
- (D) Duty to provide fair representation

18.26 Procedure on unfair labor practices
- (A) Filing charges
- (B) Remedies
- (C) Appeals

NEGOTIATIONS AND DISPUTES

18.27 Privacy of negotiations, conflict of interest

18.28 Scope of bargaining
- (A) In general
- (B) Mandatory, permissive, and prohibited subjects
- (C) Tentative agreements

18.29 Procedures for resolving disputes
- (A) In general, "time line"
- (B) Notice to negotiate, duty to bargain
- (C) Procedures for resolving deadlock
- (D) Right to strike
- (E) Bargaining procedure after "opt-in" elections

STRIKES

18.30 Legal strikes

18.31 Unauthorized strikes

18.32 Temporary injunction against strikes presenting clear and present danger

18.33 Public records issues

18.34 Defamation in connection with labor disputes
18.35 Procedural timetables

PUPILS

Chapter 19
Pupils: Desegregation and Nondiscrimination

19.01 Introduction

EVOLUTION OF DESEGREGATION CONCEPTS

19.02 School segregation to desegregation, 1867-1954
19.03 Dismantling school segregation in the South
    (A) Demise of "freedom of choice" plans
    (B) Court-ordered desegregation plans, busing
    (C) Funding court-ordered desegregation plans
19.04 Extension of desegregation to urban centers in the North and West
19.05 Urban segregation and suburban school districts
19.06 System-wide school desegregation

DESEGREGATION IN OHIO

19.07 Early demise of "separate but equal" doctrine in Ohio
19.08 Neighborhood schools
    (A) Neighborhood school concept
    (B) Use of neighborhood schools to foster segregation
19.09 State liability for local segregation
    (A) In general
    (B) "Guide for School Districts"
19.10 Other desegregation litigation in Ohio

DESEGREGATION STATUTES

19.11 Federal desegregation statutes
    (A) Civil Rights Act of 1964
    (B) Equal Educational Opportunities Act of 1974
19.12 State desegregation statutes

OTHER NONDISCRIMINATION REQUIREMENTS

19.13 Discrimination by recipients of federal financial assistance
    (A) Title VI, Civil Rights Act of 1964
    (B) Sex discrimination under Title IX, Education Amendments of 1972
    (C) Handicap discrimination under the Rehabilitation Act of 1973
    (D) Age discrimination under the Age Discrimination Act of 1975
    (E) Enforcement
19.14 Sex discrimination in education
    (A) In general
    (B) Scope of extracurricular activities and athletics
    (C) Proof of discrimination under Title IX, damages

19.14 Sex discrimination in education—*continued*
    (D) Sex discrimination and the Fourteenth Amendment
19.15 Bilingual education
19.16 Aliens

Chapter 20
Pupils: Compulsory Education and School Attendance

COMPULSORY SCHOOL ATTENDANCE LAW

20.01 Compulsory school age and free education
    (A) In general
    (B) Age of entrance into school

20.02 Compulsory school attendance
    (A) In general
    (B) Attendance at private or parochial school or special high school
    (C) Attendance by handicapped children at special programs

20.03 Excuse from compulsory attendance
    (A) Constitutionally compelled excuses
    (B) Statutory reasons for excuse
    (C) Home-based instruction

20.04 Attendance of married and pregnant pupils

SCHOOL DAY AND YEAR

20.05 Regular school day and year
    (A) In general
    (B) Division of school year
    (C) Split schedules for economic reasons
    (D) Emergency closings

20.06 Holidays and commemorative days

TRUANCY

20.07 Duty to enforce school attendance

20.08 Attendance officers
    (A) Appointment
    (B) Compensation and expenses
    (C) Powers and duties

20.09 Enforcement procedures
    (A) Investigation
    (B) Liability of parent
    (C) Liability of employer of school-age child

20.10 Attendance and withdrawal reports

AGE AND SCHOOLING CERTIFICATES AND EMPLOYMENT OF SCHOOL-AGE CHILDREN

20.11 Schooling and the child labor laws
    (A) Restrictions on employment of minors
    (B) Summer employment

20.12 Hours and terms of employment of minors

20.13 Age and schooling certificates
- (A) In general, duties of superintendent of schools
- (B) Requirements for certificate
- (C) Application, reissuance
- (D) Denial of certificate, appeal
- (E) Revocation of certificate

20.14 Special age and schooling certificates
- (A) Limited certificate
- (B) Conditional certificate
- (C) Part-time and vacation certificates
- (D) Over-age certificate

20.15 Part-time day school for certificate holders

20.16 Employer responsibility respecting minors
- (A) In general
- (B) Records
- (C) Agreement as to compensation
- (D) Return of certificate

20.17 Enforcement, penalties

Chapter 21
Pupils: Health and Safety

HEALTH SERVICES

21.01 Responsibilities of board of education

21.02 Employment of health care professionals
- (A) Physicians and dentists
- (B) Nurses

21.03 Medical examinations
- (A) In general
- (B) Examination by family physician
- (C) Tuberculosis testing
- (D) Children or staff found to have communicable disease
- (E) AIDS
- (F) Early screening for health or developmental disorders

21.04 Medical treatment
- (A) In general, parental consent, emergencies
- (B) Administration of prescription drugs
  - (1) Adoption of policy by board
  - (2) Requirements for administration
  - (3) Limitations on liability

21.05 Immunizations
- (A) Required immunizations generally
- (B) Exclusion of students not immunized
- (C) Parental objections

21.06 Dental examinations and treatment
21.07 Health records
    (A) Examination records
    (B) Immunization records
    (C) Emergency treatment authorization
21.08 Duties of board of health
    (A) Delegation of duties to board of health
    (B) Building inspection, disease prevention
21.09 Volunteer medical services at athletic events, nonliability

SAFETY MEASURES AND PROGRAMS
21.10 School building requirements
    (A) Safety and sanitation in general
    (B) Asbestos removal
    (C) Architectural barriers to handicapped
21.11 Traffic protection for students
    (A) Crossing guards
    (B) Duties of local government in traffic control
    (C) School zones and signs
21.12 Eye protection
21.13 Fire and tornado drills
21.14 Safety instruction
21.15 Fostering a drug-free environment
    (A) Drug-Free Schools and Communities Act
    (B) Drug-Free Workplace Act
    (C) Confidentiality requirements for drug counseling programs
    (D) Anabolic steroid warnings in athletic facilities
21.16 Conveyance or possession of deadly weapons or dangerous ordnance on school premises

Chapter 22
Transportation of Pupils

22.01 Introduction
22.02 Transportation coordinators and supervisors

PROVIDING TRANSPORTATION
22.03 Transportation of pupils generally
    (A) Pupils in kindergarten through eighth grade
    (B) High school and joint vocational school students
    (C) Private and parochial school students
    (D) Payment in lieu of providing transportation
22.04 Transportation of nonresident pupils
22.05 Transportation of special students
22.06 When transportation need not be provided

TRANSPORTATION COSTS

22.07 Financing transportation
    (A) Duties of state board of education
    (B) Reimbursement of school districts
        (1) In general
        (2) Distance requirements
    (C) Subsidies for school bus purchases

22.08 Insurance

22.09 Purchase of school buses

EQUIPMENT STANDARDS

22.10 Duties of department of education and director of public safety

22.11 School bus markings and equipment

22.12 Vehicles transporting preschool children

SCHOOL BUS DRIVERS

22.13 Driver qualifications
    (A) In general
    (B) Drug and alcohol testing

22.14 Medical disqualification of school bus drivers

22.15 School bus driver training

OPERATION OF SCHOOL BUSES

22.16 Bus routes, stops and depots

22.17 Driver responsibilities and pupil behavior
    (A) Driver's responsibilities generally
    (B) Driver's duty to maintain order
    (C) Pupil behavior

22.18 Traffic laws and operation of school buses
    (A) Responsibilities of driver
    (B) Responsibilities of other drivers
    (C) Accident reports

PUPIL SAFETY PROGRAMS

22.19 Instructing younger children in safety

22.20 Emergency plans and drills

22.21 Volunteer rider assistance programs

USE OF SCHOOL BUSES

22.22 Routine and nonroutine use of school buses in general

22.23 Leasing school buses for senior citizens and adult education

22.24 Leasing school buses to nonpublic schools

INDEPENDENT CONTRACTORS AND MASS TRANSIT

22.25 Contracts for transportation of pupils
    (A) Pre-existing contracts
    (B) Mandatory provisions, violation

22.26 Safety requirements for mass transit systems

ENFORCEMENT, PENALTIES
22.27 Violation of state rules on pupil transportation, penalties

Chapter 23
Pupils: Tuition and Fees

23.01 Introduction

TUITION
23.02 Admission requirements and tuition liability
- (A) Statutory requirements in general
    - (1) Admission tuition-free in district where parent resides
    - (2) Child in custody of agency or person other than parent
    - (3) Child whose parent is institutionalized or imprisoned
    - (4) Child who resides in a "home"
    - (5) Child who requires special education
    - (6) Child who has been placed for adoption
    - (7) Child participating in particular special education programs
    - (8) Child in care of shelter for victims of domestic violence
    - (9) Child admitted under interdistrict contract
    - (10) Permissive admissions, tuition required
    - (11) Child admitted under state board criteria
    - (12) Students from adjacent districts
    - (13) Special rule for certain projects or facilities
    - (14) Permanently excluded pupils
    - (15) Payment of tuition to non-Ohio schools
- (B) Determining residence
- (C) Special tuition exemptions and waivers
    - (1) Child for whom custody proceedings initiated
    - (2) Emancipated children
    - (3) Married children
    - (4) Child who may need emergency medical attention
    - (5) Child whose parent is in military service
    - (6) Child whose parent dies
    - (7) Child whose parent is building a new home
    - (8) Child whose parent is purchasing a home
    - (9) Child whose parent works in the district
    - (10) High school senior whose parent moves
    - (11) Child who resides with grandparent
    - (12) Exchange students
- (D) Computation and payment
- (E) Special programs

ACTIVITY FEES AND FUNDS
23.03 Student activity programs, fees, and funds
- (A) In general
- (B) Limitation on expenditures
- (C) State and local policies

23.04 Expenditures from student activity funds
    (A) In general, authority for expenditures
    (B) Particular expenditures

23.05 Failure to pay activity or school fees

NEEDY CHILDREN

23.06 Poverty and compulsory attendance

23.07 Special programs for needy children
    (A) Free meals
    (B) Dental care, immunizations
    (C) Instructional materials
    (D) Disadvantaged pupil programs
    (E) Preschool programs

Chapter 24
Care and Protection of Pupils, Offenses Against Minors

24.01 Introduction

DUTIES OF SCHOOL PERSONNEL TOWARD PUPILS

24.02 Teachers and parental duties and authority, in loco parentis
    (A) Civil law
    (B) Criminal law

24.03 Duty to exercise due care toward students
    (A) Due care in general
    (B) Shaping due care according to circumstances
    (C) Foreseeability of risk
    (D) Violations of duty to exercise due care toward students
        (1) Failure to instruct, or improper instruction
        (2) Inadequate supervision
        (3) Inadequate safety precautions

24.04 Duty to protect students

24.05 Duty to report suspected child abuse or neglect
    (A) In general
    (B) Recognizing child abuse and neglect
    (C) Definition of child abuse
    (D) Definition of child neglect

24.06 Duty to report crimes
    (A) General duty with respect to felonies
    (B) Principal's duty with respect to certain offenses

24.07 Notice to board of certain crimes committed by employees

OFFENSES AGAINST MINORS

24.08 Offenses against minors generally

24.09 Endangering children
    (A) Violating duty of care, protection, or support
    (B) Physical abuse, improper discipline

24.09 Endangering children—*continued*
    (C) Sexually oriented violations
    (D) Transporting children while under the influence
    (E) Riot
    (F) Improperly discharging firearm at or into school

24.10 Hazing, permitting hazing

24.11 Contributing to the delinquency or unruliness of a minor

24.12 Disseminating matter harmful to juveniles

24.13 Sex offenses in general

24.14 Drug abuse offenses in general

24.15 Alcohol and tobacco offenses involving minors
    (A) Alcohol offenses
    (B) Tobacco offenses

MISSING CHILDREN

24.16 Missing children informational programs
    (A) Fingerprinting
    (B) Photographs

Chapter 25
Conduct and Discipline of Pupils

25.01 Introduction

STANDARDS OF CONDUCT

25.02 Statutory standards for student conduct

25.03 Policy on student conduct
    (A) Requirement for policy, scope
    (B) Interpretation and application

25.04 Dress and appearance codes

25.05 Regulating student expression

DUTY TO MAINTAIN DISCIPLINE

25.06 Duties of teachers to maintain discipline

25.07 Duties of nonteaching employees to maintain order

DISCIPLINARY MEASURES

25.08 Serious disciplinary measures

25.09 Due process requirements for serious disciplinary measures
    (A) Fundamental fairness
    (B) Criminal law standards not applicable
    (C) Violation of constitutional rights

25.10 Suspension and expulsion
    (A) Authority to suspend or expel student
    (B) Suspension: procedure
    (C) Expulsion: procedure
    (D) Community service alternative

25.10 Suspension and expulsion—*continued*
- (E) Permanent exclusion for certain offenses
- (F) Denial of admission to expelled student

25.11 Emergency removal

25.12 Review of suspension or expulsion by board, appeal to common pleas court
- (A) Appeal to board
- (B) Appeal to court of common pleas

25.13 Disciplinary transfers

25.14 Checklist for suspension, expulsion, or removal
- (A) School policy on conduct
- (B) Suspension
- (C) Expulsion
- (D) Emergency removal
- (E) Appeal to board

25.15 Removal from extracurricular activities
- (A) In general
- (B) Question of due process

25.16 Corporal punishment
- (A) In general, requirement of reasonableness
- (B) Constitutional considerations
- (C) Excessive or unreasonable punishment

PROGRAMS

Chapter 26
Curriculum and Educational Programs

26.01 Introduction

STANDARDS FOR ELEMENTARY AND SECONDARY EDUCATION

26.02 State minimum standards
- (A) Curriculum
  - (1) Statutory requirements
  - (2) Rules
- (B) Educational resources
- (C) Competency-based education programs

26.03 Standards adopted by school board

GENERAL CURRICULUM

26.04 Requirement and content of curriculum

26.05 Curriculum for kindergarten through grade eight
- (A) Kindergarten
- (B) Grades one through six
- (C) Grades seven and eight

26.06 High school curriculum
- (A) In general, courses offered
- (B) Graduation requirements

26.07 Curriculum options, alternative schools, college preparatory courses and schools
- (A) In general
- (B) Alternative schools, college preparatory schools
- (C) Post-secondary enrollment options program

SPECIAL COURSES AND PROGRAMS

26.08 Disadvantaged pupils and children of migrant workers

26.09 Programs for gifted children

26.10 Special instruction, adult education
- (A) In general
- (B) Evening schools
- (C) Part-time classes for employed children
- (D) Adult high school continuation programs
- (E) Adult education diplomas

26.11 Other special courses and programs
- (A) Technical training, advanced studies
- (B) Vocational training
- (C) Cultural enrichment
- (D) Child day-care centers
- (E) Americanization schools
- (F) Vacation period activities
- (G) Educational broadcasting network, educational computer network
- (H) Business advisory councils

DRIVER TRAINING

26.12 Driver training programs
- (A) In general, minimum standards
- (B) Standard course, teachers

26.13 Costs, student requirements, equipment and safety requirements
- (A) Subsidy, course fees
- (B) Student requirements
- (C) Vehicles, lease, equipment
- (D) Limit on teacher's instruction time

26.14 Alternative driver training methods, commercial instruction

ACADEMIC ACHIEVEMENT, PROMOTION, AND GRADUATION

26.15 Criteria for student performance and promotion
- (A) In general
- (B) Educational malpractice

26.16 Awarding high school diploma
- (A) In general
- (B) Guaranteed competency of graduates

REVIEW AND EVALUATION, ENFORCEMENT OF STANDARDS

26.17 Requirements for review and evaluation

26.18 Accreditation evaluations
26.19 School charter, revocation
26.20 Student rights in research, experimental activities, and testing

Chapter 27
Vocational Education and Programs

VOCATIONAL TRAINING PROGRAMS
27.01 State and federal emphasis on vocational education
27.02 Providing vocational education
27.03 Vocational course offerings
27.04 Implementation of vocational education program, federal funding
27.05 Production of goods in vocational education programs
27.06 Payment of wages in occupational work adjustment
27.07 In-service training for vocational child-care students

JOINT VOCATIONAL SCHOOL DISTRICT
27.08 Formation of joint vocational school district
    (A) In general
    (B) Expansion of district
    (C) Consolidation of districts
    (D) Dissolution of districts
27.09 Administration of joint vocational school district
    (A) Board of education of joint vocational district
    (B) Superintendent of joint vocational district
    (C) Evaluation by state
27.10 Vocational school facilities
    (A) In general
    (B) Cooperation with technical college district
27.11 Funding joint vocational school districts
27.12 Pupils, special education, transportation

VOCATIONAL REHABILITATION
27.13 Rehabilitation services commission
    (A) Composition
    (B) Duties, organization
27.14 Ohio rehabilitation center
27.15 Records

Chapter 28
Education for Children with Disabilities

FEDERAL AND STATE REQUIREMENTS IN GENERAL
28.01 Legislation on education for children with disabilities
    (A) Federal and state acts

28.01 Legislation on education for children with disabilities—*continued*
    (B) Definitions
28.02 Individualized education program
28.03 "Free appropriate public education" (FAPE)
28.04 Extended school year services
28.05 Least restrictive environment
    (A) Preference for mainstreaming
    (B) Need for special programs or facilities
28.06 Twenty-four-hour care
28.07 Related services for children with disabilities
28.08 Bringing education to children with disabilities
    (A) Home instruction, tuition, and boarding
    (B) Education of children in hospitals
    (C) Tubercular children
28.09 Discipline of children with disabilities
    (A) In general
    (B) Advisability of developing district policy
    (C) Temporary suspension, emergency suspension
    (D) Discipline for bringing firearms to school
28.10 Discrimination in testing
    (A) In general
    (B) Meeting graduation requirements

PARENTAL RIGHTS
28.11 Parental involvement in educational decisions affecting disabled child
    (A) In general, supremacy of federal requirements
    (B) Right to notice of matters affecting identification, evaluation, placement, programs, or services
    (C) Hearing
    (D) Burden and degree of proof
    (E) Costs of hearing
    (F) Decision, appeal

ACTIONS AND REMEDIES UNDER FEDERAL LAW
28.12 Causes of action for violations
    (A) In general
    (B) Limitations on right of action
28.13 Relief, damages, compensatory education, attorney fees
    (A) Remedies for violations
    (B) Compensatory education
    (C) Damages under section 504 of Rehabilitation Act of 1973
    (D) Attorney's fees

ADMINISTRATION OF EDUCATION FOR CHILDREN WITH DISABILITIES IN OHIO
28.14 Planning and evaluation
    (A) State and district plans

28.14 Planning and evaluation—*continued*
    (B) Reports on programs and services

28.15 Funding, sharing facilities and costs
    (A) Foundation program
    (B) Cooperative agreements among school districts
    (C) Residency requirements and tuition reimbursement

28.16 Teachers of children with disabilities

28.17 Special classes, requirements for facilities
    (A) Special classes or special instruction
    (B) Eliminating architectural barriers

28.18 Assisting deaf and hard of hearing children and their parents

28.19 State schools for the deaf and blind
    (A) In general, control and supervision, personnel
    (B) Admission, return of child to parents

28.20 Role of county MR/DD boards
    (A) In general
    (B) Placement of child

Chapter 29
Administration of Programs for the Retarded and Developmentally Disabled

29.01 County MR/DD boards
    (A) In general, purpose and role
    (B) "Mental retardation" and "developmental disability"

29.02 Organization of board
    (A) Members, appointment
    (B) Qualifications
    (C) Persons disqualified from membership
    (D) Terms, vacancies, expenses
    (E) Removal

29.03 Meetings of board

29.04 Powers and duties of board
    (A) In general
    (B) Coordinating with boards of education
    (C) Fees for services
    (D) Eligibility of family members for services
    (E) Ethics councils
    (F) Regional councils
    (G) Residential facility linked deposit programs
    (H) Limitations
    (I) Complaints

29.05 Compliance with state regulations

29.06 Transportation of pupils
    (A) Costs
    (B) Transportation safety

29.07 Contracts of board with other agencies

29.08 Property, gifts and grants
    (A) Gifts, grants, devises, and bequests
    (B) Disposition of unneeded personal property

29.09 Funding and tuition
    (A) Funding
    (B) Reimbursements to families
    (C) Tuition

BOARD EMPLOYEES

29.10 Superintendent
    (A) In general
    (B) Duties

29.11 Certification and registration of employees

29.12 Civil service status of employees; contract system for management employees

29.13 Compensation and fringe benefits
    (A) Salary schedules, pay periods
    (B) Health insurance and sick leave
    (C) Vacation
    (D) Retirement
    (E) Resignation

29.14 Criminal disqualifications and background checks

29.15 Nondiscrimination and affirmative action

29.16 Liability insurance

29.17 Collective bargaining

LEGAL COUNSEL
29.18 Legal adviser, other counsel

RECORDS
29.19 Restrictions on disclosure and release

Chapter 30
Physical Education, Athletics, and Recreation

30.01 Introduction

PHYSICAL EDUCATION
30.02 Curriculum requirements for physical education

30.03 Physical education and interscholastic athletics distinguished

30.04 Physical education facilities

30.05 Physical education teachers, coaches, and trainers

INTERSCHOLASTIC ATHLETICS

30.06 Interscholastic sports, introduction

30.07 Ohio High School Athletic Association (OHSAA)
- (A) Purposes
- (B) Membership
- (C) Government and administration
- (D) National federation affiliation

30.08 Legal status of OHSAA
- (A) OHSAA as unincorporated association
- (B) OHSAA as quasi-governmental agency

30.09 Recognized sports, equality of athletic opportunity
- (A) Individual and team sports recognized by OHSAA
- (B) Boys' and girls' sports, participation by both sexes
- (C) Recognition of sport by individual school
- (D) Nonrecognized sports

30.10 Funding interscholastic athletics
- (A) OHSAA policy on financing athletics
- (B) School board authority to fund costs of athletic programs
- (C) Other sources of funding, pupil activity fund
- (D) Club sports
- (E) Rulings on use of sports funds

30.11 OHSAA rules, enforcement
- (A) Scope of rules
- (B) Penalties for violation, imposition, administrative appeal
- (C) Enforceability of rules and penalties

30.12 Sports injuries, OHSAA insurance program

RECREATIONAL PROGRAMS

30.13 Recreational programs

30.14 Joint recreational facilities and districts

30.15 Joint recreation board

Chapter 31
Schools, Parents, and Community Affairs

PUBLIC PARTICIPATION IN SCHOOL AFFAIRS

31.01 Public meetings

31.02 Annual report of school progress

31.03 Parent-educator relations

31.04 Public use of school facilities

SCHOOL PARTICIPATION IN COMMUNITY AFFAIRS

31.05 Contracts and cooperation with public institutions

31.06 Providing meals for the elderly

31.07 Field trips

31.08 Soliciting funds for charities
31.09 Registering persons to vote

Chapter 32
Religion and the Public Schools

32.01 Introduction, tests under First Amendment religion clauses
32.02 Free exercise of religion and compulsory state educational standards
32.03 Free exercise limits on compelled patriotic observances
32.04 Establishment restrictions on released time for religious instruction
32.05 Establishment through prayer and similar activity
32.06 Establishment problems from the use of public schools for religious purposes
    (A) Equal access
    (B) Traditional observances
32.07 Curriculum decisions

TEXTBOOKS—LIBRARIES—SUPPLIES—SERVICES—PROPERTY

Chapter 33
Textbooks

33.01 Introduction
33.02 Textbooks and workbooks to be furnished free
    (A) Books included
    (B) Purchase by pupil or parent
33.03 Selection and adoption of textbooks
    (A) Procedure
    (B) Adoption to last four years
    (C) Requirement that texts be current
33.04 Discretion of board in choosing books, constitutional limitations
33.05 Administrator or teacher acting as sales agent for publisher
33.06 Copyright considerations
    (A) In general
    (B) Fair use
    (C) Works made for hire

Chapter 34
Libraries

34.01 Introduction

LIBRARIES SERVING SCHOOLS
34.02 School board's authority to provide library service, in general

34.03 School district public libraries

34.04 Community library service for schools
    (A) Other libraries in school districts
    (B) Public library service for schools

STATE LIBRARY

34.05 Role of state library board

34.06 Composition of state library board

34.07 State librarian

34.08 Application for permission to establish library service

LIBRARY TRUSTEES AND STAFF

34.09 Library boards, in general
    (A) Board members, officers
    (B) Board of trustees as an entity
    (C) Quorum, open meetings

34.10 Powers of library board
    (A) In general
    (B) Specific applications

34.11 Financial transactions of library boards

34.12 Library employees, clerk of board
    (A) Employees: compensation and fringe benefits
    (B) Clerk of library board

BUDGET AND REVENUE

34.13 Library budget, annual appropriation

34.14 Income tax

34.15 Tax levies, in general
    (A) School board tax levy for library purposes
    (B) Tax levies by community libraries
    (C) No requirement to levy

34.16 Ten-mill limitation, special levies
    (A) Special levy within ten-mill limitation
    (B) Property tax in excess of ten-mill limitation

34.17 Bond issues

Chapter 35
School Supplies and Food Service

SUPPLIES

35.01 Purchase of school supplies

35.02 Charging pupils for items other than textbooks
    (A) Authority of board
    (B) Sales by school, use of proceeds for school purposes
    (C) Sales by activity groups, accounting for proceeds, pupil activity fund
    (D) Revolving account for purchase and sale of supplies

35.02 Charging pupils for items other than textbooks—*continued*
    (E) Sales tax
35.03 Vending machines, use of proceeds

FOOD SERVICES

35.04 Operation of food service by school district
    (A) In general
    (B) Meals for the elderly
    (C) Use of facilities by outside groups
35.05 Cooperative food service operations among districts
35.06 Sanitation and safety of food service operations
35.07 Breakfast and lunch programs

Chapter 36
Acquiring and Disposing of Property

ACQUIRING PROPERTY

36.01 Authority of school board to deal with property
36.02 Purchase of real property
    (A) In general
    (B) Incidental costs, terms of purchase
    (C) Option to purchase
36.03 Eminent domain and appropriation of real property
36.04 Purchase of personal property
    (A) In general
    (B) Competitive bidding
    (C) Specific property or equipment
        (1) Office equipment
        (2) Energy conservation measures
        (3) School buses
        (4) Other personal property
36.05 Lease, trade, or exchange of real or personal property
    (A) Lease
    (B) Trade or exchange
36.06 Acquisition of property by gift, devise, or bequest
36.07 Acquisition of property by educational service centers
36.08 Joint acquisition of property

DISPOSING OF SCHOOL PROPERTY

36.09 Power to dispose of property
36.10 Lease of property
    (A) In general
    (B) Mineral leases
36.11 Sale of real or personal property
    (A) In general

36.11 Sale of real or personal property—*continued*

    (B) Sale procedure

36.12 Granting option to purchase

36.13 Gift of school property prohibited

36.14 Use of sale proceeds and rentals

Chapter 37
Construction and Repair of School Buildings

CONSTRUCTION AND REPAIR OF BUILDINGS AND FACILITIES

37.01 Authority of school board

    (A) In general, board discretion

    (B) Contracting procedures, building standards

37.02 Exemption from zoning fees and building permit fees

37.03 Plans and specifications

    (A) Preparation of plans and cost estimates, changes

    (B) Approval by building department

37.04 Competitive bidding requirement

    (A) In general

    (B) Procedure

    (C) Exceptions to competitive bidding requirements

37.05 Form of bids, bidder's security for performance

37.06 Examination, acceptance, and rejection of bids

    (A) In general

        (1) RC 3313.46 requirements

        (2) The RC 9.312 option

    (B) Award of contract, performance bonds, notice to surety on performance bonds

37.07 Costs of construction

    (A) Availability of funds, certification

    (B) Funds from which payment may be made

37.08 Construction, progress payments

    (A) In general, notice to proceed

    (B) Mandatory contract provisions on payment

    (C) Progress payments

37.09 Construction and maintenance: safety and sanitation standards, supervision and inspection

37.10 Authority to employ construction manager

APPLICATION OF PREVAILING WAGE ACT

37.11 Duty to observe prevailing wage standards in school board projects

37.12 Prevailing wages

    (A) In general

    (B) Mandatory contract provisions, posting wage rates

37.13 Designating wage coordinator

37.14 Enforcement of the Prevailing Wage Act, penalties and remedies

Chapter 38
Management and Use of School Property

38.01 Introduction

MAINTENANCE

38.02 Maintenance of school property

SECURITY

38.03 Restricting access to school property, trespass
    (A) Rules on access and use, posting
    (B) Criminal trespass

38.04 Offenses against school property
    (A) Arson and related offenses
    (B) Disrupting public services
    (C) Vandalism and lesser offenses
    (D) Theft offenses
    (E) Disorderly conduct

38.05 Rewards posted by board of education for property offenses

38.06 Parental liability for property damage, theft, or assault by children
    (A) Statutory liability
    (B) Common-law liability

USE OF SCHOOL PROPERTY

38.07 Primary use of school property for school purposes

38.08 Use of school property by others, in general
    (A) Discretion of board
    (B) Equal access requirement
    (C) Liability insurance
    (D) Fees

38.09 Use of school property for educational and recreational purposes
    (A) Use by "responsible" organization
    (B) Duty of board to adopt rules on use

38.10 Use of school property for public meetings and entertainments

38.11 Use of school property for political meetings

38.12 Use of school property for religious purposes

38.13 Payment for use of school property, expenses, damages

REGULATION OF SMOKING

38.14 Bans on indoor smoking

FINANCES—RECORDS

Chapter 39
Sources of Revenue

39.01 Introduction, sources of revenue
- (A) In general
- (B) Current constitutional imbroglio

LOCAL PROPERTY TAX REVENUES

39.02 Taxing power, authority of board to levy taxes

39.03 Ten-mill limitation, voted and unvoted levies

39.04 Changes in property valuations, tax exemptions, notice to board, tax abatement

39.05 Collection of taxes

SCHOOL FOUNDATION PROGRAM

39.06 State aid for school operating expenses
- (A) Purposes of school foundation program
- (B) Constitutional issues
- (C) Administration of school foundation program, appropriations

39.07 Prerequisites for participation in foundation program
- (A) Minimum school year
- (B) Minimum tax levy
- (C) Minimum teachers' salaries, tax certificates

39.08 Nonoperating uses for foundation funds
- (A) Education for the handicapped
- (B) Vocational education
- (C) Transportation facilities

39.09 Records and reports
- (A) In general
- (B) Average daily membership
- (C) Number of classes or units for handicapped
- (D) Information on certified employees
- (E) Information on tax values and rates
- (F) Information on uncollectible taxes

MISCELLANEOUS SOURCES OF REVENUE

39.10 Fines and forfeitures

39.11 Estate and inheritance taxes

39.12 Income tax

39.13 Bequests and gifts, school foundations

39.14 Tuition

39.15 Income from athletic events, activity fees, miscellaneous income

Chapter 40
Tax Budget, Tax Levies, and Appropriations

TAX BUDGET

40.01 Duty to prepare annual tax budget

40.02 Fiscal year and school year

40.03 Tax budget timetable

40.04 Form of tax budget
- (A) Required contents
- (B) Contingent expenses and reserve
- (C) Spending reserve

40.05 County budget commission
- (A) Powers and duties of commission
- (B) Reviewing need for each tax
- (C) Levies approved by voters

40.06 Appeal from decision of budget commission

PROPERTY TAX LEVIES

40.07 Basis for tax levies

40.08 Requirement for separate levies

40.09 General and special levies within ten-mill limitation
- (A) General levy for current expenses
- (B) Special levy

40.10 Special levies outside ten-mill limitation
- (A) Nonemergency tax levies
- (B) Emergency tax levies
- (C) Incremental tax levies
- (D) County school financing district levies for special education

40.11 Renewal tax levies

40.12 Replacement tax levies

40.13 Election on tax levy outside of ten-mill limitation

40.14 Reduction in effective rate of additional tax levy

APPROPRIATIONS

40.15 Annual appropriation resolution
- (A) Necessity for annual appropriation
- (B) Certificate of resources, amendment
- (C) Temporary resolution
- (D) Limitations on amount appropriated

40.16 Amending or supplementing appropriation resolution

40.17 Adoption of spending plan concurrent with adoption of appropriation resolution

40.18 Filing requirements
- (A) Documents to be filed with state department of education
- (B) Documents to be filed with county auditor

40.18　Filing requirements—*continued*
  (C) Procedure when documents reveal district may have financial shortfall
40.19　Auditor's certificate that appropriations do not exceed estimate

Chapter 41
Borrowing Money

GENERAL AUTHORITY TO BORROW MONEY

41.01　Authority to borrow money

41.02　Other types of borrowing

UNIFORM BOND LAW RESTRICTIONS ON ISSUING BONDS AND NOTES

41.03　Uniform Bond Law

41.04　Purposes of school borrowing

41.05　Limits on unvoted debt
  (A) Statutory limitations
  (B) Constitutional limitation

41.06　Limit on voted debt

41.07　Special needs district

41.08　Other limits on debt

GENERAL PROCEDURES FOR ISSUING BONDS AND NOTES

41.09　Election procedures for voted debt

41.10　Step one: determining estimated life of permanent improvement

41.11　Step two: calculating maturity of bonds, treasurer's certificate
  (A) Calculation generally
  (B) Weighted average for multiple classes of improvements
  (C) Transfer of funds among classes

41.12　Step three: resolution of necessity
  (A) In general
  (B) Contents
  (C) Consents required when debt will exceed certain amount
  (D) Certification of resolution to county auditor
  (E) Auditor's duties and certificate

41.13　Step four: resolution to proceed
  (A) In general
  (B) Contents

41.14　Step five: election
  (A) Notice of election
  (B) Form of ballot
  (C) Certification of election results

41.15　Step six: tax levy for debt service

41.16 Step seven: authorization of bonds or notes
- (A) Procedure in general
- (B) Resolution authorizing notes
- (C) Notes in anticipation of bonds
- (D) Maturity of notes, renewal
- (E) Resolution authorizing bonds
- (F) Capitalized interest and other costs included in the bond or note issue

41.17 Step eight: sale of bonds or notes
- (A) Timing
- (B) Types of sale
- (C) Disclosure, official statement
- (D) Award
- (E) Proceeds of sale
- (F) Delivery of bonds or notes
- (G) Transcript of proceedings

41.18 Refunding or advance refunding bonds or notes

41.19 Federal tax law provisions
- (A) Form of bonds, coupons, registration
- (B) Arbitrage bonds, loss of tax advantage
- (C) Use of proceeds, rebate
- (D) Qualified tax-exempt obligations

41.20 Miscellaneous state law provisions
- (A) Lost or destroyed bonds
- (B) Incontestability
- (C) Validation of questioned securities

BORROWING FOR CURRENT EXPENSES

41.21 Borrowing in anticipation of collection of current revenue
- (A) In general
- (B) Borrowing in anticipation of future revenues

41.22 Tax anticipation notes
- (A) In general
- (B) Limits on amount

JOINT VOCATIONAL SCHOOL DISTRICT BONDS AND LEVIES

41.23 Borrowing by joint vocational school district
- (A) Voted bond issues
- (B) Tax levy over ten-mill limitation
- (C) Tax anticipation notes

STATE ASSISTANCE FOR CLASSROOM FACILITIES

41.24 Classroom Facilities Law

41.25 Net bonded indebtedness and conditions of state assistance

41.26 Application for state assistance, approval

41.27 Conditional approval, proceedings to qualify for assistance
- (A) In general
- (B) Bond issue, approval by voters

41.28 Proceedings for election
    (A) Resolution declaring necessity
    (B) Consents required if debt will exceed certain amount
    (C) Certification of resolution
    (D) Duties of county auditor
    (E) Election, time, notice
    (F) Certification of election results

41.29 Agreement for construction and sale of project
    (A) General requirements
    (B) Supplemental agreement to adjust tax levied

41.30 Issuance of bonds or notes, proceeds of sale

41.31 Suspending authority to issue bonds or notes

41.32 Certification of tax levies

EMERGENCY LOANS

41.33 Emergency loans
    (A) In general
    (B) Eligibility for emergency loan
    (C) Processing applications
    (D) Controlling board approval
    (E) Repayment

Chapter 42
Deposits and Investments

INTRODUCTION

42.01 Uniform Depository Act

42.02 Liability for undeposited funds and securities

42.03 Cash reserve

PUBLIC FUNDS AND ELIGIBLE DEPOSITORIES

42.04 Public funds, types of deposits
    (A) "Public moneys"
    (B) Active, inactive, and interim deposits

42.05 Eligible depositories
    (A) In general, participation in Ohio guaranteed student loan program
    (B) Branch located in school district
    (C) Minority banks

42.06 Maximum amount which may be deposited in given institution

PROCEDURE FOR DESIGNATING PUBLIC DEPOSITORIES

42.07 Designating depositories, in general

42.08 Separate treatment of active, inactive, and interim deposits

42.09 Resolution estimating inactive deposits, publication

42.10 Application to act as depository

42.11 Award of deposits
    (A) Meeting of board of education
    (B) Award of deposits
        (1) Inactive deposits
        (2) Interim deposits
        (3) Active deposits
42.12 Conflict of interest in award, discrimination in apportioning deposits
42.13 Evidence of deposits
42.14 Transfer of inactive or interim funds to active funds
42.15 Service charges

SECURITY FOR PUBLIC DEPOSITS
42.16 Depositories required to post security, types of security
42.17 Securities eligible for pledge
42.18 Sale of pledged securities to recover public funds
42.19 Exchange, release, and substitution of securities
42.20 Deposit of pledged securities with trustee
    (A) In general
    (B) Eligible trustees
    (C) Compensation of trustee

INTEREST, ALLOCATION
42.21 Interest, payment
42.22 Allocation of interest among funds

INVESTMENT OF PUBLIC FUNDS
42.23 Investment of interim funds
    (A) In general
    (B) Classifying funds as interim
42.24 Duties of treasurer, deposit of investments with trustee

Chapter 43
Financial Transactions and Accounting

SPENDING PUBLIC MONEY
43.01 General considerations in spending school funds
43.02 Requirement for authorization to spend money
    (A) In general
    (B) Specific authorization
    (C) Authorization by necessary implication
43.03 Requirement for public purpose
43.04 Restrictions on earmarked funds
43.05 Examples of authorized and unauthorized expenditures
    (A) Influencing vote on levy or bond issue
    (B) Certain expenses of employees
    (C) Legal expenses

(D) Miscellaneous expenses

PROCEDURE FOR EXPENDITURES

43.06 Overview of procedure for expenditures

43.07 Requisition and purchase order
- (A) Requisition
- (B) Purchase order
- (C) Disposition of purchase order

43.08 Voucher and warrant
- (A) Voucher
- (B) Warrant

43.09 Procedure for payment of purchases and contracts

43.10 Procedure for payment of wages and salaries

FINANCIAL RECORDS

43.11 Appropriation and authorization ledger

43.12 Receipts and deposits
- (A) Receipts
- (B) Receipts ledger
- (C) Bank deposit slip

43.13 Cash journal

43.14 Individual payroll record

SCHOOL FUNDS

43.15 School funds
- (A) In general
- (B) Required funds
- (C) Transfer of money among funds

43.16 Interest earned on funds

43.17 General fund

43.18 Bond funds

43.19 Bond retirement fund

43.20 Replacement fund

43.21 Permanent improvement fund

43.22 Service fund

43.23 Food service fund

43.24 School supplies fund

43.25 Student activities fund

ACCOUNTING

43.26 Uniform system of accounting
- (A) Duties of state auditor
- (B) Annual financial reports by board of education

43.27 Audits
- (A) Examination of accounts and financial reports
- (B) Irregularities found in examination

43.28 Duties of district treasurer
43.29 Data processing
43.30 Retention of records

Chapter 44
Records of Employees and Pupils

44.01 Introduction

PUBLIC RECORDS ACT

44.02 Definition of public records

44.03 Availability of public records

OHIO PRIVACY ACT

44.04 Introduction

44.05 Scope

44.06 Personal information and personal information systems

44.07 Interconnected or combined personal information systems

44.08 School district responsibility for personal information systems
- (A) Introduction
- (B) Liability and criminal penalties
- (C) System security
- (D) Ensuring that information is accurate, timely, complete, necessary, and relevant

44.09 Types, uses, and collection of information

44.10 Right to inspect personal information

44.11 Disputing accuracy, relevance, timeliness, or completeness of personal information

EMPLOYEE RECORDS

44.12 Required employee records

STUDENT RECORDS

44.13 Required student records

44.14 Access to and release of student records
- (A) Comparison and scope of state and federal law
- (B) Restrictions
- (C) Conditions of release
- (D) Records of victims of domestic violence

44.15 Administrative use of student records
- (A) Introduction
- (B) Consent

44.16 Use of records in missing child investigation

44.17 Record of persons requesting or obtaining access to student records

44.18 Student and parent inspection rights

- 44.19 Federal and state resolution of disputes over the contents of student records
  - (A) Federal and state rights
  - (B) Hearings
  - (C) School district as final decision-maker
- 44.20 Annual notice of rights to parents and pupils
- 44.21 Formulation of school district policy and procedures

DISPOSAL OF RECORDS
- 44.22 Records commission
- 44.23 Procedure for disposal of records

PUBLIC DUTY—SEARCH AND SEIZURE—LIABILITY

Chapter 45
Ethics Requirements and Education Personnel

OHIO ETHICS LAW
- 45.01 Introduction, applicability of ethics laws
  - (A) In general
  - (B) Ohio ethics commission, advisory opinions
  - (C) Applicability of ethics laws to education personnel
    - (1) In general
    - (2) Education personnel
    - (3) Financial disclosure
- 45.02 Financial disclosure
- 45.03 Restrictions on activities during and after employment
- 45.04 Unauthorized compensation and transactions
- 45.05 Conflict of interest with respect to public contracts
  - (A) Prohibited conduct
  - (B) Public contract, family members and business associates, interest in contract
  - (C) Exemption, limited interest as shareholder or creditor
  - (D) Exemption, arm's length transaction
- 45.06 Examples of permitted and prohibited transactions involving public contracts
  - (A) Permitted transactions
  - (B) Prohibited transactions
- 45.07 Conflict of interest with respect to textbooks and publishers
- 45.08 Compatible and incompatible offices
  - (A) In general
  - (B) Incompatibility arising from potential conflict of interest involving public contracts

MISCELLANEOUS PROHIBITIONS AFFECTING EDUCATION PERSONNEL

45.09　Ethics violations in criminal code, generally
45.10　Theft in office
45.11　Soliciting or receiving improper compensation
45.12　Dereliction of duty
45.13　Interfering with civil rights
45.14　Political activity by classified civil servants

Chapter 46
Liability of Schools, Officers, and Employees

LIABILITY UNDER STATE LAW

46.01　School district liability for tort claims
　　　(A) Sovereign immunity
　　　(B) Ohio Public Liability Act
　　　(C) Liability of school districts
　　　(D) Governmental and proprietary functions
46.02　Defenses to claims
46.03　Immunity of personnel
46.04　School board's duty to defend and indemnify employees
46.05　Limitation of actions, limits on damages, pleading
46.06　Damages
46.07　Payment of judgments
46.08　Contract claims
46.09　Injunctive relief
46.10　Liability for hazing
46.11　Liability to recreational users
46.12　Moral obligation doctrine

LIABILITY FOR FEDERAL CIVIL RIGHTS VIOLATIONS

46.13　Federal civil rights violations
　　　(A) In general
　　　(B) Scope of 42 USCA 1983
　　　(C) State and federal claims, limitation of actions, damages
46.14　Violation of constitutional rights giving rise to section 1983 liability
　　　(A) Procedural due process
　　　　　(1) Students
　　　　　(2) Employees
　　　(B) Substantive due process
　　　(C) First Amendment freedoms
　　　(D) Freedom from discrimination
　　　(E) Right to privacy
46.15　Liability of board members, officers, and employees for civil rights violations
　　　(A) Board members and officers

46.15 Liability of board members, officers, and employees for civil rights violations—*continued*
  (B) Teachers and employees
  (C) Qualified immunity
46.16 Recovery of attorney fees

INSURANCE AND INDEMNIFICATION
46.17 Authority of school board to provide for insurance, in general
  (A) Purchase of insurance
  (B) Self-insurance
  (C) Providing for insurance not waiver of immunity or defense
46.18 Joint self-insurance pool
  (A) In general
  (B) Reserves, report to superintendent of insurance
  (C) Administration of pool
  (D) Costs and funding, bond issue
  (E) Property and casualty insurance
  (F) Effect of collective bargaining agreement
46.19 Liability insurance for personnel
46.20 Automobile insurance
46.21 Student accident insurance

Chapter 47
Search and Seizure

47.01 Fourth Amendment standards
  (A) Standards for student searches by school officials
  (B) Police involvement in search
  (C) Use of drug-detecting dogs
  (D) Standards for employee searches by school officials
47.02 Locker searches
47.03 Liability for unlawful search

NONPUBLIC SCHOOL SYSTEM

Chapter 48
Private and Parochial Schools

48.01 Private and parochial schools defined
  (A) In general
  (B) Proprietary schools distinguished

STATE REGULATION
48.02 Right of private and parochial schools to exist
48.03 Minimum state standards for private and parochial schools
  (A) In general

48.03 Minimum state standards for private and parochial schools—*continued*
    (B) Requirement that standards be reasonable
48.04 Compulsory school attendance, employment of minors
    (A) In general
    (B) School calendar
    (C) Report of students in attendance
    (D) Age and schooling certificates
48.05 Annual progress reports to state department of education

STATE AID

48.06 State aid to parochial schools, constitutional limitations
    (A) Constitutional limitations, generally
    (B) Aid for testing and reporting
    (C) Teaching on parochial school premises
    (D) Aid to disadvantaged students
48.07 Aid provided in Ohio
48.08 Transportation of private and parochial school students
    (A) Transportation at public expense
    (B) Transportation by school

ADMISSION TO PRIVATE SCHOOLS, RECORDS

48.09 Admission, nondiscrimination
    (A) In general
    (B) Post-secondary options program
48.10 Records upon admission
48.11 Enrollment contracts
    (A) Contents
    (B) Interpretation
48.12 Tuition: payment and recovery
48.13 Withholding transcript for nonpayment of tuition and fees
48.14 Inspection and release of student records

CONDUCT AND DISCIPLINE OF STUDENTS

48.15 Conduct and discipline in general
48.16 Private schools and the requirement of due process
48.17 Search and seizure
48.18 Freedom of speech and press

EMPLOYMENT

48.19 Employment of teaching and nonteaching personnel, generally
48.20 Verification of identity and work authorization
48.21 Teacher certification
48.22 Compensation, fringe benefits, retirement
48.23 Unemployment compensation, workers' compensation
48.24 Breach of employment contract
    (A) In general

48.24 Breach of employment contract—*continued*
    (B) Breach induced by third party
48.25 Dismissal of employee under contract
48.26 Dismissal of employee not under contract
48.27 Nonrenewal of contract
48.28 Collective bargaining
    (A) In general
    (B) Parochial schools

DISCRIMINATION BY PRIVATE AND PAROCHIAL SCHOOLS
48.29 Discrimination in programs and activities
48.30 Discrimination in employment

TAX EXEMPTION OF PRIVATE AND PAROCHIAL SCHOOLS
48.31 Federal tax-exempt status of nonpublic schools
48.32 Taxation of unrelated business income
48.33 Exemption from state taxes

LIABILITY
48.34 Tort liability of private schools, officers, and employees
    (A) In general
    (B) Tort liability of private school employees
    (C) Tort liability of trustees of private schools

ENVIRONMENTAL ISSUES
48.35 Asbestos in schools

STUDENT ATHLETE ELIGIBILITY
48.36 Ohio High School Athletic Association (OHSAA)

PARENT PROGRAMS
48.37 Block parent program

INTRODUCTION—GOVERNANCE

Chapter 1

Historical Perspective

1.01 The new republic and the idea of universal education
1.02 Northwest Territory and school lands
1.03 First schools in Ohio
1.04 Ohio Constitution of 1802
1.05 Inadequacy of school lands income and advent of school taxes
1.06 Early education for the handicapped
1.07 Horace Mann and the common school movement
1.08 Common school movement in Ohio
1.09 Ohio Constitution of 1851
1.10 Secondary education and completion of the public school framework

1.01 The new republic and the idea of universal education

The need for education for all was one of the more pervasive themes in the politics of the new nation following the Revolution. It was widely held that education was a necessary ingredient to the success of the new republic. George Washington touched on this point in his farewell address in 1796: "Promote then as an object of primary importance institutions for the general diffusion of knowledge. In proportion as the structure of a government gives force to public opinion, it is essential that public opinion should be enlightened." In promoting a scheme for universal education in Virginia (which failed), Thomas Jefferson noted that it would enable the people to "understand their rights, to maintain them, and to exercise with intelligence their parts in self-government."[1]

The more radical thinkers, such as Jefferson, stumped for universal education paid for out of the public purse. John Adams agreed: "The whole people must take upon themselves the education of the whole people, and must be willing to bear the expenses of it."[2] Others were not willing to go quite this far. Jefferson's plan for a public school system supported by taxation was turned down in Virginia twice in his lifetime.[3]

1.02 Northwest Territory and school lands

The famous Northwest Ordinance of 1787 succinctly stated the fundamental republican tenet on education: "Religion, morality, and knowledge being necessary to good government and the happiness of mankind, schools and the means of education shall be forever encouraged."[4]

The means for encouraging education were provided in the land ordinances of 1784 and 1787, which directed the survey and disposition of the land in the Northwest Territory, and which mandated that section 16 in every township (or an equivalent amount of land elsewhere) be set aside for the support of schools.

The hope was, of course, that the income from these lands would be sufficient to operate a school system without the necessity for levying taxes. Experience had demonstrated the unpopularity (and political dangers) of taxation. Massachusetts had required each of its towns and districts to maintain a school with public funds since as early as 1642, but the local inhabitants proved reluctant to dip very deeply into their pockets. Some towns shirked the duty altogether, having found that it was cheaper to pay the fine for non-

---

[1] Quoted in Lawrence A. Cremin, *American Education: The National Experience 1783-1876*, at 107 (Harper & Row 1980).
[2] Letter from John Adams to John Jebb (September 10, 1785), 9 *Works of John Adams* 540.

[3] 2 *Adams-Jefferson Letters* 477-78 (Lester J. Cappon ed 1959).
[4] "Ordinance for the Government of Territory Northwest of the River Ohio," passed by the United States Congress, July 13, 1787.

compliance than to hire a schoolmaster.[5] Thomas Jefferson's plan (as well as similar plans proposed by others) for a tax-supported school system in Virginia could not garner the necessary support for adoption.

1.03 First schools in Ohio

The first schools in the Northwest Territory, and in Ohio after it became a state, were private ventures or sectarian schools rather than public institutions.

In 1789, some of the more well-to-do families in Belpre hired a schoolmarm to teach their younger children and later in the year hired a man to teach the older boys and girls. The first schoolhouse was built by John Reily at Columbia (near present-day Cincinnati), who opened his school in 1790.[6]

The early Ohio schools in fact followed the general pattern in the settled East. That is, they charged tuition, although sometimes they accepted the children of the poor free of charge.[7] Tuition more often than not was paid in kind, such as by providing room and board to the schoolmaster.

1.04 Ohio Constitution of 1802

When Ohio became a state, its new Constitution echoed the mandate of the Northwest Ordinance that schools and the means of instruction be encouraged forever.[8] In addition, the Bill of Rights of the new Constitution contained a provision which strongly suggests that the private venture and sectarian schools of the time had not been living up to the ideal of providing universal education:

> [N]o law shall be passed to prevent the poor in the several counties and townships within this state from an equal participation in the schools, academies, colleges and universities within this state which are endowed, in whole or in part, from the revenue arising from donations made by the United States, for the support of schools and colleges; doors of the said schools, academies and universities, shall be open for the reception of scholars, students and teachers, of every grade, without any distinction or preference whatever, contrary to the intent for which said donations were made.

Apparently, the poor were being shut out, as they had largely been shut out of education in the East for several generations, except where benevolent societies or churches provided free schools (often called "pauper schools"). In fact, the first free school was not opened in Ohio until 1836, in Cleveland.[9] The message to the schools in the Constitution of 1802 was, therefore, "If you want public money, you must do your part to provide universal education for rich and poor alike."

1.05 Inadequacy of school lands income and advent of school taxes

The idea of using the income from public lands in lieu of taxes to support the schools was a good one, but it did not work well in practice.

In 1817, the Ohio General Assembly authorized leasing the school lands for ninety-nine years, renewable forever, for rents fixed at six per cent of value, with the proceeds to be placed in a permanent trust fund for distribution to the schools. Unfortunately, some land was poor and its value low. Also, since abundant land was available for purchase, many people preferred to buy their own land rather than rent school lands.

In any case, the income from school lands was inadequate. Moreover, management of the school lands was a considerable burden. As a consequence, Congress (with some arm twisting) in 1826 authorized their sale, with the proceeds to be placed in a permanent trust fund and the income doled out for support of the schools in the area in which the lands were located.[10] The proceeds were disappointing—some land was

---

[5]Adolphe E. Meyer, *An Educational History of the Western World* 200 (McGraw-Hill 1972).
[6]James J. Burns, *The Educational History of Ohio* (Historical Publishing Co of Columbus 1905).
[7]James J. Burns, *The Educational History of Ohio* (Historical Publishing Co of Columbus 1905).

[8]O Const of 1802, Art VIII, § 3.
[9]James J. Burns, *The Educational History of Ohio* (Historical Publishing Co of Columbus 1905).
[10]IV US Stat at Large 138.

sold for as little as five cents per acre, when it could be sold at all.[11] As late as 1917, the school lands trust fund contained only $4.3 million.[12]

The general assembly reluctantly bowed to the inevitable and began to authorize school taxes. In 1825, county commissioners were directed to levy a real property tax of one-half mill for the use of the schools.[13] In 1829, the City of Cincinnati was granted a school charter providing for an organized, tax-supported system of free schools.[14] And, in 1838, the first law authorizing a tax to purchase land to build a schoolhouse was enacted.[15]

1.06 Early education for the handicapped

Ohio was one of the pioneering states in education for handicapped persons and began providing for such education even before the public school system as a whole was organized along modern lines.

In 1827, the general assembly permitted the incorporation of the Ohio Asylum for Educating the Deaf and Dumb. Its eight trustees were directed to investigate the proper location, construction, and plan of organization and government for schools to be built by public funds.

In 1835, a census was taken of the blind persons in the state, and in 1837 a school for the blind was opened in Columbus, with five pupils present in a classroom in the Presbyterian Church. That same year money was appropriated to build a school and to begin operation.

1.07 Horace Mann and the common school movement

Simply stated, the idea of the common schools was to provide a system of tax-supported schools, free to all, subject to compulsory attendance laws, and supervised by the state to insure achievement of educational goals. In short, the common schools were the genesis of the public school system we know today.[16]

The movement was largely the result of the work of Horace Mann in Massachusetts. The school system first ordained by the Puritans in 1642 had fallen into decay, largely (it was believed) because control had been decentralized and placed in the hands of local towns and districts with no oversight from higher authority. To find solutions, the Massachusetts legislature in 1837 created a state board of education, and Horace Mann was appointed as its executive secretary.[17]

Mann's investigations showed that the district schools lacked trained teachers and that the town and district school committees generally shirked their duties to prescribe textbooks, enforce attendance, and regularly oversee the operation of the schools in their jurisdiction. He prescribed a number of remedial measures which were enacted into law, but not without bitter opposition. It was not until 1841 that his reforms were firmly in place.[18]

Much of the opposition to Mann's reforms arose from the fact that they imposed supervision from the state level at the expense of local autonomy and also cost more money. Mann overcame this opposition by his knack for equating a public school system with republican traditions of providing equal opportunity for all and by stressing the importance of education in a self-governing society.[19]

---

[11] 3rd Annual Report of Superintendent of Common Schools, 36th Ohio General Assembly, Doc 17, at 41.

[12] Edward Alanson Miller, *The History of Educational Legislation in Ohio from 1803 to 1850* (University of Chicago Press 1920).

[13] 23 Laws of Ohio 36.

[14] 27 Laws of Ohio 33.

[15] Edward Alanson Miller, *The History of Educational Legislation in Ohio* (University of Chicago Press 1920).

[16] See Adolphe E. Meyer, *An Educational History of the Western World* 395 (McGraw-Hill 1972).

[17] Henry J. Perkinson, *Two Hundred Years of American Educational Thought* 62 (David McKay Co 1976).

[18] Henry J. Perkinson, *Two Hundred Years of American Educational Thought* 62, at 71 (David McKay Co 1976).

[19] Henry J. Perkinson, *Two Hundred Years of American Educational Thought* 62, at 78 (David McKay Co 1976).

1.08 Common school movement in Ohio

Horace Mann was indefatigable in writing about his ideas and in corresponding with other "friends of education" throughout the country. In Ohio, these "friends of education" included a number of influential citizens, such as Catherine Beecher and her brother-in-law, Calvin Stowe, a clergyman and husband of Harriet Beecher Stowe.

The "friends of education" began a campaign to adopt a common school system in Ohio. Their first effort was aimed at providing supervision of the schools, and by a close vote the office of state superintendent of schools was created in 1837.[20]

The politics of education were highly volatile, although they did not follow party lines. The vote in the Ohio House on the superintendent's bill included nearly equal numbers of Whigs and Democrats on both sides of the issue.[21] As time went on, and it became evident that the common school system in Massachusetts was working, both parties embraced the idea—the Democrats because they saw the common schools as the means by which the poor could advance in life, and the Whigs because they saw education as the means for civilizing the baser instincts of the people.[22]

1.09 Ohio Constitution of 1851

The common school movement culminated in Ohio with adoption of a constitutional mandate to create and maintain a "thorough and efficient" system of common schools. When the revised Constitution was adopted in 1851, the original requirements of the Northwest Ordinance and the Constitution of 1802 to "encourage schools and the means of instruction" were retained.[23] In addition, the new Constitution contained the following measures:

> VI § 1 Funds for education and religious purposes
>
> The principal of all funds, arising from the sale, or other disposition of lands, or other property, granted or entrusted to this State for educational and religious purposes, shall be used or disposed of in such manner as the General Assembly shall prescribe by law.
>
> VI § 2 Common school fund to be raised; how controlled
>
> The General Assembly shall make such provisions, by taxation, or otherwise, as, with the income arising from the school trust fund, will secure a thorough and efficient system of common schools throughout the State; but, no religious or other sect, or sects, shall ever have any exclusive right to, or control of, any part of the school funds of this State.
>
> VI § 3 Public school system
>
> Provision shall be made by law for the organization, administration and control of the public school system of the state supported by public funds; provided, that each school district embraced wholly or in part within any city shall have the power by referendum vote to determine for itself the number of members and the organization of the district board of education, and provision shall be made by law for the exercise of this power by such school districts.
>
> VI § 4 State board of education; superintendent of public instruction
>
> There shall be a state board of education which shall be selected in such manner and for such terms as shall be provided by law. There shall be a superintendent of public instruction, who shall be appointed by the state board of education. The respective powers and duties of the board and of the superintendent shall be prescribed by law.

These sections include the key features of the common school movement: a statewide, free public school system, supported by taxation (and, in Ohio, the income from the school lands trust fund), plus supervision from the state level of the local schools.

---

[20]Lawrence A. Cremin, *American Education: The National Experience 1783-1876,* at 173 (Harper & Row 1980).

[21]Lawrence A. Cremin, *American Education: The National Experience 1783-1876,* at 173-74 (Harper & Row 1980).

[22]Henry J. Perkinson, *Two Hundred Years of American Educational Thought* 71-72 (David McKay Co 1976).

[23]O Const Art I §7.

Section 2 laid to rest an argument that had been raging since 1789—the use of public money to maintain sectarian schools. A given religious body was not adverse to receiving public support, and many such bodies claimed (and usually received) a share of the public largesse. The several sects disapproved, however, of distributing public funds to other sects, on the grounds that the money was being used to spread false doctrine. Moreover, a considerable body of opinion maintained that supporting sectarian schools out of the public treasury violated the spirit if not the letter of the prohibition in the federal Constitution against the establishment of religion.[24] The controversy was widespread in the first years of the republic and was addressed in most states by prohibiting sectarian control of public schooling and school funds.[25] The effect was to insure that the common schools would be secular.

With the adoption of Article VI in the Constitution of 1851, the foundation of the public school system of today was laid.

1.10 Secondary education and completion of the public school framework

During most of the colonial period, secondary education was limited to a few "Latin grammar schools" which taught Latin and Greek (and sometimes Hebrew), plus the classics. They were, in essence, college preparatory schools, whose narrow curriculums appealed mainly to those planning to enter the ministry or the law. By the middle of the eighteenth century, the Latin grammar schools were being replaced by private venture schools or academies catering to the sons (and daughters) of the new merchant class and offering a range of subjects more attuned to their wants and needs. These subjects included commercial courses, modern languages, geography, and history, and, for the girls, art, music, needlework, and penmanship.[26] By the nineteenth century, these academies in their turn began to yield to the public high schools, partly because they remained in private or sectarian hands and were available only to the children of the well-to-do, and partly because their curriculums did not keep pace with the needs of a burgeoning industrial society.[27] By the 1840s, the demand had become insistent for education beyond the elementary level in the public schools, offering more utilitarian and practical instruction than the academies. Public high schools thus began to appear in increasing numbers.

The first public high school in Ohio—Central Public High School in Cleveland—opened its doors in 1846 in the basement of the Universalist Church. Its first principal was paid the grand sum of $500 per year.[28]

The real growth of secondary education in public high schools came on the heels of the growth of the national industrial complex following the Civil War. In 1890, approximately seven per cent of children age fourteen to seventeen in the United States attended a public high school; in 1930, the percentage was fifty per cent; and in 1970, it was ninety-four per cent. As one authority points out, this very nearly amounts to universal secondary education.[29]

Thomas Jefferson worked hard to achieve universal elementary education but did not live to see it.[30] His vision did not extend to universal secondary education, since he saw education beyond the elementary level as limited to the more promising students.[31]

Given his profound belief in the necessity of education to maintain a free society, however, Jefferson would doubtless be pleased to see that the public school system today includes both elementary and secondary education for all.

---

[24]US Const Am 1.

[25]R. Freeman Butts, *The Education of the West* 410-11 (McGraw-Hill Co 1973).

[26]R. Freeman Butts, *The Education of the West* 414-16 (McGraw-Hill Co 1973).

[27]R. Freeman Butts, *The Education of the West* 414-16 (McGraw-Hill Co 1973).

[28]James J. Burns, *The Educational History of Ohio* (Historic Publishing Co of Columbus 1905).

[29]R. Freeman Butts, *The Education of the West* 435 (McGraw-Hill 1973).

[30]See Text 1.01, The new republic and the idea of universal education.

[31]2 *Adams-Jefferson Letters* 477-78 (Lester J. Cappon ed 1959).

Chapter 2

Ohio's School System: An Overview

2.01 Introduction

OHIO'S SCHOOLS
2.02 Public schools and pupils
2.03 Nonpublic schools and pupils
2.04 School personnel
2.05 Curriculums and special programs

FUNDING THE SCHOOL SYSTEM
2.06 Cost of education
2.07 Sources of revenue

GOVERNING THE SCHOOLS
2.08 Role of school districts and boards of education
2.09 Roles of the state board of education and superintendent of public instruction
2.10 Interaction between Ohio and other states

EDUCATION AND THE FEDERAL GOVERNMENT
2.11 Role of the federal government
2.12 Federal aid
2.13 Conditions of federal aid, nondiscrimination

SCHOOL LAW AND ITS SOURCES
2.14 Constitutional mandates
2.15 Statutes
2.16 Court decisions
2.17 Attorney general opinions

2.01 Introduction

The structure of Ohio's school system reflects the key features of the "common schools" advocated by Horace Mann beginning in 1837 and mandated by the Ohio Constitution in 1851. The system provides education for all at public expense and is characterized by local control and state supervision.[1] Elementary and secondary education in Ohio today is a mammoth undertaking. A total of 4,609 public and nonpublic schools served 2,061,921 elementary, secondary, and vocational students in the 1994-95 school year.

OHIO'S SCHOOLS

2.02 Public schools and pupils

Ohio's public schools include elementary schools, junior high and middle schools, senior high schools, and vocational and technical high schools, organized to provide both elementary and secondary education, plus special education. During the 1994-95 school year, over 1.8 million students were served in the Ohio public schools, based on information from the Ohio Department of Education, Division of Computer Information Management Services.

Elementary schools are reserved for grades kindergarten through six, which embrace pupils aged approximately five through twelve. Junior high schools usually include grades seven and eight, or pupils aged approximately thirteen and fourteen. Middle schools usually include grades six, seven, and eight, and occasionally grades seven, eight, and nine. Senior high schools normally include grades nine through twelve, or students aged approximately fifteen through eighteen. The nomenclature of the schools does not affect curriculums, since courses of study are prescribed according to grades.[2] Elementary schools comprise nearly two-thirds of the total number of public schools. This reflects the usual (but not universal) practice of having two or more lower schools feed a single high school.

Schools devoted to vocational and technical training may be maintained by a general school district or by a joint vocational school district. These schools are for grades

---

[1] See Text 1.06, Early education for the handicapped; Text 1.08, Common school movement in Ohio.

[2] See Text 26.04, Requirement and content of curriculum; Text 26.05, Curriculum for kindergarten through grade eight; Text 26.06, High school curriculum.

nine through twelve, although many also offer post-secondary training.

2.03 Nonpublic schools and pupils

Elementary and secondary education is not the exclusive province of the public schools—a significant number of children attend private and parochial schools.[3] During the 1994-95 year, over 225,000 students were educated in non-public schools in Ohio. About one in every six elementary school children and about one in every ten high school students attend a private or parochial school.

Of the total number of elementary school students in Ohio, 15.50% attend nonpublic schools. The total number of junior high/middle school and high school students in the state includes 6.82% in private or parochial schools. Overall, 11.46% of the elementary and secondary school students in Ohio attend nonpublic schools.

2.04 School personnel

During the 1994-95 school year there were 104,118 teachers in Ohio public schools, providing a student-teacher ratio of approximately 17.4 to 1. Teachers must be certified by the state department of education,[4] and the required qualifications for the different types and grades of certificates include various combinations of undergraduate and postgraduate education, continuing education, and experience.[5] Minimum salaries for teachers are prescribed by statute,[6] although school boards can, and typically do, provide higher salaries. The average salary of a public school teacher in Ohio during 1994-95 was $36,957. Teachers are hired by contract and may acquire tenure after a specified number of years of service.[7]

Each school is authorized one principal and each school district one superintendent. Assistant principals and superintendents may also be employed, as well as other administrators. Administrators also must be certified and hired by contract.[8]

In addition to teachers and administrators, schools may employ clerical staff, maintenance personnel, food service workers, and other personnel as necessary. In the public schools, nonteaching personnel are also hired by contract.[9]

2.05 Curriculums and special programs

Ohio schools must provide a "graded course of study" from kindergarten through grade twelve. Minimum standards are prescribed in some detail by the state board of education and include the courses to be taught, the length of the school day, and the number of days in the school year. Boards of education have considerable leeway in supplementing, as well as implementing, the basic instruction provided by the minimum standards. A comparatively new feature is the requirement for "competency-based education," an intensive program designed to increase student skills in reading, composition, and mathematics and insure that they actually attain competence in these skills.[10]

In addition to the regular course of study, Ohio public schools also provide vocational and technical education and maintain special programs for the handicapped.[11]

FUNDING THE SCHOOL SYSTEM

2.06 Cost of education

By any standard, Ohio's school system is a massive enterprise. This is strikingly demonstrated by its cost. The Ohio Department of Education, Division of Information Management Services compiles finan-

---

[3]See Text Ch 48, Private and Parochial Schools.

[4]See Text Ch 8, Teachers: Certification and Appointment.

[5]See Text Ch 8, Teachers: Certification and Appointment.

[6]See Text Ch 10, Teachers: Compensation, Fringe Benefits, and Leave.

[7]See Text Ch 9, Teachers: Contracts and Tenure.

[8]See Text Ch 7, School Administrators.

[9]See Text Ch 12, Nonteaching Personnel: Introduction.

[10]See Text Ch 26, Curriculum and Educational Programs.

[11]See Text Ch 27, Vocational Education and Programs; Text Ch 28, Education for Children with Disabilities; Text Ch 29, Administration of Programs for the Retarded and Developmentally Disabled.

cial data for the school system. According to the Department, expenditures in the 1993-94 school year were $4,640 per pupil from general funds and $5,035 per pupil from all funds, excluding joint vocational high school pupils, nonpublic transportation, and auxiliary service money. Vocational education is more expensive. In the 1993-94 school year expenditures by joint vocational high schools were $6,959 per pupil from general funds and $7,177 per pupil from all funds. Per pupil expenditures vary from district to district.

In 1993-94, a total of $8.7 billion was spent on elementary and secondary education in Ohio public schools, with an additional $272 million spent on education in the joint vocational high schools. These figures include aid to private and parochial schools, which is administered through the public school districts.[12] Although significant, this aid represents a comparatively small item in nonpublic school budgets, so that the total spent on elementary and secondary education in Ohio is, in reality, significantly higher than the amounts given above for the public schools.

RC 103.143 requires the legislative budget office of the legislative service commission to review any bill introduced in either house of the general assembly and given second consideration under the rules of that house and to determine whether the bill would result in a net additional cost to, among other specified entities, school districts from any new or expanded program or service districts would be required to perform or administer under the bill. If such a net additional cost would result, a local impact statement giving the "most accurate probable estimate possible" of the additional cost in dollars must be prepared and considered before the bill is voted out of committee, unless voted out by a two-thirds vote of the committee's membership. To assist in preparing the local impact statement, school districts may be required to provide certain information. RC 103.143 also provides for an annual report on the local impact of all laws passed by both houses of the general assembly in the preceding year.

In addition, RC 105.46 requires the state and local government commission of Ohio to report on December 31, 1996 and every fourth year thereafter on existing mandates affecting, among other specified entities, school districts, the cost of such mandates, the need for eliminating or modifying obsolete mandates, and suggestions for funding mandates. Provisions also appear in RC 199.03 and RC 127.18, pertaining to the adoption and implementation of administrative regulations, that require taking into account the fiscal effect on school districts.

2.07 Sources of revenue

The major sources of funding for the schools are local property taxes, state foundation program and other state funds, and federal aid.[13] The Department of Education, Division of Information Management Services, shows the following revenue per pupil and sources for the 1993-94 school year.

Source	Revenue (1993-94) Schools other than Joint Vocational Schools	Joint Vocational Schools
Local taxes and other local sources	$4,356,121,673	$169,945,061
State foundation program and other state aid	$3,767,391,841	$124,844,763
Federal aid	$ 522,662,332	$ 5,049,532
Total	$8,646,175,846	$299,839,356

According to the above table, local revenues for schools other than joint vocational schools were 50% of the total. State aid provided 43% and federal aid 6%. The relative percentages furnished by local and state revenues actually vary considerably from district to district. Wealthier districts have higher property valuations and tend to vote higher school taxes, and the school revenue generated locally is therefore higher. State funds are allocated according to a formula designed partly to smooth out inequalities in local funding, so that the

---

[12]See Text Ch 32, Religion and the Public Schools; Text Ch 48, Private and Parochial Schools.

[13]See Text Ch 39, Sources of Revenue.

poorer districts receive a higher proportion of state funds than wealthier districts.[14]

GOVERNING THE SCHOOLS

2.08 Role of school districts and boards of education

School districts are the basic building blocks of the state school system. There are several types, listed in the table below. City, exempted village, and local school districts are self-contained units, each offering a complete course of both elementary and secondary education to the community it serves. School district boundaries are fixed by, or subject to the approval of, the state board of education and in some cases may be subject to referendum.[15]

The governing body of a school district is the board of education, composed of members elected from the district. For educational service centers, which replaced county school districts in 1995, the governing board serves this function. The board has broad authority to govern the schools within the district and to acquire, manage, and dispose of property for the operation of the schools. The board holds the purse strings and has the power to levy taxes and borrow, appropriate, and spend the money necessary to operate the schools in its district.[16]

2.09 Roles of the state board of education and superintendent of public instruction

The state board of education and the superintendent of public instruction are offices created by the Ohio Constitution.[17] The state board has broad policy-making powers and is charged with overall planning, implementation, and evaluation of the school system.[18] The superintendent of public instruction is responsible for carrying out the policies and programs of the state board. The Ohio department of education is the administrative unit for the state, and the superintendent of public instruction acts as its executive head.[19]

2.10 Interaction between Ohio and other states

RC 3301.48 and RC 3301.49 authorize Ohio to join the interstate compact for education. The stated purposes of the compact are to establish and maintain cooperation among educational leaders, to provide a forum for discussion and a clearinghouse for information on educational matters, and to facilitate improvement in state and local educational systems. Each state which is a party to the compact is granted seven seats on the governing commission.

In addition, under RC 3333.40 and RC 3333.41 Ohio is a party to the Midwestern Higher Education Compact whose purpose is to provide for greater higher educational opportunities and services in the Midwest. Each state which is a party to the Compact is granted five seats on the governing commission.

EDUCATION AND THE FEDERAL GOVERNMENT

2.11 Role of the federal government

(A) In general

The US Constitution does not mention education. This does not mean that the federal government has no role in education. On the contrary, it has an important role and considerable impact, primarily through financial aid.

Notable among past federal programs benefiting education are (1) land grants under the Northwest Ordinance of 1787; (2) the Morrill Act of 1862, setting up land-grant colleges, chiefly to promote agriculture and the mechanical arts; (3) government-financed vocational training in high

---

[14]See Text 39.06 to 39.09.
[15]See Text Ch 4, School Districts.
[16]See Text Ch 5, Boards of Education; Text Ch 35, School Supplies and Food Service; Text Ch 36, Acquiring and Disposing of Property; Text Ch 37, Construction and Repair of School Buildings; Text Ch 38, Management and Use of School Property; Text Ch 40, Tax Budget, Tax Levies, and Appropriations; Text Ch 41, Borrowing Money.
[17]O Const Art VI §4.
[18]See Text 3.03, Powers and duties of state board of education.
[19]See Text Ch 3, State Administration of Elementary and Secondary Education.

schools during World War I; and (4) the extensive training and education provided under the GI Bill of Rights after World War II, for which $14.5 billion was appropriated. Current programs are discussed below.[20]

In 1979, Congress created a separate department of education in the executive branch of the federal government. The apparent purposes of the legislation were to eliminate confusing lines of authority and administration and to improve the federal effort in education, which Congress determined was hampered by its burial in the department of health, education and welfare. Nonetheless, Congress reiterated a determination to stick to the constitutional principle that the federal role is limited to supplementing, not supplanting, state and local prerogatives in determining their educational programs.[21] The department of education is administered by the secretary of education, appointed by the President with the advice and consent of the Senate.[22]

(B) Goals 2000: Educate America Act

The Goals 2000: Educate America Act of 1994[23] constitutes a rather grandiose effort at the federal level to provide a national framework for education reform throughout the United States. It authorizes the certification of voluntary national education standards as to what students should know and emphasizes the need for comprehensive, "systemic" reform.

Goals 2000 establishes the following "national education goals" to be realized by the year 2000:

(1) All children in America will start school ready to learn;

(2) The national high school graduation rate will increase to at least 90%;

(3) All students will leave grades 4, 8, and 12 with demonstrated competency in certain specified subject areas;

(4) Teachers will have access to programs for improving their skills and the opportunity to acquire the knowledge and skills to instruct and prepare students for the next century;

(5) American students will be first in the world in mathematics and science achievement;

(6) Every adult American will be literate and able to compete in a global economy and exercise the rights and responsibilities of citizenship;

(7) Every school will be free of illicit drugs, violence, and the unauthorized presence of firearms and alcohol, and will offer a disciplined environment conducive to learning; and

(8) Every school will promote partnerships with parents that will ensure parental involvement and participation in educating their children.

To further these programs and monitor progress, a national education goals panel is created. Goals 2000 also creates a national education standards and improvement council charged with the responsibility to certify and review voluntary national content standards (that is, content-based descriptions of knowledge and skills that students should acquire in particular subject areas), student performance standards, and "opportunity-to-learn" standards, and to certify state standards in these areas. To promote higher student achievement through the use of technology, the department of education is responsible for developing a national long-range technology plan. Goals 2000 also creates a national skills standards board to stimulate the development and adoption of a voluntary national system of skill standards for various "occupational clusters." The secretary of education is also obligated to carry out an international education program that provides for the study of international education programs and delivery systems and an international education exchange program. Within the education department, an office of educational research and improvement is established to coordinate federal efforts to improve education.

New funding allotments are provided to state educational agencies that successfully apply and furnish certain required assurances. Ultimately, an applicant must, as a condition of ongoing participation, develop a comprehensive and systemic state

---

[20]See Text 2.12, Federal aid.
[21]1979 US Code Cong & Admin News 1529.
[22]20 USCA 3411.
[23]20 USCA 5801 et seq.

improvement plan for elementary and secondary education in the state. To foster improved parental awareness and involvement, grants are made available to non-profit organizations or such organizations in consortium with local educational agencies.[24]

2.12 Federal aid

The federal government administers numerous programs which provide financial assistance for elementary and secondary education. A listing is contained within the "Catalog of Federal Grant and Aid Programs to State & Local Governments," published by the Advisory Commission on Intergovernmental Relations. In addition, the Omnibus Budget Reconciliation Act of 1981 consolidated some thirty programs, formerly administered by the federal government, into a block grant to be administered through state departments of education. The consolidated programs include Elementary and Secondary Education Act Titles II-IX and Title V of the Higher Education Act of 1965.

The block grant presently involves two types of aid. Chapter I provides funds for disadvantaged students and Chapter II for all public and private school students between the ages of five and seventeen. Congress also provides specific assistance for the education of handicapped children and has prescribed stringent requirements for distribution of the assistance.[25]

2.13 Conditions of federal aid, non-discrimination

Title VI of the Civil Rights Act of 1964[26] prohibits discrimination on the basis of race, color, or national origin by any recipient under any federally funded program. Title IX of the Education Amendments of 1972[27] prohibits discrimination on the basis of sex by any program or activity receiving federal financial aid. Similarly, age discrimination in programs or activities receiving federal aid is forbidden by the Age Discrimination Act of 1975.[28]

The Family Educational Rights and Privacy Act of 1974[29] requires, as a condition of federal financial assistance, that a school district afford parents a right to inspect and review the education records of their children. The Act prescribes stringent requirements with respect to access and disclosure of student records.

Recipients of federal aid and contractors and grantees of federal agencies have affirmative statutory responsibilities to foster a drug-free environment.[30]

SCHOOL LAW AND ITS SOURCES

2.14 Constitutional mandates

Article VI, section 2 of the Ohio Constitution requires the general assembly to make provision for "a thorough and efficient system of common schools throughout the State."[31] In carrying out this mandate, the Ohio Supreme Court has declared the general assembly must be granted "wide discretion" although the discretion is not absolute.[32]

---

[24]For provisions of Goals 2000 applicable to school prayer, the expulsion of students who bring weapons to school, and smoking in indoor facilities, see, respectively, Text 32.05, Establishment through prayer and similar activity; Text 25.10(A), Authority to suspend or expel student; and Text 38.14, Bans on indoor smoking.

[25]See Text Ch 28, Education for Children with Disabilities; Text Ch 29, Administration of Programs for the Retarded and Developmentally Disabled.

[26]42 USCA 2000d to 2000d-4. See Text 19.13(A), Title VI, Civil Rights Act of 1964.

[27]20 USCA 1681 et seq. See Text 19.14, Sex discrimination in education.

[28]42 USCA 6101 et seq. See Text 19.13, Discrimination by recipients of federal financial assistance.

[29]20 USCA 1232g. See Text 44.14 to 44.21.

[30]See Text 21.15, Fostering a drug-free environment.

[31]See Text 1.08, Common school movement in Ohio.

[32]Cincinnati City School Dist Bd of Ed v Walter, 58 OS(2d) 368, 390 NE(2d) 813 (1979), cert denied 444 US 1015, 100 SCt 665, 62 LEd(2d) 644 (1980). A challenge to the state's current funding system, successful at the common pleas level, was reversed by the appeals court. De Rolph v State, No. CA-477, 1995 WL 557316 (5th Dist Ct App, Perry, 8-30-95). The matter is pending in the Ohio Supreme Court.

Article VI, section 4 of the Ohio Constitution requires a state board of education and a state superintendent of public instruction appointed by the state board.[33] Also, the Constitution requires the general assembly to make provision for the organization, administration, and control of a public school system of the state.[34] Article I, section 7 also directs the legislature to "pass suitable laws ... to encourage schools and the means of instruction."

2.15 Statutes

In addition to constitutional provisions, Ohio school law derives from common law (general rules and legal principles established by Ohio's courts), state and federal statutes, rules and regulations of state and federal administrative agencies, including the state board of education, and rules and regulations of local boards of education.

The Ohio Supreme Court has concluded that Ohio's system of local control of education, as mandated by the general assembly, provides a "rational basis supporting the disparity in per-pupil expenditures in Ohio school districts." Taxpayers within each school district determine how much money they are willing to authorize to support education and determine how the tax dollars are spent through the process of electing a board of education. Thus, "each school district can develop programs to meet perceived local needs."[35]

2.16 Court decisions

(A) State courts

Courts do not interfere in legislative matters except where legislative enactments violate basic law. Under the doctrine of judicial review, courts may determine whether the enactments of the general assembly are valid. The courts may use their judicial power to require other branches of government and public officers to conform to basic law and to compel the performance of duties imposed on them.[36]

Judicial decisions establish legal precedents which are followed within the jurisdiction of the court until the rule has been changed by the court or a higher court. One court has noted that "legal precedents provide a guiding principle in the presenting and arguing of cases, as well as in their decisions."[37] Many decisions of common pleas courts and courts of appeals are not published. Nevertheless, such unreported decisions may be cited as authority, and those within the jurisdiction to which a decision applies are considered to be on notice of the decision's legal determinations.[38]

While a common pleas court or court of appeals is not bound to follow the decisions of a court in another jurisdiction, some nonbinding decisions may be persuasive. Likewise, decisions of courts of other states, while not binding on Ohio courts, will sometimes be considered.[39] Frequently, however, the statutes of other states are so markedly different that judicial decisions of such states provide no assistance in interpreting Ohio statutes.

(B) Federal courts

While education remains primarily a function of state and local government, the federal courts have increasingly become a forum for persons challenging the actions of school officials.[40] The impact of these courts on education will continue to be significant in such areas as student rights, desegregation, employment opportunity, and education of the handicapped.

Education per se is not among the rights afforded explicit or implicit protection by the federal Constitution.[41] Nevertheless, the US Supreme Court and federal courts

---

[33]See Text Ch 3, State Administration of Elementary and Secondary Education.
[34]O Const Art VI §3.
[35]Cincinnati City School Dist Bd of Ed v Walter, 58 OS(2d) 368, 380, 390 NE(2d) 813 (1979), cert denied 444 US 1015, 100 SCt 665, 62 LEd(2d) 644 (1980).
[36]State ex rel Scott v Masterson, 173 OS 402, 405, 183 NE(2d) 376 (1962).
[37]State v George, 50 App(2d) 297, 308, 362 NE(2d) 1223 (Franklin 1975).
[38]State v George, 50 App(2d) 297, 308, 362 NE(2d) 1223 (Franklin 1975).
[39]State ex rel Nead v Nolte, 111 OS 486, 491, 146 NE 51 (1924).
[40]Florian v Highland Local School Dist Bd of Ed, 570 FSupp 1358 (ND Ohio 1983).
[41]San Antonio Independent School Dist v Rodriguez, 411 US 1, 93 SCt 1278, 36 LEd(2d) 16 (1973).

have consistently applied the due process and equal protection clauses of the Fourteenth Amendment to invalidate legislation or action by state or local governmental authorities which deprives any person of a constitutional right or a protected liberty or property interest. For example, in a landmark decision, the Supreme Court held that separate education facilities for minority students were inherently unequal and deprived them of equal protection under the Fourteenth Amendment.[42]

The role of the federal judiciary has become increasingly important in recent years, with many cases arising under 42 USCA 1983, enacted as section 1 of the Civil Rights Act of 1871.[43]

2.17 Attorney general opinions

The Ohio attorney general is the chief law officer or other authorized official of the state and all of its departments. Upon request by a county prosecuting attorney, the attorney general must advise the requesting official with respect to his duties in all complaints, suits, and controversies in which the state of Ohio is, or may become, a party.[44] A board of education may request the city law director or county prosecuting attorney for a written opinion from the attorney general.[45] In the absence of judicial precedent, these opinions serve as a guide to school officials and others in ambiguous areas of the law.

The attorney general has no judicial power. Thus, his opinions are not binding on the courts, although they are entitled to careful consideration and may be persuasive in construing statutes. In actual practice, the opinions are usually followed.

---

[42]Brown v Topeka Bd of Ed, 347 US 483, 74 SCt 686, 98 LEd 873 (1954). See Text Ch 19, Pupils: Desegregation and Nondiscrimination.

[43]See Text Ch 46, Liability of Schools, Officers, and Employees.

[44]RC 109.14.
[45]RC 109.12, RC 3313.35.

Chapter 3

State Administration of Elementary and Secondary Education

3.01 Introduction
3.02 State board of education
3.03 Powers and duties of state board of education
3.04 Department of education
3.05 Superintendent of public instruction: appointment and qualifications
3.06 Duties of superintendent of public instruction
3.07 Other personnel of department of education

3.01 Introduction

The rule-making and executive machinery for state administration of elementary and secondary education consists of the state board of education and the superintendent of public instruction, both of which are offices mandated by the Ohio Constitution,[1] plus a department of education created by the general assembly as the administrative unit.[2] The state board exercises policy-making and supervisory authority over elementary and secondary education in Ohio, through the superintendent of public instruction and the state department of education. The superintendent is the executive head of the department and secretary to and the executive and administrative officer of the state board. RC 103.141 requires the legislative budget office of the legislative service commission, in October of each even-numbered year, to report to specified elected representatives an estimate of the cost to school districts of each school law and state board rule that became effective during the preceding two calendar years.

3.02 State board of education

The Ohio Constitution requires that the state board of education be selected in such manner, for such terms, and have such powers and duties as are prescribed by the general assembly.[3]

(A) Members and qualifications

The state board of education consists of eleven elected and eight appointed members.[4] Each elected member must be a qualified elector residing in and elected from the district he represents.[5] Removal from that district during his tenure creates a vacancy in his office.[6] The appointed members are appointed by the governor with the advice and consent of the senate. Of the eight appointed members, four must represent rural districts. Evidence of satisfaction of that requirement will be established by the appointee's current place of residence and at least one of the following:

- the appointee's child attends or at one time attended school in a rural district;
- the appointee's past or present occupation is associated with one or more rural areas of the state; or
- the appointee has other credentials or experiences demonstrating knowledge and familiarity with rural school districts.[7]

During his term of office, a member may not hold any other public position of trust or profit, such as appointment by a municipal judge as a substitute during the judge's vacation period[8] or service as an administrative law judge in the Social Security Administration;[9] nor may he be an employee or officer of any public or private school, college, university, or other institu-

---

[1] O Const Art VI §4.
[2] RC 3301.13.
[3] O Const Art VI §4.
[4] RC 3301.01, RC 3301.02. In addition, the chairmen of the Ohio Senate and House of Representatives Committees that primarily deal with education are nonvoting ex officio members.
[5] RC 3301.03, RC 3503.01.
[6] RC 3301.06.
[7] RC 3301.03.
[8] RC 3301.03; OAG 65-61.
[9] OAG 91-001. See also Brickner v Voinovich, 977 F(2d) 235 (6th Cir Ohio 1992), cert denied ___ US ___, 113 SCt 2965, 125 LEd(2d) 665 (1993) (rejecting due process claim of member ousted on the basis of the attorney general's opinion).

tion of higher education.[10] No board member, whether elected or appointed, may hold that office for a period longer than two successive terms of four years. Terms are considered successive unless separated by a period of four years or more. The term limit requirement becomes effective January 1, 1996.[11]

(B) Oath of office, term, compensation

Before taking office, each member must subscribe to the official oath of office.[12] The term of office begins on the first day of January immediately following his election or appointment.[13]

The salary of board members is fixed under RC 124.15(J), and each member is entitled to actual and necessary expenses incurred while engaged in the performance of official duties or authorized board business, and while en route to and from his home for such purpose.[14]

(C) Board members as public officials

Members of the state board are public officials subject to applicable provisions of the Ohio Ethics Law[15] and criminal law provisions applying to public officials,[16] including those relating to unlawful interest in contracts.[17]

(D) Business of board, vacancies

The general assembly has made provision for meetings and records to be kept,[18] the manner of transacting business,[19] and the filling of vacancies on the board.[20] The governor is required to appoint a replacement to fill an elected or appointed state board seat within 30 days after the vacancy occurs. A replacement for an elected member serves until the next general election, while the appointed replacement member serves the remainder of the term. The board meets in Columbus[21] unless it chooses to meet elsewhere in Ohio as provided in RC 3301.04. A board member who fails to attend at least three-fifths of the regular and special meetings held by the board during any two-year period forfeits his position.[22]

3.03 Powers and duties of state board of education

Under RC 3301.07 and various other statutes, the state board of education is given several powers, which in sum make it the penultimate authority—after the general assembly—over public education in Ohio.

(A) Policy-making and administration

Planning, policy-making, supervision, and finance of public education head the list of the board's chief functions. With regard to Ohio's public schools generally, as well as adult education, the board is authorized to engage in planning, policy-making, and evaluation of broad scope.[23] It is entrusted with a leadership role in improving public education, and is charged with administering state policies regarding public schools, including the development of a standard of financial reporting to be used by all school districts to make the districts' financial information available to the public in an understandable format that facilitates year-to-year comparisons.[24]

The board must prepare and submit to the budget director biennial budget requests for the state board and its agencies, and for the public schools.[25] In addition, while the general assembly and the United States Congress hold the purse strings, the board (in accordance with statutory requirements) administers and supervises the allocation and distribution of, and accounting for, all state and federal funds in aid of public education. The board may require county auditors and treasurers, as well as school district boards of education, treasurers, teachers, other school officials and employees, and other public officers and employees to submit reports the board

---

[10]RC 3301.03.
[11]RC 3301.02(D).
[12]RC 3.20, RC 3.22, RC 3.23, RC 3301.03.
[13]RC 3301.02.
[14]RC 3301.03.
[15]RC Ch 102.
[16]RC Ch 2921.
[17]RC 2921.42. See Text Ch 45, Ethics Requirements and Education Personnel.

[18]RC 3301.04, RC 3301.05.
[19]RC 3301.05.
[20]RC 3301.06.
[21]RC 3301.13.
[22]RC 3.17.
[23]RC 3301.07(A).
[24]RC 3301.07(B).
[25]RC 3301.07(G).

prescribes concerning the management and condition of such funds.[26]

RC 3301.0717 requires the board to establish and submit to the governor and general assembly "clear and measurable" goals (with specific timetables for their achievement) for programs designed to reduce rates of retention in grade, the need for remedial courses, the student dropout rate, and to improve standardized test scores and the rate of college entry. A progress report to the governor and general assembly must be submitted in July of each odd-numbered year. House Bill 117, the 1995 Budget Act, also requires the state board of education to prepare and submit to the governor and chairs of the house and senate education committees by July 1, 1996 and annually thereafter upon the governor's request by October 1 of the preceding year, a report providing detailed information on the board's efforts to focus its attention on major policy issues and to delegate administrative responsibilities to the state superintendent.[27]

(B) Prescribing standards

The state board's impact on education is perhaps greatest through its power to prescribe minimum standards for all important aspects of elementary and secondary education in the state, including education in private and parochial schools, having due regard to the special needs, methods, and objectives of these schools but only to the extent they do not interfere with providing a high quality, general education.[28] This power includes establishing standards for curricula; competency programs; the certification and assignment of teachers, school administrators, and other professional personnel; instructional materials and equipment; libraries; the organization, supervision, and administration of individual schools; buildings and grounds; health and sanitation services and facilities; admission and promotion or retention of pupils; graduation requirements; "and such other factors as the board finds necessary."[29] The 1995 Budget Bill also provides that the state board may not amend its minimum standards without notice of the proposed changes to the chairs of the house and senate education committees, and unless the proposed changes are approved through the adoption of a concurrent resolution by a majority in both the house and the senate.

The general assembly has also granted the state board broad power to prescribe minimum standards for preschool programs and rules for school child day-care programs operated by boards of education, county MR/DD boards, and certain chartered nonpublic schools.[30] In addition, the state board is required to establish standards of qualification for prekindergarten teaching or associate certification[31] and for the teaching of community service education for credit.[32]

The power to formulate standards is also conferred with respect to specialized areas of education. The board prescribes standards for driver education courses in the high schools.[33] It provides procedures, standards, and guidelines for the education of handicapped children,[34] including programs and services operated by county boards of mental retardation and developmental disabilities, and promotes development of special programs for gifted children.[35]

---

[26]RC 3301.07(C). State aid to individual school districts is calculated in accordance with RC Ch 3317. See Text Ch 39, Sources of Revenue.

[27]RC 3301.111, eff. 9-29-95.

[28]RC 3301.07(D). See Text Ch 26, Curriculum and Educational Programs; Text Ch 48, Private and Parochial Schools.

[29]RC 3301.07(D). The board has discretion in determining whether the daily or regular use of privately produced television programming that contains commercial advertising satisfies the minimum standards the board promulgates. OAG 91-004.

[30]RC 3301.53. By virtue of RC 3301.521, RC 3301.53 to RC 3301.59 do not apply to certain child day care provided on a part-time basis exclusively for participants in an adult education program where a parent is on the premises and readily accessible.

[31]RC 3301.50, RC 3301.51.

[32]RC 3319.231. The statute also requires the state board to provide technical assistance to school districts that provide community service instructional programs for teachers.

[33]RC 3301.07(E). See Text 26.12, Driver training programs.

[34]RC 3301.07(J). See Text Ch 28, Education for Children with Disabilities.

[35]RC 3301.07(K). See Text 26.09, Programs for gifted children.

(C) Organizing and reorganizing school districts

In accordance with statutory procedures and requirements, the state board classifies and charters school districts and individual schools and may revoke charters and dissolve school districts;[36] orders, approves, or disapproves the transfer of territory between certain school districts; makes or supervises an equitable division of funds, property, and indebtedness in connection with such transfers; and proposes the reorganization of certain school districts by consolidation or transfer.[37]

Uncodified § 45.32 of the 1995 Budget Bill requires the number of educational service centers to be reduced. Specifically, by June 1, 1997 any educational service center which serves only one local district, and by June 1, 1999 any service center with an ADM of less than 8,000 must notify the state superintendent of the name of one or more adjacent service centers with which such service centers will merge to form a joint service center.[38] Where the state superintendent does not receive such notice by the required date, the superintendent shall determine one or more suitable adjacent centers for such a merger and shall notify the superintendents and governing boards of all centers involved of his determination. The centers named in the notification, whether voluntarily or as determined by the state superintendent, shall form a joint center pursuant to RC 3311.053.

(D) Evaluation of district and building education performance

City, local, exempted village, and joint vocational school districts are subject to performance evaluations by the state board of education. There are serious repercussions for districts or buildings that come up short and potential rewards, in the form of deregulation, for districts or buildings that especially shine.

The state board must adopt rules that include standards defining "measurable" indicators (such as graduation, attendance, and dropout rates, and levels of literacy and basic competency as assessed by required statewide student proficiency tests) for assessing district and building performance and standards using such indicators for determining whether any district or building is "educationally excellent" or "educationally deficient."[39]

(1) Significance of educational excellence

The state board must annually identify each district and building that meets its adopted standards for educational excellence. If a district or building is so identified, the district board may submit to the state board a list of specific statutory provisions or rules from which the district board desires an exemption for the identified district or building. If the district board employs union-represented teachers, the list must include written consent of the teachers' employee representative designated under RC 4117.04(B). In addition, the list must be limited to any requirement of RC Title 33 or any state board rule adopted under Title 33, except the list may not include any requirement or rule under RC Chapter 3307 (the state teachers retirement system), RC Chapter 3309 (the school employees retirement system), RC 3319.07 to RC 3319.21 (pertaining generally to the employment of teachers and nonteaching employees), or RC Chapter 3323 (pertaining generally to education of the handicapped).

The state board must approve or disapprove each of the requested exemptions in accordance with its approval standards. Approval cannot be for a period of more than five years. Approval must be revoked if the district or building fails for two consecutive years to meet state board standards for educational excellence.[40]

(2) Significance of educational deficiency

The state board must annually identify each district or building that is educationally deficient under its adopted standards. If a district or building is so identified, the district board must be notified of the fact and nature of the deficiency.

---

[36]RC 3301.16, RC 3301.161. See Text 26.19, School charter, revocation.
[37]RC 3301.16, RC Ch 3311. See Text Ch 4, School Districts.
[38]RC 3311.051, RC 3311.053, RC 3311.054.
[39]RC 3302.01. The rules appear in OAC 3301-15-01 et seq.
[40]RC 3302.02.

Within ninety days after receiving notice, the district board, in accordance with state board standards and procedures, must develop and submit to the state board for its approval a "corrective action plan." If the board employs union-represented teachers, the plan must include written consent of the teachers' designated employee representative. The law is not clear on what happens if consent is unreasonably withheld. Upon request, the state board must assist the district board in developing its plan. The plan may request exemptions from specific statutory provisions or rules the district board thinks necessary in order to implement its plan timely and effectively. Any exemption request must include "specific and detailed reasons" why the exemption is necessary. The exemptions that can be requested are restricted in precisely the same ways as the exemptions that may be requested under a finding of educational excellence. The state board must approve or disapprove the submitted plan in accordance with its approval standards. Any exemption from a statutory provision or rule cannot be granted for a period beyond the time the district board is subject to the plan.[41]

Upon approval, the district board must "immediately" implement the plan. In accordance with state board standards and procedures, the district board must evaluate implementation and the effect on educational performance in the district or building, as applicable. The district board must also submit a progress report on implementation 180 days after plan approval and a separate progress report on the effect on educational performance one year after plan approval.

Based on these reports, the state board must determine whether the district board is making satisfactory progress toward eliminating district or building deficiencies, as applicable. If the district board fails to submit either required report, the state board may assume a lack of satisfactory progress.

If the state board determines satisfactory progress is being made, the district board must continue implementation and submit semiannual progress reports. The state board must annually continue to determine whether satisfactory progress is being made. At any time the plan is in effect, the district board may submit revisions for state board approval or disapproval. Again, written consent of the teachers' designated employee representative, if any, is required.

The district board's obligation to maintain implementation and submit semiannual reports continues until the state board either determines that satisfactory progress is not being made (which may be assumed if the district board fails to submit a required report) or releases the district board from its corrective action plan upon state board determination that the district or building is no longer educationally deficient.[42]

If the board of a district or building identified as educationally deficient fails to develop and submit an approved corrective action plan, the state board, with the consent of the district board, will assign one or more "educational experts" to the district to assist in developing a plan. Similarly, if the state board determines (or is entitled to assume) that a district board subject to an approved plan is not making satisfactory progress, the state board will disapprove the existing plan and, with the consent of the district board, assign one or more experts to the district to assist in developing another corrective action plan that meets state board standards. Each expert assigned serves at the district's expense, and the state board will subtract the cost from the foundation program funds paid to the district under RC 3317.022.

Within ninety days after assignment of the first expert, the district must submit a corrective action plan (with written consent of the teachers' designated employee representative, if any). The state board must approve or disapprove the plan. If approved, the district board must immediately implement the plan, and the previously described procedures and requirements for implementation and ultimate release from the plan come into play.[43]

If a district board subject to the assignment of experts fails to consent to such

---

[41]RC 3302.03.
[42]RC 3302.04.

[43]RC 3302.05.

assignment, or fails to submit an approved plan even with such consent, or if the state board determines (or is entitled to assume) the district board subject to an approved plan developed with the assistance of assigned experts is not making satisfactory progress, the district board becomes subject to "monitoring" by the state superintendent of public instruction. Specifically, the state board, upon the recommendation of the state superintendent and after a hearing, may issue an order placing the district board under monitoring. Those entitled to appear at the hearing are district board members, the district superintendent, and the teachers' designated employee representative, if any.

If the state board orders monitoring, the state superintendent must appoint a state monitor to act on his behalf and ensure that an approved corrective action plan is developed and implemented and that satisfactory progress toward eliminating educational deficiencies is made. The state monitor serves at the district's expense, and the state board will subtract the cost from foundation program funds paid to the district under RC 3317.022. On behalf of the district, the state monitor is to develop and implement a corrective action plan that meets state board standards and evaluate its implementation and effect on educational performance in the district or building, as applicable.

While subject to state monitoring, the district board can take no action without the monitor's written approval. Any action taken without such approval is void. In addition, no district employee can take action inconsistent with the corrective action plan in effect. State monitoring will continue until either (1) the state board issues a written order that stipulates monitoring is no longer necessary to ensure district compliance with the corrective action plan in effect and satisfactory progress is being made, releases the district board from monitoring, and requires the district board to implement the corrective action plan in effect; or (2) the state board determines the district or building is no longer educationally deficient, in which case it must release the district board from both monitoring and the corrective action plan to which it is subject.

The district board is entitled to appeal a state board order for monitoring to the Franklin County Court of Common Pleas on questions of fact or law.[44]

Any action taken under these education performance evaluation provisions cannot abrogate any provision of a collective bargaining agreement or relieve the district board of its duty to comply with the Public Employees Collective Bargaining Act (RC Chapter 4117).[45]

(E) Innovative education pilot programs

Any school district board of education may submit to the state board of education an application proposing an "innovative education pilot program" whose implementation requires exemption from specific statutory requirements or rules. The application must include written consent of the teachers' designated collective bargaining representative, if any. Requested exemptions must be limited to any requirement of RC Title 33 or any state board rule adopted under Title 33, except the application may not propose an exemption from any requirement or rule under RC Chapter 3307 (the state teachers retirement system), RC Chapter 3309 (the school employees retirement system), RC 3319.07 to RC 3319.21 (pertaining generally to the employment of teachers and nonteaching employees), or RC Chapter 3323 (pertaining generally to education of the handicapped).

The state superintendent of public instruction must approve or disapprove the application in accordance with its adopted approval standards. Any approved exemption cannot exceed the period during which the pilot program is implemented plus "a reasonable period to allow for evaluation of the effectiveness of the program."[46]

Any action taken under an innovative education pilot program cannot abrogate any provision of a collective bargaining agreement or relieve the district board of its duty to comply with the Public Employees Collective Bargaining Act (RC Chapter 4117).[47]

---

[44]RC 3302.06.
[45]RC 3302.08.

[46]RC 3302.07.
[47]RC 3302.08.

(F) Statewide education management information system

RC 3301.0714 requires that the state board of education formulate guidelines for the establishment and maintenance of a statewide education management information system. It will facilitate comparative statistical analysis of Ohio school districts on a number of levels. The data to be compiled must include, among other things, student participation and performance data (for each grade in each school district as a whole and for each grade in each building in the district) in various categories of instruction; the number of students involved in each of the district's extracurricular programs and support services; average student grades by subject in grades nine through twelve; academic achievement levels as assessed by statutorily required student proficiency tests and, in grades one through eight, by locally developed competency programs; the number of students designated as having handicapping conditions under RC 3301.071(C)(1) and the number of students reported to the state board under RC 3301.071(C)(2); attendance rates and the average daily attendance for the year, and expulsion, suspension, dropout, and graduation rates; the percentage of students receiving corporal punishment; rates of retention in grade; and, for grades nine through twelve, the average number of Carnegie units calculated in accordance with state board rules.

The data will also include (1) personnel and classroom enrollment data for each district, including the number of employees and pupils in various categories and cost accounting data for each district as a whole and each building in each district in various categories (including administrative costs, instructional costs, and support or extracurricular costs, and sub-categories within these areas), and (2) student demographic data for each district, including the gender ratio and racial make-up of pupils and an appropriate measure of the number of pupils who come from economically disadvantaged households.[48]

Every school district board must annually collect and report such data to the state board in accordance with state board guidelines. The data may be collected and reported notwithstanding RC 2151.358 or RC 3319.321, and any such data that identifies an individual pupil is not a public record for purposes of RC 149.43.[49] The state board is obligated annually to compile furnished data and profile each district as a whole and each building within a district in a way that (1) facilitates comparison among districts and buildings within a district, and (2) presents data on academic achievement levels as assessed by statutorily required student proficiency tests so that the levels of those special education students excused from testing under RC 3301.0711(C)(1) are distinguished from the levels of those not so excused. It must then prepare an annual statewide report (including district profiles) and annual individual district reports (including building profiles).

Copies of the statewide report and the applicable district report must be available to the public for inspection at the district's offices. Upon request and payment of a reasonable fee for the cost of reproduction, the district board must furnish a copy of either report to any person. During the two weeks prior to the week in which the reports will first be available, the board must annually publish at least twice in a newspaper of general circulation in the district a notice giving the address where reports are available and the date they will be available. RC 3301.0714 subjects to RC 2913.42 (a statute that makes tampering with records a crime) any person who removes data from the system in order to release such data to any person not entitled by law to access.

An appeals court has rejected arguments that RC 3301.0714 constitutes an unlawful delegation of legislative authority and that it conflicts with the federal Family Educational Rights and Privacy Act of 1974, 20 USCA 1232g.[50]

---

[48] Whenever a school district collects racial data on enrolled students, the data must include a multiracial category. RC 3313.941.

[49] See Text 44.02, Definition of public records.

[50] Princeton City School Dist Bd of Ed v Ohio State Bd of Ed, 96 App(3d) 558, 645 NE(2d) 773 (Hamilton 1994), appeal dismissed 71 OS(3d) 1444, 644 NE(2d) 407 (1995).

(G) Other powers and duties

RC 3301.07 also confers a number of ancillary powers and duties on the state board. The board is empowered to require any reports from school districts, officers, and employees which it considers necessary and desirable.[51] It is given rule-making powers with respect to any function conferred on the board by law, and may delegate the administration and management of board functions to the superintendent of public instruction.[52] The board may cooperate with federal, state, and local agencies having duties concerning the health and welfare of children.[53] Also, the board is permitted to prepare an annual report to the governor and general assembly on the state of Ohio's public schools, with recommendations for necessary legislative action and a ten-year projection of public and nonpublic school enrollment.[54]

In addition, the state board of education is required to do the following:

(1) Conform standards for certification of teachers and administrators in non-tax-supported schools to the requirements of RC 3301.071;

(2) Establish continuing in-service training programs in school district budget and finance for local school officials;[55]

(3) Provide technical assistance in financial matters to a school district upon request, which assistance may include grants, consultants, or the temporary assignment of employees;[56]

(4) Establish and administer standards for licensing school district treasurers and business managers;[57]

(5) Adopt rules governing purchase and lease of data processing services and equipment for all school districts and administer the Ohio education computer network;[58]

(6) Adopt rules for the establishment and maintenance of block parent programs by school districts, whereby volunteers provide temporary places of refuge for school children;[59]

(7) Prescribe standards for a statewide program to assess student achievement including adopting and furnishing to school district boards of education a list of approved tests to be administered by district boards to students in grades four, six, and eight in accordance with rules adopted by the department of education on dates designated by the state board;[60]

(8) Adopt a standard limiting to twenty-five pupils the size of any class in a bilingual multicultural program;[61]

(9) Adopt rules establishing a statewide program to test the proficiency of public school students (and nonpublic school students at the option of the institution) for the purpose of ensuring that high school graduates demonstrate at least ninth grade levels of literacy and basic competency in reading, writing, mathematics, science, and citizenship, including prescribing five statewide proficiency tests (one each designed to measure skills in reading, writing, mathematics, science, and citizenship) to be administered by school district boards of education in accordance with rules adopted by the department of education;[62]

---

[51] RC 3301.07(I).
[52] RC 3301.07.
[53] RC 3301.07(H).
[54] RC 3301.07(F).
[55] RC 3301.072.
[56] RC 3301.073.
[57] RC 3301.074.
[58] RC 3301.075.
[59] RC 3301.076.
[60] RC 3301.077, RC 3301.078. No testing of fourth grade students is required under these statutes after June 30, 1994, and no testing of sixth and eighth grade students is required in any school year in which tests are administered under RC 3301.0711(B)(2). 1992 H 55, § 7. By virtue of RC 3301.0724, no board is required to test, or report the results of the testing of, any students in grade eight in any school year in which the board, pursuant to RC 3301.0711(M), administers the tests prescribed under RC 3301.0710(B) to at least a majority of the district's eighth grade students. The applicable administrative rules appear in OAC 3301-12-01 et seq. See also Text 5.08, Rule-making and regulatory power. RC 3301.077, RC 3301.078, and RC 3301.0724 were repealed effective July 1, 1995.
[61] RC 3301.079.
[62] RC 3301.0710, RC 3301.0711. Unless the state board finds it feasible to administer the science proficiency test earlier, it will first be administered in the 1995-96 school year. 1992 H 55, § 9. The applicable administrative rules appear in OAC 3301-13-01 et seq. Provision is made in RC 3301.0711(C) for excusing a special education student from taking any particular

(10) Conduct annual inspections of various institutions employing teachers, including institutions under the control of the departments of human services, mental health, mental retardation and developmental disabilities, and rehabilitation and correction;[63]

(11) Administer the foundation program;[64]

(12) Adopt minimum standards under which each county board of education must develop a "plan of service" to school districts within the county; charter each county district whose "plan of service" is approved; evaluate each county board and the services it provides every five years; and dissolve a county district that fails to submit a "plan of service," fails to comply with its "plan of service," or fails to correct violations found in state board evaluations, transferring its territory to one or more adjacent county districts;[65]

(13) Monitor and, in some cases, take control of districts which are in financial distress;[66]

(14) Monitor districts to ensure compliance with the law on open enrollment policies[67] and policies for the enrollment of students from adjacent districts;[68]

(15) Prescribe standards requiring the use of phonics in teaching reading in grades kindergarten through three and provide in-service training programs on the use of phonics as a teaching technique;[69]

(16) Develop and modify as necessary a state plan to encourage and promote the use of technological advancements in education;[70]

(17) Prepare a plan for modernizing the vocational curriculum in order to furnish students with basic academic and technological skills needed to participate successfully in the work force of the future;[71]

(18) Prescribe standards for and administer the Ohio scholarship fund for teacher trainees established by RC 3315.33;

(19) Establish a teacher education loan program for students enrolled in teacher preparation programs at state-approved institutions who indicate an intent to teach in a geographic region of Ohio or in a subject identified by the superintendent of public instruction as a region or subject in which a shortage of qualified Ohio teachers exists or is projected;[72]

(20) During the first two weeks of July of each school year, determine each school district that is "at-risk" and that receives at least $300,000 under RC 3317.023(B)(3), and notify the district of that fact and of its consequent spending obligations under RC 3317.023(B)(4);[73]

(21) Recommend to school districts, in connection with teaching secondary school sciences, (1) a suggested curriculum for chemistry, physics, biology, and such additional services as the board elects, (2) lists of minimum supplies and

---

test if the student's individualized education program excuses him; such student cannot be prohibited from taking the test, however. By virtue of RC 3301.0711(J), statewide proficiency testing does not apply to joint vocational school districts, except that, in accordance with state board rules, the board of any other school district with territory in a joint vocational district may contract with the joint vocational district board for administering any prescribed test to students of the other district who attend school in the joint vocational district.

[63] RC 3301.15.
[64] RC 3317.01.
[65] RC 3301.0712.
[66] RC 3313.488.
[67] RC 3313.97. See Text 5.08(C), Open enrollment policies.
[68] RC 3313.98, RC 3313.981. See Text 5.08(D), Enrollment of students from adjacent districts.

[69] RC 3301.07(M).
[70] RC 3301.07(N).
[71] RC 3313.901.
[72] RC 3315.36, which further provides that at least ten per cent of the total dollar amount of all loans in a given year must go toward loans to minority students, and, in the case of minority students, loans may be made only to those who indicate an intent to teach in Ohio.
[73] RC 3301.0719. An "at-risk" district is one with a dropout rate (as defined in the statute) of 30% or more and that either has an aid-to-dependent children rate (as defined in the statute) of over 30% or has an average personal income per tax return in the district below 80% of the statewide average. In the school year in which a district is initially defined as "at-risk," the statute imposes special spending and reporting requirements in lieu of the requirements of RC 3317.023(B)(4).

equipment necessary for teaching each such science with special emphasis on recommended safety equipment, (3) acquisition and replacement schedules for such supplies and equipment, and (4) suggested safety procedures including training in the safe handling, use, storing, and disposal of hazardous and potentially hazardous materials;[74]

(22) Develop a plan to assist districts in providing community service education under RC 3313.605 and develop model community service programs, teacher training courses, and community service curricula and materials;[75]

(23) Adopt rules for the establishment of an education information advisory committee in accordance with RC 3301.0723; and

(24) Adopt standards for attaining a certificate to teach students with visual disabilities that require demonstrated competency in reading and writing braille.[76]

3.04 Department of education

The department of education of Ohio consists of the state board of education, the superintendent of public instruction, and a staff of professional and clerical employees necessary to perform the duties and exercise the required functions of the department.

(A) Department as administrative unit

Although it is not one of the administrative departments headed by directors appointed by the governor,[77] the department of education is nevertheless the organization through which the policies, directives, and powers of the state board and the duties of the superintendent of public instruction are administered by the superintendent, who is the board's executive and administrative officer. In the exercise of its powers and functions, the department, and its officers and agencies, are subject to the administrative procedure law.[78] In addition to acting as the administrative unit for the state board, the general assembly has delegated certain other functions directly to the department, including functions relating to educating deaf or hard of hearing handicapped children,[79] driver education programs,[80] desegregation,[81] programs for children of migrant agricultural laborers,[82] inspecting and licensing preschool and school child day-care programs,[83] and funding head start agencies for the purpose of expanding their programs to serve more eligible children.[84]

RC 3301.131 requires the department affirmatively to seek and publicize "innovative and exemplary" school-parent and school-business partnerships (defined, respectively, as programs that actively involve parents or students in educational decision-making, and programs in which businesses, labor unions, or other persons assist schools in preparing children for employment or higher education). A school board involved in such a partnership is obligated to cooperate with the department by providing information.

RC 3301.27 requires the department to conduct research (which may include requiring school districts to administer tests in addition to those otherwise required by law) on the factors that improve educational effectiveness and to make the results available to all districts.

(B) Headquarters

The department must maintain its headquarters in Columbus, where proper office space must be provided by the department of administrative services.[85] Records must be maintained there in charge of the superintendent of public instruction.[86]

---

[74]RC 3301.0720. The statute also requires the state board to recommend provisions for a biennial assessment of each high school's safety equipment and procedures by someone other than the school personnel directly responsible for them, and to recommend procedures for making the results of such assessments available to the public.
[75]RC 3301.70. See also Text 5.09(N), Community service education programs.
[76]RC 3319.232.

[77]RC Ch 121, RC 3301.13.
[78]RC Ch 119, RC 3301.13.
[79]RC 3323.17.
[80]RC 3301.17.
[81]RC 3301.18, RC 3301.19.
[82]RC 3301.30.
[83]RC 3301.55, RC 3301.57 to RC 3301.59.
[84]RC 3301.31.
[85]RC 123.01, RC 3301.13.
[86]RC 3301.13.

(C) Chief administrative officer

The superintendent of public instruction is the chief administrative officer of the department and, subject to the policies and rules of the state board, exercises general supervision of the department.[87] It is the superintendent's responsibility to recommend, for approval by the state board, the organization of the department and the assignment of work within the department.[88]

(D) Education data management unit

RC 3301.133 requires that the organization of the department include an identifiable organizational unit that deals with the management of educational data the department gathers or uses. With the advice of the education information advisory committee established under RC 3301.0723, this unit is charged with responsibilities to review forms, in accordance with statutory criteria, work with other agencies to increase the efficiency and coordination of data collection, assist the education information advisory committee, and perform other duties assigned by the superintendent of public instruction.

3.05 Superintendent of public instruction: appointment and qualifications

The Ohio Constitution requires that the state board of education appoint a state superintendent of public instruction, and that the powers and duties of that office be prescribed by law.[89]

The superintendent is appointed by and serves at the pleasure of the state board; no fixed term of office is prescribed. The board is authorized to fix the superintendent's compensation, which may not exceed the compensation fixed for the chancellor of the Ohio board of regents.[90] During his tenure, the superintendent may not hold any other office or employment, nor may he be an officer or employee of any public or private school, college, university, or other institution of higher education. Also, he may not have any financial interest in a book publishing or selling concern.[91]

3.06 Duties of superintendent of public instruction

As chief administrative officer of the department of education, the superintendent exercises general supervision of that department, subject to the policies and rules of the state board of education.[92] He also serves as secretary to the state board[93] and acts as its executive and administrative officer, charged with the execution of all its policies, orders, and directives, with all the administrative functions of that board, and with the direction of all department employees.[94]

In addition, the superintendent is directed as follows:

(1) To provide technical and professional assistance and advice to all school districts in reference to all aspects of education, including finance, buildings and equipment, curriculum and instruction, transportation of pupils, personnel problems, and the interpretation of school laws and state rules;

(2) To prescribe and require the preparation and filing of such financial and other reports from school districts, officers, and employees as are necessary or proper, and to prescribe and require the installation by school districts of such standardized reporting forms and accounting procedures as are essential to the business-like operations of the public schools;

(3) To conduct studies and research projects for the improvement of public school education in Ohio;

(4) To prepare and submit annually to the state board a report of the activities of the department of education, and

---

[87]RC 3301.13.
[88]RC 3301.13.
[89]O Const Art VI §4.
[90]RC 3301.08.
[91]RC 3301.08. See also RC Ch 102, RC Ch 2921; Text Ch 45, Ethics Requirements and Education Personnel.

[92]RC 3301.13.
[93]RC 3301.09.
[94]RC 3301.11, RC 3301.13.

the status, problems, and needs of education in the state;

(5) To supervise all agencies over which the board exercises administrative control, including schools for the education of handicapped persons;[95] and

(6) To issue, after following prescribed procedures, adjudication orders that permanently exclude from all public schools students age sixteen or older convicted of or adjudicated delinquent for committing certain offenses on school property or at a school activity.[96]

The superintendent is required to calculate and certify the amounts payable pursuant to the foundation program.[97] He is also charged with the responsibility of administering emergency loan approvals;[98] is permitted to enforce the statutory prohibition on closing schools for financial reasons;[99] is required to analyze certain school districts' financial condition;[100] is required to enforce certain state board orders;[101] and is required to make recommendations regarding reductions in expenses,[102] to approve a schedule of maximum expenditures,[103] to act on behalf of a school district board of education under certain circumstances,[104] and upon request of the state board of education, to report to the state board on any matter.[105] He may also annually inspect and analyze, in accordance with state board rules, the expenditure of each school district and determine as to the efficiency of each district's costs relative to other districts for instructional, administrative, and student support services. A district must be notified of any such determination and the reasons for it.[106]

3.07 Other personnel of department of education

(A) Assistant superintendents and division heads

The appointment, number, and salaries of assistant superintendents and division heads are determined by the state board of education after recommendation of the superintendent of public instruction. These assistant superintendents and division heads serve at the pleasure of the board.[107]

(B) Employees

The superintendent is charged with the appointment, fixing of salaries, and termination of employment of all employees, except assistant superintendents and division heads.[108] Each employee is entitled to sick leave, payment for sick leave upon separation, disability leave, personal leave, bereavement leave, administrative leave with pay,[109] and paid holidays.[110] Prior service with the state or with any political subdivision of the state, other than as an elected officer, must be used in granting vacation credits.[111]

---

[95]RC 3301.12.
[96]RC 3301.121, RC 3313.662. Permanent exclusion of students is given expansive treatment in Text 25.10(E), Permanent exclusion for certain offenses.
[97]RC 3317.01.
[98]RC 3317.63.
[99]RC 3313.483.
[100]RC 3313.487, RC 3313.489.
[101]RC 3313.487, RC 3313.488.
[102]RC 3313.487(A).
[103]RC 3313.4811.
[104]RC 3313.487(C).
[105]RC 3301.11.
[106]RC 3301.12.
[107]RC 3301.13.
[108]RC 3301.13.
[109]RC 124.382 to RC 124.388.
[110]RC 124.19.
[111]RC 9.44.

Chapter 4
School Districts

4.01 Introduction
4.02 School districts and boundaries of other political subdivisions

CLASSIFICATION OF SCHOOL DISTRICTS
4.03 Classification of school districts

CREATION AND REORGANIZATION OF SCHOOL DISTRICTS
4.04 Authority to create or reorganize school districts
4.05 General factors in creating or reorganizing school districts
4.06 Reclassification of school districts without transfer of territory

REORGANIZATIONS INVOLVING TRANSFERS OF TERRITORY
4.07 Transfer of territory, in general
4.08 Transfers of school district territory following municipal annexation
4.09 Territorial transfers initiated by state board of education
4.10 Transfers of territory from local school districts
4.11 Transfers from city and exempted village school districts

DIVISION OF ASSETS AND LIABILITIES ON REORGANIZATION; GOVERNANCE
4.12 Allocation of state funds, minimum guarantee
4.13 Fair division of assets and liabilities
4.14 Effect of reorganization on tax levies
4.15 Board of education in reorganized district

4.01 Introduction

The school district is the basic building block of the Ohio public school system. The system is organized into territories called school districts, each with its own board of education acting as the governing and administrative unit for the schools within the district. Each school district in its own right is a political subdivision of the state. Because school districts are creatures of the legislature, their powers, duties, and liabilities are limited to those prescribed by statute or necessarily implied from the statutes.

The types of school districts which may be organized under current law are designated as city, local, joint vocational school districts, and educational service centers. Exempted village and joint high school districts may no longer be created as such, although many such districts organized under former law are still in existence.

School districts and their boundaries may be redrawn, and the Revised Code contains elaborate provisions for organizing and reorganizing districts and adjusting their territories. These provisions vary, depending on the nature of the change and the type of district involved. Reorganizations may result either from changes in circumstances—e.g., the annexation of territory by a municipality or a significant demographic change—or from action taken by a particular party. The state board of education, the county boards of education, and the qualified electors and school boards of the affected territory each have the power to initiate school district reorganizations under special circumstances. These powers are discussed in greater detail below.

4.02 School districts and boundaries of other political subdivisions

School districts may be constituted without reference to other political subdivisions. That is, the territory of a district need not coincide with the boundaries of a county, city, or township. The district is a completely separate political subdivision of the state. For example, even when the territorial limits of a city and a city school district are exactly the same, the district retains its separate identity.

Moreover, a number of city school districts encompass all or part of the territory of two or more cities. Educational service centers invariably include all or part of various villages or cities within their territories. There is even provision for an Ohio school district to join forces for certain purposes with a school district in another state.[1]

---

[1] RC 3313.42. See College Corner Local School Dist Bd of Ed v Walker, 68 App(3d) 63, 587 NE(2d) 419 (Butler 1990).

CLASSIFICATION OF SCHOOL DISTRICTS

4.03 Classification of school districts

RC 3311.01 provides that Ohio school districts shall be styled as (1) city school districts; (2) local school districts; (3) exempted village school districts; (4) cooperative education school districts; and (5) joint vocational school districts, which also may be styled vocational school districts. Exempted village school districts have been "grandfathered" into the current system and cannot be newly created today. In addition,m the entities formerly known as county school districts arenow known as educational service centers. Combinations of educational serivce centers are permitted by RC 3311.053.

(A) City school district

The territory within the corporate limits of a city, but excluding territory detached for school purposes and including territory attached for school purposes, constitutes a city school district.[2] The district may lose its status as a city school district either by a vote of the city board of education or by a decline in population. If a city is reduced in size to village status, that is, having a population of less than 5,000,[3] the city school district generally becomes a local school district. However, if the city school district includes within its boundaries all or part of two or more municipal corporations with a combined population of 5,000 or more as determined by the preceding federal census, it may, by a majority vote of the school board, remain a city school district.[4] If a majority of any city school district's board vote to declare that the district will be supervised by the county board of education, the city school district may, with the approval of the county board, become a local school district.[5]

An exempted village school district that includes all or part of two or more municipal corporations having an aggregate population of 5,000 or more may, with the approval of the state board of education, become a city school district.[6] Where the state board has created a school district from all or part of two or more contiguous local or exempted village school districts, it may designate the newly created district as a city school district so long as its population is 5,000 or more and all or part of a municipal corporation is contained within its boundaries.[7]

(B) Educational service center

An educational service center consists of the territory within the territorial limits of a county, excluding territory embraced in any city or exempted village school district, and excluding territory detached for school purposes, but including territory attached for school purposes.[8]

If an educational service center contains only one local school district, the governing board shall be the only board of education, and in addition to its own powers and duties, it shall have the powers and duties of a local board.[9] Such a governing board may exercise its discretion in determining the extent to which governing board and local board functions will be consolidated, provided that all legal requirements are satisfied.[10] In such a service center, the superintendent has the powers and duties of a local superintendent in addition to those of a service center superintendent.[11]

When a governing board employs any teacher, assistant superintendent, principal, assistant principal, or other administrator to perform services for a local school district, such persons retain rights granted to local district employees by RC Chapter 3319, and the governing board shall exercise all powers and duties of a local board.[12] One court has held, however, that

---

[2]RC 3311.02. See RC Ch 707 for conditions whereby territory within a school district may become incorporated as a city and thus the school district may likewise become eligible for advancement to city school district status pursuant to RC 3311.07.
[3]RC 703.01.
[4]RC 3311.02.
[5]RC 3311.09.
[6]RC 3311.02, RC 3311.10.
[7]RC 3311.10, RC 3311.37.

[8]RC 3311.05(A). For treatment of a county school financing district, a taxing district (with different territory) created under RC 3311.50, see Text 40.10(D), County school financing district levies for special education.
[9]RC 3311.051; OAG 86-108.
[10]OAG 86-108.
[11]RC 3311.051.
[12]RC 3311.051.

employment by a county (now governing) board is not employment in a "school district" for purposes of RC 3319.11 giving continuing service status to an administrator who has two years of service in the district and who had continuing service status as a teacher in another district previously.[13]

(C) New educational service centers

RC 3311.053 authorizes the voluntary consolidation of up to five adjoining educational service centers. To effect a consolidation, within any sixty-day period a majority of the members of each participating governing board must adopt identical resolutions stating the name of the new educational service centers (which may be styled a "joint educational service centers") and indicating which of two alternative statutory governance structures[14] the new service center will use. A copy of each resolution must be filed with the state board of education. The procedures to be followed in dissolving the preexisting service centers and establishing a new board of education are specified in RC 3311.053(B) and RC 3311.054, whichever applies. Funds and property of the dissolved service centers pass to the new board, which must also honor contracts made by the former governing boards.

The new board designates the site of the service center's offices, which must be provided and equipped by the board of county commissioners of the county in which the site is located, but costs are apportioned among the boards of county commissioners of all counties having territory in the new service center according to the proportion of pupils residing in the respective counties. In case of dispute, the probate judge of the county with the greatest number of pupils will apportion the costs.[15]

Under 1995 House Bill 117, educational service centers composed of one local school district must merge with an adjacent service center by June 1, 1997. Governing boards serving less than 8,000 students as of June 1, 1999 also must merge with an adjacent service center. Where the service centers do not notify the state superintendent of their merger plans, the state superintendent is authorized to identify and designate a suitable merger candidate.[16]

(D) Local school district

Each school district, other than a city, exempted village, joint vocational district or educatioal centers, in existence on September 16, 1943, continues to be known as a local school district until it loses its identity as a separate district or acquires a different legal status. All school districts created after September 16, 1943, other than city, exempted village (created on or before June 1, 1954, and not thereafter reclassified),[17] joint vocational districts, or educational service centers, are classified as local school districts.[18]

As previously noted, when the population of a city falls below 5,000, the city school district may become a local school district.[19] Furthermore, a board of education of an exempted village or a city school district may, by a majority vote of the full membership, declare that such exempted village or city school district is to be supervised by the governing board of the educational service center. If the governing board approves, the school district becomes a local school district under the supervision of the governing board.[20] If there is no governing board, the board of education of an exempted village or city school district may, by majority vote of the full membership, adopt a resolution declaring that such an exempted village or city school district shall become a local school district.[21] The resolution must be filed with the state board of education, and the board of education for the exempted village or city school district shall become a governing board.[22]

(E) Joint vocational school district

Management of a joint vocational school district is vested in a joint vocational school

---

[13]State ex rel Wilson v Lucas County Office of Ed, No. L-94-279, 1995 WL 244212 (6th Dist Ct App, Lucas, 4-26-95).
[14]RC 3311.053(B), RC 3311.054.
[15]RC 3319.19(B).
[16]1995 H 117, § 45.32, eff. 9-29-95.
[17]See Text 4.03(F), Exempted village school district.
[18]RC 3311.03.
[19]RC 3311.02.
[20]RC 3311.09.
[21]RC 3311.09(B).
[22]RC 3311.09(B).

district board of education.[23] The creation, consolidation, powers, and attributes of joint vocational school districts are discussed elsewhere.[24]

(F) Exempted village school district

Exempted village school districts fall into two categories: (1) those in existence on September 16, 1943,[25] and (2) those created on or before June 1, 1954, by being declared exempt from the supervision of the county board of education by the board of education of any local school district that contained within its territorial boundaries (a) all of the territory lying within the corporate limits of a village having a population of 3,000 or more according to the last federal census, or (b) all of the territory lying within the corporate limits of a village having a population of 2,000 or more according to the last federal census and a population outside of the corporate limits of the village, as determined by a census of the board, sufficient to make the total population 3,000 or more.[26]

After June 1, 1954, no new exempted village school district could be created.[27] Thus, even if a plan of reorganization of school districts includes the entire territory of a village, and even if the plan is approved by the electors, the new district so formed cannot be or become an exempted village school district.[28]

The board of any exempted village school district may, by a majority vote of the entire board, declare that the district is to be supervised by the governing board of the educational service center. Upon approval by the governing board, the exempted village school district is then known as a local school district until its status as a local school district changes.[29] If an exempted village school district organized as such on or after June 1, 1943, fails to contain territory lying within the corporate limits of a village having a population of 2,000 or more, it automatically becomes a local school district subject to supervision by the governing board.[30] Once an exempted village school district has become a local district, it cannot thereafter regain exempted village status.[31]

(G) Cooperative education school district

A cooperative education school district may be established under either RC 3311.52 or RC 3311.521.

RC 3311.52 authorizes such establishment by adoption within a sixty-day period of identical resolutions[32] by the boards of each city, local, and exempted village school district within the territory of a county school financing district.[33] Upon completion of the procedure prescribed in the statute, the county school financing district is dissolved and a new cooperative education school district is created. The governing board of the educational service center that created the county school financing district becomes the new cooperative education district's board, except that provision may be made in the initiating resolutions for an alternative board, which must include at least one member selected from or by members of the board of each city, local, exempted village, and educational service center district within the new district's territory.

Similarly, the superintendent and treasurer of the educational service center that created the county school financing district become the new cooperative education district's superintendent and treasurer, except that provision may be made in the initiating resolutions for the selection of a superintendent and treasurer in accordance with one of two options specified in RC 3311.52(B)(2).

The initiating resolutions must contain a statement of the educational program the new district will conduct, including the type of program, the grade levels proposed for inclusion, the timetable for beginning operations, and the facilities proposed to be used or constructed. Any student included

---

[23]RC 3311.19.
[24]See Text 27.08 to 27.12.
[25]RC 3311.04.
[26]RC 3311.08.
[27]RC 3311.08, RC 3311.34.
[28]1955 OAG 5736.
[29]RC 3311.09.
[30]RC 3311.10.

[31]OAG 80-105.

[32]The resolutions must contain the items specified in RC 3311.52(B).

[33]For treatment of a county school financing district, a taxing district created under RC 3311.50, see Text 40.10(D), County school financing district levies for special education.

in the average daily membership certified for any city, exempted village, or local school district under RC 3317.03 by virtue of being counted, in whole or in part, in the average daily membership of a cooperative education school district under RC 3317.03(A)(4) is construed as enrolled in both districts, but may not be counted more than once for purposes of determining the average daily membership of any one district.

Under RC 3313.521, the board of any two or more contiguous city, exempted village, or local school districts may establish a cooperative education school district for the purpose of operating a joint high school in lieu of each board operating a high school. Such a district is established by adoption within a sixty-day period of identical resolutions by each participating board.[34] When all such resolutions are adopted, a copy of each must be filed with the state board of education.

The territory of the cooperative education district thus created is the territory of all participating school districts. Upon establishment of the new district and its board, the board must give written notice of the creation of the district to the county auditor and board of elections of each county having territory in the district. RC 3311.29(C) provides that if the new district fails to maintain the grades it is specified to operate, it shall be dissolved by the state board of education unless previously dissolved under RC 3311.54. Similarly, if any participating city, exempted village, or local district fails to maintain the grades it is specified to operate, the cooperative education district must be dissolved, and, upon such dissolution, a participating district that fails to maintain grades kindergarten through twelve becomes subject to the dissolution provisions of RC 3311.29(A).

Except for the powers and duties appearing in RC Chapters 124, 3311, 3317, 3318, 3323, and 3331, a cooperative education school district (whether established under RC 3311.52 or RC 3311.521) and its board, superintendent, and treasurer generally have the powers and duties of a city school district and its board, superintendent, and treasurer.[35]

A cooperative education school district may levy taxes pursuant to RC 3311.21, RC 5705.194, and RC 5705.21. The calculation of foundation program aid for a cooperative education school district is governed by RC 3317.19.

RC 3311.53 spells out the procedure under which a city, exempted village, or local school district may become part of a cooperative education district already established under RC 3311.52 or RC 3311.521.

CREATION AND REORGANIZATION OF SCHOOL DISTRICTS

4.04 Authority to create or reorganize school districts

Education is a state function over which the state has vast power, and the general assembly has the power to enact legislation creating and reorganizing school districts as circumstances may require. However, the Ohio Constitution provides that a school district that either entirely or partially lies within the borders of a city has the power to determine for itself the size and organi-

---

[34]The resolutions must contain the items specified in RC 3311.521(B). These items pertain, among other things, to the composition of the board (which must include two members selected from or by the board of each participating district), the selection of a superintendent and treasurer (the statute provides two options: that one person may act as both, and may be required to be the superintendent or treasurer of a participating district; alternatively, that one person may be selected as superintendent and another person as treasurer, and one or both may be required to be a superintendent or treasurer of a participating district), a statement of the high school education program to be operated, a statement that no participating board will operate a high school education program of its own for the affected grade levels, a statement of how special education and related services will be provided, a statement of how transportation of students will be provided, a statement on funding of the new district by participating districts, and a procedure for amending the above provisions.

[35]RC 3311.52(D). Various statutes outside these specified Chapters that pertain to city school districts and their boards expressly do not apply to cooperative education school districts, however; thus, the only safe course in analyzing a cooperative education district board's powers and duties is to examine the specific statute in question.

zation of its board of education.[36] The statutory procedures governing the creation and reorganization of school districts and the transfer of territory are specified in detail in the Revised Code, and there is no other way to change the composition of a school district.

Functionally, the power to reorganize school districts is vested in educational service center governing boards, school district boards of education, and the state board of education. In addition, the qualified electors of the affected area have the right to petition for any change they consider expedient and also to express by referendum their opposition to any proposed change.

Although the state board may both propose and oppose reorganizations and transfers of territory, this does not affect the authority of the school boards to administer the schools within their respective districts. For example, assignments of grades to school buildings and the operation of those buildings are matters within the control and discretion of the district board of education.[37]

4.05 General factors in creating or reorganizing school districts

School districts are the basic units of the school system, and the fundamental object in organizing them and fixing their boundaries is to form self-contained units providing full elementary and secondary education in each locality. The statutes governing the creation and reorganization of school districts show that four factors are involved in accomplishing this object: efficiency, geography, demography, and money.

(A) Efficiency of school system: maintenance of kindergarten through grade twelve

The constitutional mandate to provide a "thorough and efficient" public school system in the state[38] provides the main principle on which school districts are constituted or reorganized. The objective is to organize school districts of optimum size, shape, and location capable of providing a complete and viable system of elementary and secondary schools.

Providing a complete educational system for the locality is a principal requirement. Except for a joint vocational school district or a cooperative education school district established under RC 3311.52, no school district may be created or continue to exist that does not maintain within its borders public schools offering grades kindergarten through twelve. Any nonconforming existing district must be dissolved and its territory joined with one or more other school districts by order of the state board of education if no agreement is made among the surrounding districts voluntarily.[39]

Where compliance with the complete system rule is impracticable due to topography, sparsity of population, and other factors, the state board of education may authorize exceptions.[40] The superintendent of public instruction has no authority to distribute foundation program funds to any school district that does not maintain schools with grades kindergarten through twelve unless an exception has been granted by the state board.[41]

(B) Geography: contiguous territory, neighborhood schools

A second major factor in organizing and reorganizing school districts is the need to provide compact territories with conveniently located facilities, calculated to serve the greatest number of students. Therefore, the reorganization statutes must be interpreted in light of statutory requirements with regard to contiguous territory and neighborhood schools.

In general, the territory within the boundaries of a city, local, exempted village, or joint vocational school district must

---

[36] O Const Art VI §3.
[37] RC 3313.47; Ferris v Paulding Exempted Village School Dist Bd of Ed, 7 App(3d) 163, 7 OBR 208, 454 NE(2d) 957 (Paulding 1982).
[38] O Const Art VI §2.
[39] RC 3311.29; Stromberg v Bratenahl Bd of Ed, 64 OS(2d) 98, 413 NE(2d) 1184 (1980). See also Ferris v Paulding Exempted Village School Dist Bd of Ed, 7 App(3d) 163, 7 OBR 208, 454 NE(2d) 957 (Paulding 1982). For special rules applicable to a cooperative education school district established under RC 3311.521, see RC 3311.29(C).
[40] RC 3311.29.
[41] RC 3311.29.

be contiguous.[42] The statute provides four exceptions. First, contiguous territory is not required where an island forms an integral part of the district. This exception refers, of course, to the Lake Erie islands, where the permanent population is too small to make separate island districts feasible. Second, the state board of education is authorized to grant exceptions to the contiguous territory rule, although no guidelines for granting exceptions are given. Third, any school district or group of districts may enter into an annexation agreement with a city school district having an average daily membership for the 1985-86 school year in excess of 20,000 and serving a city that contains annexed territory. The annexation agreement may provide for, or negotiation between the parties to such an agreement may result in, the transfer of territory between the agreeing districts whether the territory is contiguous or not.[43] The contiguous territory rule does not apply to educational service centers but does apply to local school districts included within the service center. Fourth, a local school district may be created pursuant to RC 3311.26 from one or more local school districts, one of which has entered into an agreement under RC 3313.42 and is therefore noncontiguous.[44]

The neighborhood school concept complements the contiguous territory rule. The board of education of each city, exempted village, local, and joint vocational school district is bound to provide educational facilities "at such places as will be most convenient for the attendance of the largest number [of students]."[45] The US Constitution adds another requirement—the schools must also be located so as to avoid any continuing effects of intentional racial segregation.[46]

(C) Demography: population shifts

Population and the characteristics of local population are dynamic rather than static, and it is both costly and inefficient to continue to maintain a school district when population decline reaches the point where a separate district is no longer practical. It can be equally inefficient and expensive to attempt to serve a growing population without making some changes in the school district structure in the locality. Several statutes consider population in creating or reorganizing school districts. For example, one of the grounds on which the state board of education may authorize an exception to the rule that a school district must maintain schools with kindergarten through grade twelve is "sparsity of population."[47] Changes in school districts based on population changes are required or permitted in the following circumstances: when a city is reduced to village status;[48] when a village is advanced to city status;[49] when an exempted village school district no longer contains within its borders territory of a village with a population of 2,000 or more;[50] or when an exempted village school district contains all or part of two or more villages with an aggregate population of 5,000 or more.[51]

(D) Finances: transfer of territory because of eroded tax base

Perhaps the most important factor in organization and reorganization of a school district is the district's financial ability to provide educational services meeting the minimum standards established by the state board of education or otherwise demanded of it. Local property taxes are one of the two main sources of revenue for both capital expenditures and operating expenses, and it would be futile to organize or maintain a district in which the tax resources cannot support its schools. Accordingly, the state board of education may initiate a transfer of territory when the assessed value of property within a district falls below $4,000 per pupil. In such case, the state board may transfer all or part of the district's territory to any city, exempted vil-

---

[42]RC 3311.06. But see State ex rel Pioneer Joint Vocational School Dist Bd of Ed v Schumann, 7 OS(2d) 41, 218 NE(2d) 180 (1966).

[43]RC 3311.06(E)(1).

[44]RC 3311.06(B).

[45]RC 3313.48.

[46]For a discussion of the constitutional implications of the neighborhood school concept, see Text 19.08, Neighborhood schools.

[47]RC 3311.29.

[48]RC 703.01, RC 3311.02.

[49]RC 703.01, RC 3311.07.

[50]RC 3311.10.

[51]RC 3311.10, RC 3311.02. See also Text 4.06, Reclassification of school districts without transfer of territory.

lage, or local school district that has more than 25,000 pupils in average daily membership.[52] The transfer requires the recommendation of the superintendent of public instruction or receipt of a resolution adopted by majority vote of the full membership of the board of any city, local, or exempted village school district requesting that the entire district be transferred[53] and the approval of both the county board of education and the board of education of the district receiving the transferred territory.

4.06 Reclassification of school districts without transfer of territory

Loss or gain in population, incorporation as a municipality, or surrender of corporate rights may trigger a change in the classification of a school district. These situations do not necessarily involve school district boundary changes, although such changes are not precluded.

(A) Change from city school district to local school district when city reduced to village

When a city's population falls below 5,000, the city becomes a village[54] and the city school district becomes a local school district[55] and thus comes under the supervision of the educational service center governing board. The district may remain a city school district, however, upon majority vote of the school board, where the district contains all or part of two or more municipalities having a combined population of 5,000 or more.[56]

(B) Change from exempted village school district to local school district

When an exempted village school district organized as such on or after June 1, 1943, no longer includes within its boundaries territory of a village having a population of 2,000 or more, the district becomes a local school district and is subject to the supervision of the educational service center governing board beginning July 1 after publication of the federal census demonstrating that fact.[57]

(C) Change from local or exempted village school district to city school district

While population loss may require reclassification of an exempted village school district as a local district, population gain may permit changing the district into a city school district. When an exempted village school district includes all or part of two or more municipalities with a combined population of 5,000 or more, it may be redesignated as a city school district by its board of education, provided the state board of education approves the change.[58]

If a village's population increases to above 5,000, the village is advanced to a city[59] and, if the major portion of the territory lying within its corporate limits (without regard to population) is contained within the territorial boundaries of a local or exempted village school district, that district may be redesignated by its board of education as a city school district.[60] If a minor portion of the territory of such a village advanced to a city is contained in a different local or exempted village school district, such territory is not affected by such advancement.[61]

(D) Change to city school district on incorporation as municipality

Ohio law contains elaborate provisions whereby previously unincorporated territory may become a municipal corporation, i.e., a village or city.[62] If the territory encompassed by a school district is incorporated, and the population of the territory is 5,000 or more, the municipal corporation is a city.[63] In such case, the school district is reclassified as a city school district.[64]

A municipal corporation may also surrender its corporate rights and revert to unincorporated status.[65] As a result of this action the affected school district may no longer qualify for city or exempted village

---

[52]RC 3311.38(B).
[53]RC 3311.38(A).
[54]RC 703.01.
[55]RC 3311.02.
[56]RC 3311.02.
[57]RC 3311.10.
[58]RC 3311.10, RC 3311.02.

[59]RC 703.01.
[60]RC 3311.07.
[61]RC 3311.07.
[62]RC Ch 707.
[63]RC 703.01.
[64]RC 3311.02.
[65]RC 703.08 to RC 703.21.

school district status, and reclassification as a local district would be required.[66]

REORGANIZATIONS INVOLVING TRANSFERS OF TERRITORY

4.07 Transfer of territory, in general

A school district reorganization may take the form of a redistribution of territory among districts, or the creation of a new district from neighboring districts, or the dissolution of a district and the distribution of its territory among adjoining districts. Such a transfer may result from the annexation of all or part of the territory of a school district to a municipal corporation or may be initiated by the state board of education, by the county board of education, by a district board of education, or, in some cases, by voter petition.

(A) Types of transfers, initiation, and approval

The types of transfers, how they may originate, and the power to approve them are as follows:

(1) Annexation of *all* of the territory of a school district to a city or village, automatically merging the annexed territory into the school district serving the municipality.[67] When only part of the territory of a school district is annexed, the annexed territory becomes part of the city's or village's school district only upon the approval of the state board of education unless there is an annexation agreement.[68] If there is an annexation agreement between any type of school district and a city school district with an average daily membership in excess of 20,000 pupils, the transfer is governed by the agreement or, if not specified by the agreement, by negotiation between the boards of education of such school districts, in which case the territory will be transferred automatically unless both boards resolve, within ninety days of the annexation, not to transfer the territory and so inform the state board.[69]

(2) Consolidation of contiguous districts or parts of such districts into a new district, or transfer of territory between contiguous districts, initiated by the state board of education or by resolution of the board of any city, local, or exempted village school district.[70] These proposals may be submitted for voter approval and, if approved, become effective prior to the next school year subject, in the case of a transfer, to approval of the board of education of the school district to which the territory is to be transferred.

(3) Transfer of all or part of one or more local school districts to one or more other local school districts in the same county, to an adjoining city or exempted village school district in the same county, or to an adjoining educational service center.[71] Such transfers may be made only to local school districts adjoining the school district that is proposed to be transferred, unless the board of education of the district proposed to be transferred has entered into an agreement pursuant to RC 3313.42, in which case the transfer may be to any local school district within the educational service center.[72] Each of these

---

[66]RC 3311.02, RC 3311.10.
[67]RC 3311.06(C)(1).
[68]RC 3311.06(C)(2). An "annexation agreement" within the meaning of RC 3311.06 necessarily involves a city school district with an average daily membership in excess of 20,000 pupils (called an "urban school district" by the statute) and is entered into pursuant to RC 3311.06(F). Any district, other than an urban district, that desires state board approval of a transfer under RC 3311.06(C)(2) must make a good faith effort to negotiate the terms with any other district whose territory would be affected. RC 3311.06(D) requires the state board to adopt rules governing negotiations held by any district except an urban district. Before the state board can approve any transfer of territory to a district, except an urban district, the state board must receive (1) a resolution requesting approval from at least one of the affected districts; (2) evidence that negotiations took place or that the district requesting the transfer made a good faith effort to hold negotiations; and (3) if negotiations took place, a statement signed by all participating boards of the terms agreed on and any points on which agreement could not be reached. See also OAC 3301-89-01 et seq.
[69]RC 3311.06(E).
[70]RC 3311.37, RC 3311.38(A). See also Text 4.09, Territorial transfers initiated by state board of education.
[71]RC 3311.22, RC 3311.231. See also Text 4.10, Transfers of territory from local school districts.
[72]RC 3311.22.

changes may be initiated by either the educational service center governing board or by voter petition. All of these changes are subject to voter referendum. A transfer to an adjoining city, exempted village, or educational service center governing board, and a transfer to an adjoining local school district initiated by petition, are subject to acceptance or rejection by the board of the district to which the transfer is proposed to be made. The board of such an adjoining local school district, in the case of a transfer initiated by the educational service center governing board, is permitted to appeal such a proposed transfer to the state board of education, which may approve or disapprove the transfer.[73] If the proposed transfer is submitted to the voters and is not approved by at least a majority of the voting electors, the issue may not be resubmitted to the electors prior to the first election occurring at least two years later.

(4) Creation initiated by resolution of the county board of education of a new educational service center governing board from all or part of one or more local school districts. Unless qualified electors in the proposed new district, equal in number to thirty-five per cent of the qualified electors voting at the last general election, petition for referendum, the new district is created. If a proper petition for referendum is filed, the educational service center governing board must certify the proposal to the county board of elections to be placed on the ballot at the next appropriate election.[74]

(5) Transfer of territory from a city or exempted village school district to an adjoining city or exempted village school district or to a educational service center proposed by the board of the district seeking to transfer its territory or by voter petition.[75] These transfers are subject to the approval of the state board of education and acceptance by the board of the transferee school district. If proposed by a board of education, as opposed to voter petition, good faith negotiations on terms of the transfer with any other district whose territory would be affected are required before filing a proposal with the state board, and the state board may not act unless it receives (a) a resolution requesting approval passed by the initiating board; (b) evidence that negotiations took place or that the district requesting the transfer made a good faith effort to hold negotiations; and (c) if negotiations took place, a statement signed by all participating boards of the terms agreed on and any points on which agreement could not be reached.[76]

(B) Agreements among school districts as to boundaries

Reorganization of school districts can be a sensitive matter in any case, but it is particularly sensitive with respect to territorial transfers brought about by municipal annexations, especially in urban areas. Contracts between school districts can be helpful in resolving potential disputes, insofar as they remove uncertainties concerning future territorial boundaries and potential claims of other school districts. In areas of growth, particularly areas undergoing suburban growth at the expense of an urban center, a city and the city school district may both be prompted to attempt to obtain territory in order to improve their respective tax bases. In such cases, as an aid to long-range planning and in the interest of avoiding future controversy, it may be desirable for all school boards involved to reach an accommodation on how district boundaries will be adjusted to make an acceptable division of pupils and tax revenues. Such agreements can also be coordinated with the annexation plans of the various municipalities involved. As bodies "politic and corporate," school boards have the power of "suing and being sued, contracting and being contracted with."[77] Thus, agreements regarding school district boundaries will bind the parties and be

---

[73] RC 3311.22.
[74] RC 3311.26. See also Text 4.10, Transfers of territory from local school districts.
[75] RC 3311.24(A). See also Text 4.11, Transfers from city and exempted village school districts.

[76] RC 3311.24(B). Such negotiations are governed by the rules adopted by the state board pursuant to RC 3311.06(D). See OAC 3301-89-01 et seq.
[77] RC 3313.17.

enforceable by court action—at least to the extent the agreements do not restrict the state's power to organize and reorganize school districts and comply with specific statutory requirements such as those appearing in RC 3311.06.

(C) Requirement of acceptance by transferee board

A school board may seek to divest the district of territory because it is difficult or uneconomical to administer. For the same reasons, school boards may be unwilling to accept the territory. Except in the case of annexation, the statutes generally condition transfer on acceptance by the board of the district to which territory is to be transferred or provide another procedure for such board to contest the transfer.[78] For example, the transfer of territory under RC 3311.24 from a city or exempted village school district to an adjoining city or exempted village school district or to an educational service center is not complete until a resolution accepting the transfer has been passed by a majority of the full membership of the board of the district to which the territory is transferred. This statutory principle was affirmed by the Ohio Supreme Court in a 1995 decision, where the court held that under RC 3311.24, the board of education of the receiving school district may reject the transfer of territory from another district even after that territory transfer proposal has been approved by the Ohio Department of Education.[79] Similarly, a transfer of territory from a local school district within the county to a contiguous an educational service center or to a contiguous city or exempted village school district may be effected only upon the approval of the receiving district board.[80]

4.08 Transfers of school district territory following municipal annexation

Ohio law contains elaborate annexation procedures whereby either unincorporated or incorporated territory may be added to the territory of an existing municipality.[81] When all of the territory of a school district is annexed to a city or village, the territory is also automatically transferred for school purposes to the board of the school district that serves the city or village. However, when only part of a school district is annexed, the transfer must be approved by the state board of education unless the board of such school district is a party to an annexation agreement with the board of the city school district serving the annexing city.[82] The act of the state board in approving or disapproving such a transfer is a quasi-judicial act and is appealable under RC Chapter 119.[83] Where a trial court, upon review, affirms the state board's order as supported by reliable, probative, and substantial evidence and in accordance with law, an appeals court, upon further review, may reverse only on a finding that the lower court abused its discretion.[84]

4.09 Territorial transfers initiated by state board of education

Proposals to reorganize school districts may be initiated either at the local or the state level. The state board of education is the central authority for the organization and reorganization of school districts. As such it is empowered to study the need for district reorganizations and to propose the consolidation of districts or the adjustment of district boundaries and is permitted to dissolve any district that fails to meet the standards for elementary and high schools as prescribed by that board and to transfer such district's territory to one or more adjacent districts.

---

[78] RC 3311.22, RC 3311.231, RC 3311.24, RC 3311.38.
[79] Garfield Heights City School District v State Board of Education, 71 OS(3d) 590 (1995).
[80] RC 3311.231.
[81] RC 709.02 to RC 709.37.
[82] RC 3311.06. For more extended treatment of RC 3311.06 procedure, see Text 4.07(A), Types of transfers, initiation, and approval.

[83] Union Title Co v State Bd of Ed, 51 OS(3d) 189, 555 NE(2d) 931 (1990). See also Rossford Exempted Village School Dist Bd of Ed v State Bd of Ed, 45 OS(3d) 356, 544 NE(2d) 651 (1989).
[84] Rossford Exempted Village School Dist Bd of Ed v State Bd of Ed, 63 OS(3d) 705, 590 NE(2d) 1240 (1992).

(A) Study of possible consolidation or transfer: scope

Where there is evidence that consolidation of school districts or transfer of territory among districts may be advisable, the state board is empowered to conduct studies into the possibility of improving district organization in the area. Any such study and any resulting recommendation must give due consideration to the wishes of the residents of the affected districts.[85]

The statutory language that directs the state board to consider the desires of the residents of the affected districts, when studying the needs and proposing consolidation of such districts, does not specify how the state board is to do so. Rather, the statute commits to the board's discretion the means by which those desires may be determined and the extent to which they affect the judgment of the board.[86]

Alternatively, upon receipt of a resolution adopted by a majority vote of the full membership of the board of any city, local, or exempted village school district requesting that the entire district be transferred, the state board may propose, by resolution, the transfer of territory.[87]

(B) Proposed reorganization

Where the state board concludes that a consolidation is appropriate, the board may propose creating a new school district, "which may consist of all or a part of the territory of two or more contiguous local, exempted village, or city school districts, or any combination of such districts."[88] Alternatively, the state board may propose transferring "part or all of the territory of a local, exempted village, or city school district to a contiguous local, exempted village, or city school district."[89]

The statutes grant the state board considerable flexibility. A new district may be created from parts of the territories of two or more adjoining districts, but otherwise leaving the adjoining districts in existence. Alternatively, a new district may be created from all of the territory of one district and part of the territory of one or more others, thus adjusting boundaries without changing the number of districts in the area. The board may also propose to consolidate all of the territory of two or more districts into one new district, thereby reducing the number of districts and eliminating the status of at least one of the existing districts as separate entities.

(C) Election

To implement any such proposed change, the state board must certify the proposal to the boards of elections of the counties involved for placement on the ballot at the next primary or general election occurring at least seventy-five days after such certification.[90] The proposal cannot be placed on the ballot, however, while an election is pending on any proposal to transfer all or part of the territory of a local school district to an adjoining district or to create a new local district.[91] Any electors residing in the proposed new district[92] or residing in the district containing territory proposed to be transferred[93] are qualified to vote on a proposal by the state board.

(D) Dissolution on failure to meet standards

Subject to the right of the qualified electors residing in the area to be transferred and equal in number to a majority of the qualified electors voting at the last general election to file a petition of referendum contesting any such order, the state board may order the dissolution of any school district which fails to meet the standards for elementary and high schools as prescribed by the state board and the transfer of any dissolved district's territory to one or more adjacent districts.[94] The receiving districts are required to accept such territory pursuant to the order of the state board.[95] The filing of a petition of referendum with respect to such an order suspends both the transfer order and the order of dissolution pending the outcome of the vote.[96] If a majority of qualified electors voting on the

---

[85] RC 3311.37, RC 3311.38.
[86] Davis v State Bd of Ed, 13 OS(2d) 24, 233 NE(2d) 321 (1968).
[87] RC 3311.38.
[88] RC 3311.37.
[89] RC 3311.38.
[90] RC 3311.38, RC 3311.37.

[91] RC 3311.38, RC 3311.37, RC 3311.22, RC 3311.231, RC 3311.26.
[92] RC 3311.37.
[93] RC 3311.38.
[94] RC 3301.16, RC 3301.161.
[95] RC 3301.16.
[96] OAG 71-036.

question do not vote in favor, the order becomes void.[97]

4.10 Transfers of territory from local school districts

Apart from the power of the state board of education to propose changes in local school district structure,[98] such changes may also be initiated at the local level. Proposed changes may include the transfer of all or part of one or more local school districts as follows: (1) to one or more other local school districts in the county;[99] (2) to an adjoining city or exempted village school district or to an adjoining county district;[100] or (3) to a new local school district to be created.[101] Such transfers may be made only to local school districts adjoining the district that is proposed to be transferred unless the board of the district proposed to be transferred has entered into an agreement pursuant to RC 3313.42, in which case the transfer may be to any local school district within the educational service center.[102] All of these changes may be proposed by resolution of the governing board of the educational service center and, except for creation of a new local school district, may also be proposed by voter petition. All are subject to approval by electors residing in the district or districts containing territory that is proposed to be transferred or residing in the proposed new district on filing of an appropriate petition of referendum.

(A) Initiating proposals, governing board resolution, voter petition

The procedure for initiating the transfer of local school district territory within a educational service center[103] and the procedure for initiating the transfer of local district territory to an adjoining city, exempted village, or educational service center[104] are similar. In either case, the proposal may be made by resolution of the educational service center governing board or by petition signed by electors in the territory proposed to be transferred equal to at least fifty-five per cent of the number voting in the last general election in that portion of the school district. It is not necessary for the signers actually to have voted in the previous election, provided the number equals the requisite percentage of those who did vote.[105] A petition is invalid if it does not include the required circulator's affidavit.[106] Any signature may be withdrawn from the petition only by order of the educational service center governing board on testimony of the signer that his signature was obtained by fraud, duress, or misrepresentation.[107]

The procedure for creating a new local school district differs from the procedure for transferring local school district territory in that the proposal can be initiated only by the governing board, not by voter petition, and in that a petition of referendum need be signed by electors equal to only thirty-five per cent of the number voting in the last general election.[108]

If the governing board imposes qualifications or conditions on its proposal and such conditions are not fulfilled, such resolution is void and will not support further transfer proceedings.[109] Also, an attorney general's opinion concludes that a governing board may rescind a resolution proposing a transfer to an adjoining educational service center, provided the adjoining governing board has not acted in reliance on the resolution.[110]

(B) Procedure on proposals, referendum

When the governing board proposes to transfer territory or create a new local school district, the board must, at its next regular meeting at least thirty days thereafter, adopt a subsequent resolution making the proposal effective at any time prior to the next July 1 unless, during the thirty-day period, a petition of referendum against the proposal is filed. If the proposal is

---

[97]RC 3301.161.
[98]See Text 4.09, Territorial transfers initiated by state board of education.
[99]RC 3311.22.
[100]RC 3311.231.
[101]RC 3311.26.
[102]RC 3311.26, RC 3311.22.
[103]RC 3311.22.
[104]RC 3311.231.

[105]OAG 69-088.
[106]RC 3501.38(E); OAG 68-074.
[107]RC 3311.22, RC 3311.231. See also State ex rel Muter v Mercer County Bd of Ed, 112 App 66, 175 NE(2d) 305 (Mercer 1959). But see 1964 OAG 1043.
[108]RC 3311.26.
[109]Emmert v Hardin County Bd of Ed, 7 App(2d) 116, 219 NE(2d) 50 (Hardin 1966).
[110]OAG 67-075 (LC).

merely to transfer territory from a local school district, the petition of referendum requires the signatures of electors residing in the territory proposed to be transferred equal to a majority voting in the last general election.[111] If the proposal is to create a new local school district, the referendum petition only requires signatures of electors residing in the territory of the proposed new district equal to thirty-five per cent of the number voting in the last general election.[112]

When the proposal to transfer territory is by voter petition or when a referendum petition against a transfer or new district is filed, the governing board must certify the transfer or referendum petition to the boards of election in the counties containing affected school districts for placement on the ballot at the next primary or general election, or at a special election on a specified date, in any case occurring at least seventy-five days after certification.[113] However, the governing board is not required to take any action with respect to any petition to transfer territory to another local school district within the county (1) if a petition of transfer was previously filed relating to all or any part of the territory included in such petition, or (2) if a resolution proposing the transfer of all or any part of the territory included in such petition was previously adopted by the governing board unless (a) a petition of referendum is filed with respect to such resolution, and (b) the proposed transfer is defeated at the ensuing election relating to the petition of referendum.[114] The governing board is also not required to take any action relating to a petition to transfer territory from a local school district to an adjoining city, exempted village, or educational service center if a petition of transfer has been previously filed or a resolution of transfer has been previously adopted relating to part or all of the territory included in such petition as long as the previously initiated proposal is pending before the governing board or is subject to an election.[115]

The persons qualified to vote on a proposal to transfer territory are the electors residing in the school districts that will be affected by the transfer.[116] The persons entitled to vote on a proposal to create a new district are the electors who reside within the proposed new district.[117] When a vote on a proposed transfer is taken, there is no provision for offering the electors a choice of school districts to which the subject territory may be transferred.[118]

The state board of education also may initiate reorganizations of local school districts.[119]

(C) Effect of consolidation, challenge

If an entire district is transferred, the district board of education is abolished.[120] When a local school district in one county is transferred to an adjoining educational service center, it cannot retain its status as an independent district but must be attached to an existing city, exempted village, or local school district.[121] Also, after two districts have been merged, electors in the districts do not have standing to challenge the previous action by the governing board of education.[122]

4.11 Transfers from city and exempted village school districts

(A) Proposal to transfer territory, hearing

Transfers of territory from a city or exempted village school district to an adjoining district may be proposed by the board of education of the district seeking to divest itself of the territory or by petition signed by seventy-five per cent of the elec-

---

[111] RC 3311.22, RC 3311.231.
[112] RC 3311.26.
[113] RC 3311.22, RC 3311.231, RC 3311.26.
[114] RC 3311.22.
[115] RC 3311.231.
[116] RC 3311.231, RC 3311.22. Both statutes permit the board of education of the district receiving territory to accept or reject the transfer.
[117] RC 3311.26. See also State ex rel Erwin v Jackson County School Dist Bd of Ed, 17 OS(2d) 63, 245 NE(2d) 730 (1969).
[118] OAG 68-100.
[119] See Text 4.09, Territorial transfers initiated by state board of education.
[120] RC 3311.22, RC 3311.231.
[121] OAG 68-100.
[122] McKinney v Brown, 31 App(2d) 25, 285 NE(2d) 385 (Brown 1972).

tors residing in the territory to be transferred who voted in the last general election.[123] An elector may withdraw his signature from the petition at any time before official action is taken with respect to it.[124] The state board of education may provide for a public hearing on the proposal, but there is no provision for a referendum.[125] The state board may initiate a similar proposal under RC 3311.37 or RC 3311.38, but is required to submit the question to the voters.[126] Pursuant to RC 3311.38, any city, local, or exempted village school district may initiate a request by resolution adopted by majority vote of the full membership of its school board that the entire district be transferred.[127]

(B) Approval of state board, completion of transfer

The state board of education must either approve or disapprove the proposed transfer by September 1 and notify the boards of the districts affected. If the state board disapproves, the proposed transfer fails. If the state board approves, the board of the district in which the territory is located must adopt a resolution transferring the territory.[128] As with cases under RC 3311.06,[129] the state board's action in an RC 3311.24 case is appealable under RC Chapter 119.[130] Where a trial court, upon review, affirms the state board's order as supported by reliable, probative, and substantial evidence and in accordance with law, an appeals court, upon further review, may reverse only on a finding that the lower court abused its discretion.[131] After the transferring board adopts a resolution transferring the territory, a resolution accepting the transfer is to be adopted by the board of the district to which the territory is transferred. The board of the receiving district may reject the transfer,[132] by a majority vote, even after the transfer has been approved by the Ohio Department of Education.

DIVISION OF ASSETS AND LIABILITIES ON REORGANIZATION; GOVERNANCE

4.12 Allocation of state funds, minimum guarantee

Foundation program funds accruing to a school district created under RC 3311.26 or RC 3311.37 may not be less than the sum of the amounts received by the former districts separately in the year in which the creation of the district became effective. When an entire school district is transferred to another district or districts pursuant to RC 3311.22, RC 3311.231, or RC 3311.38, foundation program funds accruing to the district accepting the transferred territory may not be less than the sum of the amounts allocated to the districts separately under RC Chapter 3317 in the year in which the transfer was consummated. However, that minimum guarantee may not affect the amount of aid received by a district for more than three consecutive years.[133]

---

[123]RC 3311.24. See also OAC 3301-89-01 et seq.; 1964 OAG 1043. In the case of a petition, the board of the district in which the proposal originates must file the petition with the state board of education prior to April 1 in any even-numbered year. The district board need only send a petition determined to have sufficient valid signatures. The base figure from which the required percentage of signers is to be determined is the number of voting qualified electors within the territory, not the number of electors who were eligible to vote. Moreover, a petition under RC 3311.24 does not require a circulator's affidavit (required in other contexts by RC 3501.38(E)) since the petition does not lead to an election. State ex rel Harrell v Streetsboro City School Dist Bd of Ed, 46 OS(3d) 55, 544 NE(2d) 924 (1989).

[124]State ex rel Fairview Park School Dist Bd of Ed v Rocky River School Dist Bd of Ed, 40 OS(3d) 136, 532 NE(2d) 715 (1988).

[125]See OAC 3301-89-01 et seq.

[126]See Text 4.09, Territorial transfers initiated by state board of education.

[127]RC 3311.38.

[128]RC 3311.24.

[129]See Text 4.08, Transfers of school district territory following municipal annexation.

[130]Rossford Exempted Village School Dist Bd of Ed v State Bd of Ed, 45 OS(3d) 356, 544 NE(2d) 651 (1989). See also Garfield Heights City School Dist v State Bd of Ed, 62 App(3d) 308, 575 NE(2d) 503 (Franklin 1990).

[131]Rossford Exempted Village School Dist Bd of Ed v State Bd of Ed, 63 OS(3d) 705, 590 NE(2d) 1240 (1992).

[132]Garfield Heights City School Dist v State Bd of Ed, 71 OS(3d) 590, 646 NE(2d) 163 (1995).

[133]RC 3317.04.

4.13 Fair division of assets and liabilities

In any school district reorganization involving transfer, consolidation, or the creation of a new district, there must be an equitable distribution of money, debts, and property between or among the districts involved. When an entire district is transferred (including to a newly created district), the indebtedness of the district transferred must be assumed in full by the acquiring district, and all of the funds of the district transferred must be paid in full to the acquiring district. As of the effective date of transfer, legal title to all property of the transferred district vests in the board of education of the district or districts to which the territory is transferred.[134]

When the territory transferred to a particular district includes only a part of a local school district, the funds of the district from which territory was transferred must be divided equitably by the educational service center governing board or the state board of education (depending on who initiated the transfer), or, in the case of a transfer of territory resulting from an annexation, under the supervision of the state board (whose decision is final), between the acquiring district and that part of the original district remaining after the transfer.[135]

In the case of territory transferred from a city or exempted village school district, an equitable division of funds must be made by the district board making the transfer or by the state board (depending on who initiated the transfer) between the acquiring district and that part of the former district remaining after the transfer.[136]

On the creation of a new local school district initiated by the educational service center governing board from part or all of one or more local school districts, the funds of each former district contributing only a part of the new district must be divided equitably by the county board between the new district and that part of the former district not included in the new district.[137]

On the creation of a new district initiated by the state board of education, the funds of each former district must be apportioned equitably by the state board between the new district and that part of the original district not included in the new district.[138]

In general, when a new school district is created, or when the territory transferred includes only part of a district, the net indebtedness of each original district of which only a part is taken by the new or acquiring district must be divided between the new or acquiring district and the original district in the ratio that the assessed valuation of the part taken by the new or acquiring district bears to the assessed valuation of the original district as of the effective date of the transfer.[139] If an entire district is transferred, any indebtedness of the former district incurred as a result of a loan made under RC 3317.64 shall be canceled, and such indebtedness shall not be apportioned among any of the districts acquiring the territory.[140] When the board of a city district, or an exempted village school district, or the qualified electors thereof, initiate a transfer of territory to a city, exempted village, or educational service center, the transferring board must make an equitable division of the indebtedness of the transferring district.[141] When a transfer of part of the territory of a district to another district results from annexation, an equitable division of funds and indebtedness must be made between the districts involved under supervision of the state board of education whose decision is final.[142]

When a school district is dissolved and its property transferred by the state board for failure to meet standards, the state board must make an equitable division of the funds, property, and indebtedness of the district among the receiving districts.[143]

---

[134]RC 3311.06, RC 3311.22, RC 3311.231, RC 3311.24, RC 3311.26, RC 3311.37, RC 3311.38.
[135]RC 3311.06, RC 3311.22, RC 3311.231, RC 3311.38.
[136]RC 3311.24, RC 3311.38.
[137]RC 3311.26.
[138]RC 3311.37.
[139]RC 3311.22, RC 3311.231, RC 3311.26, RC 3311.37, RC 3311.38.
[140]RC 3311.22, RC 3311.231, RC 3311.38.
[141]RC 3311.24.
[142]RC 3311.06(G).
[143]RC 3301.16.

4.14 Effect of reorganization on tax levies

(A) In general

An additional levy voted outside the ten-mill tax limitation[144] in one school district is valid as to the combined district where the voting district is combined with another district not included in the taxing district at the time of the vote.[145] When a new local school district is created pursuant to RC 3311.26, there may be spread over the entire new district the larger of any levies voted and authorized in the districts out of which the new district was created, to the extent necessary to meet the obligations for which the levies were authorized.[146]

The board of education of a district to which another district is to be transferred pursuant to RC 3311.231 may, subsequent to the election in the district to be transferred, approve the transfer, and prior to the effective date of the transfer, levy a tax outside the ten-mill limitation and, subsequent to the effective date of the transfer, levy the tax against the whole of the new taxing district.[147] After such a transfer, the tax levy of the receiving district for school purposes inside the ten-mill limitation would apply to the entire consolidated district unless the application of such rate would force an infringement of the ten-mill limitation.[148] Where the legal existence of a district is terminated by consolidation prior to the date of the election with respect to a tax levy proposed by its taxing authority, submission of the proposal to the electors of the original district or the consolidated district is not authorized.[149]

(B) Annexation

An appeals court's decision concerning the allocation of tax levies within the ten-mill limitation after annexation of one school district to another is binding when the identical issue is appealed to the board of tax appeals from the order of the county budget commission allocating the levies for the next tax year.[150]

The transfer of school district territory or division of funds and indebtedness incident to a transfer may only be completed as prescribed by RC 3311.06. The statute requires that funds received by a district for real property lost to the district by reason of annexation must be deposited in the district's bond retirement fund.[151]

The statutes pertaining to transfers of public funds, such as RC 3311.06, RC 5705.14, and RC 5705.15, must be construed together. Accordingly, where the funds received for property lost to a district have been properly deposited in the bond retirement fund, any application for an order to transfer money from the fund must be brought pursuant to RC 5705.14.[152]

4.15 Board of education in reorganized district

(A) Abolition of board or membership on board

If an entire school district is transferred, the district board of education is abolished. If part of a district is transferred, any board member who is a resident of the transferred part ceases to be a member of the board of the district from which the transfer was made.[153]

(B) Board of new local district

When a new local school district is created by the state board of education, the state board must appoint five electors residing in the district to be members of an interim board of education. A district board must be elected at the next general election held in an odd-numbered year that occurs not less than ninety days after the appointment of the initial board members.

---

[144]See Text 39.03, Ten-mill limitation, voted and unvoted levies.
[145]Kellenberger v Ross County Bd of Ed, 173 OS 201, 180 NE(2d) 834 (1962).
[146]OAG 66-098.
[147]OAG 66-040.
[148]1960 OAG 1373.
[149]1957 OAG 1212.
[150]Cambridge City School Dist v Guernsey County Budget Comm, 13 Misc 258 (BTA 1967). See also Cambridge City School Dist v Guernsey County Budget Comm, 11 App(2d) 77, 228 NE(2d) 874 (Guernsey 1967), affirmed by 13 OS(2d) 77, 234 NE(2d) 512 (1968).
[151]RC 3311.06(G).
[152]In re Margaretta Local School Dist, Transfer of Funds, 20 Misc 243, 253 NE(2d) 836 (CP, Erie 1969).
[153]RC 3311.22, RC 3311.231, RC 3311.38.

At such election, two members must be elected for a term of two years and three members for a term of four years. Thereafter, successors are elected in the same manner for the same terms as members of a local school district board.[154]

On creation of a new local school district by the initiative of a educational service center, an interim board must be appointed by the governing board. A district board must be elected at the next general election held in an odd-numbered year occurring more than thirty days after the appointment of the initial board members. At such election, two members must be elected for a term of two years and three members for a term of four years. Thereafter, successors are elected in the same manner and for the same terms as members of a local school district board.[155]

(C) Board of new city district

On creation of a new city school district by the initiative of the state board of education, the state board must determine the number of members that will comprise the district board of education, subject to RC 3313.02. The state board must then appoint that number to hold office until their successors are elected and qualified. A district board is to be elected at the next general election held in an odd-numbered year that occurs not less than ninety days after the appointment of the initial board members. If the number of members is even, half are elected for two years and half for four years. If the number is odd, half the number less one are elected for two years and the remaining number for four years. Thereafter, successors are elected as provided in RC 3313.08.[156]

(D) Duties of educational service center governing board as to dissolved local school district board

As previously described, if a county school district contains only one local school district, RC 3311.051 mandates that "there shall be only one board of education which shall be the governing board of the educational service center which shall have all the powers and duties of a local board of education in addition to those of a governing board of an educational service center." At the first general election occurring more than seventy-five days after the above provisions become applicable in a educational service center, a five-member governing board must be elected. The term of office of each member shall be determined by lot at the board's initial organizational meeting in accordance with the statutes, and all subsequent terms are for four years.[157] When a local district board loses its identity, and its powers and duties are assumed by the governing board, any pending lawsuit the local board had capacity to bring may be continued by the governing board in the name of the former board.[158]

---

[154]RC 3311.37.
[155]RC 3311.26.
[156]RC 3311.37.
[157]RC 3311.052.

[158]Miami Trace Local School Dist Bd of Ed v Marting, 7 Misc 64, 217 NE(2d) 712 (CP, Madison 1966).

Chapter 5

Boards of Education

5.01 Introduction

COMPOSITION OF BOARDS OF EDUCATION; MEMBERS

5.02 Composition of board of education
5.03 Members of board of education
5.04 Compensation and expenses of board members
5.05 Removal from office

POWERS OF BOARD OF EDUCATION

5.06 General powers of board of education
5.07 Capacity to sue and be sued
5.08 Rule-making and regulatory power
5.09 Miscellaneous powers
5.10 Authority of probate court or educational service center governing board to exercise powers of defaulting board of education

MEETINGS AND PROCEDURES

5.11 Board meetings in general
5.12 Open meetings: the sunshine law
5.13 Board action, resolutions

5.01 Introduction

The board of education, made up of resident citizens, is the governing body of the school district. With the change from county boards of education to governing boards of educational service centers, the general assembly adopted legislation which specifies, throughout Title 33, that the terms "school board" or "board of education," unless expressly stated otherwise, include governing boards of educational service centers.[1] Although the state board of education has plenary authority in the supervision of the public school system generally,[2] the actual job of establishing and maintaining public schools belongs to the school districts and their respective boards.

A board of education is considered a quasi corporation, acting for the public as one of the state's agencies, for the organization, administration, and control of the public school system of the state.[3] One court has defined a board of education as the administrative, quasi-legislative and quasi-judicial agency charged with management and control of the school system of its district.[4]

COMPOSITION OF BOARDS OF EDUCATION; MEMBERS

5.02 Composition of board of education

(A) Local and exempted village school districts, and educational service centers

In each local and exempted village school district and educational service center, the board of education or governing board consists of five members, who must be electors residing in the territory composing the district and elected at large in the district.[5] In a joint educational service center, the governing board consists of either five members to be appointed or elected in accordance with a procedure specified in RC 3311.053[6] if the board is formed under that statute, or an odd number not to exceed nine members to be appointed or elected in accordance with a procedure specified in RC 3311.054 if the board is formed under that statute.

If an educational service center contains only one local school district, there is only one board of education, the governing board, which has the powers and duties of a local board in addition to those of a governing board.[7]

> Note: For the composition of joint vocational and cooperative education school district boards of education, see, respectively, Text 27.09(A), Board of education of joint vocational district, and Text 4.03(G), Cooperative education school district.

---

[1] RC 3311.055.
[2] RC 3301.07.
[3] Wayman v Akron City School Dist Bd of Ed, 5 OS(2d) 248, 215 NE(2d) 394 (1966).
[4] Rumora v Ashtabula Area City School Dist Bd of Ed, 43 Misc 48, 335 NE(2d) 378 (CP, Ashtabula 1973).

[5] RC 3313.01.
[6] See Text 4.03(C), New educational service centers.
[7] RC 3311.051; OAG 86-108.

(B) Boards of city school districts

The number of board members in a city school district is determined according to a combination of the district's population as established by the last federal census and the board's plan of organization. If the population is:

(1) Less than 50,000, the board may consist of not less than three or more than five members elected at large from the district;

(2) Fifty thousand or more, but less than 150,000, the board may consist of not less than two or more than seven members elected at large, plus not more than two members elected from separate subdistricts; and

(3) One hundred and fifty thousand or more, the board may consist of not less than five or more than seven members elected at large.[8]

(1) Referendum to determine composition of city school district board

Article VI, section 3 of the Ohio Constitution confers on each school district within any city the power to determine for itself the number of members and organization of its board of education. The general assembly has provided the following mechanism for the exercise of that power:[9]

If a petition signed by ten per cent of the electors (calculated pursuant to the statute) in any city school district is filed with the district treasurer, asking that the question of the number of members and organization of the board be submitted to the electors, the board must, within thirty days after the date the petition was filed, adopt a resolution requiring submission of that question at a designated regular municipal election (by statutory definition, that election held in November of an odd-numbered year) and providing for the appointment of a seven-member commission, except in those cases in which a district has territory in more than one city, to frame at least two plans of organization.[10]

Three of the commission members are appointed by the board president, two by the mayor of the city in which the district is located, and two by the president of the city's board of sinking fund trustees. If the city does not have a board of sinking fund trustees (and most do not), the city treasurer or the officer who exercises the functions of a treasurer appoints two members.[11] When a district has territory in more than one city, the number of commission members depends on the number of cities. In this case, the board president appoints three members, the mayor of each city in which the district has territory appoints one member, and the president of the board of sinking fund trustees (or the treasurer or fiscal officer) of each such city appoints one member.

A certified copy of the resolution must be transmitted to the mayor and president of the board of sinking fund trustees immediately after passage, and the commission must be appointed and is required to organize within sixty days after passage of the resolution.[12] The board must make any necessary provisions for meeting the expenses of the commission, but the commissioners themselves are to receive no compensation.[13]

Each of the plans prepared by the commission must provide for the number of board members, the term of the members, and the organization of the board. One plan must provide for a board with the same number and organization as the existing board.

The plans are submitted to the electors on separate, nonpartisan ballots.[14] If one receives a majority of the votes cast for all plans, that plan becomes the law governing the number of members and organization of the board, and members are to be elected pursuant to the plan at the next general election held in an odd-numbered year. Members elected at that time take office on the first Monday of the January following their election, and their term of office will be as provided in the plan, but not less than two years.[15]

The question of the number of members and organization of the district board may

---

[8] RC 3313.02.
[9] RC 3313.04 to RC 3313.07.
[10] RC 3313.04.
[11] RC 3313.04.
[12] RC 3313.04.
[13] RC 3313.06.
[14] RC 3313.05.
[15] RC 3313.07.

not be submitted to a referendum vote more than once every four years.[16]

(2) Subdistricts of city school district

Within three months after official announcement of the result of each federal census, the board of each city school district that has elected to have subdistricts and which has a population of at least 50,000 but less than 150,000 is required to redistrict. The subdistricts must be as equal in population as possible and composed of adjacent and as compact territory as practicable. The superintendent of public instruction is required to redistrict if the board fails to do so.[17]

5.03 Members of board of education

(A) Nomination and election

Members of a board of education must be electors of the territory composing the school district and are elected in that district on a nonpartisan ballot[18] on the first Tuesday following the first Monday in November, in the odd-numbered years.[19]

Nominations of candidates for local and exempted village boards are authorized only by petition signed by twenty-five qualified electors of the district. With respect to a city school district, a candidate's petition must be signed by 25 qualified electors if the district has a population of less than 20,000 as ascertained by the next preceding federal census, 75 electors if the district population is at least 20,000 but less than 50,000, 150 electors if the district population is at least 50,000 but less than 100,000, and 300 electors if the district population is at least 100,000.

Nominating petitions must be filed with the board of elections not later than 4 p.m. of the seventy-fifth day before the day of the general election. The board of elections is required by statute to refuse a petition for filing if it appears to contain more than three times the minimum number of signatures required; however, when a petition has been accepted for filing, it will not be deemed invalid if, upon verification of the signatures, the number of signatures accepted exceeds the required minimum. A board of elections may discontinue verifying petitions when the number of verified signatures equals the minimum required number.[20]

Where the number of members of a board of education of a city school district to be elected at large is even, half are elected in the year preceding and the remaining half the year following the calendar year divisible by four. If the number to be elected is odd, half the remainder, after diminishing the number by one, are elected in the year preceding, and the remaining number elected in the year following the calendar year divisible by four. All members to be elected from odd-numbered subdistricts are elected at one election, and all members from even-numbered subdistricts are elected at the alternate election.[21]

Included among campaign and election provisions applicable to members of a board of education are the following:

(1) A requirement that all campaign finances of a candidate be handled through a single campaign committee;[22]

(2) Certain prohibited activities;[23]

(3) The establishment of times for filing reports of contributions and expenditures by any campaign committee that has received $1,000 or more in total contributions;[24]

(4) The creation of the Ohio elections commission with power to investigate campaign finance complaints;[25]

(5) Permission to make payroll deductions for political contributions;[26] and

---

[16]RC 3313.04.
[17]RC 3313.03.
[18]RC 3505.04, RC 3513.254.
[19]RC 3501.02(D).
[20]RC 3513.254.
[21]RC 3313.08.
[22]RC 3517.081.
[23]RC 3517.13.
[24]RC 3517.10.

[25]RC 3517.14, RC 3517.15.
[26]RC 3599.031. In 1995 S 8, eff. August 23, 1995, the legislature amended RC 3599.031 to prohibit any public employer from deducting political contributions from its employees' paychecks. A federal court, however, enjoined this provision as violating the US Constitution. Toledo Area AFL-CIO Council v Pizza, 898 FSupp 554 (ND Ohio 1995). As this edition went to print, this litigation was still pending.

(6) Prohibition against unfair political activities.[27]

(B) Term, oath of office

Terms of office of elected members of each board of education begin on January 1 after their election, and each member's term is for four years, expiring on December 31, except as otherwise provided by law.[28]

Before taking up the duties of office, a member is required to take an oath to support the Constitution of the United States and the Constitution of Ohio and to perform faithfully the duties of office. This oath may be administered by, among others, the district treasurer or any board member.[29]

(C) Filling vacancies

A board vacancy may be caused by death, nonresidence, resignation, removal from office, failure of a person to qualify within ten days after organization of the board or after the person's appointment or election, removal from the district, acceptance by a board member of an office the duties of which are incompatible with those of a board member, or absence from board meetings for a period of ninety days if the absence is caused by a reason declared insufficient by a two-thirds vote of the remaining board members. In the latter case, the vote must be taken and recorded not less than thirty days after the absence. Any vacancy of this nature must be filled by the board at its next regular or special meeting, but not earlier than ten days after the vacancy occurs.[30]

A majority vote of all the remaining members is necessary to fill a vacancy. Immediately after such a vote, the district treasurer must give written notice to the responsible board of elections that a vacancy has been filled and the name of the person appointed.[31]

Each person selected to fill a board vacancy by the board itself, or by the probate court upon a board's failure to act to fill a vacancy, holds office until the completion of the unexpired term, or until the January 1 immediately following the next regular board of education election more than ninety days after the person is selected, whichever period is shorter. A special election to fill the vacancy must be held unless the unexpired term ends on or before the January 1 immediately following the regular board of education election. The term of a person chosen at a special election begins on the January 1 immediately following the election.[32]

The term of a board member may not be lengthened by resignation and subsequent selection by the board or probate court.[33] Similarly, prospective vacancies cannot be filled prospectively if the appointing authority's term will expire before the vacancy arises.[34]

Upon the death of the board president, the board should adopt a resolution naming the vice-president to the presidency and then elect a new vice-president, with both new officers to serve for the balance of the year. When the president of a county board of education resigns, the vice-president automatically becomes president for the remainder of the term of that office; the board appoints a new member to the board; and the board elects one of its members vice-president for the remainder of the term of the office.[35]

5.04 Compensation and expenses of board members

(A) Compensation and retirement

Each member of a board of education, other than a county school district board or a joint vocational school district board, may be paid compensation as the board provides by resolution, not exceeding $80 per meeting attended.[36] Members of a county board may be paid such compensation as the board provides by resolution, not exceeding $80 per day, plus mileage at the rate provided by resolution of the board.[37]

---

[27]RC 3599.091, RC 3599.092.
[28]RC 3313.09.
[29]O Const Art XV §7; RC 3313.10; 1959 OAG 37.
[30]RC 3313.11. This statute expressly does not apply to joint vocational and cooperative education school districts.
[31]RC 3313.11.
[32]RC 3313.11.
[33]RC 3313.11.
[34]State ex rel Norman v Viebranz, 19 OS(3d) 146, 19 OBR 369, 483 NE(2d) 1176 (1985).
[35]OAG 68-113.
[36]RC 3313.12.
[37]RC 3313.12.

Members of a joint vocational board are compensated as the board provides by resolution, not exceeding $80 per meeting for up to twelve meetings per year and may also receive mileage to and from each meeting at the rate of twenty cents per mile.[38]

Except as provided by law, no board member may receive compensation for his services as a member.[39] The knowing solicitation or receipt by a public servant or the promise to give or giving to a public servant of any compensation, other than as allowed by law, to perform his official duties or any other act or service in the public servant's public capacity is a criminal act under RC 2921.43.[40]

Board members may authorize the deduction from their compensation of the cost of group insurance payable by them under RC 3313.202.[41]

A board member is a "public officer" as that term is used in Article II, section 20 of the Ohio Constitution and, therefore, may not receive an increase in compensation during the existing term of office. A board may vote to increase the compensation of its members to the maximum permitted by RC 3313.12, but any such increase may not constitutionally become effective with respect to a particular board member during that member's current term.[42]

A school board member may elect to become a member of the school employees retirement system (SERS).[43] In addition, a member of the public employees retirement system (PERS), the state teachers retirement system (STRS), or SERS may purchase credit for service as a school board member if the conditions spelled out in, respectively, RC 145.299, RC 3307.311, or RC 3309.311 are satisfied.

(B) Reimbursement for expenses

Members of a governing board of an educational service center may be paid for mileage at the rate per mile provided by resolution of the board to cover actual and necessary expenses incurred during attendance at any board meeting[44] but are prohibited from receiving an increase in that rate during their term in office.[45] Members of city, local, and exempted village boards of education are not entitled to payment for mileage. Members of joint vocational boards may be paid for mileage at the rate of twenty cents per mile to and from board meetings.[46] Members of educational service center governing boards and local boards within the county are also eligible to be paid their regular meeting rates, plus expenses incurred for educational meetings called by the county board. Expenses include the cost of meals served.[47]

The amount that may be set aside in a service fund to be used in paying expenses of board members actually incurred in the performance of their duties, or of members-elect, is $2 per pupil or $20,000, whichever is greater; the maximum sum for a county board is $20,000. No school district may appropriate or spend more than $60,000 from such a service fund in any one school year.[48]

There is no authority for payment to be made in advance of incurring travel expenses.

5.05 Removal from office

A board member is subject to removal from office for misconduct pursuant to RC 3.07 to RC 3.10. Grounds for removal include willfully and flagrantly exercising authority or power not authorized by law, refusing or neglecting to perform any official duty, gross neglect of duty, gross immorality, drunkenness, misfeasance, malfeasance, or nonfeasance.[49] A board member who voted on contracts to employ his spouse as an assistant school nurse, thereby violating RC 2921.42(A)(1), was guilty of malfeasance in office.[50]

---

[38]RC 3311.19.
[39]RC 3313.86.
[40]See Text 45.11, Soliciting or receiving improper compensation.
[41]RC 3311.19, RC 3313.12.
[42]OAG 78-018; OAG 80-050.
[43]RC 3309.012. See also Text Ch 14, Nonteaching Personnel: Retirement.
[44]RC 3313.12.

[45]OAG 85-036.
[46]RC 3311.19(F).
[47]RC 3315.06.
[48]RC 3315.15.
[49]RC 3.07.
[50]In re Steed, No. 1909, 1989 WL 411471 (4th Dist Ct App, Lawrence, 7-27-89). See Text 45.06(B), Prohibited transactions. See also Scherer v Rock Hill Local School Dist Bd of Ed, 63 App(3d) 555, 579

Proceedings for removal must be commenced by filing a complaint in the form of a recall petition stating the charges with sufficient precision so that the board member can adequately prepare his defense.[51] Since the complaint must be signed by the percentage of qualified electors set forth in RC 3.08, any amendment to the complaint requires recirculation and filing a new action.[52] Removal proceedings under RC 3.07 to RC 3.10 are quasi-penal in nature, so procedural requirements should be strictly construed. In an action to remove board members, a court concluded the requirements of RC 3.08 had not been met when petitioners had filed a civil complaint signed by their three attorneys and not by the petitioners.[53]

POWERS OF BOARD OF EDUCATION

5.06 General powers of board of education

(A) Statutory origin of powers

A board of education is a body politic and corporate created by the general assembly, and has only such authority and jurisdiction as the general assembly has expressly provided, plus such implied or incidental powers as are reasonably necessary to carry out the express powers.[54] A board cannot increase its power or confer upon itself additional jurisdiction through its statutory rule-making authority,[55] and it cannot take any action which is inconsistent with its powers under statutory law. While a board is given statutory authority to make necessary rules and regulations, the decision as to what rules are necessary is a policy decision involving the exercise of discretion and judgment.[56]

A board has the power to sue and be sued, contract and be contracted with, acquire, hold, possess, and dispose of real and personal property, and take and hold in trust for the use and benefit of its district any grant or devise of land and any donation or bequest of money or other personal property.[57]

Even these general grants of power, however, are subject to restrictions. For example, although boards are given the power to acquire, hold, possess, and dispose of property, a board may not acquire a building through a lease-purchase agreement.[58]

As for a board's contracting authority, RC 3313.33 states that no contract is binding on the board unless made or authorized at a regular or special board meeting. Thus, for example, an individual board member, district superintendent, assistant superintendent, principal, or superintendent of buildings and grounds cannot bind the board to a contract.[59] While no contract is binding upon the board unless approved by it, there is no prohibition against delegating to an officer of the board power to terminate an agreement.[60]

(B) Construing powers of board

The general assembly has empowered boards of education to exercise wide discre-

---

NE(2d) 525 (Lawrence 1990), a related case arising from the same facts in which the court refused to void the spouse's contract of employment.

[51]In re Recall of Each Member of the Saint Clairsville-Richland Bd of Ed, No. 83-B-34, 1984 WL 7706 (7th Dist Ct App, Belmont, 5-8-84).

[52]2,867 Signers v Mack, 66 App(2d) 79, 419 NE(2d) 1108 (Medina 1979).

[53]Petitioners v Stringer, No. 3664, 1986 WL 3532 (11th Dist Ct App, Trumbull, 3-21-86).

[54]Board of Education v Best, 52 OS 138, 39 NE 694 (1894).

[55]Verberg v Cleveland City School Dist Bd of Ed, 135 OS 246, 20 NE(2d) 368 (1939).

[56]Jones v Fairland Local School Dist, No. 1747, 1985 WL 8302 (4th Dist Ct App, Lawrence, 8-20-85).

[57]RC 3313.17.

[58]OAG 86-031.

[59]Wolf v Cuyahoga Falls City School Dist Bd of Ed, 52 OS(3d) 222, 556 NE(2d) 511 (1990); Walker v Lockland City School Dist Bd of Ed, 69 App(2d) 27, 429 NE(2d) 1179 (Hamilton 1980); Egypt, Inc v Akron Bd of Ed, No. 14687, 1990 WL 209693 (9th Dist Ct App, Summit, 12-19-90); Tirpack v Beavercreek Bd of Ed, No. 91 CA 0070, 1992 WL 172160 (2d Dist Ct App, Greene, 7-24-92).

[60]Deryck v Akron City School Dist, No. 14660, 1990 WL 203178 (9th Dist Ct App, Summit, 12-12-90) (upholding assistant superintendent's termination of independent bus driver's service contract). *Deryck* involved a service contract, and does not go so far as to suggest that termination of an employee's contract need not be by the board. Compare Rumora v Ashtabula Area City School Dist Bd of Ed, 43 Misc 48, 335 NE(2d) 378 (CP, Ashtabula 1973), which *Deryck* expressly distinguished.

tion in certain areas as to the manner in which they fulfill their duties and responsibilities. However, statutes that are mandatory or prohibitive in nature have been strictly construed.

If there is doubt as to the authority of a board to expend public funds, that doubt must be resolved against the grant of power.[61]

(C) Board discretion in exercising powers

A court generally will not restrain a board from carrying into effect its determination of any question within its discretion, unless there is an abuse of discretion, fraud, or collusion on the part of the board in the exercise of its statutory authority.[62] The exercise of an honest judgment, however erroneous it may seem to be, is not an abuse of discretion.[63] Although a court cannot control how the discretion of a board is exercised, it may compel the exercise itself.[64]

It has been said, in a case involving the nonrenewal of a principal's contract, that a court cannot substitute its judgment for that of the board, absent a claim that a statutory right or a constitutional obligation was violated.[65] Nor, absent an abuse of discretion, can a court substitute its judgment for that of a board on whether, for economic reasons, to discontinue providing bus transportation to secondary level students.[66]

To obtain injunctive relief with respect to the award of a contract in connection with the operation of a school system, a plaintiff-taxpayer must prove, by clear and convincing evidence, that the award of the contract constituted an abuse of discretion resulting in some tangible harm to the public in general or to the plaintiff as an individual.[67]

5.07 Capacity to sue and be sued

Boards of education have express power to sue and be sued.[68] Implied power has also been inferred from other grants of authority. For instance, the statute authorizing a board to acquire, hold, and dispose of property has been construed as consent to be sued with respect to the property, and a private litigant can rely on adverse possession to obtain title to land held by a board.[69]

Boards may also be sued for tort claims. Since 1983, the defense of sovereign immunity has not been available to a board in an action seeking damages for injuries allegedly caused by negligence of the board's employees.[70] As a result of court decisions and the enactment of new statutes, a board may purchase liability insurance coverage to protect individual board members or employees and the board as an entity against liability on account of damages or injury to persons or property.[71]

A vestige of sovereign immunity remains, however, in that boards remain exempt from payment of prejudgment interest in contractual wage disputes absent a specific statute or express contractual provision to the contrary.[72]

---

[61]State ex rel A. Bentley & Sons Co v Pierce, 96 OS 44, 117 NE 6 (1917).

[62]Brannon v Tiro Consolidated School Dist of Crawford County Bd of Ed, 99 OS 369, 124 NE 235 (1919). See also In re Appeal of Suspension of Huffer from Circleville High School, 47 OS(3d) 12, 546 NE(2d) 1308 (1989).

[63]Tice v Southern Local School Dist Bd of Ed, No. 80-C-48, 1983 WL 6744 (7th Dist Ct App, Columbiana, 1-21-83).

[64]State ex rel Masters v Beamer, 109 OS 133, 141 NE 851 (1923).

[65]Ross v Board of Education, 52 App(2d) 28, 367 NE(2d) 1209 (Cuyahoga 1977).

[66]Russell v Gallia County Local School Bd, 80 App(3d) 797, 610 NE(2d) 1130 (Gallia 1992).

[67]Hines v Cleveland School Dist Bd of Ed, 26 Misc(2d) 15, 26 OBR 348, 499 NE(2d) 39 (CP, Cuyahoga 1985).

[68]RC 3313.17.

[69]Brown v Monroeville Local School Dist Bd of Ed, 20 OS(2d) 68, 253 NE(2d) 767 (1969).

[70]Carbone v Overfield, 6 OS(3d) 212, 6 OBR 264, 451 NE(2d) 1229 (1983). Prior cases had allowed the defense, in the absence of a statute creating liability. See, e.g., Cincinnati Bd of Ed v Volk, 72 OS 469, 74 NE 646 (1905).

[71]RC 3313.203.

[72]Beifuss v Westerville Bd of Ed, 37 OS(3d) 187, 525 NE(2d) 20 (1988); State ex rel Brown v Milton-Union Exempted Village Bd of Ed, 40 OS(3d) 21, 531 NE(2d) 1297 (1988). Boards may, however, be assessed prejudgment interest in other contexts, such as in tort actions. Ziegler v Wendel Poultry Services, Inc, 67 OS(3d) 10, 615 NE(2d) 1022 (1993). Boards may also be liable for post-judgment interest. State ex rel Tavenner v Indian Lake Local School Dist Bd of Ed, 62 OS(3d) 88, 578 NE(2d) 464 (1991).

The right to seek an injunction to abate a nuisance created by the positive act of a board of education has been judicially recognized.[73]

A board of education is not a "person" within the meaning of RC 1331.01(A) when operating within its clear legal authority, and was therefore immune from suit in an antitrust action based on the Valentine Act, RC Chapter 1331.[74]

A board lacks capacity to sue for malicious prosecution against a taxpayer and his attorneys whose prior suit was dismissed as frivolous and vexatious, even if the board suffered special injury as a result of the suit.[75]

In a libel suit brought against, among others, a school board and a local newspaper, the court held that board members were protected by qualified privilege and may not be held liable absent a showing of actual malice.[76] The actual malice standard to be applied is that enunciated by the US Supreme Court in *New York Times v Sullivan.*[77]

5.08 Rule-making and regulatory power

(A) Management of schools

A board of education is charged with the management and control of the public schools that it operates in its district[78] and is required to make any rules that are necessary for its government and for the government of its employees, pupils, and all persons entering on school premises.[79]

A board of education's authority to manage the schools extends particularly to discretion in matters relating to the opening, closing, and use of school buildings.[80] This includes the authority to consolidate small schools into a larger one.[81] A board may suspend particular grades within a school and reassign those grades to other schools.[82] Also, a board may adopt a rule requiring that an investigator from a county children's services board obtain parental consent or permit a school official to be present before allowing the investigator to interview a child on school property in the course of an investigation conducted under RC 2151.421.[83]

(B) Regulations affecting pupils and teachers

A school board is required to adopt a policy specifying the types of misconduct for which a student may be suspended, expelled, removed or permanently excluded.[84]

Pursuant to RC 3313.20 and RC 3313.47, a board may adopt a policy that permits high school students to be excused from attendance during regular school hours for the purpose of receiving religious instruction off school property. Such a religious instruction released-time policy must comport with federal and state constitutional provisions.[85]

A board's rule-making authority was sustained against constitutional challenge in connection with a policy that prohibited out-of-state and foreign trips by school-sponsored performing groups. The consti-

---

[73]Wayman v Akron City School Dist Bd of Ed, 5 OS(2d) 248, 215 NE(2d) 394 (1966).

[74]Thaxton v Medina City Bd of Ed, 21 OS(3d) 56, 21 OBR 357, 488 NE(2d) 136 (1986).

[75]Miami Trace Local School Dist Bd of Ed v Marting, 7 Misc 64, 217 NE(2d) 712 (CP, Madison 1966).

[76]Christian v Beacon Journal Publishing Co, No. 12368, 1986 WL 6668 (9th Dist Ct App, Summit, 6-11-86). See also McCartney v Oblates of St. Francis de Sales, 80 App(3d) 345, 609 NE(2d) 216 (Lucas 1992) (applying privilege to statements by teacher and principal to parents of students about their former teacher).

[77]New York Times v Sullivan, 376 US 254, 84 SCt 710, 11 LEd(2d) 686 (1964) (knowledge that the statement is false or reckless disregard of whether it is false or not). See also Dale v Ohio Civil Service Employees Assn, 57 OS(3d) 112, 567 NE(2d) 253 (1991), cert denied 501 US 1231, 111 SCt 2853, 115 LEd(2d) 1021 (1991). That a statement can be labeled "opinion," as opposed to "fact," does not automatically preclude application of the actual malice standard and a finding of defamation. Milkovich v Lorain Journal Co, 497 US 1, 110 SCt 2695, 111 LEd(2d) 1 (1990).

[78]RC 3313.47.

[79]RC 3313.20.

[80]RC 3313.49.

[81]Tice v Southern Local School Dist Bd of Ed, No. 80-C-48, 1983 WL 6744 (7th Dist Ct App, Columbiana, 1-21-83).

[82]Allmandinger v Now, No. 84-CV-5-40, 1985 WL ____ (CP, Van Wert, 3-18-85). See Text 5.06(C), Board discretion in exercising powers.

[83]OAG 82-029.

[84]RC 3313.661. See Text 25.03, Policy on student conduct.

[85]OAG 88-001. See Text 32.04, Establishment restrictions on released time for religious instruction.

tutionality of the policy was unsuccessfully challenged when the school band was not allowed to participate in an out-of-state competition and parade.[86]

A board is responsible for employing teachers[87] and may impose qualifications and conditions of employment in addition to the minimum state standards.

(C) Open enrollment policies

RC 3313.97, which expressly does not apply to joint vocational or cooperative education school districts, requires that the board of each city, local, and exempted village school district adopt an "open enrollment policy" under which students entitled to attend school in the district may enroll in an "alternative school," defined as a school other than the one to which the student is assigned by the district superintendent. The board must provide information about the policy to parents and the general public. The state board of education is required to "monitor" school districts to ensure compliance with such policies and the law.[88]

The policy must include application procedures that specify deadlines for making application and for notice to students and principals of alternative schools when an application is accepted. A student who does not wish to attend an alternative school cannot be required to apply.

The policy must also include admissions procedures that contain capacity limits by grade, building, and education program, and provisions to ensure "an appropriate racial balance." Students enrolled in a building or living in a building attendance area established by the superintendent or board must be given a preference over applicants.

The admission procedures cannot include any requirement of academic ability or level of athletic, artistic, or other extracurricular skill; any limitation on admitting handicapped applicants (except a student may be required to attend school where services described in his individualized education program (IEP) are available); or any requirement of proficiency in English. Nor can an applicant be rejected because of disciplinary proceedings (except admission may be denied if the applicant was suspended or expelled for at least ten consecutive days in the term for which admission is sought or the immediately preceding term).

An exception to this rule was made by RC 3313.982. Those districts operating a school as of October 1, 1989 which restricted admission to students based on their possession of certain academic, athletic, artistic or other skills are entitled to continue such restrictive admissions. Districts which seek to begin restricted admissions on similar bases after that date may submit a plan with respect to such restricted admission to the state board, which may approve the plan if the state board finds it would generally promote "increased educational opportunities for students in the district and will not unduly restrict opportunities for some students.[89]

The board is not required to transport a handicapped student enrolled in an alternative school unless the student can be picked up and dropped off at a regular designated bus stop or transportation is required under a court-approved desegregation plan.

(D) Enrollment of students from adjacent districts

RC 3313.98 requires that the board of each city, local, and exempted village school district adopt a resolution that either entirely prohibits the enrollment of students from adjacent districts (i.e., abutting city, local, or exempted village districts), other than students for whom tuition is paid in accordance with RC 3317.08, or permits enrollment from all adjacent districts tuition-free in accordance with a policy contained in the resolution.[90] The board must provide information about the policy to the board and superintendent of each adjacent district and, upon request, to

---

[86]Park Hills Music Club v Fairborn Bd of Ed, 512 FSupp 1040 (SD Ohio 1981).
[87]RC 3319.07.
[88]See OAC 3301-48-01.
[89]RC 3313.982.
[90]A resolution entirely prohibiting the enrollment of students from adjacent districts does not abrogate any agreement under RC 3313.841 or RC 3313.92 or any contract under RC 3313.90 between the board and the board of an adjacent district or prohibit those boards from entering into such agreements or contracts. RC 3313.98(H).

the parent[91] of any adjacent district student.

A policy permitting enrollment must include application procedures that specify deadlines for making application and for notice to the student and adjacent district superintendent when an adjacent district student's application is approved.

The policy must also include admission procedures that contain capacity limits by grade, building, and education program, provisions to ensure "an appropriate racial balance," and a requirement that all native students (i.e., students statutorily entitled to attend school in the district) who wish to be enrolled[92] in the district will be enrolled and all adjacent district students previously enrolled will receive a preference over first-time applicants.

The admission procedures for enrollment of students from adjacent districts are subject to the same restrictions as the admission procedures for open enrollment within a district under RC 3319.97.

The board cannot adopt a policy discouraging or prohibiting its native students from applying under an adjacent district's policy except a district can object to enrollment of a native student in an adjacent district in order to maintain "an appropriate racial balance." If a board objects, an adjacent district cannot enroll such native students unless tuition is paid under RC 3317.08.

The board must accept all credits toward graduation earned in adjacent district schools by adjacent district students or native students.

The state board of education is required to "monitor" school districts to ensure compliance with districts' policies and the law. In addition, the state board can require uniform application procedures (including deadlines and notification procedures) and record-keeping requirements for all boards that adopt policies permitting the enrollment of adjacent district students.[93]

RC 3313.983 requires that each joint vocational school district board adopt a policy pertaining to the enrollment of students who, upon enrollment, will be "adjacent district joint vocational students," a term defined in RC 3313.98(A)(5) as an adjacent district student who enrolls in a city, exempted village, or local school district under an RC 3313.98 policy and also enrolls in a joint vocational district that does not contain territory of the district for which that student is a native student and does contain territory of the city, exempted village, or local district in which the student enrolls.

The board must provide information about the policy, including the application procedures, to the superintendent and board of each city, exempted village, and local district with territory in the joint vocational district and, upon request, to the parent[94] of any student who could become an adjacent district joint vocational student of the district. The policy must include application procedures (including procedures for notifying any future adjacent district joint vocational students and the superintendent of the city, exempted village, or local districts in which they are enrolled as adjacent district students whenever their applications are approved) and procedures for admitting applicants who will become adjacent district joint vocational students. The latter must include district capacity limits by grade level, school building, and education program, a requirement that all students entitled under RC 3313.64 or RC 3313.65 to attend school in a district that has territory in the joint vocational district will be enrolled in the district, and a requirement that any previously enrolled adjacent district joint vocational student shall be preferred over first-time applicants to become adjacent district joint vocational students.

The procedures for admitting students to adjacent district joint vocational schools are subject to the same restrictions as those applicable to RC 3313.97 and RC 3313.98.

RC 3313.981 requires that the state board adopt rules requiring each city,

---

[91]"Parent" is defined in RC 3313.98(A).
[92]RC 3313.98(I) specifically underscores that the statute does not permit or require the board to exclude any native student.

[93]See OAC 3301-48-02.
[94]The definition of "parent" appearing in RC 3313.98(A) applies.

exempted village, and local district board to report annually the number of adjacent district students and adjacent district joint vocational students enrolled in the district and the number of native students enrolled in adjacent districts under RC 3313.98 policies, and further requires that each joint vocational district board annually report the number of adjacent district joint vocational students enrolled in the district and, for each such student, the district in which the student enrolled as an adjacent district student. Payments to a district under the foundation program will be adjusted by the department of education in accordance with a formula set forth in the statute. Reported adjacent district students enrolled in the city, exempted village, or local district cannot be counted in the district's average daily membership (ADM) certified under RC 3317.03, but reported native students enrolled in adjacent districts are counted. A joint vocational district cannot count adjacent district joint vocational students enrolled in the district in its ADM.[95]

If a parent requests, and if the board offers transportation to native students of the same grade level and distance from school, the city, exempted village, or local district board must provide transportation for a student enrolling from an adjacent district within the boundaries of the receiving district. A nonhandicapped student can be required to use a regular designated bus stop. If the student's family's income is below the federal poverty line, the board may reimburse, in accordance with state board rules, the parent for the cost of transportation from the student's home to the designated bus stop, from funds received under RC 3317.024(K).

RC 3313.98 and RC 3313.981 to RC 3313.983 do not apply to joint vocational or cooperative education school districts except as expressly otherwise specified.

(E) Administrative due process

In exercising its regulatory powers, a board is subject to the requirements of administrative due process. Thus, for example, a statute requiring the board to honor a contract for private school transportation "if economically feasible"[96] requires a public hearing, notice to the contractor, and an opportunity to be heard on the question of economic feasibility.[97]

5.09 Miscellaneous powers

(A) Employing consultants

Boards of education may spend public funds for consultant services for any purpose related to the business administration of the school district under their supervision, and for studies or surveys pertaining to district organization and building needs, curriculum and instructional needs, and needs for improved or additional services that may be rendered by the board.[98] There is no authority, however, to pay for dinners or other expenses involved in connection with studies or surveys.[99]

A board may contract for consultant services relating to workers' compensation.[100]

Upon request, the state board of education must furnish technical assistance to a school district on certain budgetary and financial matters. The assistance may be in the form of grants, consultants, or the temporary assignment of employees.[101]

(B) Contracting for mechanical, clerical, or record-keeping services

Boards of education may enter into contracts for the performance of certain ministerial duties, such as issuing checks, keeping books and records, and preparing payroll.[102]

---

[95] See Text 39.09(B), Average daily membership.
[96] RC 3327.011.
[97] State ex rel Ruple Bus Service v Wickliffe Bd of Ed, 11 Misc 127, 229 NE(2d) 762 (CP, Lake 1967).
[98] RC 3313.171, RC 3315.061.
[99] 1965 Syllabi 16. Syllabi are unpublished determinations made by the Auditor of State's Office from approximately 1945 to 1970. During that time, brief one-sentence references to the determinations had some limited circulation outside the Auditor's Office and were sometimes referenced by the Auditor and others. Although they may not be of precedential value outside of the Auditor's Office, they are often the only authority for the specific proposition for which they are cited and so this reference has been retained.
[100] OAG 83-076.
[101] RC 3301.073.
[102] RC 9.35.

(C) Operating preschool programs

The board of education of any school district except a cooperative education district established under RC 3311.521 may, upon demonstrated need, establish and operate preschool programs.[103] A board may charge fees or tuition for such programs, which may be graduated in proportion to family income or waived in a case of hardship.[104] Transportation for participating children may be provided.[105]

Criminal records checks on applicants for employment in a preschool program are governed by RC 3301.541, which is patterned after the procedure applicable to boards of education generally under RC 3319.39.[106]

(D) Cooperation with other agencies

Boards of education may cooperate with those public officials in charge of public parks, libraries, museums, buildings, and grounds to provide additional facilities for educational, social, civic, and recreational activities.[107] They may also contract for a term not exceeding one year with trustees of colleges or universities for special technical, professional, or other advanced instruction for their students. Such contracts may also be made with boards of other school districts, or with private organizations not for profit, for educational services which the board could not otherwise furnish in the fields of art, music, science, or history.[108]

Broad authorization has been given to contract with other boards of education for joint or cooperative establishment and operation of any educational program, including any class, course, or program that may be included in a graded course of study and staff development programs.[109]

The governing bodies of any two or more counties, municipal corporations, townships, special districts, school districts, or other political subdivisions are authorized to contract with one another for the establishment of a regional council to study area governmental problems, promote cooperative arrangements, agreements, and contracts, coordinate actions, make recommendations for review and action, and perform various planning functions.[110]

Additional authority is provided for cooperation among boards of education with regard to the joint or cooperative construction, acquisition, improvement, management, operation, occupancy, use, maintenance, or repair of any building, structure, or facility or for joint or cooperative participation in programs, projects, activities, or services.[111]

A school district that contracts with a licensed proprietary school to provide vocational training under RC 3313.90 should give high school credit for courses provided by the proprietary school.[112]

(E) Membership in associations

By majority vote, a board of education may join a school boards' association and may appropriate from its general fund an amount sufficient to pay the annual dues.[113] No funds received from a board of education by a school boards' association may be used for political activity.[114]

A board may subscribe to an educational and trade periodical only if the subscription is taken in the name of the school district.

(F) Training new board members and personnel

Any board of education may use money from its service fund to pay expenses of members-elect actually incurred in training and orientation to the performance of their duties from the date of election to the date of administration of the oath of office.[115] The state board of education must maintain continuing programs of in-service training in school district budget and finance for superintendents, business managers, board members, and treasurers.[116] Each superintendent or his designee, trea-

---

[103] RC 3313.646.
[104] RC 3313.646.
[105] RC 3327.013. See also Text 22.03, Transportation of pupils generally.
[106] See Text 5.09(H), Criminal background checks.
[107] RC 3313.59.
[108] RC 3315.09.
[109] RC 3313.842.
[110] RC 167.01 to RC 167.08.
[111] RC 3313.92.
[112] OAG 72-081.
[113] RC 3313.87.
[114] RC 3313.87.
[115] RC 3315.15.
[116] RC 3301.072.

surer, and business manager must attend one such training program each year.[117]

(G) Disseminating information

Boards of education are allowed to compile, make available, or publish the following materials necessary for effective administration of the schools: student handbooks, dress codes, curriculum guides, school policy bulletins, newsletters, board meeting summaries or minutes, financial reports, annual reports, and other reports concerning school operations. Such materials may be published to further public awareness of all aspects of the district's educational program and operation including (1) board policies, procedures, administration, finance, and state and federal requirements; (2) district programs, activities, and plans; (3) student achievement and employee information; and (4) any other information the board considers helpful in keeping students, parents, employees, and district residents aware of district operations. A board may assign one or more employees the duty of producing authorized information.[118]

A board may *not* use public funds to support or oppose the passage of a school levy or bond issue or to compensate any district employee for activity intended to influence the outcome of such issues.[119] Thus, a board cannot publish and distribute publicly financed newsletters and other printed materials supporting or opposing passage of a levy.[120] Nor can a board compensate its employees for distributing privately financed materials, although such persons may perform such activity on their own time.[121] Board employees may, however, attend public meetings during working hours to present information about school finances and activities and board actions, even if the purpose of the meeting is to discuss or debate passage of a levy or bond issue.[122]

(H) Criminal background checks

RC 3319.39 requires the appointing or hiring officer of any board of education to request the superintendent of the bureau of criminal identification and investigation to conduct a criminal records check with respect to any applicant (defined as one under final consideration for employment but excluding one already employed who is being considered for a different position) for a job as a person responsible for the care, custody, or control of a child.[123] The procedure to be followed by the bureau superintendent appears in RC 109.572, which imposes a thirty-day time limit within which the superintendent is to respond and obligates the board of education to pay the fee prescribed for the check.[124] The superintendent's determination is valid for one year. If, during that year, another request is made on the same person, the superintendent is to provide the information that was the basis of the initial determination, at a lower fee than the fee applicable to the initial check.

The school district's appointing or hiring officer must inform the person, at the time of his initial application, that he is required to provide a set of fingerprints and that a criminal records check must be conducted and satisfactorily completed if he comes under final consideration for employment as a precondition to employment in the position. If the applicant does not present proof of Ohio residency for the five-year period immediately prior to the date the records check is requested or does not provide evidence that within that period the bureau superintendent has requested information about him from the Federal Bureau of Investigation (FBI) in a criminal records check, the appointing or hiring officer must

---

[117]RC 3301.072.
[118]RC 3315.07.
[119]RC 3315.07.
[120]OAG 91-064.
[121]OAG 91-064.
[122]RC 3315.07. See also Text 38.10, Use of school property for public meetings and entertainments.
[123]RC 3319.39(H) provides that if a local school district board of education adopts a resolution requesting the assistance of the county school district in which the local district has territory in conducting background checks of substitute teachers, the appointing or hiring officer of the county district board is the local district's appointing or hiring officer for the purpose of hiring substitute teachers for service in the local district.

[124]The board of education may charge the applicant a fee (not to exceed what the board paid to the bureau) for the cost it incurs in obtaining the check. If a fee is charged, the applicant, at the time of initial application, must be told the amount and also told that, unless the fee is paid, he will not be considered for employment. RC 109.572.

also request that the superintendent obtain information from the FBI as part of the check. If the applicant presents proof of Ohio residency during the five-year period, the officer may (but is not required to) request the superintendent to include information from the FBI.

The person requesting the check must furnish the applicant a copy of the form prescribed under RC 109.572(C) and a standard impression sheet (prescribed by the bureau superintendent under RC 109.572) to obtain fingerprints. An applicant who is requested to complete the form and provide fingerprints must do so (or, with respect to the former, provide the information necessary to complete the form). An applicant who refuses to comply may not be hired for any position for which a check is required. The person requesting the check is to obtain the completed form and impression sheet from the applicant and forward them to the bureau superintendent when requesting the criminal records check.

Except as provided by RC 3319.39(B)(3)[125] and rules adopted by the department of education under RC 3319.39(E), the board of education may not employ one as a person responsible for the care, custody, or control of a child if the applicant previously has been convicted of or pleaded guilty to certain specified criminal offenses.[126] The applicant may be employed conditionally until the criminal records check is completed and the results received. The person must be released from employment if subsequently disqualified by the check.

The report of any criminal records check conducted by the bureau superintendent in response to the request of a school district's appointing or hiring officer is expressly not a public record under RC 149.43 and cannot be made available to any person other than the job applicant or his representative, a court, hearing officer, or other necessary individual involved in a case dealing with the denial of employment to the applicant.[127]

The superintendent of the bureau of criminal identification and investigation is required by RC 109.57 to maintain "pertinent" information on persons convicted of serious crimes in Ohio and other "well known and habitual criminals." The statute authorizes a board of education, in addition to or in conjunction with any request required under RC 3319.39, to request, with respect to any applicant for employment, that the superintendent determine whether the bureau has such information on the person. The applicant also may request such information with respect to himself. The superintendent, if requested, must then ask the Federal Bureau of Investigation for any criminal records it has on the individual. The superintendent is then obligated to furnish a certified copy of all such information, the dissemination of which is not prohibited by law, for which a reasonable fee may be charged. Information and materials thus obtained "shall not be released or disseminated" and must be destroyed if the applicant is not employed. They expressly are not public records under RC 149.43. If the board requires the receipt of such information as a prerequisite to employment, it may accept a certified copy of any records issued by the bureau and presented by the applicant in lieu of requesting such information itself, but only if the applicant submits the copy

---

[125] This provision precludes a board of education from employing a teacher who previously pleaded guilty to or was convicted of an offense listed in RC 3319.31, a statute treated in Text 8.07, Revocation or suspension of certificate.

[126] The offenses are aggravated murder; murder; voluntary manslaughter; involuntary manslaughter; felonious assault; aggravated assault; assault; failing to provide for a functionally impaired person; aggravated menacing; patient abuse or neglect; kidnapping; abduction; child stealing; criminal child enticement; rape; sexual battery; corruption of a minor; gross sexual imposition; sexual imposition; importuning; voyeurism; public indecency; felonious sexual penetration; compelling prostitution; promoting prostitution; procuring; prostitution; disseminating matter harmful to juveniles; pandering obscenity; pandering obscenity involving a minor; pandering sexually oriented matter involving a minor; illegal use of a minor in nudity-oriented material or performance; aggravated robbery; robbery; aggravated burglary; burglary; unlawful abortion; endangering children; contributing to unruliness or delinquency of a child; domestic violence; carrying concealed weapons; having weapons while under disability; improperly discharging a firearm at or into a habitation or school; corrupting another with drugs; trafficking in drugs; or placing harmful objects in food or confection.

[127] RC 3319.39.

within one year after the date of issuance by the bureau.[128]

(I) Agreements with educational service center governing boards for services

RC 3313.843 authorizes the board of a city or exempted village school district to contract with the board of an educational service center (with territory in the same county), through adoption of identical resolutions, for certain services to be provided by the governing board. The services, which must be specified in the resolutions, may include supervisory teachers, in-service and continuing education for district personnel, curriculum services as provided by the educational service center to local school districts, research and development programs, academic instruction for which the governing board employs teachers under RC 3319.02, and assistance in accommodating and educating handicapped students. Unless otherwise specified in the resolutions, services must be provided in the same manner as they are provided to local school districts. The city or exempted village board must reimburse the educational service center pursuant to RC 3317.11. An agreement is valid only if a copy is filed with the department of education by the first day of the school year for which it is in effect. RC 3313.843 expressly does not apply to a cooperative education school district or to any city or exempted village district with an average daily membership[129] of 13,000 or more that has not entered into one or more agreements under the statute prior to July 1, 1993.

(J) Agreements with educational service center governing boards for supplies and equipment

Boards of local school districts and, subject to approval by the educational service center governing boards of city and exempted village school districts located at least partly in the county in which the educational service center is located may authorize the governing board to purchase or accept upon donation supplies and equipment for such districts. The governing board must be reimbursed in full for its expenditures on a district's behalf.[130]

(K) Teacher education loan programs

A board of education may establish and fund a teacher education loan program to make loans to students who are district graduates or residents and enrolled in teacher preparation programs at state-approved institutions and who indicate an intent to teach in the district. The board must adopt rules governing operation of the program and may contract with certain outside entities to administer the program.[131]

(L) Latchkey programs

A board of education of a city, local, or exempted village school district may operate a latchkey program, defined as a program under which children in kindergarten or of compulsory school age are provided care outside school hours (except any program that in any way promotes or furthers religious beliefs is not a latchkey program).[132] The program must be maintained and operated, and pupils admitted, under rules adopted by the board. Fees or tuition may be charged and deposited in a special fund. General fund money may not be spent for the program unless it results from an appropriation of the general assembly that specifically permits the expenditure of such appropriated funds for a latchkey program; also, the board may provide ancillary services for the program notwithstanding that some portion of the services may be supported by general fund money.[133]

A board that does not operate a latchkey program may provide ancillary services and make payments to any program provider[134] that operates a latchkey program in which district children are

---

[128]RC 109.57(F). If the bureau superintendent receives a request from the state board of education or superintendent of public instruction for information authorized under RC 3319.291, he proceeds as if the request came from a school board. See also Text 44.02, Definition of public records.

[129]See Text 39.09(B), Average daily membership.

[130]RC 3315.07(D).

[131]RC 3315.37.

[132]RC 3313.207, RC 3313.208.

[133]RC 3313.208. "Ancillary services" means space in a school district building used for other district purposes than latchkey programs; utilities furnished in conjunction with such space; or transportation to a latchkey program on regular school buses. RC 3313.207.

[134]"Program provider" means any entity or individual licensed under RC Ch 5104 or exempted from that Chapter's licensing requirements. RC 3313.207.

enrolled. Alternatively, such board may furnish to any person or entity that operates a latchkey program ancillary services or employees for use solely in conjunction with the program. The board must contract with a program provider as a condition for making any payments or furnishing any ancillary services or employees. In any case, general fund money may not be spent unless it results from an appropriation of the general assembly that specifically permits the expenditure of such appropriated funds for latchkey programs; also, the board may provide ancillary services notwithstanding that some portion of the services may be supported by general fund money.[135]

Before operating any latchkey program, making any payments, or providing any employees or ancillary services, the board must notify parents and other interested parties that the board is considering district participation in latchkey programs and adopt a policy ensuring public input on the board's decision as well as any decisions on the district's role in implementing and funding programs if the board decides to participate. The policy must also provide for regular, periodic public input in the evaluation of the district's participation in latchkey programs.[136]

(M) Healthcheck programs

At the request of the state department of human services a board of education must establish and conduct a healthcheck program for enrolled pupils who receive medical assistance under RC Chapter 5111. At the request of a board of education, the state department may enter into an agreement with the board under which the board provides medical services to a recipient of medical assistance that are reimbursable under the medical assistance program but not under the healthcheck program. RC 3313.714 specifies required components of a program and contains requirements that parents (or the pupil, if age eighteen or older) be notified that the pupil will be examined under the program and provisions for the withholding of consent. Costs of the program are reimbursed by the department of human services in accordance with the statutory formula.

Under RC 3313.715, a board of education may request from the director of mental retardation and developmental disabilities the appropriate identification numbers for all students residing in the school district who are medical assistance recipients under RC Chapter 5111. Upon such request, the numbers must be furnished. RC 3319.321 does not apply to the release of student names and other data to the director for purposes of the statute.[137] Similarly, RC Chapter 1347 does not apply to information required to be kept under the statute to the extent necessary to comply with it and RC 3313.714; however, such information must be used only for such specific legal purposes and must not be released to any unauthorized person.[138]

(N) Community service education programs

By resolution, a board of education may include community service education in the district's educational program.[139] A board that so elects must establish a community service advisory committee and develop and implement a community service plan for pupils in all grades, which plan must be based upon the recommendations of the advisory committee and provide for certain specified features.[140] Upon adoption, a copy of the plan must be submitted to the state department of education. High school credit for a community service education course may be granted only if roughly half of the course is devoted to classroom study of such matters as civic responsibility, the history of volunteerism, and community service training with approximately the other half devoted to community service.[141]

---

[135] RC 3313.209.

[136] RC 3313.208.

[137] For treatment of RC 3319.321, see Text 44.14, Access to and release of student records.

[138] For treatment of RC Chapter 1347, see Text 44.04 to 44.11.

[139] RC 3313.605. In the case of a local school district, the board may either adopt such a resolution and provide a community service education program directly or the county school district board of education, upon request of the local board, may provide a program for the local district. *Id.*

[140] For specific requirements as to the makeup of the committee and plan features, see RC 3313.605(B).

[141] "Civic responsibility," "voluntariness," and "community service" are specifically defined in RC 3313.605(A).

A board that wishes to include community service education in its program may be assisted by the governor's community service commission established under RC 121.40.

(O) Policy on parental involvement

RC 3313.472 requires the board of education of each city, exempted village, local, and joint vocational school district to adopt a policy on parental involvement designed to build consistent and effective communication between parents of students and the district's teachers and administrators. The policy must provide an opportunity for parents to be actively involved in their children's education and to be informed of (1) the importance of parental involvement to the success of their child's educational efforts, (2) how and when to assist and support the child's learning activities, and (3) techniques, strategies, and skills for use at home to improve the child's academic performance and development as a future responsible adult.

(P) Assessing skills of students with visual disabilities

RC 3323.031 requires every board of education annually to assess the reading and writing skills of each student with a visual disability enrolled in the district in each medium in which instruction is specified as appropriate under RC 3323.011(A)(2). The results of each assessment must be provided in a written statement that specifies the student's strengths and weaknesses in each medium assessed.

(Q) Tuition credit scholarship programs

RC 3334.17 authorizes the board of education of any school district, the principal of any public high school, or the chief administrative officer of any chartered nonpublic high school to establish a scholarship program to award scholarships consisting of tuition credits to students enrolled in the district or high school. The program must specify whether a beneficiary may receive payment for awarded tuition credits directly from the Ohio tuition trust authority or whether the amount of such credits shall be paid by the authority to the institution of higher learning in which the student is enrolled. It must also be registered with the tuition trust authority, which must be notified of the name and address of each beneficiary, the number of credits awarded, and the institution of higher learning in which the beneficiary is enrolled. Any person or governmental entity may purchase credits on behalf of an established program at the same price as established under the other provisions of RC Chapter 3334, and the purchaser may register the program at the time of purchase. Beneficiaries are selected in accordance with criteria established by the board, principal, or chief administrative officer, and no beneficiary may receive more than 400 credits. If a beneficiary does not use the credits within the time limit established under the program, they may be awarded to another beneficiary.

(R) Career planning

RC 3313.607(A) authorizes any board of education to assist any student in developing a written career plan. If developed utilizing state funds appropriated for the purposes of the statute, the plan must: be completed before the end of the eighth grade year; identify career goals and educational goals to prepare for those career goals; be updated periodically as high school coursework is completed; and culminate in a "career passport." RC 3313.607(B) authorizes any board of education to provide an individual career passport to any student upon successful completion of the coursework of any high school. If the district receives state money for the purposes of the statute, a passport must be provided to each such student. The passport must document the student's knowledge and skills, including the student's coursework and employment, community, or leadership experiences. The passport must also include the competency levels the student achieved, disclose the student's attendance record, and identify the career credentials the student gained.

(S) School savings banks

RC 3313.82 provides that the principal or superintendent of any public school, or any person designated by the board of education, may collect weekly or from time to time "small amounts of savings" from pupils to be deposited "on the day of collection" in a bank, building and loan association, or trust company that has an interest department. These collections are to be placed in individual pupil accounts (or, if the amount collected is insufficient to open an individual account, in the name of the collector to be held in trust until eventually transferred to the credit of the pupil). The collector must furnish the bank or institution a list giving the names, signatures, addresses, ages, birthplaces, parents' names, and such other data concerning the pupils as the bank or institution requires. The words "system of school savings" or "school savings banks" may be used in circulars and other written documents pertaining to the program. Where a program is instituted, the board must, by resolution, provide for the giving of bond by the collector and is authorized to pay the premium for the bond.[142]

(T) Other powers

The general assembly has granted boards of education many other specific powers, including the power to provide educational television courses and programs secured from nonprofit educational television corporations;[143] purchase motor vehicles;[144] compound or release claims due from banks;[145] purchase motor vehicle liability insurance;[146] purchase group life, medical, disability, dental, vision, hearing aids, prescription drugs, sickness and accident insurance and group legal services (any elected board member and the member's spouse and dependent children may be covered if the member pays the amount charged for the coverage);[147] purchase, without competitive bidding, long-term care insurance covering board members and employees who may elect to participate by paying, through payroll deduction, the entire premium charged;[148] purchase liability insurance and indemnify employees, the board, and board members against liability;[149] enter into an installment payment contract for the purchase and installation of energy conservation measures,[150] which contract may be a shared-savings contract;[151] and enter into contracts for the exploration for, and production of, iron ore, coal, petroleum, gas, or other minerals on property owned by the board.[152] Specific provisions have been enacted regulating the manner in which some of these powers may be exercised.[153]

5.10 Authority of probate court or educational service center governing board to exercise powers of defaulting board of education

If the board of any city, exempted village school district or educational service center fails to perform the duties imposed on it or fails to fill a board vacancy within thirty days, the probate court of the county in which the district is located, upon being advised and satisfied of such failure, is required to perform all duties imposed on the board. In the case of a local school district, the governing board of the educational service center in which the district is located is directed to perform all duties imposed on the board.[154]

RC 3313.85 is concerned primarily with certain mandatory board duties, such as providing free education for at least the minimum required period each year and the redistricting of subdistricts when appropriate. The section does not impose a duty on a board of education or probate court to terminate segregation within a school district.[155]

MEETINGS AND PROCEDURES

5.11 Board meetings in general

(A) Organizational meeting

The board of education of each city, exempted village, and local school district must hold its organizational meeting some

---

[142]RC 3313.83.
[143]RC 3313.606.
[144]RC 3313.172.
[145]RC 3313.19.
[146]RC 3313.201.
[147]RC 3313.202.
[148]RC 124.841.
[149]RC 3313.203. If the board purchases liability insurance that covers a "school support entity" (defined as any nonprofit entity formed for the support of a district program), the board must require the entity to reimburse the board for the cost.
[150]RC 3313.372.
[151]RC 3313.373.
[152]RC 3313.45.
[153]RC 3313.33 to RC 3313.46.
[154]RC 3313.85.
[155]Lynch v Kenston School Dist Bd of Ed, 229 FSupp 740 (ND Ohio 1964).

time during the first fifteen days of January of each year. The district treasurer must canvass the members of the new board no later than December 31 to establish the date of the organizational meeting. At the meeting, the board is to elect one of its members president and another vice-president, both to serve for one year. Similarly, in educational service centers, the board is required to meet in January of each year to organize by electing one of its members president and another vice-president, both to serve for one year.[156]

(B) Regular and special meetings

At the time of the organizational meeting the board is required to fix the time for holding its regular meetings, which must be held at least once every two months.[157]

A special board meeting may be called by the president, treasurer, or any two members of the board by serving written notice of the time and place on each member at least two days prior to the date of the meeting. The notice must be signed by the official or members calling the meeting. Service by mail is adequate for this purpose.[158] The written notice requirement is waived if all board members attend the special meeting.[159]

(C) Quorum

A majority of board members constitutes a quorum.[160] RC 121.22(C) requires a member to be present in person at a meeting open to the public in order to be considered present or to vote and for purposes of determining whether a quorum is present.

(D) Minutes

Minutes of all regular and special meetings of the board and of any covered committee or subcommittee of the board must be promptly prepared, filed, and maintained, and open to public inspection. Boards typically review and approve minutes, but failure to do so will not void actions taken during the meeting covered in the minutes.[161]

The law does not define exactly what should appear in minutes.[162] The law does provide that where an executive session is held, the minutes need only reflect the general subject of discussion.[163] Presumably minutes of public sessions must reflect something more.

5.12 Open meetings: the sunshine law

RC 121.22, commonly known as the Sunshine Act, applies to boards of education as well as other public bodies. Boards are required as a general rule to open all meetings to the public. Executive sessions are prohibited except for limited purposes specifically authorized by law.

A meeting is defined as any prearranged discussion of the public business of the public body by a majority of its members.[164] It does not, however, apply to an audit conference conducted by the state auditor or independent certified public accountants with board officials and members concerning an audit of the board's financial records.[165]

RC 121.22(B)(1)(a) expressly includes within the definition of "public body" any "board, commission, committee, agency, or

---

[156]RC 3313.14.
[157]RC 3313.15.
[158]RC 3313.16.
[159]Indian Hill Exempted Village School Dist Bd of Ed v Hamilton County Bd of Ed, 64 Abs 371, 108 NE(2d) 387 (CP, Hamilton 1952), affirmed by 62 Abs 545, 108 NE(2d) 225 (App, Hamilton 1952); 1933 OAG 314.
[160]RC 3313.18.
[161]Davidson v Hanging Rock, 97 App(3d) 723, 647 NE(2d) 527 (Lawrence 1994), dismissed, appeal not allowed 71 OS(3d) 1476, 645 NE(2d) 1256 (1995).
[162]White v Clinton County Bd of Commrs, No. CA94-08-020, 1995 WL 128394 (12th Dist Ct App, Clinton, 3-27-95) (finding that RC 121.22 was not implicated in suit contending that public body minutes must include a record of who appeared, the discussions and debates, and any actions taken).
[163]RC 121.22(C).
[164]RC 121.22(B)(2). It has been held that the statute only applies where some actual formal deliberations concerning the public business occurs, and that information-gathering and fact-finding for ministerial purposes does not implicate the Act. Holeski v Lawrence, 85 App(3d) 824, 621 NE(2d) 802 (Geauga 1993). See also Springfield Local School Dist Bd of Ed v Ohio Assn of Public School Employees Local 530, No. 17128, 1995 WL 608419 (9th Dist Ct App, Summit, 10-18-95).
[165]RC 121.22(D).

similar decision-making body of any ... school district ...." In 1994, RC 121.22(B)(1)(b) was added; it states that a "public body" includes "any committee or subcommittee of a body described in division (B)(1)(a) of this section." Thus, it is clear that the Sunshine Act applies not just to a school district's board of education itself, but also to "committees" and "subcommittees." The precise meaning of the latter terms, however, is anything but clear. A committee or subcommittee arguably does not even have to have some "decision-making" authority to be covered; presumably, it must at least be board-authorized. Whether its participants must be composed of board members themselves, in whole or in part, is not readily apparent either. The courts appear to be taking a fairly expansive view of this provision's scope.[166]

(A) In general

All boards of education and other public bodies are required to establish by rule a reasonable method whereby any person may determine the time and place of regularly scheduled meetings, and the time, place, and purpose of all special meetings. A special meeting cannot be held unless twenty-four-hour advance notice is given to the news media that have requested notification, except in case of an emergency requiring immediate action. In the event of an emergency, the members calling the meeting must notify the news media immediately of the time, place, and purpose of the meeting.[167] When faced with an emergency requiring immediate action, a public body substantially complies with RC 121.22 when it gives notice of an emergency meeting as quickly as possible, even if the news media were notified within ten minutes *after* the start of that meeting.[168] Note, however, that RC 3313.16 imposes an additional requirement that written notice of a special meeting must be served on each board member at least two days before that meeting. This requirement is waived if all board members attend the special meeting.[169]

The attorney general has concluded that, while RC 121.22 "does not directly address the right to electronically record a public meeting," the First Amendment to the US Constitution and Article I, section 11 of the Ohio Constitution preclude a "blanket prohibition" on recording. The public body may regulate audio and video recording equipment requiring that it "be silent, unobtrusive, self-contained and self-powered to avoid interference with the ability of those present to see, hear and participate in the proceedings," but the regulations "must be precisely and narrowly drawn to be no broader than necessary to insure the order of the proceedings."[170]

(B) Executive sessions

Executive sessions may be held on statutorily authorized subjects, but only after a majority-of-a-quorum roll call vote at a regular or special meeting. The motion and vote specifically must state which one or more[171] of the following permitted subjects

---

[166]Weissfeld v Akron Public School Dist, No. 16410, 1994 WL 502534 (9th Dist Ct App, Summit, 4-27-94) (holding that "building leadership team" authorized by collective bargaining agreement as a form of site-based management where teachers and building administrators engage in building-level decision-making qualifies as a public body); Thomas v White, 85 App(3d) 410, 620 NE(2d) 85 (Summit 1992) (holding that citizens advisory committee of county children services board qualifies as a public body and stating that a "strict reading" of the statute "leads us to the conclusion that a committee need not be a decision-making body in order to be a public body" although, in any event, this committee was a decision-making body).

[167]RC 121.22(F). Where a resolution for a special meeting called for it to begin at 6:00 p.m. but the minutes wrongly indicated the meeting was set for 7:00 p.m., and where the correct starting time was reported to a newspaper but mispublished in that paper as 7:00 p.m., no violation occurred when the meeting began prior to 7:00 p.m. Black v Mecca Twp Bd of Trustees, 91 App(3d) 351, 632 NE(2d) 923 (Trumbull 1993).

[168]State ex rel Brookfield Federation of Teachers v Brookfield Local School Dist Bd of Ed, No. 3515, 1985 WL 4614 (11th Dist Ct App, Trumbull, 12-20-85).

[169]Indian Hill Exempted Village School Dist Bd of Ed v Hamilton County Bd of Ed, 64 Abs 371, 108 NE(2d) 387 (CP, Hamilton 1952), affirmed by 62 Abs 545, 108 NE(2d) 225 (App, Hamilton 1952); 1933 OAG 314.

[170]OAG 88-087. See also OAG 92-032.

[171]Stating one valid basis for executive session in the motion does not constitute compliance with the law for purposes of discussing other subjects, even topics that are permissible subjects of executive sessions. Vermilion Teachers' Assn v Vermilion Local

are to be considered at the executive session:

(1) Consideration of the appointment, employment, dismissal, discipline, promotion, demotion, or compensation of an employee, student, or school official, or to investigate charges or complaints against any such person, unless the person in question requests a public hearing (when an executive session is held under this provision, the motion and vote must state which one or more of these purposes is involved but need not state the name of any person to be considered);

(2) Consideration of the purchase of property for public purposes, or sale of property at competitive bidding, but only if premature disclosure of information would give an unfair competitive or bargaining advantage to a person whose personal, private interest is adverse to the general public interest;

(3) Conferences with an attorney involving pending or imminent court action;

(4) Preparing for, conducting, or reviewing negotiations with employees regarding their compensation or other terms and conditions of their employment;

(5) Matters required to be kept confidential by state or federal law; and/or

(6) Specialized details of security arrangements.[172]

Generally, the executive session exceptions are narrowly construed by courts. The Ninth District Court of Appeals, for example, determined that an executive session discussion which addressed both subcontracting of transportation and the board's collective bargaining obligations arising from subcontracting possibilities invalidated the board's subsequent decision to enter into a private bussing contract. The court concluded that discussion of the two matters, subcontracting and bargaining, were not "inextricably linked".[173]

Prior to entering an executive session, the board should first meet in a properly called open session and then adjourn to executive session. Similarly, upon leaving the executive session, the board should return to the open session and either conduct business or adjourn.[174]

The Sunshine Act's provision for executive sessions to discuss personnel matters has been the subject of frequent litigation. The provision "permits a public body to enter into executive session when its *sole* purpose is the consideration of a *specific* employee's employment" and not a general need to prune "an aggregate number of positions from the system payroll."[175] Thus, for example, a board of education faced with a budget crunch wrongly called an executive session to debate a general cost containment proposal that would adversely affect personnel. However, a board of education may still be able to go into executive session to discuss the collective bargaining implications of cost containment provisions. Of course, an executive session is permissible to discuss termination of a *particular* employee's employment because of budgetary considerations.[176] *Matheny v Frontier Local Bd of Ed*[177] held that the Act did not create a new substantive right to a hearing where none existed previously, as in the case of considering contracts of non-tenured teachers. Where a statutory right to a hearing does exist, however, and a public hearing is requested, an executive session to consider the dismissal of a public employee is unlawful.[178]

School Dist Bd of Ed, 98 App(3d) 524, 648 NE(2d) 1384 (Erie 1994).

[172]RC 121.22(G).

[173]Springfield Local School Dist Bd of Ed v Ohio Assn of Public School Employees, Local 530, No. 17128, 1995 WL 608419 (9th Dist Ct App, Summit, 10-18-95).

[174]OAG 86-091.

[175]Gannett Satellite Information Network, Inc v Chillicothe City School Dist Bd of Ed, 41 App(3d) 218, 534 NE(2d) 1239 (Ross 1988).

[176]Davidson v Sheffield-Sheffield Lake Bd of Ed, No. 89CA004624, 1990 WL 72316 (9th Dist Ct App, Lorain, 5-23-90).

[177]Matheny v Frontier Local Bd of Ed, 62 OS(2d) 362, 405 NE(2d) 1041 (1980).

[178]Connor v Village of Lakemore, 48 App(3d) 52, 547 NE(2d) 1230 (Summit 1988). Here, all evidence was taken in public as was a vote on the dismissal. But, after hearing the evidence, an executive session was held to review the evidence before acting. That, said the court in voiding the dismissal of a village police

(C) Notice to interested persons

The Act provides that any person may, upon request and payment of a reasonable fee, obtain advance notification of any matter to be discussed in a board meeting.[179] As this provision gives employees a method to ensure that they will be notified that possible nonrenewal of their contracts will be discussed, the board is under no other affirmative duty to personally notify such employees.[180]

(D) Consequences of violation

A resolution, rule, or formal action of any kind is invalid unless adopted in an open meeting. A resolution, rule, or formal action adopted in an open meeting but that results from deliberations that took place in a meeting not open to the public is invalid unless the deliberations were properly conducted in executive session. A resolution, rule, or formal action adopted in an open meeting is also invalid if notice of the meeting was not given in accordance with RC 121.22(F).[181] However, improper procedures under the law likely can be cured by subsequent compliance with the statute.[182]

RC 121.22(I) requires, upon proof of a violation or threatened violation of the Act, that a court issue an injunction to compel compliance and order the offending public body to pay a $500 civil forfeiture to the party seeking the injunction and also to pay court costs and reasonable attorney fees. A court may reduce the penalty under certain circumstances. Furthermore, the statute provides that proof of a violation creates an irrebuttable presumption of irreparable harm and prejudice to a party suing for injunctive relief, and any person may bring an enforcement action within two years after an alleged violation or threatened violation.[183] A board of education member who willfully violates a court's injunction may be removed from office.

One who frivolously sues a board of education alleging a violation of RC 121.22 is liable for the board's court costs and reasonable attorney's fees.[184]

5.13 Board action, resolutions

(A) In general, roll call

Certain motions to adopt resolutions require the district treasurer to publicly call the roll of members and to enter on the records the names of those voting "aye" and the names of those voting "no." These include resolutions for the following:

(1) Authorization of the purchase or sale of real or personal property;

(2) Employment of a superintendent, teacher, janitor, or other employee;

---

chief, was unlawful. See also Text 25.12(A), Appeal to board. Since *Matheny*, RC 3319.11 has been amended to allow a nontenured teacher to demand a hearing, to be held in executive session unless the teacher and board of education agree to a public hearing, on the nonrenewal of a limited contract. See Text 9.13(C), Right to hearing.

[179]RC 121.22(F).

[180]Amigo v Cloverleaf Local School Dist Bd of Ed, 59 App(2d) 231, 394 NE(2d) 331 (Medina 1978).

[181]RC 121.22(H). See, e.g., State ex rel Delph v Barr, 44 OS(3d) 77, 541 NE(2d) 59 (1989); Hardesty v River View Local School Dist Bd of Ed, 63 Misc(2d) 145, 620 NE(2d) 272 (CP, Coshocton 1993); Schank v Hegele, 36 Misc(2d) 4, 521 NE(2d) 9 (CP, Morgan 1987). Inadvertent mistake by the public body in denying public access does not excuse noncompliance. State ex rel Randles v Hill, 66 OS(3d) 32, 607 NE(2d) 458 (1993). See also Text 25.12(A), Appeal to board.

[182]Moraine v Board of County Commrs, 67 OS(2d) 139, 423 NE(2d) 184 (1981) (refusing to invalidate rural zoning commission decision on basis of allegedly invalid executive session where "such deliberations were laid before the public eye"); Fox v Lakewood, 39 OS(3d) 19, 528 NE(2d) 1254 (1988) (failure to conduct public deliberations on charter amendment cured when amendment later placed on ballot); Kuhlman v Leipsic, No. 12-94-9, 1995 WL 141528 (3d Dist Ct App, Putnam, 3-27-95) (initial violation of committee meeting addressing employee termination without public notice cured by later village council meeting and properly held executive session).

[183]Thus, it has been held that the issuance of an injunction upon finding a violation of the Act is mandatory. Fayette Volunteer Fire Dept No. 2 v Fayette Twp Bd of Trustees, 87 App(3d) 51, 621 NE(2d) 855 (Lawrence 1993). It has also been held that the injunction proceedings contemplated by RC 121.22(I) are not exclusive. In Hardesty v River View Local School Dist Bd of Ed, 63 Misc(2d) 145, 620 NE(2d) 272 (CP, Coshocton 1993), a school board's disciplinary suspension of certain students was declared illegal on the basis of a RC 121.22 violation in an administrative appeal pursuant to RC 2506.04; that an injunction under RC 121.22(I) was not sought was deemed irrelevant.

[184]RC 121.22(I). McIntyre v Westerville City School Dist Bd of Ed, Nos. 90AP-1024, 90AP-1063, 1991 WL 101587 (10th Dist Ct App, Franklin, 6-6-91).

(3) Election or appointment of an officer;

(4) Payment of any debt or claim; and

(5) Adoption of any textbook.

If a majority vote aye, the president must declare the motion carried. Upon any motion or resolution, a member may demand a roll call vote, requiring the treasurer to call the roll and record the names and votes.[185]

In an 1894 decision, the Ohio Supreme Court held that the requirement for a roll call vote was mandatory and failure to adhere to the prescribed procedure rendered the action taken void.[186] Several courts, however, have since allowed some slight variation from the literal wording of RC 3313.18. Where board minutes listed the names of members in attendance and showed that a motion not to re-employ a teacher was adopted unanimously by roll call vote, so there was no uncertainty as to the results, it was not necessary to list the affirmative vote of each board member by name.[187] Similarly, a vote on a resolution to offer limited supplemental contracts to eighty-two individuals substantially complied with RC 3313.18 when a majority of board members supported the measure with the exception that a majority specifically voted against the resolution as it related to the offer of a contract to the basketball coach.[188]

(B) Vote required for passage

The affirmative vote of a majority of all board members is required for adoption of resolutions pertaining to matters calling for a roll call vote. A specific affirmative vote is required by other statutes for particular purposes (such as those relating to tax levies and bond issues, and findings of disabilities). A majority of the quorum is sufficient to pass all other motions or resolutions.[189]

When a board has adopted *Robert's Rules of Order* for procedural guidance, it has been held that an otherwise valid act of the board will not be nullified for a technical failure to follow such parliamentary procedure.[190]

(C) Dispensing with resolutions in certain cases

When a board has adopted an annual appropriations resolution providing money therefor, the board may then by general resolution dispense with adoption of specific resolutions authorizing the following:

(1) The purchase or sale of property (except real estate);

(2) The employment, appointment, or confirmation of officers and employees (except as otherwise provided by law);

(3) The payment of debts or claims;

(4) The salaries of superintendents, teachers, or other employees; or

(5) The approval of warrants for payment of any claim from school funds.[191]

---

[185]RC 3313.18.

[186]Board of Education v Best, 52 OS 138, 39 NE 694 (1894).

[187]State ex rel Cox v Crestview Local School Dist Bd of Ed, Nos. 82-C-33, 82-C-34, 1983 WL 6616 (7th Dist Ct App, Columbiana, 3-10-83); State ex rel Stafford v Clay Local School Dist Bd of Ed, No. 1331, 1982 WL 3348 (4th Dist Ct App, Scioto, 1-20-82); Clark v Board of Education, No. 389 (12th Dist Ct App, Clinton, 1-30-80).

[188]Savarese v Buckeye Local School Dist Bd of Ed, No. 94-J-30, 1995 WL 138925 (7th Dist Ct App, Jefferson, 3-21-95).

[189]State ex rel Ach v Evans, 90 OS 243, 107 NE 537 (1914).

[190]Hami v Youngstown Bd of Ed, No. 91-CV-1448 (CP, Mahoning, 7-29-91) (upholding board's hiring of assistant superintendent notwithstanding failure strictly to conform to *Robert's Rules*).

[191]RC 3313.18.

PERSONNEL

Chapter 6

Treasurer of the Board of Education, Business Manager, Legal Counsel

6.01 Introduction

TREASURER OF THE BOARD OF EDUCATION

6.02 Election or appointment of treasurer, qualifications
6.03 Removal from office, nonrenewal of contract, resignation
6.04 Absence or incapacity, temporary treasurer
6.05 Compensation
6.06 Duties of treasurer as board secretary
6.07 Duties of treasurer as fiscal officer
6.08 Miscellaneous duties of treasurer
6.09 Duties of treasurer at end of term: audit

BUSINESS MANAGER

6.10 Business manager, qualifications
6.11 Election or appointment, term, salary, bond
6.12 Suspension or removal, vacancy, resignation
6.13 Powers and duties of business manager

LEGAL COUNSEL

6.14 Legal adviser: county prosecutor, city law director, house counsel
6.15 Legal adviser: outside counsel

6.01 Introduction

A board of education *must* employ a treasurer and may employ a business manager. By law, either the city law director (in the case of a city school district) or the county prosecutor (in all other cases) is the legal counsel for a board of education, although a board may employ house counsel and also may secure the services of private counsel to replace or supplement the services of statutory counsel or house counsel.

The treasurer serves not only as fiscal officer for the school district but also as secretary. In general, he may serve the board only in those capacities and cannot be a member of the board nor an administrator, teacher, or other board employee. The business manager has various duties, particularly property management. Both the treasurer and business manager must be licensed and must meet specified educational requirements for licensure and renewal.

TREASURER OF THE BOARD OF EDUCATION

6.02 Election or appointment of treasurer, qualifications

(A) In general, incompatible offices, joint employment

The board of education of each city, exempted village, local, and joint vocational school district is required to elect a treasurer at an organizational meeting.[1]

The treasurer may not be a member of the board or otherwise regularly employed by the board.[2] In other words, as a general rule a board member, administrator, teacher, or other employee is not allowed to do double duty as treasurer. However, where an educational service center governing board has been designated to serve as the board of a joint vocational school district, that board may appoint the superintendent of the educational service center as treasurer of the joint vocational school district.[3]

---

[1] RC 3313.22. This statute, and RC 3313.222 to RC 3313.25, expressly do not apply to a cooperative education school district and its treasurer if that treasurer is also the treasurer of another school district pursuant to RC 3311.52 or RC 3311.521. See Text 4.03(G), Cooperative education school district.
[2] RC 3313.22.
[3] RC 3311.19(E).

Except for a joint vocational school district governed by an educational service center governing board that has appointed the service center superintendent to serve as treasurer, the boards of two or more school districts may, by agreement, jointly employ a treasurer.[4]

An educational service center governing board which is the taxing authority for a county school financing district that levies a tax pursuant to RC 5705.215 or chooses to act as the governing board of the educational service center pursuant to RC 135.01(D) is required to appoint a treasurer. In case the governing board is neither the taxing authority that levies such a tax nor chooses to act as a governing board pursuant to RC 135.01(D), the service center superintendent then serves as the treasurer, but the tenure and removal provisions applicable to treasurers generally do not apply to him.[5]

(B) Licensure, continuing education

The importance the general assembly attaches to the position of district treasurer is illustrated by the requirement that a treasurer must be trained and licensed for the job.

The state board of education must establish standards for licensing district treasurers and for the renewal, revocation, and issuance of duplicate copies of such licenses.[6] A grandfather clause provides that any person employed as a treasurer on July 1, 1983, is considered to meet the standards for licensure and renewal. Any person who was not a treasurer on that date may not be elected or appointed treasurer unless licensed under RC 3301.074.

To obtain an initial four-year treasurer's license, the applicant must either (1) hold a bachelor's degree, or associate degree in accounting, public administration, or finance, have 300 hours of field experience in specified subject areas (or its equivalent), and have nine semester hours or twenty-seven department of education approved continuing education units distributed over specified subject areas; or (2) be certificated as a school superintendent.[7]

The state board must also establish continuing programs of in-service training in school district budget and finance for school officials. Each treasurer or treasurer pro tempore is required to attend one of these training programs each year.[8]

To obtain a four-year renewal of a treasurer's license, the applicant must demonstrate completion of nine semester hours or twenty-seven department of education approved continuing education units (if holding a bachelor's degree, or an associate degree in accounting, public administration, or finance), or six semester hours or eighteen continuing education units (if he holds a master's degree). Alternatively, the applicant must hold a valid school superintendent's certificate. Persons employed as school treasurers on January 1, 1984, are considered to meet the requirements for licensing and renewal.[9]

(C) Term

The treasurer initially serves for a two-year probationary period and thereafter, if reappointed, serves for four-year terms. If the treasurer is reappointed, the board is required to execute a written contract of employment for each successive four-year term.[10]

When a treasurer resigns during term, the board may appoint a treasurer to hold office until the next organizational meeting, when the board must elect a treasurer to serve the initial two-year probationary term. The board of a local school district may appoint a treasurer to serve a term less than the two-year probationary term, but the treasurer must serve a full two-year probationary term before being eligible for reappointment for the four-year term also provided in RC 3313.22.[11]

(D) Bond

Before taking up the duties of office, the treasurer must execute a bond, in an amount and with surety approved by the

---

[4]RC 3313.222.
[5]RC 3313.22, RC 3313.24.
[6]RC 3301.074. The statute expressly makes the holder of a license subject to RC 3319.31 and RC 3319.311, which are discussed in Text 8.07, Revocation or suspension of certificate.

[7]OAC 3301-5-01.
[8]RC 3301.072.
[9]OAC 3301-5-01.
[10]RC 3313.22.
[11]OAG 70-075.

board, payable to the state, conditioned on the faithful performance of all the official duties required of him. The bond must be deposited with the board president and a certified copy filed with the county auditor.[12] The premium of the bond must be paid by the board.[13]

The treasurer must furnish a bond for each term of office and may not continue an old bond.[14] The amount of the bond must bear a reasonable relationship to the amount of money and property coming into the treasurer's control during term of office.[15]

If public funds are handled by an assistant treasurer, the board may require a bond and fix the amount, as required for the treasurer. The assistant treasurer could be included in a blanket bond covering employees such as secretaries and cafeteria managers, who handle public funds.

6.03 Removal from office, nonrenewal of contract, resignation

(A) In general

The treasurer may be removed at any time for cause by a two-thirds vote of the entire board. A treasurer who fails to maintain a valid license, *must* be removed. A treasurer is, of course, protected like other school district employees by general equal employment opportunity laws, the First Amendment, and Ohio's whistleblower statute.[16]

Although not statutorily required, as a constitutional matter the treasurer is entitled to notice of the charges and an informal pretermination hearing where he can present his side of the story.[17]

A board of education that does not intend to reappoint its treasurer, either after the treasurer's probationary term or after a four-year term, must give the treasurer written notice of the board's intention not later than the first regularly scheduled board meeting of October. If the board does not give timely notice, the treasurer is considered re-employed for a four-year term at a salary to be determined by the board at its next organizational meeting.[18]

Resignation of a treasurer is generally governed by the same principles as apply to teachers.[19]

(B) Appointment of substitute to make reports

Upon the failure of a treasurer within a county district to make any report required by law, the county superintendent must appoint some suitable person to make the reports. The replacement must receive reasonable compensation from the county board of education.[20] The substitution also may be initiated by the bureau of inspection and supervision of public offices on discovery of the default.[21]

6.04 Absence or incapacity, temporary treasurer

If a treasurer is absent from any meeting of the board, the members present must choose one of their number to serve in his place pro tempore.[22] But, an otherwise valid decision by the board is not rendered void because its treasurer is absent and the board fails to choose a member to serve in his place temporarily.[23]

Each board of education must adopt written standards for determining whether the treasurer is incapacitated. The treasurer may request a hearing before the board on any such action, and has the same rights as are afforded to a teacher in a teacher's contract termination hearing under RC 3319.16. If a determination is made that the treasurer is so incapacitated as to be unable to perform duties, the

---

[12] RC 3313.25.
[13] RC 3929.17.
[14] 1955 OAG 4711.
[15] 1957 OAG 706.
[16] See Text Ch 17, Equal Employment Opportunity, Family and Medical Leave; Text 9.21(E), Constitutionally protected conduct; Text 9.21(F), Protection of whistleblowers.
[17] See Cleveland Bd of Ed v Loudermill, 470 US 532, 105 SCt 1487, 84 LEd(2d) 494 (1985). See also Text 12.17(B), Notice to employee, removal order.
[18] RC 3313.22.
[19] See Text 9.17, Resignation (except for first paragraph, which applies only to teachers).
[20] RC 3319.37.
[21] 1953 OAG 2484.
[22] RC 3313.23.
[23] Crabtree v Wellston City School Dist Bd of Ed, 26 App(2d) 237, 270 NE(2d) 668 (Jackson 1970), cert denied 408 US 943, 92 SCt 2847, 33 LEd(2d) 766 (1972).

board may appoint a treasurer pro tempore.[24]

6.05 Compensation

The board of each school district must fix the compensation of its treasurer, to be paid from the general fund of the district. No order for payment of the treasurer's salary may be drawn until the treasurer presents to the board evidence of a valid license.[25] When a treasurer is jointly employed by two or more boards of education, the treasurer must be compensated according to the agreement between the boards.[26]

The treasurer's contract should authorize only mandatory statutory duties, and should fix compensation for a period of four years after the original two-year probationary period has elapsed.[27] The treasurer's salary may be increased during his term to compensate for increased duties or for experience and efficiency.[28]

Since a treasurer's contract is provided for by RC 3313.22 to RC 3313.32, a treasurer is not a "nonteaching employee" and cannot claim rights guaranteed to nonteaching employees by RC 3319.081 to RC 3319.088.[29] For instance, a retiring treasurer is not entitled under RC 3319.084 to pay for unused accrued vacation time for up to two years.[30]

6.06 Duties of treasurer as board secretary

The position of treasurer might more appropriately be termed secretary-treasurer, insofar as the duties include a number of functions normally associated with the position of secretary. These include recording the board's proceedings and miscellaneous duties such as reporting school district boundary changes.[31]

The treasurer is required to record the proceedings of each meeting of the board in a minute book to be provided by the board for that purpose, which is a public record. The record must be read at the next meeting, corrected and approved, and the approval noted in the proceedings. After approval, the record must be signed by the president and attested by the treasurer.[32] The treasurer may not delegate the duty to record, transcribe, or attest the minutes.[33]

By resolution, the board may waive the reading of the record provided it has been distributed to the members at least two days prior to the next meeting and copies are made available to the public and news media.[34]

6.07 Duties of treasurer as fiscal officer

(A) In general

As the title clearly implies, the chief function of the treasurer is keeper of the public purse. In every school district he is the treasurer of school funds.

All money received by the treasurer from any source whatever must immediately be placed in a depository designated by the board of education.[35]

No money of the district can be paid out except by a check signed by the treasurer. If the treasurer is incapacitated, the board may appoint an officer of the district to sign checks during the incapacity.[36] Payroll disbursements are an exception and, if otherwise provided by law, may be paid in any manner authorized by the board.[37] Note, however, that the secretary to the superintendent may not serve as payroll clerk, since the effect would be to remove fiscal responsibility from the hands of the treasurer. The board may employ an administrative assistant to perform mechanical payroll functions only.[38]

---

[24] RC 3313.23.
[25] RC 3301.074, RC 3313.24.
[26] RC 3313.222.
[27] 1961 OAG 2013.
[28] 1963 Inf OAG 102.
[29] Erkkila v Painesville Twp Bd of Ed, 41 App(3d) 283, 535 NE(2d) 385 (Lake 1987).
[30] Erkkila v Painesville Twp Bd of Ed, 41 App(3d) 283, 535 NE(2d) 385 (Lake 1987).

[31] See Text 6.08, Miscellaneous duties of treasurer.
[32] RC 3313.26.
[33] OAG 80-060.
[34] RC 3313.26.
[35] RC Ch 135. See also Text Ch 42, Deposits and Investments.
[36] RC 3313.51.
[37] RC 3313.51, RC 3315.08; 1931 OAG 3790.
[38] 1958 Inf OAG 106 and 1956 OAG 7107.

All functions of the county auditor, county treasurer, or other officer, relating to the money of a school district, must be carried out by dealing with the district treasurer.[39]

(B) Accounts

The treasurer must keep an account of all school funds of the board, using forms approved by the state auditor. All vouchers for payments and disbursements to and by the board must be preserved, and a monthly statement to the board and district superintendent showing receipts from all sources, the various appropriations made by the board, disbursements and their purposes, the balance remaining in each appropriation, and the assets and liabilities of the school district must be rendered by the treasurer. These statements must be made available for examination by the public.[40]

Sixty days after the close of the fiscal year, the treasurer must prepare an annual financial statement for the preceding year. The report must be published in a newspaper of general circulation in the school district.[41]

(C) Certifying availability of money

(1) Fiscal officer certificate

Before the board of education may make a contract or give any order involving the expenditure of money, the treasurer must certify that the amount required to be paid under the contract or order (or, in the case of a continuing contract, the amount required to be paid in the next fiscal year) is available or in the process of collection and appropriated for that purpose.[42] Any contract entered into without the required certification is void.[43]

The treasurer is required to encumber appropriations and complete certification. Payment of interest or service charges for unpaid past due bills could indicate non-compliance with the statutory requirements or false certification and result in a finding for recovery. The treasurer may not delegate to another the authority to certify contracts or orders for expenditures pursuant to RC 5705.41(D)(1) and RC 5705.412.[44]

(2) Treasurer, superintendent, and board president certificate

A certificate signed by the treasurer, superintendent, and board president must be attached to every contract, appropriation measure, order involving the expenditure of money, or increase in a wage or salary schedule, showing that the school district has in effect for the remainder of the school fiscal year and the succeeding fiscal year the authorization to levy taxes, including the renewal of existing levies which, when combined with the estimated revenue from all other sources available to the district at the time of certification, are sufficient to enable the district to operate an adequate educational program on all days in its school calendar for the current fiscal year and for a number of days in the succeeding fiscal year equal to the number of days instruction was held or is scheduled for the current fiscal year. A certificate attached to an appropriation measure must cover only that fiscal year.[45]

This certificate says in effect that if the money is not on hand or in process of collection, there is an expectancy of having enough money because the available sources of future revenue are adequate. Levy renewals may not be considered as available revenue unless approved by the voters.

The certificate is not required for a temporary appropriation if the measure will not be in effect on or after the thirtieth day after the earliest date the district may pass its annual appropriation, the amount of the appropriation does not exceed twenty-five per cent of the total amount of the previous year, and an amended certificate of estimated resources for the current year has not been certified to the board of education under RC 5705.36.[46]

Absence of the certificate when required renders the contract, order, or schedule void. However, if a purchase order or current payroll of, or contract of employment

---

[39] RC 3313.31.
[40] RC 3313.29. See also discussion of school finance in Text Ch 43, Financial Transactions and Accounting.
[41] RC 117.06.
[42] RC 5705.41.
[43] RC 5705.41, RC 5705.412.
[44] OAG 80-060.
[45] RC 5705.412.
[46] RC 5705.412.

with, a regular employee or officer is accompanied by the treasurer's certificate that the amount required to meet the contract or order in that fiscal year has been approved and is in the treasury or in process of collection, as required by RC 5705.41, then no additional certification is required under RC 5705.412.

One Ohio appeals court has held that only routine purchase orders could be accompanied by a treasurer's certificate under RC 5705.41.[47] In the absence of any board policy as to which types of orders came under which statute, the court held that a purchase order for at least $133,000 for three new business machines which was not accompanied by a certificate under RC 5705.412 was void. A federal district court has suggested that, with the enactment of RC 5705.412 in 1971, RC 5705.41 no longer applies to contracts entered into by a board of education.[48] Because these decisions may be limited to their particular facts, prudence suggests that these procedures be discussed with the board's legal counsel.

Any officer, employee, or other person who knowingly spends or authorizes the expenditure of public money, or the execution of a contract, order, or schedule contrary to RC 5705.412, or knowingly issues a certificate containing false statements, is jointly and severally liable for the money personally and on his bond in an amount not exceeding $20,000. No person is liable for a good faith mistake based on reasonable grounds.[49]

RC 5705.412 does not apply to any contract, order, or increase in wage or salary schedule necessary to comply with the state minimum salary schedule for teachers pursuant to RC 3317.13(B). However, RC 5705.412 does apply to all other teachers' contracts for the next school year, as distinguished from current contracts. Funds for current contracts presumably have been certified by a previous certificate.[50]

The treasurer must forward a copy of each certificate required by RC 5705.412 to the auditor of any county in which a part of the district is located. The county auditor may not distribute property taxes or any state school foundation payment to a school district that has not filed copies of all certificates required under RC 5705.412.

A school district may attach a conditional certificate to a collective bargaining agreement that contains alternative teacher salary schedules, expressly making the certificate contingent on the passage of an operating levy or the receipt of some other contingent revenue. To make the certification, the treasurer, board president, and superintendent must make two factual findings. First, they must determine that in the absence of contingent revenue the school district will be able to operate an adequate educational program during the current and subsequent fiscal years while paying teachers according to the current salary schedule. Second, they must determine that if contingent revenue is received, the district can implement the increased salary schedules and still operate an adequate educational program.[51]

(D) Certifying accuracy of reports needed to calculate state funding

The treasurer and district superintendent must certify the accuracy of all required reports containing information necessary for calculation of state funding.[52] Detailed provisions on the calculation of student enrollments for funding purposes are given in RC 3317.03.

6.08 Miscellaneous duties of treasurer

(A) Payment of teachers' salaries

The treasurer may not pay a teacher compensation until the treasurer has received from the teacher (1) all reports required of the teacher by the state and district boards of education and the district superintendent; and (2) unless the teacher is engaged part-time under a permit issued pursuant to RC 3319.301, a written state-

---

[47] CADO Business Systems of Ohio, Inc v Cleveland City School Dist Bd of Ed, 8 App(3d) 385, 8 OBR 499, 457 NE(2d) 939 (Cuyahoga 1983).

[48] Tri-County North Local Schools Bd of Ed v McGuire & Shook Corp, 748 FSupp 541 (SD Ohio 1989).

[49] RC 5705.412.

[50] Maple Heights School Dist Bd of Ed v Maple Heights Teachers Assn, 41 Misc 27, 322 NE(2d) 154 (CP, Cuyahoga 1973).

[51] OAG 81-070.

[52] RC 3301.07(I).

ment from the county, city, or exempted village district superintendent that the teacher has filed a legal teacher's certificate, or true copy, to teach the subject or grades taught, with the dates of its validity.[53] An exception to the second requirement applies to new teachers holding at least bachelor's degrees whose applications for provisional (or higher grade) certificates are pending during the first two months of initial employment with the district.[54]

(B) Receiving and recording bids

Where competitive bidding is required, the treasurer is required to enter advertisements for bids in the board records and to receive bids submitted for that work. The bids must be opened and publicly read by the treasurer, and entered in board records.[55]

(C) Reporting school district boundary changes

The treasurer must notify the board of elections in writing of all changes in boundaries of the school district, including a plat showing those changes, not later than ten days after the changes become effective.[56]

(D) Executing conveyances

All conveyances made by a board of education must be executed by the treasurer and the board president.[57]

6.09 Duties of treasurer at end of term: audit

When the term of office expires, the treasurer must deliver to the successor all books and papers relating to district affairs, including certificates and copies, and reports of school statistics filed by teachers.[58]

Also at the expiration of the treasurer's term, or before the board approves the surety of any treasurer, the board is directed to require that the treasurer produce all money, bonds, or other securities in the treasurer's hands. These must be counted by the board or a committee of the board, or by a representative of the state auditor. A certificate stating the exact amounts of money, bonds, or other securities, and signed by the representatives making the count, must be entered into board records, and constitutes prima facie evidence that the amount stated was actually in the treasury at that date.[59]

BUSINESS MANAGER

6.10 Business manager, qualifications

The board of education of a city, exempted village, or local school district may create the position of business manager, whose duties are in essence those of a property and personnel manager. At the time of election, the board must direct whether the business manager is to be responsible directly to the board or to the district superintendent.[60]

A board may not employ a person as business manager who does not hold a license issued pursuant to RC 3301.074, which authorizes the state board of education to adopt rules establishing standards for licensing business managers.[61]

Persons employed as business managers on July 1, 1983, are considered to meet the standards for licensure as a business manager.[62] OAC 3301-6-01 extends the grandfather provision to any person employed as a business manager on January 1, 1984. It also gives the standards for licensing business managers and provides for an initial four-year license subject to renewal every four years upon completion of specific requirements.

---

[53] RC 3319.30, RC 3319.36.

[54] RC 3319.30, RC 3319.36.

[55] RC 3313.46. For extended treatment of competitive bidding requirements, see Text 37.04 to 37.06. See also Text 36.04, Purchase of personal property.

[56] RC 3313.261.

[57] RC 3313.33.

[58] RC 3313.28.

[59] RC 3313.27.

[60] RC 3319.03.

[61] RC 3301.74 expressly makes the holder of a license subject to RC 3319.31 and RC 3319.311, which are discussed in Text 8.07, Revocation or suspension of certificate.

[62] RC 3301.074.

6.11 Election or appointment, term, salary, bond

The business manager is elected by the board, unless the board determines the business manager is to be responsible to the district superintendent, in which case the business manager is appointed by the superintendent and confirmed by the board. In either case, the business manager serves for a term determined by the board but not exceeding four years.[63]

The board fixes the compensation of the business manager before election or appointment. The compensation may not be decreased during the term of office.[64]

The business manager is required to give bond as prescribed by the board for the faithful discharge of his duties.[65]

6.12 Suspension or removal, vacancy, resignation

A board of education may, by a two-thirds vote, suspend or remove a business manager for cause. The charges must be stated in writing, and he must be given an opportunity to offer pertinent testimony in defense. The testimony must be received and considered by the board and made a part of the records.[66] A business manager is, of course, protected like other school district employees by general equal employment opportunity laws, the First Amendment, and Ohio's whistleblower statute.[67]

A vacancy in the office of business manager may be filled only for the unexpired term.[68]

Resignation of a business manager is generally governed by the same principles as apply to teachers.[69]

6.13 Powers and duties of business manager

The business manager is charged with the care and custody of all property of the school district, real or personal, except money.[70] Because the custody of money is excluded, the positions of business manager and treasurer in the same district are incompatible and may not be held by the same person at the same time.[71]

The business manager is required to supervise the construction, maintenance, operation, and repair of all school buildings, advertise for bids when required, purchase and have custody of supplies and equipment, assist in the preparation of the annual appropriations resolution, appoint and discharge (subject to confirmation by the board) noneducational employees, and prepare and execute all contracts necessary in carrying out his duties.[72]

However, a short term (three days or less) suspension of a civil service employee may be properly executed by the business manager under the authority in RC 3319.04.[73]

LEGAL COUNSEL

6.14 Legal adviser: county prosecutor, city law director, house counsel

(A) In general

Ohio law specifies that certain public officials have the duty to act as legal counsel for boards of education, although boards may and often do engage the services of other counsel.

The prosecuting attorney of the county is the legal adviser of all boards of education in the county, except boards of city, joint vocational, and cooperative education school districts.[74] The city law director is

---

[63]RC 3319.03.
[64]RC 3319.05.
[65]RC 3319.05.
[66]RC 3319.06.
[67]See Text Ch 17, Equal Employment Opportunity, Family and Medical Leave; Text 9.21(E), Constitutionally protected conduct; Text 9.21(F), Protection of whistleblowers.
[68]RC 3319.03.

[69]See Text 9.17, Resignation (except for first paragraph, which applies only to teachers).
[70]RC 3319.04.
[71]1920 OAG 53. See also RC 3313.22.
[72]RC 3313.51, RC 3319.04.
[73]State ex rel Specht v Oregon City Bd of Ed, 66 OS(2d) 178, 420 NE(2d) 1004 (1981).
[74]RC 3313.35. If a consolidation of county school districts occurs under RC 3311.053, the legal advisor

the legal adviser for the board of a city school district.[75] In the case of a charter city, the law director is not the legal adviser unless the duty is imposed by the charter.[76] If the duty is imposed by the charter, however, whether directly or indirectly, it may be enforced by writ of mandamus.[77]

The statutory duty to serve a board as legal counsel devolves on the official serving in a capacity similar to that of prosecuting attorney or city law director regardless of the title of that official.[78]

For a joint vocational or cooperative education school district, the legal adviser is the prosecuting attorney of the most populous county containing a member district of the joint vocational or cooperative education district.[79]

Under RC 309.10, a school board may hire "in-house" counsel, provided such counsel is paid from school funds.[80]

(B) Duties of statutory legal advisers

Actions against a board member or officer for malfeasance or misfeasance in office are to be prosecuted by the prosecuting attorney, except in city school districts, and the prosecuting attorney is to act as legal counsel for the board and its officers in all civil actions brought by or against them. In case of civil litigation between boards of education in the same county for which the prosecuting attorney is the legal adviser, the prosecuting attorney is not required to act for either of them. In city school districts these duties are the responsibility of the city law director.[81]

(C) Compensation of statutory legal counsel

No compensation in addition to the regular salary of the prosecuting attorney or city law director is allowed for services to a board of education required by law.[82] In the case of a charter city in which the law director does not have the duty of acting as legal counsel to the board, a fee arrangement between the city law department and the board which provides for reasonable compensation (as determined by the board) for legal services is permissible.[83]

The furnishing of the city law director with a reference text, such as this book, by the board of a city school district which encompasses an area greater than the city itself, for use in dealing with legal questions related to the board, is not "compensation" for purposes of RC 3313.35 and is impliedly authorized.[84]

6.15 Legal adviser: outside counsel

(A) In general, authority to employ private counsel

Any board of education may retain the services of private legal counsel in place of, or to supplement or assist, the prosecuting attorney or city law director.[85]

The power to retain legal counsel to assist the legal adviser is apparently without limit,[86] except that the board must have a legal interest in the matter for which the services are retained.[87]

(B) Services

Specific examples of purposes for which retention of private counsel has been approved include the following:

---

of the new district is the prosecuting attorney of the county in which the largest number of pupils supervised by the new district board resides.

[75] RC 3313.35.

[76] 1954 OAG 3644.

[77] State ex rel Grandview Heights City School Dist Bd of Ed v Morton, 44 OS(2d) 151, 339 NE(2d) 663 (1975).

[78] RC 3313.35.

[79] RC 3313.35.

[80] OAG 83-038.

[81] RC 3313.35.

[82] RC 3313.35. See also State ex rel Grandview Heights City School Dist Bd of Ed v Morton, 44 OS(2d) 151, 339 NE(2d) 663 (1975); Ethics Op 89-012 (city law director prohibited by RC 2921.43(A) from accepting or soliciting additional compensation from city school district for legal services provided).

[83] OAG 70-081.

[84] OAG 73-088.

[85] RC 309.10; Knepper v French, 125 OS 613, 183 NE 869 (1932); OAG 80-064; 1961 OAG 2678; 1958 OAG 2685; 1954 OAG 3644.

[86] Knepper v French, 125 OS 613, 183 NE 869 (1932); 1954 OAG 3644.

[87] Marion Local School Dist Bd of Ed v Marion County Bd of Ed, 167 OS 543, 150 NE(2d) 407 (1958); OAG 65-66; 1955 OAG 4734.

(1) Defending a school board in a suit involving the transfer of territory from one district to another;[88]

(2) Representing a school board in an action for damages against a contractor on a contingent fee basis;[89]

(3) Preparing necessary documents for the issuance of bonds;[90] and

(4) Passing on the legality of a transcript of proceedings relating to the issuance of bonds.[91]

---

[88] Knepper v French, 125 OS 613, 183 NE 869 (1932).
[89] 1961 OAG 2678.
[90] 1938 OAG 3441.
[91] 1933 OAG 1392.

Chapter 7

School Administrators

7.01 Introduction

SUPERINTENDENT OF SCHOOLS

7.02 Superintendent of schools as chief executive
7.03 Qualifications of superintendent
7.04 Appointment of superintendent, term
7.05 Superintendent's contract, compensation
7.06 Duties of superintendent
7.07 Temporary superintendent
7.08 Educational service center superintendent's offices and equipment

OTHER SCHOOL ADMINISTRATORS

7.09 Assistant superintendents, principals, and other administrators
7.10 Employment of administrators
7.11 Administrators' contracts
7.12 Supervisors and special teachers in educational service centers
7.13 Teacher employed as administrator, tenure
7.14 Evaluation of school administrators

7.01 Introduction

Subject to limited exceptions applicable only to island or cooperative education school districts, the board of each school district and educational service center is required to appoint a superintendent to be the chief executive officer of the district, charged with the duty to oversee all educational and business affairs of the district. A person must possess a valid superintendent's certificate to be eligible for appointment to the position. The experience and education requirements for obtaining the certificate are designed to assure that holders are well qualified to be chief administrators. In addition to a superintendent, a board may appoint assistant superintendents, principals, assistant principals, supervisors, administrative specialists, and other school administrators as it considers necessary. A board must follow specific statutory requirements to employ, reemploy, or nonrenew superintendents and other administrators.

---

[1] RC 3319.01. See also Text 4.03(F), Cooperative education school district.

[2] See Text 6.02, Election or appointment of treasurer, qualifications.

SUPERINTENDENT OF SCHOOLS

7.02 Superintendent of schools as chief executive

Except in an island district where the superintendent of the educational service center may serve as superintendent and except as otherwise provided for cooperative education districts, the board of education in each school district *must* appoint a qualified person to act as superintendent.[1] The overall responsibility for operation of the schools lies in the board of education, but the superintendent is the overseer of daily operations.

In the exercise of its overall responsibilities, the board delegates to the superintendent the administration, both business and educational, of the district. The superintendent answers to the board for all instructional and supervisory aspects of education, as well as for financial and business affairs of the district. Note, however, that his financial responsibilities complement, but cannot supplant, the statutory functions and duties of the district treasurer.[2] Similarly, in a district which has created the position of business manager, some of the business responsibilities of the superintendent may be shared with or delegated to the business manager.[3]

7.03 Qualifications of superintendent

The one indispensable qualification for a superintendent is possession of a valid superintendent's certificate issued by the state department of education. Possession of the certificate assures that the superintendent has met training and experience qualifications to be the chief administrator of the district.

---

[3] See Text 6.10, Business manager, qualifications.

(A) Statutory requirement that candidate possess certificate

RC 3319.01 explicitly requires that the superintendent hold a valid superintendent's certificate, issued under RC 3319.22(J) (as to superintendents in city or exempted village school districts or educational service centers), or under RC 3319.22(N) (as to superintendents in local school districts). A grandfather clause dispenses with the certificate requirement for persons employed or qualified as superintendents in any district other than a local district prior to August 1, 1939, and in any local district prior to September 16, 1957.

Although the statutes distinguish among types of superintendent's certificates based on the type of school district,[4] there is no distinction in practice. RC 3319.22, governing types of certificates, permits but does not require the distinction, and the state board of education has chosen to impose uniform requirements for certification.[5] A board of education may employ a superintendent conditioned upon his obtaining a certificate before beginning employment.[6]

(B) Requirements for obtaining certificate

OAC 3301-23-19 states the requirements for obtaining a provisional superintendent's certificate. OAC 3301-23-22 governs renewal of provisional certificates and conversion to professional and then permanent certificates.[7] Provisional and professional certificates are subject to additional requirements for renewal after initial issuance. The permanent certificate does not require renewal.

Candidates for the higher grades of certificates "go through the chairs," so to speak, since each higher grade must be converted from the next lower grade, and additional education and experience are required. Moreover, certificate holders must be assiduous in their professional growth—even renewal for the lower grades requires additional education and experience. Until a permanent certificate is obtained, either renewal or upgrading is necessary to retain a certificate and, hence, to retain a job as superintendent.

When the experience requirements for the different grades are added up, the candidate for a permanent certificate must have a minimum of eleven years in supervisory or administrative positions, of which the last eight must be as a superintendent of schools. The cumulative educational requirements add up to a minimum of eighteen semester hours (twenty-seven quarter hours) of college credit after receiving a master's degree (for some of which continuing education units may be substituted). A doctorate is not required for certification as a superintendent, but the minimum requirements make a Ph.D. program attractive to those who aspire to the office.

(1) Provisional certificate, renewal

To be eligible for a provisional superintendent's certificate, "valid for all administrative positions," a person must hold a master's degree with sixty semester hours "well distributed" over courses in administration, curriculum and instructional leadership, and "foundations." The applicant must also have "three years of satisfactory experience in an administrative or supervisory position under a standard certificate."[8] In addition, the applicant admitted to a certification program after July 1, 1987, or who completes a program after July 1, 1991, must successfully complete an examination prescribed by the department of education. A provisional certificate is valid for four years and is renewable for four years[9] on completion of additional experience and educational requirements.[10] Some flexibility is allowed in the mix of requirements.

(2) Professional certificate, renewal

A provisional certificate may be converted to a professional certificate with additional satisfactory experience of three years under the provisional certificate and completion of an individualized "entry year program" for superintendents, plus six semester hours of graduate course work in educational administration or related disci-

---

[4] RC 3319.01, RC 3319.22.
[5] OAC 3301-23-19, OAC 3301-23-22.
[6] Beisel v Monroe County Bd of Ed, No. CA-678, 1990 WL 125485 (7th Dist Ct App, Monroe, 8-29-90).
[7] RC 3319.22, RC 3319.24 to RC 3319.26.
[8] OAC 3301-23-19.
[9] RC 3319.24.
[10] OAC 3301-23-22(A).

plines.[11] A professional certificate is valid for eight years[12] and may be renewed if the applicant has satisfactory experience in an administrative position and additional education consisting of thirty-six continuing education units or twelve semester hours of graduate course work. Each year of experience under the certificate reduces the education requirements by one semester hour or three continuing education units.[13]

(3) Permanent certificate

A professional certificate may be converted to a permanent certificate with an additional five years of satisfactory experience under the professional certificate, plus an additional twelve semester hours of graduate course work in educational administration or related disciplines.

7.04 Appointment of superintendent, term

(A) In general, time of appointment, term

As previously noted, subject to very limited exceptions, a superintendent is indispensable since the board of education or governing board must appoint one. The appointment must be made by May 1 and is for any term not longer than five years, beginning August 1 and expiring July 31.[14] The superintendent may not be transferred to any other position during the term of employment except by mutual agreement of the superintendent and the board.

(B) Reemployment and nonrenewal

Like teachers, superintendents are entitled to notice of nonrenewal of their contracts. Unless the board, on or before March 1 of the year in which the superintendent's contract expires, either reemploys for a successive term or gives written notice of its intention not to reemploy, the superintendent is reemployed at the expiration of the current term for an additional term of one year at the same salary plus any increments authorized by the board.[15]

A board of education must comply with the notice requirement. The only exception, as with teachers, is where a superintendent deliberately evades the notice (which, a court has held, may be included in board minutes routinely sent to the superintendent, although the court acknowledged this is by no means the best way of serving notice).[16] Board action by resolution declaring the board's intention not to reemploy a superintendent must precede the nonrenewal notice.

Thus, a notice of intent not to reemploy executed by a majority of board members, but not acted upon or executed at a properly scheduled regular or special board meeting, does not comply with RC 3319.01 and is a nullity.[17] The Ohio Supreme Court, however, has held that the failure of a board to comply with its own policies with respect to nonrenewal deadlines, which policies called for notice prior to the March 1 statutory date, did not create an automatic right of reemployment which could be enforced in mandamus.[18]

A board may reemploy the superintendent at any regular or special meeting beginning January 1 of the calendar year immediately preceding the year in which his contract expires, for a succeeding term not longer than five years beginning August 1 of the year his term expires and ending on July 31. Failure to follow the time lines and procedure incorporated into RC 3319.01 in attempting to execute a new multi-year contract renders the contract invalid.[19]

(C) Employment of local school district superintendent

Except for the automatic reemployment of a superintendent if a board fails to act, the employment or reemployment of a

---

[11]OAC 3301-23-22(B)(2).
[12]RC 3319.25.
[13]OAC 3301-23-22(C).
[14]RC 3319.01. In the case of a cooperative education school district, see Text 4.03(F), Cooperative education school district.
[15]RC 3319.01. In the case of a cooperative education school district, see Text 4.03(F), Cooperative education school district.
[16]Pavkov v Barberton Bd of Ed, No. CA-11570, 1984 WL 6149 (9th Dist Ct App, Summit, 5-2-84).

[17]OAG 66-085. See also RC 121.22.
[18]State ex rel Stiller v Columbiana Exempted Village School Dist Bd of Ed, No. 94-C-13, 1995 WL 43646 (7th Dist Ct App, Columbiana, 1-30-95), affirmed by 74 OS(3d) 113, 656 NE(2d) 679 (1995).
[19]Hess v James A. Garfield Local School Dist Bd of Ed, No. 1651, 1986 WL 14320 (11th Dist Ct App, Portage, 12-5-86).

superintendent of a local school district can only be on the recommendation of the superintendent of the educational service center. However, a local board of education by a three-fourths vote may, after considering two nominations for the position of a local superintendent made by the service center superintendent, employ or reemploy a person not nominated for the position.[20] A recommendation is required and may be compelled whenever a local board takes affirmative action with respect to employment or reemployment of a superintendent.[21] The acceptance or rejection of the service center superintendent's recommendation may be by a simple majority vote of the local board.[22]

(D) Superintendent of joint vocational school district

The service center superintendent is the executive officer for a joint vocational school district for which the county board of education serves as the joint vocational school district board and may be paid compensation for that additional position by the joint vocational school district.[23] The service center superintendent may be appointed superintendent of a joint vocational school district even though the educational service center governing board is not also serving as the joint vocational school board, provided it is physically possible for one person to perform the duties of both offices.[24]

(E) Vacancy

If a vacancy occurs in the office of superintendent during the term of employment, the board must promptly appoint a superintendent for a term not exceeding five years from the prior August 1.[25]

7.05 Superintendent's contract, compensation

(A) Contract, termination

When the superintendent is appointed, the board must execute a written contract.[26] The contract conditions (except as to compensation) are the same for all superintendents in all types of school districts.

Since superintendents usually (if not always) come up from the ranks, they are given the benefit of the teachers' tenure law[27] regarding salary notice, sick leave, leave of absence, military leave, and related matters,[28] except as otherwise provided by law. For example, superintendents are exempt from the evaluation requirements applicable to certain teachers under RC 3319.11 and RC 3319.111.[29]

Contracts of superintendents may include provisions for vacations. If the superintendent is separated from employment, a board may compensate the superintendent for accrued and unused vacation at the superintendent's current rate of pay, up to the amount accrued within three years before separation. If a superintendent dies, any such payment for unused vacation must be made to the superintendent's estate or in accordance with RC 2113.04.[30]

Termination of a superintendent's contract for cause must be in accordance with RC 3319.16,[31] which provides for notice, hearing, and appeal. A superintendent is also, of course, protected like other school employees by general equal employment opportunity laws, the First Amendment, and Ohio's whistleblower statute.[32] Resignation of a superintendent is generally governed by the same principles as apply to teachers.[33]

---

[20] RC 3319.01.
[21] OAG 76-034.
[22] OAG 79-003.
[23] RC 3311.19.
[24] OAG 66-135.
[25] RC 3319.01.
[26] RC 3319.01.
[27] RC 3319.08 to RC 3319.18. See Text 9.04 to 9.09.
[28] RC 3319.09.
[29] RC 3319.111(C).

[30] RC 3319.01.

[31] RC 3319.01. See Text 9.21, Termination for cause, in general; Text 9.22, Termination for cause, procedure.

[32] See Text Ch 17, Equal Employment Opportunity, Family and Medical Leave; Text 9.21(E), Constitutionally protected conduct; Text 9.21(F), Protection of whistleblowers.

[33] See Text 9.17, Resignation.

(B) Compensation, expenses

At the time a superintendent is appointed, the board is required to fix compensation. Salary and compensation may be increased or decreased during the term of employment, but any decrease must be part of a uniform plan affecting salaries of all district employees.[34] The position of superintendent of an educational service center is not considered a public office for purposes of Article II, section 20 of the Ohio Constitution and is not subject to the prohibition against in-term increases in compensation.[35] If the educational service center governing board serves as the board for a joint vocational school district, the superintendent of the educational service center serves as executive officer for the joint district and may be paid additional compensation by the joint district.[36]

The governing board of an educational service center may allow the service center superintendent a sum determined by the board for traveling expenses.[37] No express statutory provision is made for travel expense allowances for city and exempted village superintendents, but it has been held that boards in those districts may authorize payments from public funds for expenses incurred by their superintendents in the performance of their official duties. The superintendent is entitled to payment for actual mileage when traveling on official business and for reimbursement of related lodging and real costs. An itemized statement of expenses should be filed with the district treasurer.[38]

7.06 Duties of superintendent

(A) In general

The superintendent attends all board meetings as executive officer of the district. He administers the schools following policies adopted by the board, rules of the state board of education, and the law. He provides the board with information needed to formulate school policies and presents other information as necessary to appraise existing policies.

The superintendent of a joint vocational school district exercises the duties and authority vested in a superintendent pertaining to the operation of a school district and employment of its personnel.[39]

(B) Assignment of personnel

The superintendent of a city or exempted village school district nominates, for appointment by the board of education, all teachers, principals, assistant principals, assistant superintendents, and other necessary administrative officers. In local school districts and educational service centers, those nominations are made by the service center superintendent.[40] The superintendent is authorized to direct and assign teachers and other school employees under his supervision, except that the superintendent exercises responsibility for teacher assignment for local school districts under the supervision of the educational service center.[41] Effective November 15, 1995, local boards of education are authorized to enter into agreements with governing boards to require local superintendents to nominate local teachers for employment and assign teachers and other employees and pupils.[42]

(1) Teachers and administrators

The superintendent's right to assign and transfer teachers has been challenged with a variety of legal arguments. Most have been unsuccessful.

---

[34]RC 3319.01, RC 3319.12. The extent to which economic fringe benefits qualify as salary and compensation for purposes of the prohibition against a decrease except under a uniform plan is unclear. Two cases decided under civil service statutes illustrate the ambiguity. Compare Ebert v Stark County Bd of Mental Retardation, 63 OS(2d) 31, 406 NE(2d) 1098 (1980) (finding it "obvious that sick leave credits, just as other fringe benefits, are forms of compensation") with State ex rel Bassman v Earhart, 18 OS(3d) 182, 18 OBR 250, 480 NE(2d) 761 (1985) (holding that free parking privileges, absent a statute requiring that they be provided, is a mere "gratuity," the cessation of which is not a reduction in pay).

[35]OAG 77-014.
[36]RC 3311.19.
[37]RC 3315.06.
[38]1952 OAG 186; 1931 OAG 1920; 1921 OAG 11.
[39]RC 3311.19(E).
[40]RC 3319.02, RC 3319.07.
[41]RC 3319.01.
[42]RC 3319.07.

In *Bohmann v West Clermont Local School Dist Bd of Ed*,[43] the Ohio Supreme Court, emphasizing a superintendent's prerogative to assign teachers, upheld the reassignment of an OWE instructor to the position of study hall teacher and also held that the seniority provisions of RC 3319.17 (which governs a reduction in force) do not apply to the mere reassignment of a teacher from one instructional area to another where no overall reduction in the number of teachers occurs. It has also been held that the assignment of a continuing contract teacher to full-time study hall supervision does not constitute a constructive termination of the contract under RC 3319.16 since a superintendent has discretionary authority to assign under RC 3319.01.[44] Similarly, a teacher assigned as a guidance counselor does not acquire a vested right to perform exclusively as a guidance counselor and may be reassigned back to the classroom.[45] When a special education teacher with a continuing contract voluntarily surrendered his special education certificate, he was not automatically entitled to be reassigned to his former position in the district as a guidance counselor; rather, the superintendent had discretion under RC 3319.01 to assign him to any position for which he was certified.[46]

Since the superintendent of a city school district has sole power to assign or reassign principals to schools within the district under RC 3319.01, the district board does not have authority under RC 3313.20 to adopt rules governing the assignment or reassignment of principals.[47]

By virtue of RC 4117.10, a collective bargaining agreement may limit a superintendent's authority under RC 3319.01 to direct and assign employees.[48]

(2) Nonteaching personnel

The responsibility for assignment of noneducational employees may be delegated to a business manager in city, exempted village, and local school districts.[49] However, where a superintendent retains the right to assign nonteaching employees, the superintendent has no authority to modify a written contract. Thus, where a nonteaching employee was issued a two-year limited contract providing for 191 four-hour work days each year, he could not be reassigned to two-hour days in the second year of the contract.[50]

(C) Assignment of pupils

The superintendent of a city or exempted village school district is charged with the assignment of pupils in the district to the proper schools and grades. The serv-

---

[43]Bohmann v West Clermont Local School Dist Bd of Ed, 2 OS(3d) 136, 2 OBR 683, 443 NE(2d) 176 (1983).

[44]Thompson v Fostoria City School Dist Bd of Ed, No. 13-80-19, 1981 WL 6797 (3d Dist Ct App, Seneca, 2-26-81). Relying on *Thompson*, another court upheld the assignment of a physical education teacher to teach health, agreeing that RC 3319.16 does not apply to reassignments and rejecting the notion that an assignment, even if made maliciously or in bad faith, violates RC 3319.01. Duer v Berea Bd of Ed, No. 45245, 1983 WL 5868 8th Dist Ct App, 3-24-83). See also Cook v Berger, No. C81-1170 (ND Ohio, 7-9-84), in which a federal court found that a teacher's reassignment, even if arbitrary and in bad faith, was not a deprivation of a property interest and not a violation of RC 3319.16. Relying on *Thompson, Duer,* and *Cook*, another court held that a continuing contract teacher could be reassigned as a permanent substitute. Baisden v Oak Hill Union Local School Dist Bd of Ed, No. 491, 1985 WL 11146 (4th Dist Ct App, Jackson, 6-7-85). But see Silavent v Buckeye Central Local School Dist Bd of Ed, 27 App(3d) 189, 27 OBR 228, 500 NE(2d) 315 (Crawford 1985), in which a superintendent was denied authority to reassign a guidance counselor to a position of reading teacher on the ground that the teacher had attained continuing contract status under an employment contract identifying him as a guidance counselor. In an opinion many believe open to serious challenge, a common pleas court has held that one with substantial service as a classroom teacher cannot, without a hearing, be reassigned as a permanent substitute. Mroczek v Beachwood City School Dist Bd of Ed, 61 Misc 6, 400 NE(2d) 1362 (CP, Cuyahoga 1979).

[45]State ex rel Fox v Springfield Bd of Ed, 11 App(2d) 214, 229 NE(2d) 663 (Clark 1966). See also Kolopp v South Range Local School Dist Bd of Ed, 47 App(2d) 208, 353 NE(2d) 642 (Mahoning 1974).

[46]Carter v Orrville City School Dist Bd of Ed, No. 2694, 1992 WL 139986 (9th Dist Ct App, Wayne, 6-17-92).

[47]OAG 72-072; 1958 OAG 2457.

[48]Alexander Local School Dist Bd of Ed v Alexander Local Ed Assn, 41 App(3d) 13, 534 NE(2d) 107 (Athens 1987). See generally Text 18.20, Supremacy of contract over certain laws.

[49]RC 3319.01, RC 3319.03, RC 3319.04. See Text 6.13, Powers and duties of business manager.

[50]Miner v Lake Local School Dist Bd of Ed, No. CA-6322, 1984 WL 4930 (5th Dist Ct App, Stark, 6-18-84).

ice center superintendent exercises responsibility for pupil assignment for local school districts, except after November 15, 1995 that responsibility may be shifted to the local superintendent where the local board of education enter into such an agreement with the educational service center governing board. The assignment of a pupil to a school district outside the pupil's district of residence must, however, be approved by the board of the district where the pupil resides.[51]

The redrawing of school attendance boundaries to promote racial balance in schools and the most efficient use of school resources is a proper discharge of a superintendent's duty to assign pupils under RC 3319.01.[52]

In addition, where two districts have merged in accordance with law, there is no restriction on the authority of a board to terminate certain grades at one school and transfer them to another within the resulting district. The reassignment of pupils is within the authority of a superintendent under RC 3319.01, and the termination of entire grades is fully within the authority of a board of education under RC 3313.47 to RC 3313.49.[53]

A superintendent's discretion in assigning pupils within a district is qualified by the district's "open enrollment" policy required by RC 3313.97.[54]

7.07 Temporary superintendent

When a board of education determines the superintendent is incapacitated, it may appoint a person to serve in his place pro tempore. A written policy is required, setting standards to determine if the superintendent is incapacitated and providing for sick leave or leave of absence status during the period of incapacity and for return to active duty. The superintendent may request a hearing before the board on a proposed action to declare him incapacitated, and he has the same rights as a teacher during a board hearing under RC 3319.16.[55]

The superintendent pro tempore performs all the duties and functions of the superintendent. His compensation is fixed by the board in accordance with RC 3319.01.[56] He serves until the board determines the incapacity of the superintendent is removed or until the superintendent's term of employment expires, whichever is sooner. The board may remove the superintendent pro tempore at any time for cause by two-thirds vote.[57]

7.08 Educational service center superintendent's offices and equipment

In most school districts, the district is required to furnish facilities, equipment, supplies, and necessary services for the use of the superintendent. This is not the case with the superintendent of an educational service center. The board of county commissioners is required to provide and equip offices as permanent headquarters for the use of the educational service center superintendent and his staff, which are also to be used by the governing board when it is in session, and to provide heat, light, water, and janitorial services for those offices.[58] The county commissioners must also provide telephone equipment, but the cost of telephone service is an operating expense of the service center governing board.[59] Some type of conference facility must be provided, but it need not also be suitable for use as a training facility. The county

---

[51]RC 3319.01.

[52]Dodd v Rue, 64 Misc 21, 411 NE(2d) 201 (CP, Hamilton 1979).

[53]Ferris v Paulding Exempted Village School Dist Bd of Ed, 7 App(3d) 163, 7 OBR 208, 454 NE(2d) 957 (Paulding 1982).

[54]Open enrollment policies are discussed in Text 5.08(C), Open enrollment policies.

[55]RC 3319.011.

[56]RC 3319.011.

[57]RC 3319.011.

[58]RC 3319.19; OAG 84-095. Each county in which the office of a county school district is located has a county board of education office fund created under RC 307.031 whose moneys are used for this purpose. Special provision is made in RC 3319.19(D) for a grant program under which additional funds may be provided.

[59]OAG 83-053; OAG 78-042. If a consolidation of county school districts occurs under RC 3311.053, costs of providing and equipping offices not covered by funds received under RC 307.031 are apportioned among the boards of county commissioners of all counties having territory in the new district. See Text 4.03(C), New educational service centers.

commissioners are not required to create and maintain a library for the use of area schools.[60] The offices must be located at the county seat unless another location in the county is approved by the county board.[61]

The county commissioners are further required to provide and equip offices for the superintendent's staff members who assist him in fulfilling his duties and responsibilities.[62]

Where a service center is made up of territories in more than one county under RC 3311.053, the governing board must designate the site of its offices. Essentially, the cost of such offices is apportioned, based on student average daily membership and the number of full-time certificated employees of each service center, under a complicated statutory formula.[63]

OTHER SCHOOL ADMINISTRATORS

7.09 Assistant superintendents, principals, and other administrators

(A) In general, authority to hire

A board of education may appoint assistant superintendents, principals, assistant principals, supervisors, administrative specialists, and other administrators as are necessary, pursuant to RC 3319.02. That section also applies to any noncertified employee who is considered a "supervisor" or "management level employee" as defined in RC 4117.01. That section also includes pupil personnel workers, including school psychologists, if they spend less than fifty per cent of their time teaching or working with students.[64] The positions of a county board of education member, now an educational service center governing board member, and administrator of a local school district within the same county are incompatible.[65]

In converting the employment of noncertified administrators who were formerly in the classified civil service or under continuing contract to RC 3319.02 contracts, the question arises whether such supervisors or management level employees also retain their classified civil service or continuing contract status. As to the former, the answer is no, it being reasonably clear that a statute moving a position from the classified to the unclassified service applies to incumbent employees in affected positions without violating constitutional prohibitions against the taking of property, the impairment of contract rights, or the enactment of retroactive laws.[66] As to the latter, the attorney general has opined that supervisors and management level employees of a non-civil service district retain contractual rights that vested before September 10, 1987, the effective date of the amendment to RC 3319.02.[67]

The teachers' tenure law[68] regarding salary notice, sick leave, leave of absence, military leave, and other matters generally applies to these administrators, except as otherwise provided by statute. However, such administrators are exempt from the evaluation requirements applicable to certain teachers under RC 3319.11 and RC 3319.111.[69]

(B) Assistant superintendents

One or more assistant superintendents may be appointed by a board of education.[70]

(C) Principals and assistant principals

Principals must be, and assistant principals may be, employed by the board of edu-

---

[60]OAG 81-005.
[61]RC 3319.19.
[62]OAG 81-005; OAG 84-095.
[63]See RC 3319.19. See also Text 4.03(C), New educational service centers.
[64]The Ohio Supreme Court has held that "teaching or working with students" requires the physical presence of students when the job activity is performed. It is not sufficient that the job activity is merely in the interest of students. State ex rel Donah v Windham Exempted Village School Dist Bd of Ed, 69 OS(3d) 114, 630 NE(2d) 687 (1994).

[65]OAG 83-070.
[66]Lawrence v Edwin Shaw Hospital, 34 App(3d) 137, 517 NE(2d) 984 (Franklin 1986); Shearer v Cuyahoga County Hospital, 34 App(3d) 59, 516 NE(2d) 1287 (Cuyahoga 1986).
[67]OAG 88-059.
[68]RC 3319.08 to RC 3319.18.
[69]RC 3319.111(C).
[70]RC 3319.02.

cation for all high schools, and principals and assistant principals may be employed for any other schools designated by the board.[71]

As is the case with other administrators, principals may not serve in certain dual capacities because of the conflicting responsibilities of the positions. Pursuant to RC 340.02, a principal may not serve on a community mental health board when his employing school board has contracted with the mental health board. The positions of full-time principal and county commissioner are incompatible when it is physically impossible for one person to perform adequately the duties of both positions.[72]

7.10 Employment of administrators

The employment or reemployment of administrators in city and exempted village school districts and educational service centers is made under nominations by the superintendent. In local school districts, employment and reemployment require nominations by the service center superintendent, subject to the possibility of an agreement between the governing board and local board of education authorizing the local superintendent to make such nomination.[73] A city, exempted village, and governing board (by a three-fourths vote) and a local board (by a majority vote) may reemploy an administrator whom the applicable superintendent refuses to nominate, after considering two nominees for the position. Reemployment of an administrator may take place at any regular or special board meeting between January 1 of the year preceding and March 31 of the year in which his contract expires.[74]

7.11 Administrators' contracts

(A) In general

The term of employment may not exceed three years, unless the administrator has been employed for three years or more. In that case, the contract may be for not more than five years and, unless the superintendent recommends otherwise, not less than two years. If the superintendent so recommends, the contract term may be one year,[75] but all subsequent contracts must be of not less than two years' nor more than five years' duration.

Employment must be under a written contract specifying the position and duties, salary and other compensation, days to be worked, vacation leave if any, and paid holidays.

A board may establish vacation leave for administrators and may compensate an administrator for accrued and unused leave at separation at his current rate of pay, up to the amount accrued within three years prior to separation. If an administrator dies, any such payment for his unused vacation leave must be made to his estate or in accordance with RC 2113.04.[76]

Except by mutual agreement of the parties, the administrator may not be transferred during the term of the employment contract to a position of lesser responsibility. The contract may be terminated or suspended only pursuant to RC 3319.16 or RC 3319.17, relating to termination for cause and reduction in force.[77] The administrator is also, of course, protected like other school district employees by general equal employment opportunity laws, the First Amendment, and Ohio's whistleblower statute.[78] Resignation of an administrator

---

[71]RC 3319.02.
[72]OAG 81-010.
[73]RC 3319.07(B).
[74]RC 3319.02.
[75]Where the superintendent does thus recommend reemployment for one year and the board of education follows that recommendation, there is no requirement that the prior contract be nonrenewed before issuance of the new one-year contract. State ex rel Willbond v Oberlin School Dist, 94 App(3d) 419, 640 NE(2d) 1179 (Lorain 1994), dismissed for failure to prosecute 70 OS(3d) 1419, 637 NE(2d) 927 (1994) (rejecting transportation supervisor's contention that absence of nonrenewal resulted in automatic reemployment under multi-year contract).

[76]RC 3319.02.

[77]RC 3319.02; RC 3319.12. See Text 9.19, Layoff; Text 9.21, Termination for cause, in general; Text 9.22, Termination for cause, procedure.

[78]See Text Ch 17, Equal Employment Opportunity, Family and Medical Leave; Text 9.21(E), Consti-

is generally governed by the same principles as apply to teachers.[79]

The salary and compensation prescribed by the contract may not be reduced unless the reduction is a part of a uniform plan affecting the entire district.[80] Notwithstanding that an administrator may meet the expansive definition of "teacher" that appears in the Ohio Teachers' Tenure Act at RC 3319.09, the salary to be paid, and any entitlement to a raise, are governed by RC 3319.02.[81]

(B) Reemployment and nonrenewal

An administrator is, at the expiration of his current term of employment, considered reemployed at the same salary plus any increments that may be authorized by the board, unless he notifies the board in writing to the contrary on or before June 1, or unless the board, on or before March 31 of the year in which his contract expires, either reemploys him for a succeeding term or gives him written notice of its intention not to reemploy him. The term of such "automatic" reemployment is one year, unless the person has been employed in the district as an administrator for three years or more; then it is two years.[82]

RC 3319.02(D) states that, before taking action to renew or nonrenew the contract of an administrator, the board must notify the administrator in writing, on or before March 31 in the year his contract expires, of the date the contract expires and of his right to request a meeting with the board; if a meeting is requested, the board must grant a meeting in executive session to discuss the board's reasons for considering renewal or nonrenewal. This meeting apparently is to occur before the board acts upon the administration's contract. Neither written nor oral reasons need to be furnished prior to the meeting; a meeting to discuss the reasons is all that is required.[83] An appeals court has held that an administrator who receives the required notice and requests a meeting may also seek reinstatement and back pay if the board refuses at the meeting to discuss the reasons for the nonrenewal.[84] Another appeals court, however, has expressly rejected this notion that reinstatement and back pay are required for the failure to discuss reasons; rather, this court maintains the appropriate remedy is merely to grant the administrator a meeting to discuss the reasons.[85] However, in light of the Ohio Supreme Court's decisions in *State ex rel Cassels v Dayton City School Dist Bd of Ed*[86] and *State ex rel Martines v Cleveland City School Dist Bd of Ed*[87] with respect to the evaluation procedures

---

tutionally protected conduct; Text 9.21(F), Protection of whistleblowers.

[79]See Text 9.17, Resignation.

[80]RC 3319.02, RC 3319.12. The extent to which economic fringe benefits qualify as salary and compensation for purposes of the prohibition against a decrease except under a uniform plan is unclear. Two cases decided under civil service statutes illustrate the ambiguity. Compare Ebert v Stark County Bd of Mental Retardation, 63 OS(2d) 31, 406 NE(2d) 1098 (1980) (finding it "obvious that sick leave credits, just as other fringe benefits, are forms of compensation") with State ex rel Bassman v Earhart, 18 OS(3d) 182, 18 OBR 250, 480 NE(2d) 761 (1985) (holding that free parking privileges, absent a statute requiring that they be provided, is a mere "gratuity," the cessation of which is not a reduction in pay).

[81]State ex rel Whitehead v Circleville City School Dist Bd of Ed, No. 90-CI-000062 (CP, Pickaway, 3-29-91) (rejecting claim of assistant principal, whose salary was frozen, for salary increase based on RC 3317.13, RC 3319.08, RC 3319.09, and RC 3317.14).

[82]RC 3319.02(C).

[83]State ex rel Smith v Etheridge, 65 OS(3d) 501, 605 NE(2d) 59 (1992).

[84]Phillips v West Holmes Local School Dist Bd of Ed, No. CA-407, 1990 WL 41584 (5th Dist Ct App, Holmes, 3-20-90). In this case, however, the court went on to conclude the administrator waived his right to reinstatement and back pay by voluntarily retiring under the board's early retirement incentive plan.

[85]State ex rel Brown v Columbus City Schools, No. 90AP-847, 1991 WL 325781 (10th Dist Ct App, Franklin, 10-10-91), affirmed in part and reversed in part sub nom State ex rel Smith v Ethridge, 65 OS(3d) 501, 605 NE(2d) 59 (1992). While agreeing that the statute requires a board to discuss reasons, the court went on to declare it does not require a "full-blown hearing" or imply that nonrenewal may only be for cause. The purpose of disclosure is simply to afford the administrator an opportunity to respond. *Brown's* rejection of *Phillips* is expressly approved in State ex rel Cassels v Dayton City School Dist Bd of Ed, No. 13607, 1993 WL 278133 (2d Dist Ct App, Montgomery, 7-22-93), affirmed on other grounds by 69 OS(3d) 217, 631 NE(2d) 150 (1994).

[86]State ex rel Cassels v Dayton City School Dist Bd of Ed, 69 OS(3d) 217, 631 NE(2d) 150 (1994).

[87]State ex rel Martines v Cleveland City School Dist Bd of Ed, 70 OS(3d) 416, 639 NE(2d) 80 (1994).

mandated by RC 3319.02(D),[88] it appears that a board of education's nonrenewal decision is immune to attack even if the requirements of RC 3319.02(D) are not observed, as long as timely notice of nonrenewal is provided.

Because the nonrenewal of an administrator is not the product of a quasi-judicial proceeding, an administrator whose contract is nonrenewed has no right of appeal under RC 2506.01.[89] However, a nonrenewed administrator who does not receive the written notice required by RC 3319.02 can seek reinstatement with back pay in court by way of an action in mandamus.[90] It has been held that, as long as a board follows the statute, the board's failure to follow board policies relating to nonrenewal does not invalidate the nonrenewal.[91]

While an administrator whose contract is improperly nonrenewed is considered reemployed as an administrator, he nevertheless has a duty to mitigate damages by seeking employment elsewhere if the board refuses to employ him. However, he need only accept similar employment. Thus, a principal need not accept employment as a physical education teacher.[92]

It is not clear whether a board may rescind action to reemploy an administrator once the administrator has accepted reemployment. One court has held rescission was improper. Where a board voted to renew the limited contract of a supervisor, and the supervisor accepted the renewal by letter, the board's subsequent reconsideration and vote not to renew the contract violated the supervisor's vested interest in the contract, and she was entitled to her position for the next school year.[93]

7.12 Supervisors and special teachers in educational service centers

The governing board of an educational service center may, on nomination by the governing superintendent, employ under written contracts for terms not to exceed five years supervisors, special instruction teachers, special education teachers, and teachers of academic courses in which there are too few students in each of the constituent local school districts or in city or exempted village school districts entering into an agreement under RC 3313.843 to warrant each district's employing teachers for those courses.[94] However, where a local school district board and governing board are comprised of the same members, the limitation of RC 3319.02(E) for hiring special education teachers for terms not to exceed five years does not apply, since, under RC 3311.051, the governing board has all the powers and duties of a local board. Thus, the governing board is obligated to issue a continuing contract to a special education teacher who meets the eligibility requirements of RC 3319.08.[95] When a governing board acting pursuant to RC 3311.051 employs any teacher, assistant superintendent, principal, assistant principal, or other administrator to perform services for a local school district, such persons retain all rights granted to local employees by RC Chapter 3319, and the board must exercise all powers and duties of a local board in accordance with the requirements of that chapter.[96]

Contracts for teachers entered into under RC 3319.02(E) may be terminated by the board under RC 3319.16 (termination for cause) and may be terminated by

---

[88]See Text 7.14(B), Evaluation of other administrators.

[89]Martines v Cleveland City School Dist Bd of Ed, No. 64263, 1993 WL 526696 (8th Dist Ct App, Cuyahoga, 12-16-93).

[90]State ex rel Donaldson v Athens City School Dist Bd of Ed, 68 OS(3d) 145, 624 NE(2d) 709 (1994); State ex rel Smith v Etheridge, 65 OS(3d) 501, 605 NE(2d) 59 (1992); State ex rel Luckey v Etheridge, 62 OS(3d) 404, 583 NE(2d) 960 (1992); State ex rel Brennan v Vinton County Local School Dist Bd of Ed, 18 OS(3d) 208, 18 OBR 271, 480 NE(2d) 476 (1985).

[91]State ex rel Floyd v Rock Hill Local School Bd of Ed, No. 1862, 1988 WL 17190 (4th Dist Ct App, Lawrence, 2-10-88).

[92]Frith v Princeton City School Dist Bd of Ed, No. C-810789, 1982 WL 8619 (1st Dist Ct App, Hamilton, 7-14-82).

[93]Migra v Warren City School Dist Bd of Ed, No. 3048, 1982 WL 5776 (11th Dist Ct App, Trumbull, 6-4-82).

[94]RC 3319.02(E).

[95]State ex rel Tschappat v Monroe County Bd of Ed, No. 583, 1984 WL 3769 (7th Dist Ct App, Monroe, 10-16-84).

[96]RC 3311.05.

the employee at the end of a school year upon at least thirty days' written notice to the board prior to termination. Such contracts may be suspended for the remainder of the contract term on the recommendation of the service center superintendent if there is a reduction in the number of approved supervisory or special instruction teacher units allocated to the district under RC 3317.05.[97]

7.13 Teacher employed as administrator, tenure

Supervisory and administrative employees cannot acquire tenure as supervisors or administrators.[98]

When a teacher with continuing service status in a district becomes an administrator in the same district, the employee retains continuing service status in the nonadministrative position.[99] An administrator employed under RC 3319.02 is entitled to a continuing contract as a teacher, if the employee previously held a continuing contract in another district and has served two years in the current district as an administrator.[100]

An assistant principal, whose two-year limited contract was renewed for three years on a form used for granting teachers' contracts and subsequently nonrenewed at the end of the three-year term, had no right to a continuing contract as a teacher, where he had not taught for three of the last five years or attained continuing contract status elsewhere, simply on the basis of the teachers' contract form. The mistake was mutual, and neither he nor the board understood he was hired in any other capacity than assistant principal.[101]

However, where a principal's administrative contract is not renewed and he is wrongfully denied a continuing contract as a teacher, the board is liable for back pay, which is computed from the salary schedule for teachers. The back pay due may not be offset by the money earned at a night laborer's job because it is not a job of a "similar nature," or by any amounts received from the state teachers' retirement system (STRS). In addition, a board is liable for unused sick leave and personal leave, but not for lost health benefits, absent evidence of actual cost of replacement. A board is also not liable for pension benefits withdrawn from STRS voluntarily or for interest on the judgments.[102]

A person employed on a part-time basis as an assistant service center superintendent or service center supervisor may also be employed by a local board as a teacher.[103]

7.14 Evaluation of school administrators

(A) Evaluation of superintendent

RC 3319.01 states that a board of education must adopt evaluation procedures for its superintendent and assess job performance in accordance with those procedures. The statute goes on to say the board must consider the evaluation in deciding whether to renew the superintendent's contract. However, the statute also states that the establishment of an evaluation procedure does not create an expectancy of continued employment, and the board is not prevented from making the final determination as to renewal or nonrenewal of the superintendent's contract. The Ohio Supreme Court has held that noncompliance with any or all of the RC 3319.02(D) evaluation requirements does not invali-

---

[97]RC 3319.02(E).
[98]See Text 8.02, Meaning of "teacher"; Text 9.07, Eligibility for continuing contract: teaching requirement.
[99]RC 3319.02(C).
[100]State ex rel Specht v Painesville Twp Local School Dist Bd of Ed, 63 OS(2d) 146, 407 NE(2d) 20 (1980); State ex rel Kelley v Clearcreek Local School Dist Bd of Ed, 52 OS(3d) 93, 556 NE(2d) 173 (1990). A county board of education is not a "school district" and thus an administrator, who was employed by the board for at least two years and who previously held a continuing contract in another district, was not entitled under RC 3319.02 to a continuing contract as a teacher with the county board. State ex rel Wilson v Lucas County Office of Education, No. L-94-279, 1995 WL 244212 (6th Dist Ct App, Lucas, 4-26-95).

[101]State ex rel Cook v Paulding Exempted Village School Dist Bd of Ed, No. 11-82-12, 1983 WL 7310 (3d Dist Ct App, Paulding, 7-27-83).
[102]Schlotterer v Coldwater Exempted Village School Dist Bd of Ed, No. 10-82-2, 1983 WL 7248 (3d Dist Ct App, Mercer, 4-26-83).
[103]RC 3319.02.

date a board's action not to renew a superintendent's contract.[104]

(B) Evaluation of other administrators

Similarly, RC 3319.02(D) states that a board of education must adopt procedures for evaluating the job performance of administrators and evaluate them in accordance with those procedures. The statute goes on to say the evaluation must be considered by the board in deciding whether to renew the administrator's contract and must measure his effectiveness in performing the duties included in his job description.

The procedures must provide for at least annual written evaluations conducted by the superintendent or his designee. To provide time to show progress in correcting deficiencies, the completed evaluation must be received by the administrator at least sixty days prior to any action by the board on his contract.

However, RC 3319.02(D) also states that the establishment of an evaluation procedure does not create an expectancy of continued employment and that the board is not prevented from making the final determination regarding the renewal or nonrenewal of the administrator's contract. This effectively renders the evaluation requirements toothless. The Ohio Supreme Court has squarely held that noncompliance with any or all of the evaluation requirements of RC 3319.02(D) does not invalidate a board's action not to renew an administrator's contract.[105]

---

[104] State ex rel Stiller v Columbiana Exempted Village School Dist Bd of Ed, No. 94-C-13, 1995 WL 43646 (7th Dist Ct App, Columbiana, 1-30-95), affirmed by 74 OS(3d) 113, 656 NE(2d) 679 (1995).

[105] State ex rel Cassels v Dayton City School Dist Bd of Ed, 69 OS(3d) 217, 631 NE(2d) 150 (1994); State ex rel Martines v Cleveland City School Dist Bd of Ed, 70 OS(3d) 416, 639 NE(2d) 80 (1994). See also State ex rel Butler v Fort Frye Local School Dist, No. 93CA31, 1995 WL 129168 (4th Dist Ct App, Washington, 4-13-95).

Chapter 8

Teachers: Certification and Appointment

8.01 Introduction
8.02 Meaning of "teacher"
8.03 Qualifications and certification in general
8.04 Grades of certificates
8.05 Types of certification
8.06 Education and experience requirements, renewing and upgrading certificates
8.07 Revocation or suspension of certificate
8.08 Nomination and appointment
8.09 Reemployment of teachers

8.01 Introduction

As with administrators,[1] a teacher generally must possess an appropriate certificate issued by the state board of education. The requirements for obtaining, renewing, and upgrading certificates are detailed in regulations adopted by the state board.[2]

A certificate may be revoked for cause or for conviction of certain crimes, is subject to forfeiture for conflict of interest, and may be suspended for breach of contract. A certificate may be reinstated when it is demonstrated that the applicant has been rehabilitated and reissuance of the certificate will not be detrimental to the schools.

Possession of a certificate does not guarantee a job. Rather, it is evidence only that the holder has the minimum qualifications required for the type of position for which the certificate was granted. Each school district may impose stricter standards for its personnel.

8.02 Meaning of "teacher"

"Teacher" is defined to include all persons certified to teach and who are employed in the public schools of Ohio as instructors, principals, supervisors, superintendents, or in any other educational position for which certification is required.[3] Although this definition sometimes is applied in other contexts, it is expressly applicable only to teaching contracts and conditions of employment set forth in RC 3319.08 to RC 3319.18, the current codification of the Ohio Teachers' Tenure Act of 1941, as amended.[4]

(A) Administrators

One consequence of this broad definition is that many of the statutory provisions concerning classroom teachers apply to other certificated employees, e.g., principals and assistant superintendents. Courts have held, however, that administrators may not acquire tenure in their administrative positions.[5] Administrators can earn tenure as teachers while serving in administrative capacities if they have already earned tenure in another district.[6]

(B) Tutors, guidance counselors, school nurses

The definition of "teacher" includes certain certificated tutors[7] and guidance coun-

---

[1] See Text 7.03(A), Statutory requirement that candidate possess certificate.
[2] OAC Ch 3301-23. See also RC 3319.291, authorizing the state board and the superintendent of public instruction to initiate criminal background checks on applicants for a certificate.
[3] RC 3319.09(A).
[4] The definition of "teacher" in RC 3319.09(A) does not automatically apply, for example, for purposes of salary placement on the teachers' salary schedule required by RC 3317.13 and RC 3317.14. RC 3317.13 contains its own definition of "teacher" which has been construed as having the ordinary meaning of one who actually teaches or instructs. Wood v Trotwood Madison Bd of Ed, No. CA 11836, 1990 WL 80622 (2d Dist Ct App, Montgomery, 6-12-90) (salary of food service supervisor not governed by RC 3317.13 and RC 3317.14); Chavis v Sycamore City School Dist Bd of Ed, 70 OS(3d) 26, 641 NE(2d) 188 (1994) (salary of tutors governed by RC 3317.13 and RC 3317.14). See also Text 10.02, Pay scales.
[5] State ex rel Saltsman v Burton, 154 OS 262, 95 NE(2d) 377 (1950); State ex rel Saltsman v Burton, 156 OS 537, 103 NE(2d) 740 (1952); Bennett v Lorain County School Dist Bd of Ed, 23 App(3d) 136, 491 NE(2d) 742 (Lorain 1985); Ross v Board of Education, 52 App(2d) 28, 367 NE(2d) 1209 (Cuyahoga 1977). See also State ex rel Donah v Windham Exempted Village School Dist Bd of Ed, 69 OS(3d) 114, 630 NE(2d) 687 (1994).
[6] See Text 9.07, Eligibility for continuing contract: teaching requirement.
[7] State ex rel Brown v Milton-Union Exempted Village Bd of Ed, 40 OS(3d) 21, 531 NE(2d) 1297 (1988); State ex rel Tavenner v Indian Lake Local School Dist Bd of Ed, 62 OS(3d) 88, 578 NE(2d) 464 (1991). See

selors.[8] School nurses would appear to meet the statutory definition,[9] although contrary authority can be cited.[10]

(C) Substitute teachers, educational aides

For purposes of certification, at least, the attorney general has stated that the term "teacher" includes substitute teachers.[11]

Educational aides are not teachers within the meaning of RC 3319.09(A) and do not perform duties for which a certificate issued pursuant to RC 3319.22 to RC 3319.30 is required. An educational aide, however, must hold an educational aide permit.[12]

8.03 Qualifications and certification in general

To be qualified to serve as a teacher, one generally must hold a certificate as provided by RC 3319.22. The certificate must certify to the holder's good moral character.[13]

(A) Certification generally mandatory

RC 3319.30 and RC 3319.36 provide that no person, unless engaged part-time under a permit issued pursuant to RC 3319.301, may receive any compensation as a teacher, in any school supported wholly or in part by the state or by federal funds, who has not obtained a certificate for that position as provided by RC 3319.22 and filed a copy of that certificate with the superintendent of the county, city, or exempted village school district, whichever is applicable. RC 3319.36 provides an exception with respect to the first two months of initial district employment of new teachers who hold bachelor's degrees or higher and have applied for a provisional (or higher grade) certificate.

A teacher must hold a valid certificate with respect to the subjects or grades taught.[14] If the district treasurer discovers that a teacher does not hold proper certification, the treasurer's duty is to withhold payment of that teacher's salary,[15] and payment to a teacher without a certificate is subject to a finding for recovery.[16] A civil action against the teacher must be brought by the board within six years from the time the certified audit by the bureau of inspection and supervision of public offices disclosing the improper payment is filed with the appropriate authorities listed in RC 117.10.[17]

A board of education is not authorized to use uncertificated persons as substitute teachers in the absence of regular teachers.[18]

Notwithstanding that certification is generally mandatory, RC 3319.301 requires the state board of education to issue permits to persons not certificated, but otherwise qualified, to teach classes for not more than twelve hours per week. The qualifications for such a permit are set by state board rules, and application for such a permit is made under RC 3319.29. By rule, the state board must authorize the board of

---

also State ex rel Fink v Grandview Hts City School Dist Bd of Ed, No. 93APE10-1462, 1994 WL 183592 (10th Dist Ct App, Franklin, 5-12-94); State ex rel Siers v Beaver Local School Dist Bd of Ed, No. 89-C-39, 1990 WL 167575 (7th Dist Ct App, Columbiana, 10-29-90); Price v Newbury Local School Dist Bd of Ed, No. 91-G-1626, 1992 WL 268795 (11th Dist Ct App, Geauga, 12-13-91), appeal dismissed by 63 OS(3d) 1421, 587 NE(2d) 302 (1992); Chavis v Sycamore City School Dist Bd of Ed, 70 OS(3d) 26, 641 NE(2d) 188 (1994).

[8]Krolopp v South Range Local School Dist Bd of Ed, 47 App(2d) 208, 353 NE(2d) 642 (Mahoning 1974).

[9]Navin v Tallman, No. WD-83-53, 1983 WL 6991 (6th Dist Ct App, Wood, 11-11-83) (school nurse a teacher for purposes of reduction in force).

[10]Beiting v Cincinnati City School Dist Bd of Ed, No. C-830105, 1983 WL 5254 (1st Dist Ct App, Hamilton, 10-19-83) (school nurse not a teacher for tenure purposes). In view of subsequent court decisions on the status of tutors, reliance on *Beiting* is thought by many to be highly suspect.

[11]1941 OAG 4204.

[12]See Text 12.19, Employment of educational aides.

[13]RC 3319.30.

[14]RC 3319.36. A valid elementary teaching certificate, unlike a high school teaching certificate, is valid for teaching without limitation as to subject matter. Chavis v Sycamore City School Dist Bd of Ed, 70 OS(3d) 26, 641 NE(2d) 188 (1994); Fisler v Mayfield City School Dist Bd of Ed, No. 49548, 1985 WL 8508 (8th Dist Ct App, Cuyahoga, 10-31-85).

[15]1934 OAG 2557.

[16]RC 117.10.

[17]Portage Lakes Joint Vocational School Dist Bd of Ed v Bowman, 14 App(3d) 132, 14 OBR 148, 470 NE(2d) 233 (Summit 1984).

[18]1964 OAG 903.

education of each school district to engage individuals holding permits to teach classes for not more than twelve hours per week. The state board's rules must include provisions regarding:

(1) That a board of education shall engage a noncertificated person to teach under the statute on a volunteer basis or under a contract with the person or his employer on such terms as are agreed to between the board and the person or his employer; and

(2) That a certificated board employee shall directly supervise the noncertificated person until the district superintendent is satisfied that the noncertificated person is competent to teach without supervision.

A noncertificated person engaged to teach under RC 3319.301 is a "teacher" for purposes of RC Title 33 except for purposes of RC Chapters 3307 and 3317 and RC 3319.07 to 3319.31; such person is not a district employee for purposes of RC Titles 1 or 41 or RC Chapter 3309. A board of education is flatly prohibited from engaging one or more noncertificated persons under the statute if such employment displaces from employment an existing certificated district employee.

(B) Adopting standards for teacher training and certification

RC 3319.23 requires the state board of education to establish standards and courses of study for the preparation of teachers, to provide for the inspection of institutions designed to prepare teachers and approve those institutions that maintain satisfactory training procedures, and to certify the qualified graduates of approved courses and institutions. Certification has state-wide validity.

The state board also must establish and publish standards and courses of study for the preparation of teachers, together with standards and rules for each grade and type of certificate and for the renewal and conversion of certificates.[19] In view of this mandate, the state board's rules governing certification have the effect of law.[20]

(C) Interstate certification

The superintendent of public instruction, with the approval of the state board, is authorized to enter into agreements with other states concerning the qualifications of teachers and other professional educational employees leading to interstate certification. These interstate agreements are intended to facilitate the movement of professional educational personnel among the states.[21]

Tenure is not recognized across state lines in the absence of an interstate agreement. Experience earned by a teacher in another state prior to formation of an interstate agreement cannot be counted as years of experience in determining eligibility for tenure.[22]

8.04 Grades of certificates

RC 3319.22 provides for five grades of teachers' certificates: temporary, one-year vocational, provisional, professional, and permanent. A "life" certificate is no longer issued and has been supplanted by the permanent certificate. Provisional, professional, and permanent certificates are normally used for certifying career teachers. Temporary and one-year vocational certificates are usually reserved for situations where there is a shortage of fully qualified teachers. An additional type of certificate, called an "internship" certificate, has been created by RC 3319.282.

(A) Temporary certificate

The superintendent of public instruction may grant temporary certificates for compliance with state board of education standards set below those set for provisional certificates. A temporary certificate is valid for one year and may be renewed for one-year periods. It may be granted with respect to any type of certification listed in RC 3319.22. With regard to supervisor certificates described in RC 3319.22(I), the superintendent may grant in accordance with state board standards a temporary certificate for a period not to exceed two years to an otherwise certificated teacher actively

---

[19] RC 3319.23.
[20] See OAC Ch 3301-23 for state board standards.
[21] RC 3319.42, RC 3319.43.

[22] Bickel v Carrollton Exempted Village School Dist Bd of Ed, No. 445, 1982 WL 6185 (7th Dist Ct App, Carroll, 9-15-82).

engaged in a program designed to qualify the teacher for a supervisor certificate.

The superintendent of public instruction may receive applications for temporary certificates only upon the request of the superintendent of a city, county, or exempted village school district or, except with regard to supervisor certificates described in RC 3319.22(I), the chief administrative head of any non-public school, and upon evidence of a scarcity of suitable teachers otherwise certified. Such a certificate is only valid for teaching in the school or schools in the administrative jurisdiction of the official signing the request, or, where a supervisor certificate is involved, for the purpose of fulfilling a contract to which the district that made the request is a party.[23] As no provision is made for applications upon request of a local superintendent, local school districts must act through the educational service center superintendent.

(B) One-year vocational certificate

A certificate valid for one year may be issued to those who meet the criteria for occupational competency in a skilled or technical occupation, or who meet the state board of education's qualifications as an occupational work experience, work adjustment, or cooperative coordinator. The holder of a one-year vocational certificate also must satisfy the pre-service teacher education requirements of an institution approved by the state board for vocational teacher education.[24] The certificate may be issued only on request of the employing local administrator or his agent. It may be renewed, not to exceed three times, for secondary program teachers.[25]

(C) Provisional certificate

A provisional certificate is valid for four years. It is issued to those who have completed in an approved institution the courses prescribed by the state board. Graduation from a four-year course is required for all types of certification, except kindergarten-primary and elementary, where the minimum requirement is shortened to two years, and vocational trade and industrial certification, where the specific training is prescribed by the state board.[26]

The state board may renew a provisional certificate upon satisfactory evidence of the applicant's professional standing and teaching success.[27]

(D) Professional certificate

A professional certificate is valid for eight years and is granted by the state board by converting any provisional certificate into a professional certificate of like type, when the applicant meets the standards of preparation, experience, and teaching success established by the board for conversion.

(1) Tenure

A teacher who holds a professional certificate is eligible for a continuing contract, i.e., tenure, provided the service requirement of RC 3319.11 is satisfied.[28] The presence of record cards in the offices of the local and county superintendents indicating that a teacher has a professional certificate, effective prior to the start of the school year, provides sufficient notice that the teacher is eligible for a continuing contract.[29]

(2) Duty of teacher to apply for certificate

One court has held that a board of education is *not* required to forward to the state board a teacher's application for a professional certificate.[30] The court found no regulation, rule, or statute from which such a duty could be inferred. This decision should be read with caution in light of the well-established practice that local boards do in fact process applications for certification.

---

[23] RC 3319.28.
[24] RC 3319.281.
[25] RC 3319.281.
[26] RC 3319.24.
[27] RC 3319.24.
[28] RC 3319.11.
[29] State ex rel Gandy v Continental Local School Dist Bd of Ed, 26 OS(2d) 115, 269 NE(2d) 605 (1971); Woodrum v Rolling Hills Bd of Ed, 66 OS(2d) 284, 421 NE(2d) 859 (1981); Pascoe v Huron Bd of Ed, No. E-82-32, 1983 WL 13842 (6th Dist Ct App, Erie, 2-18-83).

[30] Carter v Princeton Bd of Ed, No. C-800891, 1981 WL 10112 (1st Dist Ct App, Hamilton, 11-18-81).

(E) Permanent certificate

A permanent certificate is valid for the lifetime of its holder. The state board may convert any professional certificate into a permanent certificate of like type, provided the applicant has met the standards of preparation, experience, and teaching success established by the board.[31] One who possesses a permanent teaching certificate is eligible for a continuing contract, provided the service requirement of RC 3319.11 has been satisfied.

The state board no longer issues life certificates. However, a life certificate issued prior to September 5, 1935, retains its validity for the kinds of positions for which it was valid when issued.[32]

(F) Internship certificate

RC 3319.282 establishes an "internship" certificate valid for one year and renewable for one additional year for teaching subjects named in the certificate in grades seven to twelve. The applicant must have a bachelor's degree in the subject area for which certification is sought, at least three years of "successful experience deemed essential for effective teaching," pass examinations (the same way as any examinations required for a provisional certificate), and complete at least six semester hours or its equivalent course work in a board-approved "pre-service course of study."[33]

One can apply for an initial internship certificate or renewal only if the district superintendent has (1) offered the applicant a one-year limited contract of employment (made expressly contingent upon the applicant performing certain statutorily specified requirements), and (2) has established a "program of internship supervision and evaluation" approved by the state board in accordance with its standards.[34] No holder of an internship certificate can be required "to participate in any clinical or field-based teaching experience other than the experience completed while employed for one year under an internship certificate."[35] Renewal of the certificate requires, among other things, completion of one year of teaching under an initial certificate with satisfactory evaluations under the district's program of internship supervision and evaluation.

Any internship certificate is valid only in the district where the limited contract of employment was offered. The state board must adopt standards pursuant to which one who has taught at least one year under an internship certificate may qualify for a provisional certificate valid for four years.[36] Finally, every three years the state board must evaluate district programs of internship supervision and evaluation and the teaching quality and effectiveness of persons with internship certificates and who receive provisional certificates under the new statute.

8.05 Types of certification

RC 3319.22 lists seventeen different types of certification for which the state board of education *may* issue temporary, provisional, professional, or permanent certificates. The statutory list is permissive rather than mandatory, and in practice the state board's certification scheme is considerably more complex, with dozens of different certificate types provided for by administrative regulations.[37]

8.06 Education and experience requirements, renewing and upgrading certificates

OAC Chapter 3301-23 provides specific training and experience requirements for obtaining, renewing, and upgrading the various certificates.

8.07 Revocation or suspension of certificate

(A) In general

Under RC 3319.31, the state board of education may refuse to issue or may limit, suspend, or revoke a teacher's certificate[38]

---

[31] RC 3319.26.
[32] RC 3319.27.
[33] See OAC 3301-23-30.
[34] See OAC 3301-21-10 et seq.
[35] RC 3319.282(G).
[36] See OAC 3301-23-31 et seq.

[37] OAC Ch 3301-23 comprehensively regulates teacher certification standards.
[38] "Certificate" is broadly defined by RC 3319.31 to include educational aide permits, treasurer and business manager licenses, pre-kindergarten teaching certificates and associate certificates, permits for part-

for engaging in an immoral act, incompetence, negligence, or conduct unbecoming to the certificated position.[39] The statute also authorizes such action with respect to a person found guilty of or pleading guilty to any felony; any violation of RC 2907.04 (corruption of a minor), RC 2907.06 (sexual imposition), or RC 2907.07(A) or (C) (soliciting a person under age thirteen to engage in sexual conduct, or soliciting to engage in sexual conduct by one age eighteen or older of a person, other than a spouse, who is over twelve but not over fifteen and at least four years younger than the offender); any offense of violence, as defined in RC 2901.01; any theft offense, as defined in RC 2913.01; any drug abuse offense, as defined in RC 2925.01, that is not a minor misdemeanor; or any substantively comparable offense of a municipal corporation.[40] The state board may also take such action on the basis of substantially comparable conduct occurring in a jurisdiction outside Ohio or before a person applies for or receives a certificate.[41]

The state board, or superintendent of public instruction on its behalf, is authorized by RC 3319.311 to investigate any information about a person that reasonably appears to be a basis for action under RC 3319.31. Any information obtained during an investigation is confidential and expressly not a public record under RC 149.43. If no action is taken within two years after completion of an investigation, all records of the investigation must be expunged.

The superintendent of public instruction is to review the results of each investigation and determine, on behalf of the state board, whether action under RC 3319.31 is warranted. He is to advise the state board of his determination at a meeting of the board. Within fourteen days of the next meeting of the board, any board member may ask that the question of initiating action under RC 3319.31 be placed on the board's agenda for that next meeting. Prior to initiating such action against a person, the person's name and any other personally identifiable information must remain confidential.

Before acting under RC 3319.31, the state board must notify the person of the charges and provide an opportunity for hearing under RC Chapter 119. The state board may automatically suspend any certificate without a hearing, however, if the holder is found guilty of or pleads guilty to the following Ohio crimes (or any substantially comparable crimes of a municipal corporation or another state): aggravated murder; murder; aggravated arson; aggravated robbery; aggravated burglary; voluntary manslaughter; felonious assault; kidnapping; rape; sexual battery; gross sexual imposition; or corruption of a minor. In such a case, the state board must issue a written order of suspension to the certificate holder and provide a hearing upon request. If a hearing is not requested within the time limits set by RC 119.07 (thirty days from the time of mailing the notice), a final order revoking the certificate will be issued.

Any order of suspension remains effective unless reversed on appeal[42] or until a final order of the state board becomes effective. A final order must be issued

---

time teaching service under RC 3319.301, as well as certification of administrators and the various grades and types of teaching certificates described in Text 8.04, Grades of certificates, and Text 8.05, Types of certification.

[39]In assessing the level of discipline, the state board should give considerable deference to the findings and recommendations of the hearing officer. Winters v State Bd of Ed, No. 93-C-3, 1995 WL 9261 (7th Dist Ct App, Columbiana, 1-10-95), dismissed, appeal not allowed 72 OS(3d 1528, 649 NE(2d) 837 (1995) (finding state board, without further justification, could not revoke a principal's certificate contrary to the recommendation of the hearing officer). Other courts have simply required a showing of a nexus between the teacher's conduct and duties before revoking a teaching certificate. Johnson v State Bd of Ed, No. CA-8019, 1990 WL 62988 (5th Dist Ct App, Stark, 5-14-90); Sayers v State Bd of Ed, No. 66578, 1994 WL 676869 (8th Dist Ct App, Cuyahoga, 12-1-94).

[40]If a certificate holder is found guilty of any of these offenses, RC 3319.52 requires the prosecutor in the case promptly to notify the state board and, if known, the employing school district of the holder's name, address, and the fact that he pleaded guilty to or was convicted of the offense.

[41]RC 3319.31(B).

[42]A reviewing court must review the record and determine if the state board's order is based on reliable and substantial evidence. If so, the court must defer and not simply substitute its judgment for that of the board. Johnson v State Bd of Ed, No. CA-8019, 1990 WL 62988 (5th Dist Ct App, Stark, 5-14-90); Crumpler v State Bd of Ed, 71 App(3d) 526, 594 NE(2d) 1071 (Franklin 1991). See also Lucci v State

within sixty days of the suspension order or any hearing on such order, whichever is later. If a final order is not timely issued, the suspension order is dissolved, but such dissolution does not invalidate any subsequent final order of the state board.

The superintendent of public instruction, on behalf of the state board, may enter into a consent agreement with any person against whom action is being taken under RC 3319.31. No surrender of a certificate is effective until accepted by the state board unless the surrender is pursuant to a consent decree.[43]

Under RC 3319.151, the state board, on finding after an investigation that a certificated employee revealed to a student any specific question known to be part of a state-required proficiency test[44] or otherwise assisting a student to cheat on such a test, must suspend the certificate for one year.

(B) Conflict of interest

RC 3329.10 provides that a teacher may not act as sales agent, either directly or indirectly, for any person, firm, or corporation whose school textbooks are filed with the superintendent of public instruction, or for school apparatus and equipment of any kind for use in the public schools. A teacher who violates RC 3329.10 forfeits his certificate.

(C) Suspension for breach of contract

A teacher's certification may be suspended for up to one year if he terminates his teaching contract after July 10 or during the school session without the employing board's consent or at any other time without giving five days' notice to the board. The suspension can be imposed only after the filing of a complaint by the employing board to the state board of education and an investigation by the state board.[45]

(D) Reinstatement

The state board must consider the application for certification of a person whose certificate has been revoked, or an individual who has committed one of the above-mentioned crimes. The applicant is entitled to notice and an opportunity for a hearing if the state board intends to deny certification.[46]

8.08 Nomination and appointment

The responsibility for employing teachers rests with the board of education.[47] No new teacher or principal may be employed, however, unless he is nominated for the position by the superintendent of the district. In a local school district, the county superintendent must make the nomination.[48]

8.09 Reemployment of teachers

In making appointments, a board must consider teachers already employed in the district before choosing new teachers in their places.[49] However, the Ohio Supreme Court has held that RC 3319.07 does not grant a preference to nontenured teachers when a board is making employment decisions for a coming school year. Rather, RC 3319.07 applies to the situation where a vacancy occurs and a currently employed teacher may be transferred to fill it.[50] In other words, teachers operating under continuing contracts or limited contracts that will not expire until after the school year for which the appointments are being made should be considered first. In city and exempted village school districts, no teacher or principal may be employed unless nominated by the district superin-

---

Bd of Ed, No. 90-B-23, 1991 WL 97811 (7th Dist Ct App, Belmont, 6-5-91); Sayers v State Bd of Ed, No. 66578, 1994 WL 676869 (8th Dist Ct App, Cuyahoga 12-1- 94). However, a court may reverse the state board's order if it contradicts the manifest weight of evidence in the record. Winters v State Bd of Ed, No. 93-C-3, 1995 WL 9261 (7th Dist Ct App, Columbiana, 1-10-95), dismissed, appeal not allowed 72 OS(3d 1528, 649 NE(2d) 837 (1995) (board's order contradicted hearing officer's findings that principal's misdemeanor drug convictions did not warrant revocation of teaching certificate).

[43] RC 3319.311.

[44] For treatment of such tests, see Text 26.06(B), Graduation requirements; Text 3.03(G), Other powers and duties.

[45] RC 3319.15.

[46] OAC 3301-23-23.

[47] RC 3319.07, RC 3319.11.

[48] RC 3319.07.

[49] RC 3319.07.

[50] Matheny v Frontier Local Bd of Ed, 62 OS(2d) 362, 405 NE(2d) 1041 (1980).

tendent. However, the board, by three-fourths vote, may reemploy any teacher whom the superintendent refuses to appoint or recommends not be appointed.[51] An assignment of additional duties under a supplemental contract to a teacher already employed in the district is reemployment for purposes of RC 3319.07. Such supplemental contracts require a three-fourths vote by the board.[52]

A teacher employed in a local school district may be reemployed by a majority vote of the full membership, even though the teacher is not nominated by the county superintendent, but only after the local board has considered and rejected two nominations made for the position by the county superintendent.[53]

---

[51] RC 3319.07; Miller v Wayne County Joint Vocational School Dist Bd of Ed, 69 App(2d) 66, 430 NE(2d) 475 (Wayne 1980).

[52] A teacher's supplemental contract as a boys' basketball coach required a three-fourths vote by the board under RC 3319.07. Mason v Conneaut Area City School Dist Bd of Ed, No. 93-A-1842, 1994 WL 590282 (11th Dist Ct App, Ashtabula, 8-19-94).

[53] RC 3319.07.

Chapter 9

Teachers: Contracts and Tenure

INTRODUCTION
9.01 Requirement for contract, contents
9.02 Types of contracts: continuing, limited, extended limited, and supplemental
9.03 Contract employing relative of board member

CONTINUING CONTRACTS AND TENURED TEACHERS
9.04 Continuing contracts and tenure
9.05 Eligibility for continuing contract: introduction
9.06 Eligibility for continuing contract: certificate requirement
9.07 Eligibility for continuing contract: teaching requirement
9.08 Eligibility for continuing contract: service requirement
9.09 Employment options where teacher is eligible for continuing service status

LIMITED CONTRACTS AND NONTENURED TEACHERS
9.10 Employment options where teacher is not eligible for continuing service status
9.11 Notice of nonrenewal, timeliness, form
9.12 Nonrenewal and reemployment as means to change contract terms
9.13 Statutory evaluation and due process requirements
9.14 Supplemental contracts
9.15 Substitute teacher contracts
9.16 Exchange teachers

SUSPENSION AND TERMINATION OF CONTRACTS
9.17 Resignation
9.18 Retirement
9.19 Layoff
9.20 Disciplinary suspension
9.21 Termination for cause, in general
9.22 Termination for cause, procedure
9.23 Appeal of termination
9.24 Nonrenewal of teacher limited (or extended limited) contract
9.25 Teacher termination

INTRODUCTION

9.01 Requirement for contract, contents

Much of what follows derives from the Ohio Teacher Tenure Act of 1941, as amended, which currently appears in RC 3319.08 to RC 3319.18 and generally governs the employment of Ohio public school teachers. As remedial legislation, the Act is liberally construed in favor of teachers.[1]

(A) Necessity for written contract

When a teacher is employed in any school district, Ohio law requires the district board of education to execute a written contract with the teacher and presumes that it has done so.[2] There is no provision for employment of teachers at will.

Failure to execute a written agreement does not mean there is no contract, since one is created by operation of law when a teacher accepts employment pursuant to board resolution.[3] Likewise, a contract is presumed if the board fails to give timely written notice to a teacher of its intention not to renew his contract or if the board has not evaluated the teacher in accordance with RC 3319.111.[4] The automatic reemployment provision does not apply, however, to contracts suspended by layoff under RC 3319.17.[5]

Although the superintendent's nomination is necessary before the board can hire a teacher,[6] this does not mean the superintendent has authority to hire. Since RC

---

[1] See, e.g., Kiel v Green Local School Dist Bd of Ed, 69 OS(3d) 149, 630 NE(2d) 716 (1994); Naylor v Cardinal Local School Dist Bd of Ed, 69 OS(3d) 162, 630 NE(2d) 725 (1994).

[2] RC 3319.08. In other than educational service centers, Ohio law simply authorizes the board of education to employ "teachers." In the case of a service center, RC 3319.07 authorizes the employment of "special instruction teachers, special education teachers, and teachers of academic courses in which there are too few students in each of the constituent local school districts or in city or exempted village school districts entering into agreements pursuant to section 3313.843 of the Revised Code to warrant each district's employing teachers for those courses."

[3] RC 3319.08.

[4] RC 3319.11, RC 3319.111. See also O'Hare v North Central Local School, No. 2277, 1987 WL 19450 (9th Dist Ct App, Wayne, 10-28-87) (statute of frauds inapplicable to teacher's contract).

[5] State ex rel Hlynsky v Osnaburg Local School Dist Bd of Ed, 11 OS(3d) 194, 11 OBR 506, 464 NE(2d) 569 (1984). See also Text 9.19, Layoff.

[6] RC 3319.07. In all but local school districts, the nomination is made by the superintendent of the district. Where a local school district is involved, the

3319.08 specifically requires the board to enter into written contracts with teachers, it follows that a teacher had no contract where the superintendent and a principal orally informed him he had been hired but the board did not approve a contract.[7]

(B) Terms of contract

At a minimum, a teacher's contract must state the duties to be performed and the initial salary to be paid.[8] Where the contract is for more than one year, a notice indicating the salary to be paid for the coming year must be issued on or before July 1.[9] Neither the board nor the teacher is limited to the minimum statutory terms but may include other terms or conditions as appropriate.

9.02 Types of contracts: continuing, limited, extended limited, and supplemental

Teachers' contracts in all school districts are classified either as continuing, limited, or extended limited.[10] As the name implies, a continuing contract continues in force from year to year and can be terminated only for certain reasons.[11] A limited contract, on the other hand, is for a specified period that may not exceed five years and may be nonrenewed by the board of education, in compliance with RC 3319.11.[12] An extended limited contract is awarded in lieu of a continuing contract and is defined as a limited contract issued to a teacher who is otherwise eligible for continuing service status.[13]

The statutes also recognize supplemental contracts under which a teacher is paid extra compensation for duties in addition to those stated in his base contract.[14] Supplemental contracts are always limited contracts[15] and are typically used where a teacher contracts to coach a school athletic team, teach special classes, or assume some other extraordinary duty.

9.03 Contract employing relative of board member

When a board member votes for, or participates in making, a teaching contract with a person to whom he is related as father, brother, mother, or sister, the contract is void under RC 3319.21. This section does not prohibit a member from participating in hiring a spouse or other relative not specified in the statute,[16] nor does it apply if the contract is for services other than as a teacher or instructor.[17] A newer statute, however, RC 2921.42(A)(1), does prohibit a board member whose spouse is a teacher from authorizing, voting, or otherwise using the influence of his office to secure a contract with his spouse. According to the Ohio Ethics Commission, this same statute *does not* prohibit a board member whose spouse is a teacher from voting on a collective bargaining agreement between the district and the teacher's union.[18]

CONTINUING CONTRACTS AND TENURED TEACHERS

9.04 Continuing contracts and tenure

The holder of a continuing contract has continuing service status or "tenure."[19] A continuing contract remains in effect, unless terminated for cause under RC 3319.16, until the teacher resigns, elects to retire, or is laid off pursuant to RC 3319.17.

---

nomination is made by the educational service center superintendent. But see RC 3319.07(B), permitting local and governing boards to agree to allow such nominations to be made by the local superintendent.

[7]Fisher v Brooklyn Bd of Ed, No. 42947 (8th Dist Ct App, Cuyahoga, 4-9-81).
[8]RC 3319.08.
[9]RC 3319.12.
[10]RC 3319.11.
[11]See Text 9.04 to 9.09; Text 9.17 to 9.23.
[12]See Text 9.10 to 9.13.
[13]RC 3319.11(A)(3).
[14]RC 3319.08.

[15]RC 3319.08; Tate v Westerville Bd of Ed, 4 OS(3d) 206, 4 OBR 524, 448 NE(2d) 144 (1983).
[16]Zaleski School Dist Bd of Ed v Boal, 104 OS 482, 135 NE 540 (1922).
[17]In re Ron Steed, No. 1909, 1989 WL 411471 (4th Dist Ct App, Lawrence, 7-27-89) (statute not applicable to employment of spouse as assistant school nurse). See also Scherer v Rock Hill Local School Dist Bd of Ed, 63 App(3d) 555, 579 NE(2d) 525 (Lawrence 1990) (a related case in which the court refused to void the spouse's contract of employment).
[18]Ethics Op 82-003; Ethics Op 89-005.
[19]RC 3319.09(C).

During a layoff, the teacher's contract rights, except the right of recall in the case of a continuing contract teacher, are suspended.

Although a continuing contract assures tenure, it does not entitle the holder to individualized contract terms, such as extended service during the summer recess.[20] In addition, a continuing contract does not entitle a teacher to perform specific teaching duties. Thus, a court held that a continuing contract teacher could be reassigned from math to permanent substitute duty, provided there was no reduction in salary.[21] However, a court has also held that when a continuing contract specifically states the person is employed as a guidance counselor, the superintendent has no authority to reassign that person to a classroom teaching position.[22]

9.05 Eligibility for continuing contract: introduction

(A) In general

The eligibility requirements for continuing service status appear in RC 3319.11. Because RC 3319.11 "is a teacher-protection statute and not a law pertaining to minimum educational requirements under R.C. 4117.10(A)," tenure requirements may be modified by a collective bargaining agreement.[23] What follows describes the statutory scheme in the absence of any such contractual deviations.

To be eligible for a continuing contract, a teacher must hold a professional, permanent, or life certificate.[24] In addition, he must have taught in the district for at least three of the last five years, or must have served two years in the district if continuing contract status has been attained elsewhere.[25] In the latter situation, the board of education, upon recommendation by the superintendent, may at the time of initial employment, or at any time within the two-year period, declare a teacher eligible for a continuing contract.[26]

The board, however, is not required to confer continuing contract status, nor does a teacher automatically achieve such status by becoming eligible for a continuing contract during the term of a limited contract.[27] The board may decline to reemploy the teacher when the limited contract expires.[28] The board is not bound by any prior practice of regularly granting a continuing contract to teachers who become eligible for one.[29] Nor is the board required to follow a principal's recommendation to offer a continuing contract.[30] Moreover, a teacher is not entitled to a public hearing when the board is discussing whether to renew his employment, irrespective of whether he is ineligible[31] or eligible[32] for a continuing contract. However, a teacher whose employment is not renewed is entitled, upon timely written request, to a written description of the circumstances leading to his nonrenewal *and* a hearing before the board on the nonrenewal itself.[33]

---

[20]Haws v Dayton City Bd of Ed, No. CA 6242 (2d Dist Ct App, Montgomery, 7-26-79).

[21]Baisden v Oak Hill Union Local School Dist Bd of Ed, No. 491, 1985 WL 11146 (4th Dist Ct App, Jackson, 6-7-85). For other cases on this point, see Text 8.02(C), Substitute teachers, educational aides.

[22]Silavent v Buckeye Central Local School Dist Bd of Ed, 27 App(3d) 189, 27 OBR 228, 500 NE(2d) 315 (Crawford 1985).

[23]State ex rel Rollins v Cleveland Hts-University Hts City School Dist Bd of Ed, 40 OS(3d) 123, 532 NE(2d) 1289 (1988). See also Text 18.20, Supremacy of contract over certain laws.

[24]RC 3319.08. "Life" certificates are no longer issued; some senior teachers, however, may still have them. See Text 8.04, Grades of certificates.

[25]RC 3319.11(B).

[26]RC 3319.11(B).

[27]State ex rel Paul v Van Buren Local School Dist Bd of Ed, 44 OS(2d) 5, 335 NE(2d) 703 (1975).

[28]State ex rel Paul v Van Buren Local School Dist Bd of Ed, 44 OS(2d) 5, 335 NE(2d) 703 (1975); State ex rel Hura v Brookfield Local School Dist Bd of Ed, 51 OS(2d) 19, 364 NE(2d) 864 (1977); State ex rel Bell v North Union Local School Dist Bd of Ed, No. 14-84-5, 1985 WL 3730 (3d Dist Ct App, Union, 11-19-85).

[29]Millhoff v Manchester Local School Dist Bd of Ed, No. 11941, 1985 WL 11071 (9th Dist Ct App, Summit, 8-28-85).

[30]Casperson v Bexley City School Dist Bd of Ed, No. 85AP-680, 1985 WL 4949 (10th Dist Ct App, Franklin, 12-31-85).

[31]Matheny v Frontier Local Bd of Ed, 62 OS(2d) 362, 405 NE(2d) 1041 (1980).

[32]Seiler v Vantage Joint Vocational School Dist Bd of Ed, No. 15-83-23, 1985 WL 9067 (3d Dist Ct App, Van Wert, 1-25-85).

[33]RC 3319.111. See Text 9.13, Statutory evaluation and due process requirements.

A supplemental contract for the performance of duties in addition to regular duties may not be, or become, a continuing contract.[34]

(B) Burden on teacher to give notice of eligibility

A teacher must provide a board with sufficient notice of his possession of a professional, permanent, or life certificate for a continuing contract. As long as the records of the district or service center superintendent indicate the teacher has the requisite certification, however, the board has sufficient notice, even if the certificate itself is not on file.[35] Boards must exercise caution in considering the renewal of a limited contract at a time when the teacher has begun the process of upgrading a provisional certificate to a professional certificate.[36]

9.06 Eligibility for continuing contract: certificate requirement

(A) Professional, permanent, or life certificate

Continuing contract status can only be granted to a teacher who holds a professional, permanent, or life certificate.[37] Thus, only teachers with advanced education and substantial experience are eligible.[38]

A board of education has no authority to grant a continuing contract to someone who does not meet the requirements established in RC 3319.11. Thus, a board could nonrenew a teacher, even though for twenty-four years he had been treated as having tenure, because he did not have an upgraded certificate as required.[39] Likewise, a board is not bound by an invalid grant of continuing service status by a previous employer.[40]

(B) Time of issuance of certificate, filing

As long as the teacher has the necessary certificate on file and it takes effect prior to the first day of the new contract, the teacher is entitled to a continuing contract even though he did not have the certificate at the time the contract was executed.[41]

However, a teacher was not eligible for continuing contract status where the employer did not know of the qualifying certificate at the time the contract was entered into and, in any event, she did not receive the certificate until *after* the start of the school year, even though it was predated to be effective before the start of the school year.[42] Where a teacher was awarded a limited contract in April and applied for a professional certificate in mid-May, which was ultimately issued effective July 1, she was not entitled to a continuing contract since the board had no notice she would qualify as to certification when the board made its employment decision.[43]

9.07 Eligibility for continuing contract: teaching requirement

RC 3319.11 limits eligibility for continuing contracts to those "teachers who have taught" for at least three out of the last five

---

[34]RC 3319.08; Tate v Westerville Bd of Ed, 4 OS(3d) 206, 4 OBR 524, 448 NE(2d) 144 (1983).

[35]Woodrum v Rolling Hills Bd of Ed, 66 OS(2d) 284, 421 NE(2d) 859 (1981); State ex rel Gandy v Continental Local School Dist Bd of Ed, 26 OS(2d) 115, 269 NE(2d) 605 (1971).

[36]See Text 9.06(B), Time of issuance of certificate, filing.

[37]RC 3319.08. See also RC 3319.22.

[38]See Text 8.06, Education and experience requirements, renewing and upgrading certificates.

[39]Thompson v Fostoria City School Bd of Ed, No. 13-80-19, 1981 WL 6797 (3d Dist Ct App, Seneca, 2-26-81).

[40]Bickel v Carrollton Exempted Village School Dist Bd of Ed, No. 445, 1982 WL 6185 (7th Dist Ct App, Carroll, 9-15-82).

[41]State ex rel Peet v Westerville City School Dist Bd of Ed, 66 OS(2d) 287, 421 NE(2d) 861 (1981); State ex rel Price v Wauseon Exempted Village School Dist Bd of Ed, No. F-83-8 (6th Dist Ct App, Fulton, 1-6-84); State ex rel Gildersleeve v Whitehall City School Dist Bd of Ed, No. 82AP-455, 1983 WL 3330 (10th Dist Ct App, Franklin, 1-27-83).

[42]Pascoe v Huron Bd of Ed, No. E-82-32, 1983 WL 13842 (6th Dist Ct App, Erie, 2-18-83). See also Shuba v Austintown Bd of Ed, No. 83-CA-81, 1985 WL 10371 (7th Dist Ct App, Mahoning, 1-25-85).

[43]State ex rel Spires v Maceyko, No. CA-673, 1988 WL 42609 (5th Dist Ct App, Morrow, 4-27-88). See also State ex rel Fraysier v Bexley City School Dist Bd of Ed, 65 App(3d) 245, 583 NE(2d) 1000 (Franklin 1989) (district superintendent's signing of teacher's application for professional certificate does not constitute notice to board of teacher's eligibility for continuing contract at time board offered limited contract).

years in the district or have been granted tenure in another district and "have served two years in the district."

(A) Who are "teachers"

(1) Statutory definition, teachers per se

By statute, a teacher is any person who is certified to teach and is employed in the public schools as an instructor, or as a superintendent, principal, supervisor, or in any other educational position for which certification is required.[44] Clearly, a certificated person employed as a teacher comes within the definition, and may be eligible for continuing contract status under RC 3319.11.

(2) Administrators

Administrators also meet the statutory definition. Administrators, however, are not entitled to continuing contract status as such, in light of the requirement that an administrator's contract be for a specific term and the fact that an administrator exercises executive and discretionary power.[45] Nevertheless, service as administrators may, under some circumstances, entitle them to continuing contract status as teachers.

Even though an administrator cannot obtain a continuing administrator's contract, he may be entitled to tenure as a teacher, to the extent that service as an administrator can count toward continuing teacher's contract status. In *State ex rel Specht v Painesville Twp Local School Dist Bd of Ed*,[46] the employee attained continuing contract status as a teacher in one school district, then was employed for four years as an assistant principal in another district. The second district's board refused to renew his assistant principal contract and also refused to award a continuing contract as a teacher. While reaffirming that continuing contracts are not available for administrative positions, the Ohio Supreme Court held that an administrator who otherwise meets the certificate and service requirements of RC 3319.11 is entitled to tenured status as a teacher. The Court pointed to the general assembly's choice of the words "serve" and "teach" in RC 3319.11 and ruled that "service" need not be confined to the classroom. Thus, the employee met the requirements for a continuing contract as a teacher because he had attained tenure in another district and *served* more than two years in his current district as an administrator.[47]

The corollary is that three years of combined service as a teacher and administrator in the same district will not, standing alone, qualify one for continuing contract status as a teacher. The three-year experience standard in RC 3319.11 is pegged to *teaching* only, and the two-year *service* standard requires that tenure first be acquired elsewhere.

(3) Other certificated persons

Certain certificated tutors[48] and guidance counselors[49] are teachers within the meaning of RC 3319.09(A) and may be eligible for continuing contract status under RC 3319.11. With respect to certificated school nurses, authority can be cited for the proposition that they are not teachers for purposes of obtaining tenure,[50] but subse-

---

[44]RC 3319.09(A).

[45]RC 3319.01, RC 3319.02. See also State ex rel Donah v Windham Exempted Village School Dist Bd of Ed, 69 OS(3d) 114, 630 NE(2d) 687 (1994); State ex rel Saltsman v Burton, 154 OS 262, 95 NE(2d) 377 (1950); State ex rel Saltsman v Burton, 156 OS 537, 103 NE(2d) 740 (1952); Ross v Board of Education, 52 App(2d) 28, 367 NE(2d) 1209 (Cuyahoga 1977).

[46]State ex rel Specht v Painesville Twp Local School Dist Bd of Ed, 63 OS(2d) 146, 407 NE(2d) 20 (1980).

[47]That *Specht* has in no way been diminished by subsequent changes in the text of RC 3319.02 is clear. See State ex rel Kelley v Clearcreek Local School Dist Bd of Ed, 52 OS(3d) 93, 556 NE(2d) 173 (1990).

[48]State ex rel Brown v Milton-Union Exempted Village Bd of Ed, 40 OS(3d) 21, 531 NE(2d) 1297 (1988); State ex rel Tavenner v Indian Lake Local School Dist Bd of Ed, 62 OS(3d) 88, 578 NE(2d) 464 (1991). See also State ex rel Fink v Grandview Hts City School Dist Bd of Ed, No. 93APE 10-1462, 1994 WL 183592 (10th Dist Ct App, Franklin, 5-12-94); State ex rel Siers v Beaver Local School Dist Bd of Ed, No. 89-C-39, 1990 WL 167575 (7th Dist Ct App, Columbiana, 10-29-90); Price v Newbury Local School Dist Bd of Ed, No. 91-G-1626, 1992 WL 268795 (11th Dist Ct App, Geauga, 12-13-91), appeal dismissed by 63 OS(3d) 1421, 587 NE(2d) 302 (1992).

[49]Kralopp v South Range Local School Dist Bd of Ed, 47 App(2d) 208, 353 NE(2d) 642 (Mahoning 1974).

[50]Beiting v Cincinnati City School Dist Bd of Ed, No. C-830105, 1983 WL 5254 (1st Dist Ct App, Hamilton, 10-19-83). But see Navin v Tallman, No. WD-83-53, 1983 WL 6991 (6th Dist Ct App, Wood,

quent court decisions on the status of tutors make reliance on such authority highly suspect.

(B) Teaching not limited to certificated areas

A teacher with the required years of district service is eligible for continuing contract status if he holds a professional, permanent, or life certificate in *any* teaching area. His teaching experience need not be in the area of certification.[51]

9.08 Eligibility for continuing contract: service requirement

(A) Service in district

Eligibility for tenure rests primarily on service *within the district* in which continuing contract status is sought and only tangentially on service in other districts. To be eligible under RC 3319.11, a teacher must either have "taught" for three years "in the district," or have "served" for two years "in the district" after "having attained continuing contract status elsewhere."

(B) Tenure acquired elsewhere

As used in RC 3319.11, "elsewhere" means another Ohio school district. Accordingly, a teacher who achieved tenure at a private university never achieved "continuing contract status elsewhere" within the meaning of the statute.[52] Likewise, a teacher who acquired continuing contract status in another state cannot invoke the two-year service standard to obtain tenure in Ohio,[53] unless the respective state boards of education have a reciprocity agreement.[54]

(C) Time served, school year, teaching days

As applied to a teacher's service, a year means actual teaching service of not less than 120 days within a school year.[55] A board of education may classify its teachers as either full-time or part-time for purposes of determining salary and fringe benefits, provided the classification does not reduce any minimum benefit or status required by law.[56] Years spent teaching less than full school days will be counted in determining eligibility for a continuing contract if the part-time duties were substantial and were performed on a regular basis.[57] The part-time teacher, of course, is not entitled to a continuing contract if the board has properly delivered notice of its intent not to reemploy.[58]

(D) Service as substitute teacher

It has been held that days served under a substitute's contract do not count toward years of service for the purpose of continuing contract eligibility and may not be added to days taught under a limited contract to accumulate 120 days in a school year.[59] This is so even though the Ohio Supreme Court has held that days taught as a substitute may count toward years of service for placement on the teachers' salary schedule.[60] The reason is that distinguishing between substitute and regular teachers for tenure purposes is necessary to carry out the intent of the general assembly with respect to tenure eligibility. Evaluating substitute teachers effectively and uniformly would be difficult since they do not initially prepare and plan classroom activities, do not have any prolonged interaction

---

11-11-83) (school nurses are teachers for layoff purposes).

[51]State ex rel Voss v Northwest Local Bd of Ed, 66 OS(2d) 274, 421 NE(2d) 516 (1981).

[52]Ritter v Fairfield Local School Dist, No. 389 (4th Dist Ct App, Highland, 8-5-80).

[53]Anthony v Ada Exempted Village School Dist Bd of Ed, No. 6-94-2, 1994 WL 265876 (3d Dist Ct App, Hardin, 6-16-94); Bickel v Carrollton Exempted Village School Dist Bd of Ed, No. 445, 1982 WL 6185 (7th Dist Ct App, Carroll, 9-15-82).

[54]See Text 8.03(C), Interstate certification.

[55]RC 3319.09(B).

[56]OAG 83-098.

[57]State ex rel Garay v Hubbard Local School Dist Bd of Ed, 11 OS(3d) 20, 11 OBR 53, 462 NE(2d) 1219 (1984) (four hours per day sufficient); State ex rel Rogers v Hubbard Local School Dist Bd of Ed, 10 OS(3d) 136, 10 OBR 458, 461 NE(2d) 1308 (1984) (five hours and fifteen minutes per day sufficient); State ex rel Brown v Milton-Union Exempted Village Bd of Ed, 40 OS(3d) 21, 531 NE(2d) 1297 (1988) (six hours per day sufficient).

[58]State ex rel Garay v Hubbard Local School Dist Bd of Ed, 11 OS(3d) 20, 11 OBR 53, 462 NE(2d) 1219 (1984).

[59]State ex rel Gron v Euclid City School Dist Bd of Ed, No. 46594, 1983 WL 2683 (8th Dist Ct App, Cuyahoga, 10-20-83).

[60]Crawford v Barberton City Schools Bd of Ed, 6 OS(3d) 324, 6 OBR 382, 453 NE(2d) 627 (1983).

with the students, and do not participate in regularly scheduled activities.

(E) Interrupted service

An appeals court has held that a teacher who resigned after attaining continuing status and then returned to the same district more than ten years later could not take advantage of RC 3319.11's "having attained continuing contract status elsewhere" provision in applying the service requirement of the statute toward tenure eligibility. Rather, the teacher starts from scratch and must teach in the district for at least three of the last five years before being eligible for tenure.[61] However, if a continuing contract teacher resigns only to shortly return to the same district as a teacher, the years taught in the district within the last five years are counted toward service eligibility for a new continuing contract.[62]

9.09 Employment options where teacher is eligible for continuing service status

(A) Impact of 1988 House Bill 330

1988 House Bill 330, which became effective in 1989, substantially altered Ohio law with respect to the employment and reemployment of teachers. Its provisions appear in a significantly revised RC 3319.11 and a wholly new RC 3319.111. Some familiarity with its terminology and requirements is essential to understanding how continuing service status is attained.

The Bill created a new type of teacher's employment contract, called an "extended limited contract," that arises under certain specified circumstances, either automatically by operation of law or by affirmative action of the board of education. RC 3319.11(A)(3) defines "extended limited contract" as a limited contract that a board enters into with a teacher eligible for continuing service status. The Bill also established evaluation and hearing procedures applicable to teachers under limited or extended limited contracts whose employment is not renewed.[63]

(B) When continuing contract mandatory

If the teacher is eligible for continuing service status (that is, if the teacher satisfies certification and teaching/service requirements[64]), RC 3319.11 expressly covers the following contingencies:

(1) If the superintendent recommends that the teacher be reemployed and the board does not reject that recommendation by a three-fourths vote of its full membership, the teacher is reemployed under a continuing contract.[65]

(2) If the superintendent recommends that the teacher not be reemployed, the board may sever employment by giving the teacher written notice, on or before April 30, of its intention not to reemploy the teacher. If the board does not give timely written notice,[66] or if the teacher has not been evaluated in accordance with RC 3319.111(A),[67] the teacher is automatically reemployed under a one-year extended limited contract at the same salary plus any increment provided in the district's salary schedule unless the teacher, on or before June 1, gives the board written notice of his intention not to accept the contract.[68]

(3) If the superintendent recommends that the teacher be reemployed and the board rejects that recommendation by a three-fourths vote of its full membership, there are these possibilities:

(a) If the superintendent makes no recommendation that the teacher be reemployed under an extended limited contract with reasons directed at

---

[61]State ex rel Gron v Euclid City School Dist Bd of Ed, No. 46594, 1983 WL 2683 (8th Dist Ct App, Cuyahoga, 10-20-83).

[62]Wiseman v River View Coral School Dist Bd of Ed, No. 91-CA-37, 1992 WL 195357 (5th Dist Ct App, Coshocton, 7-24-92).

[63]These evaluation and hearing procedures are discussed at, respectively, Text 9.13(A), Mandatory evaluation procedures, and Text 9.13(C), Right to hearing.

[64]See Text 9.05 to 9.08.

[65]RC 3319.11(B)(1).

[66]The elements of "timely written notice" are discussed in Text 9.11, Notice of nonrenewal, timeliness, form.

[67]See Text 9.13(A), Mandatory evaluation procedures.

[68]RC 3319.11(B)(2).

professional improvement under RC 3319.11(C)(1),[69] the board may sever employment by giving the teacher written notice, on or before April 30, of its intention not to reemploy the teacher. If the board does not give timely notice, or if the teacher has not been evaluated in accordance with RC 3319.111(A), the teacher is automatically reemployed under a one-year extended limited contract at the same salary plus any increment provided in the district's salary schedule unless the teacher, on or before June 1, gives the board written notice of his intention not to accept the contract.[70]

(b) If the teacher has not previously attained continuing service status elsewhere,[71] the superintendent may recommend reemployment under an extended limited contract for a term of not more than two years, provided written notice of the superintendent's intention to make the recommendation is given to the teacher with reasons directed at professional improvement on or before April 30.[72] In such a case, there are these possibilities:

(i) If the board acts affirmatively on the superintendent's recommendation, and gives the teacher written notice of its action, on or before April 30, the teacher is reemployed under an extended limited contract in accordance with the superintendent's recommendation.

(ii) If the board acts affirmatively on the superintendent's recommendation, but does not give the teacher written notice, on or before April 30, of its action, the teacher is automatically reemployed under a continuing contract at the same salary plus any increment provided in the district's salary schedule unless the teacher, on or before June 1, gives the board written notice of his intention not to accept the contract.[73]

(iii) The board can reject the superintendent's recommendation by a three-fourths vote of its full membership. In that case, the board may sever employment by giving the teacher written notice, on or before April 30, of its intention not to reemploy the teacher. If the board does not give timely written notice, or if the teacher has not been evaluated in accordance with RC 3319.111(A), the teacher is automatically reemployed under a one-year extended limited contract at the same salary plus any increment provided in the district's salary schedule unless the teacher, on or before June 1, gives the board written notice of his intention not to accept the contract.[74]

(4) Upon the expiration of a teacher's extended limited contract, irrespective of whether the contract arose automatically by operation of law or pursuant to board action on the superintendent's recommendation for the contract with reasons directed at professional improvement, the teacher is automatically reemployed under a continuing contract at the same salary plus any increment provided in the district's salary schedule unless the teacher has been evaluated in accordance with RC 3319.111(A) and the board, acting on the superintendent's recommendation that the teacher not be reemployed, gives the teacher written notice, on or before April 30, of its intention not to reemploy the teacher. If both these requirements are satisfied, the teacher's employment is severed. Otherwise, unless the teacher, on or before June 1, gives the board written notice of his intention not to accept the contract, a continuing contract must be executed.[75]

---

[69]Extended limited contracts with reasons directed at professional improvement are discussed at Text 9.09(C), Extended limited contract for professional improvement.

[70]RC 3319.11(B)(1).

[71]For the meaning of "elsewhere," see Text 9.08(B), Tenure acquired elsewhere.

[72]RC 3319.11(C)(1). See also Text 9.09(C), Extended limited contract for professional improvement.

[73]RC 3319.11(C)(2).

[74]RC 3319.11(C)(3).

[75]RC 3319.11(D). If the superintendent recommends that the teacher be reemployed or makes no

There are contingencies not expressly addressed in RC 3319.11. The statute obviously contemplates that the superintendent will recommend that a teacher eligible for continuing service status either be reemployed or not reemployed. If the superintendent fails to recommend either for or against reemployment, what happens is, at least in some cases, simply unclear. In 1975, in *Justus v Brown*,[76] the Ohio Supreme Court held that the board of education retains ultimate responsibility for the employment and reemployment of teachers and that a unanimous vote not to reemploy a tenure-eligible teacher whom the superintendent had not recommended one way or the other severed the teacher's employment. *Justus*, however, has been badly undercut, if not jettisoned completely, by *Farmer v Kelleys Island Bd of Ed*.[77] Based on *Farmer*, it is reasonably clear in the context of RC 3319.11(D) that a failure by the superintendent to recommend would foreclose the board from ending the employment relationship, but a superintendent's failure to recommend at all pursuant to RC 3319.11(B) is at least arguably left untouched by *Farmer* even by implication. Still, whether *Justus* retains any viability even in this context is doubtful. What *Farmer* really underscores is the need legislatively to overhaul RC 3319.11 and make clear in all contexts whether it is the board or the superintendent that calls the shots.

To reemploy a teacher the superintendent has recommended *not* be reemployed, the board must vote to reemploy by a three-fourths vote.[78]

In all of the above situations, if the board decides against reemployment, the nonrenewed teacher is entitled to the due process procedures spelled out in RC 3319.11(G).[79]

(C) Extended limited contract for professional improvement

Under RC 3319.11, the superintendent's option to recommend reemployment of a teacher eligible for continuing service status who has not previously attained tenure elsewhere under a one-time contract with reasons directed at professional improvement arises only if the board rejects, by a three-fourths vote of its full membership, the superintendent's recommendation that the teacher be reemployed. At that point, the superintendent may (but is not required to) recommend reemployment under an extended limited contract for a term of not more than two years, provided written notice of his intention to make the recommendation is given, on or before April 30, to the teacher with reasons directed at professional improvement.[80]

Case law that evolved prior to the revision of RC 3319.11 effected by 1988 House Bill 330 presumably still controls as to the adequacy of any notice or reasons given. The notice cannot be vague but must clearly delineate reasons that would direct the teacher on how to improve work performance during the extended limited contract period. Otherwise, the teacher may acquire tenure by operation of law.[81]

The determination, extent, and implementation of professional standards expected of teachers are vested solely within the board's discretion. Thus, a board may establish improvement of relations

---

recommendation one way or the other, the board is apparently precluded from severing employment and the teacher is entitled to a continuing contract; in essence, in this limited context the superintendent, not the board, has the ultimate employment authority. See Farmer v Kelleys Island Bd of Ed, 70 OS(3d) 1203, 638 NE(2d) 79 (1994), clarifying 69 OS(3d) 156, 630 NE(2d) 721 (1994) (construing identically worded statutory language with respect to the superintendent's recommendation not to reemploy that appears in RC 3319.11(E) and effectively to this extent overruling Justus v Brown, 42 OS(2d) 53, 325 NE(2d) 884 (1975)). See also Text 9.10, Employment options where teacher is not eligible for continuing service status.

[76]Justus v Brown, 42 OS(2d) 53, 325 NE(2d) 884 (1975).

[77]Farmer v Kelleys Island Bd of Ed, 70 OS(3d) 1203, 638 NE(2d) 79 (1994), clarifying 69 OS(3d) 156, 630 NE(2d) 721 (1994).

[78]Miller v Wayne County Joint Vocational School Dist Bd of Ed, 69 App(2d) 66, 430 NE(2d) 475 (Wayne 1980) (relying on RC 3319.07).

[79]RC 3319.11(B)(3), (C)(3), (D), (G). The due process procedures are discussed in Text 9.13, Statutory evaluation and due process requirements.

[80]RC 3319.11(C)(1).

[81]McKita v Canton City School Dist Bd of Ed, No. CA-7684, 1989 WL 64032 (5th Dist Ct App, Stark, 5-30-89); State ex rel Suitts v Mississinawa Valley Local School Dist Bd of Ed, No. CA 1131 (2d Dist Ct App, Darke, 4-18-85); Adler v Yellow Springs Exempted Village School Dist, No. 82 CA 21, 1982 WL 3821 (2d Dist Ct App, Greene, 10-14-82).

with administrators and other teachers as a professional standard.[82]

Generalized statements do not satisfy the statutory obligation. The teacher must be provided with clear, understandable, and focused guidelines for professional improvement.[83] These must describe the teacher's professional problems and outline techniques or materials the teacher should apply to remedy the problems. Moreover, both administrators and the teacher must work cooperatively in good faith to remedy deficiencies.[84]

The notice must come directly from the superintendent[85] and must be given *before* the board acts on it.[86] Prior notice from an authorized agent of the superintendent, such as the building principal, is insufficient.[87] However, in a local school district, the notice requirement is satisfied where a local superintendent notifies a teacher of the intention to recommend an extended limited contract; RC 3319.11 does not require that the county superintendent give the notice.[88] In addition, the board must act on the superintendent's recommendation and notify the teacher of its action in writing on or before April 30.[89] In a 2-1 decision, an appeals court has held that the board may delegate to the local district superintendent the responsibility of executing the notice required of the board.[90]

(D) Nonrenewal followed by reemployment

A board may nonrenew a teacher's contract and then reemploy the teacher after April 30.[91] Thus, where a limited contract teacher eligible for a continuing contract receives timely notice of nonrenewal and is subsequently reemployed for the following year with a limited contract, the teacher is not entitled to a continuing contract.[92] If the teacher was eligible for a continuing contract, reemployment may be under either a limited contract for less than two years or a continuing contract, but thereafter reemployment must be under a continuing contract.[93]

It is crucial that the proper order be followed. The board's notice to reemploy under different terms at the end of a limited contract is invalid, and the old contract will be considered renewed, unless preceded by a timely notice of intent not to renew the limited contract.[94]

(E) Waiver of continuing contract status

Continuing service status may be waived. Where a teacher resigned and later voluntarily entered into a limited contract without withdrawing his resignation, he waived any right to a continuing contract.[95] Further, a teacher may waive eligibility for

---

[82]Casperson v Bexley City School Dist Bd of Ed, No. 85AP-680, 1985 WL 4949 (10th Dist Ct App, Franklin, 12-31-85); Rea v North Central Local School Dist Bd of Ed, No. 2295, 1988 WL 34591 (9th Dist Ct App, Wayne, 3-23-88).

[83]Biesterfeldt v Bay Village City School Dist Bd of Ed, No. 83-064424-CV (CP, Cuyahoga, 2-4-86).

[84]Biesterfeldt v Bay Village City School Dist Bd of Ed, No. 83-064424-CV (CP, Cuyahoga, 2-4-86).

[85]State ex rel Lee v Bellefontaine City Bd of Ed, 17 OS(3d) 124, 17 OBR 271, 477 NE(2d) 1135 (1985).

[86]State ex rel Suitts v Mississinawa Valley Local School Dist Bd of Ed, No. CA 1131 (2d Dist Ct App, Darke, 4-18-85).

[87]State ex rel Suitts v Mississinawa Valley Local School Dist Bd of Ed, No. CA 1131 (2d Dist Ct App, Darke, 4-18-85).

[88]Rea v North Central Local School Dist Bd of Ed, No. 2295, 1988 WL 34591 (9th Dist Ct App, Wayne, 3-23-88).

[89]RC 3319.11(C)(2); Balog v Western Brown Local School Dist Bd of Ed, No. CA84-10-013, 1985 WL 3869 (12th Dist Ct App, Brown, 11-25-85).

[90]State ex rel Remley v Licking Heights Local School Dist Bd of Ed, No. CA3489, 1990 WL 79034 (5th Dist Ct App, Licking, 6-1-90).

[91]Russell v Springfield Local School Dist Bd of Ed, No. 12163, 1985 WL 10872 (9th Dist Ct App, Summit, 10-2-85).

[92]State ex rel Mezak v Berkshire Local School Dist Bd of Ed, No. 1364, 1987 WL 32739 (11th Dist Ct App, Geauga, 12-31-87).

[93]State ex rel Hura v Brookfield Local School Dist Bd of Ed, 51 OS(2d) 19, 364 NE(2d) 864 (1977); Mate v Stow City School Dist Bd of Ed, 62 App(3d) 265, 575 NE(2d) 477 (Summit 1988).

[94]Marchand v North Canton City School Dist Bd of Ed, No. CA-6182, 1983 WL 7085 (5th Dist Ct App, Stark, 10-11-83); Beifuss v Westerville Bd of Ed, No. 83AP-775, 1984 WL 6036 (10th Dist Ct App, Franklin, 12-18-84).

[95]State ex rel Brubaker v Hardy, 5 OS(2d) 103, 214 NE(2d) 79 (1966). See also State ex rel Gildersleeve v Whitehall City School Dist Bd of Ed, No. 82AP-455, 1983 WL 3330 (10th Dist Ct App, Franklin, 1-27-83).

a continuing contract by withdrawing from the state teachers' retirement system.[96]

Waivers are not judicially favored, however. Silence or inaction alone will not waive a statutory right unless one has an obligation to speak or act.[97] Mere acceptance of a limited contract by an employee eligible for a continuing contract does not constitute a waiver.[98] Nor was a waiver found when a teacher eligible for a continuing contract signed a two-year contract with reasons directed toward professional improvement, but was not given proper notice from the superintendent under RC 3319.11,[99] notwithstanding that the teacher waited until after the limited contract had been nonrenewed. Waiver also did not occur when a teacher eligible for a continuing contract was confused by the superintendent's directions for professional improvement contained in the two-year probationary limited contract.[100] Another court refused to find waiver when the teacher failed to follow the district's procedural requirement that he request to be considered for a continuing contract.[101] Moreover, a teacher of a federally funded adult education course did not waive a continuing contract when he signed, with reservations, a contract stating that continued employment was contingent on the availability of federal funds.[102]

LIMITED CONTRACTS AND NONTENURED TEACHERS

9.10 Employment options where teacher is not eligible for continuing service status

(A) When limited contract required

Under RC 3319.11, teachers not eligible for tenure must be employed under limited contracts. This includes all teachers who hold temporary and provisional certificates, regardless of how long they have been employed, plus all teachers who hold professional, permanent, or life certificates but have not met the teaching/service requirement for tenure eligibility.[103]

(B) Duration, automatic reemployment, nonrenewal after evaluation and notice

A limited contract is limited in time; five years is the maximum term permitted.[104] If the teacher is not eligible to be considered for a continuing contract, upon expiration of his limited contract the teacher is automatically reemployed at the same salary plus any increment provided in the district's salary schedule unless the teacher has been evaluated in accordance with RC 3319.111(A)[105] and the board, acting on the superintendent's written recommendation that the teacher not be reemployed, gives the teacher written notice, on or before April 30, of its intention not to reemploy the teacher.[106] If both these requirements are satisfied, the teacher's

---

[96]State ex rel Gildersleeve v Whitehall City School Dist Bd of Ed, No. 82AP-455, 1983 WL 3330 (10th Dist Ct App, Franklin, 1-27-83).

[97]State ex rel Madden v Windham Exempted Village School Dist Bd of Ed, 42 OS(3d) 86, 537 NE(2d) 646 (1989).

[98]State ex rel Brown v Milton-Union Exempted Village Bd of Ed, 40 OS(3d) 21, 531 NE(2d) 1297 (1988). See also State ex rel McMillan v Lexington Local School Dist Bd of Ed, No. CA-2842, 1991 WL 208060 (5th Dist Ct App, Richland, 9-26-91) (waiver not found in case involving nonteaching employee).

[99]State ex rel Suitts v Mississinawa Valley Local School Dist Bd of Ed, No. CA 1131 (2d Dist Ct App, Darke, 4-18-85).

[100]Biesterfeldt v Bay Village City School Dist Bd of Ed, No. 83-064424-CV (CP, Cuyahoga, 2-4-86).

[101]State ex rel Hendricks v Canfield Local School Dist Bd of Ed, No. 84-CA-112, 1985 WL 10370 (7th Dist Ct App, Mahoning, 1-24-85).

[102]State ex rel Livingston v Belmont-Harrison Joint Vocational School Dist Bd of Ed, No. 83-B-42, 1984 WL 3804 (7th Dist Ct App, Belmont, 12-12-84).

[103]See Text 9.07, Eligibility for continuing contract: teaching requirement; Text 9.08, Eligibility for continuing contract: service requirement.

[104]RC 3319.08.

[105]See Text 9.13(A), Mandatory evaluation procedures.

[106]RC 3319.11(E). The superintendent's recommendation *not* to reemploy is *essential* to severing employment. If the superintendent recommends reemployment, the Ohio Supreme Court has declared a board of education is powerless to effect a nonrenewal and the teacher is entitled to reemployment. Farmer v Kelleys Island Bd of Ed, 70 OS(3d) 1203, 638 NE(2d) 79 (1994), clarifying 69 OS(3d) 156, 630 NE(2d) 721 (1994). Presumably, if the superintendent makes no recommendation one way or the other, the board is likewise powerless to act and reemployment

employment is severed. Otherwise, unless the teacher, on or before June 1, gives the board written notice of his intention not to accept such reemployment, "a written contract for the succeeding school year shall be executed accordingly."[107]

(C) Reemployment despite superintendent's nonrenewal recommendation

When the superintendent recommends that a teacher not be reemployed, the board may override the recommendation. In a city, exempted village, county, or joint vocational school district, a vote to reemploy despite the superintendent's recommendation requires a three-fourths majority of the board.[108] In a local school district, the board may override a nonrenewal recommendation by a simple majority *after* it has first considered and rejected two of the county superintendent's nominees for the position.[109]

(D) Waiver of right to automatic renewal

One court has found that a teacher may waive his right to automatic reemployment under a limited contract. A teacher voluntarily relinquished a known right to reemployment for a full year under RC 3319.11 where he accepted without protest or reservation a contract clearly and unequivocally restricted to one month.[110] Generally, however, waivers are not judicially favored.[111]

9.11 Notice of nonrenewal, timeliness, form

The requirement that a board give written notice by April 30 of its intention not to renew a teacher's contract is judicially construed to mean that the teacher must actually receive written notice on or before April 30.

(A) Time of notice, actual receipt required, method of service

In one case, the teacher was present when the board voted not to renew his contract. Written notice was sent by certified mail on April 29, but not delivered until May 2. Since the teacher received the notice after April 30, the board was compelled to reemploy him.[112]

Similarly, notice was deficient when it was mailed on April 14 but not received until May 1,[113] when it was delivered to the teacher's residence by April 30 but not actually received until May 1,[114] and when it was not received until after April 30 even though the teacher received a postal notice on April 28 that certified mail addressed to him was at the post office but the notice did not identify the sender.[115]

Where a teacher contended the board failed to give timely written notice and in a hearing under RC 3319.11(G) on the nonrenewal the board presented no evidence of his receipt of timely notice, the teacher was deemed reemployed in *Kiel v Green Local School Dist Bd of Ed*.[116]

RC 3319.11(H) specifies how a board's written notice of nonrenewal is to be served. The board of education or the superintendent must either deliver the notice by personal service on the teacher or deliver the notice by certified mail to the teacher at *both* his place of employment and his residence.

(B) Evasion of service

The requirement that notice actually be received on or before April 30 does not apply where the employee deliberately evades service of notice.[117] Since RC 3319.11 now specifies a method for serving

---

is automatic. The elements of timely written notice are discussed in Text 9.11, Notice of nonrenewal, timeliness, form.

[107]RC 3319.11(E).

[108]RC 3319.07; Miller v Wayne County Joint Vocational School Dist Bd of Ed, 69 App(2d) 66, 430 NE(2d) 475 (Wayne 1980).

[109]RC 3319.07.

[110]State ex rel Johnston v Cincinnati Bd of Ed, 64 App(2d) 146, 411 NE(2d) 833 (Hamilton 1979).

[111]See Text 9.09(E), Waiver of continuing contract status.

[112]State ex rel Peake v South Point Local School Dist Bd of Ed, 44 OS(2d) 119, 339 NE(2d) 249 (1975).

[113]State ex rel Kellner v Field Local School Dist Bd of Ed, No. 1153, 1982 WL 5838 (11th Dist Ct App, Portage, 3-1-82).

[114]State ex rel Gray v Springfield City School Dist Bd of Ed, No. 1713, 1983 WL 4805 (2d Dist Ct App, Clark, 2-8-83).

[115]State ex rel Francu v Windham Exempted Village School Dist Bd of Ed, 25 OS(3d) 351, 25 OBR 403, 496 NE(2d) 902 (1986).

[116]Kiel v Green Local School Dist Bd of Ed, 69 OS(3d) 149, 630 NE(2d) 716 (1994).

[117]State ex rel Peake v South Point Local School Dist Bd of Ed, 44 OS(2d) 119, 339 NE(2d) 249 (1975).

notice,[118] cases of evasion are less likely. Still, they can arise, and principles established by case law prior to amendment of the statute by 1988 House Bill 330 retain relevance.

In one case, notice was sent by certified mail April 26. The post office left notice in the teacher's mailbox, but the teacher did not pick it up until May 13. Also, on April 26, a copy of the notice was put in his school mailbox, which he was required to (and did) check daily, although he claimed he did not know the notice was in his box until May 2 or 3. The court found the evidence showed that he purposely avoided notice and ruled notice was timely given.[119]

Intentional evasion was found when the teacher was continuously absent from the day after the board voted to nonrenew his contract until May 7; the teacher never informed the administration of his whereabouts; and numerous attempts to deliver the notice through certified mail, personal service at the school and the teacher's residence, and telephone calls had all failed.[120]

Where a board voted not to renew the superintendent's contract, and he instructed his secretary to route the minutes of the meeting to the assistant superintendent instead of himself, he deliberately evaded service of the notice.[121]

The evidence must affirmatively show deliberate evasion.[122] That the teacher took a trip out of state, knowing the board had voted not to reemploy her, was insufficient in itself to show evasion.[123] Failure to pick up a certified letter containing notice until May 2, after receiving notice of the letter's existence on April 28, was also held not to constitute evasion.[124]

(C) Form of notice

The statute now specifies a method of service but does not specify the form of the notice itself, so that reasonable notice in writing in any form generally should be sufficient. In a case involving a superintendent's nonrenewal, a copy of the minutes of the meeting at which the board voted not to renew his contract was sufficient.[125]

(D) Burden of proof

A board has the burden of proving by a preponderance of the evidence that it gave the notice required by RC 3319.11.[126] However, where a board votes to nonrenew a teacher and gives timely notice, the inadvertent failure to include the teacher's name in the board minutes among the names of teachers nonrenewed does not invalidate the board's action and may be corrected by later amendment to the minutes.[127]

---

[118]See Text 9.11(A), Time of notice, actual receipt required, method of service.

[119]State ex rel Scharlotte v East Franklin Local School Dist Bd of Ed, 63 App(2d) 1, 407 NE(2d) 1389 (Summit 1978). See also Mauchamer v Covington Exempted Village School Dist Bd of Ed, No. 84-CA-5, 1984 WL 3843 (2d Dist Ct App, Miami, 9-4-84).

[120]State ex rel Boyd v Canton City School Dist Bd of Ed, No. CA-6457, 1985 WL 4709 (5th Dist Ct App, Stark, 12-23-85).

[121]Pavkov v Barberton Bd of Ed, No. CA-11570, 1984 WL 6149 (9th Dist Ct App, Summit, 5-2-84). The method of service used in this case would plainly be deficient under RC 3319.11, as amended. Whether the method would still be effective in not renewing a superintendent's contract, which is governed by RC 3319.01, not RC 3319.11, is debatable. In any event, service of notice merely by sending a copy of board minutes, even with respect to administrators whose contracts are not governed by RC 3319.11, is certainly not the preferable course. The best, and safest, course in *all* cases is to follow the method now described in RC 3319.11(H).

[122]State ex rel Kellner v Field Local School Dist Bd of Ed, No. 1153, 1982 WL 5838 (11th Dist Ct App, Portage, 3-1-82).

[123]State ex rel Curry v Grand Valley Local Schools Bd of Ed, 54 OS(2d) 67, 375 NE(2d) 48 (1978). Compare State ex rel Fraysier v Bexley City School Dist Bd of Ed, 65 App(3d) 245, 583 NE(2d) 1000 (Franklin 1989) (evasion found where teacher knew time for notice was short, i.e., Friday afternoon and Saturday, and teacher made himself incommunicado by leaving home).

[124]State ex rel Francu v Windham Exempted Village School Dist Bd of Ed, 25 OS(3d) 351, 25 OBR 403, 496 NE(2d) 902 (1986).

[125]Pavkov v Barberton Bd of Ed, No. CA-11570, 1984 WL 6149 (9th Dist Ct App, Summit, 5-2-84).

[126]Zartman v Lakota Local School Dist Bd of Ed, 33 Misc 217, 293 NE(2d) 575 (CP, Seneca 1972); State ex rel Gray v Springfield City School Dist Bd of Ed, No. 1713, 1983 WL 4805 (2d Dist Ct App, Clark, 2-8-83).

[127]State ex rel Harper v Bath-Richfield Local School Dist Bd of Ed, 7 OS(2d) 49, 218 NE(2d) 616 (1966).

9.12 Nonrenewal and reemployment as means to change contract terms

A board may vote not to renew a teacher's contract, then offer him a new contract on different terms. The vote not to renew and offer of a new contract may be made at the same meeting.[128] However, the board is still required to give the teacher notice of nonrenewal in accordance with RC 3319.11. Failure to do so will result in an automatic renewal of the old contract, even though the board informs the teacher of the different contract terms.[129] If the teacher accepts the new contract, the right to automatic renewal of the previous contract is waived.[130]

9.13 Statutory evaluation and due process requirements

(A) Mandatory evaluation procedures

RC 3319.111 requires that a board of education which is considering not reemploying a limited or extended limited contract teacher complete at least two evaluations of the teacher during the school year in which the contract expires. Failure to comply results in the teacher's automatic reemployment under a one-year limited, one-year extended limited, or continuing contract, whichever is applicable.[131]

One evaluation must be conducted on or before January 15, with the teacher receiving a written report of the evaluation no later than January 25. A copy of the evaluation must be given to the teacher. Merely showing a copy is not sufficient to comply with RC 3319.111(A).[132] Another evaluation must be conducted between February 10 and April 1, with the teacher receiving a written report no later than April 10. These evaluations must be conducted by a certificated administrator, vocational director or educational supervisor employed under RC 3319.02, or a person designated by a peer review agreement between the board and representatives of teachers in the board's employ.[133]

The board must adopt and apply evaluation procedures that include, but are not limited to the following:

(1) Criteria of job performance expectations in the teacher's areas of responsibility;

(2) At least two thirty-minute observations of the teacher for each evaluation; and

(3) A written evaluative report that includes specific recommendations for necessary improvements in job performance and the means by which the teacher may obtain assistance in making such improvements.[134]

With respect to the ratio of thirty-minute observations to written evaluations, the Ohio Supreme Court has clarified the "minimum statutory requirements" as follows: there must be two timely evaluations predicated upon at least two observations for *each* such evaluation; should the teacher be evaluated more frequently, however, any *additional* evaluations need *not* comply with the two-observation

---

[128] Graves v Youngstown City School Dist Bd of Ed, No. 82-CA-40, 1983 WL 6734 (7th Dist Ct App, Mahoning, 1-11-83).

[129] Marchand v North Canton City School Dist Bd of Ed, No. CA-6182, 1983 WL 7085 (5th Dist Ct App, Stark, 10-11-83); Beifuss v Westerville Bd of Ed, No. 83AP-775, 1984 WL 6036 (10th Dist Ct App, Franklin, 12-18-84).

[130] Kehoe v Brunswick City School Dist Bd of Ed, 24 App(3d) 51, 24 OBR 103, 493 NE(2d) 261 (Medina 1983).

[131] See Text 9.09, Employment options where teacher is eligible for continuing service status; Text 9.10, Employment options where teacher is not eligible for continuing service status.

[132] Haupricht v Rossford Exempted Village School Dist Bd of Ed, No. 93WD066, 1994 WL 262543 (6th Dist Ct App, Wood, 6-10-94).

[133] RC 3319.111(A). If a peer review process is used, the employer enjoys no common-law or First Amendment privilege against disclosure of peer review materials that are relevant to charges of discrimination under equal employment opportunity laws. See University of Pennsylvania v EEOC, 493 US 182, 110 SCt 577, 107 LEd(2d) 571 (1990). See also State ex rel James v Ohio State University, 70 OS(3d) 168, 637 NE(2d) 911 (1994) (holding that promotion and tenure records maintained by a state university are public records subject to disclosure under RC 149.43).

[134] RC 3319.111(B).

formula.[135] Further, the Supreme Court has held that a second evaluation complies with RC 3319.11(B)(3) where it specifically incorporates by reference recommendations for improvement contained in the first evaluation received by the teacher.[136]

These evaluation procedures do *not* apply to superintendents, administrators employed under RC 3319.02, or substitute teachers employed under RC 3319.10 for less than 120 days during a school year.[137] Nor do they apply to teachers working under internship certificates[138] or continuing contract teachers.

Unless a collective bargaining agreement specifically states otherwise, a board of education must fully comply with the evaluation requirements of RC 3319.111.[139] This effectively means that, in a case where the agreement provides for an evaluation procedure but does not specifically and expressly state that the procedure supersedes RC 3319.111, the board is obligated to follow *both* its labor contract and the statute.[140]

(B) Right to written statement of circumstances

RC 3319.11(G) gives a limited or extended limited contract teacher whom the board has determined not to reemploy the right, upon written demand, to a written statement describing the circumstances leading to the board's decision. The demand must be filed with the district treasurer within ten days of the teacher's receipt of the board's written notice of nonrenewal.[141] The treasurer must provide the teacher the board's response within ten days of his receipt of the demand.

The statement of circumstances must provide the teacher with a "clear and substantive basis for its decision not to reemploy the teacher for the following school year."[142] This effects a clear change from prior law, when reasons for nonrenewal were not required either as a matter of statutory or constitutional construction.[143] Where a board fails to describe the circumstances, a court cannot order reinstatement of the teacher but may award the teacher back pay until an adequate statement is provided.[144]

Even before enactment of RC 3319.11(G), the courts had concluded a collective bargaining agreement between a board and a teachers' union could require disclosure of reasons and condition nonrenewal upon compliance with negotiated procedural requirements.[145] That a collective bargaining agreement may procedurally and substantively deviate from statu-

---

[135] Farmer v Kelleys Island Bd of Ed, 70 OS(3d) 1203, 638 NE(2d) 79 (1994), clarifying 69 OS(3d) 156, 630 NE(2d) 721 (1994).

[136] Thomas v Newark City School Dist Bd of Ed, 71 OS(3d) 251, 643 NE(2d) 131 (1994).

[137] RC 3319.111(C). See also Text 7.14, Evaluation of school administrators.

[138] RC 3319.111(A).

[139] Naylor v Cardinal Local School Dist Bd of Ed, 69 OS(3d) 162, 630 NE(2d) 725 (1994).

[140] Naylor v Cardinal Local School Dist Bd of Ed, 69 OS(3d) 162, 630 NE(2d) 725 (1994). See also Text 18.20, Supremacy of contract over certain laws.

[141] In computing the ten days, it has been held hat the general time provisions of RC 1.14 apply. State ex rel Pusztay v Buckeye Joint Vocational School Dist Bd of Ed, No. 93AP070048, 1993 WL 544423 (5th Dist Ct App, Tuscarawas, 12-13-93); King v Rossford Exempted Village School Dist Bd of Ed, No. 92-CV-218 (CP, Wood, 4-7-93).

[142] Naylor v Cardinal Local School Dist Bd of Ed, 69 OS(3d) 162, 630 NE(2d) 725 (1994).

[143] See, e.g., Matheny v Frontier Local Bd of Ed, 62 OS(2d) 362, 405 NE(2d) 1041 (1980); Depas v Highland Local School Dist Bd of Ed, 52 OS(2d) 193, 370 NE(2d) 744 (1977); DeLong v Southwest School Dist Bd of Ed, 36 OS(2d) 62, 303 NE(2d) 890 (1973).

[144] Gerner v Salem City School Dist Bd of Ed, 69 OS(3d) 170, 630 NE(2d) 732 (1994). See also Naylor v Cardinal Local School Dist Bd of Ed, 69 OS(3d) 162, 630 NE(2d) 725 (1994); Barbuto v Salem City School Dist Bd of Ed, Nos. 92-C-30, 92-C-31, 1994 WL 583090 (7th Dist Ct App, Columbiana, 10-19-94); Haupricht v Rossford Exempted Village School Dist Bd of Ed, No. 93WD066, 1994 WL 262543 (6th Dist Ct App, Wood, 6-10-94).

[145] Tracy v Otsego Bd of Ed, 6 OS(3d) 305, 6 OBR 366, 453 NE(2d) 610 (1983); Struthers City Schools Bd of Ed v Struthers Ed Assn, 6 OS(3d) 308, 6 OBR 368, 453 NE(2d) 613 (1983). An interesting twist as to remedies appears in Smith v Upper Sandusky Exempted Village School Dist Bd of Ed, No. 16-88-24, 1990 WL 25066 (3d Dist Ct App, Wyandot, 3-6-90), where the board had followed RC 3319.11 (as it existed before enactment of RC 3319.11(G)) in not renewing the contract of a teacher eligible for tenure but failed to observe the evaluation procedure of its collective bargaining agreement with the teachers' union. Finding the board's breach of contract "entirely separate" from the decision not to reemploy under the statute, the court rejected the teacher's claim to a continuing contract by operation of law; rather, the court upheld the lower court's remedy under which the board could issue either a limited

tory requirements is now clear by virtue of the Ohio Public Employees' Collective Bargaining Act, specifically RC 4117.10.[146]

(C) Right to hearing

Within five days of receipt of the board's written statement of circumstances, the teacher may file with the treasurer a written demand for a hearing before the board. The treasurer, on behalf of the board, must then provide the teacher with written notice of the time, date, and place of the hearing within ten days. The hearing must be conducted within forty days of the date on which the treasurer received the demand. The hearing must be conducted by a majority of board members in executive session unless the board and teacher agree to a public hearing. Either party may be represented,[147] and either party may take a record of the hearing at its expense. The superintendent, assistant superintendent, teacher, and person designated to take a record, if any, are entitled to be present.

The Ohio Supreme Court has held that RC 3319.11(G) requires "more than an informal session between a school board and the teacher, where the teacher makes a verbal presentation protesting nonrenewal of his or her contract." Rather, "some formality" is required which "necessarily includes the presentation of evidence, confrontation and examination of witnesses and the review of the arguments of the parties."[148] In short, a substantially more sophisticated and formal proceeding is required than many observers, including a host of lower courts, had previously thought. One appellate court has held that evidence relating to the evaluation of a teacher could not be considered in determining compliance with RC 3319.111(A) where the board refused to permit cross-examination of those who wrote the evaluations.[149] The use of affidavits in lieu of live testimony has also been found deficient because it deprives the teacher of an opportunity to cross-examine.[150]

The board must issue a written decision within ten days of the conclusion of the hearing. The decision must contain an order affirming the board's intention not to reemploy the teacher or vacating the intention and expunging any record of the intention, notice of intention, and the hearing.[151]

Within thirty days of its receipt, the teacher may appeal the board's decision and order to a court of common pleas. The statute prohibits reversal of a board decision because it was not warranted by the results of an evaluation or on any other basis except failure to comply with the evaluation procedures prescribed by RC 3319.111(A) or failure by the board to give timely written notice of nonrenewal.[152] The

---

contract for one or two years with reasons directed at professional improvement or a continuing contract.

[146]See Text 18.20, Supremacy of contract over certain laws.

[147]RC 3319.11 states that a "board may be represented by counsel and the teacher may be represented by counsel or a designee." Where a teacher elected to have an Ohio Education Association Uniserv Representative serve as her designee, she was not entitled to have her union president present as well, since multiple designees are not contemplated by the statute. Gorham-Fayette Local Schools Bd of Ed v Lavens, No. 90-00128 (CP, Fulton, 5-17-91), affirmed on other grounds by No. 91FU000009, 1992 WL 173243 (6th Dist Ct App, Fulton, 7-24-92).

[148]Naylor v Cardinal Local School Dist Bd of Ed, 69 OS(3d) 162, 630 NE(2d) 725 (1994). See also Hunt v Westlake City School Dist, 100 App(3d) 233, 653 NE(2d) 732 (1994).

[149]Sparer v Evergreen Local School, No. 94FU000003, 1994 WL 602940 (6th Dist Ct App, Fulton, 11-4-94).

[150]Smithers v Rossford Exempted Village School Dist Bd of Ed, No. 93WD070, 1994 WL 262542 (6th Dist App Ct, Wood, 6-10-94).

[151]RC 3319.11(G). A court of appeals has concluded that a board's technical failure to meet the ten-day deadline is not in and of itself fatal; applying the harmless error doctrine, the court, noting the teacher was present when the board's decision was announced in public session within the deadline, found a teacher bent on this procedural challenge must demonstrate prejudice. Rickel v Cloverleaf Local School Dist Bd of Ed, 79 App(3d) 810, 608 NE(2d) 767 (Medina 1992).

[152]RC 3319.11(G)(7). The failure of a board to comply with the requirements of RC 3319.111(B) inherently constitutes a failure to comply with RC 3319.111(A) and triggers the judicial right to reverse the board's nonrenewal decision. Farmer v Kelleys Island Bd of Ed, 69 OS(3d) 156, 630 NE(2d) 721 (1994), clarified on other grounds by 70 OS(3d) 1203, 638 NE(2d) 79 (1994). If the board is ordered to reemploy, the teacher is entitled to back pay. *Id.* One court has held that the thirty-day time period for filing

appeal is governed by the procedural provisions of RC Chapter 2506.[153]

9.14 Supplemental contracts

(A) In general

Boards of education are authorized to enter into supplemental contracts with respect to duties in addition to regular teaching duties. Supplemental contracts must state the additional duties and the compensation for such duties. They are, by statutory definition,[154] limited contracts.

While a board has discretion in deciding whether to award supplemental contracts, once compensation for duties performed in addition to regular teaching duties is authorized, issuance of a supplemental contract is required by RC 3319.08.[155] Moreover, arbitrarily issuing supplemental contracts to some teachers who perform additional duties while not awarding contracts to others who also perform additional duties is an abuse of discretion.[156]

It is not necessary that the supplemental contract be a separate document. Thus, separate compensation for extended service constitutes a supplemental contract if such a provision appears as part of the regular teaching contract.[157] The extended time provision is a limited contract, notwithstanding that the teacher is employed under a continuing contract.[158]

Failure to execute a written agreement does not void the contract. Thus, where a board adopts a policy of supplemental compensation for teachers who complete graduate courses in their fields of certification and a teacher accepts employment under that policy and complies with its terms, it is unnecessary for the contract to be in writing.[159] Obviously, written supplemental contracts are preferable.

Absent a specified term, the supplemental contract has the same duration as the underlying regular teaching contract.[160] If the underlying contract is a continuing contract, the supplemental contract, unless otherwise specified, has a duration of five years.[161]

(B) Reemployment under supplemental contract

RC 3319.11(I), enacted as part of 1988 House Bill 330, states, "The provisions of this section [i.e., RC 3319.11] shall not apply to any supplemental written contracts

---

an appeal did not commence where the notice of the board's intention to nonrenew did not comply with the requirements of RC 3319.11. Hunt v Westlake City School Dist, 100 App(3d) 233, 653 NE(2d) 732 (1994).

[153]Kiel v Green Local School Dist Bd of Ed, 69 OS(3d) 149, 630 NE(2d) 716 (1994).

[154]RC 3319.08. Because supplemental contracts are not merely assignments of additional duties to employed teachers, if a teacher is not nominated by the superintendent for a supplemental contract, the board can grant the contract only upon a vote of three-fourths of its full membership. Mason v Conneaut Area City School Dist Bd of Ed, No. 93-A-1842, 1994 WL 590282 (11th Dist Ct App, Ashtabula, 8-19-94).

[155]Wolf v Cuyahoga Falls City School Dist Bd of Ed, 52 OS(3d) 222, 556 NE(2d) 511 (1990).

[156]Wolf v Cuyahoga Falls City School Dist Bd of Ed, 52 OS(3d) 222, 556 NE(2d) 511 (1990). The Court distinguished Ballard v Goshen Local School Dist Bd of Ed, 13 App(3d) 439, 13 OBR 528, 469 NE(2d) 951 (Clermont 1984), where the board's collective bargaining agreement with the teachers' union appeared to incorporate the board's policy of requiring teachers to perform extra duties without compensation. In that case, issuance of supplemental contracts was not mandatory.

[157]Hamilton Local Teachers Assn v Hamilton Local Bd of Ed, No. 83AP-32, 1983 WL 3651 (10th Dist Ct App, Franklin, 8-16-83); Beifuss v Westerville Bd of Ed, No. 83AP-775, 1984 WL 6036 (10th Dist Ct App, Franklin, 12-18-84); Guchemand v Carrollton Exempted Village School Dist Bd of Ed, No. 479, 1985 WL 10412 (7th Dist Ct App, Carroll, 4-11-85).

[158]Beifuss v Westerville Bd of Ed, No. 83AP-775, 1984 WL 6036 (10th Dist Ct App, Franklin 12-18-84).

[159]OAG 74-083.

[160]Swaykus v East Holmes Local School Dist Bd of Ed, No. CA-338, 1983 WL 6368 (5th Dist Ct App, Holmes, 2-7-83); Hamilton Local Teachers Assn v Hamilton Local Bd of Ed, No. 83AP-32, 1983 WL 3651 (10th Dist Ct App, Franklin, 8-16-83); Beifuss v Westerville Bd of Ed, No. 83AP-775, 1984 WL 6036 (10th Dist Ct App, Franklin, 12-18-84); Buckles v Granville Exempted Village School Dist Bd of Ed, No. CA-3358, 1988 WL 82144 (5th Dist Ct App, Licking, 7-27-88); Hara v Montgomery County Joint Vocational School Dist, Nos. 13636, 13937, 1994 WL 603196 (2d Dist Ct App, Montgomery, 11-4-94).

[161]Swaykus v East Holmes Local School Dist Bd of Ed, No. CA-338, 1983 WL 6368 (5th Dist Ct App, Holmes, 2-7-83); Beifuss v Westerville Bd of Ed, No. 83AP-775, 1984 WL 6036 (10th Dist Ct App, Franklin, 12-18-84); Buckles v Granville Exempted Village School Dist Bd of Ed, No. CA-3358, 1988 WL 82144 (5th Dist Ct App, Licking, 7-27-88).

entered into pursuant to section 3319.08 of the Revised Code."

On its face, this provision supports the following propositions: (1) a supplemental contract employee who is not reemployed upon expiration of the contract is *not* entitled, on request, to a written statement of circumstances and hearing pursuant to RC 3319.11(G); (2) a board decision not to reemploy is *not* conditioned on evaluation of the employee in accordance with RC 3319.111(A); and (3) in a departure from prior case law,[162] a board decision not to reemploy does *not* require service of written notice of nonrenewal on or before April 30 of the year in which the supplemental contract expires.

While the statute seems clear on these points, there are, to date, no confirming cases. As to whether a supplemental contract employee must be evaluated under RC 3319.111, the issue is arguably muddied somewhat by RC 3319.111(C), which explicitly excludes administrators and certain substitute teachers, but does not mention supplemental contracts. On the other hand, under the first sentence of RC 3319.111(A), the statute's evaluation procedures are mandatory only as to those teachers with whom the board has limited or extended limited contracts entered into "pursuant to section 3319.11 of the Revised Code," whereas RC 3319.11(I) expressly refers to supplemental contracts executed "pursuant to section 3319.08 of the Revised Code." The implication is that, for evaluation purposes, supplemental contracts are totally divorced from regular limited teaching contracts. Given the explicit exclusionary language of RC 3319.11(I) and both the structure and underlying purpose of RC 3319.111, any notion that supplemental contracts are subject to the evaluation requirements of RC 3319.111 does violence to normal principles of statutory construction.

As to whether a board of education is still obligated to give timely written notice of nonrenewal with respect to a supplemental contract the board chooses not to renew, again the statutory language rationally lends itself to but one conclusion: such notice is no longer required. At least until cases address the point, however, many boards—in an abundance of caution or simply as a matter of managerial policy—are likely to continue the practice of giving written notice on or before April 30.[163]

Two courts have held that a board cannot cancel or reduce a multi-year supplemental contract during the term of the agreement.[164] Another court has held that the extended service portion of a continuing contract could be reduced from one school year to the next.[165]

(C) Athletics

Supplemental contracts are commonly used for coaches and trainers. A certificated employee must meet the qualifications to direct, supervise, or coach a pupil activity program set forth in OAC 3301-27-01(B). Although the attorney general has ruled that the state board of education does not have authority to *certify* athletic trainers pursuant to RC 3319.22, the department of education has promulgated OAC 3301-27-02, which establishes minimum qualifications for certificated and noncertificated persons employed as athletic trainers.[166] The regulation requires satisfactory completion of 800 clock hours of supervised clinical experience, possession of a valid instructor's certificate in first aid and cardiopulmonary resuscitation, and satisfactory completion of specified college

---

[162]Tate v Westerville Bd of Ed, 4 OS(3d) 206, 4 OBR 524, 448 NE(2d) 144 (1983).

[163]The statutory issue was raised but skirted in Holthaus v Cincinnati Bd of Ed, 76 App(3d) 443, 602 NE(2d) 360 (Hamilton 1991), where the court upheld a provision in a collective bargaining agreement that provided for the automatic nonrenewal of supplemental contracts without notice. See Text 18.20, Supremacy of contract over certain laws. In Hara v Montgomery County Joint Vocational School Dist, Nos. 13636, 13937, 1994 WL 603196 (2d Dist Ct App, Montgomery, 11-4-94), the court applied RC 3319.11 to supplemental contracts, holding that the supplemental contract was automatically renewed for a term of one year. That case, however, addressed issues that arose prior to July 1, 1989, the effective date of 1988 H 330.

[164]Hamilton Local Teachers Assn v Hamilton Local Bd of Ed, No. 79CV-04-1989 (CP, Franklin, 6-26-79); Beifuss v Westerville Bd of Ed, No. 83AP-775, 1984 WL 6036 (10th Dist Ct App, Franklin, 12-18-84).

[165]Guchemand v Carrollton Exempted Village School Dist Bd of Ed, No. 479, 1985 WL 10412 (7th Dist Ct App, Carroll, 4-11-85).

[166]OAG 80-053.

and university course work in related subjects.

9.15 Substitute teacher contracts

(A) In general

A teacher may be employed as a substitute under a written, limited contract for a term not exceeding one year, to be assigned as needed.[167] Where the board adopted a resolution recording the names of substitute teachers and their compensation, and the teachers accepted employment, a contract was in force even though the parties failed to execute a written agreement.[168]

(B) Compensation, fringe benefits

Employment as a substitute does not, in itself, entitle the teacher to compensation under the regular teachers' salary schedule. Where a substitute is not assigned to one specific position, and has not completed sixty days of service, the board may establish different compensation from that provided in the schedule.[169]

If, however, the substitute is assigned to one specific teaching position and serves for sixty days, he becomes entitled to the minimum salary on the current salary schedule, plus sick leave, visiting days, and other local privileges.[170] Whether the salary to which such a substitute is entitled is the minimum base salary on the entire teachers' salary schedule irrespective of the substitute's educational credentials and prior years of teaching experience or the minimum salary to which the substitute would be entitled if given credit for such credentials and experience is not clear. In a 2-1 decision, an appeals court has held that credit must be given on the salary schedule for education and experience in determining the minimum salary due.[171] When the assignment to a specific position is terminated after sixty days, the teacher reverts to casual substitute status and is paid accordingly.

When a retired teacher is hired as a substitute, he may not be paid more than other substitutes.[172]

(C) Nonrenewal, reemployment, conversion to regular contract

Substitute teachers employed day-to-day or on a casual basis are not entitled to the written notice of nonrenewal normally required to end limited contracts.[173] Accordingly, renewal of a substitute's contract is not automatic but requires affirmative board action. The key words are day-to-day or casual. The Ohio Supreme Court has held that long-term substitutes—those employed for clearly defined periods to replace specific individuals and compensated according to the regular teachers' pay schedule—are entitled to notice of nonrenewal.[174]

When a teacher is employed as a substitute for 120 days or more during the school year, and is reemployed for or assigned to a specific teaching position for the coming year and meets all the local educational requirements for the position, he must be given a contract as a regular teacher.[175] Affirmative action by the board is required for a substitute teacher to receive regular employment. If the board does not nonrenew, the teacher is entitled only to renewal of his substitute teaching contract.[176]

(D) Tenure

Although days spent teaching as a substitute may count for purposes of salary schedule placement,[177] it has been held that they do not count as service toward eligibility for tenure.[178]

---

[167] RC 3319.10; OAG 70-042.

[168] OAG 70-042; OAG 70-129.

[169] OAG 70-042.

[170] RC 3319.10.

[171] Malina v Springfield City School Dist Bd of Ed, No. CA 2347, 1988 WL 2434 (2d Dist Ct App, Clark, 1-6-88).

[172] RC 3307.381(A).

[173] RC 3319.10. See Text 9.11, Notice of nonrenewal, timeliness, form.

[174] State ex rel Dennis v Hillsdale Local School Dist Bd of Ed, 28 OS(3d) 263, 28 OBR 341, 503 NE(2d) 748 (1986).

[175] RC 3319.10.

[176] State ex rel Dennis v Hillsdale Local School Dist Bd of Ed, 28 OS(3d) 263, 28 OBR 341, 503 NE(2d) 748 (1986). See also State ex rel Dennis v Hillsdale Local School Dist Bd of Ed, 39 OS(3d) 158, 529 NE(2d) 1248 (1988).

[177] Crawford v Barberton City Schools Bd of Ed, 6 OS(3d) 324, 6 OBR 382, 453 NE(2d) 627 (1983).

[178] State ex rel Gron v Euclid City School Dist Bd of Ed, No. 46594, 1983 WL 2683 (8th Dist Ct App, Cuyahoga, 10-20-83). See also Text 9.08(D), Service as substitute teacher.

(E) Regular teacher acting as substitute

It is sometimes expedient to have regular teachers fill in for teachers who are absent. When a regular teacher acts as a substitute in addition to his other duties, he is entitled to a supplemental contract and additional compensation, unless his base contract, board policy, or a collective bargaining agreement provides that his regular duties include possible assignments as a substitute.[179]

9.16 Exchange teachers

Under RC 3313.84, boards of education may participate in an exchange teacher program to provide for the interchange of ideas on educational methods and to promote international understanding and good will. To this end, a board may contract with other boards of education or other educational authorities, in Ohio or in other states or foreign countries, to exchange teaching services. Under such contracts, a board may send teachers to serve in other districts, in exchange for similar services from the other districts. Exchange teachers may be continued on the payroll under contract, the same as if they were working in their regular district. In taking part in any exchange program, the statute does not authorize the board to spend money except in payment of salaries.

SUSPENSION AND TERMINATION OF CONTRACTS

9.17 Resignation

A teacher's resignation, if made in accordance with statutory requirements, terminates a contract. No teacher may terminate his contract after July 10 of any school year or during the school year, before the annual session is over, without the consent of the board. However, a teacher who has either a limited or continuing contract may resign up to and including the July 10 preceding that school year by giving five days' written notice to the board.[180]

A teacher may resign at other times, and the resignation is effective if and when accepted by the board. A tender of resignation may be withdrawn at any time before its effective date if the employer has not accepted it. Acceptance occurs when the employer initiates affirmative action, preferably in writing, that clearly indicates to the employee that the tender is accepted.[181] Moreover, if the employer takes action in reliance on a tendered resignation—by hiring a replacement, for example—the withdrawal may well be ineffective even if attempted prior to board acceptance.[182] Further, if the teacher effectively abandons his teaching position—by, for example, accepting other employment—his subsequent attempts to withdraw a resignation may fail.[183]

What purports to be a resignation may be judicially viewed as a constructive discharge when the employer makes working conditions so intolerable that the employee is forced into what is in reality an involuntary resignation.[184]

When a teacher resigns, the employer sometimes agrees not to disclose the circumstances that led to the resignation. An appeals court held such a separation agreement was void as against public policy to

---

[179]OAG 69-025.

[180]RC 3319.15.

[181]See Davis v Marion County Engineer, 60 OS(3d) 53, 573 NE(2d) 51 (1991). Where the employee's resignation is accepted by vote at a public meeting, it is not necessary for the act of acceptance to be communicated to the employee before it is effective. Davidson v Hanging Rock, 97 App(3d) 723, 647 NE(2d) 527 (Lawrence 1994), dismissed, appeal not allowed 71 OS(3d) 1476, 645 NE(2d) 1256 (1995).

[182]See State ex rel Mullen v Fayetteville-Perry Local School Dist Bd of Ed, 53 App(3d) 59, 557 NE(2d) 1235 (Brown 1988).

[183]See State ex rel Mullen v Fayetteville-Perry Local School Dist Bd of Ed, 53 App(3d) 59, 557 NE(2d) 1235 (Brown 1988).

[184]See Riddle v Newton Falls Exempted Village Bd of Ed, No. 4004, 1988 WL 105556 (11th Dist Ct App, Trumbull, 10-7-88). A teacher's attempt to have her resignation disregarded as involuntary failed in Starlin v Morgan Local School Dist Bd of Ed, No. CA-93-10, 1994 WL 395859 (5th Dist Ct App, Morgan, 7-13-94).

the extent it precluded disclosure of the teacher's propensity toward pedophilia.[185]

9.18 Retirement

A teacher's contract is terminated when the teacher elects to retire. Termination occurs when a board accepts a teacher's unqualified letter of intention to retire even if the letter is subsequently withdrawn. In this situation, RC 3319.16 has no application.[186] Mandatory retirement because of age is unlawful.[187]

9.19 Layoff

(A) Reduction in force

RC 3319.17 provides that any board of education may reasonably reduce its teaching staff by reason of the return to duty of regular teachers after leaves of absence, the suspension of schools, or territorial changes affecting the district when the board decides such a reduction is necessary. In all but county school districts, decreased enrollment of pupils in the district is expressly an additional ground for reducing teaching staff. Where a county district is involved, such a reduction may be made based upon (1) where a particular service is provided directly to pupils under one or more interdistrict contracts requiring the service, a reduction in the total number of pupils the county board is required to provide with the service under all interdistrict contracts as a result of the termination or nonrenewal of one or more of these contracts, or (2) where a particular service is not provided directly to pupils under one or more interdistrict contracts requiring the service, a reduction in the total level of the service the county board is required to provide under all interdistrict contracts as a result of the termination or nonrenewal of one or more of these contracts. In all cases, what constitutes a reasonable reduction is left to the judgment of the board.[188]

In certain situations RC 3319.17 may not be applicable. For example, the Ohio Supreme Court has ruled that a board acted properly where it eliminated a course offering and then dismissed two continuing contract teachers who were not certified to teach any course other than the cancelled course.[189] The Court reasoned that the employment of a continuing contract teacher is subject to state certification requirements, and neither RC 3319.17 nor RC 3319.16 (pertaining to termination of teachers for misconduct) was involved. Further, RC 3319.17 does not apply to the transfer or reassignment of a teacher from one teaching area to another in order to reduce teachers in an area due to decreased enrollment in that area.[190] On the other hand, a board may not use RC 3319.17 to reduce a full-time teacher to part-time status, since an actual reduction in the number of teachers is required.[191]

The statutory ground of decreased pupil enrollment has proved troublesome in application. Emphasizing that the Teachers' Tenure Act (of which RC 3319.17 is a part) is to be liberally construed in favor of teachers and "narrowly against boards of education," the Ohio Supreme Court, by a 4-3 margin, has held that teachers' contracts cannot be suspended on the basis of a long-term decline in enrollment unless

---

[185]Bowman v Parma Bd of Ed, 44 App(3d) 169, 542 NE(2d) 663 (Cuyahoga 1988).

[186]King v Norwood School Dist Bd of Ed, No. C-860247, 1987 WL 10037 (1st Dist Ct App, Hamilton, 4-22-87).

[187]See Text 11.18(B), Mandatory retirement.

[188]1962 OAG 2935.

[189]State ex rel Cutler v Pike County Joint Area Vocational School Dist, 6 OS(3d) 138, 6 OBR 195, 451 NE(2d) 800 (1983). See also Merry v Perry Local School Dist Bd of Ed, Nos. 7732, 7733, 1989 WL 82234 (5th Dist Ct App, Stark, 7-10-89) (no duty to continue employment when subject teachers certified to teach no longer offered; moreover, collective bargaining agreement's evaluation procedure inapplicable since it applies only to nonrenewals for poor job performance); Antram v Jonathan Alder Local School Dist Bd of Ed, No. CA-92-08-021, 1993 WL 38096 (12th Dist Ct App, Madison, 2-16-93) (upholding termination of teacher's contract under RC 3319.16 where teacher failed to acquire required certificate). But see Boehm v Rolling Hills Local School Dist Bd of Ed, Nos. 93-CA-19, 93-CA-20, 1994 WL 202193 (5th Dist Ct App, Guernsey, 5-5-94) (distinguishing *Cutler* on the basis that the teacher there did not possess a certificate for any offered course and holding that termination of teachers as part of cost reduction effort implicated RC 3319.16).

[190]Bohmann v West Clermont Local School Dist Bd of Ed, 2 OS(3d) 136, 2 OBR 683, 443 NE(2d) 176 (1983).

[191]Millhoff v Manchester Local School Dist Bd of Ed, No. 11941, 1985 WL 11071 (9th Dist Ct App, Summit, 8-28-85).

"an actual and current decline in enrollment is shown to exist at the time of the reduction in the number of teachers."[192] Thus, notwithstanding a significant decline over a ten-year period, the suspension of a teacher's contract was overturned because there was no actual decline during the year of contract suspension. Ironically, the majority's holding effectively encourages boards of education to suspend contracts *sooner* than they otherwise might: because enrollment must still be declining during the year of suspension, boards can no longer wait until the student population has stabilized before making decisions on the appropriate level of staffing.[193]

The majority's opinion also states that RC 3319.17 cannot be applied to a decline in enrollment attributable to a board's own decision to consolidate or eliminate particular course offerings. Plainly, this area calls for extreme caution.

(B) Continuing contracts, seniority

In making a reduction in force, the board must suspend contracts in accordance with the recommendation of the superintendent. Within "each teaching field affected," the superintendent must give preference first to teachers on continuing contracts and next to limited contract teachers who have greater seniority.[194] "Seniority" means length of continuous service in the district.[195] A teacher on a continuing contract has a preference over a teacher on a limited contract with greater seniority.[196] Under RC 3319.17, the "teaching field affected" is determined with reference to fields of certification, as designated on the certificates of the teacher involved and is not limited to the teacher's current area of assignment.[197] However, a reduction in force provision in a collective bargaining agreement that limits teaching fields to the teacher's current area of assignment is permissible since, pursuant to RC 4117.10(A), it supersedes RC 3319.17.[198]

(C) Reduction by nonrenewal

Several courts have ruled that a board may reduce staff by nonrenewal under RC 3319.11 even if the underlying reasons are enumerated in RC 3319.17. Thus, a board may suspend and nonrenew contracts in combination to achieve a needed reduction.[199] However, when the collective bar-

---

[192]Phillips v South Range Local School Dist Bd of Ed, 45 OS(3d) 66, 543 NE(2d) 492 (1989).

[193]Significantly, *Phillips*'s construction of RC 3319.17 does *not* apply in interpreting the layoff provisions of a collective bargaining agreement. Declaring that "provisions in a collective bargaining agreement arrived at mutually should not be narrowly construed against either party," and that the contracting parties "will be assumed to stand on equal footing with one another unless otherwise provided for in the agreement," the Ohio Supreme Court, by a 4-3 margin, upheld a reduction in force that plainly would not have withstood *Phillips*'s analysis in Cuyahoga Falls Ed Assn v Cuyahoga Falls City School Dist Bd of Ed, 61 OS(3d) 193, 574 NE(2d) 442 (1991). However, a teacher not made a party to the appeal in *Cuyahoga Falls* was held to be entitled to reinstatement. Cuyahoga Falls Ed Assn v Cuyahoga Falls City School Dist Bd of Ed, 71 OS(3d) 171, 642 NE (2d) 1085 (1994).

[194]RC 3319.17. In the case of a county school district, these preferences apply "within each teaching field or service area affected."

[195]1962 OAG 2935.

[196]State ex rel Reams v Maplewood Local School Dist Bd of Ed, No. 3305, 1984 WL 7381 (11th Dist Ct App, Trumbull, 6-15-84). An unusual twist appears in Blubaugh v Jefferson County Joint Vocational School Dist Bd of Ed, No. 88-J-9, 1989 WL 71093 (7th Dist Ct App, Jefferson, 6-26-89). The board, because of a decline in pupil enrollment, suspended a limited contract social studies teacher who had greater seniority than a continuing contract social studies teacher. The suspended teacher was then given a part-time contract for the following school year during which he became qualified for and was awarded a continuing contract. The board subsequently suspended the continuing contract of the teacher who was initially spared in favor of the more senior teacher who now also had continuing contract status. Thus, for the next school year, the roles were reversed: the teacher whose contract was initially suspended was now employed full-time, while the teacher initially spared was suspended and then recalled to part-time work. The court found that suspension of the continuing contract did not violate RC 3319.17.

[197]Bitting v Cuyahoga Falls City School Dist Bd of Ed, No. 12042, 1985 WL 10877 (9th Dist Ct App, Summit, 10-9-85).

[198]Lilley v Cuyahoga Falls City School Dist Bd of Ed, No. 12489, 1986 WL 6346 (9th Dist Ct App, Summit, 6-4-86). See Text 18.20, Supremacy of contract over certain laws.

[199]Buchheit v Hamilton City Bd of Ed, 15 App(3d) 148, 15 OBR 240, 473 NE(2d) 61 (Butler 1984); Hamilton Classroom Teachers Assn v Hamilton City School Dist Bd of Ed, No. 82-03-0028, 1983 WL 4368 (12th Dist Ct App, Butler, 5-18-83); Strock v Barberton City School Dist Bd of Ed, No. 10516, 1982 WL 5035 (9th Dist Ct App, Summit, 6-2-82); Mans-

gaining agreement addresses layoff situations, the provisions of the agreement must be followed.

(D) Reduction by termination for cause

One court has held that a board may not reduce staff by terminating contracts pursuant to RC 3319.16, because a program to eliminate excess personnel does not constitute "other good and just cause" for termination under that statute.[200]

(E) Layoff procedure

Suspension of a contract under RC 3319.17 does not deprive a teacher of a constitutionally protected property interest, and a due process hearing is therefore not required.[201] Moreover, a suspended teacher has no statutory right to bump another teacher from another job.[202]

Where a board has negotiated a "reduction in force" procedure in a collective bargaining agreement, it has been held that the procedure pertains to reduction of teachers by suspension of contracts under RC 3319.17, absent contractual language to the contrary. Thus, a reduction which "occurs" because of voluntary retirement or resignation (attrition) does not constitute a "reduction in force" contemplated by RC 3319.17 or the contract. A reduction in force contemplates a "necessary" reduction, not simply the occurrence of a reduction.[203]

(F) Recall after layoff

Teachers whose continuing contracts are suspended have a right of restoration to continuing service status in order of seniority in the district if and when teaching positions become vacant or are created for which any of them are or become qualified.[204] A teacher is "qualified" for a position if he is certificated in that position.[205] Timing problems can arise because of the department of education's practice of issuing certificates with a backdated effective date. Construing a collective bargaining agreement, the Ohio Supreme Court has ruled the teacher must be deemed certificated as of the certificate's effective date, unless the contract specifically provides otherwise. In this case a certificate issued on October 30, 1984, stated it was valid from July 1, 1984.[206]

(G) Reducing teacher from full-time to part-time status

There is authority for the proposition that the partial suspension of a teacher's contract is unauthorized under RC 3319.17.[207] This is not to say a partial reduction of a contract cannot effectively be achieved, however. The safest way to proceed is fully to suspend the contract (thus effecting an actual reduction in the number of teachers), and then to recall the teacher to a part-time position.[208]

9.20 Disciplinary suspension

Although RC 3319.16 permits suspension of a teacher pending the outcome of proceedings to terminate his contract for cause, it is unsettled whether suspension can be used as a disciplinary measure in lieu of termination, at least in the absence of a collective bargaining agreement

---

field Ed Assn v Mansfield Bd of Ed, No. CA-1997, 1982 WL 2952 (5th Dist Ct App, Richland, 3-3-81); Hamilton Local Teachers Assn v Hamilton Local Bd of Ed, No. 79CV-04-1989 (CP, Franklin, 6-26-79). See also Bivens v West Clermont Local Bd of Ed, No. CA 871, 1981 WL 5175 (12th Dist Ct App, Clermont, 8-19-81).

[200]Tucker v Boardman Bd of Ed, No. 79 CA-150 (7th Dist Ct App, Mahoning, 12-9-80).

[201]Dorian v Euclid Bd of Ed, 62 OS(2d) 182, 404 NE(2d) 155 (1980); Lacy v Dayton Bd of Ed, 550 FSupp 835 (SD Ohio 1982).

[202]Novak v Muskingum County Area Joint Vocational School Dist Bd of Ed, No. CA-85-29, 1986 WL 3374 (5th Dist Ct App, Muskingum, 3-14-86).

[203]Stow Teachers Assn v Stow Bd of Ed, 2 App(3d) 82, 2 OBR 91, 440 NE(2d) 827 (Summit 1981); Mogadore Ed Assn v Mogadore Local School Dist Bd of Ed, No. 80-8-2227 (CP, Summit, 2-22-82).

[204]RC 3319.17. In many cases, a collective bargaining agreement will go beyond the statute and accord recall rights in some form even to limited contract teachers who have been laid off.

[205]Thus, construing a collective bargaining agreement patterned after the statute, an appeals court concluded a board had no obligation to offer a vacant position to a laid off teacher not certified for the position. Cuyahoga Falls Ed Assn v Cuyahoga Falls City School Dist Bd of Ed, No. 14035, 1989 WL 111805 (9th Dist Ct App, Summit, 9-27-89).

[206]Whitley v Canton City School Dist Bd of Ed, 38 OS(3d) 300, 528 NE(2d) 167 (1988).

[207]Millhoff v Manchester Local School Dist Bd of Ed, No. 11941, 1985 WL 11071 (9th Dist Ct App, Summit, 8-28-85) (invalidating partial suspension of 32% of teacher's contract).

[208]State ex rel Van Dorn v Mt. Gilead Exempted Village School Dist Bd of Ed, 78 App(3d) 238, 604

allowing it. An appeals court has held that RC 3319.16 provides only for suspension during the pendency of termination procedures.[209] A federal district court, however, has held that a disciplinary suspension without instigation of termination proceedings is permissible.[210]

That issue disappears if a collective bargaining agreement permits disciplinary suspensions since RC 4117.08 and RC 4117.10(A) permit such agreements.

9.21 Termination for cause, in general

RC 3319.16 empowers a board of education to terminate a teacher's contract at any time for cause, regardless of whether the contract is continuing, limited, or extended limited.[211] The same statute applies by reference to administrators' contracts.[212]

The statute defines cause to include gross inefficiency, immorality, willful and persistent violations of reasonable board regulations, or "other good and just cause." In addition, the statute expressly states that the commission of sexual battery in violation of RC 2907.03(A)(7) is grounds for termination of a teacher's contract.[213] RC 3319.151 states that revealing to a student any specific question known to be part of a statewide student proficiency test, or otherwise assisting a student to cheat on such a test, is also grounds for termination under RC 3319.16. Additional or different causes for termination may be negotiated in a collective bargaining agreement,[214] but in the absence of such an agreement, termination must be for one of the statutory reasons.

The statutory reasons provide only broad, nonspecific guidelines. Reference to the numerous cases interpreting the statute is necessary for illumination on those acts or omissions which have been sufficient (or insufficient) to support termination for cause. The cases do not, however, provide any ironclad guarantee that terminations based on similar acts or omissions will be upheld in the future. Teacher and administrator terminations are decided case by case. Decisions often turn on the reliability of the evidence that specific conduct occurred, rather than on the nature of the conduct itself. Moreover, termination cases often involve multiple derelictions rather than a single act or omission, and in such cases the decisions typically do not indicate whether any one dereliction by itself would justify termination.

(A) Gross inefficiency

Termination for gross inefficiency under RC 3319.16 requires proof of serious deficiencies and teaching performance far below that normally and reasonably expected in the district.[215] Gross inefficiency "does not consist of a separate act, but embraces a course of conduct, a lack of integrity, or limitation of capacity."[216] In the context of a superintendent's contract, it has been held that the inefficiency must be flagrant, extreme, and complete.[217]

Gross inefficiency can include a teacher's inability to maintain classroom

---

NE(2d) 239 (Morrow 1992) (upholding board's action even when part-time contract offered at same meeting as action to suspend); Ott v Buckeye Local School Dist Bd of Ed, No. 1494, 1986 WL 9353 (9th Dist Ct App, Medina, 8-27-86). See also Blubaugh v Jefferson County Joint Vocational School Dist Bd of Ed, No. 88-J-9, 1989 WL 71093 (7th Dist Ct App, Jefferson, 6-26-89); Demos v Worthington City School Dist Bd of Ed, No. 85AP-454, 1985 WL 4152 (10th Dist Ct App, Franklin, 12-3-85).

[209]Stewart v Margaretta Local Bd of Ed, No. E-81-35, 1981 WL 5839 (6th Dist Ct App, Erie, 11-27-81).

[210]Rowland v Mad River Local School Dist, No. C-3-75-4 (SD Ohio, 6-25-78). In Deal v Vandalia Butler City Schools Bd of Ed, No. 12302, 1991 WL 116644 (2d Dist Ct App, Montgomery, 6-28-91), the court expressly declined to address this issue but did find the district superintendent had authority to suspend under both the terms of a collective bargaining agreement and RC 3319.01. The latter point strikes some observers as dubious.

[211]The transfer or reassignment of a teacher is generally not regarded as a termination and does not implicate the statute. See Text 8.02(C), Substitute teachers, educational aides.

[212]RC 3319.01, RC 3319.02.

[213]See also Text 24.13, Sex offenses in general.

[214]RC 4117.08, RC 4117.10(A).

[215]Giering v Parma Bd of Ed, No. 38399 (8th Dist Ct App, Cuyahoga, 4-16-79).

[216]Huelskamp v Trotwood-Madison City School Dist Bd of Ed, No. 83-2635, at 3 (CP, Montgomery, 9-18-84), affirmed by No. 9085, 1985 WL 8730 (2d Dist Ct App, Montgomery, 6-19-85).

[217]Rumora v Ashtabula Area City School Dist Bd of Ed, 43 Misc 48, 335 NE(2d) 378 (CP, Ashtabula 1973).

discipline.[218] Termination also is proper when a teacher is reassigned to a different grade level and is unable to perform adequately in the new assignment.[219] It may also include insubordination and lack of cooperation toward the superintendent and board.[220] In addition, a teacher's inconsistent and arbitrary grading system, inaccurate attendance records, inability to follow proper disciplinary procedures, consistent tardiness at staff meetings, and occasional failure to perform nonteaching supervisory duties were grounds for termination where several remedial suggestions were made beforehand.[221] Gross inefficiency was also found when a teacher had physically abused a student, disregarded several directions from the building principal as well as board policy, failed to improve problems in recording grades, and failed to maintain adequate, regular lesson plans.[222] Taking an unauthorized leave of absence or failing to work after a requested leave has been refused may also justify termination.[223]

Where a teacher on continuing contract is charged with "gross inefficiency," it is proper to consider evidence of conduct that occurred prior to granting the contract. However, such evidence may not be the sole ground for termination. Its purpose is to show a continuing pattern.[224] Similarly, a prior adjudication does not preclude termination for gross inefficiency where the district seeks to dismiss a teacher on the basis of inefficiency which existed prior to a contract awarded as a matter of law.[225]

Although formal evaluations of job performance are often useful in establishing gross inefficiency, there is no requirement of written evaluations before termination of a teacher's contract on this ground.[226]

(B) Immorality

Termination for immorality requires a showing that the conduct involved adversely affects fitness to teach. The nexus between the immoral conduct and the person's suitability to teach is for the referee or board to determine.[227] It has been stated that sufficient grounds do not exist if the conduct is a private act which does not impact the teacher's professional duties.[228] Termination for immorality was inappropriate where there was no evidence of immoral conduct on the part of a teacher

---

[218]Baker v Twin Valley Community Local School Dist Bd of Ed, No. CA89-05-008, 1989 WL 139467 (12th Dist Ct App, Preble, 11-20-89); Medley v Springfield Local Schools Bd of Ed, No. L-84-317, 1985 WL 7088 (6th Dist Ct App, Lucas, 4-5-85); Goldsmith v Elida City Local Bd of Ed, No. 1-80-35, 1981 WL 6776 (3d Dist Ct App, Allen, 1-28-81); Clements v Mad River Twp Bd of Ed, No. 7712, 1982 WL 3775 (2d Dist Ct App, Montgomery, 8-16-82); Giering v Parma Bd of Ed, No. 38399 (8th Dist Ct App, Cuyahoga, 4-16-79).

[219]Medley v Springfield Local Schools Bd of Ed, No. L-84-317, 1985 WL 7088 (6th Dist Ct App, Lucas, 4-5-85); Huelskamp v Trotwood-Madison City School Dist Bd of Ed, No. 9085, 1985 WL 8730 (2d Dist Ct App, Montgomery, 6-19-85).

[220]Spirtos v Struthers City School Dist Bd of Ed, No. 78 CA 34 (7th Dist Ct App, Mahoning, 1979); Myers v Waverly City School Dist Bd of Ed, No. 380, 1985 WL 9388 (4th Dist Ct App, Pike, 7-12-85).

[221]Huelskamp v Trotwood-Madison City School Dist Bd of Ed, No. 9085, 1985 WL 8730 (2d Dist Ct App, Montgomery, 6-19-85). See also Wolford v Newark City School Dist Bd of Ed, No. 92-CA-5, 1992 WL 238436 (5th Dist Ct App, Licking, 9-8-92) (finding gross inefficiency where evidence showed teacher's failure to maintain discipline, failure effectively to communicate with students, failure to take recommended actions to improve job performance, failure to record student attendance, failure to prepare lesson plans, arbitrary grading, and failure to use effective testing methods).

[222]Aldridge v Huntington Local School Dist Bd of Ed, No. 84-CI-683 (CP, Ross 1965).

[223]Wetzel v Elyria City School Dist Bd of Ed, No. C74-682 (ND Ohio, 11-27-84); Thompson v West Clermont Local Bd of Ed, No. CA-967, 1981 WL 5235 (12th Dist Ct App, Clermont, 10-28-81).

[224]Powell v Young, 148 OS 342, 74 NE(2d) 261 (1947); Goldsmith v Elida City Local Bd of Ed, No. 1-80-35, 1981 WL 6776 (3d Dist Ct App, Allen, 1-28-81).

[225]Sylvania Ed Assn v Sylvania City Schools, 44 App(3d) 140, 541 NE(2d) 1060 (Lucas 1988).

[226]Baker v Twin Valley Community Local School Dist Bd of Ed, No. CA89-05-008, 1989 WL 139467 (12th Dist Ct App, Preble, 11-20-89). Note, however, that written evaluations are mandatory under RC 3319.111 prior to the *nonrenewal* of a teacher's limited or extended limited contract. See Text 9.13(A), Mandatory evaluation procedures.

[227]Duncan v Greenhills-Forest Park City School Dist Bd of Ed, No. C-840182, 1985 WL 9287 (1st Dist Ct App, Hamilton, 1-31-85) (upholding termination of tenured teacher convicted of crime of public indecency).

[228]Wells v Madison Local School Dist Bd of Ed, No. CA84-10-116, 1985 WL 7682 (12th Dist Ct App, Butler, 7-15-85).

arrested for public indecency apart from that involved in a "no contest" plea to the reduced charge of disorderly conduct.[229]

Homosexual contact with a student has been determined to constitute immorality justifying termination.[230] A teacher's improper and unconsented physical contact with students constituted immorality,[231] as did conducting a love affair with a student replete with sexually explicit love letters.[232] Similarly, a music teacher's sexual relationship with two of his students, twin daughters of the teacher's social friends, was immorality justifying termination.[233] Conviction of the third degree misdemeanor of illegal restraint, where the surrounding circumstances suggested that a school psychologist made sexual advances toward a teen-age boy, also justified termination.[234]

"Immorality" is not limited to sexual immorality. Termination for immorality was upheld, for example, where a wrestling coach ordered one student to weigh in for another before a tournament,[235] and where a teacher falsified sick leave applications and otherwise lied about his absence from school.[236]

(C) Willful and persistent violations of board regulations

This statutory ground has received little attention in the courts. Termination of a teacher (with twenty-three years of otherwise satisfactory service) for intentional failure on two occasions to evacuate his classroom promptly in accordance with the board of education's fire drill regulation has been upheld,[237] as has termination for repeated failures for personal gain to follow work order procedures.[238]

Repeated violations of administrative rules and regulations regarding day-to-day work activities has been held to justify termination even though such rules and regulations were not formally adopted by the board of education.[239]

(D) "Other good and just cause"

Predictably, the vagueness of this standard has spawned a mixed bag of cases. Often, conduct considered "good and just cause" for termination might as well have been the subject of other, more specific charges. For example, criminal conduct might be considered immoral in addition to being just cause for firing the offender.[240]

Normally, to justify termination for "other good and just cause," the conduct must be flagrant or outrageous, or at least persistent. Thus, when a teacher left the scene of a traffic accident without stopping and leaving his name and address, such isolated conduct, together with some inefficient classroom conduct, did not constitute cause for termination.[241] Similarly, the use of an expletive and the wearing of a holster and toy gun in a skit are insufficient to terminate for "other good and just cause."[242]

---

[229]Shie v Hamilton City School Dist Bd of Ed, No. CA79-10-0098, 1981 WL 5259 (12th Dist Ct App, Butler, 11-25-81).

[230]Snyder v Miami East Local School Dist, No. 79-CA-59 (2d Dist Ct App, Miami, 7-3-80).

[231]Wells v Madison Local School Dist Bd of Ed, No. CA84-10-116, 1985 WL 7682 (12th Dist Ct App, Butler, 7-15-85).

[232]Sellers v Logan-Hocking City School Dist Bd of Ed, No. 91 CA 12, 1992 WL 37785 (4th Dist Ct App, Hocking, 2-24-92).

[233]Carothers v Tri-Valley Local School Dist Bd of Ed, No. CA-92-21, 1993 WL 95621 (5th Dist Ct App, Muskingum, 3-29-93). See also Cremeens v Gallia County Local School Dist Bd of Ed, No. 92 CA 12, 1993 WL 49468 (4th Dist Ct App, Gallia, 2-17-93).

[234]Ricchetti v Cleveland City School Dist Bd of Ed, No. 64833, 1994 WL 66227 (8th Dist Ct App, Cuyahoga, 3-3-94).

[235]Florian v Highland Local School Dist Bd of Ed, 24 App(3d) 41, 24 OBR 218, 493 NE(2d) 249 (Medina 1983).

[236]Swinderman v Dover City School Dist Bd of Ed, No. 91AP110092, 1992 WL 91655 (5th Dist Ct App, Tuscarawas, 4-20-92).

[237]Calhoun v Madison Bd of Ed, No. CA-2623, 1989 WL 28690 (5th Dist Ct App, Richland, 3-24-89).

[238]Spencer v Vantage Joint Vocational School Dist Bd of Ed, No. 90-8-80 (CP, Van Wert, 3-25-91).

[239]Wolford v Newark City School Dist Bd of Ed, No. 92-CA-5, 1992 WL 238436 (5th Dist Ct App, Licking, 9-8-92).

[240]Conversely, good and just cause obviously means more than what are specifically enumerated as grounds in the statute. It is both broader than and inclusive of the other enumerated grounds. See Greco v Roper, 145 OS 243, 61 NE(2d) 307 (1945).

[241]Hale v Lancaster Bd of Ed, 13 OS(2d) 92, 234 NE(2d) 583 (1968).

[242]Imm v Newbury Local School Dist Bd of Ed, No. 1308, 1986 WL 14335 (11th Dist Ct App, Geauga, 12-5-86).

The nature of criminal conduct, such as falsification of refund slips constituting grand theft, may of itself be sufficient to sustain a termination without showing a specific impact on the teacher's classroom performance.[243]

It was also proper to terminate a teacher convicted of drug-related offenses where students were directly involved.[244] Termination was also upheld when a teacher provided nonprescription diet pills to a student who had psychological problems with weight loss.[245]

Sexually suggestive conduct may warrant termination. Good and just cause was found when a teacher made sexually suggestive remarks to students of the opposite sex and engaged in unconsented rubbing, grabbing, and biting of students,[246] and when a teacher conducted a love affair with a student replete with sexually explicit love letters.[247]

A board may consider, as cause for termination, conduct of a teacher which amounts to condonation of her husband's flagrant violation of drug laws, which resulted in arrests, reports in the news media, and adverse public reaction.[248] A principal's attempts to question the key witness in an investigation against the principal's son for violation of liquor laws, his threats when she declined to discuss the incident upon advice of school counsel, and his subsequent attack on her credibility are relevant to proceedings to terminate the principal.[249]

Where, as part of a labor dispute, a teacher willfully refuses, over several days, to report and perform duties set forth in her contract of employment and ignores the board's order to return to work, there is good and just cause for termination.[250] Similarly, a teacher was properly terminated when he allowed students to violate school rules in taking standardized tests.[251]

A termination was upheld when a teacher requested an extension of a medical leave while simultaneously accepting employment in an out-of-state school district without disclosing such other employment.[252] A teacher's failure to obtain the certification required under his contract has also been deemed just cause for termination.[253]

Noting that RC 3319.141 contemplates a range of possible sanctions for falsifying a sick leave request, an appeals court has held a board of education must take into account a teacher's total past employment record prior to imposing a particular sanction. In this case, the court overturned a board's termination decision in favor of a disciplinary suspension recommended by a referee.[254]

(E) Constitutionally protected conduct

A teacher (or other school employee) may not be fired for public or private conduct protected by the First Amendment of the US Constitution. There can be no recrimination for exercising rights of free speech or the press, of peaceful assembly, or to petition for the redress of grievances.[255] Examples of protected conduct

---

[243]Espie v Columbus City School Dist, No. 79 AP-886 (10th Dist Ct App, Franklin, 6-12-80).

[244]Houck v Greenhills-Forest Park City School Dist Bd of Ed, No. C-800358, 1981 WL 9862 (1st Dist Ct App, Hamilton, 6-24-81).

[245]Wells v Madison Local School Dist Bd of Ed, No. CA84-10-116, 1985 WL 7682 (12th Dist Ct App, Butler, 7-15-85).

[246]York v New Richmond Exempted Village School Dist Bd of Ed, No. CA85-04-023, 1986 WL 5498 (12th Dist Ct App, Clermont, 5-12-86).

[247]Sellers v Logan-Hocking City School Dist Bd of Ed, No. 91 CA 12, 1992 WL 37785 (4th Dist Ct App, Hocking, 2-24-92).

[248]Kinser v West Branch Local Bd of Ed, No. 78 CA 57 (7th Dist Ct App, Mahoning, 12-7-78).

[249]Myers v Waverly City School Dist Bd of Ed, No. 315-CIV-82 (CP, Pike, 5-3-84), affirmed by No. 380, 1985 WL 9388 (4th Dist Ct App, Pike, 7-12-85).

[250]Wheeler v Mariemont Dist Bd of Ed, 12 App(3d) 102, 12 OBR 408, 467 NE(2d) 552 (Hamilton 1983).

[251]Hopkins v Indian Hill Bd of Ed, No. C-850035, 1986 WL 796 (1st Dist Ct App, Hamilton, 1-15-86).

[252]McClelland v Cincinnati School Dist Bd of Ed, No. C-840468, 1985 WL 8878 (1st Dist Ct App, Hamilton, 6-19-85).

[253]Antram v Jonathan Alder Local School Dist Bd of Ed, No. CA-92-08-021, 1993 WL 38096 (12th Dist Ct App, Madison, 2-16-93).

[254]Katz v Maple Heights City School Dist Bd of Ed, 87 App(3d) 256, 622 NE(2d) 1 (Cuyahoga 1993).

[255]Givhan v Western Line Consolidated School Dist, 439 US 410, 99 SCt 693, 58 LEd(2d) 619 (1979); Pickering v Board of Education, 391 US 563, 88 SCt 1731, 20 LEd(2d) 811 (1968).

include union activity,[256] public criticism of the board of education,[257] and alleging, in response to a news reporter's inquiries, that the employer has engaged in unlawful discrimination.[258] A rule prohibiting cafeteria workers from talking to anyone but the school principal about school problems has been deemed an unconstitutional prior restraint on employees' complaints about allegedly unsanitary practices in the cafeteria.[259] A teacher's decision to show high school students an R-rated film spiced with explicit scenes of sexual conduct and vulgar language, however, is not constitutionally protected expression.[260] While "academic freedom" has been warmly embraced at the highest level of the judiciary with respect to colleges,[261] no court has stretched this concept to permit teachers to choose their own curriculum or classroom management techniques and procedures in defiance or contravention of school policy. Moreover, the extent to which academic freedom applies in secondary and elementary schools is not settled.[262]

The initial burden is on the terminated or nonrenewed employee to show that his conduct was constitutionally protected, and that it was a substantial or motivating factor in the board's decision.[263] At that juncture, the burden shifts to the board to show that even without the protected conduct, the employee would still have been terminated or nonrenewed. If the board fails, the employee's contract may not be canceled.[264] A federal district court in Virginia has held that where only a minority of the board is shown to have been improperly motivated, that illicit motive will not be imputed to the entire board where the board's action required a majority vote, at least where the untainted majority supports the employment decision.[265]

Thus, there is no First Amendment violation where a teacher fails to establish a causal connection between the decision to nonrenew or terminate and statements the employee maintains are protected.[266] There is also no violation when the employee is nonrenewed for poor work performance and not for filing a grievance protesting work assignments.[267] Likewise, there is no protection for an employee's remarks concerning only a private interest and not a public one.[268] Whether speech may be "fairly characterized" as addressing

---

[256]Hickman v Valley Local School Dist Bd of Ed, 619 F(2d) 606 (6th Cir Ohio 1980).

[257]Ratliff v Wellington Exempted Village Schools Bd of Ed, 820 F(2d) 792 (6th Cir Ohio 1987).

[258]Matulin v Lodi, 862 F(2d) 609 (6th Cir Ohio 1988).

[259]Luethje v Peavine School Dist of Adair County, 872 F(2d) 352 (10th Cir Okla 1989).

[260]Krizek v Cicero-Stickney Twp High School Dist No. 201 Bd of Ed, 713 FSupp 1131 (ND Ill 1989).

[261]Keyishian v University of New York Bd of Regents, 385 US 589, 87 SCt 675, 17 LEd(2d) 629 (1967) (striking down loyalty oaths).

[262]See Miles v Denver Public Schools, 944 F(2d) 773 (10th Cir Colo 1991) (expressly suggesting a secondary school teacher has no constitutionally protected academic freedom, a conclusion some observers find dubious); Ward v Hickey, 996 F(2d) 448 (1st Cir Mass 1993) (school board may regulate teacher's classroom speech if regulation reasonably related to legitimate pedagogical concern and teacher given notice of what conduct is prohibited).

[263]For an example of a nonrenewed teacher failing to show that protected conduct was a substantial or motivating factor, see Menchhofer v Hoffer, No. C-930169, 1994 WL 176910 (1st Dist Ct App, Hamilton, 5-11-94). See also Cromley v Lockport Twp High School Dist 205 Bd of Ed, 17 F(3d) 1059 (7th Cir Ill 1994), cert denied ___ US ___, 115 SCt 74, 130 LEd(2d) 28 (1994) (report to state officials of sexual misconduct by fellow teacher toward students protected, but (1) the conduct was not shown to be a motivating factor in school board's decision not to promote, and (2) in any event, the teacher would not have been promoted anyway).

[264]Mt. Healthy City School Dist Bd of Ed v Doyle, 429 US 274, 97 SCt 568, 50 LEd(2d) 471 (1977); Buchheit v Hamilton City Bd of Ed, 15 App(3d) 148, 15 OBR 240, 473 NE(2d) 61 (Butler 1984). See also Bradley v Pittsburgh Bd of Ed, 913 F(2d) 1064 (3d Cir Pa 1990) (board must show not merely that it could have properly terminated the employee, but that it would have acted in the absence of the protected activity).

[265]Flickinger v School Bd of Norfolk, Va, 799 FSupp 586 (ED Va 1992).

[266]Vukadinovich v Michigan City Area Schools Bd of School Trustees, 978 F(2d) 403 (7th Cir Ind 1992), cert denied ___ US ___, 114 SCt 133, 126 LEd(2d) 97 (1993); Brandon v Coldwater Exempted Village School Dist Bd of Ed, No. 10-80-6, 1981 WL 6822 (3d Dist Ct App, Mercer, 4-1-81); Norman v Harrison Hills City School Dist Bd of Ed, No. 367, 1981 WL 4729 (7th Dist Ct App, Harrison, 6-19-81); Buchheit v Hamilton City Bd of Ed, 15 App(3d) 148, 15 OBR 240, 473 NE(2d) 61 (Butler 1984).

[267]Robinson v Lebanon City School Dist Bd of Ed, 29 App(3d) 103, 503 NE(2d) 541 (Warren 1985).

[268]Connick v Myers, 461 US 138, 103 SCt 1684, 75 LEd(2d) 708 (1983); Rowland v Mad River Local

a matter of public concern is often a difficult question that must be determined by the content, form, and context of a given statement as revealed by the whole record.[269] Even if it does touch on a matter of public concern, the inquiry is not ended: the employee's interests in commenting on matters of public concern must then be balanced against the employer's interests in promoting the efficient delivery of public services.[270]

Further muddying these already murky waters is *Waters v Churchill*,[271] in which the US Supreme Court tried to determine whether the "public concern" test should be applied to what the public employer *thought* was said or to what was *actually* said. Since none of the four opinions spawned by this case commanded majority support, distilling a controlling principle is difficult, to say the least. What ultimately appears to emerge is a "reasonableness" test along these lines: courts will look to the facts as the public employer, in light of all the relevant circumstances, *reasonably* found them to be. Thus, the mere fact that what the employer thought was said turns out, after a full-blown trial, to differ from what was actually said is not necessarily fatal. By the same token, the employer does not have carte blanche unreasonably and erroneously to simply assume what was said based on no evidence or manifestly flimsy evidence. The key is whether, at the time of the employer's action, the employer's conclusions as to what was said, whether ultimately shown to be right or wrong, were reasonably arrived at in light of the circumstances. Needless to add, such a slippery test further fosters the proliferation of lawsuits in this area.

Given the inherent difficulty, it is not surprising that many disgruntled employees have tried to bootstrap their way to a constitutional claim. Even a cursory look at some of the many cases in this area reveals the difficulties and the fine distinctions courts have drawn.[272] The need for compe-

---

School Dist, 730 F(2d) 444 (6th Cir Ohio 1984), cert denied 470 US 1009, 105 SCt 1373, 84 LEd(2d) 392 (1985); Szymczak v Berger, No. C81-1392 (ND Ohio, 7-23-82). See also Rankin v McPherson, 483 US 378, 107 SCt 2891, 97 LEd(2d) 315 (1987).

[269]Connick v Myers, 461 US 138, 147-48, 103 SCt 1684, 75 LEd(2d) 708 (1983). Whether *Connick's* "public concern" test encompasses freedom of association claims under the First Amendment as well as free speech claims is not settled. The US Court of Appeals for the Sixth Circuit says yes. Boals v Gray, 775 F(2d) 686 (6th Cir Ohio 1985). But the Eleventh Circuit has found *Connick* "inapplicable to freedom of association claims." Hatcher v Bibb County Bd of Public Ed and Orphanage, 809 F(2d) 1546 (11th Cir Ga 1987). See also Kinsey v Salado Independent School Dist, 950 F(2d) 988 (5th Cir Tex 1992), cert denied 504 US 941, 112 SCt 2275, 119 LEd(2d) 201 (1992). Griffin v Thomas, 724 FSupp 587 (ND Ill 1989), affirmed without opinion by 929 F(2d) 1210 (7th Cir Ill 1991) expressly eschews *Hatcher* in favor of *Boals*. Without referring to *Connick*, Adkins v Magoffin County, Kentucky Bd of Ed, 982 F(2d) 952 (6th Cir Ky 1993) held that the discharge of a secretary based on her marriage to another district employee would violate freedom of association rights. In Montgomery v Carr, 848 FSupp 770 (SD Ohio 1993), the court, without reference to *Connick* and distinguishing *Adkins*, refused to issue a preliminary injunction against the *transfer* of a teacher under an anti-nepotism policy against spouses working on the same campus.

[270]Pickering v Board of Education, 391 US 563, 88 SCt 1731, 20 LEd(2d) 811 (1968). At least one court has held that, while *Pickering* applies to speech in a general public setting, a teacher's classroom speech is governed by the less stringent standard set forth in Hazelwood School Dist v Kuhlmeier, 484 US 260, 108 SCt 562, 98 LEd(2d) 592 (1988), which dealt with the regulation of student expression. Specifically, in this court's view, the school board could regulate speech so long as the regulation reasonably related to a legitimate pedagogical interest. Miles v Denver Public Schools, 944 F(2d) 773 (10th Cir Colo 1991) (teacher's classroom criticism of decline in school quality and repetition of rumors that two students had sex on tennis court during school hours not protected). Where a black teacher's aide was not rehired because of her comments at a PTA meeting about Black History Month, the court, applying *Pickering*, rejected the notion that a school district's interest in avoiding divisive public criticism outweighed the employee's free speech rights in Belyeu v Coosa County Bd of Ed, 998 F(2d) 925 (11th Cir Ala 1993).

[271]Waters v Churchill, ___ US ___, 114 SCt 1878, 128 LEd(2d) 686 (1994).

[272]See, e.g., Hall v Marion School Dist No. 2, 31 F(3d) 183 (4th Cir SC 1994) (teacher's letters to editor criticizing school board and administrators and public records requests to district protected); Tompkins v Vickers, 26 F(3d) 603 (5th Cir Miss 1994) (teacher's complaints about eliminating art class protected); Durant v Independent School Dist No. 16 of Leflore County, Oklahoma, 990 F(2d) 560 (10th Cir Okla 1993) (openly campaigning against incumbent board member protected); Stroman v Colleton County School Dist, 981 F(2d) 152 (4th Cir SC 1992) (teacher's advocacy of "sick out" during exam week, even if protected, was outweighed by interests of the public and the employer); Sanguigni v Pittsburgh Bd

(F) Protection of whistleblowers

RC 4113.52 generally shields good-faith whistleblowers against disciplinary or other retaliatory action by their employers. Specifically, if, in the course of employment, an employee reasonably believes his employer is violating an Ohio or federal statute or local ordinance or regulation, and that the violation is either a criminal offense likely to cause an imminent risk of physical harm or a hazard to public health or safety or a felony, the employee is orally to notify his supervisor of the violation and subsequently file a written report describing the violation. The failure to file a written report is fatal, and removes the employee from the statute's protective scope.[273] Within twenty-four hours after oral notification or receipt of the report, or by the close of the next regular business day, whichever is later, the employer must notify the employee in writing of any corrective effort or of the absence of the alleged violation or hazard.[274] Except for civil service

---

tent counsel in cases of this type cannot be exaggerated.

of Public Ed, 968 F(2d) 393 (3d Cir Pa 1992) (coach's statements in faculty newsletter on employee morale not a matter of public concern); Knowlton v Greenwood Independent School Dist, 957 F(2d) 1172 (5th Cir Tex 1992) (cafeteria workers' protest over serving meals after hours without pay to school board members not a matter of public concern); Cox v Miller County R-I School Dist, 951 F(2d) 927 (8th Cir Mo 1991) (bus driver's vocal opposition to tax levy protected but relief denied since it was not motivating factor in dismissal); Kinsey v Salado Independent School Dist, 950 F(2d) 988 (5th Cir Tex 1992), cert denied 504 US 941, 112 SCt 2275, 119 LEd(2d) 201 (1992) (superintendent's vigorous speech in support of and affiliation with particular slate of candidates for election to school board not protected in view of his high-level policymaking and confidential position and the need to work in close relationship with the board); Bradley v Pittsburgh Bd of Ed, 910 F(2d) 1172 (3d Cir Pa 1990) (teacher's out-of-class advocacy of particular teaching technique protected, but in-class conduct is not protected; teacher has no right to use technique board has banned); Fyfe v Curlee, 902 F(2d) 401 (5th Cir Miss 1990), cert denied 498 US 940, 111 SCt 346, 112 LEd(2d) 310 (1990) (school secretary's decision to transfer daughter to private school protected); Johnsen v Tulsa County, Oklahoma Independent School Dist No. 3, 891 F(2d) 1485 (10th Cir Okla 1989) (school nurse's crusade to change school board's medication policy involved matter of public concern but not protected, on balance, because of its disruptive effect on district's health service program); Kirkland v Northside Independent School Dist, 890 F(2d) 794 (5th Cir Tex 1989), cert denied 496 US 926, 110 SCt 2620, 110 LEd(2d) 641 (1990) (teacher's substitution of own reading lists for those approved by school administrators is matter of private concern and not protected); Copp v Unified School Dist No. 501, 882 F(2d) 1547 (10th Cir Kan 1989) (school custodian's speech at board meeting on behalf of principal being transferred after charge of sexual harassment protected); Ware v Butler County, Kansas Unified School Dist No. 492, 881 F(2d) 906 (10th Cir Kan 1989), modified on other grounds by 902 F(2d) 815 (10th Cir Kan 1990) (nonteaching employee's vocal opposition to school bond issue protected); Vukadinovich v Bartels, 853 F(2d) 1387 (7th Cir Ind 1988) (claim that dismissal as teacher was based on comment to press after resignation as basketball coach constituted nothing more than "self-serving statement on a matter of private concern"; teacher was not trying to expose any wrongdoing or raise issue of public concern because it was a public concern but merely articulating private dissatisfaction with his dismissal); Seemuller v Fairfax County School Bd, 878 F(2d) 1578 (4th Cir Va 1989) (teacher's satirical letter to school newspaper in response to allegation of sex discrimination in physical education program is protected speech on matter of public concern); Fowler v Lincoln County, Kentucky, Bd of Ed, 819 F(2d) 657 (6th Cir Ky 1987), cert denied 484 US 986, 108 SCt 502, 98 LEd(2d) 501 (1987) (teacher's showing of R-rated film to high school students not protected); Daniels v Quinn, 801 F(2d) 687 (4th Cir NC 1986) (teacher's aide who asked board member about course materials not speaking on matter of public concern); Cox v Dardenelle Public School Dist, 790 F(2d) 668 (8th Cir Ark 1986) (teacher's comments criticizing principal's administrative style and educational theories protected); Gonzales v Galveston Independent School Dist, 865 FSupp 1241 (SD Tex 1994) (school district employee's conversations with attorney general regarding allegedly illegal behavior of former supervisor touched on matter of public concern); Blackburn v Floyd County Bd of Ed, 749 FSupp 159 (ED Ky 1990) (teacher's vocal criticism of school management protected); Thompson v Chicago Bd of Ed, 711 FSupp 394 (ND Ill 1989) (school librarian's remarks on quality of education and problems in district that were published in newspaper constituted legitimate comment on matter of public concern); Adkins v Stow City School Dist Bd of Ed, 70 App(3d) 532, 591 NE(2d) 795 (Summit 1990) (nonrenewed coach's comments on team's poor performance did not address matter of public concern); Petrie v Forest Hills School Dist Bd of Ed, 5 App(3d) 115, 5 OBR 231, 449 NE(2d) 786 (Hamilton 1982) (teacher's spending of class time discussing her displeasure of police handling of car accident in which she was involved not protected).

[273] Bear v Geetronics, Inc, 83 App(3d) 163, 614 NE(2d) 803 (Butler 1992).

[274] For certain criminal violations relating to hazardous wastes and air and water pollution control and

employees who file reports under RC 124.341[275] an employee unlawfully disciplined or retaliated against may bring a civil action against the offending employer for injunctive relief, reinstatement with back pay, attorney's fees, and litigation costs. Where the employer's unlawful retaliation is deliberate, interest may be added to any award of back pay.

9.22 Termination for cause, procedure

Termination of a teacher or administrator for cause is a serious matter, and the statutes mandate various procedural safeguards, including a requirement for specific written charges, a hearing, and an opportunity for the employee to appear and defend himself. The procedure is given in RC 3319.16 and RC 3319.161.

(A) Written charges, temporary suspension

Before terminating a teacher's contract, the board must furnish written notice of its intention to consider termination. The notice must include full specification of the grounds on which the board intends to rely.

The board may suspend a teacher pending final action to terminate the contract if, in the board's judgment, the character of the charges warrants such action.[276] The statutes impose no requirements of notice and reasons in a suspension action.[277] A federal court in Ohio has held that the portion of RC 3319.16 dealing with suspension is not facially unconstitutional.[278] However, the US Supreme Court's decision in *Cleveland Bd of Ed v Loudermill*[279] requiring a pretermination hearing as a matter of constitutional due process before the discharge of a public employee clearly suggests a hearing may be required before a suspension without pay.[280] The prudent course, accordingly, would be to provide a pre-suspension hearing. *Loudermill* does not require a full evidentiary hearing or the appointment of a neutral hearing officer in a predisciplinary context.[281] Notice of the charges and an opportunity to respond should satisfy any due process requirements. This assumes, of course, that an opportunity for a full evidentiary hearing will follow; if that is not the case, a more formal hearing is desirable if not necessary.[282]

---

safety, the employee may directly notify any appropriate public official or agency with regulatory authority over the employer. In any case, if the employer does not make a reasonable good-faith effort to correct the violation within twenty-four hours after oral notification or receipt of the report, the employee may file a written report with the prosecuting attorney or other appropriate public official or agency with regulatory authority over the employer. RC 4113.52(A)(3) provides that an employee who reasonably believes a fellow employee is violating a statute, local regulation, or employer work rule, and that the violation is either a criminal offense likely to cause an imminent risk of physical harm or a hazard to public health or safety or a felony, shall orally notify his supervisor of the violation and subsequently file a written report.

[275]See Text 12.17, Termination: civil service employees.

[276]RC 3319.16; Thomas v Akron City School Dist Bd of Ed, No. 10915, 1983 WL 4024 (9th Dist Ct App, Summit, 3-16-83).

[277]Weinstein v Canton City School Dist Bd of Ed, No. 6047, 1983 WL 7382 (5th Dist Ct App, Stark, 5-23-83).

[278]Crago v Olentangy Local School Dist Bd of Ed, No. C-2-86-0419 (SD Ohio, 1-4-88).

[279]Cleveland Bd of Ed v Loudermill, 470 US 532, 105 SCt 1487, 84 LEd(2d) 494 (1985).

[280]See Bradley v Pittsburgh Bd of Ed, 913 F(2d) 1064 (3d Cir Pa 1990) (hearing required but court declined to decide whether it must be pre- or post-suspension since in *Bradley* there was no hearing at all). In Deal v Vandalia-Butler City Schools Bd of Ed, No. 12302, 1991 WL 116644 (2d Dist Ct App, Montgomery, 6-28-91), the court stressed that something less is required than in a termination case. Here, the employee had notice of the charges and an opportunity to respond, albeit no formal hearing. The court found the procedure sufficient, noting the grievance procedure in the collective bargaining agreement had been used. It has been held, as *Loudermill* itself suggests, that no due process hearing is required where the imposed suspension is *with* pay. Watkins v McConologue, 820 FSupp 70 (SD NY 1992), affirmed without opinion by 978 F(2d) 706 (2d Cir NY 1992). See also Starlin v Morgan Local School Dist Bd of Ed, No. CA-93-10, 1994 WL 395859 (5th Dist Ct App, Morgan, 7-13-94).

[281]Jones v Walton, No. CA87-09-117, 1987 WL 20377 (12th Dist Ct App, Butler, 11-23-87); Crago v Olentangy Local School Dist Bd of Ed, No. C-2-86-0419 (SD Ohio, 1-4-88). For a fuller treatment of *Loudermill*, see Text 12.17(B), Notice to employee, removal order.

[282]See Winegar v Des Moines Independent Community School Dist, 20 F(3d) 895 (8th Cir Iowa 1994), cert denied ___ US ___, 115 SCt 426, 130 LEd(2d) 340 (1994) (suspension based on stigmatizing charge of child abuse with no opportunity for a post-deprivation hearing required more than a *Loudermill*-style informal hearing).

(B) Demand for hearing, scheduling hearing

Within ten days after receiving notice, the teacher may file with the board treasurer a written demand for a hearing before either the board or a referee. The board also has the right to demand that the hearing be before a referee.

The hearing must be scheduled within thirty days from receipt of the demand, and the treasurer must give the teacher at least twenty days' written notice of the time and place. The hearing need not be commenced within the thirty-day time frame if the superintendent of public instruction fails to designate a list of potential referees in enough time for the hearing to be conducted within that limit.[283] If the hearing is before a referee, the treasurer must also give at least twenty days' notice to the superintendent of public instruction. No hearing may be held during summer vacation without the teacher's consent.

(C) Hearing by board or referee

If the hearing is before the board, it must be conducted by a majority of board members. The board must confine the hearing to the grounds given in the notice for termination.

If a referee has been demanded, the referee must be selected by mutual agreement from a list supplied by the superintendent of public instruction. If, within five days of receipt, the board and teacher are unable to agree on one of the three, the superintendent of public instruction must select the referee. This five-day period has been held to be the *maximum* time which can elapse before the superintendent must make an appointment.[284] However, there is nothing to prevent the superintendent from making an appointment before expiration of the five-day period if one party states it will not agree to selection of a referee.[285] In either event, the selection must be entered on the board's minutes.

(D) Rules of procedure, privacy, record of proceedings

The Rules of Civil Procedure, including rules governing discovery, do *not* apply to termination procedures.[286] A termination hearing is private unless the teacher requests a public hearing. Both parties may be present, be represented by counsel, require witnesses to be under oath, cross-examine witnesses, and require the presence of witnesses on subpoenas issued by the district treasurer. The board must provide for a complete stenographic record of the proceedings, a copy of which must be furnished to the teacher. The board also must pay the referee's fee.

(E) Referee's report

Where the hearing takes place before a referee, he must file a report with the board within ten days. The ten-day limit, however, is directory rather than mandatory.[287] The board, after consideration of the report, may accept or reject the referee's recommendation by a majority vote. The Ohio Supreme Court has ruled a board must accept a referee's findings of fact unless they are against the preponderance of the evidence.[288] The board still retains, however, the responsibility of interpreting the significance of the facts.[289]

(F) Decision by board

A teacher is entitled to only one hearing, before either the board or a referee, so the board, after reviewing the referee's report, may immediately vote to accept or reject the referee's recommendation without fur-

---

[283]State ex rel Webb v Bryan City School Dist Bd of Ed, 10 OS(3d) 27, 10 OBR 178, 460 NE(2d) 1121 (1984).

[284]Wheeler v Mariemont Dist Bd of Ed, 12 App(3d) 102, 12 OBR 408, 467 NE(2d) 552 (Hamilton 1983).

[285]Wheeler v Mariemont Dist Bd of Ed, 12 App(3d) 102, 12 OBR 408, 467 NE(2d) 552 (Hamilton 1983).

[286]Wheeler v Mariemont Dist Bd of Ed, 12 App(3d) 102, 12 OBR 408, 467 NE(2d) 552 (Hamilton 1983).

[287]Duncan v Greenhills-Forest Park City School Dist Bd of Ed, No. C-840182, 1985 WL 9287 (1st Dist Ct App, Hamilton, 1-31-85).

[288]Aldridge v Huntington Local School Dist Bd of Ed, 38 OS(3d) 154, 527 NE(2d) 291 (1988).

[289]Aldridge v Huntington Local School Dist Bd of Ed, 38 OS(3d) 154, 527 NE(2d) 291 (1988). See also Brownfield v Warren Local School Dist Bd of Ed, No. 89 CA 26, 1990 WL 127054 (4th Dist Ct App, Washington, 8-28-90); Ricchetti v Cleveland City School Dist Bd of Ed, No. 64833, 1994 WL 66227 (8th Dist Ct App, Cuyahoga, 3-3-94).

ther hearing.[290] But where there is conflicting evidence, due deference must be accorded to the findings and recommendation of the referee because it is the referee who is best able to observe the demeanor of the witnesses and weigh their credibility.[291] When a board determines to reject the recommendation, the board should, consistent with the spirit of due process, articulate its reasons.[292] Indeed, a board's failure sufficiently to articulate reasons has resulted in reversal of a board's decision to reject.[293] Due process does not require that a teacher be permitted to appear before the board to interpose objections to the referee's report, nor does it preclude the board from basing its decision solely on the referee's report.[294] Further, the board need not read the transcript of the hearing before making its decision.[295] However, when the board considers only the referee's findings and does not review the transcript, its decision must be consistent with those findings. The referee's recommendation carries less weight if the board independently considers all of the evidence and testimony.[296]

The board, by a majority vote, may enter its determination in its minutes. An order to terminate a contract must state the grounds. If the decision is against termination, the charges and record of the hearing must be physically expunged from the minutes and, if the teacher has suffered a loss of salary by reason of suspension, he must be paid full salary for the period of suspension.

9.23 Appeal of termination

(A) Perfecting appeal to common pleas court

A teacher affected by an order of termination may appeal to the court of common pleas within thirty days after receiving notice of the entry of the order. The appeal is commenced if a petition against the board is timely filed. Service of summons on the board may occur after the thirty-day period.[297] The petition must allege the facts on which the teacher relies for a reversal or modification of the board decision. Failure to recite the facts will prevent the court from obtaining subject-matter jurisdiction.[298]

(B) Scope of review

While not authorizing a trial de novo (i.e., a new trial), RC 3319.16 specifically directs the common pleas court to examine the record of the hearings and hold additional hearings as it considers advisable. It is within the court's discretion to admit additional evidence.[299]

The court may reverse a board order terminating a teacher where it finds the order is not supported by the weight of the evidence.[300] This requirement has been interpreted as meaning the board's decision must be supported by manifest, substantial, probative evidence.[301] One court

---

[290] Jones v Mt. Healthy City School Dist Bd of Ed, 60 App(2d) 138, 395 NE(2d) 1337 (Hamilton 1978).

[291] Graziano v Amherst Exempted Village School Dist Bd of Ed, 32 OS(3d) 289, 513 NE(2d) 282 (1987).

[292] Graziano v Amherst Exempted Village School Dist Bd of Ed, 32 OS(3d) 289, 513 NE(2d) 282 (1987).

[293] Katz v Maple Heights City School Dist Bd of Ed, 87 App(3d) 256, 622 NE(2d) 1 (Cuyahoga 1993).

[294] Jones v Morris, 541 FSupp 11 (SD Ohio 1981), affirmed by 455 US 1009, 102 SCt 1699, 72 LEd(2d) 127 (1982).

[295] Charles v Princeton City School Dist Bd of Ed, No. C-820132, 1982 WL 8722 (1st Dist Ct App, Hamilton, 9-15-82); Riccheti v Cleveland City School Dist Bd of Ed, No. 64833, 1994 WL 66227 (8th Dist Ct App, Cuyahoga, 3-3-94).

[296] See Shie v Hamilton City School Dist Bd of Ed, No. CA79-10-0098, 1981 WL 5259 (12th Dist Ct App, Butler, 11-25-81).

[297] In re Moore, 14 App(3d) 264, 14 OBR 293, 470 NE(2d) 916 (Franklin 1984).

[298] White v Greenhills-Forest Park City School Dist Bd of Ed, No. C-840646, 1985 WL 8960 (1st Dist Ct App, Hamilton, 7-31-85).

[299] Houck v Greenhills-Forest Park City School Dist Bd of Ed, No. C-800358, 1981 WL 9862 (1st Dist Ct App, Hamilton, 6-24-81); Douglas v Cincinnati Bd of Ed, 80 App(3d) 173, 608 NE(2d) 1128 (Hamilton 1992).

[300] Hale v Lancaster Bd of Ed, 13 OS(2d) 92, 234 NE(2d) 583 (1968). For an example of reversal, see Douglas v Cincinnati Bd of Ed, 80 App(3d) 173, 608 NE(2d) 1128 (Hamilton 1992).

[301] Giering v Parma Bd of Ed, No. 38399 (8th Dist Ct App, Cuyahoga, 4-16-79); Baker v Twin Valley Community Local School Dist Bd of Ed, No. CA89-05-008, 1989 WL 139467 (12th Dist Ct App, Preble, 11-20-89); Duncan v Greenhills-Forest Park City School Dist Bd of Ed, No. C-840182, 1985 WL 9287 (1st Dist Ct App, Hamilton, 1-31-85).

has held the board's determination should be upheld if the evidence consists of conflicting testimony of approximately equal weight.[302]

If the court affirms the board, it is not required to make any specific finding. This is true irrespective of whether the board has rejected or accepted the referee's recommendation.[303] One court has concluded that whatever one calls the reviewing standard for determining the sufficiency of the evidence—"competent substantial evidence," "competent and substantial evidence," or "the weight of the evidence"—the standard is still that called for in civil proceedings, "the preponderance of the evidence."[304] As noted in *Jones v Morris*,[305] if a common pleas court does not find the board's order is supported by reliable, probative, and substantial evidence and in accordance with law, it should reverse, vacate, or modify the order.

While a common pleas court may weigh the evidence and credibility of witnesses, an appellate court reviewing that determination is under a limited scope of review. Absent an abuse of discretion, the court of appeals may not substitute its judgment for that of the lower court.[306]

(C) Waiver of defects

Any alleged defects in termination proceedings must be raised at the first opportunity. Thus, for example, if procedural defects are not raised before the referee, they are waived and may not be raised in a subsequent appeal.[307]

9.24 Nonrenewal of teacher limited (or extended limited) contract

Summary of Deadlines Required by RC 3319.11 and RC 3319.111

Action	Requirements
Evaluation procedures	At least two evaluations:
	Evaluation No. 1—conducted and completed no later than *January 15*; written report provided no later than *January 25*.
	Evaluation No. 2—conducted and completed between *February 10* and *April 1*; written report provided no later than *April 10*.
Notice	Written notice of nonrenewal must be received on or before *April 30*.
Due process hearing	Teacher, within *ten days* after receipt of written notice of nonrenewal, must file with district treasurer a written demand for a written statement describing circumstances leading to nonrenewal.
	Treasurer must provide the board's written statement within *ten days* after receipt of demand.
	Teacher, within *five days* after receipt of the board's statement, may file with the treasurer a written demand for a hearing.

---

[302]Myers v Waverly City School Dist Bd of Ed, No. 380, 1985 WL 9388 (4th Dist Ct App, Pike, 7-12-85).

[303]Goldsmith v Elida City Local Bd of Ed, No. 1-80-35, 1981 WL 6776 (3d Dist Ct App, Allen, 1-28-81) (referee's recommendation rejected); Sellers v Logan-Hocking City School Dist Bd of Ed, No. 91 CA 12, 1992 WL 37785 (4th Dist Ct App, Hocking, 2-24-92) (referee's recommendation accepted).

[304]Weinstein v Canton City School Dist Bd of Ed, No. 5303 (5th Dist Ct App, Stark, 7-3-80).

[305]Jones v Morris, 541 FSupp 11 (SD Ohio 1981), affirmed by 455 US 1009, 102 SCt 1699, 72 LEd(2d) 127 (1982).

[306]Graziano v Amherst Exempted Village School Dist Bd of Ed, 32 OS(3d) 289, 513 NE(2d) 282 (1987). For an example where an abuse of discretion was found, see Cephus v Dayton Bd of Ed, No. 13884, 1993 WL 435583 (2d Dist Ct App, Montgomery, 10-27-93).

[307]Shie v Hamilton City School Dist Bd of Ed, No. 79-04-0041, 1981 WL 5217 (12th Dist Ct App, Butler, 10-7-81).

Summary of Deadlines Required by RC 3319.11 and RC 3319.111

Action	Requirements
	Within *ten days* after receipt of demand, treasurer, on behalf of the board, must provide teacher with written notice of time, date, and place of the hearing.
	Hearing must be concluded within *forty days* of receipt of demand.
	Board must issue a written decision and order within *ten days* of conclusion of the hearing.
Judicial review	Appeal must be filed within *thirty days* after teacher's receipt of board's decision and order.

9.25 Teacher termination

The following steps must be followed to terminate a continuing, extended limited, or limited contract in-term:[308]

(1) Teacher receives informal hearing before administrator prior to any action on termination by board *if* contract is to be suspended while the termination is pending;

(2) Board, after enacting resolution, sends written notice to teacher of intent to consider termination, such notice containing full specification of the grounds for such consideration;

(3) Within ten days after receipt of notice, teacher may file with treasurer a written demand for hearing before the board or a referee;

(4) If teacher does not request a hearing, ten days after teacher's receipt of notice from the board, board formally votes to terminate by vote of majority; and

(5) If teacher does request a hearing, board sets time for hearing, which must be within thirty days of board's receipt of teacher's demand for a hearing *and* must give the teacher and state superintendent (if referee requested) twenty days' notice of hearing, provided such date is not during the summer vacation:

If Board Conducts Hearing	If Referee Conducts Hearing
(a) Majority of members conduct hearing; and	(a) Conducted upon request of either board or teacher;
(b) Board determination by majority vote.	(b) Notice to superintendent of public instruction;
	(c) Superintendent of public instruction to designate immediately three persons from whom referee will be selected and to notify immediately the designees, teacher, and board of such;
	(d) Board and teacher to select referee from list within five days of receipt of notice or else superintendent of public instruction shall choose;
	(e) Referee conducts hearing;
	(f) Referee files report within ten days after termination of hearing; and
	(g) Board accepts or rejects referee's recommendation of termination by majority vote;

(6) Appeal to common pleas court within thirty days of receipt of notice of entry of determination in the board's minutes.

---

[308] RC 3319.16, RC 3319.161.

Chapter 10

Teachers: Compensation, Fringe Benefits, and Leave

COMPENSATION
- 10.01 Teachers' salaries in general
- 10.02 Pay scales
- 10.03 Service credit for salary purposes
- 10.04 Service credit established by school board
- 10.05 Training credit for salary purposes
- 10.06 Preconditions to payment of salary
- 10.07 Underpayment and overpayment of salary
- 10.08 Payroll deductions

FRINGE BENEFITS, PAID DAYS, AND INSURANCE
- 10.09 Paid days, continuing education, lunch period
- 10.10 Group insurance
- 10.11 Board payment for continuing insurance coverage during illness or pending separation
- 10.12 Payment for continuing health insurance coverage by terminated employees

SICK LEAVE
- 10.13 Accumulating sick leave
- 10.14 Adopting state standards on sick leave, caveat
- 10.15 Advance of unearned sick leave
- 10.16 Use of sick leave
- 10.17 Severance pay on basis of accumulated sick leave
- 10.18 Enforced leave for certain illnesses

LEAVES OF ABSENCE
- 10.19 Requested leave
- 10.20 Unrequested disability leave
- 10.21 Miscellaneous leaves of absence

COMPENSATION

10.01 Teachers' salaries in general

(A) Salary as mandatory contract provision, annual salary notice

A board of education is required to enter into written contracts with all teachers, and the contracts must detail "the salaries and compensation to be paid for regular teaching duties and additional teaching duties, respectively."[1] Not later than July 1, the board must notify each teacher who holds a contract for the next school year of the salary to be paid.[2]

(B) Salary decreases

The salary stated in the notice may not be less than the salary paid during the preceding year, unless the reduction is part of a uniform reduction plan throughout the district. Similarly, the compensation stated in the contract for regular or additional duties, or both, may not be decreased during the contract term except under a uniform reduction plan throughout the district.[3] This restriction does not apply when the reduction results from nonrenewal of a supplemental contract,[4] nor does it prevent a reduction when a teacher goes on half-time status,[5] or a reduction proportionate to reduction of the school year from eleven months to nine.[6] In other words, the salary reduction limitation protects continuity of service, and does not guarantee income for teachers.[7]

(C) Salary increases, bonuses

RC 3319.12 expressly allows a salary increase, in whatever amount, after the

---

[1] RC 3319.08.
[2] RC 3319.12.
[3] RC 3319.12. The extent to which economic fringe benefits qualify as compensation for purposes of the prohibition against a decrease except under a uniform plan is unclear. Two cases decided under civil service statutes illustrate the ambiguity. Compare Ebert v Stark County Bd of Mental Retardation, 63 OS(2d) 31, 406 NE(2d) 1098 (1980) (finding it "obvious that sick leave credits, just as other fringe benefits, are forms of compensation") with State ex rel Bassman v Earhart, 18 OS(3d) 182, 18 OBR 250, 480 NE(2d) 761 (1985) (free parking privileges, in absence of statute requiring that they be granted, is mere "gratuity," the cessation of which is not a reduction in pay).
[4] Stroud v Dayton City School Dist, No. 6328 (2d Dist Ct App, Montgomery, 8-28-79).
[5] Graves v Youngstown City School Dist Bd of Ed, No. 82-CA-40, 1983 WL 6734 (7th Dist Ct App, Mahoning, 1-11-83).
[6] Shields v Dayton Bd of Ed, No. CA 8583, 1984 WL 5374 (2d Dist Ct App, Montgomery, 7-11-84).
[7] Shields v Dayton Bd of Ed, No. CA 8583, 1984 WL 5374 (2d Dist Ct App, Montgomery, 7-11-84).

notice has been given.[8] Also, salary increases may be retroactive.[9]

One means of providing bonuses is to grant temporary salary increases, followed by decreases to the original contract levels. This is allowed as long as the decreases uniformly apply throughout the district.[10]

10.02 Pay scales

(A) State minimum salary schedule

The Revised Code puts a floor under teachers' salaries with a minimum salary schedule, with levels varying according to training and years of service. The minimum salaries are exclusive of retirement and sick leave.[11]

Training increments are based on a teacher's education level and include (1) less than a bachelor's degree, (2) a bachelor's degree, (3) 5 years of training but no master's degree, and (4) a master's degree or higher. Increments based on years of service range from 0 to 11 or more (0 to 5 for teachers with no bachelor's degree). Each salary level is calculated as a percentage of the base salary, which is currently $17,000 for a beginning teacher with a bachelor's degree and no prior service. The lowest minimum is 86.5% of the base salary, or $14,705 per year, for a teacher with no prior service and no bachelor's degree. The highest minimum salary is 162.3% of the base salary, or $27,591 per year, for a teacher with 11 or more years of service and a master's or higher degree.

(B) Salary schedule adopted by school board

Each year, every board of education must adopt a teachers' salary schedule with increments based on education and years of service. The schedule must be filed with the superintendent of public instruction on or before October 15. Local school districts must, in addition, file the schedule with the service center superintendent, who must then certify back to each local district board the proper salary for each teacher.[12]

Teachers' salary schedules set forth in collective bargaining agreements may apply to "teaching" positions excluded from the bargaining unit.[13] The Ohio Supreme Court awarded tutors back pay based on the teachers' salary schedules, even though the collective bargaining agreement specifically excluded tutors from the bargaining unit.[14]

However, when tutors' pay scales are specifically set forth in a collective bargaining agreement, an appellate court refused

---

[8] RC 3319.12.

[9] OAG 81-011. See also Ojalvo v Ohio State University Bd of Trustees, No. 88AP-773, 1989 WL 106340 (10th Dist Ct App, Franklin, 9-14-89).

[10] OAG 75-048.

[11] RC 3317.13. The statute defines "teacher," rather circularly, as "all teachers employed by the board of education of any school district, including any county, cooperative education, or joint vocational school district." This definition has been construed as meaning only those who teach or instruct. Thus, a food service supervisor was not entitled to be compensated under the teachers' salary schedule notwithstanding that she met the more expansive definition of "teacher" that appears in the Ohio Teachers' Tenure Act at RC 3319.09. Wood v Trotwood Madison Bd of Ed, No. CA 11836, 1990 WL 80622 (2d Dist Ct App, Montgomery, 6-12-90). Similarly, an assistant principal's compensation and entitlement to any increase is governed by RC 3319.02, not RC 3317.13 and RC 3317.14, even though he meets the definition of "teacher" in RC 3319.09. State ex rel Whitehead v Circleville City School Dist Bd of Ed, No. 90-CI-000062 (CP, Pickaway, 3-29-91). Certain certificated tutors have been held entitled to compensation under the teachers' salary schedule unless a collective bargaining agreement applicable to them provides otherwise. State ex rel Brown v Milton-Union Exempted Village Bd of Ed, 40 OS(3d) 21, 531 NE(2d) 1297 (1988); State ex rel Tavenner v Indian Lake Local School Dist Bd of Ed, 62 OS(3d) 88, 578 NE(2d) 464 (1991); State ex rel Fink v Grandview Hts City School Dist Bd of Ed, No. 93APE10-1462, 1994 WL 183592 (10th Dist Ct App, Franklin, 5-12-94); Price v Newbury Local School Dist Bd of Ed, No. 91-G-1626, 1992 WL 268795 (11th Dist Ct App, Geauga, 12-13-91), appeal dismissed by 63 OS(3d) 1421, 587 NE(2d) 302 (1992); State ex rel Siers v Beaver Local School Dist Bd of Ed, No. 89-C-39, 1990 WL 167575 (7th Dist Ct App, Columbiana, 10-29-90); Cuyahoga Falls Ed Assn v Cuyahoga Falls City School Dist Bd of Ed, No. 14962, 1991 WL 244501 (9th Dist Ct App, Summit, 11-20-91). But see Eversole v Tuslaw Local School Dist, No. 90-755-3 (CP, Stark, 4-18-91), an anomalous case difficult to reconcile with the tenor of *Brown*. See also Text 8.02, Meaning of "teacher."

[12] RC 3317.14.

[13] See Text 8.02, Meaning of "teacher."

[14] State ex rel Chavis v Sycamore City School Dist Bd of Ed, 71 OS(3d) 26, 641 NE(2d) 188 (1994). Tutors were "teachers" for purposes of statute governing teachers' salary schedules, requiring board to pay tutors in accordance with teachers' schedules adopted through collective bargaining.

to award a tutor pay premised on teachers' salary schedules.[15]

(C) Board discretion as to salaries, restrictions

In adopting its own salary plan, a board of education is not bound to duplicate the state minimum schedule but is accorded considerable leeway. There are, however, several important restrictions on the board's discretion, the net effect of which is to insure that the board's pay scale can be more generous in a given case than the state minimum, but not less. The requirements for a board's salary schedule are as follows:

(1) The schedule must provide for increments based on both education and years of service.[16]

(2) A board cannot adopt or enforce any rule which would restrict credit as provided in the state minimum schedule for academic levels achieved by teachers.[17] That is, the board must at least recognize training short of a bachelor's degree, a bachelor's degree, five years of college training but no master's degree, and a master's degree. This does not prevent a board from providing more credit.[18]

(3) While a board is specifically authorized to adopt its own requirements for years of service, it is bound to provide full credit for at least five years of service. It can, of course, provide credit for more years or for partial years of service.[19]

(4) Most important, the salary schedule may not in any case result in a lower salary than the appropriate minimum provided in the state schedule.[20]

(D) Failure to adopt schedule or to pay at least minimum

If a board fails to adopt an annual salary schedule or fails to pay a teacher at least the minimum salary provided in the state schedule, then on written complaint the superintendent of public instruction must launch an immediate investigation. If the complaint is well founded, he must order the board to correct the deficiency within ten days. No foundation program money can be paid to the district until the order is obeyed.[21]

10.03 Service credit for salary purposes

(A) Years of service

For purposes of both the state minimum salary schedule and the annual salary schedule adopted by a board of education,[22] salary increments for service are based on "years of service" as defined in RC 3317.13(A)(1), which includes both teaching and military service. Years of service include the following:

(1) Years of teaching as a certified teacher in the same school district under a teacher's contract;

(2) Years of teaching as a certified teacher in another Ohio school district, or in a chartered nonpublic school in Ohio, under a teacher's contract;

(3) Years of teaching as a certified teacher in a chartered school, institution, or special education program operated by the state or a subdivision or other local governmental unit. Chartered schools, institutions, or special education programs include unchartered ones which are subsequently chartered; and

(4) Years of active military duty in the US armed forces, up to a maximum of five years of service.

In calculating the minimum salary payable under RC 3317.13, a teacher is credited with the sum of all years of service described above, except a teacher new to a

---

[15]State ex rel Burch v Sheffield Lake City School Dist Bd of Ed, No. 94CA005832, 1995 WL 230892 (9th Dist Ct App, Lorain, 4-19-95) (holding tutors not automatically entitled to minimum salary requirements of RC 3317.13 and "collective bargaining agreement can distinguish between different employees who instruct students and can provide different salary rates for those employees").

[16]RC 3317.14.

[17]RC 3317.13.

[18]See Text 10.04, Service credit established by school board.

[19]RC 3317.14. See Text 10.03, Service credit for salary purposes.

[20]RC 3317.13, RC 3317.14.

[21]RC 3317.13.

[22]RC 3317.13, RC 3317.14.

district may be granted not more than ten years of service under (2), (3), and (4) above.[23]

(B) Years of teaching service

A year of teaching service is 120 days.[24] Although a board may within certain limits establish its own service requirements,[25] the 120-day rule was invoked where a collective bargaining agreement provided that teachers would advance to the next salary step on completion of a year of service, and a teacher worked 129 days before going on unpaid leave for the remaining 55 days of the school year. It was held that the board violated the agreement by requiring the teacher to work 55 days in the succeeding school year before being advanced a salary step.[26]

An appeals court has held "days" must be full days, not the accumulation of parts of days worked.[27] The Attorney General has concluded a board is not required to pay a teacher full increments on the salary schedule for half-time or part-time teaching[28] and may classify its teachers as either full-time or part-time for purposes of salary and fringe benefits, provided the classification does not interfere with any minimum benefit or status required by law.[29] The extent, if any, to which these principles survive subsequent Ohio Supreme Court decisions in the context of counting part-time service toward tenure eligibility[30] is, however, an open question.

Service as a substitute is teaching service within the meaning of RC 3317.13(A)(1). Since all teachers, including substitutes, must be employed pursuant to contract,[31] a substitute who teaches more than 120 days in the year has taught "under a teacher's contract" and is entitled to a year of service credit.[32] Moreover, days teaching as a casual substitute may be combined with days teaching under a regular contract during the year to determine if the teacher is entitled to credit for a year of service.[33] A teacher is not entitled to a year of service credit, however, where the substitute teaching in a school year was in different school districts and the 120 days can be satisfied only by adding days of service for multiple districts together.[34]

(C) Teaching service in Ohio or elsewhere

The *minimum* requirement is that teaching service in Ohio must be credited. A board is not bound to recognize teaching service outside Ohio, but it may do so. It is constitutional for a board to credit teaching service in public schools in another state as well as Ohio, and service in chartered private schools in Ohio, but to exclude service in private schools outside Ohio.[35]

(D) Military service

All years of active duty with US armed forces, up to a maximum of five, must be credited as years of service. A partial year of active duty must be counted as a full year if it consists of at least eight continuous months.[36] Moreover, a board may give credit for less than eight months, even if there is no written policy to that effect.[37] But, if a teacher has been credited with a fractional year of military service and the board adopts a new salary schedule, the teacher need not be given the same credit under the new schedule if it provides a salary increase.[38]

---

[23] RC 3317.13(B).

[24] RC 3317.13(A)(1)(a) to (c).

[25] RC 3317.14. See Text 10.04, Service credit established by school board.

[26] Daubenmire v Lancaster City Schools, No. 66-CA-82, 1983 WL 6524 (5th Dist Ct App, Fairfield, 7-1-83).

[27] Oney v Westerville City School Dist Bd of Ed, No. 81 AP-171, 1981 WL 3488 (10th Dist Ct App, Franklin, 9-29-81).

[28] OAG 69-069.

[29] OAG 83-098.

[30] See Text 9.08(C), Time served, school year, teaching days.

[31] RC 3319.08.

[32] Crawford v Barberton City Schools Bd of Ed, 6 OS(3d) 324, 6 OBR 382, 453 NE(2d) 627 (1983); Bigelow v Youngstown Bd of Ed, No. 77CA52 (7th Dist Ct App, Mahoning, 10-4-77).

[33] Goldman v Princeton City School Dist Bd of Ed, No. 800810, 1981 WL 10123 (1st Dist Ct App, Hamilton, 11-25-81).

[34] State ex rel Filipiak v Midview Local School Dist Bd of Ed, 95 App(3d) 139, 641 NE(2d) 1380 (Lorain 1993), appeal dismissed by 70 OS(3d) 1222, 640 NE(2d) 842 (1994).

[35] Steppe v Columbus Bd of Ed, No. C-2-82-1151 (SD Ohio, 11-1-84).

[36] RC 3317.13(A)(1)(d).

[37] OAG 68-085.

[38] OAG 68-085.

Military service must be credited regardless of when performed. Credit must be given, for example, for service prior to graduation and certification as a teacher.[39]

10.04 Service credit established by school board

RC 3317.14 expressly authorizes a board of education to adopt its own service requirements and permits the granting of service credit for such activities as teaching in public or nonpublic schools in Ohio or another state, for service as an educational aide, and for service in the military or in an appropriate state or federal governmental agency. The statute adds a proviso that no teacher can be paid less than the amount to which he would be entitled according to the state minimum salary schedule, and a further proviso that increments in the board's schedule must give full credit for at least five years of service.

(A) Minimum service credit

The board is bound by the statutory limitations in establishing its own service requirements, but it is also bound by its own salary schedule. Where the board's schedule exceeds the state minimum, a teacher must still be credited with all years of service up to the statutory minimum of five years in determining his salary on the board's schedule, even though his salary would be more than the state minimum if less credit were given.[40]

(B) Service credits exceeding statutory minimum

A board is free to give service credit above the minimum of five years. A board may also provide only the minimum credit for service outside the district and full credit for years of service in the district. Thus, in *Maple Heights Teachers Assn v Maple Heights Bd of Ed*,[41] the board's salary schedule included twenty-eight service increments. The board's policy provided that service credit would be computed as years of service in the district, plus the service credit granted the teacher at the time of employment for experience gained elsewhere. Accordingly, a teacher who was granted five years' credit for seventeen years of teaching outside the district, and who had twenty-one years of service in the district, was only entitled to twenty-six years of total service credit, since the five years' credit for outside service met the statutory minimum.

Once service credit beyond the statutory minimum is granted, it is retained even if the teacher resigns and later returns to the district. In *State ex rel Madden v Windham Exempted Village School Dist Bd of Ed*,[42] a teacher was granted one year of a prior service credit upon being hired even though she taught less than 120 days during that year. The board was not permitted to withdraw the prior service credit when the teacher resigned and then returned to her position eight years later.

(C) Credit for partial service, excluding leave time

A board may grant service credit for military service of less than eight months;[43] i.e., it may provide more credit than required by statute. On the other hand, a board may adopt a policy whereby time spent on an unpaid leave of absence, including maternity leave, is not counted for service credit purposes.[44]

(D) Failure to establish local service requirements

If a board does not adopt its own service requirements, it is bound by the service increments provided in the state minimum schedule. Where a board had a practice of limiting advancement along its salary tracks to a single increment, but the policy was unwritten and there was no evidence as to how it originated, how uniformly it had been applied, or that teachers in the district knew or should have known of its existence, it was held that the board had failed to establish its own service requirements and

---

[39]Bernardini v Conneaut Area City School Dist Bd of Ed, 58 OS(2d) 1, 387 NE(2d) 1222 (1979).

[40]Rauhaus v Buckeye Local School Dist Bd of Ed, 6 OS(3d) 320, 6 OBR 379, 453 NE(2d) 624 (1983).

[41]Maple Heights Teachers Assn v Maple Heights Bd of Ed, 6 OS(3d) 314, 6 OBR 374, 453 NE(2d) 619 (1983).

[42]State ex rel Madden v Windham Exempted Village School Dist Bd of Ed, 42 OS(3d) 86, 537 NE(2d) 646 (1989).

[43]OAG 68-085.

[44]White v Columbus Bd of Ed, 2 App(3d) 178, 2 OBR 195, 441 NE(2d) 303 (Franklin 1982).

was compelled to fully credit a teacher for all years of prior service.[45]

On the other hand, when a written policy, duly promulgated among teachers, restricted advancement to a single increment upon movement horizontally from one salary lane to another regardless of the number of years of teaching experience, a local service requirement was established, and, so long as affected teachers received at least the statutory minimum salary, teachers were bound by it and RC 3317.14 was not violated.[46]

10.05 Training credit for salary purposes

(A) In general

The salary schedule adopted by a board must provide increments based on both training and years of service.[47] Although a board may adopt more restrictive service requirements than those provided in the state minimum salary schedule,[48] it is expressly forbidden from adopting or enforcing more restrictive academic requirements than the state schedule.[49] That is, the board's salary schedule must provide increments for at least (1) less than a bachelor's degree, (2) a bachelor's degree, (3) five years of training, but no master's degree, and (4) a master's or higher degree.[50]

This does not mean the board's credits for training must duplicate those in the state schedule. The prohibition is against *restricting* academic credit, so that a board may provide more generous training increments. For example, the board might grant education credit for work experience or completion of specialized courses, or provide increments for college work beyond a master's degree, or for earning a Ph.D. Thus, although it has been held that nurses with degrees as registered nurses were not entitled to placement in the bachelor's degree column of a board's salary schedule,[51] a board could nevertheless credit nurses with actual nursing experience in determining their salary bracket.[52] When there is no clear board policy as to when additional credit must be earned, a teacher is entitled to academic credit beyond a master's degree even though the additional credit was not earned after earning a master's degree.[53]

(B) Duty of teacher to inform board of completed training

A teacher who completes training which entitles him to horizontal movement on the schedule to a higher salary bracket has the burden of filing satisfactory evidence of the training with the board treasurer no later than September 15.[54] Thus, the teacher must provide evidence of completion of training when he obtains a bachelor's degree, again when he completes a fifth year of college, and again when he obtains a master's degree. If the salary schedule provides more training increments, the teacher must also provide evidence that he has met the requirements for the extra increments.

When the teacher files the required evidence, the district treasurer must place the teacher in the appropriate salary bracket immediately.[55]

10.06 Preconditions to payment of salary

A teacher cannot be paid until he files with the district treasurer all reports required by the state and district boards of education and by the district superintendent. Also, unless engaged part-time under a permit issued under RC 3319.301, all teachers must possess the appropriate cer-

---

[45]Basler v Princeton City School Dist Bd of Ed, No. C-800305, 1981 WL 9764 (1st Dist Ct App, Hamilton, 5-6-81). See also Hummel v Buckeye Local School Dist Bd of Ed, No. 1787, 1990 WL 1760 (9th Dist Ct App, Medina, 1-10-90).

[46]Basler v Princeton City School Dist Bd of Ed, 64 App(3d) 71, 580 NE(2d) 805 (Hamilton 1989).

[47]RC 3317.14.

[48]RC 3317.14.

[49]RC 3317.13(B).

[50]RC 3317.13(B) to (D).

[51]Rivers v Barberton City School Dist, No. CV 82 92856 (CP, Summit, 2-22-83).

[52]Youngstown Ed Assn v Youngstown City School Dist Bd of Ed, No. 81 CA 171, 1983 WL 6737 (7th Dist Ct App, Mahoning, 1-12-83).

[53]Bialek v Bloom-Carroll Local School Dist Bd of Ed, No. 42-CA-86, 1987 WL 11068 (5th Dist Ct App, Fairfield, 4-21-87).

[54]RC 3317.14.

[55]RC 3317.14.

tificate, and before a teacher can be paid, his certificate (or a true copy) must be on file with the superintendent. The certificate must show the date of validity and authority to teach the subjects or grades taught. An exception to the certificate requirement applies to a new teacher, holding a bachelor's degree or higher, whose application for a provisional or higher grade certificate is pending during the first two months of initial employment in the district.[56]

10.07 Underpayment and overpayment of salary

Underpayments or overpayments of salary may be recovered in an appropriate civil action. Recovery of overpayments through payroll deduction has also been upheld.

Typically, underpayment or overpayment occurs because of a mistake of fact as to, or error in calculating, service credit.[57] Underpayment or overpayment can, of course, occur for other reasons, such as clerical errors in the salary notice.[58]

(A) Recovery of underpayment, statute of limitations, laches, waiver

Mandamus is the appropriate remedy for a teacher to recover back pay because of salary underpayments, as well as to compel the board to pay the proper salary, and the Ohio Supreme Court has held that a six-year statute of limitations applies.[59] The Court has also held that a separate claim arises each year that a teacher is underpaid.[60] Thus, an underpayment caused by an error occurring more than six years before is not barred. However, a back pay award is limited to a maximum of six years.[61]

Despite the Supreme Court's adoption of a six-year statute, an appeals court has held the applicable limitations period is fifteen years for suits based upon written contracts of employment. A concurring opinion by one judge acknowledged the six-year period would apply for claims not premised on contracts but on statutes.[62]

An appeals court has barred the claim of a teacher who waited twelve years to claim compensation for an allegedly wrong placement on the salary schedule under the doctrine of laches, finding her delay both unreasonable and prejudicial to the school board's defense.[63]

A teacher may waive his right to recover. In *White v Columbus Bd of Ed*,[64] the board asserted a teacher was wrongly credited with a year of service during which she taught less than 120 days because of mandatory maternity leave. She agreed to

---

[56] RC 3319.36.

[57] See, e.g., Crawford v Barberton City Schools Bd of Ed, 6 OS(3d) 324, 6 OBR 382, 453 NE(2d) 627 (1983). See Text 10.03, Service credit for salary purposes.

[58] Stow City School Dist Bd of Ed v Swearingen, No. 10742, 1982 WL 5193 (9th Dist Ct App, Summit, 12-22-82); Boggs v Southeastern Local School Dist Bd of Ed, No. CA 1744 (2d Dist Ct App, Clark, 2-28-83); Elmwood Local School Dist Bd of Ed v Yodzis, No. WD-84-70, 1985 WL 8381 (6th Dist Ct App, Wood, 2-1-85). See Text 10.01, Teachers' salaries in general.

[59] State ex rel Gingrich v Fairfield City School Dist Bd of Ed, 18 OS(3d) 244, 18 OBR 300, 480 NE(2d) 485 (1985). The Court applied the six-year statute (RC 2305.07) applicable to suits pertaining to liability created by statute, rejecting an argument that the two-year statute (RC 2305.11) applicable to suits to recover minimum wages should apply.

[60] State ex rel Madden v Windham Exempted Village School Dist Bd of Ed, 42 OS(3d) 86, 537 NE(2d) 646 (1989).

[61] For an example of the six-year limitations period in operation, see State ex rel Fink v Grandview Hts City School Dist Bd of Ed, No. 93APE10-1462, 1994 WL 183592 (10th Dist Ct App, Franklin, 5-12-94).

[62] Tapo v Columbus Bd of Ed, No. 85AP-687, 1986 WL 2492 (10th Dist Ct App, Franklin, 2-18-86), affirmed by 31 OS(3d) 105, 31 OBR 268, 509 NE(2d) 419 (1987) (applying RC 2305.06). The limitations issue in this case was not appealed and, accordingly, not considered by the Supreme Court. *Tapo* did not have occasion to consider the provision in RC 4117.10(A) that makes the grievance procedure of a collective bargaining agreement an employee's sole remedy if that procedure culminates in final and binding arbitration and the complaint alleges a violation of some term of the agreement. Presumably, where the claim is premised upon a collective bargaining agreement that provides for binding arbitration, the contractual remedy (including any time limits imposed by that remedy) applies. See Text 18.22, Grievance procedure and arbitration.

[63] State ex rel Stuckey v Washington Court House City School Dist, No. CA89-07-018, 1990 WL 14806 (12th Dist Ct App, Fayette, 2-20-90). In the absence of prejudice, however, the doctrine of laches cannot successfully be invoked. State ex rel Madden v Windham Exempted Village School Dist Bd of Ed, 42 OS(3d) 86, 537 NE(2d) 646 (1989).

[64] White v Columbus Bd of Ed, 2 App(3d) 178, 2 OBR 195, 441 NE(2d) 303 (Franklin 1982).

repay the overpayment, then tried to recover the amount repaid, alleging the leave policy was unconstitutional. The court agreed that the policy was unconstitutional but denied recovery, holding that by agreeing to repay she waived her right to assert a violation of the statute prohibiting a decrease in salary during the contract term.[65]

However, the same court has held that no waiver occurred when a teacher cashed a check covering part of the back payment after being advised by the board that such action would be a complete settlement of the matter.[66] The mere execution of a contract for a lower salary than that required by statute under the teachers' salary schedule does not constitute a waiver.[67]

(B) Recovery of overpayment, statute of limitations

Salary overpayments resulting from a mistake of fact as to years of service may be recovered from the teacher.[68] One court has held that overpayment resulting from arithmetical miscalculation may be recovered through unilateral deductions from the remaining paychecks in the relevant year. Although this method is not encouraged, under the particular facts such "self-help" did not violate state law or constitutional due process.[69] The decisions are split on whether a board can recover overpayments resulting from an error in the salary notice. Three courts have held a board is bound by the notice and must pay the stated salary even if it results in overpayment.[70] One court has held such overpayment can be recovered.[71]

The bureau of inspection and supervision of public offices is required to examine public agencies, including school boards, once every two years and render a report.[72] If the audit reveals public money has been paid illegally, suit to recover must be instituted. The procedure applies to salary overpayments, although the board does not have to wait for the report to attempt to recover funds found to have been wrongly paid.[73]

The six-year statute of limitations for recovery on a liability created by statute[74] applies to actions instituted under RC 117.10.[75] Presumably, the same statute would apply if suit for recovery of overpayment were not grounded on RC 117.10.[76]

10.08 Payroll deductions

(A) In general

Deductions from a teacher's salary are either required or authorized for the following:

(1) Social security and federal income tax withholding;[77]

(2) US savings bonds;[78]

(3) Municipal income tax;[79]

(4) Credit union contributions;[80]

(5) Charitable contributions, to charities which are nonprofit corporations,

---

[65]RC 3319.08.

[66]Tapo v Columbus Bd of Ed, No. 85AP-687, 1986 WL 2492 (10th Dist Ct App, Franklin, 2-18-86), affirmed by 31 OS(3d) 105, 31 OBR 268, 509 NE(2d) 419 (1987). The waiver issue in this case was not appealed and, accordingly, not considered by the Supreme Court.

[67]State ex rel Fink v Grandview Hts City School Dist Bd of Ed, No. 93APE10-1462, 1994 WL 183592 (10th Dist Ct App, Franklin, 5-12-94).

[68]Giammarco v Columbus Bd of Ed, No. 80CV-02-794 (CP, Franklin 1981).

[69]Green Local Teachers Assn v Blevins, 43 App(3d) 71, 539 NE(2d) 653 (Scioto 1987).

[70]Stow City School Dist Bd of Ed v Swearingen, No. 10742, 1982 WL 5193 (9th Dist Ct App, Summit, 12-22-82); Boggs v Southeastern Local School Dist Bd of Ed, No. CA 1744 (2d Dist Ct App, Clark, 2-28-83); Mansfield City School Dist Bd of Ed v Krizan, No. CA-2327, 1985 WL 4194 (5th Dist Ct App, Richland, 11-25-85).

[71]Elmwood Local School Dist Bd of Ed v Yodzis, No. WD-84-70, 1985 WL 8381 (6th Dist Ct App, Wood, 2-1-85).

[72]RC 117.09, RC 117.10.

[73]White v Columbus Bd of Ed, 2 App(3d) 178, 2 OBR 195, 441 NE(2d) 303 (Franklin 1982) (recovery of overpayment by means of payroll deductions upheld where employee agreed to this procedure).

[74]RC 2305.07.

[75]Portage Lakes Joint Vocational School Dist Bd of Ed v Bowman, 14 App(3d) 132, 14 OBR 148, 470 NE(2d) 233 (Summit 1984).

[76]See State ex rel Gingrich v Fairfield City School Dist Bd of Ed, 18 OS(3d) 244, 18 OBR 300, 480 NE(2d) 485 (1985).

[77]26 USCA 3102, 26 USCA 3402.

[78]RC 9.40.

[79]RC 9.42.

[80]RC 9.43.

community chests, united funds, or similar community fund organizations;[81]

(6) Retirement contributions;[82]

(7) Contributions to political organizations and parties, and for nonpartisan issues;[83]

(8) Insurance premiums, for life, health, accident, and other kinds of insurance, annuities, and payroll savings plans;[84] and

(9) Union dues and fair share fees of nonunion members.[85]

Of the foregoing, payroll deductions for social security and federal income tax withholding, municipal income tax, and retirement contributions are mandatory. If fair share fees for nonunion members are in effect, payroll deduction is mandatory. All other payroll deductions, including union dues, require written authorization from the employee.

(B) Union dues checkoff, fair share fees

(1) Dues checkoff

A collective bargaining agreement between a school board and a union *must* authorize the deduction of union dues, fees, and assessments from the wages of union members.[86] Although this provision is mandatory, actual dues checkoff requires written authorization by the employee.

Whether the employee can rescind authorization and, if so, whether the collective bargaining agreement can restrict the right of rescission are unsettled under current statutes. Former RC 9.41 provided for union dues checkoff on written authorization and specifically stated the "authorization may be revocable by written notice upon the will of the employee." It was held that a contractual provision prohibiting an employee from withdrawing checkoff authorization except during the ten days ending August 31 each year did not conflict with RC 9.41 and was enforceable.[87] RC 9.41 was repealed by the Public Employees Collective Bargaining Act,[88] and it is uncertain if that holding still applies, since the Act requires employee authorization for dues checkoff but omits the former language allowing revocation.

(2) Agency shop fees checkoff

The checkoff provisions are reversed with respect to fees from employees who are not union members. The contract *may*, but is not required to, contain an agency shop provision, but if there is such a provision, payroll deduction of a "fair share fee" is automatic and does not require the employee's written authorization.[89] The "fair share fee" cannot exceed the dues payable by union members, and the teacher cannot be compelled to join the union.

FRINGE BENEFITS, PAID DAYS, AND INSURANCE

10.09 Paid days, continuing education, lunch period

(A) Emergency school closings

RC 3319.08, dealing with teachers' contracts, provides that teachers must be paid for all days lost when the schools are closed because of "an epidemic or other public calamity."

The board of health of a city or a general health district may close any school because of danger from rapidly spreading communicable disease.[90] Sometimes, a very high absence rate among students and teachers because of a prevalent contagion will prompt local school authorities to close schools temporarily, without the intervention of the health department, and such closings also probably constitute closing due to epidemic.

What constitutes a closing due to a "public calamity" is not defined, although

---

[81]RC 9.80, RC 9.81.
[82]RC 3307.51, RC 3307.62.
[83]RC 3313.262. As of the date of publication, enforcement of 1995 S 8, which purported to prohibit payroll deduction of employee contributions to political action committees, has been enjoined by the U.S. District Court for Northern Ohio.
[84]RC 3917.04.
[85]RC 4117.09.

[86]RC 4117.09(B)(2). See Text 18.19, Requirements for contract.
[87]Franklin v Columbus Bd of Ed, 1 App(3d) 134, 1 OBR 441, 439 NE(2d) 950 (Franklin 1981).
[88]RC Ch 4117. See generally Text Ch 18, Collective Bargaining.
[89]RC 4117.09(C). See Text 18.21, Agency shop.
[90]RC 3313.48, RC 3317.01, RC 3707.26.

its meaning is apparently broad. In connection with another statute,[91] it was held to be within the discretion of the superintendent of public instruction to determine if a condition amounting to a public calamity in fact existed and justified a school board in closing schools.[92]

(B) Jury duty

School employees are not exempt from jury duty.[93] Boards of education are required to pay a full-time employee the difference between his regular compensation and the remuneration received for serving as a juror.[94] A board cannot fire or threaten to fire any permanent employee who is summoned to serve as a juror if the employee gives reasonable notice of his pending jury duty and is absent because of actual jury service.[95]

(C) Continuing education, professional days

A board of education may establish a professional development program for teachers and reimburse them for all or part of the cost incurred in successful completion of a course or training program which is part of the program.[96]

Likewise, any employee may receive compensation and expenses for days when he is excused to attend professional meetings, in accordance with board policy. The board may provide and pay the salary of a substitute for those days. Each board is required to adopt a policy governing attendance of school employees at professional meetings.[97]

The attorney general has concluded that a teacher who is on a committee or is an official of a local teachers union may be paid full salary and expenses for attending state, county, or local union meetings, if the board determines the meeting is a professional meeting and authorizes attendance by resolution.[98]

(D) Lunch period

RC 3319.072 guarantees each teacher a daily duty-free lunch period of at least thirty minutes which "shall not be cause for lengthening the school day." The "school day" is subject to the minimum period set forth by RC 3313.48, during which students are required to be in attendance.[99] An exception authorizes the governing board of an educational service center to require that the teacher in a one-teacher school remain on duty if granting a duty-free period would work a hardship.

10.10   Group insurance

(A) In general

RC 3313.202 authorizes a board of education to pay all or part of the cost of group term life, hospitalization, surgical, or major medical insurance, or a combination of these, for teaching and nonteaching employees. For dependent children and spouses of employees a board may pay all or part of the cost of hospitalization, surgical, and major medical insurance. A board may restrict health insurance coverage to those employees not covered by any other health insurance plan.[100]

Board members may also obtain group insurance coverage, at their own expense, for themselves and their spouses. Payments for coverage must be made in advance. The exercise of this option must be in writing, and be announced at a regular public meeting and recorded in board minutes.[101]

RC 3313.202 obviously overlaps to some extent with RC 9.90, which allows a board to purchase, for its employees, life insurance or sickness, accident, annuity, endowment, health, medical, hospital, dental, or

---

[91] RC 3317.01.
[92] OAG 66-030.
[93] RC 2313.34.
[94] RC 3313.211.
[95] RC 2313.18.
[96] RC 3319.071.
[97] RC 3313.20.
[98] OAG 74-012.
[99] See Text 20.05, Regular school day and year. The terms "school day" and "work day" may have different applications to teachers' allocated preparation time, depending on the collective bargaining agreement. Norwood City School Dist v Norwood Teachers Assn, No. C-930676, 1994 WL 667212 (1st Dist Ct App, Hamilton, 11-30-94). The court reinstated the arbitrator's award which interpreted the collective bargaining agreement as allocating preparation time to teachers during the "school day," rather than during the longer "work day" as the board argued.

[100] Lake Ed Assn v Lake Local Schools Bd of Ed, No. WD-83-21, 1983 WL 6873 (6th Dist Ct App, Wood, 7-15-83).

[101] RC 3313.202(D).

surgical coverage and benefits, or any combination of these, by means of insurance plans or other types of coverage. The board may pay all or any portion of the cost. A board also may assess processing fees against the insurance carrier for administration costs incurred from operating the insurance program.[102]

A board that offers employees a health benefit plan and employs at least twenty-five employees is required by RC 1742.33 to make available to and inform employees of the option to enroll in at least one health maintenance organization (HMO) certified to provide health care services in the geographic area where a substantial number of employees reside.

(B) Classification of employees for insurance purposes

A board may pay a higher percentage of health insurance premiums for its superintendent, assistant superintendent, and principals than it pays for other "teaching employees" under RC 3313.202.[103] A board may also classify its teachers as "full-time" or "part-time" for purposes of determining fringe benefits, as long as the board acts reasonably and does not reduce any minimum benefit conferred by statute.[104]

(C) Deductible feature

RC 9.90 and RC 3313.202 permit a board to provide benefits to employees under an insurance plan which obligates the board to pay claim costs up to a predetermined level with the insurance company assuming the indeterminable risks inherent in the employee coverage.[105]

(D) Self-insurance, trust funds

RC 3313.202 states that a board may provide the benefits described in that statute through an individual or joint self-insurance program as provided in RC 9.833, which contains detailed provisions on the operation and funding of such programs.[106]

RC 3313.202 also provides that a board may agree with an employee collective bargaining representative to establish a jointly administered trust fund to self-insure risks in providing fringe benefits similar to the group insurance coverages described above. A trust fund may also be created to provide insurance benefits. The types of benefits and insurance authorized include hospitalization, surgical care, major medical care, disability, dental care, vision care, medical care, hearing aids, prescription drugs, group life insurance, sickness and accident insurance, and group legal services. Competitive bidding requirements do not apply to the purchase of insurance through a trust.[107]

10.11 Board payment for continuing insurance coverage during illness or pending separation

A board of education must continue to carry on its payroll records all school employees whose sick leave accumulation has expired or who are on an approved leave of absence, for the purpose of providing them with group term life, hospitalization, surgical, or major medical insurance. The board may pay all or part of the cost of coverage, except when the employees are on an approved leave of absence or on a disability leave of absence for a period exceeding two years.[108]

A board is required to continue paying the premiums on insurance covering a teacher, purchased under RC 3313.202, after the teacher submits his resignation or applies for retirement, until the effective date of the resignation or retirement.[109]

The board is not, however, required to pay for insurance after the effective date of the teacher's resignation.[110] A common pleas court has also held that a board is not required to pay after the express June expiration date of a teacher's nonrenewed lim-

---

[102]Tax Deferred Annuities Corp v Cleveland Bd of Ed, 24 App(3d) 105, 24 OBR 176, 493 NE(2d) 305 (Cuyahoga 1985).
[103]OAG 76-078.
[104]OAG 83-098.
[105]OAG 81-045.
[106]If health care benefits are provided pursuant to RC 9.833, the HMO option mandated by RC 1742.33 still applies. See OAG 92-006.

[107]RC 3313.202(B), (C).
[108]RC 3313.202.
[109]OAG 74-050.
[110]Snyder v New Boston School Dist Bd of Ed, No. CIV 85-40 (CP, Scioto 7-16-85) (teacher who resigned effective June 4 not entitled to board-paid medical insurance for succeeding summer months).

ited contract unless a collective bargaining agreement specifically establishes a different period during which coverage will occur.[111]

10.12 Payment for continuing health insurance coverage by terminated employees

(A) Federal law

(1) Introduction, applicability

Title X of the Consolidated Omnibus Budget Reconciliation Act of 1986 (COBRA), as amended, requires employers to offer continued group health coverage to covered employees and their dependents who would otherwise face loss of coverage under an employer's group health plan because of certain qualifying events.[112] Employees and their dependents may continue coverage for a limited period by paying the group insurance rate.[113]

Although Ohio law also requires continuation of coverage for certain employees,[114] the Ohio statute is effectively preempted to the extent COBRA applies to an employer. Employers with fewer than twenty employees are exempt from COBRA's continuation requirements.[115] Whether application of COBRA to state and local government employees is constitutional has not been decided.

Virtually identical COBRA provisions were incorporated into the Employee Retirement Income Security Act (ERISA), the Internal Revenue Code (IRC), and the Public Health Service Act (PHSA). Public schools are subject to COBRA by reason of the PHSA. (A private school may be subject to COBRA by reason of ERISA, the IRC, or both.) Currently, the only regulations that assist in interpreting COBRA's continuation provisions are proposed under the IRC. The US Department of Public Health Service, which has enforcement responsibility for COBRA under the PHSA, looks to these proposed regulations for guidance.

(2) Coverage provided

Unlike the Ohio statute, which limits coverage to group major medical and hospitalization insurance policies, COBRA's requirements apply to most types of group medical, prescription drug, dental, and vision plans sponsored by employers, whether insured or self-insured, including health maintenance organizations (HMOs) and voluntary employees' beneficiary associations (VEBAs). Multiemployer plans, including plans jointly sponsored by employers and labor unions, are also covered.[116]

The extended coverage that must be offered to an eligible employee or dependent is the same coverage provided under the group plan to "similarly situated" individuals who remain eligible for regular coverage.[117]

The proposed regulations break the continued health coverage subject to a COBRA election into "core" and "noncore" coverage. Core coverage refers to the coverage that a covered employee, covered spouse, or dependent child was receiving immediately prior to the time the qualifying event occurred *other* than noncore coverage. Noncore coverage generally means vision and dental benefits.[118] An individual must be permitted to elect either the core plus noncore coverage he had immediately before the election *or* core coverage only (even if the individual previously had core plus noncore coverage).[119] An employer need not permit an election of noncore coverage only, and generally is not required to permit an election of some but not all noncore coverage. (There may be exceptions if an active employee could elect only one part of the noncore coverage—e.g., vision care only—independent of whether he also received core coverage.)[120] In general, once an election is made, the individual need not be permitted to change

---

[111] Manchester Ed Assn v Manchester Local School Dist Bd of Ed, No. CV-85-4-1166 (CP, Summit 1985), appeal dismissed as moot by No. 12481, 1986 WL 9126 (9th Dist Ct App, Summit, 8-20-86).

[112] 42 USCA 300bb-1(a); Proposed Treas. Reg. 1.162-26, Q&A-1 (hereafter, the proposed regulations will be referred to by the appropriate Q&A number).

[113] 42 USCA 300bb-2(3); Q&A-1.

[114] RC 3923.38.

[115] 42 USCA 300bb-1(B)(1); Q&A-8, Q&A-9.

[116] Q&A-8.

[117] 42 USCA 300bb-2(1); Q&A-23.

[118] Q&A-25

[119] Q&A-26

[120] Q&A-27.

the election; however, if the employer permits active employees to change health plans or options in an "open enrollment season," the COBRA-covered individual must also be given the right.[121] Similarly, the COBRA-covered individual may add new dependents (or previously uncovered dependents) only if active employees are permitted to do so.[122]

The period of COBRA coverage depends on the type of qualifying event. If an employee covered by a group health plan incurs a termination of employment, whether voluntary or involuntary (other than for "gross misconduct") or a reduction of hours which would result in loss of coverage, he (and his dependents currently covered under the plan) must be offered extended coverage for up to eighteen months (twenty-nine months if the employee is determined to have been disabled for purposes of Social Security at the time of the termination or reduction in hours, provided notice of such determination is given to the plan administrator before the end of eighteen months). If an employee's spouse or children covered as dependents under the employer's group health plan would lose coverage because of the employee's death, divorce, or legal separation, or the employee's becoming eligible for Medicare, the spouse and children must be offered extended coverage for up to thirty-six months. If an employee's dependent child who is covered by the employer's group health plan ceases to be a dependent child under the terms of the plan and thereby loses coverage, the child must be offered extended coverage for up to thirty-six months.[123]

If, during an eighteen-month coverage period, a second qualifying event occurs (for example, death or divorce), the original eighteen-month period will be extended to a maximum of thirty-six months.[124]

(3) Notice requirements

COBRA requires that the plan administrator provide written notice describing extended coverage rights to new employees and their spouses when they become covered by the plan.[125] The notice may be mailed directly to the residence of the employee, addressed to both the employee and spouse. If the employee and spouse reside at separate addresses, a separate notice should be sent to each.

Thereafter, the employer is responsible for notifying the plan administrator, within thirty days (or in the case of a multiemployer plan, such longer period as may be provided by the plan), of the death, termination of employment, or reduction of hours (leading to loss of coverage) of an employee, or of an employee's entitlement to Medicare benefits.[126] The employee or beneficiary is responsible for notifying the plan administrator of the divorce or legal separation of the employee and spouse and of the termination of eligibility of a dependent child within sixty days of any such circumstance.[127] In the case of one who is determined under Title II or XVI of the Social Security Act to be disabled at the time of the termination or reduction in hours, the employee or beneficiary is responsible for notifying the plan administrator of such determination within sixty days after the date of determination and within thirty days after any final determination that the person is no longer disabled.[128]

Thereafter, the plan administrator must notify the affected employee and dependents of their extended coverage rights. The notice must be given within fourteen days (or in the case of a multiemployer plan, such longer period as may be provided by the plan) after the administrator is informed of the event.[129] The employer may be liable for failure of the plan administrator to comply with COBRA require-

---

[121] Q&A-30.

[122] Q&A-30, Q&A-31.

[123] 42 USCA 300bb-2(2), 42 USCA 300bb-3; Q&A-18, Q&A-19, Q&A-38, Q&A-39.

[124] 42 USCA 300bb-2(2)(A)(ii); Q&A-40. A recent technical correction to the statute inadvertently extended coverage for an *additional* thirty-six months after first eligibility for Medicare. Presumably this will be corrected.

[125] 42 USCA 300bb-6(1).

[126] 42 USCA 300bb-6(2); Q&A-33.

[127] 42 USCA 300bb-6(3); Q&A-33.

[128] 42 USCA 300bb-6(3).

[129] 42 USCA 300bb-6(4).

ments.[130] Therefore, when contracting out for plan administration, the employer should include a provision expressly stating the plan administrator is responsible for complying with the notice requirements. The contract should also include an indemnification clause, holding the employer harmless if the administrator fails to provide adequate notice.

Several courts have held an employer is not required to assure receipt of the COBRA notice, provided the employer made good-faith efforts to comply with the notice requirements.[131]

(4) Payment for coverage

The employee or dependent must be given at least sixty days from the date coverage would otherwise end to elect extended coverage.[132] The election is retroactive to the date of the qualifying event, and a covered individual must pay all past due premiums within forty-five days of the date of the election.[133]

The employee or dependent may be charged up to 102% of the cost for continued coverage. In the case of a Social Security disabled individual, the employer may charge 150% of the premium for the nineteenth through the twenty-ninth months of extended coverage.[134] An employer may adopt reasonable rules for payment of premiums; however, a monthly payment option must be provided.[135]

(5) Termination of coverage

Extended coverage may be terminated before expiration of the relevant eighteen-, twenty-nine-, or thirty-six-month period if the covered individual (1) becomes covered by another employer-sponsored group health plan (which does not exclude or limit coverage with respect to any "preexisting condition"); (2) becomes covered by Medicare; or (3) fails to pay for the coverage.[136] The individual must be permitted at least a thirty day grace period to pay any missed premiums.[137] Coverage may also be terminated if the employer ceases to provide any group health plan to employees.[138] Extended coverage for a qualified beneficiary who was disabled at the time of a qualifying event will be terminated the month that begins more than thirty days after the final determination that the individual is no longer disabled.[139]

(6) Penalties

Public sector employers can be sued to enforce compliance and may also be subject to private actions for losses incurred by eligible persons not given the opportunity to elect extended coverage.[140]

(7) Conversion Option

COBRA specifically requires that a covered individual be permitted to exercise any right of conversion (i.e., to individual, rather than group, coverage) otherwise available under a plan within the 180-day period ending with expiration of the COBRA continuation coverage.[141]

(B) Coverage provided under Ohio law

Employers not subject to COBRA must still follow state law. In Ohio, certain involuntarily terminated employees have the right to maintain coverage under a group insurance policy for up to six months. The employee may continue coverage by paying the group insurance rate. Dental care, vision care, and prescription drug benefits which are provided in addition to the basic hospitalization and major medical coverage need not be continued. The coverage provided, however, may include both the terminated employee and his eligible dependents.[142]

(1) Eligible employees

Only employees eligible for unemployment compensation benefits under RC Chapter 4141 are entitled to continued cov-

---

[130]See Kidder v H & B Marine, Inc, 734 FSupp 724 (ED La 1990), affirmed in part and reversed in part by 932 F(2d) 347 (5th Cir La 1991). But see Bruno v United Steelworkers of America, 784 FSupp 1286 (ND Ohio 1992), dismissed by 959 F(2d) 233 (6th Cir 1992), affirmed by 983 F(2d) 1065 (6th Cir 1993).
[131]E.g., Jachim v KUTV Inc, 783 FSupp 1328 (D Utah 1992); Truesdale v Pacific Holding Co/Hay Adams Div, 778 FSupp 77 (D DC 1991).
[132]42 USCA 300bb-5; Q&A-32.
[133]42 USCA 300bb-2(3); Q&A-47, Q&A-48.
[134]42 USCA 300bb-2(3); Q&A-44.
[135]42 USCA 300bb-2(3); Q&A-46.
[136]42 USCA 300bb-2(2); Q&A-38.
[137]42 USCA 300bb-2(2)(C); Q&A-46.
[138]42 USCA 300b-2(2)(B); Q&A-38.
[139]42 USCA 300bb-2(2)(E).
[140]42 USCA 300bb-7.
[141]42 USCA 300bb-2(5); Q&A-43
[142]RC 3923.38.

erage. Thus, employees who are on strike, have voluntarily resigned, or are discharged for just cause are generally not eligible.[143]

Continued coverage is subject to two other restrictions. First, the employee must have been covered by the employer's group insurance plan for the three-month period before the termination. Second, double coverage is not required.[144] Thus, former employees who either obtain other employment and become covered by the new employer's group plan, or are covered by Medicare, should be dropped from coverage.[145]

(2) Obtaining continuing coverage

It is the employer's responsibility to notify the employee of the right of continuation, and the contributions required to maintain coverage, when notice of termination is given. Although an employer may increase the former employee's contribution if the insurer raises rates, the employee must be informed of this possibility in the initial notice.[146]

To continue coverage, the former employee must file a written election of continuation with the employer and pay the employer the contribution required within ten days after the date the employee's coverage would otherwise terminate (if the employee has been notified of the right of continuation before that date), but in no case may the payment be received more than thirty-one days after the date the employee's coverage would otherwise terminate. To maintain coverage after the first payment, the former employee must pay the employer, monthly and in advance, the amount of contribution required by the employer. This contribution should not exceed the group rate for the insurance being continued under the policy.[147]

SICK LEAVE

10.13 Accumulating sick leave

(A) Annual entitlement, monthly accumulation, rate

Employees of a board of education are entitled to fifteen days of paid sick leave for each year under contract, which are accumulated at the rate of 1.25 days per month.[148] Sick leave accumulates monthly even if school is not in session.[149]

(B) Part-time employees, substitute teachers

Employees whose services are part-time, seasonal, intermittent, per diem, or hourly are also to accumulate paid sick leave for the time actually worked, at the same rate applicable to full-time employees.[150]

Substitute teachers are not entitled to sick leave (or other fringe benefits) until they have served sixty days in one specific teaching assignment.[151] A board may nevertheless adopt regulations for entitlement, crediting, and use of sick leave by substitute teachers not otherwise eligible.[152] Thus, a board may credit sick leave to substitute teachers who have not taught for sixty days and whose assignments are casual or nonspecific.

(C) Maximum accumulation, transfer of sick leave credit

Unused sick leave may be accumulated up to 120 days. If an employee is credited with the full annual allowance each year, the maximum allowable unused sick leave will take eight years to accumulate. The statutory maximum is not mandatory, however, and a board may allow a larger accumulation.[153]

Accumulated sick leave up to the maximum remains with an employee who transfers from one public agency to another, or

---

[143] RC 3923.38.
[144] RC 3923.38.
[145] RC 3923.38.
[146] RC 3923.38, RC 3923.38(C)(2).
[147] RC 3923.38, RC 3923.38(C)(2), RC 3923.38(C)(3).
[148] RC 3319.141.
[149] 1954 OAG 3575.
[150] RC 3319.141.
[151] RC 3319.10.
[152] RC 3319.141.
[153] RC 3319.141.

who leaves and then reenters public service within ten years.[154] Thus, a public employee who becomes a teacher, or a teacher who goes to work for another public agency, takes his accumulated sick leave with him.

(D) Uniform application of sick leave policy

Boards are required to administer sick leave uniformly.[155] Thus, when a board increases the amount that may be accumulated, the increase must apply to all employees covered by the statute.[156] RC 4117.10(A), however, may eliminate this requirement for employees covered by a collective bargaining agreement.[157]

10.14 Adopting state standards on sick leave, caveat

RC 124.39 allows, but does not require, a board of education, as a political subdivision, to adopt policies "similar" to those applicable to state employees regarding sick leave, personal leave, and disability leave benefits.[158] If employees are represented by a union, a board must bargain about any such changes.

Boards should exercise extreme caution in considering whether to adopt such policies. Wholesale adoption could greatly increase the board's liability for employee benefits.

Two unanswered questions are, Can the board selectively adopt only the sick leave provisions of RC 124.382 (an apparent advantage) and ignore the other policies regarding personal leave and disability benefits which might increase the board's liability? What does the word "similar" mean? Most probably, the legislature intended that "similar" be given its ordinary meaning of "nearly corresponding; resembling in many respects; somewhat like; having a general likeness."[159] It may be, however, that a "similar" policy must provide benefits at least equal to the statutory benefits.[160]

A board should carefully review any question of adoption with counsel, especially before entering into any collective bargaining agreement which calls for adoption.

10.15 Advance of unearned sick leave

A board of education may, by regulation, allow its full-time employees an advance of sick leave which has not yet actually been earned. There is no distinction between new employees who have not yet earned sick leave and old employees who have exhausted the leave they had. Allowing an advance of sick leave to full-time employees is discretionary, although the board is limited by the requirement of RC 3319.08 that not less than five days paid leave annually be granted for time lost due to illness or otherwise.[161] Unearned sick leave advanced is charged against the sick leave the employee subsequently accumulates.[162]

10.16 Use of sick leave

An employee may use sick leave, on approval of the responsible district administrator, for absence due to personal illness, pregnancy, injury, exposure to contagious disease which could be communicated to other employees, and absence due to illness, injury, or death in the employee's immediate family.[163] The administrator's discretion in approving or not approving a particular use of sick leave is not unlimited. An appeals court has concluded that, once it is factually determined the leave is being used for one of the statutory reasons, refusal to approve is an abuse of discretion.[164]

Subject to its collective bargaining obligations, a board of education may adopt a rule defining immediate family, which may

---

[154]RC 3319.141.
[155]RC 3319.141.
[156]OAG 75-028.
[157]See Text 18.20, Supremacy of contract over certain laws.
[158]RC 124.382 to RC 124.386.
[159]Scott v State, 107 OS 475, 141 NE 19 (1923).
[160]OAG 84-071; OAG 84-061.
[161]OAG 72-032.

[162]OAG 72-032.
[163]RC 3319.141.
[164]Hannan v Chesapeake Union Exempted Village School Dist Bd of Ed, 41 App(3d) 221, 535 NE(2d) 392 (Lawrence 1988). See also Steinhour v Ohio State University, 62 App(3d) 704, 577 NE(2d) 413 (Franklin 1989) (university rule requiring doctor's certificate for use under RC 124.38 of sick leave due to illness of family member struck down).

limit immediate family to those persons residing in the same household.[165]

RC 3319.141 allows a teacher to use sick leave during pregnancy even though there is no illness or incapacity attributable to the pregnancy.[166] Thus, normal pregnancy is an instance when sick leave properly can be used.[167]

An employee must furnish a signed statement, on forms prescribed by the board, to justify the use of sick leave. If medical attention is required, the statement must give the name and address of the attending physician and the dates when he was consulted. But, unless its collective bargaining agreement provides otherwise, a board may not adopt a rule requiring a physician's statement to justify the use of sick leave.[168]

Falsification of a statement is grounds for suspension or termination.[169] One court has held that suspension or termination is not the exclusive remedy for improper use of sick leave. A board may withhold pay for a day when leave was wrongfully taken.[170]

10.17 Severance pay on basis of accumulated sick leave

(A) In general, payment on retirement, amount payable

An employee may elect to be paid for unused sick leave upon service or disability retirement under the employee's retirement system, provided he has at least ten years of service with the board or another public agency.[171] In calculating whether the ten-year service requirement is satisfied, years of part-time service are included.[172] An employee who terminates service before retirement is not entitled to such payment.[173]

The amount payable is one-fourth the value of his unused sick leave, based on his pay rate at the time of retirement.[174] Thus, if the retiree's unused leave amounts to twenty days, he is entitled to payment for five days. The employee may choose to be paid in installments, but the total may not exceed payment for thirty days of unused leave.[175] When payment is made, *all* accrued sick leave is eliminated.[176]

Payment is at the election of the employee and is in cash. Thus, an employee who is eligible for disability retirement benefits may exhaust all sick leave before receiving the benefits.[177]

(B) Adoption of liberalized severance pay plan

A board may adopt a more generous policy.[178] Specifically, the board may (1) authorize payment for more than one-fourth the value of unused leave; (2) fix eligibility at less than ten years of service; (3) permit more than one payment; or (4) provide for payment on termination of

---

[165]RC 3319.141, RC 3313.20; Blust v Madison Local School Dist Bd of Ed, No. CA-2022, 1982 WL 3006 (5th Dist Ct App, Richland, 7-7-82).

[166]Sloan v Warren City School Dist Bd of Ed, No. 2391 (11th Dist Ct App, Trumbull, 3-28-77).

[167]Sylvania Ed Assn v Sylvania Bd of Ed, No. C-74-517, 1976 WL 718 (ND Ohio, 12-21-76); Hoeflinger v West Clermont Local Bd of Ed, 17 App(3d) 145, 17 OBR 245, 478 NE(2d) 251 (Clermont 1984).

[168]OAG 75-015. See also Hoeflinger v West Clermont Local Bd of Ed, 17 App(3d) 145, 17 OBR 245, 478 NE(2d) 251 (Clermont 1984) (physician's statement cannot be required to justify leave because of pregnancy); Steinhour v Ohio State University, 62 App(3d) 704, 577 NE(2d) 413 (Franklin 1989) (university rule requiring doctor's certificate for use under RC 124.38 of sick leave due to illness of family member struck down).

[169]See Swinderman v Dover City School Dist Bd of Ed, No. 91AP110092, 1992 WL 91655 (5th Dist Ct App, Tuscarawas, 4-20-92) (falsification was immorality and other good and just cause for termination under RC 3319.16). Because the statute provides for a range of sanctions, one court has held a board of education must take into account a teacher's total past work record prior to imposing a particular sanction. Katz v Maple Heights City School Dist Bd of Ed, 87 App(3d) 256, 622 NE(2d) 1 (Cuyahoga 1993) (reversing board decision to terminate in favor of disciplinary suspension as recommended by a referee under RC 3319.16). See also Text 9.21, Termination for cause, in general.

[170]Martin v Washington Local Bd of Ed, No. 80-0075 (CP, Lucas, 11-9-81).

[171]RC 124.39. The election may be made by the employee only at the time of his service or disability retirement from active service. OAG 94-009.

[172]See OAG 92-015.

[173]OAG 91-026.

[174]RC 124.39(B).

[175]RC 124.39(B).

[176]RC 124.39(B).

[177]State ex rel Runyan v Henry, 34 App(3d) 23, 516 NE(2d) 1261 (Miami 1986).

[178]RC 124.39(C).

employment other than by retirement. However, a board may not provide cash payments for unused sick leave at the end of a school year.[179] Again, such payments could be authorized under a collective bargaining agreement.

Whether to go beyond minimum statutory requirements is discretionary. Thus, requiring at least ten years of service before an employee could become entitled to severance pay was permissible even though at the time no employed teacher could qualify.[180] A collective bargaining agreement may incorporate a policy, but where the agreement limited severance pay to retired employees (as in the statute), a teacher who resigned was not entitled to severance pay.[181]

10.18 Enforced leave for certain illnesses

If a teacher (or other school employee or student) is found ill with "tuberculosis in a communicable stage or other communicable disease," the school physician is bound to send him home immediately with advice to the parents, in the case of a student, to consult the family physician. Further, if a teacher or other employee has communicable tuberculosis or another communicable disease, "his employment shall be discontinued or suspended upon such terms as to salary as the board deems just until the school physician has certified to a recovery from such disease."[182]

This provision first appeared in 1913,[183] when tuberculosis was far more prevalent and isolation of persons with the active pulmonary form of the disease was necessary to prevent its spread. The difficulty is that the statute includes *any* communicable disease, literally anything from pneumonic plague to the common cold. Obviously, in applying the statute, a board of education needs carefully to assess the danger posed to students and other employees. In addition, a board's discretion in this area must be exercised in light of more modern antidiscrimination laws that generally require an employer reasonably to accommodate an employee's handicap or disability.[184]

LEAVES OF ABSENCE

10.19 Requested leave

(A) In general, return to service after leave

RC 3319.13 is the basic (but not the only) provision governing leaves of absence. It provides that on written request of a teacher the board of education *may* grant a leave for up to two consecutive school years "for educational or professional or other purposes," and *must* grant the leave if it is because of illness or other disability. A leave may be renewed on subsequent request.

If leave for other than illness or disability is denied, the teacher resorts to self-help at his peril. Failure to return to work following denial of a request for nonmedical leave is grounds for termination under RC 3319.16.[185]

Upon returning from leave under RC 3319.13, the employee has the contract status held prior to leave. If he is not yet eligible for tenure, the board may choose not to renew his limited contract, and he is not entitled to reemployment if the required notice of nonrenewal is given.[186]

(B) Leave with partial pay for professional growth

A teacher who has completed five years of service with the district may be granted a leave of absence with part pay for purposes of professional growth.[187] The service must be teaching service. A teacher with three years of teaching service and two years of

---

[179]OAG 81-052.

[180]McLaughlin v Mahoning County Joint Vocational School Dist Bd of Ed, No. 81 CA 45, 1982 WL 6122 (7th Dist Ct App, Mahoning, 4-22-82).

[181]Sayen v Toledo Bd of Ed, No. L-82-189, 1982 WL 6664 (6th Dist Ct App, Lucas, 12-3-82).

[182]RC 3313.71.

[183]GC 7692-1, 103 Ohio Laws 897.

[184]See Text 17.13, Discrimination against the handicapped.

[185]Thompson v West Clermont Local Bd of Ed, No. CA-967, 1981 WL 5235 (12th Dist Ct App, Clermont, 10-28-81).

[186]Murray v Washington Local School Dist Bd of Ed, No. L-85-159, 1986 WL 7629 (6th Dist Ct App, Lucas, 7-11-86).

[187]RC 3319.131.

military service was not eligible for leave under the statute.[188]

To obtain leave, the teacher must present a plan for professional improvement to the superintendent, and leave must be approved by the superintendent and the board. The board may grant leave only for one or two semesters, and only if there is a satisfactory substitute available to take the teacher's place while on leave. The maximum partial salary permissible for the teacher on leave is the difference between the teacher's contract salary and the substitute teacher's pay.[189]

As a condition to granting leave, the board may require the teacher to return to the district for at least one year, unless the teacher has taught for twenty-five years in Ohio. When the teacher returns, he must present evidence that he followed the plan for professional growth presented when leave was requested.[190]

While the board may grant leave to the same teacher more than once, the teacher must complete another five years of service before a subsequent leave. Also, a subsequent leave may not be granted if others have filed for leave. In any case, the board may not allow leave to more than five per cent of its professional staff at one time.[191]

10.20 Unrequested disability leave

(A) In general, hearing

A board of education may grant a leave of absence to an employee for physical or mental disability, even if leave has not been requested.[192] An employee who objects to a forced leave is entitled to the procedural safeguards provided in cases of termination for cause.[193]

The provision on disability leave in RC 3319.13 overlaps the provision on communicable disease leave in RC 3313.71. The latter statute, however, makes no mention of administrative due process for an employee who objects.

(B) Pregnancy and child care

It was once common practice arbitrarily to force female employees to take leave for pregnancy and child care after delivery. The US Supreme Court found this practice unconstitutional in *Cleveland Bd of Ed v LaFleur*.[194]

Discrimination on the basis of pregnancy is now prohibited under both state and federal law.[195] Ohio Civil Rights Commission guidelines on employment policies with respect to pregnancy and childbirth[196] make any policy or practice which excludes employees from working because of pregnancy prima facie evidence of unlawful sex discrimination. Where insufficient maternity leave is available, termination of an employee temporarily disabled because of pregnancy is unlawful. Employment policies on the commencement and duration of maternity leave must be structured so as to take individual capacity and medical status into account; and policies on seniority, reinstatement, and other benefits (except sickness and accident insurance plans) must be applied to disability due to pregnancy and childbirth on the same terms as they are applied to other leaves of absence.[197] These regulations are similar to federal regulations on the subject.[198]

10.21 Miscellaneous leaves of absence

(A) Military leave: active duty, reserve training

Any teacher who leaves to enter the armed services of the United States and returns to his position after discharge (except dishonorable discharge) must be reemployed under the same type of contract he held when he left.[199] For public employees in general (including teachers), such reemployment rights are indepen-

---

[188] 1963 OAG 347.

[189] RC 3319.131.

[190] RC 3319.131.

[191] RC 3319.131.

[192] RC 3319.13.

[193] RC 3319.16. See Text 9.22, Termination for cause, procedure.

[194] Cleveland Bd of Ed v LaFleur, 414 US 632, 94 SCt 791, 39 LEd(2d) 52 (1974).

[195] RC 4112.01(B), RC 4112.02(A); 42 USCA 2000e-2(a).

[196] OAC 4112-5-05.

[197] OAC 4112-5-05.

[198] 29 CFR 1604.10.

[199] RC 3319.14. The statute, which expressly applies to "teachers" and not school employees generally, is triggered only if the teacher enters the armed

dently affirmed, irrespective of whether the employee voluntarily or involuntarily entered active duty, in RC 5903.03.[200] Application for reemployment must be made within ninety days of discharge.[201] If a teacher's application is received not less than thirty days prior to the first day of a semester, the teacher must be reemployed the next semester, and years of absence in the armed services must be counted as though teaching service had been performed during that time.[202]

RC 5903.02 entitles a public employee to a leave of absence to be inducted or to enlist in military duty, during which leave he is "for all purposes, ... considered as having rendered service and as having received his regular rate of pay." RC 5903.05 provides that all permanent public employees[203] who are members of the Ohio National Guard, the Ohio Military Reserve, the Ohio Naval Militia, or other reserve components of US armed forces must be given leave without loss of pay for the time they are performing military duty, for periods not exceeding twenty-two eight-hour work days or one hundred seventy-six hours in any one calendar year, for each calendar year in which military duty is performed. If such an employee is called to active duty for a period in excess of this amount in a calendar year because of an executive order of the President or an act of Congress, he is entitled to receive, during each month of that excess period, the lesser of (1) the difference between his gross monthly wage or salary and the sum of his gross military pay and allowances received that month, or (2) $500 (unless his military pay and allowances for the month exceeds his gross wage or salary, in which case there is no obligation to pay). He is also entitled to receive such additional pay as the employer elects to pay and authorizes. Before being credited with leave, the employee must submit the published order authorizing the military duty or a written statement from the appropriate miliary commander authorizing such leave. Finally, if the employee is covered by a collective bargaining agreement that provides for military leave, the employee must abide by the terms of that agreement with respect to military leave.[204]

(B) Assault leave, injury in line of duty

A board of education may adopt a policy whereby an employee absent due to physical disability resulting from an assault occurring in the course of employment will be maintained on full pay during the absence.

A board electing such a policy must establish rules for entitlement, crediting, and use of assault leave and file a copy with the state board of education. The policy must require the employee to furnish a signed statement on forms prescribed by the board justifying the leave. Likewise, the policy must require the employee to furnish a doctor's certificate stating the nature of the disability and its duration if medical attention is required.[205]

Assault leave cannot be charged against sick leave or any other leave.

(C) Personal leave

Unlike the situation with respect to regular nonteaching employees,[206] no statute specifically addresses personal leave for teachers. That a board of education may adopt a personal leave policy, however, is clear.[207]

---

forces within forty school days after leaving his position.

[200]See OAG 86-050. See also 38 USCA 2021 et seq. for federal treatment of veterans' reemployment rights that overlaps Ohio law.

[201]RC 3319.14, RC 5903.03. See also RC 124.29 as to employees covered by civil service.

[202]RC 3319.14.

[203]A "permanent public employee" is defined as one holding a position in public employment that requires working a regular schedule of twenty-six consecutive bi-weekly pay periods, or any other regular schedule of comparable consecutive pay periods, not limited to a season or duration. Intermittent or seasonal employees, student help, and individuals covered by personal services contracts are excluded. RC 5903.01(A).

[204]RC 5923.05. The reference to collective bargaining agreements appears in RC 5923.05(F) and must be read in conjunction with RC 4117.10, which states that RC 5923.05 prevails over any conflicting provisions of an agreement if the terms of that agreement contain benefits less than those contained in the statute.

[205]RC 3319.143.

[206]See Text 13.10(A), Personal leave.

[207]OAG 73-084 (relying on statutory language that now appears in RC 3319.08).

(D) Family and Medical Leave Act

The federal Family and Medical Leave Act of 1993 is treated in Text 17.16, Family and Medical Leave Act of 1993.

Chapter 11

Teachers: Retirement

INTRODUCTION
11.01 State teachers retirement system (STRS)
11.02 State teachers retirement board
11.03 Funds and investments

MEMBERS OF SYSTEM
11.04 Membership in STRS
11.05 STRS membership and teachers' contracts
11.06 Certifying teachers' names and payroll reports to STRS

CONTRIBUTIONS TO SYSTEM
11.07 Mandatory contributions by members
11.08 Voluntary contributions by members
11.09 Mandatory contributions by employers
11.10 Additional contributions by employers
11.11 Withdrawal of contributions from STRS

SERVICE CREDIT
11.12 Importance of service credit, accumulation
11.13 Purchasing service credit
11.14 Military service credit
11.15 Prior service credit, certificate

DISABILITY COVERAGE
11.16 Entitlement to disability benefit
11.17 Termination of disability benefit

SERVICE RETIREMENT
11.18 Eligibility for service retirement
11.19 Amount of retirement benefits
11.20 Health benefits for retirees
11.21 Early retirement incentive plans
11.22 Employment of retired teachers
11.23 Optional compensation deferral plans

SURVIVORS' BENEFITS
11.24 Death before retirement
11.25 Death after retirement
11.26 Lump sum burial payment

INTRODUCTION

11.01 State teachers retirement system (STRS)

The state teachers retirement system of Ohio was established in 1920 for the teachers of the public schools, in recognition that their public service warranted benefits over and above the payment of wages. Several funds were created and placed under the management of the state teachers retirement board for the payment of retirement allowances and other benefits.[1]

The state system was intended to replace pension plans maintained locally, and the statutes provided for the merger of local district pension systems into STRS.[2]

Retirement, death, and disability benefits are funded by both employer and employee contributions. Retirement benefits are determined by a formula based upon the age, service, and final average salary of the retirant. A retirant enjoys several optional payment plans to receive his benefits.

Provision is made in RC 3307.751 for the recovery of erroneously paid benefits.

11.02 State teachers retirement board

(A) In general, composition

The state teachers retirement board is composed of the superintendent of public instruction, the state auditor, the attorney general, five teachers, and one retired teacher who is receiving service retirement benefits under RC 3307.38 or RC 3307.39.[3] Members serve without compensation but must be reimbursed from the expense fund for all actual necessary expenses incurred while serving. The employer of a teacher member may not reduce the teacher's compensation because of absence to attend a meeting. The board may secure and pay for indemnity insurance coverage for members and employees.[4]

(B) Conflict of interest

RC 3307.14 and RC 3307.18 contain specific prohibitions against an employee or fiduciary of the system having any interest, direct or indirect, in business involving the system except as specifically authorized by these statutes. The statutes should be reviewed in detail before a fiduciary or

---

[1] RC Ch 3307.
[2] RC 3307.68 to RC 3307.70.
[3] RC 3307.05.
[4] RC 3307.10.

employee engages in any transaction with the system.[5]

(C) Powers and duties

In addition to the general administration and management of the system and the authority to make necessary rules,[6] the board receives and acts on all applications for retirement, provides for the payment of all retirement allowances and other benefits, and makes other necessary expenditures.[7]

The board may sue and be sued, contract and be contracted with, and do all things necessary to carry out the duties delegated to it.[8] The board has standing to bring declaratory judgment actions.[9] All of its business must be transacted, all of its funds invested, all warrants for money drawn and payments made, and all of its cash, securities, and other property held in the name of the board or certain specified nominees of the board.[10]

The board is authorized to employ an executive director (who serves as secretary) and must employ other persons necessary to operate the system.[11] Board employees are not in the state civil service and are not entitled to the civil service protection of RC Chapter 124.[12]

11.03 Funds and investments

(A) Sources and purposes of separate funds

As an aid to the efficient operation of the retirement system, six different funds have been established, each as a separate legal entity:[13]

(1) Teachers' savings fund, in which the contributions of teacher members are accumulated for the purchase of annuities;

(2) Employers' trust fund, in which reserves are accumulated from employers' contributions for the payment of pensions or other benefits to members;

(3) Annuity and pension reserve fund, from which must be paid all pensions and annuities for which reserves have been transferred from the teachers' savings fund and the employers' trust fund;

(4) Survivors' benefit fund, from which survivor benefits are paid;

(5) Guarantee fund, used to facilitate crediting uniform interest on the amounts in the various other funds except the expense fund, and to provide a contingent fund out of which special requirements of any of the other funds may be covered; and

(6) Expense fund, from which administrative expenses of the system are paid.[14]

(B) Investments

As with pension plans generally, one of the actuarial assumptions in STRS is that the plan's assets will be invested and the yield applied to increase the amount available to pay benefits. Investments are under the board's control, subject to detailed statutory requirements on the composition of the STRS investment portfolio. The board is the trustee of the system's funds[15] and may invest in certain described investments.[16]

MEMBERS OF SYSTEM

11.04 Membership in STRS

(A) Persons required to be members

Any teacher or other person employed in Ohio's public schools is required to be a member of STRS if he is (1) employed under a type of contract described in RC 3319.08, (2) paid from public funds, and (3)

---

[5]Conflicts of interest are discussed in more detail in Text Ch 45, Ethics Requirements and Education Personnel.
[6]RC 3307.04.
[7]RC 3307.11.
[8]RC 3307.03.
[9]State Teachers Retirement System Bd v Cuyahoga Falls City School Dist Bd of Ed, No. CA 10871, 1983 WL 4071 (9th Dist Ct App, Summit, 4-27-83).
[10]RC 3307.03.
[11]RC 3307.11.
[12]In re Appeal of Ford, 3 App(3d) 416, 3 OBR 484, 446 NE(2d) 214 (Franklin 1982).
[13]RC 3307.66.
[14]RC 3307.65.
[15]RC 3307.65.
[16]RC 3307.15.

required to have a certificate issued pursuant to RC 3319.22 to RC 3319.31.[17] This requirement extends to certificated employees employed in educational positions under federal programs but for which no certification requirements can be made under federal law.[18] Substitute teachers and home instructors are required to be STRS members,[19] as are educational employees of the state department of education, but a student, intern, or resident employed part-time at a school, college, or university in which he is regularly attending classes is generally excluded.[20]

The attorney general has concluded that teachers employed in education programs operated by county boards of mental retardation and developmental disabilities under RC Chapter 3323 are members of STRS.[21]

In cases where required membership is in doubt, the state teachers retirement board has final authority to determine whether any person is a teacher for purposes of the retirement laws.[22]

(B) Exclusion from membership

The state teachers retirement board is authorized to deny the right to contribute or membership to any class of teachers whose compensation is partly paid by the state, who are not serving on a yearly basis, or who are on a temporary basis, who are not required to have a teacher's certificate. The board may also make optional with teachers in any such class their right to contribute or their entrance into membership.[23]

The board may deny membership to any teacher whose compensation, although disbursed by an employer, is reimbursed to the employer in whole or in part from other than public funds.[24]

11.05 STRS membership and teachers' contracts

Employers must notify prospective teachers of their duties and obligations under the state retirement system laws.[25] Any appointment or reappointment of a teacher, or service on a continuing contract, must be conditioned on the teacher's acceptance of the statutes as part of the contract to teach.[26] This condition is usually incorporated as a part of the written contract with teachers under RC 3319.08.

11.06 Certifying teachers' names and payroll reports to STRS

During September or at such other time as the retirement board approves, each employer must certify the names of all teachers to the board.[27] The employer must also notify the board monthly of the employment of new teachers, removals, withdrawals, and changes in the salaries of teachers that have occurred since the last notification.[28]

Each employer must transmit payroll reports to its treasurer and to the secretary of the retirement board, indicating the amounts of employee contributions deducted from the payroll.[29] Based on these reports, the treasurer must transmit to the board the amounts deducted, together with the normal contribution and deficiency contribution payable by the employer.[30]

CONTRIBUTIONS TO SYSTEM

11.07 Mandatory contributions by members

(A) Contribution rate, payroll deduction

Each member must contribute a minimum of 8 per cent of his compensation to the teachers' savings fund. The state teach-

---

[17]RC 3307.01(B), (E).
[18]RC 3307.012.
[19]State Teachers Retirement Bd v Cuyahoga Falls City School Dist Bd of Ed, 26 App(3d) 45, 26 OBR 218, 498 NE(2d) 167 (Summit 1985).
[20]RC 3307.01(B), (E).
[21]OAG 88-069.
[22]RC 3307.01(B).

[23]RC 3307.27.
[24]RC 3307.27.
[25]RC Ch 3307.
[26]RC 3307.58.
[27]RC 3307.59.
[28]RC 3307.60.
[29]RC 3307.61.
[30]RC 3307.62.

ers retirement board can increase the rate to not more than 10 per cent; the current rate is 9.25 per cent.[31]

For purposes of computing employee contributions, compensation generally includes all salary, wages, and other earnings paid to a member by reason of his employment. However, it does not include (1) any payments for accrued but unused sick leave or personal leave; (2) vacation pay for concurrent periods for which other salary or compensation is also paid; (3) amounts the employer pays for insurance, or payments to the employee in lieu of insurance; (4) payments attributable to retirement or agreement to retire, with certain exceptions; or (5) certain other incidental or military-related payments specified by statute.[32]

(B) Contributions while on disability leave

A member who is not a state employee need not make contributions while on disability leave, pursuant to an employer-sponsored program under which he receives a percentage of salary while on leave. Instead, the employer must make both the employer and employee contributions based on the teacher's rate of pay at the time leave was granted.[33] However, a state employee on approved disability leave must pay the employee contribution during the first three months of leave; thereafter, both the employer and employee contributions must be paid by the state.[34]

11.08 Voluntary contributions by members

(A) Contributions while on leave of absence

Any member prevented from making contributions because of a leave of absence may purchase up to two years of service credit. Contributions are based on the compensation the member would have earned, and the contribution rates that would have been applied, had the member been paid throughout the leave period. The member pays the employee contribution, and the employer pays the employer contribution.[35]

The member can choose among several methods of paying his contribution. First, if the leave began and ended in the same year, he may pay through payroll deductions in that year if certain conditions are met.[36] Second, he can pay all or part of the total contributions in one or more lump sums within a two-year "grace period," which begins at the end of the year in which the leave terminated.[37] Finally, he may pay all or part of the total contributions after the grace period has expired; however, he must pay interest on both the employer and employee contributions.[38]

A member who requests a discretionary leave of absence and promises not to purchase service credit for the period covered by the leave, if leave is granted, is bound by the agreement.[39]

(B) Extra deposits to increase annuity income

Any member may make additional direct deposits, subject to rules of the retirement board, which must be credited to the member's account to be used at

---

[31] RC 3307.51.

[32] RC 3307.01(U); OAG 86-041. Backpay awards are included as compensation. State ex rel Cicero v State Teachers Retirement Bd, 77 App(3d) 823, 603 NE(2d) 1102 (Franklin 1991) (arbitrator had awarded back pay for amount teacher would have received under supplemental contract for athletic director job had position been properly posted under collective bargaining agreement).

[33] RC 3307.511.

[34] RC 124.385(D).

[35] RC 3307.512. A collective bargaining agreement between a board of education and a union that purports to insulate the board against liability for its contributions is unenforceable since, under RC 4117.10, laws pertaining to the retirement of public employees prevail over any conflicting provision of such an agreement. Streetsboro Ed Assn v Streetsboro City School Dist Bd of Ed, 68 OS(3d) 288, 626 NE(2d) 110 (1994). See also Text 18.20, Supremacy of contract over certain laws.

[36] RC 3307.512(C).

[37] RC 3307.512(D).

[38] RC 3307.512(E).

[39] State ex rel Fox v Montgomery County Joint Vocational School Dist, No. 11355, 1990 WL 107837 (2d Dist Ct App, Montgomery, 7-31-90) (rejecting teacher's argument that such an agreement is contrary to public policy).

retirement to provide additional annuity income. Such deposits, with interest, may be refunded to the member before retirement, or to the beneficiary or estate in the event of death prior to retirement, and must be refunded if the member withdraws his refundable account.[40]

11.09 Mandatory contributions by employers

Each employer must pay to the employers' trust fund a certain percentage of the earnable compensation of each teacher. The amount is to be computed by the actuary and approved by the retirement board, but may not exceed fourteen per cent of the earnable compensation of all members.[41] The present employer contribution rate is the maximum fourteen per cent.

The board of education must pay the employer contribution for a teacher who purchases service credit while on leave as provided in RC 3307.512.[42] In addition, the board may be required to pay both the employer and employee contributions for a teacher on disability leave.[43]

Employer contributions are deducted from the monthly school foundation payments owed each school district pursuant to RC Chapter 3317. The secretary of the retirement board is required to certify monthly, to the state superintendent of public instruction, the amount each district owes to the retirement system. The superintendent then deducts that amount from the total owed to the district, and that amount is transmitted directly to STRS.[44]

11.10 Additional contributions by employers

Employers can make additional contributions by "picking up" the employees' portion of required contributions. There are two types of pickups: fringe benefit pickups and salary reduction pickups. They can be used independently or in combination. If the fringe benefit pickup is implemented, the employing board incurs an additional cost depending on the pickup amount. If a pure salary reduction pickup is implemented, the employing board incurs no additional cost.

In either case, a properly implemented pickup plan may allow employees to defer state and federal income taxes on the pickup amounts until withdrawal.[45] STRS guidelines suggest ways to ensure favorable IRS treatment. According to the guidelines, an employer may pick up contributions for any of three groups: superintendent, administrator, and teacher. The pickup must be applicable to all members of a group without exception, and no member may have the option to receive a cash payment in lieu of the pickup.

STRS guidelines also require that employers file a notification form with the retirement board when implementing a pickup plan. Changes in the amount of pickup must also be reported to the board.

(A) Fringe benefit pickup

An employer may pick up all or part of the required teacher contributions to STRS without reducing employees' salaries.[46] The amount picked up is included in calculating final average salary for retirement purposes.[47] "Final average salary" is one factor in computing service retirement benefits; it means the sum of the annual earnings for the three highest years of compensation for which contributions were made, divided by three.[48]

(B) Pickup through salary reduction

An employer may implement a salary reduction pickup,[49] under which the employer assumes and pays the teacher's retirement contribution and reduces the employee's salary by an equal amount. The employer incurs no additional expense

---

[40] RC 3307.51.
[41] RC 3307.53.
[42] See Text 11.08(A), Contributions while on leave of absence.
[43] RC 3307.511. See Text 11.07(B), Contributions while on disability leave.
[44] RC 3307.56.
[45] Rev Rul 81-35, 81-36; 1981-1 CB 255, 256; OAG 78-065. See also STRS Bull Vol 1, No. 2A (December 1983). City taxes, however, may continue to be levied against the pickup portion of a member's salary. See Williams v Columbus, 40 App(3d) 71, 531 NE(2d) 1336 (Franklin 1987).
[46] OAG 78-049.
[47] RC 3307.01(V)(1).
[48] RC 3307.01(J).
[49] OAG 84-036.

under this option. It benefits the employee by reducing his current income, thus deferring federal and state income taxes on the amount of the pickup.[50] For STRS purposes, however, compensation is determined as though the employee's income had not been reduced by the amount of the pickup.[51]

11.11 Withdrawal of contributions from STRS

When an STRS member leaves teaching, he may leave his contributions in STRS to provide for his future retirement, but he is also entitled to withdraw his contributions. A contributor who ceases to be a teacher for any reason other than death, retirement, or receipt of a disability benefit must be paid on application the accumulated contributions standing to the credit of his individual account in the teachers' savings fund.[52] The sole exception is where the contributor has been charged with a theft offense against the employer. Payment will be delayed while such a charge is pending to enforce any restitution order.[53] A member who has ceased to be a teacher, and who is also a member of either the public employees retirement system or the school employees retirement system, or both, may not withdraw his accumulated contributions unless he also withdraws his contributions from the other system(s).[54]

SERVICE CREDIT

11.12 Importance of service credit, accumulation

(A) In general

Service credit is a primary factor in determining both eligibility for retirement and the amount of retirement benefits, and therefore it is vital that the credit be properly accumulated. One year of service must be credited to any teacher who is employed on a full-time basis in a school district for the number of months district schools were in session in a given year.[55] Full-time service is defined as 120 days or two quarters of contributing service according to retirement board rules. Partial credit is given for less than full-time service and is computed as actual days of teaching service divided by 180.[56] Not more than one year of service may be credited for all service rendered in any year.[57]

At retirement the total service credited to a teacher consists of all his service as a teacher since last becoming a member, plus all certified prior service, including military service and all purchased service credit.[58]

(B) Combining credits from other public employees retirement systems

At the option of a member, or of a beneficiary, total contributions and service credit in the public employees retirement system and the school employees retirement system and STRS must be used in determining the eligibility and total allowance for the purpose of service retirement and a disability benefit. Where total contributions and service credit are combined, special provisions of law apply.[59]

11.13 Purchasing service credit

(A) In general

Members may purchase service credit for various types of state or federal employment not covered by STRS. Service for which credit may be purchased includes (1) military service; (2) time spent as a prisoner of war;[60] (3) service in an Ohio police or fire department, in the state highway patrol, in the public employees retirement system, or in the school employees retirement system;[61] (4) service for which contributions were made to a municipal retire-

---

[50] OAG 84-036.
[51] RC 3307.01(V)(1).
[52] RC 3307.46.
[53] RC 3307.72.
[54] RC 3307.47.
[55] RC 3307.31.
[56] OAC 3307-1-08.
[57] RC 3307.31.
[58] RC 3307.01(C), RC 3307.021, RC 3307.32, RC 3307.36.

[59] RC 3307.41. See also RC 3307.021(F), RC 3307.32(D).
[60] RC 3307.021. See Text 11.14, Military service credit.
[61] RC 3307.411. A service credit purchase was permitted under RC 3307.22 rather than RC 3307.411 where the STRS member had not exempted herself from the school employees retirement system, and the school employees retirement system board of directors did not validly promulgate a policy treating such

ment system in Ohio;[62] and (5) teaching service in a public or private school, college, or university of Ohio or another state, or in a school or entity operated by or for the United States government, or in certain capacities for another state or for the federal government.[63] Purchased service in each category, except the police, fire, and highway patrol category, is limited to five years or the member's total years of Ohio service, whichever is less. Provision is also made for purchasing credit for each year or portion of a year for which a member exempted himself from membership, except that a member may not purchase credit for service exempted from contributions under RC 3307.27.[64]

Purchased service credit in all the above categories is included in "total service credit" for the purpose of determining retirement eligibility and benefits.[65] Members may also purchase additional credit for certain types of nonteaching or non-Ohio public service.[66] This credit, however, can only be used in computing eligibility for service retirement.[67]

The retirement board has authority to determine and fix the amount of the payment that must be made for service credit purchased under RC 3307.33.[68] With respect to a member who established STRS membership on or after July 1, 1989, or if the credit is for service that began on or after July 1, 1989, the amount cannot be less than fifty per cent of the additional liability that results from the credit as specified by a board-employed actuary.[69]

The purchase of credit for service as a school board member (at the rate of one-quarter of a year's credit for each year of service) is authorized by RC 3307.311, which spells out certain conditions that must be satisfied.

(B) Redeposit of withdrawn contributions

A teacher or former teacher with at least one and one-half years of contributing service credit in STRS or any other retirement system specified in RC 3307.28 who withdraws his account may restore credit by redepositing in the teachers' saving fund the amount withdrawn plus interest.[70]

(C) Contributions by part-time personnel

A part-time teacher or employee may, with the consent of the appropriate system, make additional contributions to one of the retirement system funds to equal his normal full-time contributions.[71]

(D) Payroll deduction plans

RC 3307.281 authorizes the retirement board to establish by rule payroll deduction plans for paying the cost of purchasing or restoring service credit[72] or paying charges for participation in a long-term health care insurance program established pursuant to RC 3307.741.

11.14 Military service credit

Military service credit is a component of "total service credit" used to determine retirement eligibility and benefits.[73]

(A) Military service credit acquired without purchase

Any member who has left active service as a teacher to become a member of the armed forces of the United States on active duty or service, including full-time service with the American Red Cross in a combat zone, must be considered on indefinite leave of absence. Members of the Ohio National Guard, the Ohio Military Reserve, the Ohio Naval Militia, or other reserve components of US armed forces called to active duty by an executive order of the President or an act of Congress are

---

service as exempt. State ex rel Ryan v State Teachers Retirement System, 71 OS(3d) 362, 643 NE(2d) 1122 (1994).

[62]RC 3307.32.

[63]RC 3307.32. Part-time service as a graduate teaching assistant at a public university does not qualify as teaching service under the statute. State ex rel Palmer v State Teachers Retirement Bd, 90 App(3d) 497, 629 NE(2d) 1377 (Franklin 1993).

[64]RC 3307.22. See also State ex rel Brown v Public Employees Retirement Bd, No. 93AP-290, 1993 WL 387252 (10th Dist Ct App, Franklin, 9-30-93).

[65]RC 3307.01(D).

[66]RC 3307.33.

[67]RC 3307.01(D).

[68]RC 3307.33(D).

[69]RC 3307.33(D). See also RC 3307.021(D)(2), RC 3307.32(B)(2), RC 3307.411(B)(2).

[70]RC 3307.28.

[71]1964 OAG 1421.

[72]See OAC 3307-1-28.

[73]RC 3307.01(D).

accorded the same protection. On presenting an honorable discharge or certificate of service, and subject to rules adopted by the retirement board, the member must have such service considered as the equivalent of prior service up to a maximum of ten years. To receive such credit, the member must return to active service as a teacher within two years after the effective date of discharge and must establish one year of service credit. The member can also establish eligibility by becoming a member of either the public employees or school employees retirement system within the two-year period, and establishing one year of service credit in that system.[74]

(B) Purchasing service credit

A member who does not qualify for the no-cost military service credit described above may nonetheless purchase credit for military service on active duty. He may purchase one year's credit for each year of service up to five years and in addition may purchase credit for up to five years spent as a prisoner of war. The member may purchase both active-duty credit and POW credit for the same year where both categories are applicable. The combined credit purchased for both types of service may not exceed ten years or the member's total accumulated years of Ohio service, whichever is less.[75]

11.15 Prior service credit, certificate

Prior service includes certain types of service before September 1, 1920, as well as military service credit and service credit purchased under RC 3307.33 before June 25, 1945.[76]

A prior service certificate certifying the aggregate length of all prior service as a teacher is a final and conclusive record for retirement purposes, unless modified by the retirement board. The board may modify the certificate, on application of the member or on its own initiative, within one year of issuance or within one year of discovery of a mistake in the certificate.[77]

DISABILITY COVERAGE

11.16 Entitlement to disability benefit

(A) Who is eligible

STRS offers liability coverage to any member who has at least five years of total service credit.[78] For persons who become members after July 29, 1992, coverage is provided under RC 3307.431, which provides for an annual disability allowance in accordance with a specified formula. RC 3307.431 also governs the disability benefit available to persons who became STRS members on or before July 29, 1992, who validly elected pursuant to an election procedure appearing in RC 3307.42 to have coverage under RC 3307.431.

For persons who became STRS members on or before July 29, 1992, disability coverage is provided under RC 3307.43 unless a valid election was made to have coverage provided under RC 3307.431. Under RC 3307.43, a member under age sixty who is determined by the retirement board to qualify for a disability benefit goes on disability retirement and receives an annual amount in accordance with a specified formula. If disability retirement terminates, the member, when eligible, may apply for service retirement under RC 3307.38.

Application for a disability benefit may be made by the member, by a person acting on his behalf, or by the member's employer.[79] Application must be made within two years from the date the member's contributing service terminated, unless the board determines that medical records demonstrate conclusively that, at the end of this two-year period, the member was physically or mentally incapacitated for duty and unable to make application. However, a member who has withdrawn his or her contributions from the system or who is receiving service

---

[74]RC 3307.02.
[75]RC 3307.021.
[76]RC 3307.01.

[77]RC 3307.34.
[78]RC 3307.42.
[79]RC 3307.42.

retirement benefits under RC 3307.38 or RC 3307.39 may not apply for disability benefits.[80]

Once application has been made, the member must undergo a medical examination by a doctor selected by the retirement board. Following this examination, and after completion of statutory administrative procedures that may include medical review and internal appeal, the retirement board must decide whether to grant a disability benefit. The decision turns on whether the member is mentally or physically incapacitated by a disabling condition which is either permanent or presumed to be permanent for the twelve months following the application.[81]

If the member's employer made the application, and the board denies disability retirement, then the employer must restore the member to his previous position and salary or to a similar position and salary.[82]

(B) Relationship to accrued sick leave

An appeals court has ruled that an employee eligible for a disability benefit is entitled to exhaust accrued sick leave before receiving the benefit; he cannot be forced to accept a fraction of accrued sick pay as severance pay instead.[83]

11.17 Termination of disability benefit

A disability benefit may be terminated at the recipient's request or when the retirement board determines, based on a medical examination, that the recipient is capable of resuming service similar to that from which he was found disabled.[84] A conditional release to return to work is not sufficient to show the recipient is capable of resuming service.[85] A disability benefit terminates if the recipient becomes employed as a teacher in any public or private school in or out of Ohio.[86] A disability allowance under RC 3307.431 expressly terminates at the earliest of (1) the effective date of service retirement under RC 3307.38 or RC 3307.41; (2) the date the allowance is terminated under RC 3307.44; or (3) for recipients age sixty or older at the effective date of the allowance, the later of the last day of the month in which the recipient reaches age sixty-five or the last day of the month in which the applicable benefit period (which ranges from twelve to sixty months, depending upon the recipient's age) ends. A recipient subject to the last provision may apply for service retirement under RC 3307.39, in which case an annual allowance in accordance with the specified formula will be paid.

During the first five years following the effective date of a disability benefit, the recipient retains membership in the system and is considered on leave from his position. Thus, if the disability benefit terminates during this period, the member is entitled to be restored to the same or similar position and salary.[87] One court has held that "similar" in this context means any position the retirant was certified to teach at the time of retirement.[88]

If a former disability benefit recipient again becomes a contributor (other than as another system retirant under RC 3307.381) to STRS (or to the school employees retirement system or the public employees retirement system), and completes at least two additional years of service credit, he also receives service credit for

---

[80]RC 3307.42.

[81]RC 3307.42.

[82]RC 3307.42.

[83]State ex rel Runyan v Henry, 34 App(3d) 23, 516 NE(2d) 1261 (Miami 1986).

[84]RC 3307.44. So long as evidence—even if conflicting—supports the board's findings, a reviewing court will not disturb them. State ex rel Ruby v STRS, No. 13844, 1989 WL 147983 (9th Dist Ct App, Summit, 2-6-89).

[85]Bennett v Newbury Local Bd of Ed, 16 App(3d) 391, 16 OBR 460, 476 NE(2d) 366 (Geauga 1984).

[86]RC 3307.44.

[87]RC 3307.44.

[88]Bennett v Newbury Local Bd of Ed, No. 82 M 485 (CP, Geauga, 6-7-83), reversed on other grounds by 16 App(3d) 391, 16 OBR 460, 476 NE(2d) 366 (Geauga 1984).

the period spent as a disability benefit recipient.[89]

SERVICE RETIREMENT

11.18 Eligibility for service retirement

(A) In general

A member may qualify for a lifetime income at age fifty-five with twenty-five or more years of service credit, or at age sixty with at least five years of service credit, or at any age with thirty or more years of service credit.[90]

Service retirement becomes effective on the first day of the month following either the last day for which compensation was paid or the attainment of minimum age or service credit eligibility for benefits under RC 3307.38, whichever is later.

(B) Mandatory retirement

RC 3307.37 authorizes a board of education to terminate a teacher's contract by superannuation at age seventy, except as otherwise provided by the federal Age Discrimination in Employment Act of 1967 (ADEA).[91] Since the the ADEA prohibits mandatory retirement because of age, the Ohio statute currently has no significance.

11.19 Amount of retirement benefits

(A) Payment options

A member who retires under RC 3307.38 or RC 3307.39 after attaining the minimum age and service requirements may choose among six types of retirement benefits. The principal benefit, which provides the greatest monthly payment of the six options, is the "annual single lifetime benefit." This consists of monthly payments to the retirant for life, and it terminates at his death.[92]

The remaining five options permit the retirant to take a lesser monthly benefit for his lifetime in order to provide continuing income to a beneficiary after his death. Option 1 provides the named beneficiary with monthly payments equal to those the retirant had been receiving before his death. Option 2 permits the retirant to designate the monthly payment his beneficiary will receive, either as a specific dollar amount or as a percentage of the retirant's benefit. In either case, the beneficiary's monthly payment may not exceed the retirant's. Under Option 3, the lesser monthly benefit established under Option 1 or Option 2 is paid to the beneficiary except that, upon death of the beneficiary or termination of a marital relationship between the retirant and the beneficiary, the retirant may elect to return to his single lifetime benefit equivalent as determined by the retirement board; in the case of termination of a marital relationship, the election must be made with the beneficiary's written consent or pursuant to a court order. Option 4 allows the retirant to designate a specific period (subject to the retirement board's approval), within which his death will trigger equal monthly payments to his beneficiary for the remainder of the period. If the retirant lives beyond the specified period, the payments will continue to him for life. Finally, Option 5 allows a plan of payment established by the retirement board combining any of the features of Options 1, 2, and 4.[93]

A married retirant is presumed to elect a benefit under Option 2 under which one-half of the lesser benefit payable during the retirant's life will be paid after his death to his spouse for life as sole beneficiary unless (1) the retirant has selected an optional plan paying a higher amount to such spouse, or (2) the retirant submits a written statement to the board signed by the spouse attesting the spouse's awareness that the retirant has elected a single lifetime annuity or an optional plan under which the surviving spouse will receive less than would have been payable to the spouse under the presumption.[94]

---

[89]RC 3307.44.
[90]RC 3307.38.
[91]29 USCA 623.
[92]RC 3307.38.
[93]RC 3307.50.
[94]RC 3307.50. The statute authorizes the board to provide by rule for waiver of the statement (and payment of benefits other than in accordance with the presumption) if the retirant cannot obtain the statement due to the spouse's absence or incapacity "or other cause specified by the board."

If, prior to September 15, 1989, the retirant elected an optional plan providing a survivor benefit, the retirant may cancel that optional plan on the divorce, annulment, marriage dissolution, or death of a spouse beneficiary, or on the death of any other named beneficiary. In such a case the retirant returns to his single lifetime benefit equivalent as determined by the board. In the case of termination of a marital relationship, the cancellation must be made with the beneficiary's written consent or pursuant to a court order.[95]

(B) Computation

All of the available benefit options are computed as the actuarial equivalent of the single lifetime benefit. This in turn is dictated by a formula set forth in RC 3307.38, providing two alternative computation methods. The single lifetime benefit is the greater of the amounts resulting from these two computations: either (1) two and one-tenth per cent of final average salary (except that if the member has more than thirty years service credit earned under RC 3307.31 or purchased under RC 3307.512, two and five-tenths per cent of final average salary for each year or fraction of a year of credit earned or purchased under those sections that is in excess of thirty years), multiplied by a figure based on retirant's age and service credit; or (2) an annuity with a reserve equal to the member's accumulated contributions, plus a pension in the same amount, plus additional pension amounts for prior service, military service, and extended Ohio service.[96]

The annual single lifetime allowance under age and service retirement cannot exceed the lesser of one hundred per cent of final average salary or the limit established by section 415 of the Internal Revenue Code, except that retirants with thirty or more years of service are entitled to a minimum of $6,000 per year regardless of final average salary.[97] An additional allowance is paid to retirees based on increases in the consumer price index.[98] Teachers who retired prior to June 29, 1955, are granted a cost-of-living adjustment.[99]

(C) Final average salary

For purposes of computing retirement benefits, the member's final average salary is the sum of the compensation during the three highest-paid years for which STRS contributions were made, divided by three.[100] If the member has a partial year of contributing service in the year of retirement and the compensation for the partial year is at a higher rate than any of the three highest-paid full years, the partial year rate must be substituted for a pro rata portion of the lowest-paid of the three years.[101]

In determining final average salary, one court found that where a board of education provided a written salary notice for a specified amount, the full amount must be considered salary despite a claim by the retirement board that part of the compensation was in fact converted sick leave, which cannot be included in final average salary. The court held that where a salary notice refers only to salary, it is a plain and unambiguous agreement and therefore other evidence regarding the source of compensation cannot be considered.[102]

11.20 Health benefits for retirees

The retirement board provides hospital and medical insurance coverage at no charge to those receiving service retirement benefits or a disability or survivor benefit, and their eligible dependents, provided

---

[95] RC 3307.50. The statute authorizes the board to provide by rule for waiver of the statement (and payment of benefits other than in accordance with the presumption) if the retirant cannot obtain the statement due to the spouse's absence or incapacity "or other cause specified by the board." The statute further provides that following marriage or remarriage, a retirant may elect a new optional plan except that if the retirant is receiving a retirement allowance under an optional plan that provides for continuation of benefits after his death to a former spouse, the new plan may be elected only with the written consent of the former spouse or pursuant to a court order.

[96] RC 3307.38.

[97] RC 3307.38, RC 3307.384.

[98] RC 3307.403, RC 3307.401.

[99] RC 3307.401.

[100] RC 3307.013(C). "Compensation" is defined by RC 3307.01(U), as qualified by RC 3307.013(B).

[101] RC 3307.013(C).

[102] Hager v State Teachers Retirement System, No. 85AP-475, 1985 WL 10161 (10th Dist Ct App, Franklin, 9-17-85).

their benefits are based on at least one and one-half years of credit for Ohio service. Certain recipients may elect to participate in a health maintenance organization instead. Benefit recipients over age sixty-five are required to certify participation in the medicare "B" insurance program, but the board will reimburse the basic premiums paid for such participation.[103]

11.21 Early retirement incentive plans

(A) In general

Employers of STRS members may establish early retirement incentive plans for their STRS-member employees.[104] Any such plan must provide that the employer purchase service credit for eligible employees who choose to participate. Such a plan remains in effect until terminated by the employer, but once established it must remain in effect for at least one year. The plan may contain a "window" period under which an eligible employee must elect to participate by some date certain (e.g., within thirty days after the plan's effective date). [105] The employer must bear the entire cost of the purchased credit. Consequently, the cost to the employer is equal to the additional liability of STRS for retirement benefits resulting from the purchase. This amount is calculated by STRS actuaries and is binding on the employer.[106] Under STRS regulations, an employer may elect to pay for the purchased credit in equal installments payable over the number of years purchased, plus interest.[107]

In theory, a district establishing an early retirement incentive plan will save money since it will be replacing more experienced teachers with beginning teachers who are paid much less. In practice, each district must carefully compute whether a plan will in fact save money. This analysis must include consideration of many variables including the cost of purchasing the credit for those likely to retire, severance pay eligibility, the payment schedule to STRS, the salary cost of replacements, and other similar factors.

(B) Eligibility

To be eligible to participate in a retirement incentive plan, an STRS-member employee must be at least fifty years old and eligible for retirement after the purchase of service credit. Thus, if an employer offers to purchase three years of credit, an employee age fifty with twenty-seven years of credit would be eligible to participate and retire with thirty years of credit.[108]

Employee participation in a retirement incentive plan is completely voluntary. An employee who chooses to participate must agree to retire and in fact retire under RC 3307.38 within ninety days after receiving notice from STRS that service credit has been purchased for him.[109] Apparently, an employee who decides not to retire during the ninety-day period forfeits the service credit purchased under the plan.

The statute permits an employer to limit availability of early retirement to a specified percentage of those employees who are STRS members as of January 1 of that year. The percentage may not be less than five per cent of such employees. If participation is limited, employees with greater length of service with the employer can participate before those with lesser length of service.[110]

(C) Purchase of additional service credit

The retirement incentive plan may provide purchases of up to five years of service credit or twenty per cent of the participant's total service credit, whichever is less. The amount of service credit purchased for any participant must be uniformly determined.[111] Purchase of partial years is not permitted, and STRS has established form and notice requirements for participating employers and employees.[112]

---

[103]OAC 3307-1-22, implementing RC 3307.405, RC 3307.74. See also OAG 87-060.
[104]RC 3307.35.
[105]Fincher v Canton City School Dist Bd of Ed, 62 OS(3d) 228, 581 NE(2d) 523 (1991).
[106]RC 3307.35.
[107]OAC 3307-1-25.
[108]See RC 3307.01(D).
[109]RC 3307.35.
[110]RC 3307.35.
[111]RC 3307.35.
[112]OAC 3307-1-25.

(D) Checklist for establishing plan

(1) Carefully analyze the cost/benefit to the school district of the plan proposed.

(2) Fulfill any bargaining obligation with the employee organization which is the exclusive representative of the bargaining unit.

(3) The plan should be established for a definite period but must remain in effect for at least one year. The effective date of the plan will determine when the first payment to STRS is due.

(4) The plan should indicate what percentage of eligible employees may participate. This must be at least five per cent of employees eligible to participate as of January 1 of the calendar year in which credit is purchased.

(5) The plan must indicate the number of years to be purchased, which may not exceed the lesser of five years or one-fifth of the member's credited service.

(6) If more than an allowable number of employees apply, priority must be given to teachers with greater district (not total) service.

(7) Therefore, an application deadline should be established prior to the plan's effective date so that the school district can learn who the applicants are prior to approving the retirements.

(8) All retirement dates should be subject to board of education approval so as to minimize interference with the educational program.

(9) The district must notify the retirement system of the establishment of the plan on the official form.

(10) Employees must likewise make application on official retirement system forms.

11.22 Employment of retired teachers

A teacher receiving a service retirement allowance under RC 3307.38 or RC 3307.39 from the system or a combined service retirement benefit under RC 3307.41 may be employed for temporary teaching service for not more than eighty-five school days, or the equivalent in fractional service, without loss of his pension allowance. Two months must have elapsed since the teacher's retirement. A superannuate may also be employed as a full-time teacher if he has received a retirement allowance for at least eighteen months and the employment has been authorized by the retirement board.[113]

A person receiving a disability benefit may not be employed as a teacher under any circumstances.[114]

Individuals receiving emeritus compensation from state-assisted institutions of higher learning receive such pay as a supplemental retirement benefit and are not subject to the employment restrictions described above.[115]

11.23 Optional compensation deferral plans

Boards of education and public institutions of higher learning such as state universities and community colleges may establish income deferral plans for employees, which plans are eligible for favorable tax treatment under section 403(b) of the Internal Revenue Code of 1954.[116] These plans must provide a reasonable number of options for investment of the deferred funds, including annuities, variable annuities, and regulated investment trusts, which qualify for favorable tax treatment.[117]

Independent of any income deferral plan established by a board of education, STRS members are eligible to participate in the deferred compensation program offered by the Ohio public employees

---

[113] RC 3307.381. A retirant from certain other public retirement systems may also be employed as a teacher if at least two months have elapsed since retirement. The statute goes on to recite procedures to be followed in the event of such employment.

[114] RC 3307.44.

[115] OAG 65-207.

[116] RC 9.90.

[117] RC 145.73(E).

deferred compensation board pursuant to RC 145.71 to RC 145.73.[118]

SURVIVORS' BENEFITS

11.24 Death before retirement

(A) Lump sum payment

If a member dies before retirement, the balance of his accumulated account must be paid to his designated beneficiary. If no designated beneficiary survives him, his account will be paid to survivors in the order and in accordance with the procedure prescribed by statute.[119]

(B) Monthly benefits

Under certain circumstances, eligible survivors may elect a monthly benefit in lieu of the lump sum payment. If the member was eligible for a service retirement allowance, his surviving spouse or qualified dependent designated as the sole beneficiary, or an individual designated as the sole beneficiary who received one-half or more of his support from the member during the twelve-month period preceding the member's death, may choose to receive a monthly benefit equivalent to the Option 1 joint-survivor allowance previously described.[120]

Alternatively, a surviving spouse or other qualified dependent beneficiary may receive monthly benefits according to a special statutory formula set forth in RC 3307.49(C)(2). Formula benefits are payable even though the deceased member may not have been eligible for retirement, provided the member was receiving a disability benefit under RC 3307.43 or RC 3307.431 at his death or had completed at least one and one-half years' Ohio service credit, with at least one quarter year in the last two and one-half years before death.[121]

Qualified dependents in this context include (1) a surviving spouse; (2) dependent children; and (3) dependent parents, all as defined in RC 3307.49(B).[122]

(C) Termination of monthly payments

Formula benefits to a qualified dependent must be terminated on the conditions set forth in RC 3307.49(E).

11.25 Death after retirement

If a member dies while receiving service retirement benefits, the rights of survivors depend on which payment option the member had selected. If he was receiving the single lifetime allowance, no monthly benefit will be payable to any survivor. However, any sum due and unpaid to him at death will be paid to his beneficiary or, if there is none, to his eligible survivors according to statutory succession.[123] If, on the other hand, the retirant had chosen one of the optional plans that provides a monthly survivor benefit, then the named beneficiary will receive benefits in accordance with the option chosen.[124]

11.26 Lump sum burial payment

On the death of a retirant or disability benefit recipient who at the time of death was receiving a service retirement allowance or disability benefit, a lump sum payment of $1,000 must be paid to any designated or qualified beneficiary. If there is no such beneficiary, the retirement board may approve payment either to the person responsible for the burial expenses or to the retirant's or recipient's estate.[125]

---

[118]RC 145.71(A).

[119]RC 3307.48. The statute's automatic revocation of a designation of beneficiary upon, among other things, a member's marriage has been held constitutional. White v McGill, 67 App(3d) 1, 585 NE(2d) 945 (Montgomery 1990). However, this case strongly suggested the statute's then existing provision for payment of survivor benefits and accrued unpaid benefits to the older parent (if there are no persons with higher priority under the statute) unconstitutionally discriminated against women since in most marriages the man is the older spouse. The statute has since been amended to cure any arguable constitutional infirmity.

[120]RC 3307.49(A). See Text 11.19(A), Payment options.

[121]RC 3307.49(B).

[122]RC 3307.49(B)(2). The attorney general has concluded "child" as used in the statute does not include stepchildren. OAG 88-090, overruling OAG 73-065.

[123]RC 3307.48(D).

[124]See RC 3307.50. See Text 11.19(A), Payment options.

[125]RC 3307.40(A).

The retirement board may establish a death benefit plan that provides for an additional lump sum payment to eligible beneficiaries. Any such plan is to be separately administered with the additional liability cost to be covered by charges paid by participants (who must be receiving a service retirement allowance or disability benefit). The board is to establish charges (to be deducted from allowances payable to those who elect to participate) and conditions of eligibility for participation.[126]

---

[126] RC 3307.40(B).

Chapter 12

Nonteaching Personnel: Introduction

12.01 Authority to hire nonteaching employees

CIVIL SERVICE AND NON-CIVIL SERVICE EMPLOYEES
12.02 Civil service and non-civil service employees
12.03 Civil service commission, sharing cost of administration
12.04 Classified and unclassified civil service

APPOINTMENT OF EMPLOYEES
12.05 Appointment of classified civil service employees
12.06 Appointing authority for civil service positions
12.07 Probationary period for civil service employees
12.08 Hiring independent contractors in lieu of civil service personnel
12.09 Appointment of non-civil service employees
12.10 Employment of noncertificated persons to direct extracurricular activity

PROMOTION AND TRANSFER
12.11 Promotion
12.12 Transfer

LAYOFF
12.13 Layoff or job elimination: non-civil service employees
12.14 Layoff or job elimination: civil service employees

DEMOTION, REDUCTION, SUSPENSION, TERMINATION, AND RESIGNATION
12.15 Demotion, reduction, and suspension
12.16 Termination: non-civil service employees
12.17 Termination: civil service employees
12.18 Resignation

EDUCATIONAL AIDES
12.19 Employment of educational aides

12.01 Authority to hire nonteaching employees

A board of education is vested with the management and control of all the public schools that it operates in its district, including the authority to hire nonteaching employees. The authority may be delegated; the board may by general resolution empower the superintendent or another officer to hire janitors, building superintendents, and such other employees as are provided for in the annual appropriation resolution.[1] Also, if the board elects to appoint a business manager, his duties include hiring and firing nonteaching employees, subject to board confirmation.[2]

CIVIL SERVICE AND NON-CIVIL SERVICE EMPLOYEES

12.02 Civil service and non-civil service employees

(A) School districts covered by civil service: effect of coverage and noncoverage

Nonteaching employees in city school districts are covered by civil service, whereas nonteaching employees in other districts are not.[3] There are significant differences between civil service and non-civil service employees with respect to hiring procedures, tenure, discipline and discharge, and other matters. The civil service laws are elaborate, and, on the whole, civil service employees enjoy marginally greater job protection. Non-civil service employees do not serve at the whim of the employer, however, since statutes and court rulings also provide them a measure of job security.

(B) Effect of new school district or transfer of territory

If a school district or part of a district is transferred to another district, or if a new district is created, the nonteaching school employees in the district immediately prior to transfer or creation have civil service status in the new district if it is a city school district. If the new district is not a city school district, the employees are employed under RC 3319.081, and their seniority is calculated from the date of last employment in the district from which the territory is transferred.

---

[1] RC 3313.47.
[2] RC 3319.04. See also Text 6.13, Powers and duties of business manager.

[3] RC 124.11. For the anomalous status of educational aides in city school districts, see Text 12.19, Employment of educational aides.

(C) Variations arising from city charter or collective bargaining agreement

Many cities have city charters and civil service commission rules which deviate from the statutory provisions discussed in this chapter. Also, the Ohio Public Employees' Collective Bargaining Act authorizes parties to bargain contract provisions that conflict with and override state legislation, including (with specific exceptions) the civil service laws and the nonteaching employee laws.[4]

12.03 Civil service commission, sharing cost of administration

(A) Commission in single- and multi-city school districts

In a city school district which encompasses only one city, the civil service commission of that city serves as the commission for the district.[5] When the territory of a city school district encompasses more than one city, the civil service commission of the city providing the greatest number of pupils serves as the commission for the district.[6] However, if another civil service commission served such a district prior to June 20, 1983 (the effective date of RC 124.011), that commission may continue to serve the district if authorized by the legislative authority of the city and if continued service is requested by the board of education.[7] If the city with the greatest number of pupils changes for any reason, the commission servicing the district prior to the change may continue to serve the district if so requested by the board and authorized by the legislative authority of the city whose commission previously served the district.[8]

Prior to June 20, 1983, the Ohio Supreme Court had held that no one civil service commission in a multi-city school district had a clear duty to take jurisdiction over an appeal by a classified employee of the multi-city school district.[9] However, a court of appeals has applied the jurisdiction determined by RC 124.011 *retroactively* on grounds the statute is remedial in nature.[10]

(B) School district's share of costs

The board of a city school district whose territory is located in only one city may appropriate funds to meet its proportionate share of the cost of civil service administration, as determined by the ratio of the number of the board's classified employees to the entire number of classified employees under the civil service commission's jurisdiction.[11] A board may, however, decline to contribute or may pay less than the amount specified in the ratio established by RC 124.54.[12]

Where a civil service commission serves a city school district whose territory is located in more than one city, the board must pay to the commission's city an amount mutually agreed upon by the board and commission.[13] If agreement cannot be reached, the amount is determined by the ratio of the number of board employees in the classified service to the entire number of classified employees in all political subdivisions served by the commission.[14]

12.04 Classified and unclassified civil service

Under RC 124.11, the civil service is divided into unclassified and classified civil service. Positions in the unclassified service are expressly listed, and all other positions are declared to be in the classified service. The classified service is further subdivided into a competitive class and an unskilled labor class. Persons in the classified service

---

[4] See Text 18.20, Supremacy of contract over certain laws.

[5] RC 124.011(A). See also RC 124.40

[6] RC 124.011(A). The Ohio Supreme Court has held that a chartered municipality, under its home rule authority, may enact an ordinance limiting jurisdiction of its civil service commission to only city employees. The Court found the Ohio Constitution does not require that public school employees be covered by civil service laws. The municipality enacted the ordinance because the multi-city school district refused to pay its share of civil service commission administrative costs. The Court upheld the ordinance, notwithstanding RC 124.011(A). OAPSE v Twinsburg, 36 OS(3d) 180, 522 NE(2d) 532 (1988).

[7] RC 124.011(B).

[8] RC 124.011(C).

[9] State ex rel Alford v Willoughby Civil Service Comm, 67 OS(2d) 260, 423 NE(2d) 457 (1981).

[10] Ludwig v Willoughby-Eastlake City School Dist Bd of Ed, 10 App(3d) 229, 10 OBR 324, 461 NE(2d) 919 (Lake 1983).

[11] RC 124.54.

[12] OAG 78-061.

[13] RC 124.54.

[14] RC 124.54.

enjoy tenure and job security not accorded those in the unclassified service.

(A) School personnel in the unclassified civil service

(1) Administrative and professional personnel, library staff

The unclassified civil service of a city school district embraces the superintendent, assistant superintendents, business manager, principals, assistant principals, other administrative officers, teachers, instructors, persons employed in educational or research duties, and library staff.[15] Factors to be considered in determining whether an employee is "administrative" or "fiduciary" pursuant to RC 124.11(A)(9) include whether the appointing authority relies on the employee's personal judgment and he is not closely supervised, and whether the employee's duties are not the type that can be delegated to anyone possessing the technical skill to perform the job functions.[16]

(2) Clerical and administrative support personnel

Three clerical administrative support employees for each of a city school district's "principal appointive executive officers, boards, or commissions ... that are authorized to appoint such clerical and administrative support employees" are in the unclassified civil service.[17] It is not entirely clear what is meant by "principal appointive executive officers" and whether the use of the disjunctive "or" in the statute precludes more than three unclassified clerical and administrative support employees in a district. The language might be construed as allowing three such unclassified employees for the board itself, plus three more for the superintendent, and possibly an additional three for each principal. The attorney general, however, maintains that only the board of education itself qualifies under the statute.[18] If so, each city school district may have a total of only three clerical and administrative support employees in the unclassified service. All other such personnel, as skilled persons, are in the competitive classified civil service.[19]

(3) Unskilled labor

Unskilled laborers may be either unclassified or classified. If the civil service commission determines that it is impractical to include an unskilled labor position in the competitive classified service, the position is in the unclassified service.[20] Otherwise, the position is in the classified service.[21] To exempt an unskilled position from the classified service, the underlying reasons as to why inclusion in the classified service is impractical must be stated.[22] The bald statement that it is impractical to include the position of grounds attendant in the classified service, for example, is not enough to exempt the position.[23]

Determination of whether a particular position is unskilled and thus in the unclassified service depends upon the job description as applied to a particular job and not upon the title of the position or number of hours worked.[24] A position is not in the unclassified service solely because it is part-time.[25]

(B) Tenure

An employee in the unclassified service does not have the job security and tenure provided to the classified civil service.[26] Library aides are in the unclassified service

---

[15]RC 124.11(A)(7).

[16]Brown v Cuyahoga Falls, No. 13049, 1987 WL 18686 (9th Dist Ct App, Summit, 10-14-87).

[17]RC 124.11(A)(8).

[18]OAG 72-045.

[19]RC 124.11(B)(1).

[20]RC 124.11(A)(12).

[21]RC 124.11(B)(2).

[22]Adams v Canton Civil Service Comm, No. CA-6823, 1986 WL 5258 (5th Dist Ct App, Stark, 5-5-86).

[23]North Olmsted City School Dist Bd of Ed v North Olmsted Civil Service Comm, 13 App(3d) 201, 13 OBR 249, 468 NE(2d) 749 (Lorain 1983).

[24]Adams v Kettering City School Dist Bd of Ed, No. 8226, 1984 WL 5431 (2d Dist Ct App, Montgomery, 1-20-84).

[25]State ex rel OAPSE v Girard Civil Service Comm, 45 OS(2d) 295, 345 NE(2d) 58 (1976).

[26]An appeals court has held a board of education cannot, as a matter of law, contractually confer continuing contract status on an unclassified civil servant. A city school district superintendent's secretary had been employed under a contract patterned after continuing contracts. She urged unsuccessfully that she was thus effectively removed from the unclassified civil service and given a right to continued employment. Davidson v Sheffield-Sheffield Lake Bd of Ed,

and therefore are not entitled to a hearing before being laid off.[27]

An unclassified civil servant is not entitled to the due process protection of a hearing before discharge unless he can establish a constitutionally cognizable liberty or property interest.[28] An employee is not deprived of a liberty or property interest when he is not retained in a particular unclassified position. Therefore, such an employee is not entitled to a due process hearing in connection with his demotion.[29] However, where a public employer creates and disseminates a false and defamatory impression about an unclassified employee in connection with his termination such that the employee's reputation in the community is damaged or future employment opportunities are foreclosed, the employee is entitled to a name-clearing hearing to refute the impression.[30]

RC 3319.02, governing the employment of school district administrators, was amended in 1987[31] to include nonteaching employees who are "supervisors" or "management level" employees under RC 4117.01. Under this definition, some city school district employees who had classified civil service status are now administrators whose employment is governed by limited contracts under RC 3319.02(C). In effect, this amendment removed such employees from the classified to the unclassified service.[32]

APPOINTMENT OF EMPLOYEES

12.05 Appointment of classified civil service employees

(A) Competitive classified civil service

(1) Examination

In city school districts covered by civil service, applicants for tested positions in the classified service must be given an examination. The examination may be written or oral, and it must relate directly to those matters which fairly test the relative capacity of the person examined to discharge the duties of the position. It may include an evaluation of such factors as education, capacity, training, knowledge, manual dexterity, and physical or psychological fitness. If minimum or maximum requirements are established for any examination, they must be specified in the examination announcement.[33]

The Ohio Supreme Court has held that, where local civil service rules and state law do not prohibit an appeal from a civil service commission's declaring one ineligible to take an examination, the decision may be appealed to common pleas court under RC 2506.01.[34]

No. 89CA004624, 1990 WL 72316 (9th Dist Ct App, Lorain, 5-23-90). Similarly, continuing contract status could not, as a matter of law, be conferred on a maintenance supervisor even if the board had purported to incorporate into his contract the provisions of RC Ch 3319. Hart v Sheffield-Sheffield Lake Bd of Ed, No. 89CA004708, 1990 WL 177195 (9th Dist Ct App, Lorain, 11-7-90).

[27]Duplaga v North Ridgeville Civil Service Comm, No. 3502, 1983 WL 4228 (9th Dist Ct App, Lorain, 9-21-83).

[28]State ex rel Trimble v State Bd of Cosmetology, 50 OS(2d) 283, 364 NE(2d) 247 (1977); Eudela v Ohio Dept of Mental Health & Mental Retardation, 30 App(3d) 113, 30 OBR 213, 506 NE(2d) 947 (Franklin 1986); Davidson v Sheffield-Sheffield Lake Bd of Ed, No. 89CA004624, 1990 WL 72316 (9th Dist Ct App, Lorain, 5-23-90).

[29]Coons v Ohio State University, No. 80AP-918, 1981 WL 3293 (10th Dist Ct App, Franklin, 6-25-81).

[30]State ex rel Kilburn v Guard, 5 OS(3d) 21, 5 OBR 81, 448 NE(2d) 1153 (1983), cert denied 464 US 893, 104 SCt 240, 78 LEd(2d) 230 (1983).

[31]1987 H 107.

[32]A statute that thus moves an incumbent employee from the classified to the unclassified service does not violate constitutional prohibitions against the taking of property, the impairment of contractual rights, or the enactment of retroactive laws. Lawrence v Edwin Shaw Hospital, 34 App(3d) 137, 517 NE(2d) 984 (Franklin 1986); Shearer v Cuyahoga County Hospital, 34 App(3d) 59, 516 NE(2d) 1287 (Cuyahoga 1986).

[33]RC 124.23.

[34]Nuspl v Akron, 61 OS(3d) 511, 575 NE(2d) 447 (1991).

(2) Eligibility list

An eligibility list must be prepared[35] in city school districts covered by civil service, and the appointing authority must appoint from the top three names on the list.[36] Veterans are given preference over persons with an equal rating.[37]

The preparation of eligibility lists apparently is appealable pursuant to RC Chapter 2506.[38] To perfect an appeal, however, a written notice of appeal must be filed with the civil service commission within ten days after the filing of the final order, adjudication, or decision as required by RC 2505.04.[39]

(3) Effect of rank on list

A board of education is not required to select the highest ranking applicant on the eligibility list. A board is free to exercise its discretion as long as it bases its decision on merit and fitness.[40] A city school district board is not required to appoint the third person on an eligibility list where two persons on the list, having been offered the position, declined. The board can request a second list of three qualified persons from whom one may be selected.[41]

(B) Classified unskilled labor positions

Applicants for positions as unskilled laborers do not take a competitive examination. Rather, they are required to furnish evidence or take tests as the civil service director considers proper to determine "age, residence, physical condition, ability to labor, honesty, sobriety, industry, capacity, and experience" in the work of the position. If found qualified, laborers are placed on the eligibility list according to their relative ratings from the evidence or tests. When positions open, the civil service commission must furnish double the number of names needed to the appointing authority, beginning with the names at the top of the list. The appointments are made from the certified names.[42]

12.06 Appointing authority for civil service positions

For purposes of civil service, the "appointing authority" is the officer or board having the power to hire and fire with respect to civil service positions in his jurisdiction.[43] In a city school district the board itself is the appointing authority, unless the board authorizes the superintendent to hire and fire janitors, building superintendents, and other employees as authorized by the annual appropriation resolution.[44] If the board has appointed a business manager, he hires and discharges nonteaching employees, subject to the confirmation of the board.[45]

12.07 Probationary period for civil service employees

(A) In general, probationary period

In city school districts covered by civil service, a probationary period of between sixty days and one year must be fixed by civil service commissions for positions in the classified service. While still within the probationary period, but after sixty days or one-half of the probationary period, whichever is greater, the employee may be removed or reduced from his position by the board provided that the board informs the commission in writing of the decision.[46]

The removal of a probationary employee who has completed sixty days or one-half of his probationary period, whichever is greater, may not be appealed to the civil service commission.[47] An employee who is terminated orally on the fifty-ninth

---

[35]RC 124.26.
[36]RC 124.27.
[37]RC 124.23.
[38]But see State ex rel Hreha v Lorain Civil Service Comm, No. 3626, 1984 WL 5167 (9th Dist Ct App, Lorain, 7-5-84).
[39]In re Stokes, No. CA-7040, 1981 WL 2800 (2d Dist Ct App, Montgomery, 5-19-81).
[40]Seward v State ex rel Kratt, 129 OS 296, 195 NE 241 (1935).
[41]State ex rel Hreha v Lorain Civil Service Comm, No. 3626, 1984 WL 5167 (9th Dist Ct App, Lorain, 7-5-84).

[42]RC 124.11(B)(2).
[43]RC 124.01(D).
[44]RC 3313.47.
[45]RC 3319.04.
[46]RC 124.27.
[47]Walton v Montgomery County Welfare Dept, 69 OS(2d) 58, 430 NE(2d) 930 (1982). See also State ex rel Canfield v Frost, 53 OS(3d) 13, 557 NE(2d) 1206 (1990); Hanes v Smith, No. 87AP-1067, 1988 WL 70444 (10th Dist Ct App, Franklin, 6-28-88).

day of his probationary period with written confirmation of the termination on the sixty-second day is entitled to compensation for the balance of the sixty-day protected period of probationary employment and no more.[48]

Subject to the time frames set forth above, the decision as to what constitutes satisfactory probationary service lies solely with the appointing authority, and a civil service commission does not have appellate jurisdiction over such a finding. The decision of the appointing authority, made after one-half or sixty days of the probationary period, whichever is greater, to terminate a probationary employee is *final* and *not* subject to administrative or judicial review.[49]

(B) Permanent employee status

After serving his probationary period, a civil service appointee becomes a permanent employee and may not be removed or suspended for more than three days, except for cause, as provided in RC 124.34.[50]

A provisional appointment made without competitive examination does not become permanent because of a delay in obtaining an eligibility list. A provisional appointee holds a position until an employee is selected from the eligibility list.[51] A provisional employee who completes six months of service or his probationary period, and has passed the competitive examination, becomes a permanent appointee.[52]

When an employee is provisionally appointed and remains that way for two continuous years, during which no competitive exam is held, he then becomes a permanent employee.[53] But where an employee fills a position on an "acting" basis and is clearly told it is temporary, that employee has not received a provisional appointment.[54] RC 124.271, insofar as it applies to city school districts, does not contravene Article XV, section 10 of the Ohio Constitution, which requires merit and fitness in state, county, and city civil service to be determined, insofar as is practicable, by competitive examination.[55] Temporary and provisional appointments to the classified service without competitive examination may only be made in accordance with RC 124.30.

12.08 Hiring independent contractors in lieu of civil service personnel

In the absence of intent to thwart the civil service system, a public employer subject to civil service may contract with an independent contractor to perform services which might also be performed by civil service employees.[56] However, contracting out work formerly done by civil service employees because of a hiring freeze premised on a lack of funds is contrary to Ohio law.[57] Where contracting custodial work that otherwise might be performed by civil servants has definite benefits that would not ultimately eradicate the civil service system and is based on (1) cost savings, (2) greater supervision, and (3) comparable quality of services, the contracting does not violate civil service laws.[58]

12.09 Appointment of non-civil service employees

(A) Introduction, limited and continuing contracts for regular employees

In districts other than city school districts, a regular nonteaching employee must be employed initially by contract for not more than one year. If the employee is

---

[48]Medburg v Lancaster City School Dist Bd of Ed, No. 42-CA-82, 1983 WL 6420 (5th Dist Ct App, Fairfield, 5-3-83).

[49]Vonderau v Parma Civil Service Comm, 15 App(3d) 44, 15 OBR 71, 472 NE(2d) 359 (Cuyahoga 1983).

[50]RC 124.27.

[51]RC 124.30(A); State ex rel Higgins v George, 147 OS 165, 70 NE(2d) 370 (1946); State ex rel Dahmen v Youngstown, 40 App(2d) 166, 318 NE(2d) 433 (Mahoning 1973).

[52]RC 124.26(B).

[53]RC 124.271.

[54]State ex rel Aldridge v Portsmouth, No. 1642, 1987 WL 12461 (4th Dist Ct App, Scioto, 6-4-87).

[55]Cleveland Classified School Employees Civil Service Assn v Cleveland City School Dist Bd of Ed, 50 OS(2d) 31, 361 NE(2d) 1342 (1977).

[56]State ex rel Sigall v Aetna Cleaning Contractors of Cleveland, Inc, 45 OS(2d) 308, 345 NE(2d) 61 (1976).

[57]Communications Workers of America Local 4501 v Ohio State University, 12 OS(3d) 274, 12 OBR 350, 466 NE(2d) 912 (1984).

[58]OAPSE, Chapter 227 v Sylvania City School Dist, No. 85-2505 (CP, Lucas, 1-30-87).

reemployed thereafter, the contract must be for two years and if reemployed once again, the contract must be a continuing one.[59]

For contract eligibility purposes, a contract of only eighteen days has been held to be a contract of "not more than one year" under RC 3319.081(A) and so entitling the employee to a two-year contract upon reemployment.[60] A nonteaching employee may hold a continuing contract in more than one position, and a teacher may also hold a continuing contract as a nonteaching employee.[61]

A nonteaching employee who completes three years of service in the middle of a limited contract is not then eligible for a continuing contract. Where the employee has voluntarily accepted a two-year contract, he cannot change his status until the contract expires and the board can then exercise its discretion not to renew his employment.[62] A nonteaching employee employed under a series of three one-year contracts is not entitled to a continuing contract, since RC 3319.081(B) only provides for a continuing contract if the employee's contract is renewed after three years of limited contracts.[63]

RC 3319.02, governing contracts of school district administrators, was amended in 1987[64] to include employees who are "supervisors" or "management level employees" as defined in RC 4117.01. Such employees are to be given limited contracts pursuant to RC 3319.02(C). The attorney general has concluded that such employees retain any continuing contract rights that vested pursuant to RC 3319.081 before September 10, 1987, the amendment's effective date. Thus, an employee serving under a continuing contract on that date retains the right to continued employment on the same terms as before the amendment.[65] Districts employing new persons in supervisory or management level capacities should be sure to issue contracts under RC 3319.02.

(B) Who are considered regular employees

A noontime playground aide who works only part-time and whose position is funded on a year-to-year basis is not a regular nonteaching school employee to whom RC 3319.081 is applicable.[66]

A substitute bus driver who is paid less than a regular bus driver, did not receive a regular contract, and worked less than forty hours per week (thirty-five hours) is not a regular nonteaching employee and is therefore not entitled to credit for time worked as a substitute towards continuing contract status.[67] Similarly, a substitute bus driver employed on an "as needed" basis is not a regular nonteaching employee.[68]

Where a person is hired exclusively for the purpose of replacing a nonteaching employee on a leave of absence, he is *not* a regular nonteaching employee. But should he be continued in employment as a regular nonteaching employee after the return of the employee from leave, he receives credit for the time spent as a replacement for purposes of RC 3319.081. One court has stated that a person hired as a *substitute* could, under the right circumstances, be considered a *de facto* replacement. But the court held that the employee's bare assertion that he was a replacement, absent other evidence, was not sufficient.[69]

(C) Wages and hours

The salary offered each nonteaching employee must be no lower than the preceding year's salary unless a reduction is part of a uniform plan affecting nonteaching employees of the entire district.[70]

---

[59]RC 3319.081(A), (B).

[60]Toth v Kenston Local School Dist Bd of Ed, No. 1015 (11th Dist Ct App, Geauga, 12-30-82).

[61]OAG 71-021.

[62]Allen v Minford Local School Dist Bd of Ed, No. 1279, 1981 WL 5926 (4th Dist Ct App, Scioto, 5-8-81); Shankle v Ontario Local School Dist Bd of Ed, 54 App(2d) 41, 374 NE(2d) 648 (Richland 1977).

[63]Wilson v Hubbard Exempted Village School Dist Bd of Ed, No. 3129, 1983 WL 6168 (11th Dist Ct App, Trumbull, 6-24-83).

[64]1987 H 107.

[65]OAG 88-059.

[66]State ex rel Borders v Jefferson Local School Dist, 59 OS(2d) 109, 391 NE(2d) 1040 (1979).

[67]Wilson v Hubbard Exempted Village School Dist Bd of Ed, No. 3129, 1983 WL 6168 (11th Dist Ct App, Trumbull, 6-24-83).

[68]Blair v Milford Exempted Village School Dist Bd of Ed, 62 App(3d) 424, 575 NE(2d) 1190 (Clermont 1989).

[69]Robinson v Symmes Valley Local School Dist Bd of Ed, No. 1806, 1987 WL 6761 (9th Dist Ct App, Lawrence, 2-19-87).

[70]RC 3319.081(B), RC 3319.082.

As used in RC 3319.081(B) and RC 3319.082, the term "salary" means "rate of pay." Although the pay rate cannot be reduced, hours may be cut. Unless otherwise contractually specified, the *number* of hours to be worked is not statutorily guaranteed.[71]

A nonteaching employee may sue for breach of contract where a board unilaterally attempts to modify a contract specifically calling for 191 four-hour days by reducing the number of hours to be worked.[72]

(D) Right to express contract

A nonteaching employee employed pursuant to RC 3319.081 has the right to demand and receive an express contract from the board. When the board does not enter into an express contract, the employee assumes certain rights in the nature of a quasi-contract.[73]

(E) Indeterminate contracts

RC 3319.081 does not prevent a board of education from employing nonteaching personnel for an indeterminate period, to be measured by the work required. In the absence of a contract, either written or oral, between a board and a nonteaching employee clearly expressive of the terms and conditions of employment, such features must be determined from the conduct and statements of the parties and the surrounding circumstances.[74]

A board need not continue to compensate a nonteaching employee whose contract is for an indeterminate period after the board determines no further work is required, assuming that no conditional or substitute employees are engaged to perform the same work which would have been done by the employee. This is so even though the employee was engaged in actual service for more than 120 days of the school year in which the employment was discontinued and for each of the five consecutive years immediately prior.[75]

(F) Reemployment

A nonteaching employee under contract is considered reemployed unless notified by June 1 of the board's intention not to reemploy him.[76] A separate provision in the unemployment compensation law requires that school employees be notified of nonrenewal on or before April 30,[77] and the safest practice is to notify the employee by that date.

(G) Supplemental contracts not authorized

No statute authorizes supplemental contracts for nonteaching employees, and the Ohio Supreme Court has held that a board of education that tries to issue one exceeds its authority.[78] However, a board can agree in a collective bargaining agreement to issue supplemental contracts.[79] A regular nonteaching employee could also be employed to direct, supervise, or coach extracurricular programs under a separate contract issued pursuant to RC 3313.53, provided all requirements of the section were met.[80]

---

[71]OAPSE v Twin Valley Local School Dist Bd of Ed, 6 OS(3d) 178, 6 OBR 235, 451 NE(2d) 1211 (1983); Hale v Hudson Local School Dist, No. 11229, 1984 WL 5151 (9th Dist Ct App, Summit, 6-27-84).

[72]Miner v Lake Local School Dist Bd of Ed, No. CA-6322, 1984 WL 4930 (5th Dist Ct App, Stark, 6-18-84).

[73]Gates v River Local School Dist Bd of Ed, 8 App(2d) 76, 220 NE(2d) 715 (Monroe 1966), affirmed by 11 OS(2d) 83, 228 NE(2d) 298 (1967).

[74]Gates v River Local School Dist Bd of Ed, 11 OS(2d) 83, 228 NE(2d) 298 (1967).

[75]Gates v River Local School Dist Bd of Ed, 11 OS(2d) 83, 228 NE(2d) 298 (1967).

[76]RC 3319.083; Frantz v Green Local School Dist Bd of Ed, No. 1925, 1984 WL 5157 (9th Dist Ct App, Wayne, 7-5-84).

[77]RC 4141.29(I)(1)(e).

[78]Hall v Lakeview Local School Dist Bd of Ed, 63 OS(3d) 380, 588 NE(2d) 785 (1992). Here, the board had issued supplemental contracts to a custodian that labelled him a head custodian. While finding such contracts unauthorized, the Court went on to hold the employee had effectively been promoted to the head custodian job classification and could not be demoted to the classification of custodian except for cause under RC 3319.081(C).

[79]See Text 18.20, Supremacy of contract over certain laws.

[80]See Text 12.10, Employment of noncertificated persons to direct extracurricular activity.

12.10 Employment of noncertificated persons to direct extracurricular activity

(A) Introduction, preconditions to hiring noncertificated person

In certain circumstances, a city, exempted village, or local school district may employ a noncertificated person to direct, supervise, or coach a pupil-activity program. Such employment must be in accordance with standards and rules adopted by the state board of education and may only occur after the district board has adopted a resolution stating as follows:

(1) It has offered the position to certificated district employees and no such qualified employee has accepted it; and

(2) It then advertised the position as available to any certificated person qualified to fill the position, but not employed by the board, and no such person applied for and accepted the position.[81]

Whether a certificated employee "qualified to fill the position" is available is a discretionary determination to be made by a board. Thus, a board is *not* required to hire a certificated employee who desires a position if the board determines he is not qualified. The board's determination will be overturned only if a court finds an abuse of discretion.[82]

A certificated employee who applies for a coaching position is not entitled to the position even though the board failed to comply strictly with the requirements of RC 3313.53 prior to hiring a noncertificated person for the position.[83] Where a board failed to adopt a separate resolution as required by the statute, but its minutes reflected the facts a resolution should have included, there was "sufficient compliance" to justify the board's hiring of a noncertificated person.[84]

(B) What constitutes pupil-activity program

RC 3313.53 does not define "pupil-activity program," but does state that any class or course offered or required for credit toward a pupil's promotion or graduation or any activity conducted as a part of the course is not a pupil-activity program. The statute also requires the state board to adopt rules to insure the competency of certificated persons involved in directing, supervising, or coaching a pupil-activity program.[85]

(C) General qualifications

The Ohio Administrative Code requires a person employed to direct, supervise, or coach a pupil-activity program to meet the following qualifications:

(1) A noncertificated individual must demonstrate good moral character as evidenced by absence of conviction of a felony, theft offense, offense of violence, offense involving drug abuse, or a sex offense. Alternatively, the candidate must demonstrate to the board's satisfaction that complete rehabilitation occurred subsequent to the conviction.

(2) A person must demonstrate the ability to work with students. This ability must be documented by recent successful experience determined by the board and knowledge of the activity program evidenced by successful completion of a college or university course (or successful actual experience determined by the board), knowledge of applicable board rules, and knowledge of the health and safety aspects of the program.[86]

(D) Additional qualifications for coaches

The Administrative Code imposes additional requirements for a pupil-activity program involving vigorous physical activity or contact. The individual directing such an activity must demonstrate successful completion of the requirements for the volun-

---

[81]RC 3313.53(B).

[82]Harrah v Harrison Hills City School Dist Bd of Ed, No. 369, 1981 WL 4753 (7th Dist Ct App, Harrison, 8-11-81); State ex rel Stuckey v Clearcreek Local School Dist Bd of Ed, No. CA87-12-097, 1988 WL 94035 (12th Dist Ct App, Warren, 9-12-88).

[83]Gardner v Liberty Center Local Schools Bd of Ed, No. 7-81-14, 1982 WL 6802 (3d Dist Ct App, Henry, 6-1-82).

[84]State ex rel Stuckey v Clearcreek Local School Dist Bd of Ed, No. CA87-12-097, 1988 WL 94035 (12th Dist Ct App, Warren, 9-12-88).

[85]RC 3313.53.

[86]OAC 3301-27-01.

tary "Interscholastic Coaching Certificate," or have completed a college or university course on the health and safety of the participants in the activity program, or have completed an appropriate sports-related first aid training course and cardiopulmonary resuscitation training conducted pursuant to guidelines of the superintendent of public instruction. Additionally, the individual must complete at least annually a seminar relating to the health and safety of participants in the pupil-activity program conducted pursuant to guidelines approved by the superintendent of public instruction.[87]

(E) Compensation

The compensation of a noncertificated person employed pursuant to RC 3313.53 must be the same amount offered to the district's certificated employees. The compensation cannot be reduced unless the reduction is part of a uniform plan affecting the entire district. A noncertificated person so employed is considered a nonteaching employee and is not an educational aide. He may only perform the duties of director, supervisor, or coach of the pupil-activity program for which he was hired. The board must enter into a written contract with the employee for a term not exceeding one year. The contract must specify the compensation, duration, and other terms of employment. Contracts issued under RC 3313.53 can only be terminated or suspended pursuant to RC 3319.081(C). However, RC 3319.081 and RC 3319.083 (notice of nonrenewal) do not apply to the extent that they conflict with RC 3313.53. Therefore, when a district fills a coaching position with a certificated person, the prior noncertificated coach employed under RC 3313.53 has no right to continued employment even though he met the service requirements for tenure under RC 3319.081. However, one court has held that filling a coaching position pursuant to RC 3313.53 does not relieve a school district from notifying a noncertificated coach by June 1 of his nonrenewal.[88]

PROMOTION AND TRANSFER

12.11 Promotion

There are no statutory provisions governing the promotion of nonteaching employees in non-civil service school districts. In city school districts covered by civil service, vacancies and positions in the classified service must be filled as far as possible by promotions. Promotions must be based on merit, to be ascertained as far as practicable by promotional examinations, by conduct and capacity in office, and by seniority and service. All examinations for promotions must be competitive. The rules governing examinations and appointments to the vacant positions must be the same as those provided for original examinations.[89] A name on an eligible list certified to the employer may be removed at any time, even after such certification, if one becomes unqualified for a vacant position.[90]

A promotional appointment triggers a probationary period,[91] and in the event of unsatisfactory performance the employee may be returned to his former position during such period after the completion of sixty days or one-half of the period, whichever is greater.[92]

12.12 Transfer

In city school districts covered by civil service, prescribed procedures must be followed to transfer an employee. An employee may be transferred to a position having similar pay and duties. However, no transfer may be made to another classification nor may a person be transferred to an

---

[87]OAC 3301-27-01.

[88]Pistone v Canfield Local Bd of Ed, No. 87 CA 13, 1987 WL 13256 (7th Dist Ct App, Mahoning, 6-23-87).

[89]RC 124.31. Unless prohibited by local civil service rules, a civil service commission's decision that one is ineligible to take a promotional examination may be appealed to common pleas court under RC 2506.01. Nuspl v Akron, 61 OS(3d) 511, 575 NE(2d) 447 (1991).

[90]Richards v Akron Public Schools Bd of Ed, No. 15461, 1992 WL 188661 (9th Dist Ct App, Summit, 8-5-92) (upholding removal of name of one who, after certification, was suspended for drinking during work time).

[91]RC 124.27. See also Text 12.07, Probationary period for civil service employees.

[92]Clark v Ohio Dept of Transportation, 89 App(3d) 96, 623 NE(2d) 631 (Fayette 1993).

office or position which has a different examination or a different salary than is the case for the original entrance to a position or office held by the employee.[93]

Where a civil servant alleges his rights were violated when a fellow employee was transferred to a different classification without testing, the time limit for challenging the transfer runs from the date of the transfer, not the date the challenger learns of the transfer.[94] A move from one work shift to another within the same position is not a transfer but simply a job reassignment.[95]

No statutory procedures are given with respect to transfers in non-civil service school districts.

LAYOFF

12.13 Layoff or job elimination: non-civil service employees

There are no statutory provisions governing layoffs in non-civil service school districts. *DeRemer v Akron City School Dist Bd of Ed*[96] held that boards of education have a right to reduce their work force by layoffs to prevent deficiencies in public funds. Likewise, *Mash v Westerville City Bd of Ed*[97] held that, absent bad faith, a board may abolish a particular position. *DeRemer* and *Mash* involved city school districts, and legal issues concerning other districts' authority to lay off nonteaching employees are not completely resolved. In many districts, a collective bargaining agreement will specify when and how layoffs may be made. An appeals court has upheld a local school district's right to abolish a bus mechanic job classification and opined that RC 3319.081 has no applicability at all to such a decision. The affected employee was entitled to no pre-termination due process hearing either as a matter of statutory or constitutional law.[98] Another appeals court, however, has suggested that RC 3319.081 does apply to such decisions and further concluded that a local school district may not suspend or terminate a continuing contract under RC 3319.081 by means of abolishing a job classification if others remain employed under limited contracts to perform tasks which could be performed by the continuing contract employee.[99]

12.14 Layoff or job elimination: civil service employees

(A) In general

The Ohio Supreme Court has consistently upheld the authority of a public body to lay off classified civil service employees. In *State ex rel Buckman v Munson*,[100] the Court held civil service laws do not restrict public authorities in their bona fide efforts to effect necessary economies, or prevent laying off an unessential employee for reasons of economy. Thus, a board can lay off noncertificated employees for reasons of economy.[101] Where the charter or ordinances of a city do not establish a priority for layoffs of classified employees due to reasons of economy, the power to lay off is within the discretion of the appropriate public officer(s) or body to be exercised in accordance with law.[102] In a noncharter city, layoffs must be made in accordance

---

[93]RC 124.32(A).

[94]Hatton v Middletown, No. 87-06-068, 1987 WL 30339 (7th Dist Ct App, Butler, 12-21-87).

[95]State ex rel Hallinan v Tallmadge City School Dist Bd of Ed, No. 14480, 1990 WL 167021 (9th Dist Ct App, Summit, 10-31-90) (holding no right to appeal denial of request for new assignment to civil service commission).

[96]DeRemer v Akron City School Dist Bd of Ed, 72 App 283, 51 NE(2d) 303 (Summit 1943).

[97]Mash v Westerville City School Dist Bd of Ed, No. 80AP-950, 1981 WL 3443 (10th Dist Ct App, Franklin, 8-27-81).

[98]Graham v Triway Bd of Ed, 82 App(3d) 34, 610 NE(2d) 1185 (Wayne 1992), dismissed, jurisdictional motion overruled by 65 OS(3d) 1495, 605 NE(2d) 949 (1993).

[99]Ferdinand v Hamilton Local Bd of Ed, 17 App(3d) 165, 17 OBR 296, 478 NE(2d) 835 (Franklin 1984). *Graham* relies heavily on State ex rel Cutler v Pike County Joint Area Vocational School Dist, 6 OS(3d) 138, 6 OBR 195, 451 NE(2d) 800 (1983) and expressly eschews *Ferdinand* as being "in conflict" with *Cutler*.

[100]State ex rel Buckman v Munson, 141 OS 319, 48 NE(2d) 109 (1943).

[101]OAG 68-156.

[102]Gannon v Perk, 46 OS(2d) 301, 348 NE(2d) 342 (1976).

with the requirements of RC Chapter 124.[103]

Hourly employees not guaranteed a certain number of hours per day, reduced in hours worked but not in hourly rate, have not been laid off and have no right of appeal.[104]

Employees who are wrongfully laid off or otherwise excluded from employment are entitled to sue for lost wages by means of a writ of mandamus.[105]

(B) Reasons for layoff

Employees may be laid off for lack of funds.[106] A statement of rationale and supporting documentation must be filed with the civil service commission prior to sending the layoff notice.[107] While an explicit statement is preferred, a court has held that enclosing a copy of a board resolution that includes the reasons for layoff constitutes substantial and sufficient compliance.[108] Where a city sent its documentation to the commission twenty-one days after sending notice to employees, a court reversed the commission's affirmance of the layoff on this procedural ground.[109] However, in a case involving layoffs due to job abolishment for economic reasons under RC 124.321(D), where the statement to the commission was sent two days after sending notice to employees, the court found the school board's compliance was substantial and adequate.[110] Contemporaneously sending the statement to the commission and to the employees has also been held to be substantial compliance.[111] For purposes of layoff, a lack of funds exists when the district has a current or projected deficiency of funding to maintain current or to sustain projected levels of staffing and operations.[112]

Employees may also be laid off for lack of work.[113] A statement of rationale and supporting documentation must be filed with the civil service commission prior to sending the notice of layoff.[114] For purposes of layoff, a lack of work exists when the district has a current or projected temporary decrease in the work load, expected to last less than one year, which requires a reduction of current or projected staffing levels.[115]

Employees may also be laid off as a result of abolishment of positions.[116] A statement of rationale and supporting documentation must be filed with the civil service commission prior to sending the notice of a job abolishment. Where the statement to the commission was sent two days after sending notice to employees, the court found the school board's compliance was substantial and adequate.[117] An abolishment means the permanent deletion of a position due to lack of continued need for that position. Job abolishments may be accomplished as a result of reorganization for efficient operation, for reasons of economy, or for lack of work.[118] An appeals court has held that a position may not be abolished on the premise of a prospective lack of work alone; nor may abolishment be accomplished simply by transferring the duties of a classified employee to those of an unclassified employee.[119] While the burden of proving procedural defects in the layoff process rests with the employee, the burden of proving the sufficiency of the

---

[103] Treska v Trumble, 4 OS(3d) 150, 4 OBR 394, 447 NE(2d) 1283 (1983).

[104] Davies v Newark City School Dist Bd of Ed, No. CA-3180, 1986 WL 7737 (5th Dist Ct App, Licking, 7-2-86).

[105] State ex rel Bush v Spurlock, 63 OS(3d) 453, 588 NE(2d) 840 (1992).

[106] RC 124.321(B).

[107] RC 124.321(B).

[108] Grenig v Brooklyn Civil Service Comm, No. 54217, 1988 WL 86759 (8th Dist Ct App, Cuyahoga, 6-16-88).

[109] Romeo v Campbell Civil Service Comm, No. 86 CA 36, 1987 WL 20086 (7th Dist Ct App, Mahoning, 11-10-87).

[110] Leonardi v Wickliffe Civil Service Comm, No. 12-176, 1988 WL 61473 (11th Dist Ct App, Lake, 6-10-88).

[111] Aksterowicz v Lancaster, No. 43-CA-88, 1989 WL 67291 (5th Dist Ct App, Fairfield, 6-7-89).

[112] RC 124.321(B).

[113] RC 124.321(C).

[114] RC 124.321(C).

[115] RC 124.321(C).

[116] RC 124.321(D).

[117] Leonardi v Wickliffe Civil Service Comm, No. 12-176, 1988 WL 61473 (11th Dist Ct App, Lake, 6-10-88).

[118] RC 124.321(D).

[119] Esselburne v Ohio Dept of Agriculture, 49 App(3d) 37, 550 NE(2d) 512 (Franklin 1988). See also Swepston v Ohio Bd of Tax Appeals, 89 App(3d) 629, 626 NE(2d) 1006 (Franklin 1993).

substantive reasons for abolishing a job rests with the appointing authority.[120] Where an employer abolishes a job purportedly for increased efficiency but an examination of operations before and after abolishment reveals no efficiency gains, the appointing authority has not met its burden.[121] Where data entry jobs were abolished and the data entry function was contracted out at a savings of $140,000 per fiscal year, the jobs were properly abolished for reasons of economy.[122] The documentation required to support the abolishment of a position need not be highly technical but need only state the factual basis for the statutory reason for abolishment of the positions.[123]

(C) Layoff procedure

RC 124.321 to RC 124.324 contain detailed procedures for the layoff and displacement of employees within each classification and each classification series. When a reduction in the work force is necessary, a board of education must determine which classifications are to be affected and the number of employees to be laid off within each classification. Employees must be laid off using systematic consideration of length of continuous service (seniority) and efficiency. Within each primary appointment category (i.e., first temporary, then intermittent, part-time, seasonal, and finally full-time) employees must be laid off in the following order: (1) provisional employees who have not completed their probationary periods; (2) provisional employees who have completed their probationary periods; (3) employees appointed from eligibility lists who have not completed their probationary periods; and (4) employees appointed from eligibility lists who have completed their probationary periods.[124]

Employees subject to layoff are assigned retention points based upon seniority and efficiency.[125] Credit for relative efficiency may not exceed ten per cent of total retention points.[126] Retention points for efficiency are determined by averaging the employee's latest two annual performance evaluations.[127] Seniority prevails where employees have identical retention points.[128]

(D) Bumping rights

Employees whose positions are abolished or who are laid off may displace employees with fewer retention points within the same classification or a lower classification within the same classification series.[129] RC 124.324(A)(3), providing displacement rights to laid-off employees beyond their immediate classifications or classification series, is inapplicable to city school district employees.[130] A laid-off employee may also displace an employee in a classification held immediately prior to the classification from which the employee was laid off if the laid-off employee was certified in the position. Employees must notify the appointing authority of intention to exercise displacement rights within five days of notice of layoff.[131] If the position does not exist, the employee may bump into the position next previously held and so on if he meets the minimum qualifications for the position and has held it within five years of layoff.[132] Local civil service commissions may promulgate specific rules for the implementation of the layoff provisions. Employees who are laid off must be placed on layoff lists and retain reinstatement rights for a period of one year.[133]

(E) Appeal

An employee may appeal a layoff or displacement to the civil service commission no later than ten days after receipt of the layoff notice or the date the employee is displaced.[134] The commission's decision may be appealed by the employee to the

---

[120] State ex rel Bispeck v Trumbull County Bd of Commrs, 37 OS(3d) 26, 523 NE(2d) 502 (1988).

[121] State ex rel Bispeck v Trumbull County Bd of Commrs, 37 OS(3d) 26, 523 NE(2d) 502 (1988).

[122] Carter v Ohio Dept of Health, 28 OS(3d) 463, 28 OBR 511, 504 NE(2d) 1108 (1986).

[123] Berndsen v Westerville Personnel Review Bd, 14 App(3d) 329, 14 OBR 396, 471 NE(2d) 527 (Franklin 1984).

[124] RC 124.322, RC 124.323.

[125] RC 124.322.

[126] RC 124.322.

[127] RC 124.325(C).

[128] RC 124.325(D).

[129] RC 124.321, RC 124.323, RC 124.324.

[130] State ex rel Bentley v Middletown City School Dist Bd of Ed, 20 App(3d) 223, 20 OBR 270, 485 NE(2d) 768 (Butler 1984).

[131] RC 124.324.

[132] RC 124.324.

[133] RC 124.327.

[134] RC 124.328.

common pleas court in the county in which the employee resides pursuant to RC 119.12.[135] A failure to certify lack of funds until after the effective date of layoffs and a failure to verify retention points will not invalidate a layoff where the employee fails to prove that he was thereby prejudiced.[136] A job is not abolished where the appointing authority simply transfers the duties of that job to a new employee and gives the job a new title.[137]

DEMOTION, REDUCTION, SUSPENSION, TERMINATION, AND RESIGNATION

12.15 Demotion, reduction, and suspension

(A) Demotion or suspension, appeal

In non-civil service school districts, suspension or demotion of nonteaching employees is permitted, but the board of education must comply with the termination procedure outlined below.[138] In civil service school districts, the same procedures must be followed as for removal, when the suspension is for more than three working days. There is no authority under RC 124.34 to suspend an employee indefinitely after his indictment for a criminal offense pending the outcome of criminal proceedings.[139] An employee in a district covered by civil service has no right to appeal a suspension for three days or less.[140] An administrator in the city school district, as well as the board, can impose suspensions of three days or less.[141]

A nonteaching employee in a civil service school district may appeal the decision of the civil service commission affirming a suspension of more than three days to the common pleas court of the county in which the district is located pursuant to RC 2506.01.[142] The appeal must be taken within ten days of the commission's decision, pursuant to RC 2505.07(B), and must be filed with the commission under RC 2505.04.[143]

(B) Pay reduction, appeal

Involuntary reductions in pay in a civil service school district must comply with RC 124.34.[144] This statute provides that reductions in pay are permitted only for disciplinary reasons. The Ohio Supreme Court has twice held that a reduction of hours constitutes a reduction in pay within the meaning of RC 124.34. In one case, the Court held that such a reduction, whether or not for disciplinary reasons, could be appealed to the civil service commission under RC 124.40.[145] Later that same year, the Court held that only reductions for disciplinary reasons may be further appealed to court pursuant to RC 124.34, and then only to the common pleas court in the county where the employee resides.[146] Whether an

---

[135]Ludwig v Willoughby-Eastlake City School Dist Bd of Ed, 10 App(3d) 229, 10 OBR 324, 461 NE(2d) 919 (Lake 1983).

[136]Yates v Wallingford, 7 App(3d) 316, 7 OBR 411, 455 NE(2d) 687 (Franklin 1982).

[137]In re Appeal of Woods, 7 App(3d) 226, 7 OBR 288, 455 NE(2d) 13 (Franklin 1982).

[138]See Text 12.16, Termination: non-civil service employees. See also State ex rel O'Dell v Scioto Valley Local School Dist Bd of Ed, No. 1498, 1990 WL 34123 (4th Dist Ct App, Ross, 3-13-90) (demotion of non-civil service nonteaching employee on continuing contract would trigger right to constitutional due process).

[139]State ex rel Baran v Fuerst, 65 OS(3d) 413, 604 NE(2d) 750 (1992). See also OAC 124-9-08.

[140]RC 124.34.

[141]State ex rel Specht v Oregon City Bd of Ed, 66 OS(3d) 178, 420 NE(2d) 1004 (1981).

[142]Sutherland-Wagner v Brook Park Civil Service Comm, 32 OS(3d) 323, 512 NE(2d) 1170 (1987). See also Nuspl v Akron, 61 OS(3d) 511, 575 NE(2d) 447 (1991).

[143]Burns v Middletown Civil Service Comm, No. 82-06-0062, 1983 WL 4414 (12th Dist Ct App, Butler, 6-30-83). As to what constitutes an "entry" of a municipal civil service commission's order, thus triggering the appeal period, see Swafford v Norwood Bd of Ed, 14 App(3d) 346, 14 OBR 414, 471 NE(2d) 509 (Hamilton 1984).

[144]The extent to which economic fringe benefits qualify as pay for purposes of the statute is unclear. Compare Ebert v Stark County Bd of Mental Retardation, 63 OS(2d) 31, 406 NE(2d) 1098 (1980) (finding it "obvious that sick leave credits, just as other fringe benefits are forms of compensation") with State ex rel Bassman v Earhart, 18 OS(3d) 182, 18 OBR 250, 480 NE(2d) 761 (1985) (free parking privileges, in absence of statute requiring that they be granted, is mere "gratuity," the cessation of which is not a reduction in pay).

[145]State ex rel Vukovich v Youngstown Civil Service Comm, 69 OS(2d) 16, 430 NE(2d) 452 (1982).

[146]Harris v Lewis, 69 OS(2d) 577, 433 NE(2d) 223 (1982). See also Garfield Heights City Dist Bd of Ed v

appeal to court of a reduction, even for nondisciplinary reasons, is permitted pursuant to RC 2506.01 is simply not clear.[147]

12.16 Termination: non-civil service employees

(A) Introduction, grounds for termination

In non-civil service school districts, a nonteaching employee may be terminated for violation of written rules of a board of education, incompetency, inefficiency, dishonesty, drunkenness, immoral conduct, insubordination, discourteous treatment of the public, neglect of duty, or any other acts of misfeasance, malfeasance, or nonfeasance. In addition, the commission of sexual battery in violation of RC 2907.03(A)(7) is grounds for termination.[148] One court, stating an act of misfeasance must consist of a breach of a clearly defined duty, reinstated a suspended bus driver who inaccurately estimated hours. The job description requiring drivers to keep the transportation coordinator informed of changes needed in bus routes was determined not to be a clearly defined standard.[149] Also, isolated instances of incompetency without evidence of clear instructions to correct job performance will not support a termination for incompetency, inefficiency, and neglect of duty.[150] However, where a custodian's failure to secure entrances to a building resulted in a break-in, a court upheld the termination, noting the custodian had received poor evaluations and memoranda pointing out various problems with his work.[151]

Courts have upheld the termination of a bus driver for failure to report a conviction for driving under the influence of alcohol and the suspension of his license,[152] for striking a student on a school bus,[153] for speeding and subsequently making a false statement to a police officer that the speedometer on the bus was malfunctioning,[154] and for a failure to yield the right of way that resulted in a collision, even though the employee's driving record was free of citations.[155] Removal was warranted where a bus driver collided with the school bus in front of her and evidence showed she drove too fast, tailgated, and, on the date of the accident, failed to report that the brakes were not operating properly.[156] Removal of a driver with twenty years' experience for insubordination was upheld where the driver threatened and shoved a board member and hung up the phone on the

---

Gillihan, 17 App(3d) 86, 17 OBR 147, 477 NE(2d) 681 (Cuyahoga 1984).

[147]See Nuspl v Akron, 61 OS(3d) 511, 575 NE(2d) 447 (1991).

[148]RC 3319.081(C). The abolishment of a nonteaching position is not a termination within the meaning of RC 3319.081, and, accordingly, the statute does not apply to such a decision and no pre-termination hearing or notice is required. Graham v Triway Bd of Ed, 82 App(3d) 34, 610 NE(2d) 1185 (Wayne 1992), dismissed, jurisdictional motion overruled by 65 OS(3d) 1495, 605 NE(2d) 949 (1993). Similarly, the transfer or reassignment of an employee is generally not regarded as a termination and does not implicate the procedural safeguards contained in RC 3319.081. A transfer may amount to a demotion, however, which would trigger a right to constitutional due process. See State ex rel O'Dell v Scioto Valley Local School Dist Bd of Ed, No. 1498, 1990 WL 34123 (4th Dist Ct App, Ross, 3-13-90). A move from night to day shift in the same job is not a transfer but merely a job reassignment. See State ex rel Hallinan v Tallmadge City School Dist Bd of Ed, No. 14480, 1990 WL 167021 (9th Dist Ct App, Summit, 10-31-90).

[149]Mansfield v Cardinal Local School Dist Bd of Ed, No. 1195, 1985 WL 7791 (11th Dist Ct App, Geauga, 2-15-85).

[150]Panek v Chardon Local School Dist Bd of Ed, No. 1182, 1985 WL 7794 (11th Dist Ct App, Geauga, 2-15-85).

[151]Scyoc v Wellington Exempted Village School Dist, No. 4014, 1986 WL 10585 (9th Dist Ct App, Lorain, 9-24-86).

[152]McMaster v Chesapeake Union Exempted Village School Dist Bd of Ed, No. 91CA14, 1992 WL 97804 (4th Dist Ct App, Lawrence, 5-11-92).

[153]Shukert v Woodridge Local School Dist Bd of Ed, No. 12162, 1985 WL 10918 (9th Dist Ct App, Summit, 10-30-85).

[154]Ashbaugh v Paulding Exempted Village School Dist Bd of Ed, Nos. 11-86-5, 11-86-6, 1988 WL 91312 (3d Dist Ct App, Paulding, 8-29-88).

[155]Wilson v Upper Sandusky Exempted Village School Dist Bd of Ed, No. 16-85-5, 1986 WL 7728 (3d Dist Ct App, Wyandot, 7-3-86). See also Kunkelman v Elida Local School Dist Bd of Ed, No. CV93 01 0021 (CP, Allen, 7-7-93). In Finfrock v Spencerville Local School Dist Bd of Ed, No. 1-81-64 (3d Dist Ct App, Allen, 7-16-82), a twenty-day suspension for driving recklessly (thus causing another driver to drive off the road to avoid an accident) was upheld.

[156]Wills v Rossford Exempted Village School Dist, No. WD-86-76, 1987 WL 9935 (6th Dist Ct App, Wood, 4-17-87).

superintendent.[157] Removal was also upheld where a driver's recurring back trouble kept him off the job over a two-year period for most of his scheduled work days, thus establishing an inability to discharge his duties as an employee.[158]

A board may terminate a bus driver for "improper conduct" within the meaning of RC 3327.10 where the finding was based on conviction for driving while under the influence of alcohol.[159] Discharge of a bus driver whose driving record is such that the employer's insurance carrier refuses to cover him has also been upheld.[160] A board may not suspend/terminate a continuing contract for layoff purposes under RC 3319.081 if others remain employed under limited contracts to perform tasks which could be performed by the continuing contract employee.[161]

As with teachers, nonteaching employees are, of course, protected by general equal employment opportunity laws, the First Amendment, and Ohio's whistleblower statute.[162]

RC 3319.151 expressly makes the revealing to a student of any specific question known to be part of a state-required proficiency test, or otherwise assisting a student to cheat on such a test, grounds for termination under RC 3319.081(C).

(B) Notice of termination, due process

There is no express statutory requirement that a board of education afford a nonteaching employee a hearing prior to termination; however, some courts have implied one on constitutional due process grounds.[163] In light of the US Supreme Court's decision in *Cleveland Bd of Ed v Loudermill*,[164] affording civil service employees the constitutional right to a pretermination hearing, boards of education are well advised to afford such rights to all nonteaching employees.[165]

Where a hearing was held but the principal witness against the employee, who had also initiated the termination decision, was permitted to be present after the hearing while the board considered the issue but during which time the employee was excluded, the termination was found unconstitutional.[166]

(C) Hearing, evidence, board action

In determining whether to terminate a nonteaching employee's contract, a board of education may properly consider an employee's conduct in previous years as long as it is used in conjunction with evidence of misconduct in the immediate past.[167] Excessive absenteeism, tardiness, insubordination, and violation of state board of education regulations are cause for termination.[168]

---

[157]Cole v Cardington-Lincoln Local School Dist, No. CA-670, 1987 WL 19089 (5th Dist Ct App, Morrow, 10-23-87).

[158]Winners v Berea City School Dist Bd of Ed, No. 56458, 1990 WL 3156 (8th Dist Ct App, Cuyahoga, 1-18-90).

[159]Crain v Hamilton County Bd of Ed, No. C-830324, 1984 WL 6732 (1st Dist Ct App, Hamilton, 2-8-84).

[160]Thornton v Meigs Local School Dist Bd of Ed, No. 436, 1990 WL 85176 (4th Dist Ct App, Meigs, 6-15-90); Mayes v Employment Services Bureau Bd of Review, 32 App(3d) 68, 513 NE(2d) 818 (Franklin 1986). See also O'Harra v Columbus City School Dist Bd of Ed, No. 88AP-149, 1989 WL 27163 (10th Dist Ct App, Franklin, 3-23-89).

[161]Ferdinand v Hamilton Local Bd of Ed, 17 App(3d) 165, 17 OBR 296, 478 NE(2d) 835 (Franklin 1984).

[162]See Text Ch 17, Equal Employment Opportunity, Family and Medical Leave; Text 9.21(E), Constitutionally protected conduct; Text 9.21(F), Protection of whistleblowers.

[163]Mervine v Margaretta Local School Dist Bd of Ed, No. E-89-4, 1989 WL 130872 (6th Dist Ct App, Erie, 11-3-89); Pack v West Clermont Local School Dist Bd of Ed, 24 Misc(2d) 1, 24 OBR 64, 492 NE(2d) 1259 (CP, Clermont 1985) (involving three-day suspension); In re Sergent, 49 Misc 36, 360 NE(2d) 761 (CP, Montgomery 1976); Pertuset v Northwest Local School Dist Bd of Ed, 33 Misc 161, 293 NE(2d) 887 (CP, Scioto 1972).

[164]Cleveland Bd of Ed v Loudermill, 470 US 532, 105 SCt 1487, 84 LEd(2d) 494 (1985).

[165]See Text 12.17(B), Notice to employee, removal order.

[166]Shaffer v Minerva Local School Dist Bd of Ed, No. CA-8591, 1991 WL 302421 (5th Dist Ct App, Stark, 12-16-91). The mere presence of the principal accuser during board deliberations, said the court, was "inherently contradictory to basic principles of fairness and integrity." The presence of the board's legal counsel during deliberations, however, was not unconstitutional.

[167]In re Shadley, No. 6-80-11, 1981 WL 6795 (3d Dist Ct App, Hardin, 2-26-81).

[168]Powell v Jefferson Local School Dist Bd of Ed, No. 772, 1983 WL 4459 (12th Dist Ct App, Madison, 8-31-83).

However, where a board's decision is not supported by a preponderance of the evidence, it will be reversed.[169] A court may affirm, disaffirm, or modify the board's action, but, some cases have held, has no authority to remand the case to the board for further proceedings.[170]

Some courts have held that the failure to swear witnesses and provide a stenographic record of the proceedings requires reversal of a board's decision to terminate a nonteaching employee.[171]

The board must act by majority vote; the action must then be served by certified mail; and the employee may then file a written appeal with the common pleas court within ten days. Courts have applied the procedure of RC Chapter 2506 to such appeals, although the matter is not wholly free of doubt.[172] Failure to appeal within the ten-day deadline precludes a subsequent suit challenging the termination on any ground that was asserted or could have been asserted before the board.[173]

12.17 Termination: civil service employees

(A) Introduction, grounds for termination

In any school district a nonteaching employee may be terminated for incompetency, inefficiency, dishonesty, drunkenness, immoral conduct, insubordination, discourteous treatment of the public, neglect of duty, or other acts of misfeasance, malfeasance, or nonfeasance. In addition, the commission of sexual battery in violation of RC 2907.03(A)(7) is grounds for termination. In a city school district, a nonteaching employee may also be terminated for violation of the civil service rules, any other failure of good behavior, or a violation of the Ohio Ethics Code.[174] Nonteaching employees of a city district where civil service applies are included within the provisions of RC 124.34, and any change in employment must be made pursuant to the statute, notwithstanding the fact that original contracts of employment may have been drawn pursuant to RC 3319.081.[175] Advocacy or willfully retaining membership in an organization which advocates the overthrow of the government of the United States or the state by force, violence, or other unlawful means is also cause for removal.[176] In addition, RC 3319.151 expressly makes the revealing to a student of any specific question known to be part of a state-required proficiency test, or otherwise assisting a student to cheat on such a test, grounds for termination under RC 124.34.

RC 124.341 provides protection for civil servant "whistleblowers." Under this section, no disciplinary action may be taken against an employee who reports to appropriate authorities his good faith belief that there has been a violation of federal or state statutes, rules, or regulations, or a misuse of public resources. Whistleblowers

---

[169]Powell v Jefferson Local School Dist Bd of Ed, No. 772, 1983 WL 4459 (12th Dist Ct App, Madison, 8-31-83).

[170]Powell v Meigs Local School Dist, No. 502, 1993 WL 379085 (4th Dist Ct App, Meigs, 9-8-93); Crabtree v West Clermont Local School Dist Bd of Ed, No. CA84-05-038, 1985 WL 8173 (12th Dist Ct App, Clermont, 2-19-85); Smith v Clermont Northeastern Local School Dist Bd of Ed, No. CA90-10-103, 1991 WL 164577 (12th Dist Ct App, Clermont, 8-26-91).

[171]Bolek v Chardon Bd of Ed, No. 1057, 1983 WL 6211 (11th Dist Ct App, Geauga, 3-25-83); Kenney v South Range Local School Dist Bd of Ed, No. 82-CA-35, 1983 WL 6618 (7th Dist Ct App, Mahoning, 3-23-83) (remanding case to board for hearing upon sworn record).

[172]See Woerner v Mentor Exempted Village School Dist Bd of Ed, 84 App(3d) 844, 619 NE(2d) 34 (Lake 1993) and the cases cited therein; Powell v Meigs Local School Dist, No. 502, 1993 WL 379085 (4th Dist Ct App, Meigs, 9-8-93). The case for not applying RC Chapter 2506 to RC 3319.081 is stated by Judge Nader in his concurring opinion in *Woerner*. Assuming RC Chapter 2506 applies, *Woerner* and the cases cited therein reveal that the courts are divided on whether a failure to file a transcript of proceedings before the board of education permits the reviewing court to proceed or deprives the court of jurisdiction. *Powell* held that the common pleas court should have taken evidence pursuant to RC 2506.03 in the absence of a transcript rather than remand the matter back to the board.

[173]Gilbert v Trumbull County Bd of Ed, No. 92-T-4761, 1993 WL 417125 (11th Dist Ct App, Trumbull, 9-30-93) (applying legal doctrines of res judicata and collateral estoppel).

[174]RC 124.34.

[175]State ex rel Proctor v Alliance Public School Dist Bd of Ed, 60 App(2d) 396, 398 NE(2d) 805 (Stark 1978).

[176]RC 124.36.

are also protected under Ohio's general whistleblower statute, RC 4113.52.[177]

Authority is split as to whether the reason for an employee's dismissal must be job-related. One court of appeals has stated there must be a nexus between the conduct an employer seeks to regulate and a person's employment.[178] Another has held a civil service employee may be discharged for dishonesty although there is no relationship between the dishonest act and the employment.[179] That court has also held no nexus need be proved where the discharged employee was convicted of a felony involving moral turpitude.[180]

An employee who is insubordinate and refuses to assist in resolving job-related problems may be removed.[181] A school bus driver who violates Ohio traffic laws by instructing a student to raise the gates at a railroad crossing and driving the bus over that crossing is guilty of misconduct warranting removal.[182] Removal is warranted where a bus driver is involved in three work-related accidents within a four-month period and the third accident was two days after a reprimand to improve her driving performance.[183] An employee may be removed where, after requesting leave due to the illness of his wife and daughter, he is found conducting a landscaping business, conduct necessarily inconsistent with the request for leave.[184]

In assessing the propriety of a penalty, a commission does not act unreasonably when it reduces a removal to a suspension where the employee's dishonest act was the only blemish on a ten-year work record.[185]

Nonteaching employees covered by civil service, like teachers and nonteaching employees not covered by civil service, are, of course, protected by general equal employment opportunity laws and the First Amendment.[186]

(B) Notice to employee, removal order

In *Cleveland Bd of Ed v Loudermill*,[187] the US Supreme Court held that the due process clause of the Fourteenth Amendment requires that a nonprobationary public employee be afforded an opportunity to respond *before* being removed under RC 124.34. Prior to removal, the employee must be given oral or written notice of the charges, an explanation of the employer's evidence, and an opportunity to present his side of the story, either orally or in writing. One court has concluded that failure to specify precisely when adverse administrative action will occur renders the notice legally insufficient.[188]

Courts have emphasized that the pretermination hearing need not be elaborate. Thus, a full evidentiary hearing is unnecessary. Employees should, after notice and an explanation of the evidence, simply be allowed to tell their side of the story.[189] There is no constitutional right to tape record or have a stenographic record of the hearing,[190] or to confront and cross-

---

[177]RC 4113.52 receives expansive treatment in Text 9.21(F), Protection of whistleblowers.

[178]In re Chase, 50 App(2d) 393, 364 NE(2d) 292 (Ross 1976).

[179]Craddolph v Ackerman, 57 App(2d) 150, 385 NE(2d) 1091 (Franklin 1978); Watson v Schwenker, 8 App(3d) 294, 8 OBR 389, 456 NE(2d) 1243 (Franklin 1982).

[180]Stover v Bureau of Motor Vehicles, No. 87AP 569, 1987 WL 31256 (10th Dist Ct App, Franklin, 12-21-87).

[181]Renner v East Liverpool Civil Service Comm, No. 81-C-34, 1982 WL 3647 (7th Dist Ct App, Columbiana, 2-26-82).

[182]Lamb v Norton City School Dist Bd of Ed, No. 10643, 1982 WL 2738 (9th Dist Ct App, Summit, 9-1-82).

[183]Graham v Wooster City School Dist Bd of Ed, No. 2193, 1987 WL 11529 (9th Dist Ct App, Wayne, 5-20-87).

[184]Hutt v Chillicothe Correctional Institute, No. 398, 1983 WL 3096 (4th Dist Ct App, Vinton, 1-18-83).

[185]Karg v Wyandot County Engineer, No. 16-86-15, 1988 WL 33668 (3d Dist Ct App, Wyandot, 3-11-88).

[186]See Text Ch 17, Equal Employment Opportunity, Family and Medical Leave; Text 9.21(E), Constitutionally protected conduct.

[187]Cleveland Bd of Ed v Loudermill, 470 US 532, 105 SCt 1487, 84 LEd(2d) 494 (1985).

[188]Seltzer v Cuyahoga County Dept of Human Services, 38 App(3d) 121, 528 NE(2d) 573 (Cuyahoga 1987).

[189]See Manning v Clermont County Bd of Commrs, 55 App(3d) 177, 563 NE(2d) 372 (Clermont 1989).

[190]Local 4501, Communications Workers of America v Ohio State University, 49 OS(3d) 1, 550

examine witnesses.[191] The purpose of the pretermination hearing is not to resolve whether the removal is justified, but to provide an initial check against mistaken decisions—a determination of whether there are reasonable grounds to believe the charges are true and support the proposed removal. Where pretermination procedures are abbreviated, the post-termination hearing must be substantially more meaningful. At a minimum the employee must be able to attend the hearing, have the assistance of counsel, call witnesses, and produce evidence on his own behalf.[192] There is, however, no absolute due process right to face-to-face confrontation, only a right to a meaningful opportunity to challenge the adverse evidence.[193]

The nonteaching employee must be furnished with a written copy of the order stating the reasons for his removal. The order must be sufficiently detailed so that the employee is afforded the opportunity to refute the case made against him.[194]

Although an employee may waive his right to a pretermination hearing, one court has held that where a lawyer waives the pretermination hearing without the express approval of the employee, the waiver is invalid.[195]

(C) Appeal to civil service commission

The removal order must be filed with the civil service commission. The employee then has ten days to file a written appeal with the commission. Filing a removal order is not a jurisdictional prerequisite to the right of appeal before the commission.[196] However, any decision which is not filed in the manner prescribed by the civil service laws must be disaffirmed.[197] A civil service appeal must be heard within thirty days by the commission or by a trial board appointed by the commission. One court has held that the commission's failure to conduct a hearing within the thirty-day period does not deprive it of jurisdiction to proceed to hold the hearing.[198] A party may appeal to the court of common pleas in the county where the employee resides in any case involving reduction in pay for disciplinary reasons or removal.[199]

The civil service commission hearing is to determine whether statutory grounds for the action taken are present. However, court decisions have reversed commission affirmances of terminations where employees were not afforded *Loudermill* rights.[200]

Where the business manager discharges an employee, actual removal does not take place until the action is confirmed by the board of education. There is no order of removal subject to appeal to the civil service commission until the employee is given a copy of the board's order of confirmation and it is filed with the commission.

When an employee who is being removed appeals to a civil service commission and the commission denies jurisdiction, the commission's decision is a final appealable order which may be appealed to the court of common pleas pursuant to RC 119.12 or RC 2506.01.[201] If the employee fails to pursue such appellate remedies, he may not collaterally attack the commis-

---

NE(2d) 164 (1990), cert denied 497 US 1025, 110 SCt 3274, 111 LEd(2d) 783 (1990).

[191]See OAPSE v Lakewood City School Dist Bd of Ed, 68 OS(3d) 175, 624 NE(2d) 1043 (1994).

[192]Carter v Western Reserve Psychiatric Habilitation Center, 767 F(2d) 270 (6th Cir Ohio 1985). Even if a pretermination *Loudermill* hearing is given, a procedural due process violation may be found if post-termination review under RC 124.34 is denied. Sutton v Cleveland Bd of Ed, 958 F(2d) 1339 (6th Cir Ohio 1992).

[193]OAPSE v Lakewood City School Dist Bd of Ed, 68 OS(3d) 175, 624 NE(2d) 1043 (1994) (finding no due process violation where witness testified by closed circuit television that an employee had aided her as a student in obtaining illicit drugs and was cross-examined).

[194]LeClain v Logan Civil Service Comm, No. 358, 1982 WL 3345 (4th Dist Ct App, Hocking, 1-19-82).

[195]Riordin v Lakewood Civil Service Comm, No. 52398, 1987 WL 16536 (8th Dist Ct App, Cuyahoga, 9-3-87).

[196]State ex rel Shine v Garofalo, 69 OS(2d) 253, 431 NE(2d) 680 (1982).

[197]RC 124.03(A).

[198]In re Appeal of Gardner, 40 App(3d) 99, 531 NE(2d) 741 (Franklin 1987).

[199]RC 124.34.

[200]Csanyi v Cuyahoga County Commrs, 29 App(3d) 37, 29 OBR 38, 502 NE(2d) 700 (Cuyahoga 1986); Jones v Cleveland Civil Service Commrs, No. 49226, 1985 WL 6862 (8th Dist Ct App, Cuyahoga, 6-13-85); Fairley v State Personnel Bd of Review, 29 App(3d) 113, 29 OBR 129, 504 NE(2d) 75 (Franklin 1986).

[201]Walker v Eastlake, 61 OS(2d) 273, 400 NE(2d) 908 (1980); Beare v Eaton, 9 App(3d) 142, 9 OBR 207, 458 NE(2d) 895 (Preble 1983).

sion's jurisdictional determination.[202] When an employee fails to appeal the commission's denial of jurisdiction to the court of common pleas, he has no recourse to the state personnel board of review.[203] Likewise, a court of common pleas has no jurisdiction over the indefinite suspension of a civil service employee when the employee fails to file an available administrative appeal.[204]

An employer may secure a noncoercive voluntary resignation from an employee as an alternative to removal. However, where the charges of misconduct are unfounded, a resignation does not deprive the civil service commission of jurisdiction to review the matter.[205] When an employer secures a conditional resignation and fails to comply with the agreed conditions, the affected employee may maintain an action for reinstatement.[206] Where an employee tenders a resignation from an "acting" supervisory position, but not his underlying classified position, he may sue to regain his classified position when the board terminates his employment entirely.[207]

(D) Appeal to common pleas court

A party may seek review of the civil service commission's decision in the court of common pleas.[208] The court is to decide whether the record shows the order appealed from is supported by substantial evidence and is in accordance with law.[209] In so doing, a court should not search beyond the record submitted to it.[210]

A classified employee has a choice of appealing pursuant to RC 119.12 or RC 2506.01.[211] It has been held that where one files a notice of appeal with the common pleas court instead of the civil service commission, the court has no jurisdiction to hear the appeal.[212]

In an appeal filed pursuant to RC 119.12, laid-off classified employees of a city school district must appeal an order of the civil service commission to the court of common pleas of the county in which the employees reside.[213] Notice of appeal under RC 119.12 must be filed with the court within fifteen days of mailing of the civil service commission order.[214] In such an appeal, a record of the hearing before the civil service commission must be certified in common pleas court. The commission must file the record within thirty days.[215] If the record is not timely filed, the court may enter a finding in favor of the party adversely affected.[216] The moving party may also request and pay for a stenographic transcript of testimony in the administrative proceeding.[217]

It has been held that a civil service commission, in filing the record of the administrative proceeding, is not required to furnish a stenographic transcript of testimony in the proceeding when an employee appeals under RC 119.12, since the commission is not an agency as defined in RC 119.01(A) for purposes of the appeal. While the appellate provisions of RC

---

[202] State ex rel Henderson v Maple Heights Civil Service Comm, 63 OS(2d) 39, 406 NE(2d) 1105 (1980). See also State ex rel OAPSE v Orange City School Dist Bd of Ed, No. 47242, 1984 WL 5027 (8th Dist Ct App, Cuyahoga, 3-29-84).
[203] Adkins v State Personnel Bd of Review, 32 App(3d) 32, 513 NE(2d) 808 (Cuyahoga 1986).
[204] Noernberg v Brook Park, 63 OS(2d) 26, 406 NE(2d) 1095 (1980).
[205] Kinney v Department of Administrative Services, 14 App(3d) 33, 14 OBR 37, 469 NE(2d) 1007 (Franklin 1984).
[206] State ex rel Carter v Cleveland City School Dist Bd of Ed, 17 OS(3d) 105, 17 OBR 224, 477 NE(2d) 1134 (1985).
[207] Monico v Girard Bd of Ed, No. 3716, 1987 WL 26711 (11th Dist Ct App, Trumbull, 12-4-87).
[208] RC 119.12, RC 124.34, RC Ch 2506.
[209] RC 119.12, RC 2506.04.
[210] Hawkins v Marion Correctional Institution, No. 9-85-33, 1987 WL 32148 (3d Dist Ct App, Marion, 12-18-87).

[211] Walker v Eastlake, 61 OS(2d) 273, 400 NE(2d) 908 (1980).
[212] Jacobs v Marion Civil Service Comm, 27 App(3d) 194, 27 OBR 233, 500 NE(2d) 321 (Marion 1985).
[213] Thompson v Bryan Civil Service Comm, No. WMS-86-15, 1987 WL 11032 (6th Dist Ct App, Williams, 5-15-87); Ludwig v Willoughby-Eastlake City School Dist Bd of Ed, 10 App(3d) 229, 10 OBR 324, 461 NE(2d) 919 (Lake 1983).
[214] RC 119.12.
[215] RC 119.12.
[216] RC 119.12. As to what constitutes an "entry" of a civil service commission's order, thus triggering the appeal period, see Swafford v Norwood Bd of Ed, 14 App(3d) 346, 14 OBR 414, 471 NE(2d) 509 (Hamilton 1984).
[217] RC 119.12.

119.12 are made applicable to an appeal from a civil service commission by the third paragraph of RC 124.34, those provisions in RC 119.12 that particularly relate to an "agency" are inapplicable to a commission. It is therefore sufficient if the commission in its decision reviews the evidence and makes specific findings of fact upon which its ultimate conclusion can be tested.[218]

Nevertheless, every effort should be made to file a complete record and a stenographic transcript of testimony is generally desirable. It has been held that RC 119.12 makes a finding for the appellant mandatory upon a failure to prepare and certify the record.[219]

An appeal under RC 2506.01 is lodged in the court of common pleas of the county in which the school district's principal office is located.[220] A certified record of the hearing must be filed by the civil service commission within forty days of the appeal.[221] In an appeal pursuant to RC 2506.01 to the court of common pleas by a city school district school bus driver from a civil service commission decision, the only jurisdictional requirement under RC 2505.04 is the filing of the notice of appeal. RC 2505.05 then sets out what information must be designated in the notice of appeal. These, however, are not jurisdictional prerequisites, and failure to comply with them does not defeat an appeal.[222]

The determination of whether an appeal brought in a court of common pleas, under RC 124.34, involves the removal of an employee from his job, or concerns a reduction in his pay for disciplinary reasons, should be based on the action of the board of education, not on the action of the civil service commission acting as an appellate tribunal.[223] Thus, the "nature" of a case is determined by the original action taken by a board of education even if subsequently modified by a civil service commission.[224]

An appeals court has held there is no statutory right of appeal conferred upon the appointing authority from a decision of a civil service commission reinstating a classified employee terminated for "lack of funds."[225]

12.18 Resignation

The resignation of nonteaching employees, whether in a civil service or non-civil service school district, is generally governed by the same principles as apply to teachers.[226]

EDUCATIONAL AIDES

12.19 Employment of educational aides

The employment of educational aides is governed by RC 3319.088. An educational aide is a nonteaching employee who directly assists a teacher by performing duties for which a teaching certificate is not required. With limited exceptions specified in the statute, a nonteaching employee may not serve as an educational aide without first obtaining an educational aide permit issued by the state board of education. A person applying for or holding a permit is subject to RC 3319.31 and RC 3319.311.[227]

An educational aide must at all times be under the supervision and direction of a teacher and may assist the teacher to whom assigned in supervising and instructing pupils. The duties need not be performed in the physical presence of the teacher. An educational aide may not assign grades to

---

[218]Gross v Lima Civil Service Comm, No. 1-81-20, 1981 WL 6694 (3d Dist Ct App, Allen, 10-2-81). But see Martin v Bexley Civil Service Comm, No. 83AP-1067, 1984 WL 5862 (10th Dist Ct App, Franklin, 8-9-84) (declaring a transcript necessary for adjudication of appeal under RC 119.12).

[219]Lowe v Grove City Civil Service Comm, No. 80AP-47 (10th Dist Ct App, Franklin, 7-29-80).

[220]RC 2506.01.

[221]RC 2506.02.

[222]Moore v Cleveland Civil Service Comm, 11 App(3d) 273, 11 OBR 453, 465 NE(2d) 482 (Cuyahoga 1983).

[223]In re Stanley, 56 App(2d) 1, 381 NE(2d) 212 (Franklin 1978).

[224]Scott v Reinier, 58 OS(2d) 67, 388 NE(2d) 1226 (1979).

[225]Poole v Maloney, 9 App(3d) 198, 9 OBR 309, 459 NE(2d) 247 (Franklin 1983).

[226]See Text 9.17, Resignation (except for first paragraph, which applies only to teachers).

[227]See Text 8.07, Revocation or suspension of certificate.

pupils or administer corporal punishment. An educational aide may be assigned to assist more than one teacher, but cannot be subject to simultaneous supervision or direction by more than one teacher.

Educational aides may not be used in place of teachers or other employees, and the teacher-pupil ratio in the school district may not be decreased by the use of educational aides. The district may employ up to one full-time equivalent educational aide for each six full-time equivalent certificated employees in the district. Educational aides are not counted as certificated employees for purposes of the foundation program, and pupils with educational aides cannot be counted as a class or unit for foundation program purposes. Educational aides must be paid according to a salary plan adopted annually by the board of education.

The mere fact that one employed as an educational aide possesses a teaching certificate does not elevate the employee to the position of a teacher for pay or other purposes; however, if such a person occasionally performs the work of a teacher, contrary to RC 3319.088, the board of education may be required to pay for those days at the daily rate and benefits applicable to a teacher.[228]

RC 3319.088 provides that educational aides "shall have all rights, benefits, and legal protection available to other non-teaching employees in the school district," except RC Chapter 124 (pertaining to civil service) "shall not apply" to any educational aide. Thus, in other than city school districts, the statutes applicable to non-civil service employees generally apply. With respect to city school districts, the Ohio Supreme Court has held that educational aides are entitled to the rights, benefits, and legal protection available to other non-teaching employees in the *unclassified* service of the district.[229] More particularly, the tenure provisions of RC 3319.081 to RC 3319.083 do *not* apply.[230]

---

[228]State ex rel White v Marion City Bd of Ed, No. 9-87-48, 1989 WL 71125 (3d Dist Ct App, Marion, 6-27-89).

[229]OAPSE v Columbus Bd of Ed, 28 OS(2d) 58, 275 NE(2d) 610 (1971).

[230]OAPSE v Columbus Bd of Ed, 28 OS(2d) 58, 275 NE(2d) 610 (1971).

Chapter 13

Nonteaching Personnel: Compensation, Fringe Benefits, and Leave

COMPENSATION
- 13.01 Pay scales and job classifications
- 13.02 Work week: overtime and compensatory time
- 13.03 Holiday pay
- 13.04 Vacation pay
- 13.05 Other paid days
- 13.06 Payroll deductions

INSURANCE AND LEAVE
- 13.07 Insurance
- 13.08 Sick leave
- 13.09 Severance pay on basis of accumulated sick leave
- 13.10 Personal and other leaves of absence

COMPENSATION

13.01 Pay scales and job classifications

(A) In general

All boards of education receiving state foundation program funds under RC Chapter 3317 are required to adopt a salary schedule for nonteaching employees. Each board is also required to prepare job classifications for nonteaching employees.

(B) Notice of job classification and pay scale

All nonteaching employees are to be notified of the classification to which they are assigned and the salary for the classification. Compensation for like positions must be uniform except as affected by increments based on length of service. Under the federal Fair Labor Standards Act (FLSA) and state law, the current minimum wage is $4.25 per hour.[1]

On October 15 of each year the salary schedule and the list of job classifications and salaries in effect on that date must be filed with the superintendent of public instruction.[2] The failure to give experience credit on the salary schedule, vacation leave, and seniority for previous service in a similar position in the school district amounts to an abuse of discretion.[3]

In districts where the civil service laws do not apply, each board must give notice annually, not later than July 1, to each nonteaching employee holding a contract valid for the succeeding school year, as to the salary to be paid during that school year. The salary may not be lower than during the preceding school year unless the reduction is a part of a uniform plan affecting nonteaching employees of the entire district. Increases in salary may be given after the board's annual notice.[4]

There is no express requirement that the salary notice include the hourly rate paid or a specific designation of the number of hours to be worked.[5] The Ohio Supreme Court has held that employees compensated on an hourly basis must be notified no later than July 1 of the compensation to be paid during the ensuing school year, and the rate may not be cut unless the reduction is part of a uniform plan affecting all the nonteaching employees in the district, but the number of hours to be worked is not statutorily guaranteed.[6] This ruling set-

---

[1] 29 USCA 206; RC 4111.02. That the federal Act's applicability to political subdivisions, including school districts, is constitutional was established by Garcia v San Antonio Metropolitan Transit Authority, 469 US 528, 105 SCt 1005, 83 LEd(2d) 1016 (1985).

[2] RC 3317.12.

[3] Sarra v Girard City School Dist Bd of Ed, No. 3252, 1983 WL 6066 (11th Dist Ct App, Trumbull, 12-30-83).

[4] RC 3319.082. The extent to which economic fringe benefits qualify as salary for purposes of the prohibition against a decrease except under a uniform plan is unclear. Two cases decided under civil service statutes illustrate the ambiguity. Compare Ebert v Stark County Bd of Mental Retardation, 63 OS(2d) 31, 406 NE(2d) 1098 (1980) (finding it "obvious that sick leave credits, just as other fringe benefits, are forms of compensation") with State ex rel Bassman v Earhart, 18 OS(3d) 182, 18 OBR 250, 480 NE(2d) 761 (1985) (free parking privileges, in absence of statute requiring that they be granted, is mere "gratuity," the cessation of which is not a reduction in pay).

[5] OAPSE v Mentor Exempted Village School Dist Bd of Ed, No. 8-129, 1981 WL 3790 (11th Dist Ct App, Lake, 9-28-81).

[6] OAPSE v Twin Valley Local School Dist Bd of Ed, 6 OS(3d) 178, 6 OBR 235, 451 NE(2d) 1211 (1983).

tled a conflict among lower courts on whether a reduction in hours, without a reduction in hourly rate, violated RC 3319.081(B) and RC 3319.082.

(C) Duty of civil service commission

In city school districts covered by civil service, the civil service commission must certify that the persons named in the payroll have been appointed, promoted, reduced, suspended, laid off, or are being employed in accordance with civil service law. Any sum paid contrary to statutory certification requirements may be recovered from the officer making the payment or from the sureties on his bond in an action maintained by a resident citizen.[7]

13.02 Work week: overtime and compensatory time

(A) In general

In all school districts, forty hours per week is the standard work week for nonteaching employees. If an employee is required to work in excess of forty hours in any seven-day period or to work on days declared by the employing board to be legal holidays, he must be either paid time and one-half or granted compensatory time off.[8]

Under the FLSA, if the employee, at his option, works for the district in a different type of job from his regular work on an occasional or sporadic basis, the part-time hours will count toward overtime.[9] Volunteers who are paid expenses, reasonable benefits, or a nominal fee are not considered employees subject to minimum wage or overtime requirements.[10]

(B) Overtime or compensatory time

The FLSA permits public employers to use compensatory time off in lieu of overtime pay, within certain maximum limits. Where employees have designated a representative (such as a union) with authority to enter into agreements with the employer, compensatory time may be provided only if authorized by an agreement between the representative and the employer; in the absence of any such designated representative, the employer and individual employee must agree, *before* performance of the work, to compensatory time. One and one-half hours of compensatory time must be provided for each hour of overtime.[11] When an employee has accrued 240 hours of unused compensatory time, he must be paid overtime compensation for additional overtime.[12] Upon termination of employment, the employee receives payment for unused compensatory time at the higher of his average rate over the last three years or his final regular rate.[13]

An employee must be permitted to use accrued compensatory time within a "reasonable period" of his request if the use does not "unduly disrupt" the operation of the district. Compensatory time used will not count as hours worked during the applicable work period for purposes of determining overtime.[14] Employees may "trade time" with fellow employees performing the same type of work, substituting for each other without affecting overtime calculations. Trading time must be at the employee's option with the employer's consent. Employers will not be required to keep records of the hours of substitute work.[15]

13.03 Holiday pay

(A) In general

All regular nonteaching school employees employed on an eleven- or twelve-month basis are entitled to a minimum of the following holidays for which they must

---

[7] RC 9.41.

[8] RC 3319.086, RC 4111.03. The conflict between RC 3319.086, which does not require time and one-half for overtime, and RC 4111.03, which does, is resolved in favor of RC 4111.03 because it is a specific provision with later adoption. Fort Jennings Education Assn v Fort Jennings Local Bd of Ed, No. 85-37 (CP, Putnam, 7-21-86).

[9] 29 USCA 207(p)(2). RC 4111.03 requires payment of overtime "in the manner and methods provided in and subject to the exemptions of" FLSA.

[10] 29 USCA 203(e).

[11] 29 USCA 207(o). See Moreau v Klevenhagen, ___ US ___, 113 SCt 1905, 123 LEd(2d) 584 (1993). For regulations on compensatory time, see 29 CFR Part 553.

[12] 29 USCA 207(o).

[13] 29 USCA 207(o).

[14] 29 USCA 207(o).

[15] 29 USCA 207(p)(3). See also 29 CFR 553.31.

be paid their regular rate, provided the employee actually worked on his next preceding and next following scheduled work days before and after the holiday or was properly excused from attendance on either or both days: New Year's Day, Martin Luther King Day, Memorial Day, Independence Day, Labor Day, Thanksgiving Day, and Christmas Day.[16] For regular nonteaching employees employed on a nine- or ten-month basis, the holidays are the same except Independence Day is excluded. Regular nonteaching school employees employed less than nine months are entitled to a minimum of paid holidays enumerated in RC 3319.087, which fall during the employees' time of employment.

(B) Overtime and compensatory time

A nonteaching employee who is required to work on any of these holidays must be given compensatory time off at his regular rate or the board of education may establish a premium rate for working on the holiday. With respect to Labor Day, a less than twelve-month employee's last scheduled work day of his preceding period of employment is counted as his last scheduled day for holiday pay purposes.[17]

13.04 Vacation pay

(A) Allowable vacation time

Full-time nonteaching employees who have worked at least one year but less than ten years are entitled to two weeks' vacation, excluding legal holidays. Those who have worked from ten to twenty years are entitled to three weeks, and those who have worked at least twenty years are entitled to four weeks.[18] In calculating years worked for vacation purposes, an employee is not entitled to count years in which he worked less than full time.[19] On separation from employment, a nonteaching employee must be paid for all accrued and unused vacation leave accumulated for the two years immediately preceding separation. The same is true if the nonteaching employee dies.

A full-time employee for vacation purposes is one who is in service for not less than eleven months per calendar year.[20] One court has held an employee must work for the full duration or throughout each of the eleven months to qualify.[21] Since merely working within each month is insufficient, holidays and other interruptions in the work schedule must be taken into account.[22]

In computing service credit for purposes of vacation under RC 3319.084, a district must credit the employee with years served with the state or another political subdivision so long as such service immediately precedes the employee's service with the school district.[23]

(B) Using accrued vacation before full amount earned

A board of education has discretion to allow a nonteaching employee to use the accrued portion of his vacation before the full annual amount has been earned.[24]

(C) Effect of contract provision

A board's failure to honor an agreement to provide vacation benefits for less than eleven months' service may violate an employee's contractual, as opposed to statutory, rights.

13.05 Other paid days

(A) Emergency school closings

RC 3319.081 provides that when schools are closed due to "an epidemic or other public calamity" employees must be paid for the time lost. If an employee works during this time, the board is not required to pay a premium rate.[25]

---

[16]RC 3319.087.
[17]RC 3319.087.
[18]RC 3319.084.
[19]Welsh v Trotwood-Madison Bd of Ed, No. 6381 (2d Dist Ct App, Montgomery, 1-28-80).
[20]RC 3319.084.
[21]O'Dell v Preble-Shawnee Local School Dist Bd of Ed, No. 241 (12th Dist Ct App, Preble, 1-10-77).
[22]O'Dell v Preble-Shawnee Local School Dist Bd of Ed, No. 277, 1981 WL 5035 (12th Dist Ct App, Preble, 1-6-81).
[23]OAG 83-077.
[24]OAG 73-114.
[25]As to what constitutes "an epidemic or other public calamity," see Text 10.09(A), Emergency school closings.

(B) Jury duty

Nonteaching employees stand on the same footing as professional personnel with respect to jury duty.[26]

(C) Professional days

Any employee may be excused and receive pay and expenses to attend professional meetings. The board is authorized to hire and pay a substitute for such time. Each board is required to adopt a policy dealing with attendance at professional meetings.[27]

13.06 Payroll deductions

A number of deductions from a nonteaching employee's wages are either required or authorized and are the same as for teachers.[28]

INSURANCE AND LEAVE

13.07 Insurance

Nonteaching employees, like teachers, may receive group insurance fringe benefits.[29]

13.08 Sick leave

(A) In general

Sick leave is provided to nonteaching employees of school districts not covered by civil service in accordance with RC 3319.141 on the same basis as with teachers.[30]

There is some confusion as to whether nonteaching employees in city school districts covered by civil service are subject to RC 3319.141 or RC 124.38. The statutes are admittedly opaque on the point. RC 124.38 expressly applies to "[e]mployees of any board of education for whom sick leave is not provided by section 3319.141 of the Revised Code." RC 3319.141 entitles "[e]ach person who is employed by any board of education in this state" to fifteen paid days of sick leave "for each year under contract ... ." Seizing on the words "under contract," an appeals court has concluded RC 3319.141 applies only to teachers in all types of school districts and nonteaching employees in school districts other than city school districts who are not in the classified civil service. As for a city school district's classified civil service employees, the court held that they are not "under contract" within the meaning of RC 3319.141 and, accordingly, their sick leave is governed by RC 124.38.[31]

One of the chief differences between RC 3319.141 and RC 124.38 is that sick leave accumulation under the latter is unlimited. Also, leave is accrued under RC 124.38 at the rate of 4.6 hours for each 80 hours of service. The Ohio Supreme Court has determined that RC 124.38 establishes a minimum sick leave benefit, and an employer is not precluded from providing additional sick leave credits. Moreover, said the Court, while such additional credits cannot be retroactively revoked, they can be reduced prospectively to the level prescribed by RC 124.38.[32]

(B) Use of sick leave

Sick leave must be deducted from the employee's accumulation on the basis of one hour for every one hour of absence from previously scheduled work pursuant to RC 124.38. Reasons for use of sick leave and procedures to be followed in applying for leave are the same under RC 124.38 and RC 3319.141.

Subject to its collective bargaining obligations, a board of education may adopt a rule defining immediate family, which may limit immediate family to those persons residing in the same household.[33]

Pursuant to RC 124.38, an employer has discretion to approve or disapprove requests for sick leave, and denial of leave will not be reversed by a court absent an abuse of discretion.[34] An appeals court,

---

[26] See Text 10.09(B), Jury duty.
[27] RC 3313.20.
[28] See Text 10.08, Payroll deductions.
[29] See Text 10.10 to 10.12.
[30] See Text 10.13 to 10.16.
[31] Rudolph v Cincinnati City School Dist Bd of Ed, No. C-790480 (1st Dist Ct App, Hamilton, 7-9-80).

[32] Ebert v Stark County Bd of Mental Retardation, 63 OS(2d) 31, 406 NE(2d) 1098 (1980).
[33] Blust v Madison Local School Dist Bd of Ed, No. CA-2022, 1982 WL 3006 (5th Dist Ct App, Richland, 7-7-82).
[34] State ex rel Britton v Scott, 6 OS(3d) 268, 6 OBR 334, 452 NE(2d) 1312 (1983).

construing RC 3319.141, has concluded that, once it is factually determined the leave is being used for one of the statutory reasons, refusal to approve is an abuse of discretion.[35] Construing the same statute, the attorney general has concluded a board of education may not adopt a rule requiring a physician's statement to justify the use of sick leave.[36]

A school bus driver is qualified to receive accumulated sick pay from the time he fails to pass the required physical examination.[37] Likewise, one court has ruled that a driver who fails to pass the required examination to receive certification for the ensuing school year is entitled to use sick leave on commencement of the school year until leave is exhausted.[38]

Falsification of the reasons for taking sick leave can be cause for termination.[39]

13.09 Severance pay on basis of accumulated sick leave

Nonteaching employees are entitled to severance pay on the same basis as teachers.[40]

13.10 Personal and other leaves of absence

(A) Personal leave

Each board of education is required to adopt rules granting regular nonteaching employees a minimum of three days' personal leave each school year. If a board fails to adopt rules, the employee is entitled to three days of unrestricted leave during each school year.[41] A board may, but is not required to, adopt the state standards regarding personal leave.[42]

(B) Other leaves of absence

Nonteaching employees are entitled, on essentially the same basis as teachers, to military leave, assault leave, or leave for educational or professional purposes or for illness or other disability. Also, an employee may be placed on unrequested disability leave.[43]

For treatment of the federal Family and Medical Leave Act of 1993, see Text 17.16, Family and Medical Leave Act of 1993.

---

[35]Hannan v Chesapeake Union Exempted Village School Dist Bd of Ed, 41 App(3d) 221, 535 NE(2d) 392 (Lawrence 1988).

[36]OAG 75-015. See also Hoeflinger v West Clermont Local Bd of Ed, 17 App(3d) 145, 17 OBR 245, 478 NE(2d) 251 (Clermont 1984) (physician's statement cannot be required to justify leave because of pregnancy).

[37]OAG 70-071; OAG 69-057.

[38]Adams v Edison Local School Dist Bd of Ed, No. 1180 (7th Dist Ct App, Jefferson, 1-27-81).

[39]RC 3319.141; Judd v Madison Local School Dist Bd of Ed, No. 83 Civ 0232 (11th Dist Ct App, Lake, 1984). See also Swinderman v Dover City School Dist Bd of Ed, No. 91AP110092, 1992 WL 91655 (5th Dist Ct App, Tuscarawas, 4-20-92) (upholding termination of teacher for falsified sick leave applications). But see Katz v Maple Heights City School Dist Bd of Ed, 87 App(3d) 256, 622 NE(2d) 1 (Cuyahoga 1993) (reducing termination of teacher who falsified sick leave applications to disciplinary suspension in light of employee's past employment record).

[40]See Text 10.17, Severance pay on basis of accumulated sick leave.

[41]RC 3319.142.

[42]See Text 10.14, Adopting state standards on sick leave, caveat.

[43]See Text 10.19 to 10.21.

Chapter 14

Nonteaching Personnel: Retirement

INTRODUCTION
14.01 School employees retirement system (SERS)
14.02 School employees retirement board
14.03 Sources and purposes of separate funds

MEMBERS OF SYSTEM
14.04 Membership in SERS

CONTRIBUTIONS TO SYSTEM
14.05 Mandatory contributions by members
14.06 Voluntary contributions by members
14.07 Mandatory contributions by employers
14.08 Additional contributions by employers

SERVICE CREDIT
14.09 Service credit: definition
14.10 Purchasing service credit

BENEFITS
14.11 Disability coverage
14.12 Service retirement
14.13 Early retirement incentive plans
14.14 Employment of retired members
14.15 Optional compensation deferral plans
14.16 Survivor benefits

INTRODUCTION

14.01 School employees retirement system (SERS)

The Ohio school employees retirement system was established in 1937 for school employees other than teachers. The system includes the several funds created and managed by the school employees retirement board for the payment of retirement allowances and other benefits.[1]

With some exceptions, the system is similar to the state teachers retirement system and is subject to similar requirements and rules.[2]

Provision is made in RC 3309.70 for the recovery of erroneously paid benefits.

14.02 School employees retirement board

(A) In general, composition

The school employees retirement board is composed of the state auditor, the attorney general, four employee members elected by ballot by the members of the system, and one retired employee member who is elected by ballot by former employees who are receiving service retirement benefits or a disability benefit.[3] Members serve without compensation, but they must be reimbursed from the expense fund for all actual necessary expenses and for any loss of salary or wages they may suffer through serving on the board.[4]

The board elects a chairman from its own membership; it also employs an executive director, who serves as secretary and who may be a member of the board.[5] The state treasurer is custodian of the system's funds,[6] and the attorney general is the board's legal adviser.[7]

(B) Conflict of interest

RC 3309.19 contains specific prohibitions against a fiduciary or employee of the retirement board having any interest, direct or indirect, in the gains or profits of any investment made by the board. In addition, RC 3309.155 and RC 3309.156 severely restrict transactions between the system and any fiduciary or "party in interest," including anyone who within the past three years has been an employee, board member, or officer of the system. RC 3309.156 makes fiduciaries responsible for forbidden transactions under certain circumstances. These statutes should be reviewed in detail before any employee or fiduciary is involved in any business transaction involving the system.[8]

(C) Powers and duties

The board may sue and be sued, contract and be contracted with, and do every-

---
[1] RC Ch 3309.
[2] See Text Ch 11, Teachers: Retirement.
[3] RC 3309.05.
[4] RC 3309.10.
[5] RC 3309.11.
[6] RC 3309.12.
[7] RC 3309.13.
[8] See Text Ch 45, Ethics Requirements and Education Personnel.

thing necessary to carry out the statutory requirements. All of its business must be transacted, all of its funds invested, all warrants for money drawn and payments made, and all of its cash, securities, and other property held in the name of the board or certain specified nominees of the board.[9]

The board is also charged with the duty to invest the assets of the system.[10] The board may secure the services of such technical and administrative employees as are necessary to transact system business.[11]

In addition to the general administration and management of the system, and the authority to make necessary rules,[12] the board receives and acts upon all applications for retirement, provides for the payment of all retirement allowances and other benefits, and makes other necessary expenditures as are required or authorized.[13]

14.03 Sources and purposes of separate funds

Members of the retirement board are trustees of the system's funds[14] and may invest the funds in certain described investments.[15]

The funds created, together with their purposes, are as follows:

(1) Employees' savings fund, in which the contributions of employee members are accumulated for the purchase of annuities;

(2) Employers' trust fund, in which reserves are accumulated from employers' contributions for the payment of pensions or other benefits to members;

(3) Annuity and pension reserve fund, from which must be paid all pensions and annuities for which reserves have been transferred from the employees' savings fund and the employers' trust fund;

(4) Survivors' benefit fund, from which survivor benefits are paid;

(5) Guarantee fund, used to facilitate crediting uniform interest on the amounts in the various other funds except the expense fund, and to provide a contingent fund out of which special requirements of any of the other funds may be covered; and

(6) Expense fund, from which administrative expenses of the system are paid.[16]

MEMBERS OF SYSTEM

14.04 Membership in SERS

All public school employees in positions for which a certificate is not required under RC 3319.22 to RC 3319.31 are required to be members of SERS with exceptions for certain students, emergency temporary employees, and persons employed under certain federally authorized job training programs.[17] Any person who works for a contractor but who performs service common to the daily operation of the educational unit is considered to be an employee for SERS purposes. Retirement board policy includes in this category the employees of contractors who perform food service, transportation, and custodial or maintenance services.

Employers must give a written statement (prepared and furnished to the employer by the retirement board) to prospective employers of their duties and obligations under SERS laws. Acceptance of the statutes is a condition of employment of a school employee.[18]

Certificated employees employed in educational positions under federal pro-

---

[9] RC 3309.03.
[10] RC 3309.15.
[11] RC 3309.14.
[12] RC 3309.04.
[13] RC 3309.14.
[14] RC 3309.15. This statute does not create a fiduciary duty on the part of SERS to exercise reasonable care and diligence with regard to applicants for disability benefits. State ex rel McMaster v School Employees Retirement System, 69 OS(3d) 130, 630 NE(2d) 701 (1994).

[15] RC 3309.15 to RC 3309.17. See Text 11.03(B), Investments.

[16] RC 3309.60.

[17] RC 3309.01(B), RC 3309.23. Educational aides are expressly included by RC 3319.088.

[18] RC 3309.53.

grams but for which no certification requirements can be made under federal law are not SERS members.[19]

CONTRIBUTIONS TO SYSTEM

14.05 Mandatory contributions by members

Each member must contribute a minimum of eight per cent of his compensation to the employees' savings fund. The retirement board can increase the rate to not more than ten per cent; at present the rate for employee contributions is nine per cent.[20]

For purposes of computing employee contributions, compensation generally includes all salary, wages, and other earnings paid to a member by reason of his employment. However, it does not include (1) any terminal pay, including unused or converted sick leave pay; (2) vacation pay for concurrent periods for which other salary or compensation is also paid; (3) amounts the employer pays for insurance, or payments to the employee in lieu of insurance; or (4) certain other incidental or military-related payments specified by statute.[21] In addition, SERS rules specify that contributions will not be deducted from payments covering accrued but unused compensatory time for overtime worked, from bonuses not reflecting additional services rendered, nor from payments in consideration of agreements to retire.[22]

14.06 Voluntary contributions by members

(A) Contributions while on leave

SERS members under contract are permitted to make contributions for time spent on approved absences for illness, accident, or other reason. These contributions may be made directly to the employer or by payroll deduction following the member's return to contributing service.[23] Members who are not state employees need not make contributions while on paid disability leave; instead the employer must make both the employer and employee contributions during this time.[24] State employees, however, must pay the employee share of retirement contributions during the first three months of approved disability leave; thereafter both the employer and employee contributions must be paid by the state.[25]

(B) Extra deposits to increase annuity income

Members are permitted to make extra deposits to provide additional annuity income. These deposits may be refunded to the member before retirement and must be refunded if the member withdraws his refundable amount. The deposits may also be refunded to the beneficiary or estate if the member dies before retirement. The retirement board must determine whether interest should be credited to such refunded deposits.[26]

14.07 Mandatory contributions by employers

Employers are required to make contributions to SERS at an actuarially established rate. This rate may not exceed fourteen per cent of the earnable compensation of all members, which is the rate currently in effect.[27]

14.08 Additional contributions by employers

Employers can make additional contributions by "picking up" the employees' portion of required contributions.[28] There are two types of pickups: fringe benefit pickups and salary reduction pickups.[29]

---

[19] RC 3309.011.
[20] RC 3309.47.
[21] RC 3309.01(V).
[22] OAC 3309-1-02.
[23] RC 3309.47.
[24] RC 3309.471.
[25] RC 124.385.
[26] RC 3309.47.

[27] RC 3309.49.
[28] Employers are not obligated to pick up their employees' contributions to SERS. State ex rel Willbond v Oberlin School Dist, 94 App(3d) 419, 640 NE(2d) 1179 (Lorain 1994), dismissed for failure to prosecute 70 OS(3d) 1419, 637 NE(2d) 927 (1994).
[29] For more extended treatment, see Text 11.10, Additional contributions by employers.

(A) Fringe benefit pickups

An employer may pick up all or part of the required employee contributions to SERS without reducing employees' salaries.[30] The amount picked up is included in calculating final average salary for retirement purposes.[31]

(B) Pickup through salary reduction

An employer may implement a salary reduction pickup[32] under which the employer assumes and pays the employee's retirement contribution and reduces the employee's salary by an equal amount. The employer incurs no additional expense under this option. It benefits the employee by reducing his current income, thus deferring federal and state income taxes on the amount of the pickup. For SERS purposes, however, compensation is determined as though the employee's income had not been reduced by the amount of the pickup.[33]

SERVICE CREDIT

14.09 Service credit: definition

Service credit is a primary factor in determining both eligibility for retirement and the amount of retirement benefits under RC 3309.34 and RC 3309.36. One year's service is credited for 120 or more days of service during the school year. Service of less than 120 days is prorated on the basis of 180 days in a school year. That is, a fraction of a year is credited by dividing the actual number of days worked by 180.[34] Service credit for military service is governed by RC 3309.02. Service credit earned in certain Ohio retirement systems may be combined in order to determine eligibility for retirement and to compute benefits.[35]

14.10 Purchasing service credit

(A) In general

Members may purchase service credit for various types of state or federal employment not covered by SERS. Service for which credit may be purchased includes (1) military service; (2) time spent as a prisoner of war;[36] (3) service in an Ohio police or fire department or in the state highway patrol;[37] and (4) service in a public or private school, college, or university of Ohio or another state, or in a school or entity operated by or for the United States government, or in certain capacities for another state or the federal government.[38] Purchased service in each category, except the police, fire, and highway patrol category, is generally limited to the five years or the member's total years of Ohio service, whichever is less.[39] Provision is also made for purchasing credit for each year or portion of a year for which a member exempted himself from membership, except that a member may not purchase credit for service exempted from contribution under RC 3309.23.[40]

The purchase of credit for service as a school board member (at the rate of one-quarter of a year's credit for each year of service) is authorized by RC 3309.311, which spells out certain conditions that must be satisfied.

(B) Redeposit of withdrawn contributions

A member or former member with at least one and one-half years of contributing service credit in SERS or any other retirement system specified in RC 3309.26 who withdraws his account may restore credit by redepositing in the employees' savings fund the amount withdrawn plus interest.[41]

(C) Payroll deduction plans

RC 3309.27 authorizes the retirement board to establish by rule payroll deduction

---

[30] OAG 79-001.
[31] RC 3309.01(V)(1).
[32] OAG 84-036.
[33] RC 3309.01(K), (V)(1).
[34] RC 3309.30; OAC 3309-1-12(D).
[35] RC 3309.35. See Text 11.12(B), Combining credits from other public employees retirement systems.
[36] RC 3309.021; OAC 3309-1-28.
[37] RC 3309.351; OAC 3309-1-39.
[38] RC 3309.31; OAC 3309-1-29.
[39] RC 3309.21, RC 3309.31.
[40] RC 3309.301.
[41] RC 3309.26.

plans for paying the cost of purchasing or restoring service credit or paying charges for participation in a long-term health care insurance program established pursuant to RC 3309.691.

BENEFITS

14.11 Disability coverage

SERS offers disability coverage to any member who has at least five years of total service credit.[42] For persons who become members after July 29, 1992, coverage is provided under RC 3309.401, which provides for an annual disability allowance in accordance with a specified formula. RC 3309.401 also governs the disability benefit available to persons who became SERS members on or prior to July 29, 1992, who validly elected pursuant to an election procedure appearing in RC 3309.39 to have coverage under RC 3309.401.

For persons who became SERS members on or prior to July 29, 1992, disability is provided under RC 3309.40 unless a valid election was made to have coverage provided under RC 3309.401.[43] Under RC 3309.40, a member under age sixty who is determined by the retirement board to qualify for a disability benefit goes on disability retirement and receives an annual amount in accordance with a specified formula.

The determination of whether a SERS member is entitled to a disability benefit is solely within the province of the retirement board pursuant to RC 3309.39.[44] Thus, the board's decision is conclusive unless shown to be an abuse of discretion,[45] and the board is not bound by the rules or determinations of other agencies regarding whether an individual is disabled.[46]

In general, eligibility for and termination of a disability benefit for SERS members parallel the criteria applicable to teachers.[47] The attorney general has concluded that since a member of a board of education is an officer, not an employee, for purposes of RC Chapter 3309, the allowance of a disability benefit to one who serves as a board member need not be terminated under language in RC 3309.41 that says an allowance shall cease if the benefit recipient becomes employed by an SERS employer.[48]

14.12 Service retirement

Mandatory retirement based on age is prohibited by the federal Age Discrimination in Employment Act of 1967.[49] Voluntary retirement is available to SERS members who attain eligibility pursuant to RC Chapter 3309.

A member is eligible for service retirement if he has at least five years of total service credit and has attained sixty years of age, or if he has at least thirty years of service credit at any age. A member is eligible for commuted service retirement, providing lesser benefits, if he has at least twenty-five years' service credit and is at least fifty-five years of age. A member may retire effective the first day of the month following the later of the last day of employment for which compensation was paid or the attainment of minimum age and service credit eligibility for service or commuted service retirement. Application for retirement must be made on a form provided by the retirement board.[50]

Retirants under SERS may choose from options similar to those available to teach-

---

[42]RC 3309.39.

[43]Where a member over age 60 with five years service credit became disabled in December 1991 and applied for disability benefits on October 1, 1992, mandamus would lie to compel SERS to pay disability benefits beginning February 1, 1992, the first day of the month following the last day she received compensation, rather than the first day of the first month RC 3309.39 became effective. State ex rel Plavcan v School Employees Retirement System, 71 OS(3d) 122, 643 NE(2d) 240 (1994).

[44]Fair v School Employees Retirement System, 53 OS(2d) 118, 372 NE(2d) 814 (1978).

[45]State ex rel McMaster v School Employees Retirement System, 69 OS(3d) 130, 630 NE(2d) 701 (1994) (stating that judicial review by way of mandamus is appropriate and finding no abuse of discretion in the denial of benefits in this case).

[46]Fair v School Employees Retirement System, 53 OS(2d) 118, 372 NE(2d) 814 (1978).

[47]RC 3309.39, RC 3309.40, RC 3309.401, RC 3309.41. See Text 11.16, Entitlement to disability benefit; Text 11.17, Termination of disability benefit.

[48]OAG 91-046.

[49]29 USCA 623.

[50]RC 3309.34.

ers for dividing benefits between a retirant and his designated beneficiary.[51] As under the teachers' system, the annual single lifetime allowance is the basic benefit from which all others are calculated. This allowance, which provides lifetime income with no monthly survivor benefits, is computed according to a statutory formula and may not exceed the lesser of ninety per cent of the member's final average salary or the limit established by section 415 of the Internal Revenue Code.[52] An additional allowance is paid to retirees based on increases in the consumer price index.[53] Statutes enacted from time to time have provided for recalculations and additional benefits to various groups of retirants.[54]

14.13 Early retirement incentive plans

Employers of SERS members may establish early retirement incentive plans for their SERS-member employees. RC 3309.33 is the authorizing statute, and relevant SERS regulations appear in OAC 3309-1-43. In all material respects, these plans are patterned after early retirement plans permitted for teachers.[55]

14.14 Employment of retired members

A retirant from SERS other than a disability retirant or a retirant from certain other public retirement systems may be employed without forfeiting his pension allowance in accordance with the procedures appearing in RC 3309.341.

14.15 Optional compensation deferral plans

Boards of education and public institutions of higher learning such as state universities and community colleges may establish income deferral plans for employees eligible for favorable tax treatment under section 403(b) of the Internal Revenue Code of 1954.[56] These plans must provide a reasonable number of options for investment of the deferred funds, including annuities, variable annuities, and regulated investment trusts which qualify for favorable tax treatment.[57]

Independent of any income deferral plan established by a board of education, SERS members are eligible to participate in the deferred compensation program offered by the Ohio public employees deferred compensation board pursuant to RC 145.71 to RC 145.73.[58]

14.16 Survivor benefits

Survivor benefits and options are available with respect to SERS members similar to those applicable to teachers.[59]

---

[51] RC 3309.46. See also Text 11.19, Amount of retirement benefits.
[52] RC 3309.36.
[53] RC 3309.374.
[54] RC 3309.361 to RC 3309.3710.
[55] See Text 11.21, Early retirement incentive plans.
[56] RC 9.90.
[57] RC 145.73(E).
[58] RC 145.71(A).
[59] RC 3309.44, RC 3309.45, RC 3309.50. See also Text 11.24 to 11.26. The lump sum burial payment authorized on behalf of SERS members by RC 3309.50 is $500, as opposed to the $1,000 payment authorized on behalf of STRS members by RC 3307.40(A).

Chapter 15
Unemployment Compensation

15.01 School participation in unemployment compensation system
15.02 Eligibility for unemployment compensation benefits
15.03 Benefits
15.04 Student eligibility for unemployment compensation
15.05 Work gap between school terms not considered unemployment
15.06 Unemployment arising from labor dispute
15.07 Voluntary resignation
15.08 Suspension or discharge for cause

15.01 School participation in unemployment compensation system

An employee of a board of education who has been separated from employment may be eligible to receive unemployment compensation. Each board is required either to contribute to the unemployment compensation fund or to reimburse the fund for amounts paid to former employees. Substitute teaching as well as the performance of regular employment duties falls within the statutory definition of employment. However, publicly elected officials, i.e., school board members, are not entitled to benefits,[1] nor are student employees if they are enrolled and regularly attending classes.[2]

15.02 Eligibility for unemployment compensation benefits

Benefits are paid only as compensation for loss of remuneration due to "involuntary total or partial unemployment." An individual is not eligible for benefits unless he (1) has filed a valid application for benefits; (2) has registered at an employment office maintained by or designated by the bureau of employment services; (3) is able to work, available for work, and is actively seeking "suitable work"; (4) is unable to obtain suitable work; and (5) has satisfied the requirement of employment in the "base period."[3]

(A) Unemployment

A person is "totally unemployed" in any week during which he performs no service and with respect to which no remuneration is payable to him.[4]

A person is "partially unemployed" in any week if, due to involuntary loss of work, his earnings for that week are less than his weekly benefit amount.[5] Benefits for a person who is partially unemployed are in the amount of his weekly benefit less his actual earnings for that week to the extent they exceed twenty per cent of his weekly benefit amount.

A laid-off teacher who continues to receive paychecks as deferred compensation for work already performed is not precluded from being totally or partially unemployed within the meaning of RC 4141.01(M) or (N) since such remuneration is not for the weeks with respect to which benefits are claimed.[6]

(B) Actively seeking suitable work

The administrator may waive the requirement that a claimant be actively seeking work when the employer has notified the administrator within ten days of layoff that work is expected to be available within forty-five calendar days of the claimant's last day of work.

Whether work is "suitable" within the meaning of RC 4141.29 is a question of fact.[7] Obviously, the more dissimilar the work to a claimant's former work, the less likely it will be considered "suitable." An employer's offer of work paying roughly fifteen per cent less than the job from which the employee is being laid off has been deemed suitable.[8] A teacher is "available for suitable work" where he is eligible to

---

[1] RC 4141.01(B)(3)(c)(i).
[2] RC 4141.01(B)(3)(e).
[3] RC 4141.29.
[4] RC 4141.01(M).
[5] RC 4141.01(N).
[6] Mt. Healthy Bd of Ed v Cook, 28 OS(3d) 1, 28 OBR 1, 501 NE(2d) 615 (1986).

[7] Pennington v Dudley, 10 OS(2d) 90, 226 NE(2d) 738 (1967).
[8] Pennington v Dudley, 10 OS(2d) 90, 226 NE(2d) 738 (1967).

teach pursuant to a second renewal of a one-year vocational teaching certificate and renewal has not been denied.[9]

Despite similarity of work, rates of pay and hardships imposed can defeat a conclusion that offered work is suitable. A teacher's refusal to accept a similar position offering less than half the earnings in previous full-time employment as a substitute was not a refusal of suitable work.[10] However, when a substitute teacher is entitled by law to a contract as a regular teacher, but refuses substitute work, the teacher is not entitled to benefits because substitute teaching is suitable work.[11]

(C) Minimum employment prior to separation

The "base period" is the first four of the last five completed calendar quarters immediately preceding the first day of an individual's benefit year.[12] During that base period, the individual must have earned at least 27.5% of the statewide average weekly wage as computed each January 1 under RC 4141.30(B)(3), rounded down to the nearest dollar, during each of twenty calendar weeks. That amount is currently $135. An "alternate base period" is defined as the four most recently completed calendar quarters preceding the benefit year if there are insufficient qualifying weeks and wages.[13] This provision primarily affects substitute and part-time employees. A substitute bus driver was found to be entitled to benefits under the alternate base period, where the standard base period would have resulted in a denial of benefits.[14] No calendar quarter in a base period or alternate base period can be used to establish a subsequent benefit year.[15]

(D) Disqualifications

A claimant is disqualified from receiving benefits if he was discharged for just cause or quits work without just cause.[16] Resigning, rather than having the principal recommend nonrenewal to the superintendent and board of education, has been held not to constitute just cause for quitting and will result in denial of benefits.[17] A claimant is also ineligible for benefits for refusing suitable work without good cause or quitting to marry or because of marital, parental, filial, or other domestic obligations.[18] If he knowingly made a false statement to obtain benefits or became unemployed due to incarceration or dishonesty (defined as the commission of substantive theft, fraud, or deceitful acts) in connection with his most recent or any base period employment, he is barred from benefits.[19] If any individual week of unemployment was due to a labor dispute other than lockout, or disciplinary layoff for misconduct in connection with work, benefits for that week will be denied.[20]

15.03 Benefits

For a person "totally unemployed," weekly benefits are half of his average weekly wage or the statutory maximum, whichever is less. The statutory maximum is adjusted during the first week of January as the statewide average weekly wage increases or decreases, subject to statutorily specified maximum percentages of the statewide average weekly wage.[21] A person's "average weekly wage" is determined by applying a statutory formula to his earnings during the "base period."[22]

In all cases, no benefits are payable during a one-week waiting period after the

---

[9]Central Ohio Joint Vocational School Dist Bd of Ed v Ohio Bureau of Employment Services, 21 OS(3d) 5, 21 OBR 269, 487 NE(2d) 288 (1986).

[10]Watson v Employment Services Bureau Bd of Review, No. 3503, 1986 WL 2725 (11th Dist Ct App, Trumbull, 2-28-86).

[11]Trowbridge v Employment Services Bureau Bd of Review, No. L-83-057, 1983 WL 6827 (6th Dist Ct App, Lucas, 6-3-83).

[12]RC 4141.01(Q)(1).

[13]RC 4141.01(Q)(2).

[14]Ohio Bureau of Employment Services v Byers, No. 95-CA-006, 1995 WL 502246 (5th Dist Ct App, Fairfield, 8-10-95).

[15]RC 4141.01(Q)(2).

[16]RC 4141.29(D)(2).

[17]Stallings v Vanguard Joint Vocational School, No. WD-94-114, 1995 WL 428462 (6th Dist Ct App, Wood, 7-21-95).

[18]RC 4141.29(D)(2)(c).

[19]RC 4141.29(D)(2)(d).

[20]RC 4141.29(D)(1)(b).

[21]RC 4141.30(B), (E).

[22]RC 4141.01(Q).

claim for benefits is filed. However, no more than one week of waiting period is required in any benefit year.[23]

Benefits are normally payable for twenty-six weeks. Extended benefit weeks are implemented in accordance with federal law in times of high unemployment.

15.04 Student eligibility for unemployment compensation

A student who becomes unemployed while attending school may be eligible for benefits in special circumstances. A student's base period credit must have been earned partially or totally while attending school. When the student makes himself available for any shift hours for his most recent employer, other base period employer, or for any other suitable work, he meets the availability and active search work requirements.

A student has not become unemployed for purposes of unemployment compensation when he was already partially unemployed during the week he first began attending classes. Thus, the unemployment, either partial or total, must occur after the student begins attending school. Otherwise, a full-time student seeking work during the hours when he is not in school is not available for work and may not receive benefits.[24]

The unemployment compensation law does not cover students who perform services in the employ of the nonprofit or public educational institution they attend or who are enrolled full-time in a nonprofit or public school program which combines academic instruction with work experience.[25]

15.05 Work gap between school terms not considered unemployment

(A) In general

Benefits are not paid to school employees employed in an instructional, research, or principal administrative capacity for any week of unemployment between two successive academic years or terms, or during a similar period between two regular but not successive terms, or during a paid sabbatical leave, if the individual performs the services in the first of the academic years or terms and has a contract or a reasonable assurance that he will perform services in the second of the academic years or terms.[26] Likewise, benefits are denied for any week which begins during an established and customary vacation or holiday recess if there is a reasonable assurance that the individual will perform services in the period immediately following the vacation or holiday recess.[27]

Noninstructional and nonadministrative employees are subject to a similar disqualification.[28] However, RC 4141.29(I)(1)(b) provides for retroactive payment of benefits if the employee was denied benefits and then did not have an opportunity to perform services. An application for retroactive benefits must be filed prior to the end of the fourth full calendar week following the end of the period for which benefits were denied because of a reasonable assurance of employment.

An employee of a school district or county MR/DD board must be notified of nonreemployment for the following academic year by April 30.[29]

---

[23]RC 4141.29(B).

[24]Halco v Administrator, Bureau of Employment Services, 41 App(2d) 228, 325 NE(2d) 255 (Cuyahoga 1974).

[25]RC 4141.01(B)(3).

[26]RC 4141.29(I)(1)(a).

[27]RC 4141.29(I)(1)(c).

[28]RC 4141.29(I)(1)(b). See also Johnson v Brunswick City School Dist Bd of Ed, 24 App(3d) 48, 24 OBR 101, 492 NE(2d) 1252 (Medina 1983). The disqualification applies only to school district employees, however. Thus, school crossing guards employed by a city police department have been deemed qualified for summer benefits. Euclid v Administrator, Ohio Bureau of Employment Services, Nos. 60304 et al, 1992 WL 67095 (8th Dist Ct App, Cuyahoga, 4-2-92); North Olmsted v Ohio Bureau of Employment Services, 62 App(3d) 173, 574 NE(2d) 1158 (Cuyahoga 1989).

[29]RC 4141.29(I)(1)(e). But see Text 12.09(F), Reemployment, as to the nonrenewal of nonteaching employees in school districts not covered by civil service.

(B) Reasonable assurance of work in succeeding term

No between-term, holiday, or vacation disqualification will be imposed until unemployment compensation officials receive a written statement from the school district that the claimant has a contract or reasonable assurance of reemployment for the succeeding academic year or term.[30]

A substitute teacher had a reasonable assurance of employment for the next year when tendered an application for substitute assignments in the next school year.[31] The same rule has been applied to substitute[32] and regular part-time[33] bus drivers.

However, a full-time teacher whose limited contract is not renewed and who is offered a contract for substitute service in the ensuing school year on an "on call as needed" basis has been awarded benefits.[34] Similarly, a full-time school bus driver who, after being told her continuing contract would be terminated for the next year, requested and received placement on the list of substitute drivers was eligible for benefits since she was merely "on-call" with no assurance she ever would be called or have a certain amount of work.[35] Whether an individual has a "reasonable assurance" is always a factual determination dependent on the circumstances of the case.

(C) Employee with two jobs

An individual employed by both an educational and noneducational employer may be eligible for benefits during the between-term, holiday, or vacation disqualification period based on employment with the noneducational employer. The noneducational employment must be sufficient to qualify the person for benefit rights apart from his school employment. Likewise, the weekly benefit amounts must be computed based on nonschool employment.[36]

15.06 Unemployment arising from labor dispute

An employee who is otherwise eligible for benefits may be disqualified for the reasons set forth in RC 4141.29(D). When unemployment is due to a labor dispute other than a lockout occurring at the same premises where the individual is employed, he may not receive benefits.[37] The employer must notify the Ohio Bureau of Employment Services, in writing, of any unemployment due to a labor dispute other than a lockout. If the individual was laid off prior to the dispute, was separated from employment prior to the dispute for reasons other than the dispute, or obtains a job with another employer during the dispute, the labor dispute disqualification does not apply. The test is whether the individual's unemployment was caused by the labor dispute. Thus, where an employer terminates employment during a labor dispute, the dispute is no longer the proximate cause of unemployment and the disqualification no longer applies.[38]

For unemployment compensation purposes, the term "lockout" has been more broadly construed than in traditional labor relations parlance. If an employer refuses to extend an expiring collective bargaining agreement and "maintain the status quo" for a reasonable period pending agreement on a new contract, employees who engage in a work stoppage have been deemed locked out and thus eligible for benefits. In a 4-3 decision, the Ohio Supreme Court

---

[30]RC 4141.29(I)(2); Knight v Bureau of Employment Services, 28 OS(3d) 8, 28 OBR 6, 501 NE(2d) 1198 (1986).

[31]Nohl v Canton Bd of Ed, No. CA-5088 (5th Dist Ct App, Stark, 8-8-79).

[32]Johnson v Brunswick City School Dist Bd of Ed, 24 App(3d) 48, 24 OBR 101, 492 NE(2d) 1252 (Medina 1983).

[33]University of Toledo v Heiny, 30 OS(3d) 143, 30 OBR 454, 507 NE(2d) 1130 (1987).

[34]See Ash v Ohio Bureau of Employment Services Bd of Review, 26 OS(3d) 158, 26 OBR 136, 497 NE(2d) 724 (1986) (construing a former version of the statute, but the conclusion would seem to follow under the statute as currently written).

[35]Wolfe v Ohio Bureau of Employment Services Bd of Review, No. 3-81-6, 1981 WL 6757 (3d Dist Ct App, Crawford, 12-31-81). See also Watson v Employment Services Bureau Bd of Review, No. 3503, 1986 WL 2725 (11th Dist Ct App, Trumbull, 2-28-86).

[36]Minis v Unemployment Compensation Bd of Review, No. 50076, 1986 WL 1078 (8th Dist Ct App, Cuyahoga, 1-23-86).

[37]RC 4141.29(D)(1)(a). A special hearing procedure is prescribed by RC 4141.28(D)(1) if there is reason to believe the unemployment of twenty-five or more individuals relates to a labor dispute.

[38]Baugh v United Telephone Co, 54 OS(2d) 419, 377 NE(2d) 766 (1978).

has even held that a union's offer to extend an existing agreement for one year while negotiations continue transformed a work stoppage by employees when the employer refused the offer into a lockout, entitling the employees to benefits.[39]

15.07 Voluntary resignation

Voluntary resignation disqualifies the employee for benefits.[40] A teacher was found to have quit without just cause when he wrote a resignation letter at a meeting with administrators called by them to discuss their concerns about his behavior with children.[41] Similarly, a teacher is not entitled to benefits who, after learning he would not be reemployed for the following school year, submitted his resignation, to be effective on completion of his current contract.[42] Whether a resignation is voluntary or involuntary will depend on the particular circumstances.

15.08 Suspension or discharge for cause

(A) Grounds for discipline or discharge

An individual is not eligible for benefits if he received a disciplinary layoff in connection with work, quit work without just cause, or was discharged for just cause. An individual is not disqualified who separates from employment to enter the armed forces within thirty days of separation; separates under a labor agreement or employer policy that permits the employee, because of lack of work, to accept separation; has left employment to accept recall from a prior employer or to accept other employment as provided in RC 4141.291; or has left concurrent employment where remuneration and working conditions are less favorable than his other employment and the concurrent employment would not be considered suitable work.[43]

Willful or wanton negligence or misconduct will disqualify a claimant. For example, reporting to work intoxicated has been held to be just cause for discharge.[44] Likewise, a school bus driver convicted of driving while intoxicated during off work hours was discharged for just cause when the school board's insurance carrier refused to issue liability insurance for the employee.[45] The court noted his employment was contingent on the statutory requirement of being certified, one of the conditions for which was maintaining insurable status with the board's carrier. Also, a bus driver's speeding ticket while transporting students, along with other unsafe acts, constituted just cause for discharge.[46] An accident-prone driver who negligently operated her bus on an icy road, resulting in a serious accident, was discharged for just cause, not-

---

[39]Bays v Shenago Co, 53 OS(3d) 132, 559 NE(2d) 740 (1990). See also Agich v Ohio Bureau of Employment Services Bd of Review, No. 92-C-41, 1993 WL 205003 (7th Dist Ct App, Columbiana, 6-8-93) (teachers who participated in partial strike disqualified for benefits except for period during which court ordered schools to close for "cooling off" period).

[40]RC 4141.29(D)(2). Exceptions exist under the statute if an employee elects termination under a collective bargaining agreement or employer policy that permits the employee, because of lack of work, to accept a separation from employment, or if the employee is not required by such an agreement or policy to accept work offered by the employer.

[41]De La Torre v Cleveland Bd of Ed, No. 49112, 1985 WL 9004 (8th Dist Ct App, Cuyahoga, 5-16-85).

[42]Noelker v Great Oaks Joint Vocational School Dist, 8 App(3d) 327, 8 OBR 437, 457 NE(2d) 340 (Hamilton 1982).

[43]RC 4141.29(D)(2). If an employee has been given a definite layoff date and before that date quits to accept other employment, no disqualification is imposed under RC 4141.29(D). However, if the person does not meet the employment and earnings requirements of RC 4141.291(A)(2), he is ineligible for benefits for any week of unemployment that occurs prior to the layoff date. RC 4141.29(D)(2)(a)(iv).

[44]Hawkins v Leach, 115 App 259, 185 NE(2d) 36 (Franklin 1961). See also Superior Metal Products, Inc v Bureau of Employment Services, 41 OS(2d) 143, 324 NE(2d) 179 (1975). Notwithstanding that alcoholism and drug addiction are handicaps under the Ohio Fair Employment Practices Act (see Text 17.13, Discrimination against the handicapped), where such chemical dependency adversely affects job performance, the employee may be discharged and benefits will be denied. Harris v Ohio Bureau of Employment Services, 51 OS(3d) 37, 553 NE(2d) 1350 (1990).

[45]Mayes v Employment Services Bureau Bd of Review, 32 App(3d) 68, 513 NE(2d) 818 (Franklin 1986).

[46]Ashbaugh v Board of Review, No. 11-86-9, 1988 WL 100624 (3d Dist Ct App, Paulding, 9-21-88). See also Pugh v Employment Services Bureau Bd of Review, No. 89CA34, 1990 WL 178123 (4th Dist Ct App, Washington, 10-30-90) (school board had just cause to terminate bus drivers who operated bus at excessive speed).

withstanding that she was found not guilty in municipal court of failing to maintain the assured clear distance ahead; the court noted that the legal issues and burden of proof in the two contexts are substantially different.[47]

Mere inefficiency or unsatisfactory performance may not necessarily be sufficient to disqualify a claimant.[48] In *Tzangas, Plakas & Mannos v Ohio Bureau of Employment Services*,[49] however, the Ohio Supreme Court made it more difficult for employees terminated for poor performance to receive benefits. The Court held that mere unsuitability for a position constitutes fault on the part of the employee sufficient to deny benefits where: (1) the employee does not perform the required work, (2) the employer made known its expectations at the time of hiring; (3) the expectations were reasonable; and (4) the requirements of the job did not change since the original date of hire.[50]

Absenteeism and tardiness caused by bona fide illness is not, for unemployment compensation purposes, just cause for discharge.[51] An employer has cause to discharge a worker who gives a mere fifteen-minute notice of departure to temporary military service when he could have avoided such short notice.[52]

Failure to follow a mandatory progressive disciplinary procedure, such as may exist in a collective bargaining agreement, in discharging an employee generally renders the discharge without just cause and entitles the claimant to benefits.[53]

(B) Standard of proof, procedure and effect of determinations

The standard of proof necessary to support a discharge for cause is substantially lower than in a criminal case. Denial of benefits need only be supported by relevant, probative evidence, which in a hearing before a referee may consist of a copy of the transcript from a previous termination proceeding.[54] However, an arbitrator's determination upholding a discharge for just cause under a collective bargaining agreement does not preclude a conclusion that the employee was not discharged for just cause within the meaning of RC 4141.29(D)(2)(a).[55]

RC 4141.28(S) expressly provides that factual findings and legal conclusions in unemployment compensation proceedings are not controlling in any judicial, administrative, or arbitration proceeding outside the unemployment compensation context.

An employer may engage lay representatives for unemployment compensation hearings.[56]

---

[47]Casserly v Board of Review, Administrator, Ohio Bureau of Employment Services, No. 89AP-239, 1989 WL 110990 (10th Dist Ct App, Franklin, 9-26-89). See also Pugh v Employment Services Bureau Bd of Review, No. 89CA34, 1990 WL 178123 (4th Dist Ct App, Washington, 10-30-90) (school board had just cause to terminate bus drivers who operated bus at excessive speed).

[48]See Loy v Unemployment Compensation Bd of Review, 30 App(3d) 204, 30 OBR 347, 507 NE(2d) 421 (Hamilton 1986); Sellers v Ohio Bureau of Employment Services Bd of Review, 1 App(3d) 161, 1 OBR 473, 440 NE(2d) 550 (Franklin 1981); Hardman v Unemployment Compensation Bd of Review, 94 Abs 257, 200 NE(2d) 825, 826 (CP, Clark 1964).

[49]Tzangas, Plakas & Mannos v Ohio Bureau of Employment Services, 73 OS(3d) 694, 653 NE(2d) 1207 (1995).

[50]Tzangas, Plakas & Mannos v Ohio Bureau of Employment Services, 73 OS(3d) 694, 653 NE(2d) 1207 (1995).

[51]Schultz v Herman's Furniture, Inc, 52 App(2d) 161, 368 NE(2d) 1269 (Erie 1976). See also Work-connected inefficiency or negligence as "misconduct" barring unemployment compensation, 26 ALR3d 1356.

[52]Burkart v Post-Browning, Inc, 859 F(2d) 1245 (6th Cir Ohio 1988).

[53]Pickett v Unemployment Compensation Bd of Review, 55 App(3d) 68, 562 NE(2d) 521 (Cuyahoga 1989).

[54]Nordonia Hills City School Dist Bd of Ed v Unemployment Compensation Bd of Review, 11 App(3d) 189, 11 OBR 283, 463 NE(2d) 1276 (Summit 1983).

[55]Youghiogheny & Ohio Coal Co v Oszust, 23 OS(3d) 39, 23 OBR 57, 491 NE(2d) 298 (1986).

[56]Henize v Giles, 22 OS(3d) 213, 22 OBR 364, 490 NE(2d) 585 (1986).

Chapter 16

Workers' Compensation, Occupational Safety and Health

16.01 Introduction
16.02 Employees covered by workers' compensation
16.03 Compensable injuries
16.04 Compensable occupational diseases
16.05 Compensation and benefits
16.06 Filing claims
16.07 Disputed claims
16.08 Employer immunity from suit, exception for intentional torts
16.09 Occupational safety and health

16.01 Introduction

Ohio's workers' compensation system provides benefits to employees or their survivors for injury, disease, or death sustained in the course of, and arising out of, employment. The system originated in 1912, with adoption of Article II, section 35 of the Ohio Constitution.

Prior to 1912, the only way to obtain compensation for a work-related injury, disease, or death was to sue the employer for negligence. This was difficult, since the employer could assert any of three defenses: contributory negligence, negligence by a fellow servant of the injured employee, and assumption of risk. The last defense in particular often prevented recovery, since merely accepting employment in an unsafe workplace could be construed as acceptance of the risks involved.

This state of affairs changed with creation of the workers' compensation system. The system, governed by RC Chapter 4123, provides benefits for work-related injury, disease, or death without regard to fault of the employer, employee, or fellow servants. Compensation is paid from an insurance fund maintained pursuant to RC Chapter 4123 with premiums paid by employers.[1]

The workers' compensation statutes have been amended many times, including comprehensive amendments in 1979,[2] 1986,[3] 1989,[4] and 1993.[5] The law governing a claim is the law in effect on the date of injury or diagnosis of disease.

16.02 Employees covered by workers' compensation

Every person in the service of a school district, including executive officers and board of education members, under any appointment or contract for hire, oral or written, is an "employee" under the workers' compensation law. Employees of independent contractors rendering service to the board of education are not board employees. Boards should require proof of coverage by independent contractors. If the independent contractor does not have coverage, the injured employee may elect coverage by the school district.[6]

A school district may contract with the bureau of workers' compensation for coverage of members of organizations or associations who might not otherwise be district employees but who perform services for the district. A district is generally immune from damage suits by covered persons.[7]

16.03 Compensable injuries

An "injury" includes any injury, whether caused by external accidental means or accidental in character and result, received in the course of, and arising out of, the injured employee's employment.[8] Both the "in the course of" and "arising out of" elements must be satisfied.[9]

(A) In general

Purposely self-inflicted injuries are not compensable.[10] An injury need not develop from unusual circumstances, and an

---

[1] RC 4123.23 to RC 4123.50.
[2] 1978 S 545.
[3] 1986 S 307.
[4] 1989 H 222.
[5] 1993 H 107.
[6] RC 4123.01(A).
[7] RC 4123.03.
[8] RC 4123.01(C).
[9] Fisher v Mayfield, 49 OS(3d) 275, 551 NE(2d) 1271 (1990).
[10] RC 4123.54(A).

employee may sustain a compensable injury while performing usual duties.[11]

Formerly, an injury was not compensable unless it resulted from a specific, identifiable accident. Now, an injury which develops gradually over time as a result of performing job-related duties is compensable under RC 4123.01(C).[12]

A physical injury caused solely by mental or emotional stress is compensable if the stress is unusually greater than that to which all workers are occasionally subjected and such stress is established as the medical cause of the injury.[13] A mental injury caused by mental or emotional distress, however, is not compensable.[14] A pre-existing condition may be compensable if it is aggravated by a physical trauma or harm which is otherwise compensable.[15] Also, if an injury or disease causes or "substantially accelerates" an employee's death, the employee's dependents may be eligible for benefits.[16]

In *Fisher v Mayfield*,[17] a teacher was injured while collecting voluntary contributions from co-workers for a "flower fund" (a well-known tradition in the district) used to provide flowers and expressions of sympathy upon the death of a co-worker's family member or congratulations upon an employee's marriage or birth of a child. On the day in question, she, on her own volition, left home early to stop at a school on the way to the school where she worked. While leaving the school, prior to the start of her normal working hours, she fell and suffered an injury. Even though she was not at her assigned work building and the injury occurred outside her assigned working hours, benefits were allowed. The Ohio Supreme Court stressed that she was on the employer's premises, the employer controlled the premises, and the employer benefited from the "heightened [employee] morale that naturally flows" from such a flower fund. As more fully discussed below, the Court found both that the injury arose out of employment and occurred in the course of employment.

(B) Injury arising out of employment

A compensable injury must "arise out of" the employment. In other words, there must be a "causal connection" between the injury and the employment.[18] Whether that connection exists depends on all the surrounding facts and circumstances, including (1) proximity of the scene of the accident to the place of employment, (2) the employer's degree of control over the scene, and (3) the benefit the employer received from the employee's presence on the scene.[19]

A virus made worse by exposure to natural elements, such as extreme cold and wind,[20] and an injury occurring while so intoxicated that the job cannot be performed,[21] do not "arise out of" employment. An injury sustained on the employer's premises by an employee while

---

[11]Czarnecki v Jones & Laughlin Steel Corp, 58 OS(2d) 413, 390 NE(2d) 1195 (1979).

[12]Village v General Motors Corp, 15 OS(3d) 129, 15 OBR 279, 472 NE(2d) 1079 (1985), overruling Bowman v National Graphics Corp, 55 OS(2d) 222, 378 NE(2d) 1056 (1978), and any other case suggesting that, to be compensable, an injury must result from a sudden mishap at a particular place and time.

[13]Ryan v Connor, 28 OS(3d) 406, 28 OBR 462, 503 NE(2d) 1379 (1986). For an example where the unusual stress required by *Ryan* was not shown, see Small v Defiance Public Library, 85 App(3d) 583, 620 NE(2d) 879 (Defiance 1993).

[14]Harover v Northwood, 48 App(3d) 312, 549 NE(2d) 1194 (Hamilton 1988), appeal dismissed by 47 OS(3d) 607, 546 NE(2d) 931 (1988).

[15]Schell v Globe Trucking, Inc, 48 OS(3d) 1, 548 NE(2d) 920 (1990) (noting that the physical trauma or harm must have some "real adverse effect" on the condition).

[16]RC 4123.59, RC 4123.60. See also Oswald v Connor, 16 OS(3d) 38, 16 OBR 520, 476 NE(2d) 658 (1985); McKee v Electric Auto-Lite Co, 168 OS 77, 151 NE(2d) 540 (1958).

[17]Fisher v Mayfield, 49 OS(3d) 275, 551 NE(2d) 1271 (1990).

[18]Fisher v Mayfield, 49 OS(3d) 275, 551 NE(2d) 1271 (1990). See also Fox v Industrial Comm, 162 OS 569, 125 NE(2d) 1 (1955).

[19]Lord v Daugherty, 66 OS(2d) 441, 423 NE(2d) 96 (1981). Applying these criteria, and emphasizing this list is not exhaustive but illustrative of the factors to be considered, a majority of the Court in *Fisher* found the necessary causal link between the teacher's fall while soliciting flower fund contributions and her employment.

[20]Phillips v Ingersoll-Humphreys Div, Borg-Warner Corp, 32 OS(2d) 266, 291 NE(2d) 736 (1972).

[21]Phelps v Positive Action Tool Co, 26 OS(3d) 142, 26 OBR 122, 497 NE(2d) 969 (1986).

walking a picket line during a strike also does not "arise out of" employment.[22]

(C) Injury in course of employment

A compensable injury must be sustained in the course of the employment. Whereas the "arising out of" element concerns causation, the "in the course of" element relates to the time, place, and circumstances of the injury.[23]

If the employee is merely commuting to work, the injury is not within "the course of" employment.[24] On-premises injuries are compensable even if due to natural elements, such as ice and snow.[25] An injury sustained while walking to the restroom or a fellow employee's work station while on an authorized rest break arises in the course of employment and is compensable.[26] An injury is generally not compensable where the employee is injured while traveling to or from lunch away from the employer's premises irrespective of whether the meal break is paid or unpaid.[27]

(D) Exclusions

For injuries occurring after August 22, 1986, the statutes specify four exclusions from the definition of injury: (1) psychiatric conditions, except where they arise from a compensable injury or disease; (2) injuries or conditions "caused primarily by the natural deterioration of tissue, an organ or part of the body"; (3) injuries or disabilities incurred as a result of an employer-sponsored fitness or recreational activity, if the employee signs a waiver prior to engaging in the activity; and (4) injuries or diseases caused by the employee's intoxication or being under the influence of a controlled substance not prescribed by a physician.[28]

16.04 Compensable occupational diseases

Every employee who is disabled by contracting an occupational disease in the course of employment is entitled to compensation.[29] Specific occupational diseases are scheduled in RC 4123.68(A) to (AA). A scheduled disease, such as gasoline poisoning, tenosynovitis, or asbestosis, must be contracted in the course of employment by exposure to the substance listed or process described in the statute. For a nonscheduled occupational disease to be compensable, it must be contracted in the course of employment. In addition, the employment must result in a hazard which distinguishes the particular employment from employment generally; *and* the employment must create a risk of contracting the disease to a greater degree and in a different manner from the public generally.[30]

For nonscheduled occupational diseases with dates of disability or diagnosis prior to August 22, 1986, the disease must also be "peculiar" to the employment.[31] An employee is not entitled to compensation for an occupational disease where his work

---

[22]Koger v Greyhound Lines, Inc, 90 App(3d) 387, 629 NE(2d) 492 (Hamilton 1993) (also holding that such an injury does not occur in the course of employment).

[23]Fisher v Mayfield, 49 OS(3d) 275, 551 NE(2d) 1271 (1990). Under all the circumstances, with emphasis on the fact that the teacher's injury occurred just minutes before her scheduled work time at a site controlled by the board of education, a majority of the Court concluded the "in the course of" element was satisfied.

[24]MTD Products, Inc v Robatin, 61 OS(3d) 66, 572 NE(2d) 661 (1991). See also Lohnes v Young, 175 OS 291, 194 NE(2d) 428 (1963); Bralley v Daugherty, 61 OS(2d) 302, 401 NE(2d) 448 (1980).

[25]Griffin v Hydra-Matic Div, General Motors Corp, 39 OS(3d) 79, 529 NE(2d) 436 (1988).

[26]Bauder v Mayfield, 44 App(3d) 91, 541 NE(2d) 98 (Union 1988).

[27]Hill v General Metal Heat Treating, Inc, 47 App(3d) 72, 547 NE(2d) 405 (Cuyahoga 1988). See also Eagle v Industrial Comm, 146 OS 1, 63 NE(2d) 439 (1945).

[28]RC 4123.01(C), RC 4123.54(B), as amended by 1986 S 307.

[29]RC 4123.54, RC 4123.68.

[30]RC 4123.01(F). The fact that a disease is scheduled in RC 4123.68 does not preclude a claimant from proving the existence of a compensable occupational disease under the definition appearing in RC 4123.01(F). Hutchinson v Ohio Ferro Alloys Corp, 70 OS(3d) 50, 636 NE(2d) 316 (1994) (finding silicosis to be an occupational disease under RC 4123.01(F) even though there was no showing that satisfied the requirements of RC 4123.68(X)).

[31]State ex rel Ohio Bell Telephone Co v Krise, 42 OS(2d) 247, 327 NE(2d) 756 (1975).

exposure aggravates a pre-existing condition.[32]

16.05 Compensation and benefits

(A) In general

In the event of injury or death, the employee or his dependents may be entitled to benefits—for medical expenses, nursing, hospital, and other services as may be authorized by law and approved[33]—and possibly to several different types of compensation. Each form of compensation is paid at an approved rate for the year of the injury or disease.[34]

(B) Temporary total disability

Temporary total disability compensation is paid while the employee is off work for more than seven days as a direct result of an allowed injury. It is generally paid at 72% of the full weekly wage for the first twelve weeks and 66⅔% of the average weekly wage thereafter, but may not exceed the statewide average weekly wage (SAWW) for the year of the injury or disease.[35]

The test for determining whether an employee is entitled to receive temporary total disability compensation under RC 4123.56 is whether the employee can return to his former position.[36] Compensation will be terminated if the employee is found capable of returning, either by his attending physician or through an independent examination and hearing before a district hearing officer.[37] If a disability becomes medically permanent, such that it will continue for an indefinite time with no reasonable probability of recovery, temporary total disability compensation will be terminated after a hearing.[38] A doctor's report indicating a claimant suffers from a permanent partial impairment,[39] a report indicating a claimant has reached maximum recovery,[40] or a conclusion that the claimant has a "poor prognosis for any improvement"[41] is evidence to support a finding that the disability has become permanent. For injuries or diseases occurring after August 22, 1986, temporary total disability compensation may be terminated when (1) work within the physical capabilities of the employee is made available; (2) the employee reaches the "maximum medical improvement";[42] or (3) the claimant is imprisoned on conviction of a crime.[43] The finding does not, however, preclude the employee from filing for another form of compensation.

If an employee abandons his employment by becoming self-employed,[44] or by voluntarily retiring for reasons unrelated to conditions in his claim,[45] compensation may also be terminated after hearing. Incarceration is considered a voluntary abandonment of employment.[46] Mere acceptance of a light-duty job does not constitute abandonment.[47] If a claimant with two jobs is unable to return to the job at which the injury occurred, but is able and does return to the other job, compensation may be terminated.[48]

---

[32] State ex rel Miller v Mead Corp, 58 OS(2d) 405, 390 NE(2d) 1192 (1979).

[33] RC 4123.54.

[34] RC 4123.54.

[35] RC 4123.56(A).

[36] State ex rel Ramirez v Industrial Comm, 69 OS(2d) 630, 433 NE(2d) 586 (1982). See also State ex rel General American Transportation Corp v Industrial Comm, 49 OS(3d) 91, 551 NE(2d) 155 (1990).

[37] RC 4123.56; State ex rel Milburn v Industrial Comm, 26 OS(3d) 119, 26 OBR 102, 498 NE(2d) 440 (1986).

[38] Vulcan Materials Co v Industrial Comm, 25 OS(3d) 31, 25 OBR 26, 494 NE(2d) 1125 (1986). See also, e.g., State ex rel Eaton Corp v Lancaster, 40 OS(3d) 404, 534 NE(2d) 46 (1988).

[39] State ex rel Delk v Industrial Comm, 35 OS(3d) 187, 519 NE(2d) 638 (1988).

[40] State ex rel Eldridge v Industrial Comm, 35 OS(3d) 189, 519 NE(2d) 650 (1988).

[41] State ex rel Cassity v Montgomery County Dept of Sanitation, 49 OS(3d) 47, 550 NE(2d) 474 (1990).

[42] RC 4123.56(A).

[43] RC 4123.54.

[44] State ex rel Nye v Industrial Comm, 22 OS(3d) 75, 22 OBR 91, 488 NE(2d) 867 (1986).

[45] State ex rel McGraw v Industrial Comm, 56 OS(3d) 137, 564 NE(2d) 695 (1990); State ex rel Scott v Industrial Comm, 40 OS(3d) 47, 531 NE(2d) 704 (1988); State ex rel Jones & Laughlin Steel Corp v Industrial Comm, 29 App(3d) 145, 29 OBR 162, 504 NE(2d) 451 (Franklin 1985).

[46] State ex rel Ashcraft v Industrial Comm, 34 OS(3d) 42, 517 NE(2d) 533 (1987).

[47] State ex rel Diversitech General Plastic Film Div v Industrial Comm, 45 OS(3d) 381, 544 NE(2d) 677 (1989).

[48] State ex rel Johnson v Rawac Plating Co, 61 OS(3d) 599, 575 NE(2d) 837 (1991).

(C) Wage loss

For injuries or diseases occurring after August 22, 1986, a new type of compensation may be awarded when an employee suffers a wage loss from returning to a different job, or he cannot find a job consistent with his physical capabilities as a direct result of the condition allowed in his claim. The employee may receive up to 66⅔% of his weekly wage loss, up to the SAWW in the year of his injury or disease, for not more than 200 weeks.[49]

Noting that "wage loss is broader in scope than temporary total disability," the Ohio Supreme Court has held that the discharge of an employee may, but does not automatically, bar wage loss compensation under RC 4123.56(B).[50]

(D) Permanent partial disability

Another type of compensation is paid for "permanent partial disability."[51] Compensation is based on the percentage of disability to the body as a whole which is permanent and medically demonstrable as a direct result of the conditions allowed in the claim. The percentage awarded is applied to 200 weeks at 66⅔% of a claimant's average weekly wage, but not more than 33⅓% of the SAWW for the year of the injury or disease.

RC 4123.57(B) provides payment of partial disability compensation for certain scheduled losses and indicates the periods during which compensation will be paid for various specified severance or loss of use of body parts. For example, loss of a great toe is assigned thirty weeks. The statute provides that compensation is paid per week at the SAWW. For injuries or diseases prior to August 22, 1986, the limitation is 50% of the SAWW.

To prohibit a double recovery for a single injury, a claimant who receives permanent partial disability benefits under RC 4123.57(A) for an injury which later deteriorates to total loss of an appendage, or other condition qualifying for a scheduled award, may not receive scheduled benefits under RC 4123.57(B) without an offset of the benefits received under RC 4123.57(A).[52]

(E) Impairment of earning capacity

For injuries or diseases occurring prior to August 22, 1986, a claimant may elect to receive compensation for "impairment of earning capacity" but must demonstrate the impairment is the result of the allowed condition in his claim.[53] If awarded, it is paid at 66⅔% of the impairment, not exceeding the SAWW in the year of the injury or disease, up to $17,500. The compensation paid is deducted from any future award for permanent partial disability. A claimant who has elected to receive permanent partial disability payments may not thereafter collect an earnings impairment award, unless granted a change of election by a district hearing officer for good cause shown.[54]

(F) Permanent total disability

If a claimant's disability is both permanent and total, compensation may be awarded "to continue until ... death," at the rate of 66⅔% of the average weekly wage, not to exceed 66⅔% of the SAWW for the year of injury or disease.[55] The industrial commission is to examine claimant's age, education, work record, and all other physical, psychological, and sociological factors in making its determination of permanent total disability.[56] Loss of two or more bodily parts, including hands, arms, feet, legs, or eyes, results in an automatic

---

[49] RC 4123.56(B).

[50] State ex rel Watts v Schottenstein Stores Corp, 68 OS(3d) 118, 623 NE(2d) 1202 (1993).

[51] RC 4123.57(A), formerly RC 4123.57(B).

[52] State ex rel Maurer v Industrial Comm, 47 OS(3d) 62, 547 NE(2d) 979 (1989).

[53] RC 4123.57(A); State ex rel Johnson v Industrial Comm, 40 OS(3d) 384, 533 NE(2d) 775 (1988). A claimant's voluntary retirement does not automatically preclude compensation based on impaired earning capacity. State ex rel CPC Group, General Motors Corp v Industrial Comm, 53 OS(3d) 209, 559 NE(2d) 1330 (1990).

[54] Former RC 4123.57(A).

[55] RC 4123.58(A).

[56] State ex rel Stephenson v Industrial Comm, 31 OS(3d) 167, 31 OBR 369, 509 NE(2d) 946 (1987). See also, e.g., State ex rel Hopkins v Industrial Comm, 70 OS(3d) 36, 635 NE(2d) 1257 (1994). Examining physicians should confine their opinions to the question of medical impairment, with the question of disability (that is, the effect the impairment has on the claimant's ability to work) being left for the commission to decide. State ex rel Woods v Industrial Comm, 50 OS(3d) 227, 553 NE(2d) 665 (1990).

award of permanent total disability.[57] After a period of time, if a claimant receives less than a certain amount per month, as determined by statutory formula, he may receive supplemental compensation from the disabled workers' relief fund.[58]

An employee who voluntarily retires for reasons unrelated to conditions in his claim is not entitled to permanent total disability compensation.[59] Nor can permanent total disability and permanent partial disability compensation be received for the same injury.[60]

(G) Funeral expenses, payment to dependents

If an injury or occupational disease causes death, medical and funeral expenses can be paid.[61] Compensation at 66⅔% of the average weekly wage—not to exceed 100% but not less than 50% of the SAWW—may be apportioned among the dependents (if a claimant is receiving total disability compensation at the time of death, the maximum allowable compensation automatically applies).[62]

In case of death which is not compensable, any compensation to which the claimant may have been entitled while alive may be awarded and paid to dependents or to defray expenses. All claims abate on the date of the claimant's death.[63]

(H) Additional awards for violation of specific safety requirements

Under Article II, section 35 of the Ohio Constitution, the industrial commission is empowered to determine if a worker's injury, disease, or death resulted from a violation by the employer of a specific statutory requirement or commission rule for the protection of the health or safety of employees.[64] If so, the commission may award additional penalty payments to the employee of not less than fifteen per cent or more than fifty per cent of the base award established by law.

A number of statutes establish specific safety requirements.[65] Also, the division of safety and hygiene has adopted detailed regulations providing safety requirements for elevators, construction, workshops and factories, foundries, steel mills, laundry, drycleaning and dyeing operations, rubber and plastics industries, potteries, window cleaning, and electric power supply and transmission.[66]

For violations after August 22, 1986, the commission will levy a fine of up to $50,000 for more than one violation within twenty-four months.[67]

16.06 Filing claims

Claims must be filed with the bureau of workers' compensation, which is required to notify the employer of the receipt of the claim and the facts alleged. All claims are referred to a district office of the bureau for investigation. Determining the facts concerning an injury or occupational disease claim may be done in whatever manner is most appropriate. A board of education should notify the bureau of any facts adverse to the claim as soon as possible.[68]

Injury claims must generally be filed within two years.[69] Disease claims must be

---

[57]RC 4123.58(C).

[58]RC 4123.411 et seq.

[59]See State ex rel Chrysler Corp v Industrial Comm, 62 OS(3d) 193, 580 NE(2d) 1082 (1991); State ex rel Consolidation Coal Co v Yance, 63 OS(3d) 460, 588 NE(2d) 845 (1992).

[60]State ex rel Murray v Industrial Comm, 63 OS(3d) 473, 588 NE(2d) 855 (1992).

[61]For dependents to recover benefits for a death by suicide, the evidence must establish that (1) an injury was received in the course of, and arising out of, employment; (2) the injury caused such domination by disturbance of the mind as to override normal rational judgment; and (3) the disturbance resulted in the suicide. Borbely v Prestole Everlock, Inc, 57 OS(3d) 67, 565 NE(2d) 575 (1991).

[62]RC 4123.59 (as modified on constitutional grounds by State ex rel Doersam v Industrial Comm, 45 OS(3d) 115, 543 NE(2d) 1169 (1989)), RC 4123.60. The decedent's average weekly wage is based on wages for the year preceding the injury, not the year preceding the date of death. State ex rel Truslow v Industrial Comm, 58 OS(3d) 100, 568 NE(2d) 671 (1991).

[63]RC 4123.60.

[64]See State ex rel Aspinwall v Industrial Comm, 40 OS(3d) 55, 531 NE(2d) 681 (1988).

[65]See, e.g., RC Ch 4107.

[66]OAC 4121:1.

[67]RC 4121.47.

[68]RC 4123.512.

[69]RC 4123.84. See Dent v AT&T Technologies, Inc, 38 OS(3d) 187, 527 NE(2d) 821 (1988); Clementi v Wean United, Inc, 39 OS(3d) 342, 530 NE(2d) 909 (1988).

filed within two years after the disability begins, or within a longer period if it does not exceed six months from the date of the diagnosis.[70] Death claims must be filed within two years from the date of death.[71]

The industrial commission retains jurisdiction over allowed claims for six years from payment of the last medical bill if medical benefits only are paid, but for ten years from the date of the last payment of compensation if compensation has been paid for temporary total, permanent total, or permanent partial disability.[72]

Retaliation by an employer against an employee for filing a claim or testifying in a workers' compensation proceeding is expressly prohibited by RC 4123.90.

16.07 Disputed claims

The administrator of the bureau of workers' compensation issues the initial order allowing or disallowing a claim on all issues. The order may be appealed within fourteen days of its receipt. An appeal from an administrator's order must be referred to an industrial commission district hearing officer who must afford the claimant and employer an opportunity to be heard, on reasonable notice, and to present testimony and facts pertinent to the claim.[73] Most claimants and most employers are represented at workers' compensation hearings.

(A) Administrative appeals

A claimant or employer who is dissatisfied with the hearing officer's decision may appeal by filing a notice of appeal within fourteen days with the industrial commission or bureau of workers' compensation.[74]

A staff hearing officer will hear the appeal, whose decision may be appealed within fourteen days to the industrial commission, which may either refuse or accept the appeal for hearing. If the commission refuses the appeal, the hearing officer's decision can be appealed directly to the court of common pleas in the same way that an adverse decision of the commission, after acceptance of the appeal, can be appealed to the court of common pleas pursuant to RC 4123.512.

(B) Appeals to common pleas court

Only decisions not involving "the extent of disability" of the claimant can be appealed to the court of common pleas.[75] Thus, while the original allowance of a claim and subsequent physical conditions allowed in the claim may be appealed to court, the amount or type of compensation paid or denied may not.[76] However, such awards may be challenged by an action in mandamus to show that the commission abused its discretion. The relator must show that the ruling was contrary to law or that there was no evidence to support the commission's order.[77] Where the record contains "some evidence" supporting the commission's factual findings, a court will not disturb them.[78] In extent of disability cases involving multiple allowed conditions, the commission need not consider only those medical reports evaluating a claimant's total impairment resulting from the combined effect of all allowed conditions, and the reviewing court's role is limited to determining whether some evidence supports the commission's order.[79]

To facilitate judicial review, the Ohio Supreme Court has held that district hearing officers and the commission must specify the basis of a decision by stating which evidence has been relied upon to reach a conclusion. In other words, a reviewing court will not search the file for "some evi-

---

[70]RC 4123.85. See White v Mayfield, 37 OS(3d) 11, 523 NE(2d) 497 (1988).

[71]RC 4123.84.

[72]RC 4123.52.

[73]RC 4123.511.

[74]RC 4123.511.

[75]RC 4123.512.

[76]Zavatsky v Stringer, 56 OS(2d) 386, 384 NE(2d) 693 (1978).

[77]State ex rel Braswell v Industrial Comm, 25 OS(3d) 61, 25 OBR 83, 494 NE(2d) 1147 (1986); State ex rel Kramer v Industrial Comm, 59 OS(2d) 39, 391 NE(2d) 1015 (1979).

[78]State ex rel Fiber-Lite Corp v Industrial Comm, 36 OS(3d) 202, 522 NE(2d) 548 (1988). Even if the parties seem to agree that "some evidence" is present, the court may still perform its own review and make a decision. State ex rel Firestone Tire & Rubber Co v Industrial Comm, 49 OS(3d) 283, 551 NE(2d) 979 (1990).

[79]State ex rel Burley v Coil Packaging, Inc, 31 OS(3d) 18, 31 OBR 70, 508 NE(2d) 936 (1987), overruling State ex rel Anderson v Industrial Comm, 62 OS(2d) 166, 404 NE(2d) 153 (1980), which had established a combined effects evidentiary rule for the disposition of multiple-injury claims.

dence" in support.[80] In a similar vein, to facilitate determining whether a decision involving an intervening incident is appealable, the Court has held that "the exact nature of the intervening incident, including whether it was work related and whether there was a causal nexus between the intervening trauma and the claimed disability" must be "clearly and fully" stated in the administrative decision.[81]

Notice of appeal must be filed with the court of common pleas of the county in which the injury was inflicted or in which the exposure which caused the occupational disease occurred within sixty days after the date of receipt of the decision appealed from or within sixty days after the date of receipt of the order of the commission refusing to permit an appeal from the regional board of review.[82]

16.08 Employer immunity from suit, exception for intentional torts

Since the workers' compensation system was intended to be an exclusive remedy, RC 4123.74 precludes an employee from suing his employer for injuries received during the course of employment. Although this is still the general rule,[83] the Ohio Supreme Court ruled in 1982 that, despite the statute, an employee can sue for injuries received in the course of employment as a result of an employer's intentional torts.[84]

Enacted in 1986 in response to the Supreme Court's action, RC 4121.80 authorized a special action for an intentional tort, capped the amount an employee could recover, entrusted to the industrial commission the task of setting damages, and created an "intentional tort fund" from which any award and the employer's attorney fees would be paid. This statute was jettisoned, however, in *Brady v Safety-Kleen Corp*[85] where, by a 4-3 margin, the Supreme Court found it contrary in toto to Ohio's Constitution. It has since been repealed and ultimately was replaced with RC 2745.01, which created an "employment intentional tort" that required a plaintiff to "set forth specific facts supported by clear and convincing evidence to establish that the employer committed an employment intentional tort against his employee." An employer would be liable only if such evidence shows that the employer "deliberately" committed the elements of the tort. In *State ex rel AFL-CIO v Voinovich*,[86] however, the Ohio Supreme Court concluded on procedural grounds that this statute was unconstitutionally enacted.

The Ohio General Assembly has again responded. Amended House Bill 103,

---

[80]State ex rel Mitchell v Robbins & Myers, Inc, 6 OS(3d) 481, 6 OBR 531, 453 NE(2d) 721 (1983) (relying, in part, on RC 4123.515 and RC 4123.518). See also, e.g., State ex rel Noll v Industrial Comm, 57 OS(3d) 203, 567 NE(2d) 245 (1991). Notwithstanding that a case is typically returned to the industrial commission where the basis is not sufficiently specified, courts are not precluded from directly ordering the commission to award permanent total disability compensation where "there is substantial likelihood" that the claimant is permanently and totally disabled. State ex rel Gay v Mihm, 68 OS(3d) 315, 626 NE(2d) 666 (1994). See also, e.g., State ex rel Haddix v Industrial Comm, 70 OS(3d) 59, 636 NE(2d) 323 (1994).

[81]Cook v Mayfield, 45 OS(3d) 200, 543 NE(2d) 787 (1989).

[82]RC 4123.519. The requirement that an appeal be filed in the county specified is jurisdictional; an appeal filed in the wrong county will be dismissed. Hartsock v Chrysler Corp, 44 OS(3d) 171, 541 NE(2d) 1037 (1989).

[83]RC 4123.74 has been held not to provide the exclusive remedy for claims based on sexual harassment in the workplace. Kerans v Porter Paint Co, 61 OS(3d) 486, 575 NE(2d) 428 (1991).

[84]Blankenship v Cincinnati Milacron Chemicals, Inc, 69 OS(2d) 608, 433 NE(2d) 572 (1982), cert denied 459 US 857, 103 SCt 127, 74 LEd(2d) 110 (1982). See also Jones v VIP Development Co, 15 OS(3d) 90, 15 OBR 246, 472 NE(2d) 1046 (1984). The definition of an intentional tort encompasses two different levels of intent: (1) "direct intent," where the employer does something that causes the exact result intended and desired; and (2) "substantially certain" intent, where the employer does something he believes is substantially certain to cause a particular result even if that result is not desired. Most intentional torts fall in the latter category. Harasyn v Normandy Metals, Inc, 49 OS(3d) 173, 551 NE(2d) 962 (1990); VanFossen v Babcock & Wilcox Co, 36 OS(3d) 100, 522 NE(2d) 489 (1988). *Harasyn* holds that insurance against torts in the second category is not void as against public policy.

[85]Brady v Safety-Kleen Corp, 61 OS(3d) 624, 576 NE(2d) 722 (1991).

[86]State ex rel AFL-CIO v Voinovich, 69 OS(3d) 225, 631 NE(2d) 582 (1994).

effective November 1, 1995, enacted RC 2305.112 and RC 2745.01 and overruled *Blankenship v Cincinnati Milacron Chemicals, Inc*[87] by restricting the scope of employment intentional torts. This new bill defines "employment intentional tort" as one in which the employer deliberately and intentionally injures, causes an occupational disease of, or causes the death of an employee.[88]

16.09 Occupational safety and health

(A) In general

RC Chapter 4167 specifically regulates the occupational safety and health of workers in Ohio's public sector. RC 4167.04 generally requires every Ohio public employer[89] to furnish employment and a place of employment free from recognized hazards causing or likely to cause death or serious harm to employees and to comply with all Ohio employment risk reduction standards,[90] rules, and orders promulgated under RC Chapter 4167. The employer, however, is not required to take any action that would cause an undue hardship,[91] unless the action is required to prevent imminent danger of death or serious harm.

Additionally, effective November 1, 1995, a public employer can apply for a seven-year renewable exemption from compliance with RC Chapter 4167 provided certain conditions are met.[92] In addition to several procedural steps, the employer must be a member of a group-rated workers' compensation plan or have a workers' compensation premium that is 50% of the base rate.[93] RC 4167.05 generally requires every public employee[94] to comply with all relevant Ohio employment risk reduction standards, rules, and orders, and to comply with all reasonable safety rules adopted by the employer to comply with RC Chapter 4167.

RC 4167.02 empowers the Ohio Bureau of Employment Services to enforce RC Chapter 4167. RC 4167.02 also creates within the bureau the Public Employment Risk Reduction Advisory Commission (PERRAC), consisting of sixteen members equally divided between representatives of public employers and representatives of public employees and no more than half of whom may be of the same political party.

By July 1, 1994, PERRAC is required by RC 4167.07 to adopt as a rule and as an Ohio employment risk reduction standard every federal occupational safety and health standard then in effect under the Occupational Safety and Health Act of 1970.[95] Within 120 days of the adoption, modification, or revocation of any federal standard, PERRAC is to take corresponding and conforming action in Ohio unless it determines that existing Ohio rules and standards provide protection at least as effective as the federal standards would

---

[87]Blankenship v Cincinnati Milacron Chemicals, Inc, 69 OS(2d) 608, 433 NE(2d) 572 (1982), cert denied 459 US 857, 103 SCt 127, 74 LEd(2d) 110 (1982).

[88]1995 H 103, eff. 11-1-95.

[89]School districts are expressly included within "public employer." RC 4167.01(A).

[90]An "employment risk reduction standard" is defined by RC 4167.01(D) as a standard that requires conditions or the adoption or use of one or more practices, means, methods, operations, or processes reasonably necessary or appropriate to provide safe and healthful employment and places of employment. An "Ohio employment risk reduction standard" is defined by RC 4167.01(E) as any such standard adopted or issued under RC Chapter 4167. No such standard applies to any Ohio public employee until July 1, 1994, however. 1992 H 308, §3.

[91]"Undue hardship" is defined by RC 4167.01(F) as any requirement that would necessitate the employer's taking action "with significant difficulty or expense" in light of (1) the nature and cost of the action; (2) the employer's overall financial resources; (3) the number of employees at the particular location where action is required; (4) the effect on expenses and resources or other impact of the action on the employer's operations at the location; (5) the employer's overall size with respect to the number of its employees; (6) the number, type, and location of the employer's operations, including the composition, structure, and functions of the workforce; and (7) the geographic separateness, administrative, or fiscal relationship of the employer's operations to the whole public employer.

[92]RC 4167.19, as enacted by 1995 H 103, eff. 11-1-95.

[93]RC 4167.19, as enacted by 1995 H 103, eff. 11-1-95.

[94]"Public employee" includes not just those hired by the school district but also employees of a private employer with whom the district contracts if the National Labor Relations Board has declined jurisdiction over such employees under federal labor law. RC 4167.01(B).

[95]The federal OSHA is codified at 29 USCA 651 et seq.

ensure or that local conditions warrant a different standard. For these same reasons, PERRAC may adopt as a rule and Ohio standard any occupational safety and health standard that is not covered under federal law or that differs from the federal standard.

Except for the automatic incorporation of existing federal standards by July 1, 1994, all PERRAC rules must be adopted in accordance with the administrative procedure set forth in RC Chapter 119, except that the effective date may be delayed for up to ninety days beyond the otherwise required effective date to ensure that employers and employees are informed of and have an opportunity to familiarize themselves with the specific requirements.[96] In emergency or unusual situations, RC 4167.08 authorizes the chief of the division of occupational safety and health to issue emergency temporary Ohio employment risk reduction standards that take effect immediately upon publication in newspapers of general circulation in Cleveland, Columbus, Cincinnati, and Toledo.

An employer affected by a rule or employment risk reduction standard (including emergency temporary standards) may apply to the chief for a temporary variance in accordance with the detailed procedure set forth in RC 4167.09(A). The temporary variance may be granted only after notice to affected employees and their union, if any, and an opportunity for a hearing under RC 4167.15.[97] The affected employer may also apply to the chief for a variance (as opposed to a temporary variance). A variance will be granted only after notice to affected employees and their union, if any, and an opportunity for a hearing under RC 4167.15.

The employer's application must satisfy the requirements of RC 4167.09, one of which is establishing to the satisfaction of the chief that the employer's plan will be as safe and healthful as compliance without the variance. Upon application of the employer, an employee, or the union, or upon his own motion, the chief may modify or revoke the variance at any time during six months after the date of issuance. RC 4167.10(B) permits any public employee, or the employee's union, who believes that a violation of an Ohio employment risk reduction standard exists that threatens physical harm, or that an imminent danger exists, to request an inspection by filing a written notice with the chief or his designee.[98]

If, upon receipt of the notice, the chief finds no reasonable grounds to credit the allegation, the chief must inform the employee or union in writing of that determination. If the chief finds there are reasonable grounds to believe a violation or danger exists, he must within five days of receipt of the notice inform the employer by certified mail of the alleged violation or danger and that the chief or his designee will investigate and inspect the employer's workplace. A copy of the notice that prompted the action must also be furnished to the employer. The employer must respond within thirty days. If the employer does not correct the violation or danger, or fails to respond, within the thirty-day period, the investigation and inspection will ensue.[99]

Investigation and inspection authority is not limited to the alleged violation or danger: any area where the chief or his designee has reason to believe a violation or danger exists may be examined. If a workplace condition or practice is found that presents a substantial probability that the condition or practice could result in death or serious physical harm, an order will issue—after notice to the employer of the intent to issue an order—prohibiting the employment of any public employee or any

---

[96] Where toxic materials or harmful physical agents are involved, special requirements set forth in RC 4167.07(C) apply to PERRAC's adoption, modification, or revocation of any employment risk reduction standard.

[97] A temporary variance generally cannot exceed the period needed to achieve compliance or one year, whichever is shorter. However, upon timely application by the employer, the chief may renew a temporary variance up to two times. RC 4167.09(C).

[98] The notice must be signed and set forth the grounds "with reasonable particularity." The name(s) of the employee(s) making the notice or referred to in it must be kept confidential and will not appear in the copy ultimately provided to the employer. RC 4167.10(B)(1).

[99] No inspection can occur prior to the end of this thirty-day period unless requested or permitted by the employer. RC 4167.10(B)(2).

continuing operation or process under such condition or practice until necessary corrective steps are taken. Unless otherwise ordered by a court, such an order cannot be effective for more than fifteen days.

Generally, investigations and inspections occur only pursuant to an employee or union request, or a request by the public employer, or a request under RC 4167.06(B).[100] The taking of environmental samples and photographs, the examination of relevant records, the conducting of relevant tests and other studies, and the issuance of subpoenas to compel the attendance of witnesses and the production of documents all fall within the chief's investigation and enforcement authority. If a violation is found, the chief "with reasonable promptness" is to issue, by certified mail, a written citation that includes a time within which the employer is to abate the violation. No citation may be issued after six months following the final occurrence of any violation.

Upon receipt, the employer must immediately post the citation or a copy at or near each place the violation occurred. The employer has fourteen days within which to notify the chief of an intent to contest the violation. If such notice is timely given, or if within fourteen days after issuance of a citation a public employee or the employee's union files notice that the time fixed for abatement is unreasonable, the chief must hold an adjudication hearing in accordance with RC Chapter 119.[101]

Except for one who fails timely to contest a citation, any employer, employee, or union affected by an order, rule, or Ohio employment risk reduction standard proposed, adopted, or otherwise issued under RC Chapter 4167 may, within fourteen days of the proposal, adoption, or issuance of the order, rule, or standard, request a hearing from the chief. Within fourteen days of the request, the chief must appoint a hearing officer who, within fourteen days of his appointment, is to hold a hearing in accordance with RC Chapter 119. Within fourteen days of the hearing, the hearing officer is to render a decision, which may, within thirty days, be appealed to the chief. Unless timely appealed, or unless the chief on his own motion modifies or reverses the decision within the thirty-day period, the hearing officer's resolution is final and not appealable to court.[102]

A party adversely affected by a final order of the chief has thirty days within which to appeal to the court of common pleas of Franklin County or the county in which the alleged violation occurred. If the court finds an undue hardship would result pending determination of the appeal, the order may be suspended. After conducting a hearing on the appeal, the court may affirm, reverse, vacate, or modify the order or make such other ruling as the evidence supports. The court's decision may then be appealed in accordance with RC Chapter 2505.[103]

In the event of a willful failure to comply with any final order of the chief, the chief may apply to court for an order compelling compliance. The court "shall order such relief as it considers appropriate" and also impose a civil penalty of not more than $500 per day per violation up to a total of $10,000 for the violation.[104]

In addition, any court of common pleas has jurisdiction upon petition of the chief to enjoin any workplace conditions or practices that present a danger that could reasonably be expected to cause death or serious harm or contribute significantly to occupationally related illness immediately or before resolution through normal enforcement procedures. Indeed, if the chief or his designee responsible for inspections determines that the imminent danger is such that immediate action is necessary, and further determines that there is insuffi-

---

[100]For treatment of RC 4167.06(B), see Text 16.09(B), Good faith refusals to work under dangerous conditions.

[101]RC 4167.10. In fixing a time within which abatement must occur, RC 4167.10(H) requires the chief to consider costs, the size and resources of the employer, the severity of the violation, technological feasibility of the employer's ability to comply, the possible present and future detriment to an employee's health and safety associated with noncompliance, and other factors he deems appropriate. The chief, in light of such factors, may allow up to two years and may extend that period an additional year. The citation provisions of RC 4167.10 (namely, divisions (D) to (H)) do not apply, however, until January 1, 1995. 1992 H 308, §3.

[102]RC 4167.15.
[103]RC 4167.16.
[104]RC 4167.17.

cient time to seek and obtain injunctive relief, the chief or his designee may immediately file a petition with the court for such injunctive relief and issue an order requiring action to avoid, correct, or remove the imminent danger.[105]

(B) Good faith refusals to work under dangerous conditions

RC 4167.06 permits a public employee acting in good faith to refuse to work under conditions the employee reasonably believes present an imminent danger of death or serious harm, if such conditions are not normally associated with or reasonably expected to occur on the job. If the employee has requested the employer to correct the hazardous conditions but the conditions remain uncorrected, and there was insufficient time to eliminate the danger by resorting to normal enforcement methods, the employer is prohibited from disciplining or otherwise discriminating against the employee. If not reassigned to other tasks, the employee retains a right to continued employment and to full compensation for the tasks that would have been performed but for the refusal; if reassigned, the employee is entitled to full compensation as if he were not reassigned. An employee who refuses to perform assigned tasks and fails to meet all of the conditions set forth in RC 4167.06(A) for the refusal may be disciplined for a refusal to work as provided by law or in any applicable contract.

By written, signed statement, the employee is "as soon as practicable" to notify the chief of the dangerous condition. The chief or his designee is then "immediately" to inspect the premises and comply with RC 4167.10 in conducting the inspection and investigation and issuing orders and citations.[106]

(C) Retaliation prohibited

RC 4167.13 prohibits any public employer from discharging or otherwise discriminating against any employee who in good faith initiates or participates in any proceeding under RC Chapter 4167 or otherwise, on his own behalf or on behalf of others, exercises any right afforded by RC Chapter 4167.

(D) Information

The chief is to maintain an effective program of collection, compilation, and analysis of employment risk reduction statistics. To that end, PERRAC is to adopt rules requiring public employers to make, keep, and make available to the chief various reports and records and, through posting of notices or other appropriate means, to keep employees informed of their rights and obligations under RC Chapter 4167 and of applicable Ohio employment risk reduction standards.[107]

All information reported to or otherwise obtained by the chief in connection with any investigation, inspection, or proceeding under RC Chapter 4167 that reveals a trade secret is generally confidential.[108]

(E) No-fault inspection

On or before January 1, 1995, any public employer may request the chief to conduct an employment risk reduction inspection of the employer's place of employment. No information obtained from the inspection may be used in any proceeding for a violation of RC Chapter 4167 or any rule or order issued thereunder or in any other action in an Ohio court.[109]

---

[105] RC 4167.14.
[106] RC 4167.06(B).
[107] RC 4167.11.
[108] RC 4167.12.
[109] 1992 H 308, §4.

Chapter 17

Equal Employment Opportunity, Family and Medical Leave

17.01 Introduction

KEY ANTIDISCRIMINATION LAWS
17.02 The Thirteenth and Fourteenth Amendments, federal Civil Rights Acts of 1866 and 1871
17.03 Title VII, federal Civil Rights Act of 1964
17.04 Ohio Fair Employment Practices Act
17.05 Antidiscrimination requirements for contractors dealing with schools

PARTICULAR APPLICATIONS
17.06 Age discrimination
17.07 Hiring and promotion practices
17.08 Equal pay
17.09 Pregnancy
17.10 Nonrenewal of contract for discriminatory purpose
17.11 Sexual harassment
17.12 Retaliatory discharge
17.13 Discrimination against the handicapped
17.14 National origin discrimination
17.15 Religious discrimination

FAMILY AND MEDICAL LEAVE
17.16 Family and Medical Leave Act of 1993

RECORDS
17.17 Notices, record-keeping, and reports

AFFIRMATIVE ACTION
17.18 Affirmative action and reverse discrimination

WAIVERS
17.19 Waiver of claims not prohibited
17.20 Table of laws affecting equal employment opportunity

17.01 Introduction

Many constitutional provisions, statutes, and executive orders may affect a public or private Ohio school's obligation to assure nondiscrimination, equal opportunity, or affirmative action in employment. A chart identifying these sources of regulation appears at the end of this chapter. The statutes with the greatest impact on schools, some of which were significantly modified by the Civil Rights Act of 1991, are discussed below, as is the Family and Medical Leave Act of 1993.

KEY ANTIDISCRIMINATION LAWS

17.02 The Thirteenth and Fourteenth Amendments, federal Civil Rights Acts of 1866 and 1871

(A) In general

Following the Civil War, the Thirteenth Amendment, abolishing slavery, and the Fourteenth Amendment, guaranteeing equal protection of laws, were made part of the US Constitution. Congress passed the Civil Rights Acts of 1866 and 1871 to implement the constitutional guarantees.

Three sections of Title 42 of the US Code in particular have been used to remedy employment discrimination. Section 1981 prohibits race discrimination in connection with contracts, including employment contracts.[1] This prohibition has been construed to apply to discrimination based on ancestry and ethnic characteristics as well.[2] Section 1983 provides judicial redress for acts under color of state law which deprive persons of constitutional rights, including the Fourteenth Amendment right to equal protection, and rights secured by federal statutes. It does not apply to purely private conduct; nor is a privately owned school that receives public funding subject to it.[3] Section 1985(3) prohibits conspira-

---

[1] 42 USCA 1981. The statute expressly pertains only to the making and enforcing of contracts. In 1991, it was amended to expand its scope and legislatively overrule Patterson v McClean Credit Union, 491 US 164, 109 SCt 2363, 105 LEd(2d) 132 (1989), which held that a claim of racial harassment during employment after a contract was formed was not actionable. Specifically, the making, performance, modification, and termination of contracts, as well as the enjoyment of all benefits, privileges, terms, and conditions of the contractual relation are now covered.

[2] St. Francis College v Al-Khazraji, 481 US 604, 107 SCt 2022, 95 LEd(2d) 582 (1987).

[3] Rendell-Baker v Kohn, 457 US 830, 102 SCt 2764, 73 LEd(2d) 418 (1982). For extended treatment of section 1983, see Text 46.13 to Text 46.15.

cies, both private and public, to deprive a person of equal rights.[4]

These provisions are independent of any claim of discrimination under Title VII of the Civil Rights Act of 1964 and retained significance after 1972 amendments extended Title VII to public employers.[5] For example, a claim under section 1983 has a longer limitations period than applies under Title VII.[6] Further, remedies may differ. Compensatory and punitive damages are generally available under the older Acts.[7] Under section 1983, a public agency is financially liable for deprivation of constitutional or of certain other federally protected rights resulting from application of established custom or policy, and in some cases public officials may be personally liable.[8] The US Supreme Court has held that section 1983 provides the exclusive federal damages remedy for violation by a public agency, such as a public school district, of rights guaranteed by section 1981.[9]

(B) Application

(1) Disparate treatment, intent

Sections 1981, 1983, and 1985(3) prohibit only intentional discrimination.[10] Unlike Title VII, a violation cannot be proved on a disparate impact theory (that is, a theory that neutral policies or practices have an adverse impact on a protected class). Rather, disparate treatment must be shown, and direct or circumstantial proof of motive is critical.[11]

(2) Punitive damages, attorney fees

Public bodies are immune from liability for punitive damages in section 1983 actions.[12] However, punitive damages may be awarded against individual defendants in section 1983 actions whose conduct was in reckless or callous disregard of federal rights, as well as when there is actual malicious intent.[13]

The prevailing party in an action under sections 1981, 1983, or 1985 may recover attorney's fees, which may include fees for services of experts, by virtue of 42 USCA 1988,[14] and, in appropriate cases, fees may be awarded when the case is settled before trial.[15] To be considered a "prevailing party," one need not win every aspect of a lawsuit. If a party prevails on "any significant issue" and receives some of the relief sought, the statute is triggered.[16] A plaintiff who wins only "nominal" damages is a prevailing party, but under such circumstances may be entitled to no fee award at all.[17] Attorney fees are not available for legal services expended in pursuit of a state administrative remedy absent a requirement that such remedies be exhausted prior to bringing a federal suit.[18] Time spent in administrative proceedings before a school board may not be sufficiently preparatory for trial to be compensable.[19]

---

[4]Griffin v Breckenridge, 403 US 88, 91 SCt 1790, 29 LEd(2d) 338 (1971).

[5]Great American Federal Savings & Loan Assn v Novotny, 442 US 366, 99 SCt 2345, 60 LEd(2d) 957 (1979).

[6]See Owens v Okure, 488 US 235, 109 SCt 573, 102 LEd(2d) 594 (1989).

[7]Smith v Wade, 461 US 30, 103 SCt 1625, 75 LEd(2d) 632 (1983); Harris v Richards Mfg Co, 675 F(2d) 811 (6th Cir Tenn 1982).

[8]See Text 46.13 to 46.15.

[9]Jett v Dallas Independent School Dist, 491 US 701, 109 SCt 2702, 105 LEd(2d) 598 (1989).

[10]General Bldg Contractors Assn v Pennsylvania, 458 US 375, 102 SCt 3141, 73 LEd(2d) 835 (1982).

[11]International Brotherhood of Teamsters v United States, 431 US 324, 97 SCt 1843, 52 LEd(2d) 396 (1977); Washington v Davis, 426 US 229, 96 SCt 2040, 48 LEd(2d) 597 (1976); Arnold v Ballard, 448 FSupp 1025 (ND Ohio 1978).

[12]Newport v Fact Concerts, Inc, 453 US 247, 101 SCt 2748, 69 LEd(2d) 616 (1981).

[13]Smith v Wade, 461 US 30, 103 SCt 1625, 75 LEd(2d) 632 (1983).

[14]A fee award may include compensation for the work of paralegals and law clerks at market rates. Missouri v Jenkins, 491 US 274, 109 SCt 2463, 105 LEd(2d) 229 (1989). Section 1988 does not preclude a plaintiff from privately entering into a contingent-fee contract (under which he agrees to pay a specified percentage of any recovery) even if the arrangement results in a prevailing civil rights plaintiff paying his attorney more than the statutory award against the defendant. Venegas v Mitchell, 495 US 82, 110 SCt 1679, 109 LEd(2d) 74 (1990).

[15]Maher v Gagne, 448 US 122, 100 SCt 2570, 65 LEd(2d) 653 (1980).

[16]Texas State Teachers Assn v Garland Independent School Dist, 489 US 782, 109 SCt 1486, 103 LEd(2d) 866 (1989).

[17]Farrar v Hobby, 506 US 103, 113 SCt 566, 121 LEd(2d) 494 (1992).

[18]Webb v Dyer County Bd of Ed, 471 US 234, 105 SCt 1923, 85 LEd(2d) 233 (1985).

[19]Webb v Dyer County Bd of Ed, 471 US 234, 105 SCt 1923, 85 LEd(2d) 233 (1985).

Under section 1988, only time reasonably spent in litigation is compensable.[20]

17.03 Title VII, federal Civil Rights Act of 1964

Title VII of the Civil Rights Act of 1964, 42 USCA 2000e et seq., is the most comprehensive and significant of the modern federal statutes prohibiting employment discrimination. Title VII was amended in 1972 to extend its application to public agencies, including school boards.

(A) Race, color, religion, sex, or national origin

Title VII states that an employer shall not discriminate against an employee or job applicant, or "limit, segregate, or classify his employees or applicants for employment in any way which would deprive or tend to deprive any individual of employment opportunities or otherwise adversely affect his status as an employee, because of such individual's race, color, religion, sex, or national origin."[21] It further prohibits retaliation against any individual who opposes unlawful employment practices or participates in investigations and enforcement proceedings under Title VII.[22]

(B) Exceptions

Statutory exceptions to the nondiscrimination requirement allow certain activities as follows:

(1) Consideration of religion, sex, or national origin if it is a bona fide occupational qualification reasonably necessary to the employer's normal operation;[23]

(2) Consideration of religion by a private school with religious affiliation;[24]

(3) Differentiation in connection with compensation, terms, conditions, or privileges of employment pursuant to "a bona fide seniority or merit system," so long as the differences are not the result of an intention to discriminate;[25] and

(4) Reliance on professionally developed ability tests, provided the tests are not "designed, intended or used to discriminate."[26]

Courts have generally construed these exceptions narrowly.

(C) "Disparate treatment" and "disparate impact"

Title VII prohibits both intentional discrimination ("disparate treatment") and neutral practices which have a significant adverse impact on members of a protected group but are not substantially job related ("disparate impact"). The Supreme Court has described these concepts as follows:

> "Disparate treatment" ... is the most easily understood type of discrimination. The employer simply treats some people less favorably than others because of their race, color, religion, sex, or national origin. Proof of discriminatory motive is critical, although it can in some situations be inferred from the mere fact of differences in treatment. ... Claims of disparate treatment may be distinguished from claims that stress "disparate impact." The latter involve employment practices that are facially neutral in their treatment of different groups but that in fact fall more harshly on one group than another and cannot be justified by business necessity. ... Proof of discriminatory motive, we have

---

[20]Northcross v Memphis City Schools Bd of Ed, 611 F(2d) 624 (6th Cir Tenn 1979), cert denied 447 US 911, 100 SCt 2999, 64 LEd(2d) 862 (1980).

[21]42 USCA 2000e-2.

[22]42 USCA 2000e-3. The courts are not unanimous on whether a *former* employee may pursue the prior employer for retaliatory conduct (such as "blacklisting") that arises out of and is related to that employment relationship. The majority have answered in the affirmative. See Charlton v Paramus Bd of Ed, 25 F(3d) 194 (3d Cir NJ 1994), cert denied ___ US ___, 115 SCt 590, 130 LEd(2d) 503 (1994) (following majority stance and discussing cases on both sides).

[23]42 USCA 2000e-2(e)(1). In assessing whether sex is a bona fide occupational qualification in the context of hiring practices, the Ohio Supreme Court has held under Ohio's Fair Employment Practices Act that an employer seeking to use this affirmative defense must prove (1) that its gender-based criteria involve the essence of the employer's business, and (2) either that all (or substantially all) members of the excluded gender are incapable of performing the job or it is impractical to determine each applicant's qualifications nondiscriminatorily. Little Forest Medical Center of Akron v Ohio Civil Rights Comm, 61 OS(3d) 607, 575 NE(2d) 1164 (1991), cert denied 503 US 906, 112 SCt 1263, 117 LEd(2d) 491 (1992).

[24]42 USCA 2000e-2(e)(2).

[25]42 USCA 2000e-2(h).

[26]42 USCA 2000e-2(h).

held, is not required under a disparate impact theory.[27]

(D) Enforcement by Equal Employment Opportunity Commission (EEOC)

Interpretation and enforcement of Title VII is entrusted principally to the Equal Employment Opportunity Commission (EEOC). To pursue a Title VII claim, exhaustion of administrative remedies is generally required before filing suit in court.[28] An individual must file a timely[29] discrimination charge with the EEOC, which then has the authority to investigate and determine whether there is "reasonable cause" to believe the charge is true.[30] In making such determination, it must give "substantial weight to final findings and orders made by state or local authorities," but it is not bound by the finding of a state or local agency. If the EEOC determines there is reasonable cause to believe the charge, it must endeavor to conciliate the charge—that is, attempt to persuade the employer and the complainant to enter into a settlement agreement. If the EEOC finds "no reasonable cause," or if it finds "reasonable cause" but is unsuccessful in conciliation, or if the EEOC fails to complete its investigation within 180 days of the filing of the charge, it may issue a letter informing the complainant that he can file suit within ninety days of receipt of the notice. The suit must be reasonably related to what was alleged in the charge; wholly new claims are not permitted.[31] Although suit is typically filed in federal court, state courts have concurrent jurisdiction over Title VII claims.[32] In lieu of issuing this "right-to-sue" letter, the EEOC may refer the case to the attorney general to file suit against a public employer, although this procedure is not commonly used.[33]

Ohio is a "deferral state," which permits the EEOC to defer to the Ohio Civil Rights Commission (OCRC) for processing of charges asserting claims that are common to both Title VII and to the Ohio Fair Employment Practices Act.[34] The EEOC normally adopts the determination of the OCRC on such charges, but may reconsider the OCRC determination if requested by one of the parties.

(E) Actions, remedies

In addition to suits based on individual discrimination charges, the federal government may file suit against employers "engaged in a pattern or practice of resistance ... of such a nature and intended to deny the full exercise of the rights" described by Title VII.[35]

If an employer has discriminated in violation of Title VII, the court may enjoin continuance of the "unlawful employment practice, and order such affirmative action as may be appropriate, which may include, but is not limited to, reinstatement or hiring of employees, with or without back

---

[27]International Brotherhood of Teamsters v United States, 431 US 324, 335 n.15, 97 SCt 1843, 52 LEd(2d) 396 (1977).

[28]Love v Pullman, 404 US 522, 92 SCt 616, 30 LEd(2d) 679 (1972); Ang v Proctor & Gamble Co, 932 F(2d) 540 (6th Cir Ohio 1991). See also Zipes v Trans World Airlines, Inc, 455 US 385, 102 SCt 1127, 71 LEd(2d) 234 (1982).

[29]The charge must be filed with the EEOC within 180 days after the alleged unlawful employment practice occurred unless the individual first files a charge with the Ohio Civil Rights Commission, in which case the time period is extended to a maximum of 300 days. 42 USCA 2000e-5(e). If a claim is based on an employer's seniority system, adopted for an intentionally discriminatory purpose, the time period begins to run when the seniority system is adopted, when an individual becomes subject to it, or when an individual is injured by application of it.

[30]As part of its investigation, the EEOC may subpoena relevant information. The US Supreme Court, in a case involving a university that denied tenure to a faculty member, has rejected any notion of a special common-law or First Amendment privilege against the disclosure of sensitive peer review information used in tenure decisions. So long as the subpoenaed information is relevant to the charge, tenure peer review materials must be disclosed. University of Pennsylvania v EEOC, 493 US 182, 110 SCt 577, 107 LEd(2d) 571 (1990). This case has obvious meaning for Ohio school districts that use peer review procedures in evaluating teachers. See Text 9.13(A), Mandatory evaluation procedures.

[31]See, e.g., Cheek v Western & Southern Life Insurance Co, 31 F(3d) 497 (7th Cir 1994).

[32]Yellow Freight Systems, Inc v Donnelly, 494 US 820, 110 SCt 1566, 108 LEd(2d) 834 (1990); Manning v Ohio State Library Bd, 62 OS(3d) 24, 577 NE(2d) 650 (1991).

[33]42 USCA 2000e-5.

[34]42 USCA 2000e-5(c), (d); New York Gaslight Club, Inc v Carey, 447 US 54, 100 SCt 2024, 64 LEd(2d) 723 (1980). See Text 17.04, Ohio Fair Employment Practices Act.

[35]42 USCA 2000e-6.

pay" or any other equitable relief as the court deems appropriate provided that "back pay liability shall not accrue from a date more than two years prior to the filing of a charge with the Commission" and shall be reduced by interim earnings and amounts earnable with reasonable diligence.[36] The US Supreme Court has ruled that Title VII backpay awards and settlements are subject to taxation under federal income tax laws.[37]

When an employer discharges an employee for discriminatory reasons but discovers other legitimate reasons (such as resumé fraud) for the discharge after the discharge decision was made, the employee may still win a discrimination suit, but may not be entitled to reinstatement or to back pay beyond the date that the after-acquired evidence was discovered.[38]

In addition, 42 USCA 1981a, enacted in 1991, generally authorizes compensatory and punitive damages for intentional, and only intentional, discrimination in violation of Title VII. Punitive damages are not recoverable against political subdivisions, such as school districts, however. Compensatory damages do not include back pay, interest on back pay, and any other relief authorized by 42 USCA 2000e-5(g). Such damages do address future pecuniary losses, emotional pain, suffering, inconvenience, mental anguish, loss of enjoyment of life, and other nonpecuniary losses. Limits ranging from $50,000 to $300,000 are imposed, depending on the size of the employer. An express condition to any such recovery, however, is that "the complaining party cannot recover under [42 USCA] 1981 ... ." Thus, double recovery for the same harm arising out of the same set of circumstances is precluded. Relief under 42 USCA 1981 is also expressly shielded from any of the damage limitations imposed by 42 USCA 1981a. One of the latter statute's most significant features gives the party claiming damages the right to a jury trial, with a prohibition against informing the jury of the dollar limitations on damages.

The prevailing party (other than the government) in a Title VII action may be awarded reasonable attorney fees.[39] Attorney fees are awarded to prevailing plaintiffs in all but special circumstances, but a prevailing defendant is awarded attorney fees only when the court finds the plaintiff's action was frivolous, unreasonable, or without foundation.[40] Further, in appropriate cases, section 706(f) and (k) authorize a federal suit to recover attorney fees for work done by the prevailing complainant in state administrative and judicial proceedings to which the complainant was referred by the EEOC.[41] Attorney fees will not be awarded to a plaintiff for work performed resisting dismissal proceedings under state law.[42]

(F) Proof of discrimination

(1) Disparate treatment cases

The burden and order of proof in disparate treatment cases are articulated in *McDonnell Douglas Corp v Green*[43] and *Texas Dept of Community Affairs v Burdine*.[44]

A plaintiff alleging disparate treatment may initially establish a prima facie case (thereby creating a rebuttable presumption of unlawful discrimination) by introducing

---

[36] 42 USCA 2000e-5(g).

[37] United States v Burke, 504 US 229, 112 SCt 1867, 119 LEd(2d) 34 (1992); Commissioner of Internal Revenue Service v Schleier, 515 US ___, 115 SCt 2159, 132 LEd(2d) 294 (1995).

[38] McKennon v Nashville Banner Publishing Co, 513 US ___, 115 SCt 879, 130 LEd(2d) 852 (1995); Milligan-Jensen v Michigan Technological University, 975 F(2d) 302 (6th Cir Mich 1992), cert granted ___ US ___, 113 SCt 2291, 125 LEd(2d) 686 (1993), cert dismissed ___ US ___, 114 SCt 22, 125 LEd(2d) 773 (1993); Johnson v Honeywell Information Systems, Inc, 955 F(2d) 409 (6th Cir Mich 1992).

[39] 42 USCA 2000e-5(k).

[40] Christiansburg Garment Co v EEOC, 434 US 412, 98 SCt 694, 54 LEd(2d) 648 (1978). The Supreme Court has also ruled that a prevailing party is entitled to recover fees from an "intervenor" in a Title VII case only if the intervenor's action was frivolous, unreasonable, or without foundation. Independent Federation of Flight Attendants v Zipes, 491 US 754, 109 SCt 2732, 105 LEd(2d) 639 (1989).

[41] New York Gaslight Club, Inc v Carey, 447 US 54, 100 SCt 2024, 64 LEd(2d) 723 (1980).

[42] Cooper v Williamson County Bd of Ed, 820 F(2d) 180 (6th Cir Tenn 1987), cert denied 484 US 1006, 108 SCt 699, 98 LEd(2d) 651 (1988).

[43] McDonnell Douglas Corp v Green, 411 US 792, 93 SCt 1817, 36 LEd(2d) 668 (1973).

[44] Texas Dept of Community Affairs v Burdine, 450 US 248, 101 SCt 1089, 67 LEd(2d) 207 (1981). See also United Postal Service v Aikens, 460 US 711, 103 SCt 1478, 75 LEd(2d) 403 (1983) (reaffirming the *McDonnell-Burdine* standards).

evidence which, if unexplained, is sufficient to show it is more likely than not that the employer unlawfully discriminated against him. If the plaintiff succeeds, the burden of going forward then shifts to the employer, who must be given the opportunity to respond by "articulating some legitimate, non-discriminatory reason" for the challenged employment decision or condition. If the employer does proffer such a reason, the presumption of discrimination drops out of the picture. Then, the plaintiff may attempt to show that any reason advanced by the employer is a sham or pretext for discrimination. Even if every one of the employer's proffered reasons is discredited, however, it does not automatically follow that the plaintiff prevails, for the ultimate burden of proving discrimination rests at all times with the plaintiff.[45] 42 USCA 2000e-2(R), enacted as an amendment to Title VII in 1991, expressly declares that demonstrating an employment practice is required by business necessity is not a defense to intentional discrimination. Many federal court decisions apply the *McDonnell-Burdine* standards to employment discrimination actions against school districts.[46]

With respect to mixed-motive cases, where the employer has considered both discriminatory and nondiscriminatory factors in making an employment decision, 1991 amendments to Title VII significantly alter the rules established in 1989 by the US Supreme Court in *Price Waterhouse v Hopkins*,[47] 42 USCA 2000e-2(m) states that unlawful discrimination exists whenever a plaintiff demonstrates that race, color, religion, sex, or national origin was "a motivating factor for any employment practice, even though other factors also motivated the practice." However, 42 USCA 2000e-2(g) states that if the employer in such a case demonstrates the same action would have been taken in the absence of the impermissible motivating factor, the employer is exposed only to declaratory and injunctive relief, costs and fees "directly attributable only to the pursuit of a claim under section 2000e-(2)(m)" and the court is expressly barred from awarding damages or ordering "any admission, reinstatement, hiring, promotion, or payment" by way of remedy.[48]

The *McDonnell-Burdine* standards still apply without modification to disparate treatment cases other than mixed-motive cases.

(2) Disparate impact cases

The allocation and burdens of proof are significantly different in a disparate impact case. Here, 42 USCA 2000e-2(k), enacted as an amendment to Title VII in 1991 and legislatively overruling *Wards Cove Packing Co v Atonio*,[49] governs. The plaintiff must demonstrate an employer's particular employment practice causes a disparate impact on the basis of race, color, religion, sex, or national origin. The burden then shifts to the employer to prove the challenged practice is both job-related for the position in question and consistent with business necessity, phraseology lifted from the Americans with Disabilities Act of 1990.[50] If the employer can show the specific employment practice does not cause the disparate impact, that the practice is required by business necessity need not

---

[45]St. Mary's Honor Center v Hicks, ___ US ___, 113 SCt 2742, 125 LEd(2d) 407 (1993). The Court went on to explain that, while rejection of the employer's proffered reasons is a relevant factor that might, together with the elements of a prima facie case, permit an inference of discrimination, such rejection does not ipso facto compel a finding of discrimination. For an example of a plaintiff's failure to meet his ultimate burden of persuasion under *Hicks*, arising in the context of a reverse discrimination claim by a white principal who was fired, see Pilditch v Chicago Bd of Ed, 3 F(3d) 1113 (7th Cir Ill 1993), cert denied sub nom Pilditch v Gool, ___ US ___, 114 SCt 1065, 127 LEd(2d) 385 (1994).

[46]E.g., Farber v Massillon Bd of Ed, 917 F(2d) 1391 (6th Cir Ohio 1990), cert denied 501 US 1230, 111 SCt 2851, 115 LEd(2d) 1019 (1991); Daniels v Ravenna City School Dist Bd of Ed, 805 F(2d) 203 (6th Cir Ohio 1986); Lujan v Franklin County Bd of Ed, 766 F(2d) 917 (6th Cir Tenn 1985).

[47]Price Waterhouse v Hopkins, 490 US 228, 109 SCt 1775, 104 LEd(2d) 268 (1989).

[48]The Ohio Supreme Court currently follows *Price Waterhouse* in construing and applying Ohio's Fair Employment Practices Act. Cleveland Civil Service Comm v Ohio Civil Rights Comm, 57 OS(3d) 62, 565 NE(2d) 579 (1991).

[49]Wards Cove Packing Co v Atonio, 490 US 642, 109 SCt 2115, 104 LEd(2d) 733 (1989), judgment affirmed in part, reversed in part by 10 F(3d) 1485 (9th Cir Wash 1993), cert denied ___ US ___, 115 SCt 57, 130 LEd(2d) 16 (1994).

[50]See Text 17.13(B), Americans with Disabilities Act of 1990.

also be shown. The plaintiff can rebut the employer's defense by demonstrating the existence of an alternative employment practice that would fulfill the employer's interest without causing a disparate impact and the employer's refusal to adopt such an alternative employment practice. 42 USCA 2000e-2(k) goes on to declare that an employer's rule barring the employment of one who currently and knowingly uses or possesses a controlled substance (except when the substance is medically or otherwise authorized) cannot be challenged on a disparate impact theory, but may be challenged if adopted or applied with an intent to discriminate.

Although disparate impact cases typically involve objective selection procedures, such as standardized tests, this need not be the case. The Supreme Court has recognized adverse impact analysis may also apply to subjective procedures, such as committing promotion decisions to the subjective discretion of supervisors.[51] The standards of proof remain the same, although, as the Court acknowledged, employers as a practical matter have an easier time defending subjective selection criteria.

Where the work force is predominantly white, a school district's heavy reliance on nepotism and word-of-mouth hiring that operates to exclude outsiders may be found violative of Title VII on a disparate impact theory.[52]

(3) Pattern or practice cases

In so-called "pattern or practice" cases under Title VII, the plaintiff bears the initial burden of establishing that discrimination was the employer's standard operating procedure.[53] Although these cases are a variant of disparate treatment and proof of discriminatory motive is critical, the plaintiff's initial showing shifts the burden of proof to the employer to demonstrate that each hiring or promotion decision was not due to the discriminatory policy but to some other, legitimate consideration.[54]

A leading hiring discrimination case is *Hazelwood School Dist v United States*,[55] a pattern or practice suit that alleged a large, suburban St. Louis school district had discriminated against black applicants for teaching positions. The district's hiring practices consisted principally of interviews and other relatively unstructured procedures. The district had not conducted on-site recruiting interviews at either of the state's two predominantly black four-year colleges. Less than 2 per cent of teachers were black, whereas 15.4 per cent of all teachers employed in the area were black. Such evidence, the court of appeals had concluded, supported allegations that the district had engaged in a pattern or practice of discrimination. However, the Supreme Court reversed because the lower court failed to consider that the statistical disparity between the district's staff and the number of teachers in the area may not have been the proper comparison to make in evaluating hiring practices, and because any statistical disparity between the staff and the percentage of black teachers available in the relevant job market might be explained by pre-1972 practices that ended prior to the extension of Title VII to public employers.

(4) Statistical evidence

Whether the claim proceeds on a theory of disparate treatment, disparate impact, or pattern or practice, statistics are frequently used as evidence to prove or disprove discrimination.[56] They must be based on a sufficiently large sample for the results to be meaningful; the group selected for analysis must be appropriate in light of the proposition for which the statistical evidence is offered.[57] In analyzing an employer's hiring practices in a case of alleged racial discrimination, for example, the proper comparison is between the racial composition of

---

[51]Watson v Fort Worth Bank and Trust, 487 US 977, 108 SCt 2777, 101 LEd(2d) 827 (1988).

[52]Thomas v Washington County School Bd, 915 F(2d) 922 (4th Cir Va 1990).

[53]International Brotherhood of Teamsters v United States, 431 US 324, 97 SCt 1843, 52 LEd(2d) 396 (1977).

[54]International Brotherhood of Teamsters v United States, 431 US 324, 97 SCt 1843, 52 LEd(2d) 396 (1977); Craik v Minnesota State University Board, 731 F(2d) 465 (8th Cir Minn 1984).

[55]Hazelwood School Dist v United States, 433 US 299, 97 SCt 2736, 53 LEd(2d) 768 (1977).

[56]See, e.g., Simpson v Midland-Ross Corp, 823 F(2d) 937 (6th Cir Mich 1987); Lujan v Franklin County Bd of Ed, 766 F(2d) 917 (6th Cir Tenn 1985).

[57]Grano v Columbus Department of Development, 637 F(2d) 1073 (6th Cir Ohio 1980).

qualified persons in the relevant labor market with the racial composition of the persons holding the jobs at issue.[58]

(G) Pursuing state and federal remedies

Initial resort to state administrative remedies for civil rights claims does not deprive an individual of a right to trial in federal court on a Title VII claim. However, a state court judgment in an employment discrimination case will foreclose a Title VII action based on the same claim if the state proceeding afforded a full and fair opportunity to litigate the discrimination claim and the judgment would, under state law, preclude relitigating the claim in state court.[59]

17.04 Ohio Fair Employment Practices Act

(A) Race, color, religion, sex, national origin, handicap, age, or ancestry

The Ohio Fair Employment Practices Act, RC Chapter 4112, is the principal state equal employment opportunity law. RC 4112.02(A) makes it unlawful for "any employer, because of the race, color, religion, sex, national origin, handicap, age, or ancestry of any person, to discharge without just cause, to refuse to hire or otherwise to discriminate against that person with respect to hire, tenure, terms, conditions or privileges of employment, or any matter directly or indirectly related to employment." Retaliation against any person who files a charge or assists in an investigation is also prohibited.[60]

RC 4112.01(A)(2) defines "employer" to include boards of education. However, "employer" does not include, for purposes of individual liability, board members. Actions under RC Chapter 4112 should be brought against the board in its corporate capacity.[61]

(B) Parallels between Ohio and federal law

Both substantively and procedurally, RC Chapter 4112 parallels Title VII in many ways, and the Ohio Supreme Court has held that federal case law interpreting Title VII is generally applicable to cases alleging violations of RC Chapter 4112.[62]

A glaring inconsistency between the federal and state schemes was created in 1991, however, when the Ohio Supreme Court construing RC 4112.99, concluded, in a 4-3 decision, that administrative remedies need *not* be exhausted before bringing suit in state court for alleged discrimination in violation of RC Chapter 4112.[63] Thus, a victim of discrimination may opt under state law either to sue the employer in the first instance or to pursue administrative relief by first filing a charge with the Ohio Civil Rights Commission.[64] A jury trial in an action under RC 4122.99 may be demanded.[65] The statute of limitations generally applicable to claims brought under RC 4122.99 is RC 2305.07, which provides for a six-year period,[66] but a claim of age discrimination is subject to the

---

[58]Wards Cove Packing Co v Atonio, 490 US 642, 109 SCt 2115, 104 LEd(2d) 733 (1989), judgment affirmed in part, reversed in part by 10 F(3d) 1485 (9th Cir Wash 1993), cert denied ___ US ___, 115 SCt 57, 130 LEd(2d) 16 (1994). See also Hazelwood School Dist v United States, 433 US 299, 97 SCt 2736, 53 LEd(2d) 768 (1977).

[59]Kremer v Chemical Construction Corp, 456 US 461, 102 SCt 1883, 72 LEd(2d) 262 (1982). Judicially unreviewed state administrative agency findings, however, do not preclude such suits in federal court. See Astoria Federal Savings and Loan Assn v Solimino, 501 US 104, 111 SCt 2166, 115 LEd(2d) 96 (1991).

[60]RC 4112.02(I).

[61]Sowers v Ohio Civil Rights Comm, 20 Misc 115, 252 NE(2d) 463 (CP, Trumbull 1969).

[62]Plumbers & Steamfitters Joint Apprenticeship Committee v Ohio Civil Rights Comm, 66 OS(3d) 192, 421 NE(2d) 128 (1981). See also Little Forest Medical Center of Akron v Ohio Civil Rights Comm, 61 OS(3d) 607, 575 NE(2d) 1164 (1991), cert denied 503 US 906, 112 SCt 1263, 117 LEd(2d) 491 (1992).

[63]Elek v Huntington National Bank, 60 OS(3d) 135, 573 NE(2d) 1056 (1991). Although *Elek* specifically applies to a claim of discrimination on the basis of handicap, it plainly extends to cases involving discrimination on the basis of other illegitimate criteria under RC Chapter 4112.

[64]See *id.*; Text 17.04(C), Enforcement by Ohio Civil Rights Commission (OCRC). If one opts to pursue the administrative avenue with the Ohio Civil Rights Commission, it has been held that one cannot later abandon that process in favor of switching to an independent suit pursuant to RC 4112.99, however. Gallant v Toledo Public Schools, 84 App(3d) 378, 616 NE(2d) 1156 (Lucas 1992).

[65]Taylor v National Group of Companies, Inc, 65 OS(3d) 482, 605 NE(2d) 45 (1992).

[66]Cosgrove v Williamsburg of Cincinnati Management Co, Inc, 70 OS(3d) 281, 638 NE(2d) 991 (1994).

180-day limitations period that appears in RC 4112.02(N).[67]

Distinctions between the Ohio and federal schemes also exist with respect to remedies.[68]

(C) Enforcement by Ohio Civil Rights Commission (OCRC)

If one does not proceed directly to court under RC 4112.99, RC 4112.05 authorizes initiation of a proceeding by filing a timely[69] discrimination charge with the OCRC. An individual who files a charge with the EEOC may have the charge referred to the OCRC by that agency. The OCRC then investigates the charge and makes a finding of "probable cause" or "no probable cause." The OCRC has discretion in determining whether an investigation must be made. Likewise, the OCRC has discretion as to whether to issue a complaint after investigation.[70] A finding of "no probable cause" will not be second-guessed by a court unless the OCRC decision is irrational, unlawful, arbitrary, or capricious.[71]

If the OCRC finds "probable cause," it must attempt to settle the matter by negotiating a conciliation agreement. If conciliation is unsuccessful, the OCRC issues a complaint, and the employer is required to defend in a formal administrative hearing conducted in accordance with RC 4112.05 and applicable OCRC rules.[72] Such complaints must be filed within one year after the complainant files a charge,[73] and a writ of prohibition will issue to prevent the OCRC from proceeding on a complaint which is not filed within the required time period.[74] However, a writ will not issue when an employer seeks to stop an OCRC hearing merely because of alleged irregularities in the conciliation and investigation process.[75]

Under OCRC rules, after considering all sworn testimony and other evidence presented, the hearing examiner submits written findings of fact, conclusions of law, and a recommended decision to the full commission, which then may approve, disapprove or modify the recommendation.[76]

At all stages of court and administrative proceedings, the attorney general represents the complainant, except in court proceedings where the complainant is challenging an adverse OCRC decision.[77] Because of the attorney general's representation there is no statutory provision for attorney fees, although the complainant may be represented by his own counsel.

(D) Remedies

Authorized remedies for violations include requiring the employer to cease and desist from unlawful discriminatory practices and taking such further affirmative action as will effectuate the purposes of RC Chapter 4112, including, but not limited to, hiring, reinstatement or upgrading of employees, with or without back pay, less allowance for interim earnings.[78] The OCRC cannot award compensatory or

---

[67] Bellian v Bicron Corp, 69 OS(3d) 517, 634 NE(2d) 608 (1994).

[68] Compare Text 17.03(E), Actions, remedies, with Text 17.04(D), Remedies.

[69] The charge must be filed with the OCRC within six months after the alleged unlawful discriminatory practice is committed. RC 4112.05(B). Where the limited contract of a teaching or nonteaching employee is not renewed, the limitations period begins to run from the date the contract expires and employment terminates, not the date on which the board of education votes not to renew or gives notice of its intent not to renew. Lordstown Local School Dist Bd of Ed v Ohio Civil Rights Comm, 66 OS(2d) 252, 421 NE(2d) 511 (1981).

[70] State ex rel Westbrook v Ohio Civil Rights Comm, 17 OS(3d) 215, 17 OBR 452, 478 NE(2d) 799 (1985).

[71] McCrea v Ohio Civil Rights Comm, 20 App(3d) 314, 20 OBR 416, 486 NE(2d) 143 (Summit 1984); Mason v US Fidelity & Guaranty Co, 37 App(3d) 22, 523 NE(2d) 344 (Hamilton 1987).

[72] OAC 4112-3-09.

[73] RC 4112.05(B).

[74] State ex rel General Motors Corp v Ohio Civil Rights Comm, 50 OS(2d) 111, 362 NE(2d) 1221 (1977); State ex rel Republic Steel Corp v Ohio Civil Rights Comm, 44 OS(2d) 178, 339 NE(2d) 658 (1975).

[75] State ex rel State Farm Mutual Automobile Insurance Co v Ohio Civil Rights Comm, 6 OS(3d) 426, 6 OBR 471, 453 NE(2d) 601 (1983).

[76] OAC 4112-3-09.

[77] RC 4112.05(G).

[78] RC 4112.05(G). Where the amount of back pay that would have been received by the victim but for the unlawful discrimination is unclear, ambiguities are resolved against the discriminating employer. Any unemployment compensation benefits the victim may have received are not deducted from the back pay award. An award also generally includes prejudgment

punitive damages[79] or make orders of restitution.[80]

Public employees may not sue an employer to redress alleged violations of the Ohio Constitution where other reasonably satisfactory remedies are provided by statute; thus, the constitutional claim of a teacher who alleged she was disciplined for criticizing her employer's practices and for having filed discrimination charges with the OCRC and the EEOC was dismissed in *Provens v Stark County Bd of Mental Retardation and Developmental Disabilities*.[81]

(E) Appeals, standards of review

The OCRC's final order is subject to judicial review, but the findings of fact, if supported by reliable, probative, and substantial evidence, must be affirmed.[82]

Affirming that federal case law under Title VII also applies to alleged violations of RC Chapter 4112, the Ohio Supreme Court has held that an OCRC decision against an employer must be reversed when it is not supported by "reliable, probative and substantial evidence ... sufficient to support a finding of discrimination under Title VII."[83] The Court specifically approved and followed the US Supreme Court's formulation of the Title VII standard and burden of proof in *Texas Dept of Community Affairs v Burdine*.[84] Further, while a reviewing court must give "due deference" to the OCRC's resolution of evidentiary conflicts, such deference "does not contemplate uncritical acquiescence to administrative findings," and an OCRC decision must be reversed if it is based on "inferences improperly drawn from the evidence adduced."[85] However, OCRC findings are not to be upset merely because different inferences *could* have been drawn from disputed evidence.[86]

An OCRC order may be judicially enforced, modified, or set aside in whole or in part based on the record or the record and such additional evidence as the court may admit.[87]

---

interest calculated from the point of discrimination. Ohio Civil Rights Comm v Ingram, 69 OS(3d) 89, 630 NE(2d) 669 (1994). As to prejudgment interest, however, recovery against a public employer, such as an Ohio school district, is presumably not permitted. The Ohio Supreme Court has held that boards of education generally are not liable for prejudgment interest absent a statute or explicit contractual provision requiring such payment. State ex rel Brown v Milton-Union Exempted Village Bd of Ed, 40 OS(3d) 21, 531 NE(2d) 1297 (1988); Beifuss v Westerville Bd of Ed, 37 OS(3d) 187, 525 NE(2d) 20 (1988).

[79]Ohio Civil Rights Comm v Lysyj, 38 OS(2d) 217, 313 NE(2d) 3 (1974), cert denied 419 US 1108, 95 SCt 780, 42 LEd(2d) 804 (1975).

[80]Jackson v Ohio Civil Rights Comm, 50 App(3d) 13, 552 NE(2d) 237 (Cuyahoga 1989).

[81]Provens v Stark County Bd of Mental Retardation and Developmental Disabilities, 64 OS(3d) 252, 594 NE(2d) 959 (1992).

[82]RC 4112.06(E). The time limit for instituting judicial review is thirty days. RC 4112.06(H). See also Ramsdell v Ohio Civil Rights Comm, 56 OS(3d) 24, 563 NE(2d) 285 (1990) (statutory thirty-day period not extended by Ohio Rules of Civil Procedure).

[83]Plumbers & Steamfitters Joint Apprenticeship Committee v Ohio Civil Rights Comm, 66 OS(2d) 192, 421 NE(2d) 128 (1981).

[84]Texas Dept of Community Affairs v Burdine, 450 US 248, 101 SCt 1089, 67 LEd(2d) 207 (1981). See also Keene State College Bd of Trustees v Sweeney, 439 US 24, 99 SCt 295, 58 LEd(2d) 216 (1978); Furnco Construction Corp v Waters, 438 US 567, 98 SCt 2943, 57 LEd(2d) 957 (1978); McDonnell Douglas Corp v Green, 411 US 792, 93 SCt 1817, 36 LEd(2d) 668 (1973). For subsequent modification of the *Burdine* standards in mixed-motive cases, see Text 17.03(F)(1), Disparate treatment cases.

[85]Plumbers & Steamfitters Joint Apprenticeship Committee v Ohio Civil Rights Comm, 66 OS(2d) 192, 200, 421 NE(2d) 128 (1981). Also, an Ohio appeals court, reversing an OCRC decision, held that a board of education did not violate RC 4112.02 by refusing to hire a female teaching applicant because substantial evidence established that the board had legitimate nondiscriminatory reasons for preferring two male applicants and that the OCRC failed to establish these reasons were pretextual. Port Clinton City Schools v Ohio Civil Rights Comm, No. OT-80-5, 1981 WL 4225 (6th Dist Ct App, Ottawa, 11-4-80). See also Twinsburg City Schools v OCRC, No. 15651, 1993 WL 325489 (9th Dist Ct App, Summit, 2-24-93) (OCRC finding of age discrimination in refusal to hire applicant for teaching position not supported by the evidence).

[86]T. Marzetti Co v Doyle, 37 App(3d) 25, 523 NE(2d) 347 (Franklin 1987).

[87]RC 4112.06(A). See Ohio Civil Rights Comm v Ingram, 69 OS(3d) 89, 630 NE(2d) 669 (1994).

17.05 Antidiscrimination requirements for contractors dealing with schools

(A) Mandatory contract provisions

RC 125.111(A) provides that every contract for or on behalf of a school district for any purchase must contain the following equal opportunity provisions:

(1) In the hiring of employees to perform work under the contract or subcontract, no contractor shall, by reason of race, color, religion, sex, age, handicap, national origin, or ancestry, discriminate against any citizen of this state in the employment of a person qualified and available to do the work specified in the contract; and

(2) No contractor, subcontractor, or any person acting on behalf of any contractor or subcontractor shall, in any manner, discriminate against, intimidate, or retaliate against any employee hired to work under the contract on account of race, color, religion, sex, age, handicap, national origin, or ancestry.

(B) Affirmative action by contractors

All contractors from whom the district makes purchases must have a written affirmative action program for the employment and utilization of economically disadvantaged persons.[88]

PARTICULAR APPLICATIONS

17.06 Age discrimination

(A) Alternative procedures

An employee claiming age discrimination in connection with employment has five options. The federal Age Discrimination in Employment Act (ADEA)[89] prohibits discrimination on the basis of age by school districts with more than twenty employees.[90] It protects persons age forty and over and provides for a civil suit in federal court.[91] Double damages may be recovered in cases of willful violations.[92] Suit may not be brought until a charge has been filed with the OCRC.[93] This prerequisite is met, however, even though the filing with the OCRC is not timely under Ohio law.[94]

Under Ohio law, an employee claiming age discrimination may elect to file suit directly in common pleas court under RC 4101.17. There is no right to a jury trial under this statute.[95] Also, the statute expressly does not apply to employment decisions which can be challenged through a binding arbitration procedure. RC Chapter 4112 has three remedies for age discrimination. Under RC 4112.05, one may file a charge with the OCRC, which will process the charge administratively the same as other discrimination charges.[96] Under RC 4112.02(N), an employee may bypass the administrative procedure and proceed directly to court. The administrative procedure may also be bypassed in favor of a direct suit under RC 4112.99.[97]

At least some, if not all, of these state remedies—which represent a clear and senseless example of legislative overkill and have aptly been described as "creating a legal hall of mirrors"[98]—are mutually exclusive. Filing a charge under RC 4112.05 bars a civil action under RC 4112.02(N) or RC 4101.17.[99] Filing an action under RC 4112.02(N) bars an action under RC 4101.17 or administrative proceedings under RC 4112.05.[100] Likewise,

---

[88] RC 125.111(B).

[89] 29 USCA 621 et seq.

[90] 29 USCA 623(a), 29 USCA 630(b); Kelly v Wauconda Park Dist, 801 F(2d) 269 (7th Cir Ill 1986), cert denied 480 US 940, 107 SCt 1592, 94 LEd(2d) 781 (1987).

[91] 29 USCA 626, 29 USCA 631(a).

[92] 29 USCA 626(b). See also Hazen Paper Co v Biggins, 507 US ___, 113 SCt 1701, 123 LEd(2d) 338 (1993); Lee v Rapid City Area School Dist No. 51-4, 981 F(2d) 316 (8th Cir SD 1992).

[93] 29 USCA 626(d), 29 USCA 633(b); Piecuch v Gulf & Western Mfg Co, 626 FSupp 65 (ND Ohio 1985).

[94] Oscar Mayer & Co v Evans, 441 US 750, 99 SCt 2066, 60 LEd(2d) 609 (1979).

[95] Hoops v United Telephone Co of Ohio, 50 OS(3d) 97, 553 NE(2d) 252 (1990).

[96] See Text 17.04, Ohio Fair Employment Practices Act.

[97] See Elek v Huntington National Bank, 60 OS(3d) 135, 573 NE(2d) 1056 (1991); Bellian v Bicron Corp, 69 OS(3d) 517, 634 NE(2d) 608 (1994).

[98] Balent v National Revenue Corp, 93 App(3d) 419, 421, 638 NE(2d) 1064 (Franklin 1994).

[99] RC 4112.08.

[100] RC 4112.02(N).

filing suit under RC 4101.17 bars a suit under RC 4112.02(N) or administrative processing under RC 4112.05.[101] Pursuing a charge before the OCRC bars a suit under RC 4112.99.[102] Finally, a decision in a federal ADEA case is res judicata as to a state law age discrimination claim arising out of the same circumstances.[103]

A claimant who has previously filed an age discrimination action under RC 4101.17, however, is not barred from filing a claim with the OCRC pursuant to RC 4112.05 to satisfy the federal ADEA's mandatory requirement.

The statute of limitations applicable to age discrimination claims brought under RC 4101.17 is the six-year period in RC 2305.07.[104] Claims under RC Chapter 4112 must be brought within 180 days.[105] Claims under the ADEA must be brought within ninety days after receipt of a right-to-sue notice from the EEOC.[106] Under RC 4112.02(N), a cause of action for age discrimination accrues when the discriminatory practice occurs, not when the adverse consequences manifest themselves.[107]

(B) Proof of discrimination

Regardless of which avenue is chosen, federal case law developed under the ADEA generally applies.[108] Absent direct evidence of age discrimination, to establish a prima facie case, a plaintiff must prove that he was a member of the statutorily protected class (over age forty); that he was discharged, not hired for a vacancy, or otherwise subjected to an adverse employment action; that he was qualified for the position; and that he was replaced by, or that his discharge permitted the retention of, a person not belonging to the protected class. The employer may rebut this prima facie case by propounding a legitimate, nondiscriminatory reason for its action, after which the plaintiff must be allowed to show that the employer's rationale was only a pretext for unlawful discrimination. Within the context of RC 4101.17, "just cause" for a discharge is established if plaintiff was terminated for reasons other than those explicitly prohibited by the statute.[109]

ADEA violations generally are established under a disparate treatment theory. A 1993 US Supreme Court case questioned, but expressly declined to decide, whether disparate impact theory can ever apply to an ADEA action,[110] and one appellate court has since held that it should not apply.[111]

In disparate treatment cases, an isolated remark by a supervisor to the effect that "younger blood" is needed will not of itself

---

[101] RC 4101.17(B). See also Giambrone v Spalding and Evenflo Co, 79 App(3d) 308, 607 NE(2d) 106 (Miami 1992) (recognizing that RC 4112.02(N) and RC 4101.17 require an election between the two statutes but finding that dismissal of entire claim where a plaintiff filed simultaneously under both was improper; also finding that one must elect between pursuing claim under RC 4112.02(N) and RC 4112.99).

[102] Balent v National Revenue Corp, 93 App(3d) 419, 638 NE(2d) 1064 (Franklin 1994) (recognizing, however, that the cases are not consistent, while ultimately declaring that the legislature intended "to require an election of a single administrative or statutory remedy when bringing a claim for age discrimination").

[103] Borowski v State Chemical Mfg Co, 97 App(3d) 635, 647 NE(2d) 230 (Cuyahoga 1994).

[104] Morris v Kaiser Engineers, Inc, 14 OS(3d) 45, 14 OBR 440, 471 NE(2d) 471 (1984).

[105] RC 4112.02(N). See also Bellian v Bicron Corp, 69 OS(3d) 517, 634 NE(2d) 608 (1994) (applying RC 4112.02(N)'s 180-day limitations period even where suit is brought under RC 4112.99).

[106] 29 USCA 626(e).

[107] Morris v Kaiser Engineers, Inc, 14 OS(3d) 45, 14 OBR 440, 471 NE(2d) 471 (1984).

[108] Kohmescher v Kroger Co, 61 OS(3d) 501, 575 NE(2d) 439 (1991). See also Barker v Scovill, Inc, 6 OS(3d) 146, 6 OBR 202, 451 NE(2d) 807 (1983).

[109] Kohmescher v Kroger Co, 61 OS(3d) 501, 575 NE(2d) 439 (1991). See also Barker v Scovill, Inc, 6 OS(3d) 146, 6 OBR 202, 451 NE(2d) 807 (1983).

[110] Hazen Paper Co v Biggins, 507 US ___, 113 SCt 1701, 123 LEd(2d) 338 (1993).

[111] EEOC v Francis W. Parker School, 41 F(3d) 1073 (7th Cir Ill 1994), cert denied 515 US ___, 115 SCt 2577, 132 LEd(2d) 828 (1995), rejecting application of disparate impact theory and holding that a school district lawfully refused to interview teachers for a position if their experience would require paying them more than $28,000 per year, even though this practice clearly had a disparate impact on older applicants. Compare Lowe v Commack Union Free School Dist, 886 F(2d) 1364 (2d Cir NY 1989), cert denied 494 US 1026, 110 SCt 1470, 108 LEd(2d) 608 (1990), and Geller v Markham, 635 F(2d) 1027 (2d Cir Conn 1980), cert denied 451 US 945, 101 SCt 2028, 68 LEd(2d) 332 (1981), two pre-*Hazen* cases in which the courts recognized the possibility that a teacher applicant could prove age discrimination on an impact theory.

support a finding of discrimination or move the case into the "mixed-motive" category under which the burden of proof shifts to the employer to show its decision was not the product of discriminatory factors.[112] Calling one "overqualified" for a new position after one's former position has been eliminated may be viewed as a pretext that masks underlying age discrimination.[113] An employer's policy of not hiring college graduates for certain positions has withstood a claim of pretext.[114] On the other hand, the discharge of a long-time bus driver with an exemplary work record ostensibly for a two-year old minor traffic violation was pretextual.[115]

In the context of a work force reduction, a showing that one is forty or older, qualified for the job, and dismissed is not enough. There must be additional direct, circumstantial, or statistical evidence tending to indicate the employer singled one out for impermissible reasons, even if younger people were kept in other jobs the employee could have performed.[116]

An employer may base employment decisions on a facially neutral criteria, such as seniority or compensation level, even though such criteria tend to correllate with age.[117] Thus, a school district does not violate the ADEA if it interviews only applicants with relatively little experience because they are less expensive, even though this practice may disqualify most older applicants.[118] A board policy that limits salary schedule credit for years of teaching experience that occurred more than ten years ago, thus giving recent teaching experience more value, does not automatically violate the ADEA.[119]

Even if an employer has a practice of paying "market rates" to newly hired faculty but not to others, and this practice has a disparate impact on older faculty members, age discrimination will not be found if the school has a legitimate business justification for the practice, such as a need to pay such rates to attract and hire good new teachers.[120]

The bona fide occupational qualification exception (29 USCA 623(f)(1)) to the ADEA is extremely narrow and is a defense that must be affirmatively asserted and proved by an employer.[121]

(C) Retirement

(1) Mandatory retirement prohibited

The ADEA and Ohio antidiscrimination laws[122] prohibit mandatory retirement at any age. Whether mandatory retirement policies that can show that age is either a bona fide occupational qualification[123] or is rationally related to the achievement of a legitimate purpose[124] are valid remains to be seen.

Where an employee retires for a legitimate reason but is forced by the employer into a less desirable retirement plan (in this case, length of service as opposed to disability retirement), the ADEA is violated.[125]

---

[112] Gagne v Northwestern National Ins Co, 881 F(2d) 309 (6th Cir Ohio 1989). For additional discussion of mixed-motive cases, see Text 17.03(F), Proof of discrimination.

[113] Taggart v Time, Inc, 924 F(2d) 43 (2d Cir NY 1991).

[114] Stein v National City Bank, 942 F(2d) 1062 (6th Cir Ohio 1991).

[115] Hudson v Normandy School Dist, 953 F(2d) 410 (8th Cir Mo 1992) (also holding, however, that violation was not willful; hence, double damages not allowed).

[116] Barnes v GenCorp, Inc, 896 F(2d) 1457 (6th Cir Ohio 1990), cert denied 498 US 878, 111 SCt 211, 112 LEd(2d) 171 (1990). See also Murphy v East Akron Community House, 56 App(3d) 54, 564 NE(2d) 742 (Summit 1989).

[117] Hazen Paper Co v Biggins, 507 US ___, 113 SCt 1701, 123 LEd(2d) 338 (1993).

[118] EEOC v Francis W. Parker School, 41 F(3d) 1073 (7th Cir Ill 1994), cert denied 515 US ___, 115 SCt 2577, 132 LEd(2d) 828 (1995); EEOC v Atlantic Community School Dist, 879 F(2d) 434 (8th Cir Iowa 1989).

[119] Wooden v Jefferson County, Kentucky Bd of Ed, 931 F(2d) 376 (6th Cir Ky 1991).

[120] MacPherson v University of Montevallo, 922 F(2d) 766 (11th Cir Ala 1991).

[121] Tullis v Lear School, Inc, 874 F(2d) 1489 (11th Cir Fla 1989). See generally Western Air Lines, Inc v Criswell, 472 US 400, 105 SCt 2743, 86 LEd(2d) 321 (1985).

[122] 29 USCA 623; RC 4101.17, RC 4112.01, RC 4112.02.

[123] Johnson v Mayor of Baltimore, 472 US 353, 105 SCt 2717, 86 LEd(2d) 286 (1985).

[124] Vance v Bradley, 440 US 93, 99 SCt 939, 59 LEd(2d) 171 (1979).

[125] Betts v Hamilton County Bd of Mental Retardation and Developmental Disabilities, 897 F(2d) 1380 (6th Cir Ohio 1990), cert denied sub nom Public

(2) Discriminatory mortality tables

The US Supreme Court has held that use of sex-segregated mortality tables in structuring retirement benefits violates Title VII where it results in payment of lower monthly benefits to women than to men who make the same contributions.[126]

17.07 Hiring and promotion practices

(A) In general: disparate impact

Employee selection procedures, that is, the methods and criteria used to recruit and select persons for hiring and promotion, have been a major focus of employment discrimination litigation in both the public and private sectors.

In *Griggs v Duke Power Co*,[127] the US Supreme Court first used what has come to be known as the "disparate impact" theory of establishing Title VII violations in selection procedure cases. Specifically, the Court held that Title VII prohibits an employer from requiring employees to acquire a high school education or pass a standardized general intelligence test as a condition of assignment to jobs when both requirements operated to disqualify blacks at a substantially higher rate than whites, and neither standard was shown to be significantly related to successful job performance. Under this theory, an employment practice may be unlawful in the absence of intentional discrimination if it adversely affects members of a protected group.

Title VII, as amended in 1991, expressly outlaws the practice of "race-norming" employment-related tests (that is, applicants or candidates effectively compete only against members of their own race) in connection with the selection or referral of applicants or candidates for employment or promotion. Specifically, adjusting the scores of, using different cutoff scores for, or otherwise altering the results of such tests on the basis of race, color, religion, sex, or national origin is prohibited.[128]

(B) Uniform Guidelines on Employee Selection

Building on *Griggs*, the EEOC and other federal agencies have developed detailed Uniform Guidelines on Employee Selection Procedures (UGESP).[129] The Guidelines provide for evaluating an employer's selection process and individual components to determine whether the process or its components have a statistically significant adverse impact on blacks, females, and members of other protected groups. When feasible, policies which have an adverse impact must be justified as substantially job related by validation studies, which must be conducted in accordance with professionally accepted standards as prescribed by the Guidelines. The OCRC also has promulgated rules governing Employee Selection Procedures, which are generally consistent with the UGESP.[130]

17.08 Equal pay

Several statutes, with various remedial provisions, prohibit discrimination in connection with employee pay rates.

(A) In general

The Equal Pay Act of 1963 amended the Fair Labor Standards Act (FLSA)[131] and prohibits paying female employees a lower wage than male employees for performing work which is equal in skill, effort, and responsibility and is performed under similar working conditions, unless the wage differential is based on a seniority system, a merit system, a system measuring quantity and quality of production, or some factor other than sex. Once a plaintiff establishes a difference in wages paid to male and female employees for equal work within the meaning of the first part of the statute, the burden of proof then shifts to the employer to show justification for the differential on the basis of one or more of the four affirmative defenses appearing in the

---

Employees Retirement System of Ohio v Betts, 498 US 963, 111 SCt 397, 112 LEd(2d) 407 (1990).
[126]Arizona Governing Committee for Tax Deferred Annuity & Deferred Compensation Plans v Norris, 463 US 1073, 103 SCt 3492, 77 LEd(2d) 1236 (1983).

[127]Griggs v Duke Power Co, 401 US 424, 91 SCt 849, 28 LEd(2d) 158 (1971).
[128]42 USCA 2000e-2(l).
[129]29 CFR Part 1607.
[130]OAC 4112-5-03.
[131]29 USCA 206(d).

second part.[132] The Equal Pay Act was made applicable to public employers in 1974, and a subsequent Supreme Court decision validating extension of the minimum wage and overtime provisions of the FLSA to state and local government employees[133] effectively removes any doubt about the constitutionality of its application. A violation of the Equal Pay Act is also a violation of Title VII of the Civil Rights Act of 1964.[134]

In Ohio, RC 4111.17 substantially duplicates the Equal Pay Act's prohibition of wage rate sex discrimination and goes further to prohibit pay rate discrimination based on race, color, religion, age, national origin, or ancestry. A differential based on a system that measures earnings by quantity or quality of production or on any factor other than those listed in the statute is legal.[135]

(B) Actions, statutes of limitations

Both the Equal Pay Act and RC 4111.17 can be enforced by individual lawsuits as well as by appropriate administrative agencies. A damage action under the federal statute must be filed within two years (three years for willful violations).[136] An action under RC 4111.17 must be filed within one year, but recovery may be had for a longer period so long as an action is filed within one year of the last date on which the wage discrimination occurred.[137] In short, ongoing discrimination tolls running of the statute.

(C) "Equal pay for equal work" and "comparable worth"

The general nondiscrimination provisions of Title VII and RC 4112.02(A) are broad enough to prohibit wage rate discrimination based on race, sex, and other grounds covered by those provisions.[138] Title VII must be construed so as to be consistent with the Equal Pay Act.[139]

Since enactment in 1963, the Equal Pay Act consistently has been construed to require equal pay for substantially equal work, but has not been extended to require that differentials in pay rates between dissimilar jobs be in proportion to the relative degrees of skill, effort, and responsibility required.

Washington County v Gunther[140] held that Title VII sex-based wage claims are not limited to the "equal pay for equal work" standard of the Equal Pay Act. Thus, female prison guards could state a claim under Title VII by showing that part of the differential between their pay and the wages of male guards was due to intentional discrimination, even though their work was not equal to the male guards' work. However, the Court held that the four Equal Pay Act defenses (seniority, merit, quantity and quality of production, and factors other than sex) are available to Title VII defendants. Further, the Court expressly declined to consider or endorse any "so-called comparable worth theory."

Neither EEOC guidelines nor other administrative regulations have been extended to cover the "comparable worth" concept.

Public school teachers' salary schedules in Ohio, uniformly based on training and experience, comply with all statutes providing for equal pay for equal work. Salaries paid to other employees or to teaching employees pursuant to extra duty contracts may be subject to scrutiny if one of two

---

[132]E.g., Mitchell v Jefferson County Bd of Ed, 936 F(2d) 539 (11th Cir Ala 1991). As to the some-factor-other-than-sex defense, it has been held that following a gender-neutral state civil service classification system may not, in and of itself, be enough; rather, the employer must show the pay differential is justified by legitimate business-related differences in work responsibilities and qualifications. Aldrich v Randolph Central School Dist, 963 F(2d) 520 (2d Cir NY 1992), cert denied ___ US ___, 113 SCt 440, 121 LEd(2d) 359 (1992).

[133]Garcia v San Antonio Metropolitan Transit Authority, 469 US 528, 105 SCt 1005, 83 LEd(2d) 1016 (1985).

[134]Korte v Diemer, 909 F(2d) 954 (6th Cir Ohio 1990).

[135]Weidemann v Village of Smithville, No. 2247, 1987 WL 15096 (9th Dist Ct App, Wayne, 7-29-87).

[136]29 USCA 216.

[137]Featzka v Millcraft Paper Co, 62 OS(2d) 245, 405 NE(2d) 264 (1980).

[138]See Text 17.03, Title VII, federal Civil Rights Act of 1964; Text 17.04, Ohio Fair Employment Practices Act.

[139]42 USCA 2000e-2(h).

[140]Washington County v Gunther, 452 US 161, 101 SCt 2242, 68 LEd(2d) 751 (1981).

similar jobs has historically been exclusively or predominantly female.

17.09 Pregnancy

(A) In general

School employees unable to work because of pregnancy, childbirth, or related medical conditions are entitled to use their accumulated sick leave under RC 3319.141, which lists pregnancy as one of several conditions for which sick leave may be used. The Family and Medical Leave Act of 1993 also entitles eligible employees to leave for the birth of a son or daughter.[141]

In 1978, Title VII was amended to specifically state that its prohibition of discrimination "because of sex" included discrimination "on the basis of pregnancy, childbirth, or related medical conditions," and to further provide that "women affected by pregnancy, childbirth, or related medical conditions shall be treated the same for all employment-related purposes, including receipt of benefits under fringe benefit programs, as other persons not so affected but similar in their ability or inability to work."[142] However, this provision does "not require an employer to pay for health insurance benefits for abortion, except where the life of the mother would be endangered if the fetus were carried to term, or except where medical complications have arisen from an abortion."[143] The Ohio Fair Employment Practices Act has also been amended to specifically provide that discrimination because of sex includes discrimination based on pregnancy, illnesses arising from or occurring during pregnancy or childbirth, and medical conditions relating to pregnancy or childbirth.[144]

The US Supreme Court has upheld a California statute that not only requires leave for employees disabled by pregnancy but goes further than the Ohio statute or Title VII by requiring employers to reinstate employees returning from leave.[145] It is therefore likely that OCRC administrative regulations that prohibit termination of an employee who is temporarily disabled due to pregnancy based on an employment policy "under which insufficient or no maternity leave is available" will be upheld.[146]

A school district's collective bargaining agreement with a union that gave female employees, but not males, an option for a one-year child-rearing leave violated Title VII's prohibition against sex discrimination. The agreement was unlawful for any leave granted beyond the period of the mother's actual physical disability on account of pregnancy, childbirth, or related medical conditions.[147]

Where a collective bargaining agreement's sick leave provisions permitted the use of sick leave for pregnancy-related disabilities but prohibited following a period of sick leave with any other form of leave when the person was not still disabled, the refusal to grant an unpaid maternity leave immediately after a mother's pregnancy-related disability for which sick leave was requested did not violate Title VII.[148]

(B) Treatment as other temporary disability

EEOC Guidelines interpret Title VII to prohibit any employment policy or practice which excludes applicants or employees from employment opportunities because of pregnancy, childbirth, or related medical conditions.[149] Further, the Guidelines state that termination because the employee is disabled due to pregnancy or related conditions is unlawful even if the employer terminates other temporarily disabled employees, when the employer's policy has a disparate impact on the females and is

---

[141]See Text 17.16, Family and Medical Leave Act of 1993.

[142]42 USCA 2000e-2(k). A federal court in Ohio has applied this nondiscrimination provision to the nonrenewal of an unwed teacher who became pregnant through artificial insemination. See Cameron v Hillsboro, Ohio, City School Dist Bd of Ed, 795 FSupp 228 (SD Ohio 1991).

[143]42 USCA 2000e-1.

[144]RC 4112.01(B).

[145]California Federal Savings & Loan Assn v Guerra, 479 US 272, 107 SCt 683, 93 LEd(2d) 613 (1987).

[146]OAC 4112-5-05(G)(2).

[147]Schafer v Pittsburgh School Dist Bd of Public Ed, 903 F(2d) 243 (3d Cir Pa 1990). See also Text 17.16, Family and Medical Leave Act of 1993.

[148]Maganuco v Leyden Community High School Dist 212, 939 F(2d) 440 (7th Cir 1991).

[149]29 CFR 1604.10.

not justified by business necessity.[150] Otherwise, the Guidelines require all employer policies, including leave policies, benefit policies, and seniority policies, to be applied to persons disabled because of pregnancy in the same manner as they are applied to other employees with temporary physical disabilities.[151] Thus, a teacher disabled because of pregnancy, childbirth, or related medical conditions is entitled to an unpaid leave of absence under RC 3319.13, because such leaves (up to two years) are available as a right to employees with other physical disabilities. However, an RC 3319.13 unpaid leave of absence for child care, when no physical disability is involved, is discretionary with the board of education, except to the extent it is required by the FMLA.[152]

(C) Commencement and duration of maternity leave

In addition to the requirements of Title VII and RC Chapter 4112, the US Supreme Court has held that the Fourteenth Amendment prohibits arbitrarily requiring pregnant teachers to begin maternity leaves without regard to the individual's physical condition, and further prohibits requiring teachers to remain on leave until the teacher's child reaches a certain age.[153] Further, a public agency sued for a violation of the Fourteenth Amendment's equal protection clause under 42 USCA 1983 may be liable for back pay to employees wrongfully terminated because of pregnancy.[154] In *Lordstown Local School Dist Bd of Ed v Ohio Civil Rights Comm*,[155] the Ohio Supreme Court affirmed an OCRC finding that the board of education violated RC 4112.02 by not renewing two teachers' limited contracts because of their pregnancies.

17.10 Nonrenewal of contract for discriminatory purpose

A board of education cannot refuse to renew a limited contract pursuant to RC 3319.11 because of the teacher's race, sex, national origin, or membership in another protected group. The same analysis applies to employee assignment, transfer, evaluation, leaves, and other areas where a board otherwise has broad authority to make discretionary decisions.[156]

In a nonrenewal case, the statute of limitations for filing a charge begins to run when the contract expires, not when the board sends the written notice required by RC 3319.11.[157]

17.11 Sexual harassment

The EEOC has promulgated specific guidelines under Title VII of the Civil Rights Act of 1964 prohibiting sexual harassment, which is defined as "[u]nwelcome sexual advances, requests for sexual favors, and other verbal or physical conduct of a sexual nature" when (1) submission to such conduct is made either explicitly or implicitly a term or condition of employment; (2) submission to or rejection of such conduct by an individual is used as the basis for employment decisions affecting the individual; or (3) such conduct has the purpose or effect of substantially interfering with an individual's work performance or creating an intimidating, hostile, or offensive working environment.[158] In essence relief for sexual harassment may be premised on one or both of two theories: (1) quid pro quo harassment (conditioning a tangible employment benefit on sexual favors), and/or (2) harassment that gives rise to a hostile

---

[150] 29 CFR 1604.10(c).
[151] 29 CFR 1604.10(b).
[152] See Text 17.16, Family and Medical Leave Act of 1993.
[153] Cleveland Bd of Ed v LaFleur, 414 US 632, 94 SCt 791, 39 LEd(2d) 52 (1974).
[154] Monell v New York City Dept of Social Services, 436 US 658, 98 SCt 2018, 56 LEd(2d) 611 (1978).
[155] Lordstown Local School Dist Bd of Ed v Ohio Civil Rights Comm, 66 OS(2d) 252, 421 NE(2d) 511 (1981).
[156] Lordstown Local School Dist Bd of Ed v Ohio Civil Rights Comm, 66 OS(2d) 252, 421 NE(2d) 511 (1981) (nonrenewals based on pregnancy); Westerville City Schools v Ohio Civil Rights Comm, 1980 WL 4646 (App, Franklin 1980) (unlawful recall from layoff of male over female employee with equal seniority because male was sole family breadwinner); Belmont-Harrison Area Joint Vocational School Dist Bd of Ed v Hoelzer, No. 86-B-19, 1987 WL 15453 (7th Dist Ct App, Belmont, 8-10-87) (nonrenewed teacher replaced by younger employee and reasons given for nonrenewal inconsistent).
[157] Lordstown Local School Dist Bd of Ed v Ohio Civil Rights Comm, 66 OS(2d) 252, 421 NE(2d) 511 (1981).
[158] 29 CFR 1604.11(a).

or abusive work environment.[159] The US Supreme Court approved the EEOC's guidelines in holding that the reach of Title VII is not restricted only to quid pro quo harassment and that unwelcome sexual advances by a supervisor could create a cognizable hostile work environment claim.[160] A victim need not suffer psychological injury in a hostile work environment case. As the Supreme Court has explained:

> [W]hether an environment is "hostile" or "abusive" can be determined only by looking at all the circumstances. These may include the frequency of the discriminatory conduct; its severity; whether it is physically threatening or humiliating, or a mere offensive utterance; and whether it unreasonably interferes with an employee's work performance. The effect on the employee's psychological well-being is, of course, relevant to determining whether the plaintiff actually found the environment abusive. But while psychological harm, like any other relevant factor, may be taken into account, no single factor is required.[161]

In evaluating the severity and pervasiveness of the harassment, some courts have adopted a "reasonable woman" standard that focuses on the perspective of the victim. The perspective of a reasonable woman as opposed to a "reasonable person" standard is premised on the belief that the latter is male-biased and tends to ignore the experiences of women.[162] Although not addressing the issue directly, the US Supreme Court, in Harris v Forklift Systems, Inc,[163] appeared to favor a "reasonable person" approach. That the matter is not yet fully resolved, however, is apparent from a subsequent decision by the US Court of Appeals for the Ninth Circuit in which Harris is discussed but the "reasonable woman" standard is reiterated and applied.[164]

The EEOC's guidelines suggest an employer should take affirmative steps to prevent sexual harassment.[165] Failure to act may lead to liability for sexual harassment by supervisors.[166] Where a supervisor exercises authority delegated by the employer to make or threaten decisions affecting the status of subordinates, the employer is liable under basic principles of agency.[167] Where the claim is based on a hostile work environment theory, whether effective procedures for dealing with sexual harassment grievances are in place is relevant to determining if the employer should be held liable.[168]

The US Court of Appeals for the Sixth Circuit, in a case involving alleged harassment by a nonsupervisory coworker, set out a five-part test for hostile work environment cases.[169] The plaintiff must show that (1) he was a member of a protected class; (2) he was subject to unwelcome harassment; (3) the harassment was based upon sex; (4) the harassment unreasonably interfered with his work performance and produced a hostile working environment; and (5) the doctrine of respondeat superior applies to create employer liability.[170]

---

[159]A lucid explanation of the two theories appears in, among other places, Karibian v Columbia University, 14 F(3d) 773 (2d Cir NY 1994), cert denied ___ US ___, 114 SCt 2693, 129 LEd(2d) 824 (1994).

[160]Meritor Savings Bank, FSB v Vinson, 477 US 57, 106 SCt 2399, 91 LEd(2d) 49 (1986). Whether sexual advances are "unwelcome" is sometimes difficult to discern. See Trautvetter v Quick, 916 F(2d) 1140 (7th Cir Ind 1990).

[161]Harris v Forklift Systems, Inc, ___ US ___, 114 SCt 367, 126 LEd(2d) 295, 302-03 (1993).

[162]Ellison v Brady, 924 F(2d) 872 (9th Cir Cal 1991). See also Burns v McGregor Electronic Industries, 989 F(2d) 959 (8th Cir Iowa 1993). But see Radtke v Everett, 442 Mich 368, 501 NW(2d) 155 (1993) (rejecting reasonable woman test as "retrench[ing] the very sexist attitudes it is attempting to counter" and "weav[ing] great discord and unnecessary confusion into the law").

[163]Harris v Forklift Systems, Inc, ___ US ___, 114 SCt 367, 126 LEd(2d) 295 (1993).

[164]Steiner v Showboat Operating Co, 25 F(3d) 1459 (9th Cir Nev 1994), cert denied ___ US ___, 115 SCt 733, 130 LEd(2d) 636 (1995).

[165]29 CFR 1604.11(f).

[166]Meritor Savings Bank, FSB v Vinson, 477 US 57, 106 SCt 2399, 91 LEd(2d) 49 (1986).

[167]Meritor Savings Bank, FSB v Vinson, 477 US 57, 106 SCt 2399, 91 LEd(2d) 49 (1986).

[168]Meritor Savings Bank, FSB v Vinson, 477 US 57, 106 SCt 2399, 91 LEd(2d) 49 (1986). For expansive discussion of the efficacy of a grievance procedure and whether it will shield an employer against liability, see Bouton v BMW of North America, Inc, 29 F(3d) 103 (3d Cir NJ 1994).

[169]Rabidue v Osceola Refining Co, Div of Texas-American Petrochemicals, Inc, 805 F(2d) 611 (6th Cir Mich 1986), cert denied 481 US 1041, 107 SCt 1983, 95 LEd(2d) 823 (1987).

[170]Rabidue v Osceola Refining Co, Div of Texas-American Petrochemicals, Inc, 805 F(2d) 611, at

Under the hostile work environment theory, the Sixth Circuit distinguishes between cases where the harasser is a supervisor and cases where the harasser is merely a nonsupervisory co-worker. In the former, principles of agency apply, and the question is whether the act complained of took place in the course and scope of the supervisor's employment, an inquiry requiring an examination of when and where the act took place and whether it was foreseeable. This is not tantamount to a strict liability standard, however. Even if a supervisor engaged in harassing conduct in the course and scope of his employment, the employer can still negate liability by responding adequately and effectively once it has notice of the conduct.[171] On the other hand, where harassment by a nonsupervisory co-worker is involved, agency principles do not come into play. Here, the question is whether the employer, through its supervisory personnel, knew or should have known of the conduct and, if so, whether the employer took prompt and appropriate corrective action.[172]

Under EEOC guidelines, an employer may be liable for harassment by nonemployees if the employer knows or should have known of the conduct and fails to take corrective action.[173]

A victim of sexual harassment (or some other form of unlawful discrimination, for that matter) who quits a job may later pursue a claim under a theory of constructive discharge. Mere proof of discrimination in and of itself, however, does not suffice to demonstrate a constructive discharge. At least some degree of foreseeability on the part of the employer must also be shown; that is, the constructive discharge theory applies only if a reasonable employer would have foreseen that a reasonable employee (or the particular employee if facts peculiar to that employee are known) would quit as a result of the harassment.[174]

Ohio's Fair Employment Practices Act does not preempt and abolish common-law tort actions premised on sexual misconduct in an employment context.[175] Indeed, the Ohio Supreme Court appears to have recognized sexual harassment itself as a separate workplace tort, although its elements are not clearly defined.[176] A cause of action may be brought for wrongful discharge in violation of public policy based on sexual harassment/discrimination.[177]

17.12 Retaliatory discharge

Keeley v Webb[178] illustrates the obvious point that discharging a teacher for filing charges with the EEOC violates both Title VII and 42 USCA 1981. In Ohio, RC Chapter 4112 similarly prohibits retaliation, including discharge, for pursuing state discrimination remedies.

17.13 Discrimination against the handicapped

(A) Ohio and pre-ADA federal standards

The Rehabilitation Act of 1973, 29 USCA 791 to 29 USCA 794,[179] and RC 4112.02 prohibit employment discrimination against handicapped job applicants and employees. With specific reference to the blind, deaf, or mobility impaired, RC 955.43 generally provides that when such a

---

619-20 (6th Cir Mich 1986), cert denied 481 US 1041, 107 SCt 1983, 95 LEd(2d) 823 (1987).

[171]Kauffman v Allied Signal, Inc, Autolite Div, 970 F(2d) 178 (6th Cir Ohio 1992), cert denied ___ US ___, 113 SCt 831, 121 LEd(2d) 701 (1992). See also Yates v Avco Corp, 819 F(2d) 630 (6th Cir Tenn 1987). As *Kauffman* goes on to note, in a quid pro quo case, an employer is strictly liable for the conduct of a supervisor with authority over hiring, advancement, dismissal, and discipline of employees. See also Highlander v KFC Natl Management Co, 805 F(2d) 644 (6th Cir Ohio 1986).

[172]Kauffman v Allied Signal Inc, Autolite Div, 970 F(2d) 178 (6th Cir Ohio 1992), cert denied ___ US ___, 113 SCt 831, 121 LEd(2d) 701 (1992). See also Rabidue v Osceola Refining Co, Div of Texas-American Petrochemicals, Inc, 805 F(2d) 611 (6th Cir Mich 1986), cert denied 481 US 1041, 107 SCt 1983, 95 LEd(2d) 823 (1987).

[173]29 CFR 1604.11(e).

[174]Wheeler v Southland Corp, 875 F(2d) 1246 (6th Cir Ohio 1989).

[175]Helmick v Cincinnati Word Processing, Inc, 45 OS(3d) 131, 543 NE(2d) 1212 (1989).

[176]Kerans v Porter Paint Co, 61 OS(3d) 486, 575 NE(2d) 428 (1991).

[177]Collins v Rizkana, 73 OS(3d) 65, 652 NE(2d) 653 (1995).

[178]Keeley v Webb, 734 F(2d) 14 (6th Cir Tenn 1984).

[179]The Rehabilitation Act of 1973 is discussed as to children in Text Ch 28, Education for Children with Disabilities.

person is accompanied by a trained dog, the dog may be taken into public conveyances and places, including elementary and secondary schools.

Unlike most other forms of discrimination, the prohibition against discrimination on the basis of handicap is not unqualified. RC 4112.02(L) provides that the nondiscrimination requirement of RC 4112.02(A) does not require employment or training of handicapped persons when the handicap would substantially impair the person's ability to perform tasks routinely required by the job or when employment of the handicapped person would significantly increase occupational hazard. The OCRC has adopted rules defining these limitations, prescribing acceptable screening and selection procedures, and indicating what reasonable accommodations employers should make for handicapped employees.[180] Federal statutes and regulations are similarly limited in scope.[181]

Section 504 of the Rehabilitation Act[182] prohibits handicap discrimination by recipients of federal funding. The US Supreme Court has held that a section 504 suit can be maintained even if the primary purpose of the employer's federal financial assistance is unrelated to employment.[183] Insofar as section 504 relates to employment, it does not cover an alcoholic or drug abuser whose current use of alcohol or drugs prevents the individual from performing the duties of the job in question or whose employment, because of such current use, would directly threaten the safety or property of others.[184] A contagious disease such as tuberculosis can qualify as a handicap within the meaning of Section 504.[185] However, a 1988 amendment denies coverage, for employment purposes, to a person with "a currently contagious disease or infection" (such as AIDS) who, for that reason, directly threatens the health or safety of others or is unable to perform job duties.[186]

At least one federal appeals court (in a case that arose before and therefore did not consider the 1988 amendment) has ordered a school district to reinstate a teacher with AIDS, holding that he is handicapped and qualified for classroom duty.[187] The OCRC has issued a policy statement recognizing AIDS as a handicap under state law, but has not addressed the status of other contagious diseases. RC 3701.249 shields the employer of an employee with the AIDS virus from liability arising out of transmission of the virus from the infected employee to another person "unless the transmission occurs as a result of the reckless conduct of the employer." Similarly, the statute shields the employer from liability to an employee arising from any stress-related illness or injury that results from the employee having to work with one who has tested positive for the AIDS virus or has AIDS or an AIDS-related condition.

The demotion of diabetic school van drivers who were insulin-dependent and subject to hyperglycemic and hypoglycemic episodes that increased the potential for accidents did not violate Section 504 where the evidence showed the school district could not reasonably accommodate the handicap without such demotion.[188] The discharge of a teacher who suffered an allergic reaction to an airborne fungus was not violative of Section 504 where the jury concluded her ability to work was not substantially limited and, accordingly, she was not handicapped within the meaning of the statute.[189]

---

[180]OAC 4112-5-08. What is "reasonable," of course, varies from case to case. For an illustration where significant efforts to accommodate nevertheless came up short, see Kent State University v Ohio Civil Rights Comm, 64 App(3d) 427, 581 NE(2d) 1135 (Portage 1989).

[181]29 USCA 793, 29 USCA 794; 41 CFR 60.741, 45 CFR 84.1 to 45 CFR 84.14.

[182]29 USCA 794.

[183]Consolidated Rail Corp v Darrone, 465 US 624, 104 SCt 1248, 79 LEd(2d) 568 (1984).

[184]29 USCA 706(8)(B).

[185]Nassau County School Bd v Arline, 480 US 273, 107 SCt 1123, 94 LEd(2d) 307 (1987).

[186]29 USCA 706(8)(C).

[187]Chalk v United States Dist Ct Central Dist of Cal, 840 F(2d) 701 (9th Cir Cal 1988).

[188]Wood v Omaha School Dist, 25 F(3d) 667 (8th Cir Neb 1994). (In Ohio, an insulin-dependent diabetic is generally disqualified from driving a school bus except that the department of education will grant waivers to insulin users under certain circumstances. See OAC 3301-83-07.)

[189]Byrne v West Allis-West Milwaukee Bd of Ed, 979 F(2d) 560 (7th Cir Wis 1992).

Where an employee voluntarily retires, he is barred from asserting a Section 504 claim alleging discrimination in employment.[190] Where damages are requested under Section 504, it has been held that one is entitled to a jury trial.[191]

The Ohio Supreme Court has held that alcoholism and drug addiction are handicaps under RC 4112.01(A)(13), but indicated the law does not protect alcoholics or substance abusers whose current use of drugs or alcohol prevents them from performing their jobs or poses a direct threat to the safety or property of others.[192] Similarly, prior job misconduct or absenteeism of a prospective employee, even if attributable to alcoholism, may be considered in deciding whether to hire an applicant.[193]

That a divergence of medical opinion exists as to the cause of a handicapping condition does not take one outside the protective scope of RC 4112.02.[194]

(B) Americans with Disabilities Act of 1990

The Americans with Disabilities Act of 1990 (ADA), 42 USCA 12101 et seq., comprehensively prohibits discrimination on the basis of disability.[195] Its provisions supplement, but do not supplant, other laws that bar discrimination against the handicapped.

Title I of the ADA broadly proscribes discrimination by covered entities, including school districts,[196] against a qualified individual on the basis of disability[197] with respect to all aspects of employment.[198] An employer must make reasonable accommodations[199] to the individual's known physical or mental limitations unless the employer can show accommodation would impose an undue hardship.[200] An employer may not use qualification standards, tests, or employee selection criteria that screen out or tend to screen out individuals with

---

[190]Cabelli v Fort Smith School Dist, 23 F(3d) 1295 (8th Cir Ark 1994).

[191]Pandazides v Virginia Bd of Ed, 13 F(3d) 823 (4th Cir Va 1994); Waldrop v Southern Company Services, Inc, 24 F(3d) 152 (11th Cir Ala 1994).

[192]Hazlett v Martin Chevrolet, Inc, 25 OS(3d) 279, 25 OBR 331, 496 NE(2d) 478 (1986). That *Hazlett* does not insulate an employee from discharge where his chemical dependency adversely affects job performance was underscored in Harris v Ohio Bureau of Employment Services, 51 OS(3d) 37, 553 NE(2d) 1350 (1990). See also Hayes v Cleveland Pneumatic Co, 92 App(3d) 36, 634 NE(2d) 228 (Cuyahoga 1993), dismissed, jurisdictional motion overruled by 69 OS(3d) 1415, 630 NE(2d) 376 (1994).

[193]Cleveland Civil Service Comm v Ohio Civil Rights Comm, 57 OS(3d) 62, 565 NE(2d) 579 (1991).

[194]Kent State University v Ohio Civil Rights Comm, 64 App(3d) 427, 581 NE(2d) 1135 (Portage 1989).

[195]The Act defines "disability" as a physical or mental impairment that substantially limits one or more of a person's major life activities, a record of such impairment, or being regarded as having such impairment. 42 USCA 12102(2). Homosexuality, bisexuality, transvestism, pedophilia, exhibitionism, voyeurism, gender identification disorders not resulting from physical impairments, other sexual behavior disorders, compulsive gambling, kleptomania, pyromania, and psychoactive substance use disorders resulting from current use of illegal drugs are all expressly excluded from the definition of disability. 42 USCA 12211.

[196]42 USCA 12111(2), (5), (7).

[197]"Qualified individual with a disability" means one with a disability who, with or without reasonable accommodation, can perform essential functions of the job. In this connection, "consideration shall be given to the employer's judgment as to what functions of a job are essential," and a preexisting written job description "shall be considered evidence of the essential functions of the job." 42 USCA 12111(8). The term does *not* include any applicant or employee currently engaged in the illegal use of drugs. 42 USCA 12114. See also 42 USCA 12210. Noting that regular and reliable attendance is an essential job function, the court in Tyndall v National Ed Centers, 31 F(3d) 209 (4th Cir Va 1994) held that the termination of a teacher with lupus whose performance was more than adequate when she was working but whose attendance was unacceptable did not violate the Act.

[198]42 USCA 12112.

[199]"Reasonable accommodations" may include making facilities readily accessible to and usable by persons with disabilities, job restructuring, part-time or modified work schedules, reassignment, acquisition or modification of equipment, adjustment or modification of tests, training materials, or policies, provision of qualified readers or interpreters, and "other similar accommodations for individuals with disabilities." 42 USCA 12111(9).

[200]"Undue hardship" means action requiring "significant difficulty or expense" when considered in light of such factors as the nature and cost of the accommodation needed; the financial resources of the facility involved and of the employer as an entity; the number employed at the facility and by the employer overall; the impact upon operation of the facility; the number, type, and location of the employer's facilities; and the type of operations carried on by the employer, including the composition, structure, and functions of the work force and the geographic separateness, administrative, or fiscal relationship of the facility involved to

disabilities unless they can be shown to be job-related for the particular position and consistent with business necessity.[201]

An employer may not conduct a medical examination[202] or question a job applicant or employee on the existence of a disability or its nature or severity, but can question an applicant on ability to perform job-related functions.[203] After making an offer of employment, a medical examination may be required if required of all entering employees and if information obtained on the applicant's medical condition or history is kept on separate forms in separate medical files and treated as a confidential medical record.[204] However, supervisors and managers may be told of necessary restrictions on the employee's work duties and necessary accommodations; first aid and safety personnel may be told if the disability might require emergency treatment; and officials investigating compliance with the ADA must be provided relevant information upon request.[205] Subject to these same restrictions on use of information, an employer may conduct voluntary medical examinations as part of an employee health program available to employees at the work site.[206]

An employer may refuse to assign to a job involving the handling of food a person with an infectious or communicable disease (which disease must be included on a list to be compiled by the Secretary of Health and Human Services) transmitted to others through food handling where the problem cannot be eliminated by reasonable accommodation.[207]

The Act expressly permits employers to prohibit the illegal use of drugs or the use of alcohol in the workplace and to hold current drug users or alcoholics to the same performance and behavior standards as other employees.[208]

Enforcement of Title I is entrusted principally to the Equal Employment Opportunity Commission, with the remedies and procedures generally applicable to charges of discrimination under Title VII of the Civil Rights Act of 1964 incorporated by reference.[209] In cases of intentional discrimination where the provision of a reasonable accommodation is at issue, however, a specific provision of 42 USCA 1981a precludes the recovery of damages if the employer demonstrates good-faith efforts, in consultation with the disabled person who has informed the employer that accommodation is needed, to identify and make a reasonable accommodation that would provide the person with an equally effective opportunity and not cause an undue hardship on the operation of the employer's business. The EEOC's regulations that implement the ADA's employment provisions appear in 29 CFR 1630.

Title II of the ADA broadly prohibits public entities, including school districts,[210] from discriminating against a qualified individual on the basis of disability or denying such person participation in or the benefits of the services, programs, or activities of the public entity.[211] The US Attorney General's regulations that implement this provision appear in 28 CFR Part 35. Any person alleging such discrimination is

---

the employer's overall operations. 42 USCA 12111(10).

[201] 42 USCA 12112(b)(6), 42 USCA 12113(a). Qualification standards may include a requirement that one not pose a direct threat to the health or safety of other workers. 42 USCA 12113(b).

[202] A test to determine the illegal use of drugs expressly is not a medical examination. 42 USCA 12114(d). Overall, the Act takes a neutral stance on the issue of drug testing, an issue treated more fully at Text 47.03, Drug, alcohol, and weapon searches.

[203] 42 USCA 12112(c)(2), (4).

[204] 42 USCA 12112(c)(3).

[205] 42 USCA 12112(c)(3).

[206] 42 USCA 12112(c)(4).

[207] 42 USCA 12113(d).

[208] 42 USCA 12114(c). However, a person who has successfully completed or is participating in a supervised drug rehabilitation program (or has otherwise been rehabilitated successfully) and is no longer using illegal drugs is a "qualified individual with a disability." Drug testing to ensure such an individual is no longer using drugs is expressly permitted. 42 USCA 12114(b).

[209] 42 USCA 12117(a). See Text 17.03, Title VII, federal Civil Rights Act of 1964.

[210] 42 USCA 12131(1).

[211] 42 USCA 12132. "Qualified individual with a disability" means one with a disability who, with or without reasonable modifications to rules, policies, or practices; the removal of architectural, communication, or transportation barriers; or the provisions of auxiliary aids and services; meets the essential requirements for receiving services or participating in programs or activities the public entity provides. 42 USCA 12131(2). "Auxiliary aids and services" are defined in 42 USCA 12102(1).

afforded the remedies, procedures, and rights that appear in section 505 of the Rehabilitation Act of 1973, 29 USCA 294a.[212]

Retaliation against an individual who opposes any act or practice made unlawful by the ADA or because such individual made a charge, testified, assisted, or participated in an investigation, proceeding, or hearing under the ADA is prohibited, as is coercion, intimidation, or interference with respect to any person who exercises or enjoys, or encourages any other person to exercise or enjoy, any right the Act grants or protects.[213] A reasonable attorney's fee may be allowed the prevailing party in any action or administrative proceeding brought under the ADA.[214]

17.14 National origin discrimination

Vinton County Local School Dist Bd of Ed v Ohio Civil Rights Comm[215] upheld an OCRC decision that a teacher was wrongly denied tenure because of national origin.

17.15 Religious discrimination

The ban on religious discrimination is also tempered with some qualifications. The employer's obligation is to make a reasonable accommodation to the employee's religious beliefs if it can do so without undue hardship.[216] The US Supreme Court has held that Title VII does not require a school board to accept a teacher's suggested accommodation; the board need only show a reasonable accommodation was afforded to the employee.[217]

A union ran afoul of Title VII when a Roman Catholic university professor opposed to contributing to or associating with an organization that supports legalized abortion objected to paying fees under an agency shop arrangement negotiated by the union. The union's offer to reduce the fees by a percentage amount relative to the union's support of issues the professor found objectionable was insufficient accommodation since it ignored the associational element of the objection. The court suggested one reasonable accommodation might be payment of the entire fees to the local union to be used solely for local collective bargaining purposes.[218]

The First Amendment to the US Constitution guarantees the free exercise of religious convictions. This does not mean, however, that a teacher is free to disregard the school district's prescribed curriculum when to conform would conflict with religious beliefs. Thus, in a case premised not on Title VII but the Constitution, the discharge of a Jehovah's Witness who flatly refused to teach subjects involving patriotic themes has been upheld, the court noting that efforts to accommodate the teacher's beliefs had been made but failed.[219] A school district's refusal to allow a teacher to wear religious attire while teaching, in compliance with a state statute that prohibited teaching in religious clothing, has withstood challenge under Title VII.[220]

Under Article I, section 7 of the Ohio Constitution, a teacher may belong to any faith or sect, or may be a nonbeliever, and cannot be required to take a religious test.

In *Dayton Christian Schools, Inc v Ohio Civil Rights Comm*,[221] a Christian school

---

[212]42 USCA 12133. The precise implications of Title II for Ohio school districts are simply not clear. Most of the Title pertains to accommodating disabled persons with respect to public transportation. Those provisions, however, expressly do not apply to public school transportation. See 42 USCA 12141. Titles III and IV of the ADA do not apply to public school districts.
[213]42 USCA 12203.
[214]42 USCA 12205.
[215]Vinton County Local School Dist Bd of Ed v Ohio Civil Rights Comm, No. 388, 1982 WL 3476 (4th Dist Ct App, Vinton, 7-13-82).
[216]Trans World Airlines v Hardison, 432 US 63, 97 SCt 2264, 53 LEd(2d) 113 (1977). The duty to accommodate is immediate and settlement offers made in the context of administrative proceedings after a charge has been filed do not qualify as reasonable accommodation. Toledo v Nobel-Sysco, Inc, 892 F(2d) 1481 (10th Cir NM 1989), cert denied 495 US 948, 110 SCt 2208, 109 LEd(2d) 535 (1990).
[217]Ansonia Bd of Ed v Philbrook, 479 US 60, 107 SCt 367, 93 LEd(2d) 305 (1986).
[218]EEOC v University of Detroit, 904 F(2d) 331 (6th Cir Mich 1990).
[219]Palmer v Chicago Bd of Ed, 603 F(2d) 1271 (7th Cir Ill 1979), cert denied 444 US 1026, 100 SCt 689, 62 LEd(2d) 659 (1980).
[220]United States v Philadelphia School Dist Bd of Ed, 911 F(2d) 882 (3d Cir Pa 1990).
[221]Dayton Christian Schools, Inc v Ohio Civil Rights Comm, 766 F(2d) 932 (6th Cir Ohio 1985),

sought to prevent the OCRC from processing a charge of sex discrimination, claiming it would entangle government in religion contrary to the First Amendment. The Sixth Circuit Court of Appeals held the First Amendment precluded application of the Ohio Fair Employment Practices Act. The US Supreme Court reversed, holding the court should have abstained. A federal court should not interfere with ongoing state proceedings except in exceptional circumstances. Either the OCRC or the state courts could resolve any constitutional questions, so federal intervention was unwarranted.[222]

FAMILY AND MEDICAL LEAVE

17.16 Family and Medical Leave Act of 1993

Under the Family and Medical Leave Act of 1993,[223] an eligible employee[224] is entitled to a total of twelve workweeks of leave during any twelve-month period for one or more of the following reasons: (1) the birth of a son or daughter and in order to care for such son or daughter; (2) the placement of a son or daughter with the employee for adoption or foster care; (3) to care for the employee's spouse, son, daughter, or parent who has a serious health condition; or (4) because of the employee's own serious health condition that renders the employee unable to perform the functions of the job.[225] Where spouses are both employed by the same employer, the aggregate number of workweeks to which both may be entitled may be limited to twelve during any twelve-month period if leave is taken (1) for the birth of a son or daughter and in order to care for such son or daughter; (2) for the placement of a son or daughter for adoption or foster care; or (3) to care for a parent (not, however, parent-in-law) who has a serious health condition.[226]

---

reversed by 477 US 619, 106 SCt 2718, 91 LEd(2d) 512 (1986).
[222] Ohio Civil Rights Comm v Dayton Christian Schools, Inc, 477 US 619, 106 SCt 2718, 91 LEd(2d) 512 (1986).
[223] 29 USCA 2601 et seq. The Act applies to all Ohio school districts. 29 USCA 2611. Regulations under the Act appear in 29 CFR Part 825.
[224] To be eligible for any leave under the Act, an employee (male or female) must have been employed for at least twelve months by a school district that employs at least fifty employees at the employee's work site or within a seventy-five-mile radius of that work site and must also have worked at least 1,250 hours during the twelve-month period immediately preceding the leave. 29 USCA 2611. See also 29 CFR 825.108. The twelve months of employment need not be consecutive and the 1,250 hours is determined according to principles established under the Fair Labor Standards Act for determining compensable hours of work. An employer who claims an employee does not meet the 1,250-hour requirement "must be able to clearly demonstrate" that fact. A full-time teacher is "deemed to meet the 1,250 test" in the absence of an actual record of hours that clearly demonstrates otherwise. 29 CFR 825.110.
[225] 29 USCA 2612. "Son or daughter" means a biological, adopted, or foster child, stepchild, legal ward, or child of a person standing in loco parentis, who is either under eighteen or incapable of self-care because of a physical or mental disability. "Parent" means the biological parent or one who stood in loco parentis to the employee when the employee was a son or daughter. "Serious health condition" means an illness, injury, impairment, or physical or mental condition that involves inpatient care at a hospital, hospice, or residential care facility; or continuing treatment by a health care provider. 29 CFR 825.114. "Health care provider" means an MD, osteopath, or "any other person determined by the [US] Secretary [of Labor] to be capable of providing health care services." 29 USCA 2611. In 29 CFR 825.118, the secretary includes within "health care provider" state-authorized podiatrists, dentists, clinical psychologists, optometrists, chiropractors (limited to treatment consisting of manual manipulation of the spine to correct a subluxation as demonstrated by x-ray), nurse practitioners, nurse midwives, clinical social workers, and any health care provider recognized by the employer (or the employer's group health plan); also included are Christian Science practitioners listed with the First Church of Christ, Scientist in Boston, Massachusetts. 29 CFR 825.200 states that an employer may choose one of the following methods of determining the twelve-month period in which the twelve weeks of leave entitlement occurs: the calendar year; any fixed twelve-month leave year such as a fiscal year, a year required by state law, or a year starting on an employee's anniversary date; the twelve-month period measured forward from the employee's first leave under the Act; or a rolling twelve-month period measured backward from the date the employee uses leave under the Act. Whichever option the employer selects must be "applied consistently and uniformly to all employees" and sixty days' notice must be provided to all employees if a change to some other allowed alternative is made.
[226] 29 USCA 2612. See also 29 CFR 825.202. Thus, the combined total limitation for spouses does not

Where the reason for leave is the birth or placement for adoption or foster care of a son or daughter, leave is not to be taken intermittently or on a reduced leave schedule[227] unless the employer and employee mutually agree otherwise. Where a serious health condition is the reason for leave, however, leave may be taken intermittently or on a reduced leave schedule when "medically necessary," but such leave does not reduce the total amount of leave to which the employee is entitled under the FMLA beyond the amount of leave actually taken. If the need for such intermittent or reduced schedule leave is foreseeable based on planned medical treatment, the employer can require the employee to transfer temporarily to an alternative position for which the employee is qualified that both has equivalent pay and benefits and better accommodates recurring periods of leave than the employee's regular position.[228]

Leave may be unpaid. If the employer provides paid leave for fewer than twelve workweeks, the additional weeks necessary to attain twelve may be unpaid. The employee may elect, or the employer may require the employee, to substitute any of the employee's annual paid vacation leave, personal leave, or family leave for any part of the twelve-week period; in addition, where a serious health condition is the reason for leave, the employee may elect, or the employer may require the employee, to substitute any accrued medical or sick leave for any part of the twelve-week period.[229] Additionally, leave taken pursuant to a disability plan or workers' compensation can be credited against an employee's FMLA leave entitlement.[230]

If the necessity for leave is foreseeable based on expected birth or a placement for adoption or foster care, the employee must provide thirty days' notice of the intention to take leave before leave begins (if the actual date of birth or placement requires leave to begin in less than thirty days, the employee is to provide "such notice as is practicable"). If the necessity for a leave based on a serious health condition is foreseeable based on planned medical treatment, the employee must (1) make a reasonable effort to schedule treatment so as to not "disrupt unduly" the employer's operations, subject to approval of the employee's (or the son's, daughter's, spouse's, or parent's, as may be appropriate) health care provider; and (2) give thirty days' notice of the intention to take leave before leave begins (if the actual date of treatment requires leave to begin in less than thirty days, the employee is to provide "such notice as is practicable").[231]

In addition, where a serious health condition is the reason for leave, the employer may require certification of the need for leave from the relevant health care provider. Certification is sufficient if it states (1) the date on which the serious health condition began; (2) the probable duration; (3) the "appropriate medical facts" about the condition; (4) a statement that the employee is needed to care for the relevant relative and an estimate of the time that is needed for such care, or, where the employee's own health condition is involved, a statement that the employee is unable to perform the functions of the job; and (5) where intermittent or reduced schedule leave for planned medical treatment is involved, the dates of expected treatment and the duration of such treatment, and (a) where the employee's own health condition is involved, a statement of the medical necessity for the intermittent or reduced schedule leave and the expected duration of such leave; or (b) where a relative's health condition is involved, a statement that the leave is necessary for the care of the relative or will assist in the relative's recovery and the expected duration and schedule of the leave.

If the employer has reason to doubt the certification, the employer may at its expense require the employee to obtain a

---

apply where the reason for leave is the serious health condition of a son or daughter of the employee.

[227]"Reduced leave schedule" means a schedule that reduces the employee's usual number of hours per workweek, or hours per workday. 29 USCA 2611.

[228]29 USCA 2612.

[229]29 USCA 2612. The statute expressly states the employer need not provide paid medical or sick leave in any situation where the employer would not normally provide such leave. Where an employer wishes to designate and substitute paid leave for part of the twelve-week period, the requirements of 29 CFR 825.208 come into play and must be followed.

[230]29 CFR 825.702.

[231]29 USCA 2612(e)(1).

second opinion from a health care provider (other than one employed on a regular basis by the employer) designated or approved by the employer. In the event of a conflict, the employer may at its expense require the employee to obtain a third opinion from a health care provider designated or approved jointly by the employer and employee, which third opinion is final and binding. Subsequent recertifications may be required on a "reasonable basis."[232]

During leave, any pre-existing group health benefits must be maintained at the level and under the conditions coverage would have been provided but for the leave. The premium paid for maintaining coverage may be recovered by the employer if the employee fails to return upon expiration of the leave for a reason other than a serious health condition that entitles the employee to leave (in which case the employer may require certification from the relevant health care provider of such condition) or "other circumstances beyond the control of the employee."[233]

On return from leave, the employee is entitled to be restored to the position held when leave began or to an equivalent position.[234] Taking leave cannot result in the loss of any benefits accrued prior to leave, but seniority and benefits do not accrue during the period of leave. The employer can require an employee to report periodically on his status and intention to return to work.[235]

If the employee is employed "principally in an instructional capacity,"[236] special rules can come into play. Where leave is premised upon a serious health condition, and the need for intermittent or reduced schedule leave is foreseeable based on planned medical treatment and the employee could be off for more than twenty percent of the total number of workdays in the period during which leave could extend, the school district may require the employee to elect either (1) to take leave for periods of a particular duration not be exceed the duration of the planned medical treatment, or (2) to transfer temporarily to an available alternative position for which the employee is qualified that both has equivalent pay and benefits and better accommodates recurring periods of leave than the employee's regular position.[237] Moreover, where such an instructional employee takes leave for any reason under the FMLA near the end of an "academic term," these special rules apply:

(1) If leave begins more than five weeks before the end of the term, the employee may be required to continue leave until the end of the term if

(a) the leave is at least three weeks in duration, and

(b) the return to work would occur during the three-week period before the end of the term;

(2) If leave for a purpose other than the employee's own serious health condition begins five weeks or less before the end of the term, the employee may be required to continue leave until the end of the term if

(a) the leave is greater than two weeks' duration, and

(b) the return to work would occur during the two-week period before the end of the term;

---

[232] 29 USCA 2613.

[233] 29 USCA 2614. See also 29 CFR 825.209 to 29 CFR 825.218.

[234] 29 USCA 2614. See also 29 CFR 825.209 to 29 CFR 825.218. Determination of what constitutes an "equivalent position" is to be based on "established school board policies and practices ... and collective bargaining agreements." 29 USCA 2118.

[235] 29 USCA 2614. Where the employee is salaried and among the highest paid ten percent of employees employed by the employer (referred to as a "key" employee in the regulations), restoration can be denied if "necessary to prevent substantial and grievous economic injury to the operations of the employer"; the employer notifies the employee of the intent to deny restoration at the time of the determination that such injury would occur; and, if leave has already commenced, the employee elects after receipt of such notice not to return to employment. Id. See also 29 CFR 825.217 to 29 CFR 825.219.

[236] This category of employees includes teachers, athletic coaches, driving instructors, and special education assistants such a signers for those with a hearing disability. It does not include guidance counselors, psychologists, nurses, educational aides, or such obviously noninstructional employees as cafeteria and maintenance workers, custodians, and bus drivers. See 29 CFR 825.800.

[237] 29 USCA 2618. See also 29 CFR 825.601.

(3) If leave for a purpose other than the employee's own serious health condition begins three weeks or less before the end of the term, and the duration of leave is greater than five workdays, the employee may be required to continue leave to the end of the term.[238]

Investigative authority to ensure compliance with the FMLA, including subpoena power, is lodged with the US Secretary of Labor.[239] Employers are required conspicuously to post a prescribed notice of employee rights under the FMLA[240] and are also prohibited from discharging or otherwise discriminating against any person for opposing any action made unlawful by the FMLA and from interfering, restraining, or denying the exercise or attempt to exercise any right provided by the FMLA. It is likewise unlawful to retaliate against any employee for initiating or participating in enforcement proceedings under the FMLA.[241]

An aggrieved employee has the option of either filing (or having another file on his behalf) a complaint with the Secretary of Labor or directly suing the employer in federal or state court. The limitations period in either case is two years unless the violation is willful, in which case it is three years. An offending employer may be held liable for damages and such equitable relief as may be appropriate. Damages are doubled unless the employer shows to the satisfaction of the court reasonable grounds for believing its action was not a violation. Costs (including attorney fees and expert witness fees) are recoverable by a successful employee. The secretary is empowered to investigate and resolve complaints in the same manner as violations of the Fair Labor Standards Act are investigated and resolved, and may sue on behalf of an employee to recover damages, in which case the employee's right to sue terminates.[242]

RECORDS

17.17 Notices, record-keeping, and reports

Title VII,[243] the Ohio Fair Employment Practice Act,[244] the ADEA,[245] the ADA,[246] and the FMLA[247] all require employers to inform employees of their nondiscrimination rights by conspicuously posting notices in a form approved or prepared by the government agency charged with enforcing the statute. Appropriate notices can be obtained from district EEOC and OCRC offices.

Title VII requires public elementary and secondary schools to retain their personnel records for a period of one year and to retain personnel records relating to a discrimination charge or pattern or practice suit until final disposition of the charge or lawsuit.[248] Further, school systems with 100 or more employees must file an annual Elementary-Secondary Staff Information Report EEO-5 (showing the composition of the work force by race and sex), and school systems with 15 to 100 employees must file such reports if the EEOC requests them to do so.[249] School districts must maintain EEO-5 reports, and records sufficient to complete and support them, for three years.

Although RC 4112.02(E)(2) appears to prohibit maintenance of records showing the race, sex, color, national origin, or religion of job applicants, the OCRC, by rule, permits maintenance of such records where necessary to comply with government reporting requirements, so long as the data are gathered and maintained in a manner which precludes inadvertent or

---

[238] 29 USCA 2618. See also 29 CFR 825.602. The regulations equate "academic term" with a semester and flatly prohibit having more than two academic terms in a year.

[239] 29 USCA 2616.

[240] 29 USCA 2619.

[241] 29 USCA 2615.

[242] 29 USCA 2617; 29 CFR 825.400 to 29 CFR 825.404. Records pertaining to the employer's compliance with the FMLA must be kept in accordance with 29 CFR 825.500.

[243] 42 USCA 2000e-10.

[244] RC 4112.07.

[245] 29 USCA 627.

[246] 42 USCA 12115.

[247] 29 USCA 2619.

[248] 29 CFR 1602.40.

[249] 29 CFR 1602.41.

intentional discriminatory use.[250] RC 4112.04(A)(10) requires all public agencies which have undertaken affirmative action pursuant to a conciliation agreement or any state or federal statute, rule, or order to submit annual progress reports to the OCRC not later than November 1.

In addition to Title VII and the Ohio Fair Employment Practices Act, other state and federal civil rights statutes and executive orders generally require maintenance of records sufficient to provide information to investigate compliance. Personnel and payroll records normally maintained pursuant to state law and board of education policy are generally sufficient to satisfy these requirements. No civil rights statute, regulation, or order requires records retention for more than three years, except for information related to ongoing investigations or litigation.

AFFIRMATIVE ACTION

17.18 Affirmative action and reverse discrimination

"Affirmative action" encompasses all the various steps an employer may take, beyond mere nondiscrimination, to promote employment opportunities for blacks, females, Hispanics, and members of other groups protected by civil rights laws. Affirmative action concepts also have been applied to student admissions at colleges and universities and at private schools.

Affirmative action plans have several sources:

(1) They may be required by federal agencies as a condition of receipt of federal funds under a grant or government contract;

(2) They may be ordered by a court as a remedy for past discrimination in an employment discrimination suit or as part of the remedy in a desegregation suit;

(3) They may be included in a court consent decree or an agreement with the OCRC or EEOC to settle discrimination charges;[251] or

(4) They may be developed on a purely voluntary basis by the employer.

Of various provisions included in affirmative action plans, the most controversial have been numerical goals and ratios—for example, a provision requiring that one of every three persons hired, promoted, or admitted must be black until such time as a fixed percentage (the "goal") of a work force (or student body) is black. Such "race-conscious" plan components have frequently been attacked as "reverse discrimination," especially when voluntarily adopted by employers in settlement agreements or purely voluntary affirmative action plans. Several US Supreme Court decisions since 1978 offer guidance on this issue, but do not fully and finally resolve the conflicts between the rights of minorities and affected nonminorities.

In *University of California Regents v Bakke*,[252] an unsuccessful white applicant for admission to the University of California Medical School challenged a voluntary affirmative action plan under which a fixed number of admissions were reserved for minorities, whose qualifications were judged by less stringent standards than qualifications of white applicants. The Supreme Court invalidated the plan by a 5-4 vote, but, because the nine justices wrote six separate opinions presenting different rationales, the scope of *Bakke* was not entirely clear. Four justices held that Title VI of the Civil Rights Act of 1964, 42 USCA 2000d, prohibits a voluntary race-conscious plan, at least where there has been no finding of past discrimination. Five justices agreed that both Title VI and the Fourteenth Amendment require strict judi-

---

[250]OAC 4112-5-04.

[251]A litigated or consent judgment or order that resolves a claim of employment discrimination generally may not be challenged by one who, prior to entry of the judgment or order, had actual notice of the proposed judgment or order sufficient to apprise one of the adverse impact on his employment interests and a reasonable opportunity to object to the entry. Even in the absence of these factors, a challenge generally cannot be made where the person's interests were adequately represented by another who had previously challenged the judgment or order on the same legal grounds with a similar fact situation, absent an intervening change in law or fact. 42 USCA 2000e-2(n).

[252]University of California Regents v Bakke, 438 US 265, 98 SCt 2733, 57 LEd(2d) 750 (1978).

cial scrutiny of racial classifications; four of them argued the need to correct societal discrimination and increase the representation of minorities in the medical profession was sufficient to justify the plan, even in the absence of evidence that the school had discriminated in the past. The justice in the middle, Justice Powell, stated that this particular plan violated both the Constitution and Title VI, but indicated race could be considered as one factor for student admission.

In *United Steelworkers of America v Weber*,[253] the Court held that a voluntary affirmative action plan set forth in a collective bargaining agreement did not violate Title VII for the following reasons:

(1) Its race-conscious element, i.e., the reservation of fifty per cent of the openings in a craft-training program for black employees, was consistent with Title VII because it was designed exclusively to eliminate patterns of racial segregation in affected job categories evidenced by a statistical disparity between the percentage of jobs and the percentage of blacks available in the local labor force;

(2) The plan was temporary, and the ratio was to be discontinued when the percentage of blacks in affected jobs became commensurate with the percentage of blacks available in the local labor force; and

(3) The plan did not unnecessarily interfere with the interests of white employees in that

(a) the preference did not require the discharge or displacement of any white employees; and

(b) the preference did not create an absolute bar to the advancement of white employees.

In *Johnson v Transportation Agency, Santa Clara County*,[254] the Court extended its *Weber* analysis to sex discrimination cases, upholding the promotion of a female pursuant to a plan allowing specific consideration of sex as one selection factor.

However, the Court has been more troubled by affirmative action in layoff cases. *Wygant v Jackson Bd of Ed*,[255] applying the equal protection clause of the Fourteenth Amendment, struck down a collectively bargained plan which resulted in the layoff of nonminority teachers in favor of less senior minority teachers. The Court's plurality opinion held the layoffs imposed too great a burden on innocent individuals, a much greater burden than affirmative action hiring goals. "Denial of a future employment opportunity is not as intrusive as loss of an existing job."[256] Since less intrusive means, such as adoption of hiring goals, were available, the race-conscious layoff procedure could not survive.[257]

Wygant is also significant because of the emphasis some justices placed on the need to narrowly tailor specific affirmative action to specific and convincing evidence of past discrimination.[258]

The Court reemphasized these considerations in *Richmond v J.A. Croson Co*,[259] a case involving the power of a municipal government to impose affirmative action requirements on municipal contractors. The Court applied a "strict scrutiny" test to invalidate the city of Richmond's thirty per cent minority set-aside requirement for contractors who subcontract work on city construction contracts.

---

[253]United Steelworkers of America v Weber, 443 US 193, 99 SCt 2721, 61 LEd(2d) 480 (1979).

[254]Johnson v Transportation Agency, Santa Clara County, 480 US 616, 107 SCt 1442, 94 LEd(2d) 615 (1987).

[255]Wygant v Jackson Bd of Ed, 476 US 267, 106 SCt 1842, 90 LEd(2d) 260 (1986).

[256]Wygant v Jackson Bd of Ed, 476 US 267, at 282-83, 106 SCt 1842, 90 LEd(2d) 260 (1986).

[257]Cf. Firefighters Local Union No. 1784 v Stotts, 467 US 561, 104 SCt 2576, 81 LEd(2d) 483 (1984) (Title VII allows routine application of seniority system absent proof of intent to discriminate and lower court wrongly modified consent decree to require layoff of white employees when seniority system called for layoff of black employees).

[258]For an application of *Wygant* in a school setting, see Crumpton v Bridgeport Ed Assn, 993 F(2d) 1023 (2d Cir Conn 1993) (rejecting absolute preference for retaining minorities where layoff of teachers involved).

[259]Richmond v J.A. Croson Co, 488 US 469, 109 SCt 706, 102 LEd(2d) 854 (1989).

In *Adarand v Pena*,[260] the Supreme Court extended *Croson* to all government affirmative action requirements, including those imposed by Congress. It overruled *Metro Broadcasting, Inc v FCC*,[261] and held that all race-based classifications, including those which benefit minorities, are subject to a strict scrutiny test. Thus, when evaluating affirmative action, courts must determine whether the interests served by the affirmative action are compelling, whether the affirmative action program is narrowly tailored, and whether the program is limited so that it would not last longer than the discrimination it was designed to eliminate. These criteria, if applied to employment affirmative action programs, would not abolish affirmative action designed to compensate for specific acts of past discrimination, but they would cast doubt on any program which is broader than the specific acts of discrimination that require correction. The federal government is reviewing its affirmative action requirements in light of *Adarand*.[262]

The EEOC has adopted affirmative action guidelines which, although not having the force of law, offer some protection against reverse discrimination suits to employers who undertake explicitly race-conscious plans. These guidelines approve voluntary written plans reasonably related to correcting the adverse effects of neutral policies, past discrimination, or disparate treatment.[263] Neither a past violation of Title VII nor an admission of discrimination is required.[264] The plans may include goals, timetables, and other race-, color-, sex-, or ethnic-conscious elements, when reasonably related to accomplishment of legitimate objectives.[265] If a "reverse discrimination" charge is filed against an employer as a result of actions taken in reliance on a plan conforming to the guidelines, the EEOC will issue a "no reasonable cause" determination and state its determination constitutes a formal agency opinion under section 713(b) of Title VII,[266] which may be asserted as a defense in future actions. While courts regard the guidelines as persuasive, they are not conclusive, and extreme care must be used even when drafting a plan consistent with them.

An urban Ohio school district's race-conscious teacher transfer policy designed to ensure the racial balance of the teaching staff at a given school approximated the racial balance of the teaching staff of the system as a whole has withstood challenge under the equal protection clause, since the policy did not prefer one race over another and substantially related to the important governmental objective of having a system-wide racially integrated faculty.[267]

WAIVERS

17.19 Waiver of claims not prohibited

A voluntary and knowingly made waiver of employment discrimination claims does not violate public policy and will generally be enforced in the absence of fraud, duress, lack of consideration, or mutual mistake.[268]

The federal Age Discrimination in Employment Act (ADEA) expressly declares that no right or claim under the Act may be waived unless the waiver is "knowing and voluntary," which means, at a minimum, that (1) the waiver must be part of a written agreement between the individual and employer; (2) it must specifically refer to rights or claims under the Act; (3) the individual cannot waive rights or claims that may arise after the waiver is signed; (4) the waiver must be for consider-

---

[260] Adarand v Pena, 515 US ___, 115 SCt 2097, 132 LEd(2d) 158 (1995).

[261] Metro Broadcasting, Inc v FCC, 494 US 1024, 110 SCt 1467, 108 LEd(2d) 605 (1990). The majority in Metro Broadcasting held that strict scrutiny was not warranted for race-conscious measures mandated by Congress.

[262] For examples of affirmative action that ran afoul of these requirements, see Cunico v Pueblo School Dist No. 60, 917 F(2d) 431 (10th Cir Colo 1990) (finding unlawful discrimination against white female worker when school district retained junior black worker during reduction in force); United States v Piscataway Twp Bd of Ed, 832 FSupp 836 (D NJ 1993).

[263] 29 CFR 1608.4(b), (c).

[264] 29 CFR 1608.4(b).

[265] 29 CFR 1608.4(c)(1).

[266] 42 USCA 2000e-12(b).

[267] Jacobson v Cincinnati Bd of Ed, 961 F(2d) 100 (6th Cir Ohio 1992), cert denied ___ US ___, 113 SCt 94, 121 LEd(2d) 55 (1992).

[268] Shaheen v B.F. Goodrich Co, 873 F(2d) 105 (6th Cir Ohio 1989).

ation in addition to anything of value to which the individual is already entitled; (5) the individual must be advised in writing to consult with legal counsel before signing; (6) the individual must receive time (at least twenty-one days unless the waiver is requested in connection with an exit incentive or other employment termination program offered to a class or group of employees, in which case the minimum period is forty-five days) to consider the waiver agreement; and (7) the waiver agreement must provide for at least seven days after execution during which the individual may revoke the agreement.[269]

---

[269] 29 USCA 626(f). If a waiver is in settlement of a charge filed with the EEOC or a court action alleging age discrimination under the ADEA, only the first five requirements listed must be satisfied and the individual must be "given a reasonable period of time" to consider the settlement agreement. If a waiver is requested in connection with an exit incentive or other employment termination program offered to a group or class of employees, not only must all seven listed requirements be satisfied, but also the individual must be informed in writing of those covered by the program, any eligibility factors and time limits applicable to the program, the job titles and ages of all individuals eligible or selected for the program, and the ages of all individuals in the same job classification or organizational unit who are not eligible or selected for the program.

17.20 Table of laws affecting equal employment opportunity

PART I. Federal E.E.O. laws generally applicable to schools and other employers

1. Constitution, Statutes, Executive Orders or Other Basis of Authority	2. Types of Discrimination Prohibited Generally	3. Investigating Agency, if any	4. Conciliation Formal	5. Plaintiff or Equivalent in Adjudication Proceedings	6. Legal Forum for Evidentiary Hearing in Adjudication Proceedings	7. Review Forum	8. Remedy for Discrimination	9. Affirmative Action Requirements
A. U.S. Constitution—Fourteenth Amendment. No state shall deny to any person the equal protection of the laws	Any discrimination under color of state law not reasonably related to a legitimate state purpose	The Fourteenth Amendment is implemented by 42 U.S.C. §§1981, 1983 and 1985 set forth below.						
B. Title VII, Civil Rights Act of 1964, as amended, 42 U.S.C. §2000e et seq.	Discrimination in employment made on the basis of race, color, religion, sex, pregnancy, national origin by any employer, employment agency or union organization	Equal Employment Opportunity Commission (EEOC)	Yes	EEOC, aggrieved individual, Justice Department against state and local agencies	Federal District Court	Federal Court of Appeals	Injunction; declaratory judgment including equitable relief; compensatory damages where discrimination is intentional	Following adjudication
C. Equal Pay Act of 1963, as amended, 29 U.S.C. §206	Any sex-based discrimination in pay by any employer, including public bodies	EEOC	No	EEOC or aggrieved individual	Federal District Court	Federal Court of Appeals	Injunction; declaratory judgment and/or compensatory relief (damages plus equal amount as liquidated damages)	No
D. Civil Rights Act of 1866, 42 U.S.C. §1981	Discrimination by any person within the U.S. on the basis of race, color or alienage with regard to making contracts, suing and obtaining the full protection of the law	None	No	Any person within the jurisdiction of the U.S.	Federal District Court	Federal Court of Appeals	Injunction; declaratory judgment, including compensatory relief and punitive damages	Following adjudication
E. Civil Rights Act of 1871, 42 U.S.C. §1983	Any discrimination on the basis of race, color or sex under color of state law	None	No	Aggrieved individual	Federal District Court	Federal Court of Appeals	Injunction; declaratory judgment, including compensatory relief	Following adjudication
F. Civil Rights Act of 1861 and 1871, 42 U.S.C. §1985	Race, class (conspiracy only)	None	No	Aggrieved individual	Federal District Court	Federal Court of Appeals	Injunction; declaratory judgment, including compensatory relief	Following adjudication
G. Age Discrimination in Employment Act of 1967, as amended, 29 U.S.C. § 621 et seq.	Any discrimination in employment on the basis of age (40 and over) by any employer, employment agency or labor organization	EEOC	Yes	EEOC or aggrieved individual	Federal District Court	Federal Court of Appeals	Injunction; declaratory judgment including compensatory relief damages plus equal amount as liquidated damages)	No
H. Americans with Disabilities Act of 1990	Discrimination in employment on the basis of disability	EEOC	Yes	EEOC, aggrieved individual, Justice Department against state and local agencies	Federal District Court	Federal Court of Appeals	Injunction; declaratory judgment including equitable relief; compensatory damages where discrimination is intentional	Following adjudication

PART II. State E.E.O. laws generally applicable to schools and other employers

1. Constitution, Statutes, Executive Orders or Other Basis of Authority	2. Types of Discrimination Prohibited Generally	3. Investigating Agency, if any	4. Conciliation Formal	5. Plaintiff or Equivalent in Adjudication Proceedings	6. Legal Forum for Evidentiary Hearing in Adjudication Proceedings	7. Review Forum	8. Remedy for Discrimination	9. Affirmative Action Requirements
A. Ohio Fair Employment Practices Act, RC Ch 4112	Discrimination because of race, color, religion, sex, pregnancy, national origin, handicap, age, or ancestry in employment	Ohio Civil Rights Commission (OCRC)	Yes	OCRC, (Individual Complainant also may participate)	OCRC Administrative hearing	Common Pleas Court	Injunctive and declaratory relief, including reinstatement with back pay less interim earnings	Following adjudication
B. RC § 4101.17 Discrimination because of age by employers	Age discrimination, hiring and discharge only	None	No	Aggrieved individual	Common Pleas Court (Only if no contract arbitration available and no OCRC charge filed)	State Court of Appeals	Appropriate relief, including, in discharge cases, reinstatement with back pay less interim earnings	No
C. RC § 4111.17, Wage Discrimination	Wage discrimination because of race, color, religion, sex, national origin, age or ancestry	Director of Industrial Relations	No	Director of Industrial Relations; aggrieved individual	Common Pleas Court	State Court of Appeals	Back pay (double damages)	No

PART III. Federal laws generally applicable to schools

1. Constitution, Statutes, Executive Orders or Other Basis of Authority	2. Types of Discrimination Prohibited Generally	3. Investigating Agency, if any	4. Conciliation Formal	5. Plaintiff or Equivalent in Adjudication Proceedings	6. Legal Forum for Evidentiary Hearing in Adjudication	7. Review Forum	8. Remedy for Discrimination	9. Affirmative Action Requirements
A. Equal Educational Opportunities Act of 1974, 20 U.S.C. 1701, et seq.	Segregation on the basis of race, color, sex, or national origin by state and local agencies in connection with educational opportunities; may include employment discrimination	Department of Justice	No	Department of Justice	Federal District Court	Federal Court of Appeals	Injunctive, declaratory and other appropriate relief	No
B. Title IV, Civil Rights Act of 1964, 42 U.S.C. §2000c	Segregation on basis of race, color, religion, sex or national origin; may include employment discrimination	Department of Justice, Department of Education	No	Department of Justice	Federal Court	Federal Court of Appeals	Injunctive and declaratory relief	Following adjudication

PART IV. Laws applicable to schools as federal funding recipients

NOTE: Most of the federal funding statutes are not principally directed to employment discrimination. Rather, Title VI, Title IX, and similar statutes cover employment discrimination (as opposed to discrimination impacting students) only when provision of employment is a principal purpose of the funding program. There also are various other funding statutes which include non-discrimination provisions but, because of the nature of the funding programs, they are unlikely to affect schools.

1. Constitution, Statutes, Executive Orders or Other Basis of Authority	2. Types of Discrimination Prohibited Generally	3. Investigating Agency If Any	4. Conciliation, Formal	5. Plaintiff or Equivalent in Adjudication Proceedings	6. Legal Forum for Evidentiary Hearing in Adjudication Proceedings	7. Review Forum	8. Remedy for Discrimination	9. Affirmative Action Requirements
A. Title VI, Civil Rights Act of 1964, 42 U.S.C. §§ 2000d-2000d-4	Any discrimination on the basis of race, color, national origin by any recipient under any federally assisted program	Justice Department Government Agency or Dept.	No	Department of Education, other governmental agencies or any person in the United States	Agency hearing	Whatever is provided to each agency for similar action on other grounds; federal courts	Suspension or termination of assistance; refusal to grant assistance; Compensatory damages where discrimination is intentional	No
B. Title IX, Education Amendments of 1972 20 U.S.C. §§1681 et seq., as implemented by Department of Health and Human Services regulations 45 C.F.R. §86.51 et seq. and Department of Education regulations 34 C.F.R. §106.1 et seq.	Any discrimination on the basis of sex in any education program or activity receiving federal financial aid	Department of Education	No	U.S. and Department of Education, or any person who believes herself or any specific class to be subjected to discrimination prohibited by these regs.	Department hearing procedures same as those for Title VI	Federal Court of Appeals	Termination or suspension of assistance in whole or in part; compensatory damages	No
C. Rehabilitation Act of 1973, as amended 29 U.S.C. §794	No qualified handicapped individual shall be denied the benefits of, or be subjected to discrimination under program or activity receiving federal aid	Department of Education other governmental agencies	No	Other governmental agencies and individuals	Applicable agency hearing, federal courts	Federal Court of Appeals	Suspension, termination or refund to award federal assistance; compensatory damages	No
D. Age Discrimination Act of 1975, 42 U.S.C.§ 6101. et seq.	Age discrimination in programs or activities receiving federal financial assistance	Department of Education	No	Aggrieved individual, Department of Education	Agency hearing, Federal District Court	Federal Court of Appeals	Suspension or termination of funding	No

PART V. Federal laws applying to government contractors

NOTE: Statutes and Executive Orders in this section are not normally applicable to public schools, but they may be applicable to private schools and/or institutions of higher education if the private schools or institutions of higher education are involved with government contracts.

1. Constitution, Statutes, Executive Orders or Other Basis of Authority	2. Types of Discrimination Prohibited Generally	3. Investigating Agency if any	4. Conciliation, Formal	5. Plaintiff or Equivalent in Adjudication Proceedings	6. Legal Forum for Evidentiary Hearing in Adjudication Proceedings	7. Review Forum	8. Remedy for Discrimination	9. Affirmative Action Requirements
A. Executive Order 11246, as amended	Any discrimination in employment on the basis of race, color, religion, sex or national origin by any federal contractor or subcontractor	Office of Federal Contract Compliance Programs (OFCCP), Dept. of Labor	Yes	OFCCP, Justice Department	Agency hearing, federal district court	Secretary of Labor, Federal Court of Appeals	Loss of contract and ineligibility for future contracts, affected class and back pay relief; injunctive relief	Written if 50 employees and $50,000 contract or subcontract
B. Rehabilitation Act of 1973, as amended 29 U.S.C. §793	Any failure by anyone who enters a contract with the U.S. Gov't in excess of $2,500 for the procurement of personal property and nonpersonal services to employ and advance in employment handicapped individuals.	OFCCP, Department of Labor	No	OFCCP	Agency hearings, federal court	Federal Court of Appeals	Contract termination or suspension in whole or in part, affected class and back pay relief, injunctive relief	Contractor must promise to affirmatively advance and treat handicapped workers without discrimination in all phases of employment; those with contracts exceeding $50,000 and have over 50 employees must prepare and maintain an Affirmative Action Program (AAP) within 120 days of commencement of contract
C. Vietnam Era Veterans Readjustment Assistance Act of 1974, 38 U.S.C. §§2011, 2012 and 2014	Any discrimination against disabled veterans and Vietnam veteran in employment by any federal contractor or subcontractor thereof	OFCCP, Dept. of Labor	Yes	OFCCP, Justice Department	Agency hearing, federal district court	Secretary, Federal Court of Appeals	Loss of contract and ineligibility for future contracts, affected class and back pay relief and injunctive relief	Written (if 50 employees and $50,000 contractor or sub-contract
D. Executive Order 11141, Equal Employment Opportunity Age Discrimination, 5 U.S.C. § 3301 Note	Age discrimination by federal contractors and sub-contractors.	Various federal agencies	No	Federal agency	Agency hearing	Federal Court of Appeals	Contract termination, ineligibility for future contracts, relief to aggrieved individuals	No

Chapter 18
Collective Bargaining

Note: The footnotes in this chapter contain several references to opinions of SERB Hearing Officers (indicated by the abbreviation "HO"). While a Hearing Officer's analysis is often useful, extreme caution must be exercised in assessing whether it has precedential value. Unless expressly adopted by SERB itself, a Hearing Officer's reasoning is not regarded by SERB as precedent and may not be cited to SERB as authority. OAC 4117-1-15(B), OAC 4117-1-17(B). See also In re Office of Collective Bargaining (State Highway Patrol), SERB 89-016 (7-13-89). SERB's adoption of a Hearing Officer's recommendations does not necessarily include adoption of the underlying analysis. In a given case, both the Hearing Officer's opinion and SERB's subsequent action with respect to it, if any, must be carefully scrutinized to determine just what does, and what does not, carry the weight of precedent.

INTRODUCTION
18.01 Historical background
18.02 State Employment Relations Board (SERB)

COVERAGE
18.03 Public employers
18.04 Employee organizations and bargaining rights
18.05 Excluded employees: management level
18.06 Excluded employees: confidential employees
18.07 Excluded employees: casual and seasonal workers
18.08 Professional and nonprofessional employees in same bargaining unit

EMPLOYEE RIGHTS
18.09 Employee rights in general
18.10 Collective bargaining

BARGAINING UNIT
18.11 Statutory guidelines for determining bargaining unit
18.12 Teacher bargaining units
18.13 Nonteaching employee bargaining units

CERTIFICATION OF BARGAINING REPRESENTATIVE
18.14 Recognition of exclusive bargaining representative
18.15 Representation elections
18.16 Voluntary recognition
18.17 Challenges to incumbent representative
18.18 Decertification

COLLECTIVE BARGAINING AGREEMENTS
18.19 Requirements for contract
18.20 Supremacy of contract over certain laws
18.21 Agency shop
18.22 Grievance procedure and arbitration
18.23 Expiration of contracts

UNFAIR LABOR PRACTICES
18.24 Unfair labor practices by employer
18.25 Unfair labor practices by union
18.26 Procedure on unfair labor practices

NEGOTIATIONS AND DISPUTES
18.27 Privacy of negotiations, conflict of interest
18.28 Scope of bargaining
18.29 Procedures for resolving disputes

STRIKES
18.30 Legal strikes
18.31 Unauthorized strikes
18.32 Temporary injunction against strikes presenting clear and present danger
18.33 Public records issues
18.34 Defamation in connection with labor disputes
18.35 Procedural timetables

INTRODUCTION

18.01 Historical background

The collective bargaining rights of Ohio's public employees have traveled from one end of the spectrum to the other—from a prohibition against strikes to full recognition of rights to bargain collectively and to strike.

(A) Ferguson Act

In 1947, the Ferguson Act codified the early English common-law principle that striking against a public authority was unlawful. The penalties for striking were (1) upon notification that they were on strike, employees lost their jobs; (2) they could not be rehired at compensation above that being paid when they went on strike; and (3) if rehired, their jobs were probationary for two years. That same year the Ohio Supreme Court, in *Hagerman v Dayton*,[1] held that a city could not agree to deduct dues from the salaries of union members.

(B) Early denial of collective bargaining rights

When the Ferguson Act was passed, it was widely believed that collective bargaining by a public employer would constitute an unlawful delegation of authority, since the employer was elected to make employment decisions, not employees. This often led to use of a "memorandum of understanding" that set forth agreements on certain terms and conditions of employment and was then adopted as policy by the employer. Similarly, public employers maintained submission of disputes to binding arbitration would unlawfully delegate authority to an outsider not responsible to the electorate.

(C) Recognition of unions

In 1959, former RC 9.41 legislatively overruled *Hagerman v Dayton* by permitting the deduction of union dues upon employee authorization, which could be revoked at will.

Two Ohio Supreme Court decisions in the 1970s provided further impetus for public employee collective bargaining. *Dayton Classroom Teachers Assn v Dayton Bd of Ed*[2] held a public employer was bound by a collective bargaining agreement "so long as such agreement does not conflict with or purport to abrogate the duties and responsibilities imposed upon the [public employer] by law." *Loveland Ed Assn v Loveland City School Dist Bd of Ed*[3] held that a union recognition agreement outlining procedures for negotiating a labor contract was enforceable.

(D) Public Employees' Collective Bargaining Act

Finally, after two vetoes of previous attempts at legislation, a new era began on July 6, 1983, when the governor signed the Public Employees' Collective Bargaining Act, most of which became effective on April 1, 1984. This legislation created the State Employment Relations Board to oversee implementation and enforcement of provisions regulating representation elections, unfair labor practices, and dispute settlement procedures in connection with collective bargaining.

18.02 State Employment Relations Board (SERB)

The three-member State Employment Relations Board (SERB) is responsible for implementing and administering the Public Employees' Collective Bargaining Act. Members are appointed by the governor with the advice and consent of the senate and serve staggered six-year terms. No more than two members may be from the same political party, and each must be experienced in labor relations or personnel practices. Although headquartered in Columbus, SERB may exercise its powers anywhere in Ohio, and has established regional offices in Cleveland and Cincinnati.

In addition to the power to conduct representation elections, adjudicate unfair labor practices, and regulate dispute settlement procedures, SERB is responsible for creating a bureau of mediation to perform dispute resolution functions; making studies for legislative recommendations; holding hearings and making findings in connection with specific statutory duties; training employers and employees in the rules and techniques of collective bargaining; and conducting studies on conditions of employment and statistical data relating to wages, benefits, and employment practices. SERB has promulgated permanent rules governing administrative procedure and implementation of its authority.[4]

---

[1]Hagerman v Dayton, 147 OS 313, 71 NE(2d) 246 (1947).

[2]Dayton Classroom Teachers Assn v Dayton Bd of Ed, 41 OS(2d) 127, 323 NE(2d) 714 (1975).

[3]Loveland Ed Assn v Loveland City School Dist Bd of Ed, 58 OS(2d) 31, 387 NE(2d) 1374 (1979).

[4]OAC 4117-1-01 et seq.

The Ohio Supreme Court has held that SERB has a right to participate as a party in judicial appeals of its adjudications, although it is not a necessary or indispensable party to review proceedings.[5]

COVERAGE

18.03 Public employers

The Public Employees' Collective Bargaining Act's broad definition of "public employer" encompasses every public educational institution in Ohio. Thus, all public school districts, county MR/DD boards, and institutions of higher education are covered.[6]

In the case of an educational cooperative, SERB has held that the employer, for collective bargaining purposes, is the cooperative (not a board of education as the fiscal agent) since it is organized, managed, governed, and funded by the governmental organizations that serve on its board, and because it serves a public purpose.[7]

18.04 Employee organizations and bargaining rights

(A) In general

The Public Employees' Collective Bargaining Act defines an "employee organization" as "any labor or bona fide organization in which public employees participate and which exists for the purpose, in whole or in part, of dealing with public employers concerning grievances, labor disputes, wages, hours, terms, and other conditions of employment."[8] SERB has held an organization claiming to be "a non-unionized group ... formed to ensure that control of education is in the hands of the local Board of Education and the Teaching Staff" is not an employee organization.[9] However, an employee organization was found to exist when an employer established a committee to discuss matters affecting all employees, including salary, benefits, and other working conditions, thus enabling SERB to find the employer guilty of the unfair labor practice of creating and dominating a union in violation of RC 4117.11(A)(2).[10]

Organization and bargaining rights are granted to all public employees except those specifically exempted.[11] A probationary employee meets the statutory definition and has the same protected rights as other covered public employees.[12] Expressly included within the meaning of "public employee" by the statute is "any person working pursuant to a contract between a public employer and a private employer and over whom the national labor relations board has declined jurisdiction on the basis that the involved employees are employees of a public employer ...." This provision has been construed as *not* requiring an actual decision by the national labor relations board as a predicate to SERB's jurisdiction.[13] For school employers the significant exemptions are confidential employees, management level employees, supervisors, students whose primary purpose is educational training, seasonal and casual employees as determined by SERB, and part-time faculty members of institutions of higher education.[14]

(B) Bargaining with excluded employees

The Public Employees' Collective Bargaining Act does not prohibit voluntarily electing to bargain collectively with exempted employees.[15] Moreover, SERB

---

[5] Hamilton County Bd of Mental Retardation & Developmental Disabilities v Professionals Guild of Ohio, 46 OS(3d) 147, 545 NE(2d) 1260 (1989).

[6] RC 4117.01(B).

[7] In re Southeastern Ohio Voluntary Ed Cooperative, SERB 85-046 (9-24-85).

[8] RC 4117.01(D). See In re City of Port Clinton, SERB 95-002 (2-27-95).

[9] Georgetown Exempted Village Schools, No. 84-VR-07-1520 (12-19-84 (SERB)).

[10] Hamilton County Dept of Human Services, No. 85-UR-07-3939 (HO 3-20-87, adopted 11-19-87, vacated on other grounds 1-22-88 (SERB)). See also Text 18.24(E), Employer domination of union.

[11] RC 4117.01(C).

[12] In re Cleveland City School Dist Bd of Ed, SERB 89-013 (5-19-89); In re ODOT, SERB 87-020 (10-8-87).

[13] Hamilton v SERB, 70 OS(3d) 210, 638 NE(2d) 522 (1994), cert denied sub nom Hamilton v Amalgamated Transit Union, Local No. 738, ___ US ___, 115 SCt 1104, 130 LEd(2d) 1070 (1995). The Ohio Supreme Court applies a "right to control" test to determine the status of employees under this provision. *Id.*

[14] RC 4117.01(C).

[15] RC 4117.03(C). See also In re City of Canton, SERB 85-011 (4-2-85).

will not remove supervisors and management level employees included in a bargaining unit before the Public Employees' Collective Bargaining Act from the unit; they may only be removed by agreement of the parties.[16]

18.05 Excluded employees: management level

(A) In general

Employees with authority to hire, transfer, suspend, lay off, recall, promote, discharge, assign, reward, or discipline other employees or with responsibility for directing them, adjusting their grievances, or effectively recommending such action are "supervisors."[17] However, the exercise of authority must require independent judgment and not be merely of a routine or clerical nature, and the "sporadic" exercise of some supervisory authority may be insufficient to establish supervisory status.[18] Whether an employee is a supervisor is a question of fact to be decided case-by-case.[19]

To qualify, an employee must possess one or more of the listed responsibilities, and the key to supervisory status is the use of independent judgment when exercising authority.[20] Adjusting grievances, for example, involves not merely the power to deny grievances perfunctorily but the capacity for independent evaluation, with authority to assess the merits and take corrective action when necessary. The mere authority to issue verbal reprimands is not sufficient to confer supervisory status based on authority to discipline; writing letters of commendation, without evidence that they play a role in promotions, is not sufficient to qualify as rewarding employees; responsibly directing employees involves more than simply following general routines in assigning tasks.[21]

Because supervisors are excluded from coverage, an appeals court overturned a SERB order that a supervisor discharged after engaging in union activity be reinstated with back pay.[22]

(B) Educational supervisors

The Public Employees' Collective Bargaining Act also contains detailed criteria for supervisors within educational institutions. Department chairmen or consulting teachers within school districts are not supervisors,[23] but heads of departments or divisions of state institutions of higher education are. No other faculty member of an institution of higher education is a "supervisor" solely because the member participates in decisions with respect to courses, curriculum, personnel, or other matters of academic policy.

School employees are covered by a special provision that makes it difficult to exclude certificated employees from a teacher bargaining unit. No teacher may be designated a supervisor or management level employee unless he is employed under a superintendent's or administrator's contract under RC 3319.01, RC 3319.011, or RC 3319.02 and (1) is assigned to an administrative or supervisory position requiring a certificate listed in RC 3319.22(F) to (J), (L), (N), or (O); or (2) is

---

[16]In re University of Cincinnati (University Hospital), SERB 85-022 (5-24-85), affirmed by 1987 SERB 4-25 (CP, Hamilton, 2-9-87); In re University of Cincinnati Hospital, SERB 86-005 (2-14-86), affirmed by 42 App(3d) 78, 536 NE(2d) 408 (Hamilton 1988).

[17]RC 4117.01(F).

[18]RC 4117.01(F); Franklin Local School Dist, No. 84-RC-07-1681 (5-8-85 (SERB)) (head cooks not supervisors because responsibilities in assigning and directing employees were routine and required no independent judgment); In re University of Cincinnati, SERB 89-028 (10-12-89).

[19]In re Mahoning County Dept of Human Services, SERB 92-006 (6-5-92), affirmed sub nom Ohio Council 8, AFSCME v Mahoning County Dept of Human Services, 1994 SERB 4-14, 1994 WL ___ (10th Dist Ct App, Franklin, 4-26-94); In re Lucas County Recorder's Office, SERB 85-061 (11-27-85);

In re Northwest Local School Dist Bd of Ed, SERB 84-007 (10-25-84).

[20]In re Mahoning County Dept of Human Services, SERB 92-006 (6-5-92), affirmed sub nom Ohio Council 8, AFSCME v Mahoning County Dept of Human Services, 1994 SERB 4-14, 1994 WL ___ (10th Dist Ct App, Franklin, 4-26-94). This case effectively overrules In re Greater Cleveland Regional Transit Authority, SERB 86-015 (4-17-86), which held that more than one of the listed responsibilities was required.

[21]In re Ohio State University, SERB 90-005 (2-23-90), appeal dismissed by 1990 SERB 4-119 (CP, Franklin, 12-10-90).

[22]SERB v Belmont County Engineer, 1989 SERB 4-126, 1989 WL 128755 (7th Dist Ct App, Belmont, 10-30-89).

[23]RC 4117.01(F)(1).

a supervisor certified under RC 3319.22(K).[24]

A hearing officer has determined that "head teachers" (performing the role of school building principals) and the athletic director should be excluded from a teacher bargaining unit. They received more pay, benefits, and work days per year than unit members. The head teachers were certificated as principals, had authority to recommend the renewal or nonrenewal of teachers' contracts, and their recommendations were normally followed. The athletic director had authority to make recommendations for hiring coaches and setting their salaries, which were normally followed. The hearing officer's determination was not challenged on review by SERB.[25]

(C) Other managerial employees

Employees who formulate policy or who may reasonably be required to assist in preparing for collective bargaining, to administer collective bargaining agreements, or to have a major role in personnel administration are "management level employees."[26] Assistant superintendents, principals, and assistant principals whose employment is governed by RC 3319.02 are specifically included.[27] However, in a departure from federal labor law, faculty of an institution of higher education are not management level employees merely because of involvement in the formulation or implementation of academic or institutional policy.[28]

18.06 Excluded employees: confidential employees

"Confidential employees" are also excluded from coverage. The Public Employees' Collective Bargaining Act gives the term a meaning different from ordinary usage. Confidential employees are those who work in the personnel office of an employer and deal with information used in collective bargaining or those who work in a close continuing relationship with persons directly participating in collective bargaining on the employer's behalf.[29]

The statutory definition is narrowly construed. Mere contact with or access to personnel records, grievances, or tenure decisions does not confer "confidential" status.[30] Moreover, the employer's intent to assign employees confidential duties in the future is irrelevant.[31]

18.07 Excluded employees: casual and seasonal workers

Another excluded group is "casual and seasonal" employees. The Public Employees' Collective Bargaining Act leaves the determination of casual and seasonal employees to SERB,[32] which defines "casual employees" as those employees assigned on an "on call" or "as needed" basis to supplement the work force (1) who averaged in the aggregate less than 500 hours the previous year, or (2) among whom less than 60% who worked one year returned the following year. "Seasonal employees" are those employees who work a certain regular season or period of the year performing some work or activity limited to that season or period (1) who averaged in the aggregate less than 500 hours the previous year, or (2) among whom less than 60% who worked one year returned the following year.[33]

---

[24]RC 4117.01(F).

[25]In re Franklin Local School Dist Bd of Ed, SERB 84-008 (11-8-84).

[26]RC 4117.01(K).

[27]RC 4117.01(K).

[28]RC 4117.01(K). For treatment of college faculties in the private sector, see NLRB v Yeshiva University, 444 US 672, 100 SCt 856, 63 LEd(2d) 115 (1980).

[29]RC 4117.01(J); In re University of Cincinnati, SERB 86-023 (6-5-86) (construing participation in bargaining as participation in contract negotiations).

[30]In re University of Cincinnati, SERB 86-023 (6-5-86); Muskingum Vocational School Dist, No. 84-RC-07-1643 (HO 2-8-85, adopted 4-9-85 (SERB)) (executive secretaries, who occasionally typed evaluations or reprimands, not confidential employees because they did not work in the personnel office, lacked access to the personnel files, had no input into the evaluations, and had no substantial exposure to bargaining-related matters); Ashtabula Area City Schools Bd of Ed, No. 89-REP-05-0132 (HO 12-21-89, adopted 2-27-90 (SERB)) (four secretarial positions in treasurer's office not confidential employees).

[31]Holmes County Dept of Human Services, Nos. 84-RC-08-1787, 84-VR-04-0018 (HO 1-31-85, adopted 4-29-85 (SERB)). See also In re City of Toledo, SERB 90-004 (2-16-90).

[32]RC 4117.01(C)(13).

[33]In re Ohio Turnpike Comm, SERB 93-022 (12-21-93). See also In re Tallmadge Firefighters Assn, SERB 95-011 (6-30-95). These standards apply on a job classification basis. If a particular classifica-

Substitute teachers who are not entitled under RC 3319.10 to regular teaching contracts for the succeeding school year (that is, those who have taught less than 120 days during the current school year) can be excluded from a teacher bargaining unit as temporary or casual employees upon objection by the employer, since they have no reasonable expectation of continued employment.[34]

However, "daily" substitute teachers (that is, substitutes who had taught less than sixty days in a single assignment during the current school year) were not casual employees where the employer had already included "long-term" substitutes in the teacher bargaining unit.[35] Unlike substitutes in many school districts, daily substitutes in this case shared nearly identical working conditions with long-term substitutes and regular teachers.

18.08 Professional and nonprofessional employees in same bargaining unit

Although covered by the Public Employees' Collective Bargaining Act, professional employees may not be included in a bargaining unit with nonprofessional employees unless a majority of both groups vote for inclusion in a combined unit.[36] In a representation election, this unit determination question must be stated on the ballot first, followed by the question of whether employees wish to be represented.[37]

A "professional employee" is either an employee engaged in work which is predominantly intellectual, involving the consistent exercise of discretion and judgment and requiring advanced knowledge in a field of science or learning customarily acquired by a prolonged course in an institution of higher learning, or an employee who has completed the courses of specialized intellectual instruction and is performing related work under the supervision of a professional to qualify himself to become a professional employee.[38]

Because teachers are plainly professional employees, a bargaining unit of teachers and nonteaching employees may only be certified if a majority of both vote for inclusion.[39]

Where a petition does not seek an initial representation election, but only a pure bargaining unit determination election as to whether two existing units—one composed of professionals and the other composed of nonprofessionals—wish to combine, the petition must be supported by a thirty per cent showing of interest in each of the existing units, not merely the proposed combined unit as a whole as is the case in an initial representation election.[40]

EMPLOYEE RIGHTS

18.09 Employee rights in general

The Public Employees' Collective Bargaining Act guarantees public employees a wide range of rights relating to union organization and collective bargaining, including the following rights:

(1) To form, join, assist, or participate in, or refrain from forming, joining, assisting, or participating, in an employee organization;

(2) To engage in other concerted activities for the purpose of collective bargaining or other mutual aid and protection;

---

tion satisfies the applicable standard, all workers employed in that classification are deemed not to be casual or seasonal even though particular employees may or may not meet the standard. The *Ohio Turnpike* standards apply prospectively and replace the standards earlier adopted in In re Hamilton County Dept of Welfare, SERB 85-008 (3-14-85).

[34] In re Franklin Local School Dist Bd of Ed, SERB 84-008 (11-8-84).

[35] In re Toledo Bd of Ed, SERB 85-017 (5-2-85).

[36] RC 4117.06(D)(1).

[37] In re Erie County Bd of Mental Retardation & Developmental Disabilities, SERB 91-007 (9-12-91).

[38] RC 4117.01(I).

[39] In re Montgomery County Bd of Ed, SERB 90-014 (8-29-90). See also In re Stark County Bd of Mental Retardation & Developmental Disabilities, SERB 93-018 (12-16-93); In re Lake County Bd of Mental Retardation & Developmental Disabilities, SERB 90-022 (12-19-90), affirmed by 86 App(3d) 300, 620 NE(2d) 970 (Franklin 1993).

[40] In re Cuyahoga County Community Health Bd, SERB 94-006 (3-10-94). See also Text 18.15(A), Petition for election.

(3) To be represented by an employee organization;

(4) To bargain collectively with their employers over wages, hours, terms, and other conditions of employment and to enter into collective bargaining agreements; and

(5) To present grievances to the employer and have them adjusted, without the intervention of the bargaining representative, except any adjustment cannot be inconsistent with the collective bargaining agreement and the bargaining representative must have the opportunity to be present at the adjustment.[41]

These rights may be extended to employees not covered by the Public Employees' Collective Bargaining Act if the public employer so elects.[42]

One of the most important enumerated rights is the right to engage in concerted activities for mutual aid and protection. This statutory language also appears in the federal labor law applicable to private sector employers and in the public sector labor laws of a number of other states. Just how it should be construed has long been a vexing problem. In the private sector, an individual employee's assertion of a right contained in a collective bargaining agreement is viewed as inherently concerted.[43] Otherwise, however, the National Labor Relations Board maintains that an employee's activity is concerted only when "engaged in with or on the authority of other employees and not solely by and on behalf of the employee himself."[44]

SERB initially took a much broader view. In *In re Cleveland City School Dist Bd of Ed*,[45] SERB, declaring that "the requirement that an activity be concerted relates to the ends, not to the means," concluded that

what determines whether a certain activity is concerted activity ... does not hinge on whether it was done by an individual employee or a group of employees, but rather whether the end to be served by the activity at issue is a "concerted" one for the employees [sic] "mutual aid and protection," and affects all employees.[46]

SERB stressed that the existence of a collective bargaining agreement or a unionized work force is not essential to finding that the assertion of a right is protected:

[C]onduct which, in its end result will benefit other employees in their status as employees, qualifies as "concerted activity" even in the absence of a collective bargaining agreement or of union representation. Hence, even for nonorganized employees, any invocation of a rule or procedure by an individual employee contained in a manual or employee's [sic] rules of any kind is "concerted activity" because the end result of this activity is interpretation and implementation of rules and procedures which affect all employees.[47]

In *In re Cincinnati Metropolitan Housing Auth*,[48] however, SERB expressly disavowed the *Cleveland* standard and adopted the *Meyers Industries* standard that applies in the private sector. As stated by SERB:

"Concerted" by its very definition, mandates more than one and clearly anticipates group action. The concept of collective activity ... embraces the actions of employees who have joined together in order to achieve common goals. ...

Although we believe that an individual acting alone may engage in concerted activity by invoking a contract right or attempting to induce other employees to act in concert, we disavow the notion, advanced in *Cleveland*, that an individual engages in concerted activity by invoking manual policies or rules which did not have their genesis in collective

---

[41] RC 4117.03(A).
[42] RC 4117.03(C). See also In re City of Canton, SERB 85-011 (4-2-85).
[43] NLRB v City Disposal Systems, 465 US 822, 104 SCt 1505, 79 LEd(2d) 839 (1984), cited with approval in In re Cleveland City School Dist Bd of Ed, SERB 89-013 (5-19-89).
[44] Meyers Industries, Inc, 281 NLRB 882 (NLRB 1986), enforced by 835 F(2d) 1481 (DC Cir 1987), cert denied 487 US 1205, 108 SCt 2847, 101 LEd(2d) 884 (1988) (supplementing 268 NLRB 493 (1984)).

[45] In re Cleveland City School Dist Bd of Ed, SERB 89-013 (5-19-89).
[46] In re Cleveland City School Dist Bd of Ed, SERB 89-013, at 3-82, 3-83 (5-19-89).
[47] In re Cleveland City School Dist Bd of Ed, SERB 89-013, at 3-83 (5-19-89) (citations omitted).
[48] In re Cincinnati Metropolitan Housing Auth, SERB 93-002 (4-6-93).

action. Individual action does not become concerted activity simply because it affects more than one employee.[49]

SERB went on to find that even if activity is concerted, it is not necessarily protected. Concerted activity may be engaged in in such an abusive manner that the employee's legal protection is forfeited.[50] Moreover,

> the *Meyers* standard safeguards against abuse. There are obvious differences between the assertion of a contractual right and what otherwise is tantamount to a *personal* complaint. Under the *Cleveland* standard, there is no safeguard against an employee acting alone and solely in his own interest from later claiming "concerted" activity to prevent possible disciplinary measures.[51]

Finally, SERB maintains that in any claim of discrimination against an employee for participating in concerted, protected activity, it must be shown hat the employer had knowledge of the employee's activity.[52]

In the private sector and under virtually all public employee bargaining laws in other states, the concept of concerted activity has been interpreted to include the right of an employee, upon request, to union representation at any investigatory interview the employee reasonably believes may result in disciplinary action. This is known as a *Weingarten* right, after the US Supreme Court case of that name.[53] Seizing on the language of RC 4117.03(A)(3),[54] however, SERB has explicitly eschewed *Weingarten* analysis in favor of creating a much larger right to representation. *In re Trotwood-Madison School Dist Bd of Ed*[55] involved two employees who requested meetings with management to discuss their job performance and further requested union representation at the meetings. Finding the employer's refusal to hold the meetings if a union representative were present to be unlawful, SERB, in a 2-1 decision, announced a broad rule that applies even in a nondisciplinary context:

> [W]e construe the statute as providing that an employee is entitled to have an agent of the exclusive representative assist, accompany, or speak on the employee's behalf in discussions with management that: (a) are relevant to the employer-employee relationship and (b) are not routine supervisory, instructional, or directory encounters.[56]

Presumably, representation must be requested by the employee, and the employer is not required to apprise the employee of the right in the absence of a request. In the same case, SERB held that "the selection of the particular union agent to accompany the employee is a matter to be determined by the employee and his exclusive representative, without interference by the employer."[57]

In short, SERB has stretched to broaden the right of union representation substantially beyond that which exists in other jurisdictions. However, SERB has refused to extend *Trotwood-Madison* to a work force where there is no certified or recog-

---

[49]In re Cincinnati Metropolitan Housing Auth, SERB 93-002, at 3-10, 3-11 (4-6-93).

[50]For an example, see In re City of Dayton, SERB 93-014 (8-12-93) (employee's vulgar and profane individual attack on supervisor, not in context of grievance proceeding or contract negotiations, not protected and written reprimand upheld), reversed in part sub nom FOP, Captain John C. Post Lodge No. 44 v SERB, 1995 SERB 4-8 (CP, Montgomery, 1-25-95).

[51]In re Cincinnati Metropolitan Housing Auth, SERB 93-002, at 3-11 (4-6-93).

[52]In re Cincinnati Metropolitan Housing Auth, SERB 93-002, at 3-11 (4-6-93). Under its new standard, SERB has concluded that counseling or advising a co-worker on terms and conditions of employment—in this case, advising a co-worker not to sign a written reprimand—is concerted, protected activity. In re Cincinnati Metropolitan Housing Auth, SERB 93-008 (5-18-93). In a case decided before adoption of its new standard, SERB concluded a teachers' union officer's complaint to her principal about class size and teaching materials, followed up with letters to parents and school board members and the distribution of materials to other teachers, was concerted, protected activity. In re West Carrollton City School Dist Bd of Ed, SERB 88-010 (7-14-88).

[53]NLRB v J. Weingarten, Inc, 420 US 251, 95 SCt 959, 43 LEd(2d) 171 (1975).

[54]The language guarantees a public employee's right to "[r]epresentation by an employee organization."

[55]In re Trotwood-Madison School Dist Bd of Ed, SERB 89-012 (5-19-89).

[56]In re Trotwood-Madison School Dist Bd of Ed, SERB 89-012, at 3-70 (5-19-89).

[57]In re Trotwood-Madison School Dist Bd of Ed, SERB 89-012, at 3-72 (5-19-89).

nized exclusive representative.[58] SERB has expressly left open the question of whether, in an unrepresented work force, an employee has a protected right under RC 4117.03(A)(2) to have a co-worker (as opposed to an outside union agent) present during certain meetings with management.[59]

18.10 Collective bargaining

Employers are required to bargain collectively with the exclusive representatives of their employees.[60] The duty to bargain requires the employer and union to carry out the mutual obligation to negotiate in good faith at reasonable times and places with respect to wages, hours, terms, and other conditions of employment, and the continuation, modification, or deletion of an existing provision in a collective bargaining agreement, with the intention of reaching an agreement, or to resolve questions arising under the agreement. The duty does not require either party to agree to a proposal or make a concession.[61] The duty includes an employer obligation to provide requested information relevant to the union's obligation to bargain collectively, to administer the collective bargaining agreement, or to prepare for negotiations.[62] In addition, the duty continues after execution of a collective bargaining agreement, and, absent a union waiver of bargaining rights, throughout the term of the contract requires the employer to give the union notice and an opportunity to bargain on proposed changes in "mandatory" subjects of bargaining.[63]

Recognizing that the Public Employees' Collective Bargaining Act "is grounded on the premise of freedom of contract," SERB has declared that its function is to oversee the process of bargaining, not the substance of collective bargaining agreements. Accordingly, SERB "will not sit in judgment upon the substantive terms" of a contract, leaving such terms "completely to the parties themselves to negotiate, to bargain and to struggle with."[64]

BARGAINING UNIT

18.11 Statutory guidelines for determining bargaining unit

(A) Authority of SERB

SERB is statutorily vested with final and conclusive authority to determine in each case the unit appropriate for collective bargaining, and its determination is not appealable.[65] However, SERB may not decide a unit is appropriate if it includes both professional and nonprofessional employees, unless a majority of each group first votes for the combined unit.[66] Additionally, SERB may not designate as appropriate a unit that contains more than one institution of higher education or within a single institution of higher education a unit which would be inconsistent with the accreditation standards governing the institution or any department, school, or college.[67] An employer may agree to include supervisors in a unit since RC 4117.06(D) does not specifically prohibit their inclusion.[68]

Moreover, SERB's ostensibly "final and conclusive" authority in determining an appropriate bargaining unit has been watered down significantly by the Ohio Supreme Court. While a SERB determina-

---

[58]In re Pickaway County Human Services Dept, SERB 89-014 (6-16-89), remanded on another ground by 1992 SERB 4-82, 1992 WL 10137 (4th Dist Ct App, Pickaway, 1-15-92).

[59]In re Pickaway County Human Services Dept, SERB 89-014, at 3-90 n.2 (6-16-89), remanded on another ground by 1992 SERB 4-82, 1992 WL 10137 (4th Dist Ct App, Pickaway, 1-15-92).

[60]RC 4117.04(B). For discussion of how an employee becomes the exclusive representative of a bargaining unit, see Text 18.14 to 18.17.

[61]RC 4117.01(G).

[62]In re Franklin County Bd of Commrs, SERB 87-010 (5-21-87), reversed on other grounds by 1989 SERB 4-116 (10th Dist Ct App, Franklin, 9-19-89),
citing NLRB v Truitt Co, 351 US 149, 76 SCt 753, 100 LEd 1027 (1956); Martins Ferry City School Dist Bd of Ed, No. 87-ULP-03-0124 (HO 1-31-89, adopted 4-18-89 (SERB)).

[63]See Text 18.28, Scope of bargaining.

[64]In re Truck Drivers, Chauffeurs & Helpers, Local No. 100, IBT, SERB 92-011 (7-15-92).

[65]RC 4117.06(A).

[66]Thus, a unit of teachers and nonteaching employees requires majority assent by both groups. See Text 18.08, Professional and nonprofessional employees in same bargaining unit.

[67]RC 4117.06(D).

[68]In re City of Canton, SERB 85-011 (4-2-85).

tion is not directly appealable, an action in mandamus to challenge SERB's conclusion as an abuse of discretion is available.[69] And, where a union proposes the composition of a bargaining unit, the Court believes SERB abuses its discretion in finding the unit inappropriate unless "substantial evidence" of inappropriateness is presented.[70] In *In re St. Mary School Dist Bd of Ed*,[71] SERB applied for the first time the guidelines laid out by the Supreme Court in *Glass Molders*. Where both the employer and the union propose "an" appropriate unit, SERB will weigh the statutory factors in RC 4117.06(B) to determine which is "the" appropriate unit. While SERB retains significant latitude in this area, its authority is not nearly as plenary as RC 4117.06(A) declares.

(B) Factors used in determining unit

In fashioning an appropriate bargaining unit, SERB is required to consider all relevant factors, including the desires of employees; the community of interests; wages, hours, and other working conditions; the administrative structure of the employer; efficiency of the employer's operations; the effects of overfragmentation; and the history of collective bargaining.[72] SERB may certify a unit as appropriate, even though another may also be appropriate.[73] Because certification means only that the unit is *an* appropriate unit, and not necessarily the *most* appropriate unit, SERB maintains that the legal doctrines of collateral estoppel, res judicata, and equitable estoppel have no relevance to unit determinations.[74]

Early SERB decisions reveal how these factors will be applied. First, although a mutually agreed proposed unit may be instructive, SERB will not approve it if there is a question as to appropriateness.[75] Second, the statutory list of relevant factors is not exhaustive.[76] Finally, no single fact will be dispositive; rather, an appropriate unit determination requires a finding based on a totality of relevant facts.[77] The burden of establishing an exclusion of employees from a unit on grounds they are not covered public employees rests with the party seeking the exclusion.[78]

Attempts to carve out small units from within a broader unit are assessed case-by-case. Generally, where a petitioner seeks a small group within a large department, SERB insists that the small group's community of interest "is sufficiently distinct and unique in relation to other employees and administratively sensible to make their segregation appropriate."[79]

SERB rules also permit the amendment or clarification of an existing bargaining unit.[80] A petition for amendment of certification pertains to a proposed alteration of the unit's composition by adding, deleting, or changing terminology in the unit description; a petition for clarification of a unit pertains to whether a particular employee or group of employees is

---

[69]State ex rel Glass, Molders, Pottery, Plastics & Allied Workers Intl Union, Local 333 v SERB, 70 OS(3d) 252, 638 NE(2d) 556 (1994); State ex rel Glass, Molders, Pottery, Plastics & Allied Workers Intl Union, Local 333 v SERB, 66 OS(3d) 157, 609 NE(2d) 1266 (1993).

[70]State ex rel Glass, Molders, Pottery, Plastics & Allied Workers Intl Union, Local 333 v SERB, 70 OS(3d) 252, 638 NE(2d) 556 (1994) (holding that SERB abused its discretion in finding union-proposed unit inappropriate).

[71]In re St. Marys School Dist Bd of Ed, SERB 95-007 (4-21-95).

[72]RC 4117.06(B).

[73]RC 4117.06(C).

[74]In re State of Ohio Dept of Corrections, SERB 92-009 (6-25-92); In re State of Ohio, SERB 87-030 (12-17-87).

[75]Medina County Commrs, Nos. 84-RC-04-0027, 84-RC-04-0436 (8-23-84 (SERB)).

[76]In re Northwest Local School Dist Bd of Ed, SERB 84-007 (10-25-84).

[77]In re Northwest Local School Dist Bd of Ed, SERB 84-007 (10-25-84). In some circumstances, for example, the effects of overfragmentation have been accorded overriding importance. See In re City of Bowling Green, SERB 92-008 (6-17-92); In re Office of Collective Bargaining, SERB 92-007 (6-10-92).

[78]In re Franklin Local School Dist Bd of Ed, SERB 84-008 (11-8-84); Mad River Township, Nos. 84-VR-04-0854, 84-RC-04-0863 (12-5-84 (SERB)). See Text 18.05 to 18.07.

[79]In re Columbiana County Human Services Dept, Children' Services Div, SERB 93-004 (4-21-93); In In re University of Akron, SERB 95-005 (4-21-95), SERB observed that while "an employer's 'convenience' is not a statutorily enumerated factor, O.R.C. Chapter 4117 does not require an employer to reconfigure its operations to accommodate any unit proposed by an employee organization."

[80]OAC 4117-5-01(E), OAC 4117-5-02(D).

included or excluded from the unit based on the existing unit description and the duties of the employees in question.[81] A petition for amendment or clarification will not be granted, however, if a question of representation exists[82] or if the petition does not present a matter that is ripe for adjudication.[83] SERB will not recognize as binding bargaining unit changes manipulated by an employer and union without the filing and SERB approval of either a petition for amendment or clarification.[84] Moreover, only the union or the employer, not an individual employee, has standing to petition for amendment or clarification.[85] SERB has held that whether accretion of employees into an existing unit by means of a petition for amendment or clarification is proper depends on (1) degree of movement of employees between the unrepresented group and the existing unit; (2) geographic proximity of the two groups; (3) integration of operations; (4) degree of central administrative control over the two groups; (5) similarity of skills, work, and working conditions; (6) degree of common control over labor relations; (7) collective bargaining history; and (8) number of employees in each group.[86] These are not necessarily the only factors to be considered, nor must each and every factor be present to justify accretion in a particular case.[87]

Where employees are accreted into an existing unit, the employer has no obligation to bargain with respect to them if an existing collective bargaining agreement can be applied "reasonably and sensibly" to them; if an existing agreement cannot be so applied, the employer has a "very narrow" duty to bargain with respect only to those issues unique to them that are not covered and could not have been predicted when the agreement was negotiated.[88]

However, where employees are added to an existing bargaining unit by means of an "opt-in" election, as opposed to accretion without an election, the existing unit's collective bargaining agreement does not automatically apply to the added employees irrespective of whether its terms could be "reasonably and sensibly" applied. Instead, the employer and union are obligated to bargain on an interim basis for the added employees, which is ultimately followed by a single successor agreement for the entire unit.[89]

There are substantial barriers to changing the makeup of a "deemed certified" pre-Act unit.[90] Where a union has been recognized as the exclusive representative of such a unit, the unit cannot be altered until challenged by another union and subsequent certification by SERB of the rival union. Thus, a deemed certified unit will, in the absence of such a challenge, not be disturbed even if it contains a patently inappropriate combination of employees judged by standards incorporated in the Public Employees' Collective Bargaining Act for all other units, and SERB is without jurisdiction to entertain petitions that seek to alter the composition of such a unit.[91]

Although not expressly addressed in either RC Chapter 4117 or SERB's administrative regulations, SERB has recognized and approved "opt-in" elections in which a

---

[81] OAC 4117-5-01(E). When a petition to amend certification seeks to add a group of employees to an existing unit, the number of employees to be added must be "substantially smaller" than the number of existing unit employees. OAC 4117-05-01(G).

[82] OAC 4117-05-01(E), OAC 4117-5-02(D)(4); Wooster City School Dist, No. 84-AC-05-1212 (1-30-85 (SERB)).

[83] In re Ohio Dept of Development, SERB 95-003 (2-27-95).

[84] In re State of Ohio, Office of Collective Bargaining, SERB 91-008 (9-19-91); In re City of Gallipolis, SERB 94-005 (3-3-94).

[85] OAC 4117-5-01(E); In re Martin, SERB 89-023 (9-8-89).

[86] In re Ohio State University, SERB 90-005 (2-23-90), appeal dismissed by 1990 SERB 4-119 (CP, Franklin, 12-10-90).

[87] In re Office of Collective Bargaining, SERB 92-007 (6-10-92)(holding accretion appropriate where only three of the factors were present).

[88] In re Kent State University, SERB 92-002 (3-20-92), affirmed in Ohio Council 8, AFSCME v Kent State University, 93 App(3d) 728, 639 NE(2d) 868 (Franklin 1994).

[89] In re University of Cincinnati, SERB 94-001 (2-8-94). This case goes on to state that RC 4117.14 procedures apply to such interim bargaining, except only the added employees are entitled to participate in a fact-finding vote or strike. See Text 18.29, Procedures for resolving disputes.

[90] For the meaning of a "deemed certified" unit, see Text 18.14, Recognition of exclusive bargaining representative.

[91] 1983 S 133 §4(A); Ohio Council 8, AFSCME v Cincinnati, 69 OS(3d) 677, 635 NE(2d) 361 (1994)

union petitions to represent a group of employees and include them in an existing bargaining unit.[92]

18.12 Teacher bargaining units

As a general rule, all certificated teaching employees should be included in a single bargaining unit. Thus, a proposed unit that included only some teachers and other professional employees was inappropriate where their job responsibilities were substantially the same as those of professional employees who were excluded.[93] SERB has included learning disability tutors in a teacher unit,[94] but has also certified a separate unit of learning disability tutors.[95]

However, an employer may object to inclusion of substitute teachers who are not entitled under RC 3319.10 to regular teaching contracts for the succeeding school year (that is, those who have taught less than 120 days during the current school year) in a teacher unit established after the effective date of the Public Employees' Collective Bargaining Act.[96] At least one employer successfully asserted that "as needed" noncontract substitutes did not share a community of interests with full-time teachers because they did not receive fringe benefits or have regular employment.[97] A separate unit of "short term" substitutes (that is, those who have taught for less than sixty days in the same assignment during the current school year) is appropriate where the employer has already included all other substitutes in the teacher unit.[98]

18.13 Nonteaching employee bargaining units

Contrary to the general rule for teacher bargaining units, SERB has found appropriate several units that do not include all nonteaching employees covered by the Act. Units have been approved, for example, that are limited to the following:

(1) Bus drivers;[99]

(2) Bus drivers and special program drivers;[100]

(3) Bus drivers and attendants;[101]

(4) Bus drivers and bus mechanics;[102]

(5) Aides and monitors;[103]

(6) Craft employees;[104]

(7) Bus drivers, aides, secretaries, and cafeteria workers;[105]

(8) Health aides;[106] and

(9) All nonteaching employees, excluding bus drivers, bus aides, educational aides, auxiliary aides, and clerical employees.[107]

(invalidating OAC 4117-5-01(F) as being in conflict with §4(A) and effectively overruling several prior SERB decisions on this issue).

[92] See In re University of Cincinnati, SERB 94-001 (2-8-94); In re Lake County Bd of Mental Retardation & Developmental Disabilities, SERB 92-004 (4-20-92).

[93] Hamilton County Bd of Mental Retardation & Developmental Disabilities, No. 84-RC-05-1037 (HO 1-25-85, adopted 4-29-85 (SERB)).

[94] In re Franklin Local School Dist Bd of Ed, SERB 84-008 (11-8-84). Compare Wooster City School Dist, No. 84-AC-05-1212 (1-30-85 (SERB)) (amendment of certification petition to include tutors in teacher unit denied since it raised a question of representation) with In re Columbus Bd of Ed, SERB 86-051 (12-4-86) (clarification petition to accrete tutors into teacher unit did not raise question of representation and was granted).

[95] Whitehall City Schools, No. 84-VR-10-2122 (2-12-85 (SERB)).

[96] In re Franklin Local School Dist Bd of Ed, SERB 84-008 (11-8-84).

[97] In re Solon City School Dist, SERB 87-003 (3-5-87).

[98] In re Toledo Bd of Ed, SERB 85-017 (5-2-85).

[99] Canton City School Dist, No. 84-RC-10-2162 (4-11-85 (SERB)).

[100] In re St. Marys School Dist Bd of Ed, SERB 95-007 (4-21-95); Northridge School Dist, No. 89-REP-09-0207 (1-2-90 (SERB)).

[101] Cleveland City School Dist, No. 84-RC-04-0076 (4-4-85 (SERB)).

[102] Dayton City School Dist, 84-RC-09-1876 (5-2-85 (SERB)); In re Northwest Local School Dist Bd of Ed, SERB 84-007 (10-25-84).

[103] Springfield Local School Dist, No. 84-VR-04-0634 (7-3-84 (SERB)).

[104] Cincinnati Bd of Ed, Nos. 84-VR-09-1949, 84-RC-05-0915 (5-2-85 (SERB)).

[105] Southeast Local School Dist, No. 84-VR-07-1526 (2-8-85 (SERB)).

[106] Forest Hills Local School Dist Bd of Ed, No. 89-REP-05-0126 (11-28-89 (SERB)).

[107] Hamilton City School Dist, No. 84-VR-07-1547 (2-8-85 (SERB)).

CERTIFICATION OF BARGAINING REPRESENTATIVE

18.14 Recognition of exclusive bargaining representative

Under the Public Employees' Collective Bargaining Act, an employee organization can obtain or maintain recognition as the exclusive bargaining representative in one of three ways: (1) through various "grandfather" provisions, (2) by voluntary recognition by the employer, or (3) by a representation election. The Act's grandfather provisions provide that a union's exclusive status as bargaining representative for a particular bargaining unit is preserved, as of October 6, 1983, the union was recognized as the exclusive representative either explicitly or through tradition, custom, practice, election, or negotiation. Such a recognized exclusive representative is "deemed certified until challenged by another organization under the provisions of [RC Chapter 4117] and the State Employment Relations Board has certified an exclusive representative."[109] SERB refers to grandfathered bargaining units as "deemed certified" units. While a collective bargaining agreement or memorandum of understanding expressly recognizing the union as the exclusive representative is the best evidence of an employer's exclusive recognition, it is not essential, although a party claiming deemed certified status in the absence of such a document has a "substantial burden."[110]

The Public Employees' Collective Bargaining Act also codifies an established, albeit infrequently applied, principle of federal labor law by providing that SERB may certify an organization as the exclusive representative without an election if it finds that the organization at one time had the support of a majority of employees and a free and untrammeled election cannot be conducted because of the employer's serious and pervasive unfair labor practices.[111]

18.15 Representation elections

(A) Petition for election

An employee, group of employees, or employee organization may file a petition for representation election alleging that at least thirty per cent of the employees in an appropriate bargaining unit wish to be represented.[112] The petition must be accompanied by substantial evidence of a thirty per cent showing of interest;[113] otherwise, the petition will be dismissed.[114] If dismissed, the petition of an intervening employee organization (which normally would be required to satisfy only a ten per cent showing of interest)[115] will also be dismissed absent evidence of a thirty per cent interest.[116] Once the statutory showing of inter-

---

[108] See, e.g., Greenview Local School Dist Bd of Ed, No. 89-REP-05-0133 (11-28-89 (SERB)); Noble Local Bd of Ed, No. 89-REP-06-0159 (11-28-89 (SERB)); Columbiana Exempted Village Bd of Ed, 89-REP-06-0168 (11-28-89 (SERB)); Circleville City School Dist Bd of Ed, No. 87-REP-11-0273 (12-12-89 (SERB)); Lakota Local School Dist Bd of Ed, No. 86-REP-12-0376 (2-2-90 (SERB)).

[109] 1983 S 133 §4(A). If an employee organization successfully adds unrepresented employees to a deemed certified bargaining unit by means of a representation petition and subsequent election, the changed unit becomes a Board-certified unit and no longer enjoys the special protection afforded deemed certified units. In re Lake County Bd of Mental Retardation & Developmental Disabilities, SERB 92-004 (4-20-92).

[110] In re City of Akron, SERB 94-012 (7-7-94) (denying deemed certified status where there was no agreement or memorandum and the union relied on dues deductions and grievance processing). Compare In re City of Bedford Hts, SERB 87-016 (7-24-87), affirmed by 41 App(3d) 21, 534 NE(2d) 115 (Cuyahoga 1987) (deemed certified status recognized where memorandum of understanding did not expressly give union exclusive recognition but parties had history of regular, full-fledged bargaining).

[111] RC 4117.07(A)(2). The principle was established in the private sector by NLRB v Gissel Packing Co, 395 US 575, 89 SCt 1918, 23 LEd(2d) 547 (1969).

[112] RC 4117.07(A)(1); OAC 4117-5-01(B).

[113] OAC 4117-5-02(A)(6). See generally In re Cuyahoga County Community Health Bd, SERB 94-006 (3-10-94).

[114] Cuyahoga County Nursing Home, No. 84-RC-09-2035 (5-17-84 (SERB)).

[115] RC 4117.07(B). See also In re Lake County Bd of Mental Retardation & Developmental Disabilities, SERB 85-034 (7-3-85).

[116] OAC 4117-5-01(C). See In re Hocking County Sheriff's Dept, SERB 85-047 (9-24-85).

est is met, it may not be attacked by submission of evidence suggesting employees have changed their minds, such as cards revoking authorization.[117]

An employer may also petition for a representation election by alleging that one or more employee organizations have requested recognition as the exclusive representative of an appropriate unit.[118]

Upon receipt of an employer or employee petition, SERB must investigate and, if it has reasonable cause to believe that a question of representation exists, hold a hearing upon notice to the parties.[119] If the investigation shows a question of representation requiring an election exists and there are no other disputed issues, SERB may direct an election without a hearing.[120]

In the case of an employer petition, the employer has the burden of showing that a question of representation exists by, for example, introducing evidence to demonstrate the union's claim for majority support is without foundation or in some manner tainted.[121] The employer's statement that it "does not believe it is in the best interest of each and every employee to voluntarily recognize" the union is insufficient.[122] Similarly, testimony that persons who signed authorization cards were misinformed as to their use was rejected where the cards made no reference to an election, there were no representations that the cards would only be used for an election, the testimony was uncorroborated hearsay, and the union would still have majority support if the disputed cards had been disregarded.[123]

(B) Consent election agreement

At any time after filing of a petition, the parties may enter into a consent election agreement. The agreement must include a waiver of hearing, a stipulated bargaining unit, a proposed time and place for the election, and the date upon which voter eligibility will be determined.[124] If approved by SERB, the election will be conducted in the same manner as an election resulting from a hearing. SERB will determine the time and date with due consideration given to the proposals of the parties.[125] Once an employer agrees to a consent election, it cannot withdraw absent "extraordinary circumstances."[126] Although an employee organization may subsequently withdraw from a consent election, it is prohibited from filing any representation petition for the same unit for the succeeding six months.[127]

(C) Election to settle representation question, results

If SERB determines after hearing (or without a hearing, in an appropriate case) that a question of representation exists, it must order a secret ballot election.[128] A choice of "no representative" must be included on the ballot.[129] Unions designated by more than ten per cent of bargaining unit employees may be listed on the ballot,[130] but an incumbent employee organization, if challenged, will automatically be placed on the ballot without a showing of interest.[131] An employee organization is not entitled to participate in an election unless it shows a good faith organizational effort and a representative interest in the unit employees *before* SERB schedules the election.[132]

To be certified as the exclusive representative, an employee organization must

---

[117]In re Painesville Township Local Bd of Ed, SERB 86-033 (9-5-86).

[118]RC 4117.07(A)(2); OAC 4117-5-01(A).

[119]RC 4117.07(A)(2); OAC 4117-5-04, OAC 4117-5-05.

[120]OAC 4117-5-05(D).

[121]In re Franklin Local School Dist Bd of Ed, SERB 84-008 (11-8-84).

[122]Riverside Bd of Ed, Nos. 84-VR-05-1221, 84-RC-06-1339 (12-12-84 (SERB)).

[123]Franklin Local School Dist, Nos. 84-RC-04-0181, 84-RC-04-0270, 84-VR-04-0275 (HO 7-12-85, adopted 9-20-85 (SERB)).

[124]OAC 4117-5-03.

[125]OAC 4117-5-03(C).

[126]In re Wayne County Engineer, SERB 85-028 (6-17-85).

[127]In re Clermont County Commrs, Clermont County Service Dept, SERB 84-003 (9-7-84).

[128]OAC 4117-5-05(C), (D).

[129]RC 4117.07(C)(4).

[130]RC 4117.07(B).

[131]In re Lake County Bd of Mental Retardation & Developmental Disabilities, SERB 85-034 (7-3-85).

[132]Ottawa-Glandorf Local School Dist, No. 84-RE-04-0135 (5-17-84 (SERB)).

receive a majority of valid votes cast.[133] Therefore, certification does not occur where the choice is between the employee organization and "no representation" and the vote is equally divided.[134] If more than one employee organization participates in the election, and none of the choices receives a majority, a runoff election is held between the two choices receiving the most votes.[135]

If employees vote against representation, SERB may not conduct an election during the succeeding twelve months in the unit.[136] This is sometimes referred to as an "election bar."[137]

(D) Challenge to election

Any party may file objections relating to the conduct of the election or conduct affecting the results of the election within ten days after the ballots are tallied.[138] Unsupported objections may be dismissed.[139] SERB is required to conduct an investigation if objections are supported or if the number of challenged voters is sufficient to affect the election outcome.[140] After the investigation, and a hearing if there are disputed material facts, SERB may dismiss the objections or challenges and certify the result, or order the counting of some or all of the challenged ballots and then certify the result, or set aside the election and order another.[141] If a rerun election is ordered, only employees who were eligible to vote in the first election and remain eligible on the date of the rerun election may vote.[142]

In a departure from federal labor law, SERB has prohibited all "captive audience" speeches prior to an election.[143] An employer may hold *voluntary* meetings during work time to explain its views on unionization, but only if (1) voluntariness is specified in the meeting announcement, (2) voluntariness remains unrevoked either directly or implicitly, and (3) the union is afforded an opportunity to hold a paid meeting at a similar time and place. Failure to satisfy these requirements is a basis for setting aside an election.[144] An employer's untimely submission of a list of eligible voters that contains substantial inaccuracies may also result in a rerun election.[145]

SERB has adopted a general rule that no wage increases or other benefits should be granted during a representation election campaign unless the employer was obligated to provide the increase before representation became an issue or the increase follows an established practice or custom or is required by law. Announcement of such an increase should be delayed until after the election if the custom or obligation permits; in any event, it must be accompanied by an explanation of its necessity that is full, clear, and neutral.[146] If the union wins the election and is certified, the employer's obligation to grant increases is "more limited." After certification, there is no obligation to act on the basis of past practice or custom—only preannounced increases or those the employer may be obligated by law to give are required.[147]

---

[133] RC 4117.07(C)(3).

[134] OAC 4117-5-09(A); In re Butler County Bd of Mental Retardation & Developmental Disabilities, SERB 92-019 (10-2-92).

[135] RC 4117.07(C)(5); OAC 4117-5-09(B).

[136] RC 4117.07(C)(6).

[137] See In re Skufca, SERB 89-035 (12-29-89).

[138] OAC 4117-5-10(A).

[139] OAC 4117-5-10(A).

[140] OAC 4117-5-10(B). At the election, the eligibility of a voter may be challenged. If unresolved challenged ballots are sufficient to affect the outcome, supporting evidence and position statements must be filed within ten days of the election. See *id.*; OAC 4117-5-08(F).

[141] OAC 4117-5-10(B).

[142] OAC 4117-5-10(B); In re Butler County Bd of Mental Retardation & Developmental Disabilities, SERB 89-001 (1-19-89).

[143] In re Belmont County Engineer, SERB 85-049 (9-26-85); In re Noble County Engineer, SERB 85-030 (6-20-85).

[144] In re Hamilton County Bd of Mental Retardation & Developmental Disabilities, SERB 86-050 (12-11-86), appeal dismissed by 1987 SERB 4-47 (10th Dist Ct App, Franklin, 8-12-87). See also OAC 4117-5-06(D), (E).

[145] See Hamilton County Bd of Mental Retardation & Developmental Disabilities v Professionals Guild of Ohio, 46 OS(3d) 147, 545 NE(2d) 1260 (1989).

[146] Lucas County Bd of Mental Retardation & Developmental Disabilities, SERB 86-048 (12-4-86).

[147] In re Chester Twp Police Dept, SERB 92-014 (9-2-92).

SERB set aside an election when the employee organization issued sample ballots altered to suggest SERB endorsed both the union and a single unit comprised of professional and nonprofessional employees.[148] SERB refused to set aside an election when an employee organization distributed allegedly misleading campaign literature because it did not have a restraining or coercive effect on employee rights.[149]

Election misconduct may justify setting aside an election, but infractions so innocuous as to have no effect on the result will not invalidate an election.[150]

(E) Service of notice of certification

Neither RC 4117.04 nor RC 4117.05 provides how SERB is to serve notice of its certification of a union as the exclusive bargaining representative. An appeals court has held that, by virtue of RC 4117.02(M), RC 119.09 applies and notice to the employer must be by certified mail. Thus, an employer who did not receive notice by certified mail had no duty to bargain with a union SERB certified after a representation election.[151]

(F) Appealability of SERB orders

SERB's adjudications are, by virtue of RC 4117.02(M), subject to judicial review pursuant to RC Chapter 119.[152]

However, to be appealable, the order must be "final" within the meaning of RC 2505.02. Thus, a SERB order for a rerun election, being interlocutory in nature, is not appealable;[153] nor is an order for a self-determination election between professional and nonprofessional employees of a school district.[154] Because a SERB order finding that an employer is covered by the Act "is but a preliminary step in the complete process of a SERB ordered election," it, too, is not final and, hence, not appealable.[155] In general, orders directing an election are not appealable.[156]

18.16 Voluntary recognition

(A) In general

An employee organization may become the exclusive bargaining representative by being recognized voluntarily by the employer and then certified by SERB. The organization must file a request for recognition with the employer, with a copy to SERB, describing the bargaining unit, which must be an appropriate unit described with specificity,[157] and alleging that a majority of unit employees wish to be represented by the organization. The request must be supported by substantial evidence of majority support in accordance with SERB rules,[158] or it will be dismissed.[159]

(B) Procedure

The employer must either petition SERB for an election within three weeks following the request for recognition or proceed with the voluntary recognition pro-

---

[148]In re South Community, Inc, SERB 85-062 (12-6-85).

[149]In re Stark County Engineer, SERB 85-012 (4-4-85).

[150]In re Sugarcreek Local School Dist, SERB 86-027 (6-26-86).

[151]Franklin County Bd of County Commrs v SERB, 64 App(3d) 113, 1989 SERB 4-116, 580 NE(2d) 832 (Franklin 1989).

[152]South Community, Inc v SERB, 38 OS(3d) 224, 527 NE(2d) 864 (1988). See also Springfield City School Support Personnel v SERB, 84 App(3d) 294, 1992 SERB 4-85, 616 NE(2d) 983 (Franklin 1992) (SERB decision to dismiss petition for election on procedural grounds appealable).

[153]Hamilton County Bd of Mental Retardation and Developmental Disabilities v Professionals Guild of Ohio, 46 OS(3d) 147, 545 NE(2d) 1260 (1989).

[154]Trotwood-Madison Ed Assn Support Staff Personnel, OEA/NEA v Trotwood-Madison City School Dist, 1990 SERB 4-31 (CP, Franklin, 5-31-90).

[155]Ohio Historical Society v SERB, 48 OS(3d) 45, 549 NE(2d) 157 (1990).

[156]Ohio Historical Society v SERB, 48 OS(3d) 45, 549 NE(2d) 157 (1990); Five-County Joint Juvenile Detention Center v SERB, 57 OS(3d) 4, 565 NE(2d) 546 (1991).

[157]In re Columbiana County Auditor's Office, SERB 91-002 (5-21-91). Subsequently, however, SERB's refusal to certify on the particular facts of this case was rejected as an arbitrary abuse of discretion in State ex rel Glass, Molders, Pottery, Plastics & Allied Workers Intl Union, Local 333 v SERB, 66 OS(3d) 157, 609 NE(2d) 1266 (1993).

[158]RC 4117.05(A)(2); OAC 4117-3-01.

[159]Upper Scioto Valley Local School Dist, No. 84-VR-11-2336 (11-28-84 (SERB)); Springfield Bd of Ed, No. 84-VR-09-1905 (11-14-84 (SERB)).

cedures of the Public Employees' Collective Bargaining Act.[160]

Upon receipt of the voluntary recognition request, the employer must immediately post a notice in each facility at which employees in the proposed unit are employed.[161] Absent an employer election petition, SERB will certify the employee organization as the exclusive representative three weeks after the request is made unless SERB receives substantial evidence, in accordance with its rules, demonstrating that (1) a majority of employees do not wish to be represented by the organization; (2) at least ten per cent of the employees wish to be represented by another employee organization; or (3) the proposed unit is not appropriate under the Public Employees' Collective Bargaining Act.[162] Certification will occur after three weeks even if the employer fails to post the statutorily required notice.[163]

(C) Rival employee organization, objection, election

The request for voluntary recognition will be dismissed if a rival employee organization files an objection and submits substantial evidence of a ten per cent showing of interest in the proposed unit.[164] Such evidence must be filed concurrently with the objection.[165]

18.17   Challenges to incumbent representative

(A) In general, when challenge may be made

If an employee organization is certified as an exclusive bargaining representative after an election, SERB may not conduct an election within the next twelve months in the unit.[166] Moreover, RC 4117.07(C)(6) codifies the "contract bar" doctrine, developed in the private sector, that an election may not be held during the term of a lawful collective bargaining agreement (by virtue of RC 4117.09(E), the agreement must be for a term not to exceed three years).[167] Election petitions may be filed during the period from 120 to 90 days before an agreement expires[168] or at any time after an agreement expires and before a new agreement is entered into.[169] A petition filed by a rival employee organization outside this window period will be dismissed notwithstanding that the collective bargaining agreement provides for a different window period.[170] The contract bar doctrine applies to pre-Public Employees'

---

[160] RC 4117.05(A)(2); Celina City School Dist, Nos. 84-VR-10-5289, 84-RC-11-2452 (12-12-84 (SERB)); Fayetteville-Perry Local School Dist Bd of Ed, Nos. 84-VR-04-0558, 84-RC-05-1161 (HO 10-10-84 (SERB)).

[161] RC 4117.05(A); OAC 4117-3-01.

[162] RC 4117.05(A); OAC 4117-3-02; Symmes Valley Local Bd of Ed, No. 84-VR-05-0935 (7-3-84 (SERB)). If the employer does not present substantial evidence that the proposed unit is inappropriate, SERB may still find it inappropriate and dismiss the petition. In re Columbiana County Auditor's Office, SERB 91-002 (5-21-91). Subsequently, however, SERB's refusal to certify on the particular facts of this case was rejected as an arbitrary abuse of discretion in State ex rel Glass Workers Intl Union, Local #333 v SERB, 1991 SERB 4-131, 1991 WL 254886 (10th Dist Ct App, Franklin, 12-3-91), affirmed by 66 OS(3d) 157, 609 NE(2d) 1266 (1993).

[163] Hamilton City School Dist, No. 84-VR-07-1547 (2-8-85 (SERB)); Strasburg-Franklin Bd of Ed, No. 84-VR-05-1269 (12-12-84 (SERB)).

[164] Cuyahoga Heights Bd of Ed, No. 85-VR-01-2797 (4-3-85 (SERB)).

[165] East Holmes Local Bd of Ed, Nos. 85-RC-03-3127, 85-VR-03-3051 (11-7-85 (SERB)).

[166] RC 4117.07(C)(6); OAC 4117-5-11(C). Although not expressly provided in the statute as is the case with this "election bar," SERB has held that a comparable twelve-month "certification bar" should be applied to certifications that occur under RC 4117.05(A)(2) without an election. In re Skufca, SERB 89-035 (12-29-89). A union request for recognition within twelve months of an election is also untimely and will be dismissed upon an employer's objection. In re City of South Euclid, SERB 92-021 (12-23-92). See also In re Butler County Bd of Mental Retardation & Developmental Disabilities, SERB 92-019 (10-2-92) (holding neither election nor certification bar applied under particular circumstances of this case).

[167] Thus, even if all parties agree to such a procedure, SERB will not approve an election date prior to the expiration date of an existing agreement unless there is "clear and unequivocal evidence" that the agreement has legally been terminated before both its expiration date and the election date. In re Boardman Twp Trustees, SERB 93-016 (9-2-93), overruling In re City of Niles, SERB 87-029 (11-25-87).

[168] For the mechanics of calculating this window period, see In re City of Garfield Heights, SERB 90-008 (6-18-90).

[169] RC 4117.07(C).

[170] In re Brunswick City School Dist Bd of Ed, SERB 85-035 (7-3-85).

Collective Bargaining Act deemed certified units.[171] The doctrine does not apply, however, where a union petitions for a self-determination election to determine whether employees of two bargaining units represented by the union, one professional and one nonprofessional, wish to consolidate into a single unit.[172]

To act as a bar, an agreement must be in writing, executed by both parties, include a definite expiration date, and contain substantial terms and conditions of employment. An agreement that contains only salary and fringe benefits is insufficient.[173]

A petition filed after expiration of a collective bargaining agreement is valid if tentative agreement on a new contract has been reached but only one party has executed it.[174] However, ratification of the new agreement by members of the bargaining unit is not required unless the agreement, by its terms, is not effective unless so ratified.[175] In addition, an executed agreement will bar an election even if the signature pages are not attached.[176]

(B) Election petition by rival organization

A rival union that files a petition for representation election must satisfy the same requirement of a thirty per cent showing of interest that applies in an initial representation election.[177] The election will be conducted in the same manner as an initial election, except the incumbent union will automatically be on the ballot without having to satisfy any showing of interest requirement.[178]

When a valid petition for representation election, supported by the required showing of interest, has been filed by a rival employee organization, the employer may refuse to bargain with the incumbent union until the issue of representation is decided.[179] A rival union, however, lacks standing to challenge an employer decision to continue bargaining with the incumbent.[180]

Where a rival union filed a petition for representation election with respect to a deemed certified bargaining unit and the employer sought to alter the unit description, SERB refused to delay the election and review appropriateness of the unit.[181] However, a rival union can file a petition seeking to represent just one category of present unit members.[182]

While the Public Employees' Collective Bargaining Act provides for challenging an incumbent union by means of a petition for representation election, no procedure appears for challenging by means of a voluntary recognition proceeding. Thus, a rival union's request for voluntary recognition will be dismissed.[183]

---

[171] For the meaning of "deemed certified," see Text 18.14, Recognition of exclusive bargaining representative.

[172] In re Stark County Bd of Mental Retardation & Developmental Disabilities, SERB 93-018 (12-16-93); In re Montgomery County Bd of Ed, SERB 90-014 (8-29-90); In re Lake County Bd of Mental Retardation & Developmental Disabilities, SERB 90-022 (12-19-90), affirmed by 1993 SERB 4-12, 1993 WL 280814 (10th Dist Ct App, Franklin, 2-11-93). See also Text 18.08, Professional and nonprofessional employees in same bargaining unit.

[173] West Branch Bd of Ed, No. 84-VR-04-0714 (HO 12-10-84, adopted 3-15-85 (SERB)).

[174] In re Ohio University, SERB 85-053 (10-4-85).

[175] Compare In re Northeast Ohio Sewer Dist, SERB 85-031 (6-24-85) (ratification not required) with City of Franklin, No. 84-RC-05-0923 (5-23-85 (SERB)) (agreement required ratification).

[176] City of Cleveland, Nos. 84-RC-04-0075, 84-RC-04-0031 (HO 1-7-85, adopted 3-20-85 (SERB)).

[177] OAC 4117-5-01(C). See also In re Summit County Bd of Mental Retardation, SERB 85-029 (6-20-85).

[178] In re Lake County Bd of Mental Retardation & Developmental Disabilities, SERB 85-034 (7-3-85).

[179] In re North Canton City Schools, SERB 85-037 (8-2-85); In re Cleveland School Dist Bd of Ed, SERB 85-003 (2-1-85). See also In re West Carrollton City School Dist, SERB 86-026 (6-26-86).

[180] In re Summit County Bd of Mental Retardation & Developmental Disabilities, SERB 85-014 (4-18-85).

[181] In re Eaton City Bd of Ed, SERB 87-022 (11-9-87); In re Sheffield-Sheffield Lake City School Dist, SERB 87-023 (11-9-87); In re Willoughby-Eastlake Bd of Ed, SERB 87-024 (11-9-87). SERB went on to note, in these cases, that, if not rendered moot by the election results, unit appropriateness could be considered by means of a petition for unit clarification or an amendment to certification. See Text 18.11(B), Factors used in determining unit.

[182] In re Cuyahoga County Bd of Commrs, SERB 87-012 (6-10-87).

[183] In re Stow City School Dist, SERB 85-051 (9-30-85).

(C) Union affiliation votes

Occasionally, an unaffiliated local union decides to "affiliate" with a larger regional, state, or national union. Generally, this is viewed as an internal union matter that does not affect the union's status as an exclusive employee representative. Thus, an employer may not withdraw recognition from or refuse to bargain with a union simply because it has thus affiliated with another union. SERB has held an affiliating union is entitled to an amendment of certification if (1) union members were given reasonable notice of the upcoming affiliation vote and afforded an opportunity to discuss the question, (2) the vote is by secret ballot, and (3) a "substantial continuity" exists between the pre-affiliation union and the post-affiliation union.[184] The right to vote need not be granted to all members of the bargaining unit, but may be restricted to union members.[185] These same considerations govern an amendment of certification where a local union "disaffiliates" from another union.[186] Where a deemed certified[187] affiliated local union changes its affiliation from one national union to another national union, however, SERB has held that the procedures of RC Chapter 4117 changing a bargaining representative apply and that an employer's recognition of and agreement with the newly affiliated union are unlawful.[188]

18.18 Decertification

The Public Employees' Collective Bargaining Act guarantees both the right to have a collective bargaining representative and the right not to have one. Thus, employees may seek to decertify, or remove, an exclusive representative, and choose not to bargain collectively, by filing a petition for decertification with SERB. The petition must allege, together with evidence in support, that the union no longer enjoys majority support of unit employees and that at least half no longer desire such representation.[189] SERB's view that a decertification petition may not be filed where the incumbent union represents a deemed certified unit[190] has been rejected by a reviewing court.[191] SERB, however, continues to maintain that a decertification petition may only be filed with respect to a SERB-certified unit, a position that appears to be supported by implication in *SERB v Miami University*.[192] Where the unit is either deemed certified or not certified at all, a decertification petition will be dismissed.[193]

Evidence in support may consist of original signed and individually dated statements, such as cards and petitions, that clearly show the employee's intent regarding representation. A single employee may file a petition but must demonstrate an agency for others.[194]

---

[184]In re Montgomery County Joint Vocational School Dist Bd of Ed, SERB 89-010 (5-11-89).

[185]In re Montgomery County Joint Vocational School Dist Bd of Ed, SERB 89-010 (5-11-89). See also In re Mad River-Green Local Bd of Ed, SERB 86-029 (7-31-86).

[186]In re Cuyahoga County Sheriff's Dept, SERB 92-013 (9-1-92).

[187]For the meaning of "deemed certified," see Text 18.14, Recognition of exclusive bargaining representative.

[188]In re Mad River-Green Local Bd of Ed, SERB 86-029 (7-31-86).

[189]RC 4117.07(A)(1); OAC 4117-5-01(D), OAC 4117-5-02(C). See also New Miami Bd of Ed, No. 84-RD-01-2636 (2-4-85 (SERB)).

[190]OAC 4117-5-01(D)(2).

[191]New Miami Local School Dist Bd of Ed v SERB, 57 Misc(2d) 27, 1989 SERB 4-17, 566 NE(2d) 201 (CP, Butler 1989).

[192]SERB v Miami University, 71 OS(3d) 351, 643 NE(2d) 1113 (1994).

[193]In re Cuyahoga County Sheriff's Dept, SERB 93-015 (8-25-93). SERB acknowledged that the deemed certified provision in 1983 S 133, §4(A), eff. 10-6-83, "creates a legal nightmare and, worse, an unjust and unfair prohibition of employees to exercise their statutory rights to choose not to be represented by any employee organization." Nevertheless, SERB believes it is "bound by the clear language of the statute" and forced to this seemingly absurd result.

[194]OAC 4117-15-02(C); In re Rooney, SERB 89-018 (8-17-89), appeal dismissed by Miami University v SERB, 70 App(3d) 514, 1990 SERB 4-111, 591 NE(2d) 415 (Franklin 1990); In re Hocking County Engineer, SERB 86-002 (1-31-86).

The petition must be filed during the same "open window" period applicable to representation elections.[195] An employer lacks standing to challenge the dismissal of an employee's untimely petition.[196] The petition will be investigated, and an election will be conducted, with the same procedures as apply to representation elections. An incumbent union will not be decertified unless a majority of the votes cast are for "no representative."[197]

The filing of a timely decertification petition entitles the employer, upon motion to SERB, to an order that stays bargaining with the incumbent union pending the outcome; if the petition is withdrawn or dismissed, however, the employer is dutybound to bargain even if a good faith doubt exists as to whether the union maintains support among a majority of bargaining unit employees. In a departure from principles that apply in the private sector, SERB insists that an employer's unilateral withdrawal of recognition, even where a good faith doubt exists, is unlawful per se.[198] Emphasizing that under Ohio's Public Employees' Collective Bargaining Act, "certification is the benchmark which triggers a bargaining obligation," SERB believes the duty to bargain "depends not upon the majority status of the employee organization, but rather upon the certification of the employee organization by SERB as the exclusive bargaining agent" and that, therefore, the duty "is relieved only upon revocation of certification by the Board or temporarily by granting a motion to stay."[199] SERB's position has been approved by the Ohio Supreme Court in *SERB v Miami University*.[200]

COLLECTIVE BARGAINING AGREEMENTS

18.19 Requirements for contract

(A) In general

Collective bargaining agreements must be in writing and cannot be for a term greater than three years, although the parties may mutually extend an agreement.[201] All agreements must contain a grievance procedure which *may* (but need not) culminate in final and binding arbitration.[202] Agreements must also contain a dues checkoff provision authorizing the employer to deduct dues, fees, and assessments of union members upon presentation of written authorization by the employee.[203] At least in the absence of a question of representation, an employer who unilaterally insists that the authorization be signed in his presence to ensure its voluntariness commits an unfair labor practice.[204]

(B) Peer review plan

The agreement *may* (but need not) provide for a peer review plan under which teachers may, for other teachers in the unit or other teachers whom the union represents, assist in instructing, evaluating, and making recommendations or decisions regarding the termination or nonrenewal of such other teachers. The participation of a teacher or union in such a plan is expressly not an unfair labor practice.[205]

---

[195]See Text 18.17(A), In general, when challenge may be made.

[196]Miami University v SERB, 70 App(3d) 514, 1990 SERB 4-111, 591 NE(2d) 415 (Franklin 1990); Montgomery County Clerk of Courts v Ohio Council 8, AFSCME, 1991 SERB 4-18 (CP, Franklin, 3-6-91).

[197]OAC 4117-5-09(A).

[198]In re Marion County Children's Services Bd, SERB 92-017 (10-1-92).

[199]In re Marion County Children's Services Bd, SERB 92-017, at 3-58 (10-1-92).

[200]SERB v Miami University, 71 OS(3d) 351, 643 NE(2d) 1113 (1994).

[201]RC 4117.09(A), (D).

[202]RC 4117.09(B)(1). This statute goes on to say a party to an agreement may sue in common pleas court for violation of the agreement or to enforce an arbitration award. Such jurisdiction has been deemed exclusive. Moore v Youngstown State University, 63 App(3d) 238, 578 NE(2d) 536 (Franklin 1989) (holding court of claims lacks jurisdiction over alleged violation of agreement). See Text 18.22, Grievance procedure and arbitration.

[203]RC 4117.09(B)(2). For discussion of what an agreement must contain in order to trigger the contract-bar doctrine, see Text 18.17(A), In general, when challenge may be made.

[204]In re Clermont County Sheriff, SERB 89-024 (10-5-89).

[205]RC 4117.09(D).

18.20 Supremacy of contract over certain laws

The Public Employees' Collective Bargaining Act reverses the principle of Ohio law that terms of a collective bargaining agreement are valid only to the extent they do not conflict with or abrogate duties and responsibilities imposed upon boards of education by law.[206] Under RC 4117.10, a collective bargaining agreement governs wages, hours, and terms and conditions of employment and generally prevails over any conflicting law.[207] However, if there is no collective bargaining agreement, or if the agreement "makes no specification about a matter," the employer and employees remain subject to state and local laws pertaining to terms and conditions of employment.[208] The statute goes on to list specific exceptions to this "supremacy of contract": laws pertaining to civil rights,[209] affirmative action, unemployment compensation, workers' compensation, the retirement of public employees,[210] residency requirements, the minimum educational requirements in the Revised Code pertaining to public education, including the requirement of a certificate under RC 5705.41, and state board of education minimum standards under RC 3301.07(D) are expressly excepted; in addition, the law pertaining to leave and compensation for military service under RC 5923.05 prevails over a collective bargaining agreement that provides lesser benefits or no such benefits if the public employer is the state or a political subdivision that elects to provide benefits under RC 5923.05(D). Although the statute purports to state the only exceptions, courts may prevent a collective bargaining agreement from altering legal relationships between a government and the public at large. Thus, an employer and union cannot agree to make secret personnel records that are public records under the Public Records Act.[211]

Provisions of a collective bargaining agreement establishing supplemental workers' compensation or unemployment compensation benefits or exceeding minimum statutory requirements pertaining to public education or minimum state board of education standards are valid.

That a collective bargaining agreement may modify statutory teacher tenure eligibility requirements[212] is also clear. The decisive case, *State ex rel Rollins v Cleveland Hts-University Hts City School Dist Bd of*

---

[206] See Dayton Classroom Teachers Assn v Dayton Bd of Ed, 41 OS(2d) 127, 323 NE(2d) 714 (1975).

[207] It matters not whether the provision of the collective bargaining agreement at issue pertains to a permissive, as opposed to a mandatory, subject of bargaining. Cincinnati v Ohio Council 8, AFSCME, 61 OS(3d) 658, 576 NE(2d) 745 (1991). See also Text 18.28, Scope of bargaining.

[208] Thus, for a collective bargaining agreement to prevail over a statute, there must be a genuine conflict. A bare majority of the Ohio Supreme Court stretched to avoid finding a conflict in State ex rel Clark v Greater Cleveland Regional Transit Authority, 48 OS(3d) 19, 548 NE(2d) 940 (1990), wherein a group of employees of a political subdivision successfully argued they were entitled to additional prior service credit for vacation purposes by virtue of RC 9.44. Even though the agreement included vacation eligibility provisions, the majority concluded prior service credit was required under RC 9.44 since that precise issue was not specifically addressed in collective bargaining. Since the benefits provided by the statute were not specifically bargained away, the employees remained entitled to them. The three dissenting justices easily found a "clear conflict" between the agreements (under which continuing service with the employer was the sole factor in calculating vacation leave) and RC 9.44 (which required prior service with another public employer to also be counted).

Following *Clark*, the Court held in a case involving a civil service employer that where a collective bargaining agreement made no specification with respect to the probationary status of new employees, RC 124.27 and local law determined whether an employee was probationary and the procedure to be followed in dismissing him. Bashford v Portsmouth, 52 OS(3d) 195, 556 NE(2d) 477 (1990). See also State ex rel International Union of Operating Engineers v Simmons, 58 OS(3d) 247, 569 NE(2d) 886 (1990); State ex rel Caspar v Dayton, 53 OS(3d) 16, 558 NE(2d) 49 (1990); Felker v Mid-East Ohio Vocational School Dist Bd of Ed, No. 93-21, 1993 WL 545385 (5th Dist Ct App, Muskingum, 12-22-93). For an example of local law prevailing where protracted collective bargaining failed to produce an agreement, see State ex rel International Union of Operating Engineers v Cleveland, 62 OS(3d) 537, 584 NE(2d) 727 (1992).

[209] See Bettio v Stow Civil Service Comm, Nos. 12855, 12856, 1987 WL 10349 (9th Dist Ct App, Summit, 4-22-87).

[210] See Streetsboro Ed Assn v Streetsboro City School Dist Bd of Ed, 68 OS(3d) 288, 626 NE(2d) 110 (1994).

[211] State ex rel Dispatch Printing Co v Wells, 18 OS(3d) 382, 18 OBR 437, 481 NE(2d) 632 (1985); RC 149.43. See Text Ch 44, Records of Employees and Pupils.

[212] See Text 9.05 to 9.08.

Ed,[213] emphasizing that "R.C. 3319.11 is a teacher protection statute and not a law pertaining to minimum educational requirements under R.C. 4117.10(A)," refused to nullify a purely contractual requirement that the teacher be recommended for tenure by the building principal. A collective bargaining agreement may limit a district superintendent's authority under RC 3319.01 to direct and assign employees,[214] incorporate teacher evaluation procedures different from those prescribed in RC 3319.111,[215] and compensate tutors at an hourly rate that yields less pay than they would otherwise receive by operation of law.[216] A collective bargaining agreement may also enable a classified civil service employee to engage in partisan politics notwithstanding the prohibitions on such activity that appears in RC 124.57.[217]

Absent contractual language to the contrary, it is generally assumed that a word or phrase in a collective bargaining agreement is intended to have the same meaning as the word or phrase in the statute.[218]

18.21 Agency shop

(A) "Fair share" union dues for nonmembers

A collective bargaining agreement *may* (but need not) provide for an "agency shop" arrangement where, as a condition of employment, bargaining unit employees who decline to become members of the union are compelled to pay to the union a so-called "fair share" fee. If agreed to, deduction and payment of the fee by the employer to the union is automatic and does not require the employee's authorization.[219]

The Public Employees' Collective Bargaining Act specifically prohibits a union shop, under which an employee must not merely give the union financial support but also join the union as a condition of employment.[220]

(B) Rebates and exemptions

Employee organizations must establish procedures permitting rebates of that portion of the service fee allocated to support partisan political or ideological causes not germane to collective bargaining.[221] These procedures must conform to federal law and can be challenged in court. A challenger is not required to exhaust the state administrative remedies that appear in RC 4117.09(C) before going to court.[222] The union's determination of the amount of rebate is conclusive, subject to review by SERB of whether the determination was arbitrary and capricious.[223]

The Public Employees' Collective Bargaining Act permits employees who are members of a bona fide religion that has historically opposed joining or supporting a union to pay an amount equal to the service fee to a mutually agreed-upon nonreligious charitable fund.[224] A comparable provision of federal labor law, however, has

---

[213]State ex rel Rollins v Cleveland Hts-University Hts City School Dist Bd of Ed, 40 OS(3d) 123, 532 NE(2d) 1289 (1988).

[214]Alexander Local School Dist Bd of Ed v Alexander Local Ed Assn, 41 App(3d) 13, 534 NE(2d) 107 (Athens 1987).

[215]Gorham-Fayette Local Schools Bd of Ed v Lavens, No. 91FU000009, 1992 WL 173243 (6th Dist Ct App, Fulton, 7-24-92); Young v Washington Local School Dist Bd of Ed, 85 App(3d) 37, 619 NE(2d) 62 (Scioto 1993).

[216]State ex rel Siers v Beaver Local School Dist Bd of Ed, No. 89-C-39, 1990 WL 167575 (7th Dist Ct App, Columbiana, 10-29-90); Price v Newbury Local School Dist Bd of Ed, No. 91-G-1626, 1992 WL 268795 (11th Dist Ct App, Geauga, 12-13-91), appeal dismissed by 63 OS(3d) 1421, 587 NE(2d) 302 (1992).

[217]OAG 91-065.

[218]See Whitley v Canton City School Dist Bd of Ed, 38 OS(3d) 300, 528 NE(2d) 167 (1988); Cuyahoga Falls Ed Assn v Cuyahoga Falls City School Dist Bd of Ed, No. 15687, 1993 WL 21043 (9th Dist Ct App, Summit, 1-27-93).

[219]RC 4117.09(C).

[220]RC 4117.09(C).

[221]RC 4117.09(C).

[222]Gibney v Toledo Bd of Ed, 40 OS(3d) 152, 523 NE(2d) 1300 (1988).

[223]OAC 4117-11-01.

[224]RC 4117.09(C); OAC 4117-11-02. For examples of this religious exemption in operation, see In re Miller, SERB 85-027 (6-17-85); In re Cuckler, No. 84-CE-06-1388 (4-29-85 (SERB)). Where the exemption does not apply, serious issues can still arise under antidiscrimination laws that require employers and unions to reasonably accommodate an employee's religious beliefs. See Text 17.15, Religious discrimination.

been held unconstitutional on grounds it creates a "denominational preference."[225]

The expenditure of service fees for political, social, and ideological purposes, by itself, does not breach the employee organization's duty of fair representation; to prevail on such a claim, an employee must prove that (1) he followed the union's rebate procedure; (2) no such procedure was established; or (3) the procedure exists, but has been applied arbitrarily or discriminatorily.[226]

(C) Constitutional issues arising from agency shop

Whether an agency shop arrangement adequately protects the free speech and association rights of bargaining unit employees who are not union members, as well as whether various union fee assessment and rebate procedures pass constitutional muster, has been frequently litigated.

The US Court of Appeals for the Sixth Circuit has identified three minimum requirements for agency shop provisions: (1) the union must provide an adequate accounting of all union expenditures which enables the nonmember employee to appraise where his fees are being spent; (2) the union must allow an advance reduction of any money clearly expended for ideological purposes; and (3) on a nonmember's objection, any money not clearly related to the negotiation and administration of the collective bargaining agreement should be held in escrow pending resolution by an impartial decisionmaker.[227]

Under these guidelines, the agency shop provision at issue was constitutionally deficient in three areas. First, it allowed the union to collect and use full union dues before calculating the mandatory advance reduction. Second, it did not provide for an independent audit of the union's financial

---

[225] Wilson v NLRB, 920 F(2d) 1282 (6th Cir Mich 1990), cert denied ___ US ___, 112 SCt 3025, 120 LEd(2d) 896 (1992).

[226] In re Bowles, SERB 84-004 (9-13-84).

[227] Tierney v Toledo, 824 F(2d) 1497 (6th Cir Ohio 1987). This was the US Court of Appeals for the Sixth Circuit's first interpretation of the US Supreme Court's decision in Chicago Teachers Union Local No. 1 v Hudson, 475 US 292, 106 SCt 1066, 89 LEd(2d) 232 (1986) (employee wages cannot be used for activities not germane to collective bargaining). See also Ellis v Brotherhood of Railway Clerks, 466 US 435, 104 SCt 1883, 80 LEd(2d) 428 (1984) (expenditures not necessarily or reasonably incurred for the purpose of performing duties of an exclusive representative may be challenged); Abood v Detroit Bd of Ed, 431 US 209, 97 SCt 1782, 52 LEd(2d) 261 (1977) (union may not collect from dissenting employees for the support of ideological causes not germane to collective bargaining); Communications Workers of America v Beck, 487 US 735, 108 SCt 2641, 101 LEd(2d) 634 (1988) (under federal labor law applicable to private sector, union with agency shop arrangement may not use fees for purposes not germane to collective bargaining, contract administration, and grievance adjustments). Outside the Sixth Circuit, the cases are inconsistent on whether an advance reduction of fees is required or whether escrowing is sufficient. See Grunwald v San Bernardino City Unified School Dist, 994 F(2d) 1370 (9th Cir Cal 1993), cert denied ___ US ___, 114 SCt 439, 126 LEd(2d) 373 (1993) (following cases that find escrowing sufficient while expressly acknowledging that *Tierney* is to the contrary at least as to any amount clearly dedicated to ideological expenses). That the Sixth Circuit itself is having second thoughts on the issue is at least arguable given language in Weaver v University of Cincinnati, 942 F(2d) 1039 (6th Cir Ohio 1991). The US Supreme Court further clarified just what union expenses are chargeable and not chargeable to dissenting employees in Lehnert v Ferris Faculty Assn, 500 US 507, 111 SCt 1950, 114 LEd(2d) 572 (1991). Charging for legislative lobbying and other political activities unrelated to effectuation of the collective bargaining agreement, for litigation costs unrelated to the employees' bargaining unit, and for public relations activities that extended beyond the context of bargaining and grievance resolution was improper. On the other hand, dissenting employees could be charged their share for strike preparation expenses, for sending local union delegates to the state and national conventions of parent unions with which the local was affiliated, for certain informational support services, and for otherwise chargeable activities of the parent unions provided "the payment is for services that may ultimately enure to the benefit of the members of the local union by virtue of their membership in the parent organization." As to this last point, Weaver v University of Cincinnati, 942 F(2d) 1039 (6th Cir Ohio 1991) affirms that a local union must give notice of just what portion of the fair share fee goes to the union's affiliates. Mitchell v Los Angeles Unified School Dist, 963 F(2d) 258 (9th Cir Cal 1992), cert denied ___ US ___, 113 SCt 375, 121 LEd(2d) 287 (1992) holds that a dissenting employee need only be given an opportunity to opt out of paying nonchargeable expenses, with no additional requirement that the employee affirmatively consent to payment of the full fee, a position with which the Sixth Circuit agrees. Weaver v University of Cincinnati, 970 F(2d) 1523 (6th Cir Ohio 1992), cert denied sub nom Weaver v Steger, ___ US ___, 113 SCt 1274, 122 LEd(2d) 668 (1993).

information or for the distribution of financial information to nonmembers before collecting fees; it also lacked a procedure by which nonmembers could object to union expenditures. Finally, it failed to provide for a "reasonably prompt decision by an impartial decisionmaker" on whether escrowed funds should be rebated.[228]

These defects are similar to those SERB and the courts initially identified in the Ohio Education Association's fair share fee procedure.[229] SERB also held that an employee who objects to union use of his fee must object each time the contract containing the agency shop provision is renewed.[230]

SERB has since held that, in order to collect service fees, a union must first adopt a rebate determination procedure that provides for the following:

(1) Notice to nonunion employees that the collective bargaining agreement has a fair share fee provision and that dues based on advance calculation of the nonmember's fair share fee will be deducted on a predetermined date, accompanied by (a) an adequate explanation of the basis of the fee, including disclosure of the union's yearly expenditures broken down between chargeable and nonchargeable categories, and (b) an adequate explanation of how challenges may be made, allowing reasonable time for filing objections;

(2) Independent auditor to verify expenditures as represented by the union;

(3) Impartial decisionmaker to make a reasonably prompt determination upon a nonmember's challenge to the fair share fee;

(4) Reasonable time for adjudicating the validity of the fee assessment by the decisionmaker and for refund of an additional rebate, if any, to the objecting nonmember; and

(5) Escrow account for the amount reasonably in dispute.[231]

The Sixth Circuit, upholding the collection of fair share fees by the OEA under a revised procedure, has rejected any notion that a union's disclosed financial information must be audited at the "highest" level of audit service available or that the union must use the "least restrictive" procedure imaginable to collect the fees. Financial disclosure need only be "adequate" or "sufficient."[232]

A school board will be enjoined from deducting agency fees where the procedure does not meet constitutional require-

---

[228]Tierney v Toledo, 824 F(2d) 1497 (6th Cir Ohio 1987). Subsequently, a revised rebate procedure was still faulted for inadequate financial disclosure and a requirement that administrative remedies be exhausted before challenging constitutionality in the courts. Tierney v Toledo, 917 F(2d) 927 (6th Cir Ohio 1990). See also Damiano v Matish, 830 F(2d) 1363 (6th Cir Mich 1987).

[229]In re Liptak, SERB 87-006 (4-9-87); Lowary v Lexington Local Bd of Ed, 704 FSupp 1430 (ND Ohio 1987), affirmed in part, reversed in part 903 F(2d) 422 (6th Cir Ohio 1990), cert denied 498 US 958, 111 SCt 385, 112 LEd(2d) 396 (1990); Gillespie v Willard City Bd of Ed, 700 FSupp 898 (ND Ohio 1987). Lowary did say RC 4117.09 is constitutional on its face. Subsequently, a revised OEA procedure was deemed unconstitutional by the Sixth Circuit because of its "local union presumption" provision under which the percentage of chargeable expenditures by local unions would be presumed by the impartial decisionmaker to be whatever is found appropriate for chargeable OEA expenditures. This presumption, said the court, impermissibly permitted the OEA to avoid providing audited and detailed financial statements to nonmembers regarding local unions. Lowary v Lexington Local Bd of Ed, 903 F(2d) 422 (6th Cir Ohio 1990), cert denied 498 US 958, 111 SCt 385, 112 LEd(2d) 396 (1990).

[230]In re Liptak, SERB 87-006 (4-9-87).

[231]In re Gibney, SERB 89-004 (2-9-89), amended on reconsideration SERB 89-020 (8-23-89) (partially overruling In re Liptak, SERB 87-006 (4-9-87)). With respect to a union's obligation to provide a means of dispute resolution through an impartial decisionmaker, the Sixth Circuit has emphasized that objecting nonmembers cannot be forced to use and be bound by the means the union chooses. In United Food and Commercial Workers Local 951 v Mulder, 1994 WL 363891 (6th Cir Mich 1994), cert denied ___ US ___, 115 SCt 1095, 130 LEd(2d) 1064 (1995), the union's internal dispute resolution mechanism was arbitration. When the union sought judicial confirmation of certain arbitrators' awards rendered under this mechanism, the Sixth Circuit balked since the objecting nonmembers had never agreed to be bound and arbitration requires an agreement to arbitrate.

[232]Gwirtz v Ohio Education Assn, 887 F(2d) 678 (6th Cir Ohio 1989), cert denied 494 US 1080, 110 SCt 1810, 108 LEd(2d) 941 (1990). See also Lehnert v Ferris Faculty Assn, 893 F(2d) 111 (6th Cir Mich 1989), cert denied sub nom Lindsey v Ferris Faculty

ments.[233] A collective bargaining agreement that includes an agency shop provision typically includes an agreement by the union to indemnify and hold the employer harmless from any legal challenge to the agency shop arrangement. The Sixth Circuit, however, has held such clauses contrary to public policy and unenforceable.[234]

18.22 Grievance procedure and arbitration

(A) In general

A collective bargaining agreement must contain some type of grievance procedure for the resolution of disputes under the agreement.[235] The procedure *may* (but need not) culminate in final and binding arbitration. The employer must give the union notice of the date, time, and place of grievance meetings, even though the Public Employees' Collective Bargaining Act allows individuals to process grievances without union representation.[236] Where an employer does not initially challenge the "grievability" of a dispute, SERB has held that the defense is waived.[237] The failure to resolve a grievance does not trigger the impasse resolution procedures of the Public Employees' Collective Bargaining Act.[238]

Where an agreement makes a specification about a matter and provides for final and binding arbitration, the grievance procedure is exclusive,[239] and a civil service commission has no jurisdiction to receive and determine appeals relating to matters that were the subject of such a procedure.[240] Thus, in city school districts subject to RC Chapter 124, a collective bargaining agreement may govern all matters subject to civil service jurisdiction except prohibited subjects of bargaining (namely, the conduct and grading of civil service examinations, the rating of candidates, and the establishment of eligible lists and original appointments from the eligible lists) provided alleged violations of the contract are subject to final and binding arbitration.

So long as the statutory grounds for vacating or modifying an arbitration award under RC 2711.10 and RC 2711.11 do not apply and the award "draws its essence" from the parties' agreement, the courts will not disturb it.[241] The issue of arbitrability, on the other hand, is generally a question

---

Assn, 496 US 905, 110 SCt 2586, 110 LEd(2d) 267 (1990).

[233]Weaver v University of Cincinnati, 942 F(2d) 1039 (6th Cir Ohio 1991); Lowary v Lexington Local Bd of Ed, 854 F(2d) 131 (6th Cir Ohio 1988).

[234]Weaver v University of Cincinnati, 970 F(2d) 1523 (6th Cir Ohio 1992), cert denied sub nom Weaver v Steger, ___ US ___, 113 SCt 1274, 122 LEd(2d) 668 (1993).

[235]RC 4117.09(B)(1).

[236]In re New Richmond Exempted Village School Dist Bd of Ed, SERB 86-022 (6-4-86); In re City of Jackson, SERB 89-025 (10-5-89), appeal dismissed by 1990 SERB 4-51 (4th Dist Ct App, Jackson, 8-17-90). A waiver of the union's right to be present must be clear and unequivocal and will not be lightly inferred. Eastern Local School Dist Bd of Ed, No. 86-ULP-12-0504 (HO 9-1-88, adopted 10-26-88 (SERB)).

[237]In re New Richmond Exempted Village School Dist Bd of Ed, SERB 86-022 (6-4-86).

[238]In re Miamisburg School Dist Bd of Ed, SERB 86-001 (1-15-86); RC 4117.14.

[239]RC 4117.10(A); State ex rel Parsons v Fleming, 68 OS(3d) 509, 628 NE(2d) 1377 (1994). See also Brown v East Cleveland Bd of Ed, No. 65607, 1994 WL 197220 (8th Dist Ct App, Cuyahoga, 5-19-94); Cook v Maxwell, 57 App(3d) 131, 567 NE(2d) 292 (Hamilton 1989) concluded that RC 4117.10(A) was inapplicable where a contract provided for arbitration of grievances but did not affirmatively make such arbitration final and binding. Buie v Chippewa Local School Dist Bd of Ed, 93 App(3d) 434, 638 NE(2d) 1073 (Wayne 1994) concluded that RC 4117.10(A) was inapplicable where a contract addressed the termination of a teacher's contract but not the procedure to be followed; since the board of education initiated termination under RC 3319.16, the court found the teacher could appeal to court under the procedures of that statute and was not relegated to the grievance and arbitration procedure. Of course, a court action may be brought where the collective bargaining agreement itself expressly contemplates that possibility. See Herman v Tuscarawas Valley Local School Dist Bd of Ed, No. 93AP040032, 1993 WL 472871 (5th Dist Ct App, Tuscarawas, 11-1-93).

[240]RC 4117.10(A); Richards v State Personnel Bd of Review, No. CA-3393, 1989 WL 11498 (5th Dist Ct App, Licking, 1-20-89).

[241]Hillsboro v Fraternal Order of Police, Ohio Labor Council, Inc, 52 OS(3d) 174, 556 NE(2d) 1186 (1990); Findlay City School Dist Bd of Ed v Findlay Ed Assn, 49 OS(3d) 129, 551 NE(2d) 186 (1990); Mahoning County Bd of Mental Retardation & Developmental Disabilities v Mahoning County TMR Ed Assn, 22 OS(3d) 80, 22 OBR 95, 488 NE(2d) 872 (1986). An award departs from the "essence" of the agreement when (1) it conflicts with express terms of the agreement, and/or (2) it lacks rational support or cannot be rationally derived from the agreement.

for the courts, not an arbitrator, to resolve, unless the parties clearly and unmistakably provide otherwise.[242] An arbitrator who finds a violation of a collective bargaining agreement is presumed to have implicit authority to fashion an appropriate remedy absent restrictive contractual language that withdraws a particular remedy from the arbitrator's jurisdiction.[243]

Disputes often arise over whether the grievance procedure must be exhausted before filing a suit in court. When the procedure includes final and binding arbitration and the case involves the interpretation or application of the collective bargaining agreement, exhaustion of contractual remedies is required.[244] Where the procedure culminates in "advisory" arbitration, exhaustion may not be required.[245]

Where a grievance procedure afforded employees in a city school district only a limited access to arbitration (that is, a grievance could be submitted to final and binding arbitration only if a grievance panel formed at the prior step of the grievance procedure and consisting of three union and three employer representatives deadlocked on the grievance), RC 4117.10(A) was deemed inapplicable and employees were not required to follow it.[246]

The Ohio Supreme Court has held, in a case that arose prior to RC Chapter 4117 and that therefore did not consider RC

Ohio Office of Collective Bargaining v Ohio Civil Service Employees Assn, Local 11, 59 OS(3d) 177, 572 NE(2d) 71 (1991). In OAPSE v Lakewood City School Dist Bd of Ed, 68 OS(3d) 175, 624 NE(2d) 1043 (1994), the Ohio Supreme Court held that procedural due process does not entitle a discharged employee to direct face-to-face confrontation with the principal witness against him at a post-termination arbitration hearing. The employee is entitled only to a meaningful opportunity to challenge adverse evidence. Here, that opportunity was fulfilled when the employee cross-examined his accuser, who had testified by closed circuit television that the employee had aided her as a student in obtaining illicit drugs. An error of law in the arbitrator's rationale for the award does not justify setting the award aside. International Brotherhood of Firemen v Cleveland City School Dist Bd of Ed, No. 57088, 1990 WL 84299 (8th Dist Ct App, Cuyahoga, 6-21-90).

[242]Teamsters, Local Union 20 v Toledo, 48 App(3d) 11, 548 NE(2d) 257 (Lucas 1988); Tye v Polaris Joint Vocational School Dist Bd of Ed, 44 App(3d) 76, 541 NE(2d) 466 (Cuyahoga 1988); Springfield Local Assn of Classroom Teachers v Springfield Local School Dist Bd of Ed, 37 App(3d) 167, 525 NE(2d) 27 (Summit 1987); Vulcan-Cincinnati, Inc v United Steelworkers of America, 113 App 360, 173 NE(2d) 709 (Hamilton 1960). Where the dispute over arbitrability turns on construction of the contractual grievance procedure's provisions for processing a grievance (such as whether time limits for filing and appealing a grievance have been met), however, the question is for an arbitrator to decide. Reynoldsburg City School Dist Bd of Ed v Reynoldsburg School Support Assn, OEA/NEA, No. 90AP-1233, 1991 WL 101599 (10th Dist Ct App, Franklin, 6-4-91). The courts sometimes distinguish in this area between procedural arbitrability (to be decided by an arbitrator) and substantive arbitrability (to be decided by the courts).

[243]Queen City Lodge No 69, FOP v Cincinnati, 63 OS(3d) 403, 588 NE(2d) 802 (1992). But see Bucyrus City Bd of Ed v Bucyrus Ed Assn, No. 3-94-8, 1994 WL 379002 (3d Dist Ct App, Crawford, 7-20-94) (vacating award wherein arbitrator found that board did not make "every reasonable effort" to maintain a 25 to 1 student/teacher ratio in violation of contract and ordered the board to compensate all teachers in the affected grade level on a pro rata basis for every student over 25; the award of increased compensation "based on no apparent reference to, or authority derived from, the parties' collective bargaining agreement, confirms that the arbitrator exceeded his authority").

[244]RC 4117.10(A); State ex rel Wallace v West Geauga Local School Dist Bd of Ed, No. 91-G-1644, 1992 WL 276673 (11th Dist Ct App, Geauga, 5-29-92), appeal dismissed by 65 OS(3d) 1439, 600 NE(2d) 682 (1992); Albright v Jackson, No. 89AP-1215, 1990 WL 63041 (10th Dist Ct App, Franklin, 5-15-90); Tickhill v Cuyahoga Falls, No. 13603, 1988 WL 133672 (9th Dist Ct App, Summit, 12-7-88); State ex rel Williams v Belpre City School Dist Bd of Ed, 41 App(3d) 1, 534 NE(2d) 96 (Washington 1987). A procedure requiring an employee's discrimination grievance to be held in abeyance pending outcome of the employee's lawsuit under Title VII, however, violates the anti-retaliation provisions of Title VII and an employer will be compelled by the court to arbitrate the dispute. Wedding v University of Toledo, 884 FSupp 253 (ND Ohio 1995).

[245]Blair v Milford Exempted Village School Dist Bd of Ed, 62 App(3d) 424, 575 NE(2d) 1190 (Clermont 1989); Combs v Stark County Area Joint Vocational School Dist Bd of Ed, No. CA-6612, 1985 WL 6077 (5th Dist Ct App, Stark, 8-13-85). A grievance procedure without arbitration, but culminating in a proceeding before the public employer's governing body, has been held not to be reviewable in court. Local No. 2134, International Assn of Firefighters v Marion Twp Bd of Trustees, 33 App(3d) 204, 514 NE(2d) 1386 (Marion 1986). Such grievance procedures are now rare.

[246]Sutton v Cleveland Bd of Ed, 958 F(2d) 1339 (6th Cir Ohio 1992).

4117.10(A) insofar as it pertains to the exclusivity of a grievance procedure that culminates in binding arbitration, that two teachers did not need to exhaust a contractual grievance procedure when their claim of failure by the school board to compensate them at the appropriate step of the teachers' salary schedule did not relate to interpretation or application of the collective bargaining agreement and there was no dispute as to the provisions of the agreement.[247] Exhaustion has also not been required where the dispute involves a statutory or constitutional, as opposed to a purely contractual, question.[248]

The Public Employees' Collective Bargaining Act also contains provision for binding arbitration of collective bargaining disputes for safety forces and certain other employee groups.[249] In labor relations parlance, such arbitration of unresolved issues on the bargaining table is called "interest" arbitration, as distinguished from grievance arbitration that may occur under the terms of a contractual grievance procedure. Boards of education *may* (but need not) agree to binding interest arbitration. Agreements to mediate disputes, as opposed to agreements to arbitrate, are not subject to the arbitration confirmation procedure established in RC Chapter 2711. Mediation and arbitration represent separate and distinct means of attempting to resolve disputes, mediation generally being advisory, while arbitration is typically binding.[250]

Construing RC 2711.10, two appeals courts, following a host of federal precedents under an identically worded federal statute, have held that a bargaining unit employee lacks standing to seek to vacate an arbitrator's award when the parties to the arbitration were the union and the employer.[251] Another appeals court has concluded a bargaining unit employee does have standing to seek to vacate an award under the Ohio statute, however.[252] The latter court has also concluded a bargaining unit employee has standing to seek to enforce an award.[253]

(B) Arbitration and unfair labor practice proceedings

Adopting a policy similar to that developed under federal law in the private sector, SERB will often defer to arbitration if the controversy is susceptible to resolution through either a grievance procedure or an unfair labor practice proceeding. *In re Upper Arlington Ed Assn*[254] establishes the following general rules on deferral:

(1) Deferral is inappropriate where "statutory interpretation and application lie at the center of the dispute";

(2) SERB will retain jurisdiction but defer to arbitration where a refusal to bargain is alleged and the collective bargaining agreement and its meaning "lie

---

[247]Tapo v Columbus Bd of Ed, 31 OS(3d) 105, 31 OBR 268, 509 NE(2d) 419 (1987). See also Kelley v Barberton City School Dist Bd of Ed, No. 13065, 1987 WL 18685 (9th Dist Ct App, Summit, 10-14-87). Had RC 4117.10(A) come into play, a different result would presumably have been reached. See State ex rel Johnson v Cleveland Hts-University Hts City School Dist Bd of Ed, 73 OS(3d) 189, 652 NE(2d) 750 (1995); Mayfield Hts Fire Fighters Assn, Local 1500, IAFF v DeJohn, 87 App(3d) 358, 622 NE(2d) 380 (Cuyahoga 1993).

[248]State ex rel Runyan v Henry, 34 App(3d) 23, 516 NE(2d) 1261 (Miami 1986).

[249]RC 4117.14(I). A bitterly divided Ohio Supreme Court, rejecting its own earlier decision, has held this provision constitutional even as to "home-rule" charter municipalities under Article XVIII, Sections 3 and 7 of the Ohio Constitution. Rocky River v SERB, 43 OS(3d) 1, 539 NE(2d) 103 (1989) (vacating 39 OS(3d) 196, 530 NE(2d) 1 (1988) and 40 OS(3d) 606, 533 NE(2d) 270 (1988)). The Court refused to rule the entire Act unconstitutional as to home-rule municipalities in Twinsburg v SERB, 39 OS(3d) 226, 530 NE(2d) 26 (1988). See also Kettering v SERB, 26 OS(3d) 50, 26 OBR 42, 496 NE(2d) 983 (1986).

[250]Ohio Council 8, AFSCME v Ohio Dept of Mental Retardation & Developmental Disabilities, 9 OS(3d) 139, 9 OBR 388, 459 NE(2d) 220 (1984).

[251]Art v Newcomerstown Bd of Ed, No. 92AP050038, 1993 WL 34542 (5th Dist Ct App, Tuscarawas, 1-11-93); Wilson v Toledo Bd of Ed, No. L-85-425, 1986 WL 11639 (6th Dist Ct App, Lucas, 10-17-86).

[252]Barksdale v Ohio Dept of Administrative Services, 78 App(3d) 325, 604 NE(2d) 798 (Franklin 1992). See also Geist v Ohio Dept of Commerce, 78 App(3d) 404, 604 NE(2d) 1372 (Franklin 1992).

[253]Lepp v Hazardous Waste Facility Bd, 1991 SERB 4-117, 1991 WL 224181 (10th Dist Ct App, Franklin, 9-26-91).

[254]In re Upper Arlington Ed Assn, SERB 92-010 (6-30-92), which purports to clarify and supplement the deferral policy initially announced in In re Miamisburg School Dist Bd of Ed, SERB 86-001 (1-15-86).

at the center of the dispute and it appears that the arbitral interpretation of the contract will resolve both the unfair labor practice and the contract interpretation issues";[255]

(3) Deferral is inappropriate where "the grievance-arbitration process ... itself is one of the issues of a pending unfair labor practice charge";[256]

(4) SERB will never defer if the contractual grievance procedure does not include final and binding arbitration.[257]

SERB may defer to arbitration sua sponte or in response to a motion for deferral filed by a party upon receipt of an unfair labor practice charge. In either case, the parties are to file a copy of the arbitration award with the Board, which will be reviewed only if a motion for review is filed within thirty days after issuance of the award.[258]

Where SERB defers to the grievance procedure and an arbitration award ultimately issues, SERB, upon reviewing the award, will defer to it if the arbitration proceedings appear to have been fair and regular, the parties have agreed to binding arbitration, and the award is not "clearly repugnant" to the Act; as to whether the award is so repugnant, SERB will defer if the arbitrator's decision is susceptible to interpretation consistent with the Public Employees' Collective Bargaining Act.[259]

An appeals court has held that if SERB issues a complaint alleging an unfair labor practice with knowledge that the same matter is being pursued through the grievance procedure, SERB cannot summarily defer to the arbitrator's award and dismiss the complaint after the arbitration but must hold a hearing and determine whether an unfair labor practice was committed.[260]

18.23 Expiration of contracts

SERB has adopted a principle from federal labor law applicable to the private sector that during negotiations following the expiration of a collective bargaining agreement, the employer is generally required to "maintain the status quo" as to wages and working conditions and that, therefore, at least for some purposes, the agreement effectively survives its expiration date.[261] During negotiations for a successor contract following expiration of an agreement, existing terms and conditions of employment must be maintained at least until the point of ultimate impasse.[262]

Significantly, however, SERB has concluded a management rights clause does *not* survive the contract expiration date "unless it clearly and unmistakably indicates that such was the intention." Thus, an employer committed an unfair labor practice by refusing to bargain over its decision to lay off employees after expiration of its contract and while bargaining for a successor agreement even if the expired contract gave the employer an unrestricted right to lay off.[263]

An appeals court has held that, when the collective bargaining agreement expires, the employer is no longer obligated to deduct union dues and fair share fees.[264] SERB, however, maintains deductions must continue following expiration of the

---

[255]In re Upper Arlington Ed Assn, SERB 92-010 (6-30-92) expressly leaves open the question of whether deferral is appropriate in cases alleging other than a refusal-to-bargain unfair labor practice. Moreover, SERB may eschew deferral if the case involves "matters of great statutory significance ... ." *Id.* at n.2.

[256]In re Upper Arlington Ed Assn, SERB 92-010 (6-30-92). This refers, for example, to cases in which a party is alleged not to have timely processed grievances, refused to arbitrate, or withheld information needed to process a grievance.

[257]In re Upper Arlington Ed Assn, SERB 92-010 (6-30-92). SERB may elect case-by-case not to defer under other circumstances as well.

[258]In re Upper Arlington Ed Assn, SERB 92-010 (6-30-92).

[259]In re Otsego Local School Dist Bd of Ed, SERB 92-020 (10-9-92).

[260]OAPSE, Chapter 177 v Forest Hills Local School Dist Bd of Ed, 73 App(3d) 771, 1992 SERB 4-31, 598 NE(2d) 200 (Franklin 1992). See also Jefferson Technical College Ed Assn v SERB, SERB 4-59, 1992 WL 223733 (7th Dist Ct App, Jefferson, 9-10-92).

[261]In re West Carrollton City School Dist, SERB 86-026 (6-26-86), citing Peerless Roofing Co v NLRB, 641 F(2d) 734 (9th Cir NLRB 1981).

[262]See Text 18.24(C), Refusal to bargain, unilateral action at point of ultimate impasse.

[263]In re Cuyahoga County Commrs, SERB 89-006 (3-15-89).

[264]OAPSE, Chapter 762 v New Miami Local School Dist Bd of Ed, 31 App(3d) 163, 31 OBR 328, 509 NE(2d) 973 (Butler 1986).

agreement and prior to ultimate impasse.[265]

Where a collective bargaining agreement expired but both the school board and union continued to operate under its term as if it were in effect during the next school year, an appeals court held that the teacher evaluation procedures contained in the lapsed agreement superseded the procedures specified in RC 3319.111 and that, accordingly, a teacher evaluated in accordance with the contract was properly nonrenewed.[266]

UNFAIR LABOR PRACTICES

18.24 Unfair labor practices by employer

(A) In general

RC 4117.11(A) makes it an unfair labor practice for an employer, its agents, or representatives to do the following:

(1) Interfere with or coerce employees in the exercise of their rights under the Public Employees' Collective Bargaining Act or an employee organization in the selection of its representative for purposes of collective bargaining and grievance adjustment;

(2) Initiate, create, dominate, or interfere with the administration of an employee organization, except an employer may permit employees to confer with him during working hours without loss of pay and may permit employee organizations to use facilities and interoffice mails for meetings and communications with members;

(3) Discriminate in regard to hiring or tenure on the basis of organizational rights granted employees, though the public employer may enforce an agency shop agreement made with the employee organization;

(4) Discriminate against any employee who files charges or testifies under the Public Employees' Collective Bargaining Act;

(5) Refuse to bargain collectively with the employees' exclusive bargaining representative;

(6) Establish a pattern or practice of repeated failure to timely process grievances or requests for arbitration;

(7) Lock out employees to force an employee or employee organization to agree with the employer's terms in a labor dispute; or

(8) Cause or attempt to cause an employee organization or its agents to commit an unfair labor practice.

(B) Interference and coercion

SERB has stated that where a violation of RC 4117.11(A)(1) is alleged, "the appropriate inquiry is an objective rather than subjective one" and "necessarily entails a thorough review" of all the facts and circumstances to see if one can "reasonably conclude that employees were restrained or coerced."[267] This appears to be at odds with an earlier pronouncement that an employer's conduct may be deemed "inherently destructive" of employees' protected rights, in which case specific proof of antiunion motive is unnecessary to make out an unfair practice under RC 4117.11(A)(1).[268] Laying off union activists immediately after a representation election, without legitimate reason, has been deemed an example of such inherently destructive conduct.[269] Questioning an employee during a union's organizing drive about union support or activity has also been viewed as inherently coercive and a per se violation of the statute.[270]

---

[265]Western Brown Local School Dist Bd of Ed, 87-ULP-11-0537 (HO 12-1-88, adopted 1-19-89 (SERB)).

[266]Young v Washington Local School Dist Bd of Ed, 85 App(3d) 37, 619 NE(2d) 62 (Scioto 1993) (noting that any other conclusion would result in "a chaotic and unworkable situation").

[267]In re Pickaway County Human Services Dept, SERB 93-001 (3-24-93).

[268]In re Belmont County Engineer, SERB 88-007 (7-5-88), reversed on other grounds by 1989 SERB 4-14 (CP, Belmont, 1-25-89).

[269]In re Belmont County Engineer, SERB 88-007 (7-5-88), reversed on other grounds by 1989 SERB 4-14 (CP, Belmont, 1-25-89).

[270]In re Lakota Local School Dist Bd of Ed, SERB 89-019 (8-23-89).

Other examples of this unfair labor practice include retaliating (or threatening to retaliate) against an employee for filing a grievance,[271] requesting union representation,[272] or persisting in union activities.[273] Refusing to bargain so long as a particular individual is part of the union's negotiating team also violates the statute.[274]

Generally, an employer is precluded from changing the status quo between the time of a representation election and certification of a union as the employees' exclusive bargaining representative. However, SERB has held that an employer's unilateral decision for a valid managerial reason between an election and certification to convert a part-time position to a full-time position, with the consequent layoff of the part-time worker who was precluded for medical reasons from working full-time, did not violate the Public Employees' Collective Bargaining Act where the change did not affect the overall number of bargaining unit employees and the employer was not motivated by antiunion animus.[275]

An involuntary transfer that went beyond the bounds of reasonable discipline for an unprotected vulgar and profane personal attack on a supervisor has been deemed unlawful interference and coercion.[276]

(C) Refusal to bargain, unilateral action at point of ultimate impasse

Experience has borne out the expectation that many unfair labor practices would concern alleged refusals to bargain based upon unilateral action by an employer with respect to a mandatory subject of bargaining.[277] Generally, such action is an unfair labor practice, although SERB has concluded otherwise where the unilateral change was deemed trivial.[278]

To avoid a refusal-to-bargain unfair labor practice, the party desiring to make a change with respect to a mandatory subject of bargaining generally must give timely notice of the proposed change to the other party[279] and then, upon timely request, bargain over the matter in good faith.[280]

An employer may unilaterally act to implement the terms of its last offer after bargaining to ultimate impasse.[281] Accordingly, when that point occurs is a crucial question which, regrettably, is sometimes difficult to answer.

Where the parties are operating under the statutory dispute resolution procedure contained in RC 4117.14,[282] SERB has held that, in cases involving employees (such as school employees) given the right to strike under the Public Employees' Collective Bargaining Act, ultimate impasse occurs at the point a strike may lawfully be

---

[271] In re Akron Bd of Ed, SERB 86-006 (8-20-86).

[272] In re Cleveland City School Dist Bd of Ed, SERB 89-013 (5-19-89).

[273] In re West Carrollton City School Dist Bd of Ed, SERB 88-010 (7-14-88).

[274] In re Central State University, SERB 85-056 (10-28-85). A party may lawfully insist on removal if the particular individual's presence would violate RC 4117.20, however. Vandalia-Butler City School Dist Bd of Ed, SERB 87-007 (4-30-87). See Text 18.27, Privacy of negotiations, conflict of interest.

[275] In re Pickaway County Human Services Dept, SERB 93-001 (3-24-93).

[276] In re City of Dayton, SERB 93-014 (8-12-93), reversed with respect to the portion of SERB's order upholding a written reprimand for misconduct by FOP, Captain John C. Post Lodge No. 44 v SERB, 1995 SERB 4-8 (CP, Montgomery, 1-25-95).

[277] For examples of mandatory subjects of bargaining, with citations to cases in which refusals to bargain were found, see Text 18.28, Scope of bargaining.

[278] In re United Local School Dist, SERB 87-019 (10-9-87); Canfield Local School Dist Bd of Ed, No. 85-UR-04-3563 (HO 7-20-87, adopted 11-19-87 (SERB)).

[279] In re Mayfield City School Dist Bd of Ed, SERB 89-033 (12-20-89).

[280] The other party's right to bargain in a given case may be waived, either by virtue of a term in a collective bargaining agreement or by failure timely to request bargaining. See Text 18.28(B), Mandatory, permissive, and prohibited subjects.

[281] In re Youngstown City School Dist Bd of Ed, SERB 95-010 (6-30-95); In re City of Fostoria, SERB 86-037 (9-15-86); In re Vandalia-Butler City School Dist Bd of Ed, SERB 90-003 (2-9-90), affirmed by 1991 SERB 4-81, 1991 WL 355161 (2d Dist Ct App, Montgomery, 8-15-91). See also In re Central Ohio Transit Authority, SERB 89-032 (11-29-89); In re Cuyahoga County Commrs, SERB 89-006 (3-15-89). SERB uses the term "ultimate impasse" to distinguish the point at which unilateral action is permissible from the various "impasses" identified in the Act that merely trigger advancement to the next step in the statutory procedure for resolving disputes.

[282] See Text 18.29, Procedures for resolving disputes.

initiated (that is, at the end of the seven-day publication period following rejection of the fact-finding panel's recommendations).[283] SERB has also indicated that a finding of ultimate impasse is never possible if an employer has not bargained in good faith.[284]

Where the parties are operating under a mutually agreed alternative dispute resolution procedure,[285] the point of ultimate impasse can be elusive indeed. The sending of a notice to strike does not, of itself, indicate an impasse.[286] Impasse, rather, involves a question of fact to be decided case-by-case on the basis of many factors, such as bargaining history, good faith, the length of negotiations and importance of the disputed issues, the parties' understanding as to the state of negotiations, and whether continued bargaining realistically has the possibility of being fruitful.[287] Even the occurrence of a strike does not per se indicate the existence of ultimate impasse.[288] In short, ultimate impasse is a fluid concept that cannot be predetermined.

(D) Direct dealing

Bypassing the union and dealing directly with bargaining unit employees who are not designated or authorized by the union to bargain is generally an unfair labor practice. Thus, an employer's establishment of a "faculty advisory committee" to "gather input" from other faculty concerning mandatory subjects of bargaining has been deemed unlawful.[289] SERB also appears to have adopted a near-blanket rule that an employer commits an unfair labor practice by sending employees, even after receipt of a union intent to strike, a factual report on negotiations that includes a list of issues on which agreement has been reached, the parties' proposals and counter-proposals, and the status of unresolved issues.[290] Unilaterally requiring employees to sign union dues deduction authorization forms in the employer's presence, ostensibly to ensure voluntariness, has also been labelled unlawful direct dealing.[291]

(E) Employer domination of union

In assessing if an employer has dominated an employee organization, relevant factors include the relationship of the employer to the organization; the nature of discussions between the parties; the control the employer has over the organization's membership; the structure of the organization and the nature and place of its meetings; whether employees are compensated for attendance at meetings; and what part supervisory personnel play in the organization.[292] SERB has not decided whether the proper test is potential for domination or actual domination.

(F) Discrimination

An essential predicate to any finding of unlawful discrimination under RC 4117.11(A)(3) is a finding that the alleged

---

[283] In re City of Fostoria, SERB 86-037 (9-15-86). *Fostoria* expressly left open the question of when ultimate impasse occurs where the parties have opted out of the statutory dispute resolution procedures.

[284] In re Vandalia-Butler City School Dist Bd of Ed, SERB 90-003 (2-9-90), affirmed by 1991 SERB 4-81, 1991 WL 355161 (2d Dist Ct App, Montgomery, 8-15-91). See also Chairman Sheehan's opinion in In re Central Ohio Transit Authority, SERB 89-032 (11-29-89).

[285] See Text 18.29, Procedures for resolving disputes.

[286] In re Vandalia-Butler City School Dist Bd of Ed, SERB 90-003 (2-9-90), affirmed by 1991 SERB 4-81, 1991 WL 355161 (2d Dist Ct App, Montgomery, 8-15-91).

[287] In re Vandalia-Butler City School Dist Bd of Ed, SERB 90-003 (2-9-90), affirmed by 1991 SERB 4-81, 1991 WL 355161 (2d Dist Ct App, Montgomery, 8-15-91).

[288] In re Vandalia-Butler City School Dist Bd of Ed, SERB 90-003 (2-9-90), affirmed by 1991 SERB 4-81, 1991 WL 355161 (2d Dist Ct App, Montgomery, 8-15-91).

[289] SERB v Brookfield Local School Dist Bd of Ed, No. 87-ULP-3-0095 (HO 7-18-88 (SERB)).

[290] In re Vandalia-Butler City School Dist Bd of Ed, SERB 90-003 (2-9-90), affirmed by 1991 SERB 4-81, 1991 WL 355161 (2d Dist Ct App, Montgomery, 8-15-91); In re Mentor Exempted Village School Dist Bd of Ed, SERB 89-011 (5-16-89), affirmed by 76 App(3d) 465, 602 NE(2d) 374 (Lake 1991), appeal dismissed by 63 OS(3d) 1455, 590 NE(2d) 750 (1992). See also Findlay City School Dist Bd of Ed, SERB 88-006 (5-31-88); In re Central Ohio Transit Authority, SERB 89-032 (11-29-89).

[291] In re Clermont County Sheriff, SERB 89-024 (10-5-89).

[292] Hamilton County Dept of Human Services, No. 85-UR-07-3939 (HO 3-20-87, adopted 11-19-87, vacated on other grounds 1-22-88 (SERB)).

discriminatee engaged in or attempted to engage in concerted, protected activity.[293]

SERB's initial standard in discrimination cases distinctly favored employees by incorporating an "in part" test under which discrimination was found per se if an employer's action with respect to an employee was motivated in any part by antiunion animus. Subsequently, however, SERB joined the mainstream of labor relations thought by expressly scrapping the "in part" test in favor of a "but for" standard. Under this standard, upon proof that the employer's motive was at least partially illicit, the burden of proof shifts and the employer's decision survives only if the employer shows that the action still would have been taken even in the absence of the unlawful motive.[294]

The Ohio Supreme Court, however, in *SERB v Adena Local School Dist Bd of Ed*,[295] subsequently held that SERB's "but for" test "cannot be reconciled with" and "is not a reasonable interpretation of" RC Chapter 4117. A majority concluded the "in part" test is not only a permissible construction of Chapter 4117, but "mandated" by it. Curiously, however, the majority then proceeded to water down the very "in part" test they adopted, at least to some degree. Noting that SERB is not required to find an unfair labor practice if it is determined that antiunion animus played "a minuscule part" in the employer's decision, the majority fashioned the following formulation, which is currently Ohio's law on the issue:

> Under the "in part" test to determine the actual motivation of an employer charged with an unfair labor practice, the proponent of the charge has the initial burden of showing that the action by the employer was taken to discriminate against the employee for the exercise of rights protected by RC Chapter 4117. Where the proponent meets this burden, a prima facie case is created which raises a presumption of antiunion animus. The employer is then given an opportunity to present evidence that its actions were the result of other conduct by the employee not related to protected activity, to rebut the presumption. The State Employment Relations Board then determines, by a preponderance of the evidence, whether an unfair labor practice has occurred.[296]

As the two justices who concurred in the judgment but disagreed with the majority on this point noted, this effectively sounds as much like the "but for" test the majority repudiated as it does the "in part" test the majority purported to embrace. The current standard is simply muddled, at least as to label.

(G) Failure to process grievances

In the determination of whether an employer has failed to process grievances, an employer's "good faith" effort to fulfill its contractual obligation under the circumstances is a valid defense.[297] Repeated failure to process grievances an employer believes to be nonarbitrable is deemed an unfair labor practice by SERB since the employer can raise the issue of arbitrability before the arbitrator and then, if necessary, challenge the arbitrator's jurisdiction and authority under RC Chapter 2711.[298]

18.25 Unfair labor practices by union

(A) In general

RC 4117.11(B) makes it an unfair labor practice for an employee organization, its agents, or representatives to do the following:

---

[293]In re City of Dayton, SERB 93-014 (8-12-93). See also In re Warren County Sheriff, SERB 88-104 (9-28-88). For the meaning of concerted, protected activity, see Text 18.09, Employee rights in general.

[294]In re Ft. Frye Local School Dist Bd of Ed, SERB 91-005 (7-17-91), reversed by 1993 SERB 4-77 (4th Dist Ct App, Washington, 11-10-93), overruling In re Gallia-Jackson-Vinton Joint Vocational Bd of Ed, SERB 86-044 (11-13-86), affirmed by 1989 SERB 4-6 (CP, Gallia, 12-30-88). See also In re Cincinnati Metropolitan Housing Auth, SERB 93-002 (4-6-93); In re Cincinnati Metropolitan Housing Auth, SERB 93-008 (5-18-93).

[295]SERB v Adena Local School Dist Bd of Ed, 66 OS(3d) 485, 613 NE(2d) 605 (1993).

[296]SERB v Adena Local School Dist Bd of Ed, 66 OS(3d) 485, 613 NE(2d) 605 (1993).

[297]In re Cuyahoga County Sheriff's Dept, SERB 90-017 (9-28-90) (holding delays in processing grievances due to unanticipated volume not an unfair labor practice).

[298]In re Franklin County Sheriff, SERB 91-001 (1-8-91), affirmed by 78 App(3d) 158, 1992 SERB 4-16, 604 NE(2d) 189 (Franklin 1992).

(1) Restrain or coerce employees in the exercise of their rights under the Public Employees' Collective Bargaining Act;

(2) Cause or attempt to cause an employer to commit an unfair labor practice;

(3) Refuse to bargain collectively with an employer;

(4) Call, institute, or maintain a boycott against any public employer or picket any place of business of a public employer on account of a jurisdictional dispute;

(5) Induce or encourage any individual to engage in an illegal strike or to refuse to handle goods, perform services, threaten, coerce, or restrain any employer to cease doing business with a person or to force an employer to recognize an employee organization not certified by SERB;

(6) Fail to represent fairly all public employees in a bargaining unit;

(7) Induce or encourage picketing at the residence or place of private employment of a public official or representative of the public employer; or

(8) Picket or strike, unless a ten-day notice is given of the proposed action to both the employer and SERB. The notice must specifically state the date and time that the action will commence.[299]

(B) Restraint and coercion

To make out an unfair labor practice under RC 4117.11(B)(1), the union's restraint and coercion must apply to a protected public employee; thus, there is no violation if the activity is directed at a management level employee.[300]

It is not an unfair labor practice, in the context of a representation election, for a union to distribute campaign propaganda that casts the employer in an unfavorable light so long as the material does not have a restraining or coercive effect.[301] Threatening physically to prevent employees from crossing a picket line in the event of a strike is an unfair labor practice.[302]

A union that allows use of a picket sign with the word "scabs" and a nonstriking employee's name on it does not commit an unfair labor practice; telling the employee's name to a newspaper that publishes the name in an article together with a union comment that nonstrikers are generally motivated by personal economic concerns is also not prohibited.[303]

Internal union policies or practices may give rise to a violation, although SERB will not consider the merits of such a claim unless internal union remedies are exhausted. As is the case with employers under RC 4117.11(A)(1), SERB applies an "objective standard" in determining whether, under all the circumstances, one can reasonably conclude employees were restrained or coerced or that interference with their rights under RC 4117.03 occurred.[304]

(C) Refusal to bargain

Where a collective bargaining agreement expressly permitted periodic reports to other than those directly represented by the union and employer bargaining teams only with the approval of both parties, the

---

[299]SERB has held that sympathy picketing must be preceded by the ten-day notice even if a work stoppage does not occur. In re Liberty Local School Dist, SERB 85-063 (12-6-85). SERB subsequently concluded that any picketing that relates to activities regulated by RC Ch 4117 and falling within SERB's jurisdiction is subject to the ten-day notice requirement. However, purely informational picketing (such as support for political candidates) not related to labor disputes involving the public employer or employee rights under RC Ch 4117 is not subject to the notice requirement. In re Ohio Civil Service Employees Assn, Local 11, AFSCME, SERB 94-009 (5-26-94) (holding that picketing over dispute regarding holiday pay under collective bargaining agreement was unfair labor practice in absence of required notice). See also In re University of Akron, SERB 86-010 (3-14-86). For extended treatment of the ten-day notice requirement, see Text 18.29(D), Right to strike.

[300]In re AFSCME, Ohio Council 8, SERB 90-015 (9-14-90).

[301]In re Stark County Engineer, SERB 85-012 (4-4-85).

[302]See In re Pickaway County Human Services Dept, SERB 87-018 (8-31-87).

[303]In re AFSCME, Local 772, SERB 90-013 (7-20-90).

[304]See In re Amalgamated Transit Union, Local 268, SERB 93-013 (6-25-93) (noting that had complaint been fairly and timely amended, SERB would have found unfair labor practice on basis of charging party not having equal right to seek union office).

union's unilateral release of information to the news media purporting to describe the employer's position on bargaining positions has been deemed an unlawful refusal to bargain.[305]

(D) Duty to provide fair representation

The requirement that the union fairly represent all bargaining unit employees codifies a similar duty in the private sector. A union, however, is accorded substantial leeway in balancing the various, and sometimes conflicting, interests of employees. An unfair labor practice will be found only if the union's action is arbitrary; that is, it has no rational basis. The relevant inquiry is not whether the union's reason for acting or not acting was wise but "merely whether the reason is rational."[306] Even where no rational basis is apparent (as would be the case, for example, where the union has articulated no actual reason for its conduct), SERB will not assume arbitrariness; rather, there must be evidence of bad faith or discriminatory intent. Absent such intent, "arbitrariness will be found only if the [union's] conduct is so egregious as to be beyond the bounds of honest mistake or misjudgment."[307] While simple negligence is within the bounds of honest mistake or misjudgment, gross negligence is not.[308] Thus, for example, a union is given wide latitude in deciding whether to pursue a grievance to arbitration,[309] and is not liable for mistakenly misfiling a grievance that results in that grievance being procedurally barred.[310] Negotiating varying wage increases with differentials based on the nature of the work and seniority falls well within a union's "wide range of discretion."[311] A union's disagreement with an employee over interpretation of a contractual seniority provision does not, of itself, breach the duty of fair representation,[312] nor does negotiating an agency shop provision.[313] A union may restrict a contract ratification vote to members only,[314] or establish a membership eligibility date for a ratification vote, provided it acts in accordance with its internal procedures and not discriminatorily, arbitrarily, or in bad faith.[315] Indeed, a union need not submit a tentative agreement to members for a ratification vote at all, absent a provision in the union's constitution or by-laws or a collective bargaining agreement that requires such a vote.[316] That a majority of unit employees may oppose the union's actions (in this case, pursuit of a grievance) does not indicate the union has breached its duty.[317]

An employer lacks standing to allege a breach of duty of fair representation unless harmed by the alleged misconduct.[318]

SERB maintains this particular unfair labor practice necessarily involves union misconduct that affects terms of employment as opposed to conduct involving only internal union affairs.[319]

---

[305] In re South Euclid-Lyndhurst City School Dist Bd of Ed, SERB 92-005 (4-21-92), affirmed by 1993 SERB 4-82 (CP, Franklin, 12-1-93). See also Ohio Assn of Public School Employees v SERB, No 92CVF-05-3757, 1993 WL 773577 (CP, Franklin, 12-1-93).

[306] In re AFSCME, Local 2312, SERB 89-029 (10-16-89).

[307] In re AFSCME, Local 2312, SERB 89-029, at 3-203, 3-204 (10-16-89).

[308] In re Ohio Civil Service Employees Assn/AFSCME, Local 11, SERB 93-019 (12-20-93) (noting that articulation of the union's reason for its conduct is typically preferred but not per se required); In re Ohio Health Care Employees Union, Dist 1199, SERB 93-020 (12-20-93).

[309] In re Ohio Civil Service Employees Assn/AFSCME, Local 11, SERB 93-019 (12-20-93).

[310] In re Ohio Health Care Employees Union, Dist 1199, SERB 93-020 (12-20-93).

[311] In re Nicolaci, SERB 89-030 (10-16-89). See also Ohio Assn of Public School Employees (OAPSE), No. 84-UU-06-1443 (3-20-85 (SERB)).

[312] In re Williams, SERB 85-059 (11-7-85). See also In re OAPSE, SERB 93-021 (12-21-93).

[313] Fairland Assn of Classroom Teachers, No. 84-UU-11-2367 (1-4-85 (SERB)).

[314] In re Adkins, SERB 85-064 (12-31-85).

[315] Ohio Assn of Public School Employees (OAPSE), No. 84-UU-08-1829 (HO 9-20-85, adopted 11-14-85 (SERB)).

[316] In re Greater Cincinnati Building & Trades Council, SERB HO 1992-HO-026 (7-2-92).

[317] In re City of Canton, SERB 90-006 (2-16-90).

[318] In re City of Canton, SERB 90-006 (2-16-90); In re City of Middleburg Heights, SERB 85-045 (9-20-85). *Canton* goes on to say that turmoil and adverse media publicity do not constitute the sort of harm required. This does not mean, however, that an employer may not intervene in an appropriate case where one with standing has filed a charge or introduce evidence in an appropriate case. In re Ohio Civil Service Employees Assn/AFSCME, Local 11, SERB 93-019 (12-20-93).

[319] See In re Amalgamated Transit Union, Local 268, SERB 93-013 (6-25-93).

18.26 Procedure on unfair labor practices

SERB is empowered to determine whether an employer or employee organization has committed any unfair labor practices and to remedy any violations found. SERB's jurisdiction in this respect is exclusive.[320] Thus, in 1991, the Ohio Supreme Court declared that, if a claim arises from or depends on rights created by the Public Employees' Collective Bargaining Act, SERB's authority over the matter is preemptive and a court has no jurisdiction to hear the case, irrespective of whether an unfair labor practice charge has actually been filed.[321] Emphasizing that SERB's exclusive jurisdiction to determine unfair labor practices does not foreclose parties to a collective bargaining agreement from settling contractual differences under a grievance procedure that culminates in binding arbitration, the Court has more recently stated that, in essence, SERB's jurisdiction is exclusive (1) where an unfair labor practice charge has been filed, or (2) where a complaint filed in court alleges conduct that fairly falls within the unfair labor practices specifically enumerated in RC 4117.11.[322]

(A) Filing charges

An unfair labor practice charge must be filed within ninety days after the alleged unfair labor practice occurred.[323] The only statutory exception is for persons prevented from filing by reason of military service, in which case the charge must be filed within ninety days after discharge from the armed services. SERB, however, has held that the ninety-day period may be tolled under certain limited circumstances for reasons of equity.[324] Moreover, while RC 4117.12(B) states that "anyone" may file a charge, SERB has held, "This obviously means anyone with standing."[325] SERB has also concluded the ninety-day period is not jurisdictional but a statute of limitations; thus, it is an affirmative defense that may be waived.[326] The period begins to run when (1) the charging party knows or has constructive knowledge of the practice at issue, and (2) actual damage to the charging party is caused by the practice.[327] Where a genuine dispute exists over just when an unfair labor practice occurs,

---

[320] Since SERB is the only agency empowered to decide unfair labor practice claims, decisions by other state agencies (such as the Personnel Board of Review) on aspects of the same incident that gave rise to the claim are not controlling as to unfair labor practice issues. In re Ohio State University, SERB 85-057 (10-30-85).

[321] Franklin County Law Enforcement Assn v Fraternal Order of Police, Lodge No. 9, 59 OS(3d) 167, 572 NE(2d) 87 (1991); Franklin County Sheriff's Dept v Fraternal Order of Police, Lodge No. 9, 59 OS(3d) 173, 572 NE(2d) 93 (1991). See also Ohio Historical Society v SERB, 66 OS(3d) 466, 613 NE(2d) 591 (1993). On the other hand, if the underlying conduct is not even arguably an unfair labor practice, the fact that the plaintiffs have filed charges with SERB does not deprive the court of jurisdiction. Kingsbury v Southeast Local School, 58 App(3d) 94, 568 NE(2d) 752 (Wayne 1989). See also Ohio Patrolmen's Benevolent Assn v MetroHealth System, 87 App(3d) 16, 621 NE(2d) 833 (Cuyahoga 1993) (holding SERB did not have exclusive jurisdiction on whether employer was obligated to arbitrate two discharge grievances since there was no evidence of a pattern or practice of repeated failures to arbitrate and hence no unfair labor practice implicated); Myers v Riley, 98 App(3d) 133, 648 NE(2d) 16 (Huron 1994) (holding that tort claims arising out of the employment relationship were not arguably unfair labor practices and not within SERB's exclusive jurisdiction); Slauson v New Philadelphia City School Dist Bd of Ed, No. 93-AP-07-005, 1994 WL 75612 (5th Dist Ct App, Tuscarawas, 3-1-94) (dismissing claim that teacher's transfer was for unconstitutional reasons, in part because the claim could impact upon unfair labor practice proceedings).

[322] East Cleveland v East Cleveland Firefighters Local 500, IAFF, 70 OS(3d) 125, 637 NE(2d) 878 (1994).

[323] RC 4117.12(B); OAC 4117-7-01; SERB v Ohio State University, 36 App(3d) 1, 520 NE(2d) 597 (Franklin 1987). If the nonrenewal of a limited contract is involved, the limitations period begins to run from the date the contract expires and employment terminates, not the date the board of education votes not to renew or gives advance notice of its intent not to renew. See Lordstown Local School Dist Bd of Ed v Ohio Civil Rights Comm, 66 OS(2d) 252, 421 NE(2d) 511 (1981); Cincinnati Metropolitan Housing Auth v SERB, 53 OS(3d) 221, 560 NE(2d) 179 (1990).

[324] In re Central State University, SERB 89-027 (10-5-89).

[325] In re City of Canton, SERB 90-006 (2-16-90). See also In re City of Middleburg Heights, SERB 85-045 (9-20-85).

[326] In re Paulding Exempted Village School Dist Bd of Ed, SERB 90-010 (6-22-90). See also SERB v Hubbard Twp Trustees, 1990 SERB 4-79 (11th Dist Ct App, Trumbull, 10-22-90).

[327] In re City of Barberton, SERB 88-008 (7-5-88), affirmed by 1990 SERB 4-46 (CP, Summit, 7-31-90). See also SERB v Hubbard Twp Trustees, 1990 SERB

SERB is required to consider the relevant circumstances and give some explanation for a finding of untimeliness.[328]

Upon receipt of the charge, SERB will investigate to determine if there is probable cause to believe an unfair labor practice has occurred.[329] If not, the charge is dismissed, and SERB's finding is not appealable.[330] If probable cause is found, SERB will issue a complaint and conduct a hearing.[331] Issuance of the complaint is what commences the adjudicatory proceeding and SERB may consider any incidents that occurred prior to issuance of the complaint that support the allegations in the charge even if they occurred after filing of the charge.[332] Notwithstanding that RC 4117.12(B) states that, after issuance of a complaint, SERB "shall conduct a hearing," it has been held that no absolute right to a hearing exists and SERB may settle a case over a charging party's objection where the settlement substantially remedies the unfair labor practice alleged in the complaint.[333] The proper standard of proof in an unfair labor practice hearing is a "preponderance of the evidence," and a hearing officer who applies a "clear and convincing evidence" standard errs.[334] A party not named in a charge has no automatic right to introduce evidence at a hearing, but a blanket rule against such action is inappropriate.[335]

Persons not protected by the Public Employees' Collective Bargaining Act, such as supervisors, may not file charges against an employer.[336]

(B) Remedies

If SERB determines, after a hearing, that an unfair labor practice has been committed, it will issue a cease and desist order and require the offending party affirmatively to remedy the violation. This may include reinstatement of affected employees with or without back pay.[337] However,

---

4-79 (11th Dist Ct App, Trumbull, 10-22-90). For an example of constructive knowledge, see SERB v City of Cincinnati, SERB 91-003 (3-7-91), affirmed by 1994 SERB 4-16 (CP, Hamilton, 3-30-94).

[328]State ex rel OAPSE v SERB, 64 OS(3d) 149, 593 NE(2d) 288 (1992).

[329]OAC 4117-7-02. SERB files compiled during the investigation are generally public records, although information excepted under RC 4117.17 and RC 149.43 may be redacted prior to disclosure. State ex rel Eaton City School Dist Bd of Ed v SERB, 64 OS(3d) 383, 595 NE(2d) 938 (1992); Franklin County Sheriff's Dept v SERB, 63 OS(3d) 498, 589 NE(2d) 24 (1992).

[330]OAPSE, Chapter 643 v Dayton City School Dist Bd of Ed, 59 OS(3d) 159, 572 NE(2d) 80 (1991). See also State ex rel OAPSE v SERB, 64 OS(3d) 149, 593 NE(2d) 288 (1992). However, an action in mandamus to challenge a SERB determination is apparently available to correct an abuse of discretion. See State ex rel Glass, Molders, Pottery, Plastics & Allied Workers Intl Union, Local 333 v SERB, 70 OS(3d) 252, 638 NE(2d) 556 (1994); State ex rel Glass, Molders, Pottery, Plastics & Allied Workers Intl Union, Local 333 v SERB, 66 OS(3d) 157, 609 NE(2d) 1266 (1993); State ex rel Toledo Police Patrolmen's Assn, Local 10 v SERB, 1993 SERB 4-73 (CP, Franklin, 6-14-93).

[331]RC 4117.12(B); OAC 4117-7-03 to OAC 4117-7-05. The text of RC 4117.12(B)(1) is incoherent insofar as it relates to filing an answer to a complaint. The second sentence states an answer "shall" be filed within ten days from receipt of a complaint or amended complaint, whereas the third sentence states a charged party "may" file an answer. See SERB v Adena Local School Dist Bd of Ed, 1991 SERB 4-119, 1991 WL 260832 (4th Dist Ct App, Ross, 11-26-91), reversed on other grounds by 66 OS(3d) 485, 613 NE(2d) 605 (1993). A complaint may be amended only prior to the close of hearing, and an attempt to amend after hearing will be denied. RC 4117.12(B)(1). See In re Amalgamated Transit Union, Local 268, SERB 93-013 (6-25-93).

[332]SERB v Warren County Sheriff, 63 OS(3d) 69, 584 NE(2d) 1211 (1992).

[333]Metcalf v Ohio Council 8, AFSCME, , 1992 SERB 4-28 (CP, Montgomery, 3-30-90).

[334]RC 4117.12(B)(3); In re City of Sidney, SERB 86-017 (4-23-86).

[335]In re Ohio Civil Service Employees Assn/AFSCME, Local 11, SERB 93-019 (12-20-93).

[336]Cleveland Metro General Hospital, No. 84-VR-05-1087 (1984 (SERB)).

[337]RC 4117.12(B). A board of education is generally not liable for any prejudgment interest on an award of back pay absent a statute or explicit contractual provision requiring such payment. State ex rel Brown v Milton-Union Exempted Village Bd of Ed, 40 OS(3d) 21, 531 NE(2d) 1297 (1988); Beifuss v Westerville Bd of Ed, 37 OS(3d) 187, 525 NE(2d) 20 (1988). For treatment of liability for postjudgment interest and prejudgment interest in other contexts, see Text 5.07, Capacity to sue and be sued. State ex rel Martin v Bexley School Dist Bd of Ed, 39 OS(3d) 36, 528 NE(2d) 1250 (1988), which did not arise under RC Chapter 4117 but applies by analogy, holds that the amount of back pay is generally reduced by the amount the employee earned, or with due diligence could have earned, in the interim. The burden is on the employer to prove what was, or could have been, earned. SERB sets off wages earned in mitigation on a year-to-year basis. Overtime earnings are included in back pay only where the employee can show with rea-

SERB cannot order reinstatement or back pay for any individual whose suspension or discharge was for just cause unrelated to rights protected by the Public Employees' Collective Bargaining Act and in accordance with the procedure contained in the collective bargaining agreement.[338] In refusal to bargain cases involving unilateral changes in working conditions, the remedy typically requires the employer to restore the status quo (that is, reinstate the working conditions unilaterally changed) and engage in collective bargaining.[339] Where an employer unilaterally increases employees' work load, SERB may, in fashioning an appropriate remedy, require the employer to compensate employees for additional work time occasioned by the unlawful action.[340]

SERB is not empowered to issue a remedial order against a party not named in a complaint.[341]

(C) Appeals

Decisions of SERB may be appealed to the common pleas court in any county where the unfair labor practice occurred or where the person aggrieved by SERB's order resides or transacts business.[342] The notice of appeal must set forth the order appealed from and the grounds for appeal.[343] Once the notice is filed, SERB is divested of jurisdiction to reconsider, vacate, or modify its decision in the absence of express statutory language to the contrary.[344] Pursuant to RC 4117.13(B), however, the court has discretion to remand the case to SERB to take additional evidence regarding violations of the order being appealed.[345] SERB's findings of fact are binding and conclusive if supported by substantial evidence.[346] The court has jurisdiction to enforce, modify, or set aside the order in whole or in part. However, the court "must accord due deference to SERB's interpretation of R.C. Chapter 4117" in reviewing the order.[347] Moreover, an appellate court's review of the common pleas court's decision is even more limited: the court is only to determine whether the lower court abused its discretion. That the appellate court might have come to a different conclusion than SERB or the lower court is immaterial.[348]

---

sonable certainty that the overtime would have been worked. In re Warren County Sheriff, SERB 94-002 (2-9-94).

[338]RC 4117.12(B).

[339]See, e.g., In re City of Canton, SERB 94-011 (6-29-94); Findlay City School Dist, SERB 87-031 (12-17-87), affirmed by 1988 SERB 4-54 (CP, Hancock, 5-11-88).

[340]SERB v East Palestine City School Dist Bd of Ed, No. 87-C-40, 1988 WL 70884 (7th Dist Ct App, Columbiana, 6-29-88).

[341]In re Ohio Civil Service Employees Assn/AFSCME, Local 11, SERB 93-019 (12-20-93) (where union charged with breaching its duty of fair representation in withdrawing grievance, SERB cannot order unnamed employer to arbitrate the grievance).

[342]RC 4117.13(A). Where the "person aggrieved" is a union, the union may appeal to the common pleas court in the county where the union has its headquarters even if it has a local in another county where the unfair labor practice occurred. SERB v Akron City School Dist Bd of Ed, 83 App(3d) 719, 1992 SERB 4-83, 615 NE(2d) 711 (Franklin 1992). The statute does not specify a time limit for filing an appeal. An appeals court has suggested that, by virtue of RC 4117.02(M), the time limit in RC 119.12, requiring an aggrieved party to file within fifteen days after mailing of notice of an agency's order, applies. Boieru v SERB, 54 App(3d) 23, 560 NE(2d) 801 (Cuyahoga 1988).

[343]RC 4117.13(D). The statute authorizes appeal of a SERB "final order ... granting or denying, in whole or in part, the relief sought." Thus, a procedural ruling by a SERB hearing officer, being neither final nor a SERB order, is not appealable. East Cleveland v SERB, 1989 SERB 4-130 (CP, Cuyahoga, 10-13-89). A SERB order that establishes a party's liability but remands the matter to a hearing officer for consideration as to remedy is also not a final, appealable order. Office of Collective Bargaining v SERB, 1989 SERB 4-143 (CP, Franklin 11-17-89).

[344]Lorain Ed Assn v Lorain City School Dist Bd of Ed, 46 OS(3d) 12, 544 NE(2d) 687 (1989).

[345]Franklin County Sheriff's Dept v SERB, 63 OS(3d) 498, 589 NE(2d) 24 (1992).

[346]RC 4117.13(D); Lorain City School Dist Bd of Ed v SERB, 40 OS(3d) 257, 533 NE(2d) 264 (1988); Akron Bd of Ed v SERB, 38 App(3d) 95, 526 NE(2d) 115 (Summit 1987). See also University Hospital, University of Cincinnati College of Medicine v SERB, 63 OS(3d) 339, 587 NE(2d) 835 (1992) (holding that a common pleas court's conclusion that a SERB order is not supported by substantial evidence is a legal determination fully reviewable by court of appeals).

[347]Lorain City School Dist Bd of Ed v SERB, 40 OS(3d) 257, 533 NE(2d) 264 (1988). However, an appeals court has suggested such defense need not be accorded SERB's interpretation of a collective bargaining agreement. Lakewood v SERB, 66 App(3d) 387, 1990 SERB 4-35, 584 NE(2d) 70 (Cuyahoga 1990).

[348]Lorain City School Dist Bd of Ed v SERB, 40 OS(3d) 257, 533 NE(2d) 264 (1988). See also SERB v Adena Local School Dist Bd of Ed, 66 OS(3d) 485,

Court or SERB determination that an employee or public officer committed an unfair labor practice cannot be the basis of his removal or recall or discipline.[349] Neither the public officer nor the employee is subject to a suit for damages based upon a determination that an unfair labor practice has been committed.[350] However, a party to a collective bargaining agreement may enforce the agreement and seek damages for its violation.[351]

NEGOTIATIONS AND DISPUTES

18.27 Privacy of negotiations, conflict of interest

Collective bargaining sessions between the employer and the employee organization are generally private and are not subject to the Sunshine Act, RC 121.22.[352] Conducting sessions in public is permitted only by order of the mediator if a strike has been enjoined.[353] Insistence upon public sessions is an unlawful refusal to bargain.[354]

RC 4117.20 prohibits any person who is a member of the same local, state, national, or international organization as the employee organization with which the employer is bargaining or who has an interest in the outcome of the bargaining, which interest conflicts with the employer's interest, from participating in bargaining on behalf of the employer. However, such person, if entitled to vote on the ratification of an agreement, may vote. The employer must immediately remove from negotiations any person who has a conflict of interest as described in the statute. Failure to comply with the removal requirement is an unfair labor practice.[355]

18.28 Scope of bargaining

(A) In general

As a general matter, the Public Employees' Collective Bargaining Act declares that all matters pertaining to wages, hours, or terms and other conditions of employment and the continuation, modification, or deletion of an existing provision of a collective bargaining agreement are subject to collective bargaining between the employer and the exclusive representative.[356] However, the conduct and grading of civil service examinations, the rating of candidates, the establishment of eligible lists from the examinations, and the original appointments from the eligible lists are not appropriate subjects for bargaining.[357] In addition, there are a number of fundamental management rights which, unless the employer otherwise agrees in a collective bargaining agreement, are not impaired by the Public Employees' Collective Bargaining Act and over which the employer is not required to bargain except as those management rights "affect wages, hours, and terms and conditions of employment, and the continuation, modification, or deletion of an existing provision of a collective bargaining agreement."[358]

(B) Mandatory, permissive, and prohibited subjects

The Public Employees' Collective Bargaining Act thus embraces the traditional labor law concept that subjects of bargaining fall within three basic categories: (1) "mandatory," meaning those which must be bargained; (2) "permissive," meaning those which may be bargained but for which no duty to bargain exists; and (3) "prohibited" or "illegal," meaning those which may not be bargained.[359] The

---

613 NE(2d) 605 (1993); Franklin County Sheriff's Dept v SERB, 63 OS(3d) 498, 589 NE(2d) 24 (1992).

[349] RC 4117.11(C).
[350] RC 4117.11(C).
[351] RC 4117.11(C).
[352] RC 4117.21.
[353] RC 4117.16(B).
[354] In re City of Dayton, SERB 85-006 (3-14-85).
[355] In re Springfield Twp Bd of Trustees, SERB 89-015 (6-29-89), affirmed by 70 App(3d) 801, 1990 SERB 4-117, 592 NE(2d) 871 (Hamilton 1990), appeal dismissed by 59 OS(3d) 718, 572 NE(2d) 691 (1991). See also Vandalia-Butler City School Dist Bd of Ed, SERB 87-007 (4-30-87).

[356] RC 4117.08(A).
[357] RC 4117.08(B).
[358] RC 4117.08(C).

[359] See Cincinnati v Ohio Council 8, AFSCME, 61 OS(3d) 658, 576 NE(2d) 745 (1991) (insisting to the point of a bargaining impasse on the inclusion of a permissive subject in a collective bargaining agree-

mandatory subjects are wages, hours, or terms and other conditions of employment, and changes in the existing provisions of a collective bargaining agreement.

The conduct and grading of civil service examinations, the rating of candidates, the establishment of eligible lists from the examinations, and the original appointments from the eligible lists are prohibited subjects. However, all matters affecting promotions in the civil service have been held appropriate subjects for bargaining.[360]

The permissive subjects are all nonmandatory subjects whose inclusion in a collective bargaining agreement is not prohibited by law and include those basic management rights, which the Public Employees' Collective Bargaining Act identifies as the right to perform the following:

(1) Determine matters of inherent managerial policy;

(2) Direct, supervise, evaluate, or hire employees;

(3) Maintain and improve the efficiency and effectiveness of operations;

(4) Determine the overall methods, process, means, or personnel by which operations are to be conducted;

(5) Suspend, discipline, demote, or discharge for just cause, or lay off, transfer, assign, schedule, promote, or retain employees;

(6) Determine the adequacy of the work force;

(7) Determine the overall mission of the employer;

(8) Effectively manage the work force; and

(9) Take actions to carry out the mission of the employer.

SERB has also held that the tape recording of investigatory pre-disciplinary hearings mandated by a collective bargaining agreement is a permissive subject of bargaining.[361]

Under RC 4117.08(C), an employer is not required to bargain on any of these subjects "except as affect wages, hours, terms and conditions of employment, and the continuation, modification, or deletion of an existing provision of a collective bargaining agreement." This last clause has been read by some as transforming the exercise of a management right involving one of the purportedly permissive subjects into a mandatory subject. Under this view, both the managerial decision itself and its impact on bargaining unit employees become subject to bargaining. In this connection, SERB early on rejected any notion that, under RC 4117.08(C), the employer is only obligated to bargain the "effects" of the managerial decision.[362] In *Lorain City School Dist Bd of Ed v SERB*,[363] the Ohio Supreme Court, by a 4-3 margin, accepted SERB's initial view and held that the employer was obligated to bargain about its decision to restructure the work force and reassign work previously performed by bargaining unit nurses to non-unit personnel. The majority, contrary to the three dissenters, found that more than "effects" bargaining is necessary:

> In choosing the word "affect," as opposed to the word "effect," the legislature has given us a verb rather than a noun as would be the case with "effect."
>
> The word "affect" in R.C. 4117.08(C) suggests that management rights which "act upon" or "produce a material influence upon" working conditions are bargainable. See Webster's Third New International Dictionary (1986) 35. Thus, a reasonable interpretation of R.C. 4117.08(C) is that where the exercise of a management right causes a change in or "affects" working conditions or terms of a contract, then the decision to exercise that right is a mandatory subject for bargaining.[364]

---

ment is unlawful). See also In re City of Cincinnati, SERB 93-010 (6-10-93).

[360]DeVennish v Columbus, 57 OS(3d) 163, 566 NE(2d) 668 (1991). See also State ex rel Parsons v Fleming, 68 OS(3d) 509, 628 NE(2d) 1377 (1994). In In re City of Akron, SERB 94-012 (7-7-94), SERB specifically held that civil service rules governing promotions constitute a mandatory subject of bargaining.

[361]In re City of Cincinnati, SERB 93-010 (6-10-93).

[362]See In re Lorain City School Dist Bd of Ed, SERB 86-020 (5-15-86); In re City of Lakewood, SERB 88-009 (7-11-88), affirmed by 66 App(3d) 387, 1990 SERB 4-35, 584 NE(2d) 70 (Cuyahoga 1990).

[363]Lorain City School Dist Bd of Ed v SERB, 40 OS(3d) 257, 533 NE(2d) 264 (1988).

[364]Lorain City School Dist Bd of Ed v SERB, 40 OS(3d) 257, at 262, 533 NE(2d) 264 (1988).

Accordingly, under this construction of its last paragraph, RC 4117.08(C)'s purported reservation to employers of nine basic management rights is often rendered illusory upon the decision to exercise those rights.[365]

In *In re Youngstown City School Dist Bd of Ed*,[366] however, SERB, finding that its initial approach "has virtually eliminated the concept of management rights for Ohio's public employers," attempted anew to reconcile RC 4117.08's "seemingly contradictory language" by adopting a "new standard, in the form of a balancing test, to identify those subjects about which public employers must bargain in Ohio." The new test reads as follows:

> ... if a given subject is alleged to affect and is determined to have a material influence upon wages, hours, or terms and other conditions of employment *and* involves the exercise of inherent management discretion, the following factors must be balanced to determine whether it is a mandatory or permissive subject of bargaining:
>
> 1) The extent to which the subject is logically and reasonably related to wages, hours, terms and conditions of employment;
>
> 2) The extent to which the employer's obligation to negotiate may significantly abridge its freedom to exercise those managerial prerogatives set forth in and anticipated by O.R.C. 4117.08(C), including an examination of the type of employer involved and whether inherent discretion on the subject matter at issue is necessary to achieve the employer's essential mission and its obligations to the general public; and
>
> 3) The extent to which the mediatory influence of collective bargaining and, when necessary, any impasse resolution mechanisms available to the parties are the appropriate means of resolving conflicts over the subject matter.[367]

Managerial decisions found, on balance, to be within areas of management discretion may be implemented without bargaining (unless, of course, bargaining is required by a term of the employer's collective bargaining agreement with a union). However, a limited bargaining duty still remains as to "[a]ny reasonable foreseeable wages, hours or terms and other conditions of employment which are affected by those decisions," which bargaining must be undertaken "as soon as possible and, whenever reasonably practicable, before the announced implementation date if the union makes a timely request to bargain."[368]

Applying its test, SERB found that a public employer's decision to implement an early retirement incentive plan pursuant to RC 3307.35 is a mandatory subject of bargaining. Where the plan is implemented mid-term in a collective bargaining agreement, the employer "should give the union reasonable advance notice both of the policy it intends to implement and the projected date of implementation." If the union timely requests bargaining, the employer must then bargain in good faith either to an agreement or to an ultimate impasse, at which point the employer is

---

[365] Of course, if the parties have already bargained over a mandatory subject and incorporated their agreement in the labor contract, an employer may not unilaterally alter the agreement. Thus, for example, RC 4117.08(C)'s reservation of management rights does not give an employer the right to impose additional requirements for the use of sick leave (here, the requirement of a doctor's certificate) beyond those set forth in the sick leave provision of the collective bargaining agreement. Deeds v Ironton, 48 App(3d) 7, 548 NE(2d) 254 (Lawrence 1988).

[366] In re Youngstown City School Dist Bd of Ed, SERB 95-010 (6-30-95). SERB had earlier announced almost identical revisions in In re Transportation Dept, SERB 93-005 (4-29-93). However, the Tenth District Court of Appeals reversed SERB's order in In re Transportation Dept on grounds of mootness in Ohio Civil Service Employees Assn v Ohio Dept of Transportation, No. 94APE08-1252, 1995 WL326265 (10th Dist Ct App, Franklin, 6-1-95).

[367] In re Youngstown City School Dist Bd of Ed, SERB 95-010, at 3-76, 3-77 (6-30-95). Subjects that affect wages, hours, or terms and conditions of employment but do not involve the exercise of inherent management rights will not be balanced—they are mandatory subjects of bargaining per se. Similarly, areas of inherent management discretion that do not affect wages, hours, or terms and conditions of employment will not be balanced—they are permissive subjects of bargaining per se.

[368] In re Youngstown City School Dist Bd of Ed, SERB 95-010 (6-30-95).

free to implement in accordance with the agreement or its final offer to the union.[369]

In *In re Youngstown City School Dist Bd of Ed*,[370] SERB concluded the retirement incentive plan was a mandatory subject of bargaining. SERB held the following to be mandatory subjects of bargaining: (1) agency shop, (2) the school calendar, (3) employee evaluation procedures, (4) vacations and holidays, (5) length of work day and work week, (6) individual employment contracts, (7) leave policies, (8) salary advancement, (9) various payroll deductions, (10) tuition reimbursement policies, (11) retirement incentive policies, (12) leave and release time for union business, (13) leave and release time for participation in collective bargaining, (14) extra duty pay, (15) staff meetings, (16) planning time, (17) scheduling of calamity make-up days, (18) employee travel allowances, (19) the number of visits an employee is required to make to a student's home for home instruction or other purposes, and (20) eligibility for, the level of benefits provided by, and the carriers for various insurance fringe benefits. Other examples of mandatory subjects, according to SERB, include disciplinary policies,[371] changes in work schedules and hours,[372] personnel drug and alcohol policies (including drug and alcohol testing policies),[373] the number of periods in a school day,[374] the amount of student contact time,[375] layoff procedures,[376] the creation and implementation of a new position for which a supplemental teaching contract is offered,[377] the abolition of teaching positions and assignment of duties within those positions to other teachers,[378] and employee residency requirements.[379] At least some of these issues, however, might be decided differently today under SERB's new balancing test. The precise scope of an employer's duty to bargain remains, in a word, murky.

Even where an employer's decision to act results not from an exercise of managerial discretion but in response to a statutory

---

[369]In re Youngstown City School Dist Bd of Ed, SERB 95-010 (6-30-95). Whether the courts will endorse SERB's new standard remains to be seen. SERB assumes a reviewing court "will continue to afford deference" to SERB's views "based upon SERB's growing experience applying the statute to labor disputes in the public sector." In re Transportation Dept, SERB 93-005, at 3-25 n.3 (4-29-93). SERB has also characterized the Supreme Court's discussion approving SERB's old standard in Lorain City School Dist Bd of Ed v SERB, 40 OS(3d) 257, 533 NE(2d) 264 (1988) as "dicta and not precedential." In re Youngstown City School Dist Bd of Ed, SERB 95-010 (6-30-95).

[370]In re Youngstown City School Dist Bd of Ed, SERB 95-010 (6-30-95).

[371]SERB v Swanton Local School Dist Bd of Ed, SERB 89-008 (4-12-89), affirmed by 1989 SERB 4-139 (CP, Fulton, 11-1-89); Norwood Bd of Ed, No. 87-ULP-04-0144 (HO 8-29-88, adopted 12-15-88 (SERB)). Even if employee discipline is not the primary focus of a policy, bargaining may be required if the possibility of discipline is an incidental aspect of the policy. Thus, a school bus safety procedure that contemplated discipline for noncompliance was deemed a mandatory subject in United Local School Dist Bd of Ed, No. 86-ULP-10-0384 (HO 9-30-88, adopted 12-29-88 (SERB)).

[372]In re Portage Lakes Joint Vocational School Dist Bd of Ed, SERB 93-009 (6-2-93), affirmed in Portage Lakes Ed Assn v SERB, 1995 SERB 4-13 (5-3-95); SERB v Bedford Hts, 41 App(3d) 21, 534 NE(2d) 115 (Cuyahoga 1987); In re City of Lakewood, SERB 88-009 (7-11-88), affirmed by 66 App(3d) 387, 1990 SERB 4-35, 584 NE(2d) 70 (Cuyahoga 1990); Nordonia Hills City School Dist Bd of Ed, Nos. 86-ULP-7-0254, 87-ULP-4-0142 (HO 5-19-88, adopted as modified 8-24-88 (SERB)), affirmed by 1990 SERB 4-22 (CP, Summit, 4-30-90).

[373]In re City of Canton, SERB 94-011 (6-29-94). See also Findlay City School Dist, SERB 87-031 (12-17-87), affirmed by 1988 SERB 4-54 (CP, Hancock, 5-11-88); Franklin County Sheriff, SERB 90-012 (7-18-90). In *Canton*, SERB emphasized that where safety-sensitive job classifications are involved, the decision to implement a drug/alcohol testing policy may well be only a permissive subject of bargaining, but the effects of the decision would still be a mandatory subject. Of course, where testing is required by federal law (see Text 22.13(B), Drug and alcohol testing), only the effects are bargainable.

[374]In re Bowling Green Bd of Ed, SERB 88-005 (4-20-88), affirmed by 1988 SERB 4-81 (CP, Wood, 9-15-88).

[375]In re Perrysburg Bd of Ed, SERB 86-038 (9-15-86), affirmed by 1987 SERB 4-18 (CP, Wood, 1-16-87).

[376]Cuyahoga County Commissioners, SERB 89-006 (3-15-89).

[377]In re Mayfield City School Dist Bd of Ed, SERB 89-033 (12-20-89).

[378]SERB v Eaton City School Dist Bd of Ed, No. 87-ULP-10-0494 (3-22-90), affirmed by 71 App(3d) 783, 1991 SERB 4-23, 595 NE(2d) 432 (Preble 1991).

[379]In re St. Bernard, SERB 89-007 (3-15-89), affirmed by 74 App(3d) 3, 1991 SERB 4-67, 598 NE(2d) 15 (Hamilton 1991). See also City of St. Bernard v SERB, 1994 SERB 4-52 (1st Dist Ct App, Hamilton, 7-27-94).

duty to act, a limited obligation to bargain may still attach. Thus, for example, SERB has held that an employer is not required to bargain on whether to purchase liability insurance required by law but does have a duty to bargain the nature and quality of the coverage provided.[380] Similarly, in *In re Findlay City School Dist Bd of Ed*,[381] the employer's decision to schedule a legally required make-up day was not bargainable but when the day would be scheduled was.

An employee organization's legal right to bargain may be waived, although waivers will not be lightly inferred. A waiver most often occurs in one of two ways: (1) by express language in the collective bargaining agreement, or (2) by union inaction when given the opportunity to bargain.

A contractual waiver may appear anywhere in the collective bargaining agreement. A waiver will be found only where there is "clear and unmistakable" intent to relinquish bargaining rights. SERB will examine the contract language, bargaining history, and extrinsic evidence in determining whether the right to bargain has been waived.[382] Plainly, a general reservation of managerial authority or the mere existence of a "zipper" clause, without more, will not suffice with respect to a particular subject.[383]

SERB found a waiver by union inaction in *Pickaway-Ross Joint Vocational School Dist Bd of Ed*,[384] where the union slept on its rights despite repeated opportunities to bargain. Subsequent decisions, however, emphasizing "the very strict standards applicable to waiver," reveal that *Pickaway-Ross* will not be applied readily and that, as in the case of contractual waivers, the union's disinterest in bargaining must be "clear and unmistakable."[385]

Either an employer or the employee organization may insist to the point of impasse upon a proposal pertaining to a mandatory subject of bargaining. In virtually all jurisdictions, it is an unfair labor practice for either party to insist upon a permissive subject to the point of impasse. SERB indirectly addressed this axiomatic principle in *In re Stark County Bd of Mental Retardation & Developmental Disabilities*,[386] holding that a strike allegedly over a permissive bargaining subject was not illegal under RC 4117.23.[387] Rather, the employer's only recourse was to file an unfair labor charge. An employer can act unilaterally during the term of a collective bargaining agreement with respect to any "permissive" subject but may not with respect to a "mandatory" subject without first affording the employee organization an opportunity to bargain and, absent a union waiver of bargaining rights, bargaining to ultimate impasse.[388]

(C) Tentative agreements

RC 4117.10(B) provides that a legislative body[389] must approve or reject the submission of an agreement *as a whole*.[390] If the legislative body fails to act within thirty

---

[380]In re Wilmington City School Dist Bd of Ed, SERB 87-005 (4-9-87), affirmed by 1989 SERB 4-70 (CP, Franklin, 4-21-89); Willard City School Dist Bd of Ed, No. 86-ULP-3-0081 (HO 6-30-87, adopted 9-30-87 (SERB)), set aside by No. 51493 (CP, Huron, 10-3-88), reversed by 65 App(3d) 259, 1989 SERB 4-133, 583 NE(2d) 1009 (Huron 1989), set aside again on remand by 1990 SERB 4-26 (CP, Huron, 5-4-90).

[381]In re Findlay City School Dist Bd of Ed, SERB 88-006 (5-13-88).

[382] In re Youngstown City School Dist Bd of Ed, SERB 95-010 (6-30-95). See also In re City of Canton, SERB 94-011 (6-29-94). In assessing whether a waiver exists, SERB will consider bargaining history and extrinsic evidence of the parties' intent together with the relevant contractual language.

[383] In re Youngstown State University, SERB 93-011 (6-10-93) (zipper clause not sufficiently specific to waive bargaining rights with respect to employer's smoking policy).

[384]Pickaway-Ross Joint Vocational School Dist Bd of Ed, SERB 87-027 (11-19-87).

[385]Akron City School Dist Bd of Ed, No. 86-ULP-11-0438 (HO 1-10-89, adopted 2-16-90 (SERB)). See also SERB v Swanton Local School Dist Bd of Ed, SERB 89-008 (4-12-89), affirmed by 1989 SERB 4-139 (CP, Fulton, 11-1-89).

[386]In re Stark County Bd of Mental Retardation & Developmental Disabilities, SERB 85-041 (9-12-85).

[387]See Text 18.31, Unauthorized strikes.

[388]See Text 18.24(C), Refusal to bargain, unilateral action at point of ultimate impasse.

[389]The legislative body of a school district is the board of education. In the case of a county MR/DD board, the legislative body for purposes of the statute is the board of county commissioners. Stark County Educators Assn for the Training of Retarded Persons v SERB, 1989 SERB 4-119, 1989 WL 120658 (5th Dist Ct App, Stark, 10-10-89); Stark County Educators Assn for the Training of Retarded Persons v SERB, 1991 SERB 4-19 (CP, Stark, 4-1-91).

[390]RC 4117.10(B). Thus, the legislative body may not pick and choose those parts that are acceptable, thereby effectively presenting the union with a

days, the agreement shall be deemed approved.[391] The tentative agreement will become the contract if the action taken by the board is to table any vote and the tentative agreement is not approved or rejected within thirty days of the date it was originally submitted to the board.[392]

18.29 Procedures for resolving disputes

The Act includes detailed procedures for the conduct of negotiations and an extensive variety of dispute resolution procedures.

(A) In general, "time line"

These procedures are implemented according to a "time line." The statutory period for bargaining can be suspended pending resolution of a refusal-to-bargain unfair labor practice charge filed during negotiations. The duty to bargain, however, is not suspended.[393]

SERB has held these procedures do not apply to the disposition of a grievance arising under an existing contract. Consequently, SERB dismissed a notice to negotiate over an alleged change in a collective bargaining agreement with respect to which a grievance was lodged.[394]

SERB has also held these procedures do not apply to mid-term bargaining disputes (i.e., disputes involving bargainable issues that arise over the course of a collective bargaining agreement's term). SERB will deal with such disputes case-by-case and "recommends" that parties adopt procedures specially designed to deal with such disputes.[395]

(B) Notice to negotiate, duty to bargain

A party who wishes to terminate or modify a collective bargaining agreement, or negotiate a successor agreement, must notify the other party in writing at least sixty days before the current agreement expires and offer to bargain.[396] If the agreement has no expiration date, notification must be given at least sixty days prior to when the proposed changes are, or the successor agreement is, to take effect. The notifying party must also send copies of the notice and the current agreement to SERB.[397] A union's notice that is not sent to both the employer and SERB will be dismissed.[398] If the parties are negotiating for the first time, the negotiation period is ninety rather than sixty days.[399]

The parties must bargain upon receipt of the notice.[400] If they cannot reach agreement, at any time prior to forty-five days before expiration of the agreement, they may submit the issues in dispute to any mutually agreed-upon dispute settlement method which supersedes the specific procedures contained in RC 4117.14.[401] The statute specifies several such alternative dispute settlement methods which include a variety of arbitration procedures and "any other dispute settlement procedure mutually agreed to by the parties."[402] In the absence of a valid alternative dispute

---

counteroffer. In re City of Martins Ferry, SERB 89-021 (8-23-89), affirmed by 1991 SERB 4-62, 1991 WL 98694 (7th Dist Ct App, Belmont, 6-6-91). See also Stark County Educators Assn for the Training of Retarded Persons v SERB, 1989 SERB 4-119, 1989 WL 120658 (5th Dist Ct App, Stark, 10-10-89).

[391]RC 4117.10(B).

[392]East Palestine City School Dist Bd of Ed v SERB, No. 87-C-6, 1987 WL 29612 (7th Dist Ct App, Columbiana, 12-15-87).

[393]In re City of Oakwood, SERB 85-001 (1-11-85).

[394]In re Miamisburg School Dist Bd of Ed, SERB 86-001 (1-15-86).

[395]In re Franklin County Sheriff, SERB 90-012 (7-18-90). See also In re Transportation Dept, SERB 93-005 (4-29-93).

[396]RC 4117.14(B); OAC 4117-9-02(A).

[397]RC 4117.14(B); OAC 4117-9-02(A). RC 4117.14's notice requirements do not apply to mid-term bargaining (that is, limited bargaining during the term of a collective bargaining agreement not aimed at reaching an accord on the terms of a successor agreement). See In re Youngstown State University, SERB 93-011 (6-10-93). Where, prior to bargaining for a successor agreement, neither party filed the required notice, SERB refused to hold an ensuing strike unauthorized for the union's failure to file in In re University of Cincinnati, SERB 93-007 (5-13-93), noting that the employer had an equal obligation to file and was thus equally at fault for no notice having been given; SERB emphasized its conclusion was based on the particular facts of this case, however.

[398]Woodridge Ed Assn, No. 85-MF-01-2734 (1-25-85 (SERB)).

[399]RC 4117.14(B); OAC 4117-9-02(B).

[400]RC 4117.14(B)(4).

[401]RC 4117.14(C); OAC 4117-9-02(E), (F), OAC 4117-9-03.

[402]RC 4117.14(C).

settlement procedure, the procedures of RC 4117.14 apply.[403]

Thus, in *Mad River-Green Local Ed Assn*,[404] SERB found a strike following unsuccessful bargaining under a wage reopener to be unauthorized where the parties' alternative procedure—mediation—was "faulty and thus inoperative" because, by its terms, it might never be exhausted prior to the expiration of the collective bargaining agreement, thus allowing no accommodation for the employees' right to strike during the reopener period. Because the alternative procedure was deemed faulty, no dispute settlement procedure had been exhausted and the strike was thus unauthorized.[405] In another case, a strike was deemed unauthorized where the parties' alternative procedure called for a three-person consulting panel that was to submit a written report within fifteen days of the chairman's appointment or such later date as mutually agreed upon, but the procedure did not specify what would happen if the deadline passed and no extension was agreed to, which is what happened before the strike. Finding that this procedure, too, was faulty and inoperative, SERB declared that parties who opt for an alternative procedure "have a responsibility to write one that leads to the possibility of resolution and one that has finality."[406]

On the other hand, where mediation was specified as the alternative procedure, and the procedure expressly expired as of the date the collective bargaining agreement expired, the necessary finality was present and a strike after its exhaustion was authorized.[407] SERB has also concluded a contract that called for mediation "until the parties arrive at an agreement" was, in light of the parties' bargaining history and the contract read as a whole, "sufficiently exhaustive and operative under the circumstances" to validate a strike, but cautioned that the provision was neither well drafted nor a model of clarity and that "[p]arties who forego the statutory dispute resolution procedures for their own alternatives are well-advised to draft language which is clear and self-explanatory."[408]

(C) Procedures for resolving deadlock

If the parties have not reached an agreement fifty days before expiration of their agreement and an alternative dispute settlement procedure has not been agreed upon, either party may request SERB to intervene. SERB must appoint a mediator if an impasse exists or if forty-five days remain before the expiration of the current agreement.[409] If the mediator, after assisting the parties, advises SERB that the parties have reached impasse or if only thirty-one days remain in the term of the agreement, SERB must appoint, in one day, a fact-finding panel of not more than three members selected by the parties.[410] However, SERB has refused a request for fact-finding when the number and nature of unresolved issues indicated the parties had not engaged in "effective mediation."[411] In that situation, SERB refused to pay its nor-

---

[403] RC 4117.14(C); OAC 4117-9-02(F).

[404] Mad River-Green Local Ed Assn, SERB 88-016 (9-29-88).

[405] On the right to strike under a contract reopener provision, see Text 18.30, Legal strikes.

[406] In re Weathersfield Local Bd of Ed, SERB 91-009 (11-8-91), affirmed by 1992 SERB 4-89 (CP, Franklin, 10-14-92). While the common pleas court agreed with SERB that the strike was illegal, it rejected SERB's view that the procedure was faulty.

[407] In re Niles City Bd of Ed, SERB 91-010 (11-8-91).

[408] In re Springfield Local Bd of Ed, SERB 92-016 (9-30-92).

[409] RC 4117.14(C); OAC 4117-9-04.

[410] RC 4117.14(C). To facilitate appointment of the panel, SERB sends the parties a list of five fact-finders from its register of neutrals after receiving a notice to negotiate. OAC 4117-9-05(A). Not later than thirty-five days prior to expiration of the negotiating period, the parties are to submit to SERB in writing a mutually selected panel of one or three members together with the names of alternates to the preferred panel. If the parties cannot agree on the number of panel members, SERB will appoint a one-member panel. OAC 4117-9-05(B). The parties may mutually select any fact-finder from SERB's register of neutrals instead of selecting from the list provided. However, selection of a fact-finder not on SERB's register constitutes a mutually agreed upon alternative dispute settlement procedure and precludes the appointment or payment of the panel by SERB. OAC 4117-9-05(C). If the parties do not submit a selected panel within the time limits of OAC 4117-9-05, SERB, not later than thirty days prior to expiration of the negotiating period, will appoint a one-member panel. OAC 4117-9-05(D). In addition, where selected fact-finders are unavailable, SERB will appoint a panel at its discretion. OAC 4117-9-05(E).

[411] In re Elmwood Local Bd of Ed, SERB 85-043 (9-20-85).

mal share of the costs of fact-finding and only supplied a list from which the parties could select their own fact-finder.[412]

The fact-finding panel is required to gather facts and make recommendations for resolving the dispute. It may do this through written position statements and hearings, which are to be held in private. The panel's recommendations must be transmitted within fourteen days after appointment, unless the parties agree to an extension. The parties have seven days to act on the recommendations, which are binding unless the employer, or the employee organization, by a three-fifths vote of their respective total membership, rejects the report.[413] Fact finders are to refrain from public comment regarding their reports during the fact-finding voting period.[414]

An extension will be granted if delays in mailing the recommendations give the parties insufficient time to consider, but an extension will not be granted if requested after the seven-day period and a formal motion for an extension is not filed.[415] The vote results must be certified to SERB and the other party within twenty-four hours, but in no event later than twenty-four hours after expiration of the seven-day period.[416] A vote by both parties is unnecessary if one party has already rejected the report.[417] If either party rejects the recommendations, SERB must publicize the panel's report. However, one or both parties may release the report at an earlier time.[418]

(D) Right to strike

If the parties do not reach agreement within seven days after the panel report is published, or if the agreement has expired, school employees have the right to strike provided the employee organization has given a ten-day prior written notice of the date and time of the action, and that the strike is for full, consecutive work days and the beginning date of the strike is at least ten work days after the ending date of the most recent prior strike involving the same bargaining unit.[419] A strike occurring after the agreement had expired but less than seven days after the panel report was published by SERB was declared illegal.[420] However, an appeals court has held that if the agreement has expired and the statutory negotiating procedure has been exhausted by one party's rejection of the panel's report, employees can strike (provided the ten-day notice was given) even if seven days have not elapsed from SERB's publication of the report.[421]

The mandatory ten-day strike notice must be given to both the employer and to SERB[422] and, because the notice requirement implicates a public interest, it cannot be waived.[423] When the notices to SERB and the employer are mailed on the same day, a strike that occurs ten days after the employer receives the notice is permitted even if, because of mailing delays, SERB receives the strike notice less than ten days before the strike.[424] The ten-day notice requirement does not mandate ten literal twenty-four hour periods, but ten calendar days, with the first day being the day after service and the last day being the tenth day after that. If multiple, overlapping notices are given, the later-filed notice supersedes any earlier notice.[425]

---

[412]In re Elmwood Local Bd of Ed, SERB 85-043 (9-20-85).

[413]RC 4117.14(C); OAC 4117-9-05(F) to (O). See also In re Carlisle Local Bd of Ed, SERB 87-025 (11-10-87); In re Miami University, SERB 86-030 (8-7-86).

[414]In re City of Shaker Heights, SERB 93-012 (6-17-93).

[415]In re Stark County Engineer, SERB 85-058 (10-31-85).

[416]OAC 4117-9-05(M), (N).

[417]See In re City of Lima, SERB 85-002 (1-25-85); RC 4117.14(C); OAC 4117-9-05(P).

[418]See In re City of Lima, SERB 85-002 (1-25-85); RC 4117.14(C); OAC 4117-9-05(P).

[419]RC 4117.14(D), as amended by 1995 H 200, eff. 9-21-95.

[420]In re City of Springfield, SERB 85-038 (8-9-85).

[421]Ohio Council 8, AFSCME v Springfield Bd of Park Trustees, 43 App(3d) 26, 539 NE(2d) 175 (Franklin 1988).

[422]In re Summit County Dept of Human Services, SERB 85-013 (4-5-85).

[423]In re Central Ohio Transit Authority, SERB 86-047 (11-25-86).

[424]RC 4117.15(C).

[425]In re Dayton City School Dist Bd of Ed, SERB 93-003 (4-15-93).

(E) Bargaining procedure after "opt-in" elections

Where a group of employees elects a union representative during the term of a collective bargaining agreement through an "opt-in" election[426] and thus becomes included within an already represented bargaining unit, the existing collective bargaining agreement does not automatically apply to them. Instead, interim bargaining with respect to these employees is required, which will ultimately be followed by a single successor agreement covering the entire unit. For the purpose of any fact-finding vote under RC 4117.14(C)(6) or a strike permitted by RC 4117.14(D)(2), only those added to the unit by means of the opt-in election can participate if the interim bargaining breaks down.[427]

STRIKES

18.30 Legal strikes

As previously indicated, the Public Employees' Collective Bargaining Act permits school employees to strike after the appropriate negotiation procedures have been exhausted, provided the required ten-day strike notice has been given and that the strike is for full, consecutive work days beginning at least ten working days after the ending date of the most recent prior strike involving the same bargaining unit.[428] The Public Employees' Collective Bargaining Act specifically prohibits strikes during the term or extended term of a collective bargaining agreement or during the pendency of settlement procedures.[429]

SERB has held that employees are not prohibited from striking after reaching ultimate impasse during negotiations pursuant to a wage reopener in the collective bargaining agreement, declaring the union's right to bargain under the reopener without the right to strike would be an empty one.[430] No employee is entitled to compensation from the public employer for the period engaged in any strike.[431]

18.31 Unauthorized strikes

Effective September 21, 1995, an unauthorized strike[432] is an employee strike occurring prior to the completion of the negotiation process, during the term of a collective bargaining agreement, or a partial or intermittent strike whether it occurs during or after the term of a collective bargaining agreement or the completion of the negotiating process.[433]

---

[426] For treatment of "opt-in" elections, see Text 18.11(B), Factors used in determining unit.

[427] In re University of Cincinnati, SERB 94-001 (2-8-94).

[428] RC 4117.14(D), as amended by 1995 H 200, eff. 9-21-95; In re Vandalia-Butler City School Dist, SERB 86-012 (3-27-86) (involving contractual dispute resolution procedure).

[429] RC 4117.15(A). Just when the term or extended term of a contract ends can be a difficult question. See In re University of Cincinnati, SERB 93-007 (5-13-93) (finding union's notice of intent to strike tantamount to contractually required notice of intent to terminate collective bargaining agreement).

[430] In re Carlisle Local Bd of Ed, SERB 87-025 (11-10-87), citing NLRB v Lion Oil Co, 352 US 282, 77 SCt 330, 1 LEd(2d) 331 (1957).

[431] RC 4117.14(D)(2); OAC 4117-13-01.

[432] Whether a strike is, in fact, taking place is sometimes disputed. SERB has held that proof that some employees were absent for one day does not, standing alone, show that a strike occurred. In re Newton Falls Exempted Village School Dist, SERB 86-032 (9-5-86). (To the extent *Newton Falls* suggests that a single-day sick-out cannot constitute an unauthorized strike, however, it has been overruled by In re City of New Lexington, SERB 94-004 (2-8-94).) On the other hand, where twenty-eight of thirty-three employees failed to report for work, SERB had little trouble finding the "symptom's [sic] of blue-flu—a euphemism for a badly camouflaged job action," and found an illegal strike. In re City of Youngstown, SERB 87-002 (1-30-87). SERB has held that the concerted refusal of bus drivers to accept extracurricular runs in order to protest certain cost-reduction measures was a strike even though under the employees' collective bargaining agreement extracurricular runs could be refused on an individual basis. In re Shelby City Bd of Ed, SERB 93-017 (11-10-93), reversed by 1994 SERB 4-33 (CP, Franklin, 5-17-94). But SERB has also held that employees who refuse to volunteer to work overtime under a collective bargaining agreement that specifies acceptance of overtime is optional are not engaged in a strike. In re Western Reserve Transit Auth, SERB 90-007 (5-23-90). Relying on *Western Reserve Transit Auth*, a reviewing common pleas court reversed SERB in *Shelby*. Employees who do not report for work because their employer refuses to extend a collective bargaining agreement are engaged in a strike. In re Summit County Child Support Enforcement Agency and Summit County Department of Human Services, SERB 91-006 (7-18-91).

[433] RC 4117.01(I), enacted by 1995 H 200, eff. 9-21-95. See also RC 4117.15(A).

This includes strikes in response to an unfair labor practice by the employer.[434] In addition, SERB has held a strike occurring after the collective bargaining agreement expires is illegal if it occurs less than seven days after the fact-finder's report is publicized by SERB[435] or if the ten-day notice does not state the date and time that the strike will commence.[436] Simply incorporating the statute is not a legally sufficient strike notice; the notice must specifically give the employer ten days advance notice with the date and time of the projected job action.[437]

SERB refused to declare illegal a strike that was allegedly an attempt to compel bargaining over permissive subjects of bargaining. The proper method for challenging the strike, said SERB, was through an unfair labor practice charge.[438] SERB has also concluded that instances of misconduct by individual strikers are irrelevant to determining whether a strike is authorized.[439]

An employer may seek an injunction against an illegal strike in the court of common pleas of the county in which the strike is located.[440] In addition, the employer may ask SERB to determine whether a strike is authorized under the Public Employees' Collective Bargaining Act, in which case SERB must make its determination within seventy-two hours.[441] However, SERB has held it will apply RC 4117.23 only to a live, continuing work stoppage. If the strike ends before the seventy-two-hour deadline, the legality of the conduct may be determined through unfair labor practice proceedings.[442] A SERB finding of illegality under RC 4117.23 is a final order that is appealable to the courts under RC 119.12.[443]

If SERB determines that a strike is unauthorized, the employer may remove or suspend the employees involved if they continue to strike one day after they are notified of SERB's decision. Upon request, SERB may authorize the employer to impose penalties retroactive to the date the strike commenced. An employer may rehire illegal strikers on the same basis as was permitted under the Ferguson Act. Employees may only be reinstated with no salary increase at the time of reinstatement or for one year thereafter. If an employer imposes this penalty, the employees may appeal to SERB. SERB may modify, suspend, or reverse the penalty imposed by the employer if it does not find the penalties were appropriate to the situation. The imposition of a penalty is appealable to the courts. If a strike is unauthorized, the employer must deduct from each striking employee's wages the equivalent of two days' pay for each day the employee is on strike one day after receiving notice of SERB's decision. This penalty is not appealable to SERB.[444]

18.32 Temporary injunction against strikes presenting clear and present danger

An employer may seek a seventy-two-hour temporary restraining order from the court of common pleas against a strike

---

[434]RC 4117.15(B).

[435]In re City of Springfield, SERB 85-002 (1-25-85). But see Ohio Council 8, AFSCME v Springfield Bd of Park Trustees, 43 App(3d) 26, 539 NE(2d) 175 (Franklin 1988), in which the court held that if the agreement has expired and the statutory negotiating procedure has been exhausted by one party's rejection of the panel's report, employees can strike (provided the ten-day notice was given) even if seven days have not elapsed from SERB's publication of the report.

[436]In re South Euclid-Lyndhurst City School Dist Bd of Ed, SERB 84-006 (10-9-84). See also OAC 4117-13-01(B).

[437]In re Fort Frye Local School Dist Bd of Ed, SERB 87-021 (11-5-87).

[438]In re Stark County Bd of Mental Retardation & Developmental Disabilities, SERB 85-041 (9-12-85).

[439]In re Beaver Local School Dist Bd of Ed, SERB 90-002 (1-26-90).

[440]RC 4117.15(A).

[441]RC 4117.23(A); OAC 4117-13-02, OAC 4117-13-03.

[442]In re Akron City School Dist Bd of Ed, SERB 89-031 (10-27-89). SERB did say that if it appears the strike might be repeated or harassment may continue, application of RC 4117.23 may be appropriate even if the strike has ended. SERB reaffirmed *Akron* in In re Jefferson County Human Services Dept, SERB 92-015 (9-25-92), and further declared that, where a work stoppage has ceased, an employer must submit "affidavit evidence" of a likely recurrence to avoid dismissal of the case. See also In re City of New Lexington, SERB 94-004 (2-8-94).

[443]Groveport Madison Local Ed Assn, OEA/NEA v SERB, 62 OS(3d) 501, 584 NE(2d) 700 (1992).

[444]RC 4117.23(B); OAC 4117-13-05.

which constitutes "a clear and present danger to the public health or safety."[445] If granted, the employer must immediately request authorization of SERB to enjoin the strike beyond the effective period of the order. Only if SERB "finds that a clear and present danger exists" can the court further enjoin the strike, and then only for "sixty days following the end of the temporary restraining order or when an agreement is reached, whichever occurs first." Thereafter, no court may issue any further injunction.[446] During the period of the injunction, the parties must engage in collective bargaining under the auspices of a SERB-appointed mediator. The mediator may, in his discretion, order public negotiating sessions.[447] If no agreement is reached after forty-five days of bargaining, the mediator may issue a public report on the parties' positions and the efforts made for settlement, which must include a statement by each party of its position and offers of settlement.[448]

The Ohio Supreme Court has concluded RC 4117.16 does not unconstitutionally delegate judicial authority to SERB in violation of the doctrine of separation of powers and that a court has no jurisdiction to go beyond issuance of a seventy-two-hour temporary restraining order if SERB does not find that the strike creates a clear and present danger to the public.[449]

18.33 Public records issues

RC 4117.17 specifically makes charges, petitions, complaints, orders, evidence, fact-finding recommendations, and other SERB proceedings public records available for inspection and copying, and further specifies that SERB hearings are open to the public. The Ohio Supreme Court has rejected the notion that, as to SERB files, RC 4117.17 preempts the broad definition of public records that appears in RC 149.43, holding that the latter statute and its exceptions[450] apply to SERB records not designated in RC 4117.17. Accordingly, investigatory files compiled with respect to unfair labor practice charges must be disclosed upon request unless a court's in camera inspection shows that portions are excepted under RC 149.43 from disclosure, in which case excepted information may be redacted.[451]

18.34 Defamation in connection with labor disputes

In assessing defamation claims based on statements made by and about participants in a labor dispute, the Ohio Supreme Court has adopted the "actual malice" standard and broadly defined "labor dispute" to include any controversy over terms and conditions of employment, or the representation of employees for collective bargaining purposes, whether or not the dispute is subject to SERB jurisdiction.[452]

---

[445]RC 4117.16(A); OAC 4117-13-06, OAC 4117-13-07.

[446]RC 4117.16(A). SERB will find a clear and present danger "where a strike poses a risk of significant harm to the health or safety of the general public or segment of the general public, in contravention of the public interest. What constitutes a risk of significant harm to the public or any particular segment of the public will depend upon the facts and circumstances of each case." In re Napoleon City School Dist Bd of Ed, SERB 93-023 (12-22-93) (finding that protracted intermittent strike by teachers risked serious harm to students and thus posed a clear and present danger). *Napoleon* overrules the more stringent standard previously articulated by SERB in In re City of Gallipolis, SERB 90-016 (9-14-90) and In re Central Ohio Transit Authority, SERB 87-001 (2-19-87).

[447]RC 4117.16(B); OAC 4117-13-07.

[448]RC 4117.16(B); OAC 4117-13-07.

[449]Central Ohio Transit Authority v Transport Workers Union of America, Local 208, 37 OS(3d) 56, 524 NE(2d) 151 (1988).

[450]See Text 44.02, Definition of public records.

[451]Franklin County Sheriff's Dept v SERB, 63 OS(3d) 498, 589 NE(2d) 24 (1992). See also State ex rel Eaton City School Dist Bd of Ed v SERB, 64 OS(3d) 383, 595 NE(2d) 938 (1992).

[452]Dale v Ohio Civil Service Employees Assn, 57 OS(3d) 112, 567 NE(2d) 253 (1991), cert denied 501 US 1231, 111 SCt 2853, 115 LEd(2d) 1021 (1991) (holding leaflet falsely accusing union organizer of lying may have been negligently published but not published with actual malice). The Court expressly adopted the standard of New York Times v Sullivan, 376 US 254, 84 SCt 710, 11 LEd(2d) 686 (1964). See also Linn v United Plant Guard Workers, Local 114, 383 US 53, 86 SCt 657, 15 LEd(2d) 582 (1966).

18.35 Procedural timetables

REPRESENTATION TIME FRAMES

I. Objection Timeline to SERB Certification Where No Exclusive Representative Exists

Initial Recognition Petition Filed

21st DAY _____

Employer and Employee have 21 days of file objections to Recognition Request from Employee Organization.

22nd DAY _____
SERB will Certify Employee Organization UNLESS:

1) SERB receives employer petition for election.

2) SERB receives Substantial Evidence that Majority of employees DON'T want representation.

3) SERB receives Substantial Evidence that 10% of employees want different representative.

4) SERB receives Substantial Evidence that the Bargaining Unit is Inappropriate.

II. Bars to Representation Process

1) Election Bar: Only 1 valid election every 12 months.
2) Certification Bar: Exclusive Representation granted employee organization for at least 12 months following SERB Certification. — 12 MONTHS

3) Contract Bar: Collective Bargaining Agreement valid fo UP TO 3 years.
Includes Exclusive Representation for employee organization for UP TO 3 years — 3 YEARS

III. Election Timeline Where Collective Bargaining Agreement in Effect

120 Days Before Contract Expiration Date	90 Days Before Contract Expiration Date	Contract Expiration Date
	"open window"	"insulated period"	
	election petitions may be filed only during this 30 day period	incumbent union safe from rival union challenges	if new contract not signed rival union may challenge incumbent

DETERMINING AN UNFAIR LABOR PRACTICE

Steps in the Process

ULP Charge Filed with SERB → SERB Investigation → SERB Issues Complaint → SERB Holds Hearing → SERB Issues Decision → Enforcement of SERB Decision

Procedure at Each Step

SERB Investigation
- If SERB finds Probable Cause to believe ULP charge
- No SERB Hearing on ULP charge Occurring more than 90 days earlier (Armed Forces exception)
- If SERB dismisses charge as frivolous complainant can be assessed costs of investigation

SERB Issues Complaint
- SERB can petition Court of Common Pleas for appropriate Injunctive Relief (TRO) if ULP charge alleges Substantial and Irreparable injury if not granted temporary relief
- Charged party is served Notice of Complaint
- Charged party has 10 days from receipt of complaint or amended complaint to file an answer

SERB Holds Hearing
- Representative of the SERB holds hearing on charge within 10 days of service of complaint
- SERB can amend complaint at any time prior to close of Hearing
- At discretion of SERB any interested party may present evidence at Hearing
- Hearing Officer shall reduce evidence to writing, and issue an order for carrying out the decision
- All evidence and the Proposed Decision will be submitted to the SERB

SERB Issues Decision
- Parties have 20 days to file exceptions to proposed decision
- If no exceptions filed, decision becomes the Effective Order of the SERB. If exceptions are filed, SERB decides if Substantial Issues raised by Exceptions. SERB can modify decision or refuse to review decision. Decision is effective if no SERB review
- SERB ordered ULP remedies can include Cease & Desist Order and Affirmative Action to rectify ULP. Affirmative Action can include employee reinstatement and back pay. NOTE: ULP finding shall not be the basis for any charge for removal or recall from office of any public officer. ULP finding shall not be the basis for any disciplinary actions, including suspension or termination, against any public employee

Enforcement of SERB Decision
- SERB retains authority to modify or set aside, in whole or part, any ULP finding or order up to the time the record in the case is filed in a Court for judicial review
- The SERB or the Complaining Party may petition the Court of Common Pleas for enforcement of an ULP order
  △ Complaining Party may intervene
  △ Court takes jurisdiction over the ULP issue determination
  △ Court may enforce or modify, in whole or part, the order of the SERB
  △ Findings of the SERB, if supported by substantial evidence on the record as a whole, are conclusive
  △ Court may allow additional evidence to be submitted to the SERB
  △ SERB can modify original findings and submit modifications to the Court
- Findings of the Court are final subject to Appellate Review
  △ Appeals shall be expeditiously heard by the Court

STATUTORY NEGOTIATIONS/IMPASSE PROCEDURES [1]

90 DAYS	61 DAYS	60 DAYS	50 DAYS	45 DAYS
Where no Collective Bargaining Agreement exists notice to be served on SERB and other party offering to meet	Serve notice upon other party and Board of desire to terminate, modify or negotiate a successor agreement and offer to bargain collectively	Begin Negotiations	Party may request SERB intervention	Submit issues in dispute to any mutually agreed upon dispute settlement procedure or SERB appoints a Mediator

30 DAYS	16 DAYS	10 DAYS	9 DAYS	0 DAYS
SERB appoints fact-finding panel	Findings of fact and recommendations of fact-finding panel transmitted to Employer	Notice of Right to Strike	Rejection of Panel's recommendation (3/5ths vote)/report made public	Right to Strike contract expiration

1. This table excludes safety forces and other employees listed in 4117.14(D)(1), who do not have the right to strike and who must engage in mandatory conciliation.

PUPILS

Chapter 19

Pupils: Desegregation and Nondiscrimination

19.01 Introduction

EVOLUTION OF DESEGREGATION CONCEPTS

19.02 School segregation to desegregation, 1867-1954
19.03 Dismantling school segregation in the South
19.04 Extension of desegregation to urban centers in the North and West
19.05 Urban segregation and suburban school districts
19.06 System-wide school desegregation

DESEGREGATION IN OHIO

19.07 Early demise of "separate but equal" doctrine in Ohio
19.08 Neighborhood schools
19.09 State liability for local segregation
19.10 Other desegregation litigation in Ohio

DESEGREGATION STATUTES

19.11 Federal desegregation statutes
19.12 State desegregation statutes

OTHER NONDISCRIMINATION REQUIREMENTS

19.13 Discrimination by recipients of federal financial assistance
19.14 Sex discrimination in education
19.15 Bilingual education
19.16 Aliens

19.01 Introduction

In 1954, Ohio law governing desegregation and nondiscrimination consisted principally of the implicit constitutional prohibition against racially segregated schools, plus the statutory neighborhood school policy. Since then, constitutional developments have dramatically changed urban education in Ohio. Court decisions have been supplemented by statutes imposing desegregation requirements and providing federal assistance to school districts involved in desegregation activities. Further, as recipients of federal assistance, boards of education are prohibited from discrimination against students on various grounds.

EVOLUTION OF DESEGREGATION CONCEPTS

19.02 School segregation to desegregation, 1867-1954

The principal source of the obligation to maintain desegregated public schools is the equal protection clause of the Fourteenth Amendment.

Although the Fourteenth Amendment was ratified in 1867, for more than eighty years thereafter many states by statute required separation of the races in the public schools, relying on a US Supreme Court decision that allowed racially "separate but equal" public accommodations on railroads.[1]

This doctrine, as applied to de jure segregation of public schools, finally was rejected in 1954 in the landmark case of *Brown v Topeka Bd of Ed*,[2] wherein the Court stated that "separate educational facilities are inherently unequal," and held that segregation deprives minority group children of equal protection, even if physical facilities and other tangible factors are equal. In short, "separate is not equal." In a supplemental opinion,[3] the Court directed that desegregation be effected "with all deliberate speed."

---

[1] Plessy v Ferguson, 163 US 537, 16 SCt 1138, 41 LEd 256 (1896).
[2] Brown v Topeka Bd of Ed, 347 US 483, 74 SCt 686, 98 LEd 873 (1954) (*Brown I*).

[3] Brown v Topeka Bd of Ed, 349 US 294, 75 SCt 753, 99 LEd 1083 (1955) (*Brown II*).

19.03 Dismantling school segregation in the South

Subsequently, the Supreme Court principally was concerned with desegregation plans developed by school districts which, by state law, had operated dual systems for black and white students. Many had replaced the requirement for racial separation with plans permitting parents to choose which schools their children would attend.

(A) Demise of "freedom of choice" plans

In 1968, the Court rejected a freedom of choice plan which (like most such plans) had resulted in little actual desegregation.[4] "Freedom of choice" is unacceptable, the Court held, if speedier and more effective methods of desegregating are reasonably available. Under *Brown II,* districts "operating state-compelled dual systems were ... clearly charged with the affirmative duty to take whatever steps might be necessary to convert to a unitary system in which racial discrimination would be eliminated root and branch."[5] Mere "deliberate speed" was no longer enough; rather, the burden was on the "school board to come forward with a plan that promises realistically to work, and promises realistically to work *now*."[6]

(B) Court-ordered desegregation plans, busing

Three years later, the Court delineated more specific guidelines for eliminating segregation where state-enforced dual school systems had existed.[7] While school boards have primary responsibility for desegregation, when "local authority defaults" and a constitutional violation remains apparent, the remedial powers of the federal courts are very broad. In each case, "the nature of the violation determines the scope of the remedy" and the courts retain jurisdiction until the district has achieved "unitary" status.[8]

Turning to specific components of remedial plans, it is permissible, the Court held, to alter attendance zones and to pair and group noncontiguous zones. Further, while the Constitution requires no particular degree of racial balance, mathematical ratios are a useful starting point for staff and student assignment in a desegregation plan.

Also, for the first time, the Court expressly approved busing students if assignment to the school nearest their homes would not dismantle a dual system.[9]

Federal supervision of a school district, however, is only "intended as a temporary measure to remedy past discrimination," and desegregation injunctions "are not intended to operate in perpetuity."[10] In deciding whether to modify or dissolve an injunction, "a school board's compliance with previous court orders is obviously relevant," and, in assessing whether the vestiges of segregation have been "eliminated as far as practicable," a court should look to all facets of the school system, including such variables as faculty, staff, transportation, extracurricular activities, and facilities.[11]

Recognizing that the word "unitary" does not have a "fixed meaning or content," the Court has held that judicial supervision may be withdrawn with respect to "discrete categories in which the school district has achieved compliance with a court-ordered desegregation plan" and that

---

[4] Green v New Kent County School Bd, 391 US 430, 88 SCt 1689, 20 LEd(2d) 716 (1968).

[5] Green v New Kent County School Bd, 391 US 430, at 437-38, 88 SCt 1689, 20 LEd(2d) 716 (1968).

[6] Green v New Kent County School Bd, 391 US 430, at 439, 88 SCt 1689, 20 LEd(2d) 716 (1968).

[7] Swann v Charlotte-Mecklenburg Bd of Ed, 402 US 1, 91 SCt 1267, 28 LEd(2d) 554 (1971).

[8] Swann v Charlotte-Mecklenburg Bd of Ed, 402 US 1, at 16, 91 SCt 1267, 28 LEd(2d) 554 (1971).

[9] That mandatory busing is no panacea is increasingly clear, and the emphasis now is shifting more to voluntary desegregation plans. For an example where a mandatory plan that included busing ultimately failed because of "white flight" and the court approved a voluntary plan relying heavily on magnet programs that appeared likely to succeed, see Stell v Savannah-Chatham County Bd of Ed, 888 F(2d) 82 (11th Cir Ga 1989).

[10] Oklahoma City Public Schools Bd of Ed v Dowell, 489 US 237, 111 SCt 630, 112 LEd(2d) 715 (1991), affirmed sub nom Dowell by Dowell v Oklahoma City Public Schools Bd of Ed, 8 F(3d) 1501 (10th Cir 1993).

[11] Oklahoma City Public Schools Bd of Ed v Dowell, 489 US 237, 111 SCt 630, 112 LEd(2d) 715 (1991), affirmed sub nom Dowell by Dowell v Oklahoma City Public Schools Bd of Ed, 8 F(3d) 1501 (10th Cir 1993). See also Stell v Savannah-Chatham County Bd of Ed, 860 FSupp 1563 (SD Ga 1994); Tasby v Woolery, 869 FSupp 454 (ND Tex 1994).

active judicial control need not be retained "over every aspect of school administration until a school district has demonstrated unitary status in all facets of its system." In short, gradual judicial withdrawal in incremental stages where a district achieves compliance in some but not all areas is permitted.[12] Moreover, purely demographic changes in a district that are unrelated to a prior violation do not have "constitutional implications" even if resegregation results.[13] An appeals court subsequently emphasized that *Freeman* does not mean demographic changes absolve a school district of its duty to desegregate. Rather, "[w]hat matters is whether current racial identifiability is a vestige of a school system's de jure past, or only a product of demographic changes outside the school district's control."[14] Improved achievement on test scores is not necessarily required for a district to achieve partial unitary status. In 1995, *Missouri v Jenkins (Missouri II)* emphasized that external factors beyond the control of the district which affect minority student achievement are not necessarily relevant to the remedial calculus: "So long as these external factors are not the result of segregation, they do not figure in the remedial calculus."[15]

(C) Funding court-ordered desegregation plans

In *Missouri v Jenkins (Missouri I)*, the Court, by a 5-4 margin in 1990, ruled that the federal courts may constitutionally require a school district to fund the implementation of a desegregation remedy by ordering the district to levy an increase in property taxes without regard to any limitation imposed by state law.[16]

The Court later ruled in *Missouri II* that the federal district court exceeded its remedial authority by requiring the state to fund salary increases for school district employees. Although the order increasing salaries grounded itself in improving the "desegregative attractiveness" of the school district, the district court exceeded its discretion.[17]

19.04 Extension of desegregation to urban centers in the North and West

It was not until 1973 that the Supreme Court first considered a case from a state where segregation had not been maintained by explicit law.[18] The Court emphasized that a finding of intentional segregation is necessary to prove a constitutional violation, and declined to hold that a neighborhood school policy necessarily would violate the Constitution merely because it effectively reflected uneven geographical distribution of races within a district. However, the Court inferred intentional discrimination from various school board decisions, such as locating new schools and structuring attendance zones so as to maintain predominantly white schools. Further, the Court held that intentionally segregative board actions in a meaningful portion of a district create a presumption that other segregated schools in the system also resulted from intentional discrimination.

19.05 Urban segregation and suburban school districts

In *Milliken v Bradley*,[19] the Supreme Court reversed a federal judge's decision to include fifty-three suburban school districts in a plan designed to remedy unlawful segregation in Detroit city schools.

This multi-district remedy was impermissible because there were no findings that school district boundary lines had been

---

[12]Freeman v Pitts, 503 US 467, 112 SCt 1430, 118 LEd(2d) 108 (1992).

[13]Freeman v Pitts, 503 US 467, 112 SCt 1430, 118 LEd(2d) 108 (1992).

[14]Brown v Topeka Bd of Ed, 978 F(2d) 585, 591 (10th Cir Kan 1992), cert denied sub nom Unified School Dist No. 501 v Smith, ___ US ___, 113 SCt 2994, 125 LEd(2d) 688 (1993). If policies traceable to the de jure past remain in force and have a discriminatory effect, those policies must be reformed to the extent practicable. See United States v Fordice, 505 US 717, 112 SCt 2727, 120 LEd(2d) 575 (1992). For an example of a lower court grappling with the principles of *Dowell* and *Freeman*, see Hull v Quitman County Bd of Ed, 1 F(3d) 1450 (5th Cir Miss 1993).

[15]Missouri v Jenkins, ___ US ___, 115 SCt 2038, 2056, 132 LEd(2d) 63 (1995) (*Missouri II*).

[16]Missouri v Jenkins, 495 US 33, 110 SCt 1651, 109 LEd(2d) 31 (1990) (*Missouri I*).

[17]Missouri v Jenkins, ___ US ___, 115 SCt 2038, 132 LEd(2d) 63 (1995).

[18]Keyes v Denver School Dist No. 1, 413 US 189, 93 SCt 2686, 37 LEd(2d) 548 (1973).

[19]Milliken v Bradley, 418 US 717, 94 SCt 3112, 41 LEd(2d) 1069 (1974) (*Milliken I*).

drawn for a segregative purpose, that the suburban districts themselves had violated the Constitution, or that unlawful acts of either the state or suburban districts were a substantial cause of interdistrict segregation.

In short, because the constitutional violation was limited to Detroit, so too the remedy had to be limited. That the state was partially responsible could not justify a multi-district remedy.[20]

On remand, the trial court formulated a single-district remedy which, in addition to pupil reassignment and transportation, included institution of several remedial programs to be supported in part by state funds. The Supreme Court approved this remedy.[21]

In *Missouri II*,[22] the Court rejected the district court's creation of a magnet district in order to attract nonminority students from the surrounding suburban school districts, holding that the multi-district goal was beyond the scope of the intradistrict remedy.

19.06 System-wide school desegregation

The Supreme Court further refined remedial standards in *Dayton Bd of Ed v Brinkman*.[23] The board of education engaged in intentional segregation by the establishment in 1933 of an all-black high school, by maintenance of two optional high school attendance zones, and by rescission of a previous board resolution which had acknowledged the board's role in intentional segregation. In overturning a suggested district-wide remedy, the Court said the lower court

must determine how much incremental segregative effect these violations had on the racial distribution of the Dayton school population as presently constituted, when that distribution is compared to what it would have been in the absence of such constitutional violations. The remedy must be designed to redress that difference, and only if there has been a system-wide impact may there be a system-wide remedy.[24]

Ultimately, the Court revisited the case together with a similar case involving Columbus schools.[25] In both cases, the Court found intentional segregation and ordered system-wide remedies. First, the Court found that local policies and practices had resulted in system-wide intentional segregation in 1954, when *Brown I* was decided. Second, the boards' failure to eliminate the effects of this segregation continued the constitutional violation. Third, the Court found independent evidence of continuing intentional discrimination in connection with staff assignment and optional attendance zones and, in the Columbus case, with discontiguous attendance areas, boundary changes, and site selection. Particularly because of the failure to correct the effects of system-wide segregation which existed in 1954, the Court approved a system-wide remedy.

DESEGREGATION IN OHIO

19.07 Early demise of "separate but equal" doctrine in Ohio

Ohio abolished separate schools for black students by statute in 1887, and the Ohio Supreme Court first held that segre-

---

[20]See also Lauderdale County School Dist v Enterprise Consolidated School Dist, 24 F(3d) 671 (5th Cir Miss 1994), cert denied ___ US ___, 115 SCt 484, 130 LEd(2d) 397 (1994) (court cannot compel the interdistrict transfer of students to achieve desegregation in the absence of a finding of an interdistrict segregative violation).

[21]Milliken v Bradley, 433 US 267, 97 SCt 2749, 53 LEd(2d) 745 (1977) (*Milliken II*).

[22]Missouri v Jenkins, ___ US ___, 115 SCt 2038, 132 LEd(2d) 63 (1995) (district court improperly devised a remedy to accomplish indirectly the interdistrict transfer of students).

[23]Dayton Bd of Ed v Brinkman, 433 US 406, 97 SCt 2766, 53 LEd(2d) 851 (1977) (*Dayton I*).

[24]Dayton Bd of Ed v Brinkman, 433 US 406, at 420, 97 SCt 2766, 53 LEd(2d) 851 (1977) (*Dayton I*).

[25]Dayton Bd of Ed v Brinkman, 443 US 526, 99 SCt 2971, 61 LEd(2d) 720 (1979) (*Dayton II*); Columbus Bd of Ed v Penick, 443 US 449, 99 SCt 2941, 61 LEd(2d) 666 (1979).

gated schools were no longer required or permitted in the following year.[26]

19.08 Neighborhood schools

(A) Neighborhood school concept

For many years, Ohio law has required each board of education to provide for the free education of school-age youth at places most convenient for the attendance of the largest number of pupils, that is, to adhere to a "neighborhood school" policy.[27]

RC 3313.48 does not grant students an absolute right to have a neighborhood school or an absolute right to attend that school. At most, the statute confers an expectation that schools will not be located such that they are convenient only for a minority of a district's students.[28]

Adherence to the statutory neighborhood school policy does not, without more, violate the equal protection clause merely because neighborhood schools result in some racial imbalance within the district.[29]

(B) Use of neighborhood schools to foster segregation

However, under the US Supreme Court's *Dayton II* and *Columbus* decisions,[30] adherence to a neighborhood school policy may not be permissible if and to the extent that policy impairs a board's ability to carry out its affirmative duty to eliminate the continuing effects of intentional segregation in a district which was unlawfully segregated in 1954 or at any time thereafter. Further, under *Dayton II* and *Columbus,* courts must continue to scrutinize very carefully all discretionary actions taken by boards of education in avowed reliance on a neighborhood school policy, at least when the actions have a reasonably foreseeable segregative effect.

In *Reed v Rhodes,*[31] the court held that the Cleveland board had implemented its neighborhood school policy in an unconstitutional, intentionally segregative manner, based on the following findings:

(1) Existence of many predominantly black schools;

(2) Practice, from 1969 to 1973, of assigning most black teachers to predominantly black schools;

(3) Site selection for new schools and expansion of existing schools (principally prior to 1963) in a manner which had a predictable segregative effect, including, as one example, the practice of constructing elementary schools for specific public housing projects at a time when these projects were segregated by design;

(4) Temporarily busing students from overcrowded black schools to predominantly white schools, but keeping the students in separate classes at the receiving schools (1961 to 1966);

(5) Use of optional attendance zones and changes in the boundaries of attendance zones which predictably had a segregative effect; and

(6) Temporary expansion (portable classrooms) of overcrowded black schools when the overcrowding could have been alleviated by revising attendance zones to permit attendance at underutilized white schools within feasible transportation distance.

Applying *Dayton II* and *Columbus*, the court held that "the Cleveland schools in 1964 were segregated by race, and that in the years between 1964 and 1975, the Cleveland board of education had a duty to desegregate that system which it completely failed to perform."[32]

---

[26]Board of Education v State, 45 OS 555, 16 NE 373 (1888).

[27]RC 3313.48.

[28]Central High School Defense Assn v Columbus Bd of Ed, 10 App(3d) 126, 10 OBR 151, 460 NE(2d) 725 (Franklin 1983).

[29]Deal v Cincinnati Bd of Ed, 369 F(2d) 55 (6th Cir Ohio 1966), cert denied 389 US 847, 88 SCt 39, 19 LEd(2d) 114 (1967). See also Deal v Cincinnati Bd of Ed, 419 F(2d) 1387 (6th Cir Ohio 1969), cert denied 402 US 962, 91 SCt 1630, 29 LEd(2d) 128 (1971).

[30]See Text 19.06, System-wide school desegregation.

[31]Reed v Rhodes, 607 F(2d) 714 (6th Cir Ohio 1979), cert denied sub nom Cleveland Bd of Ed v Reed, 445 US 935, 100 SCt 1329, 63 LEd(2d) 770 (1980).

[32]Reed v Rhodes, 607 F(2d) 714, at 735 (6th Cir Ohio 1979), cert denied sub nom Cleveland Bd of Ed v Reed, 445 US 935, 100 SCt 1329, 63 LEd(2d) 770 (1980).

19.09 State liability for local segregation

(A) In general

The question of possible state liability for segregation has been raised in several Ohio cases. In 1956, the attorney general advised that the state board of education has the power to withhold state funds from any board operating an unlawfully segregated school system.[33] In *Penick v Columbus Bd of Ed*,[34] the court held that a general finding of state failure to affirmatively require desegregation was insufficient to establish state liability. It remanded the case for more specific findings concerning the state board's knowledge of the district's segregative practices, its continuing support in light of such knowledge, its failure to withhold funds, its motive in failing to investigate de facto segregation in Columbus, and the incremental segregative effect, if any, of the state board's actions and failure to act.[35] The same approach was adopted in the Cleveland case.[36]

Ultimately, in these cases, the state was held jointly liable for maintaining illegally segregated public schools.[37]

(B) "Guide for School Districts"

Consistent with its obligations to oversee public education, the state board of education approved a "Guide for School Districts on Constitutional Provisions, Assessment Procedures, and Monitoring Activities Pertaining to Racial Isolation." The booklet advises districts to identify schools in which the ethnic composition of the staff or student body substantially varies from the district average and, for this purpose, suggests using "plus or minus fifteen per cent" for students and "plus or minus five per cent" for staff. It further advises districts to assess the causes of any substantial variations and to prepare a plan to eliminate or alleviate racial imbalance. School districts which do not may be requested to appear before the superintendent of public instruction.

19.10 Other desegregation litigation in Ohio

In addition to the Dayton, Columbus, and Cleveland cases discussed above, Cincinnati, Youngstown, and Lorain have been involved in desegregation litigation. Cincinnati's neighborhood school policy was upheld in *Deal v Cincinnati Bd of Ed*.[38] In a related case, a state court, dismissing an action by parents of white students, held that the board of education acted lawfully when it voluntarily revised attendance boundaries to promote racial balance and to use school resources efficiently.[39]

In another case, a federal court refused to enjoin the closing of a predominantly black Cincinnati elementary school for financial reasons when no discriminatory purpose or irreparable harm was shown.[40] That same court examined the racial composition of Cincinnati schools and neighboring suburban schools and found no evidence of either a causal link between anything that happened in a suburban district and the racial distribution in Cincinnati schools or wrongful conduct with an interdistrict segregative effect.[41]

---

[33] 1956 OAG 514.

[34] Penick v Columbus Bd of Ed, 583 F(2d) 787 (6th Cir Ohio 1978), affirmed by 443 US 449, 99 SCt 2941, 61 LEd(2d) 666 (1979) (as to city defendants).

[35] Penick v Columbus Bd of Ed, 583 F(2d) 787, at 818 (6th Cir Ohio 1978), affirmed by 443 US 449, 99 SCt 2941, 61 LEd(2d) 666 (1979) (as to city defendants).

[36] Reed v Rhodes, 607 F(2d) 714, 718 (6th Cir Ohio 1979), cert denied sub nom Cleveland Bd of Ed v Reed, 445 US 935, 100 SCt 1329, 63 LEd(2d) 770 (1980).

[37] Reed v Rhodes, 662 F(2d) 1219 (6th Cir Ohio 1981), cert denied sub nom Ohio State Bd of Ed v Reed, 455 US 1018, 102 SCt 1713, 72 LEd(2d) 135 (1982); Penick v Columbus Bd of Ed, 663 F(2d) 24 (6th Cir Ohio 1981), cert denied 455 US 1018, 102 SCt 1713, 72 LEd(2d) 135 (1982).

[38] Deal v Cincinnati Bd of Ed, 369 F(2d) 55 (6th Cir Ohio 1966), cert denied 389 US 847, 88 SCt 39, 19 LEd(2d) 114 (1967). See also Deal v Cincinnati Bd of Ed, 419 F(2d) 1387 (6th Cir Ohio 1969), cert denied 402 US 962, 91 SCt 1630, 29 LEd(2d) 128 (1971).

[39] Dodd v Rue, 64 Misc 21, 411 NE(2d) 201 (CP, Hamilton 1979).

[40] Bronson v Cincinnati School Dist Bd of Ed, 550 FSupp 941 (SD Ohio 1982).

[41] Bronson v Cincinnati School Dist Bd of Ed, 578 FSupp 1091 (SD Ohio 1984). Settlement of this litigation received court approval in Bronson v Cincinnati School Dist Bd of Ed, 604 FSupp 68 (SD Ohio 1984).

In *Alexander v Youngstown Bd of Ed*,[42] it was found that school officials did not conduct an unlawfully segregated school system.

Even where desegregation litigation is voluntarily settled before an adjudication on the merits, legal hurdles can appear. Thus, for example, in *Lorain NAACP v Lorain Bd of Ed*,[43] a consent decree was entered into under which the state of Ohio was to contribute not more than $1 million over a seven-year term to help defray desegregation costs. When it became apparent that this amount was insufficient, a federal district court increased it only to be overturned by the US Court of Appeals for the Sixth Circuit, which concluded liability under such a decree cannot be enhanced in the absence of an adjudication or admitted violation of law.

DESEGREGATION STATUTES

19.11 Federal desegregation statutes

Constitutional desegregation requirements are supplemented by several federal statutes, principally Title IV of the Civil Rights Act of 1964[44] and the Equal Educational Opportunities Act of 1974.[45]

(A) Civil Rights Act of 1964

Title IV prohibits the segregation of public school students by race, color, sex, or national origin, but it does not require racial balance.[46] It authorizes the secretary of education to provide technical assistance to public schools in connection with preparing and implementing desegregation plans, to hold training institutes for educators involved in desegregation, and to make grants to school boards for in-service training in desegregation. Section 407 of Title IV[47] authorizes the US attorney general, after receiving and investigating a complaint and notifying the school board, to file suit on behalf of parents whose children are being denied equal protection, but this authorization must not be construed to empower the court "to issue any order seeking to achieve a racial balance in any school by requiring the transportation of pupils." The US Supreme Court has held that this provision does not limit the inherent power of a federal court to include transportation of pupils as an element of the remedy for unconstitutional segregation.[48]

(B) Equal Educational Opportunities Act of 1974

Like Title IV, the 1974 Act prohibits segregation of pupils by race, color, sex, or national origin.[49] It does not require racial balance, and specifically approves the nondiscriminatory application of neighborhood school policies.[50] However, the Act also requires school boards to affirmatively act to correct past segregation.[51] Further, it prohibits transfer and assignment of students in a manner that increases segregation, and specifically forbids discrimination in the employment, employment conditions, or assignment of faculty and staff.[52]

The Act provides for court enforcement by both private individuals and the attorney general,[53] and permits intervention by the attorney general in any action filed by a private individual.[54] Further, it attempts to define remedies comprehensively in desegregation cases. In this connection, it provides that school district lines may not be ignored or altered "except where it is established that the lines were drawn for the purpose, and had the effect of segregating children."[55] Further, it suggests priorities among possible remedies,[56] and prohibits transportation of students outside

---

[42]Alexander v Youngstown Bd of Ed, 675 F(2d) 787 (6th Cir Ohio 1982). The court did find that school officials acted unconstitutionally in the "narrowly circumscribed area" of assigning black teachers and administrators to predominantly black schools.

[43]Lorain NAACP v Lorain Bd of Ed, 979 F(2d) 1141 (6th Cir Ohio 1992), cert denied sub nom Lorain Bd of Ed v Ohio Dept of Ed, ___ US ___, 113 SCt 2998, 125 LEd(2d) 691 (1993).

[44]42 USCA 2000a et seq.

[45]20 USCA 1701 et seq.

[46]42 USCA 2000c(b).

[47]42 USCA 2000c-6.

[48]Swann v Charlotte-Mecklenberg Bd of Ed, 402 US 1, 91 SCt 1267, 28 LEd(2d) 554 (1971).

[49]20 USCA 1703.

[50]20 USCA 1704, 20 USCA 1705.

[51]20 USCA 1703(b).

[52]20 USCA 1703(c) to (e).

[53]20 USCA 1706.

[54]20 USCA 1709.

[55]20 USCA 1715.

[56]20 USCA 1713.

their neighborhoods to remedy a statutory violation.[57]

The Act does recognize the permissibility of busing when necessary to remedy constitutional violations,[58] but only as a last resort[59] and provides that transportation remedies must be implemented so as to coincide with the beginning of an academic school year.[60]

The Act also states that a school board found to have violated the law must have a reasonable time for developing voluntary school desegregation plans.[61]

Finally, the Act expressly does not prohibit a board from voluntarily agreeing to a remedy beyond remedies the Act prescribes.[62]

19.12 State desegregation statutes

In 1982, the US Supreme Court twice considered the constitutionality of state laws which limited the scope of desegregation remedies. In *Crawford v Los Angeles Bd of Ed*,[63] the Court upheld a California constitutional amendment which limited state court-ordered busing to instances in which a federal court would order busing to remedy a constitutional violation.

However, in *Washington v Seattle School Dist No. 1*,[64] the Court struck down a Washington statute that prohibited school boards from requiring a student to attend a school other than the school nearest or next nearest to his residence but then made exceptions for virtually all educational purposes except desegregation. The statute had the effect of invalidating certain voluntary desegregation plans.

OTHER NONDISCRIMINATION REQUIREMENTS

19.13 Discrimination by recipients of federal financial assistance

Several federal statutes prohibit discrimination by recipients of federal financial assistance.[65] The first, and the model for all subsequent statutes of this kind, is Title VI of the Civil Rights Act of 1964.[66]

(A) Title VI, Civil Rights Act of 1964

Section 601 of Title VI[67] provides that "[n]o person ... shall, on the ground of race, color, or national origin, be excluded from participation in, be denied the benefits of, or be subjected to discrimination under any program or activity receiving Federal financial assistance." Section 602 of Title VI[68] provides for enforcement by each agency administering a federal funding program. Pursuant to section 602, federal regulations prohibit specific discriminatory actions by schools receiving federal funds, require assurances by schools seeking federal funds, and provide formal procedures for investigating complaints. The regulations also compel compliance with nondiscrimination requirements as a condition of continued funding and termination of funding programs when compliance is not obtained.[69]

Practices prohibited by Title VI include racial segregation, denial of equal opportunity to non-English-speaking students, and any disparate treatment of persons intended to benefit from funded programs on the basis of race, color, or national origin.[70]

A claim under Title VI by black students in New York City that the school curriculum was biased in favor of European cul-

---

[57]20 USCA 1714.
[58]20 USCA 1718.
[59]20 USCA 1755.
[60]20 USCA 1757.
[61]20 USCA 1758.
[62]20 USCA 1716.
[63]Crawford v Los Angeles Bd of Ed, 458 US 527, 102 SCt 3211, 73 LEd(2d) 948 (1982).
[64]Washington v Seattle School Dist No. 1, 458 US 457, 102 SCt 3187, 73 LEd(2d) 896 (1982).
[65]Receipt of federal funds by any part of an educational institution subjects all operations of the institution, not just the specific program receiving funds, to the antidiscrimination provisions of these statutes. This result was effected by the Civil Rights Restoration Act of 1987, Pub L No. 100-259, 100th Cong, 2d Sess (1988).
[66]42 USCA 2000d et seq.
[67]42 USCA 2000d.
[68]42 USCA 2000d-1.
[69]34 CFR Part 100. A list of federal financial assistance programs to which these regulations apply is given in Appendix A to 34 CFR Part 100.
[70]34 CFR 100.3.

ture was dismissed as to the US Department of Education and Secretary of Education since there was no showing that these defendants exercised control over the local curriculum.[71]

(B) Sex discrimination under Title IX, Education Amendments of 1972

Prohibition of discrimination in connection with federally funded education programs was extended to sex discrimination by Title IX of the Education Amendments of 1972.[72] Like Title VI, Title IX concerns participation in, denial of benefits under, and discrimination under federally funded programs. Procedural regulations applicable to Title VI also govern administrative enforcement and investigations of Title IX complaints.[73]

(C) Handicap discrimination under the Rehabilitation Act of 1973

Similar legislation prohibits discrimination against otherwise qualified handicapped persons by recipients of federal financial assistance.[74]

(D) Age discrimination under the Age Discrimination Act of 1975

Likewise, recipients of federal funds are prohibited from discriminating on the basis of age.[75]

(E) Enforcement

Although compliance with these federal statutes depends principally on enforcement by the appropriate administrative agency in administrative proceedings, individuals may, under some circumstances, seek direct court enforcement. In *Cannon v University of Chicago*,[76] the US Supreme Court ruled there is a private right of action under Title IX, at least to enforce its nondiscrimination provisions. Courts have also discerned a private right of action under Title VI [77] and the Rehabilitation Act.[78]

In *Guardians Assn v New York City Civil Service Comm*,[79] the Supreme Court considered whether Title VI prohibits only intentional discrimination or whether it also encompasses disparate impact discrimination. The Court concluded proof of discriminatory intent is not required to prove a violation of Title VI but that, absent such proof, compensatory relief may not be awarded to private plaintiffs, thus leaving declaratory and injunctive relief as the only available remedies. That monetary damages may be sought for intentional discrimination appears to be settled in the affirmative.[80]

19.14 Sex discrimination in education

(A) In general

Nondiscrimination on the basis of sex in education is governed principally by Title IX of the Education Amendments of 1972.[81]

Title IX provides that "[n]o person in the United States shall, on the basis of sex, be excluded from participation in, be denied the benefits of, or be subjected to discrimination under any education program or activity receiving Federal financial

---

[71]Grimes v Cavazos, 786 FSupp 1184 (SD NY 1992). The court went on to dismiss the Title VI claim against state defendants since there was no allegation of intentional discrimination. In Grimes v Sobol, 832 FSupp 704 (SD NY 1993), the court held that administrative regulations under Tile VI simply do not encompass the regulation of curricular content. In Elston v Talladega County Bd of Ed, 997 F(2d) 1394 (11th Cir Ala 1993), a broadside Title VI challenge to the restructuring of a southern school district was rejected.

[72]20 USCA 1681 et seq. See Text 19.14, Sex discrimination in education.

[73]34 CFR 106.71.

[74]29 USCA 794, 794a. See also Text 17.13, Discrimination against the handicapped; Text Ch 28, Education for Children with Disabilities.

[75]42 USCA 6101 et seq.

[76]Cannon v University of Chicago, 441 US 677, 99 SCt 1946, 60 LEd(2d) 560 (1979).

[77]E.g., Neighborhood Action Coalition v Canton, Ohio, 882 F(2d) 1012 (6th Cir Ohio 1989). There is, however, no private right of action against the funding agency. Grimes v Cavazos, 786 FSupp 1184 (SD NY 1992).

[78]Consolidated Rail Corp v Darrone, 465 US 624, 104 SCt 1248, 79 LEd(2d) 568 (1984). See also Pendleton v Jefferson Local School Dist Bd of Ed, 754 FSupp 570 (SD Ohio 1990), affirmed in part, reversed in part by 958 F(2d) 372 (6th Cir Ohio 1992).

[79]Guardians Assn v New York City Civil Service Comm, 463 US 582, 103 SCt 3221, 77 LEd(2d) 866 (1983).

[80]See Franklin v Gwinnett County Public Schools, 503 US 60, 112 SCt 1028, 117 LEd(2d) 208 (1992).

[81]20 USCA 1681 et seq.

assistance."[82] Title IX does not, however, require a school to grant preferential treatment to members of one sex merely because an imbalance exists with respect to the number of persons of that sex participating in or receiving the benefit of any federally supported program or activity,[83] although evidence of such an imbalance is relevant in assessing whether a violation exists.[84]

Administrative regulations implementing Title IX prohibit schools receiving federal financial assistance from discriminating on the basis of sex in connection with both academic and extracurricular activities.[85] The following requirements are most applicable to public schools:

(1) Prohibition of sex-segregated classes, except for sex education classes, and except for permissible separation of males and females during physical education classes devoted to bodily contact sports;[86]

(2) Prohibition of sex discrimination in connection with counseling and in the use of appraisal and counseling materials;[87]

(3) Restrictions on a school's right to differentiate among students because of marital or parental status, including pregnancy;[88]

(4) Prohibition of sex discrimination in employment;[89] and

(5) Prohibition of sex discrimination in connection with interscholastic and intramural athletics.[90]

The sexual harassment of students by school district employees is actionable under Title IX,[91] and a district that takes no appropriate action to curb the sexual harassment of students by other students (often called "peer harassment") may incur Title IX liability.[92] While the educational entity may be liable, courts have held there is no individual liability.[93]

(B) Scope of extracurricular activities and athletics

Extracurricular programs are also subject to Title IX. Administrative regulations prohibit discrimination in connection with interscholastic and intramural athletics.[94] Separate teams for members of each sex may be maintained for competitive sports and bodily contact sports, but, if only one team is maintained in a particular sport, the funding recipient must allow members of the opposite sex to try out for the team, unless it is a contact sport.[95]

---

[82] 20 USCA 1681(a). The statute applies only to students involved in programs or activities receiving federal financial assistance, not employees of schools or parents of students. Romeo Community Schools v US Dept of Health, Ed, and Welfare, 600 F(2d) 581 (6th Cir Mich 1979), cert denied 444 US 972, 100 SCt 467, 62 LEd(2d) 388 (1979) (employees); R.L.R. v Prague Public School Dist I-103, 838 FSupp 1526 (WD Okla 1993) (parents).

[83] 20 USCA 1681(b).

[84] See Cohen v Brown University, 991 F(2d) 888 (1st Cir RI 1993) (enjoining university's demotion of women's gymnastics and volleyball from full varsity status to intercollegiate status). See also Kelley v University of Illinois Bd of Trustees, 35 F(3d) 265 (7th Cir 1994), cert denied 115 SCt 938, 130 LEd(2d) 883 (1995) (university's elimination for financial reasons of men's swimming team while retaining women's swimming team in order to increase disproportionately small number of women students participating in varsity athletics did not violate Title IX).

[85] 34 CFR 106.31 to 34 CFR 106.42.

[86] 34 CFR 106.34.

[87] 34 CFR 106.36.

[88] 34 CFR 106.40.

[89] 34 CFR 106.51 to 34 CFR 106.61.

[90] 34 CFR 106.41.

[91] Franklin v Gwinnett County Public Schools, 503 US 60, 112 SCt 1028, 117 LEd(2d) 208 (1992). See also Patricia H. v Berkeley Unified School Dist, 830 FSupp 1288 (ND Cal 1993).

[92] Doe v Petaluma City School Dist, 830 FSupp 1560 (ND Cal 1993), reversed on other grounds by 54 F(3d) 1447 (9th Cir Cal 1995). But see Aurelia v Monroe County Bd of Ed, 862 FSupp 363 (MD Ga 1994) (holding "no basis" for claim under Title IX for school's inaction regarding complaints of peer harassment); Seamons v Snow, 864 FSupp 1111 (D Utah 1994) (student and parents failed to state Title IX discrimination claim against school district).

[93] Doe v Petaluma City School Dist, 54 F(3d) 1447 (9th Cir Cal 1995). Prior to 1992, when the alleged sexual harassment occurred, the school counselor had no clear duty under Title IX to intervene. However, the court noted the counselor may not be entitled to the same immunity today. See also Lipsett v University of Puerto Rico, 864 F(2d) 881 (1st Cir PR 1988); Aurelia v Monroe County Bd of Ed, 862 FSupp 363 (MD Ga 1994) (dismissing claim against individual defendants on basis of qualified immunity).

[94] 34 CFR 106.41(a).

[95] 34 CFR 106.41(b). See also Kleczek v Rhode Island Interscholastic League, Inc, 768 FSupp 951 (D RI 1991) (field hockey a contact sport); Williams v

In determining whether equal opportunities in athletics are available, regulations provide for consideration of whether the selection of sport and levels of competition accommodate the interests and abilities of members of both sexes, the provision of equipment and supplies, scheduling of games and practice time, opportunities for coaching, assignment of coaches, physical facilities, and publicity. Unequal aggregate expenditures for members of each sex or unequal expenditures for male and female teams are also considered, but such inequalities do not necessarily constitute noncompliance with the regulations.[96]

In a decision interpreting Title IX sports regulations, the US Court of Appeals for the Sixth Circuit held that Ohio High School Athletic Association (OHSAA) Rule I, section 6, which prohibited girls from participating on a boys' team in any contact sport at all levels under its jurisdiction, conflicted with the Title IX regulation, which allows exclusion of girls from boys' teams only if there is another mechanism for achieving equal athletic opportunity.[97]

(C) Proof of discrimination under Title IX, damages

Whether discriminatory purpose must be shown to establish a Title IX violation is unclear. A federal appeals court has held that proof of disparate impact is not sufficient; rather, proof of discriminatory intent is necessary.[98]

That monetary damages are available for intentional violations of Title IX is clear.[99]

(D) Sex discrimination and the Fourteenth Amendment

In addition to Title IX, the equal protection clause has some impact on a school system's obligation not to discriminate on the basis of sex. However, under equal protection analysis, sex-based distinctions are impermissible only if they are not substantially related to the achievement of an important governmental objective. In *Cape v Tennessee Secondary School Athletic Assn*,[100] the court held that the defendant's rules for sex-segregated girls' basketball teams did not violate the equal protection clause. However, the US Supreme Court has ruled that a state university's policy of admitting only women to its nursing school was unconstitutional.[101]

The equal protection clause forbids intentional discrimination. For example, female student athletes in Kentucky alleged sex discrimination with respect to a Kentucky High School Athletic Association's rule that a new sport will not be recognized unless 25% of member schools indicate willingness to participate. Although the rule had a disparate impact on females, failure to show discriminatory intent precluded students' claim on equal protection grounds.[102]

19.15 Bilingual education

The rights of students whose education is impeded by language barriers were considered by the US Supreme Court in *Lau v*

Bethlehem, Pa School Dist, 998 F(2d) 168 (3d Cir Pa 1993), cert denied ___ US ___, 114 SCt 689, 126 LEd(2d) 656 (1994) (concluding that field hockey may be a contact sport and remanding case for determination on that issue).

[96] 34 CFR 106.41(c).

[97] Yellow Springs Exempted Village School Dist Bd of Ed v OHSAA, 647 F(2d) 651 (6th Cir Ohio 1981). The regulation in question now appears at 34 CFR 106.41.

[98] Cannon v University of Chicago, 648 F(2d) 1104 (7th Cir Ill 1981), cert denied 454 US 1128, 102 SCt 981, 71 LEd(2d) 117 (1981), cert denied 460 US 1013, 103 SCt 1254, 75 LEd(2d) 482 (1983). See also Pfeiffer v Marion Center Area School Dist, 917 F(2d) 779 (3d Cir Pa 1990); Fulani v League of Women Voters Ed Fund, 684 FSupp 1185 (SD NY 1988), affirmed by 882 F(2d) 621 (2d Cir NY 1989); Nagel v Avon Bd of Ed, 575 FSupp 105 (D Conn 1983). Some courts, however, have not required proof of discriminatory intent. See Sharif v New York State Ed Dept, 709 FSupp 345 (SD NY 1989); Haffer v Temple University, 678 FSupp 517 (ED Pa 1987).

[99] Franklin v Gwinnett County Public Schools, 503 US 60, 112 SCt 1028, 117 LEd(2d) 208 (1992). That the violation must be intentional is confirmed by Doe v Petaluma City School Dist, 830 FSupp 1560 (ND Cal 1993), reversed on other grounds by 54 F(3d) 1447 (9th Cir Cal 1995).

[100] Cape v Tennessee Secondary School Athletic Assn, 563 F(2d) 793 (6th Cir Tenn 1977).

[101] Mississippi University for Women v Hogan, 458 US 718, 102 SCt 3331, 73 LEd(2d) 1090 (1982).

[102] Horner v Kentucky High School Athletic Assn, 43 F(3d) 265 (6th Cir Ky 1995). Although the court rejected the students' equal protection claim, the Title

Nichols.[103] The Court held that the San Francisco school district's failure to provide English language instruction, where other instructional procedures for non-English-speaking Chinese students were inadequate, discriminated against them in violation of Title VI of the Civil Rights Act of 1964.[104] The Court held that the district was obligated to comply with federal guidelines, including in particular a guideline providing, "Where inability to speak and understand the English language excludes national origin-minority group children from effective participation in the educational program offered by a school district, the district must take affirmative steps to rectify the language deficiency in order to open its instructional program to the students."[105]

Shortly after *Lau*, Congress enacted section 204(f) of the Equal Educational Opportunity Act of 1974[106] and the Bilingual Education Act of 1974 (BEA).[107] Section 204(f) states that no person shall be denied equal educational opportunity because of race or national origin by "the failure of an educational agency to take appropriate action to overcome language barriers that impede equal participation by its students in its instructional programs."[108] The BEA provides federal funding to state and local school agencies for bilingual educational programs. These funding programs are administered by the department of education pursuant to regulations published in 34 CFR Part 500.

At least two courts of appeals have held that the phrase "appropriate action" as used in 20 USCA 1703(f) does not go beyond the essential requirement of *Lau* and does not require local educational authorities to adopt any particular type of remedial language program.[109] The phrase leaves state and local educational authorities a substantial amount of latitude in choosing the programs and techniques they would use to meet their obligations. On the other hand, a program that fails adequately to identify and place students with limited proficiency in English would violate the law.[110] The department of education has attempted to enforce the BEA against school districts deemed not in compliance by seeking refunds of bilingual education grants. At least one court has held that no such action may be taken without first conducting a proper civil audit of the school's programs.[111]

Other courts have held that there is no constitutional right to a bilingual education.[112] However, absent bilingual education, the statutes require that the student's language difficulties be addressed through remedial assistance.[113]

19.16 Aliens

In *Plyler v Doe*,[114] the US Supreme Court held that a Texas statute which required withholding state funds from local school districts for the education of children who were not "legally admitted" into the United States, and which authorized denying enrollment to such children, violated the equal protection clause of the Fourteenth Amendment.

IX claim was remanded to determine whether sanctioning fewer sports for girls than for boys resulted in discrimination.

[103]Lau v Nichols, 414 US 563, 94 SCt 786, 39 LEd(2d) 1 (1974), quoting Identification of Discrimination and Denial of Services on the Basis of National Origin, 35 Fed Reg 11,595 (Dept of Health, Education and Welfare (1970)).

[104]42 USCA 2000(b).

[105]Lau v Nichols, 414 US 563, 94 SCt 786, 39 LEd(2d) 1 (1974).

[106]20 USCA 1703(f).

[107]20 USCA 3221 et seq.

[108]20 USCA 1703(f).

[109]Gomez v Illinois State Bd of Ed, 811 F(2d) 1030 (7th Cir Ill 1987); Castaneda v Pickard, 781 F(2d) 456 (5th Cir Tex 1986). See also Teresa P. v Berkeley Unified School Dist, 724 FSupp 698 (ND Cal 1989).

[110]Gomez v Illinois State Bd of Ed, 811 F(2d) 1030 (7th Cir Ill 1987).

[111]Tangipahoa Parish School Bd v United States Dept of Ed, 821 F(2d) 1022 (5th Cir La 1987).

[112]Guadalupe Organization, Inc v Tempe Elementary School Dist No. 3, 587 F(2d) 1022 (9th Cir Ariz 1978); Heavy Runner v Bremner, 522 FSupp 162 (D Mont 1981).

[113]Idaho Migrant Council v Board of Education, 647 F(2d) 69 (9th Cir Idaho 1981).

[114]Plyler v Doe, 457 US 202, 102 SCt 2382, 72 LEd(2d) 786 (1982).

Chapter 20

Pupils: Compulsory Education and School Attendance

COMPULSORY SCHOOL ATTENDANCE LAW
20.01 Compulsory school age and free education
20.02 Compulsory school attendance
20.03 Excuse from compulsory attendance
20.04 Attendance of married and pregnant pupils

SCHOOL DAY AND YEAR
20.05 Regular school day and year
20.06 Holidays and commemorative days

TRUANCY
20.07 Duty to enforce school attendance
20.08 Attendance officers
20.09 Enforcement procedures
20.10 Attendance and withdrawal reports

AGE AND SCHOOLING CERTIFICATES AND EMPLOYMENT OF SCHOOL-AGE CHILDREN
20.11 Schooling and the child labor laws
20.12 Hours and terms of employment of minors
20.13 Age and schooling certificates
20.14 Special age and schooling certificates
20.15 Part-time day school for certificate holders
20.16 Employer responsibility respecting minors
20.17 Enforcement, penalties

COMPULSORY SCHOOL ATTENDANCE LAW

20.01 Compulsory school age and free education

(A) In general

A child between six and eighteen who is a resident of Ohio is of compulsory school age and must attend school, but may be excused by one of the statutory exemptions. In addition, a child who graduates from the twelfth grade prior to reaching eighteen is not required to attend school.[1]

Free public education complements compulsory school attendance.[2] Although attendance is required only between six and eighteen, public schools are free to residents at least five but under twenty-two and to handicapped preschool children (defined as children at least three but not of compulsory school age who have not entered kindergarten).[3] Furthermore, a board of education may make special education available to handicapped children under three years of age.[4]

(B) Age of entrance into school

A child must be five or six years old by September 30 to be admitted to kindergarten or first grade, respectively, where the school district admits pupils in August or September. If the district admits pupils at another time of year, kindergarten and first grade students must have reached age five or six on or before the first day of that term or semester.[5]

A child who will reach age five or six after September 30 but before January 1 may be admitted to kindergarten or first grade by passing a standardized test. A board of education must either establish an educationally accepted standardized testing program for determining eligibility or designate the necessary standards and testing program it will accept for the purpose of determining eligibility. The district must provide such testing on request of the parent or guardian.[6]

RC 3321.01 makes kindergarten attendance generally mandatory.[7]

20.02 Compulsory school attendance

(A) In general

Ohio's compulsory education law[8] requires the education of all children because education is fundamental to advancement of a civilized society.[9] The law is directed toward both children and the persons legally responsible for them. Parents have a duty both to their children and to the state to educate their children. Ohio may constitutionally compel school

---

[1] RC 3321.01, RC 3321.04. For discussion of the exemptions, see Text 20.03, Excuse from compulsory attendance.
[2] RC 3313.48.
[3] RC 3313.64.
[4] RC 3323.01(A), RC 3323.06 to RC 3323.091.
[5] RC 3321.01.
[6] RC 3321.01.
[7] For extended treatment, see Text 26.05(A), Kindergarten.
[8] RC Ch 3321.
[9] State v Gans, 168 OS 174, 151 NE(2d) 709 (1958), cert denied 359 US 945, 79 SCt 722, 3 LEd(2d) 678 (1959).

attendance since "the natural rights of a parent to the custody and control of his infant child are subordinate to the power of the state and may be regulated and restricted by municipal laws."[10]

Parents may fulfill their duty by enrolling their children in a public school, special education program, or private or parochial school which conforms to state minimum standards.[11] They are required to see that the child attends for the full time the school is in session.[12] Children whose residence in the state is seasonal, who have attended school in another state for the legal period required by the state, or whose parents reside in another state, must nevertheless comply with Ohio's compulsory education law.[13]

At the time of initial entry, RC 3313.672 requires that a pupil present to the school's admissions officer any records given to him by the public or nonpublic elementary or secondary school most recently attended; a certified copy of any order or decree (or modification of such an order or decree) allocating parental rights and responsibilities for the care of a child and designating a residential parent and legal custodian of the child; and a birth certificate (or such other document as the statute permits in lieu of a birth certificate). Within twenty-four hours of entry, a school official must request the pupil's official records from the public or nonpublic elementary or secondary school most recently attended.

A child of compulsory school age who receives a high school diploma, successfully completes the curriculum of any high school, successfully completes the individualized education program developed for the student under RC 3323.08, or receives an age and schooling certificate, need not attend school further. An age and schooling certificate shows that the child is at least sixteen years old, has completed an educational program adequate to prepare him for a vocation, and is regularly employed.[14]

(B) Attendance at private or parochial school or special high school

Children may attend private and parochial schools that conform to state minimum standards.[15] The hours and terms of attendance must be equivalent to the attendance required in the public schools of the district. Children may attend vocational, commercial, or other special types of schools rather than high school, provided the instruction is for a term and hours equivalent to those of a high school and provided the school offers a continuous program of education to students until they reach age sixteen.[16]

(C) Attendance by handicapped children at special programs

Physically and mentally handicapped children are subject to the compulsory education law. The board of each school district is required to place each handicapped child of compulsory school age residing within the district in an appropriate educational program.[17]

20.03 Excuse from compulsory attendance

(A) Constitutionally compelled excuses

While the state's power to compel school attendance outweighs the parents' natural right to custody and control of their child, that power "is not totally free from a balancing process when it impinges on fundamental rights and interests."[18] Accordingly, where members of the Old Order Amish proved that education beyond the eighth grade threatened their religious beliefs, the US Supreme Court held the state could not compel attendance in public school.[19]

The Ohio Supreme Court, engaging in similar balancing, found the state minimum standards for parochial schools unreasona-

---

[10] Parr v State, 117 OS 23, 157 NE 555 (1927).
[11] RC 3321.03, RC 3321.04, RC 3321.07.
[12] RC 3321.04.
[13] RC 3321.02.
[14] RC 3321.03, RC 3331.01 et seq. See Text 20.13 to 20.17. For treatment of individualized education programs under RC 3323.08, see Text Ch 28, Education for Children with Disabilities.

[15] RC 3321.04, RC 3321.07.
[16] RC 3321.07.
[17] RC 3321.04, RC 3323.04. See generally Text Ch 28, Education for Children with Disabilities.
[18] Wisconsin v Yoder, 406 US 205, 92 SCt 1526, 32 LEd(2d) 15 (1972).
[19] Wisconsin v Yoder, 406 US 205, 92 SCt 1526, 32 LEd(2d) 15 (1972).

bly comprehensive and burdensome.[20] The standards have since been amended.[21]

(B) Statutory reasons for excuse

In addition to excuses based upon attendance in an approved private or parochial school or age and schooling certificates, a child of compulsory school age may be excused from attending school under standards adopted by the state board of education.[22] These standards are authorized by RC 3321.04, which permits the superintendent to excuse a student for any of the following reasons:

(1) The student's physical or mental condition, as certified by a physician or psychologist, does not permit attendance and provision is made for appropriate instruction;

(2) The student is being taught at home by a person qualified to teach the branches in which instruction is required and which the advancement of the child may require in the superintendent's opinion;

(3) The child is over fourteen and temporarily needed to work directly and exclusively for his parents; or

(4) The student is expelled or suspended under board of education rules on discipline.[23]

(C) Home-based instruction

Where a parent files a request for excuse on account of home-based instruction, the decision is made by the superintendent of the city, exempted village, or county school district in which the child resides.[24] The superintendent must evaluate the curriculum taught and the qualifications of the person teaching the child. The superintendent must also "file in his office, with a copy of the excuse, papers showing how the inability of the child to attend school or a special education program ... [was] determined."[25] It appears, however, that the child need be under no greater inability than his parents' desire to avoid his attendance at school.[26]

The superintendent's decision has been held an "adjudication" within the meaning of RC 2506.01,[27] and a party seeking permission for home instruction must be afforded a due process hearing at which a transcript is taken.[28] Where the superintendent refuses to excuse a child, an appeal may be taken to the county juvenile judge.[29]

The in-home study excuse does not allow a child of compulsory school age to withdraw from school unilaterally and receive home instruction by correspondence course.[30] A request to be excused must be filed with the superintendent who must determine that the home instruction is provided by a person qualified to teach. A parent who fails to obtain the superintendent's approval cannot defend against a prosecution for noncompliance with the compulsory attendance law by showing his child is being taught at home in substantial compliance with state minimum standards.[31] This is true even where the parents' objections to institutional education are constitutionally grounded, since the legislature requires a parent to apply first to the superintendent for the purpose of determining the in-home instructor's quali-

---

[20]State v Whisner, 47 OS(2d) 181, 351 NE(2d) 750 (1976). See Text 20.09(B), Liability of parent; Text 32.02, Free exercise of religion and compulsory state educational standards.

[21]See OAC 3301-35-08.

[22]RC 3321.03.

[23]RC 3321.04.

[24]There is no constitutional right of parents to educate their children at home free from reasonable governmental regulation. Clonlara, Inc v Runkel, 722 FSupp 1442 (ED Mich 1989).

[25]RC 3321.04. Regulations governing the issuance of excuses, and the application process, appear in OAC 3301-34-01 et seq. OAC 3301-34-03(A) specifies the information a parent must supply to the superintendent in connection with the application.

[26]See, e.g., In re Snyder, No. 86-CA-14, 1986 WL 13825 (5th Dist Ct App, Knox, 11-20-86); Fresh v Searcy, No. 1172, 1985 WL 7842 (11th Dist Ct App, Ashtabula, 4-5-85) ("Once it is established that the curriculum contemplates reasonable education standards, and the instructor is competent to teach those subjects, home instruction is permitted."). See also OAC 3301-34-03.

[27]Fresh v Searcy, No. 1172, 1985 WL 7842 (11th Dist Ct App, Ashtabula, 4-5-85).

[28]OAC 3301-34-03.

[29]RC 3331.08.

[30]State v Oja, No. 82-11 684 SLV (Juv, Delaware, 1-7-83).

[31]Akron v Lane, 65 App(2d) 90, 416 NE(2d) 642 (Summit 1979).

fications and ensuring the continued adequate education of the child.[32]

20.04 Attendance of married and pregnant pupils

Ohio law permits marriage without parental consent of males eighteen and over and females sixteen and over. Minors who have not attained those ages may marry only with parental consent.[33] A minor who attempts to marry without the necessary consent may be adjudicated an unruly child and thus subject to the disposition of a juvenile court.[34] Married students of compulsory school age are subject to the compulsory attendance law.[35] A married student may not be excluded from any extracurricular activities solely because he is married. A married student has a constitutional right to marital privacy which the state may not invade, even for the purpose of discouraging other student marriages.[36]

It would appear that pregnant students may not automatically be excluded from classes and extracurricular activities since a blanket exclusion in disregard of the individual student's physical ability denies the constitutional guarantee of equal protection.[37] However, a board of education may, for the physical safety and well-being of the student, require that a student at an advanced stage of pregnancy not attend regular classes.[38] In such a case, the board may provide an alternative means of instruction and may assign a teacher to the home instruction of the student.[39]

SCHOOL DAY AND YEAR

20.05 Regular school day and year

(A) In general

Each school day for grades one through twelve must consist of not less than five hours with pupils in attendance. The school day for grades one to six may include fifteen-minute morning and afternoon recess periods. The school day may be shortened in an emergency, including lack of classroom space, if approved by the state board of education.[40]

A part-time school or class, if provided for children who are employed on age and schooling certificates, must be conducted not fewer than four hours but not more than eight hours per school week, and not fewer than 144 hours per calendar year.[41]

The school year must consist of at least 182 days, which may include certain days for parent-teacher conferences and professional meetings.[42] The school year begins on July 1 and ends on June 30.[43] The date on which the school term begins and ends is left to the discretion of each board of education.

The requirements of the state foundation program with regard to the minimum number of school days or hours will be waived by the superintendent of public instruction "for the school year in which a board of education initiates a [new calen-

---

[32]State v Schmidt, 29 OS(3d) 32, 29 OBR 383, 505 NE(2d) 627 (1987), cert denied 484 US 942, 108 SCt 327, 98 LEd(2d) 354 (1987). The Court observed that the judiciary has neither the time nor the resources to determine the adequacy of home study and to continually monitor it. Further, since the parents had foregone a request to the superintendent for home study, they could not maintain the superintendent would have, by some unconstitutional act, denied their application. Relying on *Schmidt*, a common pleas court has rejected an argument that RC 3321.04 is void for vagueness. Pendergrass v Columbus Public Schools, No. 88JU-03-1591 (CP, Franklin, 8-26-88).
[33]RC 3101.01.
[34]RC 2151.022(D), RC 2151.354.
[35]OAG 77-001.

[36]Davis v Meek, 344 FSupp 298 (ND Ohio 1972).
[37]Ordway v Hargraves, 323 FSupp 1155 (D Mass 1971). See also Cleveland Bd of Ed v LaFleur, 414 US 632, 94 SCt 791, 39 LEd(2d) 52 (1974); 1961 OAG 2147; OAG 68-061.
[38]OAG 68-061; 1961 OAG 2147. See also Cleveland Bd of Ed v LaFleur, 414 US 632, 94 SCt 791, 39 LEd(2d) 52 (1974).
[39]OAG 68-061; 1961 OAG 2147; RC 3319.08.
[40]RC 3313.48.
[41]RC 3313.56, RC 3321.08.
[42]RC 3313.48. See also Text 39.07(A), Minimum school year. Days for parent-teacher conferences and professional meetings are more fully treated in Text 20.05(B), Division of school year.
[43]RC 3313.62.

dar] plan of operation pursuant to section 3313.481 of the Revised Code."[44]

(B) Division of school year

RC 3313.481 provides that, with the approval of the department of education, a board of education may operate any of its schools on a schedule other than that required by RC 3313.48, specifically on a quarter, trimester, or pentamester calendar basis, or to provide a flexible school day for parent-teacher conferences and reporting periods, or to provide staggered attendance schedules.[45] A district operating a school under RC 3313.481 must have the school open for instruction at least 910 hours per school year.[46] These hours may include (1) morning and afternoon recess periods of not more than fifteen minutes per period in grades one through six; (2) ten hours for individualized parent-teacher conferences and reporting periods; (3) ten hours for teachers' attendance at professional meetings; and (4) the hours when school is closed because of a public calamity as provided in RC 3317.01.[47] In determining whether a school on a staggered attendance schedule is in compliance with RC 3313.481, the department of education may include not more than the first seventy school days of the ensuing school year, provided these days are not considered school days during such ensuing year.[48] RC 3313.481(C) explicitly prohibits a board from discriminating on the basis of race, sex, religion, or national origin when assigning pupils to attendance schedules.

For districts operating under the semester plan, the school year may include up to four half-days for parent-teacher conferences and up to two days for professional meetings of teachers.[49] School may be dismissed for the number of hours in which parent conferences are held outside of regular school hours, whether or not dismissal occurs on the same day conferences are held.[50]

(C) Split schedules for economic reasons

A board of education's decision to close its elementary school buildings due to lack of sufficient funds and to operate on split sessions in its remaining middle and high school buildings, by staggering the schedules of all students, is neither unreasonable nor prohibited by RC 3313.48.[51]

(D) Emergency closings

If school is closed due to a disease epidemic, hazardous weather conditions, inoperability of school buses or other equipment necessary to the school's operation, damage to a building, or other temporary circumstances due to utility failure rendering the school building unfit for use, the minimum school year requirement is waived by the superintendent of public instruction to the extent of the days thus missed provided the school year consists of not less than 175 school days (for schools operating under a trimester, quarter, or pentamester plan, the 175-day requirement is changed, respectively, to 79 days in any trimester, 59 days in any quarter, and 44 days in any pentamester).[52] RC 3313.482 requires that the board of education of each city, exempted village, and local school district annually adopt a resolution by September 1 specifying a contingency plan under which students will make up days when school is closed for these reasons if such days must be made up in order to comply with RC 3317.01, RC 3313.48, and RC 3313.481. The plan must provide for making up at least five full school days and the resolution cannot conflict with any collective bargaining agreement to which the board is a party. The attorney general has concluded a day may not be deducted from the minimum school year requirement if the reason for closure is fear of disruption of bus schedules and traffic con-

---

[44]RC 3317.01.
[45]RC 3313.481(A)(1) to (3).
[46]RC 3313.481(B).
[47]RC 3313.481(B).
[48]RC 3313.481(B).
[49]RC 3313.48.
[50]OAG 85-015.

[51]Tice v Southern Local School Dist Bd of Ed, No. 80-C-48, 1983 WL 6744 (7th Dist Ct App, Columbiana, 1-21-83).
[52]RC 3313.48, RC 3317.01. For discussion of the superintendent's waiver authority, see State ex rel Cleveland Bd of Ed v State Bd of Ed, 11 OS(3d) 89, 11 OBR 392, 464 NE(2d) 137 (1984).

gestion because of a scheduled political rally.[53]

The board of health of a city or general health district may close any school during an epidemic or when a dangerous communicable disease is unusually prevalent.[54] Further, a district may excuse twelfth grade students from attendance for up to three days when schools are otherwise open for instruction.[55]

20.06 Holidays and commemorative days

A board of education is authorized to dismiss students attending its schools on ten legal holidays: New Year's Day, January 1; Martin Luther King Day, the third Monday in January; Washington-Lincoln Day, the third Monday in February; Memorial Day, the last Monday in May; Independence Day, July 4; Labor Day, the first Monday in September; Columbus Day, the second Monday in October; Veterans' Day, November 11; Thanksgiving, the fourth Thursday in November; and Christmas Day, December 25.[56] If any designated holiday falls on Sunday, the next day, Monday, is the legal holiday.

The following days must be commemorated in the schools: Lincoln's birthday, February 12; Washington's birthday, February 22; Memorial Day, May 30; and Veterans' Day, November 11.[57]

TRUANCY

20.07 Duty to enforce school attendance

Although parents have a legal duty to see that their children attend school, the primary responsibility for enforcement of the compulsory education law lies with boards of education.

Every board is required to adopt a written policy for the notification of a student's parents, custodial parent, guardian, legal custodian, or any other person responsible for the student within a reasonable time after a determination that the student is absent from school. The parents (or other person responsible) must provide the school the student attends with a current address and telephone number at which the notice can be received.[58] The attorney general has concluded that, while "the quickest possible notice is desirable," a board may tailor its policy to the needs of its district and that immediate or same-day notice is not required per se; however, a procedure under which notice will not be received until some time after the day of the absence is valid only if, in light of all the circumstances, the notice is provided within a reasonable time after determination of the student's absence.[59]

20.08 Attendance officers

(A) Appointment

The board of a city or exempted village or educational service center is required to employ an attendance officer and may employ or appoint assistants as necessary.[60] In cities with a population of 100,000 or more, the board may appoint, on nomination of the superintendent, one or more pupil personnel workers and may pay traveling expenses within the district for these employees.[61]

(B) Compensation and expenses

Compensation and traveling expenses of service center attendance officers and assistants must be paid from the educational service center fund. With the consent of the judge of the juvenile court, a probation officer of the court may be designated as the service center attendance officer or assistant. The additional traveling expenses of the probation officer serving as attendance officer must be paid out of the educational service center fund. The governing board may also pay additional compensa-

---

[53]OAG 89-018.
[54]RC 3313.48, RC 3317.01, RC 3707.26.
[55]RC 3317.01.
[56]RC 1.14, RC 5.21, RC 3313.63.
[57]RC 5.23.
[58]RC 3313.205.

[59]OAG 94-028 (the attorney general went on to conclude a board could scrap its postcard method of giving notice in favor of an alternative method so long as statutory requirements were satisfied).
[60]RC 3321.14, RC 3321.15.
[61]RC 3321.14.

tion to any probation officer designated as attendance officer.[62]

(C) Powers and duties

An attendance officer or assistant may investigate (1) any case of nonattendance at a public, private, or parochial school by a child of compulsory school age who resides in the district, is enrolled in any school within the district, or is found in the district; and (2) any case of nonattendance of any person over eighteen enrolled in any school within the district. The officer or assistant may take such action as the district superintendent directs, or as the attendance officer or assistant considers proper, in the absence of specific direction.[63]

Attendance officers and assistants are vested with police powers. They may take into custody any truant of compulsory school age and conduct him to the school he should attend. They may serve warrants and enter any place where children are employed, and do whatever is necessary to investigate and enforce the compulsory education and child labor laws.[64] Inspectors of the division of workshops and factories have similar authority to deal with any child found violating school attendance laws.[65]

20.09 Enforcement procedures

(A) Investigation

Attendance officers must investigate all cases of suspected truancy. If a child is found to be truant, the officer must notify the child and his parent in writing of the legal consequences of the child's failure to attend school. If the parent fails to immediately cause the child to attend school, the officer may either file a complaint against the parent in the appropriate court or, if so directed by the school district board or superintendent, send notice requiring such person's attendance at a parental educational program established under RC 3321.19(A).[66] County, municipal, and juvenile courts have jurisdiction in these cases.[67]

(B) Liability of parent

A parent who violates the compulsory education law is subject to a fine or may be required to give a bond insuring that he will cause the child to attend school. A parent is subject to imprisonment for failure to pay the fine or give the bond.[68] An indigent parent may not be imprisoned for failure to pay the fine if the failure is not due to mere neglect.[69] An indigent parent has the right to be represented by a court-appointed attorney.[70] If a parent proves to the court his inability to cause the child to attend school, he must be discharged. The attendance officer must then initiate proceedings before the juvenile court to have the child declared delinquent or dependent, and the judge will deal with the child as provided by law.[71]

It is a valid defense to a charge of violating the compulsory attendance laws that compliance would interfere with the constitutional right to the free exercise of religion.[72]

(C) Liability of employer of school-age child

An employer is subject to criminal punishment for failure to comply with the compulsory education laws and with the laws

---

[62]RC 3321.15.

[63]RC 3321.16.

[64]RC 3321.17.

[65]RC 4113.14.

[66]RC 3321.19 to RC 3321.22. RC 3321.19(A) gives any board of education the option of requiring the parent of a truant child to attend "an educational program established pursuant to rules adopted by the state board of education for the purpose of encouraging parental involvement in compelling the attendance of the child." See OAC 3301-47-01. The parent cannot fail to attend without "good cause." Violation subjects the parent to penalties described in RC 3321.38.

[67]RC 4109.13(D).

[68]RC 3321.38, RC 3321.99. An accused parent has no right to a jury trial at least where potential incarceration in not at issue. State v Atwood, 61 App(3d) 650, 573 NE(2d) 739 (Ross 1990); State v Levy, 55 App(3d) 219, 563 NE(2d) 358 (Cuyahoga 1988).

[69]State v Bosstic, 16 App(3d) 438, 16 OBR 509, 476 NE(2d) 722 (Ross 1984).

[70]State v Bosstic, 16 App(3d) 438, 16 OBR 509, 476 NE(2d) 722 (Ross 1984).

[71]RC 3321.22.

[72]State ex rel Nagle v Olin, 64 OS(2d) 341, 415 NE(2d) 279 (1980). See Text 20.03(A), Constitutionally compelled excuses.

governing age and schooling certificates required for employed minors.[73]

20.10 Attendance and withdrawal reports

To execute the laws relating to compulsory education and employment of minors, the head of each public, private, and parochial school is required to report annually, to the treasurer of the district in which the school is located, certain information concerning all pupils below age eighteen in attendance at that school. This information, including names, ages, and places of residence, facilitates carrying out the laws relating to compulsory education and the employment of minors. Reports must be made within the first two weeks of each school year and must be supplemented monthly as required by the state board of education.[74]

When any child of compulsory school age withdraws from school, the child's teacher must ascertain the reason for withdrawal and notify the district superintendent. If the child withdraws because of change of residence, the teacher must learn the new address and notify the superintendent. The superintendent is then required to forward the essential facts regarding the child, including the child's new residence, to the superintendent of the district to which the child has moved.[75]

Upon receiving information that a child of compulsory school age has withdrawn from school for some reason other than a change of residence and is not attending in accordance with school policy an approved program to obtain a diploma or its equivalent, the district superintendent, within two weeks, must notify the registrar of motor vehicles (in the manner the registrar by rule requires) and the juvenile judge (in writing) of the county in which the district is located.[76]

If, and only if, the board of education adopts a resolution providing that RC 3321.13(B)(2) applies within the district,[77] the superintendent, upon receiving information that, during any semester or term, a child of compulsory school age has been absent from school without legitimate excuse for more than ten consecutive school days or at least fifteen total school days, is to notify the child and his parent in writing that he has such information, that as a result the child's temporary instruction permit or driver's license will be suspended (or the opportunity to obtain a permit or license will be denied), and that the child and parent may appear at a specified date, time, and place before the superintendent or his designee to challenge the information. The notification must set forth the information received. The hearing date must be no earlier than three and no later than five days after notification is given, unless an extension is requested and granted.[78]

If the child and parent do not appear, or if the superintendent or designee determines at the hearing that the information is valid, the superintendent is to notify (within two weeks after receipt of the information or, if a hearing occurs, within two weeks after the appearance) the registrar of motor vehicles (in the manner the registrar by rule requires) or the juvenile judge (in writing) of the child's habitual absence without legitimate excuse. A legitimate excuse includes, but is not limited to, that the child is enrolled in any other school or school district, that the child was excused from school attendance pursuant to RC 3321.04, or that the child received an age and schooling certificate under RC 3331.01.[79]

RC 3321.13(B)(3) provides that if a pupil is suspended or expelled from school for using or possessing alcohol and/or a drug of abuse, the district superintendent, within two weeks, may (but is not required to) notify the registrar of motor vehicles (in the manner the registrar by rule requires) or the juvenile judge (in writing).[80]

---

[73]RC 4109.02 to RC 4109.04, RC 4109.12, RC 4109.13.
[74]RC 3321.12. The reporting provisions of this statute expressly do not apply to joint vocational or cooperative education school districts.
[75]RC 3321.13(A).
[76]RC 3321.13(B)(1).

[77]RC 3321.13(B)(2) expressly does *not* apply in the absence of a resolution.
[78]RC 3321.13(B)(2).
[79]RC 3321.13(B)(2).
[80]Helmeci v Bureau of Motor Vehicles, 75 App(3d) 172, 598 NE(2d) 1294 (Ottawa 1991), confirms that the superintendent's duty is permissive, not

Any notification of withdrawal, habitual absence without legitimate excuse, suspension, or expulsion given to the registrar or juvenile judge under RC 3321.13(B) must include the child's name, address, date of birth, school, and school district. The superintendent must immediately notify the registrar or juvenile judge if a notification was given in error.[81]

Procedures for suspending a child's driving privileges (which in no event may go beyond the child's eighteenth birthday) and for lifting any suspension on the basis of RC 3321.13(B) notifications are detailed in RC 4507.061.

AGE AND SCHOOLING CERTIFICATES AND EMPLOYMENT OF SCHOOL-AGE CHILDREN

20.11 Schooling and the child labor laws

The child labor laws and the compulsory school attendance laws are complementary. The prime objective is to insure at least a minimum education. While minors are permitted to work, their employment may not interfere with their education.

Statutes regulating the employment of minors appear in RC Chapter 4109. A minor is any person less than eighteen years of age.[82] Authority to enforce the requirements is vested in the director of industrial relations or his authorized representative, the superintendent of public instruction or his authorized representative, any school attendance officer, any probation officer, the director of health or his authorized representative, and any representative of a local department of health.[83] The director of industrial relations is empowered to promulgate rules prohibiting the employment of minors in occupations determined by him to be hazardous to children.[84] Employment of minors in any hazardous occupation is expressly prohibited.[85]

(A) Restrictions on employment of minors

Where employment of minors is permitted, the state has imposed certain restrictions to protect them from the possible harmful effects of employment and to ensure compliance with compulsory education laws.[86] Thus, unless the prospective employment is exempted under RC 4109.06, an employer may not employ a minor of compulsory school age unless the minor presents an age and schooling certificate.[87] Moreover, if the age and schooling certificate becomes void, the employer may not continue to employ the minor.[88] Age and schooling certificates may be issued pursuant to RC 3331.01 as legitimate cause for issuance arises.[89] However, no certificate may be issued if the employment contemplated is prohibited by any law regulating the employment of a minor.[90] No employer or agent of an employer may participate in or acquiesce in a violation of law relating to the employment or compulsory education of a minor.[91]

(B) Summer employment

An exception is provided with respect to summer employment of sixteen- and seventeen-year-olds. No regular or part-time and vacation age and schooling certificates are required of minors sixteen and seventeen years of age who are to be employed during summer vacation. This exception applies only to nonagricultural and nonhazardous employment as defined by the Fair Labor Standards Act, 29 USCA 201, and similar state statutes, or other employment not prohibited by law to minors age sixteen or seventeen. To be hired for summer work, a minor must provide the employer with the same proof of age he would give the superintendent were he applying for a certificate, and a statement from the parent or guard-

---

mandatory, and goes on to hold that, in the case of a suspension or expulsion from a local school district, the local superintendent, not the county superintendent, must send the notice since a county superintendent has no suspension or expulsion authority under RC 3313.66.

[81] RC 3321.13(C).
[82] RC 4109.01(D).
[83] RC 4109.01(C).
[84] RC 4109.05(A).
[85] RC 4109.05(B).
[86] State ex rel Trydle v Industrial Comm, 32 OS(2d) 257, 260, 291 NE(2d) 748 (1972).
[87] RC 4109.02, RC 4109.03.
[88] RC 4109.03.
[89] OAG 67-127.
[90] RC 3331.01, RC 4109.06.
[91] RC 4109.04.

ian consenting to the employment. In the absence of a parent or guardian, an adult with whom the minor resides may sign the consent statement. Copies of the proof of age and consent statement must be retained by the employer with the minor's employment record.[92]

20.12 Hours and terms of employment of minors

Hours and the daily and weekly terms of employment of a minor are strictly controlled. No minor under age sixteen may be employed before seven a.m.[93] When school is in session, no minor under sixteen may be employed after seven p.m. or during school hours, unless specifically permitted by RC Chapter 4109.[94] Between June 1 and September 1 or during any school holiday of five or more days' duration, no minor under sixteen can be employed after nine p.m.[95] Additionally, a minor under sixteen may not be employed more than three hours in any school day or eighteen hours in any week that school is in session.[96] A minor may, however, be employed up to eight hours in any day which is not a school day and forty hours in any week school is not in session.[97] If a minor is employed for more than five consecutive hours, he must be given a thirty-minute rest period.[98]

Employment of a minor under sixteen may not exceed forty hours in any one week, nor may it occur during school hours unless the employment is incidental to a program of vocational cooperative training, work study, or other work-oriented program whose purpose is educating students. The program must also meet standards established by the state board of education.[99] A minor under sixteen may not be employed in any door-to-door sales activity unless the employer is registered under and in compliance with RC 4109.21. The minor may not be employed in such activity before seven a.m. or after seven p.m. or during school hours, unless specifically permitted by RC Chapter 4109. The same restriction applies to a minor sixteen or seventeen years of age except the seven p.m. limit is moved back to eight p.m.[100]

RC 4109.07(D) states that no person age sixteen or seventeen who is required to attend school may be employed before seven a.m. on a school day (unless the person was not employed after eight p.m. the previous night, in which case the person may be employed after six a.m.) or after eleven p.m. on the night preceding a school day. However, RC 4109.06(C) authorizes a minor to petition the juvenile court or apply to the superintendent of the school district who issued the minor's age and schooling certificate for an exemption from these particular restrictions if they will cause a substantial hardship or are not in the minor's best interests. If the minor prevails, the court or superintendent must establish hours of employment for the minor and notify the minor and the minor's employer of these hours.

20.13 Age and schooling certificates

(A) In general, duties of superintendent of schools

Age and schooling certificates are issued by the superintendent of the city or exempted village district or educational service center in which the child seeking the certificate resides.[101] Residents of other states who work in Ohio must qualify with the school authority in the school district where the place of employment is located.[102]

Whether the requirements for issuance of the certificate have been met is left to the discretion of the superintendent.[103] Thus, a superintendent is under no statu-

---

[92]RC 3331.05, RC 4109.02.
[93]RC 4109.07(A)(2).
[94]RC 4109.07(A)(1), (3).
[95]RC 4109.07(A)(3).
[96]RC 4109.07(A)(4), (5).
[97]RC 4109.07(A)(6), (7).
[98]RC 4109.07(C).
[99]RC 4109.07(B).
[100]RC 4109.21(F). Activity conducted in connection with a bona fide educational, charitable, or religious activity or for a newspaper subscription drive (if the minor delivers newspapers to the consumer for the newspaper in question and if the drive is supervised by an employee at least eighteen) is not door-to-door activity within the meaning of the statute. RC 4109.21(G).

[101]RC 3331.01. As used in RC Ch 3331, "superintendent" expressly means the superintendent or superintendent's designee.

[102]RC 3331.01.

[103]OAG 70-026.

tory duty to issue the certificate to a former student who has the assurance of employment; that is only one fact which should be considered in determining whether statutory requirements have been met.[104]

(B) Requirements for certificate

Before a certificate is issued, there must be satisfactory proof that the minor is over sixteen and has completed a vocational or special educational program adequate to prepare the student for the occupation.[105] A certified copy of a birth certificate or, in its absence, a passport or attested transcript or an attested transcript of birth or baptism or other religious record showing the date and place of birth of the child constitutes conclusive evidence of age. If no such proof of age can be produced, the superintendent may accept other documentary evidence satisfactory to him. If no documentary proof of age can be obtained, a parent or guardian can sign an application to secure a physician's certificate to establish the age of the child. The age and schooling certificate must then be granted if the school physician or a physician employed by the board of education is satisfied the child is over sixteen.[106]

An age and schooling certificate may only be issued on satisfactory proof that the employment contemplated by the child is not prohibited by law. The superintendent must also receive, approve, and file the following before issuing a certificate:

(1) The written pledge of the employer to legally employ the child and to permit him to attend school and to return the certificate or notify the superintendent within two days of the child's withdrawal or dismissal from employment;

(2) The school record of the child; and

(3) A certificate from the school physician or a physician designated by him that the child is physically fit to be employed in the specified occupation.[107]

Each certificate must be signed by the child in whose name it is issued in the presence of the officer issuing it. Blank certificates are furnished by the state board of education on request.[108]

(C) Application, reissuance

Application for an age and schooling certificate must be made to the superintendent of the district in which the student resides. A child whose district of residence is a local school district must apply to the local superintendent. The information must be forwarded to the service center superintendent for issuance of a certificate.

If the service center superintendent issues the certificate, the child must then sign it in the presence of the local superintendent. The service center superintendent may issue a certificate directly to a child when the local school district offices are closed during regular business hours. The service center superintendent must notify the local superintendent of all certificates issued directly by him.[109]

When an age and schooling certificate that has been returned by the employer as required by law is reissued, a written pledge of the new employer and a certificate from the school physician must be obtained and filed.[110]

(D) Denial of certificate, appeal

If the superintendent refuses to grant an age and schooling certificate, appeal may be taken within ten days to the juvenile judge of that county.[111]

(E) Revocation of certificate

The superintendent may revoke an age and schooling certificate because of (1) noncompliance with its stipulations, (2) physical condition of the child, or (3) other sufficient cause. In addition, the certificate may be revoked if the child fails to attend any required part-time classes.[112]

---

[104] OAG 70-026.
[105] RC 3331.01.
[106] RC 3331.02(C).
[107] RC 3331.02.
[108] RC 3331.01.
[109] RC 3331.01.
[110] RC 3331.07.
[111] RC 3331.08.
[112] RC 3331.09.

20.14 Special age and schooling certificates

(A) Limited certificate

A limited certificate may be issued to a child who, because of certain disabilities, is permitted to engage only in limited and specific types of employment. Any certificate will be made a limited certificate if issued with the word "Limited" printed or stamped diagonally across the face. The statement made by the physician examining the pupil determines whether the child is fit for employment in the specific occupation.[113]

A limited certificate may not serve as the legal age and schooling certificate for employment in any other occupation.[114]

(B) Conditional certificate

A conditional certificate may be issued for the regular employment of a child who is at least sixteen and unable to pass a seventh grade test, but who is capable of doing further school work. For the certificate to be issued, it must be proven that the child is not addicted to any habit which may detract from his reliability or effectiveness as a worker, proper use of his earnings or leisure, or carrying out the required pledge of continuing his education, plus additional requirements as follows:

(1) He has either attended school diligently for the previous two years in that district, and can read, write, or perform the fundamental operations of arithmetic; or

(2) If the child has been a resident for less than two years, he attended school diligently in the previous school district of residence the preceding school year and has been diligent in his studies in the current district; or

(3) He has moved to the present school district since the beginning of the last annual school session and that instruction adapted to his needs is not provided in regular day schools; or

(4) He is not sufficiently familiar with the English language to benefit in regular schools; or

(5) Conditions are such that he must provide for his own support or care for his family.

These facts must be acceptable to the superintendent issuing the certificate and must be agreed to in writing by the child and by persons in charge of the child. The certificate is granted on condition the child will attend an appropriate, part-time, evening or home study program directed by the superintendent until reaching eighteen. If lack of English language proficiency is the reason for granting the certificate, the superintendent may direct the child to attend classes to assist him in learning English.[115]

(C) Part-time and vacation certificates

A part-time and vacation age and schooling certificate may be issued to any child over fourteen, permitting him to be employed in any occupation not forbidden to him by law.[116] A holder of a part-time and vacation certificate may be employed whenever his school is not in session. The conditions applicable to regular age and schooling certificates apply. In addition, the superintendent may impose other requirements. The forms and directions for recording the facts on part-time and vacation certificates may be prescribed by the state board of education.[117]

(D) Over-age certificate

An over-age certificate may be issued directly to a minor who is eighteen or over and who is requested by his employer to present evidence of his age. A superintendent must issue an over-age certificate in the manner prescribed for the issuance of other age and schooling certificates if the person proves to be over eighteen. When a child holding an age and schooling certificate reaches eighteen, the certificate must be released to him by his employer and can be used as an over-age certificate.[118]

20.15 Part-time day school for certificate holders

Every child who has been granted an age and schooling certificate is required to attend a part-time school or class until the

---

[113]RC 3331.02, RC 3331.06.
[114]RC 3331.02, RC 3331.06.
[115]RC 3331.04.

[116]RC 3331.05, RC 4109.06.
[117]RC 3331.05.
[118]RC 3331.15.

age at which the certificate is no longer required, provided the board of education has made the class available.[119] This requirement does not apply to children working under vacation and part-time certificates.[120] A part-time school or class must offer minors instruction supplemental to their daily occupations, increase their civic and vocational competence, or both. Attendance at a part-time school or class provided by an employer, partnership, corporation, or individual, by a private or parochial school, by a college, or by a philanthropic or similar agency may also fulfill this requirement if approved by the state board of education.[121]

20.16 Employer responsibility respecting minors

(A) In general

Except as noted above with respect to a child sixteen or seventeen employed during summer vacation, no minor of compulsory school age can be employed unless he presents a proper age and schooling certificate. The employer must keep the certificate on file or return it or give notice to the superintendent of the minor's withdrawal or dismissal from employment within five days thereof. The employer must permit enforcement officials to examine certificates, working conditions of minors, and make reasonable inquiry of minors.[122]

(B) Records

Every employer of minors is required to keep two lists of such minors under eighteen: one on file, and one posted where such minors are employed.[123] The employer must keep written records regarding a minor's employment, including his name, address, occupation, hours worked, and wages received. The director of industrial relations or his authorized representative has access to such records and may copy them. The records must be kept for two years.[124]

Where no certificate is on file, any employer of minors may be required by an enforcement official to furnish satisfactory evidence that the employee is in fact over eighteen. The enforcement official may require the same evidence of age of the employee as is required on the issuance of an age and schooling certificate. Failure to produce this evidence is a violation of the law regarding employment of minors.[125]

(C) Agreement as to compensation

An employer must enter into an agreement with the minor as to wages or compensation. The employer must furnish the minor with written evidence of the agreement and with an earnings statement on or before each payday. An employer may not reduce a minor's earnings without a written agreement and at least twenty-four hours' notice. A minor's earnings cannot be reduced because of presumed negligence, incompetence, or failure to abide by work rules. An employer cannot receive a monetary deposit to guarantee the minor's performance.[126]

(D) Return of certificate

When an employee has made a written request for return of his age and schooling certificate, the employer's failure to return the certificate to the issuing authority within three days will render him liable to the employee for an amount equal to the wages he would have earned had he continued employment.[127]

There is an apparent conflict between RC 3331.02, which requires an employer to return an age and schooling certificate within two days of the minor's termination of employment, and RC 4109.03, which requires return within five days of termination.

20.17 Enforcement, penalties

The director of industrial relations is required to designate officials to enforce laws relating to the employment of minors.[128]

On discovery of a violation of the employment laws and after notice to the employer, an enforcement official must file

---

[119]RC 3313.56, RC 3321.08.
[120]RC 3321.08.
[121]RC 3321.09.
[122]RC 4109.02, RC 4109.03.
[123]RC 4109.02, RC 4109.08.

[124]RC 4109.11.
[125]RC 4109.08.
[126]RC 4109.10.
[127]RC 4109.09.
[128]RC 4109.13(A).

a complaint in court. Fines collected for violation of the compulsory attendance laws and laws relating to the employment of minors are paid to the school district in which the offense was committed.[129]

An employer who fails to comply with the requirements of compulsory school attendance and age and schooling certificates as to minors in his employ is subject to criminal penalty.[130]

---

[129]RC 4109.13(C), (D), (F).

[130]RC 4109.99.

Chapter 21

Pupils: Health and Safety

HEALTH SERVICES
- 21.01 Responsibilities of board of education
- 21.02 Employment of health care professionals
- 21.03 Medical examinations
- 21.04 Medical treatment
- 21.05 Immunizations
- 21.06 Dental examinations and treatment
- 21.07 Health records
- 21.08 Duties of board of health
- 21.09 Volunteer medical services at athletic events, nonliability

SAFETY MEASURES AND PROGRAMS
- 21.10 School building requirements
- 21.11 Traffic protection for students
- 21.12 Eye protection
- 21.13 Fire and tornado drills
- 21.14 Safety instruction
- 21.15 Fostering a drug-free environment
- 21.16 Conveyance or possession of deadly weapons or dangerous ordnance on school premises

HEALTH SERVICES

21.01 Responsibilities of board of education

Boards of education have explicit authority to conduct a school health service program. In addition, a board may exercise powers clearly implied and necessary for the execution of powers expressly granted.[1]

The attorney general has recognized a board's implied authority "to enact rules and regulations reasonably designed to preserve discipline, as well as to protect the morals, health and physical safety of students."[2] For example, school authorities may take steps reasonably necessary to remove pupils infected with head lice, subject to statutory limitations as to suspensions and expulsions.[3]

A board's authority in this area is not unlimited, however. A New York court, for example, has held that the due process clause of the US Constitution's Fourteenth Amendment prohibits a school district from dispensing condoms to unemancipated minors without the prior consent of their parents or an "opt-out" provision.[4]

21.02 Employment of health care professionals

(A) Physicians and dentists

School physicians and school dentists may be employed by city, exempted village, and local school district boards of education. Two or more districts may jointly employ a physician and dentist. School physicians and dentists serve one-year terms or until their successors are appointed but may be discharged at any time. Their compensation is determined by the board. Both school physicians and dentists must be licensed to practice in Ohio.[5]

A chiropractor may conduct student physical examinations to determine suitability for participation in athletic activities unless the board requires examining physicians to conduct tests that are not within a chiropractor's education, training, and experience.[6]

(B) Nurses

Boards of education may also employ registered nurses as school nurses to aid in conducting and coordinating the school health service program.[7] School nurses must be certificated pursuant to RC 3319.22(P), but any registered nurse employed on January 1, 1973, to serve full-

---

[1] See Verberg v Cleveland City School Dist Bd of Ed, 135 OS 246, 20 NE(2d) 368 (1939); Schwing v McClure, 120 OS 335, 166 NE 230 (1929).
[2] OAG 74-095.
[3] 1942 OAG 5091.
[4] Alfonso v Fernandez, 195 AD(2d) 46, 606 NYS(2d) 259 (SCt 1993), appeal dismissed by 83 NY(2d) 906, 614 NYS(2d) 388, 637 NE(2d) 279 (1994).
[5] RC 3313.68.
[6] OAG 83-002.
[7] RC 3313.68.

time as a school nurse is considered to have fulfilled the requirements for certification.[8]

21.03 Medical examinations

(A) In general

School physicians may examine for hearing and visual defects, and diagnose all children referred to them. To protect the health of the pupils and employees, physicians may examine teachers and other school employees and inspect school buildings.[9]

(B) Examination by family physician

If the parent or guardian of any pupil, or any teacher or other school employee, after notice from the board of education, within two weeks furnishes a doctor's certification of examination, additional examination by the school physician must be dispensed with. Also, any child must be exempted from a dental inspection, hearing test, or visual test, on presentation to school authorities of a certificate that he has been professionally examined during the immediately preceding twelve months.[10]

(C) Tuberculosis testing

Boards of education must require and provide examinations for tuberculosis of pupils in selected grades and of employees as may be required by the Ohio Public Health Council. All pupils with positive reactions must have chest x rays, and all positive reactions and x-ray findings must be reported promptly to the county record bureau of tuberculosis cases. Boards of education must waive the required test where a pupil presents a written statement from his family physician certifying that the pupil has been tested and is free from tuberculosis in a communicable stage, or that the test is medically inadvisable, or from his parent or guardian objecting to the test because of religious convictions.[11]

Newly employed teachers, school bus drivers, and other employees are required to present documented evidence of a negative tuberculin test within ninety days before their first day of work. All employees with positive reactions must have chest x rays and any other medical and laboratory examinations considered necessary by the school physician to determine the absence of tuberculosis in a communicable stage within ninety days before their first day of work. Currently employed teachers, drivers, and other employees who become known to have a positive reaction must have chest x rays and other examinations the school physician considers necessary.[12]

The board is required to pay for the annual tuberculosis examination of teachers and other employees pursuant to RC 3313.71.[13]

(D) Children or staff found to have communicable disease

Whenever a pupil, teacher, or other school employee is found to be suffering from tuberculosis or other communicable disease, the school physician must promptly send him home, with a statement to his parent or guardian (in the case of a pupil) briefly stating the facts and advising that the family physician be consulted. In the case of a teacher or other employee, employment must be discontinued at a salary the board considers just until the school physician has certified recovery.[14] The validity of RC 3313.71 as applied to Acquired Immune Deficiency Syndrome (AIDS) victims is highly dubious in light of court decisions finding it illegal to exclude employees and students simply because they have the disease.[15] RC 3313.71 must also be applied with caution in other types of cases where the targeted person has a disability or handicap that implicates current antidiscrimination laws.

---

[8]RC 3319.221.
[9]RC 3313.69, RC 3313.71.
[10]RC 3313.69, RC 3313.71.
[11]RC 3313.71.
[12]OAC 3701-15-02.
[13]OAG 74-069.
[14]RC 3313.71.
[15]Chalk v United States Dist Ct Central Dist of Cal, 840 F(2d) 701 (9th Cir Cal 1988); Martinez v Hillsborough County School Bd, 861 F(2d) 1502 (11th Cir Fla 1988); Doe v Dolton Elementary School Dist

No. 148, 694 FSupp 440 (ND Ill 1988); Robertson v Granite City Community Unit School Dist No. 9, 684 FSupp 1002 (SD Ill 1988); Doe v Belleville Public School Dist No. 118, 672 FSupp 342 (SD Ill 1987); Thomas v Atascadero Unified School Dist, 662 FSupp 376 (CD Cal 1986); District 27 Community School Bd v New York City Bd of Ed, 130 NY Misc(2d) 398, 502 NYS(2d) 325 (NY Sup Ct 1986); Phipps v Saddleback Valley Unified School Dist, 204 Cal App(3d) 1110, 251 Cal Rptr 720 (1988).

(E) AIDS

The Ohio department of health has issued guidelines stating that children with AIDS should be allowed to attend school in a regular classroom setting provided the status of the child, as evaluated by the child's physician, allows participation in regular school activity. The guidelines further indicate decisions should be made case-by-case. Overall, the guidelines emphasize that an AIDS-infected child is generally not a threat to other students or school personnel.[16]

RC 3701.245 prohibits a school district from withholding services to any individual solely because that individual refuses to consent to a test for the AIDS virus or to disclose the test results.

(F) Early screening for health or developmental disorders

RC 3313.673 provides that, prior to November 1 of the school year in which a pupil is enrolled for the first time in either kindergarten or first grade, the pupil must be screened for vision, hearing, speech and communications, and health and medical problems and for any developmental disorders. Prior to the preceding August 1, the board of education must furnish the pupil's parents with information on the screening program.

The board may provide the screening program, contract with some person or governmental entity to provide screening, or request parents to obtain screening from a provider selected by the parents. In the last case, the board must provide lists of providers and information about any screening services available in the community to parents who cannot afford them. A parent requested to obtain services may opt out by signing a written statement that he does not wish to have his child screened.

If the screening reveals the possibility of special learning needs, the board must provide further assessment in accordance with RC Chapter 3323 (pertaining to education of the handicapped).

21.04 Medical treatment

(A) In general, parental consent, emergencies

In the medical supervision of school children provided by a board of health of a city or general health district, no medical or surgical treatment can be administered to any minor child without the written consent of a parent or guardian. Any information regarding any diseased condition or defect found as a result of any school medical examination must be communicated only to the parent or guardian and, if in writing, must be in a sealed envelope addressed to the parent or guardian.[17] However, a minor may consent to diagnosis or treatment of venereal disease, and parental consent is not required.[18]

Under RC 3313.712, a board of education must keep on file a form signed by the parents or guardian regarding emergency treatment of their child in case of illness or injury.[19] Parents may authorize treatment or not, but if treatment is not authorized, parents must indicate the procedure they wish school authorities to follow. Where treatment is authorized, school authorities must still make a reasonable attempt to contact the parents before treating the child. School personnel who make a good faith attempt to comply are shielded from liability.

(B) Administration of prescription drugs

(1) Adoption of policy by board

RC 3313.713 requires the board of each city, local, exempted village, and joint vocational school district to adopt a policy on administering prescription drugs to students.[20] The statute allows boards one of two choices:

> (1) Except as otherwise required by federal law, no board employee may in the course of employment administer any drug prescribed by a physician to any student; or

---

[16]Ohio Department of Health Guidelines and Recommendations for Preschool, Elementary and Secondary Schools (Youth ages 3 and above) Regarding Acquired Immunodeficiency Syndrome (AIDS) and HIV Infection, issued October 1989. See also *id.*

[17]RC 3709.22.
[18]RC 3709.241.
[19]See Text 21.07(C), Emergency treatment authorization.
[20]RC 3313.713(B).

(2) Designated board employees may be authorized to administer drugs prescribed by a physician to students.

Except as otherwise required by federal law, the board's policy may provide that certain drugs or types of drugs may not be administered, or that no employee, or no employee without appropriate training, may use certain procedures (such as injection) to administer drugs.[21]

The person designated to administer drugs may be designated by name or position, training, qualifications, or similar distinguishing factors. RC 3313.713 does not require an employee to administer a drug unless required by board policy, and a board shall not require an employee who objects on religious grounds to administer a drug. RC 3313.713 does not affect application of RC 2305.23, RC 2305.231, or RC 3313.712 governing administration of emergency care or treatment to a student.[22]

(2) Requirements for administration

RC 3313.713 imposes certain requirements before any prescription drug may be administered. The board or its designee must first receive a written request, signed by the student's parent or guardian, that the drug be administered.[23] The board must also receive a statement, signed by the physician who prescribed the drug, that includes all of the following:

(1) Name and address of the student;

(2) School and class in which the student is enrolled;

(3) Name of the drug and dosage to be administered;

(4) Times or intervals at which each dosage is to be administered;

(5) Date administration of the drug is to begin;

(6) Date administration of the drug is to cease;

(7) Any severe adverse reaction that should be reported to the physician and one or more phone numbers where the physician can be reached in an emergency; and

(8) Special instructions for administration of the drug, including sterile conditions and storage.[24]

The parent or guardian must further agree to submit a revised statement signed by the prescribing physician if any information provided by the physician's statement changes.[25]

The person authorized to administer the drug must receive the physician's statement before administering the drug.[26] That person must also receive the drug in the containers in which it was dispensed by the prescribing physician or licensed pharmacist.[27] If the board's policy requires additional procedures, those must also be followed.[28]

If a prescribed drug is administered, the board must keep copies of all documents required by RC 3313.713(C)(1) to (3) and must ensure that by the next school day following receipt of the physician's statement a copy is given to the person authorized to administer the drug. The board or its designee must also establish a location in each school building for the storage of drugs. All drugs must be stored in that location in a locked storage place, except that drugs requiring refrigeration may be kept in a refrigerator in a place not commonly used by students.[29]

(3) Limitations on liability

No person who has been authorized to administer a drug and has a copy of the most recent physician's statement given to him in accordance with RC 3313.713(D) prior to administering the drug is liable in civil damages for administering or failing to administer the drug, unless the person acts

---

[21] RC 3313.713(B).
[22] RC 3313.713(F).
[23] RC 3313.713(C)(1).
[24] RC 3313.713(C)(2).
[25] RC 3313.713(C)(3).
[26] RC 3313.713(C)(4).
[27] RC 3313.713(C)(5).
[28] RC 3313.713(C)(6).
[29] RC 3313.713(D).

in a manner that constitutes gross negligence or wanton or reckless misconduct.[30]

21.05 Immunizations

(A) Required immunizations generally

A board of education is authorized to make and enforce rules to secure the immunization of pupils to prevent the spread of communicable diseases. The power extends to those eligible to attend district schools as well as to those actually in attendance. When the safety and interest of the public requires it, boards of health, legislative authorities of municipal corporations, and boards of township trustees on application of the board of education must provide, without delay and at public expense, the means of immunization to pupils not provided immunization by their parents or guardians.[31] The expense is borne by the particular board of health, municipal corporation, or township involved.[32]

(B) Exclusion of students not immunized

Except in certain instances, no pupil, at the time of his original entry or at the beginning of each school year, may be permitted to remain in school for more than fourteen days unless he presents written evidence that he has been immunized against mumps, poliomyelitis, diphtheria, pertussis, tetanus, rubeola, and rubella, or is in the process of being immunized. A student is "in the process" if he has been immunized against mumps, rubeola, and rubella and has received at least the first dose of the immunization series for poliomyelitis, diphtheria, pertussis, and tetanus. Written evidence must be presented to the child's building principal of each subsequent dose.[33]

A student admitted under the "in process" provision who has not complied with the immunization intervals prescribed by the director of health must be excluded from school on the fifteenth day of the following school year. He must be readmitted upon submitting evidence to the building principal of progress on the director of health's interval schedule. A child whose physician certifies in writing that an immunization against any disease is medically contraindicated is not required to be immunized. A child who has had natural rubeola is not required to be immunized against that disease upon presentation of a signed statement from his parent to that effect. A pupil who has had natural mumps, and presents a signed statement from his parent or physician to that effect, is not required to be immunized against mumps.[34]

(C) Parental objections

RC 3313.671 provides that a pupil who presents a written statement from his parent or guardian objecting to immunization for good cause, including religious convictions, is not required to be immunized. Ohio courts have rejected the contention that a pupil has an absolute right to enter school without immunization on the basis of written objection of his parents.[35] One court has upheld a school board's refusal to admit a child whose parents objected to the child's immunization on nonreligious grounds. The refusal did not violate the student's constitutional right to privacy, due process, or equal protection.[36] Likewise, the attorney general has stated that RC 3313.671 does not preclude boards of education from continuing to make rules and regulations to secure the immunization of pupils.[37]

21.06 Dental examinations and treatment

A school dentist is required to examine, diagnose, and render remedial or corrective treatment for school children, as prescribed by the board of education, but treatment must be limited to the children whose parents cannot otherwise provide for it, and then only with the written consent of the parents or guardian. School dentists

---

[30]RC 3313.713(E).
[31]RC 3313.67, RC 3313.671(B).
[32]1960 OAG 1099.
[33]RC 3313.671.
[34]RC 3313.671.

[35]State ex rel Mack v Covington Bd of Ed, 1 App(2d) 143, 204 NE(2d) 86 (Miami 1963).
[36]Hanzel v Arter, 625 FSupp 1259 (SD Ohio 1985).
[37]1959 OAG 890.

may also conduct oral hygiene educational work as authorized by the board.[38]

21.07 Health records

(A) Examination records

School physicians are required to keep accurate card-index records of all examinations. Records must be kept according to the form prescribed by the state board of education. These records are not open to the public and are maintained solely for the use of boards of education and the officers of boards of health.[39]

Boards of education and boards of health are required to keep accurate records of hearing and vision tests. The records must be kept on a form prescribed by the director of health and include the measures taken to correct defects. Statistical data from the records must be made available to official state and local health, education, and human services departments and agencies. Individual records, however, must be made available to these departments and agencies only where there is evidence that no measures have been taken to correct defects determined by the tests. The records must also be made available to school authorities where they are considered essential in establishing special education facilities for children with hearing and visual defects.[40]

(B) Immunization records

Boards of education are required to keep immunization records for each pupil. The records must include immunization data for poliomyelitis, diphtheria, pertussis, rubeola, rubella, and tetanus. The records must also contain the results of tuberculin tests and any immunizations required by the board. Annually, by October 15, boards of education must submit a summary, by school, of the immunization records of all initial entry pupils in the district to the director of health, on forms prescribed by the director. Records of immunization must be made available to parents or guardians on request.[41]

(C) Emergency treatment authorization

Boards of education are required to distribute annually to parents or guardians and to keep on file forms giving parents or guardians the option of authorizing emergency medical treatment for children who become ill or injured while under school authority. The form must be an identical copy of the form prescribed by RC 3313.712(B) and must be distributed to the parent within thirty days after the entry of any minor pupil into a public school for the first time. The completed form must be kept on file and sent to any school to which the student transfers. School authorities may permit a parent to make changes in a previously filed form or file a new form upon request.[42]

21.08 Duties of board of health

(A) Delegation of duties to board of health

The board of education may delegate the duties of examination, diagnosis, and treatment to the board of health or the officer performing the functions of a board of health within the school district, if the board or officer is willing to assume the duties.[43] Where a board of education has not employed a school physician, the board of health is required to conduct the health examination of all school children in the health district, report the findings, and make recommendations to parents or guardians for the correction of any defects.[44]

(B) Building inspection, disease prevention

A board of health of a city or general health district is required to make sanitary inspections of all schools and school buildings within their jurisdiction.[45] The state department of health is also required to inspect all public or private schools, to condemn all unsanitary or defective plumbing, and to order changes it deems necessary to insure public health.[46]

---

[38] RC 3313.68.
[39] RC 3313.71.
[40] RC 3313.50.
[41] RC 3313.67.
[42] See Text 21.04(A), In general, parental consent, emergencies.
[43] RC 3313.68, RC 3313.72, RC 3709.22.
[44] RC 3313.73.
[45] RC 3707.26.
[46] RC 3703.01, RC 3703.03.

Boards of education are required to cooperate with boards of health in the prevention and control of epidemics.[47] A board of health of a city or general health district may disinfect any building and has the authority to close any school during an epidemic or when a dangerous communicable disease is unusually prevalent.[48] Local boards of education may contract with a health district for services of school physicians, dentists, and nurses.

21.09 Volunteer medical services at athletic events, nonliability

No medical practitioner or registered nurse who volunteers services to a school's athletic program is liable for damages for administering emergency care to a participant in a school athletic event at the scene or while in transport to a medical facility or doctor's office for treatment, unless the acts constitute willful or wanton misconduct. "Medical practitioner" includes persons licensed or certificated by the state medical board to practice medicine, surgery, osteopathic medicine or surgery, or podiatry. This immunity does not apply if the service is rendered for a fee or the expectation of a fee.[49]

SAFETY MEASURES AND PROGRAMS

21.10 School building requirements

(A) Safety and sanitation in general

School buildings must be maintained in a safe and sanitary manner.[50] To enforce these requirements, standards and inspections are provided for by the department of health,[51] the board of building standards,[52] and the department of industrial relations.[53]

(B) Asbestos removal

The Environmental Protection Agency's final regulations implementing the Asbestos Hazard Emergency Response Act of 1986 (AHERA)[54] require schools to designate one person to be trained in each district to insure proper implementation in compliance with the regulations. The designated asbestos coordinator's training must provide a basic knowledge of the health effects of asbestos, of asbestos control techniques, and of federal and state regulations concerning asbestos.

The regulations also require (1) inspection and reinspection of schools; (2) sampling, analysis, and assessment of asbestos materials; (3) development and implementation of management plans in operations and maintenance programs; (4) performance of appropriate response actions or abatement; (5) training and periodic surveillance; and (6) maintenance of records and use of warning labels.[55]

Under the regulations, school districts must have had an accredited inspector visually inspect all areas of each school building to identify locations of all suspected asbestos-containing building materials before October 12, 1988, unless the district requested deferral. If deferral was requested and granted, the inspections must have been completed by May 9, 1989. Each school district with any asbestos must select an accredited management planner who, after review of the results of the inspection and assessment, must create a management plan for the district and recommend in writing appropriate response actions. A copy of this management plan must be maintained in the administrative office, as well as in the office of each school building having asbestos-containing building materials. The management plan was to be submitted for approval to the governor of each state or agency the governor designates by October 12, 1988, unless the district requested deferral. If deferral was requested and granted, the management plans were to have been submitted for approval by May 9, 1989. Regardless of whether deferral was granted, implementa-

---

[47]RC 3313.68.
[48]RC 3707.26.
[49]RC 2305.231.
[50]RC 3781.06.
[51]RC Ch 3703, RC Ch 3707.
[52]RC Ch 3781, RC Ch 3791.
[53]RC 4107.31 et seq.
[54]15 USCA 2641 et seq.
[55]The regulations are numerous and detailed, and each district's needs should be discussed thoroughly with legal counsel. This discussion simply highlights significant deadlines and requirements.

tion of a management plan was to have begun on or before July 9, 1989.

In addition, each school district must implement an operations, management and repair program (O and M Program) when any asbestos is present or assumed to be present in a building owned, leased, or otherwise used as a school building. The O and M Program, which must be documented in the management plan, consists of specific worker protection and training programs, and also must detail procedures for cleaning and removal.

Each school district must insure, prior to the implementation of its O and M Program and management plan, that all members of its maintenance and custodial staff who may work in an area with asbestos-containing building materials receive at least two hours of "awareness training" concerning asbestos. New custodial and maintenance employees must be trained within sixty days after the beginning of their employment.

Under Ohio law, asbestos abatement actions brought by school district boards of education are subject to the four-year limitations period established by RC 2305.091.

(C) Architectural barriers to handicapped

Standards and rules adopted by the state board of building standards pursuant to RC 3781.11 and RC 3781.111 are designed to facilitate the reasonable accommodation of and use by handicapped persons of buildings and facilities.

21.11 Traffic protection for students

(A) Crossing guards

A board of education may employ guards to protect school children while crossing streets en route to school and pay for the services from the general fund. However, a board may not contribute school funds to municipal authorities for the employment of traffic officers to act as traffic guards in school areas.[56]

(B) Duties of local government in traffic control

A board may not install traffic lights for the purpose of protecting pupils on their way to and from school. This authority is granted only to counties, municipalities, and other local boards and bodies having authority to adopt police regulations under the Constitution and laws of Ohio.[57]

(C) School zones and signs

RC 4511.21 provides for the permissive use of certain school zone signs and generally defines a school zone so that it includes the portion of the street or highway that would be within school property lines if the lines were projected into the street or highway. The zone can be enlarged by the director of transportation on request of local jurisdictions. The statute does not require the placement of flashing lights or notice of effective hours or school zone signs. Private schools are among schools for which school zones are established.

21.12 Eye protection

Industrial quality eye protective devices are required for all students, teachers, and visitors while participating in or observing courses in vocational, technical, industrial arts, fine arts, chemical, physical, or combined chemical-physical educational activities involving exposure to hot molten metals or other molten materials; milling, sawing, drilling, turning, shaping, cutting, grinding, buffing, or stamping of any solid materials; heat treatment, tempering, or kiln firing of any metal or other materials; gas or electric welding; repair or servicing of any vehicle; and caustic or explosive materials. Eye protective devices are also required for persons participating in or observing chemical, physical, or combined chemical-physical laboratories involving caustic or explosive materials, hot liquids or solids, injurious radiations, or other hazards.[58]

Pupils engaged in drawing need not wear eye protective devices unless they are close enough to a hazardous activity to be injured. Likewise, pupils temporarily away from a welder or other metal-working machine need not wear eye protective devices as long as the machines are not in operation. Eye protective devices need not be used when explosive solutions are not being used or handled. However, these

---

[56]1936 OAG 5583; 1952 Inf OAG 220.
[57]RC 4511.01(AA), RC 4511.10, RC 4511.11.

[58]RC 3313.643.

devices must be worn by pupils using hand saws, hand planes, or other hand wood- or metal-working tools.[59]

Eye protective devices may be furnished for all students and teachers, purchased and sold at cost to students and teachers, or made available at a moderate rental fee. They must be made available to all visitors to shops and laboratories. The superintendent of public instruction is required to circulate instructions and recommendations for implementing the eye safety provisions, and the industrial commission is responsible for enforcement.[60]

21.13 Fire and tornado drills

A public or private school having an average daily attendance of fifty or more pupils must conduct drills or rapid dismissals at least once each month to prepare students to leave the building in the shortest possible time without confusion in the event of sudden emergency. Doors and exits of school buildings must be unlocked during school hours.[61]

In conjunction with the drills or rapid dismissals, public and private schools must instruct pupils in safety precautions to be taken in case of a tornado or a tornado alert or warning. Appropriate shelter areas in case of a tornado or a tornado alert or warning must be designated in accordance with standards prescribed by the fire marshal. The fire alarm system may not be used to alert building occupants of a tornado or a tornado alert or warning. Facilities need not be constructed or improved for use as a shelter area.[62]

The fire marshal is required to annually inspect each school and enforce compliance with the tornado drill and shelter requirements.[63]

21.14 Safety instruction

Instruction in first aid, safety, and fire prevention is part of the mandatory graded course of study for all schools under the control of boards of education of city, exempted village, and county school districts and cooperative education districts established under RC 3311.521.[64] In grades kindergarten through six, instruction in personal safety and assault prevention is required except the pupil is to be excused upon written request of the parent or guardian.[65]

21.15 Fostering a drug-free environment

Laws at both the federal and state levels take aim at specific aspects of the plagues of illicit drugs and abuse of alcohol in a school setting.

(A) Drug-Free Schools and Communities Act

The federal Drug-Free Schools and Communities Act of 1986,[66] as amended in 1989, requires, as a condition of receiving any form of federal financial assistance, a state or local educational agency to certify it has adopted and implemented a program to prevent the unlawful possession, use, or distribution of illicit drugs and alcohol.[67] State and local educational agencies must develop separate programs targeting students and employees.

The student program must include an age-appropriate, developmentally based education and prevention program for all students served by the state or local educational agency from early childhood through grade twelve.[68] It must address the legal, social, and health consequences of using drugs and alcohol and provide information about effective techniques for resisting

---

[59] 1963 OAG 542.
[60] RC 3313.643.
[61] RC 3737.73(A).
[62] RC 3737.73(B), (C); OAC 1301:7-5-09.
[63] RC 3737.73(C).
[64] RC 3313.60.
[65] RC 3313.60. Mandatory safety programs for pupils who use school buses are treated in Text 22.19,

Instructing younger children in safety; Text 22.20, Emergency plans and drills.
[66] 20 USCA 3171 et seq.
[67] 20 USCA 3224a. Implementing regulations appear in 34 CFR Part 86.
[68] 34 CFR 86.200(a).

peer pressure to use them.[69] The agency must also provide a statement to students that the use of illicit drugs and the unlawful possession and use of alcohol are wrong and harmful.[70]

In both student and employee programs, copies of mandatory standards of conduct (prohibiting, at a minimum, the unlawful possession, use, or distribution of illicit drugs and alcohol by students or employees on school premises or as a part of any school activities) must be given to students, parents, and employees along with a clear statement of disciplinary sanctions for violations, up to and including expulsion (as applied to students) or termination of employment (as applied to employees) and referral for prosecution.[71] Completion of an appropriate rehabilitation program is an acceptable disciplinary sanction.[72] Finally, information regarding drug and alcohol counseling, rehabilitation, and re-entry programs available to students or employees must be distributed.[73] The drug prevention programs must be reviewed on a biennial basis to gauge effectiveness and ensure consistent application of disciplinary sanctions.[74]

Failure to implement a drug prevention program or to consistently enforce disciplinary sanctions subjects a violator to penalties including the repayment of federal financial assistance received and/or termination of future federal assistance.[75] Application for reinstatement of federal assistance may occur no earlier than eighteen months after termination of eligibility.[76]

(B) Drug-Free Workplace Act

The federal Drug-Free Workplace Act of 1988[77] requires contractors and grantees of federal agencies to certify that they will provide drug-free workplaces as a precondition of receiving a contract or grant. The ultimate penalty for noncompliance is debarment or suspension. Federal implementing regulations[78] indicate that all grantees are covered. A "grantee" is defined as "a person who applies for or receives a grant directly from a Federal agency," and "employee" is narrowly defined to include only those "directly engaged in the performance of work" pursuant to the grant.[79] In the required certification, the grantee represents that it will provide a drug-free workplace by (1) publishing a statement notifying employees of the employer's policy and the penalties for violating the policy, (2) establishing a drug-free awareness program, and (3) notifying employees that, as a condition of employment, an employee will tell the employer of any criminal drug conviction occurring in the workplace. This last requirement does not obligate an employee to tattle on a fellow employee, but only to give notice of his own conviction.

(C) Confidentiality requirements for drug counseling programs

Federal law restricts the disclosure and use of patient records maintained in connection with any federally assisted alcohol and drug abuse program.[80] Most school-based programs that counsel students for drug problems are covered, and students who affirmatively contact a school's program and/or participate in the program would appear to be "patients."[81] Thus, disclosure of records (any information relating to a patient) received or acquired by a school's alcohol and drug abuse program is generally prohibited absent written consent.[82] Exceptions, under limited circumstances, are made for the reporting of child abuse pursuant to state law, communications to law enforcement officers, medical emergencies, research activities, and

---

[69] 34 CFR 86.200(a).
[70] 34 CFR 86.200(b).
[71] 34 CFR 86.200(c), (d), (f), (g), 34 CFR 86.201(a), (b), (d), (e).
[72] 34 CFR 86.201(b), 34 CFR 86.200(d).
[73] 34 CFR 86.200(e), 34 CFR 86.201(c).
[74] 34 CFR 86.200(h), 34 CFR 86.201(f).
[75] 34 CFR 86.300, 34 CFR 86.301.
[76] 34 CFR 86.411.
[77] 41 USCA 701 et seq.
[78] Common regulations pertaining to grantees of various federal agencies are published in several parts of the Code of Federal Regulations. Those pertaining to the Department of Education, for example, appear at 34 CFR Part 85.
[79] 34 CFR 85.605.
[80] 42 USCA 290dd-2. Implementing regulations appear at 42 CFR Part 2.
[81] 42 CFR 2.11 defines "patient" as "any individual who has applied for or been given diagnosis or treatment."
[82] 42 CFR 2.13(a). The required elements for written consent, and a sample consent form, appear in 42 CFR 2.31(a).

responses to court orders.[83] Sanctions for violations include fines.[84]

(D) Anabolic steroid warnings in athletic facilities

RC 3313.752 sets forth the terms of a mandatory warning on the deleterious effects of anabolic steroids. The warning notes that the possession, sale, or use of anabolic steroids without a prescription is a crime. The warning must be conspicuously posted in each locker room of a public school building that includes any grade higher than sixth grade.

21.16 Conveyance or possession of deadly weapons or dangerous ordnance on school premises

A person who knowingly conveys or attempts to convey a deadly weapon or dangerous ordnance onto school property or to an activity under the auspices of a board of education of a city, local, exempted village, or joint vocational school district, or who knowingly possesses a deadly weapon or dangerous ordnance under such circumstances, is guilty of a fourth degree felony on a first offense and a third degree felony on any subsequent offense.[85]

---

[83] 42 CFR 2.12(c), 42 CFR 2.51 to 42 CFR 2.67.
[84] 42 USCA 290dd-2(f).
[85] RC 2923.122. The statute expressly does not apply to state or federal officers, agents, or employees, or to law enforcement officers authorized to carry such weapons or ordnance acting within the scope of their duties, or to any security officer employed by the board of education during duty time, or to any other person whose conduct accords with written authorization from the board.

Chapter 22
Transportation of Pupils

22.01 Introduction
22.02 Transportation coordinators and supervisors

PROVIDING TRANSPORTATION
22.03 Transportation of pupils generally
22.04 Transportation of nonresident pupils
22.05 Transportation of special students
22.06 When transportation need not be provided

TRANSPORTATION COSTS
22.07 Financing transportation
22.08 Insurance
22.09 Purchase of school buses

EQUIPMENT STANDARDS
22.10 Duties of department of education and director of public safety
22.11 School bus markings and equipment
22.12 Vehicles transporting preschool children

SCHOOL BUS DRIVERS
22.13 Driver qualifications
22.14 Medical disqualification of school bus drivers
22.15 School bus driver training

OPERATION OF SCHOOL BUSES
22.16 Bus routes, stops and depots
22.17 Driver responsibilities and pupil behavior
22.18 Traffic laws and operation of school buses

PUPIL SAFETY PROGRAMS
22.19 Instructing younger children in safety
22.20 Emergency plans and drills
22.21 Volunteer rider assistance programs

USE OF SCHOOL BUSES
22.22 Routine and nonroutine use of school buses in general
22.23 Leasing school buses for senior citizens and adult education
22.24 Leasing school buses to nonpublic schools

INDEPENDENT CONTRACTORS AND MASS TRANSIT
22.25 Contracts for transportation of pupils
22.26 Safety requirements for mass transit systems

ENFORCEMENT, PENALTIES
22.27 Violation of state rules on pupil transportation, penalties

22.01 Introduction

Provisions for transporting pupils to and from school became necessary with the consolidation of schools into larger districts. Once seen mainly in rural areas, school buses are now commonplace everywhere. Transportation for children who live relatively far from the school to which they are assigned is the predicate to Ohio's free public education and compulsory attendance laws.[1] Parents and guardians may not, however, use distance from school as a reason for evading the compulsory attendance laws.[2]

No person or business entity can transport pupils to or from school on a school bus or contract with a board of education for the transportation of pupils on a school bus without being licensed by the department of public safety.[3]

22.02 Transportation coordinators and supervisors

Coordinators of school transportation must be appointed by the superintendent of public instruction to assure that each pupil is transported to and from school safely and economically using public school collection points, routes, and schedules.[4]

Ohio department of education rules permit a school board to designate a transportation supervisor to arrange and supervise (1) personnel, (2) safety, (3) training, (4) operations, and (5) maintenance.[5] Qualifications for this supervisory position include a satisfactory driving record and work history, a report of the state bureau of criminal investigation, post-high school education or work experience in education, business administration, management or

---

[1] The US Constitution does not require a state to offer transportation service at all, much less offer it for free. Kadrmas v Dickinson Public Schools, 487 US 450, 108 SCt 2481, 101 LEd(2d) 399 (1988). In Ohio, the general assembly has chosen to provide services as detailed in this chapter.

[2] Sommers v Putnam County Bd of Ed, 113 OS 177, 148 NE 682 (1925).

[3] RC 4511.763.

[4] RC 3327.011.

[5] OAC 3301-83-05(C).

transportation, and the ability to work with a wide range of individuals.[6] In smaller school districts, the superintendent or other administrator often functions as the transportation supervisor.

PROVIDING TRANSPORTATION

22.03 Transportation of pupils generally

(A) Pupils in kindergarten through eighth grade

Boards of education of city, exempted village, and local school districts must provide transportation to resident pupils in grades kindergarten through eight who live more than two miles from the school to which they are assigned or the nonpublic school which they attend.[7] The distance between the residence of a pupil and the school must be calculated by the most direct public route.[8] In the case of a pupil attending a nonpublic school, the two-mile limitation is measured from the nonpublic school. In the case of a student attending public school, the distance is measured from the school to which the child is assigned by the board.[9]

A board of education other than the board of a cooperative education school district that operates a preschool program under RC 3313.646 is authorized to provide transportation for participating children. If the board of a cooperative education district operates a preschool program, the boards of the city, exempted village, or local districts with territory in the cooperative education district may provide transportation for children participating in the program.[10]

(B) High school and joint vocational school students

Transportation may be provided for resident pupils in grades nine through twelve to and from the high school to which they are assigned or the nonpublic high school which they attend. In determining the necessity of transportation, availability of facilities and distance to the school must be considered.[11]

A member local school board may provide transportation for its district pupils to and from a joint vocational school. Such transportation may be made available only after considerations of facilities and distance as set forth in RC 3327.01 and standards adopted by the state board of education.[12]

(C) Private and parochial school students

Whatever permissive or optional transportation is provided for students attending public schools must also be provided to students attending nonpublic schools.[13] Thus, a board of education is required to provide transportation for resident students attending nonpublic high schools whenever, in similar circumstances, transportation is provided for resident students attending public vocational high schools.[14] The constitutionality of providing such transportation at public expense to children attending nonpublic schools has been upheld.

Children attending a nonpublic school are entitled to transportation under RC 3327.01 unless their circumstances specifically except them under that section.[15] A local school board must strictly comply with the requirements of RC 3327.01 before making payment in lieu of transportation under that section to children who attend a nonpublic school. The state board of education has adopted internal guidelines governing whether to confirm a local board's decision to pay in lieu of providing transportation. The guidelines also enumerate factors to be considered by the local board in making its decision: (1) time and distance; (2) cost in terms of equipment, maintenance, personnel, and administration; (3) number of pupils; (4) whether similar or equivalent service is provided to public school pupils; (5) the extent to which

---

[6]OAC 3301-83-06(A).
[7]RC 3327.01.
[8]Eisenhut v Morrow, 124 OS 260, 178 NE 12 (1931).
[9]OAG 80-012.
[10]RC 3327.013.
[11]RC 3327.01 See also Russell v Gallia County Local School Bd, 80 App(3d) 797, 610 NE(2d) 1130 (Gallia 1992) (board decision to forego bussing secondary students not to be second-guessed by court absent an abuse of managerial discretion).
[12]OAG 68-103.
[13]OAG 68-156.
[14]OAG 74-040.
[15]Hartley v Berlin-Milan Local School Dist, 69 OS(2d) 415, 433 NE(2d) 171 (1982).

additional service would unavoidably disrupt current schedules; and (6) state board-approved alternatives not reasonably available. The guidelines also specify the procedure to be followed by the board. An appeal from the state board's confirmation of a local board's decision to make payments in lieu of transportation must be lodged against the local board, not the state board since the latter is not a proper party.[16]

A board is not required, however, to transport elementary or high school students to and from a nonpublic school where it would require more than thirty minutes of direct travel time measured from the collection point designated by the coordinator of school transportation.[17] Transportation of nonpublic school students must be provided at times when the nonpublic school is open and the public school is closed.[18]

(D) Payment in lieu of providing transportation

If it is impractical to transport a pupil, the board of education may pay a parent, guardian, or person in charge of a child an amount in lieu of providing transportation. The amount must not exceed the statewide average transportation cost per pupil in the preceding year.[19]

A board determination under RC 3327.01 that transporting a particular pupil is "impractical" is limited to a situation in which transportation generally available cannot practically be provided; it does not include the situation where a board has abandoned busing of all high school pupils because of lack of funds. The necessity of a determination of "impracticality" under RC 3327.02 applies only where the district is required by law to transport the pupils and not where the district has discretion to provide transportation, as in the case of pupils in grades nine through twelve.[20]

If a local board determines transportation of a pupil is impractical, the state board of education must concur.[21] A board wishing to make payment in lieu of transportation has the burden of establishing that transportation is impractical. In *Pushay v Walter*,[22] the Ohio Supreme Court reversed the state board's finding that provision of transportation by a local board was impractical because the local board had failed to substantiate its cost figures.

22.04 Transportation of nonresident pupils

The board of education of any city, exempted village, or local school district may contract with the board of another district for the admission or transportation, or both, of pupils into any school in the other district.[23] Before transportation is provided to a nonresident pupil, that pupil's resident district must consent in writing.[24] If the transporting board fails to receive written consent, a complaint may be filed with the state board against the transporting board. If the state board finds that transportation is being provided without consent, it may withdraw state transportation funds from the offending district.[25]

A board may provide transportation for a nonresident pupil to and from a nonpublic school if the pupil's parent or guardian agrees to pay the board all transportation costs incurred but not reimbursed by the state and the pupil's district of residence does not provide transportation for public

---

[16]Haig v State Bd of Ed, 62 OS(3d) 507, 584 NE(2d) 704 (1992).

[17]RC 3327.01; Geiger v Aurora City School Dist Bd of Ed, No. 1236, 1987 WL 20493 (11th Dist Ct App, Portage, 6-30-83). A constitutional challenge, on equal protection grounds, to application of this part of the statute was emphatically rejected in Novak v Revere Local School Dist, 65 App(3d) 363, 583 NE(2d) 1358 (Summit 1989).

[18]OAG 83-096.

[19]RC 3327.01; Geiger v Aurora City School Dist Bd of Ed, No. 1236, 1987 WL 20493 (11th Dist Ct App, Portage, 6-30-83).

[20]OAG 81-025. See also Novak v Revere Local School Dist, 65 App(3d) 363, 583 NE(2d) 1358 (Summit 1989).

[21]Shafer v Southwest Licking Local School Dist Bd of Ed, No. CA-2896, 1982 WL 5638 (5th Dist Ct App, Licking, 12-28-82).

[22]Pushay v Walter, 18 OS(3d) 315, 18 OBR 361, 481 NE(2d) 575 (1985).

[23]RC 3327.04.

[24]RC 3327.05.

[25]RC 3327.05(A).

school pupils of the same grade as the pupil being transported.[26]

22.05 Transportation of special students

Boards of education of city, exempted village, and local school districts are required to provide transportation to and from school or special education classes for educable mentally retarded children in accordance with standards adopted by the state board of education. Transportation must also be provided for students who because of the nature and severity of the disability are unable to walk to and from school. If a dispute arises as to whether a child is capable of walking, the health commissioner must resolve the dispute.[27]

A board of education may also provide for and pay the cost of transportation of children to and from special schools for persons affected with tuberculosis.[28]

A county mental retardation and developmental disabilities (MR/DD) board is required by RC 5126.03 to provide mentally retarded persons with free transportation to and from facilities operated by the board within the county. An educational service center, however, is not entitled to receive special state reimbursement for transportation costs of educable mentally retarded children of school age to and from facilities operated by the board.[29]

Students in wheelchairs must be transported in accordance with federal guidelines, including the use of wheelchair securement devices while transporting students in forward-facing positions.[30]

22.06 When transportation need not be provided

A board of education is not required to provide transportation under RC 3327.01 to students attending a school for which the state board of education does not prescribe standards pursuant to RC 3301.07(D).[31] Likewise, a board of education need not provide transportation for pupils attending a school not in compliance with state board of education rules.[32]

Pupils may not be transported to any school which discriminates on the grounds of race, color, religion, or national origin.[33]

TRANSPORTATION COSTS

22.07 Financing transportation

(A) Duties of state board of education

The state board of education is directed to approve transportation costs for each local, exempted village, and city school district in which transportation of pupils is considered necessary, in accordance with rules adopted by it and pursuant to a formula established by the board.[34] The number of pupils transported and the total number of miles traveled are among factors to be considered in determining the amount of money to be included for pupil transportation.[35]

(B) Reimbursement of school districts

(1) In general

All districts receiving foundation payments under RC Chapter 3317 are eligible for reimbursement of operating costs for transporting children who attend public or nonpublic schools.[36] A board of education providing fare support on public transportation or payments in lieu of fare support for its pupils, as authorized under RC 3327.01, is also eligible for reimbursement.[37] For purposes of reimbursement by the state board, the language of RC 3327.01, providing for situations in which "it is impractical to transport a pupil by school conveyance," covers situations

---

[26]RC 3327.05(B). This provision expressly does not apply to joint vocational and cooperative education school districts.
[27]RC 3327.01.
[28]RC 3313.55.
[29]OAG 73-014.
[30]49 CFR 571.222. See Text 28.07, Related services for children with disabilities.

[31]OAG 68-058.
[32]OAG 80-012.
[33]RC 3327.01.
[34]RC 3317.024(K); OAC 3301-83-01.
[35]RC 3317.024(K).
[36]OAC 3301-83-01.
[37]RC 3317.024(K); OAC 3301-83-01(E)(3); OAG 72-043.

where transportation is inaccessible to certain pupils.[38]

A joint vocational school district is not eligible under RC 3317.024 for reimbursement of costs incurred in the transportation of educable mentally retarded children to special classes.[39] However, a county board of education is eligible to receive state funding for approved transportation costs for physically or emotionally handicapped pupils and for educable mentally retarded pupils for whom regular school bus transportation is impractical. Educational service centers are also eligible for state school bus purchase subsidies.[40]

(2) Distance requirements

To receive reimbursement, a board must provide transportation to a pupil from a point one-half mile or less from the student's residence. The student's residence must be one mile or more from school.[41]

In districts having all or part of their transportation costs paid by the state, membership records must be kept, showing which pupils are transported to and from school, which pupils being transported live within one mile of the school they attend, and any other information prescribed by the state board.[42]

(C) Subsidies for school bus purchases

State subsidies for the purchase of school buses are provided under rules established by the state board and approved by the controlling board. No payments may be made unless the district can demonstrate that pupils residing more than one mile from the school could not be transported without the additional aid.[43]

Rules adopted under RC 3317.07 allow the department of education to withhold approval of a district's application for state subsidies to purchase new school buses. The department cannot be compelled to submit the district's application to the state controlling board.[44]

22.08 Insurance

A board of education is required to procure liability and property damage insurance covering employees who operate school buses and motor vans.[45] In addition, it may procure accident insurance for children and other authorized passengers transported[46] and for pupils participating in school athletic programs.[47]

A board is authorized to procure liability insurance under RC 3313.201 to protect employees and pupils against liability occasioned by operation of motor vehicles owned or operated by the district in auto mechanics classes.[48] Boards must purchase motor vehicle accident liability insurance on employees operating buses or other school transportation vehicles. Coverage may not be less than $100,000 per person, $300,000 per occurrence, $50,000 property damage, and $3,000 for medical payments.[49]

In addition, boards are required to purchase liability insurance protecting officers and employees from damage to persons or property arising out of the operation of board-owned or -operated vehicles. Insurance must be procured to cover vehicles operated for state board of education approved driver training courses, whether such vehicles are owned or leased by the board or donated to the board.[50] All insurance must be purchased from a company authorized to do business in Ohio and authorized by board resolution setting forth (1) the amount of the insurance, (2) the necessity for the insurance, and (3) the estimated cost. Such liability coverage may be supplemented with collision, medical

---

[38]OAG 72-043.
[39]OAG 72-049.
[40]RC 3317.11(A)(4).
[41]OAC 3301-83-01(G).
[42]RC 3317.031.
[43]RC 3317.07. See OAC 3301-85-01.
[44]State ex rel Dayton Bd of Ed v State Dept of Ed, 67 OS(2d) 126, 423 NE(2d) 174 (1981).

[45]RC 9.83, RC 3327.09.
[46]RC 3327.09.
[47]RC 3315.062.
[48]OAG 81-012.
[49]RC 3327.09.
[50]OAG 72-078.

payments, comprehensive, and uninsured motorist insurance.[51]

22.09 Purchase of school buses

Boards of education may purchase on individual contracts school buses and other equipment used in transporting pupils to and from school and school-related activities. Alternatively, buses may be purchased through a centralized purchasing system established by the department of education. State subsidy payments, however, must be based on the amount of the lowest price available to the boards by either method. All purchases must be made through competitive bidding in accordance with RC 3313.46. All bids must state that the buses, prior to delivery, will comply with safety rules of the department of education and other pertinent provisions of law.[52]

All districts eligible to receive foundation funds under RC Chapter 3317 are eligible to receive state support for the purchase of school buses.[53]

EQUIPMENT STANDARDS

22.10 Duties of department of education and director of public safety

All new school buses purchased must meet or exceed all current federal and Ohio minimum standards relating to school bus construction and design.[54] The department of education, by and with the advice and consent of the director of public safety, must adopt and enforce rules relating to the construction, design, equipment, and operation of all school buses. The rules, set forth in OAC Chapter 3301-87, apply to school buses privately owned and operated under contract with a district as well as those district-owned and district-operated. Reference must be made to the rules in each contract with a district. Every district, its officers and employees, and every person employed under contract by a district are subject to the rules. The department of public safety is also required to adopt and enforce rules relating to the construction, design, equipment, and operation of all school buses not subject to department of education rules.[55] These rules appear in OAC Chapter 4501-5.

22.11 School bus markings and equipment

A "school bus" is defined as a bus owned by a public, private, or governmental agency to carry nine or more persons to or from a school function. "School bus" does not include a municipally owned transit system or common carrier (unless the latter is devoted exclusively to transporting children). Nor does it include a van or bus used by a licensed day-care center or type A family day-care home (as those terms are defined in RC 5104.01) to transport children from the center or home to a school if the vehicle does not contain more than fifteen children at any time.[56] A school bus must be painted the distinctive yellow color known as national bus chrome number two and be marked both in the front and rear with the words "school bus" in black lettering not less than eight inches high and in the rear with the word "stop" in black lettering not less than ten inches high.[57] Every school bus must be equipped with signal lamps mounted as high and as widely spaced as practicable, which must display to the front and to the rear two alternately flashing red lights located at the same level. The lights must be visible at 500 feet in normal sunlight. Alternately flashing amber lights must be located next to the red lights.[58] In addition, all new school buses purchased, leased, or rented after May 6, 1986, must have a seat belt for the operator.[59] RC 4513.241 exempts from certain window-tinting restrictions school buses that are to be sold or operated outside Ohio and certain side and rear windows of school buses used in Ohio to transport handicapped children.

---

[51] RC 3313.201.
[52] RC 3327.08.
[53] See OAC 3301-85-01.
[54] OAC 3301-85-01.
[55] RC 4511.76.
[56] RC 4511.01(F).
[57] RC 4511.77.
[58] RC 4511.771.
[59] RC 4511.772.

Each school bus must be registered with, and inspected annually by, the state highway patrol. After registration, an identifying number is assigned to each vehicle and must appear on the front and rear of the vehicle in letters at least six inches high. The number remains unchanged as long as ownership of the vehicle remains the same.[60] The annual inspection decal issued under RC 4511.761 must also be displayed on the vehicle.

A vehicle registered as a school bus in accordance with RC 4511.764 cannot also be registered as a church bus under RC 4503.07.[61] A school bus to be used exclusively for purposes other than the transportation of children must be painted a different color, and its former markings obliterated.[62] However, the color and markings of a vehicle used as a school bus as well as for other purposes may remain intact as long as the other use is not exclusive. In addition, the flashing lights of a school bus must be made inoperable or covered when the vehicle is not being used as a school bus.[63]

22.12 Vehicles transporting preschool children

Preschool children may not be transported to and from a nursery school, kindergarten, or day-care center in a vehicle owned, leased, or hired by those institutions unless the vehicle is equipped with and is displaying two amber flashing lights mounted on a bar attached to the top of the vehicle, which includes a sign saying "Caution—Children." A vehicle displaying such lights and sign may not be used for any purpose other than the transportation of preschool children.[64]

SCHOOL BUS DRIVERS

22.13 Driver qualifications

(A) In general

A person employed as a school bus driver must first give bond and be certified (by the educational service center in the case of a local school district, or by the district superintendent in the case of a city or exempted village school district) as being at least eighteen years of age, of good moral character, and qualified physically and otherwise for the position. Qualifications include an abstract of the applicant's driving record updated annually, completion of pre-service and in-service training, the ability to handle handicapped pupils, and a report of the state bureau of criminal investigation.[65] Substitute school bus drivers must also be legally qualified and meet all licensing requirements.[66]

In addition, a driver must report in writing convictions of traffic violations and suspensions and revocations of his commercial driver's license with the superintendent or his designee. No driver may drive a school bus after conviction, suspension, or revocation until he files the notice with the appropriate administrator.[67] Failure to comply may be cause for revocation of the driver's certificate, disciplinary action, or termination of employment.[68] Where a driver's certification was revoked after suspension of his driving rights for operating a vehicle while intoxicated, the Ohio Supreme Court refused to order his reinstatement.[69] Failure to comply with RC 3327.10(D) is a minor misdemeanor.[70]

---

[60]RC 4511.764.
[61]OAG 70-158.
[62]RC 4511.762.
[63]OAG 70-158.
[64]RC 4513.182.
[65]RC 3327.10; OAC 3301-83-06, OAC 3301-83-07, OAC 4501-3-03(A), OAC 4501-3-04(A). Relying on RC 3326.10 andRC 3313.20, the Ohio Supreme Court has affirmed that a county school district board of education has broad authority to adopt bus driver certificate policies even if a particular policy deviates from the criteria spelled out in the Ohio Administrative Code for the issuance or revocation of certificates.OAPSE v Stark County Bd of Ed, 63 OS(3d) 300, 587 NE(2d) 293 (1992).

[66]OAC 4501-3-04(B).

[67]RC 3327.10(D).

[68]RC 3327.10(A). See also Mervine v Margaretta Local School Dist Bd of Ed, No. E-89-4, 1989 WL 130872 (6th Dist Ct App, Erie, 11-3-89) (upholding termination for lack of certificate after certification denied for license suspension).

[69]Patton v Springfield Bd of Ed, 40 OS(3d) 14, 531 NE(2d) 310 (1988).

[70]RC 3327.10(E).

Since boards are required to carry liability insurance coverage on all drivers, an insurance company's legitimate refusal to cover a driver may result in termination of the employee.[71]

(B) Drug and alcohol testing

Effective January 1, 1996, all school districts are required under regulations promulgated by the US Department of Transportation pursuant to the Omnibus Transportation Employee Testing Act of 1991 to conduct pre-employment/pre-duty, reasonable suspicion, random, and post-accident alcohol and controlled substances testing of all bus drivers, any other employees required to have a commercial driver's license (CDL), and applicants for driver positions.[72] Pre-employment testing is administered at the time of employment application, while pre-duty testing may be administered at any time up to the performance of the first safety-sensitive task. Districts are not authorized to conduct pre-employment alcohol testing under the regulations.[73] Districts are also required to provide return-to-duty testing, and, in some instances, follow-up testing for drivers who have engaged in conduct prohibited by transportation department rules.[74]

Under the regulations, each covered school district must impose penalties on drivers whose test results confirm prohibited alcohol concentration levels or the presence of a controlled substance; comply with extensive reporting and recordkeeping requirements; adopt an employee alcohol and controlled substances misuse policy; disseminate information on alcohol and controlled substances misuse to drivers; and provide for supervisor training and the referral of drivers who engage in prohibited conduct to substance abuse professionals (SAPs) and counselling and treatment programs.[75]

Alcohol testing must be conducted through the use of an evidential breath testing device or non-evidential alcohol screening device, and must be administered by a breath alcohol technician (BAT) who is properly trained in the use of testing devices.[76] The test location must be sufficiently private to prevent unauthorized persons from seeing or hearing test results.[77] A driver whose blood alcohol concentration is greater than 0.02 must take a second test.[78] If the result of the second test is greater than 0.02 but less than 0.04, the driver is prohibited from driving or performing any other safety-sensitive function for 24 hours.[79] If the result of the second test is 0.04 or greater, the driver may not perform a safety-sensitive function until the driver completes a return-to-duty alcohol test with a result less than 0.02;[80] is given names, addresses, and telephone numbers of resources for evaluating and resolving problems with controlled substance use; and is evaluated by a SAP to determine the need for rehabilitation or follow-up testing. Return-to-duty testing and SAP evaluations are also required for drivers who: (1) use or possess alcohol while performing a safety-sensitive function; (2) perform a safety-sensitive function within four hours after using alcohol; (3) use alcohol within

---

[71] Gaus v Westerville City School Dist, No. 94APE07-980, 1994 WL 694966 (10th Dist Ct App, Franklin, 12-8-94) (insurance company's refusal to cover driver with four violations in less than two years resulted in the legitimate termination of the driver).

[72] 49 CFR 382.103, 49 CFR 382.301 to 49 CFR 382.307. The regulations are issued pursuant to 49 USCA 2717. Districts with fifty or more employees subject to CDL requirements as of March 17, 1994 must start controlled substance testing on January 1, 1995. Pre-duty alcohol testing must start on May 1, 1995. Districts with fewer than fifty CDL employees as of March 17, 1994 must start all testing on January 1, 1996. The Federal Highway Administration has suspended indefinitely pre-employment alcohol testing requirements. 60 Fed Reg 24,765 (May 10, 1995) (to be codified at 49 CFR 382). This suspension complies with a decision by the Fourth Circuit Court of Appeals which vacated the pre-employment alcohol testing requirements since consuming alcohol before applying for a job usually is not illegal. American Trucking Association v FHWA, 51 F(3d) 405 (4th Cir 1995). This suspension only applies to pre-employment alcohol testing and does not affect requirements for controlled substance testing or alcohol testing at other times during employment (such as pre-duty testing). Employers are not barred from administering pre-employment alcohol testing but cannot use federal regulations as justification. 49 CFR 382.115.

[73] 60 Fed Reg 24,765 (May 10, 1995) (to be codified at 49 CFR 382).

[74] 49 CFR 382.309 to 49 CFR 382.311.

[75] 49 CFR 382.401 to 49 CFR 382.605.

[76] 49 CFR 40.51 to 49 CFR 40.53.

[77] 49 CFR 40.57.

[78] 49 CFR 40.51 to 49 CFR 40.53.

[79] 49 CFR 382.505.

[80] 49 CFR 382.201, 49 CFR 382.605.

eight hours following an accident that requires post-accident testing; or (4) refuse to submit to testing.[81]

The regulations require that drivers be tested for five controlled substances: marijuana, cocaine, opiates, amphetamines, and phencyclidine.[82] School districts must use the split sample method of urine testing. This requires the driver to provide at least 45 ml. of urine, which is divided into a primary specimen and a split specimen. If the primary tests positive, the driver has 72 hours (with some exceptions) to request that the laboratory that conducted the first test send the split sample to another laboratory for testing. The result of the second test is controlling. However, action required by the regulations is not stayed pending the result of the second test.[83]

Controlled substances testing must be conducted at properly equipped and staffed testing facilities and laboratories.[84] Precautions must be taken to establish a proper chain of custody[85] and to ensure that specimens are not adulterated or diluted.[86] Aural and visual privacy must be provided to the driver, except where there is reason to believe the driver may alter or substitute the specimen.[87] The regulations list the exclusive grounds for believing a driver may do so.[88]

Drug test results must be reported by the laboratory to a medical review officer (MRO), a licensed physician who reviews and interprets positive test results.[89] Before verifying a positive result to the school district, the MRO must contact the driver confidentially and afford him a chance to discuss the result. The MRO must then examine alternate medical explanations for the result. Only then may the MRO notify the school district of a positive result.[90] The district must then notify the driver of the positive result and the controlled substance for which he tested positive.[91] For pre-employment tests, the district must give notification of results only if the applicant requests it within 60 days of being notified of the disposition of the applicant's employment application.[92]

Any driver whose test is verified positive by the MRO may not perform a safety-sensitive function until the driver completes a return-to-duty test with a verified negative result, is evaluated by a SAP to determine the need for rehabilitation or follow-up testing, and is informed of resources for evaluating and resolving problems with controlled substance use. The same consequences apply to a driver who refuses to take a test or reports for or remains on duty when the driver is using any controlled substance.[93]

22.14 Medical disqualification of school bus drivers

Each driver must undergo an annual physical examination.[94] Medical grounds for disqualification are set forth in state rules.[95] A currently employed driver who is disqualified for medical reasons must be notified by the superintendent within fifteen days following receipt of the report. The driver then has fifteen days to appeal to the superintendent in writing. Upon receipt of the appeal, provision is made for re-examination, to be conducted by a physician other than the one conducting the original examination. The results of the re-examination are final.[96]

---

[81] 49 CFR 382.204 to 49 CFR 382.211, 49 CFR 382.503.
[82] 49 CFR 40.21.
[83] 49 CFR 40.25.
[84] 49 CFR 40.25 (testing facilities); 49 CFR 40.27 to 49 CFR 40.31 (laboratories).
[85] 49 CFR 40.23.
[86] 49 CFR 40.25(f). This regulation prescribes 25 minimum precautions for ensuring the integrity and identity of specimens.
[87] 49 CFR 40.25(e)(1).
[88] 49 CFR 40.25(f).
[89] 49 CFR 40.3, 49 CFR 40.33.
[90] 49 CFR 40.33.
[91] 49 CFR 382.411.
[92] 49 CFR 382.411.

[93] 49 CFR 382.501, 49 CFR 382.605.
[94] RC 3327.10.
[95] OAC 3301-83-07. A coronary condition coupled with high blood pressure may medically disqualify a driver. Miller v Summit County Bd of Ed, No. 16493, 1994 WL 511043 (9th Dist Ct App, Summit, 9-21-94). However, for insulin dependent diabetics (who are generally disqualified), the department of education will grant waivers under certain circumstances spelled out in the regulation.
[96] OAC 3301-83-07. See Miller v Summit County Bd of Ed, No. 16493, 1994 WL 511043 (9th Dist Ct App, Summit, 9-21-94) (second medical examination which found driver unfit based on heart problems and high blood pressure was final).

Any certificate issued to a bus driver may be revoked by the granting authority upon proof that the driver has been guilty of improper conduct, has failed to file all traffic convictions with the county board or superintendent, or has in some manner neglected his duty.[97] When a driver's contract is terminated for improper conduct under RC 3327.10, the driver must be given due process under RC 3319.081 in a school district where civil service laws do not apply[98] and under RC 124.34 in a district where they do apply.[99]

A driver who is disqualified medically under RC 3327.10 is entitled to use accumulated sick leave from the time he fails to pass the required physical examination to the date of disability retirement approval.[100] However, such a driver does not automatically qualify for disability benefits under RC 3309.39.[101]

22.15 School bus driver training

The department of education prescribes minimum bus driver training requirements. Each school district must train one or more persons to be responsible for on-the-bus instruction of beginning drivers. Beginning drivers must complete the program before being assigned to drive a bus with pupils on board. The eight-hour program must consist of conducting the pretrip inspection as outlined in OAC 3301-83-11(B), plus driving techniques.[102] In addition, beginning drivers must complete fifteen hours of classroom instruction on topics detailed in OAC 3301-83-10(A)(2).

Currently employed drivers are to participate in annual workshops of at least four hours on topics generated by a needs assessment and including certain mandated topics.[103] School bus maintenance personnel must be afforded an opportunity to participate in an annual workshop or training seminar with a minimum of two hours of instruction.[104]

OPERATION OF SCHOOL BUSES

22.16 Bus routes, stops and depots

When transportation of pupils is provided, the board must adopt a time and route schedule and put the schedule in force not later than ten days after the beginning of the school term.[105] Included in this plan is the location of all bus stops as determined by the superintendent.[106] Stops must provide for maximum safety, be on the residence side of all four-lane highways, and, if not visible from 500 feet on either side of the stop, a school bus stop ahead sign must be installed.[107]

School authorities must designate all stops. Stops must be limited as far as possible. When children from several homes can meet safely at a single central point, it must be the only stop. Stops must be sufficiently removed from grades or curves to allow good visibility for approaching traffic in both directions. School authorities may plan routes which allow students to be loaded and unloaded on the side of the road on which they reside where practical and advisable.[108]

Boards of education of city, exempted village, or local school districts *may* designate certain places as depots at which to gather children. Depots must be provided with a shelter and be made comfortable during inclement weather.[109] Such boards may also maintain school bus turn-around points.[110]

---

[97]RC 3327.10; OAC 4501-3-03(B). RC 3327.10 has been construed as permitting a board to promulgate standards for certificate revocation more stringent than those specified in the statute. OAPSE v Stark County Bd of Ed, 63 OS(3d) 300, 587 NE(2d) 293 (1992).
[98]Crain v Hamilton County Bd of Ed, No. C-830324, 1984 WL 6732 (1st Dist Ct App, Hamilton, 2-8-84).
[99]Csanyi v Cuyahoga County Commrs, 29 App(3d) 37, 29 OBR 38, 502 NE(2d) 700 (Cuyahoga 1986).
[100]OAG 69-057.
[101]OAG 70-103.

[102]OAC 3301-83-10.
[103]OAC 3301-83-10.
[104]OAC 3301-83-10.
[105]RC 3327.01.
[106]OAC 3301-83-13.
[107]OAC 3301-83-13.
[108]OAC 3301-83-13, OAC 4501-3-05(F) to (H).
[109]RC 3327.03.
[110]RC 3327.12. At the request of such a board, a municipal corporation, township trustees, or county commissioners may maintain turn-around points on, respectively, municipal roads, township roads, or county roads. Also at the request of the board, but

22.17 Driver responsibilities and pupil behavior

(A) Driver's responsibilities generally

A school bus driver must make a daily inspection to determine if the bus is in safe operating condition.[111] State rules specify the items which must be checked and require the reporting of deficient items to the responsible authority. Mechanical defects must be reported in writing.[112]

Every school bus must be equipped with red visual signals meeting the requirements of RC 4511.771, which must be activated by the driver of the bus when, but only when, the bus is stopped or stopping on the highway to receive or discharge school children.[113] Whenever any warning lights fail to operate, the driver must assume the responsibility of assuring safe crossing for pupils to their residence side of the highway.[114] A driver may not activate the red visual signals in designated school bus loading areas if the bus is entirely off the highway.[115]

A driver is required to follow established routes and make stops as designated by the school authority or person in charge of school bus transportation.[116] He must operate the bus on the approved time schedule and wait for pupils if he is running ahead of schedule.[117]

(B) Driver's duty to maintain order

The driver is in charge of the bus and responsible for maintaining order. He may, within the scope of his employment, use and apply such force as is reasonable and necessary.[118] A driver may not inflict corporal punishment upon a student passenger being transported to or from school.[119] He should not exclude a pupil from the bus but must report the unmanageable pupil to the proper authority. Immediate removal of a pupil is authorized when the pupil's presence poses a danger to persons or property or a threat to safe operation of the bus.[120]

(C) Pupil behavior

At bus stops, pupils must wait for the bus away from traffic and are not to threaten life, limb, or property of any individual. When the bus arrives, pupils must go directly to an assigned or available seat.[121] While on the bus, pupils must keep aisles clear, obey the driver, not smoke, eat, or drink, refrain from throwing objects, and keep head and arms in the bus.[122]

As discussed above, pupils who misbehave may be removed. If immediate removal is necessary, a hearing must be held within seventy-two hours. Whether immediate or not, removal is not to exceed ten days.[123]

22.18 Traffic laws and operation of school buses

(A) Responsibilities of driver

A driver must, of course, use care in operating the vehicle and obey all traffic laws.[124] In addition, specific rules apply to operation of school buses. A bus may not be driven backward on school grounds while children are being loaded or unloaded. Passing is prohibited, and buses must depart from a loading area at safe intervals. Before students are loaded or discharged, the bus must be driven to the right side of the roadway and brought to a full stop.[125]

Drivers operating a school bus on a divided highway or a highway with four or more traffic lanes must receive and discharge all children on their residence side of the highway.[126] No driver may proceed until a child who has left the bus has reached a place of safety on his residence

---

only after an investigation by the board has determined that such maintenance is necessary for such use, a municipal corporation, township trustees, or county commissioners may maintain turn-around points on private property; the board may provide the cost of materials for such maintenance.

[111] OAC 3301-83-11, OAC 4501-3-05.
[112] OAC 3301-83-11(B)(2).
[113] RC 4511.75.
[114] OAC 4501-3-05(B).
[115] RC 4511.75.
[116] OAC 4501-3-05.
[117] OAC 3301-83-20(C).
[118] RC 3319.41.
[119] OAG 68-161.
[120] OAC 3301-83-08.
[121] OAC 3301-83-08.
[122] OAC 3301-83-08.
[123] OAC 3301-83-08.
[124] OAC 4501-3-08 to OAC 4501-3-15.
[125] OAC 3301-83-12(D), OAC 4501-3-05(F), OAC 4501-3-06.
[126] RC 4511.75(D).

side of the road.[127] If a bus stops to discharge pupils who must cross a road not in control of a traffic officer or mechanical signal, the pupils must cross the highway ten feet in front of the standing bus.[128] Pupils may not cross the highway until the driver has activated the safety lamps and told them it is safe to cross.[129]

A driver may not operate a bus for more than eight hours in any one day. State rules further recommend that a bus driver's total number of working hours not exceed ten per day.[130]

School buses must be brought to a stop before proceeding over railroad crossings. The driver must listen through an open door and look in both directions before crossing the track. Pupils must remain silent at crossings, and the driver may not proceed until it is safe.[131]

No school bus may be operated in excess of the safe and legal speed limit given existing driving conditions. A bus may not cut in and out of moving traffic.[132] Department of public safety rules require the driver to remain at least 100 feet from the preceding vehicle when driving on school grounds and 400 feet while driving along the highway at normal speed.[133]

(B) Responsibilities of other drivers

The driver of a vehicle, upon meeting or overtaking from either direction any school bus stopped for the purpose of receiving or discharging any school child, must stop at least ten feet from the school bus and may not proceed until the bus resumes motion, or until he is signaled by the bus driver to proceed.[134] A driver of a vehicle approaching a stopped school bus from either direction must stop whether or not the driver has activated the red signals unless the bus is stopped on the opposite roadway of a divided highway.[135]

If a highway is divided into four or more traffic lanes, a driver of a vehicle need not stop for a school bus approaching from the opposite direction. The driver of a vehicle must stop on such a divided highway when overtaking a school bus.[136]

(C) Accident reports

Each school district is required to maintain a "School Bus Driver Accident Report" for each accident resulting in injury or property damage.[137]

PUPIL SAFETY PROGRAMS

22.19 Instructing younger children in safety

All pupils in grades kindergarten through three in city, exempted village, or local school districts who are regularly transported must receive instruction in the following areas within two weeks after the start of school each year: (1) safe walking habits, (2) proper clothing for increased visibility, (3) avoidance of personal risks, (4) procedure for late bus arrival, (5) safe embarking and alighting procedures, (6) safe riding practices, (7) highway crossing procedures, and (8) courtesy and respect for others.[138] Pupils in these grades who are not regularly transported must be given general safety instructions annually. Pupils in grades four through twelve who receive regular transportation should also receive general instructions in safety procedures.[139]

22.20 Emergency plans and drills

All school districts must have an emergency plan for accidents, disability of drivers, school bus failures, and weather emergencies. As part of this plan, districts must annually conduct drills during which buses are evacuated by everyone exiting through the front door, everyone exiting through the rear emergency door, and one-half the

---

[127] RC 4511.75(E).
[128] OAC 4501-3-06(G).
[129] OAC 4501-3-06(G).
[130] OAC 4501-3-04(B)(2).
[131] OAC 3301-83-12(B).
[132] OAC 4501-3-09.
[133] OAC 4501-3-15.
[134] RC 4511.75(A). In the event of a violation, the school bus driver must report the license plate number and a general description of the vehicle and its operator to law enforcement authorities; also, other persons with first-hand knowledge may report such information. RC 4511.751.
[135] OAG 74-106.
[136] RC 4511.75(C).
[137] OAC 3301-83-14(G).
[138] RC 3327.16(B); OAC 3301-83-09(A).
[139] OAC 3301-83-09(C).

passengers exiting through each door.[140] The drills should be conducted on school grounds with the driver remaining with the bus to insure that it does not move. Pupils after evacuating are to remain at least 100 feet from the bus. Evacuation of handicapped pupils may require modification of these procedures.[141]

22.21 Volunteer rider assistance programs

RC 3327.16, which expressly does not apply to joint vocational and cooperative education school districts, authorizes district superintendents to establish volunteer bus rider assistance programs. Adults or responsible older students may ride buses in order to assist younger pupils in embarking, alighting, and crossing streets, and assist the driver in maintaining order and other activities as designated by the superintendent. A corresponding statute permits superintendents of county MR/DD boards to establish such programs.[142] Boards of education are permitted to purchase liability insurance for such assistants.[143]

USE OF SCHOOL BUSES

22.22 Routine and nonroutine use of school buses in general

The main job of school buses is, of course, the regular transportation of students between their homes and school. A variety of other uses is allowed by statute and regulations of the state board of education.[144]

The district superintendent is required to issue a signed trip permit for each nonroutine use of a school bus. The permit must indicate the date, destination, purpose of the trip, name of school district, driver's name, bus registration number, and total miles of trip.[145]

Other approved nonroutine uses of school buses include (1) transportation of pupils in summer recreation programs;[146] (2) transportation of the aged under a contract with a municipal corporation or other agency delivering service to the aged;[147] (3) emergency evacuation drills; (4) civil emergencies declared by the governor; and (5) transportation of employees participating in board-approved in-service. Out-of-state trips are permitted if the total distance does not exceed 240 miles.[148]

Selection of drivers for nonroutine trips should be based on board policy.[149] Often, the selection procedures are established in a collective bargaining agreement covering bus drivers and other nonteaching employees. Pretrip inspections shall be conducted under the procedure outlined in OAC 3301-83-11.[150]

22.23 Leasing school buses for senior citizens and adult education

Boards of education are specifically authorized to lease school buses for transporting senior citizens and groups engaged in adult education activities. The lease agreement may be with a municipal corporation, or a public or nonprofit agency delivering services to the aged. In addition to the use of school buses to transport persons sixty years of age or older, a board may also contract under a similar agreement with any group, organization, or other entity engaged in adult education activity. The cost of the agreements may not exceed the actual cost to the district, including the cost of providing a properly licensed driver, the required liability and property damage insurance, and other direct and indirect

---

[140]OAC 3301-83-15(B).
[141]OAC 3301-83-15(B).
[142]RC 5126.061.
[143]RC 3313.203(A).
[144]OAC 3301-83-16.
[145]OAC 3301-83-16.
[146]RC 755.12 to RC 755.16, RC 3319.59; OAG 67-081.
[147]RC 3327.14.

[148]RC 3327.15. The attorney general has concluded a privately owned school bus that transports children to and from school may also be used for such additional, nonsimultaneous purposes as transporting adults, Christmas trees, or delivering "meals on wheels," provided it is not the board of education that puts the bus to those uses. OAG 91-032.
[149]OAC 3301-83-16.
[150]OAC 3301-83-16.

cost to the district. The charge to the lessee must be specified in the contract.[151]

All state board of education rules governing the use of buses by public schools while transporting pupils to and from school-related activities are to apply to the extent applicable to the transportation of senior citizens and persons engaged in adult education activities. Insurance coverage on each bus and passenger must be obtained.[152]

22.24 Leasing school buses to non-public schools

A board of education is authorized to contract with nonpublic schools located in the district for the use of school buses for transporting nonpublic school pupils to and from a school-related activity, provided the activity would be an approved activity if offered by the district to public school pupils. The cost to the nonpublic school, which must be specified in the contract, may not exceed the actual cost as determined by the board. All state board of education rules governing the use of buses by public schools in transporting pupils to and from school-related activities are applicable to their use by the nonpublic school.[153]

INDEPENDENT CONTRACTORS AND MASS TRANSIT

22.25 Contracts for transportation of pupils

(A) Pre-existing contracts

RC 3327.011, requiring that a board of education "shall give preference if economically feasible" to a pre-existing contract during the contract term to persons or firms providing school transportation, imposes a mandatory duty upon a board to hold a public hearing, to grant notice to the contracting party, and to give it an opportunity to appear and be heard on the question of whether it is economically feasible to continue the contract.[154]

(B) Mandatory provisions, violation

When school buses are privately owned and operated under contract, state school bus transportation rules must be incorporated by reference in the contract. Any officer or employee of any school district who violates any such rule, or who fails to include the obligation to comply with the rule in any contract executed by him on behalf of the district, is guilty of misconduct and subject to removal from office or employment. Any person operating a school bus under contract with a district who fails to comply with any such rule is guilty of breach of contract, and the contract must be canceled by the responsible officers of the district. No person may operate a school bus in violation of the rules of the department of education and department of public safety.[155]

22.26 Safety requirements for mass transit systems

Whenever a mass transit system transports children to or from a school session or school function, it must provide for periodic safety inspection of buses, safety training of drivers, and the equipping of every bus with outside rear-view mirrors.[156] Before a mass transit system transports pupils, it must apply for, in writing, a license from the director of the department of public safety.[157]

ENFORCEMENT, PENALTIES

22.27 Violation of state rules on pupil transportation, penalties

Criminal penalties are provided for the violation of certain rules promulgated by the state board of education and/or the department of public safety.[158] These pen-

---

[151] RC 3327.14.
[152] RC 3327.14.
[153] RC 3327.13.
[154] State ex rel Ruple Bus Service v Wickliffe Bd of Ed, 11 Misc 127, 229 NE(2d) 762 (CP, Lake 1967).
[155] RC 4511.76.

[156] RC 4511.78.
[157] OAC 4501-1-03.
[158] RC 4511.99. A person cited for violating RC 4511.75(A) must appear in person in court to answer the charge. RC 4511.99(G).

alties are in addition to job-related discipline which may be imposed.

Any person who permits the operation of a school bus without displaying the inspection decal issued by the state, uses a school bus for exclusive purposes other than transportation of pupils without painting it another color, fails to register the bus and display its identifying number, or who fails to operate a school bus not properly painted and marked is guilty of a minor misdemeanor on the first offense. A second offense is a misdemeanor of the fourth degree.[159] In addition to these penalties, the trial judge may suspend for up to three years or revoke the license of any person, partnership, association, or corporation engaging in the transportation of pupils.[160]

---

[159] RC 4511.99(C).

[160] RC 4511.99(E).

Chapter 23

Pupils: Tuition and Fees

23.01 Introduction

TUITION
23.02 Admission requirements and tuition liability

ACTIVITY FEES AND FUNDS
23.03 Student activity programs, fees, and funds
23.04 Expenditures from student activity funds
23.05 Failure to pay activity or school fees

NEEDY CHILDREN
23.06 Poverty and compulsory attendance
23.07 Special programs for needy children

23.01 Introduction

Free public education is the foundation of the Ohio school system. But while every child is entitled to an education through high school at public expense, the right is not without qualifications. In general, a child must attend school in the district where he resides; otherwise, tuition must be paid on his behalf. There are, however, significant exceptions.

The right to a free education extends only to the costs of basic education. Fees may be charged for instructional materials other than textbooks and for activities and programs beyond strictly educational programs. A number of programs and services may be provided at reduced costs or free to children financially unable to pay.

The general assembly has struggled mightily with the residency and tuition statutes, regularly enacting amendments as new problems emerge. This constant tinkering has contributed to their complexity.

TUITION

23.02 Admission requirements and tuition liability

(A) Statutory requirements in general

RC 3313.64 (a labyrinthine challenge to even the most sophisticated reader) and related statutes establish the following rules regarding pupil admission and tuition liability.

(1) Admission tuition-free in district where parent resides

The general rule is that a child at least five but under twenty-two years of age must be admitted tuition-free in the "district"[1] where his "parent"[2] resides.[3]

(2) Child in custody of agency or person other than parent

A child who does not reside in the district where his parent resides must be admitted in the district where the child resides if he is in the legal or permanent custody of a government agency or a person other than his natural or adoptive parent,[4] in which case tuition is to be paid to

---

[1] "District" means a city, local, or exempted village school district and excludes any school operated in an institution maintained by the department of youth services. RC 3313.64(A)(3).

[2] "Parent" generally means either parent. If parents are separated or divorced, or if the marriage has been dissolved or annulled, "parent" means the residential parent and legal custodian of the child. RC 3313.672 requires a residential parent to whom an order or decree allocating parental rights and responsibilities for the care of a child and designating a residential parent and legal custodian of the child (including a temporary or modified order or decree) is issued in connection with the breakup of a marriage to furnish a certified copy of the order or decree to the school's admissions officer (upon a pupil's initial entry to school a copy of any already existing order or decree must be furnished). If the child is in the legal or permanent custody of a government agency (defined to include a children services board or county department of human services that has assumed administration of child welfare functions, a certificated organization that assumes custody of children and places children in family homes for adoption, and comparable agencies of other states or countries that have satisfied certain Ohio requirements) or a person other than his natural or adoptive parent, "parent" means the parent with residual parental rights, privileges, and responsibilities. "Legal custody," "permanent custody," and "residual parental rights, privileges, and responsibilities" have the same meanings as in RC 2151.011. RC 3313.64(A)(1), (2). The attorney general has concluded that legal or permanent custody may be established by a court order or by evidence of the transfer of custody without a court order under RC 5103.15 or RC 5103.16. OAG 94-033.

[3] RC 3313.64(B)(1), (C).

[4] The attorney general has opined that one appointed by a probate court as guardian of a minor under RC Chapter 2111 has "legal custody" and the

415

the admitting district by (1) the district where the child's parent resided when the court removed the child from his home or when the court vested custody, whichever occurred first; (2) if the parent's residence when the child was removed or placed in custody is unknown, the district where the child resided when removed or placed in custody, whichever occurred first; or (3) if a district cannot be established under (1) or (2) above, by the district determined pursuant to RC 2151.357 by the court when it vests custody.[5] If no district can be determined under these provisions, the attorney general believes the admitting district must bear the cost of educating the child, although where the child's parents reside outside Ohio, the district may seek reimbursement from an out-of-state source under any contracts or other legal arrangements that may exist.[6] This is patently a tangled and, in some respects, unsatisfactory area of law that gives rise to vexing practical problems.

However, if at the time the court removed the child or vested custody, whichever occurred first, one parent was in a residential or correctional facility or a juvenile residential placement[7] and the other parent, if living and not in such a facility or placement, was not known to reside in Ohio, tuition is to be paid in accordance with rule (3) below.[8]

(3) Child whose parent is institutionalized or imprisoned

A child who does not reside in the district where his parent resides, and for whom a tuition obligation has not been previously established under rule (2) above, must be admitted in the district where the child resides if at least one parent is in a residential or correctional facility or a juvenile residential placement and the other parent, if living and not in such facility or placement, is not known to reside in Ohio, in which case tuition is to be paid to the admitting district as follows:

(1) If the parent is in a juvenile residential placement, by the district in which the parent resided when he became subject to the juvenile court's jurisdiction;

(2) If the parent is in a correctional facility, by the district in which the parent resided when sentence was imposed; or

(3) If the parent is in a residential facility, by the district in which the parent resided when admitted to the facility, unless transferred from another resi-

---

child must be admitted to school in the district where the child resides. (If a guardian has lesser rights that do not constitute legal or permanent custody, the guardianship does not affect the school the child is entitled to attend under RC 3313.64 even if the child resides with the guardian.) Similarly, one granted custody of a child by the domestic relations division of a common pleas court has "legal custody" and the child must be admitted to school in the district where the child resides. OAG 83-041; OAG 94-033; OAG 94-070.

[5]RC 3313.64(B)(2), (C)(2). See also Christman v Washington Court House School Dist, 30 App(3d) 228, 30 OBR 386, 507 NE(2d) 384 (Fayette 1986); OAG 89-092; OAG 89-006. There is no statutory provision addressing tuition when a child's custody changes without a court order and without placement for adoption. The attorney general believes the admitting district must bear the cost of educating the child in such a case, all the while acknowledging that this result may not have been legislatively intended. OAG 94-033. If a child is placed in a detention home established under RC 2151.34 or a juvenile facility established under RC 2151.65, RC 2151.357 requires his school district to pay the cost based on the per capita cost of the educational facility within the home or facility. If the court places a child in a private institu-

tion, school, residential treatment center, or other private facility, the state must pay the court a subsidy (pursuant to the statutory formula, not to exceed $500 per year) to defray the cost.

[6]OAG 94-033.

[7]One is "in a residential facility" if he is a resident or resident patient in a facility licensed as a nursing or rest home, community alternative home for AIDS victims, adult care facility, county or district home maintained by county commissioners, state institution for the mentally ill, institution administered by a community mental health board, facility licensed by the departments of mental health or mental retardation and developmental disabilities, facility operated by the veteran's administration or other federal agency, or the Ohio soldiers' and sailors' home. One is "in a correctional facility" if he is an Ohio resident in prison, in a community-based correctional facility, required to reside in a halfway house or similar institution as a condition of probation or release from imprisonment, or imprisoned in another state's or federal penal or reformatory institution if an Ohio resident when sentence was imposed. One is "in a juvenile residential placement" if he is an Ohio resident under twenty-one who has been removed from his residence by order of a juvenile court. RC 3313.65(A).

[8]RC 3313.64(C)(2)(d).

dential facility, in which case tuition is to be paid by the district in which the parent resided when admitted to the facility from which he was transferred.

In case of disagreement as to which district is liable, the superintendent of public instruction is to determine the issue.[9]

(4) Child who resides in a "home"

A child who does not reside in the district where his parent resides must be admitted in the district where the child resides if he resides in a "home,"[10] in which case tuition is to be paid to the admitting district by (1) the district in which the child's parent resides; or (2) if the parent is not an Ohio resident, by the home.[11]

(5) Child who requires special education

A child who does not reside in the district where his parent resides must be admitted in the district where the child resides if he requires special education, in which case tuition is to be paid in accordance with RC 3323.091, RC 3323.13, RC 3323.14, or RC 3323.141,[12] regardless of who has custody or whether the child resides in a home.[13]

(6) Child who has been placed for adoption

A child not entitled under rules (2) or (4) above to be admitted in the district where he resides and who resides with an Ohio resident with whom he has been placed for adoption[14] must be admitted tuition-free in the district where the child resides unless (1) the placement for adoption has been terminated; or (2) another district is required to admit the child under rule (1) above.[15]

(7) Child participating in particular special education programs

RC 3313.64(H) authorizes a child to attend school or participate in a special education program in a district other than the district where he is entitled to attend under rules (1) through (6) above pursuant to (1) RC 3311.211 (pertaining to attendance in a joint vocational school district of a student who is a resident of a district not part of the joint vocational district under arrangements made between such district board of education and the joint vocational district board); (2) RC 3313.90 (pertaining to vocational education programs provided by a school district); (3) RC 3319.01 (pertaining to a superintendent's assignment of a pupil to a school outside his district of residence with approval by the board of education of the district of residence); and (4) RC 3327.04 and RC 3327.06 (discussed under, respectively, rules (9) and (10) below).

(8) Child in care of shelter for victims of domestic violence

A child with his parent under the care of a shelter for victims of domestic violence (as defined in RC 3113.33) must be admitted tuition-free in the district in which he is with the parent.[16]

(9) Child admitted under interdistrict contract

RC 3327.04 authorizes the board of any city, exempted village, or local school district to contract with the board of another district for the admission of pupils in the other district on such terms as the boards agree upon. RC 3327.06(A) provides that

---

[9]RC 3313.65(B) to (D).

[10]"Home" means a home, institution, family foster home, group home, or other residential facility in Ohio that receives and cares for children and is (or is operated by a person who is, or accepted the child through a placement by a person who is) licensed, certified, or approved for such purpose by the state or maintained by the department of youth services, or that is a children's home under RC 5153.21 et seq. RC 3313.64(A)(4).

[11]RC 3313.64(B)(2), (C)(3). If a home that is liable fails to pay, the admitting district may recover the tuition, its costs of recovery, and attorney's fees in a civil action. RC 3313.64(D). See also RC 3323.141(D).

[12]See Text 23.02(D), Computation and payment.

[13]RC 3313.64(B)(2), (C)(1).

[14]A child is "placed for adoption" if an agency to which the child has been permanently committed or surrendered agrees with a person pursuant to RC 5103.06 for the care and adoption of the child, or the child's natural parent places the child pursuant to RC 5103.16 with a person who will care for and adopt the child. RC 3313.64(A)(6).

[15]RC 3313.64(B)(3), (C).

[16]RC 3313.64(F)(9). If, at the time of initial entry to a school, the child is under the care of a shelter for victims of domestic violence, the pupil or parent must notify the school of that fact and the school, upon being so informed, must inform the elementary or secondary school from which it requests the pupil's records of that fact. RC 3313.672.

in such cases tuition is to be paid in the manner provided in RC 3317.08.[17]

(10) Permissive admissions, tuition required

RC 3327.06(B) and (C) provide that when the board of a city, exempted village, or local school district admits a pupil not entitled to admission tuition-free and for whose attendance tuition is not the obligation of another district board or home, tuition is to be collected from the pupil's parents or guardian and failure to collect the required tuition renders the pupil's attendance "unauthorized."[18] Similarly, RC 3317.08 allows a district board to admit a pupil whose admission is not required "if tuition is paid for the child."

(11) Child admitted under state board criteria

RC 3313.645 allows a board of education to admit tuition-free any district resident not otherwise eligible for admission who meets criteria established by the state board of education, whose rules may restrict or limit the classes or programs in which such persons may participate.

(12) Students from adjacent districts

Students from adjacent districts must be admitted to a district's schools tuition-free if the district board has adopted a policy permitting such enrollment pursuant to RC 3313.98.[19]

(13) Special rule for certain projects or facilities

If a political subdivision owns and operates an airport, a welfare or penal institution, or other project or facility outside its corporate limits and the territory within which the facility is located is exempt from taxation by the school district within which the territory is located, and school age children reside in the territory, the subdivision must pay tuition to the district in which the children attend school.[20]

(14) Permanently excluded pupils

RC 3313.64(K) expressly declares the statute neither requires nor authorizes the admission to any Ohio public school of a pupil permanently excluded from public school attendance by the superintendent of public instruction pursuant to RC 3313.662 and RC 3301.121.[21]

(15) Payment of tuition to non-Ohio schools

The attorney general has stated that school districts are not empowered by RC 3313.64 to pay tuition to schools outside Ohio.[22] However, a juvenile court, in determining pursuant to RC 2151.357 the school district that is to bear the cost of educating a child removed from his home or placed in the legal or permanent custody of a government agency or person other than his parent, may direct tuition payments to an out-of-state school.[23] Likewise, an exception to the general prohibition on paying tuition to non-Ohio schools may arise when a disabled student is placed in an out-of-state special education program. Such tuition payments may be necessary to assure the "free, appropriate public education" mandated by the Individuals with Disabilities Education Act and RC Chapter 3323.[24]

(B) Determining residence

RC 3313.64(J) states that, in the event of a disagreement, the superintendent of public instruction must determine the district in which the pupil's parent resides. No minimum period of residency is required to trigger the right to a free education.[25]

A court has concluded that where divorced parents have joint custody of a child and live in different school districts, the child may attend school tuition-free in

---

[17] See Text 23.02(D), Computation and payment.

[18] RC 3317.03(F) expressly prohibits inclusion of pupils whose attendance is unauthorized under RC 3327.06 in calculating the district's average daily membership for foundation payment purposes and approved classroom units as provided in RC 3317.05.

[19] See Text 5.08(D), Enrollment of students from adjacent districts.

[20] RC 3317.08.

[21] Such permanent exclusions are given expansive treatment in Text 25.10(E), Permanent exclusion for certain offenses.

[22] OAG 65-16.

[23] OAG 89-092. See also OAG 89-006.

[24] See generally Text Ch 28, Education for Children with Disabilities.

[25] In re Laricchiuta, 16 App(2d) 164, 243 NE(2d) 111 (Preble 1968).

either district.[26] Where two houses in different districts were necessary for a particular family to carry out its daily activities, the child was deemed eligible to attend school tuition-free in either district.[27] Indications of district residency include being physically present and living as a householder during significant parts of each day[28] and such activities as eating, sleeping, working, relaxing, playing, eating meals, and receiving mail.[29] An Ohio prison inmate has been deemed a resident of the district in which the prison is located.[30]

With respect to special education programs for children with disabilities operated by a county MR/DD board under RC 3323.09 or by various state departments under RC 3323.091 and school district obligations for tuition or excess costs under RC 3323.13 and RC 3323.14, a child's school district of residence is specifically defined by RC 3323.01(I) as follows:

(1) The district in which the child's "parents"[31] reside; or if not so determined

(2) The last district in which the parents are known to have resided if the parents' whereabouts are unknown; or if not so determined

(3) The district determined by the court under RC 2151.357, or if no district has been so determined, the district as determined by the probate court of the county in which the child resides (the district so established on December 12, 1983, remains the district of residence until a district can be established under (1) or (2) above).

However, if a district is required by RC 3313.65 to pay tuition for a child, that district is the child's district of residence.[32]

(C) Special tuition exemptions and waivers

For several categories of pupils, exemption from tuition liability or the waiver of tuition is either required or authorized.

(1) Child for whom custody proceedings initiated

A board of education may enroll a child tuition-free for not to exceed sixty days upon the sworn statement of an adult district resident that he has initiated legal proceedings for custody of the child.[33]

(2) Emancipated children

A person at least eighteen but under twenty-two years of age who lives apart from his parents, supports himself, and has not successfully completed the high school curriculum or the individualized education program developed for the person under RC 3323.08 must be admitted tuition-free in the district in which he resides.[34]

(3) Married children

Any child under age eighteen who is married must be admitted tuition-free in the district in which the child resides.[35]

(4) Child who may need emergency medical attention

A child with a medical condition that may require emergency medical attention must be admitted tuition-free in the district in which either parent is employed; the parent must submit to the district board a statement from the child's doctor certifying that the child's condition may require emergency attention and supported by such other evidence as the board may require.[36]

---

[26] State ex rel Green v Lyden, No. 84-413 (CP, Logan, 11-21-85).
[27] Oakwood City School Dist Bd of Ed v Dille, 109 App 344, 165 NE(2d) 807 (Montgomery 1959).
[28] Oakwood City School Dist Bd of Ed v Dille, 109 App 344, 165 NE(2d) 807 (Montgomery 1959).
[29] Kenton City Schools Bd of Ed v Day, 30 Misc(2d) 25, 30 OBR 289, 506 NE(2d) 1239 (CP, Hardin 1986); Baucher v Coldwater Exempted Village School Dist Bd of Ed, 31 Misc 49, 277 NE(2d) 92 (CP, Mercer 1971).
[30] OAG 82-106.
[31] For purposes of RC 3323.01(I), "parents" means either parent. If the parents are separated or divorced, "parent" means the parent with legal custody of the handicapped child. "Parent" does not include a child's guardian or custodian. RC 3323.01(H). A grandparent thus is not a "parent" regardless of whether the grandparent is the child's guardian or custodian. OAG 93-023.
[32] RC 3323.01(I)(4).
[33] RC 3313.64(E).
[34] RC 3313.64(F)(1).
[35] RC 3313.64(F)(2).
[36] RC 3313.64(F)(3).

(5) Child whose parent is in military service

A child residing with a person other than his parent must be admitted tuition-free for a period not to exceed twelve months in the district in which that person resides provided the child's parent files an affidavit with the district superintendent stating (1) the fact that he (the parent) is serving outside Ohio in the United States armed forces, (2) his intention to reside in the district upon returning to Ohio, and (3) the name and address of the person with whom the child is living while the parent is outside Ohio.[37]

(6) Child whose parent dies

A child under age twenty-two who, after the death of a parent, resides in a district other than the district in which he attended school at the time of death may continue to attend school tuition-free in the latter district for the rest of the school year, subject to approval of that district board.[38]

(7) Child whose parent is building a new home

A child under age twenty-two who resides with a parent who is having a new house built in a district outside the district where the parent resides must be admitted tuition-free for up to ninety days (as established by the district superintendent) in the district where the house is being built if the parent provides the superintendent (1) a sworn statement explaining the situation, giving the location of the house being built, and stating the parent's intention to reside there upon its completion; and (2) a statement from the builder confirming a house is being built for the parent at the location indicated in the parent's statement.[39]

(8) Child whose parent is purchasing a home

A child under age twenty-two who resides with a parent who has a contract to purchase a house in a district outside the district where the parent resides and is awaiting the financing closing date in connection with the purchase must be admitted tuition-free for up to ninety days (as established by the district superintendent) in the district where the house is being purchased if the parent provides the superintendent (1) a sworn statement explaining the situation, giving the location of the house, and stating the parent's intention to reside there; and (2) a statement from a real estate broker or bank officer confirming that the parent has a purchase contract, is awaiting the closing, and that the house's location is as indicated in the parent's statement.[40]

(9) Child whose parent works in the district

A child whose parent works full-time for a city, exempted village, or local school district may be admitted tuition-free in the district where the parent is employed, provided the district board has established such an admission policy.[41]

(10) High school senior whose parent moves

A child under age twenty-two whose parent moves out of the district after commencement of the child's senior year in high school is entitled, subject to approval of the district board, to attend school tuition-free in the district of attendance at the time of the move for the remainder of the school year and one additional semester or equivalent term. A district board may adopt a policy specifying extenuating circumstances under which a student may attend for an additional period to complete successfully the high school curriculum or

---

[37] RC 3313.64(F)(4).
[38] RC 3313.64(F)(5).
[39] RC 3313.64(F)(6). The student may participate in interscholastic athletics under the auspices of the school to which he is admitted if the board of the district where the parent resides, by formal action, releases him to so participate at the school he is attending and if the student receives any authorization required by a public agency or private organization of which the district is a member exercising authority over interscholastic sports.

[40] RC 3313.64(F)(7). As to participation in interscholastic athletics, the same requirements as apply to a student admitted under RC 3313.64(F)(6) must be satisfied.
[41] RC 3313.64(F)(8), which further provides that any such board policy (or amendment or repeal) must take effect on the first day of the school year, be uniformly applied, and provide for admission of the child upon request of the parent. No child may be admitted under the policy after the first day of classes of any school year.

the individualized education plan developed for the student under RC 3323.08.[42]

(11) Child who resides with grandparent

A child under age twenty-two in the custody of a parent but who resides with a grandparent and who does not require special education may attend school tuition-free in the district where the grandparent resides provided the district board and the board of education of the district where the parent resides agree in advance in writing that good cause exists for such attendance. The agreement must describe such good cause and specify the boards' consent to such attendance.[43]

In lieu of a consent form signed by a parent, the district board may request the grandparent to complete any consent form the district requires, including any emergency medical or prescription drug authorizations required under RC 3313.712 and RC 3313.713. Upon request, the grandparent must complete any consent form required by the district, and the district is expressly shielded from liability because of its receipt of a form from a grandparent in lieu of a parent.[44]

(12) Exchange students

After approving admission, a district board may waive tuition for students who temporarily reside in the district and who are either (1) residents or domiciliaries of another country who request admission as foreign exchange students, or (2) residents or domiciliaries of the United States but not Ohio who request admission as participants in an exchange program operated by a student exchange organization.[45]

(D) Computation and payment

The general formula for computing tuition appears in RC 3317.08. A district's tuition charge for a school year is the quotient obtained by dividing the sum of (1) the district's total taxes charged and payable for current expenses for the preceding tax year, and (2) the district's total taxes collected for current expenses under a school district income tax adopted pursuant to RC 5748.03 that are disbursed to the district during the fiscal year (on or before June 1, the tax commissioner certifies to the department of education the amount to be used for the next fiscal year for each district that levies an income tax) by the district's average daily membership less half the kindergarten average daily membership for the preceding school year. If a child attends for only part of a school year, the district's tuition charge is computed in proportion to the number of school days the child is enrolled in the district during the school year.

Tuition is the sum of the amount computed under RC 3317.08 plus the per pupil amount a district received during the preceding school year under RC 3317.022, RC 3317.023, and RC 3317.025 to RC 3317.028 if it is payable by a "home" pursuant to RC 3313.64(C)(3)(b)[46] or if neither the child nor his parent resides in Ohio and tuition is required by RC 3327.06.[47]

Special statutes in RC Chapter 3323 apply if a disabled child with respect to whom tuition is payable is receiving special education.[48] If a school resident of one district (as determined by RC 3323.01(I))[49] receives special education from another district, the latter may require from the former a sum not to exceed the tuition that would have been payable for a child of normal needs of the same school grade.[50] However, if the per capita cost of such education exceeds the sum of the per capita amount received by the district of attendance under RC 3317.08(A) and the per capita amount received from the state board of education, such excess cost (as determined by using the formula approved by the department of education and agreed upon in contracts entered into by the school boards involved when the child was

---

[42]RC 3313.64.

[43]RC 3313.64(F)(11).

[44]RC 3313.64(F)(11).

[45]RC 3313.64(G).

[46]See Text 23.02(A)(4), Child who resides in a "home."

[47]RC 3317.081.

[48]As for children with disabilities who reside in state developmental centers operated under RC Ch 5123, the attorney general addresses a variety of placement and tuition issues (that defy quick summarization) under these statutes in OAG 91-024 and OAG 91-025.

[49]See Text 23.02(B), Determining residence.

[50]RC 3323.13. For a disabled preschool child not included in a unit under RC 3317.05(E), the tuition is as calculated under RC 3317.08(B).

accepted for enrollment) is added.[51] If a child not in the legal or permanent custody of an Ohio resident or government agency and whose parents are not known to have been Ohio residents after the child's birth resides in a "home" as defined in RC 3313.64 and receives special education from a school district or county MR/DD board, the home is to pay tuition as follows:

(1) If the special education is from a school district, tuition is the district's per capita cost of providing the education, calculated as the sum of the tuition determined under RC 3317.08, the per pupil amount received by the district under RC 3317.024(N) and (O), and such excess cost as is determined by using a formula established by the department of education (which excess cost cannot be used as excess cost computed under RC 3323.14); or

(2) If the special education is from a county MR/DD board, tuition is the board's per capita cost as determined by using a formula established by rule of the department of mental retardation and developmental disabilities.[52]

If a school district places or has placed a child with a county MR/DD board for special education, but another district is legally responsible for tuition and the child is not a resident of the territory being served by the county MR/DD board, the board may charge the responsible district with the educational costs in excess of the per pupil amount received under RC Chapter 3317, such excess cost to be determined by the formula established by the department of education under RC 3323.14.[53] Finally, RC 3323.091 provides that institutions under the jurisdiction of the departments of mental health, mental retardation and developmental disabilities, youth services, rehabilitation and correction, and the board of trustees of the Ohio veterans' children's home shall establish special education programs for children with disabilities and may apply to the department of education for unit funding. Except for the veterans' children's home, by June 30 of each year the superintendent of each institution must submit to the department of education a statement containing the name and district of residence of each child who received special education. The department will then pay to the institution an amount equal to tuition calculated under RC 3317.08(A) and deduct the same from state funds payable under RC 3317.022 and RC 3317.023 to the child's district of residence or, if the amount of such state funds is insufficient, require the district of residence to pay the institution an amount equal to tuition calculated under RC 3317.08(A).[54]

Except where RC 3313.64(I) applies, payment of tuition computed under RC 3317.08 by one school district to another is handled as follows: the treasurer of the district of attendance certifies the tuition to the district board required to pay; if that board refuses to pay or there is disagreement over the amount payable or the district liable for payment, the board of the district of attendance notifies the superintendent of public instruction who is to determine the correct amount and the district required to pay and deduct that amount, if any, under RC 3317.023(G), from the paying district and add it to the amount allocated to the district of attendance.[55]

RC 3313.64(I), which expressly does not apply to students receiving special education, establishes the following payment procedure for tuition due from a school district under RC 3313.64(C)(2) or (3) and RC 3313.65:[56]

(1) A district required to pay such tuition has an amount deducted under

---

[51] RC 3323.14, which further provides that the department of education must certify the amount of RC Chapter 3317 payments for such disabled pupils for such school year ending July 30. RC 3323.14 expressly does not apply to a disabled preschool child except if included in a unit approved under RC 3317.05(E).

[52] RC 3323.141. In both instances, the statute prescribes a special formula for calculating tuition in the case of a disabled preschool child not included in a unit under RC 3317.05(E).

[53] RC 3323.142. This statute expressly does not apply to a disabled preschool child except if included in a unit approved under RC 3317.05(E).

[54] RC 3323.091 prescribes a special formula for calculating the amount in the case of a disabled preschool child not included in a unit under RC 3317.05(E).

[55] RC 3317.08.

[56] That is, tuition due as described in Text 23.02(A)(2) to (4).

RC 3317.023(G) equal to its own tuition rate for the same period of attendance;

(2) A district entitled to receive such tuition has an amount credited under RC 3317.023(G) equal to its own tuition rate for the same period of attendance;

(3) If the tuition rate credited to the district of attendance exceeds the rate deducted from the district required to pay, the department of education pays the difference to the district of attendance; and

(4) Each district treasurer must, by January 15 and July 15, report to the superintendent of public instruction the names of each child who attended district schools under RC 3313.64(C)(2) or (3) and RC 3313.65 during the preceding six months, the duration of the attendance of those children, the district responsible for tuition on the child's behalf, and any other information the superintendent requires.[57]

(E) Special programs

Various statutes address specific questions on tuition in connection with particular programs or persons. For example, RC 3311.211 authorizes a joint vocational school district to charge tuition for pupils who are school residents of districts not part of the joint vocational district under arrangements between the pupil's district board and the joint vocational district board.

RC 3313.645 authorizes admission tuition-free and without regard to age of the following participants in vocational education programs the district operates or participates in pursuant to RC 3313.90 and RC 3313.91:[58]

(1) Any district resident who has successfully completed the individualized education plan developed for that person at any high school pursuant to RC 3323.08; and

(2) Any noncertificated district employee whom the district superintendent authorizes to be admitted to a class or program related to the employee's position in the district.

RC 3313.646 authorizes a district operating a preschool program to charge fees and tuition, which may be graduated in proportion to family income or waived in case of hardship.

RC 3313.647 prohibits charging any fee for enrollment under a district's policy guaranteeing the competency of its high school graduates.[59]

RC 3313.52, RC 3313.531, RC 3313.54, and RC 3313.641 specifically address whether, and under what circumstances, fees and tuition may be charged for special programs (such as summer schools, driver training courses, instruction in basic literacy, and adult high school continuation programs) a district operates under those statutes.[60]

ACTIVITY FEES AND FUNDS

23.03 Student activity programs, fees, and funds

(A) In general

Boards of education may collect special fees from students who participate in extracurricular activities and may spend general revenue funds for student activities included in the school district's program and authorized by the state board of education.[61]

In particular, a board may charge to participate in an extracurricular athletic program. Student fees collected totaling more than $50 per year must be paid into a student activity fund established under RC 3315.062(C).[62]

---

[57]The January 15 and July 15 dates are directory, rather than mandatory, and the superintendent has discretion to accept tuition information after the due date. OAG 87-101.

[58]See Text 27.02, Providing vocational education.

[59]See Text 26.16(B), Guaranteed competency of graduates.

[60]For treatment of the various special programs authorized by these statutes, see Text 26.10, Special instruction, adult education; Text 26.11(E), Americanization schools; Text 26.12 to 26.14.

[61]OAG 82-014.

[62]OAG 82-014; State ex rel Plain Dealer Publishing Co v Lesak, 9 OS(3d) 1, 9 OBR 52, 457 NE(2d) 821 (1984).

(B) Limitation on expenditures

Student activity fund expenditures may not exceed 0.5% of the board's annual operating budget.[63] The amount spent from the general fund under RC 3313.53 for directing, supervising, or coaching student activities should not be included in calculating the amount spent from the general fund to conform to this limitation.[64] A board's retirement contributions associated with the operation of an extracurricular program must be paid from funds allocated under RC Chapter 3317 and not from student activity funds.[65]

(C) State and local policies

The state board of education is required to develop a list of approved student activities. If more than $50 per year is received through a student activity program, it must be paid into an activity fund.[66]

Each board of education must adopt regulations governing the establishment and maintenance of the activity fund, in accordance with the System of Accounting for the Use of Student Activities Programs, as outlined by the state auditor's Circular No. 81-9. The board, under this standardized system of accounting, must verify each transaction and show the source from which the fund revenue was received, the amount collected from each source, and the amount spent for each purpose. Expenditures from each fund are subject to board approval.[67] Student activity funds must be budgeted and appropriated in accordance with the procedures in RC Chapter 5705, including the certification requirements of RC 5705.41(D)(1) and RC 5705.412.[68]

Circular No. 81-9 also prescribes the method to be followed for approving expenditures and sets out guidelines for what would and would not be acceptable expenditures and/or collections. It details how a board may make investments, separate and organize its activity funds, and control its cash flow. Finally, it gives the procedure for auditing student activity funds.

Under RC 117.17, the treasurer may delegate authority to receive custody of the funds initially. However, the treasurer may not authorize an employee to retain custody of the funds for longer than twenty-four hours or to deposit the funds himself.[69]

23.04 Expenditures from student activity funds

(A) In general, authority for expenditures

A board of education's authority in financial matters must be clearly granted by statute. Doubts over the right to spend public funds are resolved against expenditure.[70]

(B) Particular expenditures

A board may purchase accident insurance for pupils participating in athletic programs for which the district is authorized to spend public money. A board may also establish a self-insurance plan to protect pupils in athletic programs from loss resulting from accidental injury or death or for paying a deductible under an insurance policy.[71]

The attorney general has stated a board may spend funds from student activity accounts for meals to nonstudents, provided the expenditure is for a public purpose.[72] Using public funds to pay initiation fees or membership dues for participating in any association, club, society, or professional organization is prohibited.[73]

A board may also use extracurricular athletic fees to pay the supplemental salaries of teachers who work with athletic programs as well as reasonable transportation costs incurred in the programs.[74]

A board can use general fund money to purchase supplies and equipment for the

---

[63] RC 3315.062.
[64] OAG 80-060.
[65] OAG 82-014.
[66] RC 3315.062.
[67] RC 3315.062.
[68] OAG 80-060.
[69] OAG 80-060.
[70] State ex rel Locher v Menning, 95 OS 97, 115 NE 571 (1916); State ex rel Clarke v Cook, 103 OS 465, 134 NE 655 (1921); State ex rel A. Bentley & Sons Co v Pierce, 96 OS 44, 117 NE 6 (1917).
[71] RC 3315.062(D).
[72] OAG 75-008.
[73] RC 9.65.
[74] OAG 82-014.

graded course of study required by RC 3313.60. Equipment for extracurricular activities not a part of the graded course of instruction must be purchased with activity funds.

23.05 Failure to pay activity or school fees

RC 3313.642 authorizes a public school to withhold a student's grades and credits for failure to pay assessed fees for "materials used in a course of instruction" other than textbooks, which must be furnished without charge under RC 3329.06. Emphasizing that free education is the general rule, the Ohio Supreme Court has declared that this statutory exception must be construed narrowly. Thus, the Court struck down a school board's attempt to assess a per pupil fee, enforced by withholding grades and credits, to defray the cost of administrative supplies as opposed to instructional materials.[75] Since fees for extracurricular activities fall outside the statute, its sanctions probably cannot be applied to force their collection. The attorney general has ruled that grades cannot be withheld from students who failed to account for items entrusted to them for extracurricular fund-raising programs, because the activity was not instructional and the items were not intended to become school property.[76]

NEEDY CHILDREN

23.06 Poverty and compulsory attendance

Compulsory school attendance is established by RC 3321.04. Poverty does not excuse nonattendance.[77] It is the responsibility of the parent to ensure that a child attends school.[78]

23.07 Special programs for needy children

(A) Free meals

Boards of education which operate and manage lunchroom facilities may provide free breakfasts and lunches to children they determine are in need. If more than one-third of the district's children are eligible for free meals under federal programs, the board *must* provide such programs.[79] Appropriations may be transferred from the general fund or otherwise to cover the expense.[80] A state subsidy is provided pursuant to RC 3313.81 to assist in providing free lunches to needy children.[81]

(B) Dental care, immunizations

Remedial or corrective dental treatment may be provided children whose parents cannot afford it, but only with written parental consent.[82]

Upon application of a board of education, boards of health, legislative authorities of municipal corporations, and boards of township trustees must provide without delay and at public expense for the immunization of pupils not provided with immunization by their parents.[83] The expense is borne by the particular board of health, municipal corporation, or township involved.[84]

(C) Instructional materials

Boards of education may charge for instructional materials, with the exception of necessary textbooks; however, a board may furnish any such materials free to pupils determined to be in serious financial need.[85]

(D) Disadvantaged pupil programs

The state distributes foundation program funds under RC 3317.01 and RC 3317.023(B) for maintenance by a school district of a program to benefit indigent children receiving Aid to Dependent Children.

---

[75]Association for Defense of Washington Local School Dist v Kiger, 42 OS(3d) 116, 537 NE(2d) 1292 (1989).
[76]OAG 84-027.
[77]Dornette v Allais, 76 App 345, 63 NE(2d) 805 (Hamilton 1945).
[78]RC 3321.03.

[79]RC 3313.813.
[80]RC 3313.81.
[81]RC 3317.024(L).
[82]RC 3313.68.
[83]RC 3313.67, RC 3313.671(B).
[84]1960 OAG 1099.
[85]RC 3313.642.

(E) Preschool programs

The tuition and fees a school district charges for a preschool program may be graduated in proportion to family income or waived in case of hardship.[86]

---

[86]RC 3313.646.

Chapter 24

Care and Protection of Pupils, Offenses Against Minors

24.01 Introduction

DUTIES OF SCHOOL PERSONNEL TOWARD PUPILS

24.02 Teachers and parental duties and authority, in loco parentis
24.03 Duty to exercise due care toward students
24.04 Duty to protect students
24.05 Duty to report suspected child abuse or neglect
24.06 Duty to report crimes
24.07 Notice to board of certain crimes committed by employees

OFFENSES AGAINST MINORS

24.08 Offenses against minors generally
24.09 Endangering children
24.10 Hazing, permitting hazing
24.11 Contributing to the delinquency or unruliness of a minor
24.12 Disseminating matter harmful to juveniles
24.13 Sex offenses in general
24.14 Drug abuse offenses in general
24.15 Alcohol and tobacco offenses involving minors

MISSING CHILDREN

24.16 Missing children informational programs

24.01 Introduction

Teachers and other school employees have various duties toward the children in their charge. These include exercising due care to protect pupils from unreasonable, foreseeable risks, and protecting them from harm inflicted by others. Some duties arise because teachers are considered to stand in the place of a parent for at least some purposes, so that parental duties to some extent also devolve on teachers.

Specific statutes require school employees to report the misconduct or mistreatment of children. School personnel are required to report suspected child abuse or neglect, as well as any felony of which they have knowledge. Additionally, a number of offenses in the criminal code may involve minor victims, and the highlights of these are discussed in this chapter.

DUTIES OF SCHOOL PERSONNEL TOWARD PUPILS

24.02 Teachers and parental duties and authority, in loco parentis

Teachers often are characterized as standing in loco parentis—"in the place of a parent"—toward children in their charge. The doctrine analogizes the parent-child relationship to determine the duties, authority, liability, and immunity of guardians, custodians, and others toward children. In Ohio its application to teachers varies.

(A) Civil law

Prior to the enactment of RC Chapter 2744 in 1985, teachers and other employees were not immune from suits for injuries inflicted upon students. Under RC 2744.03(A)(6), an employee is immune from acts and omissions in the scope of his employment unless he acts maliciously, recklessly, or in bad faith, or liability is expressly imposed by statute. However, the employee's immunity does not affect the liability of the board of education for employee negligence in many cases.[1]

With respect to disciplinary authority, various courts have spoken of teachers as standing in loco parentis.[2]

(B) Criminal law

Teachers do not stand in loco parentis for purposes of at least one and quite possibly both of the two sections in Ohio's criminal code in which the phrase is used. RC 2907.03 defines the offense of sexual battery and among other acts prohibits engaging in sexual conduct with a person who is not the offender's spouse, when "[t]he offender is the other person's natural or adoptive parent, or a stepparent, or guardian, custodian or person in loco parentis." In 1993, the Ohio Supreme Court squarely held that this provision generally does not apply to a school teacher or athletic coach but only to a person who has assumed the

---

[1] RC Ch 2744 receives extended treatment in Text Ch 46, Liability of Schools, Officers, and Employees.

[2] See Text 25.06, Duties of teachers to maintain discipline.

dominant parental role and is relied upon by the child for support.[3] RC 2907.03 has since been amended to specifically make such conduct by a teacher, administrator, coach, or other school authority figure a criminal offense.[4] This conclusion presumably (albeit not automatically) also applies to RC 2919.22, which defines the offense of endangering children and, among other conduct, prohibits a "parent, guardian, custodian, person having custody or control, or person in loco parentis" from creating a substantial risk to the health or safety of a child under eighteen or a handicapped person under twenty-one, by violating a duty of care, protection, or support.[5]

24.03 Duty to exercise due care toward students

Teachers and other school personnel are bound to exercise due care, also referred to as ordinary care, to protect students in their charge from unreasonable risks of harm. This is the same general duty owed by every person to every other person, breach of which constitutes negligence. While school employees ordinarily are immune from suit for their negligent acts and omissions, boards of education may well be liable, and it is, accordingly, important to examine what may constitute employee negligence.[6]

(A) Due care in general

The standard of "due care" or "ordinary care" to be applied in a given situation may be imposed by statute or judicial decision, and in the absence of either is determined by considering the facts and circumstances of each case.[7] In the latter instance, the standard is that degree of care which a reasonably prudent person would exercise under the same or similar circumstances.[8] This comes close to equating due care with the use of common sense to protect others from unreasonable risks.

(B) Shaping due care according to circumstances

Due care is a flexible standard, varying according to the circumstances.[9] Although all circumstances must be taken into account, some may be of particular importance in gauging what constitutes due care in a given setting in the teacher-student relationship. These include the age and relative maturity of a student, the fact that a teacher is in authority over the student, and the degree of danger or risk involved in a particular situation or activity. As to the last factor, for example, a New York school district was not liable when a student athlete suffered a broken neck in a varsity football game since players who voluntarily join in extracurricular interscholastic sports assume the risks to which their roles expose them, and the board and its employees must exercise only reasonable care to protect them from unassumed, concealed, or unreasonably increased risks.[10]

Because the immaturity and inexperience of young people renders them less able to foresee or perceive and avoid danger, the degree of care due them is greater than the care due adults. Accordingly, the more immature and less experienced the child, the greater the degree of care required.[11]

Also, because teachers and other employees represent authority figures, students will be more inclined than adults to do what the teacher directs, even if they are unsure what to do, doubt the teacher's ability, or perceive actual danger. Since the risk is magnified under these circumstances, the degree of required care is increased.

The degree of care also increases with the foreseeable danger; the more hazardous the activity, the greater the care

---

[3]State v Noggle, 67 OS(3d) 31, 615 NE(2d) 1040 (1993) (dismissing criminal charge against teacher and coach who had consensual sexual relationship with his student who was over sixteen years of age).

[4]RC 2907.03(A)(8), (9), as amended by 1994 H 454, eff. 7-19-94.

[5]See also Text 24.09, Endangering children.

[6]For extended treatment of the tort liability of boards of education and the immunity generally available to school employees, see Text 46.01 to 46.07 (analyzing RC Chapter 2744).

[7]Eisenhuth v Moneyhon, 161 OS 367, 119 NE(2d) 440 (1954).

[8]Ward v Barringer, 123 OS 565, 176 NE 217 (1931).

[9]Palace Hotel Co v Medart, 87 OS 130, 100 NE 317 (1912).

[10]Benitez v New York City Bd of Ed, 73 NY(2d) 650, 543 NYS(2d) 29, 541 NE(2d) 29 (1989).

[11]Boaz v Ostrander, 105 App 524, 147 NE(2d) 671 (Cuyahoga 1958).

required.[12] A greater degree of care would be required of, for example, a shop teacher overseeing his students' use of power tools, or a chemistry teacher dealing with dangerous chemicals, than would be required of a study hall monitor.

Although the *degree* of care may vary with circumstances, the requirement of exercising due care or ordinary care does not change.[13]

(C) Foreseeability of risk

A school employee is not bound to protect students from all risks, only unreasonable risks. If a risk is not reasonably foreseeable, there is no liability for failing to perceive and avoid it. For example, school employees are not liable for injuries resulting from fights between students where the fights are not foreseeable.[14] That a first-grade student, on a school playground during recess, would be struck in the eye by a "dirt ball" thrown by a fourth-grade student has been deemed unforeseeable.[15] That a fifth-grade student would be struck in the eye by a piece of metal propelled by a rubber band with which a classmate was playing was also not foreseeable.[16] Nor was it foreseeable that during the school day a student would bring a pit bull terrier on school property where the dog attacked another student,[17] or that three male students released from after-school detention would attack and rape a female student working on a science project after school.[18] That an unknown student would unlatch a restraining rope used to keep spectators from walking on to a basketball court has also been deemed unforeseeable.[19] Similarly, the school and employees were not liable when a student, under the supervision of the principal while awaiting counseling, left the school and was injured while attempting to enter her home. Although the school had a duty to supervise the student, it was not foreseeable that she would leave school, go home, climb on a window sill to enter her locked home, and that the window would fall on her as she was entering.[20]

(D) Violations of duty to exercise due care toward students

Apart from suits based on excessive or improper disciplinary measures,[21] most cases in which teachers, school administrators, or other employees have been found to have breached their duty of due care toward students are based on a failure to instruct the student properly, failure to exercise adequate supervision, or failure to take reasonable safety precautions.

(1) Failure to instruct, or improper instruction

The duty to instruct requires the teacher to explain how a procedure should be performed and what the potential dangers may be. Several cases from outside Ohio illustrate the principle. A chemistry teacher was liable for injuries resulting from an explosion during a dangerous experiment performed by his students, where his instructions consisted merely of handing them a textbook and telling them to follow the directions.[22] Similarly, a shop teacher was liable for injuries after failing to tell students about the hazards of using a power grinder without a guard.[23] Actual demon-

---

[12]Scott v Marshall, 90 App 347, 105 NE(2d) 281 (Clermont 1951), appeal dismissed by 156 OS 270, 101 NE(2d) 906 (1951).

[13]Scott v Marshall, 90 App 347, 105 NE(2d) 281 (Clermont 1951), appeal dismissed by 156 OS 270, 101 NE(2d) 906 (1951).

[14]Schaeffer v Paxton, No. C-890432, 1990 WL 130182 (1st Dist Ct App, Hamilton, 9-12-90); McElroy v Painesville City School Dist Bd of Ed, No. 11-086, 1986 WL 11717 (11th Dist Ct App, Lake, 10-10-86).

[15]Allison v Field Local School Dist, 51 App(3d) 13, 553 NE(2d) 1383 (Portage 1988).

[16]Miller v Howard, No. 89CA004730, 1990 WL 102448 (9th Dist Ct App, Lorain, 7-18-90).

[17]Nottingham v Akron Bd of Ed, 81 App(3d) 319, 610 NE(2d) 1096 (Summit 1992), dismissed, jurisdictional motion overruled by 65 OS(3d) 1416, 598 NE(2d) 1168 (1992).

[18]Williams v Columbus Bd of Ed, 82 App(3d) 18, 610 NE(2d) 1175 (Franklin 1992). See also Seither v Maple Hts Bd of Ed, No. 65798, 1994 WL 24263 (8th Dist Ct App, Cuyahoga, 1-27-94).

[19]Roper v Bristolville (Bristol) Local School Dist, No. 93-T-4933, 1994 WL 197306 (11th Dist Ct App, Trumbull, 5-13-94).

[20]Guhn v Clyde-Green Springs School Dist Bd of Ed, No. S-86-23, 1987 WL 6188 (6th Dist Ct App, Sandusky, 2-6-87).

[21]See Text 25.16, Corporal punishment.

[22]Mastrangelo v West Side Union High School Dist of Mercer County, 2 Cal(2d) 540, 42 P(2d) 634 (1935).

[23]Severson v Beloit, 42 Wis(2d) 559, 167 NW(2d) 258 (1969).

stration by the teacher may be required, and where a gym teacher failed to demonstrate any stunts on the rings, he was liable for injuries to an inadequately trained student.[24] Moreover, the demonstration should illustrate required procedures. Where a shop teacher did not use the safety guard in demonstrating use of a power saw, he was liable for injuries to a student who used the saw without the guard.[25]

(2) Inadequate supervision

Many cases involving inadequate supervision are based on the teacher's absence from the classroom, although a few are based on failure to exercise proper supervision even though present. Not infrequently, claims arise from playground injuries where school employees are supervising a large group of students.

In *Hayes v Westfall Local School Dist Bd of Ed*,[26] a teacher was not liable for an assault by one student on another when the teacher did not observe the assault, because he was answering questions from other students. The court held the teacher did not breach his duty of supervision and that any arguable breach was not the primary cause of the child's injuries. In *Guy v Springfield Local Bd of Ed*,[27] the board was not liable when one student deliberately tripped and injured another while going to the locker room from a baseball field. The class physical education instructor had warned students about horseplay, and his actions were not the cause of the injury. Similarly, in *Waiters v Schowerth*,[28] the court held that neither the teacher, the administrator, nor the board was negligent when a behaviorally handicapped child assaulted a first grade student as she was walking down the hall to the restroom. In *Person v Gum*,[29] a teacher allowed a seven-year-old child to walk home for lunch, and on the way the child was chased into the street by a dog and struck by a car. The teacher was held not liable, on the ground that even if she had been negligent, her negligence was not the cause of the child's injuries. In *Boyer v Jablonski*,[30] an art teacher who was present in the classroom and the school principal were not liable for injuries suffered by a student when another student kicked a stool out from under her. In *Guyten v Rhodes*,[31] a teacher was not liable when, during his absence from a class of "defective and incorrigible youths," a pupil was assaulted by another pupil known to have violent tendencies. The court found the teacher's absence was not the cause of the injury.[32]

On the other hand, in *Black v Dayton City School Dist*,[33] the district was liable for the negligence of a teacher who, contrary to board policy, was not at his classroom door during a change in classes when a scuffle between two students, one of whom was seriously injured, occurred.

The general duty to supervise a student athlete cannot be stretched to require proof that the student has medical insurance as a condition of participating in athletic programs.[34]

(3) Inadequate safety precautions

Predictably, cases of liability for failure to take reasonable safety precautions often arise out of those activities which are potentially more dangerous.

Vocational training classes provide the background for a number of cases, with liability imposed for removal of the safety

---

[24]Armlin v Middleburgh Central School Dist Bd of Ed, 36 AD(2d) 877, 320 NYS(2d) 402 (1971).

[25]Ridge v Boulder Creek Union Junior-Senior High School Dist of Santa Cruz, 60 Cal App(2d) 453, 140 P(2d) 990 (1943).

[26]Hayes v Westfall Local School Dist Bd of Ed, No. 85 CA 30, 1986 WL 9643 (4th Dist Ct App, Pickaway, 8-27-86).

[27]Guy v Springfield Local Bd of Ed, No. 87 CA 118, 1988 WL 59822 (7th Dist Ct App, Mahoning, 6-3-88).

[28]Waiters v Schowerth, Nos. 52490, 52516, 1987 WL 16188 (8th Dist Ct App, Cuyahoga, 8-27-87).

[29]Person v Gum, 7 App(3d) 307, 7 OBR 390, 455 NE(2d) 713 (Cuyahoga 1983).

[30]Boyer v Jablonski, 70 App(2d) 141, 435 NE(2d) 436 (Cuyahoga 1980).

[31]Guyten v Rhodes, 65 App 163, 29 NE(2d) 444 (Hamilton 1940).

[32]See also Perorazio v East Liverpool City School Dist Bd of Ed, No. 86-C-2, 1986 WL 14957 (7th Dist Ct App, Columbiana, 12-30-86).

[33]Black v Dayton City School Dist, No. 12108, 1991 WL 227793 (2d Dist Ct App, Montgomery, 3-25-91).

[34]Limerick v Euclid Bd of Ed, 69 App(3d) 807, 591 NE(2d) 1299 (Cuyahoga 1990).

guard on a table saw,[35] and, in cases from outside Ohio, for failure to provide a safety guard for a press;[36] an improperly secured safety guard on a power jointer-planer;[37] improperly adjusted machinery;[38] and failure to provide a safety rail on scaffolding.[39]

Claims also surface in the context of physical education classes. In an Ohio case, a gym teacher had students jump over an inappropriate obstacle (a wooden bench) without a mat, and a student suffered a serious knee injury.[40] With respect to an injury that occurred during a wrestling practice in which a student was permitted to participate despite a prior injury, a coach was not liable because the injury, a dislocated elbow, was not caused by the coach's knowledge that the student had a prior rib injury.[41]

Although chemistry, shop, and gym teachers may be required to exercise a greater degree of care, school employees must exercise due care toward students in *any* setting.

24.04 Duty to protect students

Apart from the duty to exercise due care,[42] there may be an affirmative duty to protect students from harm by others. RC 2919.22(A) provides in part that no parent, guardian, custodian, person having custody or control, or person in loco parentis shall, by violating a duty of care, protection, or support, create a substantial risk to the health or safety of a child under eighteen or handicapped person under twenty-one. Whether school personnel are included within the proscription, either as persons having custody or control or as persons in loco parentis, is unclear.[43] If they are, the statute may impose a positive duty to protect students from harm—as distinguished from the duty to exercise due care, breach of which is negligence.

24.05 Duty to report suspected child abuse or neglect

(A) In general

A variety of persons whose duties bring them into contact with children are expressly required to report immediately instances of suspected child abuse or neglect, including attorneys; doctors, nurses, and other health care professionals; psychologists and school psychologists, speech pathologists, or audiologists; administrators and employees of public or private child care or children services agencies; teachers, school employees, and school administrators; social workers; and spiritual healers.[44]

The duty to report arises when any such person "knows or suspects" that a child under eighteen or a physically or mentally handicapped person under twenty-one "has suffered or faces a threat of suffering any physical or mental wound, injury, disability, or condition of a nature that reasonably indicates abuse or neglect."[45]

The report of suspected child abuse or neglect must be made immediately by telephone or in person to the children services board, the county department of human services exercising the children services function, or a municipal or county peace officer in the county where the child resides or where the abuse or neglect occurred.[46] The oral report must be followed up with a written report, if requested, to include the names and addresses of the child and his parents or custodian if known; the child's age and the nature and extent of the known or suspected injury, abuse, or neglect or the

---

[35]Bigley v Morrison, No. 88-T-4128, 1991 WL 206640 (11th Dist Ct App, Trumbull, 9-30-91), dismissed, jurisdictional motion overruled by 62 OS(3d) 1506, 583 NE(2d) 1318 (1992).

[36]Lehmann v Los Angeles City Bd of Ed, 154 Cal App(2d) 256, 316 P(2d) 55 (1957).

[37]Duncan v Koustenis, 260 Md 98, 271 A(2d) 547 (1970).

[38]Banks v Seattle King County School Dist No. 1, 195 Wash 321, 80 P(2d) 835 (1938).

[39]Weber v State, 53 NYS(2d) 598 (Ct of Claims 1945).

[40]Baird v Hosmer, 46 OS(2d) 273, 347 NE(2d) 533 (1976).

[41]Brasch v Listerman, No. C-850814, 1986 WL 14937 (1st Dist Ct App, Hamilton, 12-31-86).

[42]See Text 24.03, Duty to exercise due care toward students.

[43]See Text 24.02, Teachers and parental duties and authority, in loco parentis.

[44]RC 2151.421.

[45]RC 2151.421.

[46]RC 2151.421. In addition, OAC 5123:2-17-02 states that any person providing services to an individual with mental retardation or developmental disabilities must report the suspected abuse or neglect to the county board of mental retardation and developmental disabilities.

known or suspected threat of injury, abuse, or neglect; any evidence of previous injury, abuse, or neglect; and any other information which might help establish the cause. Persons required to make the report may also arrange for color photographs to be taken of "areas of trauma visible on a child" and, if medically indicated, for x rays.[47]

Once the report is made, it becomes the duty of the county department of human services or children services board, in cooperation with law enforcement authorities, to institute an investigation within twenty-four hours to determine the circumstances surrounding the injuries, abuse, or neglect, the cause, and the persons responsible.[48] A board of education may adopt a rule requiring an investigator either to obtain parental consent or to permit a school official to be present before interviewing a child on school property in an RC 2151.421 investigation.[49]

Failure to make the report is a fourth degree misdemeanor.[50] Also, the reports are confidential, and permitting or encouraging unauthorized dissemination of the contents is also a fourth degree misdemeanor.[51]

The duty imposed by RC 2151.421 is intended for the protection of individuals rather than for the public in general. In *Curran v Walsh Jesuit High School*, the school was found not liable to a student who alleged he had been assaulted due to a violation of RC 2151.421, where the alleged breach of the school's duty to report involved a different student, even though the same teacher was accused of misconduct.[52] A board of education or school officials may also be held civilly liable for negligence for failing to report under RC 2151.421. The duty to report is intended for the protection of individuals and not the general public, so only the specific child who is reportedly abused or neglected may bring a civil claim against a board of education or school official for breach of the statutory duty in RC 2151.421.[53]

(B) Recognizing child abuse and neglect

Health care professionals, social workers, and law enforcement authorities are better equipped by training and experience than school employees to determine if a child is in fact abused or neglected. The function of school personnel is merely to bring possible abuse or neglect cases to the immediate attention of the proper authorities so that the investigative and judicial machinery can begin as soon as possible.

It is important to remember that the duty to report does not require a school employee to have proof positive, but merely reason to suspect that a child is abused or neglected. In doubtful cases, it is better to err on the side of making a report. RC 2151.421 expressly shields from all civil or criminal liability a school employee who makes such a report or who participates in good faith in a judicial proceeding resulting from the report. However, if it is proved that a report or such participation was not undertaken in good faith, the court will award the prevailing party attorney's fees and costs.

While school personnel do not need to be experts in the field, it is important to be informed on what constitutes abuse and neglect and how to recognize it.[54] Indeed, Ohio law requires each elementary school nurse, teacher, counselor, school psychologist, or administrator, within the first three

---

[47] RC 2151.421.

[48] RC 2151.421. For detailed discussion of the comprehensive investigatory authority of these children services agencies, including express affirmation of their authority to undertake such investigations at public school, see OAG 89-108. For the obligations of a children services agency when a report of excessive corporal punishment of a student is received, see OAG 92-082.

[49] RC 3313.20; OAG 82-029.

[50] RC 2151.99.

[51] RC 2151.421, RC 2151.99. Thus, investigatory reports of alleged child abuse under RC 2151.421 need not be disclosed under the public records law.

State ex rel Renfro v Cuyahoga County Dept of Human Services, 54 OS(3d) 25, 560 NE(2d) 230 (1990). See also Text 44.02, Definition of public records; Text 44.03, Availability of public records.

[52] Curran v Walsh Jesuit High School, 99 App(3d) 696, 651 NE(2d) 1028 (Summit 1995).

[53] See Curran v Walsh Jesuit High School, 99 App(3d) 696, 651 NE(2d) 1028 (Summit 1995). See also Brodie v Summit County Children Services Bd, 51 OS(3d) 112, 554 NE(2d) 1301 (1990).

[54] See Darlene M. Kamine, *Child Abuse, Neglect and Dependency in Ohio* (Columbus, Ohio State Bar Foundation 1982).

years of employment with the district, to complete at least four hours of in-service training for child abuse prevention.[55] Such training is to be developed by the employing board of education in consultation with public or private experts in child abuse prevention or intervention programs.[56]

(C) Definition of child abuse

An abused child is one who (1) is the victim of a sex offense involving sexual activity;[57] (2) is the victim of a violation of the statute prohibiting endangering children;[58] (3) shows evidence of physical or mental injury or death which is nonaccidental (other than lawful corporal punishment), or of injury or death which "is at variance with the history given of it";[59] (4) as a result of acts of his parent, guardian, or custodian suffers physical or mental injury that threatens the child's health or welfare;[60] or (5) is subjected to "out-of-home care child abuse" as defined in RC 2151.011.[61]

School personnel are most likely to obtain knowledge that a minor has been sexually abused from the victim's statements. Allowance should be made for the fact that an abused child may give a confused and inarticulate account of what has happened, but if the account raises a reasonable suspicion of sexual abuse, the incident should be reported under RC 2151.421.

(D) Definition of child neglect

A child is neglected if (1) he is abandoned; (2) he lacks proper parental care because of the faults or habits of his parent, guardian, or custodian; (3) his parent, guardian, or custodian neglects or refuses to provide proper or necessary subsistence, education, medical or surgical care or treatment, or other care necessary to his health, morals, or well being; (4) his parent, guardian, or custodian neglects or refuses to provide special care required by his mental condition; (5) his parent, guardian, or custodian attempts to illegally place him for adoption; (6) he, because of an omission of his parent, guardian, or custodian, suffers physical or mental injury that harms or threatens to harm his health or welfare; or (7) he is subjected to "out-of-home care child neglect" as defined in RC 2151.011.[62]

The type of neglect most likely to come to the attention of school personnel is lack of care generally revealed by visible evidence of poor personal hygiene, malnourishment, infestation with vermin or skin diseases, dirty and poorly cared-for clothing or clothing unsuited to the season, untreated illnesses, or any combination of these. But, a child may be neglected under the statute without the appearance of neglect. School officials were held to have acted properly when they reported parents who failed to cooperate in arranging home instruction for their daughter who suffered from psychological problems.[63] Where a child's mother and her paramour engaged in sexual relations in the child's presence, the child was found to be neglected.[64] Merely having a live-in boyfriend, however, is not sufficient evidence of neglect without a showing of a detrimental impact on the children.[65]

24.06 Duty to report crimes

(A) General duty with respect to felonies

In addition to the specific duty of school personnel to report suspected child abuse or neglect, every person (school personnel included) has a duty to report to law enforcement authorities a felony he knows has been or is being committed. Failure to do so is a fourth degree misdemeanor.[66] A report is not required when it would disclose privileged information, obtained in the relationship of attorney and client, doctor and patient, psychologist (including school psychologist) and client, clergyman and person seeking counseling, or husband and wife. Also, a report is not required if it

---

[55]RC 3319.073.
[56]RC 3319.073.
[57]Sexual activity is defined to include sexual touching as well as vaginal or anal intercourse, cunnilingus, or fellatio. See RC 2907.01.
[58]RC 2919.22. See Text 24.08, Offenses against minors generally.
[59]RC 2151.031(C).
[60]RC 2151.031(D).
[61]RC 2151.031(E).
[62]RC 2151.03(A).
[63]State v Goduto, Nos. WD 86-4, WD 86-5, 1986 WL 11412 (6th Dist Ct App, Wood, 9-30-86).
[64]State v Griffin, 93 App 299, 106 NE(2d) 668 (Champaign 1952).
[65]In re Burrell, 58 OS(2d) 37, 388 NE(2d) 738 (1979).
[66]RC 2921.22.

would tend to incriminate a member of the person's immediate family.[67] Required or not, a disclosure of information under the statute cannot give rise to liability for a breach of privilege or confidence.[68]

Insofar as child abuse or neglect can be a felony, RC 2921.22 and RC 2151.421 overlap. The duty to report under RC 2921.22, however, is imposed on all persons and extends to all felonies, not merely child abuse. This includes a wide range of criminal conduct, including most homicides, serious assaults, kidnapping and abduction, many sex offenses, arson and serious vandalism, robbery, burglary, serious theft offenses, most drug offenses, and many other prohibited acts. School personnel should seek the advice of counsel when in doubt whether particular conduct that has come to their knowledge is a felony.

The attorney general has opined that RC 2921.22 does not require the reporting of acts of delinquency by a juvenile, which include acts that would be felonies if committed by adults.[69]

(B) Principal's duty with respect to certain offenses

RC 3319.45 obligates a principal of any city, local, exempted village, or joint vocational school district public school who, acting in his official or professional capacity, knows or observes a pupil (regardless of the pupil's age) committing a violation listed in RC 3313.662(A)[70] on school property or at any activity held under the auspices of the board of education to report the violation to the district superintendent (or superintendent's designee) within one school day. Within a reasonable period after obtaining knowledge of or observing the violation, the principal may report the violation to a law enforcement officer of the jurisdiction in which the violation occurred or, if the pupil is a juvenile, to either a law enforcement officer of the jurisdiction in which the violation occurred or of the jurisdiction where the pupil resides.[71]

24.07 Notice to board of certain crimes committed by employees

RC 3319.20 requires the prosecutor to notify the state board of education when any employee, other than an employee who is a certificate holder to whom RC 3319.52 applies, is convicted of or pleads guilty to any of the following:

(1) Any felony;[72]

(2) Any offense of violence, which includes a wide variety of assaultive conduct;[73]

(3) Any felony theft offense, which includes a broad range of violations involving some element of larceny or fraud;[74]

(4) Any felony drug abuse offense, which includes a majority of the offenses involving controlled substances;[75]

(5) Corruption of a minor, a sex offense;[76] and

(6) Sexual imposition, also a sex offense.[77]

Any felony is a serious crime. The list of offenses which must be reported includes not only all felonies, but two misdemeanor sex offenses which are obviously considered serious when committed by school personnel. The state board is required to revoke the certificate of any certificated person

---

[67] RC 2921.22(G).

[68] RC 2921.22(H).

[69] OAG 90-099 (concluding that school officials may, but are not required to, call law enforcement agencies to investigate suspected cases of illegal drug or alcohol use on school property, but also concluding that RC 3319.321 prohibits the release, without proper consent on behalf of the student, of information on drug and alcohol use that is personally identifiable information, other than directory information, concerning any student). See also Text 44.14, Access to and release of student records.

[70] These violations are identified in Text 25.10(E), Permanent exclusion for certain offenses.

[71] The Student Records Privacy Act, RC 3319.321, expressly states a principal is not required to obtain the consent of the pupil (or of the pupil's parent, custodian, or guardian) before making a report under RC 3319.45. RC 3319.321(H).

[72] RC 2901.02.

[73] RC 2901.01(I).

[74] RC 2913.01(K).

[75] RC 2925.01(H), (I).

[76] RC 2907.04.

[77] RC 2907.06.

who pleads guilty to any such offense. When the employee does not plead guilty but is found guilty, the state board must suspend the certificate pending appeal or until the time for appeal has expired.[78]

Where an employee is a certificate holder to whom RC 3319.52 applies, the prosecutor's duty to report is governed by that statute.[79]

OFFENSES AGAINST MINORS

24.08 Offenses against minors generally

Any offense may be committed against a minor, insofar as the offense can have a victim and the victim in a given instance is a person under eighteen. Currently, some classes of crimes have a high incidence of juvenile involvement—drug abuse offenses, for example. Also, a number of offenses specifically contemplate a minor victim, either by including age as an element of the crime, or by providing enhanced penalty provisions. The following sections discuss various offenses and classes of offenses which either have a high incidence of juvenile victims or expressly contemplate a minor victim.

School employees are required to report suspected child abuse or neglect, and all persons are required to report any felony of which they have knowledge and are subject to criminal penalties for failure to do so.[80] Thus, except for misdemeanor child abuse or neglect, there is no criminal penalty for failure to report other or lesser offenses. This does not mean, of course, that school personnel cannot or should not report misdemeanors coming to their attention.

24.09 Endangering children

RC 2919.22 prohibits various acts or omissions constituting neglect or abuse of a child under eighteen or a physically or mentally handicapped person under twenty-one. The offense can be either a serious misdemeanor or any of various degrees of felony, depending on the specific violation, the harm caused, and whether the offender has a prior conviction of the offense or any related offense. Also, school employees are required to report suspected violations of the statute.[81] Other parts of Ohio's Criminal Code address the offenses of riot and improperly discharging a firearm at or into a school.

(A) Violating duty of care, protection, or support

A parent, guardian, custodian, person having custody or control, or person in loco parentis is prohibited by RC 2919.22 from creating a substantial risk to the health or safety of a child by violating a duty of care, protection, or support. Whether teachers and other school authority figures are covered is unclear. They conceivably could be regarded under at least some circumstances as having custody or control or as standing in loco parentis, but substantial doubt exists on the question.[82] The statute imposes a positive duty on the persons listed to protect, or at least attempt to protect, their children or the children in their charge from harm.[83]

(B) Physical abuse, improper discipline

RC 2919.22 also prohibits abusing or improperly punishing a child by any person.[84] The statute uses the phrases "abuse the child" and "torture or cruelly abuse the child," which presumably refer only to physical abuse.[85] It also forbids excessive disciplinary measures which create a substantial risk of serious physical harm or unwarranted disciplinary measures which if continued pose a substantial risk of impairment of the victim's mental health or devel-

---

[78]RC 3319.31.
[79]For discussion of RC 3319.52, see Text 8.07, Revocation or suspension of certificate.
[80]See Text 24.05, Duty to report suspected child abuse or neglect; Text 24.06, Duty to report crimes.
[81]See Text 24.05, Duty to report suspected child abuse or neglect.

[82]See Text 24.02, Teachers and parental duties and authority, in loco parentis.
[83]See Text 24.04, Duty to protect students.
[84]RC 2919.22(B)(1) to (4).
[85]RC 2919.22(B)(1), (2).

opment.[86] A teacher or school administrator who unreasonably disciplines a pupil is subject to prosecution under this provision.

(C) Sexually oriented violations

Further, enticing, coercing, encouraging, allowing, employing, or using a child in any obscene, sexually oriented or nudity-oriented performance or matter is prohibited under RC 2919.22(B)(5) unless the material or performance is produced, presented, or disseminated for a bona fide medical, scientific, educational, religious, governmental, judicial, or other proper purpose by any of various professional persons listed in RC 2919.22(D)(1). These prohibitions overlap similar prohibitions in RC Chapter 2907.[87]

(D) Transporting children while under the influence

RC 2919.22(C) makes operating a vehicle while under the influence of alcohol or illicit drugs (in violation of RC 4511.19) when one or more children under eighteen years of age are in the vehicle a third or fourth degree felony, depending upon which circumstances specified in RC 2919.22(E)(5) apply.

(E) Riot

One who with four or more other persons participates in disorderly conduct in violation of RC 2917.11 with a purpose to hinder, impede, or obstruct the orderly process of administration or instruction at an educational institution or to disrupt lawful activities at such an institution is guilty of the criminal offense labeled riot, a first degree misdemeanor.[88]

(F) Improperly discharging firearm at or into school

One who, without privilege to do so, knowingly discharges a firearm at or into a school is guilty of a third degree felony (second degree felony upon a repeated offense) under RC 2923.161.

24.10 Hazing, permitting hazing

RC 2307.44 and RC 2903.31 make hazing a crime and authorize civil actions for hazing. Hazing is defined as doing any act, or coercing another to do any act, in connection with initiation into any student or other organization that causes or creates a substantial risk of mental or physical harm. School administrators, employees, and faculty members are specifically prohibited from permitting hazing.

Civil suits may be brought against schools, school administrators, and employees who reasonably should have known about hazing and made no reasonable attempts to prevent it. A school may defend against such a suit on the basis that it was actively enforcing a policy against hazing at the time the injury occurred.

24.11 Contributing to the delinquency or unruliness of a minor

RC 2919.24 prohibits aiding, abetting, inducing, causing, encouraging, or contributing to a child's becoming delinquent or unruly, or acting in a way tending to cause a child to become delinquent or unruly. The offense is a first degree misdemeanor, and each day of continuing violation constitutes a separate offense. The statute, which overlaps Ohio's compulsory education law to some extent, imposes strict criminal liability, and its violation may be prosecuted independently of any violation of or prosecution under the compulsory education law.[89]

A child is delinquent if he commits any act which, if committed by an adult, would be an offense (other than a traffic offense) under any federal or state law or municipal ordinance of the state, or if he violates an order of the juvenile court issued under RC

---

[86]RC 2919.22(B)(3), (4). Punishment and corporal punishment are discussed in more detail in Text 25.08 to 25.15.

[87]RC 2907.321 to RC 2907.323.

[88]RC 2917.03.

[89]State v Wood, 63 App(3d) 855, 580 NE(2d) 484 (Lucas 1989), appeal dismissed by 48 OS(3d) 704, 549 NE(2d) 1190 (1990), cert denied 497 US 1028, 110 SCt 3279, 111 LEd(2d) 788 (1990). For treatment of compulsory attendance law, see also Text 20.02 to 20.09.

Chapter 2151.[90] A child is unruly if he is habitually wayward or disobedient toward his parents, teachers, guardian, or custodian; is habitually truant from school; conducts himself so as to injure or endanger the health or morals of himself or others; attempts to marry without proper consent; is found in a "disreputable place"; visits or patronizes any place prohibited by law (a brothel, for instance) or associates with "vagrant, vicious, criminal, notorious, or immoral persons"; engages in an occupation prohibited to children; is in a situation which is physically dangerous or injurious to the health or morals of himself or others; or violates a law applicable only to juveniles, e.g., RC 2907.33(B).[91]

Patently, contributing to the delinquency or unruliness of a child covers a broad range of conduct. Some typical violations include aiding or causing a child to commit a crime,[92] liquor violations involving a child,[93] or contributing to the immorality of a child.[94]

It is not necessary that the child actually become delinquent or unruly, or be adjudicated a delinquent or unruly child, in order to sustain a successful prosecution of an adult.[95]

24.12 Disseminating matter harmful to juveniles

RC 2907.31 prohibits any person from recklessly disseminating or providing—or offering or agreeing to disseminate or provide—any material or performance which is obscene or harmful to juveniles, when such person has knowledge of its character or content. The statute also prohibits any person from recklessly allowing a juvenile to review or peruse any material or view any live performance that is harmful to juveniles, when such person has knowledge of its character or content. Any material or performance is considered harmful to juveniles if it is offensive to prevailing standards in the adult community with respect to what is suitable for juveniles and if it meets any one of seven criteria:

(1) Tends to appeal to the prurient interest of juveniles;

(2) Contains a display, description, or representation of various kinds of sexual activity or nudity;

(3) Contains bestiality, extreme or bizarre violence, cruelty, or brutality;

(4) Contains a display, description, or representation of human bodily functions of elimination;

(5) Makes repeated use of foul language;

(6) Contains lurid detail of violent physical torture, dismemberment, destruction, or death of a human being; or

(7) Describes criminal activity in a way that tends to glorify or glamorize the activity and has a dominant tendency to corrupt.[96]

An affirmative defense to a charge under the section is provided if the parent furnished the material or performance or consented to it being performed.[97]

The offense is a first degree misdemeanor if the material or performance is harmful to juveniles except as otherwise provided in RC 2907.31. If the material or performance is obscene, the offense is a fifth degree felony; if the juvenile is under thirteen, the offense is a fourth degree felony.[98]

24.13 Sex offenses in general

RC 2907.03 was amended in 1994 to specifically include within the offense of sexual battery, a third degree felony, sexual conduct between a teacher, administrator,

---

[90]RC 2151.02.
[91]RC 2151.022.
[92]State v Clark, 92 App 382, 110 NE(2d) 433 (Huron 1952).
[93]State v Zaras, 81 App 152, 78 NE(2d) 74 (Hancock 1947).
[94]State ex rel Meng v Todaro, 161 OS 348, 119 NE(2d) 281 (1954).
[95]State ex rel Meng v Todaro, 161 OS 348, 119 NE(2d) 281 (1954).

[96]RC 2907.01(E).
[97]RC 2907.31(B)(1), (2).
[98]RC 2907.31(D). See RC 2907.01(E) and (F) for definitions of "harmful to juveniles" and "obscene." With respect to possible application of RC 2907.31 to school textbooks and library books, see Text 33.04, Discretion of board in choosing books, constitutional limitations.

coach, or other person in authority employed by or serving in a school and a student enrolled in or attending the school. This prohibition does not apply if the student is married to the offender or if the student is not a minor and the offender is also a student enrolled in or attending the school.

A number of sex offenses include elements as to the age of the victim or have enhanced penalty provisions when the victim is a child.

The punishment for rape by force of a child under thirteen is life in prison.[99] The offense of corruption of a minor[100] is defined as sexual conduct with a child age thirteen to fifteen by a person eighteen or older. If the offender is less than four years older than the victim, the offense is a first degree misdemeanor, but if the offender is four or more years older, the offense becomes a fourth degree felony. Sexual contact with a child under thirteen is gross sexual imposition, a third degree felony,[101] while sexual contact with a child thirteen to fifteen by an adult four or more years older than the victim is sexual imposition, a third degree misdemeanor; a repeat offender is guilty of a misdemeanor of the first degree.[102] Soliciting sex with a child is importuning, a first degree misdemeanor if the child is under thirteen, and a fourth degree misdemeanor if the child is thirteen to fifteen and the offender is an adult four or more years older than the victim.[103]

So-called "child pornography" includes materials or performances in which a child is depicted or employed, and which are obscene, sexually oriented, or nudity-oriented. Various acts involving such materials, labeled collectively as pandering, are prohibited under RC 2907.321 to RC 2907.323. Pandering obscene, sexually oriented or nudity-oriented matter involving a minor generally is a second degree felony. Mere possession of child pornography is a fourth degree felony on a first offense and a third degree felony on subsequent offenses.[104] These offenses overlap portions of the statute on endangering children.[105]

24.14 Drug abuse offenses in general

Drug trafficking and abuse with or among children is a serious problem, and one drug offense involving minor victims is among the most serious crimes in the criminal code. Corrupting another with drugs is defined in part as furnishing or administering a drug of abuse to a juvenile, causing a juvenile to use a drug of abuse, or causing a juvenile to commit a felony drug abuse offense, when the offender is two or more years older than the victim and the offender either knows or is recklessly disregardful of the juvenile's age; the definition also includes using a juvenile, whether or not the offender knows the juvenile's age, to perform surveillance activity intended to prevent the detection of felony drug abuse or the arrest of one for a felony drug abuse offense.[106] The penalty varies according to the drug involved and ranges from a fourth degree felony to a first degree felony, with a mandatory minimum term of imprisonment in each case. If the offense is committed on school premises, in a school building, or within 1,000 feet of the boundaries of any school premises (as those terms are defined in RC 2925.01), the offense is more serious and carries a stiffer penalty as prescribed in the statute.[107]

Similarly, the penalties for certain drug trafficking offenses under RC 2925.03, for permitting drug abuse in violation of RC 2925.13, and for illegally dispensing drug samples in violation of RC 2925.36 are enhanced if the offense is committed on school premises, in a school building, or within 1,000 feet of the boundaries of any school premises, or if the offense is committed within 100 feet of a juvenile or within the view of a juvenile (whether or not the offender knows the age or location

---

[99]RC 2907.02.
[100]RC 2907.04.
[101]RC 2907.05.
[102]RC 2907.06.
[103]RC 2907.07.
[104]The US Supreme Court has upheld the constitutionality of this prohibition. Osborne v Ohio, 495 US 103, 110 SCt 1691, 109 LEd(2d) 98 (1990).

[105]RC 2919.22(B)(5), (6). See Text 24.09, Endangering children.
[106]RC 2925.02.
[107]The federal "schoolyard" statute pertaining to drug crimes within 1,000 feet of a school is found in 21 USCA 860.

of the juvenile or the juvenile actually views the offense). Such enhanced penalties have survived constitutional challenges on due process and equal protection grounds.[108]

Selling drug paraphernalia to a juvenile is a misdemeanor of the first degree.[109] The practice known colloquially as "glue sniffing" (which includes inhaling a number of harmful intoxicants defined in the statute) is a form of drug abuse usually committed by young juveniles.[110] Harmful intoxicants include substances which have common, legitimate uses, so that their sale or distribution is not prohibited per se, although it is an offense to dispense or distribute a harmful intoxicant to a minor without the parent's written order, when the offender knows or has reason to believe the minor intends to use it as a substance of abuse. Violation is a fourth degree misdemeanor.[111]

24.15 Alcohol and tobacco offenses involving minors

(A) Alcohol offenses

No beer or intoxicating liquor (which includes wine as well as hard liquor) may be sold to, or handled by, a person under twenty-one, except that an employee, eighteen years or older, of a permit holder may handle beer or intoxicating liquor in sealed containers in connection with wholesale or retail sales, delivery, or storage.[112] Any person nineteen years of age or older employed by a permit holder may handle intoxicating liquor when acting as a waiter or waitress.[113] However, no one under twenty-one can sell intoxicating liquor across the bar.[114] No "low-alcohol" beverage (as defined in RC 4301.01) may be sold to a person under eighteen.[115]

A person under twenty-one is prohibited from purchasing intoxicating liquor or beer.[116] No person under twenty-one shall order, pay for, share the cost of, or attempt to purchase or consume beer or liquor in a public or private place.[117] No person may sell beer or intoxicating liquor to an underage person or furnish an underage person with beer or intoxicating liquor except a doctor in the course of his practice, or a parent or legal guardian. No minor shall consume or possess alcohol in a public or private place unless provided by a parent, spouse (who is not an underage person), guardian, or doctor.[118] No person who is the owner or occupant of any public or private place shall knowingly allow an underage person to remain and consume beer or liquor unless permission is given by that person's parent, spouse (who is not an underage person), or guardian present at the time.[119] In addition, no person shall engage or use a hotel, inn, cabin, campground, or restaurant for underage alcohol use or drug use.[120]

It is also forbidden to knowingly give false information as to the name, age, or identification of an underage person, whether the information is given by another for the purpose of obtaining beer or intoxicating liquor for such person,[121] or is given by the underage person to obtain it for himself or another.[122] A permit holder is absolved of liability for selling alcohol to an underage person if in good faith he asks for and is shown apparently valid credentials (such as a driver's license) identifying the person as being of proper age and the

---

[108]See State v Ward, 92 App(3d) 631, 637 NE(2d) 16 (Hamilton 1993); State v Harris, 89 App(3d) 147, 623 NE(2d) 1240 (Cuyahoga 1993); State v Altick, 82 App(3d) 240, 611 NE(2d) 863 (Montgomery 1992).
[109]RC 2925.14.
[110]RC 2925.31.
[111]RC 2925.32.
[112]RC 4301.22.
[113]RC 4301.22.
[114]RC 4301.22.
[115]RC 4301.22.
[116]RC 4301.63.
[117]RC 4301.632.
[118]RC 4301.69.

[119]RC 4301.69. With respect to "low-alcohol" beverages, RC 4301.631 imposes as to persons under eighteen restrictions similar to those appearing in the above statutes.
[120]RC 4301.69. In the case of alcohol use, the statute excepts a person who is present at the time of consumption and who is either the spouse of the underage person (and not himself an underage person) or the parent or legal guardian of all the underage persons who consume alcohol on the premises.
[121]RC 4301.633.
[122]RC 4301.634. With respect to "low-alcohol" beverages, RC 4301.631 imposes similar restrictions as to persons under eighteen.

permit holder has reason to believe the person is of age.[123]

All permit premises must prominently display a sign giving warning with respect to age requirements in the liquor laws.

(B) Tobacco offenses

RC 3313.751 prohibits smoking and the use or possession of tobacco or tobacco products by students in any areas under control of the school district or in any activity sponsored by the district. Boards of education are directed to adopt policies to enforce the prohibition and establish disciplinary measures. RC 2927.02 provides that a person engaged in manufacturing, producing, distributing, or selling (at wholesale or retail) may not sell or distribute tobacco products to a person under eighteen years of age. In addition, persons dealing in tobacco products must prominently display a sign stating that selling, giving, or distributing tobacco products to a person under eighteen is forbidden. The statute also regulates the sale of cigarettes and other tobacco products by vending machine. Violation is a fourth degree misdemeanor on a first offense and a third degree misdemeanor on subsequent offenses.[124]

MISSING CHILDREN

24.16 Missing children informational programs

Each board of education is required to develop informational programs regarding missing children. Boards may request copies of the informational materials acquired or prepared by the missing children clearinghouse under RC 109.65 and may request clearinghouse assistance in developing school district programs.[125] Upon a board's request, the missing child educational program established under RC 109.65(E) is specifically required to provide a reasonable number of copies of the information it acquires or prepares under RC 109.65(C)(3) and to provide certain specified assistance in the development of a school district's informational programs regarding missing children.

Within twenty-four hours of a pupil's entry into school, a school official must request the pupil's official records from the public or nonpublic elementary or secondary school the pupil most recently attended. If that school claims to have no record of the pupil's attendance or the records are not received within fourteen days, or if no birth certificate (or alternative document as authorized in RC 3313.672) is presented, the principal or chief administrative officer of the school must notify the law enforcement agency with jurisdiction over the area where the pupil resides of that fact and of the possibility that the pupil may be a missing child as defined in RC 2901.30.[126]

If a board of education is notified by school personnel that a missing child is attending school, it must immediately give notice of that fact to the law enforcement agency with jurisdiction over the area where the missing child resides.[127]

(A) Fingerprinting

Boards may also develop a fingerprinting program for students and minors in the district. If a board elects to establish a fingerprinting program, it must be developed in conjunction with law enforcement agencies having jurisdiction within the district. The programs must be developed solely to locate or identify missing children. No student or minor can be required to participate. A student's participation must be authorized by the parent, guardian, custodian, or other person responsible for the student on a form prescribed for that purpose. Fingerprint cards must be given to the parent, custodial parent, guardian, legal custodian, or other responsible person and cannot be retained by the district or law enforcement agency.[128]

(B) Photographs

Principals or chief administrative officers of each public school are required to ask the school photographer to provide one free wallet-sized photograph of each

---

[123]RC 4301.639.

[124]For discussion of the Pro-Children Act of 1994, part of the federal Goals 2000: Educate America Act, and its prohibition of indoor smoking, see Text 38.14, Bans on indoor smoking.

[125]RC 3313.96(B).

[126]RC 3313.672. See also Text 20.02, Compulsory school attendance.

[127]RC 109.65(D).

[128]RC 3313.96(C).

pupil for inclusion in the student's file. The school official is to indicate the purpose is that the school will have a current photograph to show law enforcement officials if the child is determined to be missing. The photographer need not comply; but school authorities can make providing the photographs a condition to the taking of student photographs.[129]

---

[129] RC 3319.22.

Chapter 25

Conduct and Discipline of Pupils

25.01 Introduction

STANDARDS OF CONDUCT
25.02 Statutory standards for student conduct
25.03 Policy on student conduct
25.04 Dress and appearance codes
25.05 Regulating student expression

DUTY TO MAINTAIN DISCIPLINE
25.06 Duties of teachers to maintain discipline
25.07 Duties of nonteaching employees to maintain order

DISCIPLINARY MEASURES
25.08 Serious disciplinary measures
25.09 Due process requirements for serious disciplinary measures
25.10 Suspension and expulsion
25.11 Emergency removal
25.12 Review of suspension or expulsion by board, appeal to common pleas court
25.13 Disciplinary transfers
25.14 Checklist for suspension, expulsion, or removal
25.15 Removal from extracurricular activities
25.16 Corporal punishment

25.01 Introduction

Students are required to obey reasonable school rules, and teachers and administrators are bound to enforce them. A range of disciplinary measures is available to school authorities to enforce acceptable pupil behavior. Routine measures may be imposed without notice or hearing, but more serious measures such as suspension or expulsion require that due process be accorded the student and his parents.

STANDARDS OF CONDUCT

25.02 Statutory standards for student conduct

No statute specifies a student's duties. However, several indirect statutory references make it clear that students are required to obey their teachers and school administrators and conform their conduct to acceptable norms. The key statute is RC 2151.022, which defines an unruly child as, among other things, a child who fails to submit to the reasonable control of his parents, teachers, guardian, or custodian; is habitually truant from school; or conducts himself so as to injure or endanger the health or morals of himself or another. Also, RC 3313.20 gives a board of education broad powers to adopt regulations necessary for the "government" of the schools and pupils. Implicit is the duty of students to obey the rules, and the power of the board to enforce them. Further, under RC 3319.16, one of the causes for which a teacher may be fired is "gross inefficiency," which has been defined as including the failure to maintain order and discipline.[1] The duty of students to behave is implicit here as well.

25.03 Policy on student conduct

(A) Requirement for policy, scope

Every board of education is required to adopt a policy covering procedures for suspension, expulsion, emergency removal, and permanent exclusion that specifies the types of conduct for which a student may be suspended, expelled, or removed and the acts listed in RC 3313.662[2] for which a student may be permanently excluded.[3] No student may be suspended, expelled, or removed except in accordance with the policy, and no student may be permanently excluded except in accordance with RC 3313.662 and RC 3301.121. A copy of the policy must be posted in a central location in each school and made available to pupils

---

[1] See Text 9.21(A), Gross inefficiency.
[2] These acts are identified in Text 25.10(E), Permanent exclusion for certain offenses.
[3] For discussion of the federal Gun-Free Schools Act of 1994 and its requirement that a school district, as a condition of receiving assistance under the Goals 2000: Educate America Act, have in effect a policy requiring the expulsion for not less than one year of any student who brings a weapon to school and discussion of the general assembly's amendments to the student discipline statutes in response to that law, see Text 25.10(A), Authority to suspend or expel student.

upon request.[4] The school library qualifies as a central location.[5]

A board may cover other areas in its policy. The reasonableness and constitutionality of the rules are subject to judicial review. All rules must bear a reasonable relationship to a valid educational purpose and not unlawfully infringe on students' constitutional rights.[6] A school regulation prohibiting students from attending parties where alcohol is served has survived a constitutional challenge,[7] as has a rule that prohibited students from "loitering" at an entrance area adjacent to a school.[8]

Pursuant to RC 3313.20, a board may adopt rules providing for the administration of breathalyzer tests to students suspected of having consumed alcoholic beverages.[9]

(B) Interpretation and application

Boards of education and school officials have considerable latitude to interpret their policies on student conduct. A board's reasonable interpretation of its own rules is controlling unless that interpretation is so extreme as to be a violation of due process.

Thus, courts generally refrain from substituting their own notions in the construction of school rules.[10]

A school board's determination that selling illicit drugs is a more serious offense, warranting a harsher disciplinary penalty, than merely possessing or using drugs is a reasonable exercise of managerial judgment.[11]

An expulsion under a policy provision that assessed demerits for certain acts of misconduct with an accumulation of demerits constituting grounds for expulsion has been upheld.[12] Similarly, courts are reluctant to involve themselves in decisions concerning academic grading procedures.[13]

25.04 Dress and appearance codes

RC 3315.07(B) expressly authorizes any board of education to adopt, among other things, student "dress codes." School dress and grooming codes have been upheld where the regulation bears a reasonable relationship to a valid educational purpose, such as maintenance of discipline or protection of the health and safety of pupils.[14]

---

[4]RC 3313.661. Any policy adopted under the statute with regard to suspensions or expulsions applies to any student, whether or not enrolled in the district, attending or otherwise participating in any curricular program provided in a school operated by the board of education or provided on any other property owned or controlled by the board. RC 3313.661(D).

[5]See Starcher v Danbury Bd of Ed, No. CA OT-84-7, 1984 WL 7885 (6th Dist Ct App, Ottawa, 5-18-84).

[6]Gfell v Rickelman, 441 F(2d) 444 (6th Cir Ohio 1971); Jackson v Dorrier, 424 F(2d) 213 (6th Cir Tenn 1970), cert denied 400 US 850, 91 SCt 55, 27 LEd(2d) 88 (1970).

[7]Bush v Dassel-Cokato Bd of Ed, 745 FSupp 562 (D Minn 1990).

[8]Wiemerslage v Maine Twp High School Dist 207, 29 F(3d) 1149 (7th Cir Ill 1994).

[9]OAG 83-012.

[10]In re Appeal of Suspension of Huffer from Circleville High School, 47 OS(3d) 12, 546 NE(2d) 1308 (1989). See also Rohrbaugh v Elida Local Bd of Ed, 63 App(3d) 685, 579 NE(2d) 782 (Allen 1990); Kiser v Clear Fork Valley Local School Bd, No. CA-2782, 1991 WL 12806 (5th Dist Ct App, Richland, 1-25-91); Reed v Vermilion Local School Dist, 83 App(3d) 323, 614 NE(2d) 1101 (Erie 1992); Hardesty v River View Local School Dist Bd of Ed, 63 Misc(2d) 145, 620 NE(2d) 272 (CP, Coshocton 1993) (overturning students' suspensions, however, for violation of RC 121.22).

[11]Morgan v Girard City School Dist Bd of Ed, 90 App(3d) 627, 630 NE(2d) 71 (Trumbull 1993).

[12]Trautman v Waterloo Local Bd of Ed, No. 81-CV-1069 (CP, Portage, 1-5-82).

[13]Johnson v Cuyahoga County Community College, 29 Misc(2d) 33, 29 OBR 371, 489 NE(2d) 1088 (CP, Cuyahoga 1985) (student must show arbitrariness, capriciousness, or bad faith in grading procedure).

[14]Gfell v Rickelman, 441 F(2d) 444 (6th Cir Ohio 1971); Jackson v Dorrier, 424 F(2d) 213 (6th Cir Tenn 1970), cert denied 400 US 850, 91 SCt 55, 27 LEd(2d) 88 (1970). See also Pyle v South Hadley School Comm, 861 FSupp 157 (D Mass 1994) (holding that district may restrict vulgar expression on T-shirts, but that dress code provision prohibiting apparel that "harasses" was unconstitutional content-based restriction). But see McIntire v Bethel School, Independent School Dist No. 3, 804 FSupp 1415 (WD Okla 1992) (enjoining superintendent from applying dress code prohibition against wearing clothing that advertises alcoholic beverages to students wearing shirts with slogan alleged to be parody of liquor ad since district failed to prove slogan in fact advertised alcoholic beverages). In Jeglin v San Jacinto Unified School Dist, 827 FSupp 1459 (CD Cal 1993), a school policy that prohibited students from wearing clothing that identified any professional sports team or college was upheld as to high school students (where the school board successfully demonstrated the disruptive effect of such clothing) but rejected as to elementary and

One court upheld a dress code as reasonably related to the valid purpose of teaching community values.[15]

Despite rulings of the US Court of Appeals for the Sixth Circuit supporting regulation of hair length, some Ohio courts have held that such school policies unnecessarily interfere with a matter of personal preference and unlawfully discriminate against boys.[16] Other Ohio courts have upheld hair and dress codes.[17] Where hair length is based on a sincerely held religious belief, it is more likely to receive constitutional protection.[18]

25.05 Regulating student expression

The US Supreme Court has upheld the suspension of a student for giving an offensively lewd speech at a school assembly. Such speech, said the Court, has no claim to First Amendment protection. Moreover, the school rule prohibiting obscene and profane speech was neither unconstitutionally vague nor overbroad: disciplinary rules need not be as detailed as a criminal code and the rule here adequately warned the student that his speech could subject him to sanctions.[19]

The Supreme Court subsequently furnished additional guidance on how the First Amendment applies to students in a school setting in *Hazelwood School Dist v Kuhlmeier*,[20] ruling that educators may control the style and content of school-sponsored publications, theatrical productions, and other expressive activities, so long as their actions are reasonably related to legitimate pedagogical concerns. Student speech that is not consistent with the school's educational mission can be censored. Although students do not "shed their constitutional rights to freedom of speech or expression at the schoolhouse gate," their rights "are not automatically co-extensive with the rights of adults in other settings."[21] The Court distinguished *Tinker v Des Moines Independent Community School Dist*,[22] which afforded constitutional protection to personal expression (namely, the wearing of black armbands in protest of the Vietnam war) on school premises that did not significantly interfere with the work of the school or impinge on the rights of others.

While *Hazelwood* involved a student newspaper that was part of a particular course being taught as part of the curriculum, its language suggests that any school-sponsored publication is covered by its rationale. Nevertheless, one court has explicitly refused to extend *Hazelwood* to an extracurricular school-sponsored student newspaper for which students received no formal classroom instruction or academic credit, although it had a faculty advisor.[23]

---

middle school students as an unconstitutional deprivation of their First Amendment rights.

[15]Harper v Edgewood Bd of Ed, 655 FSupp 1353 (SD Ohio 1987) (no violation of First Amendment when students attending prom in clothes of opposite sex asked to leave).

[16]Jacobs v Benedict, 39 App(2d) 141, 316 NE(2d) 898 (Hamilton 1973); Warren v Perry Local School Dist Bd of Ed, 41 Misc 87, 322 NE(2d) 697 (CP, Lake 1974).

[17]Royer v C.R. Coblentz Local School Dist Bd of Ed, 51 App(2d) 17, 365 NE(2d) 889 (Preble 1977); Laucher v Simpson, 28 App(2d) 195, 276 NE(2d) 261 (Knox 1971).

[18]Alabama and Coushatta Tribes of Texas v Trustees of Big Sandy Independent School Dist, 817 FSupp 1319 (ED Tex 1993), remanded without opinion by 20 F(3d) 469 (5th Cir Tex 1994) (regulation of male Indian students' hair length unconstitutional).

[19]Bethel School Dist No. 403 v Fraser, 478 US 675, 106 SCt 3159, 92 LEd(2d) 549 (1986). See also Broussard v Norfolk School Bd, 801 FSupp 1526 (ED Va 1992) (upholding suspension of middle school student for wearing shirt printed with the words "Drugs Suck"). On the other hand, a suspension was found violative of a student's free speech rights in Lovell v Poway Unified School Dist, 847 FSupp 780 (SD Cal 1994) where the student, frustrated over efforts to change her class schedule, allegedly threatened to shoot a guidance counselor. The court found the student's statement was not a serious expression of intent to harm in light of all the circumstances and not, therefore, really a threat.

[20]Hazelwood School Dist v Kuhlmeier, 484 US 260, 108 SCt 562, 98 LEd(2d) 592 (1988).

[21]Hazelwood School Dist v Kuhlmeier, 484 US 260, at 266, 108 SCt 562, 98 LEd(2d) 592 (1988), quoting Tinker v Des Moines Independent Community School Dist, 393 US 503, 506, 89 SCt 733, 21 LEd(2d) 731 (1969) and Bethel School Dist No. 403 v Fraser, 478 US 675, 106 SCt 3159, 92 LEd(2d) 549 (1986).

[22]Tinker v Des Moines Independent Community School Dist, 393 US 503, 89 SCt 733, 21 LEd(2d) 731 (1969).

[23]Romano v Harrington, 725 FSupp 687 (ED NY 1989).

A federal appeals court has upheld the right of a school district to demand prior review of a student-authored underground paper, and to govern distribution under its policy controlling distribution of unofficial written materials on school premises.[24] Subsequent to *Hazelwood*, another court found a policy that required high school students to submit for approval all student-written materials before their distribution on school premises or at school functions to be unconstitutionally overbroad.[25] The court stressed the policy applied even to non-school-sponsored publications.

Emphasizing that a school-sponsored newspaper, a yearbook, and athletic event programs are nonpublic forums, a federal appeals court found that a school district reasonably refused to run advertisements from Planned Parenthood since they would be controversial and distract from the district's educational mission.[26]

The US Court of Appeals for the Sixth Circuit has extended *Hazelwood* to justify the disqualification of a candidate for student council president who made discourteous and rude remarks about an assistant principal during a campaign speech at a school-sponsored assembly. "Civility is a legitimate pedagogical concern," declared the court.[27] Another court concluded that the failure of teachers to approve a student's candidacy for student council president, under school regulations that required such approval, related to valid pedagogical concerns and was not in retaliation for the student's outspoken views on issues.[28]

The scope of students' rights to religious expression is a fertile area of litigation. The US Court of Appeals for the Sixth Circuit has held that teachers have broad discretion to limit free speech rights to focus class discussion and work on the assignment in question. The court affirmed the dismissal of a First Amendment claim brought by a student who received a zero grade for a research paper entitled "The Life of Jesus Christ."[29] In a case decided on free speech grounds and finding the First Amendment's prohibition of the establishment of religion inapplicable, a federal district court upheld the right of high school students to distribute to other students a free nonstudent newspaper that promoted Christian principles. The school district policy banning "[m]aterial that proselytizes a particular religion or political belief" was deemed unconstitutional on its face.[30] On the other hand, distribution of such material can be reasonably regulated as to time, place, and manner.[31]

Relying on *Hazelwood*, a federal district court in Pennsylvania found that a principal's decision to preclude a teacher's distribution of a student's survey soliciting other students' views of God as part of an independent study project, and the teacher's decision to have the student orally report on the project only before the teacher and not in the classroom, related to valid pedagogical concerns and were reasonable.[32] Similarly, prohibiting a second grader from

---

[24]Bystrom v Fridley High School, 822 F(2d) 747 (8th Cir Minn 1987).

[25]Burch v Barker, 861 F(2d) 1149 (9th Cir Wash 1988).

[26]Planned Parenthood of Southern Nevada, Inc v Clark County School Dist, 941 F(2d) 817 (9th Cir Nev 1991).

[27]Poling v Murphy, 872 F(2d) 757 (6th Cir Tenn 1989), cert denied 493 US 1021, 110 SCt 723, 107 LEd(2d) 742 (1990).

[28]Bull v Dardanelle Public School Dist No. 15, 745 FSupp 1455 (ED Ark 1990).

[29]Settle v Dickson County School Bd, 53 F(3d) 152 (6th Cir Tenn 1995).

[30]Rivera v East Otero School Dist R-1, 721 FSupp 1189 (D Colo 1989). See also Slotterback v Interboro School Dist, 766 FSupp 280 (ED Pa 1991) (finding similar school policy unconstitutional and discussing First Amendment's prohibition of establishment of religion); Clark v Dallas Independent School Dist, 806 FSupp 116 (ND Tex 1992) (prohibiting nondisruptive distribution of religious tracts by students on school property unconstitutional, but oral proselytizing and religious meetings at such times might be regulated if substantially disruptive of school operations); Bacon v Bradley-Bourbonnais High School Dist No. 307, 707 FSupp 1005 (CD Ill 1989) (decided not on religion clauses of the First Amendment but on free speech and equal protection grounds, and holding unconstitutional school policy prohibiting distribution of Gideon Bibles on public sidewalk in front of high school); Text 32.06, Establishment problems from the use of public schools for religious purposes.

[31]Hemry v School Bd of Colorado Springs School Dist No. 11, 760 FSupp 856 (D Colo 1991); Nelson v Moline School Dist No. 40, 725 FSupp 965 (CD Ill 1989).

[32]Duran v Nitsche, 780 FSupp 1048 (ED Pa 1991), appeal dismissed, order vacated by 972 F(2d) 1331 (3d Cir Pa 1992).

showing a video of herself singing a proselytizing religious song as part of a show-and-tell was related to a valid pedagogical concern and reasonable.[33] In general, as the Department of Education recognized in its guidelines on religious expression in schools issued in 1995,[34] courts tend to require schools to allow students to express their personal religious views or beliefs as they would be allowed to express non-religious views and beliefs, but leave schools the discretion to impose rules of order and other pedagogical restrictions on student activities in general.

It is otherwise difficult to discern clear general rules from the many cases in the area of student expression. One federal appeals court, in a case involving the discipline of students who supported striking teachers by wearing buttons to school that included the word "scab" in reference to replacement teachers and who refused to remove the buttons when ordered to do so, attempting to articulate a synthesis in this difficult area, has discerned three "distinct areas of student speech" governed by three standards: (1) vulgar, lewd, obscene, or offensive speech, which may be suppressed even if it does not occur during a school-sponsored event or threaten to be substantially disruptive; (2) school-sponsored speech (such as school newspapers or yearbooks) that might reasonably be seen as bearing the imprimatur of the school, in which case school authorities are entitled to greater control and the school can disassociate itself from an entire range of speech (speech, for example, that is ungrammatical, poorly written, ineptly researched, or unsuitable for immature audiences); and (3) speech that is neither lewd or offensive nor bearing the school's imprimatur, in which case the school board must show a reasonable threat of substantial disruption as a precondition to suppression. Finding the meaning of the buttons fell into the third category, and rejecting the notion that the conduct was inherently disruptive, the court remanded the case to a lower court for a determination of whether school authorities could show a reasonable threat of substantial disruption.[35]

The regulation of expression on school-controlled property is often evaluated under the forum analysis articulated by the US Supreme Court in *Perry Ed Assn v Perry Local Educators' Assn*[36] and *Cornelius v NAACP Legal Defense Fund*.[37] If the property constitutes a traditional or designated public forum, speakers can be excluded on the basis of the subject matter of their speech only when "necessary to serve a compelling state interest and the exclusion is narrowly drawn to achieve that interest."[38] If, however, the property is not a public forum, a school district can control access "based on subject matter and speaker identity so long as the distinctions drawn are reasonable in light of the purpose served by the forum and are viewpoint neutral."[39]

A Pennsylvania school district's requirement that students complete a prescribed number of hours of community service as a condition of graduation did not violate either the First Amendment's guarantee of

---

[33]DeNooyer v Livonia Public Schools, 799 FSupp 744 (ED Mich 1992), affirmed without opinion sub nom DeNooyer v Merinelli, 12 F(3d) 211 (6th Cir Mich 1993), cert denied ___ US ___, 114 SCt 1540, 128 LEd(2d) 193 (1994).

[34]Letter from Secretary of Education Richard W. Riley to superintendents, August 10, 1995.

[35]Chandler v McMinnville School Dist, 978 F(2d) 524 (9th Cir Ore 1992).

[36]Perry Ed Assn v Perry Local Educators' Assn, 460 US 37, 105 SCt 948, 74 LEd(2d) 794 (1983).

[37]Cornelius v NAACP Legal Defense and Educational Fund, Inc, 473 US 788, 105 SCt 3439, 87 LEd(2d) 567 (1985).

[38]Cornelius v NAACP Legal Defense and Educational Fund, Inc, 473 US 788, 800, 105 SCt 3439, 87 LEd(2d) 567 (1985). A traditional public forum (such as a street or park) is a public space long used for purposes of discussing public questions. A public forum by designation differs in that the government has acted to open what would otherwise be a nonpublic forum to public use, the government is not obligated to retain the open character of the forum indefinitely, and the forum may be designated for only limited uses or a limited class of speakers.

[39]Cornelius v NAACP Legal Defense and Educational Fund, Inc, 473 US 788, at 806, 105 SCt 3439, 87 LEd(2d) 567 (1985). See also, e.g., Student Coalition for Peace v Lower Merion School Dist Bd of School Directors, 776 F(2d) 431 (3d Cir Pa 1985) (upholding school board's refusal to permit student organizations to use athletic field, a nonpublic forum, for public antinuclear and peace exhibition); Brody v Spang, 957 F(2d) 1108 (3d Cir Pa 1992) (remanding to lower court for determination of whether high school graduation ceremony a designated public forum or a nonpublic forum).

free speech or the Thirteenth Amendment's guarantee against involuntary servitude.[40]

This is a difficult area where the courts often draw subtle distinctions that do not always seem consistent. The need for care and competent counsel cannot be overstated.

DUTY TO MAINTAIN DISCIPLINE

25.06 Duties of teachers to maintain discipline

The scope of a teacher's authority and responsibility with respect to pupils is not precisely defined by statute or case law. Although it has never ruled on the question directly, the Ohio Supreme Court has apparently subscribed to a limited view of the doctrine of in loco parentis.[41] The teacher stands in the parents' place in his relationship to a pupil and has such portion of the powers of the parent as are necessary to carry out his or her employment, including authority to maintain discipline.[42] Indeed, a teacher not only has the authority but also the duty to maintain order in the classroom.[43] The US Court of Appeals for the Sixth Circuit has held the teacher stands in loco parentis on field trips outside of school hours.[44] Persistent failure to maintain discipline constitutes gross inefficiency and grounds for termination.[45]

It has long been recognized that a teacher performs his or her duties under the control and direction of the board of education.[46] Boards are required to adopt rules necessary for the government of employees and pupils.[47] Teachers who persistently disobey the rules may be discharged.[48]

25.07 Duties of nonteaching employees to maintain order

In general, the role of nonteaching employees in maintaining discipline is secondary. School bus drivers are specifically required to take charge and maintain order on the bus,[49] but they may not eject or exclude an obstreperous pupil. Rather, they must report the student to the school authorities. Immediate removal of the student from transportation is authorized only if his presence poses a threat to persons or property or the safe operation of the bus.[50]

Nonteaching school employees, including bus drivers, may, within the scope of their employment, use and apply such force and restraint as is reasonable and necessary for self-defense or for protection of persons or property, to quell a disturbance threatening injury to others, or to confiscate weapons or other dangerous objects.[51]

DISCIPLINARY MEASURES

25.08 Serious disciplinary measures

Serious disciplinary measures require notice and hearing (due process) before they can be imposed. Such measures include suspension, expulsion, or permanent exclusion from school, and disciplinary transfers from one school to another.[52] Infliction of corporal punishment in a school district where such punishment is permitted may be subject to procedural safeguards, if required by the board of education, and then should be considered a serious disciplinary measure.[53]

More routine measures do not require such procedural safeguards. Denying a student the privilege of participating in extra-

---

[40]Steirer v Bethlehem Area School Dist, 987 F(2d) 989 (3d Cir Pa 1993), cert denied ___ US ___, 114 SCt 85, 126 LEd(2d) 53 (1993).

[41]Baird v Hosmer, 46 OS(2d) 273, 347 NE(2d) 533 (1976).

[42]Baird v Hosmer, 46 OS(2d) 273, at 278, 347 NE(2d) 533 (1976).

[43]Guyten v Rhodes, 65 App 163, 29 NE(2d) 444 (Hamilton 1940). See Text 24.02, Teachers and parental duties and authority, in loco parentis.

[44]Webb v McCullough, 828 F(2d) 1151 (6th Cir Tenn 1987).

[45]See Text 9.21(A), Gross inefficiency.

[46]New Antioch Special School Dist Bd of Ed v Paul, 7 NP 58, 10 D 17 (CP, Clinton 1900).

[47]RC 3313.20.

[48]RC 3319.16. See Text 9.21(A), Gross inefficiency; Text 9.21(C), Willful and persistent violations of board regulations.

[49]RC 3319.41.

[50]OAC 3301-83-08(D)(3).

[51]RC 3319.41. See also Text 25.16, Corporal punishment.

[52]Goss v Lopez, 419 US 565, 95 SCt 729, 42 LEd(2d) 725 (1975).

[53]RC 3319.41.

curricular activities can be an effective sanction, but is a nonserious measure. A student need not be given notice, a hearing, and the right to appeal in the case of "normal disciplinary procedures" in which the student is removed from a curricular or extracurricular activity for less than one school day and is not subject to suspension or expulsion.[54] If, however, the administrator concludes, after investigation, that suspension or expulsion may be warranted, written notice and a hearing must be given. Routine, day-to-day disciplinary measures, such as detention, do not require notice and hearing.

25.09 Due process requirements for serious disciplinary measures

(A) Fundamental fairness

Boards of education possess broad authority to prescribe and enforce standards of student conduct, but this authority must be exercised in a manner consistent with constitutional safeguards.

Ohio's free public education and compulsory attendance laws[55] create a property interest in a public education that may not be taken away for misconduct without employing fundamentally fair procedures, as required by the due process clause of the Fourteenth Amendment. Due process requires, with regard to a suspension of ten days or less, that the student receive notice of the charges and, if he denies them, an explanation of the evidence school officials have and an opportunity to present his version of the event.[56]

Apart from *procedural* due process, disciplinary measures may implicate *substantive* due process concerns under the Fourteenth Amendment. A federal district court in Indiana has held, for example, that reducing a student's grade for consuming alcohol during school hours was unconstitutional. An academic sanction, said the court, requires that the misconduct be related to academic performance.[57]

To the extent that information from law enforcement agencies regarding student use of drugs or alcohol is relevant to determining appropriate discipline, a board of education may request, and the agencies may share, such information as may appear in their public records.[58]

(B) Criminal law standards not applicable

Constitutional protections applicable to criminal proceedings do not necessarily apply to cases of school discipline. The right of a criminal suspect to remain silent during investigation of a crime, for example, apparently has no application in a student expulsion proceeding. Moreover, an expulsion, even if determined to be too severe under the circumstances, does not constitute cruel and unusual punishment under the Eighth Amendment.[59]

(C) Violation of constitutional rights

School officials are not immune from liability if they knowingly or maliciously disregard a student's clearly established constitutional rights in the enforcement of disciplinary rules, or if they should have known their actions would violate clearly established constitutional rights.[60]

RC 3313.66 governing suspensions and expulsions does not explicitly apply to transportation. One court has held that suspension of a student from riding the school bus for 113 days without affording him a due process hearing established a cause of action under 42 USCA 1983.[61]

25.10 Suspension and expulsion

(A) Authority to suspend or expel student

RC 3313.66 generally governs the suspension or expulsion of a student.[62] The statute applies to the suspension or expulsion of any student, whether or not the student is enrolled in the district, attending or

---

[54]RC 3313.66(E).
[55]RC 3313.48, RC 3313.64, RC Ch 3321.
[56]Goss v Lopez, 419 US 565, 95 SCt 729, 42 LEd(2d) 725 (1975).
[57]Smith v School City of Hobart, 811 FSupp 391 (ND Ind 1993).
[58]OAG 90-099.
[59]Frierott v Vandalia-Butler Schools Bd of Ed, No. CA 6629 (2d Dist Ct App, Montgomery, 6-18-80).

[60]See Text 46.13 to 46.15.
[61]Schaffer v Halloran, No. 84-B-34, 1985 WL 7042 (7th Dist Ct App, Belmont, 9-23-85).
[62]For discussion of the special problems associated with the discipline of a student with a disability, see Text 28.09, Discipline of children with disabilities.

otherwise participating in any curricular program provided in a school operated by the board of education or provided on any other property owned or controlled by the board.[63]

A district superintendent or a principal may suspend a student for not more than ten school days. If fewer than ten days remain in the school year in which the incident takes place, any remaining part or all of the suspension may be applied to the following school year.[64]

Only a superintendent may expel a student.[65] Since a suspension is a removal for ten days or less, by implication an expulsion is any removal for more than ten school days. A superintendent may expel pupils for a period of up to eighty school days or the number of school days remaining in the semester or term in which the incident takes place, whichever is greater, unless the expulsion is extended under RC 3313.66(F). If fewer than eighty days remain in the school year in which the incident takes place, any remaining part or all of the expulsion may be applied to the following school year.[66] The Gun-Free Schools Act of 1994,[67] part of the federal Goals 2000: Educate America Act,[68] states that no assistance under Goals 2000 may be provided to a school district unless the district has in effect a policy requiring the expulsion for not less than one year of any student who brings a weapon[69] to school, except that the policy may allow the district superintendent to modify this expulsion requirement on a case-by-case basis. The general assembly passed and the governor signed 1995 House Bill 64,[70] incorporating this requirement in the student discipline provisions of the revised code.[71] This law also authorizes a board of education to adopt a resolution permitting the superintendent to expel a pupil for a period not to exceed one year for bringing a knife into a school or on to other property operated, owned, or controlled by the board.[72]

RC 3313.66(F) provides for the extension of an expulsion under certain circumstances. If a student age sixteen or older is expelled for a violation listed in RC 3313.662(A),[73] and if a complaint is filed under RC 2151.27 alleging the student is a delinquent child based upon the violation or if the student is prosecuted as an adult for the violation, and if the resulting juvenile court or criminal proceeding is pending when the expulsion terminates, the district superintendent may file a motion with the court requesting an order extending the expulsion for the lesser of an additional eighty days or the number of school days remaining in the school year. If the court, after notice and hearing, determines that reasonable cause exists to believe the student committed the violation, it must grant the requested extension.

Similarly, if a student has been convicted of or adjudicated a delinquent child for a violation listed in RC 3313.662(A) committed when the child was sixteen or older and if the student has been expelled for that violation and the board of education has adopted a resolution seeking his permanent exclusion,[74] the superintendent may file a motion with the court that convicted the student or adjudicated him a delinquent child requesting an order to extend the expulsion until an order or other determination regarding permanent exclusion is

---

[63]RC 3313.66(H).
[64]RC 3313.66(A).
[65]RC 3313.66(B)(1).
[66]RC 3313.66(B)(1).
[67]20 USCA 3351.
[68]See Text 2.11(B), Goals 2000: Educate America Act. Readers should note that the decision in United States v Lopez, ___ US ___, 115 SCt 1624, 131 LEd(2d) 626 (1995), invalidating the Gun-Free School Zones Act, 18 USCA 922(q), does not invalidate state or local laws penalizing gun possession on or near school grounds nor does it eliminate the federal mandate that states which receive federal monies for education must impose specific penalties for students who carry firearms on the school property under the Gun Free Schools Act of 1994. See RC 3313.66, 3313.661, and 3313.662.

[69]"Weapon" is defined as a "firearm" as that term is defined in 18 USCA 921.
[70]Eff. September 14, 1995.
[71]RC 3313.66(B)(2).
[72]R.C. 3313.66(B)(3). The law also added the requirement that a board of education in its student conduct code (i) specify the reasons for which the superintendent may reduce a mandatory one-year expulsion and (ii) if it exercises its right to expel students for bringing a knife to school, define the term "knife." RC 3313.661(A). See Text 25.03, Policy on student conduct. For discussion of related changes in the student discipline statutes under this law, see Text 25.10(E), Permanent exclusion for certain offenses.
[73]See Text 25.10(E), Permanent exclusion for certain offenses, for listed offenses.
[74]See Text 25.10(C), Expulsion: procedure.

issued by the superintendent of public instruction. If, after notice and hearing, the court determines the student's continued attendance in the public school system may endanger the health and safety of other students or employees, it must grant the requested extension.[75] During the period of expulsion of a student from a district, any other school district may, after providing the student an opportunity for a hearing, temporarily deny admittance for the remainder of the expulsion period. After the period has expired, the student shall be admitted to school pursuant to RC 3313.64 and RC 3313.65.[76]

(B) Suspension: procedure

Before a student is suspended, the superintendent or principal must give the student written notice of the intention to suspend, including the reasons for the suspension. The notice should incorporate the date, time, and location of the action giving rise to the suspension. Failure to include the date, time, and location, however, does not constitute a violation of due process rights.[77] If the proposed suspension is based on a violation listed in RC 3313.662(A) by a student age sixteen or older, the notice must include a statement that the superintendent may seek permanently to exclude the student if the student is convicted of or adjudicated a delinquent child for that violation.[78] The student must also be given the opportunity to appear at an informal hearing before the principal, assistant principal, superintendent, or superintendent's designee to challenge the reason for the suspension or otherwise to explain his actions.[79] A principal is not disqualified from handling the suspension process when he is either the subject of the misconduct or a witness to the misconduct.[80]

No particular procedure need be followed in conducting a suspension hearing. The hearing may be held immediately after notice is given. The student should be given an opportunity to read the specification of charges and then respond. School authorities are not required to allow the student to secure legal counsel, to confront and cross-examine witnesses supporting the charges,[81] or to call his own witnesses to verify his version of the incident.[82] However, if the pupil denies the charges, other students or staff members who can either corroborate or refute the student's explanation of his conduct should be questioned. These witnesses may be interviewed as a group or out of the presence of the student at the discretion of the administrator conducting the hearing. In difficult cases the administrator may, if he wishes, permit cross-examination and representation by counsel.[83]

If the administrator determines as a result of the hearing that the pupil should be suspended, the parent, guardian, or custodian of the pupil and the district treasurer must be notified in writing within one school day of the suspension. The notice must include the reasons for the suspension and notification of the right of the pupil or his parent, guardian, or custodian to appeal to the board of education or its designee, to be represented in the appeal, to be granted a hearing before the board or its designee, to request that the board hear the appeal in executive session, and notification that the superintendent may seek the student's per-

---

[75]For expanded treatment of permanent exclusions and identification of the violations listed in RC 3313.662(A), see Text 25.10(E), Permanent exclusion for certain offenses.

[76]RC 3313.66(J). For a discussion of RC 3313.64 and RC 3313.65, see Text 23.02, Admission requirements and tuition liability.

[77]Molnar v Willoughby-Eastlake Bd of Ed, No. 80 CIV 329 (CP, Lake 1981).

[78]RC 3313.66(A). However, RC 3313.66(G) states that failure to provide information on the possibility of permanent exclusion in the notice is not jurisdictional and does not affect the validity of any suspension procedure conducted in accordance with the statute or any permanent exclusion procedure conducted in accordance with RC 3313.662 and RC 3301.121.

[79]RC 3313.66(A).

[80]Stimpert v Porter, No. CA-1808 (5th Dist Ct App, Richland, 12-4-79).

[81]Paredes v Curtis, 864 F(2d) 426 (6th Cir Mich 1988); Newsome v Batavia Local School Dist, 842 F(2d) 920 (6th Cir Ohio 1988); Beavers v Anthony Wayne Schools Bd of Ed, No. L-89-300, 1991 WL 59888 (6th Dist Ct App, Lucas, 4-19-91).

[82]Goss v Lopez, 419 US 565, 95 SCt 729, 42 LEd(2d) 725 (1975); Molnar v Willoughby-Eastlake Bd of Ed, No. 80 CIV 329 (CP, Lake 1981).

[83]See Goss v Lopez, 419 US 565, 95 SCt 729, 42 LEd(2d) 725 (1975).

manent exclusion if the suspension was based on a violation listed in RC 3313.662(A) that was committed when the child was age sixteen or older and if the student is convicted of or adjudicated a delinquent child for that violation.[84] The parental notification requirement is met where, assuming compliance with the requirements as to content, the notice is mailed to the address of the parents on the day of the suspension.[85] Failure to comply with the notification requirements of RC 3313.66(D) may result in reversal of the suspension.[86] One court, however, refused to reverse a suspension notwithstanding a total failure, in "clear violation" of RC 3313.66(D), to include in the notice of suspension any mention of the right to appeal.[87] Essentially, the court found no prejudice resulted from the omission. This case may well be anomalous. Strict compliance with the statute is the only safe course.

(C) Expulsion: procedure

Before a student is expelled, the superintendent must provide the student and his parent, guardian, or custodian written notice of the intention to expel. The notice must include the reasons for the intended expulsion and state that the student and his parent, guardian, custodian, or representative have the opportunity to appear before the superintendent or the superintendent's designee to challenge the expulsion or otherwise explain the pupil's actions. The notice must state the time and place of the hearing. If the proposed expulsion is based on a violation listed in RC 3313.662(A) by a student age sixteen or older, the notice must include a statement that the superintendent may seek permanently to exclude the student if the student is convicted of or adjudicated a delinquent child for that violation.[88]

The superintendent must then provide the pupil and his parent, guardian, custodian, or representative an opportunity to appear in person before the superintendent or his designee to challenge the reasons for the intended expulsion or otherwise explain the pupil's actions. The hearing must be held not less than three or more than five school days after the notice is given, unless the superintendent grants an extension of time. An extension may be requested by the student or his parent, guardian, custodian, or representative. If an extension is granted, the superintendent must notify the pupil and his parent, guardian, custodian, or representative of the new time and place for the hearing.[89]

At the expulsion hearing, the student and his parent, guardian, custodian, or representative must be given the opportunity to defend against the charges. This does not include the right to confront and cross-examine the student's accuser.[90] Although RC 3313.66 does not set forth any particular requirements, the seriousness of expulsion suggests that more formal procedures for expulsion hearings should be established.[91] The pupil can be represented at the hearing by any individual, whether an attorney or not.

If the superintendent determines as a result of the hearing that the pupil should be expelled, written notification of the decision and the right to appeal is required, as in the case of a suspension. The parent, guardian, or custodian of the pupil and the district treasurer must be notified in writing within one school day of the expulsion. The notice must include the reasons for the expulsion and notification of the right of the pupil or his parent, guardian, or custodian to appeal to the board of education or its designee, to be represented in the appeal, to be granted a hearing before the board or its designee, to request that the

---

[84]RC 3313.66(D).

[85]Stimpert v Porter, No. CA-1808 (5th Dist Ct App, Richland, 12-4-79).

[86]Ernst v Georgetown Bd of Ed, No. 81CV-28642 (CP, Brown, 11-20-81); Kattine v Georgetown Bd of Ed, No. 81CV-28643 (CP, Brown, 11-20-81).

[87]Brunswick City School Dist Bd of Ed v Formani, No. 1671, 1988 WL 34601 (9th Dist Ct App, Medina, 3-22-88).

[88]RC 3313.66(B)(4). However, RC 3313.66(G) states that failure to provide information on the possibility of permanent exclusion in the notice is not jurisdictional and does not affect the validity of any expulsion procedure conducted in accordance with the statute or any permanent exclusion procedure conducted in accordance with RC 3313.662 and RC 3301.121.

[89]RC 3313.66(B)(4).

[90]Newsome v Batavia Local School Dist, 842 F(2d) 920 (6th Cir Ohio 1988).

[91]See Goss v Lopez, 419 US 565, 95 SCt 729, 42 LEd(2d) 725 (1975).

board hear the appeal in executive session, and notification both that the expulsion may be extended under RC 3313.66(F) if the student is age sixteen or older and that the superintendent may seek the student's permanent exclusion if the expulsion was based on a violation listed in RC 3313.662(A) that was committed when the child was age sixteen or older and if the student is convicted of or adjudicated a delinquent child for that violation. If the expulsion is for more than twenty school days, or if it will extend into the following semester or school year, the notice must also provide information (including names, addresses, and phone numbers) about services or programs offered by public and private agencies that work toward improving those aspects of the student's attitudes and behavior that contributed to the expulsion.[92]

In *Stuble v Cuyahoga Valley Joint Vocational School Dist Bd of Ed*,[93] the court held that technical irregularities in expulsion procedures *that do not prejudice the student* do not defeat substantial compliance and do not render an expulsion void. Directing written notice of the pre-expulsion hearing to the parent rather than the student was considered insignificant since the student lived at home. Likewise, that the notice was signed by the school's director rather than the superintendent was not material since he was acting at the superintendent's direction. Omission of the grounds for expulsion did not defeat substantial compliance since those reasons were fully described in a previous suspension notice. Finally, failure to hold the hearing within the mandated three to five days was excused where the hearing was actually held during the time a ten-day suspension for the same offense was being served.[94] While substantial compliance may suffice in a particular case, strict compliance is the only safe course.

Some have suggested that RC 3313.66(E) requires a record of suspension or expulsion proceedings. However, that provision's requirement of a verbatim record applies only to an appellate hearing before the board or its designee.[95]

(D) Community service alternative

A board of education may (but is not required to) establish a program and adopt guidelines under which the superintendent may require the performance of community service in conjunction with or in the place of a suspension or expulsion other than an expulsion for bringing a firearm to school. Such guidelines, if adopted, must permit imposition of a community service requirement beyond the end of the school year in lieu of applying the suspension or expulsion into the next school year and must be included in the district's student conduct policy.[96]

(E) Permanent exclusion for certain offenses

RC 3313.662 and RC 3301.121 empower the superintendent of public instruction to issue an adjudication order that permanently excludes a student from attending any Ohio public school if the student is convicted of, or adjudicated a delinquent child for, committing, at age sixteen or older, an act that would be a criminal offense if committed by an adult and that constitutes any of the following:

(1) illegal conveyance or possession of deadly weapons or dangerous ordnance on school premises in violation of RC 2923.122;

(2) carrying concealed weapons in violation of RC 2923.12 (or a similar

---

[92]RC 3313.66(D). However, RC 3313.66(G) states that failure to provide information on the possibility of permanent exclusion in the notice is not jurisdictional and does not affect the validity of any expulsion procedure conducted in accordance with the statute or any permanent exclusion procedure conducted in accordance with RC 3313.662 and RC 3301.121.

[93]Stuble v Cuyahoga Valley Joint Vocational School Dist Bd of Ed, No. 44412, 1982 WL 5953 (8th Dist Ct App, Cuyahoga, 10-7-82).

[94]Stuble v Cuyahoga Valley Joint Vocational School Dist Bd of Ed, No. 44412, 1982 WL 5953 (8th Dist Ct App, Cuyahoga, 10-7-82).

[95]Cashdollar v Northridge Local School Dist Bd of Ed, No. CA-3004, 1984 WL 7430 (5th Dist Ct App, Licking, 4-4-84). See Text 25.12(A), Appeal to board.

[96]RC 3313.661(B). Any program or guideline adopted under the statute applies to any student, whether or not enrolled in the district, attending or otherwise participating in any curricular program provided in a school operated by the board of education or provided on any other property owned or controlled by the board. RC 3313.661(D). See also Text 25.03, Policy on student conduct.

municipal ordinance) on school property or at a school activity;

(3) selling or offering to sell or possessing a controlled substance in violation of RC 2925.03(A)(1), (4), (5), (6), (7), (9), or (10) on school property or at a school activity;

(4) aggravated murder in violation of RC 2903.01, murder in violation of RC 2903.02, voluntary manslaughter in violation of RC 2903.03, involuntary manslaughter in violation of RC 2903.04, felonious assault in violation of RC 2903.11, aggravated assault in violation of RC 2903.12, rape in violation of RC 2907.02, gross sexual imposition in violation of RC 2907.05 or felonious sexual penetration in violation of RC 2907.12 on school property or at a school function if the victim at the time of the act was a school employee; and

(5) complicity in any of the above-described violations regardless of whether the act of complicity was committed on school property or at a school activity.

Upon obtaining or receiving proof that a student attending school in his district has been convicted of, or adjudicated a delinquent child for, committing, at age sixteen or older, any of the above-described violations, the superintendent of a city, local, exempted village, or joint vocational school district may issue to the board of education a request that the student be permanently excluded from public school attendance if (1) after obtaining or receiving such proof, he or his designee determines the student's continued attendance may endanger the health and safety of other students or school employees and gives the student (and his parent, guardian, or custodian) written notice of the superintendent's intent to recommend that the board adopt a resolution requesting the superintendent of public instruction permanently to exclude the student from public school attendance, and (2) he or his designee forwards to the board the district superintendent's written recommendation that includes the aforesaid determination of a danger to health and safety and a copy of the proof he obtained or received.[97]

Within fourteen days after receiving the district superintendent's recommendation, the board, after considering certain specified information,[98] may adopt a resolution requesting the superintendent of public instruction permanently to exclude the student from public school attendance. If the board does not adopt such a resolution, it "immediately" must send written notice of that fact to the district superintendent and the student (and his parent, guardian, or custodian).[99]

If the board adopts the resolution, it, along with proof of the conviction or adjudication that is the basis of the resolution and a copy of the student's entire school record and "any other relevant information," must "immediately" be forwarded to the state superintendent of public instruction. A copy of the resolution must also be forwarded to the student (and his parent, guardian, or custodian). The board shall then "promptly" designate a representative (who may be an attorney) to present the case for permanent exclusion to the superintendent of public instruction or the referee appointed by him pursuant to RC 3301.121.[100]

After receiving a board's resolution requesting the permanent exclusion of a student, the superintendent of public instruction is to follow the adjudication procedures prescribed by RC 3301.121. That statute incorporates elaborate

---

[97] RC 3313.662(C). Where a complaint is filed in juvenile court alleging a child age sixteen or older committed an act that would be a criminal offense if committed by an adult and that is a violation listed in RC 3313.662(A), or where the juvenile court adjudicates a child to be a delinquent child on the basis of an act committed at age sixteen or older that would be a criminal offense if committed by an adult and that is a violation listed in RC 3313.662(A), the court must give written notice of such fact within ten days to the district superintendent. RC 2151.27(F), RC 2151.355(J).

[98] RC 3313.662(C)(2) requires board review of all available information on the student's academic and disciplinary record, extracurricular activities, social history, and response to prior discipline, as well as review of evidence regarding the seriousness of and aggravating factors related to the offense, the probable danger posed to health and safety, the probable disruption of teaching in the district, the availability of alternative less serious sanctions, and mitigating factors.

[99] RC 3313.662(C)(3).

[100] RC 3313.662(D).

requirements for notice and a hearing. The hearing is either before the superintendent or a referee who must report his findings to the superintendent at the conclusion of the hearing. After considering the entire school record of the student and other factors listed in the statute, the superintendent may enter an order of permanent exclusion only if a preponderance of the evidence shows, and it is found that, the student was convicted of, or adjudicated a delinquent child for, committing, at age sixteen or older, a violation listed in RC 3313.662(A) and that the student's continued attendance in the public school system may endanger the health and safety of other students or school employees. Otherwise, the superintendent must issue a written order that rejects the resolution.[101] A student may appeal an order of permanent exclusion to the common pleas court of the county in which the board that requested the permanent exclusion is located, and any such appeal is conducted in accordance with RC Chapter 2505.[102]

Where a student has been permanently excluded, the superintendent of the district in which the student desires to attend school may, upon determining that attendance by the student will no longer endanger the health and safety of other students or school employees, issue a recommendation with reasons to the board of education that the permanent exclusion be revoked.[103] The board may then by resolution request revocation by the superintendent of public instruction who, in turn and in accordance with the adjudication procedures of RC Chapter 119, will either issue an order of revocation or reject the board's resolution.[104]

A permanently excluded student may request the district superintendent to admit him on a probationary basis for not to exceed ninety school days, in which case the superintendent may enter into discussions to develop a probationary admission plan. If such a plan is agreed to, the superintendent must issue a recommendation with reasons and a copy of the plan to the board of education which, within fourteen days, may adopt or reject the recommendation. For students whose permanent exclusion resulted in whole or in part from the student bringing a firearm to school, the plan may not include an admission date less than one year after the firearm incident occurred unless the superintendent has determined on a case-by-case basis to reduce the one-year expulsion for the reasons stated in the student conduct code.[105] If probationary admission is permitted and the student fails to comply with the plan, the district superintendent may immediately remove the student from school and recommend to the board that the probationary admission be revoked. Within five days, the board may adopt the recommendation. If a majority of the board does not adopt the recommendation, the student can continue to attend school "in compliance with his probationary admission plan."[106] If probationary admission is permitted and the student complies with the plan, the district superintendent may, prior to expiration of the probationary period, be requested to extend the terms and period of the admission for not to exceed ninety days or issue a recommendation to the board that the student's permanent exclusion be revoked.[107]

Any information regarding the permanent exclusion of a student must be included in the student's official records and in any records sent to any district that requests the student's records, except that when the student either reaches age twenty-two or his permanent exclusion is revoked, all districts that have records on the exclusion must remove and destroy all references to the exclusion.[108] Such a student is expressly authorized to request the

---

[101] RC 3301.121(F), (G), RC 3313.662(D)(3).
[102] RC 3301.121(H).
[103] The superintendent of the district may not recommend revocation where the permanent exclusion resulted in whole or in part from the student bringing a firearm to school except by application on a case-by-case basis of the reasons specified in the student conduct code. See Text 25.10(A), Authority to suspend or expel student.
[104] RC 3313.662(F)(1).

[105] RC 3313.662(F)(2). For discussions of expulsions for possession of a firearm, see Text 25.10(A), Authority to suspend or expel student.
[106] RC 3313.662(F)(2).
[107] RC 3313.662(F)(2). Subsequent probationary admission periods not to exceed ninety days each may also be granted.
[108] RC 2151.358 provides that if records of one adjudicated a delinquent child are sealed, a school district that maintains records of an individual who

superintendent of any such district in writing to ensure the records are removed and destroyed, and the superintendent is obligated to follow through on such a request.[109]

A student may be suspended or expelled in accordance with RC 3313.66 prior to being permanently excluded from public school attendance.[110] A permanently excluded student is not precluded from seeking a certificate of high school equivalence, and may be permitted to participate in a course of study in preparation for the tests of general educational development, except such participation during normal school hours in any public school building or structure is prohibited.[111]

RC 3313.662 has no applicability to (1) a residential facility maintained by the department of youth services that receives and cares for children and operates a school chartered by the state board of education under RC 3301.16, (2) any on-premises school operated by an out-of-home care entity chartered by the state board under RC 3301.16, or (3) any school operated in connection with an out-of-home care entity or nonresidential youth treatment program that contracts with a school district for educational services in other than a district building or structure during normal school hours.[112]

(F) *Denial of admission to expelled student*

The General Assembly now authorizes a district to temporarily deny admission to a student who has been expelled from another district until the student's expulsion period in the expelling district expires. The district must offer the student a hearing before denying admission, and must grant admittance when the student's expulsion period is over.[113]

25.11 Emergency removal

If a student's presence poses a continuing danger to persons or property or an ongoing threat of disrupting the academic process either within a classroom or elsewhere on the school premises, the notice and hearing ordinarily required for suspension and expulsion can be temporarily waived.[114] The student may be removed immediately from any curricular or extracurricular activity or from the school premises by the superintendent, principal, or assistant principal. A teacher may remove such a student from curricular or extracurricular activities under his supervision, although not from the school premises.

If a teacher makes an emergency removal, the reasons must be submitted in writing to the principal as soon as practicable. If, prior to the hearing following removal, the superintendent or principal reinstates a student who has been removed by a teacher, the reasons must be given in writing to the teacher upon request.[115]

A hearing must be held as soon as practicable after the removal, but in no case later than three school days from the time removal is ordered. Written notice of the hearing and of the reasons for removal must be given to the student prior to the hearing. The hearing must be held in accordance with either the suspension or expulsion procedure, depending on the probable action that will be taken. The person who ordered, caused, or requested the emergency removal must be present at the hearing.[116]

---

has been permanently excluded is permitted to maintain records regarding an adjudication used as the basis of the exclusion. An order to seal does not revoke an order of permanent exclusion, but it may be presented to the district superintendent as evidence to support a contention that the superintendent should recommend revocation of the exclusion. RC 2953.32 contains substantively identical provisions with respect to the sealing of a record of a criminal conviction.

[109] RC 3313.662(G).
[110] RC 3313.662(B).
[111] RC 3313.662(H).
[112] RC 3313.662(H).
[113] RC 3313.662.
[114] RC 3313.66(C).
[115] RC 3313.66(C).
[116] RC 3313.66(C).

25.12 Review of suspension or expulsion by board, appeal to common pleas court

(A) Appeal to board

A student or his parent, guardian, or custodian may appeal a suspension or expulsion to the board of education or its designee.[117] Thus, the board may either review the case itself or appoint a hearing officer. The student has the right to representation at the hearing. A parent does not perfect an appeal to the board by merely appearing at a board meeting. A notice of appeal must be given.[118]

The hearing must be held in public unless the pupil, his parent, guardian, custodian, or attorney requests that the hearing be held in executive session. Even if an executive session is requested, formal action on the appeal must be taken in a public meeting.[119] As to whether, in the absence of a request for executive session, the board may, after receiving the evidence in public, go into executive session before acting for the purpose of reviewing the evidence and the appropriateness of the discipline, the cases are not consistent.[120] The safest course is not to hold an executive session under these circumstances. By a majority vote of the board's full membership or by action of the board's designee, the order of suspension or expulsion may be affirmed, reversed, vacated, or modified, or the student may be reinstated.

The board or its designee is required to make a "verbatim record" of appeal hearings. An appeals court has held this requirement for a verbatim record does not mean a transcript is essential; here, the court concluded everything germane to the case was recorded.[121] The safest and advisable course is to have a transcript, however. A written, tape-recorded, or stenographic record may be used. The record need not be reduced to writing unless the matter is further appealed.

Other than the requirement of a verbatim record, no particular procedure is required for an appeal hearing. Each board should adopt guidelines which assure consistency and fairness. Decisions of the board or its designee may be appealed to common pleas court under RC Chapter 2506.[122] One court has determined that when school officials fail to follow RC 3313.66, a student may pursue injunctive relief and is not limited to an appeal under RC Chapter 2506.[123]

(B) Appeal to court of common pleas

When a student suspension or expulsion is appealed to common pleas court pursuant to RC Chapter 2506, written notice of appeal must be filed with the board[124] within thirty days.[125] Filing the notice is mandatory, and an appeal may be dismissed when this requirement is not met.[126] A suspension may not be appealed to common pleas court unless the board has

---

[117]RC 3313.66(E).

[118]Stimpert v Porter, No. CA-1808 (5th Dist Ct App, Richland, 12-4-79).

[119]RC 121.22, RC 3316.66(E). The statute states that "the board or its designee may [if requested] hold the hearing in executive session but shall act upon the suspension or expulsion only at a public meeting." Where a designee has been appointed, whether the board itself is obligated to take action with respect to the designee's decision is not clear. A common pleas court has held that board action in public session is required before the designee's decision is final. In the absence of ratification by the board, the designee's decision was not a final order or decision appealable to court under RC Ch 2506. Sellers v Spencerville Local Bd of Ed, No. CV94 03 0163 (CP, Allen, 7-26-94).

[120]Armstead v Lima City Bd of Ed, 75 App(3d) 841, 600 NE(2d) 1085 (Allen 1991) (executive session permitted at least in the absence of demand that deliberations be public); State ex rel Humphrey v Adkins, 18 App(2d) 101, 247 NE(2d) 330 (Montgomery 1969) (finding expulsion was lawful where executive session held without request); Schank v Hegele, 36 Misc(2d) 4, 521 NE(2d) 9 (CP, Morgan 1987) (executive session not permitted). In Hardesty v River View Local School Dist Bd of Ed, 63 Misc(2d) 145, 620 NE(2d) 272 (CP, Coshocton 1993), the court overturned student suspensions on the ground that the suspensions resulted from unauthorized executive sessions in violation of RC 121.22 that occurred weeks prior to the meeting at which the board acted to affirm the suspensions. See also Text 5.12, Open meetings: the sunshine law.

[121]Smider v Jackson Milton Local School Dist Bd of Ed, No. 91 CA 215, 1992 WL 198080 (7th Dist Ct App, Mahoning, 8-11-92).

[122]RC 3313.66(E).

[123]Stimpert v Porter, No. CA-1808 (5th Dist Ct App, Richland, 12-4-79).

[124]RC 2505.04.

[125]RC 2505.07.

[126]Kettering Bd of Ed v Gollnitz, No. 6376 (2d Dist Ct App, Montgomery, 3-6-80). In *Gollnitz* no

entered a resolution of the suspension in its minutes.[127]

On filing a praecipe, the board or its designee must file with the court a complete transcript of all original papers, evidence, and testimony within forty days after the notice of appeal is filed.[128] The court considers the appeal on the basis of the transcript unless it appears on the face of the transcript, or the appellant files an affidavit indicating, that

- the transcript does not contain all evidence admitted or proffered;

- appellant was not permitted to appear in person or by his attorney to offer evidence and arguments and to cross-examine witnesses;

- testimony was not given under oath;

- appellant was unable to present evidence because of lack of subpoena power; or

- the board or its designee failed to file conclusions of fact supporting its decision.

If any of these five conditions is present, the court must hear additional evidence any party wishes to introduce and must consider both the supplemental evidence and the transcript in making its decision.[129] One court has held, however, that a student who fails to attend the hearing conducted by the board or its designee waives any right to supplement the transcript.[130]

The board must initially bear the cost of preparing the transcript.[131] However, RC 2506.02 provides that the cost of the transcript is to be taxed as a part of the costs of the appeal, suggesting that the losing party must ultimately pay the expense of preparing and filing the record.

The reviewing court must determine whether the board's decision was supported by the preponderance of substantial, reliable, and probative evidence on the whole record, and whether the actions were legal and reasonable.[132]

25.13 Disciplinary transfers

RC 3319.01 gives the superintendent responsibility for assigning pupils to the proper schools and grades. No due process procedure is mandated in connection with the transfer of a student. However, one Ohio court has concluded, relying on *Goss v Lopez*,[133] that minimal due process must be met when a student is given a disciplinary transfer, because the transfer puts at stake a student's good name, reputation, honor, or integrity.[134] In other words, the student must be given oral or written notice of the charges against him and, if he denies them, an explanation of the evidence and an opportunity to present his side of the story.

25.14 Checklist for suspension, expulsion, or removal

The following list should be followed when suspending, expelling, or removing a pupil. The list incorporates requirements of RC 3313.66 and RC 3313.661 and the due process clause of the Fourteenth Amendment.

"notice of appeal" was filed with the clerk of courts or the board of education. In Evans v Greenview Local School Dist, No. 88 CA 40, 1989 WL 569 (2d Dist Ct App, Greene, 1-4-89), a "notice of appeal" was filed with the clerk of courts who sent a copy to the board which the board received within the thirty-day time limit. Under those circumstances, the court concluded the filing requirement was satisfied.

[127]Cashdollar v Northridge High School Bd of Ed, No. CA 2951, 1983 WL 6527 (5th Dist Ct App, Licking, 7-7-83).

[128]RC 2506.02.

[129]RC 2506.03.

[130]Eller v Muskingum Area Joint Vocational School Dist Bd of Ed, No. 81-846 (CP, Muskingum, 4-27-82).

[131]Smith v Chester Twp Bd of Trustees, 60 OS(2d) 13, 396 NE(2d) 743 (1979).

[132]E.g., Cross v Princeton City School Dist Bd of Ed, 49 Misc(2d) 1, 550 NE(2d) 219 (CP, Hamilton 1989); Myers v Eastern Local Bd of Ed, No. 83-CV-29142 (CP, Brown, 1-7-83). See also Beavers v Anthony Wayne Schools Bd of Ed, No. L-89-300, 1991 WL 59888 (6th Dist Ct App, Lucas, 4-19-91) (noting appeals court's role even more limited and consists of determining whether common pleas court abused its discretion in finding as it did).

[133]Goss v Lopez, 419 US 565, 95 SCt 729, 42 LEd(2d) 725 (1975).

[134]Waite v Columbus Bd of Ed, No. 79 AP-668 (10th Dist Ct App, Franklin, 3-27-80). See also Everett v Marcase, 426 FSupp 397 (ED Pa 1977) (distinguishing between administrative transfers and disciplinary transfers and requiring a hearing for the latter).

(A) School policy on conduct

(1) Before taking disciplinary action, be sure the action is in accordance with the policy on conduct adopted by the board of education.

(2) The policy on conduct should specify when and where it applies.

(3) The policy must also specify the types of misconduct for which a pupil may be suspended, expelled, or removed.

(4) The policy must spell out the offenses in sufficient detail to put students on notice of actions which result in disciplinary action.[135]

(5) A copy of the policy must be posted in a central location at each school and made available to pupils upon request.

(B) Suspension

(1) The superintendent or principal must give written notice of the intention to suspend and the reasons for the intended suspension (and, if applicable, notice that the superintendent may seek permanent exclusion) to the pupil. The notice should include all rules violated.

(2) The pupil must be given an informal hearing to challenge the reasons for the intended suspension or otherwise explain his actions.

(3) If the student has been suspended, the superintendent or principal must notify the parent, custodian, or guardian and the board's treasurer in writing within one school day of the suspension and such notice must include (a) the reasons for the suspension; (b) the right to appeal the action to the board or its designee; (c) the right to a hearing; (d) the right to request the hearing be held in executive session; and (e) if applicable, notice that the superintendent may seek permanent exclusion.

(C) Expulsion

(1) The pupil and his parent, guardian, or custodian must be given written notice of the intention to expel.

(2) The written notice must include (a) the reasons (and, if applicable, notice that the superintendent may seek permanent exclusion); (b) the opportunity to appear before the superintendent or his designee to challenge the reasons; (c) the date of the hearing; (d) apprisement of the right to be represented; and (e) the right to request an extension of time.

(3) The hearing must be no sooner than three but no later than five school days after the notice, unless an extension is granted.

(4) If an extension is granted, the parties must be notified of the new time and place.

---

[135]Unless the policy is drafted carefully, it may be attacked as overly broad or too vague. In In re Appeal of Suspension of Huffer from Circleville High School, 47 OS(3d) 12, 546 NE(2d) 1308 (1989), the Ohio Supreme Court, reversing an appeals court, upheld a suspension under a policy provision that defined "under the influence" of narcotics and intoxicants with reference to physical symptoms (such as odor of the substance or dozing in class) that might be just as apparent with ingestion of lawful and permissible substances. Emphasizing that alleged overbreadth must be considered case by case, the Court found the provision not overbroad with respect to a student suspended for attending a high school wrestling practice smelling of alcohol and who, upon questioning, admitted drinking beer earlier in the day. This case, with its broad endorsement of school board authority in this area, casts serious doubt on Evans v Greenview Local School Dist, No. 88 CA 40, 1989 WL 569 (2d Dist Ct App, Greene, 1-4-89), wherein the court overturned the suspensions of students accused of being "under the influence" of alcohol within the meaning of the school's policy. The students indisputably had come to school after drinking beer, but exhibited no symptoms. The court declared that "[i]n the absence of any definition of 'under the influence' in the School District's policy, the phrase should retain its commonly understood meaning and should not be extended to the situation here." See also Rohrbaugh v Elida Local Bd of Ed, 63 App(3d) 685, 579 NE(2d) 782 (Allen 1990) (upholding suspensions of students who admitted using alcohol before boarding a school bus to a football game and reversing lower court's holding that "under the influence" requires evidence that conduct be actually influenced as improper substitution of court's view for that of the board in construing its own student conduct policy); Connors v Fairview Park Bd of Ed, No. 245435 (CP, Cuyahoga, 5-26-93) (affirming board's right to promulgate rule obligating students to inform on others using alcohol at school event but overturning suspension of two students for failure to inform on fellow students who drank in out-of-town hotel room after volleyball tournament since that location was not within reach of rule under its terms).

(5) If the student has been expelled, the superintendent must notify the parent, guardian, or custodian and the board's treasurer in writing of the action within one school day. The notice must include (a) the reasons for the expulsion (and, if applicable, notice that the superintendent may seek permanent exclusion); (b) the right to appeal the action of the board of education or its designee; (c) the right to be represented in appeal proceedings; (d) the right to a hearing before the board or its designee; and (e) the right to request the hearing be held in executive session. If the expulsion is for more than twenty school days, or will extend into the next semester or school year, it must also contain information on services or programs that work toward improving the student's attitudes and behavior.

(D) Emergency removal

(1) Determine whether the removal really is emergency in nature or a routine disciplinary action. That is, does the pupil's presence truly impose a continuing danger to persons or property or an ongoing threat of disrupting the academic process?

(2) If the removal is by a teacher, the removal must be confined to the curricular/extracurricular activities under his control.

(3) If the removal is by a teacher, the teacher must submit the reasons in writing as soon as practicable after the removal to the principal.

(4) A hearing must be scheduled to be held as soon as practicable but not later than three school days after the initial removal.

(5) Notice and hearing requirements applicable to suspensions or expulsions must be followed, as appropriate.

(6) The individual who ordered, caused, or requested the removal must be present at the hearing.

(7) If the pupil was reinstated to a curricular/extracurricular activity prior to the hearing, the teacher must be given the reasons for the reinstatement in writing upon request.

(E) Appeal to board

(1) The appeal must be filed within a reasonable time limit established by school rules.

(2) A verbatim record of the appeal hearing must be made. That record will have to be reduced to writing and filed with the common pleas court in the event of further appeal.

(3) The hearing should be held in accordance with a board-prescribed procedure which gives the student and administration a fair opportunity to present the arguments against and for the discipline. The student, as the appealing party, should go forward first.

(4) Final action taken by the board or its designee must occur at an open meeting.

25.15 Removal from extracurricular activities

(A) In general

A student may be suspended or expelled solely from participation in extracurricular activities while being allowed to continue to attend regular classes.[136]

(B) Question of due process

RC 3313.66 is unclear as to whether a student suspended or expelled solely from an extracurricular activity is entitled to due process. The last sentence of RC 3313.66(E) can be interpreted to require notice and hearing whenever a student is removed from a curricular or extracurricular activity for one full school day or more. However, RC 3313.66(A) and (B) can be fairly read to require notice and hearing when, and only when, a student is suspended or expelled from "school," meaning *all* curricular *and* extracurricular activities.

As a matter of constitutional as opposed to statutory right, a student does not have a protected liberty or property interest in extracurricular activities. In *Glenn v*

---

[136]Holroyd v Eibling, 116 App 440, 188 NE(2d) 797 (Franklin 1962), appeal dismissed by 174 OS 27, 186 NE(2d) 200 (1962); McNaughton v Circleville Bd of Ed, 46 Misc 12, 345 NE(2d) 649 (CP, Pickaway 1974).

Harper,[137] the court determined that "although the right to education is constitutionally protected, due process protection need not reach a component part of education."[138] The court did not address the issue of whether RC 3313.66 requires due process for dismissals from extracurricular activities.

The right to dismiss a student from an activity may turn upon the regulations established for the activity. For example, a pregnant student's dismissal from the National Honor Society was upheld, because the handbook of the organization provided that a member can be removed without warning for flagrant violations of the organization's standards.[139] Courts in other states have also held that membership in the Society does not implicate a property interest entitling one to due process in the admission process.[140] Similarly, conditioning participation in a special vocational program on maintenance of "good citizenship" within the community has withstood constitutional challenge.[141] Where a board has established particular procedures for disciplining a student in an activity (e.g., an athletic code), it will usually be bound to follow its own rules.

Courts have also upheld state and district regulations suspending students from participating in extracurricular activities due to low grades.[142] These "no pass, no play rules" reflect the position that there is no fundamental right to participate in extracurricular activities, and therefore they need only satisfy the standard that the rule be rationally related to their intended purpose.

25.16 Corporal punishment

(A) In general, requirement of reasonableness

Ohio's law on corporal punishment was substantially revised by 1993 Senate Bill 29, a complex attempt to discourage, but not prohibit, corporal punishment in Ohio's public schools.

RC 3319.41(A) provides that no teacher, principal, administrator, noncertificated school employee, or bus driver in a public school may use corporal punishment as a means of pupil discipline unless the district's board (1) adopted a resolution by September 1, 1994, to permit corporal punishment,[143] and (2) has not adopted a resolution prohibiting corporal punishment under RC 3319.41(B).[144] Where corporal punishment is thus permitted under RC 3319.41(A), a teacher, principal, or administrator may use reasonable corporal pun-

---

[137]Glenn v Harper, 620 F(2d) 302 (6th Cir Ohio 1980).

[138]See also, e.g., McFarlin v Newport Special School Dist, 980 F(2d) 1208 (8th Cir Ark 1992).

[139]Elliot v Rice, No. 83-CV-316 (CP, Greene, 5-23-83).

[140]Dangler v Yorktown Central Schools, 771 FSupp 625 (SD NY 1991); Price v Young, 580 FSupp 1 (ED Ark 1983); Karnstein v Pewaukee School Bd, 557 FSupp 565 (ED Wis 1983); Dallam v Cumberland Valley School Dist, 391 FSupp 358 (MD Pa 1975).

[141]Felton v Fayette School Dist, 875 F(2d) 191 (8th Cir Mo 1989) (upholding dismissal of student from off-campus vocational program after he was involved in theft of auto parts).

[142]Spring Branch Independent School Dist v Stamos, 695 SW(2d) 556 (Tex 1985), appeal dismissed by 475 US 1001, 106 SCt 1170, 89 LEd(2d) 290 (1986); Abraham v Firelands Local School Dist Bd of Ed, No. 97443-86 (CP, Lorain 1986).

[143]No such resolution permitting corporal punishment could be adopted before receiving and studying the written report of a task force appointed under RC 3319.41(A)(2).

[144]RC 3319.41(B) states that the board of any city, local, exempted village, or joint vocational school district in which corporal punishment is permitted may at any time after September 1, 1996, adopt a resolution to prohibit corporal punishment. Thereafter, the board may adopt a resolution permitting corporal punishment only after receiving and studying the written report of a local discipline task force. Task force members must include teachers, administrators, noncertificated school employees, school psychologists, members of the medical profession, pediatricians when available, and representatives of parents' organizations. The task force must hold meetings regularly, give public notice of any meeting in newspapers or other periodicals of general circulation in the district, and produce a written report of findings and recommendations. All task force meetings must be open to the public, and at least one meeting must be for the purpose of inviting public participation. RC 3319.41(B)(3)(b). In addition, RC 3319.41(B) states that the board of any city, local, exempted village, or joint vocational district that has not permitted corporal punishment under RC 3319.41(A) may at any time after September 1, 1998, adopt a resolution permitting corporal punishment only after receiving and studying the written report of such a local discipline task force.

ishment upon a student attending the school to which the employee is assigned whenever such punishment "is reasonably necessary in order to preserve discipline while the student is subject to school authority."[145] Moreover, in a district that permits corporal punishment the board must, as part of its disciplinary policy, permit the parents, guardian, or custodian of a student to request that corporal punishment not be used on that child, in which case an alternative disciplinary measure must be applied; a procedure for the exercise of this option must be included in the board's resolution that permits the use of corporal punishment.[146]

RC 3319.41(D) provides that, if the board of a city, local, exempted village, or joint vocational district elects to prohibit corporal punishment, the board must, before the effective date of the prohibition, (1) adopt a policy on discipline that includes alternative disciplinary measures; and (2) consider what in-service training, if any, employees might need as part of implementing that policy.

Where corporal punishment is prohibited, teachers, principals, administrators, noncertificated school employees, and bus drivers remain free, within the scope of their employment, to use and apply reasonable force and restraint as necessary to quell a disturbance that threatens physical injury, to obtain weapons or other dangerous objects from a pupil, to protect persons or property, or for self-defense.[147]

Where corporal punishment is authorized, it is specifically unlawful for a teacher or other person to administer excessive corporal punishment or physical discipline. Only reasonable corporal punishment, force, and restraint are permitted.[148] The areas examined in determining reasonableness are the decision to administer corporal punishment, the method used, and the results of the punishment as applied.[149] The characteristics of the particular child, including any developmental disabilities, are also relevant.[150] The state carries the burden of proving the punishment was conducted in a reckless manner.[151] Absent aggravating circumstances, such as producing serious physical harm or a repeated offense, a violation is a third degree felony.[152]

The attorney general has opined that the Children's Trust Fund Board, which, among other things, makes grants to schools for establishing child abuse and child neglect prevention programs, lacks authority to prohibit a school that allows corporal punishment from receiving such funds.[153]

(B) Constitutional considerations

The due process clause of the Fourteenth Amendment does not require notice or hearing prior to the infliction of corporal punishment.[154] A board of education may, however, adopt rules requiring procedural safeguards before punishment is administered. The safeguards approved in *Baker v Owen*[155] suggest that students should be informed in advance of the specific misbehavior that will merit corporal punishment and that the punishment should be administered in the presence of a second school official (teacher or principal), who should be informed beforehand and in the student's presence of the reason. Finally, *Baker* indicates the school official who administered the punishment should provide the child's parent, upon request, a written explanation of the reasons and the name of the second official who was present.

---

[145] RC 3319.41(E).

[146] RC 3319.41(F).

[147] RC 3319.41(C), (G).

[148] RC 2919.22(B), RC 3319.41; Chrysinger v Decatur, 3 App(3d) 286, 3 OBR 331, 445 NE(2d) 260 (Franklin 1982); Dixon v Youngstown City Bd of Ed, No. 73-1188-4 (ND Ohio, 11-19-75). See also Jackson v Wooster Bd of Ed, 29 App(3d) 210, 29 OBR 254, 504 NE(2d) 1144 (Wayne 1985) (requiring push-ups not outrageous and did not constitute infliction of emotional distress). The use of reasonable corporal punishment consistent with the statute precludes a finding of child abuse of a school child. OAG 92-082.

[149] State v Albert, 8 Misc(2d) 13, 8 OBR 149, 456 NE(2d) 594 (County Ct, Belmont 1983).

[150] OAG 92-082.

[151] OAG 92-082.

[152] RC 2919.22(E).

[153] OAG 89-053.

[154] Ingraham v Wright, 430 US 651, 97 SCt 1401, 51 LEd(2d) 711 (1977).

[155] Baker v Owen, 395 FSupp 294 (MD NC 1975), affirmed by 423 US 907, 96 SCt 210, 46 LEd(2d) 137 (1975).

Reasonable corporal punishment is not contrary to the Eighth Amendment's prohibition against cruel and unusual punishment.[156] Paddling was deemed reasonable when a student was struck twice, no objective evidence indicated the paddling was unreasonable, the child had been a discipline problem, and the parents had twice been informed, without objection, of the intention to inflict corporal punishment.[157]

(C) Excessive or unreasonable punishment

Infliction of excessive or unreasonable corporal punishment may entitle the student to damages.[158]

For a teacher who inflicts corporal punishment to be convicted of criminal assault, the state must prove not only that the elements of an assault were present but also that the corporal punishment was excessive and unnecessary. Whether corporal punishment is reasonable requires examination of the standards set forth in RC 2919.22(B).[159]

---

[156]Ingraham v Wright, 430 US 651, 97 SCt 1401, 51 LEd(2d) 711 (1977). See also Sims v Waln, 536 F(2d) 686 (6th Cir Ohio 1976), cert denied 431 US 903, 97 SCt 1693, 52 LEd(2d) 386 (1977).

[157]Traub v Wasem, No. CA16-85, 1985 WL 7274 (5th Dist Ct App, Fairfield, 10-16-85).

[158]For cases and analysis, see Text 46.14(B), Substantive due process.

[159]State v Hoover, 5 App(3d) 207, 5 OBR 470, 450 NE(2d) 710 (Ottawa 1982).

PROGRAMS

Chapter 26

Curriculum and Educational Programs

26.01 Introduction

STANDARDS FOR ELEMENTARY AND SECONDARY EDUCATION
26.02 State minimum standards
26.03 Standards adopted by school board

GENERAL CURRICULUM
26.04 Requirement and content of curriculum
26.05 Curriculum for kindergarten through grade eight
26.06 High school curriculum
26.07 Curriculum options, alternative schools, college preparatory courses and schools

SPECIAL COURSES AND PROGRAMS
26.08 Disadvantaged pupils and children of migrant workers
26.09 Programs for gifted children
26.10 Special instruction, adult education
26.11 Other special courses and programs

DRIVER TRAINING
26.12 Driver training programs
26.13 Costs, student requirements, equipment and safety requirements
26.14 Alternative driver training methods, commercial instruction

ACADEMIC ACHIEVEMENT, PROMOTION, AND GRADUATION
26.15 Criteria for student performance and promotion
26.16 Awarding high school diploma

REVIEW AND EVALUATION, ENFORCEMENT OF STANDARDS
26.17 Requirements for review and evaluation
26.18 Accreditation evaluations
26.19 School charter, revocation
26.20 Student rights in research, experimental activities, and testing

26.01 Introduction

Each board of education is required to establish a curriculum in the schools under its jurisdiction. The board's discretion is circumscribed, however, by statutory minimum standards and department of education regulations. In addition to the general curriculum, a board of education is authorized or directed to conduct a number of special education programs.

STANDARDS FOR ELEMENTARY AND SECONDARY EDUCATION

26.02 State minimum standards

(A) Curriculum

(1) Statutory requirements

Required courses in elementary and secondary schools are specified both by statutes and rules.

Under the statutes, courses in districts under the control of boards of education of city and exempted village districts and educational service centers must include language arts (reading, writing, spelling, English, and literature), geography, Ohio and United States history, government (national, state, and local), mathematics, natural science, health education, physical education, the fine arts, and first aid.[1] Pupils may participate in courses involving the study of social problems, economics, foreign affairs, United Nations, world government, socialism, and communism only after basic instruction in geography, United States history, government, the Declaration of Independence, and the Ohio and United States Constitutions.[2] Boards may contract with townships, corporations, or counties for the assignment of police officers to dis-

---

[1] RC 3313.60.

[2] RC 3313.60. This statute generally does not apply to a cooperative education school district established under RC 3311.52. Such a district is separately treated under RC 3313.60(F). Specifically, the board of a cooperative education district must prescribe a curriculum for subject areas and grade levels offered in any school under its control. Where a cooperative education district exists under RC 3311.521, RC 3313.60(E) provides that the curriculum shall only include the

trict schools to work with students and counselors to help reduce substance abuse.[3] Boards must also develop and implement a program which explains the counterfeit drug laws to pupils.[4]

RC 3313.602 requires the board of each city, local, exempted village, and joint vocational school district to adopt a policy stating whether recitation of the pledge of allegiance to the flag is part of the school's program and, if so, establishing a time and manner for the recitation.[5] The statute also requires the board, in developing its graded course of study, to ensure that democratic and ethical principles are emphasized and discussed whenever appropriate throughout the curriculum in all grades. The board is also required to adopt policies that encourage all district employees to be cognizant of their roles in instilling ethical principles and ideals in pupils.

(2) Rules

The department of education has detailed basic requirements for curriculum in OAC 3301-35-02. A course of study must be adopted for each subject taught and be based on the philosophy and educational goals adopted by the board of education. Further, the course of study must prescribe what is to be taught, specify subject matter objectives, establish a scope and sequence, and provide a basis for pupil evaluation. Career education, citizenship, human relations education, multi-cultural education, energy and resource conservation education, and instruction in study skills must be part of each course of study. Courses of study must be reviewed and updated at least once every five years.[6]

(B) Educational resources

OAC 3301-35-03 provides a wide range of standards and requirements for delivering education, amounting to a thumbnail blueprint for staffing, equipping, and operating a school. Covered subjects include minimum requirements for staffing with administrators, teachers, and nonteaching personnel; instructional materials and equipment; facilities; pupil health and safety; pupil records, admission, placement, and withdrawal; pupil attendance and conduct; guidance services; extracurricular activities; and community relations.

(C) Competency-based education programs

RC 3301.0715 requires the board of each city, local, and exempted village school district to "implement a competency-based education program for composition, mathematics, science, citizenship, and reading in grades one through twelve," except that if RC 3311.29(C)(1)(b) applies to the district, the program must be implemented in all grades the board is required to operate under that statute. The board of each joint vocational and cooperative education school district must "implement a competency-based education program for composition, mathematics, science, citizenship, and reading in each grade that the district provides." The aim is to ensure that students actually achieve competence in these basic skills, rather than merely be exposed to courses in those subjects.

The program must contain for each grade level in each subject pupil performance objectives, curricula and instructional methods to ensure those objectives can be met, provisions for periodic assessment of pupil performance,[7] availability of intervention services for pupils who fail to make satisfactory progress, written policies and procedures on the participation or exemption of handicapped pupils, procedures for evaluating the program at least every five years, and provisions for annually making certain information about the program's operation during the preceding school year available to the state board of education upon request, which information must be available for public inspection at the district's offices and be furnished to any per-

---

study of subjects applicable to the grades operated by it and participating districts.

[3]RC 3313.95.

[4]RC 2925.01, RC 2925.37.

[5]Constitutional issues under the religion clauses of the First Amendment are discussed at Text 32.03, Free exercise limits on compelled patriotic observances.

[6]OAC 3301-35-02(B).

[7]A district may elect a proficiency test administered under RC 3301.0711 for a particular grade level as the assessment for that grade level. RC 3301.0715. See Text 26.06(B), Graduation requirements.

son upon request and payment of a reasonable fee for the cost of reproduction.[8]

To help districts develop their programs, the state board of education is required to establish model programs, which districts must "seriously consider ... together with other relevant resources, standards, and models" in developing their programs. The models must include for grades pre-kindergarten through twelve: board-recommended performance objectives at each grade level in composition, mathematics, science, citizenship, and reading and in any additional area of study identified by the state board; model curricula at each grade level for instruction in composition, mathematics, science, citizenship, and reading and in any additional area of study identified by the state board; recommended assessment methods for measuring progress in meeting performance objectives; and a recommended program of intervention services by grade level for pupils who do not satisfactorily progress toward performance objectives.[9]

The state board may establish model competency-based education programs for any grade level in areas of study other than composition, mathematics, science, citizenship, and reading, which, if established, must contain performance objectives, a model curriculum, recommended assessment methods, and a suggested intervention program as in the case of required model programs.[10]

26.03 Standards adopted by school board

The standards prescribed for courses of study, staffing, materials and facilities, and related matters in the statutes and rules are minimum standards. The actual course of study for the schools in a school district is prescribed by the board of education, and the board is free to exceed the minimum standards if it chooses.[11] For example, the board may elect to employ more teachers than the minimum required by the prescribed teacher-student ratio of 1:25 or hire more educational service personnel than the minimum of 5 for every 1,000 students.[12] Or, the board might choose to provide competency testing more often than the minimum specified by the state board of education.[13] Or, instead of three units of English language arts, the board might specify that four units are required for graduation from high school.[14]

GENERAL CURRICULUM

26.04 Requirement and content of curriculum

Boards of education must prescribe a curriculum for all schools under their control.[15] The state board formulates and prescribes minimum standards applicable to all elementary and high schools in the state for the purpose of requiring a general education of high quality for all school children.[16]

The kindergarten through twelfth grade educational programs must be implemented in accordance with adopted board policies, which must be available to parents, pupils, and school personnel. The educational program must be evaluated at least once every five years.[17]

The US Supreme Court has upheld the right of school officials to regulate curriculum. *Hazelwood School Dist v Kuhlmeier*[18] held that school officials did not violate the free speech rights of students by removing objectionable material from a school-sponsored newspaper for legitimate educational reasons.[19] *Hazelwood* has been interpreted to allow boards of education to make con-

---

[8]A district may elect a proficiency test administered under RC 3301.0711 for a particular grade level as the assessment for that grade level. RC 3301.0715. See Text 26.06(B), Graduation requirements.

[9]RC 3301.0716(A).
[10]RC 3301.0716(B).
[11]See RC 3313.60.
[12]OAC 3301-35-03(A)(3), (4).
[13]OAC 3301-35-02(B)(2)(b).
[14]OAC 3301-35-02(B)(6)(a).
[15]RC 3313.60.

[16]RC 3301.07.
[17]OAC 3301-35-02.
[18]Hazelwood School Dist v Kuhlmeier, 484 US 260, 108 SCt 562, 98 LEd(2d) 592 (1988).
[19]Similarly, the Sixth Circuit Court of Appeals upheld a teacher's right to regulate the curriculum by rejecting a research paper on the life of Jesus Christ, which was outside the scope of the assignment. Settle v Dickson County School Bd, 53 Fd(3d) 152 (6th Cir Tenn 1995), cert denied ___ SCt ___, 63 USLW 3800 (1995). For more expansive treatment of *Hazelwood*

tent-based decisions regarding curriculum as long as they reasonably relate to legitimate pedagogical goals. Thus, a school district did not violate students' First Amendment rights by removing a humanities textbook from the curriculum on the ground that two works in the book contained vulgarity and sexuality inappropriate for high school students.[20]

Content-based discrimination is to be distinguished from viewpoint-based discrimination, however. Once it is decided that students should be furnished with information on a particular subject, school officials may not distinguish between particular speakers simply on the basis of their views about the matter. Thus, when an organization of peace activists challenged, on free speech grounds, a school board's regulations on who could participate and what information could be presented to high school students during a "career day" program, the court upheld a requirement that presenters have direct knowledge of the career opportunities about which they speak but rejected as unreasonable an additional requirement that the presenter have "some present affiliation with that career field." The board, continued the court, could legitimately prohibit a presenter from denigrating or denouncing certain careers (e.g., military service), but could not constitutionally ban a presenter from giving negative factual information about the disadvantages of a particular job.[21]

26.05 Curriculum for kindergarten through grade eight

(A) Kindergarten

All city, exempted village, and local school districts are required to offer kindergarten, unless exempted by the state board. To be eligible to enroll, a child must be five years old on or before September 30 of the year of admittance, or by the first day of a term or semester other than one beginning in August or September in districts granting admittance at the beginning of such term or semester. A child who does not meet the age requirement must be admitted if the child meets standards determined by the board's testing program. Upon request of the parent, a child who will be the proper age by January 1 of the school year for which admission is requested must be so tested.[22]

RC 3321.01 generally makes kindergarten attendance mandatory. Specifically, no district can admit to the first grade any child who has not successfully completed kindergarten unless, upon parental request, this requirement is waived by the district's "pupil personnel services committee."[23] A waiver is permissible only in the case of a child who is at least six years old by September 30 of the year of admittance and who demonstrates to the committee's satisfaction the possession of the "social, emotional, and cognitive skills necessary for the first grade."[24]

The board of each city, local, and exempted village school district must establish a pupil personnel services committee whose only authority is the issuing of waivers to the mandatory kindergarten requirement. The committee must be composed of the following "to the extent such personnel are either employed by the district or employed by the board of education of the county district within which the district is located and the county district generally furnishes the services of such personnel to the district": the director of pupil personnel services, an elementary counselor, an elementary principal, a school psychologist, and a first grade teacher.[25]

A kindergarten class "shall be developmentally appropriate," with times for classes and length of the school day to be

---

and related cases, see Text 25.05, Regulating student expression.

[20]Virgil v Columbia County, Fla School Bd, 862 F(2d) 1517 (11th Cir Fla 1989). Similarly, a board properly censored a guest lecturer's film clip showing bare-chested women to tenth grade students without violating the lecturer's free speech and due process rights. Silano v Sag Harbor Union Free School Dist Bd of Ed, 42 F(3d) 719 (2d Cir NY 1994), cert denied ___ US ___, 115 SCt 2612, 132 LEd(2d) 856 (1995).

[21]Searcey v Harris, 888 F(2d) 1314 (11th Cir Ga 1989).
[22]RC 3301.16, RC 3311.29, RC 3313.64, RC 3321.01(A).
[23]RC 3321.01(C).
[24]RC 3321.01(D).
[25]RC 3321.01(D).

determined by the board.[26] A child has successfully completed kindergarten within the meaning of the statute if the child has completed kindergarten requirements at a public or chartered nonpublic school, or completed a kindergarten class offered by a licensed day-care provider which is directly taught by the holder of a kindergarten-primary certificate issued under RC 3319.22(A), a Montessori preprimary credential or age-appropriate diploma (or certification deemed by the department of education upon written request of the provider to be equivalent), or certification for teachers in non-tax-supported schools pursuant to RC 3301.071.[27]

Kindergarten pupils must be provided scheduled classes, supervised activities, or approved educational options for the equivalent of at least two and one-half hours a day.[28] A minimum of 200 minutes per week must be allocated to readiness activities in handwriting, mathematics, and reading, and the balance of the time must be allocated for art, English, language arts, health, music, physical education, science, and social studies.[29]

(B) Grades one through six

A five-hour school day, exclusive of lunch, consisting of scheduled classes, supervised activities, or approved educational options, is required for pupils in grades one through six. A minimum of 1,100 minutes per week must be allocated at each grade level for planned instruction in English language arts, health, mathematics, reading, science, and social studies. Foreign language instruction may be included in the 1,100 minutes. A minimum of 200 minutes per week is required at each grade level for planned instruction in art, music, and physical education. Except for English language arts, mathematics, and reading, these weekly time allocations may be modified. Pupils will complete an equivalent amount of time on an annual basis.[30]

(C) Grades seven and eight

The school day for pupils in grades seven and eight must consist of scheduled classes, supervised activities, and approved educational options for at least five and one-half hours exclusive of lunch and interscholastic athletics. At least 1,000 minutes per week must be scheduled for planned instruction in English language arts, mathematics, reading or foreign language, science, and social studies.[31] Additionally, seventh and eighth grade pupils must be scheduled for the equivalent of at least eighty minutes per week in physical education and for eighty minutes per week in art, health, and music. The remainder of the minimum school week for seventh and eighth graders may be divided among any of the foregoing subjects, or in such subjects as business education, typewriting or keyboarding, computer science, home economics, or industrial arts.[32] Pupils below the ninth grade may take advanced work for credit, but such credit may not be considered in calculating the units required for high school graduation.[33]

A statutory requirement for promotion to the ninth grade is one year's course of study in American history and one-half year of Ohio studies for promotion from the eighth grade.[34] Promotion and retention decisions regarding pupils in kindergarten through eighth grades who select an educational option must consider performance relative to the objective of the option.[35]

26.06 High school curriculum

(A) In general, courses offered

The school day for pupils in grades nine through twelve must consist of scheduled

---

[26]RC 3321.01(E), (F).
[27]RC 3321.01(B), (G).
[28]OAC 3301-35-02(B)(10).
[29]OAC 3301-35-02(B)(10).
[30]OAC 3301-35-02(B)(11).
[31]OAC 3301-35-02(B)(12). For treatment of American sign language as a foreign language, successful completion of which entitles a pupil to credit toward satisfaction of a school's foreign language requirement, see Text 26.06(A), In general, courses offered.
[32]OAC 3301-35-02(B)(12). For treatment of American sign language as a foreign language, successful completion of which entitles a pupil to credit toward satisfaction of a school's foreign language requirement, see Text 26.06(A), In general, courses offered.
[33]OAC 3301-35-02(B)(8)(e).
[34]OAC 3301-35-02(B)(5).
[35]OAC 3301-35-02(C).

classes, supervised activities, or approved educational options for at least five and one-half hours exclusive of interscholastic activities and lunch period.[36] A minimum of forty-five units must be scheduled and operated by each board in separately organized classes each year, distributed as follows: (1) business or vocational business, two units, of which at least one-half unit is to be typewriting or keyboarding; (2) economics, one-half unit; (3) English language arts, four and one-half units; (4) fine arts, four units, of which at least one must be art and one music; (5) foreign language, three units if one foreign language is scheduled; two units each if two foreign languages are scheduled; (6) health, one-half unit; (7) home economics or vocational home economics, two units; (8) industrial arts, two units; (9) mathematics, four units; (10) physical education, one-half unit; (11) reading, one-half unit; (12) science, four units, including at least two laboratory courses; (13) social studies, one and one-half units, including one-half unit of American history and one-half unit of American government; and (14) fifteen additional units which may include up to twelve units in vocational courses either at the home school or a vocational school.[37]

RC 3313.604 expressly recognizes American sign language as a foreign language that any school may offer, and successful completion of a course in American sign language entitles a student to credit toward satisfaction of a school's foreign language requirement.[38]

(B) Graduation requirements

To be eligible for graduation from high school, a pupil must successfully earn eighteen credits in grades nine through twelve, including at least three units in the English language arts, one-half unit in health, two units in mathematics, one-half unit in physical education, one unit in science, two units in social studies including at least one-half unit in American history and one-half unit in American government, and nine elective units. Additionally, each pupil is required to complete three units in another subject in addition to the English language arts requirement.[39]

No credit may be awarded unless the course of study is scheduled for a minimum of 120 hours, except that laboratory courses must be scheduled for a minimum of 150 hours and physical education courses scheduled for a minimum of 120 hours for one-half unit of credit. Each credit course must have at least two meetings per week.[40]

Statewide proficiency testing to measure skill in reading, writing, mathematics, science, and citizenship is required in city, exempted village, and local school districts by RC 3301.0710 and RC 3301.0711.[41] In accordance with rules adopted by the state board of education, the board of a city, exempted village, or local district with territory in a joint vocational school district or cooperative education school district established under RC 3311.52 may enter into an agreement with the board of the joint vocational or cooperative education district for administering a prescribed test to students of the city, exempted village, or local district who are attending school in the joint vocational or cooperative education district. Where the city, exempted village, or local district has territory in a cooperative education district established under RC 3311.521, an agreement with the cooperative education district is required that provides for the administration of any test required under RC 3301.0711 to (1) students attending school in the cooperative education district and who, if such district were not established, would be entitled to attend school in the city, exempted village, or local district; and (2) persons who have successfully completed the high school curriculum (or the individualized education program developed for the student by the high school pursuant to RC 3323.08) but

---

[36]OAC 3301-35-02(B)(13).

[37]OAC 3301-35-02(B); RC 3313.60.

[38]See also Text 28.18, Assisting deaf and hard of hearing children and their parents.

[39]OAC 3301-35-02(B)(6).

[40]OAC 3301-35-02(B)(8).

[41]A student receiving special education under RC Ch 3323 is excused from taking any particular test if the student's individualized education plan excuses him; such student cannot be prohibited from taking the test, however. RC 3301.0711(C). If a person is not a United States citizen or permanent resident and does not intend to reside in the United States after completing high school, he is exempted from having to attain the applicable score on the test in citizenship. RC 3313.61(H). See also Text 3.03(G), Other powers and duties.

not received a diploma and who request to take such test at any time it is administered in the district. Any testing under such an agreement is in lieu of any testing of such students or persons pursuant to RC 3301.0711.[42]

If a student successfully completes the high school curriculum (or an individualized education plan developed for the student by the high school pursuant to RC 3323.08) and achieves at least a ninth grade level of literacy and basic competency in the measured skill, he must be granted a diploma under RC 3313.61. A diploma cannot be granted except as provided in the statute. An honors diploma will be issued to a student who, in addition, satisfies the criteria established by the state board of education for such diplomas.[43]

26.07 Curriculum options, alternative schools, college preparatory courses and schools

(A) In general

Boards of education are permitted to offer certain educational options to pupils, except that no pupil under eighteen may participate without parental approval.[44]

Each educational option must have an instructional plan which includes the objectives, instructional activities, and description of criteria to assess pupil performance. A certified teacher must provide instruction and evaluate the pupil performance in tutorial programs and independent studies and must evaluate pupil performance in correspondence courses, educational, travel, and mentor programs. A maximum of six units of credit through educational options may be applied toward the eighteen units required for graduation from high school with only four of the six being applied to requirements in English, language arts, health, mathematics, physical education, science, and social studies.[45]

(B) Alternative schools, college preparatory schools

A school district may establish a special purpose college preparatory high school or an alternative school, provided the school complies with the minimum standards specified in OAC 3301-35-01 to OAC 3301-35-03 and pupils have the option of attending a high school which operates in compliance with the minimum standards.[46] The provisions for competency-based education do not apply to college preparatory high schools.[47]

Colleges and universities have widely varying entrance requirements, and many look for students whose academic preparation has been more intense than that provided by completion of only the minimum requirements for a high school diploma. Although a high school graduate in Ohio is entitled to admission without examination to any state-supported university or college in Ohio, unconditional admission may require completion of various courses and units in addition to the minimum required for graduation.[48] Ohio State University, for example, now requires graduates to have completed a college preparatory program to qualify for unconditional admission.

A college preparatory program can be completed in a regular high school or in a school devoted exclusively to a college preparatory education. A typical curriculum includes additional required units in English, science, and social studies, plus two units in foreign languages, and allows fewer electives than the minimum requirements for high school graduation.

(C) Post-secondary enrollment options program

RC 3365.02 establishes a post-secondary enrollment options program under which a secondary (defined as eleventh or twelfth) grade student may enroll in a state-assisted college or university (or private institution holding a certificate of authorization under

---

[42]RC 3301.0711(J).
[43]RC 3313.61. See also RC 3301.0711 and OAC 3301-13-01 et seq. Section 10 of 1992 H 55 provides that failure to satisfy proficiency testing requirements with respect to science will not preclude the granting of a diploma until September 15, 1998 unless the state board finds it feasible to apply such requirements earlier.

[44]OAC 3301-35-02(C).
[45]OAC 3301-35-02(C).
[46]OAC 3301-35-05.
[47]OAC 3301-35-05(A)(3).
[48]RC 3345.06; 1958 OAG 1749.

RC Chapter 1713) and complete nonsectarian courses for high school and college credit.

State board of education rules governing the program[49] include requirements that school districts provide tenth and eleventh grade students with information about the program by March 1 of each year; that a student or his parent inform the district board by March 30 of the student's intent to participate in the following school year (a student who misses the deadline may not participate in the program during the following school year without the district superintendent's written consent); that districts provide counseling (which must include a number of prescribed elements) to tenth and eleventh grade students before participation to ensure awareness of risks and consequences; and that the student and parent sign a district form stating they have received counseling and understand the responsibilities they must assume.[50] Notwithstanding any other provision of law, a district student may apply to enroll in a college during his eleventh or twelfth grade school year.[51]

The student must exercise either of these options: (1) he may elect at the time of enrollment to receive only college credit for the course; the student is responsible for all tuition, textbooks, materials, and associated fees; if the student successfully completes the course, the college must award him full credit, but the district cannot award him high school credit; or (2) he may elect at the time of enrollment for each course to receive both college credit and high school credit; the college will furnish the student textbooks and materials free of charge and will then be reimbursed by the department of education under a formula set forth in RC 3365.07, with a negative adjustment to state foundation program payments to the student's district; if the student successfully completes the course, the college must award him full credit and the district must award him high school credit.[52]

Under the second option, if a dispute develops between the district board and the student over how much high school credit for a course is granted, the student may appeal to the state board, whose decision is final. The student's district record must include evidence of successful completion of each course, the high school credits awarded, and the name of the college. The district board is to determine how the grade received will be counted in calculating any cumulative grade point average.[53]

A student in grade eleven may not enroll in courses for which he elects under the second option to receive credit toward high school graduation for more than the equivalent of two academic school years. For a student in grade twelve enrolling for the first time under the program, the limit is the equivalent of one year, These restrictions are reduced proportionately in accordance with state board rules if the student enrolls in the program during the course of a school year.[54]

In considering admission of a secondary student applicant, the college must give priority to its other students regarding enrollment in courses; however, once accepted, the participant cannot be displaced by another student.[55]

No student enrolled in a course for which credit toward high school graduation is awarded is eligible for student financial assistance under RC Chapter 3351.[56] If the district board provides transportation for resident eleventh and twelfth grade students, the parent of a pupil who exercised the second option (i.e., opted for both college credit and high school credit) may apply to the board for full or partial reimbursement of the cost of transporting the student between his secondary school and the college. The state board is to establish guidelines, based on financial need, under which a district board may provide reimbursement, which may be paid solely from funds received under RC 3317.024(K).[57] However, both this transportation provision and provisions for reimbursing a college for tuition, textbooks, materials, and

---

[49] OAC 3301-44-01 et seq.
[50] RC 3365.02.
[51] RC 3365.03.
[52] RC 3365.04.
[53] RC 3365.05.

[54] RC 3365.06(A).
[55] RC 3365.06(B).
[56] RC 3365.08(B).
[57] RC 3365.08(C).

fees do not apply to any college course in which a student is enrolled if at the same time he is a full-time student in his district school. State board rules are to prescribe a method for determining whether a student is enrolled full-time in his district school.[58]

SPECIAL COURSES AND PROGRAMS

26.08 Disadvantaged pupils and children of migrant workers

State funds are made available to eligible school districts for the design and operation of special programs to improve the educational and cultural status of disadvantaged pupils. The maximum amount that may be received by the district is $200 times the number of children between the ages of five and seventeen who reside in the district and receive Aid to Dependent Children. A district must have fifty or more resident eligible children or have the qualifying children make up five per cent of the district's average daily membership in order to receive funds.[59]

The state board of education may establish standards and rules for the operation by city, exempted village, or local boards of education of classes for the children of migrant workers who are unable to attend an Ohio school during the entire regular school year. State financial support for the instruction is limited to the subjects regularly offered by the district providing the classes.[60]

26.09 Programs for gifted children

RC 3313.21 requires that every city, local, and exempted village school district formulate a written policy for the identification of gifted children in accordance with the state board of education's definition of "gifted child."[61] In accordance with this policy, gifted students shall be identified annually. The district board must also annually report the number of students identified as gifted and the number receiving services in units approved under RC 3317.05(C) to the state board.[62] The department of education has promulgated guidelines for the identification of gifted children. A gifted child is one who is superior in one or more of four areas: (1) cognitive ability, (2) specific academic ability, (3) creative thinking ability, or (4) visual and/or performing arts ability.[63]

Each school district must also have written procedures for the placement of gifted children in approved programs and services. The procedures must comply with state board rules, provide criteria for placement or withdrawal of students, and provide a process for notification and review of placement decisions.[64] State rules provide for a variety of gifted program alternatives.[65] The state board is required to employ individuals for the purpose of promoting and developing programs for the academically "gifted child"; for researching, advising, and counseling boards of education; and for encouraging the training of teachers in the special instruction of gifted children. Financial assistance is available to boards for the design and implementation of experimental programs for the education of such children upon approval of the state board.[66] Special education support units for gifted children may be requested under RC 3317.024(O)(2). State rules set forth standards for the approval of units or fractional units.[67]

School districts may contract with each other or with the trustees of any college or university to provide special educational services for gifted children.[68]

---

[58] RC 3365.09.
[59] RC 3317.024(F).
[60] RC 3317.024(C).
[61] OAC 3301-51-15. This rule also provides specific means for determining superior ability.
[62] RC 3313.21. This statute expressly does not apply to joint vocational or cooperative education school districts.

[63] OAC 3301-51-15(B).
[64] OAC 3301-51-15(C).
[65] OAC 3301-51-15(D).
[66] RC 3301.07(K).
[67] OAC 3301-51-15(E).
[68] RC 3315.09.

26.10 Special instruction, adult education

(A) In general

The board of education of a city, exempted village, or local school district may operate a summer school, an evening or day school for adults and out-of-school youth, a technical school or institute for instruction beyond the high school, driver training courses as a part of the regular curriculum, or offer post-graduate work in any course of instruction to pupils who have completed the twelfth grade, which may be open to any pupil irrespective of age on such terms and payment of tuition as the board prescribes. Further, a board may offer instruction in basic literacy, with or without tuition.[69]

A board that operates an educational program under RC 3313.641, except for summer school, may authorize the district superintendent to assign to the program any student at least eighteen years old who has not successfully completed the curriculum of any high school or the individualized education plan developed for the student pursuant to RC 3323.08 and who is being readmitted following expulsion or commitment to the department of youth services. Tuition may not be charged if the student is entitled under RC 3313.64 to attend district schools tuition-free.[70]

A board may not, under either RC 3313.531[71] or RC 3313.641, contract with and pay a private nonprofit association for the instruction of secondary school-age pupils who have dropped out of school and desire to complete a general curriculum designed to lead toward a diploma.[72]

(B) Evening schools

A board of education may organize evening schools, and any person over eighteen may be permitted to attend on such terms and payment of tuition as the board prescribes.[73] Reasonable terms and conditions of a withdrawal and refund policy will be enforced.[74] Adult residents of the district may be required to pay tuition. Nonresident adults should be charged an amount sufficient to cover the additional cost entailed by their admission.[75]

(C) Part-time classes for employed children

A board may also establish and maintain part-time schools or classes for the further education of children employed on age and schooling certificates and may provide for the expense of such schools and classes the same as for ordinary elementary schools. These schools and classes must be conducted under standards prescribed by the state board of education.[76]

(D) Adult high school continuation programs

A board of education may operate adult high school continuation programs consisting of organized instruction for persons sixteen and older. Such programs must be limited to courses for which credit may be granted toward a diploma. The state board of education is required to adopt rules and standards under which any school district or combination of districts may operate the programs and receive reimbursement from state funds.[77]

Any student enrolled in such an adult high school continuation program who is twenty-two or more years of age may request an evaluation by the board of education operating the program to determine if the person is handicapped. If found to be handicapped, the board must determine whether to excuse the person from taking any of the tests prescribed by RC 3301.0710. Such determination must be made in the same manner as it would be for special education students in the district.[78]

The district board may authorize the district superintendent to assign any student eighteen or older who has not received a high school diploma and who is being readmitted following expulsion or commitment to the department of youth services.

---

[69]RC 3313.641.
[70]RC 3313.641, RC 3313.531.
[71]See Text 26.10(D), Adult high school continuation programs.
[72]OAG 81-002.
[73]RC 3313.52.

[74]Reineck v Randall, 20 App(3d) 97, 20 OBR 119, 484 NE(2d) 1061 (Sandusky 1984).
[75]1954 OAG 64.
[76]RC 3313.56.
[77]RC 3313.531. See OAC 3301-43-01 et seq.
[78]RC 3313.532.

Tuition may not be charged if the student is entitled under RC 3313.64 to attend district schools tuition-free.[79]

An adult high school may be chartered in accordance with minimum standards specified in OAC 3301-35-01 to OAC 3301-35-03, subject to exceptions approved by the state board based on recommendations by the superintendent of public instruction.[80]

A board may pay to advertise district offerings of adult education classes as provided for in RC 3313.52, RC 3313.531, RC 3313.641, and RC 3313.644.[81]

(E) Adult education diplomas

RC 3313.611 requires the state board of education to adopt standards "for awarding high school credit equivalent to credit for completion of high school academic and vocational education courses" to applicants for a diploma of adult education. The standards may permit credit for work experiences or experiences as a volunteer, completion of academic, vocational, or self-improvement courses, and "other life experiences considered by the board to provide knowledge and learning experiences comparable to that gained in a classroom setting."[82]

The board of each city, exempted village, or local school district that operates a high school must grant an adult education diploma to any applicant over twenty-one who is a district resident, has not received a high school diploma under RC 3313.61, has attained (unless excused under an individualized education plan developed under RC 3323.08 or exempted under the provisions of RC 3313.61(H) applicable to the test in citizenship) the scores designated pursuant to RC 3301.0710(B) for demonstrating ninth grade proficiency in certain measured skills, and has attained sufficient high school credits, including equivalent credits, to qualify for graduation.[83]

If an applicant is found ineligible, the board must inform him of the reason and provide a list of courses required for a diploma for which he has not received credit. The applicant may reapply at any time.[84]

An adult education diploma is paid for out of the district's general fund and must be dated and signed by the board president, district superintendent, and treasurer.[85]

26.11 Other special courses and programs

(A) Technical training, advanced studies

A board of education may contract with any legally organized college or university to obtain instruction in special, technical, professional, or other advanced studies beyond the scope of the public high school. Such a contract to obtain instruction or other educational services may also be entered into with a private corporation or nonprofit association maintaining and furnishing a museum of art, science, or history, or providing musical instruction.[86]

(B) Vocational training

A board may establish and maintain, in connection with the public school systems, manual training, industrial arts, domestic science, and commercial departments and agricultural, industrial, vocational, and trade schools.[87]

(C) Cultural enrichment

A board may cooperate (including contributions of funds, equipment, or personnel) with boards of county commissioners and boards or other public officials having the custody and management of public parks, libraries, museums, and public buildings and grounds. These cooperative activities are to provide for educational, social, civic, and recreational activities, in buildings and on grounds under the manage-

---

[79]RC 3313.531.
[80]OAC 3301-35-05(D).
[81]RC 3313.204.
[82]RC 3313.611(A). See OAC 3301-43-01 et seq.
[83]RC 3313.611(B). RC 3313.611 does not apply to joint vocational school districts or to cooperative education school districts established under RC 3311.52. RC 3313.61(I). Any applicant for an adult education diploma under RC 3313.611 may request an evaluation by the board to determine if the person is handi-

capped. If found to be handicapped, the board must determine whether to excuse the person from taking any of the tests prescribed by RC 3301.0710. Such determination must be made in the same manner as it would be for special education students in the district. RC 3313.532.
[84]RC 3313.611(C).
[85]RC 3313.611(D).
[86]RC 3315.09.
[87]RC 3313.53.

ment of the boards or other public officials.[88]

A board may employ competent persons to lecture or give instruction on any educational subject and provide for the further education of adult persons in the community.[89]

(D) Child day-care centers

The director of human services is required to license child day-care centers.[90] Child day-care programs conducted by boards of education or by chartered nonpublic schools in school buildings and for school children only are exempt from the licensing requirement, as are preschool programs and school child programs subject to licensure by the department of education.[91]

(E) Americanization schools

A board may establish and maintain, on application of not less than fifteen adult persons born outside the territorial limits of the United States (including Hawaii and Alaska), Americanization schools, open to all persons eighteen or over, who are residents of that district or an adjoining district and are of foreign birth. The board may charge a fee for this school.[92]

(F) Vacation period activities

A board may provide summer vacation activities for children, subject to parental approval, which will promote their health, civic interest, vocational competence, industry, recreation, character, or thrift. The board must provide the service necessary for such activities, and may pay the necessary expenses. The district superintendent is to keep records of activities assigned and completed. With state board of education approval, the successful completion of such vacation activities may be required for a promotion or diploma of graduation but not for the issuance of an age and schooling certificate.[93]

(G) Educational broadcasting network, educational computer network

Ohio has a network of television and radio facilities and base stations incorporated into a statewide system, which is an integral part of the nationwide system, under the overall guidance of the Ohio Educational Broadcasting Network Commission.[94]

The state board of education is required to adopt rules governing the purchasing and leasing of data processing services and equipment for all school districts. These rules must include provisions for the establishment of an Ohio education computer network consisting of no more than twenty-seven data acquisition sites.[95]

(H) Business advisory councils

RC 3313.174 requires that the board of each city, exempted village, and county school district appoint a "business advisory council" (whose membership and organization the board determines) to advise and provide recommendations on board-specified matters including the development of curriculum to instill employment skills, the types of employment where future jobs are most likely to be available, and development of a "working relationship" among businesses, labor unions, and district educational personnel.

DRIVER TRAINING

26.12 Driver training programs

(A) In general, minimum standards

The board of education of a city, exempted village, or local school district may offer driver training courses as a part of the regular curriculum.[96] The state board of education must formulate and prescribe minimum standards for driver education courses conducted at high schools in the state, with the advice and assistance of the director of public safety. Energy conservation and financial responsibility information must be included as part of the curriculum.[97]

(B) Standard course, teachers

A district board that makes available a driver training course under RC 3301.17

---

[88] RC 3313.59.
[89] RC 3313.58.
[90] RC 5104.02, RC 5104.05.
[91] RC 5104.02(B)(6), (7).
[92] RC 3313.54.
[93] RC 3313.57.
[94] RC Ch 3353.
[95] RC 3301.075.
[96] RC 3313.641.
[97] RC 3301.07(E).

must make available the standard sixty-hour course unless an exception is approved by the department of education.[98] State rules set the minimum requirements for course content.[99] Driver education teachers in public schools and laboratory aid instructors must meet certain minimum qualifications. Teachers must hold a provisional or higher grade certificate with driver education endorsed on the certificate. Substitute teachers must meet all of the qualifications of a regular teacher.[100]

26.13 Costs, student requirements, equipment and safety requirements

(A) Subsidy, course fees

Public schools are subsidized $50 for each student who completes the driver education course.[101] Parental consent is required before a student can be enrolled in the behind-the-wheel phase of driver education. A temporary driving permit is also required for behind-the-wheel instruction.[102] A board may require pupils enrolled in the course to pay a fee not exceeding the lesser of $50, or the actual cost per pupil of providing driver education less the state driver education reimbursement per pupil.[103]

(B) Student requirements

A board is required to make driver education courses available during the semester or term of a child's sixteenth birthday or the immediate succeeding semester or term. Each board is required to develop a driver education course of study. Pupils must be at least sixteen before actual behind-the-wheel instruction is started. Behind-the-wheel instruction cannot begin until completion of nine hours of classroom instruction. Pupils must be provided instruction in both the classroom and laboratory phases during the same semester or the following semester. The complete course must be completed within nine months.[104]

(C) Vehicles, lease, equipment

A board may pay a service or lease charge for driver education vehicles. All vehicles obtained or used in driver education must be used exclusively for that purpose and properly equipped with dual controls, instructor's inside mirror, seat belts for all occupants, and outside rear view mirrors installed on the right and left sides of the vehicle.[105]

(D) Limit on teacher's instruction time

A teacher may spend no more than four consecutive hours in behind-the-wheel instruction after which a minimum one-half hour break must be taken before further instruction is given.[106]

26.14 Alternative driver training methods, commercial instruction

A board is required to pay to each commercial driver training school from state funds an amount per pupil not exceeding the amount received from the state if a driver training course is not available at the pupil's high school or the pupil was unable to enroll in a driver's education course at another high school or a course conducted by the county board of education, or if a student cannot avail himself of such a course during the semester or term of his sixteenth birthday due to scheduling difficulties. A student is considered to have scheduling difficulties if he is employed or is traveling to or from his employment at the time the course is offered. The student is also considered to have scheduling difficulties if the principal determines the student is involved in a hardship situation or if

---

[98] RC 3301.17; OAC 3301-81-01, OAC 3301-81-02. Boards are no longer required to offer driver education courses. Districts that opt to continue offering courses are not able to require enrollment in lieu of taking a course from a licensed commercial driver training school. Each high school principal is required to notify students annually in writing that they may elect to take a course from a commercial driver training school or, if available, enroll in a course offered by the district.

[99] OAC 3301-81-03.
[100] OAC 3301-81-04.
[101] OAC 3301-81-01(C), OAC 3301-81-08.
[102] OAC 3301-81-06.
[103] RC 3301.171.
[104] OAC 3301-81-01.
[105] OAC 3301-81-07.
[106] OAC 3301-81-12.

there are scheduling conflicts with other courses.[107]

The inability of a pupil to obtain a driver training course or the unavailability of a course must be confirmed by completion of a department of education form which must be signed by the principal of the pupil's high school and submitted by the pupil to the operator of the commercial training school prior to the time the pupil enrolls in the training course. Each licensed private driver training school seeking reimbursement must submit statements to the board of the pupil's school district. A board must then pay to the commercial school $50 for each student, from state board of education funds it has received for that purpose.[108]

The department of education must contract for the use of public school and county boards of education facilities wherever possible to provide driver education courses. Such courses may also be established and operated by the department of education under the supervision of transportation coordinators.[109] A board of education may contract for a one-year term with another board of education or with a driver training school, licensed under RC 4508.03, for providing instruction in driver education. The driver training school must meet course content standards of the state board.[110]

ACADEMIC ACHIEVEMENT, PROMOTION, AND GRADUATION

26.15 Criteria for student performance and promotion

(A) In general

Neither the statutes nor the rules contain specific requirements for gauging student performance. School boards are required to establish procedures for evaluating and monitoring student achievement,[111] but the grading system and standards for achievement are within the board's discretion under its general authority.[112]

The procedures for monitoring performance must provide for making progress reports to parents at established intervals. If progress is unsatisfactory, interim reports are required, and parents must be notified of any attendance or deportment problems. Criteria for decisions on promotion or retention must include a requirement that pupils complete one year of American history and one-half year of Ohio studies to be promoted from the eighth grade.[113]

(B) Educational malpractice

A board of education or teacher does not guarantee that every graduate has mastered basic skills. Thus, Ohio courts have refused to recognize a cause of action for educational malpractice.[114]

26.16 Awarding high school diploma

(A) In general

A high school diploma must be granted by the board of education of any city, exempted village, or local school district that operates a high school to one who satisfies the requirements set forth in RC 3313.61.[115] The diploma must be signed by the board president, district superintendent, treasurer, and high school principal. The diploma must be dated and in a form prescribed by the board, and its cost is paid out of the district's general fund.[116]

Under RC 3313.642, credits may be withheld for nonpayment of school fees, if the board has previously adopted a written

---

[107]RC 3301.17.
[108]RC 3301.17.
[109]RC 3301.17.
[110]RC 3315.091.
[111]OAC 3301-35-02(B)(1), (4).
[112]RC 3313.20, RC 3313.47.
[113]OAC 3301-35-02(B)(5).
[114]Poe v Hamilton, 56 App(3d) 137, 565 NE(2d) 887 (Warren 1990); Denson v Steubenville Bd of Ed, No. 85-J-31, 1986 WL 8239 (7th Dist Ct App, Jefferson, 7-29-86).

[115]These requirements are treated in Text 26.06(B), Graduation requirements. RC 3313.61 does not apply to joint vocational school districts or to cooperative education school districts established under RC 3311.52.

[116]RC 3313.61.

schedule of fees.[117] A board may not withhold the grade or credits of pupils who fail to account for items for which they voluntarily assumed responsibility in connection with school-sponsored or school-approved fund-raising activities.[118]

A school district that contracts with a licensed proprietary school to provide vocational training should give high school credit for courses provided by the proprietary school.[119]

A diploma must be granted to an Ohio resident who has earned credits while an inmate of a correctional institution by both the school district in which the inmate resided prior to his incarceration and the correctional institution. If a nonresident inmate is eligible to receive a diploma, it must be issued by the correctional institution only.[120]

(B) Guaranteed competency of graduates

RC 3313.647 states that the board of a city, local, exempted village, or joint vocational school district may (but is not required to) establish, pursuant to state board of education rules,[121] a policy guaranteeing a specific level of competency of certain of the district's high school graduates. The policy must state that any graduate meeting board-specified criteria is capable of performing indicated functions at a level established in the policy. If an employer or potential employer submits a written statement stating the guaranteed graduate does not meet that level, the board must provide free additional educational opportunity, regardless of the graduate's age or residence, until the guaranteed level is attained. School funds may be spent on a guarantee program, but a student participant cannot be included in the district's average daily membership under RC 3317.03[122] or counted in any other program if inclusion would result in additional state funds for the district.

REVIEW AND EVALUATION, ENFORCEMENT OF STANDARDS

26.17 Requirements for review and evaluation

Evaluation of educational programs and resources is an integral part of the requirements for curriculum and educational resources. Curriculum and instruction must include systematic planning, articulation, implementation, and evaluation.[123] Each course of study must, among other matters, provide a basis for pupil evaluation. As earlier noted, courses of study must be reviewed and updated at least once every five years.[124] Similarly, the allocation of educational resources must be evaluated at least once every five years, "according to professionally recognized criteria and procedures."[125]

The department of education is required to collect and analyze information annually on each new educational program and activity administered by or through it, to determine the degree to which the program or activity achieves its goals and objectives and meets the state's educational needs. Any resident of the state must, upon request, be granted access to the information and analysis.[126]

Comparative statistical analysis of Ohio school districts on a number of levels will be facilitated by the statewide education management information system to be established and maintained by the state board of education under RC 3301.0714.[127]

26.18 Accreditation evaluations

A board of education may appropriate from the general fund an amount sufficient to pay annual membership dues and a service fee to one or more accrediting associations which have the purpose of improving education. The annual dues and service fees may not exceed a total of $400 per

---

[117]RC 3313.642 renders 1960 OAG 1860 obsolete, at least in part; arguably, the part of the opinion that prohibits refusal of a diploma for nonpayment of fees has continuing vitality.
[118]OAG 84-027.
[119]OAG 72-081.
[120]RC 3313.61.
[121]See OAC 3301-49-01.

[122]See Text 39.09(B), Average daily membership.
[123]OAC 3301-35-02(B).
[124]OAC 3301-35-02(B)(1).
[125]OAC 3301-35-03(K).
[126]RC 3301.132.
[127]See Text 3.03(F), Statewide education management information system.

public school evaluated for accreditation. In addition, a board may pay the necessary and proper expenses associated with accreditation activities and school evaluations. Also, a board may pay an employee his regular salary during his service as an evaluator in another school district.[128]

26.19 School charter, revocation

Based upon its established standards for elementary and high schools, the state board of education is directed to classify and charter school districts and individual schools within each district and must revoke the charter of any district or school which fails to meet the standards prescribed. The procedure to be followed in the issuance and revocation of charters is governed by the Administrative Procedure Act, RC 119.01 et seq.[129]

RC 3301.16 charter requirements do not limit a district board's authority to terminate particular grades at one school and transfer the grades and pupils to another school in the district.[130]

If a district's charter is revoked, the state board may dissolve the district and transfer its territory to one or more adjacent districts.[131]

The filing of a referendum petition pursuant to RC 3301.161 against the transfer of a local school district suspends not only the transfer order made by the department of education, pending the outcome of the vote, but also the companion order of dissolution of the district.[132]

26.20 Student rights in research, experimental activities, and testing

20 USCA 1232h, popularly known as the Hatch Amendment, requires that all instructional materials used in connection with any survey, analysis, or evaluation as part of any program or project funded by the US department of education be available for inspection by the parents or guardians of the children.[133] In addition, no student can be required without prior written consent of the parent or guardian to participate in any such survey, analysis, or evaluation that reveals information regarding (1) political affiliations, (2) potentially embarrassing mental and psychological problems, (3) sex behavior and attitudes, (4) illegal, anti-social, self-incriminating, and demeaning behavior, (5) critical appraisals of others with whom the student has close family relationships, (6) legally recognized privileged and analogous relationships, or (7) income (other than as required for determining eligibility for financial assistance). Parents and students must be given effective notice of their rights under the statute. Only a directly affected student or parent (or guardian) may file a complaint under this statute, which must include evidence of attempted resolution at the local level.[134] If the recipient of department funds does not comply with the statute, funds may be withheld or terminated.[135]

---

[128] RC 3313.871.
[129] RC 3301.16.
[130] Ferris v Paulding Exempted Village School Dist Bd of Ed, 7 App(3d) 163, 7 OBR 208, 454 NE(2d) 957 (Paulding 1982).
[131] RC 3301.16, RC 3301.161. See State ex rel Bratenahl Local School Dist Bd of Ed v State Bd of Ed, 53 OS(2d) 173, 373 NE(2d) 1238 (1978), cert denied 439 US 865, 99 SCt 190, 58 LEd(2d) 175 (1978) (discussion of dissolution and transfer procedure).

[132] OAG 71-036.
[133] The statute defines "instructional materials" to include "teacher's manuals, films, tapes, or other supplementary instructional material ... " Regulations under the statute appear at 34 CFR Part 98.
[134] 34 CFR 98.7.
[135] 34 CFR 98.10.

Chapter 27

Vocational Education and Programs

VOCATIONAL TRAINING PROGRAMS
27.01 State and federal emphasis on vocational education
27.02 Providing vocational education
27.03 Vocational course offerings
27.04 Implementation of vocational education program, federal funding
27.05 Production of goods in vocational education programs
27.06 Payment of wages in occupational work adjustment
27.07 In-service training for vocational child-care students

JOINT VOCATIONAL SCHOOL DISTRICT
27.08 Formation of joint vocational school district
27.09 Administration of joint vocational school district
27.10 Vocational school facilities
27.11 Funding joint vocational school districts
27.12 Pupils, special education, transportation

VOCATIONAL REHABILITATION
27.13 Rehabilitation services commission
27.14 Ohio rehabilitation center
27.15 Records

VOCATIONAL TRAINING PROGRAMS

27.01 State and federal emphasis on vocational education

As society advances in technological achievement, the need for skilled employees increases. To encourage states to make vocational training available to more young people, Congress has provided for federal subsidies. Legislation has been adopted and implemented in Ohio to create programs which provide vocational education to as many students as possible.[1]

27.02 Providing vocational education

Each city, exempted village, and local school district must provide vocational education adequate to prepare enrolled pupils for an occupation. A school board may meet its obligation through several methods (provided state board of education standards are met):

(1) Establishing and maintaining a vocational education program of its own (this is the preferred method if it is feasible);

(2) Being a member of a joint vocational school district; or

(3) Contracting for vocational education with a joint vocational school or another school district.[2] Criteria for a contract between school districts are specified by regulation.[3]

A board also may contract with approved private parties.[4] The state board of education may require that a school district enter into a contract to supply vocational education and that an appropriate fee be paid for such services.[5]

The state board may assign a district that does not supply adequate vocational services to a joint vocational school district.[6] When the state board makes an assignment, it must also direct the districts to contract so as to provide suitable vocational services.[7] Where districts are involuntarily assigned to a joint vocational school district, the county auditor and treasurer are not obligated to extend the joint vocational district's tax levies to the involuntarily assigned school districts.[8] Both state law and rules alternatively provide that contracting districts pay a participation fee to the district providing the vocational program.[9] If the assignment is opposed by a

---

[1] RC 3303.02, RC 3313.90.
[2] RC 3313.90.
[3] OAC 3301-61-06.
[4] RC 3313.91.
[5] RC 3313.91; OAC 3301-61-06.
[6] RC 3313.91, RC 3313.911.
[7] Eastland Joint Vocational School Dist v Department of Education, 50 OS(2d) 91, 362 NE(2d) 654 (1977).

[8] State ex rel Vantage Joint Vocational School Dist Bd of Ed v Hoffman, 54 OS(2d) 384, 377 NE(2d) 758 (1978).
[9] RC 3313.91; OAC 3301-61-06.

majority of the electorate in a referendum conducted pursuant to RC 3313.911, the state board may thereafter require the district to contract for vocational education under RC 3313.91.

A school district which contracts with a licensed proprietary school to provide vocational training under RC 3313.90 should give high school credit for courses provided by the school.[10]

RC 3317.21 creates within the state treasury a vocational school building assistance fund to be used solely to provide interest-free loans to school districts, including joint vocational school districts, to assist in funding the construction of new or the renovation of existing vocational classroom facilities or the purchase of vocational education equipment or facilities. Application procedures and priorities to be used in evaluating applications appear in RC 3317.22, which, among other things, requires the repayment of any loan for the construction, acquisition, or renovation of facilities within a maximum of fifteen years and the repayment of any loan for equipment within a maximum of five years. A loan agreement must be entered into between the state board of education and the school district it approves for a loan as prescribed in RC 3317.23.

27.03 Vocational course offerings

Neither the statutes nor the regulations specify the courses or units which make up given vocational training programs. State board of education rules provide that each school district must provide, by one of the means outlined above,[11] for a minimum of twelve different vocational education job training offerings and twenty classes of vocational education, with no more than four of the twelve training offerings provided through cooperative education (i.e., on-the-job training).[12] Present and future labor market trends, plus the recommendations of local advisory committees of employer and employee representatives from several fields, must be taken into account in constructing a vocational program.[13]

The state board is statutorily charged with the task of developing a "plan of action" to modernize the vocational curriculum.[14]

27.04 Implementation of vocational education program, federal funding

Some federal funds currently are provided for the salaries and training of teachers and administrators of vocational subjects.[15] The federal department of education is available for cooperation in the program, which is under the direction of the state board of education.[16]

Any school, department, or class giving instruction in vocational education subjects approved by the state board, and any approved school or college training teachers in such subjects and receiving federal funds, are entitled to receive a matching amount of state funds for the year.[17]

The state treasurer is the custodian of all federal funds received under the program, and all such federal funds and all state appropriations are disbursed on the order of the state board of education.[18] All approved vocational education instruction programs are eligible for extended service funding and may be approved for state subsidy support based on application from a local education agency.[19] Extended service funding allows the district to increase the work year of certain personnel beyond the regular school calendar. State regulations specify the number of weeks of funding allotted for certain categories of employees.[20]

27.05 Production of goods in vocational education programs

When implementing vocational education programs authorized under RC

---

[10]OAG 72-081.
[11]See Text 27.02, Providing vocational education.
[12]OAC 3301-61-03.
[13]OAC 3301-61-03.
[14]RC 3313.901.
[15]RC 3303.03.
[16]RC 3303.04.
[17]RC 3303.05.
[18]RC 3303.06.
[19]OAC 3301-61-13.
[20]OAC 3301-61-13.

3313.90, a school may compete in private enterprise, even at a profit, so long as the program is reasonably necessary to fulfill the requirements of the school's curriculum.[21] The school district must comply with applicable state laws in regard to the acquisition, use, and sale of property.[22]

A school with vocational education programs involving the retail sale of goods, whether purchased with public funds or otherwise, is subject to the Sales Tax Act on the transfer of such goods to another and must obtain a vendor's license as provided in RC 5739.17.[23]

A joint vocational school district, as a part of its educational program, may construct and sell single family residences on school land no longer needed for other school purposes, and the land may be subdivided for this purpose.[24] A district also has authority to contract with a board of county commissioners for construction by district students, as part of their vocational training, of a juvenile treatment center for the county.[25] A district also may enter into an agreement with a nonprofit corporation whereby students construct a building on property owned by the corporation with materials and equipment supplied by the corporation, so long as the program is reasonably necessary to fulfill the requirements of the school's curriculum.[26] The district must comply with the sale at auction requirements of RC 3313.41 with respect to any property exceeding $10,000 in value.

A board of education is prohibited from entering into a joint venture with a commercial oil company to construct and operate for profit a service station on school property.[27]

27.06 Payment of wages in occupational work adjustment

Students in occupational work adjustment laboratories, where students produce items on a contract basis, may be paid wages by a board of education. Under the Fair Labor Standards Act, students in approved vocational training programs may make seventy-five per cent of the minimum wage. A special student-learner certificate must be obtained in advance from the wage and hour division of the department of labor.[28]

27.07 In-service training for vocational child-care students

An exception is made to the general requirement that all child-care center staff members have completed high school or an approved training program. A student enrolled in the second year of a vocational child-care training program, which is approved by the state board of education and leads to high school graduation, may be designated or employed as a child-care staff member provided the student performs duties in the child day-care center under the continuous supervision of an experienced child-care staff member; receives periodic supervision from the vocational child-care training program teacher-coordinator in his high school; and meets all other requirements of RC Chapter 5104.[29]

JOINT VOCATIONAL SCHOOL DISTRICT

27.08 Formation of joint vocational school district

Although the preferred method for providing vocational education is for a school district to maintain its own program,[30] circumstances may dictate that a high quality program can be maintained more easily and economically if two or more school districts join forces. One vehicle for doing this is the joint vocational school district.

(A) In general

Any combination of local, exempted village or city boards of education or governing boards of educational service centers may make or commission a study of

---

[21]OAG 71-068.
[22]See Text Ch 35, School Supplies and Food Service; Text Ch 36, Acquiring and Disposing of Property.
[23]See Text Ch 35, School Supplies and Food Service; Text Ch 36, Acquiring and Disposing of Property.
[24]OAG 76-065; OAG 81-092.
[25]OAG 89-061.
[26]OAG 81-092.
[27]OAG 78-040.
[28]RC 3313.93. See 29 CFR Part 520.
[29]RC 5104.011.
[30]See Text 27.02, Providing vocational education.

the need for a joint vocational school district within the county or adjoining counties and for preparing a plan to establish and operate the district. Joint vocational school districts also may be called vocational school districts. Local, exempted village, and city school districts in the service center territories involved may share the cost of the study and plan. The plan is submitted to the state board of education by the initiating district(s).[31]

On approval by the state board, the plan is filed with the board of education of each district proposed to be included in the new joint vocational school district.[32] Subject to the consent of those districts, the initiating district(s) may create a joint vocational school district composed of the territory of the consenting districts.[33] RC 3311.16 does not require that districts forming a joint vocational school district be contiguous.[34]

A joint vocational school district is an entity separate and apart from any other school district; however, the participating school districts do not lose their separate identity or legal existence.[35] A joint vocational school district board of education generally has the same powers and duties as a city school district board of education.[36] However, a city civil service commission has no jurisdiction over the personnel of a joint vocational school district when its facilities are located in the city but its territory is spread over several counties.[37]

(B) *Expansion of district*

With the approval of the joint vocational school district board, any other school district in the county or counties comprising the district, or in an adjacent county, may become part of the joint vocational district. RC 3311.213 sets forth the procedure for joinder, for remonstrance petitions, and for adjustment of the membership of the board of the joint vocational school district.

A new local school district created under RC 3311.26 by combining two local school districts, each of which was a participating member of separate joint vocational school districts, does not automatically become a participating district of either joint vocational school district.[38]

The state board of education may assign school districts to joint vocational districts and must require districts to enter into agreements under RC 3313.90 so that special education students as well as others may receive suitable vocational services.[39] The assignment by the state board of a school district to a joint vocational district is a reviewable administrative decision.[40] County auditors and treasurers are not required to extend the joint vocational district tax levy to the districts involuntarily assigned to the joint district.[41]

(C) *Consolidation of districts*

RC 3311.214 expressly authorizes the consolidation of two or more joint vocational school districts, subject to approval by the state board of education. A majority of each participating joint vocational district board must adopt identical resolutions proposing that one new joint vocational school district be created. A copy of each resolution must be filed with the state board for its approval or disapproval. The resolutions must contain a provision, prescribed in the statute, on the make-up of the new district board.

If the resolutions are approved, the statute prescribes a procedure under which electors in a district to be dissolved can file with the state board a petition of remonstrance against creation of the proposed new district. Otherwise, a new district is created under a statutory timetable. Funds, property, and the "net indebtedness" (as defined in the statute) of the dissolved districts pass to the new board which must also honor contracts made by the former

---

[31]RC 3311.01, RC 3311.16.
[32]RC 3311.17.
[33]RC 3311.18.
[34]State ex rel Pioneer Joint Vocational School Dist Bd of Ed v Schumann, 7 OS(2d) 41, 218 NE(2d) 180 (1966).
[35]OAG 65-167; RC 3311.18.
[36]RC 3311.19(D). See Text 27.09(A), Board of education of joint vocational district.
[37]OAG 73-062.

[38]OAG 66-098.
[39]RC 3313.91; Eastland Joint Vocational School Dist v Department of Education, 50 OS(2d) 91, 362 NE(2d) 654 (1977).
[40]See RC Ch 119. See also In re Assignment of New Riegel Local School Dist, 8 App(3d) 306, 8 OBR 414, 456 NE(2d) 1245 (Franklin 1982).
[41]State ex rel Vantage Joint Vocational School Dist Bd of Ed v Hoffman, 54 OS(2d) 384, 377 NE(2d) 758 (1978).

boards. The new district board must notify the county auditor of each district in which a dissolved district was located that a new district has been created and certify to each auditor any changes that might be required in the tax rate as a result of creation of the new district.

(D) Dissolution of districts

RC 3311.217 provides that, upon either approval of a majority of the full membership of the joint vocational school district board or receipt of resolutions adopted by a majority of the boards of districts participating in the joint vocational district, the joint vocational district board shall adopt and send to the state board of education a resolution requesting dissolution of the district. This resolution must state the reasons for dissolution, include a plan for the equitable allocation of assets and obligations, and provide that the tax duplicate of each participating district shall be bound for and assume its share of the joint vocational district's outstanding indebtedness. Upon approval by the state board, the joint vocational district is dissolved.

27.09 Administration of joint vocational school district

(A) Board of education of joint vocational district

Management and control of a joint vocational school district is vested in a joint vocational school district board of education. Except for the powers, duties, and authority granted by RC Chapters 124, 3311, 3317, 3323, and 3331, the board has the same powers and duties and authority for the management and operation of the district as a city school district board of education and is subject to all provisions of law applicable to a city school district.[42]

Considerable flexibility is allowed in the composition of the board.[43] However, when a person desires to hold two conflicting positions, e.g., health commissioner of the general health district of a county and member of the board of a joint vocational school district, it is clear that he may only hold one position.[44] In general, the board is composed of representatives from each of the boards participating in the joint district. If the participating districts are all local school districts in the same county, the service center governing board acts as the joint district board. Also, participating districts (including city, exempted village, and local districts) all in the same county may agree to have the governing board act as the joint board. Under a procedure spelled out in RC 3311.19(B), governing board members may be replaced or supplemented by local board members for service on the joint vocational board.

A local school district is not entitled to direct representation on the board of a joint vocational district except in accordance with RC 3311.19.[45] The appointment of a member of a joint vocational district board by a participating school district is made by a resolution adopted by a majority of the members of the appointing board.[46]

(B) Superintendent of joint vocational district

The board of a joint vocational district may appoint any qualified administrator to serve as district superintendent. However, if the educational service center governing board acts as the joint vocational district board, then the service center superintendent serves as the superintendent.[47] The service center superintendent may be appointed superintendent of a joint vocational district even if the governing board is not also serving as the joint vocational board, provided it is physically possible for one person to perform the duties of both offices.[48]

(C) Evaluation by state

By October 30 of each year, the state superintendent of public instruction is required to determine and certify to the superintendent of each city, exempted village, and local school district whether that

---

[42] RC 3311.19(D). Various statutes outside these specified Chapters that pertain to city school districts and their boards expressly do not apply to joint vocational districts, however; thus, the only safe course in analyzing a joint vocational district board's powers, duties, and authority is to examine the specific statute in question.

[43] RC 3311.19(A).
[44] OAG 86-038.
[45] OAG 71-015.
[46] OAG 70-111.
[47] OAG 70-111.
[48] OAG 66-135.

district is in compliance with the laws regarding providing vocational education. If a district is not in compliance, the superintendent must notify the district board of the actions necessary to accomplish compliance.[49]

27.10 Vocational school facilities

(A) In general

A joint vocational school district may construct and equip the buildings and other facilities necessary to operate its programs and may levy taxes and issue bonds; both require approval of the electorate.[50] Joint vocational district facilities may be used for post-high school training, technical training, and retraining programs. A district may construct, maintain, and operate dormitories and other facilities for any students.[51]

A participating member district of a joint vocational school district by agreement may permit the use of its buildings for a vocational school program, either without cost or at a stipulated rental.[52]

(B) Cooperation with technical college district

A coterminous joint vocational school district and technical college district may, by resolutions adopted by their respective boards, enter into written agreements for sharing the use of physical facilities or equipment owned or used by either district. The agreement also may provide for the contribution by the joint vocational district of a portion of its funds for current operating expenses to the technical college district, to be spent by the latter for any lawful purpose.[53] Copies of the agreement must be filed with the board of regents and state board of education.

"Coterminous" for this purpose means "having the same or coincident boundaries; covering or involving the same area."[54]

27.11 Funding joint vocational school districts

A joint vocational school district's eligibility for foundation program payments under RC Chapter 3317 is limited to the allowances listed in RC 3317.16 and is further qualified by the nature of the class units for which funds are sought.[55]

The board of a joint vocational district, by a two-thirds vote of its full membership, may adopt a resolution declaring it necessary to levy a tax in excess of the ten-mill limitation,[56] but the period of the tax cannot be more than ten years. Any levy whose purpose is limited to any of the purposes of an existing levy must be designated as a "renewal" levy on the ballot.[57]

A joint vocational district is solely responsible for the costs of a special election called at its request; if it is unable to pay the board of elections with current operating funds, then the amount is to be subsequently withheld by the county auditor from money payable to the district at the next tax settlement.[58]

27.12 Pupils, special education, transportation

When a student is in full-time attendance at a joint vocational school, within the meaning of "full-time attendance,"[59] he must be included in the average daily membership of the public school district of his residence for purposes of state support under the school foundation program. The definition of "full-time attendance" must take into consideration auxiliary services provided to nonpublic school pupils under RC 3317.06. When a pupil attends classes at a joint vocational school under RC 3313.90, but receives auxiliary services through a nonpublic school under RC 3317.06, he should be included in the average daily membership for the nonpublic school under RC 3321.12 on a pro rata basis.[60]

---

[49]RC 3313.90.
[50]RC 3311.20, RC 3311.21.
[51]RC 3311.215.
[52]RC 3311.212.
[53]RC 3311.218.
[54]OAG 72-089.
[55]OAG 72-049.

[56]See Text 39.03, Ten-mill limitation, voted and unvoted levies.
[57]RC 3311.21.
[58]RC 3501.17; OAG 71-012.
[59]RC 3313.48, RC 3313.90, RC 3317.03.
[60]OAG 72-083.

Special education classes for handicapped pupils and driver education courses may be approved for state funding in joint vocational school districts.[61]

A local member school board of a joint vocational school district may provide transportation for the pupils of its local district to and from the joint vocational school, provided the transportation could be made available after consideration of facilities and distance as outlined in RC 3327.01 and the standards adopted by the state board of education.[62]

VOCATIONAL REHABILITATION

27.13 Rehabilitation services commission

(A) Composition

The rehabilitation services commission created by RC 3304.12 consists of a bureau of services for the visually impaired and a bureau of vocational rehabilitation, and may consist of other administrative subdivisions under its control as it considers necessary.[63] The commission consists of seven members appointed by the governor, no more than four of whom can be members of the same political party. At least one member must be from the field of services for the blind, and at least four members must be handicapped. At least two but not more than three of the members must have received vocational rehabilitation services from a state agency or the veterans administration. The handicapped members must be representative of the major categories of persons served by the commission.[64]

(B) Duties, organization

The duties of the commission include establishing and operating vocational rehabilitation programs and activities, research, rule-making, reporting and certifying the disbursement of funds for vocational rehabilitation activities, consulting, and acting as an advocate for the rights of handicapped persons. The commission is specifically authorized to cooperate and contract with any other public or private agencies for the establishment of vocational rehabilitation programs.[65]

The rehabilitation services commission is the sole state agency that can administer the plan provided for by the Rehabilitation Act of 1973, 29 USCA 701. The commission is composed in part of three bureaus:

(1) Bureau of vocational rehabilitation, which provides services to persons with disabilities other than visual;

(2) Bureau of services for the visually impaired, which provides services to the legally blind or visually impaired; and

(3) Bureau of disability determination, which makes determinations on all claims for social security benefits and supplementary security income payments.[66]

27.14 Ohio rehabilitation center

The Ohio rehabilitation center was created to develop and encourage the application of means and methods of restoring physically handicapped persons to positions of improved social and economic usefulness. The center is under the control of the board of trustees of Ohio State University, through the regular administrative and fiscal officers of the university.[67]

The objectives of the center are to rehabilitate handicapped or disabled persons whose rehabilitation requires extended residential care or intensive study and services; to cooperate with similar institutions in the state; to provide training in the field of rehabilitation; to conduct research; to disseminate information; and to afford such other rehabilitation services as the center may develop for the benefit of Ohio citizens.[68]

27.15 Records

Client records held by the rehabilitation services commission in connection with the state vocational rehabilitation services program are not public records for purposes of

---

[61] RC 3317.16.
[62] OAG 68-103.
[63] RC 3304.15.
[64] RC 3304.12.
[65] RC 3304.16.
[66] RC 3304.16(D); OAC 3304-1-01.
[67] RC 3335.50 et seq.
[68] RC 3335.51, RC 3335.55.

RC 149.43, because the general release of such records is prohibited.[69]

The rehabilitation services commission may implement a requirement that a state or federal legislator seeking disclosure of client information present a written consent to such disclosure, signed by the person to whom the information relates. The commission has no general authority to disclose such records to a state or federal legislator without such consent.[70]

---

[69]OAG 84-084. See also RC 3304.21; 34 CFR 361.49.

[70]OAG 84-084.

Chapter 28
Education for Children with Disabilities

FEDERAL AND STATE REQUIREMENTS IN GENERAL
28.01 Legislation on education for children with disabilities
28.02 Individualized education program
28.03 "Free appropriate public education" (FAPE)
28.04 Extended school year services
28.05 Least restrictive environment
28.06 Twenty-four-hour care
28.07 Related services for children with disabilities
28.08 Bringing education to children with disabilities
28.09 Discipline of children with disabilities
28.10 Discrimination in testing

PARENTAL RIGHTS
28.11 Parental involvement in educational decisions affecting disabled child

ACTIONS AND REMEDIES UNDER FEDERAL LAW
28.12 Causes of action for violations
28.13 Relief, damages, compensatory education, attorney fees

ADMINISTRATION OF EDUCATION FOR CHILDREN WITH DISABILITIES IN OHIO
28.14 Planning and evaluation
28.15 Funding, sharing facilities and costs
28.16 Teachers of children with disabilities
28.17 Special classes, requirements for facilities
28.18 Assisting deaf and hard of hearing children and their parents
28.19 State schools for the deaf and blind
28.20 Role of county MR/DD boards

FEDERAL AND STATE REQUIREMENTS IN GENERAL

28.01 Legislation on education for children with disabilities

(A) Federal and state acts

Signaling the federal government's interest in the rights of those with disabilities, section 504 of the Rehabilitation Act of 1973[1] provides that "[n]o otherwise qualified individual with a disability in the United States, as defined in section 706(8) of this title, shall, solely by reason of her or his disability, be excluded from the participation in, be denied the benefits of, or be subjected to discrimination under any program or activity receiving Federal financial assistance or under any program or activity conducted by any Executive agency or by the United States Postal Services."

This policy of nondiscrimination was specifically applied to education by the Education for All Handicapped Children Act of 1975, now known as the Individuals with Disabilities Education Act (IDEA),[2] which mandates that *all* children of compulsory school age, regardless of physical, mental, or emotional disability, are entitled to a "free, appropriate public education" (FAPE) in the least restrictive environment.[3] It requires the states to adopt and implement special education programs by imposing specific administrative, coordinating, and reporting responsibilities on each state education agency. Regulations for administration of IDEA are found at 34 CFR Part 300. By conditioning each state's receipt of federal funds on compliance with required procedures, IDEA seeks to ensure a FAPE which emphasizes special education and related services designed to meet the unique needs of each child with a disability.

Since 1986, IDEA has authorized early childhood intervention services for infants and toddlers with disabilities (defined as children from birth to age two, inclusive, who need early intervention services because they are developmentally delayed or have a diagnosed physical or mental condition that may result in developmental

---

[1] 29 USCA 794, as amended.
[2] 20 USCA 1400 et seq.
[3] Embracing a "zero reject" policy, a federal appeals court has emphatically declared that no child is too disabled to qualify for a public education under IDEA and that a lower court erred in concluding a child must be able to benefit from special education in order to be eligible for it. Timothy W. v Rochester, N.H., School Dist, 875 F(2d) 954 (1st Cir NH 1989), cert denied 493 US 983, 110 SCt 519, 107 LEd(2d) 520 (1989). See also Thomas v Cincinnati Bd of Ed, 918 F(2d) 618 (6th Cir Ohio 1990); RC 3323.02 (special education and related services required "regardless of the severity" of the disability). The FAPE may, in appropriate cases, however, involve less than full school days for the disabled child. Christopher M. v Corpus Christi Independent School Dist, 933 F(2d) 1285 (5th Cir Tex 1991).

delay) and their families to be carried out in each state through comprehensive, multi-disciplinary efforts. Federal grants are available to states to assist in developing early childhood intervention programs.[4]

The companion legislation to IDEA in Ohio is RC Chapter 3323. State regulations are found at OAC Chapter 3301-51 and, for preschool children, OAC Chapter 3301-31.

While 20 USCA 1412 and 34 CFR 300.1 et seq. mandate a FAPE for all children with disabilities between the ages of three and twenty-one, IDEA expressly states that, with respect to children aged three to five, this requirement does not apply in any state where its application would be inconsistent with state law. That is not the case in Ohio because Ohio law requires "that all handicapped children three to twenty-one years of age in this state shall be provided with an appropriate public education."[5]

Benefits under IDEA are generally targeted at children enrolled in public schools or placed in private schools by state or local officials. Where parents voluntarily place a disabled child in a private school, the parents are generally responsible for paying for the child's education but special education and related services must be provided to such private school children.[6] Where a parochial school is involved, providing a sign language interpreter to a profoundly deaf child whose parents enrolled him in a Roman Catholic school did not run afoul of the First Amendment's establishment clause.[7]

(B) Definitions

"Children with disabilities" means children under age twenty-two who are mentally retarded, hearing impaired, speech impaired, visually impaired, seriously emotionally disturbed, orthopedically impaired, autistic, traumatic brain injured, multi-handicapped, otherwise health impaired, or who have specific learning disabilities, and therefore require special education.[8] A child whose educational performance is adversely affected by a communicable disease such as tuberculosis, Acquired Immune Deficiency Syndrome (AIDS), or Hepatitis B undoubtedly qualifies.[9] Likewise, a child with severe emotional problems who is unable to derive any benefit from a regular education program is covered, despite the fact that the child has an above-average IQ.[10] On the other hand, the statute is not triggered merely because a child is socially maladjusted or is experiencing some behavioral or emotional problems that do not adversely affect educational performance.[11]

A "special education" program means instruction specifically designed to meet the unique needs of a child with a disability, including classroom instruction, home instruction, instruction in hospitals and institutions, and required related services. For a complete listing of definitions, see 20 USCA 1401 and RC 3323.01.

28.02 Individualized education program

Both state and local education agencies have a duty to identify, locate, and evaluate children with disabilities.[12] Those children who, after completion of a multifactored evaluation, are deemed to be eligible for special education must be educated consistent with an "individualized education program" (IEP). The IEP must be written by an IEP Team composed of: (1) a represen-

---

[4] 20 USCA 1471 et seq.
[5] RC 3323.02.
[6] 34 CFR 300.403, 34 CFR 300.452.
[7] Zobrest v Catalina Foothills School Dist, ___ US ___, 113 SCt 2462, 125 LEd(2d) 1 (1993). The religion clauses are more fully discussed in Text Ch 32, Religion and the Public Schools.
[8] 20 USCA 1401(a)(1). See also RC 3323.01(A).
[9] E.g., Nassau County School Bd v Arline, 480 US 273, 107 SCt 1123, 94 LEd(2d) 307 (1987) (tuberculosis); New York State Assn for Retarded Children, Inc v Carey, 612 F(2d) 644 (2d Cir NY 1979) (Hepatitis B); Martinez v Hillsborough County School Bd, 861 F(2d) 1502 (11th Cir Fla 1988) (AIDS). See also Robertson v Granite City Community Unit School Dist No. 9, 684 FSupp 1002 (SD Ill 1988) (AIDS victim covered only if ability to learn and do required work is impaired).
[10] Antkowiak v Ambach, 653 FSupp 1405 (WD NY 1987), reversed on other grounds by 838 F(2d) 635 (2d Cir NY 1988), cert denied sub nom Doe v Sobol, 488 US 850, 109 SCt 133, 102 LEd(2d) 105 (1988).
[11] A.E. v Independent School Dist No. 25 of Adair County, Oklahoma, 936 F(2d) 472 (10th Cir Okla 1991); Lyons v Smith, 829 FSupp 414 (D DC 1993); Doe v Connecticut Bd of Ed, 753 FSupp 65 (D Conn 1990).
[12] 34 CFR 300.128(a)(1), 34 CFR 300.220.

tative of the district other than the teacher, qualified to provide or supervise special education; (2) the child's teacher; and (3) one or both of the child's parents.[13] The IEP Team must develop an IEP for the child,[14] defined as a written statement for each child with a disability, designed to meet the unique needs of the child. The IEP must include the following:

(1) Statement of the present levels of educational performance of the child;

(2) Statement of annual goals, including short-term instructional objectives;

(3) Statement of the specific educational services to be provided, and the extent to which the child will be able to participate in regular educational programs;

(4) Statement of needed transition services (defined in 20 USCA 1401(19)) beginning no later than age sixteen and annually thereafter (and, when appropriate, at age fourteen or younger) including, when appropriate, a statement of the interagency responsibilities or linkages (or both) before the child leaves the school setting;

(5) Projected date for initiation and anticipated duration of such services; and

(6) Appropriate objective criteria and evaluation procedures and schedules for determining, at least annually, whether instructional objectives are being achieved.[15]

The IEP for a student with a visual disability must, in addition, include certain statements required by RC 3323.011 regarding instruction in braille and other reading and writing media. Where instruction in braille reading and writing is specified as appropriate, RC 3323.18 requires that the entity providing the instruction integrate braille "into the student's entire curriculum and other classroom activities in such a manner that braille reading and writing becomes an effective learning tool for the student."

IDEA directs that the educational placement be reviewed at least once a year. A school district is required to give proper written notice to the child's parents before changing the educational placement of their child.[16] The state board of education has established procedures and standards to assure that, to the maximum extent appropriate, disabled children, including children in public or private institutions or other care facilities, are educated with children who are not disabled.

The precise interrelationship between IDEA and section 504 of the Rehabilitation Act of 1973 is still evolving. Because the definition of "individual with a disability" that applies under section 504[17] is somewhat broader than IDEA's definition of "children with disabilities," a school district may have evaluative and special services obligations under the antidiscrimination requirements of section 504 even if the child in question is not eligible for special education under IDEA.[18]

28.03 "Free appropriate public education" (FAPE)

For a state to qualify for federal financial assistance, IDEA requires a state to demonstrate it has in effect a policy that assures all children with disabilities the right to a FAPE.[19]

The US Supreme Court clarified the obligation to provide a FAPE in *Hendrick Hudson Central School Dist Bd of Ed v Rowley*:[20]

> Insofar as a state is required to provide a handicapped child with a "free appro-

---

[13] 34 CFR 300.344(A)(1)-(3).

[14] At least one court has held that the parents do not have a vote equal to the collective votes of the district representatives. Buser v Corpus Christi Independent School Dist, 51 F(3d) 490 (5th Cir Tex 1995), rehearing denied, 56 F(3d) 1387 (5th Cir Tex 1995), cert denied ___ US ___, 116 SCt 305, ___ LEd(2d) ___ (1995).

[15] 20 USCA 1401(20). See also RC 3323.01(E), (L). Where a participating agency, other than an educational agency, fails to provide agreed upon services, the IEP team must reconvene to identify alternative strategies to meet transition objectives. 20 USCA 1401(20). See also RC 3323.08(C).

[16] 34 CFR 300.504(a).

[17] See 29 USCA 706(8).

[18] See Lyons v Smith, 829 FSupp 414 (D DC 1993).

[19] 20 USCA 1412(1).

[20] Hendrick Hudson Central School Dist Bd of Ed v Rowley, 458 US 176, 102 SCt 3034, 73 LEd(2d) 690 (1982).

priate public education," we hold that it satisfies this requirement by providing personalized instruction with sufficient support services to permit the child to benefit educationally from that instruction.[21]

Rowley explicitly rejected the notion that school districts and states are required to maximize the potential of disabled children commensurate with the opportunity afforded other children.[22] The Court found that Congress did not intend a strict equality of opportunity or services for disabled and nondisabled children.

The Court also specified a methodology for courts to follow in interpreting IDEA: (1) the court first must decide whether the school district and state have complied with IDEA's procedural requirements;[23] and (2) the court must then determine whether the IEP developed through the statutorily required procedures is "reasonably calculated" to enable the disabled child to receive educational benefits.[24] If these two requirements are met, the function of the reviewing court is fulfilled.

The Court cautioned lower courts to defer to educational program decisions made by local and state officials, if made in compliance with IDEA's procedures, warning them not "to substitute their own notions of sound educational policy for those of the school authorities which they review."[25]

---

[21]Hendrick Hudson Central School Dist Bd of Ed v Rowley, 458 US 176, 203, 102 SCt 3034, 73 LEd(2d) 690 (1982).

[22]See also, e.g., Gallagher v Pontiac School Dist, 807 F(2d) 75 (6th Cir Mich 1986); Sherri A.D. v Kirby, 975 F(2d) 193 (5th Cir Tex 1992); Angevine v Smith, 959 F(2d) 292 (DC Cir 1992); In re Conklin, 946 F(2d) 306 (4th Cir Md 1991); Todd D. v Andrews, 933 F(2d) 1576 (11th Cir Ga 1991). On the other hand, IDEA calls for and requires more than a "trivial" educational benefit, even if *Rowley* says the benefit need not be optimal. Polk v Central Susquehanna Intermediate Unit 16, 853 F(2d) 171 (3d Cir Pa 1988), cert denied sub nom Central Columbia School Dist v Polk, 488 US 1030, 109 SCt 838, 102 LEd(2d) 970 (1989). Whether the educational benefits are adequate is to be assessed case-by-case in light of the disabled child's individual needs. JSK v Hendry County School Bd, 941 F(2d) 1563 (11th Cir Fla 1991). Furthermore, *Rowley*'s rejection of a potential-maximizing standard does not preclude consideration of the appropriateness of an educational setting on the basis of, among other things, the progress or educational advancement of the child. Chris D. v Montgomery County Bd of Ed, 753 FSupp 922 (MD Ala 1990).

[23]Failure to satisfy IDEA's procedural requirements has been deemed in and of itself to be an adequate ground for holding a school district has failed to provide a FAPE. Cabell County Bd of Ed v Dienelt, 843 F(2d) 813 (4th Cir WVa 1988); Jackson v Franklin County School Bd, 806 F(2d) 623 (5th Cir Miss 1986); Hall v Vance County Bd of Ed, 774 F(2d) 629 (4th Cir NC 1985). Most courts, however, including the US Court of Appeals for the Sixth Circuit, require that the procedural error be prejudicial. E.g., Thomas v Cincinnati Bd of Ed, 918 F(2d) 618 (6th Cir Ohio 1990); Cordrey v Euckert, 917 F(2d) 1460 (6th Cir Ohio 1990), cert denied 499 US 938, 111 SCt 1391, 113 LEd(2d) 447 (1991); W.G. v Board of Trustees of Target Range School Dist No. 23, Missoula, Montana, 960 F(2d) 1479 (9th Cir Mont 1992); Doe v Alabama State Dept of Ed, 915 F(2d) 651 (11th Cir Ala 1990); Amann v Stow School System, 982 F(2d) 644 (1st Cir Mass 1992); Andersen v District of Columbia, 877 F(2d) 1018 (DC Cir 1989). In assessing whether an IEP constitutes a FAPE, the Sixth Circuit has opined that the procedural requirements at issue pertain to "the process by which an IEP is produced, rather than the myriad of technical items that must be included in the written document." Thus, although two items technically required by 20 USCA 1401(20) to be included in an IEP were omitted, the procedural requirements were still satisfied (the court emphasized that the missing information was in fact known to all parties). Doe v Defendant I, 898 F(2d) 1186 (6th Cir Tenn 1990).

[24]The IEP has been called "the centerpiece of the statute's education delivery system for disabled children." Honig v Doe, 484 US 305, 108 SCt 592, 98 LEd(2d) 686 (1988). Absent truly extraordinary circumstances, the IEP must be developed *prior* to placement of the disabled child. A decision to place that precedes development of the IEP is generally a procedural error sufficient in and of itself to warrant a finding of no FAPE. Spielberg v Henrico County Public Schools, 853 F(2d) 256 (4th Cir Va 1988), cert denied 489 US 1016, 109 SCt 1131, 103 LEd(2d) 192 (1989).

[25]Thus, questions of educational methodology or whether a particular service or method can feasibly be provided in a specific setting are to be resolved by educational authorities, not the courts. The Sixth Circuit has recognized that courts should not "substitute the plaintiffs' notions of sound educational policy for those of the school system." McWhirt v Williamson County Schools, 28 F(3d) 1213 (6th Cir Tenn 1994) (no reason to dispute the school's decision to place student in comprehensive development classroom at another school farther away from home because the school had complied with IDEA's procedural requirements and had examined the academic and nonacademic benefits to the child). See Lachman v Illinois State Bd of Ed, 852 F(2d) 290 (7th Cir Ill 1988), cert denied 488 US 925, 109 SCt 308, 102 LEd(2d) 327 (1988), which upheld the placement of a hearing-

The Court's treatment of FAPE does not address all questions concerning IDEA's substantive requirements. It does, however, further define a school district's responsibility. In giving meaning to the statutory definition of a FAPE,[26] the Court focused on the requirement that educational instruction be *specifically designed* to meet the unique needs of the disabled child and that such instruction be supported by services necessary to permit the child to *benefit* from the instruction. However, minimal academic achievement, as evidenced, for example, by regular promotion from grade to grade, may be insufficient to demonstrate that a disabled student has been provided a FAPE.[27]

The US Court of Appeals for the Sixth Circuit relied upon *Rowley* in determining that a school district was not obligated to provide extracurricular activities to disabled students. The court found that 34 CFR 300.306, upon which a lower court had relied in ordering one hour of extracurricular activities per week, "requires a strict equality of opportunity, and accordingly is in conflict with the pronouncements of *Rowley*." The court further held that the district was not obligated to provide extracurricular activities from which the disabled student "would receive no significant educational benefit."[28]

That cost can be given consideration in devising a FAPE for an individual child is clear.[29] However, "cost considerations are only relevant when choosing between several options, all of which offer an 'appropriate' education." Thus, where the only placement that afforded a FAPE was highly expensive, the school district could not rely on cost in urging an alternative placement.[30]

In assessing whether an IEP is reasonably calculated to enable a disabled child to benefit educationally, a court may consider the parents' hostility to the proposed placement and if that hostility undermines its

---

impaired child in a setting that relied primarily on sign language over the parents' preference for a cued speech technique. Relying on *Rowley*, the court declared that, once IDEA's requirements are met, a court should not become embroiled in questions of methodology that are fairly debatable. See also Petersen v Hastings Public Schools, 31 F(3d) 705 (8th Cir Neb 1994) (district's choice of sign-language system for hearing-impaired students provided FAPE); Dreher v Amphitheater Unified School Dist, 22 F(3d) 228 (9th Cir Ariz 1994) (district's proposed placement of deaf child appropriate notwithstanding parents' preference for different methodology); Johnson v Westmoreland County School Bd, 19 IDELR 787 (ED Va 1993) (requiring residential placement over parent's objection); G.D. v Westmoreland School Dist, 930 F(2d) 942 (1st Cir NH 1991) (public school not required to place child in more restrictive school parents prefer if adopted IEP provides FAPE); Goodall v Stafford County School Bd, 930 F(2d) 363 (4th Cir Va 1991), cert denied 502 US 864, 112 SCt 188, 116 LEd(2d) 149 (1991) (district's offer to provide cued speech interpreter at public school sufficient; parents cannot insist such services be provided at sectarian school); Barnett v Fairfax County School Bd, 927 F(2d) 146 (4th Cir Va 1991), cert denied 502 US 859, 112 SCt 175, 116 LEd(2d) 138 (1991) (district not required to duplicate cued speech program for single student merely because high school he would rather attend exists closer to his home); Bertolucci v San Carlos Elementary School Dist, 721 FSupp 1150 (ND Cal 1989) (court refused to choose between competing methodologies for child with dyslexia); Brougham v Town of Yarmouth, 823 FSupp 9 (D Me 1993) (district's placement of deaf child appropriate notwithstanding parents' preference for different methodology); Bonnie Ann F. v Calallen Independent School Dist, 835 FSupp 340 (SD Tex 1993), affirmed by 40 F(3d) 386 (5th Cir Tex 1994), cert denied ___ US ___, 115 SCt 1796, 131 LEd(2d) 723 (1995) (district's placement of deaf child appropriate notwithstanding parents' preference for different methodology).

[26]20 USCA 1401(18).

[27]Hall v Vance County Bd of Ed, 774 F(2d) 629 (4th Cir NC 1985). See also In re Conklin, 946 F(2d) 306 (4th Cir Md 1991) (noting that the converse is also true: a child who does not receive passing marks and advance from grade to grade is not ipso facto being denied a FAPE—grades and advancement are simply "important factors to be considered").

[28]Rettig v Kent City School Dist, 788 F(2d) 328 (6th Cir Ohio 1986), cert denied 478 US 1005, 106 SCt 3297, 92 LEd(2d) 711 (1986).

[29]E.g., Roncker v Walter, 700 F(2d) 1058 (6th Cir Ohio 1983), cert denied sub nom Cincinnati School Dist Bd of Ed v Roncker, 464 US 864, 104 SCt 196, 78 LEd(2d) 171 (1983); Age v Bullitt County Public Schools, 673 F(2d) 141 (6th Cir Ky 1982).

[30]Clevenger v Oak Ridge School Bd, 744 F(2d) 514 (6th Cir Tenn 1984). See also Cremeans v Fairland Local School Dist Bd of Ed, 91 App(3d) 668, 633 NE(2d) 570 (Lawrence 1993).

value to the child an alternative placement may be warranted.[31]

28.04 Extended school year services

Ohio law requires that schools provide education to students for an academic year of not less than 182 days.[32] However, several courts have held that, in some instances, IDEA may require special education programs extending beyond a state's normal school year, known as "extended school year (ESY) services," and that these programs may not otherwise be categorically limited in duration.[33]

An Ohio federal court, in *Rettig v Kent City School Dist*,[34] explained that a year-round program would be required only where it would be more than merely beneficial to the child; extended programming must be a necessary component of an appropriate IEP and needed to prevent significant regression. In *Cordrey v Euckert*,[35] the US Court of Appeals for the Sixth Circuit refined this standard. Beginning with the proposition that an extended school year is the exception, not the rule, *Cordrey* held that the *Rettig* regression standard does not necessarily require proof that a child has regressed in the past and that, in the absence of empirical data, the need for an extended school year may be shown by expert opinion based on a professional individual assessment. More specifically, it must be shown "in a particularized manner relating to the individual child" that an extended school year is "necessary to avoid something more than adequately recoupable regression" and also necessary to permit the child to benefit in more than a de minimus way from his instruction.[36] If the child benefits from instruction under a proper IEP in a regular school year, an extended school year is not required unless the benefits during the year are significantly jeopardized in the absence of an extended school year.[37]

Whether ESY services should be provided is a matter to be determined by the IEP Team at a properly noticed IEP Team Meeting.[38]

28.05 Least restrictive environment

(A) Preference for mainstreaming

In addition to assuring a FAPE, IDEA also requires that participating states establish procedures to assure that, "to the maximum extent appropriate," disabled children, including children in public or private institutions or other care facilities, are educated with children who are not disabled.[39] Special classes, separate schooling, or other removal of disabled children from the regular educational environment should occur only when the nature or severity of the disability is such that education in regular classes with the use of supplementary aides and services cannot be achieved satisfactorily. This "mainstreaming" preference is

---

[31]Community Consolidated School Dist No. 21 Bd of Ed v Illinois State Bd of Ed, 938 F(2d) 712 (7th Cir Ill 1991), cert denied 502 US 1066, 112 SCt 957, 117 LEd(2d) 124 (1992). This is a 2-1 decision with an especially vigorous (and, many believe, correct) dissenting opinion.

[32]RC 3313.48. See Text 20.05, Regular school day and year.

[33]E.g., Battle v Pennsylvania, 629 F(2d) 269 (3d Cir Pa 1980), cert denied sub nom Scanlon v Battle, 452 US 968, 101 SCt 3123, 69 LEd(2d) 981 (1981); Crawford v Pittman, 708 F(2d) 1028 (5th Cir Miss 1983); Yaris v St. Louis County Special School Dist, 558 FSupp 545 (ED Mo 1983), affirmed by 728 F(2d) 1055 (8th Cir Mo 1984); Alamo Heights Independent School Dist v Texas Bd of Ed, 790 F(2d) 1153 (5th Cir Tex 1986). See also Johnson v Independent School Dist No. 4 of Bixby, 921 F(2d) 1022 (10th Cir Okla 1990), cert denied 500 US 905, 111 SCt 1685, 114 LEd(2d) 79 (1991).

[34]Rettig v Kent City School Dist, 539 FSupp 768 (ND Ohio 1981), affirmed in part and vacated in part by 720 F(2d) 463 (6th Cir Ohio 1983), cert denied 467 US 1201, 104 SCt 2379, 81 LEd(2d) 339 (1984) (extended school year unnecessary since child regressed during year even after attending summer program).

[35]Cordrey v Euckert, 917 F(2d) 1460 (6th Cir Ohio 1990), cert denied 499 US 938, 111 SCt 1391, 113 LEd(2d) 447 (1991).

[36]For a discussion of other factors to consider, see Johnson v Independent School Dist No. 4 of Bixby, 921 F(2d) 1022 (10th Cir Okla 1990), cert denied 500 US 905, 111 SCt 1685, 114 LEd(2d) 79 (1991).

[37]Cordrey v Euckert, 917 F(2d) 1460 (6th Cir Ohio 1990), cert denied 499 US 938, 111 SCt 1391, 113 LEd(2d) 447 (1991). For an Ohio example of an extended school year under these standards, see Cremeans v Fairland Local School Dist Bd of Ed, 91 App(3d) 668, 633 NE(2d) 570 (Lawrence 1993).

[38]See Reusch v Fountain, 872 FSupp 1421 (D Md 1994).

[39]20 USCA 1412(5). See also RC 3323.04.

further evidenced by the requirement, spelled out in IDEA's implementing regulations, that disabled children receive special education and related services "in the least restrictive environment."[40] This includes a requirement that the child's educational placement be as close as possible to the child's home.[41] Neither IDEA nor Ohio law requires mainstreaming when it is not appropriate. *Roncker v Walter*[42] deals at length with mainstreaming and the "difficult burden" it imposes on the courts.

Factors the courts consider include the costs of the mainstreaming programming, the impact, both positive and negative, which the presence of the disabled child has on nondisabled peers, and the level of educational benefit the disabled child would receive in a "mainstream" as opposed to a more restrictive setting.

(B) Need for special programs or facilities

Despite this preference for mainstreaming, IDEA acknowledges that "the nature or severity of the disability [may be] such that education in regular classes with the use of supplementary aides and services cannot be achieved satisfactorily," and provides for the education of some disabled children in separate classes or institutional settings.[43]

Roncker v Walter,[44] an Ohio case decided by the US Court of Appeals for the Sixth Circuit, emphasizes the strong congressional preference for mainstreaming, noting the requirement also applies to non-academic activities such as lunch, gym, recess, and transportation to and from school, and then discusses placement of a disabled child this way:

> In some cases, a placement which may be considered better for academic reasons may not be appropriate because of the failure to provide for mainstreaming. The perception that a segregated institution is academically superior for a handicapped child may reflect no more than a basic disagreement with the mainstreaming concept. ... In a case where the segregated facility is considered superior, the court should determine whether the services which make that placement superior could be feasibly provided in a nonsegregated setting. If they can, the placement in the segregated school would be inappropriate under [IDEA]. Framing the issue in this manner accords the proper respect for the strong preference in favor of mainstreaming while still realizing the possibility that some handicapped children simply must be educated in segregated facilities either because the handicapped child would not benefit from mainstreaming, because any marginal benefits received from mainstreaming are far outweighed by the benefits gained from services which could not feasibly be provided in the nonsegregated setting, or because the handicapped child is a disruptive force in the nonsegregated setting.[45]

---

[40] 34 CFR 300.550 to 34 CFR 300.556.

[41] 34 CFR 330.552; Remis v New Jersey Dept of Human Services, 815 FSupp 141 (D NJ 1993).

[42] Roncker v Walter, 700 F(2d) 1058 (6th Cir Ohio 1983), cert denied sub nom Cincinnati School Dist Bd of Ed v Roncker, 464 US 864, 104 SCt 196, 78 LEd(2d) 171 (1983).

[43] 20 USCA 1412(5).

[44] Roncker v Walter, 700 F(2d) 1058 (6th Cir Ohio 1983), cert denied sub nom Cincinnati School Dist Bd of Ed v Roncker, 464 US 864, 104 SCt 196, 78 LEd(2d) 171 (1983).

[45] Roncker v Walter, 700 F(2d) 1058, 1063 (6th Cir Ohio 1983), cert denied sub nom Cincinnati School Dist Bd of Ed v Roncker, 464 US 864, 104 SCt 196, 78 LEd(2d) 171 (1983). See also Doe v Tullahoma City Schools Bd of Ed, 9 F(3d) 455 (6th Cir Tenn 1993), cert denied ___ US ___, 114 SCt 2104, 128 LEd(2d) 665 (1994). The US Court of Appeals for the Fifth Circuit has expressly rejected this mode of analysis in evaluating mainstreaming questions as "necessitat[ing] too intrusive an inquiry into the educational policy choices that Congress deliberately left to state and local school officials." Daniel R.R. v State Bd of Ed, 874 F(2d) 1036 (5th Cir Tex 1989). For the Fifth Circuit, the initial question is "whether education in the regular classroom, with the use of supplemental aids and services, can be achieved satisfactorily for a given child." If that question is answered in the negative, and the district intends to provide special education or remove the child from regular education, then a second question arises: "whether the school has mainstreamed the child to the maximum extent appropriate." Daniel R.R. v State Bd of Ed, 874 F(2d) 1036, 1048 (5th Cir Tex 1989). This standard was also expressly adopted in Greer v Rome City School Dist, 950 F(2d) 688 (11th Cir Ga 1991), opinion withdrawn by 956 F(2d) 1025 (11th Cir Ga 1992), opinion reinstated in relevant part by 967 F(2d) 470 (11th Cir Ga 1992), and Oberti v Borough of Clementon School Dist Bd of Ed, 995 F(2d) 1204 (3d Cir NJ 1993). The Eighth and Fourth Circuits, however, follow *Roncker*. A.W. v Northwest R-1 School Dist, 813 F(2d) 158 (8th Cir Mo 1987), cert denied 484 US 847, 108 SCt 144, 98 LEd(2d) 100 (1987); Devries v Fairfax County School Bd, 882 F(2d) 876 (4th Cir Va 1989). The Ninth Cir-

Other courts have also recognized the central significance of mainstreaming in the structure of IDEA. In *Springdale School Dist v Grace*,[46] for example, even though education of a profoundly deaf child could be obtained at a school for the deaf where she "might learn more quickly," the court, heeding IDEA's command to integrate disabled children to the greatest extent appropriate, placed the child in a regular public classroom. Similarly, in *Kerkam v Superintendent, D.C. Public Schools*,[47] placement of a severely retarded child in a local school extended-day program that conferred at least some educational benefit satisfied IDEA even if the child would have made more progress in the more restricted environment of a residential placement.

In *Wilson v Marana Unified School Dist No. 6 of Pima County*,[48] however, the school district was permitted to relocate a disabled student from her neighborhood school to another, thirty minutes away, where she could be taught by special education teachers certified in physical disabilities. The child, who possessed normal intelligence but had difficulty learning to read and write due to a physical disability, had failed to make satisfactory progress after receiving remedial instruction from a learning disabilities teacher. The court declared: "We are well aware of the importance of this [mainstreaming] policy; however it is a policy which must be balanced with the primary objective of providing handicapped children with an 'appropriate' education."[49]

While IDEA creates a "clear preference" for an integrated, public education "to the maximum extent appropriate," it does not compel a state to establish entire new levels of education services to satisfy that requirement. *Mark A. v Grant Wood Area Education Agency*[50] declined to require a school district to establish an entirely new program for preschool disabled students which would integrate disabled preschoolers with their nondisabled peers.

Nor does IDEA require a district to make costly structural changes to the school nearest the paralyzed student's home where a fully accessible school (to which the child is assigned) exists in the district and provides the child with a FAPE.[51]

Indeed, RC 3323.08 expressly provides that a district may, by cooperative agreement or contract with one or more districts, provide for the identification, location, and evaluation of handicapped children, and for classes or other suitable programs that meet state board of education standards. A district may also contract for the provision of related services that meet state board standards. If, when an IEP is approved for a child, a district is not providing a program or related service required by the IEP, the district may contract with a nonpublic entity for the provision of the program or service if the program or service meets state board of education standards and is provided in Ohio. IDEA only expresses a preference, not a mandate, for placement at a neighborhood school.[52] Neither the

---

cuit has approved a balancing test drawn from both lines of cases. Sacramento City Unified School Dist Bd of Ed v Rachel H., 14 F(3d) 1398 (9th Cir Cal 1994), cert denied ___ US ___, 114 SCt 2679, 129 LEd(2d) 813 (1994).

[46]Springdale School Dist No. 50 of Washington County v Grace, 693 F(2d) 41 (8th Cir Ark 1982), cert denied 461 US 927, 103 SCt 2086, 77 LEd(2d) 298 (1983).

[47]Kerkam v Superintendent, D.C. Public Schools, 931 F(2d) 84 (DC Cir 1991).

[48]Wilson v Marana Unified School Dist No. 6 of Pima County, 735 F(2d) 1178 (9th Cir Ariz 1984).

[49]For other examples of judicial recognition that mainstreaming is not an absolute preference, see, e.g., Briggs v Connecticut Bd of Ed, 882 F(2d) 688 (2d Cir Conn 1989); DeVries v Fairfax County School Bd, 882 F(2d) 876 (4th Cir Va 1989); Lachman v Illinois State Bd of Ed, 852 F(2d) 290 (7th Cir Ill 1988), cert denied 488 US 925, 109 SCt 308, 102 LEd(2d) 327 (1988); A.W. v Northwest R-1 School Dist, 813 F(2d) 158 (8th Cir Mo 1987), cert denied 484 US 847, 108 SCt 144, 98 LEd(2d) 100 (1987).

[50]Mark A. v Grant Wood Area Education Agency, 795 F(2d) 52 (8th Cir Iowa 1986), cert denied 480 US 936, 107 SCt 1579, 94 LEd(2d) 769 (1987).

[51]Schuldt v Mankato Independent School Dist No. 77, 937 F(2d) 1357 (8th Cir Minn 1991), cert denied 502 US 1059, 112 SCt 937, 117 LEd(2d) 108 (1992).

[52]Urban v Jefferson County School Dist R-1, 870 FSupp 1558 (D Colo 1994).

ADA nor section 504 requires placement at a neighborhood school.[53]

28.06 Twenty-four-hour care

Because of the severity of their disabilities, some disabled children require and are afforded residential treatment under 20 USCA 1401(16). Conflicts arise when the IEP calls for a day program only, yet the parents demand twenty-four-hour residential placement because of disruption in the home.

Kruelle v New Castle County School Dist[54] distinguished between residential placement necessary for learning and residential placement in response to medical or emotional problems that are segregable from the learning process. In effect, the question was whether placement is required for emotional problems, and is therefore the responsibility of parents or social service agencies, or whether placement is a necessary ingredient for learning. In *Krulle*, involving a profoundly retarded child whose learning ability was impeded by the transition from home to school and school to home, residential placement was appropriate.

Likewise, *North v District of Columbia Bd of Ed*[55] enjoined a school board from denying an epileptic child free placement in a residential program. The court found the social, emotional, medical, and educational problems were so intertwined "that realistically it is not possible for the court to perform the Solomon-like task of separating them."[56]

Matthews v Davis[57] upheld a school district's termination of a residential placement where (1) it was unlikely the student would benefit further from the placement; and (2) other aspects of the educational program could be implemented while the student lived at home. The court concluded the residential program served primarily custodial and not educational purposes, and that the student "has probably reached a point of diminishing marginal returns and would not be able to learn much more."[58]

28.07 Related services for children with disabilities

The precise scope of related services that must be provided under IDEA is not always easily discerned. "Related services" means

---

[53]Urban v Jefferson County School Dist R-1, 870 FSupp 1558 (D Colo 1994). See also Murray v Montrose County School Dist RE-1J, 51 F(3d) 921 (10th Cir Colo 1995), cert denied ___ US ___, 116 SCt 278, ___ LEd(2d) ___ (1995).

[54]Kruelle v New Castle County School Dist, 642 F(2d) 687 (3d Cir Del 1981).

[55]North v District of Columbia Bd of Ed, 471 FSupp 136 (D DC 1979).

[56]For other examples of residential placements, see, e.g., Ojai Unified School Dist v Jackson, 4 F(3d) 1467 (9th Cir Cal 1993), cert denied ___ US ___, 115 SCt 90, 130 LEd(2d) 41 (1994); Drew P. v Clarke County School Dist, 877 F(2d) 927 (11th Cir Ga 1989), cert denied 494 US 1046, 110 SCt 1510, 108 LEd(2d) 646 (1990); Ash v Lake Oswego School Dist No. 7J, 766 FSupp 852 (D Ore 1991), affirmed by 980 F(2d) 585 (9th Cir Ore 1992); Vander Malle v Ambach, 667 FSupp 1015 (SD NY 1987). See also Mark Z. v Mountain Brook Bd of Ed, 792 FSupp 1228 (ND Ala 1992) (holding public residential facility, rather than private residential facility offering substantially similar program, was least restrictive environment); Woods v New Jersey Dept of Ed, 823 FSupp 254 (D NJ 1993) (state agencies need not fund residential placement cost where it is not yet determined that residential placement is required); Slack v Delaware Dept of Public Instruction, 826 FSupp 115 (D Del 1993) (parents entitled to reimbursement for costs of twenty-four-hour residential placement even though decision at due process hearing left open what type of residential placement was appropriate); Hall v Shawnee Mission School Dist (USD No. 512), 856 FSupp 1521 (D Kan 1994) (parents not entitled to reimbursement for costs of son's unilateral placement at private residential facility since school district had offered FAPE). In Cremeans v Fairland Local School Dist Bd of Ed, 91 App(3d) 668, 633 NE(2d) 570 (Lawrence 1993), a 24-hour per day extended school year residential placement was required for an autistic and possibly retarded child whose behavioral problems were especially severe.

[57]Matthews v Davis, 742 F(2d) 825 (4th Cir Va 1984).

[58]See also Burke County Bd of Ed v Denton, 895 F(2d) 973 (4th Cir NC 1990) (where IEP without residential services appropriate, residential educational program not required, and school board not required to fund habilitative services for child in his home); Swift v Rapides Parish Public School System, 812 FSupp 666 (WD La 1993), affirmed without opinion by 12 F(3d) 209 (5th Cir La 1993) (residential placement not required where meaningful educational benefit being received in school placement even though residential placement might increase benefit).

transportation, and such developmental, corrective, and other supportive services (including speech pathology and audiology, psychological services, physical and occupational therapy, recreation, including therapeutic recreation, social work services, counseling services, including rehabilitation counseling, and medical services except that such medical services shall be for diagnostic and evaluation purposes only) as may be required to assist a child with a disability to benefit from special education, and includes the early identification and assessment of disabling conditions in children.[59]

Several definitional issues are readily apparent. Does, for example, "psychological services" or "counseling services" include psychotherapy to be paid by the local educational agency? Or, is psychotherapy a "medical service" and therefore not paid by the local agency because it is not "diagnostic or evaluative"? In Ohio, psychotherapy may be practiced by psychologists licensed under RC 4732.01, as well as by psychiatrists, who must be doctors of medicine, and whether the local agency must pay arguably depends on just who is providing the service.[60]

In *Irving Independent School Dist v Tatro*,[61] the US Supreme Court held that providing clean, intermittent catheterization to a disabled child is a "supportive service," not a "medical service," and therefore must be provided and paid for by the school district as a necessary related service. The Court listed three criteria for determining whether a service, though not expressly listed in IDEA, is a related service:

> First, a child must be handicapped so as to require special education;

> Second, only those services necessary to aid a handicapped child to benefit from special education must be provided (i.e., if the procedure may just as easily be performed before or after the school day, the district need not provide it); and,

> Third, services must be provided only if they can be performed by a nurse or other qualified person, not if they must be performed by a physician.

It is important to note that the parents did not ask the district to provide the equipment, but only the services through equipment they made available.

In *Detsel v Auburn Enlarged City School Dist Bd of Ed*,[62] parents sought to have the school board provide care for a child who required the use of a respirator monitored constantly by a licensed practical nurse. Holding the board was not required to provide constant in-school nursing care, the court concluded such services "more closely resemble" excluded medical services than "supportive services" and distinguished *Tatro* by noting the services requested were more substantial and of a more permanent nature.[63]

Stressing that the question was whether a placement was necessary for educational purposes or in response to medical, social, or emotional problems apart from the learning process, the US Court of Appeals for the Ninth Circuit concluded hospitalization of a disabled child at an expensive acute care psychiatric hospital was an excluded "medical service" under IDEA since it was primarily for medical reasons.[64]

The transportation of a disabled child is also a "related service," to be paid for by the school district.[65] However, there must

---

[59]20 USCA 1401(17). See also RC 3323.01(C).

[60]See Doe v Anrig, 651 FSupp 424 (D Mass 1987) (individual psychotherapy and group therapy provided by psychologist constitutes related services); Darlene L. v Illinois State Bd of Ed, 568 FSupp 1340 (ND Ill 1983) (psychiatric treatment by psychiatrist does not constitute related services). See also In re Family "A", 184 Mont 145, 602 P(2d) 157 (1979) (psychotherapy falls within "psychological services").

[61]Irving Independent School Dist v Tatro, 466 US 923, 104 SCt 1703, 80 LEd(2d) 176 (1984).

[62]Detsel v Auburn Enlarged City School Dist Bd of Ed, 637 FSupp 1022 (ND NY 1986), affirmed by 820 F(2d) 587 (2d Cir NY 1987), cert denied 484 US 981, 108 SCt 495, 98 LEd(2d) 494 (1987).

[63]See also Granite School Dist v Shannon M., 787 FSupp 1020 (D Utah 1992); Bevin v Wright, 666 FSupp 71 (WD Pa 1987). Notwithstanding these cases, a full-time nurse to give tracheostomy care to a child with a rare breathing disorder was deemed a supportive, not excluded medical, service in Neely v Rutherford County Schools, 851 FSupp 888 (MD Tenn 1994), reversed by 68 F(3d) 965 (6th Cir Tenn 1995).

[64]Clovis Unified School Dist v California Office of Administrative Hearings, 903 F(2d) 635 (9th Cir Cal 1990).

[65]Alamo Heights Independent School Dist v Texas Bd of Ed, 790 F(2d) 1153 (5th Cir Tex 1986); Macomb County Intermediate School Dist v Joshua S., 715 FSupp 824 (ED Mich 1989); Felter v Cape Girardeau

be a relationship between the related service and the "unique needs" of the child to trigger district responsibility. Thus, where a hearing-impaired child did not require any special transportation needs, the district was not required to provide transportation to a private school in which the child was voluntarily placed by her parents.[66] Where a district offers an appropriate placement and the parents unilaterally place the child elsewhere, it has been held that reimbursement for transportation expenses incurred because of the unilateral placement is not required,[67] but several cases suggest a contrary result as to the district's obligation to provide related services at least under some circumstances.[68]

A blanket rule against providing hands-on physical therapy, a related service, violates IDEA and contradicts the requirement that an IEP be truly individualized.[69]

28.08 Bringing education to children with disabilities

(A) Home instruction, tuition, and boarding

If a disabled child cannot attend school, even with the help of special transportation, the district of residence must provide home instruction. The board of education may do so itself or in cooperation with another district, a county MR/DD board, or other educational agency. If a child is capable of being transported to school, it does not automatically follow that home instruction, as opposed to school instruction, is precluded; indeed if home instruction provides a FAPE, that is what should be provided.[70] The district board is required to pay tuition in accordance with RC 3323.12 to RC 3323.15.

The state board of education may arrange to pay to any board of education for any disabled children who are not residents of the district but for whom the district is providing special education.[71]

(B) Education of children in hospitals

When a public hospital for children with tuberculosis or epilepsy or any public institution (except state institutions for the care of delinquent, unstable, or socially maladjusted children) is located in a school district, that board must provide for the education of all children in such institutions. If another school district within the same county or in an adjoining county is the source of sixty per cent or more of the children in the hospital or institution, the board of that district must provide for the education of all the children.[72]

(C) Tubercular children

A board of education may establish such schools as it deems necessary for persons with tuberculosis, which causes their exclusion from the regular schools,[73] and pay for their transportation to special schools.[74]

28.09 Discipline of children with disabilities

(A) In general

The US Supreme Court has held that IDEA prohibits the expulsion of a student whose misconduct is attributable to the child's disability.[75] Indefinite expulsions and suspensions of students for conduct attributable to their disabilities deprives them of their right to a FAPE. Further, IDEA clearly was "meant to strip schools of the *unilateral* authority they had traditionally employed to exclude disabled students, particularly emotionally disturbed students, from the school."[76] In short,

---

School Dist, 810 FSupp 1062 (ED Mo 1993); OAG 87-026.

[66]McNair v Oak Hills Local School Dist, 872 F(2d) 153 (6th Cir Ohio 1989).

[67]Barwacz v Michigan Dept of Ed, 681 FSupp 427 (WD Mich 1988).

[68]See Felter v Cape Girardeau School Dist, 810 FSupp 1062 (ED Mo 1993); Work v McKenzie, 661 FSupp 225 (D DC 1987).

[69]Polk v Central Susquehanna Intermediate Unit 16, 853 F(2d) 171 (3d Cir Pa 1988), cert denied sub nom Central Columbia School Dist v Polk, 488 US 1030, 109 SCt 838, 102 LEd(2d) 970 (1989).

[70]Thomas v Cincinnati Bd of Ed, 918 F(2d) 618 (6th Cir Ohio 1990).

[71]RC 3323.15.

[72]RC 3313.55.

[73]RC 3313.71.

[74]RC 3313.55.

[75]Honig v Doe, 484 US 305, 108 SCt 592, 98 LEd(2d) 686 (1988).

[76]Honig v Doe, 484 US 305, 323, 108 SCt 592, 98 LEd(2d) 686 (1988).

IDEA's "stay-put" provision[77] prohibits school authorities from unilaterally excluding disabled children for dangerous and disruptive conduct growing out of their disabilities while proceedings initiated under IDEA are pending.[78]

IDEA indicates that prior to suspending or expelling a disabled child, a group of persons knowledgeable about the child must determine whether the misconduct is a manifestation of the child's disability.[79] If the misconduct is not related to the disability, the school district may expel or suspend the child after giving proper notice under IDEA, including notice of procedural safeguards.[80] The school district must still provide appropriate educational services to the child during the period of the disciplinary exclusion.[81] If the misconduct is related to the child's disability, the student may not be expelled or suspended for more than ten school days in a school year without triggering IDEA's procedural protections.[82]

In extreme cases, a school district may seek a court order to remove a disabled student from school or change the student's current educational placement if the student is substantially likely to cause injury to himself or others.[83] Prior to seeking the assistance of the court, however, the district should make reasonable efforts to reduce the risk that the student will cause injury.[84]

A federal court in Ohio, in a pre-*Honig* decision, ruled that severely behaviorally disabled students barred from the classroom and given a private tutor were subjected to a change in placement without the approval of their guardians. As a result they were returned to the classroom.[85] The US Court of Appeals for the Sixth Circuit has held that expulsion is a change of placement that, if carried out without first

---

[77]20 USCA 1415(e)(3) requires that a disabled child remain in his then current educational placement during review proceedings under IDEA unless the parents and educational authorities agree otherwise. The stay-put provision applies only to services included within the child's IEP. Cordrey v Euckert, 917 F(2d) 1460 (6th Cir Ohio 1990), cert denied 499 US 938, 111 SCt 1391, 113 LEd(2d) 447 (1991); Gregory K. v Longview School Dist, 811 F(2d) 1307 (9th Cir Wash 1987). The stay-put is determined at the time due process is requested. Clyde K. v Puyallup School Dist No. 3, 35 F(3d) 1396 (9th Cir Wash 1994) (at the time parents requested due process they had consented to the district's removal of the child to an off-campus self-contained program, so the off-campus program was the stay-put). The proper stay-put for a student who has not been identified as disabled likely is the post-suspension or expulsion placement and there is no obligation to reinstate the student pending a determination of eligibility. See OSEP Memorandum 95-16, 22 IDELR 531; Burke County Public School System, 22 IDELR 743 (SEA GA 1995); Deborah V. v Leonard, 21 IDELR 979 (D Mass 1993). See also Thomas v Cincinnati Bd of Ed, 918 F(2d) 618 (6th Cir Ohio 1990) (stay-put is the operative placement under which the child is receiving instruction at the time of the dispute not an unimplemented IEP).

[78]The *Honig* Court insisted this conclusion "does not leave educators hamstrung," noting procedures for dealing with problem children "may include the use of study carrels, timeouts, detention, or the restriction of privileges." In more drastic cases, the child can be suspended for up to ten school days, and if parents refuse to agree to a change in placement school officials may seek to have a court "temporarily enjoin a dangerous disabled child from attending school." Honig v Doe, 484 US 305, 325-27, 108 SCt 592, 98 LEd(2d) 686 (1988). For an example of an injunction, see Texas City Independent School Dist v Jorstad, 752 FSupp 231 (SD Tex 1990) (enjoining student from attending regular classes as provided in IEP and limiting attendance to participation in behavioral management class or home care).

[79]See 34 CFR 300.533(a)(3) (composition of the placement team); 34 CFR 300.344(a)(1)-(5) (composition of IEP Team).

[80]See 34 CFR 300.504(a) and 34 CFR 300.505.

[81]Metropolitan School Dist of Wayne Twp v Davila, 969 F(2d) 485 (7th Cir Ind 1992), cert denied ___ US ___, 113 SCt 1360, 122 LEd(2d) 740 (1993) (school district is required to continue educational services even if a student's misconduct is unrelated to his or her disability).

[82]Honig v Doe, 484 US 305, 108 SCt 592, 98 LEd(2d) 686 (1988).

[83]Honig v Doe, 484 US 305, 108 SCt 592, 98 LEd(2d) 686 (1988). See Light v Parkway C-2 School Dist, 41 F(3d) 1223 (8th Cir Mo 1994), cert denied ___ US ___, 115 SCt 2557, 132 LEd(2d) 811 (1995).

[84]Light v Parkway C-2 School Dist, 41 F(3d) 1223 (8th Cir Mo 1994), cert denied ___ US ___, 115 SCt 2557, 132 LEd (2d) 811 (1995) (in addition to showing a student is substantially likely to cause injury, the school district must show it took reasonable steps to accommodate the student's disabilities). See J.B. v Independent School Dist No. 191, 21 IDELR 1157 (D Minn 1995) (dissolving a prior TRO because the district failed to establish that the student's presence would create a substantial likelihood of harm to himself or others and there was no showing that the district took reasonable steps to mitigate the risk of harm).

[85]Lamont X. v Quisenberry, 606 FSupp 809 (SD Ohio 1984).

affording the student the procedural safeguards of 20 USCA 1415, violates the IDEA.[86] The court also reaffirmed that a child may not be expelled if the disruptive behavior is a manifestation of his disability. At the same time, a disabled child is not totally immunized from disciplinary action since the child may be temporarily suspended without employing section 1415 procedures and may be expelled in appropriate circumstances so long as the procedural safeguards are observed and the child's disruptive behavior is not a manifestation of his disability. However, there cannot be a complete cessation of educational services during the expulsion period.[87] This analysis is arguably consistent with *Honig* and therefore still relevant.

In a case arising under section 504 of the Rehabilitation Act, the expulsion of a student because of her emotional reaction to a cut (the student had a rare disease that made her susceptible to life-threatening bleeding and that qualified as a handicap) was enjoined where the school failed reasonably to accommodate her condition.[88]

(B) Advisability of developing district policy

In light of these decisions, districts should develop a policy on discipline of disabled students which, at a minimum, requires consideration of the relationship between the misconduct and the child's disability *before* expulsion. Because the district cannot completely terminate educational services, the district may want to modify the student's IEP to a more restrictive environment, such as home instruction. However, such a significant change in the program could be challenged by the parents through a due process proceeding. In that event, and unless the child's behavior presents a danger to himself or others, under IDEA's "stay-put" provision the current program must continue unchanged pending the outcome. If the IEP is found inappropriate, the program must be altered to reflect the special needs of the child.

(C) Temporary suspension, emergency suspension

Under Ohio law, students may be suspended temporarily for a maximum of ten days.[89] Such a temporary suspension does not constitute a change in placement requiring compliance with procedures under 20 USCA 1415.[90] Some argue, however, that cumulative suspensions that total more than ten days in a school year might constitute a change of placement. When the due process requirements of RC 3313.66 and 20 USCA 1415 are not met, disciplinary action may be enjoined.[91]

(D) Discipline for bringing firearms to school

1994 amendments to IDEA give school districts greater flexibility in responding to students with disabilities who bring a "weapon" to school.[92] Prior to determining whether the behavior is a manifestation of the student's disability, the school district may place the student in an interim alternative educational setting for 45 calendar days as designated by the IEP Team.[93]

The Gun-Free Schools Act also applies to disabled students, although the state law must allow for modification of the expulsion requirement on a case-by-case basis. Educational services must be continued

---

[86]Kaelin v Grubbs, 682 F(2d) 595 (6th Cir Ky 1982). See also S-1 v Turlington, 635 F(2d) 342 (5th Cir Fla 1981), cert denied 454 US 1030, 102 SCt 566, 70 LEd(2d) 473 (1981).

[87]See also Metropolitan School Dist of Wayne Twp v Davila, 969 F(2d) 485 (7th Cir Ind 1992), cert denied ___ US ___, 113 SCt 1360, 122 LEd(2d) 740 (1993).

[88]Thomas v Davidson Academy, 846 FSupp 611 (MD Tenn 1994) (also finding this private school violated the public accommodation provisions of the Americans with Disabilities Act; those provisions do not apply to public school districts).

[89]RC 3313.66.

[90]Peoria School Dist 150 Bd of Ed v Illinois Bd of Ed, 531 FSupp 148 (CD Ill 1982); Kaelin v Grubbs, 682 F(2d) 595 (6th Cir Ky 1982). Honig v Doe, 484 US 305, 108 SCt 592, 98 LEd(2d) 686 (1988) plainly agrees. See 484 US at 325 n.8.

[91]Goodwin v Clermont Northeastern School Dist, No. C-1-85-137 (SD Ohio 1985).

[92]"Weapon" means firearm as defined in 18 USCA 921(a)(3).

[93]20 USCA 8921.

28.10 Discrimination in testing

(A) In general

An evolving area of the law is found in cases challenging standardized intelligence tests as racially and culturally biased in violation of section 504 of the Rehabilitation Act of 1973 and IDEA.

In 1994, the Ninth Circuit vacated a 1986 decision which banned IQ testing of all African-American children and restricted the decision only to IQ tests for admission to class for the educable mentally retarded (EMR). The earlier decision had determined that the test had not been validated for the populations and purposes for which it was being used, and its use resulted in the overidentification of black children as mentally retarded, in violation of Section 504 and IDEA. In its most recent ruling, the court ordered supplemental proceedings to determine whether all special education classes were substantially equivalent to EMR.[94]

Conversely, *Parents in Action on Special Ed v Hannon*[95] found that evidence of racial bias in standardized IQ tests was insufficient to preclude their use as part of a classification procedure for placing children in "educably mentally handicapped" classes. Acknowledging some children are misplaced in such classes, the court stated the erroneous placements had not been shown to be due to racial bias in the tests.

(B) Meeting graduation requirements

A New York decision[96] deals with a different aspect of the testing issue, holding as follows:

(1) State adoption of regulations respecting graduation requirements, including minimum competency testing, does not violate section 504 because disabled children are not "otherwise qualified handicapped individuals" within the meaning of the statute;

(2) IDEA does not mitigate against withholding a diploma from a disabled student who is unable to pass a basic minimum competency test, when the student has been provided a FAPE;

(3) Since the institute conferring the diploma certifies that the recipient possesses the knowledge and skills expected of individuals exposed to a rigorous academic discipline, disabled students who cannot pass minimum competency tests have no legitimate expectation approximating a constitutionally protected property or liberty right in a diploma; and

(4) Requiring all diploma recipients to successfully complete a basic competency test is not state action which intentionally discriminates against disabled children; protection of the integrity of a diploma is a legitimate state interest and one to which the testing program is reasonably related.[97]

PARENTAL RIGHTS

28.11 Parental involvement in educational decisions affecting disabled child

(A) In general, supremacy of federal requirements

IDEA and RC 3323.05 assure disabled students and their parents procedural safeguards with respect to the identification, evaluation, educational placement, or educational program of a disabled child.[98] Where conflict occurs, federal law prevails. IDEA's emphasis on parental involvement is unmistakable. It is important to observe

---

[94]Crawford v Honig, 37 F(3d) 485 (9th Cir Cal 1994).

[95]Parents in Action on Special Ed v Hannon, 506 FSupp 831 (ND Ill 1980).

[96]Northport-East Northport Union Free School Dist Bd of Ed v Ambach, 90 AD(2d) 227, 458 NYS(2d) 680 (3d Dept 1982), affirmed by 60 NY(2d) 758, 469 NYS(2d) 669, 457 NE(2d) 775 (1983), cert denied 465 US 1101, 104 SCt 1598, 80 LEd(2d) 129 (1984).

[97]See also Brookhart v Illinois Bd of Ed, 697 F(2d) 179 (7th Cir Ill 1983) (requiring disabled students to pass minimal competency test in order to receive high school diplomas does not violate IDEA or section 504, but here procedural due process rights violated because of lack of adequate notice).

[98]See OAC 3301-51-02; 20 USCA 1415; 34 CFR 300.500 et seq.

closely the procedural rights under IDEA because " 'adequate compliance' with the procedures will, in most cases, assure the disabled child's substantive right to free appropriate public education has been met."[99] Failure to meet these requirements may alone show that the district failed to provide FAPE.[100]

Congress chose to enforce IDEA by providing due process safeguards and review in the state and federal courts. 20 USCA 1415 dictates the procedures to be followed *even if they conflict with the state's provisions.* Briefly, parents or guardians may request conferences and reviews or file complaints concerning the child's IEP. These requests and complaints must be acted upon by the local education agency, meaning, in Ohio, the appropriate board of education, and are subject to judicial review. 20 USCA 1416 also allows the secretary of education to withhold funds whenever he finds a state is not in substantial compliance with IDEA.

A child need not have been identified as disabled before the procedural safeguards of 20 USCA 1415 may be invoked; to the contrary, the question of whether a child is in fact disabled within the meaning of IDEA may be raised at a due process hearing under the statute.[101]

(B) Right to notice of matters affecting identification, evaluation, placement, programs, or services

Both federal and Ohio law require prior written notice to the parents of a disabled child whenever the school proposes to initiate or change, or refuses to initiate or change, the identification, evaluation, or placement of the child or the provision of special education programs or services. The requirements for contents of the notices are found in 34 CFR 300.505 and OAC 3301-51-02. Parental consent must be obtained before conducting a preplacement evaluation and before making the initial placement in a special education program.

The mere transfer of a disabled child from one school to another that does not significantly affect the educational program is not a change in placement under IDEA that triggers the notice requirement.[102]

Modifications to short-term objectives in an IEP prepared by the IEP Team, following notice to and input from the parents, does not constitute a change of placement.[103]

Courts may deem that parents who refuse an offer to schedule a procedurally proper IEP meeting have waived their right to such a meeting.[104]

(C) Hearing

Both federal and Ohio law entitle parents to an impartial due process hearing to resolve complaints concerning the special education of their child. The hearing may be initiated by either the school or the parent with respect to any matter regarding identification, evaluation, educational placement, or special education services to a disabled child.

Though the Ohio rules provide for intermediate procedures, including case conferences and administrative review, a parent's right to a hearing cannot be conditioned upon completion of these procedures.[105]

---

[99] Buser v Corpus Christi Independent School Dist, 51 F(3d) 490, 493 (5th Cir Tex 1995), rehearing denied, 56 F(3d) 1387 (5th Cir Tex 1995), cert denied ___ US ___, 116 SCt 305, ___ LEd(2d) ___ (1995), citing Board of Ed v Rowley, 458 US 176, 102 SCt 3034, 73 LEd(2d) 690 (1982). See also Brimmer v Traverse City Area Public Schools, 872 FSupp 447 (WD Mich 1994).

[100] Buser v Corpus Christi Independent School Dist, 51 F(3d) 490, 493 (5th Cir Tex 1995), rehearing denied, 56 F(3d) 1387 (5th Cir Tex 1995), cert denied ___ US ___, 116 SCt 305, ___ LEd(2d) ___ (1995), citing Jackson v Franklin County School Bd, 806 F(2d) 623 (5th Cir Miss 1986).

[101] Hacienda La Puente Unified School Dist of Los Angeles v Honig, 976 F(2d) 487 (9th Cir Cal 1992).

[102] Weil v Board of Elementary & Secondary Ed, 931 F(2d) 1069 (5th Cir La 1991), cert denied 502 US 910, 112 SCt 306, 116 LEd(2d) 249 (1991); Middlebrook v Knox County, Tennessee School Dist, 805 FSupp 534 (ED Tenn 1991). See also Tilton v Jefferson County Bd of Ed, 705 F(2d) 800 (6th Cir Ky 1983), cert denied 465 US 1006, 104 SCt 998, 79 LEd(2d) 231 (1984) (finding change in placement where programs not "comparable").

[103] Buser v Corpus Christi Independent School Dist, 51 F(3d) 490 (5th Cir Tex 1995), rehearing denied, 56 F(3d) 1387 (5th Cir Tex 1995), cert denied ___ US ___, 116 SCt 305, ___ LEd(2d) ___ (1995).

[104] Cordrey v Euckert, 917 F(2d) 1460 (6th Cir Ohio 1990), cert denied 499 US 938, 111 SCt 1391, 113 LEd(2d) 447 (1991) (parents claimed IEP meeting improper since teacher not in attendance and then refused district's offer to schedule proper meeting).

[105] 20 USCA 1415.

The hearing officer may be selected by the parents and the educational agency. If agreement is not reached, the hearing officer will be appointed by the state superintendent of public instruction.[106] The hearing may not be conducted by an employee of the educational agency responsible for educating the child.

At the hearing, parents may be accompanied by counsel and by individuals with special knowledge or training with respect to disabled children.[107] Any party has the right to present testimony and other evidence and to confront, cross-examine, and compel the attendance of witnesses. Under federal regulations, at least five days prior to the hearing the parties must exchange witness lists and the written materials to be introduced at the hearing. If potential witnesses or evidentiary matters are not revealed to the opposing party within that time frame, their introduction at the hearing will be prohibited.

(D) Burden and degree of proof

Federal and Ohio law are silent as to who bears the burden of proof. Some courts have suggested the school district has the burden of showing its proposal is appropriate, while others have said the party proposing a change in placement must prove the propriety of a new plan.[108] The US Court of Appeals for the Sixth Circuit has held that the party challenging the terms of the IEP must prove the educational placement established by the IEP is inappropriate.[109] Most courts hold the party challenging an administrative determination has the burden of persuading the reviewing court that the decision was wrong,[110] but the US Court of Appeals for the Third Circuit believes that where IDEA's mainstreaming requirement is at issue, the burden always falls on the school district.[111]

As to procedural compliance with IDEA, the Sixth Circuit has rejected an argument that the burden of proof falls on the school district, although procedural issues are subject to "strict review."[112]

That placement decisions by school officials are entitled to at least some deference is clear. The US Supreme Court has rejected the notion that IDEA gives courts broad power to review and upset placement decisions, declaring IDEA's provision authorizing review "is by no means an invitation to the courts to substitute their own notions of sound educational policy for those of the school authorities which they review."[113] Subsequent decisions confirm that *Rowley* requires due deference to the final results of prior administrative proceedings.[114]

---

[106] OAC 3301-51-01(G)(3).
[107] 34 CFR 300.508(a)(1); OAC 3301-51-02(G)(7)(a).
[108] See generally Note, *Burden of Proof Under the Education for All Handicapped Children Act*, 51 Ohio St LJ 760 (1990).
[109] Doe v Tullahoma City Schools Bd of Ed, 9 F(3d) 455 (6th Cir Tenn 1993), cert denied ___ US ___, 114 SCt 2104, 128 LEd(2d) 665 (1994); Cordrey v Euckert, 917 F(2d) 1460 (6th Cir Ohio 1990), cert denied 499 US 938, 111 SCt 1391, 113 LEd(2d) 447 (1991); Doe v Defendant I, 898 F(2d) 1186 (6th Cir Tenn 1990). See also Christopher M. v Corpus Christi Independent School Dist, 933 F(2d) 1285 (5th Cir Tex 1991); Johnson v Independent School Dist No. 4 of Bixby, 921 F(2d) 1022 (10th Cir Okla 1990), cert denied 500 US 905, 111 SCt 1685, 114 LEd(2d) 79 (1991).
[110] E.g., Community Consolidated School Dist No. 21 Bd of Ed v Illinois State Bd of Ed, 938 F(2d) 712 (7th Cir Ill 1991), cert denied 502 US 1066, 112 SCt 957, 117 LEd(2d) 124 (1992); Hampton School Dist v Dobrowolski, 976 F(2d) 48 (1st Cir NH 1992); Kerkam v McKenzie, 862 F(2d) 884 (DC Cir 1988); Barnett v Fairfax County School Bd, 927 F(2d) 146 (4th Cir Va 1991), cert denied 502 US 859, 112 SCt 175, 116 LEd(2d) 138 (1991); Roland M. v Concord School Committee, 910 F(2d) 983 (1st Cir Mass 1990), cert denied 499 US 912, 111 SCt 1122, 113 LEd(2d) 230 (1991); Gerstmyer v Howard County Public Schools, 850 FSupp 361 (D Md 1994).
[111] Oberti v Borough of Clementon School Dist Bd of Ed, 995 F(2d) 1204 (3d Cir NJ 1993). See also Mavis v Sobol, 839 FSupp 968 (ND NY 1993).
[112] Cordrey v Euckert, 917 F(2d) 1460 (6th Cir Ohio 1990), cert denied 499 US 938, 111 SCt 1391, 113 LEd(2d) 447 (1991).
[113] Hendrick Hudson Central School Dist Bd of Ed v Rowley, 458 US 176, 102 SCt 3034, 73 LEd(2d) 690 (1982).
[114] E.g., Doe v Tullahoma City Schools Bd of Ed, 9 F(3d) 455 (6th Cir Tenn 1993), cert denied ___ US ___, 114 SCt 2104, 128 LEd(2d) 665 (1994); Gillette v Fairland Bd of Ed, 932 F(2d) 551 (6th Cir Ohio 1991); Thomas v Cincinnati Bd of Ed, 918 F(2d) 618 (6th Cir Ohio 1990). However, findings at administrative proceedings are not conclusive and a reviewing court may take additional evidence and reach independent conclusions. Teague Independent School Dist v Todd L., 999 F(2d) 127 (5th Cir Tex 1993).

(E) Costs of hearing

Generally, costs of the hearing are borne by the school district of the child's residence. This includes any cost associated with the hearing officer, and a written or electronic verbatim record must be made at the district's expense.[115] Parents who prevail in the hearing are usually entitled to recover attorney fees.[116]

(F) Decision, appeal

The parties must be given a written decision, including findings of fact, within forty-five days of receipt of the hearing request, unless an extension is granted.[117] Pending the outcome, the disabled child must remain in his placement, unless the parties agree otherwise. However, in the instance of a complaint regarding a child's initial application to public school, the child must be admitted to public school, if the parents so desire, pending the outcome of the proceedings.[118]

Either party may appeal within forty-five days of notification of the decision to the state board of education for impartial review.[119] A final written decision must be rendered within thirty days.[120] Under RC 3323.05, the state board of education appoints a reviewing officer who reviews the case and issues a final order. Courts have held IDEA precludes appointment of an employee of the state agency, since such review would not be impartial.[121]

Under Ohio law, an appeal from a state level decision may be taken, within forty-five days of notification of the decision, to the common pleas court of the county in which the school district is located.[122] Federal law permits appeal through either state or federal court. A federal appeals court has concluded that once a reviewing court approves a change in placement, IDEA's "stay-put" provision, 20 USCA 1415(e)(3), does not automatically require maintenance of the status quo pending further judicial appeals.[123]

ACTIONS AND REMEDIES UNDER FEDERAL LAW

28.12 Causes of action for violations

(A) In general

Under 20 USCA 1415(e)(2), an aggrieved parent or guardian of a child with a disability may sue the appropriate educational agencies to enforce rights afforded by IDEA. Before suing under IDEA (or any other law that protects the

---

[115] A district that employs its own court reporter to make an unofficial record of the proceedings does not violate the due process rights of the parent or child. Caroline T. v Hudson School Dist, 915 F(2d) 752 (1st Cir NH 1990).

[116] See Text 28.13(D), Attorney fees.

[117] OAC 3301-51-02(G)(10)(i); 34 CFR 300.512(a).

[118] 20 USCA 1415(e)(3), commonly referred to as the IDEA's "stay-put" provision. But see Logsdon v Pavilion Central School Dist Bd of Ed, 765 FSupp 66 (WD NY 1991) (rejecting parents' demand that disabled child was entitled to be enrolled in regular public kindergarten class pending completion of administrative appeals of initial placement determination in special education program). In Cronin v East Ramapo Central School Dist Bd of Ed, 689 FSupp 197 (SD NY 1988), the court found that a decision to graduate a student from a vocational program, over the parents' objection, constituted a change in placement that triggered IDEA's procedural safeguards. Removal as a result of graduation was deemed a violation of the "stay-put" requirement. Compare Knight v District of Columbia, 877 F(2d) 1025 (DC Cir 1989) (where student's current placement becomes unavailable, district obligated to provide "similar" placement pending administrative and judicial approval of its eventual plans; moreover, a public placement is not inherently dissimilar to a private placement). See also McKenzie v Smith, 771 F(2d) 1527 (DC Cir 1985); McClain v Smith, 793 FSupp 756 (ED Tenn 1989). Where a school district contracts with another district for placement of a disabled child in the other district's special education program, the district lacks standing to invoke the stay-put provision to prevent the other district from later unilaterally removing the child. Seneca Falls Central School Dist Bd of Ed v Liverpool Central School Dist Bd of Ed, 728 FSupp 910 (WD NY 1990).

[119] RC 3323.05; OAC 3301-51-02(G)(12); 34 CFR 300.510.

[120] OAC 3301-51-02(G)(12); 34 CFR 300.512(b).

[121] Muth v Central Bucks School Dist, 839 F(2d) 113 (3d Cir Pa 1988), cert denied 488 US 838, 109 SCt 103, 102 LEd(2d) 78 (1988), cert granted sub nom Gilhool v Muth, 488 US 815, 109 SCt 52, 102 LEd(2d) 30 (1988), reversed on other grounds sub nom Dellmuth v Muth, 491 US 223, 109 SCt 2397, 105 LEd(2d) 181 (1989); Helms v McDaniel, 657 F(2d) 800 (5th Cir Ga 1981), cert denied 455 US 946, 102 SCt 1443, 71 LEd(2d) 658 (1982); Colin K. v Schmidt, 715 F(2d) 1 (1st Cir RI 1983).

[122] RC 3323.05.

[123] Andersen v District of Columbia, 877 F(2d) 1018 (DC Cir 1989).

rights of disabled children if the relief sought is also available under IDEA), administrative remedies must be exhausted, unless resort to such remedies would be futile or inadequate[124] or in an emergency situation where a child faces irreversible damage.[125]

Although section 504 of the Rehabilitation Act does not expressly provide for a private right of action, the courts have inferred one.[126]

(B) Limitations on right of action

Monahan v Nebraska[127] determined that section 504 authorizes a private right of action for damages but only under limited circumstances. Specifically, one must show more than a mere failure to provide the FAPE required by IDEA. Rather, there must be proof of either bad faith or gross misjudgment: "So long as the state officials involved have exercised professional judgment, in such a way as not to depart grossly from accepted standards among educational professionals, we cannot believe that Congress intended to create liability under § 504."[128]

Strongly criticizing *Monahan*, however, a federal district court has held that a special education student who alleged he was not receiving the proper amount of occupational and physical therapy, or receiving the therapy in the proper manner, stated a cognizable section 504 claim.[129]

In *Smith v Robinson*,[130] the US Supreme Court concluded IDEA is the "exclusive avenue" through which a disabled child can pursue a FAPE and that its procedures and remedies can neither be circumvented nor enlarged by resort to section 504 or the assertion of constitutional claims. Attorney fees were denied because IDEA, as it then existed, did not provide for them.

In response, Congress legislatively overruled *Smith* in 1986 by amending 20 USCA 1415 to specifically reserve a right to attorney fees,[131] and to allow one to pursue related federal claims under the US Constitution, the Rehabilitation Act of 1973, and "other federal statutes" protecting the rights of disabled children, except that, if the relief sought is available under IDEA, the administrative procedures mandated by IDEA must be exhausted before bringing court action.[132]

28.13 Relief, damages, compensatory education, attorney fees

(A) Remedies for violations

20 USCA 1415(e)(3) authorizes "such relief as the court determines is appropriate." Most courts have concluded damages, outside of reimbursement for tuition, transportation, or other essential services, are

---

[124]20 USCA 1415(f). See, e.g., Doe v Smith, 879 F(2d) 1340 (6th Cir Tenn 1989), cert denied sub nom Doe v Sumner County Bd of Ed, 493 US 1025, 110 SCt 730, 107 LEd(2d) 749 (1990); Crocker v Tennessee Secondary School Athletic Assn, 873 F(2d) 933 (6th Cir Tenn 1989). For an example of the futility exception in operation, see Lester H. v Gilhool, 916 F(2d) 865 (3d Cir Pa 1990), cert denied sub nom Chester Upland School Dist v Lester H., 499 US 923, 111 SCt 1317, 113 LEd(2d) 250 (1991). For an example of the inadequacy exception in operation, see Marcus X v Adams, 856 FSupp 395 (ED Tenn 1994).

[125]Kominos v Upper Saddle River Bd of Ed, 13 F(3d) 775 (3d Cir NJ 1994) (cautioning that this exception "is to be sparingly invoked").

[126]See, e.g., Miener v Missouri, 673 F(2d) 969 (8th Cir Mo 1982), cert denied 459 US 909, 103 SCt 215, 74 LEd(2d) 171 (1982); Pushkin v University of Colorado Regents, 658 F(2d) 1372 (10th Cir Colo 1981). Although the US Supreme Court has not expressly decided the issue, there is no reason to think any question remains. See Consolidated Rail Corp v Darrone, 465 US 624, 104 SCt 1248, 79 LEd(2d) 568 (1984); Nassau County School Bd v Arline, 480 US 273, 107 SCt 1123, 94 LEd(2d) 307 (1987).

[127]Monahan v Nebraska, 687 F(2d) 1164 (8th Cir Neb 1982), cert denied sub nom Rose v Nebraska, 460 US 1012, 103 SCt 1252, 75 LEd(2d) 481 (1983).

[128]Monahan v Nebraska, 687 F(2d) 1164, 1171 (8th Cir Neb 1982), cert denied sub nom Rose v Nebraska, 460 US 1012, 103 SCt 1252, 75 LEd(2d) 481 (1983). See also Marvin H. v Austin Independent School Dist, 714 F(2d) 1348 (5th Cir Tex 1983); Barnett v Fairfax County School Bd, 721 FSupp 755 (ED Va 1989), affirmed on other grounds by 927 F(2d) 146 (4th Cir Va 1991), cert denied 502 US 859, 112 SCt 175, 116 LEd(2d) 138 (1991).

[129]Howell v Waterford Public Schools, 731 FSupp 1314 (ED Mich 1990).

[130]Smith v Robinson, 468 US 992, 104 SCt 3457, 82 LEd(2d) 746 (1984).

[131]For further analysis, see Text 28.13(D), Attorney fees.

[132]For cases on the exhaustion requirement, see Text 28.11(A), In general, supremacy of federal requirements.

not available.[133] IDEA emphasizes procedural safeguards without mentioning compensatory or punitive damages. The courts have concluded Congress did not intend that money designated for educating children with disabilities be spent for that purpose.

The US Supreme Court has ruled that, under 20 USCA 1415, parents are entitled to reimbursement for expenditures made to place their child in private special education settings whenever the school district's proposed placement is found inappropriate. As long as the parents ultimately prevail, reimbursement is mandated, even if they unilaterally placed the child during the pendency of administrative or legal proceedings. However, if the parents ultimately lose, they are not entitled to reimbursement for any interim period in which the child's placement violated statute.[134]

Reimbursement for the cost of transportation or other services which are determined to be essential to the child's IEP may also be "appropriate relief" under IDEA. In *Hurry v Jones*,[135] the court held that reimbursement could include not only out-of-pocket expenses but also nominal compensation for reasonable time and effort. In that case, the child's parents not only received out-of-pocket costs for driving the child to school, but also received a nominal reimbursement for their time and effort in personally providing that transportation.

States, by virtue of a 1990 amendment to IDEA, are not immune from suit under the Eleventh Amendment to the US Constitution.[136]

(B) Compensatory education

Numerous courts have concluded that compensatory education, whether in the form of additional years of schooling beyond the mandatory school age or special services at public expense, may be an appropriate remedy for violations of IDEA.[137]

---

[133]E.g., Crocker v Tennessee Secondary School Athletic Assn, 980 F(2d) 382 (6th Cir Tenn 1992); Hall v Knott County Bd of Ed, 941 F(2d) 402 (6th Cir Ky 1991), cert denied 502 US 1077, 112 SCt 982, 117 LEd(2d) 144 (1992); Powell v Defore, 699 F(2d) 1078 (11th Cir Ga 1983); Miener v Missouri, 673 F(2d) 969 (8th Cir Mo 1982), cert denied 459 US 909, 103 SCt 215, 74 LEd(2d) 171 (1982); Stacey G. v Pasadena Independent School Dist, 695 F(2d) 949 (5th Cir Tex 1983); Ezratty v Puerto Rico, 648 F(2d) 770 (1st Cir PR 1981). But see Quackenbush v Johnson City Central School Dist, 716 F(2d) 141 (2d Cir NY 1983), cert denied 465 US 1071, 104 SCt 1426, 79 LEd(2d) 750 (1984); Mason v Schenectady City School Dist, 879 FSupp 215 (D NY 1993) (parents who brought action for violation of the IDEA under 42 USCA 1983 could recover punitive damages against individual defendants in their individual capacities).

[134]Burlington School Committee v Massachusetts Dept of Ed, 471 US 359, 105 SCt 1996, 85 LEd(2d) 385 (1985). See also, e.g., Doe v Tullahoma City Schools Bd of Ed, 9 F(3d) 455 (6th Cir Tenn 1993), cert denied ___ US ___, 114 SCt 2104, 128 LEd(2d) 665 (1994); Babb v Knox County School System, 965 F(2d) 104 (6th Cir Tenn 1992), cert denied ___ US ___, 113 SCt 380, 121 LEd(2d) 290 (1992); Gillette v Fairland Bd of Ed, 932 F(2d) 551 (6th Cir Ohio 1991); Doe v Defendant I, 898 F(2d) 1186 (6th Cir Tenn 1990); Teague Independent School Dist v Todd L., 999 F(2d) 127 (5th Cir Tex 1993); Ash v Lake Oswego School Dist No. 7J, 980 F(2d) 585 (9th Cir Ore 1992); Hampton School Dist v Dobrowolski, 976 F(2d) 48 (1st Cir NH 1992). As an Ohio federal district court put it, to be entitled to reimbursement it must be shown that (1) private placement by the parents was proper under IDEA, and (2) the IEP calling for placement in a public school was inappropriate. Matta v Indian Hill Exempted Village Schools Bd of Ed, 731 FSupp 253 (SD Ohio 1990). Reimbursement has been granted even where parents placed their child in a private school that did not have state approval. Florence County School Dist Four v Carter, ___ US ___, 114 SCt 361, 126 LEd(2d) 284 (1994) (holding that requirements of 20 USCA 1401(a)(18) do not apply to parental placements).

[135]Hurry v Jones, 734 F(2d) 879 (1st Cir RI 1984).

[136]20 USCA 1403, legislatively overruling Dellmuth v Muth, 491 US 223, 109 SCt 2397, 105 LEd(2d) 181 (1989).

[137]E.g., Hall v Knott County Bd of Ed, 941 F(2d) 402 (6th Cir Ky 1991), cert denied 502 US 1077, 112 SCt 982, 117 LEd(2d) 144 (1992); Pihl v Massachusetts Dept of Ed, 9 F(3d) 184 (1st Cir Mass 1993); Lester H. v Gilhool, 916 F(2d) 865 (3d Cir Pa 1990), cert denied sub nom Chester Upland School Dist v Lester H., 499 US 923, 111 SCt 1317, 113 LEd(2d) 250 (1991); Mrs. C. v Wheaton, 916 F(2d) 69 (2d Cir Conn 1990); Jefferson County Bd of Ed v Breen, 853 F(2d) 853 (11th Cir Ala 1988); Cremeans v Fairland Local School Dist Bd of Ed, 91 App(3d) 668, 633 NE(2d) 570 (Lawrence 1993). Because compensatory education is a possible remedy, the Ohio Supreme Court ruled in Strongsville City School Dist Bd of Ed v Theado, 57 OS(3d) 162, 566 NE(2d) 667 (1991) that where a due process hearing to challenge the appropriateness of an IEP was requested the day before the student turned twenty-two, the hearing officer had

(C) Damages under section 504 of Rehabilitation Act of 1973

That compensatory damages are recoverable under section 504 is clear in light of the US Supreme Court's decision in *Franklin v Gwinnett County Public Schools* and subsequent rulings.[138] Where damages are requested, it has been held that one is entitled to a jury trial.[139]

(D) Attorney fees

20 USCA 1415 gives a court discretion to "award reasonable attorney fees as part of the costs to the parents or guardian of a child or youth with a disability who is the prevailing party." In administering the adjudication of attorney fees, courts look both to cases decided under IDEA and other similar legislation.[140] The Supreme Court determined that a party prevails "... when actual relief on the merits of his claim materially alters the legal relationship between the parties by modifying the defendant's behavior in a way that directly benefits the plaintiff."[141] A party need not prevail on the "central issue" but only succeed on any "significant issue" and achieve some of the benefits sought to receive attorney fees.[142]

Attorney fees may be awarded to parents who prevail in administrative proceedings under IDEA, in addition to those decided by court.[143] Indeed, in cases resolved prior to a due process hearing, recovery of attorney fees for pre-hearing services may be appropriate.[144] How much should be awarded can itself give rise to protracted wrangling.[145] Merely prevailing on preliminary injunctive relief, however, may not be sufficient to entitle plaintiff to the status of a "prevailing plaintiff"; thus, such a plaintiff cannot recover attorney fees.[146]

Where there is no final court proceeding by which to judge the changes in the legal relationship between the parties, the action taken at the administrative level must be causally related to the recovery

---

jurisdiction to proceed and the case had not become moot.

[138]Franklin v Gwinnett County Public Schools, 503 US 60, 112 SCt 1028, 117 LEd(2d) 208 (1992) (damages available under Title IX of the Education Amendments of 1972). Relying on *Franklin*, compensatory damages were deemed available under section 504 in Tanberg v Weld County Sheriff, 787 FSupp 970 (D Colo 1992). For pre-*Franklin* cases finding that damages are recoverable, see, e.g., Smith v Barton, 914 F(2d) 1330 (9th Cir Idaho 1990), cert denied 501 US 1217, 111 SCt 2825, 115 LEd(2d) 995 (1991) (also holding, where compensatory damages sought, that constitutional right to jury trial exists); Miener v Missouri, 673 F(2d) 969 (8th Cir Mo 1982), cert denied 459 US 909, 103 SCt 215, 74 LEd(2d) 171 (1982).

[139]Pandazides v Virginia Bd of Ed, 13 F(3d) 823 (4th Cir Va 1994); Waldrop v Southern Company Services, Inc, 24 F(3d) 152 (11th Cir Ala 1994).

[140]Krichinsky v Knox County Schools, 963 F(2d) 847 (6th Cir Tenn 1992).

[141]Farrar v Hobby, 502 US 1090, 112 SCt 1159, 117 LEd(2d) 407 (1992). See also Hewitt v Helms, 482 US 755, 107 SCt 2672, 96 LEd(2d) 654 (1987) (there must be some relief on the merits of the claim); Rhodes v Stewart, 488 US 1, 109 SCt 202, 102 LEd(2d) 1 (1988) (per curiam) (relief must affect the party requesting attorney fees); Texas State Teachers Assn v Garland Independent School Dist, 489 US 782, 109 SCt 1486, 103 LEd(2d) 866 (1989) (relief must materially alter the legal relationship between the two parties); Beard v Teska, 31 F(3d) 942 (10th Cir Okla 1994).

[142]Krichinsky v Knox County Schools, 963 F(2d) 847 (6th Cir Tenn 1992). See also, e.g., Mitten v Muscogee County School Dist, 877 F(2d) 932 (11th Cir Ga 1989), cert denied 493 US 1072, 110 SCt 1117, 107 LEd(2d) 1024 (1990); Angela L. v Pasadena Independent School Dist, 918 F(2d) 1188 (5th Cir Tex 1990). For an example of how knotty the problems in this area can become, see Phelan v Bell, 8 F(3d) 369 (6th Cir Mich 1993).

[143]E.g., Eggers v Bullitt County School Dist, 854 F(2d) 892 (6th Cir Ky 1988); Moore v Crestwood Local School Dist, 804 FSupp 960 (ND Ohio 1992); Moore v District of Columbia, 907 F(2d) 165 (DC Cir 1990), cert denied 498 US 998, 111 SCt 556, 112 LEd(2d) 563 (1990).

[144]Barlow-Gresham Union High School Dist No. 2 v Mitchell, 940 F(2d) 1280 (9th Cir Ore 1991); Angela L. v Pasadena Independent School Dist, 918 F(2d) 1188 (5th Cir Tex 1990); Shelly C. v Venus Independent School Dist, 878 F(2d) 862 (5th Cir Tex 1989), cert denied 493 US 1024, 110 SCt 729, 107 LEd(2d) 748 (1990); E.M. v Millville Bd of Ed, 849 FSupp 312 (D NJ 1994); Masotti v Tustin Unified School Dist, 806 FSupp 221 (CD Cal 1992); Fischer v Rochester Community Schools, 780 FSupp 1142 (ED Mich 1991); Mr. D. v Glocester School Committee, 711 FSupp 66 (D RI 1989); Rossi v Gosling, 696 FSupp 1079 (ED Va 1988). But see Brown v Griggsville Community Unit School Dist No. 4, 12 F(3d) 681 (7th Cir Ill 1993).

[145]See Moore v Crestwood Local School Dist, 804 FSupp 960 (ND Ohio 1992).

[146]Fischer v Rochester Community Schools, 780 FSupp 1142 (ED Mich 1991) (attorney unnecessarily "aggrandized" and protracted the misunderstanding between the parties).

obtained.[147] Limited success on a claim justifies a reduction in fees.[148]

IDEA allows all attorneys, whether private or part of publicly funded agencies, to be awarded fees "based on rates prevailing in the community in which the action or proceeding arose for the kind and quantity of services furnished."[149] It stipulates that no award may be made for services subsequent to a written offer of settlement if the relief finally obtained by the parents is "not more favorable" than the rejected offer.[150] A fee request may be trimmed if a court determines the parents "unreasonably" extended proceedings or the request is excessive, but not if the school board "unreasonably" protracted proceedings or violated IDEA's procedural requirements.[151] IDEA prohibits payment of awards with part B funds, which are to be used for direct funding of special education (for example, teacher salaries and educational materials).

ADMINISTRATION OF EDUCATION FOR CHILDREN WITH DISABILITIES IN OHIO

28.14 Planning and evaluation

(A) State and district plans

The state board of education must adopt a state plan for the education of disabled children three to twenty-one years of age and for the availability of educational placement and special education for disabled children under three years of age, develop and implement a plan for in-service training of instructional and support personnel, and select competent personnel to inspect all classes or programs.[152] The board has codified its standards and rules for education of the disabled at Chapter 3301-51 of the Ohio Administrative Code. Reference should also be made to local plans required by the board.

Each school district must submit, for the approval of the state board, a comprehensive plan for the education of children with disabilities. The plan must satisfy the standards set forth in RC 3323.08.

(B) Reports on programs and services

No school district, county MR/DD board, or other educational agency is eligible to receive state or federal funds for a special education program unless the program is operated in accordance with procedures, standards, and guidelines adopted by the state board. Not later than February 1 each year, the superintendent of public instruction is required to furnish the chairmen of the education committees of the house of representatives and the senate with a report on the status of implementation of programs and service for children with disabilities.[153]

28.15 Funding, sharing facilities and costs

(A) Foundation program

Under the foundation program each approved special education program for teaching the disabled, gifted children, or for child study relating to exceptional children may be approved, in full or in part, for state funding by the state board of education.[154]

No unit for deaf children may be disapproved for funding under RC 3317.024(N) on the basis of methods of instruction used in educational programs in the school district or institution to teach deaf children to communicate, and no preference in approving units for funding may be given

---

[147]Brown v Griggsville Community Unit School Dist No. 4, 817 FSupp 734 (CD Ill 1993), affirmed by 12 F(3d) 681 (7th Cir Ill 1993). See also Hall v Detroit Public Schools, 823 FSupp 1377 (ED Mich 1993) (finding that the demand for injunctive relief materially contributed to the decision to schedule an IEP meeting).
[148]Johnson v Bismarck Public School Dist, 949 F(2d) 1000 (8th Cir ND 1991).
[149]20 USCA 1415(e)(4)(C).
[150]20 USCA 1415(e)(4)(D). Examples of this provision in operation are Hyden v Wilson County Bd of Ed, 714 FSupp 290 (MD Tenn 1989); Fischer by Fischer v Rochester Community Schools, 780 FSupp 1142 (ED Mich 1991); Mr. L. & Mrs. L. v Woonsocket Ed Dept, 793 FSupp 41 (D RI 1992).
[151]20 USCA 1415(e)(4)(F). See Fischer by Fischer v Rochester Community Schools, 780 FSupp 1142 (ED Mich 1991) (attorney unnecessarily "aggrandized" and protracted the misunderstanding between the parties).
[152]RC 3323.06.
[153]RC 3323.02.
[154]RC 3317.024, RC 3317.05.

by the state board for teaching deaf children by the oral, manual, total communication, or other method of instruction.[155]

(B) Cooperative agreements among school districts

Two or more boards of education may enter into contracts for sharing, on a cooperative basis, the services of supervisory teachers, special instruction teachers, special education teachers, and other certificated personnel, to conduct classes for physically, emotionally, or mentally disabled pupils. For this purpose one of the contracting districts is designated as the funding agent.[156]

(C) Residency requirements and tuition reimbursement

The state may not impose a residency requirement on a disabled child covered by IDEA if that child lives in the state with a bona fide intention of remaining there, regardless of the residence of the parent or legal guardian.[157] In *Wise v Ohio Dept of Ed*,[158] the United States District Court for the Northern District of Ohio held that the irrebuttable presumption in RC 3323.141 and RC 3323.09(C)(1) that a child is a nonresident if his or her parents or legal guardians have never lived in Ohio is inconsistent with IDEA. Thus, the MR/DD board could not charge the state-licensed residential facility providing long-term care to the child or the child's parents for tuition at an Ohio public school, as provided by RC 3323.141.

28.16 Teachers of children with disabilities

The state board is authorized to arrange with the education department of any college or university for the classroom and in-service training of teachers for disabled children. Provision is made for payment for such teacher education services.[159]

Teachers in education programs under RC Chapter 3323 must possess the usual qualifications required of special education teachers in the public schools. Any instruction in braille reading and writing provided under RC 3323.011 to a student with a disability must be provided by a teacher certified to teach students with visual disabilities.[160]

28.17 Special classes, requirements for facilities

(A) Special classes or special instruction

All children of compulsory school age are required to attend school or participate in a special education program that conforms with minimum standards until a diploma or work permit is granted, unless otherwise excused from attendance.[161]

A statewide continuing identification system for disabled children and youth is required, and no placement of a disabled child may be made on the basis of a single criterion.[162]

Special education classes for disabled pupils may be approved for state funding in joint vocational school districts.[163]

(B) Eliminating architectural barriers

Standards and rules adopted by the state board of building standards pursuant to RC 3781.11 and RC 3781.111 are designed to facilitate the reasonable accommodation of and use by handicapped persons of buildings and facilities.[164]

Similarly, regulations promulgated under section 504 of the Rehabilitation Act require districts to make their programs "readily accessible" to disabled persons.[165] As to existing facilities, districts may comply through redesign of equipment, reassignment of classes to accessible buildings, use of aides, etc. New construction must make the facility readily accessible to the disabled. Alteration must be undertaken in a manner that, "to the maximum extent feasible," makes the altered portion readily accessible to and usable by disabled persons.[166]

---

[155] RC 3323.16.
[156] RC 3313.841, RC 3317.05.
[157] See 20 USCA 1412(1), (2)(B), and (2)(C).
[158] Wise v Ohio Dept of Ed, 863 FSupp 570 (ND Ohio 1994).
[159] RC 3317.024, RC 3323.01.
[160] RC 3323.011(D).

[161] RC 3321.03, RC 3321.04, RC 3321.08.
[162] RC 3323.03.
[163] RC 3317.16.
[164] See OAC Ch 4101:2-11.
[165] 34 CFR 104.22.
[166] 34 CFR 104.23.

In general, both IDEA and section 504 require that educational facilities for special education programs be comparable (albeit not necessarily "precisely equivalent") to those enjoyed by nondisabled pupils.[167]

28.18 Assisting deaf and hard of hearing children and their parents

The state board of education may use various methods to carry out RC 3325.06 to aid and assist parents of deaf or hard of hearing children in affording such children optimum communication. The methods of instruction may include classes for parents of preschool children, a nursery school where parents and child enter as a unit, correspondence courses, personal consultation and interviews, and such other means deemed advisable to assist such children to construct a pattern of communication at an early age.

A program to provide training for the parents of preschool children who are deaf or hard of hearing is established to give such children the very best possible facilities for learning to communicate at an early age.[168]

The department of education is responsible for supervising and giving technical assistance to school districts on all accepted methods (with no bias toward one over another) of educating deaf or hard of hearing children.[169] This includes consulting with school employees who confer with parents of such children about the children's education, assisting districts interested in integrating sign language into their curricula or offering American Sign Language as a foreign language, and consulting with districts on the use of interpreters in the classroom and how interpreters can improve the children's skills.[170]

With specific reference to the blind, deaf, or mobility impaired, RC 955.43 generally provides that when such a person is accompanied by a dog trained to assist the person, the dog may be taken into public conveyances and places, including elementary and secondary schools.

A federal appeals court has held that section 504 of the Rehabilitation Act requires a school district to provide sign language interpreter service to deaf parents of non-hearing impaired children at school-initiated conferences incident to academic or disciplinary aspects of their children's education. As for participation in voluntary extracurricular activities, the Americans With Disabilities Act might obligate a school district to provide, at public expense, a sign language interpreter or some other form of reasonable accommodation for the disabled person.

28.19 State schools for the deaf and blind

(A) In general, control and supervision, personnel

The control and supervision of the state schools for the deaf and the blind are the responsibility of the state board of education. Superintendents for both schools are appointed by recommendation of the state superintendent of public instruction and serve at the board's pleasure.[171]

The superintendents have the authority to employ teachers, nurses, and such other employees as necessary to provide proper care and instruction for pupils, subject to civil service rules and the approval of the superintendent of public instruction.[172]

Statewide proficiency tests are administered to students in accordance with RC 3301.0711(L), and diplomas and honors diplomas are granted in accordance with RC 3325.08.

(B) Admission, return of child to parents

Under state rules for the education of disabled children,[173] children referred for placement at the Ohio School for the Deaf or the Ohio School for the Blind first receive a multi-factored evaluation. Upon completion of that evaluation and receipt of a placement team conference report, the

---

[167]See Hendricks v Gilhool, 709 FSupp 1362 (ED Pa 1989).
[168]RC 3325.06, RC 3325.07.
[169]RC 3323.17.
[170]RC 3323.17.
[171]RC 3325.01.
[172]RC 3325.04.
[173]OAC 3301-51-20.

superintendent of the child's home school district makes a placement decision.

If the superintendent of the residential school determines the program is not appropriate for the child, he must inform the superintendent of the school district of residence and the parents in writing of the intent to dismiss the child from the residential school.[174] Thereafter, either the parents or the school district of residence may challenge the intended dismissal through an appeal procedure.[175] The rules expressly provide that "the educational status of the child shall not change until all appeal proceedings are completed."

28.20 Role of county MR/DD boards

(A) In general

The department of mental retardation and developmental disabilities is required to establish special education programs for disabled or developmentally delayed preschool children to be operated and maintained by county MR/DD boards in accordance with a plan submitted to and approved by the director.[176] Reimbursement for providing such special education is to be made in accordance with RC 3323.09 and RC 3317.08.

(B) Placement of child

The disabled child's district of residence remains responsible for insuring that a child placed in a program run by a county MR/DD board receives an appropriate special education.[177]

Roncker v Walter[178] vacated a district court's judgment that upheld placement of a disabled child in a county MR/DD board program, based in part on the lower court's use of a wrong standard in reviewing placement decision but also emphasizing IDEA's strong preference for mainstreaming. Yet, the fact that some disabled children simply must be educated in segregated facilities cannot be denied.

The state department of education places the burden of proof for placing a child in a county MR/DD board facility with the school district. A memorandum of the superintendent of public instruction points out that the following factors do *not*, by themselves, justify the placement of a disabled child in a separate facility:

(1) Classroom unit for multi-handicapped children may not be available;

(2) Needed related services may not be currently available through the school district; or

(3) Child meets the eligibility criteria for the programs of the county MR/DD board.[179]

Roncker pointed out that cost is a proper factor to consider, because excessive spending for one disabled child deprives other disabled children of needed program elements. Cost is no defense, however, if the school district has failed to provide a proper continuum of alternative placements for disabled children.[180]

---

[174] OAC 3301-51-20(B).
[175] See Text 25.12, Review of suspension or expulsion by board, appeal to common pleas court.
[176] RC 3323.09.
[177] RC 3323.04.
[178] Roncker v Walter, 700 F(2d) 1058 (6th Cir Ohio 1983), cert denied sub nom Cincinnati School Dist Bd of Ed v Roncker, 464 US 864, 104 SCt 196, 78 LEd(2d) 171 (1983).
[179] Memorandum of Superintendent of Public Instruction, "Placement of Handicapped Children in the Least Restrictive Environment" (July 14, 1981).
[180] Age v Bullitt County Public Schools, 673 F(2d) 141 (6th Cir Ky 1982).

Chapter 29

Administration of Programs for the Retarded and Developmentally Disabled

29.01 County MR/DD boards
29.02 Organization of board
29.03 Meetings of board
29.04 Powers and duties of board
29.05 Compliance with state regulations
29.06 Transportation of pupils
29.07 Contracts of board with other agencies
29.08 Property, gifts and grants
29.09 Funding and tuition

BOARD EMPLOYEES

29.10 Superintendent
29.11 Certification and registration of employees
29.12 Civil service status of employees; contract system for management employees
29.13 Compensation and fringe benefits
29.14 Criminal disqualifications and background checks
29.15 Nondiscrimination and affirmative action
29.16 Liability insurance
29.17 Collective bargaining

LEGAL COUNSEL

29.18 Legal adviser, other counsel

RECORDS

29.19 Restrictions on disclosure and release

29.01 County MR/DD boards

(A) In general, purpose and role

The legislature has created in each county a board of mental retardation and developmental disabilities (county MR/DD board) to provide comprehensive education and habilitation programs for mentally retarded and developmentally disabled children and adults residing in the county.[1] These boards are sometimes referred to as "169" boards because they were created by 1967 Senate Bill 169.

(B) "Mental retardation" and "developmental disability"

"Mental retardation" means mental impairment during the developmental period characterized by significantly subaverage general intellectual functioning coupled with deficiencies in the effectiveness or degree with which one meets expected standards of personal independence and social responsibility in light of one's age and cultural group.[2]

"Developmental disability" means having a severe, chronic disability manifested before age twenty-two, likely to continue indefinitely, and attributable to mental and/or physical impairments not caused solely by mental illness. The disability must result in at least one developmental delay or an established risk in the case of a person under age three; at least two developmental delays or an established risk in the case of a person age three to six; and a substantial functional limitation in at least three specified major life activities in the case of a person age six or over. It must also cause the person to need a combination of special care, treatment, or services for an extended period that is individually planned and coordinated.[3]

29.02 Organization of board

(A) Members, appointment

Each county MR/DD board consists of seven county residents, five appointed by the board of county commissioners, and two by the county probate judge. The board membership as nearly as possible must reflect the composition of the county population.[4]

(B) Qualifications

At least two of the members appointed by the board of county commissioners must be parents of persons eligible for and currently receiving services provided by the county MR/DD board. Whenever possible, one should be the parent of a person currently receiving adult services, and the other the parent of a person currently receiving services for pre-school or school-age children. At least one of the members

---

[1] RC 3323.09, RC 5126.01 et seq.
[2] RC 5126.01(E).
[3] RC 5126.01(B)(1) to (5). "Developmental delay" and "established risk" are defined in RC 5126.01(B) by reference to RC 5123.011.

[4] RC 5126.02.

appointed by the probate judge must be a family member of a person eligible for or currently receiving services in a public or private residential facility, licensed pursuant to RC 5123.19 and RC 5123.20. All persons appointed must be interested and knowledgeable in the field of mental retardation and other allied fields.[5]

(C) Persons disqualified from membership

Certain persons are specifically disqualified to be board members, such as designated public officials, immediate family members of another board member, board employees and immediate family members of board employees, and former board employees within one year after termination of employment with the board.[6] The attorney general has determined that an assistant county prosecutor may not serve since the county prosecutor's office is the legal advisor of the board.[7] Similarly, a city council member may not serve since the prohibition against elected public officials serving is not limited to county officials.[8] Likewise, one may not serve simultaneously in the positions of superintendent of the county MR/DD board and member of a city school district board of education.[9] RC 5126.03(D) prohibits one from being a member or an employee of a county MR/DD board if an immediate family member is a county commissioner of the county served by the board unless the person was a member or employee before October 31, 1980.[10] One may not be a county MR/DD board member if he or an immediate member of his family serves on the board of a contract agency of that county board unless there is no conflict of interest, and in no event may a county MR/DD board member vote on any matter concerning a contract agency of which he or a member of his immediate family is also a board member or employee. Any questions relating to the existence of a conflict of interest must be submitted to the local prosecuting attorney and the Ohio Ethics Commission for resolution.[11] Finally, no employee (or immediate family member of the employee) of an agency contracting with a county MR/DD board may serve as a county board member or employee, except that the county board may by resolution employ an immediate family member.[12]

(D) Terms, vacancies, expenses

All appointments are for four-year terms. A member who has served during two consecutive terms may not be reappointed for a subsequent term until one year after he ceases to be a board member, except that a member who has served for six years or less within two consecutive terms may be reappointed for another full term before becoming ineligible for reappointment for one year. The membership of a person appointed as the parent of a recipient of services may not be terminated because the child or adult no longer receives services.[13]

Sixty days after a vacancy occurs, it must be filled by the appointing authority for the unexpired term. Any member appointed to fill a vacancy holds office for the remainder of that term. Appointment other than appointment to fill a vacancy must be made no later than November 30 of each year, and the term of office begins on the date of the annual organizational meeting.[14]

Board members serve without compensation but are reimbursed for necessary expenses incurred in the conduct of board business, including those incurred within the county of residence.[15]

(E) Removal

RC 5126.04 provides that the appointing authority must remove a board member for neglect of duty, misconduct, malfeasance, failure to attend at least one in-service training session each year,[16] violating RC 5126.03(A) to (D), or upon the absence of

---

[5] RC 5126.02.

[6] RC 5126.03. According to the attorney general, an individual who was not an immediate family member when appointed but who later becomes an immediate family member of another board member is in violation of the statute and subject to removal pursuant to RC 5126.04. OAG 89-057.

[7] OAG 83-030.

[8] OAG 83-028.

[9] OAG 86-016.

[10] See also OAG 81-067.

[11] RC 5126.03.

[12] RC 5126.03.

[13] RC 5126.02.

[14] RC 5126.02.

[15] RC 5126.02.

[16] The attorney general has concluded "year" is not measured from the time of a member's appointment but, rather, denotes a calendar year. OAG 89-057.

the member from four regularly scheduled meetings within one year or from two regularly scheduled board meetings if the member gave no prior notice of his absence. This removal provision does not apply to absences from special meetings or work sessions. The board must supply the board member and his appointing authority with written notice of the charges against the member, and the appointing authority must afford an opportunity for a hearing, in accordance with its adopted procedures. Upon determining the charges are accurate, the authority must remove the member and appoint another person to complete the member's term. A removed member is ineligible for reappointment for at last one yer. The appointing authority must specify the time during which the removed member is ineligible for reappointment and, if the reason for removal was failure to attend in-service training, also specify the training that must be completed before any reappointment.

29.03 Meetings of board

Each county MR/DD board must hold an organizational meeting no later than January 31 of each year and elect a president, vice-president, and recording secretary. After the organizational meeting, the board must meet as prescribed by its rules but at least ten times annually, in regularly scheduled sessions, not including in-service training sessions.[17]

Board meetings must be conducted in accordance with RC 121.22.[18] A majority constitutes a quorum. The board is required to adopt rules for the conduct of its business, and a record must be kept of board proceedings, which must be open for public inspection.[19]

29.04 Powers and duties of board

(A) In general

The powers and duties of a county MR/DD board are mainly set forth in RC 5126.05 and may be generally described as those necessary for:

(1) Administering and operating facilities, programs, and services as provided by RC Chapters 3323 and 5126 and establishing policies for their administration and operation;

(2) Assessing the facility and service needs of the mentally retarded and developmentally disabled residents of the county and of certain former residents of the county;

(3) Planning and setting priorities based on available funds to provide for both facilities and services to meet the needs of county residents and certain former residents;

(4) Coordinating, monitoring, and evaluating existing services and facilities;

(5) Providing early childhood services, supportive home services, and adult services;

(6) Providing special education programs according to RC Chapter 3323, and ensuring that related services, as defined in RC 3323.01, are available as required;

(7) Requiring individual habilitation or service plans for mentally retarded or developmentally disabled individuals who are being served or are awaiting service after having been determined eligible for services;

(8) Providing for a qualified superintendent as defined by rules of the director of the department of mental retardation and developmental disabilities by either employing a superintendent or obtaining the services of the superintendent of another county MR/DD board pursuant to RC 5126.05(B);[20]

(9) Adopting a budget, authorizing expenditures, and exercising such other powers and duties as are prescribed by the director of mental retardation and developmental disabilities;

(10) Submitting annual reports to the director and to the board of county commissioners at the close of the fiscal year and at such other times as may be reasonably requested;

(11) Authorizing all positions of employment (including the establish-

---

[17]RC 5126.04.
[18]See Text 5.12, Open meetings: the sunshine law.
[19]RC 5126.04.
[20]See Text 29.10, Superintendent.

ment of compensation and fringe benefits) and employing legal counsel;

(12) Providing case management services in accordance with RC 5126.15;

(13) Certifying respite care homes pursuant to rules adopted under RC 5123.171;

(14) Providing for or arranging residential services and supported living for mentally retarded or developmentally disabled individuals, subject to availability of resources;[21]

(15) Planning and developing supported living for mentally retarded and developmentally disabled county residents as provided in RC 5126.41 to RC 5126.47;[22]

(16) Purchasing liability insurance;[23]

(17) Making eligibility determinations in accordance with criteria in RC 5126.011; and

(18) Where available resources are insufficient to meet the needs of those it serves, establish waiting lists in accordance with RC 5126.052.

(B) Coordinating with boards of education

County MR/DD boards are to consult with boards of education and assist in the identification, location, and evaluation of all disabled children residing within the districts and to help in determining which such children are not receiving appropriate special education and related services.[24]

In addition, a county MR/DD board provides special education for disabled children and disabled or developmentally delayed preschool children.[25] Disabled children and their parents are entitled to the full range of procedural safeguards provided by RC 3323.05 when placement is made in county MR/DD boards under RC 3323.04 and RC 3323.09.[26] RC 3323.09 also requires reports and statements to appropriate school districts and homes where disabled children reside.

(C) Fees for services

A county MR/DD board must establish fees for services rendered to eligible persons if such fees are required by federal regulation and by rule adopted by the director of mental retardation and developmental disabilities.[27] A board may provide services to ineligible persons, and may establish fees for these services.[28]

(D) Eligibility of family members for services

Membership on or employment by a county MR/DD board does not affect the eligibility of any member of such person's family for services provided by the board or any entity under contract with the board.[29]

(E) Ethics councils

RC 5126.032 requires the president of the county MR/DD board to appoint, at the annual organizational meeting, three board members to an ethics council. The president may be one of those appointed, but may not appoint a member to the council if that member or a person from his family will have any interest in any client services contract the council reviews. If, during the member's service or the one-year period thereafter, the member or a person from his family has or will have such an interest, the president must replace the member with another. The board superintendent is a nonvoting council member. The council is to review, approve, or disapprove all direct services contracts in accordance with standards set forth in the statute and develop, in consultation with the prosecuting attorney, and recommend ethical standards, contract audit procedures, and grievance procedures regarding the award and reconciliation of direct services contracts. Under certain specified circumstances, the board itself may assume the

---

[21] RC 5126.051.
[22] RC 5126.40.
[23] RC 5126.09.
[24] RC 3323.03.
[25] RC 3323.04, RC 3323.09. See also Austintown Local School Dist Bd of Ed v Mahoning County Bd of Mental Retardation and Developmental Disabilities, 66 OS(3d) 355, 613 NE(2d) 167 (1993) (holding, among other things, that where school district places disabled child in county MR/DD board program, county board may not veto decision but must resolve any disagreement under procedure contained in RC 3323.04); OAG 80-009.
[26] See Text 28.11, Parental involvement in educational decisions affecting disabled child.
[27] RC 5126.054.
[28] RC 5126.053.
[29] RC 5126.031.

responsibilities and perform the duties of the council.[30]

(F) Regional councils

RC 5126.13 authorizes a county MR/DD board to contract with one or more county MR/DD boards to establish a regional council in accordance with RC Chapter 167. The agreement must specify the council's functions and duties, which may include any functions and duties a county MR/DD board is authorized to perform. By resolution, a county MR/DD board that is a member of a regional council may direct the department of mental retardation and developmental disabilities to distribute money for that county for the functions or duties performed by the council, that would otherwise be distributed to the county board, to the council's fiscal officer.

RC 5126.13 also authorizes a county MR/DD board to contract with one or more school districts in other political subdivisions to establish a regional council in accordance with RC Chapter 167.

(G) Residential facility linked deposit programs

A residential facility linked deposit program is intended to provide low-cost funds for lending that will effectively reduce high interest rates and materially help to remedy the shortage of suitable residential facilities for county residents with mental retardation or developmental disabilities.[31]

A county MR/DD board may, by resolution, request the board of county commissioners to implement a program if the MR/DD board finds (1) a shortage of residential facilities in the county for persons with mental retardation or developmental disabilities; (2) eligible organizations willing and able to develop residential facilities in the county have been unable to do so because of high interest rates; and (3) placement of residential facility linked deposits will assist financing development of residential facilities in the county that otherwise would not be developed because of high interest rates. A certified copy of the resolution must be transmitted to the board of county commissioners.[32]

A board of county commissioners that receives a requesting resolution from the county MR/DD board may, by resolution, implement a residential facility linked deposit program for the county if it makes the same findings as the MR/DD board and further finds that county public moneys are available for the program and at least one eligible lending institution[33] has an office in the county into which county public moneys may be deposited.[34] In its implementing resolution, the county commissioners must include (1) specific findings of fact that justify the program; (2) guidelines to be followed by the county MR/DD board in establishing standards under RC 5126.49 for approving applications for linked deposit loans; (3) instructions to the county's investing authority[35] as necessary for the placement and monitoring of, and reporting with respect to, deposits under the program; and (4) any information the county commissioners require an applicant for a loan to provide to the county MR/DD board that would not otherwise be provided to that board under RC 5126.51 to RC 5126.62. A certified copy of the resolution must be transmitted to the county MR/DD board and the county's investing authority (unless the board of county commissioners is that authority).[36] The program is not operative unless this implementing resolution is adopted.[37]

An eligible organization that seeks a loan under the program must obtain approval of the proposed project by the county MR/DD board of the county in which the facility will be developed.[38] The county MR/DD board must, by resolution, approve or disapprove the project. Approval requires a finding, based on the application and evaluation of the applicant,

---

[30]See also RC 5126.033, which imposes certain conditions for direct services contacts.

[31]RC 5126.52.

[32]RC 5126.49.

[33]A lending institution is "eligible" if, among other things, it can make commercial loans and holds itself out as participating in the residential facility linked deposit program. RC 135.801(A), RC 5126.51(B).

[34]RC 135.801(B).

[35]RC 5126.51(D) defines "investing authority" by reference to RC 135.31. It is typically the county treasurer.

[36]RC 135.802.

[37]RC 5126.53.

[38]RC 5126.54. The statute includes specific requirements as to the form of the application for approval.

that the project is consistent with the board's plan and priorities for providing residential services. In addition, either approval or disapproval requires inclusion in the resolution of specific findings of fact justifying the decision. A certified copy of the resolution must be transmitted to the applicant and the board of county commissioners.[39]

On receiving a resolution of approval, the board of county commissioners must determine if the county public moneys are available for a residential facility linked deposit and certify to the county MR/DD board either that moneys are or are not available. If moneys are not available, the certification must indicate the date, if any, on which it is anticipated that moneys will be available.[40]

On receiving a resolution of approval, the eligible organization may apply to an eligible lending institution for a residential facility linked deposit loan to finance all or part of the project. The application must include a copy of the resolution of approval and a resolution, adopted by the organization's board of trustees, certifying that if the application is approved and accepted, the loan will be used solely for the project as approved by the county MR/DD board.[41]

The lending institution, applying its customary standards for residential property loans, must approve or disapprove the application within a reasonable time, in accordance with commercial practice. If approved, the institution must prepare and transmit to the county MR/DD board certain information specified in RC 5126.57. If disapproved, it must promptly notify the MR/DD board.[42] The MR/DD board must also approve or disapprove the application, by resolution. Disapproval is required unless the board makes certain findings specified in RC 5126.58. The resolution must include specific findings of fact justifying acceptance or rejection of the application. If accepted, the resolution must also specify the amount of the residential facility linked deposit. A certified copy of the resolution must be transmitted to the applicant, lending institution, and county investing authority.[43]

On acceptance of a loan by the county MR/DD board, the county investing authority is to enter into an agreement with the lending institution that must contain all of the terms specified in RC 5126.59. These must include an agreement by the investing authority to place certificates of deposit with the institution in the amount of the residential linked deposit at an interest rate up to five per cent per year below current market rates and an agreement by the institution to lend the value of the certificates to the eligible organization at an annual interest rate that is the same number of percentage points below the current borrowing rate for similar loans as the rate for the certificates is below current market rates. On complying with the agreement and making the loan, the institution is to transmit to the investing company a certification of its compliance.[44]

The county investing authority is to monitor compliance with the statutes by lending institutions and organizations receiving loans and annually report on operation of the program, listing organizations receiving loans, to the board of county commissioners and the county MR/DD board.[45] Neither of these boards, nor the county or county investing authority, is liable for repaying the laon, and delay in payment or default by the organization receiving the loan does not affect the deposit agreement between the county investing authority and the lending institution.[46]

(H) Limitations

The attorney general has found that a county MR/DD board lacks authority to independently purchase real estate. The board may purchase real estate with approval of the board of county commissioners pursuant to RC 5705.19(L) or by the board of county commissioners under RC 307.02.[47] An appeals court has also held that a county MR/DD board has no

---

[39] RC 5126.55.
[40] RC 135.803.
[41] RC 5126.56.
[42] RC 5126.57.
[43] RC 5126.58.

[44] RC 5126.60.
[45] RC 5126.61.
[46] RC 5126.62.
[47] OAG 82-018.

power independently to contract for the purchase of real estate.[48]

The attorney general has concluded that a county MR/DD board may establish a cash payment retirement incentive program as a form of compensation for employees.[49]

(I) Complaints

RC 5126.041 provides that any person, except employees of a county MR/DD board, who has a complaint involving programs, services, policies, or administrative practices of the board or any entity under contract with the bord may file a complaint with the board. Before filing any civil action regarding the matter, the administrative resolution process established in rules adopted under RC 5123.043 must be exhausted.

29.05 Compliance with state regulations

A county MR/DD board must comply with rules adopted by the director of mental retardation and developmental disabilities governing all services provided by the board. These rules without limitation include as follows:

(1) Determination of what constitutes a program or service;

(2) Procedures for approval of all forms used;

(3) Standards for determining the nature and degree of mental retardation and developmental disability;

(4) Standards for determining eligibility for programs and services other than case management services;

(5) Procedures for obtaining consent for services under RC 5126.31 in connection with an abused or neglected adult who is mentally retarded or developmentally disabled; and

(6) Specification of case management services to be provided, standards for determining the eligibility of clients for case management services, and standards for resolving grievances in connection with such services.[50]

29.06 Transportation of pupils

(A) Costs

In accordance with RC 5126.14, the department of mental retardation and developmental disabilities pays a county MR/DD board for transportation operating costs for children under age three enrolled in the board's early childhood education program or persons enrolled in adult programs. RC 3323.09 provides that a county MR/DD board may combine transportation for children and adults enrolled in certain programs. The department pays the board fifty per cent of its reported transportation costs for the previous calendar year for such persons.[51]

(B) Transportation safety

The superintendent may establish a volunteer bus rider assistance program under which qualified persons may be authorized to ride with pupils. The volunteers may be assigned to assist pupils in embarking and disembarking and in crossing streets and to perform other duties as the superintendent determines will aid in the safe and efficient transportation of pupils. The volunteers may not be compensated.[52]

The superintendent must ensure that each pupil is instructed in school bus safety, proper bus rider behavior, and the potential problems and hazards associated with school bus ridership. This instruction must be given within two weeks after the pupil first receives transportation.[53]

The board can insure volunteer bus rider assistants against liability arising from the performance of their official duties.[54]

29.07 Contracts of board with other agencies

A county MR/DD board may contract with other such boards and with public or private, nonprofit, or profit-making agencies or organizations of the same or

---

[48]Dietrich & Hoover v Circleville Recreation Center, Inc, No. 81-CA-19, 1984 WL 4261 (4th Dist Ct App, Pickaway, 2-28-84).
[49]OAG 90-075.
[50]RC 5126.08; OAC 5123:2.
[51]RC 5126.14.
[52]RC 5126.061.
[53]RC 5126.061.
[54]RC 5126.09.

another county, to provide authorized or required facilities, programs, and services; however, a county MR/DD board cannot contract with an agency whose board includes a commissioner of the county served by the MR/DD board.[55]

A county MR/DD board is bound by the competitive bidding requirements of RC 307.86 when entering into contracts where dollar amounts exceed $10,000.[56] However, contracts for the purchase of certain services, including case management and residential, are not required to be put up for bid.[57] If the amount exceeds $10,000, RC 307.88 requires the bid be accompanied by a bond or certified check as security.[58]

29.08 Property, gifts and grants

(A) Gifts, grants, devises, and bequests

A county MR/DD board may receive by gift, grant, devise, or bequest any money, land, or property for purposes for which the board is established and may hold, apply, and dispose of the same according to the terms of the gift, grant, or bequest. All money or disposition of land or property received must be deposited in the county treasury to the credit of the board and must be available for purposes determined or stated by the donor or grantor, but may not be used for personal expenses of board members.[59] Interest earned on gifts, grants, or bequests made to a county MR/DD board must be deposited in the county treasury to the credit of the board and must be available for any purpose stated by the donor or grantor.[60]

A county MR/DD board may give money received under a testamentary bequest to a nonprofit foundation established to aid the mentally retarded, provided the gift bears restrictions designed to assure the money is used to further the board's statutory purposes and further provided the gift complies with terms of the bequest.[61]

(B) Disposition of unneeded personal property

When a county MR/DD board has personal property, acquired other than by gift, grant, devise, or bequest, and such property is no longer needed or obsolete, the board may sell or lease the property in accordance with procedures set forth in RC 307.12 and OAG 84-054.

29.09 Funding and tuition

(A) Funding

The board of county commissioners must levy taxes and make appropriations sufficient to enable the county MR/DD board to perform its functions and duties as provided in RC 5126.05 and may use any available local, state, or federal funds for such purpose.[62] A county MR/DD board may sue in mandamus to compel the commissioners to meet their financial obligations.[63] Proceeds from a special levy passed for the purpose of supporting the county MR/DD board and for the construction and operation of new facilities must be placed in a special account within the county mental retardation and developmental disabilities general fund.[64] The pro-

---

[55]RC 5126.05, RC 5126.03. "Agency" includes nonprofit corporations created under RC Ch 1702. OAG 92-069. See also Text 29.04(F), Regional councils.

[56]OAG 81-050. See also Text 37.06(A)(2), The RC 9.312 option.

[57]RC 307.86.

[58]OAG 84-064.

[59]RC 5126.05.

[60]RC 5126.05; OAG 92-075; OAG 85-055.

[61]OAG 85-031.

[62]RC 5126.05.

[63]See Cuyahoga County Bd of Mental Retardation v Cuyahoga County Bd of Commrs, 41 OS(2d) 103, 322 NE(2d) 885 (1975). In Jackson County Bd of Mental Retardation and Developmental Disabilities v Jackson County Bd of Commrs, 49 OS(3d) 63, 551 NE(2d) 133 (1990), the Ohio Supreme Court held that if the commissioners do levy a tax and appropriate funds but simply cannot supply sufficient funds, RC 5126.05 does not require the appropriation of funds for the agency from the county general fund. Rather, said the Court, when a county is unable to fund all its MR/DD needs, the state is to augment county appropriations pursuant to RC 5123.351. The provisions of RC 5123.351 upon which the Court relied have since been repealed, however.

[64]RC 5705.19(L) and RC 5705.222 authorize voter approved tax levies to fund services and facilities. Revenue thus received must be deposited in accordance with RC 5705.091 and RC 5705.10. With respect to a special election for a tax levy for community mental retardation and developmental disabilities programs and services held under RC 5705.19(L), the board of county commissioners, not the county MR/DD board,

ceeds must be used for the specific purpose for which the taxes were levied.[65] Any unexpended balance at the end of the fiscal year must be appropriated the next fiscal year to the same fund.[66] A mental retardation and developmental disabilities capital fund may be established for the acquisition, construction, or improvement of facilities or equipment used in providing services.[67] General funds not needed for current operating expenses may be transferred by the county commissioners from the general fund to a capital fund or any other fund created for the purposes of county MR/DD boards.[68] After satisfying all outstanding obligations, any unexpended balance may be transferred back to the general fund.[69]

In addition, each board receives state financial assistance based on average daily membership, excluding those receiving home-based services, by submitting to the department of mental retardation and developmental disabilities the certifications required by RC 5126.12.

Enrollment in approved educational programs provided by other public or private, nonprofit or for-profit agencies, pursuant to contract under RC 5126.05, will be considered by the state board of education in appropriating state funds.[70]

(B) Reimbursements to families

Subject to rules adopted by the director of mental retardation and to the availability of state and federal funds, a county MR/DD board must make payments to a mentally retarded or developmentally disabled person or the family of such a person, if they reside in the county, for all or part of costs incurred or estimated to be incurred for promoting self-sufficiency or normalization, preventing or reducing inappropriate institutional care, and furthering family unity. No payments may be made to a person or family of a person living in a residential facility which provides services under a contract with the department of mental retardation or county board. Payments may be made for:

(1) Respite care;

(2) Counseling, training, and education of the family of a mentally retarded or developmentally disabled person;

(3) Special diets, modification of home, and purchase or lease of special equipment if necessary to improve or facilitate the care of a mentally retarded or developmentally disabled person; or

(4) Any other services consistent with RC 5126.11(B).

The mentally retarded or developmentally disabled person must be in need of habilitation. Further, payments are adjusted for income. The applicant must prove eligibility and submit a statement of expenses. A county board's refusal to approve a service may be appealed.[71]

(C) Tuition

Tuition obligations with respect to a handicapped child who receives special education from a county MR/DD board are treated in Text Chapter 23, specifically at Text 23.02(D), Computation and payment.

BOARD EMPLOYEES

29.10 Superintendent

(A) In general

The superintendent of a county MR/DD board is employed by the board by contract, for a term of one to five years. At the expiration of his current term, the superintendent must be reemployed for a term of one year at the same salary plus any increments that may be authorized by the board, unless the board, on or before ninety calen-

---

must pay election costs as provided in RC 3501.17. OAG 91-042.

[65]OAG 86-103. See also OAG 92-027, wherein the Attorney General not only reaffirmed this point but went on to state no authority exists for automatically transferring proceeds to a school district when that district assumes responsibility for educating persons previously educated by the county MR/DD board; however, the board may pay proceeds from a voted levy to a school district in exchange for facilities, programs, goods, or services to the extent the board has authority to carry out the purposes of the levy by acquiring those facilities, programs, goods, or services from a school district.

[66]RC 5705.091.
[67]RC 5705.091.
[68]RC 5705.14(H), RC 5705.222.
[69]RC 5705.14(H).
[70]OAG 86-040.
[71]RC 5126.11.

dar days prior to the current contract expiration date, either reemploys the superintendent for a succeeding term or gives him written notification of its intention not to reemploy him. The board must give a superintendent in his first year of employment such written notification sixty days prior to his current contract expiration date if the contract is for one year.[72] If the superintendent is reemployed, the board may designate that he is to continue for a term not exceeding five years. The superintendent may be removed, suspended, or demoted for cause pursuant to RC 5126.23, which prescribes a procedure for written notice of charges, a predisciplinary conference where the superintendent is afforded an opportunity to refute the charges, and, if requested, a postdisciplinary hearing before an impartial referee.[73] Alternatively, the parties may submit issues regarding the removal, suspension, or demotion to binding arbitration.[74]

The board is required to review the performance of the superintendent. The superintendent has no voting privileges on the board. In addition to his compensation as fixed by the board, the superintendent must be reimbursed for actual and necessary expenses.[75]

The superintendent must meet the certification standards set by the department of mental retardation and developmental disabilities in OAC 5123:2-5-03.

Two or more county MR/DD boards may agree that the superintendent of one board will also act as the superintendent of the other boards, provided each board adopts a resolution specifying the duration of the arrangement, the functions the superintendent is to perform for the additional boards he serves, and the contribution each board is to make to his compensation.[76]

(B) Duties

The superintendent's duties include the following:

(1) Administration of the work of the board subject to its rules;

(2) Recommendation to the board of the changes necessary to increase the effectiveness of the programs and services offered;

(3) Employment of persons for all positions authorized by the board, approval of contracts of employment for management employees that are for a term of one year or less, and approval of personnel actions that involve employees in the classified civil service as may be necessary for the work of the board;

(4) Approval of compensation for employees within the limits set by the salary schedule and budget set by the board and in accordance with RC 5126.26 and ensuring that all employees and consultants are properly reimbursed for actual and necessary expenses incurred in the performance of official duties; and

(5) Provision of consultative services to public agencies as defined in RC 102.01(C), including other county MR/DD boards, and to individuals, agencies, or organizations providing services supported by the board.[77]

The superintendent may authorize the payment of board obligations by the county auditor.[78] Further, the superintendent may enter into a written employment contract with a person holding the position of instructor, or instructor's assistant, but is not required to do so.[79]

29.11 Certification and registration of employees

Under RC 5126.20 and RC 5126.22, county MR/DD board employees fall into three categories. "Management employees" include those positions specifically listed in RC 5126.22(A) (e.g., an assistant superintendent, director of personnel, plant manager, or case management supervisor) and any other positions having managerial or supervisory responsibilities or designated by the county MR/DD board

---

[72] RC 5126.05(C).
[73] RC 5126.23(C) to (G).
[74] RC 5126.23(H).
[75] RC 5126.05(C).

[76] RC 5126.05(C).
[77] RC 5126.06.
[78] RC 5126.06.
[79] OAG 81-036.

under RC 5126.22(D).[80] "Professional employees" include those positions specifically listed in RC 5126.22(B) (e.g., a psychologist, physical therapist, registered nurse, or dentist) and any other position that requires either a bachelor's (or higher) degree from an accredited college or university or a license of certificate issued under RC Title 47.[81] Employees who hold neither management nor professional positions are "service employees."[82] RC 5126.22(E) prescribes a procedure for designating a particular position not listed in the statute as a management, professional, or service position, and RC 5126.22(F) provides that no employee can be terminated solely because a position is added (or designated) or eliminated (or no longer designated) from the positions listed in the statute.

RC 5126.25 requires that the director of mental retardation and developmental disabilities adopt rules establishing uniform standards and procedures for the certification of persons for employment by county MR/DD boards as superintendents, management employees, and professional employees. The rules shall specify the professional positions that require certification. If an applicant for a certificate has not completed the courses necessary under the certification standards, he will receive at least one year to complete the courses and cannot be required to complete more than four courses in any one year. RC 5126.27 requires a county MR/DD board that hired a professional employee before July 17, 1990, who does not meet the certification standards for his position as of July 17, 1990, to allow the employee to elect (1) to accept an available position, with no cut in pay, for which he meets certification standards; or (2) to remain in the position held on July 17, 1990, and comply with a professional development plan prescribed by the director of mental retardation and developmental disabilities under RC 5126.27(B). Notwithstanding any certification standards established under RC 5126.25, if the employee successfully and timely completes the plan, the director must grant the appropriate certificate for the position he holds. RC 3323.11 requires that teachers assigned to education programs under RC Chapter 3323 have the qualifications required of special education teachers in the public schools.

RC 5126.25 also requires that the director adopt rules establishing uniform standards and procedures for the registration of persons for employment by county MR/DD boards as registered service employees. The rules shall specify the service positions that require registration. No standard can require a service employee to have a bachelor's (or higher) degree.

The certification and registration rules adopted under RC 5126.25 apply to those who directly provide, or supervise persons who directly provide, services or instruction to or on behalf of individuals with mental retardation or developmental disabilities except that the rules do not apply to (1) persons certificated under RC Chapter 3319 who perform no duties other than teaching or supervision of a teaching program, or (2) persons licensed or certificated under RC Title 47 who perform only those duties governed by the license or certificate.

RC 5126.25(D) provides that a certificate or evidence of registration must be denied, suspended, or revoked if the applicant or holder is found guilty of intemperate, immoral, or other conduct unbecoming to his position, or guilty of incompetence or negligence within the scope of his duties, or has been convicted or pleaded guilty to any offense described in RC 5126.28(E).

Pending the issuance of an initial certificate or registration, an applicant for employment may be employed if he meets the applicable requirements, has applied for certification or registration, and the application has not been denied. Otherwise, no person can be employed by a county MR/DD board who does not hold the certificate, evidence of registration, or license required for the position.[83]

---

[80]RC 5126.20(C), RC 5126.22(A). For the meaning of managerial or supervisory responsibilities, see RC 5126.20(F), (G).

[81]RC 5126.20(B), RC 5126.22(B).

[82]RC 5126.22(C). Service employee positions expressly include workshop specialist, workshop specialist assistant, contract procurement specialist, community employment specialist, and any assistant to a professional employee certified to provide or supervise the provision of adult services or case management.

[83]RC 5126.26.

29.12 Civil service status of employees; contract system for management employees

Employees of a county MR/DD board, as county employees, are members of the civil service, and their employment is governed by RC Chapter 124.[84] However, if the employees are union-represented, terms and conditions of their employment will also be set by the collective bargaining agreement.[85]

The superintendent and management employees as defined in RC 5126.20 are specifically included in the unclassified civil service.[86] These positions, therefore, are not entitled to the protection afforded members of the classified civil service regarding tenure, reduction, suspension, removal, and demotion. Management employees, other than the superintendent, are employed under limited contracts for a term of one to five years. A management employee is automatically reemployed for one year unless, at least ninety days prior to expiration of his contract, he receives notice of the superintendent's intention not to rehire him.[87] Any management employee given continuing contract status before the effective date of RC 5126.21 (June 24, 1988) retains that status so long as he is employed by the board.[88] If he was a probationary employee on the effective date of the statute, he is entitled to continuing contract status if reemployed at the end of his probationary period.[89] Salaries and fringe benefits are determined by the board,[90] which is also required to establish and follow a lay-off policy in the event a reduction of management employees is necessary.[91] A management employee may be removed, suspended, or demoted in accordance with RC 5126.23. That statute prescribes a procedure for written notice of charges, a predisciplinary conference where the employee is afforded an opportunity to refute the charges, and, if requested, a postdisciplinary hearing before an impartial referee.[92] Alternatively, the parties may submit issues regarding the removal, suspension, or demotion to binding arbitration.[93]

All other positions within a county MR/DD board, with the exception of teaching positions, which may be in the unclassified service, are in the classified civil service. RC 124.241 expressly provides, however, that professional and registered service employees[94] may be hired on the basis of qualifications rather than on the basis of the results of an examination.

The attorney general has ruled a county MR/DD board employee performing his official duties may not receive a fee from a private nonprofit corporation which has contracted with the board.[95]

29.13 Compensation and fringe benefits

(A) Salary schedules, pay periods

RC 5126.24 requires each county MR/DD board annually to adopt separate salary schedules for teachers and nonteaching employees. No teacher may be paid less than the salary he would be paid under RC 3317.13, and no nonteaching employee may be paid less than the salary in effect on July 1, 1985.

Pursuant to its authority to establish compensation levels for employees, a county MR/DD board may pay its employees in twenty-six biweekly installments, extended over a calendar year, whether the employees work twelve months or only nine months during the year. However, being paid in twenty-six installments does not per se entitle a full-time nine-month employee to accrue sick leave or vacation benefits during the time the employee is not actually scheduled for work.[96]

---

[84] RC 124.01, RC 124.11; OAG 81-036; OAG 73-077.
[85] See Text 18.20, Supremacy of contract over certain laws.
[86] RC 124.11(A)(19).
[87] RC 5126.21(A).
[88] RC 5126.21(E).
[89] RC 5126.21(F).
[90] RC 5126.21(A), (C).

[91] RC 5126.21(G).
[92] RC 5126.23(C) to (G). The reasons for which a management employee may be disciplined are specified in RC 5126.23(B).
[93] RC 5126.23(H).
[94] See Text 29.11, Certification and registration of employees.
[95] OAG 84-109.
[96] OAG 82-055.

(B) Health insurance and sick leave

The county MR/DD board has the authority to contract for employee benefits, including health insurance.[97] However, a board is not a political subdivision within the meaning of RC 9.833 and thus is not authorized by that statute to participate in establishing and maintaining a joint self-insurance program to provide health care benefits.[98]

Sick leave for board employees, other than the superintendent and management employees as defined in RC 5126.20, is provided by RC 124.38 and is based on 4.6 hours of sick leave with pay for each 80 hours of service. This represents the minimum sick leave benefit. The board can adopt a more generous policy.[99] Full-time employees who work during only nine months of the year are not entitled to accrue sick leave benefits pursuant to RC 124.38 for the three months during which they are not scheduled to work, unless the board has adopted a policy specifically authorizing accrual.[100] RC 124.38 authorizes the board, upon notification to the board of county commissioners, to establish alternative sick leave schedules for employees not within a bargaining unit established by the State Employment Relations Board under RC 4117.06, provided the alternative schedules are not inconsistent with a collective bargaining agreement covering other board employees.

A county board may adopt a policy which provides for cash payment to employees for accrued sick leave benefits upon termination of employment other than retirement, so long as the board's policy provides benefits at least as great as any benefits to which the employees may otherwise be entitled pursuant to statute or a policy adopted by the board of county commissioners under RC 124.39(C). The board may also adopt a policy which provides for cash payment to employees at the end of each school year for the past year's accrued sick leave benefits, provided the board's policy provides benefits at least as great as any benefits to which the employees may otherwise be entitled pursuant to statute or a policy adopted by the county commissioners.[101]

(C) Vacation

Vacation benefits for board employees, other than the superintendent and management employees as defined in RC 5126.20, are earned pursuant to RC 325.19, which provides that on completion of the first year of employment, vacation leave accrues according to the statutory schedule. A board may adopt a more generous benefit.[102] Full-time employees who work during only nine months of the year are not entitled to accrue vacation leave benefits for the three months during which they are not scheduled to work, unless the board has adopted a policy specifically authorizing it.[103] An employee who is awarded a position categorized as full time may have a right to seek both vacation and holiday pay benefits pursuant to a mandamus petition.[104]

(D) Retirement

Membership in the public employees retirement system (PERS) is mandatory for employees of a county MR/DD board under RC 145.01 et seq.[105] In addition, the attorney general has since concluded that all teachers employed in education programs operated by county MR/DD boards under RC Chapter 3323 are members of the state teachers retirement system (STRS) by virtue of the definition of "teacher" in RC 3307.01(B).[106]

PERS members are eligible to participate in the deferred compensation program offered by the Ohio public employees deferred compensation board pursuant to RC 145.71 to RC 145.73.[107]

(E) Resignation

RC 5126.29 provides that no certificated professional or management employee may

---

[97] RC 5126.05; OAG 79-064.
[98] OAG 92-061.
[99] OAG 82-055; Ebert v Stark County Bd of Mental Retardation, 63 OS(2d) 31, 406 NE(2d) 1098 (1980).
[100] OAG 82-055.
[101] OAG 84-071.
[102] See Ebert v Stark County Bd of Mental Retardation, 63 OS(2d) 31, 406 NE(2d) 1098 (1980).
[103] OAG 82-055.
[104] State ex rel LanFranchi v Summit County Bd of Mental Retardation & Developmental Disabilities, 46 App(3d) 71, 545 NE(2d) 1308 (1988).
[105] RC 145.01, RC 145.03; OAG 80-063.
[106] OAG 88-069.
[107] RC 145.71(A).

terminate an employment contract with a county MR/DD board without advance written board consent or thirty days' written notice. Failure to comply may result in suspension of one's certificate for up to one year.

29.14 Criminal disqualifications and background checks

RC 5126.28, which is patterned largely after the procedure applicable to school boards under RC 3319.39, generally precludes the employment of an applicant who has been convicted of or pleaded guilty to certain specified crimes.[108] The applicant must submit a signed statement attesting that he has not been convicted of or pleaded guilty to such an offense.

In addition, the registrar of motor vehicles must be asked to supply a certified abstract regarding convictions for violations of motor vehicle laws for any applicant who will drive board vehicles or transport persons with mental retardation or developmental disabilities. The applicant must be supplied with a copy of any report or abstract obtained.[109] Each entity within which a county MR/DD board contracts for services to persons with mental retardation or developmental disabilities must conduct substantially similar background investigations of applicants for positions that involve providing services directly to such individuals.

29.15 Nondiscrimination and affirmative action

No county MR/DD board or any agency, corporation, or association under contract with the board may discriminate in the services provided under its authority or contract on the basis of race, color, sex, creed, disability, national origin, or the ability to pay for services received.

Each board must provide a plan of affirmative action describing its goals and methods to provide for equal employment opportunities for all persons under its authority and must ensure nondiscrimination in employment under its authority or in contracting on the basis of race, color, sex, creed, disability, or national origin.[110]

29.16 Liability insurance

A county MR/DD board is authorized to purchase liability insurance for board members, employees, or agencies with which it contracts.[111]

29.17 Collective bargaining

County MR/DD boards, like other public employers, are required to bargain collectively with their employees' duly certified representative, if any, over wages, hours, terms, or conditions of employment.[112] However, the legislative body for the board, for purposes of funding and approving collective bargaining agreements under RC 4117.10(B), is the board of county commissioners.[113]

LEGAL COUNSEL

29.18 Legal adviser, other counsel

RC 305.14(C) authorizes a county MR/DD board to employ legal counsel for advice or representation in any matter of public business or in litigation to which the board or board member or employee in his official capacity is a party. In "any legal proceeding" in which the county prosecutor is able to represent the board without a conflict of interest, such other counsel may

---

[108] Any substantially equivalent offense under existing or former Ohio, other state, or federal law is also included. For treatment of RC 3319.39, see Text 5.09(H), Criminal background checks. RC 5126.281 similarly requires criminal background checks under certain circumstances by entities under contract with a county MR/DD board for the provision of direct services to mentally retarded or developmentally disabled persons.

[109] An applicant may be employed for up to sixty days pending receipt of reports under the statute.

[110] RC 5126.07.

[111] RC 5126.09. For discussion of a board's tort liability, see the extended treatment of the Ohio Public Liability Act, RC Ch 2744, that appears in Text Ch 46, Liability of Schools, Officers, and Employees.

[112] RC 4117.01(B). See also Text Ch 18, Collective Bargaining.

[113] Stark County Educators Assn for the Training of Retarded Persons v SERB, 1989 SERB 4-119, 1989 WL 120658 (5th Dist Ct App, Stark, 10-10-89).

be employed only with the prosecutor's written consent. If the prosecutor is unable to represent the board in a legal proceeding for any reason, he must notify the board and it may employ other counsel without further permission.

In practice, county MR/DD boards are commonly represented, in certain matters, by counsel other than the county prosecutor.

RECORDS

29.19 Restrictions on disclosure and release

RC 5126.38 generally precludes any person from disclosing the identity of one who requests programs or services under RC Chapter 5126 or releasing a record or report regarding an eligible person that is maintained by a county MR/DD board or an entity under contract with a board unless (1) the individual or eligible person (or his guardian or, if he is a minor, his parent or guardian) makes a written request to the board or entity for or approves in writing disclosure of the person's identity or release of the record or report; (2) disclosure of one's identity is needed for approval of a direct services contract under RC 5126.032 or RC 5126.033 (in which case only the person's name and the general nature of the services to be provided is to be released); or (3) disclosure of one's identity is needed to ascertain that the board's waiting lists for programs or services are being properly maintained (in which case only the person's name, the general nature of the services to be provided, the person's rank on each waiting list that includes him, and any circumstances under which the person was given priority when placed on a waiting list are to be released).[114]

At the request of an eligible person (or his guardian or, if he is a minor, his parent or guardian) the county board or entity under contract with the board must provide access to records and reports regarding the person. On written request, copies of such records and reports must be provided, for which a reasonable fee to cover the costs of copying may be charged (the fee may be waived in cases of hardship). A county board must provide access to any waiting list or record or report regarding an eligible person that the board maintains to any state agency responsible for monitoring and reviewing the board's programs and services, any state agency involved in the coordination of services for an eligible person, or any agency under contract with the department of mental retardation and developmental disabilities for the provision of protective services under RC 5126.56.

A county board or entity under contract with the board that discloses an individual's identity or releases a record or report regarding an eligible person must maintain a record of when and to whom the disclosure or release was made. In addition, a county board must notify an eligible person (or his guardian or, if he is a minor, his parent or guardian) prior to destroying any record or report regarding the person.

---

[114]One who makes a disclosure or release in violation of the statute is guilty of a first degree misdemeanor. RC 5126.99. See also RC 5123.62(T), which guarantees the right of mentally retarded persons or developmentally disabled persons to "confidential treatment of all information in their personal and medical records" except as otherwise provided in RC 5123.89 and RC 5126.38.

Chapter 30

Physical Education, Athletics, and Recreation

30.01   Introduction

PHYSICAL EDUCATION

30.02   Curriculum requirements for physical education
30.03   Physical education and interscholastic athletics distinguished
30.04   Physical education facilities
30.05   Physical education teachers, coaches, and trainers

INTERSCHOLASTIC ATHLETICS

30.06   Interscholastic sports, introduction
30.07   Ohio High School Athletic Association (OHSAA)
30.08   Legal status of OHSAA
30.09   Recognized sports, equality of athletic opportunity
30.10   Funding interscholastic athletics
30.11   OHSAA rules, enforcement
30.12   Sports injuries, OHSAA insurance program

RECREATIONAL PROGRAMS

30.13   Recreational programs
30.14   Joint recreational facilities and districts
30.15   Joint recreation board

30.01   Introduction

A school district engages in athletics, sports, and related activities on three levels. First, physical education is a required part of the curriculum for all students.[1] Second, junior high and middle schools and senior high schools may maintain an interscholastic sports program. Such a program is an extracurricular activity but very often (particularly in senior high schools) is one of the most highly visible of a school's activities and engenders lively interest in the community.[2] Third, school boards may maintain community recreational programs throughout the year. Such programs and the supporting facilities may be maintained by a school district jointly with other political subdivisions.[3]

PHYSICAL EDUCATION

30.02   Curriculum requirements for physical education

Physical education is mandatory from kindergarten through high school. With some exceptions, the requirements are the same for both public and nonpublic schools.[4]

Scheduled classes, supervised activities, and approved educational options for kindergarten pupils must occupy the equivalent of a minimum of two and one-half hours per day and include at least 200 minutes per week in readiness activities for reading, writing, and mathematics. The balance of the scheduled time must be allocated among various other subjects, including physical education.[5] In grades one through six, scheduled classes, supervised activities, and optional educational activities must include a minimum of 200 minutes per week in art, music, and physical education.[6]

Pupils in grades seven and eight in public schools must be "scheduled for planned instruction the equivalent of at least eighty minutes per week in physical education."[7] Nonpublic schools are not required to schedule physical education instruction for seventh and eighth grade pupils.[8]

The minimum requirement for graduation from high school is eighteen units earned in grades nine through twelve, including one-half unit in physical education.[9] At least 120 hours of scheduled time is required to earn credit for one-half unit in physical education.[10] (In other subjects, 120 hours earns one full credit.)

Text 26.05, 26.06

---

[1] See Text 30.02 to 30.05.
[2] See Text 30.06 to 30.12.
[3] See Text 30.13 to 30.16.
[4] See generally OAC 3301-35-03, OAC 3301-35-04.
[5] OAC 3301-35-02(B)(10).
[6] OAC 3301-35-02(B)(11)(b).
[7] OAC 3301-35-02(B)(12)(b).
[8] OAC 3301-35-04(A).
[9] OAC 3301-35-02(B)(6)(d).
[10] OAC 3301-35-02(B)(8)(a)(ii).

30.03 Physical education and interscholastic athletics distinguished

Two main goals of physical education are to promote physical fitness and instill life-long habits of maintaining physical fitness. Interscholastic sports promotes these goals very well but only for the limited number who participate. Physical education, on the other hand, reaches all students. Consequently, department of education regulations make it plain that interscholastic athletics are *not* part of the curriculum at any level. The phrases "physical education" and "interscholastic athletics" are used in different contexts, and although physical education must be part of the planned instruction during the school day, interscholastic sports are expressly excluded from the school day.[11] Instead, interscholastic athletics are school-sponsored, noncredit, extracurricular activities.[12]

30.04 Physical education facilities

There is no requirement that any school construct and maintain special facilities for physical education. The lack of such facilities does not prevent physical education or preclude an interscholastic sports program. Older elementary schools, for example, may have no specialized indoor facilities at all and have outdoor facilities consisting only of a playground. Many high schools maintain swimming and diving teams using natatoriums maintained by a municipality, YMCA, or another school.

Although gymnasiums, playing fields, tracks, and related facilities are not required, they are a decided convenience that enhances physical education and interscholastic sports programs. Such facilities may be provided by a board of education under its general authority to build, equip, and maintain buildings and other facilities necessary to the district's educational programs.[13]

30.05 Physical education teachers, coaches, and trainers

Teachers, including physical education teachers, must be certificated.[14] Teachers may also coach or direct an interscholastic team, provided they meet certain minimum requirements in addition to certification.[15] Coaching is normally the subject of a supplemental contract.

In certain enumerated circumstances and after following the prescribed procedures,[16] noncertificated persons may be employed as coaches in interscholastic sports. Such persons must be of good moral character and meet the same requirements imposed on certificated teachers for coaching.[17] In general, the requirements for both certificated and noncertificated persons to coach are an ability to work with children, training or experience in the sport, knowledge of the rules, and knowledge of the health and safety aspects of the sport.[18]

Similarly, certificated and noncertificated persons may be employed as athletic trainers, provided they have experience as athletic trainers, possess an instructor's certificate in cardio-pulmonary resuscitation, and have completed certain college courses in the health sciences and related disciplines.[19]

INTERSCHOLASTIC ATHLETICS

30.06 Interscholastic sports, introduction

Interscholastic athletics are heavily regulated to coordinate competition, prevent abuses, and insure health and safety. The regulations are not, however, created pursuant to statute or by a state agency. Rather, they are promulgated by the Ohio High School Athletic Association, a private association composed of member schools.

---

[11] OAC 3301-35-02(B)(12), (13).
[12] OAC 3301-35-01(I).
[13] RC 3313.37. See Text 30.10(B), School board authority to fund costs of athletic programs.
[14] RC 3319.30; OAC 3301-35-03(A)(4). See Text 8.03, Qualifications and certification in general.
[15] OAC 3301-27-01(B).
[16] RC 3313.53.
[17] OAC 3301-27-01(A), (B).
[18] OAC 3301-27-01(B). See Text 9.14(C), Athletics.
[19] OAC 3301-27-02.

30.07 Ohio High School Athletic Association (OHSAA)

(A) Purposes

The stated purpose of OHSAA is "to regulate, supervise and administer interscholastic athletic competition among its member schools to the end that the interscholastic program be an integral factor in the total educational program of the schools."[20] The purpose has also been described as "to promote and maintain pure wholesome amateur athletics among its members."[21]

(B) Membership

Membership is voluntary and open to any chartered Ohio school[22] which contains a combination of grades seven through twelve. Membership is annual, beginning August 1 and ending the following July 31.[23] Dues may be levied by the board of control as considered necessary.[24] During the 1994-95 school year, there were 815 member high schools, plus 845 member schools in the 7th-8th igh grade division.[25]

Although members are individual junior high schools, middle schools, and senior high schools in Ohio, authority to become a member necessarily is conferred by the board of education of the district to which the school belongs, because the board is vested with plenary power to govern all schools in its district.[26] The corollary to the board's power to authorize a school to join OHSAA is the power to forbid a school to join. The OHSAA constitution makes a board resolution authorizing membership a prerequisite for initial or renewed membership of a school.[27]

Although not mandatory, membership in OHSAA is a practical necessity if a school wishes to have a viable interscholastic sports program, since competition with nonmember schools is forbidden absent OHSAA permission.[28] The great majority of middle schools and junior and senior high schools in Ohio are members, so that OHSAA could, by withholding permission, severely limit the opportunities of nonmember schools for interscholastic contests.

(C) Government and administration

Management of OHSAA is vested in a board of control, district boards, a commissioner, and any other person(s) designated by the board of control.[29] The board consists of one representative from each of six district boards, and one 7th-8th grade representative, a nonvoting ex-officio member representing the state department of education, and a nonvoting ex-officio member from the Ohio Interscholastic Athletic Administrators Association.[30] Members of the district boards and the board of control are elected by the members of the Association. All board members must be members of the teaching profession and employed by a member school, and elections are organized so that the current members of a district board and the board of control are evenly divided among representatives of large, medium, and small schools (designated as AAA, AA, and A schools). The districts are organized geographically.[31] Duties of the several district boards include assisting the board of control and the commissioner in promoting the association's purposes, organizing and conducting interscholastic athletic tournaments, and accepting any additional assigned duties.[32]

The commissioner, appointed by the board of control, is OHSAA's chief executive officer. His duties include promoting the purpose of the association; enforcing the association's bylaws and regulations; deciding questions and interpretations of the association's constitution, bylaws, and regulations; imposing and enforcing penalties; managing the association's administra-

---

[20]OHSAA Const 2-1-1.
[21]State ex rel Ohio High School Athletic Assn v Stark County Common Pleas Court Judges, 173 OS 239, 240, 181 NE(2d) 261 (1962).
[22]See RC 3301.16 for the definition of a chartered school.
[23]OHSAA Const 3-1-5.
[24]OHSAA Const 4-1-1.
[25]OHSAA 1995-1996 Handbook, p. 3.

[26]State ex rel OHSAA v Stark County Common Pleas Court Judges, 173 OS 239, 181 NE(2d) 261 (1962).
[27]OHSAA Const Art 3.
[28]OHSAA Bylaw 9-1-1.
[29]OHSAA Const 5-1-1.
[30]OHSAA Const 5-2-1.
[31]OHSAA Const Art 5, 7.
[32]OHSAA Const 7-7-1.

tive and financial affairs; and supervising association staff.[33]

(D) National federation affiliation

Since 1924, OHSAA has been a member of the National Federation of State High School Associations (NFSHSA), which is made up of the state school athletic associations in the fifty states and the District of Columbia, ten provincial associations from Canada plus the Canadian School Sports Federation, and associations from the Philippines, Okinawa, Guam, and St. Thomas.[34]

30.08 Legal status of OHSAA

(A) OHSAA as unincorporated association

OHSAA is an unincorporated, voluntary, not-for-profit association.[35] As such, it has the power to contract or to sue on behalf of members and to be sued as an entity.[36] Further, OHSAA property is subject to judgment and execution. A money judgment may be enforced only against OHSAA, however, and not against the property of any member.[37]

(B) OHSAA as quasi-governmental agency

OHSAA has no powers or duties conferred by statute and indeed is not mentioned in the revised code. Courts have nevertheless upheld OHSAA rules and its power to enforce them on numerous occasions.[38] This creates an anomaly—a private, unincorporated association which has neither statutory authority nor recognition, yet regulates a school activity as completely and effectively as could be done by the state board of education.

The anomaly can be explained by conceiving of OHSAA as the alter ego of the schools with respect to interscholastic athletics. As such, it operates as an agent of the government. Insofar as its rules affect the activities of governmental entities—the schools—OHSAA has been held to act in a governmental capacity. In *Yellow Springs Exempted Village School Dist Bd of Ed v Ohio High School Athletic Assn*,[39] a challenge was made to an OHSAA rule which prohibited girls from participating on a boys' team in any contact sport, claiming sex discrimination in violation of a federal regulation dealing with equal athletic opportunity.[40] OHSAA asserted that since the regulation affected only the actions of agencies receiving federal aid, it was inapplicable. The court rejected this argument, holding that OHSAA acts as a public school agency to the extent it regulates a school activity.

For purposes of RC Chapter 2744, however, OHSAA is not a political subdivision.[41]

30.09 Recognized sports, equality of athletic opportunity

(A) Individual and team sports recognized by OHSAA

Only certain sports are "recognized," i.e., adopted, by the OHSAA board of control.[42] These are

(1) baseball (boys),

(2) basketball (boys and girls),

(3) cross country (boys and girls),

(4) field hockey (girls),

(5) football (boys),

(6) golf (boys and girls),

(7) gymnastics (boys and girls),

(8) ice hockey (boys),

(9) soccer (boys and girls),

(10) softball—fast pitch (girls),

(11) swimming and diving (boys and girls),

(12) tennis (boys and girls),

---

[33]OHSAA Const Art 6.

[34]OHSAA 1995-1996 Handbook, p. 22-23.

[35]State ex rel OHSAA v Stark County Common Pleas Court Judges, 173 OS 239, 181 NE(2d) 261 (1962); OHSAA 1995-1996 Handbook, p. 3.

[36]RC 1745.01.

[37]RC 1745.02.

[38]See Text 30.11, OHSAA rules, enforcement.

[39]Yellow Springs Exempted Village School Dist Bd of Ed v OHSAA, 647 F(2d) 651 (6th Cir Ohio 1981).

[40]Former 45 CFR 86.41, now 34 CFR 106.41.

[41]Wissel v OHSAA, 78 App(3d) 529, 605 NE(2d) 458 (Hamilton 1992). For extended treatment of RC Ch 2744, see Text Ch 46, Liability of Schools, Officers, and Employees.

[42]OHSAA Bylaw 1-5-1.

(13) track and field (boys and girls),

(14) volleyball (girls), and

(15) wrestling (boys).[43]

Many team and individual sports seen in college or Olympic competition are missing from the list. Schools generally can support only a limited number of team and individual sports, and since the more esoteric sports generate less interest, the mainstream sports tend to be favored.

The list also reflects the fact that opportunities for students to participate in interscholastic athletics must be spread over the school year and balanced between boys and girls. Although the list can and does change, sports tend to be added only when it appears they have won sufficient popularity to support a viable interscholastic program. Soccer, for example, was not recognized until the 1970s.

(B) Boys' and girls' sports, participation by both sexes

The foregoing list shows that under OHSAA rules some sports are available to boys only, some to girls only, and some to both boys and girls. OHSAA rules provide that girls may play on a boys' team if there is no girls' team, or if the overall opportunities for interscholastic competition by girls is limited.[44] Lack of overall opportunity also allows boys to play on girls' teams, with the additional proviso that the competing schools must agree.[45] Competition between teams of the opposite sex is flatly prohibited.[46]

A former OHSAA rule prohibiting participation by girls on a boys' team in a contact sport was challenged under a federal regulation designed to provide equality of athletic opportunity for boys and girls.[47] It was held that the OHSAA rule conflicted with the regulation, which the court construed to permit exclusion of girls from boys' teams only if other means are available to provide equal athletic opportunity.[48] Equality of athletic opportunity does not require that separate boys' and girls' teams be maintained in every sport sponsored by a school but does require balance in the availability of suitable sports for boys and girls. The mix of sports recognized by OHSAA for boys only, girls only, and both boys and girls is partly designed to provide this balance.

A school can lose its federal funding if found guilty of sex discrimination under Title IX of the Education Amendments of 1972.[49] Even though a school's athletic programs might not receive federal assistance directly, they are considered to be covered by Title IX under the theory that the students receive some benefit from the federal government from any aid to the school.[50]

The equal protection clause of the Fourteenth Amendment prohibits sex discrimination, unless such discrimination is substantially related to achievement of an important governmental objective. Under this standard a school athletic association rule in another state, providing for basketball teams segregated by sex, was held not to violate the clause.[51]

(C) Recognition of sport by individual school

Schools are not required to participate in all (or even any) sports recognized by OHSAA. Money, or the lack of it, availability of qualified coaching personnel and facilities, size and makeup of the student body, student interest, community support—to name some of the more important factors—combine to dictate the structure and extent of a school's interscholastic sports program. Few, if any, schools sponsor teams in all recognized sports.

(D) Nonrecognized sports

The fact that a sport is not recognized by OHSAA does not prevent a school from participating in it as a club sport.[52] If a member school participates in a nonrecognized sport, it is nevertheless subject to OHSAA bylaws and regulations.[53]

---

[43]OHSAA Bylaw 1-5-1.
[44]OHSAA Bylaw 1-7-1.
[45]OHSAA Bylaw 1-7-4.
[46]OHSAA Bylaw 1-8-1.
[47]Former 45 CFR 86.41, now 34 CFR 106.41.
[48]Yellow Springs Exempted Village School Dist Bd of Ed v OHSAA, 647 F(2d) 651 (6th Cir Ohio 1981).

[49]See Text 19.14, Sex discrimination in education.
[50]Haffer v Temple University, 688 F(2d) 14 (3d Cir Pa 1982). See also Grove City College v Bell, 465 US 555, 104 SCt 1211, 79 LEd(2d) 516 (1984).
[51]Cape v Tennessee Secondary School Athletic Assn, 563 F(2d) 793 (6th Cir Tenn 1977).
[52]See Text 30.10(D), Club sports.
[53]OHSAA Bylaw 1-6-1.

30.10 Funding interscholastic athletics

Adequate funding is critical to school participation in a sport and is a key factor in determining school sponsorship. A board of education is authorized to fund sports facilities and the cost of coaching. A board may also fund an interscholastic athletics program, subject to a statutory limitation on the amount. Additional sources of funding are also available.

(A) OHSAA policy on financing athletics

OHSAA policy states, "The [interscholastic athletics] program should be financed by budgeted organizational and school funds rather than solely by admission charges."[54] Practices, games, previews, and other interscholastic contests in recognized sports are declared to be the financial responsibility of the participating schools.[55] Moreover, the entire salary of the coach must be paid by the board of education or the corresponding body for private schools.[56]

(B) School board authority to fund costs of athletic programs

School boards are authorized to acquire land and to build, equip, and maintain the facilities necessary to carry out the educational programs in the district, and funds for the purpose may be the subject of a tax levy.[57] Since physical education is part of the required curriculum in both public and private schools,[58] a board necessarily may fund the construction, equipment, and maintenance of gymnasiums, exercise rooms, locker rooms, playing fields, and related facilities. These same facilities, of course, can serve interscholastic athletics as well as curricular programs.

A board is also empowered to pay the expenses of directing, supervising, or coaching athletics.[59] Money derived from a tax levy for current expenses may be used for this purpose.[60]

Interscholastic athletics are classified as a "pupil activity program" because they receive school supervision and support but are noncredit activities not in the curriculum.[61] Consequently, the direct expenses of interscholastic sports must be funded under RC 3315.062, which limits the amount which may be paid out of the general fund for student activity programs. The amount appropriated from the general fund for uniforms, supplies, game officials, security, and related expenses of interscholastic competition cannot exceed 0.5% of the operating budget.[62] Since other student activity programs also have claims for funding within this limitation, the amount available for interscholastic sports may be even less. The amount spent under RC 3313.53 for coaching is not counted in calculating the 0.5% limit[63] and presumably money spent for athletic facilities under RC 3313.37 should not be counted either.

(C) Other sources of funding, pupil activity fund

Money available from the general fund for an interscholastic sports program may be augmented from various sources. Admission to athletic events may be charged, and students may be assessed a reasonable fee to participate in an extracurricular athletics program.[64]

If more than $50 per year "is received through a student activity program," the money must be deposited in an activity fund established by the school board.[65] The board must also adopt rules governing administration of the fund, including a system of accounting for receipts and expenditures. Disbursements are subject to board approval[66] and may be made for a variety of purposes in support of student activity programs,[67] including supplemental salaries and transportation costs incurred in operating an interscholastic athletics program.[68]

---

[54] OHSAA 1995-1996 Handbook, p. 18.
[55] OHSAA Bylaw 1-2-1.
[56] OHSAA Bylaw 6-2-1.
[57] RC 3313.37.
[58] OAC 3301-35-02, OAC 3301-35-04.
[59] RC 3313.53.
[60] OAG 84-083.
[61] OAC 3301-35-01(I).
[62] OAG 84-083.

[63] OAG 80-060.
[64] OAG 84-083; OAG 82-014; 1939 OAG 356.
[65] See State ex rel Plain Dealer Publishing Co v Lesak, 9 OS(3d) 1, 9 OBR 52, 457 NE(2d) 821 (1984).
[66] RC 3315.062.
[67] OAG 86-013 (student activity funds are public funds which board can expend, in its discretion, for any reasonable, valid, and proper public purposes).
[68] OAG 82-014. See Text 23.10 to 23.12.

Fund-raising activities by students and others to support an extracurricular activity are common. It is unclear if the proceeds are "received through a student activity program" and therefore must be deposited in the student activity fund under RC 3315.062. As a matter of school policy, however, it is advisable to require that the proceeds of student activity fund-raisers be administered through the activity fund. Such a policy is within the school board's general authority to govern the schools.[69]

(D) Club sports

The fact that a sport is not recognized by OHSAA, or that a school provides limited financial support for a recognized sport, does not necessarily prevent school participation in the sport. If there is sufficient interest, if a qualified coach can be found, and if the school authorities allow it, a sports club can be formed to field a team. A student club is a pupil activity program[70] and therefore eligible for at least limited support from the school activity fund.

As an example, lacrosse is not recognized by OHSAA, but a number of schools maintain teams through lacrosse clubs which have school sponsorship but derive their support mainly from donations, activity fees, fund-raisers, and services contributed by parents or teachers. Member schools that sponsor nonrecognized sports must still comply with the OHSAA bylaws and regulations.[71]

(E) Rulings on use of sports funds

School officials should be aware of various rulings and attorney general opinions that govern school athletic activities and expenditures. For example, the attorney general has ruled that money raised from athletic event ticket sales and contributed to student activity funds may not be used to purchase accident insurance for high school athletics.[72] The attorney general also has issued an opinion authorizing school boards to sell football equipment back to their student athletes for $1.[73] A board may not assume payments for equipment donated by a booster club that was unable to pay for the equipment but can pay for the equipment out of the athletic account of the student activities fund.[74] Normally, boards can accept funds earmarked for athletic purposes through the adoption of a resolution.[75]

30.11 OHSAA rules, enforcement

(A) Scope of rules

The impact of OHSAA on interscholastic scholastic sports comes chiefly through promulgation and enforcement of rules governing interscholastic competition. General and specific rules are provided in OHSAA bylaws and sports regulations, which are compiled in a handbook published annually by the association.[76]

The bylaws and sports regulations provide, among other matters, for the following: classifying schools by size; age and grade limitations on students for participation in school sports; student enrollment and residence requirements for eligibility; transfer of students and eligibility; defining amateur status; qualifications of coaches; leagues; competition, including out-of-state competition; tournaments; contracts for games; requirements for good sportsmanship; conduct, character, and discipline of students; sport seasons and calendars; limitations on pre-season and out-of-season practice and competition, out-of-season coaching, and student participation on independent teams; game rules; and qualifications, training, and conduct of game officials.

In a sense, OHSAA regulates all sports, not merely "recognized" sports,[77] since it requires member schools that sponsor a nonrecognized sport to adhere to OHSAA bylaws and regulations.[78] Thus, for example, if a school sponsors a girls' fencing team (a nonrecognized sport), and the

---

[69]RC 3313.20, RC 3313.47.
[70]OAC 3301-35-01(I).
[71]OHSAA Bylaw 1-6-1.
[72]OAG 76-008. See Text 30.12, Sports injuries, OHSAA insurance program.
[73]OAG 86-062.
[74]1932 OAG 4622.
[75]1962 OAG 3246.

[76]Persons interested in obtaining a copy should write or call Ohio High School Athletic Association, 4080 Roselea Place, Columbus, Ohio 43214; (614) 267-2502.

[77]See Text 30.09, Recognized sports, equality of athletic opportunity.

[78]OHSAA Bylaw 1-6-1.

team has a male coach, the school must obey the OHSAA rule requiring an adult female to accompany the team at all contests.[79] Similarly, OHSAA regulations may affect nonmember schools and independent teams. If OHSAA grants permission for a member school to compete with a nonmember school or an independent team, the member school must observe all Ohio eligibility and contest rules in the contest.[80]

(B) Penalties for violation, imposition, administrative appeal

The sanctions that may be imposed for violation of the OHSAA constitution, bylaws, and sports regulations include suspension, forfeiture of games or championship rights, probation, public censure, denial of participation, fines not to exceed $1,000 per occurrence, "or such other penalties as the Commissioner may deem appropriate."[81] Penalties are imposed by the commissioner.[82] Penalties for certain infractions are specified, e.g., all regular season games in which an ineligible player has participated must be forfeited.[83] Sometimes further penalties may be imposed in addition to game forfeiture for eligibility violations at the discretion of the commissioner.[84]

The commissioner's decision may be appealed to the board of control[85] under a rather elaborate procedure.[86]

(C) Enforceability of rules and penalties

The courts on many occasions have upheld OHSAA rules and the power to enforce them. A bylaw or regulation, or a particular application of it, will be upheld if it is not illegal or arbitrary, does not violate the association's own constitution or rules, and involves no mistake, fraud, or collusion.

The leading case involved a recruiting violation—specifically, the use of influence (apparently by the boosters' club) to obtain two football players from another school by inducing their family to move into the recruiting school's district. After investigation and hearing, OHSAA declared the students ineligible and suspended the offending school from football for an entire season. An attempt to prevent enforcement was thwarted by the Ohio Supreme Court, which affirmed the board of education's power to authorize schools under its jurisdiction to join OHSAA, and held that in the absence of mistake, fraud, collusion, or arbitrariness the courts will accept association decisions respecting its internal affairs. The Court acknowledged the penalty was "indeed harsh and most severe" but ruled it was not arbitrary, since all who wished to be heard were given the opportunity before the suspension was confirmed.[87]

The OHSAA rule that prohibited students who turn nineteen before September 1 (now August 1)[88] from participating in interscholastic sports was upheld because it is designed to avoid inherent risks when students as young as fourteen compete against more experienced and mature players.[89] The rule making students whose parents live out of state ineligible to play for Ohio schools has been sustained,[90] as has a soccer rule limiting out-of-season play or play for independent teams,[91] and a rule restricting a school swimmer from indepen-

---

[79]OHSAA Bylaw 3-2-2.
[80]OHSAA Bylaw 9-1-2.
[81]OHSAA Bylaw 12-1-2.
[82]OHSAA Bylaw 12-1-1.
[83]OHSAA Bylaw 11-2-1.
[84]OHSAA Bylaw 11-3-1.
[85]OHSAA Const Art 5-7-1.
[86]OHSAA 1995-1996 Handbook, p. 20-21.
[87]State ex rel OHSAA v Stark County Common Pleas Court Judges, 173 OS 239, 248, 181 NE(2d) 261 (1962). In Bowles v OHSAA, No. 92 CA 94, 1992 WL 384401 (7th Dist Ct App, Mahoning, 12-21-92), however, OHSAA's application of its recruiting rules was enjoined as to three students found to have been recruited illegally on the ground that OHSAA acted arbitrarily.

[88]OHSAA Bylaw 4-2-1, which now denies eligibility to students who turn nineteen before August 1.
[89]Woods v OHSAA, No. 80 CA 30, 1981 WL 6063 (4th Dist Ct App, Pickaway, 11-9-81).
[90]Menke v OHSAA, 2 App(3d) 244, 2 OBR 266, 441 NE(2d) 620 (Hamilton 1981). See also Alerding v OHSAA, 779 F(2d) 315 (6th Cir Ohio 1985). OHSAA Bylaw 4-6-9 sets forth this rule and several exceptions to its application.
[91]Anderson v OHSAA, 754 F(2d) 372 (6th Cir Ohio 1984); Pecoraro v OHSAA, No. C-800865, 1981 WL 10126 (1st Dist Ct App, Hamilton, 11-25-81). See also Burrows v OHSAA, 891 F(2d) 122 (6th Cir Ohio 1989) (upholding constitutionality of OHSAA bylaw pertaining to administration of the soccer regulation).

dent competition.[92] The rule forbidding recruiting of student athletes has been upheld as rationally related to the legitimate goal of maintaining the wholesomeness of high school athletics.[93]

A rule prohibiting girls from participating on boys' teams was declared in conflict with a federal regulation requiring equality of athletic opportunity between the sexes.[94]

30.12 Sports injuries, OHSAA insurance program

The risk of injury is an unpleasant constant in athletics. School districts and their employees and agents can be sued for negligence resulting in athletic injuries. Doctors and nurses who volunteer services to a school athletic program are immune from liability under most circumstances,[95] and school board members and administrators have a qualified good faith immunity.[96]

As a service to its members, OHSAA purchases catastrophic accident insurance covering students injured in connection with interscholastic athletics. The policy pays medical benefits exceeding a deductible amount, plus excess medical, rehabilitation, and other benefit payments in the event of catastrophic injury.[97] The coverage is subject to various exclusions and provisos, and school authorities should examine it carefully to determine if the purchase of additional coverage is indicated. Also, the policy terms may change from year to year.

RECREATIONAL PROGRAMS

30.13 Recreational programs

Boards of education of city, exempted village, or local school districts may provide activities for children which will promote their health or recreation or other stated needs during summer vacation and may employ personnel and purchase equipment necessary for such activities.[98]

A board may, upon nomination of the superintendent, employ persons to supervise, organize, direct, and conduct social and recreational work in the district, whether during the school year or vacation periods.[99] A board may propose a levy for recreational purposes to the electors of the district.[100]

30.14 Joint recreational facilities and districts

Municipalities, townships, counties, and school districts are permitted to form joint recreation districts, with taxing and bond issuing power.[101]

Any school district may join with any other school district, or municipal corporation, county, township or township park district, and a joint recreation district, in equipping, operating, and maintaining recreational facilities, and may appropriate money for such purposes. A school district, municipal corporation, township, township park district, or county, jointly with any one or more other school districts, municipal corporations, townships, township park districts, or counties, in any combination, and joint recreation districts, may acquire property and operate and maintain parks, playgrounds, playfields, gymnasiums, public baths, swimming pools, or indoor recreation centers. A school district may include joint facilities in building or enlarging any school building or school premises. The parties to the joint venture may contribute

---

[92]Kaufman v OHSAA, No. 81AP-51, 1981 WL 3011 (10th Dist Ct App, Franklin, 2-19-81). See also Palmisano v Willoughby-Eastlake Bd of Ed, No. 8-177, 1981 WL 3792 (11th Dist Ct App, Lake, 1981) (no constitutional right to participate in sports; unfairness must be remedied through OHSAA procedural changes).

[93]Massillon City School Dist Bd of Ed v OHSAA, No. CA 7247, 1987 WL 19827 (5th Dist Ct App, Stark, 11-5-87).

[94]See Text 30.09(B), Boys' and girls' sports, participation by both sexes.

[95]See Text 21.09, Volunteer medical services at athletic events, nonliability.

[96]Kropf v Vermilion Bd of Ed, No. E-85-48, 1986 WL 8652 (6th Dist Ct App, Erie, 8-8-86).

[97]OHSAA 1995-1996 Handbook, p. 16-17.

[98]RC 3313.57.

[99]RC 3313.58.

[100]RC 5705.21.

[101]RC 133.01, RC 755.14 to RC 755.181, RC 5705.01, RC 5705.19, RC 5705.194.

lands, money, other personal property, or services, as may be agreed.[102]

30.15 Joint recreation board

The legislative authorities of municipal corporations, boards of township trustees, boards of township park commissioners, boards of county commissioners, and boards of education that have joined in creating joint recreational facilities may establish a joint recreation board.[103]

---

[102]RC 755.16.

[103]RC 755.14.

Chapter 31

Schools, Parents, and Community Affairs

PUBLIC PARTICIPATION IN SCHOOL AFFAIRS
31.01 Public meetings
31.02 Annual report of school progress
31.03 Parent-educator relations
31.04 Public use of school facilities

SCHOOL PARTICIPATION IN COMMUNITY AFFAIRS
31.05 Contracts and cooperation with public institutions
31.06 Providing meals for the elderly
31.07 Field trips
31.08 Soliciting funds for charities
31.09 Registering persons to vote

PUBLIC PARTICIPATION IN SCHOOL AFFAIRS

31.01 Public meetings

Ohio law generally requires that meetings of public bodies, including boards of education, be open to the public. A public body must establish a reasonable method whereby any person can determine the time and place of a regularly scheduled meeting and in the case of a special meeting must give twenty-four hours' notice to any news media that have requested advance notice.[1]

The minutes of a regular or special meeting of a public body shall be promptly recorded and open to inspection as public documents.[2] However, minutes of a particular meeting do not exist as minutes until approved and entered in the permanent record of the board at the next meeting.[3]

31.02 Annual report of school progress

A board of education is required to issue an annual progress report for each school under its control and for the district, based on guidelines established by the state board of education. The report must contain a ten-year projection of enrollment, by year and by grade level; the names, addresses, and home telephone numbers of the members of the state board of education, the Ohio House of Representatives, and the Ohio Senate elected from districts within which the school district has territory; and information about achievements, problems, plans, and improvements in the district.[4]

In addition, on or before each August 1, school statistics are to be reported by each board of a city and exempted village district (to the state board) and local district (to the county superintendent) on forms furnished by the state board. The reports must include information on civil proceedings in which a board is either a defendant or a party and in which another party is a board of education or an officer, board, or official of the state. The report must include the nature of the proceeding, the capacity in which the board is a party, the total expenses incurred by the board, and those incurred during the reporting period.[5] Boards of city and exempted village school districts may also publish an annual report of the condition and administration of district schools. This report must include an exhibit on the district's financial affairs and the above information on pending litigation.[6]

The board of any district may compile, make available, or publish any of the following: student handbooks, dress codes, curriculum guides, school policy bulletins, newsletters, board meeting summaries or minutes, financial reports, annual reports, and other reports concerning operation of the district's schools.[7]

31.03 Parent-educator relations

A school may dismiss classes one-half day early up to four school days per year (two school days each trimester, one school day each quarter, or one school day each pentamester), or use the equivalent amount of time on a different number of

---

[1] RC 121.22(F). See generally Text 5.12, Open meetings: the sunshine law.
[2] RC 121.22(C).
[3] 1962 Inf OAG 489.

[4] RC 3313.94. See also OAC 3301-11-01 et seq.
[5] RC 3319.33.
[6] RC 3319.33.
[7] RC 3315.07.

days, for individualized parent-teacher conferences and reporting periods.[8] Dismissal for the number of hours in which parent-teacher conferences are held outside of regular school hours is allowed whether or not the dismissal occurs on the same day on which the conferences are held.[9]

RC 3313.472 requires the board of education of each city, exempted village, local, and joint vocational school district to adopt a policy on parental involvement designed to build consistent and effective communication between parents of students and the district's teachers and administrators.[10]

When, in the context of divorce, marriage dissolution, separation, or annulment proceedings, a court allocates parental rights and responsibilities for the care of a child, the parent who is not the residential parent is entitled to the same access as the residential parent to "any student activity" unless the court determines otherwise, in which case the court must specify the terms and conditions under which the parent is to have access to student activities.[11] School officials and employees who knowingly fail to allow such access may be found in contempt of court.[12]

31.04 Public use of school facilities

Ohio law allows use of school facilities by community groups for various purposes and for adult education.[13]

SCHOOL PARTICIPATION IN COMMUNITY AFFAIRS

31.05 Contracts and cooperation with public institutions

Boards of education are authorized to contract with each other or with colleges or universities for special, technical, professional, or other advanced studies beyond the scope of the high school. Similarly, boards may contract with each other or a private nonprofit association or corporation providing a museum of art, science, history, or musical instruction. Such contracts may not exceed one year.[14] Boards may not contract with a private nonprofit association for the instruction of high school dropouts who desire instruction designed to lead to a high school diploma.[15]

Boards of education are likewise authorized to cooperate with boards of county commissioners and other public officials who operate parks, libraries, museums, and other public facilities providing educational, social, civic, and recreational activities. Boards may contribute funds, equipment, or personnel to both public and private nonprofit corporations maintaining museums available to the district's pupils.[16]

County and city boards of education may make payments to symphony associations, area arts councils, or similar nonprofit organizations. The annual payments, in quarterly installments, may not exceed one-half cent on each $100 of taxable property of the district. A recipient must adopt a resolution accepting all applicable provisions of RC 757.03 to RC 757.08 and file a certified copy with the board in order to qualify for payment. The resolution must include the right to nominate to the trustees of the governing body three members, consisting of a member of the board of education, superintendent or assistant superintendent, and member of the music department of the public schools; the right to nominate one of the three foregoing trustees to the executive committee; and the right to require feasible performances in the public schools.[17]

31.06 Providing meals for the elderly

A board of education that operates a food service program may provide meals at cost to district residents who are age sixty or older or may contract with public or private organizations providing services to the elderly to provide meals for such persons. Records of receipts and expenditures must

---

[8] RC 3313.48, RC 3313.481.
[9] OAG 85-015.
[10] For extended treatment of RC 3313.472, see Text 5.09(O), Policy on parental involvement.
[11] RC 3109.051(J).
[12] RC 3109.051(J).

[13] RC 3313.641. See Text 38.08 to 38.12.
[14] RC 3315.09.
[15] OAG 81-002.
[16] RC 3313.59.
[17] RC 757.03, RC 757.04.

be separately maintained, in accordance with RC 3313.29.[18]

31.07 Field trips

To enrich instruction, districts may arrange field trips to community industries and institutions. Transportation may be financed out of public funds when the trip falls within the educational purposes of the curriculum.

The state department of natural resources is authorized to acquire a system of nature preserves for, among other purposes, the teaching of biology, natural history, ecology, geology, conservation, and other subjects.[19]

31.08 Soliciting funds for charities

A board of education may permit or prohibit soliciting funds within the schools for charitable purposes provided it does so on a uniform, nondiscriminatory basis.[20] A district may establish a payroll deduction plan for nonprofit charities, with deductions to be voluntarily authorized by employees in writing.[21]

31.09 Registering persons to vote

Each public high school and vocational school is to have one person selected by the board of education to serve as coordinator for voter registration within the school. The coordinator cannot receive additional compensation for such duties. The board is required to establish a schedule of school days and hours during such days when the coordinator shall provide registration assistance.[22]

---

[18]RC 3313.81. See Text 43.28, Duties of district treasurer.
[19]RC 1517.05.
[20]RC 3313.20.
[21]RC 9.80, RC 9.81.
[22]RC 3503.10. The statute also addresses certain training and other requirements that occur under the auspices of the secretary of state. It expressly does not limit the authority of a board of education, superintendent, or principal to allow, sponsor, or promote voluntary election registration programs within a high school or vocational school, provided no pupil is required to participate.

Chapter 32

Religion and the Public Schools

Note: This chapter focuses on constitutional issues relevant to schools. For treatment of religious discrimination in employment under federal and state equal employment opportunity laws, see Text Ch 17, Equal Employment Opportunity, Family and Medical Leave.

32.01 Introduction, tests under First Amendment religion clauses
32.02 Free exercise of religion and compulsory state educational standards
32.03 Free exercise limits on compelled patriotic observances
32.04 Establishment restrictions on released time for religious instruction
32.05 Establishment through prayer and similar activity
32.06 Establishment problems from the use of public schools for religious purposes
32.07 Curriculum decisions

32.01 Introduction, tests under First Amendment religion clauses

The First Amendment to the US Constitution forbids the establishment of religion by public bodies (including school districts) on the one hand, and protects the free exercise of personal religious convictions on the other. An inherent tension exists between the "establishment" and "free exercise" clauses, and courts have struggled mightily and often to reconcile their sometimes conflicting commands.

The establishment clause prohibits state actions that foster or support religious beliefs. It is not, however, a precise provision capable of ready application. Thus, each case calls for an individualized inquiry.[1]

A law or policy challenged under the establishment clause must pass a three-point test. First, it must have a secular purpose. Second, its primary effect must neither advance nor inhibit religion. Third, it must not excessively entangle government in religion.[2]

Unconstitutionally excessive entanglement and advancement of religion occur most frequently in the area of state aid to parochial schools.[3] Other cases do arise, however. For example, a Missouri school district's rule prohibiting dances on school premises has passed the constitutional test.[4] Where a school district leased classroom space from a facility owned by the Catholic church, the lease required that the space be used consistent with Catholic teachings, and children were regularly exposed to crosses and religious statues, a constitutional violation was found.[5] A school district's use of mobile classrooms parked outside parochial schools in providing remedial services to students, however, was found not to promote religion or create impermissible symbolic union between church and state.[6] In a case arising under the Individuals with Disabilities Education Act,[7] the provision of a sign language interpreter to a profoundly deaf child whose parents voluntarily enrolled him in a paro-

---

[1] See, e.g., Grand Rapids School Dist v Ball, 473 US 373, 105 SCt 3216, 87 LEd(2d) 267 (1985) ("Establishment Clause jurisprudence is characterized by few absolutes."); Illinois ex rel McCollum v Champaign County School Dist No. 71 Bd of Ed, 333 US 203, 226, 68 SCt 461, 92 LEd 649 (1948) (stressing "the importance of detailed analysis of the facts to which the constitutional test of separation is to be applied").

[2] Lemon v Kurtzman, 403 US 602, 91 SCt 2105, 29 LEd(2d) 745 (1971). See also Grand Rapids School Dist v Ball, 473 US 373, 105 SCt 3216, 87 LEd(2d) 267 (1985). The *Lemon* test badly splinters the current US Supreme Court, and its continued viability is open to some question. It remains, however, the current standard. See Kiryas Joel Village School Dist v Grumet, ___ US ___, 114 SCt 2481, 129 LEd(2d) 546 (1994).

[3] For extended treatment of this subject, see Text 48.06 to 48.08.

[4] Clayton v Place, 884 F(2d) 376 (8th Cir Mo 1989), cert denied 494 US 1081, 110 SCt 1811, 108 LEd(2d) 942 (1990).

[5] Spacco v Bridgewater School Dept, 722 FSupp 834 (D Mass 1989).

[6] Walker v San Francisco Unified School Dist, 46 F(3d) 1449 (9th Cir Cal 1995).

[7] IDEA is given expansive treatment in Text Ch 28, Education for Children with Disabilities.

chial school did not run afoul of the establishment clause.[8] The establishment of a separate school district for a distinctive religious enclave populated only by practitioners of a strict form of Judaism known as the Satmar Hasidic sect does violate the establishment clause.[9]

Under the free exercise clause, governmental regulation of religious beliefs, as such, is flatly prohibited. The problem becomes more ticklish where the exercise of religion involves not only the belief but the performance of (or abstention from) some act. In *Employment Div, Dept of Human Resources of Oregon v Smith*,[10] the US Supreme Court held that the free exercise clause does not relieve one from complying with laws of general applicability not aimed at religion and whose effect on the exercise of religious beliefs is only incidental. Thus, *Smith* concluded that a state may, as part of a general prohibition on using hallucinogenic drugs, prohibit the sacramental use of peyote in ceremonies of the Native American Church.[11]

Believing that *Smith* had significantly weakened the constitutional protection afforded the free exercise of religion, Congress enacted the Religious Freedom Restoration Act of 1993 (RFRA).[12] It provides that government—which is defined to include not only federal agencies and officials but also the states and the political subdivisions of each state (such as Ohio school districts)—may not "substantially burden a person's exercise of religion, even if the burden results from a rule of general applicability" unless the burden demonstrably (1) "is in the furtherance of a compelling governmental interest," and (2) "is the least restrictive means of furthering that compelling governmental interest."[13] The RFRA generally applies to all federal and state laws, including the implementation of such laws through administrative regulations.[14] A prevailing plaintiff under the RFRA may recover attorney fees under 42 USCA 1988.[15]

Just what constitutes a religious belief or practice can be a delicate question. In *Wisconsin v Yoder*,[16] the Court seemed to suggest that protection of the religion clauses depended, at least in part, on membership in an organized, established denomination or sect. Elsewhere, however, the Court has found that a sincere belief rooted in religion suffices even if it is not based on a tenet or teaching of an organized religious body.[17]

Scheduling high school graduation exercises on Saturday does not violate the free exercise rights of a student sabbatarian so long as attendance is not required for receipt of a diploma.[18] Refusing, in compliance with state statutes, to permit a teacher to teach in religious attire has also withstood scrutiny under the free exercise clause.[19]

---

[8] Zobrest v Catalina Foothills School Dist, ___ US ___, 113 SCt 2462, 125 LEd(2d) 1 (1993).

[9] Kiryas Joel Village School Dist v Grumet, ___ US ___, 114 SCt 2481, 129 LEd(2d) 546 (1994).

[10] Employment Div, Dept of Human Resources of Oregon v Smith, 494 US 872, 110 SCt 1595, 108 LEd(2d) 876 (1990).

[11] *Smith* was widely viewed as an abandonment of the "compelling governmental interest test" previously articulated by the Court in Sherbert v Verner, 374 US 398, 83 SCt 1790, 10 LEd(2d) 965 (1963) and its progeny. In *Sherbert*, a facially neutral South Carolina law requiring all persons seeking unemployment compensation benefits to be available to work every day of the week except Sunday was viewed as unconstitutionally placing undue pressure on a Seventh-day Adventist sabbatarian to abandon the precepts of her religion.

[12] 42 USCA 2000bb et seq.

[13] 42 USCA 2000bb-1. Students relying on the Religious Freedom Restoration Act unsuccessfully challenged a nondiscrimination school policy which conditioned formation of a Christian club upon allowing non-Christians as officers. Hsu v Roslyn Union Free School Dist No. 3, 876 FSupp 445 (D NY 1995).

[14] 42 USCA 2000bb-3.

[15] For extended discussion of 42 USCA 1988, see Text 17.02(B)(2), Punitive damages, attorney fees.

[16] Wisconsin v Yoder, 406 US 205, 92 SCt 1526, 32 LEd(2d) 15 (1972).

[17] Frazee v Illinois Dept of Employment Security, 489 US 829, 109 SCt 1514, 103 LEd(2d) 914 (1989). See also Welsh v United States, 398 US 333, 90 SCt 1792, 26 LEd(2d) 308 (1970).

[18] Smith v North Babylon Union Free School Dist Bd of Ed, 844 F(2d) 90 (2d Cir NY 1988).

[19] Cooper v Eugene School Dist No. 4J, 301 Or 358, 723 P(2d) 298 (1986), appeal dismissed by 480 US 942, 107 SCt 1597, 94 LEd(2d) 784 (1987) (upholding Oregon statutes prohibiting public school teachers from wearing religious dress while teaching). See also United States v Board of Education for School District of Philadelphia, 911 F(2d) 882 (3d Cir Pa 1990) (rejecting challenge under Title VII of the Civil Rights Act of 1964 to Pennsylvania statute prohibiting public

In a case decided on free speech and equal protection grounds, a school policy prohibiting distribution of Gideon Bibles on a public sidewalk in front of a high school was found unconstitutional.[20] By comparison, a school district's policy allowing Bibles to be distributed to students outside school buildings after school hours did not violate the establishment clause of the First Amendment.[21]

32.02 Free exercise of religion and compulsory state educational standards

While the state's power to compel school attendance outweighs the parents' natural rights to custody and control of their child,[22] that power "is not totally free from a balancing process when it impinges on fundamental rights and interests."[23] Accordingly, where certain Amish parents proved that mandatory education of their children beyond the eighth grade would endanger, if not destroy, the free exercise of their religious beliefs, the US Supreme Court held the state could not compel attendance in public school.[24] Courts must balance the state interest in an educated citizenry against the interest of parents in the religious upbringing of their children.

The Ohio Supreme Court, in 1976, similarly balanced free exercise rights favorably against the burden imposed on parochial schools by then existing minimum state standards issued by the state board of education.[25] The standards were so comprehensive in scope and effect that any distinction between public and nonpublic education was effectively eradicated. In light of the Court's objections, the standards were subsequently revised.[26]

On the other hand, given the state's "compelling" interest in making certain that its children receive an adequate secular education, less intrusive and comprehensive procedures for approving the private education being provided have generally survived constitutional challenge.[27]

32.03 Free exercise limits on compelled patriotic observances

Students cannot be forced to salute or pledge allegiance to the flag in violation of their religious beliefs.[28] However, the state's interest in teaching its curriculum may override the freedom of a teacher with similar beliefs. A teacher thus may be discharged for refusing to teach patriotic observances to kindergarten students where he knew this would be a job duty.[29]

Even as to students, the issue is not so cut and dried as some believe. Under an Illinois statute that required the pledge of allegiance to be recited by elementary students, the US Court of Appeals for the Seventh Circuit okayed the practice so long as pupils were free to not participate.[30] The court distinguished two other cases that reached the opposite result where dissenting students were required to stand at attention while others recited the pledge.[31]

---

school teachers from wearing religious dress while teaching).

[20]Bacon v Bradley-Bourbonnais High School Dist No. 307, 707 FSupp 1005 (CD Ill 1989).

[21]Schanou v Lancaster County School Dist No. 160, 863 FSupp 1048 (D Neb 1994), order vacated by 62 F(3d) 1040 (8th Cir Neb 1995).

[22]Parr v State, 117 OS 23, 157 NE 555 (1927).

[23]Wisconsin v Yoder, 406 US 205, 92 SCt 1526, 32 LEd(2d) 15 (1972).

[24]Wisconsin v Yoder, 406 US 205, 92 SCt 1526, 32 LEd(2d) 15 (1972).

[25]State v Whisner, 47 OS(2d) 181, 351 NE(2d) 750 (1976). See also State ex rel Nagle v Olin, 64 OS(2d) 341, 415 NE(2d) 279 (1980).

[26]See OAC 3301-35-01 et seq. See also Text Ch 20, Pupils: Compulsory Education and School Attendance.

[27]See, e.g., New Life Baptist Church Academy v Town of East Longmeadow, 885 F(2d) 940 (1st Cir Mass 1989), cert denied 494 US 1066, 110 SCt 1782, 108 LEd(2d) 784 (1990); Fellowship Baptist Church v Benton, 815 F(2d) 485 (8th Cir Iowa 1987).

[28]West Virginia State Bd of Ed v Barnette, 319 US 624, 63 SCt 1178, 87 LEd 1628 (1943).

[29]Palmer v Chicago Bd of Ed, 444 US 1026, 100 SCt 689, 62 LEd(2d) 659 (1980).

[30]Sherman v Community Consolidated School Dist 21 of Wheeling Twp, 980 F(2d) 437 (7th Cir Ill 1992), cert denied ___ US ___, 113 SCt 2439, 124 LEd(2d) 658 (1993).

[31]Lipp v Morris, 579 F(2d) 834 (3d Cir NJ 1978); Goetz v Ansell, 477 F(2d) 636 (2d Cir NY 1973).

32.04 Establishment restrictions on released time for religious instruction

The state may not release students from classes to attend voluntarily religious instruction *within the building* taught by instructors employed by private religious groups.[32] The state can release students, however, to *leave the public school grounds* and voluntarily go to religious centers for religious education or exercises.[33]

The "released time" program may not discriminate among sects. An Ohio court struck down an off-campus program in which "one religious sect, to the exclusion of all others, [was] the recipient of instruction in its religious faith through the 'released time' program."[34]

32.05 Establishment through prayer and similar activity

Recitation of a denominationally neutral official state prayer in public schools is not permitted, even if students who do not wish to participate can remain silent or be excused.[35] This prohibition on prayer extends even to ceremonial invocations and benedictions at graduation exercises,[36] and to a basketball coach's practice of leading the team in the Lord's prayer at practices and games.[37] The US Court of Appeals for the Fifth Circuit upheld a Texas school district's resolution that permitted the students in the graduating senior class to decide on whether to use an invocation and benediction by a student volunteer at graduation exercises, provided the prayers are nonsectarian and nonproselytizing.[38] The Supreme Court vacated a decision by the US Court of Appeals for the Ninth Circuit which held that prayers at school-sponsored events, such as graduation ceremonies, violated the establishment clause despite a class vote to include prayer in the ceremony.[39] In states such as Ohio, the issue remains unclear. A state or school board cannot require that a passage from the Bible be read daily.[40] The US Supreme Court has also struck down a statute authorizing a one-minute period of silence for meditation or voluntary prayer.[41]

No funds provided under the Goals 2000: Educate America Act[42] may be used by a school district "to adopt policies that prevent voluntary prayer and meditation in public schools."[43] Similarly, state or local educational agencies that willfully violate federal court orders with respect to prayer in public schools are ineligible for federal funds under the Improving America's Schools Act of 1994.[44]

Under a specific Ohio statute, RC 3313.601, a teacher may provide a reasonable period for programs or meditation on a moral, philosophical, or patriotic theme. No student may be required to participate if participation is contrary to the student's or his parents' religious convictions. Finally, a public school teacher may belong to any faith or sect, or be a nonbeliever,

---

[32]Illinois ex rel McCollum v Champaign County School Dist No. 71 Bd of Ed, 333 US 203, 68 SCt 461, 92 LEd 649 (1948). *McCollum* controls even if the religious instruction is nondenominational and taught by lay people. Doe v Human, 725 FSupp 1503 (WD Ark 1989), affirmed without opinion by 923 F(2d) 857 (8th Cir Ark 1990), cert denied 499 US 922, 111 SCt 1315, 113 LEd(2d) 248 (1991).

[33]Zorach v Clauson, 343 US 306, 72 SCt 679, 96 LEd 954 (1952). See also OAG 88-001.

[34]Moore v Board of Education, 4 Misc 257, 212 NE(2d) 833 (CP, Mercer 1965).

[35]Engel v Vitale, 370 US 421, 82 SCt 1261, 8 LEd(2d) 601 (1962).

[36]Lee v Weisman, 505 US 577, 112 SCt 2649, 120 LEd(2d) 467 (1992).

[37]Doe v Duncanville Independent School Dist, 994 F(2d) 160 (5th Cir Tex 1993).

[38]Jones v Clear Creek Independent School Dist, 977 F(2d) 963 (5th Cir Tex 1992), cert denied ___ US ___, 113 SCt 2590, 124 LEd(2d) 697 (1993). A federal district court in Florida followed *Jones* in Adler v Duval County School Bd, 851 FSupp 446 (MD Fla 1994). While a federal district court in Mississippi adhered to *Jones*, the court distinguished between graduation ceremonies and other school-related activities such as student assemblies and sporting events. Ingebretsen v Jackson Public School Dist, 864 FSupp 1473 (SD Miss 1994).

[39]Harris v Joint School Dist No. 241, 41 F(3d) 447 (9th Cir Idaho 1994), cert granted and judgment vacated by ___ US ___, 115 SCt 2604, 132 LEd(2d) 849 (1995).

[40]Abington Twp School Dist v Schempp, 374 US 203, 83 SCt 1560, 10 LEd(2d) 844 (1963).

[41]Wallace v Jaffree, 472 US 38, 105 SCt 2479, 86 LEd(2d) 29 (1985).

[42]See Text 2.11(B), Goals 2000: Educate America Act.

[43]20 USCA 6061.

[44]20 USCA 8900.

and cannot be required to take a religious test.[45]

32.06 Establishment problems from the use of public schools for religious purposes

RC 3313.77 authorizes a board of education to permit private and parochial schools to use public school facilities when those facilities are not being used for public school purposes. This statute has been construed to mean a board cannot permit religious instruction on school property during instructional time or during the school day immediately before or after actual instructional time.[46]

(A) Equal access

The federal Equal Access Act (EAA)[47] makes it unlawful for any public secondary school which receives federal funds and which has a limited open forum to deny access on the basis of "the religious, political, philosophical, or other content" of speech to students who wish to conduct a meeting.[48] A limited open forum exists "whenever such school grants an offering to or opportunity for one or more noncurriculum related student groups to meet on school premises during noninstructional time." A school is deemed to have fairly offered students an opportunity to meet if the school uniformly provides that meetings are voluntary and student-initiated; there is no school sponsorship; school employees are present at religious meetings only in a nonparticipatory capacity; meetings do not significantly interfere with the school's educational activities; and nonschool persons do not direct, conduct, control, or regularly attend student groups' activities.[49] In essence, the EAA extends to public secondary schools the reasoning of *Widmar v Vincent*,[50] wherein the US Supreme Court invalidated a state university regulation that generally made school facilities available to all registered student groups except religious groups.

In *Westside Community Schools Bd of Ed v Mergens*,[51] the Supreme Court upheld the EAA against a constitutional attack premised on the establishment clause. School policy in this case permitted students voluntarily to join various student clubs that met after school hours on school property. School officials refused, however, to permit the formation of a Christian club that would have allowed students to read and discuss the Bible, have fellowship, and pray together. Membership in the club was to be voluntary and open to all students irrespective of religious affiliation.

Holding this prohibition of the Christian club violated the Act, the Court sought to shed light on the troublesome term "noncurriculum related student group." That "crucial phrase," said the majority,

> is best interpreted broadly to mean any student group that does not *directly* relate to the body of courses offered by the school. In our view, a student group relates to a school's curriculum if the subject matter of the group is actually taught, or will soon be taught, in a regularly offered course; if the subject matter of the group concerns the body of courses as a whole; if participation in the group is required for a particular course; or if participation in the group results in academic credit.

Finding that the school's existing school groups included non-curriculum-related student groups (for example, chess and scuba diving clubs), the Court concluded the school maintained a limited open

---

[45]O Const Art I §7.

[46]Ford v Manuel, 629 FSupp 771 (ND Ohio 1985). See also Quappe v Endry, 772 FSupp 1004 (SD Ohio 1991), affirmed by 979 F(2d) 851 (6th Cir Ohio 1992) (upholding board's decision to permit Bible study club to meet at elementary school at 6:30 p.m. but not directly after school).

[47]20 USCA 4071 to 20 USCA 4074.

[48]In the absence of a "meeting" within the meaning of 20 USCA 4071(a), the EAA does not apply. See Clark v Dallas Independent School Dist, 806 FSupp 116 (ND Tex 1992) (distribution of religious tracts before and after school on school property not a meeting).

[49]The EAA effectively gives a school district two choices: either create a limited open forum open to all students on an equal basis or refuse access to all noncurricular student groups. There is also a third choice: to forego federal funding, in which case the EAA has no applicability. See Pope v East Brunswick Bd of Ed, 12 F(3d) 1244 (3d Cir NJ 1993); Student Coalition for Peace v Lower Merion School Dist Bd of School Directors, 776 F(2d) 431 (3d Cir Pa 1985).

[50]Widmar v Vincent, 454 US 263, 102 SCt 269, 70 LEd(2d) 440 (1981).

[51]Westside Community Schools Bd of Ed v Mergens, 496 US 226, 110 SCt 2356, 110 LEd(2d) 191 (1990).

forum under the EAA and therefore could not discriminate on the basis of the content of the speech against students wishing to meet on school property during noninstructional time.[52]

Subsequent to *Mergens*, a school district's contention that a plainly religious "Gospel Choir" violated the EAA where it had school sponsorship, a school employee was present in a participating capacity, and nonschool persons regularly attended its activities has been judicially upheld.[53] Relying on *Mergens*, another court emphasized that only noncurriculum related activities are implicated by the EAA and that, accordingly, the EAA has no applicability to extracurricular activities such as school-sponsored athletic teams.[54]

A school board policy requiring that all student activities be board-sponsored rather than student-initiated does not exempt a district from the Act; there simply is no requirement that a "noncurriculum related student group" be student-initiated.[55]

Where the EAA is not at issue, a similar requirement of nondiscrimination has evolved in the courts under the First Amendment. In *Lamb's Chapel v Center Moriches Union Free School Dist*,[56] the US Supreme Court confirmed that a school district is not constitutionally compelled to make school property available to non-school groups for nonschool purposes at all. Once a district opens its property to such uses, however, it cannot discriminate against some users merely on the basis of their religious viewpoint. Thus, a district that permitted the use of its property for civic and social purposes unconstitutionally denied a request from an evangelical church for permission to use school facilities to show a religious film series on family issues and child rearing, there being no question that a film series on these topics without a religious perspective would have been approved.[57]

Following *Lamb's Chapel*, a school district's policy of charging churches a higher rental rate for using school property than other users during off-duty hours has been

---

[52] Under the supremacy clause of the US Constitution, the EAA takes precedence over state constitutions that more rigorously separate church and state than the First Amendment. Garnett v Renton School Dist No. 403, 987 F(2d) 641 (9th Cir Wash 1993), cert denied ___ US ___, 114 SCt 72, 126 LEd(2d) 41 (1993).

[53] Sease v Philadelphia School Dist, 811 FSupp 183 (ED Pa 1993).

[54] Doe v Duncanville Independent School Dist, 994 F(2d) 160 (5th Cir Tex 1993) (striking down basketball coach's practice of leading team in Lord's prayer at practices and games).

[55] Pope v East Brunswick Bd of Ed, 12 F(3d) 1244 (3d Cir NJ 1993) (holding that since Key Club, a student service organization affiliated with the Kiwanis, was noncurriculum related student group, district's refusal to recognize Bible club violated the Act; also noting that a district with a limited open forum may choose to close it, but that did not happen here).

[56] Lamb's Chapel v Center Moriches Union Free School Dist, ___ US ___, 113 SCt 2141, 124 LEd(2d) 352 (1993).

[57] Prior to *Lamb's Chapel*, several lower courts had reached a similar conclusion. See Gregoire v Centennial School Dist, 907 F(2d) 1366 (3d Cir Pa 1990), cert denied 498 US 899, 111 SCt 253, 112 LEd(2d) 211 (1990); Grace Bible Fellowship, Inc v Maine School Administrative Dist No. 5, 941 F(2d) 45 (1st Cir Me 1991); Travis v Owego-Apalachin School Dist, 927 F(2d) 688 (2d Cir NY 1991); Randall v Pegan, 765 FSupp 793 (WD NY 1991); Verbena United Methodist Church v Chilton County Bd of Ed, 765 FSupp 704 (MD Ala 1991). See also Berger v Rensselaer Central School Corp, 982 F(2d) 1160 (7th Cir Ind 1993), cert denied ___ US ___, 113 SCt 2344, 124 LEd(2d) 254 (1993) (district's practice, under its content-neutral policy on the distribution and display of materials on school premises, of annually permitting the Gideon Society to distribute bibles in elementary and middle schools found unconstitutional under First Amendment's establishment clause); Slotterback v Interboro School Dist, 766 FSupp 280 (ED Pa 1991) (finding unconstitutional school policy that prohibited distribution in schools of nonschool materials that proselytize a particular religious or political belief); DeNooyer v Livonia Public Schools, 799 FSupp 744 (ED Mich 1992), affirmed without opinion sub nom DeNooyer v Merinelli, 12 F(3d) 211 (6th Cir Mich 1993), cert denied ___ US ___, 114 SCt 1540, 128 LEd(2d) 193 (1994) (elementary school classroom a nonpublic forum and prohibiting second grader from showing video of herself singing proselytizing religious song during show-and-tell constitutional). In Brody v Spang, 957 F(2d) 1108 (3d Cir Pa 1992), the court did not rule on the validity of certain restrictions on religious speech at a high school graduation ceremony, electing instead to remand the case to a lower court for determination of whether the ceremony qualified as a designated public forum (in which case the restrictions would be subject to "strict scrutiny" and have to qualify as "narrowly drawn to further a compelling state purpose") or was merely a nonpublic forum (in which case the restrictions need be only "reasonable" and "viewpoint neutral").

held unconstitutional,[58] as has a school board's refusal to rent a school facility for a privately sponsored baccalaureate ceremony where religious activity would occur.[59] A policy of closing school facilities from 3:00 to 6:00 p.m. to all community groups except Scouts and athletic groups unconstitutionally discriminated on the basis of viewpoint against a club that sought the use of the facilities to foster the moral development of junior high school students from a Christian perspective.[60] On the other hand, allowing Scouts to use school facilities, to distribute literature during school hours, and to have posters on school grounds has passed constitutional muster.[61] A school policy that prohibited the distribution by students of religious materials that others might reasonably believe to be sponsored or endorsed by the school has been struck down, although parts of the policy that restricted distribution of written materials to a table near the school entrance and that prohibited the distribution of materials primarily prepared by non-students survived.[62]

While *Mergens* and *Lamb's Chapel* resolve several issues in this difficult area of law, significant problems obviously remain and the need for competent counsel in establishing access policies is clear.

(B) Traditional observances

Establishment questions also arise when school activity borders between that which is recognizably religious and that considered merely traditional and without an effect of endorsing or favoring religion.

The performance of Christmas music with religious content under a school holiday policy that emphasized religion was to be neither promoted nor disparaged has withstood challenge,[63] On the other hand, where the "pre-eminent purpose" is "plainly religious in nature" and no credible secular purpose is discernible, as in the case of a state statute requiring posting of a copy of the Ten Commandments (purchased with private contributions) in each public school classroom, the establishment clause is violated.[64] Similarly, the permanent display of a student painting with a religious theme (the crucifixion of Christ) in a high school auditorium has been held unconstitutional,[65] as has the prominent display of an artist's portrait of Christ at the intersection of the main hallways of a school.[66]

The inherent constitutional difficulty in this kind of case is apparent in *Allegheny County v American Civil Liberties Union Greater Pittsburgh Chapter*,[67] wherein a bitterly fragmented US Supreme Court struck down a county-sponsored holiday display consisting of a nativity scene while simultaneously allowing a city-sponsored display that included a Chanukah menorah together with a Christmas tree and sign saluting liberty. Distillation of a guiding and workable principle from the justices' five different opinions is anything but easy. Ultimately, one concludes that display of a religious symbol (however traditional), standing alone, runs afoul of the establishment clause, but a combined display that includes purely secular symbols (especially

---

[58]Fairfax Covenant Church v Fairfax County School Bd, 17 F(3d) 703 (4th Cir Va 1994), cert denied ___ US ___, 114 SCt 2166, 128 LEd(2d) 888 (1994).

[59]Shumway v Albany County School Dist No. One Bd of Ed, 826 FSupp 1320 (D Wyo 1993).

[60]Good News/Good Sports Club v Ladue School Dist, 28 F(3d) 1501 (8th Cir Mo 1994), cert denied ___ US ___, 115 SCt 2640, 132 LEd(2d) 878 (1995).

[61]Sherman v Community Consolidated School Dist 21 of Wheeling Twp, 8 F(3d) 1160 (7th Cir Ill 1993), cert denied ___ US ___, 114 SCt 2109, 128 LEd(2d) 669 (1994).

[62]Hedges v Wauconda Community Unit School Dist No. 118, 9 F(3d) 1295 (7th Cir Ill 1993) (emphasizing that school authorities should remind pupils and parents that they do not necessarily endorse the private views expressed in the schools "rather than squelch the speaker").

[63]Florey v Sioux Falls School Dist 49-5, 619 F(2d) 1311 (8th Cir SD 1980), cert denied 449 US 987, 101 SCt 409, 66 LEd(2d) 251 (1980). See also Clever v Cherry Hill Twp Bd of Ed, 838 FSupp 929 (D NJ 1993) (upholding district policy requiring certain classrooms to maintain calendars that depicted national, ethnic, and religious holidays and permitting seasonal displays that contained religious as well as secular symbols).

[64]Stone v Graham, 449 US 39, 101 SCt 192, 66 LEd(2d) 199 (1980).

[65]Joki v Schuylerville Central School Dist Bd of Ed, 745 FSupp 823 (ND NY 1990).

[66]Washegesic v Bloomingdale Public Schools, 33 F(3d) 679 (6th Cir Mich 1994).

[67]Allegheny County v American Civil Liberties Union Greater Pittsburgh Chapter, 492 US 573, 109 SCt 3086, 106 LEd(2d) 472 (1989).

if the religious symbol is not the display's predominant element) may withstand judicial scrutiny.[68] A conspicuous disclaimer that a display does not constitute endorsement of any religion or religious tenet may help insulate against a constitutional attack.[69] Each case must be evaluated in its own context and the key inquiry is what message is likely to be conveyed. If that message is religious, there is constitutional trouble brewing.

32.07   Curriculum decisions

The US Supreme Court long has recognized that "public education in our nation is committed to the control of state and local authorities" and "local school boards have broad discretion in the management of school affairs."[70] While curriculum decisions generally fall within the discretion of state and local education authorities, the courts will not hesitate to overturn efforts to inculcate religious beliefs.

A prohibition against teaching the theory of biological evolution violates the establishment clause.[71] So does a state law requiring the public schools to give balanced treatment to creation-science and evolution-science.[72] The US Supreme Court inescapably concluded that the theory of creation constitutes a religious belief, not science. The state's requirement had a religious purpose, in violation of the establishment clause.

Whether students can successfully object to sex education classes based on the First Amendment is still a question in Ohio. Courts in other states have upheld noncompulsory sex education classes.[73]

The First Amendment issues involved in selection of textbooks and library books are treated in Chapter 33.[74]

---

[68]See also Lynch v Donnelly, 465 US 668, 104 SCt 1355, 79 LEd(2d) 604 (1984); Americans United for Separation of Church and State v Grand Rapids, 980 F(2d) 1538 (6th Cir Mich 1992); Doe v Clawson, 915 F(2d) 244 (6th Cir Mich 1990); American Civil Liberties Union of Central Ohio v Delaware County, 726 FSupp 184 (SD Ohio 1989).

[69]See American Civil Liberties Union of Kentucky v Wilkinson, 895 F(2d) 1098 (6th Cir Ky 1990).

[70]Island Trees Union Free School Dist No. 26 Bd of Ed v Pico, 457 US 853, 102 SCt 2799, 73 LEd(2d) 435 (1982).

[71]Epperson v Arkansas, 393 US 97, 89 SCt 266, 21 LEd(2d) 228 (1968).

[72]Edwards v Aguillard, 482 US 578, 107 SCt 2573, 96 LEd(2d) 510 (1987). See also Webster v New Lenox School Dist No. 122, 917 F(2d) 1004 (7th Cir Ill 1990) (social studies teacher had no constitutional right to teach nonevolutionary theory of creation and stray from established curriculum by injecting religious advocacy in classroom); Peloza v Capistrano Unified School Dist, 37 F(3d) 517 (9th Cir Cal 1994), cert denied ___ US ___, 115 SCt 2640, 132 LEd(2d) 878 (1995) (rejecting biology teacher's argument that teaching theory of evolution amounts to an unconstitutional state-supported religion but suggesting that school district cannot force teacher to teach evolution without a creator as a fact but only as a scientific theory).

[73]Citizens for Parental Rights v San Mateo County Bd of Ed, 51 Cal App(3d) 1, 124 Cal Rptr 68 (1975), appeal dismissed by 425 US 908, 96 SCt 1502, 47 LEd(2d) 759 (1976) (students could be excused from portions of courses that conflicted with parents' religious beliefs or used materials to which parents objected). See also Smith v Ricci, 446 A(2d) 501 (NJ 1982), appeal dismissed by 459 US 962, 103 SCt 286, 74 LEd(2d) 272 (1982); Medeiros v Kiyosaki, 52 Haw 436, 478 P(2d) 314 (1970); Hobolth v Greenway, 52 Mich App 682, 218 NW(2d) 98 (1974). There is no constitutionally protected parental right, however, for students to opt out of curriculum for purely secular reasons. Immediato v Rye Neck School Dist, 873 FSupp 846 (SD NY 1995) (holding mandatory community service program was not in violation of constitutional rights).

[74]See Text 33.04, Discretion of board in choosing books, constitutional limitations.

TEXTBOOKS—LIBRARIES—SUPPLIES—SERVICES—PROPERTY

Chapter 33

Textbooks

33.01 Introduction
33.02 Textbooks and workbooks to be furnished free
33.03 Selection and adoption of textbooks
33.04 Discretion of board in choosing books, constitutional limitations
33.05 Administrator or teacher acting as sales agent for publisher
33.06 Copyright considerations

33.01 Introduction

Selection of textbooks and other printed materials for use in schools is made by the local boards of education. The selection process often provokes controversy as some interest groups seek adoption of books supporting their positions, while others seek to have particular books banned or removed from schools.

In selecting instructional materials, copyright issues can also come into play.

33.02 Textbooks and workbooks to be furnished free

(A) Books included

The board of each local, exempted village, and city school district must furnish, free of charge, necessary textbooks to pupils attending public schools. The textbooks remain district property and are considered loaned to pupils on terms prescribed by each board.[1]

A board is not required to furnish instructional materials other than textbooks and may charge for use of supplementary supplies, such as a musical instrument.[2] Boards may prescribe fees for these materials and enforce payment by withholding grades and credits of pupils who fail to pay. An exception may be made for pupils in serious financial need.[3] The Ohio Supreme Court has emphasized that the authorization of fees in RC 3313.642 is contrary to the general rule of a free education and must be construed narrowly. Thus, the Court rejected a board's attempt to assess a per pupil fee, enforced by withholding grades and credits, to defray the cost of administrative supplies as opposed to instructional materials.[4]

(B) Purchase by pupil or parent

A board must sell textbooks to a pupil or parent who requests to buy at a price not to exceed cost plus ten per cent.[5]

33.03 Selection and adoption of textbooks

(A) Procedure

Any United States publisher desiring to offer school books for use in Ohio public schools first must file in the office of the superintendent of public instruction a list of the published wholesale prices on or before January 1 of each year. The filing must state that the list wholesale price of a textbook to Ohio school districts will not exceed the lowest list price to districts in any other state. Otherwise, the books may not be purchased by any school board.[6]

If a publisher offers a school book after January 1, a supplementary list must be filed showing the published wholesale

---

[1] RC 3329.06; 1938 OAG 3545; 1938 OAG 3545. See also OAG 65-89.
[2] 1962 OAG 3438.
[3] RC 3313.642. See Text 23.05, Failure to pay activity or school fees.
[4] Association for Defense of Washington Local School Dist v Kiger, 42 OS(3d) 116, 537 NE(2d) 1292 (1989).
[5] RC 3329.09.
[6] RC 3329.01.

price, subject to the same "best price" statement.[7]

In all cases, the publisher must file with the wholesale price of the book the wholesale price of a computer diskette that contains the text of the book in the American standard code for information interchange (ASCII) or in another computer language approved by the superintendent of public instruction for translating the text into braille. The latter wholesale price cannot exceed the wholesale price filed for the printed version of the book.[8]

Boards must choose, by majority vote at a regular meeting, textbooks from the list approved by the superintendent of public instruction, except local school districts select from lists adopted by the county board of education.[9]

A board must include in its annual budget as a separate item the amount necessary to administer the textbook statutes, and that amount is not subject to transfer to any other fund.[10]

The above procedure does not apply to supplementary reading books, library books, reference books, or any other books except textbooks. Such books must be purchased in the same way as other supplies and equipment.[11]

The maximum price for textbooks is fixed by the superintendent of public instruction. If the publisher agrees in writing to furnish books at that price during stated periods, the publisher may sell the books to boards of education.

(B) Adoption to last four years

No textbook may be changed, revised, or substituted within four years after the date of adoption, except by consent at a regular meeting of four-fifths of all board members. Books substituted must themselves be adopted for the full four-year term.[12]

(C) Requirement that texts be current

Boards are required to adopt policies to ensure that texts are up-to-date. These policies must be available to parents, pupils, and school personnel.[13]

33.04 Discretion of board in choosing books, constitutional limitations

Within the statutory guidelines, boards may exercise discretion in selecting textbooks. The discretion granted by RC 3329.07 has stirred much debate that is far from settled. Court decisions appear to afford boards somewhat greater latitude in selecting textbooks than has been the case with library books.

In *Hazelwood School Dist v Kuhlmeier*,[14] the US Supreme Court held that the First Amendment of the Constitution allows educators to exercise control over the style and content of student newspapers, so long as their actions are reasonably related to legitimate pedagogical concerns. In view of that standard, a Florida school board's decision to remove a humanities text deemed inappropriately sexual and vulgar survived a constitutional challenge.[15]

In *Minarcini v Strongsville City School Dist*,[16] the court found that an Ohio school board did not act arbitrarily or capriciously or deny parents or pupils their constitutional rights by refusing to purchase certain novels recommended by teachers for an English course. The board is empowered to make the ultimate decision on whether a book should be used.

However, a board's discretion in selecting library books may be more circumscribed. In *Island Trees Union Free School Dist No. 26 Bd of Ed v Pico*,[17] the US Supreme Court stated a school board lacks authority to ban library books because they contain ideas members find repugnant. This holding, while dealing with removal of

---

[7]RC 3329.01.
[8]RC 3329.01.
[9]RC 3329.08.
[10]RC 3329.06.
[11]RC 3329.05.
[12]RC 3329.08.
[13]OAC 3301-35-03(B).
[14]Hazelwood School Dist v Kuhlmeier, 484 US 260, 108 SCt 562, 98 LEd(2d) 592 (1988).

[15]Virgil v Columbia County, Fla School Bd, 862 F(2d) 1517 (11th Cir Fla 1989).
[16]Minarcini v Strongsville City School Dist, 541 F(2d) 577 (6th Cir Ohio 1976).
[17]Island Trees Union Free School Dist No. 26 Bd of Ed v Pico, 457 US 853, 102 SCt 2799, 73 LEd(2d) 435 (1982).

library books, suggests a board may not remove a textbook merely because it dislikes the book's substance.

Minarcini also involved the removal of books from the school library. While the board could not remove books because members did not like the message or language, the court noted that books could be removed on the good-faith belief that they were outdated, worn out, or there was a lack of shelf space.[18]

While removal of the Bible and other religiously oriented books from a school library is not constitutionally required, at least where the collection shows no preference for a particular religion or religion in general, school officials could order removal of religious books from a particular teacher's classroom library and require that the teacher keep his Bible out of sight and refrain from silently reading it during classroom hours.[19]

In most of these cases, the board, on its own, was making decisions about particular books. Situations also arise where the board is pressured from the outside to take action. For example, parents may object to a book as offensive to them and their children. In *Grosser v Woollett*,[20] the court found that even though the books— *Manchild in the Promised Land* and *One Flew Over the Cuckoo's Nest*—were offensive and harmful to juveniles within the meaning of RC 2907.31, their use upon written parental consent was permissible.

Mozert v Hawkins County Public Schools[21] involved reading textbooks that some parents objected to on religious grounds. There was no showing that requiring students to read the books entailed affirmation or denial of a religious belief or the performance of a religious exercise. Accordingly, the court found the books did not impermissibly burden the free exercise of religion under the First Amendment.

An earlier case arising in West Virginia reached a similar conclusion,[22] while subsequent cases arising in Illinois and California rejected a claim that certain elementary school reading materials containing stories relating to wizards, sorcerers, and other beings with supernatural powers either fostered a particular religious belief or interfered with the free exercise of religion.[23] And, in a case that received wide publicity, a federal appeals court refused to prohibit numerous textbooks objected to by fundamentalist Christian parents as promoting "secular humanism." While some material in the books might be offensive to some parents, "the message conveyed is one of a governmental attempt to instill in Alabama public school children such values as independent thought, tolerance of diverse views, self-respect, maturity, self-reliance, and logical decision-making. This is an entirely appropriate secular effect."[24]

33.05 Administrator or teacher acting as sales agent for publisher

A superintendent, supervisor, principal, or teacher may not act as sales agent, directly or indirectly, for any person or firm whose textbooks are filed with the superintendent of public instruction, or for school apparatus or equipment. The penalty for violation is forfeiture of certification.[25]

A teacher may act as sales agent for publishers of general reference works, selling to private individuals, provided the publisher has not filed with the superinten-

---

[18]Minarcini v Strongsville City School Dist, 541 F(2d) 577 (6th Cir Ohio 1976).

[19]Roberts v Madigan, 921 F(2d) 1047 (10th Cir Colo 1990), cert denied ___ US ___, 112 SCt 3025, 120 LEd(2d) 896 (1992).

[20]Grosser v Woollett, 74 OO(2d) 243 (App, Cuyahoga 1975).

[21]Mozert v Hawkins County Bd of Ed, 827 F(2d) 1058 (6th Cir Tenn 1987), cert denied 484 US 1066, 108 SCt 1029, 98 LEd(2d) 993 (1988).

[22]Williams v County of Kanawha Bd of Ed, 388 FSupp 93 (SD WVa 1975), affirmed by 530 F(2d) 972 (4th Cir WVa 1975).

[23]Fleischfresser v Directors of School Dist 200, 15 F(3d) 680 (7th Cir Ill 1994); Brown v Woodland Joint Unified School Dist, 27 F(3d) 1373 (9th Cir Cal 1994).

[24]Smith v Mobile County Bd of School Commrs, 827 F(2d) 684 (11th Cir Ala 1987). See also Grove v Mead School Dist No. 354, 753 F(2d) 1528 (9th Cir Wash 1985), cert denied 474 US 826, 106 SCt 85, 88 LEd(2d) 70 (1985) (rejecting claim that curriculum book entitled *The Learning Tree* unconstitutionally promoted "secular humanism").

[25]RC 3329.10.

dent of public instruction any textbooks for use in the schools.[26]

33.06 Copyright considerations

(A) In general

A copyright gives the owner of an original work of authorship[27] exclusive rights to copy that work in various forms.[28] One who infringes a copyright may be liable for damages.[29] In cases of willful infringement for purposes of commercial advantage or private financial gain, criminal penalties may be imposed.[30] However, it is not an infringement of copyright for a library or archives to reproduce or distribute one copy of a copyrighted work if it is done without any purpose of commercial advantage, the institution's collections are open to the public or generally available to persons doing research in a specialized field, and a notice of copyright is included.[31]

(B) Fair use

Of the several exceptions under federal law to a copyright owner's exclusive rights in a copyrighted work, the most notable is the "fair use" exception. The Copyright Act expressly states the fair use of a copyrighted work for such purposes as "teaching (including multiple copies for classroom use), scholarship, or research" does not constitute infringement.[32] In determining fair use, factors to be considered include (1) the purpose and character of the use, including whether it is commercial in nature or for nonprofit educational purposes; (2) the nature of the copyrighted work; (3) the amount and substantiality of the portion used relative to the copyrighted work as a whole; and (4) the effect on the potential market for or value of the copyrighted work.[33] The US Supreme Court has indicated that fair use analysis must be tailored to the individual case.[34] By way of example, a school teacher who incorporated a substantial portion of another teacher's copyrighted booklet on cake decorating into her own booklet on the subject for use in her classroom was guilty of infringement.[35]

Although not part of the copyright law itself and not controlling on the courts, Congressional guidelines published in connection with a substantial revision of the Copyright Act in 1976 are helpful in assessing fair use copying of copyrighted works by public school districts for instructional purposes.[36] Purporting to state "minimum" standards for educational fair use, the guidelines authorize a teacher to make, in connection with teaching or preparing to teach a class, a single copy of a chapter from a book; an article from a periodical or newspaper; a short story, short essay, or short poem, whether or not from a collective work; or a chart, graph, diagram, drawing, cartoon, or picture from a book, periodical, or newspaper.[37] Multiple copies (not to exceed more than one per pupil in a course) may be made for classroom use or discussion if the copying meets specified brevity, spontaneity, and cumulative effect tests, and each copy includes a notice of copyright.[38] No charge to the pupil is authorized beyond the actual cost of copying. Repeated copying of the same item by the same teacher from term to term, copy-

---

[26] 1948 OAG 4251.

[27] Defined by 17 USCA 102 to include literary, musical, and dramatic works; pantomimes and choreographic works; pictorial, graphic, and sculptural works; motion pictures and audiovisual works; and sound recordings. That computer programs are also copyrightable is clear. See, e.g., Whelan Associates, Inc v Jaslow Dental Laboratory, Inc, 797 F(2d) 1222 (3d Cir Pa 1986), cert denied 479 US 1031, 107 SCt 877, 93 LEd(2d) 831 (1987); M. Kramer Mfg Co v Andrews, 783 F(2d) 421 (4th Cir SC 1986). See also 17 USCA 117.

[28] Specifically, the copyright owner has exclusive rights to reproduce the work, to prepare derivative works based upon the copyrighted work, to distribute copies of the work to the public, to perform the work publicly, and to display the work publicly. 17 USCA 106.

[29] 17 USCA 501, 17 USCA 504. Reasonable attorney's fees may also be awarded the prevailing party in a suit for copyright infringement. 17 USCA 505.

[30] 17 USCA 506.

[31] 17 USCA 108.

[32] 17 USCA 107.

[33] 17 USCA 107.

[34] Harper & Row Publishers, Inc v Nation Enterprises, 471 US 539, 105 SCt 2218, 85 LEd(2d) 588 (1985).

[35] Marcus v Rowley, 695 F(2d) 1171 (9th Cir Cal 1983).

[36] See 1976 US Code Cong & Admin News 5678 et seq.

[37] See 1976 US Code Cong & Admin News at 5681-82.

[38] "Brevity," for prose, means a complete article, story, or essay of less than 2,500 words or an excerpt

ing as a substitute for purchasing books and periodicals, and copying from "consumable" works (such as workbooks and standardized tests and answer sheets) is generally prohibited.[39]

(C) Works made for hire

Ownership of a copyright vests initially in the author or authors of the work.[40] An exception is made for authorship of a "work made for hire." Here, the author is the "employer or the person for whom the work was prepared," not the person who actually created or developed the work.[41] A work made for hire is defined by 17 USCA 101 as (1) a work prepared by an employee within the scope of his employment; or (2) a work specially ordered or commissioned for one of nine specified uses[42] if the parties expressly agree in writing that the work will be considered a work made for hire.

As to who is an "employee" under the first prong of the definition, the US Supreme Court has looked to the common law of agency to determine whether the preparer is an employee or independent contractor,[43] which requires examination of the hiring party's right to control the manner and means by which the work is accomplished.[44]

---

from any work of not more than 1,000 words or ten per cent of the work, whichever is less. Separate brevity rules govern poetry, illustrations, and "special" works. "Spontaneity" requires that the copying be at the instance and inspiration of the particular teacher, so close in time to the moment of its use for maximum teaching effectiveness that it would be unreasonable to expect a timely reply to a request for permission. The "cumulative effect" test requires that copying be for only one course; that not more than one short poem, article, story, essay, or two excerpts be copied from the same author, nor more than three from the same collective work or periodical volume in one class term; and that the total instances of multiple copying for one course during one class term not exceed nine. These last two limitations do not apply, however, to current news periodicals and newspapers and current news sections of other periodicals. See 1976 US Code Cong & Admin News at 5682-83.

[39]See 1976 US Code Cong & Admin News at 5683.
[40]17 USCA 201(a).
[41]17 USCA 201(b).

[42]Specifically, "for use as a contribution to a collective work, as part of a motion picture or other audiovisual work, as a translation, as a supplementary work, as a compilation, as an instructional text, as a test, as answer material for a test, or as an atlas." 17 USCA 101. The statute goes on explicitly to amplify the meanings of "supplementary work" and "instructional text."

[43]Community for Creative Non-Violence v Reid, 490 US 730, 109 SCt 2166, 104 LEd(2d) 811 (1989). The Court rejected arguments that the test is whether the hiring party retains the right to control the product or actually controlled creation of the product. It also rejected an argument that "employee" means "formal, salaried" employees.

[44]For a nonexhaustive list of factors relevant to determining whether a hired party is an employee, no one of which is determinative, see Community for Creative Non-Violence v Reid, 490 US 730, 109 SCt 2166, 2178-79, 104 LEd(2d) 811 (1989). See also Restatement (2d) of Agency § 228 (1958).

Chapter 34

Libraries

34.01	Introduction
	LIBRARIES SERVING SCHOOLS
34.02	School board's authority to provide library service, in general
34.03	School district public libraries
34.04	Community library service for schools
	STATE LIBRARY
34.05	Role of state library board
34.06	Composition of state library board
34.07	State librarian
34.08	Application for permission to establish library service
	LIBRARY TRUSTEES AND STAFF
34.09	Library boards, in general
34.10	Powers of library board
34.11	Financial transactions of library boards
34.12	Library employees, clerk of board
	BUDGET AND REVENUE
34.13	Library budget, annual appropriation
34.14	Income tax
34.15	Tax levies, in general
34.16	Ten-mill limitation, special levies
34.17	Bond issues

34.01 Introduction

Title 33 of the Ohio Revised Code governs libraries as well as education generally. RC Chapter 3375 covers all types, ranging from the state library to public libraries to law libraries. This chapter focuses on school libraries and aspects of the public library system directly affecting education. The duties and responsibilities of library trustees and staff are also discussed.

LIBRARIES SERVING SCHOOLS

34.02 School board's authority to provide library service, in general

Until 1947, the board of education of a city, exempted village, or local school district could establish and maintain school libraries for pupils. A board may also contract with any organization operating a public library in a community to furnish school library service.[1] The board must pay all or such part of the expense, including the salaries of school librarians, as the parties may agree, but the organization may still provide classroom collections, bookmobiles, branches, or its main library even if branches or the main library are located within a school building. Boards of education are also authorized to purchase, construct, or improve buildings for library purposes and to furnish the buildings.[2]

The board of a city, exempted village, or local school district may purchase, construct, improve, or furnish buildings and acquire real estate to render free public library service to the people of the district.[3] These facilities must be operated by the board of library trustees of the district if a free public library was established by the school board prior to September 4, 1947; otherwise, they may be operated by the board of trustees of any free public library, library association, or corporation on such terms as may be agreed upon provided the school board finds such operation will benefit the district and its residents.[4]

Also, the board of any school district may convey or lease any district property suitable for public library purposes to the board of trustees of any free public library rendering free library service to the people of the district, upon mutually agreed terms.[5]

Further, a board of a city, exempted village, or local school district may purchase, construct, enlarge, improve, equip, and furnish buildings and acquire necessary real estate to provide free library service to the people of the district and may issue bonds for the purpose in accordance with the Uniform Bond Law.[6]

34.03 School district public libraries

In any school district in which a free public library was established by the board of education prior to September 4, 1947,

---

[1] RC 3375.14, RC 3375.42.
[2] RC 3375.14, RC 3375.42.
[3] RC 3375.18.

[4] RC 3375.18.
[5] RC 3375.16.
[6] RC Ch 133.

the library must be managed by a seven-member board of library trustees appointed by the board of education. If the board of education does not act within forty-five days after a member's term expires or a vacancy occurs, the appointment will be made by the county probate court. A majority must be qualified electors in the district; a minority may be qualified electors of the county who reside outside the district. Terms are for seven years. Current members of the board of education, or persons who have served as members of the board of education within a year, are ineligible.[7] A majority of the trustees must not be employed by school districts or other political subdivisions.[8]

There can be only one school district public library system per district. When, therefore, two or more districts having school district public libraries consolidate, the successor district must appoint a board of trustees for the consolidated system.[9]

The board of a local school district may arrange with the board of trustees of a school district public library established by the district before September 4, 1947, to spend part of the proceeds of a bond issue for school purposes to construct a new library building.[10] The building may be built on land of the school district public library owned or held under a perpetual lease.[11]

34.04 Community library service for schools

(A) Other libraries in school districts

In addition to school district public libraries whose trustees are appointed by the board of education, certain other public libraries have boards of trustees appointed by other authorities, but which may also render library service to schools and the people of the school districts:

(1) County free libraries (RC 3375.06);

(2) Free public township libraries (RC 3375.10);

(3) Municipal libraries (RC 3375.12);

(4) County libraries (RC 3375.22); and

(5) Regional libraries (RC 3375.30).[12]

(B) Public library service for schools

A public library is expected to provide normal public library service to all inhabitants of the county on equal terms as a condition to tax entitlement[13] but is not required to provide special library service within the schools or any one particular school. Boards of education must provide their own library service or may contract with an existing public library for that service, paying all or part of the cost.[14]

A political subdivision may appropriate funds for library services under RC 3375.42 only pursuant to a contract with the board of library trustees, private corporation, or library association, which provides library services to all inhabitants of the political subdivision.[15] A board of county commissioners has no duty to create a library for use of area schools.[16]

STATE LIBRARY

34.05 Role of state library board

The state library board manages the state library and exercises certain powers to improve and coordinate library services throughout the state. The board administers federal, state, and private funds contributed for library purposes. It has authority to, among other things, approve, disapprove, or modify resolutions to redefine and adjust library boundaries when school districts are consolidated.[17]

---

[7]RC 3375.15.
[8]RC 3375.63. The authority of the board of trustees is treated in Text 34.10, Powers of library board.
[9]OAG 65-119.
[10]OAG 67-090 (LC).
[11]OAG 67-090 (LC); 1953 OAG 2485. See also Text 34.17, Bond issues.

[12]The authority of such boards of trustees is treated in Text 34.10, Powers of library board.
[13]RC 5705.28.
[14]RC 3375.14, RC 3375.42.
[15]OAG 73-058.
[16]OAG 81-005.
[17]RC 3375.01, RC 3375.04.

34.06 Composition of state library board

The state library board consists of five members appointed by the state board of education. One member is appointed each year for a term of five years. No one is eligible who is, or within the previous year was, a member of the state board of education. A member of the state library board may not be a member of the board of library trustees for any library in any political subdivision.[18]

Members receive no compensation but are paid their actual and necessary expenses incurred in the performance of their duties within or without the state. The board may purchase liability insurance covering its members, officers, employees, and agents of the state library.[19]

34.07 State librarian

The state library board appoints the state librarian, who serves as board secretary and as executive officer of the state library during the pleasure of the board.[20]

The state librarian has the power to appoint and remove state library employees. He administers the state library and executes board policies; provides technical assistance and maintains a clearinghouse of information, data, and other materials in the field of library service to public libraries and other agencies and organizations; collects, compiles, and publishes statistics and information; makes studies of library problems; assists and cooperates with other state agencies and officials, with organizations, and with local and federal agencies in carrying out programs involving library service; maintains a collection of documents and publications; issues official lists of publications and bibliographical and informational publications; and disposes of unneeded items. Under RC 3375.02(H), he is authorized to make appropriate transfers or disposition of books and materials no longer needed in the state library without regard to RC 125.12.[21]

34.08 Application for permission to establish library service

Application may be made to the state library board by the board of trustees of any public library receiving public tax support to establish library service to the inhabitants of any school district (other than a district located within the subdivision or district over which that board has jurisdiction of free public library service) by means of library stations, branches, or traveling library service. The state board's decision on the application is final.[22]

LIBRARY TRUSTEES AND STAFF

34.09 Library boards, in general

(A) Board members, officers

The board of trustees of a county free public library is appointed by the county court of common pleas;[23] township library trustees are appointed by the township trustees;[24] municipal public library trustees are appointed by the mayor;[25] school district public library trustees are appointed by the district board of education;[26] in a county library district, three trustees are appointed by the county court of common pleas and four by the county commissioners;[27] and regional district library trustees are appointed by the boards of county commissioners of the participating counties, in rotation.[28]

Each board must meet in January of each year and organize by selecting a president, vice-president, secretary, and clerk, who serve for terms of one year.[29]

Board members serve without compensation[30] but in some instances (not includ-

---

[18]RC 3375.01. The library board is not part of the state department of education. 1956 OAG 6359.
[19]RC 3375.01. The library board is not part of the state department of education. 1956 OAG 6359.
[20]RC 3375.02.
[21]See OAG 73-037. RC 125.12 et seq. deal with the disposition by state agencies of excess and surplus supplies.
[22]RC 3375.05.

[23]RC 3375.06.
[24]RC 3375.10.
[25]RC 3375.12.
[26]RC 3375.15.
[27]RC 3375.22.
[28]RC 3375.30.
[29]RC 3375.32.
[30]RC 3375.06, RC 3375.10, RC 3375.12, RC 3375.15, RC 3375.22, RC 3375.30.

ing a school district public library board) are expressly entitled to reimbursement for expenses incurred in performing their duties.[31]

Board members may not have any pecuniary interest in any contract entered into by their respective boards.[32] In addition, the criminal code and the ethics law contain broad prohibitions against conflicts of interest.[33]

(B) Board of trustees as an entity

Boards of library trustees may sue and be sued, execute contracts, own and dispose of property, and exercise such other powers as are conferred on them by law.[34]

(C) Quorum, open meetings

For the purpose of transacting business, a quorum is a majority of the full board. The purchase of real property requires a two-thirds vote of the full board.[35] Library boards are subject to the Sunshine Act (RC 121.22).[36]

34.10 Powers of library board

(A) In general

Each board of library trustees may for the free public library under its jurisdiction:

(1) Own and keep real and personal property;

(2) Spend money for library purposes and generally do whatever is necessary to establish, maintain, and improve the library;

(3) Purchase, construct, or lease buildings or parts of buildings, and other real property, and purchase automobiles and other personal property necessary to operate and maintain libraries (financing may be secured through issuance of a promissory note, an installment sale, or a lease-purchase agreement);

(4) Purchase, lease, lease with an option to purchase, or erect buildings or parts of buildings;

(5) Establish and maintain a main library, branches, library stations, and traveling library service within the subdivision or district;

(6) Establish and maintain branches, library stations, and traveling library service in any school district outside the subdivision or district over which it has jurisdiction of free public library service, on approval of the state library board;

(7) Appoint and fix the compensation of employees;

(8) Make and publish rules;

(9) Establish and maintain a museum as an adjunct to a library;

(10) Accept any bequest, gift, or endowment according to the limitations imposed by law;

(11) By a two-thirds vote, at the end of any fiscal year, set aside any unencumbered surplus remaining in the general funds of the library for the purpose of creating a special building and repair fund, or for the purpose of operating the library or acquiring equipment and supplies;

(12) Procure and pay all or part of the cost of various specified group insurance benefits for employees, their spouses, and dependents; and

(13) Pay reasonable dues and expenses for library trustees in library associations.[37]

In addition, a board may purchase certain types of liability insurance,[38] contract with a nonprofit corporation to establish a museum for the general public in the territory served,[39] and contract for library service with other library boards and with boards of education of school districts within the territory to provide library service.[40]

(B) Specific applications

Library trustees have no powers except those expressly granted by statute. In the absence of statutory authority, the trustees

---

[31] RC 3375.06, RC 3375.22, RC 3375.30.
[32] RC 3375.35.
[33] See Text Ch 45, Ethics Requirements and Education Personnel.
[34] RC 3375.33, RC 3375.34. See also Text 34.10, Powers of library board.

[35] RC 3375.35.
[36] See Text 5.12, Open meetings: the sunshine law.
[37] RC 3375.40.
[38] RC 3375.401.
[39] RC 3375.402.
[40] RC 3375.403.

may not disassociate libraries from school districts.[41]

Libraries must advertise for bids when $15,000 or more is involved to build, demolish, alter, or repair library property, except in cases of urgent necessity or for the security and protection of the property. The lowest responsible bid must be accepted.[42]

A public library may employ a special police officer to be on duty several hours each evening to protect library property and prevent disturbances. A county sheriff may contract with library districts for these services.

Library trustees may not spend public funds under an agreement or contract with a university or private corporation for sharing the costs of training in library science.[43]

A school district public library board of trustees may not borrow money from a bank to purchase real property, nor can it secure the loan by its promissory note and a mortgage on the property.[44] But, the board may purchase the property through a land contract entered into with the seller under RC 3375.40.[45]

Library trustees may lawfully sell unneeded real property without advertising for bids.[46]

Public library funds may not be used for voter registration without reimbursement by the board of elections to the library for the costs incurred. Library trustees and a board of elections may contractually agree that library personnel and facilities may be used for voter registration with such reimbursement.[47]

A public library may become a member of a regional council of governments created under RC Chapter 167 and may participate in a self-funded health care benefit program authorized by RC 9.833(B).[48]

34.11 Financial transactions of library boards

No money credited to a free public library may be paid out except by check signed by the clerk of the board of library trustees and the board president, vice president, or secretary.[49]

At the end of the fiscal year, each board is required to submit a report to the state librarian and to the officer or board that appointed the trustees, on forms provided by the state library board. The report must include a complete financial statement showing receipts and expenditures in detail.[50] An annual financial report to the state auditor must also be prepared and published in a newspaper of general circulation in the district.[51]

34.12 Library employees, clerk of board

(A) Employees: compensation and fringe benefits

The board of library trustees may appoint and fix the compensation of all employees of the free public library under its jurisdiction.[52] A library trustee may not be employed part time, on an hourly basis, to work in a library.[53]

The staff of any library in the state, supported wholly or in part at public expense, are in the unclassified civil service.[54] This does not apply, however, to employees who work in the library of a college or university.[55]

---

[41]1933 OAG 1509.
[42]RC 3375.41.
[43]1963 Inf OAG 27.
[44]1965 Inf OAG 29.
[45]1965 Inf OAG 29.
[46]OAG 70-162.
[47]OAG 77-091.
[48]OAG 93-031.
[49]RC 3375.35.
[50]RC 3375.35.
[51]RC 117.06.
[52]RC 3375.40(G). The board's authority with respect to insurance fringe benefits is discussed in Text 34.10, Powers of library board.

[53]1965 Syllabi 2. Syllabi are unpublished determinations made by the Auditor of State's Office from approximately 1945 to 1970. During that time, brief one-sentence references to the determinations had some limited circulation outside the Auditor's Office and were sometimes referenced by the Auditor and others. Although they may not be of precedential value outside of the Auditor's Office, they are often the only authority for the specific proposition.
[54]RC 124.11(A)(7)(b).
[55]Lynch v Ohio State University, No. 84AP-258, 1985 WL 9888 (10th Dist Ct App, Franklin, 3-5-85).

RC 124.38, a civil service statute dealing with sick leave, does not apply to library employees. Library trustees have power under RC 3375.40 to make rules governing sick leave benefits.[56]

(B) Clerk of library board

At the organizational meeting in January each board must elect and fix the compensation of a clerk, who may be a member of the board, and who serves for a term of one year. Before assuming duties, the clerk must execute a bond in an amount and with surety to be approved by the board, payable to the board, and conditioned on the faithful performance of his duties.[57]

As treasurer of the library's funds, the clerk's duties include placing all money in a depository designated by the board, keeping accounts, rendering a monthly financial statement, and submitting a complete financial statement at the end of each fiscal year.[58]

A librarian may not use collected fines for incidental expenses, since the clerk is responsible for collecting all money and immediately placing it in a designated depository. Library trustees may authorize a petty cash fund to be held only by the clerk, with all disbursements to be supported by proper receipts.

The clerk must submit a monthly financial report, which should be approved by the board and the approval reported in the minute record. It is not necessary for the report itself to be filed in the minute record, but the clerk must retain the report in his files.

The Attorney General has concluded that the position of clerk of a school district public library and membership on the legislative authority of a village within the jurisdiction of that public library are incompatible.[59]

BUDGET AND REVENUE

34.13 Library budget, annual appropriation

Each public library entitled to participate in any appropriations or revenue of a subdivision is required to file its budget with the taxing authority of the subdivision before June 1 in each year, estimating contemplated revenue and expenditures for the next year. The taxing authority must include in its budget of receipts the full amounts specified by the library board of trustees as contemplated revenue from classified property taxes and must include in its budget of expenditures the full amounts requested by the board.[60]

Although the tax budget of a school district public library does not become a part of the tax budget of the school district, the procedures (but not the timeliness) concerning public inspection and hearing on the budget, its adoption, submission to the county auditor and his presentation of it to the county budget commission, appearance of a representative before the commission to explain needs, and appeal to the state board of tax appeals are the same as those of a school district.[61]

A library is not a taxing authority.[62] However, most library districts are political subdivisions[63] and must follow RC 117.06[64] in connection with their annual financial reports.

Library trustees must pass an annual appropriation resolution, showing classifications of appropriations for which expenditures are to be made in the fiscal year. Thereafter the board is not required to

---

[56]1950 OAG 2077.
[57]RC 3375.32.
[58]RC 3375.36 et seq.
[59]OAG 90-059.
[60]RC 5705.28.

[61]The annual budget process for school districts is discussed more fully in Text 40.01 to 40.06.
[62]1937 OAG 909.
[63]1953 OAG 2994.
[64]See Text 6.07(B), Accounts.

34.14 Income tax

RC 5747.03(A)(1)(b) establishes a credit of six and three-tenths per cent of the Ohio income tax collected during the preceding month for the library and local support fund for distribution in accordance with RC 5747.47.

The board of trustees of any public library, except a school district public library, wishing to share in the proceeds of the county library and local government support fund is required to adopt rules extending the benefits of its library services to all people of the county on equal terms, unless by law the service is available to all inhabitants.[65] The county budget commission is empowered to allocate the proceeds of the county library and local government support fund to library boards on the basis of need.[66]

34.15 Tax levies, in general

(A) School board tax levy for library purposes

The library trustees of a school district public library may annually, during May, certify to the district board of education the amount of money needed to maintain and operate the library during the next fiscal year and the amount of revenue anticipated from all sources other than a tax levy on the taxable property of the school district. The board of education may annually levy a tax not exceeding one and one-half mills on the taxable property of the district, which is in addition to all other levies authorized by law.[67] Because this tax has not been approved by the voters, it is levied within the ten-mill limitation.

(B) Tax levies by community libraries

The library trustees of a county library district may annually, during May, certify its needs to the county commissioners, whereupon the commissioners may levy a tax of up to one mill, in addition to all other levies authorized by law.[68] Also, where a county free public library has been created, the county commissioners may levy a tax not exceeding one mill on each dollar of taxable property for the purpose of maintaining the library.[69]

In any township where a public library has been created before September 4, 1947, the township trustees may annually levy a tax of up to one mill to maintain the library and procure suitable rooms.[70]

(C) No requirement to levy

Although the taxing authorities of the appointing political subdivisions are authorized to levy tax upon the taxable property of the respective districts, irrespective of the library's participation in the proceeds of classified property taxes, the taxing authority is not required to provide by tax levy the full amount certified by the library trustees as needed to maintain and operate the library.[71]

34.16 Ten-mill limitation, special levies

(A) Special levy within ten-mill limitation

A special levy within the ten-mill limitation for library purposes of a subdivision is authorized without a vote of the people, but the levy must be within other statutory authorizations and is subject to the control of the county budget commission.[72] This type of levy is very uncommon since it either has to utilize millage not being levied by any other subdivision or be deducted from the school district's inside millage.

(B) Property tax in excess of ten-mill limitation

The taxing authority of any subdivision, by vote of two-thirds of all the members of the authority, may at any time declare by resolution that the taxes which may be raised within the ten-mill limitation will not be enough to provide for the necessary requirements of the subdivision and that it is necessary to levy a tax in excess of the ten-mill limitation for a public library supported by that subdivision.[73]

---

[65] RC 5705.28.
[66] RC 5705.32. See also OAG 92-028.
[67] RC 3375.17.
[68] RC 3375.23.
[69] RC 3375.07.
[70] RC 3375.09.
[71] 1947 OAG 2148.
[72] RC 5705.06.
[73] RC 5705.19.

A special levy for library purposes must be submitted by the board of education to a vote of the electors of the school district if requested by the library trustees of a school district public library.[74] The levy may be in effect for any specified number of years or for a continuing period as stated in the resolution. This is the most common type of levy submitted by school district libraries. Also, a board may submit to the electors of a district a tax levy in excess of the ten-mill limitation for library purposes.[75]

34.17 Bond issues

Library trustees of a school district public library may request the board of education to place a bond issue on the ballot for consideration by the electors of the school district.[76] If so requested, the board must submit the question to the electors.[77] The ballot form is prescribed by law.[78] After approval by the voters and issuance of the bonds by the board, the proceeds are delivered to the library trustees for the acquisition and construction of permanent improvements in accordance with the purpose stated on the ballot.[79]

A board of education that does not have a school district public library is also authorized to assist any library by issuing bonds for the purpose of purchasing, constructing, improving, and furnishing library facilities, and acquiring real estate and interests in real estate.[80]

---

[74] RC 5705.23.
[75] RC 5705.19(D), RC 5705.21; OAG 84-083.
[76] RC 3375.43.
[77] OAG 88-013.
[78] RC 133.18(F)(1)(b).
[79] RC 3375.43.
[80] RC 3375.431.

Chapter 35
School Supplies and Food Service

SUPPLIES
- 35.01 Purchase of school supplies
- 35.02 Charging pupils for items other than textbooks
- 35.03 Vending machines, use of proceeds

FOOD SERVICES
- 35.04 Operation of food service by school district
- 35.05 Cooperative food service operations among districts
- 35.06 Sanitation and safety of food service operations
- 35.07 Breakfast and lunch programs

SUPPLIES

35.01 Purchase of school supplies

The board of education of any school district, except a county school district, may purchase books, supplies, and equipment necessary to pupil instruction and administration of the schools.[1]

The board of a county school district may provide supplies and equipment for special education and driver training programs and for the county superintendent's use in furthering the district's instructional program.[2]

35.02 Charging pupils for items other than textbooks

(A) Authority of board

Except for textbooks, which must be furnished free of charge, a board may prescribe fees for instructional materials and enforce payment by withholding grades and credits of pupils who fail to pay. Exceptions may be made for students in serious financial need, and must be made for students who receive aid under RC Chapter 5107, Aid to Dependent Children, or RC Chapter 5115, Disability Assistance. Such exceptions need only be provided for materials needed for the student to participate fully in a course of instruction, but not for materials needed to participate in extracurricular activities or in a pupil enrichment program that is not part of a course of instruction.[3] The Ohio Supreme Court has emphasized that the authorization of fees in RC 3313.642 is contrary to the general rule of a free education and must be construed narrowly. Thus, the Court rejected a board's attempt to assess a per pupil fee, enforced by withholding grades and credits, to defray the cost of administrative supplies as opposed to instructional materials.[4]

A board may elect to furnish, or not furnish, free of charge, supplies or materials needed for home economics, industrial arts, or vocational training courses, except that if a completed project is taken home, the pupil should be charged for materials used.[5]

An appeals court has held that a board may require students who drive to school and park on school property to obtain a parking permit for which a fee is charged.[6] A board may also charge for participation in extracurricular activities.[7]

(B) Sales by school, use of proceeds for school purposes

A board of education, principal, teacher, or class organization may not sell or supervise the sale for profit of uniform school supplies, foods, candies, or similar items on school premises, unless the profit is to be used for school purposes. The state board of education enforces this provision.[8]

---

[1] RC 3313.37, RC 3315.07, RC Ch 3329.
[2] RC 3313.37, RC 3315.06.
[3] RC 3313.642. See Text 23.05, Failure to pay activity or school fees.
[4] Association for Defense of Washington Local School Dist v Kiger, 42 OS(3d) 116, 537 NE(2d) 1292 (1989).
[5] OAG 65-089.
[6] Picklesimer v Southwestern City Bd of Ed, No. 80 AP-195 (10th Dist Ct App, Franklin, 9-30-80). But see OAG 74-063, wherein the attorney general concluded a board may charge students and others a fee for parking on school property for school functions (such as athletic events and graduation exercises) but may not charge such a fee to students who are attending classes.
[7] OAG 82-014. See Text 43.25, Student activities fund.
[8] RC 3313.811. See Text 23.03, Student activity programs, fees, and funds; Text 23.04, Expenditures from student activity funds; Text 30.10(C), Other sources of

(C) Sales by activity groups, accounting for proceeds, pupil activity fund

Activity groups may sell uniform school supplies with board authorization. All income and expenses must be handled through the group or activity account, and profits may be used for school purposes that fall within the rules of the board.[9] If more than $50 annually is received, the board must establish a student activity fund and adopt rules for its administration.[10] Moneys in the fund are "public funds" and may be disbursed only upon board appropriation and determination that the expenditures will serve a proper public purpose.[11]

(D) Revolving account for purchase and sale of supplies

A board is required to provide revolving accounts for the purchase and sale to pupils of uniform school supplies either by appropriation from the general fund or accumulation from sales and receipts. Those accounts are to be kept separate from other transactions.[12]

(E) Sales tax

When the board requires pupils to pay for uniform school supplies, it is exempt from the Ohio sales tax if the transactions are not for profit.[13] RC 5739.02 specifically exempts from the sales tax sales to and occasional sales by parent-teacher associations, booster groups, or similar organizations primarily engaged in promoting and supporting curricular or extracurricular school activities.

35.03 Vending machines, use of proceeds

A board of education may purchase and install vending machines that dispense uniform school supplies, food, candy, or refreshments. Profits from board-installed machines must be deposited in the uniform school supply fund or the lunchroom fund. If a class organization sponsors the installation, profits must be applied to some school purpose for the benefit of all pupils.[14]

FOOD SERVICES

35.04 Operation of food service by school district

(A) In general

A board of any school district, except the governing board of an educational service center, may establish a food service operation to prepare and serve meals or refreshments to pupils, employees, and other persons taking part in or patronizing any school activity.[15] A board may provide free lunches to teaching employees at the school cafeteria.[16] Any restrictions on the use of facilities must be applied equally to all pupils, all employees, or all persons taking part in or patronizing a school activity, respectively, except the board may expend school funds other than funds from federally reimbursed moneys or student payments to provide free meals to senior citizens performing volunteer services in accordance with a board approved volunteer program. The facilities must be managed and controlled by the board, and not operated for profit.[17] RC 5739.02 specifically exempts from the Ohio sales tax sales of food to students in a cafeteria maintained by a school.

(B) Meals for the elderly

The food service operation may provide meals at cost to district residents who are sixty or older and may contract for such service with nonprofit organizations that provide services to the elderly.[18] Records of the program must be separately maintained.

(C) Use of facilities by outside groups

A board may allow the PTA or other outside groups to use the lunchroom if the group pays for the food and does its own serving.[19]

---

funding, pupil activity fund; Text 43.25, Student activities fund.

[9] 1964 OAG 1285.
[10] RC 3315.062.
[11] OAG 86-013.
[12] RC 3313.811.
[13] RC Ch 5739; 1935 OAG 4617.

[14] RC 3313.811; 1964 OAG 1285.
[15] RC 3313.81.
[16] OAG 81-052.
[17] RC 3313.81.
[18] RC 3313.81.
[19] 1938 OAG 3486.

35.05 Cooperative food service operations among districts

A board may provide food service to one or more school districts on a contract basis. Two or more boards may establish a central kitchen to provide food service to schools within the districts. Boards of education may also form cooperatives and establish revolving accounts for purchasing food, supplies, and equipment used in food service operations.[20]

35.06 Sanitation and safety of food service operations

A food service operation cannot be operated without a license, which must be displayed at the licensed location.[21] Boards of health of cities or general health districts regularly inspect food service operations pursuant to RC 3732.08. A license may be suspended or revoked in accordance with RC 3732.11. A failure to comply with any provision of RC Chapter 3732 is a criminal offense.[22]

35.07 Breakfast and lunch programs

Pursuant to RC 3313.813, the state board of education requires the board of each school district to maintain a school breakfast and lunch program under the federal National School Lunch and Child Nutrition Acts.[23] The requirements are as follows:

(1) A board must establish a breakfast program in every school where at least one-third of the pupils are eligible for free breakfasts and a lunch program in every school where one-third are eligible for free lunches; and

(2) A board must establish a breakfast program in every school where the parents of at least one-half of the children enrolled have requested that a breakfast program be established.

Any board required to establish a program under (2) may charge for meals to cover all or part of the costs. If a board cannot for good cause comply with these requirements at the time the state board determines the district is subject to them, the state board may grant a reasonable extension of time.[24]

Each board must adopt and enforce standards for the types of foods sold on school premises and specify the time and place each type may be sold. The state board is required to adopt guidelines that local boards may follow.[25]

---

[20] RC 3313.812.

[21] RC 3732.03. "Food service operation" is defined by RC 3732.01 as any area where food intended to be served in individual portions is prepared or served for a charge or required donation. Among other listed exclusions from the definition are schools preparing or serving food intended for individual portion service on their premises for not more than seven consecutive days or twelve separate days during an annual licensing period (March through February). Certain vending machine locations are also excluded.

[22] RC 3732.99.

[23] The federal Acts were amended to comply with the Healthy Meals for Healthy Americans Act of 1994. PL 103-448. School meals must comply with new federal dietary guidelines by the 1996-97 school year, unless a waiver not to exceed two years is authorized by the state agency. 42 USCA 1751 et seq. and 42 USCA 1771 et seq. See also 7 CFR 210, 7 CFR 220; Text 23.07(A), Free meals.

[24] RC 3313.813.

[25] RC 3313.814.

Chapter 36

Acquiring and Disposing of Property

ACQUIRING PROPERTY
36.01 Authority of school board to deal with property
36.02 Purchase of real property
36.03 Eminent domain and appropriation of real property
36.04 Purchase of personal property
36.05 Lease, trade, or exchange of real or personal property
36.06 Acquisition of property by gift, devise, or bequest
36.07 Acquisition of property by educational service centers
36.08 Joint acquisition of property

DISPOSING OF SCHOOL PROPERTY
36.09 Power to dispose of property
36.10 Lease of property
36.11 Sale of real or personal property
36.12 Granting option to purchase
36.13 Gift of school property prohibited
36.14 Use of sale proceeds and rentals

ACQUIRING PROPERTY

36.01 Authority of school board to deal with property

Boards of education may acquire and possess real and personal property.[1] They may acquire property by purchase, lease, or grant,[2] by lease-purchase,[3] by gift, devise, or bequest,[4] by exchange,[5] by appropriation,[6] by dedication,[7] and by adverse possession.[8] Property acquired is held in a fiduciary capacity and must be used for school purposes.[9]

36.02 Purchase of real property

(A) In general

The board of education of any school district, except a county school district, may purchase or lease real property and interests in real property for school sites and playgrounds, either within or outside the district, and may purchase or lease-purchase buildings for any school district purpose.[10] A board may select sites it considers most suitable at the time,[11] and courts will not interfere absent an abuse of discretion or failure to act in good faith.[12]

(B) Incidental costs, terms of purchase

A board has implied authority to pay incidental costs incurred in acquiring real property, including real estate broker's fees and expert appraisal fees.[13]

The purchase price of land may be paid in "cash, by installment payments, with or without a mortgage, by entering into lease-purchase agreements or by leasing property with an option to purchase."[14] However, the authority to make deferred payments is strictly limited.[15] Payments may not extend over more than five years, and future payments must be provided for by a special tax levy approved by school district electors.[16] These provisions do not limit a board's authority to issue bonds and notes for the purchase of real property under RC Chapter 133.[17]

Prior to the enactment of RC 3313.375, the attorney general had determined a board of education is without authority to

---

[1] RC 3313.17.
[2] RC 3313.17, RC 3313.37.
[3] RC 3313.375.
[4] RC 3313.36, RC 3313.37.
[5] RC 3313.40, RC 3313.41.
[6] RC 3313.37, RC 3313.39.
[7] RC 721.18.
[8] Wapakoneta Bd of Ed v Unknown Heirs of Aughinbaugh, 99 App 463, 134 NE(2d) 872 (Auglaize 1955).
[9] Weir v Day, 35 OS 143 (1878); OAG 79-043.

[10] RC 3313.37, RC 3313.375.
[11] RC 3313.37. The statute also authorizes the rental of schoolrooms.
[12] State ex rel Clarke v Jefferson Twp Rural School Dist Bd of Ed, 11 App 146, 30 CC(NS) 365 (Clinton 1919); 1956 OAG 6451; 1931 OAG 3087.
[13] 1956 OAG 7225.
[14] RC 3313.37(B)(2).
[15] RC 3313.37(B)(2).
[16] RC 3313.37; 1964 OAG 1522.
[17] See Text Ch 41, Borrowing Money.

purchase a building under a lease-purchase agreement.[18]

Boards of education (except governing boards of educational service centers) may acquire federal land either at its fair market value or at a discount by lease-purchase agreement, gift, grant, or otherwise.[19]

(C) Option to purchase

A board may also enter into an option agreement for the purchase of land. This power is implied from the greater power to acquire property.[20]

36.03 Eminent domain and appropriation of real property

Boards of education have the power of eminent domain. A board may appropriate real property within the territorial limits of its school district, but only in accordance with RC Chapter 163, and only when necessary to obtain or enlarge sites to be used for any of the following purposes:

(1) Buildings used for public school purposes (classrooms, an auditorium, or for technical training, administrative, storage, or other educational purposes);

(2) Agricultural purposes, athletic fields, or playgrounds;

(3) Housing for teachers, when the cost of erecting the buildings has been contributed by private donations; or

(4) Sewage disposal facilities for school buildings or grounds.[21]

A board has no authority to appropriate real property outside of the school district,[22] or to appropriate real property for any purpose other than those listed above.[23]

36.04 Purchase of personal property

(A) In general

Boards of education, except governing boards of educational service centers, may "furnish" schools and "provide the necessary apparatus and make all other necessary provisions" for the schools under its control.[24] In addition, these boards may purchase, among other items, school buses,[25] other motor vehicles,[26] and schoolbooks.[27]

(B) Competitive bidding

Generally, boards of education have discretion in determining whether to follow competitive bidding procedures in the purchase of supplies. While recognizing this discretion, the state auditor recommends that competitive bidding procedures be followed. Boards of education must follow competitive bidding procedures in improving school property including the purchase of office equipment and a telephone system where the cost exceeds the $25,000 threshold specified in RC 3313.46.[28]

The competitive bidding requirement of RC 3313.46 is expressly qualified by RC 125.04 and RC 713.23. RC 125.04(A) authorizes the department of administrative services to determine what supplies, equipment, and services required by elective and appointive state officers, boards, and commissions shall be purchased and furnished for their use. RC 125.04(B) then authorizes the department to permit a school district to participate in contracts the department enters into "for the purchase of supplies, services, material other than printing materials, and equipment."

Any school district desiring to participate in such purchase contracts must file with the department a certified copy of a resolution of its board of education requesting that the district be authorized to participate and agreeing that the district will be bound by such terms and conditions as the department prescribes and that the district will pay the vendor under each purchase contract. The department may

---

[18]OAG 86-031.

[19]RC 9.26, RC 3313.37(B)(4).

[20]Stanley v Like, 90 Abs 587, 190 NE(2d) 697 (CP, Scioto 1962).

[21]RC 3313.39.

[22]Sterkel v Mansfield Bd of Ed, 172 OS 231, 175 NE(2d) 64 (1961).

[23]OAG 69-006.

[24]RC 3313.37.

[25]RC 3327.08.

[26]RC 3313.172.

[27]RC Ch 3329.

[28]OAG 90-085; OAG 84-046. For extended treatment of RC 3313.46 advertising and bidding requirements, see Text 37.04 to 37.06.

charge the district a reasonable fee to cover administrative costs.

Purchases under RC 125.04 are exempt from any competitive bidding required by law for the purchase of supplies, services, materials, and equipment. A district is prohibited from making any purchase under the statute when bids have been received unless the purchase can be made at a lower price under the statute. The department may require participating school districts to file a report as often as the department finds it necessary stating how many such contracts school districts participate in within a specified period and such other information as the department requires. RC 713.23(D) contains similar provisions under which a political subdivision, such as a school district, can participate without competitive bidding in purchase contracts of a regional planning commission for supplies, services, materials, and equipment on behalf of political subdivisions.

If a board determines that personal property can be obtained from the federal government at prices less than could be had by taking bids from private persons, it has express authority to purchase the property directly without taking bids.[29]

Boards of education must follow RC 3313.46 and RC 3327.08 advertising and bidding procedures in the purchase of school buses.[30]

(C) Specific property or equipment

(1) Office equipment

Boards of education and governing boards of educational service centers may acquire necessary office equipment and computer hardware and software for instructional purposes by purchase, lease, or installment payments, by entering into lease-purchase agreements, or by leasing the equipment with an option to purchase.[31] "Office equipment" includes without limitation typewriters, copying and duplicating equipment, and computer and data processing equipment.[32] Contracts for the acquisition of office equipment and computer hardware and software for instructional purposes may be considered to be "continuing contracts" under RC 5705.41 if the purchase price is to be paid over a period of time.[33] Payments under any of the types of purchase plans listed in RC 3313.37(B)(5), which may be made from operating funds, may not extend beyond five years. Any proposed purchase plan should be carefully structured to avoid improper incurrence of "debt" by the board. RC 3313.371 provides that a county board may borrow money to purchase computer equipment subject to terms and conditions agreed to by the board and the lender.

(2) Energy conservation measures

Boards of education (except governing boards of educational service centers) may enter into installment payment contracts for the purchase and installation of certain energy conservation measures.[34] These include insulation, storm windows and coatings that reduce energy consumption, automatic energy control systems, heating, ventilating, and air conditioning system modifications, caulking and weatherstripping, certain energy-saving lighting modifications, energy recovery systems, cogeneration systems, and other conservation measures approved by the state department of education.[35] Generally, a board must follow RC 3313.46 advertising and bidding procedures, unless the board waives those requirements by vote of at least two-thirds of its members. Any provisions of these contracts relating to interest and financing terms must comply with specific requirements in RC 3313.372 but are not subject to the advertising and bidding requirements of RC 3313.46.

Any such contract must require that the board pay not less than one-tenth of the costs within two years, and the remaining balance within ten years, from the date of purchase.[36] Boards of education may issue notes to secure the installment payments

---

[29] RC 9.25.
[30] OAG 70-105.
[31] RC 3313.37(B)(5). RC 3313.46 expressly exempts the acquisition under RC 3313.37(B)(5) of computer hardware for instructional purposes and computer software for instructional purposes from competitive bidding requirements.

[32] RC 3313.37(B)(5).
[33] RC 3313.37(B)(5).
[34] RC 3313.372(B).
[35] RC 3313.372(A).
[36] RC 3313.372(B).

and apply revenues from local taxes or otherwise for the purpose of conserving energy or paying current expenses to pay interest and retire the notes. The notes may be sold at private sale or given as consideration for the contract and are not to be included in calculating district net indebtedness under RC 133.04.

Boards of education (except governing boards of educational service centers) may also enter into shared-savings contracts with any person experienced in the design and implementation of certain "energy saving measures" for buildings owned or rented by the board without complying with the advertising and bidding requirements of RC 3313.46.[37] "Energy saving measures" include the acquisition and installation by purchase, lease, lease-purchase, lease with option to buy, or installment purchase of an "energy conservation measure" and any attendant architectural and engineering consulting services related to energy conservation.[38] A "shared-savings contract" is generally a contract for one or more energy saving measures which provides that all payments, except payments for maintenance and repairs and obligations on termination of the contract prior to its expiration, are to be a stated percentage of calculated savings of energy costs attributable to the energy saving measure over a defined period of time and are to be made only to the extent that such savings occur.[39] A contract that requires any additional capital investment or contribution of funds, other than funds available from state or federal energy grants, or that is for an initial term of longer than ten years is not a shared-savings contract.[40] Shared-savings contracts for purchase of energy saving measures are considered "continuing contracts" under RC 5705.41.[41]

These provisions do not limit a board's authority to issue bonds and notes for the purchase of personal property constituting "permanent improvements" pursuant to RC Chapter 133.[42]

(3) School buses

The purchase of school buses must be competitively bid in accordance with RC 3313.46 and all bids must state that upon delivery the buses will comply with all applicable safety regulations.[43]

(4) Other personal property

A board of education may not enter into installment purchase or lease-purchase agreements in connection with the acquisition of other personal property, such as musical instruments[44] or portable buildings to be used as classrooms.[45]

36.05 Lease, trade, or exchange of real or personal property

(A) Lease

Boards of education, except county district boards, may lease sites for schoolhouses, suitable schoolrooms, and real estate for playgrounds.[46] This authority includes the power to lease suitable buildings to be used for school purposes.[47] A lease of real property may extend for a "reasonable time" and is considered a "continuing contract" under RC 5705.41, provided it is not coupled with a firm contract to purchase the property.[48] Incidental to leasing real property, a board may make reasonable repairs and alterations to make the property suitable for school purposes.[49]

Under RC 3313.37, a board may also lease personal property to provide necessary apparatus for the operation of its schools,[50] such as office equipment[51] or musical instruments.[52]

(B) Trade or exchange

A board may trade an item of personal property, as a part or all of the consideration for the purchase of an item of similar

---

[37] RC 3313.373(B).
[38] RC 3313.373(A).
[39] RC 3313.373(A).
[40] RC 3313.373(A)(2).
[41] RC 3313.373(B).
[42] See Text Ch 41, Borrowing Money.
[43] RC 3327.08. See also Text 22.09, Purchase of school buses.
[44] OAG 65-030.
[45] 1963 OAG 501.
[46] RC 3313.37.
[47] 1958 OAG 1604.
[48] 1958 OAG 1604; 1960 OAG 1304.
[49] 1947 OAG 1672.
[50] RC 3313.37.
[51] RC 3313.37(B)(5).
[52] OAG 65-030.

personal property, on terms and conditions agreed by the parties to the trade.[53]

A board's authority to trade real property is more limited. Under RC 3313.40, a board may exchange real property only with a municipal corporation and only if the exchange is "mutually beneficial."

36.06 Acquisition of property by gift, devise, or bequest

A board of education may accept a grant, devise, gift, endowment, or bequest of real property on certain conditions or stipulations, provided they do not interfere with the board's control of the public schools.[54] If a gift of the use of real property for a limited time is made, the board may spend funds necessary to temporarily repair or convert the property to use for school purposes.[55]

A board may accept any donation or bequest of money or other personal property that it will hold in trust for the use and benefit of the school district.[56] For example, a board may accept a donation of money made on condition that it be used to purchase equipment for interscholastic athletics.[57]

36.07 Acquisition of property by educational service centers

A governing board of an educational service center may purchase or lease real estate and suitable facilities for conducting special education and driver education programs and may "furnish" these facilities and provide "the necessary apparatus" for them.[58]

Except as provided in RC 3313.37(B)(5) with respect to office equipment and computer hardware and software for instructional purposes,[59] and RC 3313.371 with respect to computer equipment, a governing board may not enter into installment or lease-purchase agreements when acquiring property.[60]

A board of county commissioners is required by RC 3319.19 to provide and equip offices for the educational service center and its staff.[61]

36.08 Joint acquisition of property

Subject to approval of the state superintendent of public instruction, the boards of any two or more school districts may enter into agreements for the joint or cooperative acquisition of any building, structure, or facility, together with furniture, furnishings and equipment, and real estate and interests in real estate.[62] Any such agreement must meet requirements given in RC 3313.92(B) or RC Chapter 167.

DISPOSING OF SCHOOL PROPERTY

36.09 Power to dispose of property

Among the powers of a board of education specified in RC 3313.17 is the power to "dispose" of real and personal property. RC 3313.40 and RC 3313.41 implement this general authority. RC 3313.40 allows a board to "exchange" real property with municipal corporations, and RC 3313.41 provides specific authority and procedures for the sale of real and personal property.

While RC 3313.75 to RC 3313.78 authorize a board to make its real property available for the temporary use of others for certain purposes when it is not in actual use for school purposes, and to charge a reasonable fee for such use,[63] there is no express authority for a board to lease real property (apart from mineral rights) over a substantial period of time. In general, the authority to lease is implied, under certain

---

[53] RC 3313.41(D).
[54] RC 3313.17, RC 3313.36(A).
[55] 1961 OAG 2658.
[56] RC 3313.17, RC 3313.36.
[57] 1962 OAG 3246.
[58] RC 3313.37.
[59] See Text 36.04, Purchase of personal property.

[60] RC 3313.37.
[61] See Text 7.08, Educational service center superintendent's offices and equipment.
[62] RC Ch 167, RC 3313.92.
[63] For a discussion of temporary use of board property by others, see Text Ch 38, Management and Use of School Property.

circumstances, from a board's authority to sell property.

36.10 Lease of property

(A) In general

The lease by a board of eduction of real property to a private party does not violate Ohio's Constitution where the lease does not effect a union of private and public property. A board thus may lease real property not presently needed for school purposes and which cannot be advantageously sold, provided the lease permits the board to terminate the arrangement upon a determination that the property is needed for school purposes. Such a lease may provide for automatic renewal solely at the option of the lessee if the board determines, prior to execution, that the lease (including its renewal periods) will be advantageous to the school district and that the property is not anticipated to be needed for school use.[64]

(B) Mineral leases

A board may enter into contracts or leases to mine iron ore, stone, coal, petroleum, gas, salt, or other minerals located on school property, on such terms and conditions as the board determines.[65] These contracts and leases (except those for exploration for and production of petroleum or gas) may be for terms not exceeding fifteen years and must provide for the payment of rents or royalties to the board at least annually.[66]

Under certain circumstances a board may also employ a geologist to report on the feasibility of exploring for petroleum and gas on board property and, by two-thirds vote of all members, may appropriate funds and enter into contracts with others to investigate, explore, prospect, or drill for petroleum and gas and their constituent components and mineral by-products. Thereafter, the board may also appropriate funds and enter into contracts with others to extract, produce, sell, use, or transport those items.[67]

36.11 Sale of real or personal property

(A) In general

Pursuant to RC 3313.17 and RC 3313.41, boards of education may sell real and personal property. Strict procedural requirements apply to a sale of school property valued in excess of $10,000, and failure to comply renders a sale and conveyance void.[68] The sale procedures apply even to the sale of a residential dwelling built by students of a joint vocational school district as part of a vocational education program[69] and to the sale of football equipment purchased with funds from a student fund-raising activity.[70] School property with a value of $10,000 or less may be sold under procedures of the individual board. A board may sell real property as an entire tract or divide it into parcels.[71]

(B) Sale procedure

The first requirement under RC 3313.41 is that "a board of education which proposes to sell ... must decide to do so. This is tantamount to saying that it must determine that it has no present or probable future need for the property in question."[72]

The next step is to offer the property for sale at public auction after thirty days' published or posted notice. The notice may be given by publication in a newspaper of general circulation in the school district or by posting in five of the most public places in the district. A board may reserve the right to reject all bids. If the property is at least once offered at public auction and not sold, a board may then sell at a negotiated private sale on such terms as the parties agree, except the sale must be for cash.[73]

A board is not required to follow the auction procedure in selling to certain public bodies. RC 3313.41 authorizes a sale, "upon such terms as are agreed upon," to the adjutant general; any subdivision or taxing authority as defined in RC 5705.01(A) and (C), which includes boards of education; township park district; board of park commissioners established under

---

[64]OAG 92-016.
[65]RC 3313.45.
[66]RC 3313.45.
[67]RC 3313.451.
[68]RC 3313.41; 1934 OAG 2474.

[69]OAG 76-065; OAG 81-092.
[70]OAG 86-062.
[71]RC 3313.41.
[72]1963 OAG 662.
[73]RC 3313.41; 1933 OAG 1027.

RC Chapter 755; park district established under RC Chapter 1545; tax-supported institution of higher education; or board of trustees of a school district library.

In connection with a sale of property, a board may employ an appraiser[74] and an auctioneer. Unless he is a board member, employee, or officer, the auctioneer must be licensed as an auctioneer and real estate broker.[75]

The board president and treasurer are required to execute and deliver all deeds and other necessary conveyances to complete any sale under RC 3313.41.

36.12 Granting option to purchase

Under certain circumstances boards of education may grant options to purchase real or personal property not needed for school purposes. An option may be granted to any public entity with which a board is empowered, pursuant to RC 3313.41(C), to negotiate a private sale. The option must provide that it will terminate upon board determination that the property is needed for school purposes.[76]

36.13 Gift of school property prohibited

A board has no authority to give away property. The attorney general has determined that a board may not turn over a tract of land to a township without consideration.[77] Similarly, the state auditor has advised that a board cannot donate an unused school building to a civic group.[78]

36.14 Use of sale proceeds and rentals

Proceeds from the sale of a "permanent improvement" (any property with an estimated life or usefulness of five years or more, including land) are, in the discretion of the board of education, to be paid into its bond retirement fund or into a special fund for the construction or acquisition of permanent improvements. These proceeds are not to be paid into the general fund.[79] Proceeds from the sale of property that is not a "permanent improvement" are to be paid into the fund from which the property was acquired or maintained; if there is no such fund, proceeds are to be paid into the general fund.[80]

Rental payments received under leases of property by a board to others, as revenue for which no particular purpose is prescribed by law, are to be paid into the general fund.[81]

---

[74] OAG 74-002.
[75] Auditor's Messenger, Winter 1982.
[76] 1953 OAG 2534; 1932 OAG 4588; 1965 Syllabi 59. Syllabi are unpublished determinations made by the Auditor of State's Office from approximately 1945 to 1970. During that time, brief one-sentence references to the determinations had some limited circulation outside the Auditor's Office and were sometimes referenced by the Auditor and others. Although they may not be of precedential value outside of the Auditor's Office, they are often the only authority for the specific proposition for which they are cited and so this reference has been retained.
[77] OAG 83-082.
[78] 1968 Syllabi 16.
[79] RC 5705.10.
[80] RC 5705.10.
[81] RC 5705.10.

Chapter 37

Construction and Repair of School Buildings

CONSTRUCTION AND REPAIR OF BUILDINGS AND FACILITIES
37.01 Authority of school board
37.02 Exemption from zoning fees and building permit fees
37.03 Plans and specifications
37.04 Competitive bidding requirement
37.05 Form of bids, bidder's security for performance
37.06 Examination, acceptance, and rejection of bids
37.07 Costs of construction
37.08 Construction, progress payments
37.09 Construction and maintenance: safety and sanitation standards, supervision and inspection
37.10 Authority to employ construction manager

APPLICATION OF PREVAILING WAGE ACT
37.11 Duty to observe prevailing wage standards in school board projects
37.12 Prevailing wages
37.13 Designating wage coordinator
37.14 Enforcement of the Prevailing Wage Act, penalties and remedies

CONSTRUCTION AND REPAIR OF BUILDINGS AND FACILITIES

37.01 Authority of school board

(A) In general, board discretion

Boards of education (except county boards) may build, enlarge, repair, and improve any schools[1] and other buildings for school purposes, such as a garage for school buses[2] or a bell tower.[3] In addition, with the approval of the superintendent of public instruction, the boards of two or more school districts may agree to act jointly or cooperatively to construct or improve any building, structure, or facility that will benefit all parties.[4] County boards may build, enlarge, repair, and furnish facilities for conducting special education and driver education programs.[5]

Generally, a board's determination of where construction will take place will not be disturbed in the absence of an abuse of discretion.[6] RC 713.02 provides that a board may, by a two-thirds vote of its members, overrule a municipal zoning commission's determination as to proper locations for schools and select sites it deems necessary and proper.[7]

(B) Contracting procedures, building standards

In constructing and improving facilities, a board must follow contracting procedures in RC 3313.46 and certain of the procedures and requirements of RC Chapter 153. Also, RC Chapters 3781 and 3791 and RC 4733.17 prescribe standards of construction and sanitation and safety features that must be met in all public buildings, including schoolhouses.

The board of building standards cannot require alteration or repair of a city, local, exempted village, or joint vocational school district building operated in conjunction with a primary or secondary school program if the building meets all applicable building code requirements in existence when the building was constructed, the part of the building altered or repaired conforms to all building rules in existence when the alteration or repair was made, and the building otherwise satisfies RC 3781.06.[8]

37.02 Exemption from zoning fees and building permit fees

Boards of education are exempt from municipal building permit fees[9] and, as political subdivisions of the state, are also exempt from any municipal zoning fees[10] in locating, acquiring, constructing, and using buildings. In the absence of a specific stat-

---

[1] RC 3313.37.
[2] 1936 OAG 5977.
[3] 1940 OAG 1698.
[4] RC 3313.92.
[5] RC 3313.37.
[6] State ex rel Berry v Board of Education, 11 Abs 254 (App, Adams 1932). Cf. Watkins v Hall, 13 CC 255, 7 CD 434 (Licking 1896), appeal dismissed by 38 WLB 198 (CC, Licking 1897) (abuse of discretion); Robinson v McDonald, 5 App 376, 26 CC(NS) 137 (Coshocton 1916) (no abuse of discretion).
[7] 1956 OAG 6451.
[8] RC 3781.11(A)(5).
[9] 1956 OAG 6326.
[10] 1945 OAG 495.

ute to the contrary, no fee may be charged to a board by a building department for the inspection or approval of plans.[11]

This is not to say boards are exempt from all local regulation. For example, one board was prohibited from contracting for electrical power with a private utility company not franchised to operate in the municipality, where that contract would have interfered substantially with the municipality's power to control public utilities.[12]

37.03 Plans and specifications

(A) Preparation of plans and cost estimates, changes

A board of education must have plans, specifications, and an estimate of cost prepared by a licensed engineer or architect for the construction, repair, enlargement, demolition, or furnishing of a school, or for any improvements or repairs, that will cost in excess of $5,000, unless the board determines other information is sufficient to inform bidders of the board's requirements.[13] If the board makes such a determination, it may not engage in the construction of any project involving the practice of professional engineering, surveying, or architecture for which plans, specifications, and estimates have not been made by, and the construction inspected by, a licensed professional engineer, licensed professional surveyor, or registered architect.[14] Procedures for the selection of professional design services for projects with an estimated design fee of $25,000 or more are specified by RC 153.65 through RC 153.71.

Except in cases of "urgent necessity," if the estimated cost of the project is over $25,000, the board may enter into a contract only after competitive bidding.[15] Notice of any change in the plans and specifications or estimate of cost must be given to persons who have obtained plans and specifications for the project. If the change occurs within seventy-two hours before the published time for opening bids (excluding Saturdays, Sundays, and legal holidays), the time for opening bids must be extended for one week.[16]

(B) Approval by building department

RC 3791.04 and OAC 4101:2 provide that plans, specifications, and data prepared for the construction or improvement of certain buildings, including any building that may be used for public education, must be submitted to the certified municipal, township, or county building department having jurisdiction (or in the absence of a certified department to the chief of the state's division of factory and building inspection) for approval prior to execution of a contract for the project. The plans and specifications will be approved only if the building would, if constructed, repaired, or equipped according to the plans, comply with RC Chapters 3781 and 3791 and rules adopted under those chapters.

The building department may approve, reject, or conditionally approve the project. Construction of any portion of a project that has not been approved may not proceed.

37.04 Competitive bidding requirement

(A) In general

Generally, boards of education are required to follow the competitive bidding procedures in RC 3313.46 when letting contracts to build, repair, enlarge, improve, or demolish any school building. For example, contracts for painting and for the purchase and installation of a telephone system have been deemed contracts for repairs or improvements under RC 3313.46.[17]

The state auditor maintains that lease-purchase arrangements are subject to competitive bidding under the statute,[18] and has even suggested, in what strikes some

---

[11] 1965 Inf OAG 100.
[12] Lucas v Lucas Local School Dist, 2 OS(3d) 13, 2 OBR 501, 442 NE(2d) 449 (1982).
[13] RC 153.01(A), RC 3313.46(A)(1), RC 4733.17.
[14] RC 3313.46(A)(1).
[15] RC 3313.46. See Text 37.04, Competitive bidding requirement.
[16] RC 153.12.
[17] State ex rel Kuhn v Smith, 92 Abs 527, 194 NE(2d) 186 (CP, Monroe 1963) (painting); OAG 84-046 (telephone system). For additional discussion of the scope of RC 3313.46, see Text 36.04, Purchase of personal property.
[18] Audit Bulletins 89-003, 89-004.

observers as a case of overreaching, that true leases are covered as well.[19] This issue awaits further clarification.

RC 3313.46 expressly exempts the acquisition of computer hardware for instructional purposes and computer software for instructional purposes under RC 3313.37(B)(5) from the competitive bidding requirements of the statute. In addition, the statute exempts the acquisition of educational materials used in teaching and, if determined by a two-thirds vote of all board of education members, items available only from a single source and energy conservation measures undertaken pursuant to RC 3313.372.

(B) Procedure

The competitive bidding procedures are calculated to preserve the integrity of public contracts and are strictly construed and enforced by the courts.[20] These procedures include the following:

(1) Public advertising for bids once each week for four consecutive weeks by placing a notice in a newspaper of general circulation in the school district;

(2) Unless the board extends the time, opening of bids at the time and place specified in the notice;

(3) Consideration of only those bids that meet statutory and board requirements, including requirements that the bid contain the name of every person interested in it and be accompanied by an appropriate bid guaranty; and

(4) Acceptance by the board of only the lowest responsible bid.[21] If each of two bids is the lowest responsible bid, either may be accepted. The work may not be split between the two lowest bidders.

Implicit in the competitive bidding procedure is the requirement that all bidders bid on the same plans, specifications, and estimates of cost.[22] Customarily, an advertisement for bids will recite that the plans, specifications, and estimates are on file in the administrative offices of the board.

(C) Exceptions to competitive bidding requirements

There are two instances (other than those discussed at the beginning of this section) in which boards are not required to let such contracts by competitive bidding:

(1) When a board declares an "urgent necessity" or that a contract is necessary for "the security and protection of school property"; or

(2) When the dollar amount of the contract does not exceed $25,000.[23]

A board's declaration of "urgent necessity" must be adequately supported by the facts and circumstances.[24]

Any attempt to divide projects piecemeal to avoid bidding requirements is improper.[25]

37.05 Form of bids, bidder's security for performance

Bids for the construction, alteration, repair, demolition, or reconstruction of an improvement must include the name of every person interested in them and must be accompanied by a bid bond for the full amount of the bid or by a certified check, cashier's check, or letter of credit in an amount equal to ten per cent of the bid.[26]

When the work bid upon includes both labor and materials, a board may require labor and materials to be listed separately in each bid, with the price of each specified, or alternatively may require that each bid be submitted without such separation.[27] A board must require separate proposals for each separate trade or kind of mechani-

---

[19]Audit Bulletin 89-008.

[20]Chillicothe City School Dist Bd of Ed v Sever-Williams Co, 22 OS(2d) 107, 258 NE(2d) 605 (1970), cert denied 400 US 916, 91 SCt 175, 27 LEd(2d) 155 (1970); H.R. Johnson Construction Co v Painesville Twp Local School Dist Bd of Ed, 16 Misc 99, 241 NE(2d) 403 (CP, Lake 1968).

[21]For the meaning of "responsible bid," see Text 37.06(A), In general.

[22]1929 OAG 605.

[23]RC 3313.46.

[24]Mueller v Board of Education, 11 NP(NS) 113, 25 D 195 (CP, Hamilton 1911); Bolce v Cincinnati School Dist Bd of Ed, 22 Abs 363 (CP, Hamilton 1934).

[25]State ex rel Kuhn v Smith, 92 Abs 527, 194 NE(2d) 186 (CP, Monroe 1963).

[26]RC 153.54, RC 3313.46.

[27]RC 153.50, RC 3313.46.

cal labor, business, or employment entering into an improvement.[28]

It is important that the forms of bids received be closely examined. A board is without authority to award a contract to a bidder who does not meet the board's formal bid requirements.[29]

37.06 Examination, acceptance, and rejection of bids

(A) In general

(1) RC 3313.46 requirements

A board of education may consider all timely bids that are in proper form, and only the "lowest responsible" bid may be accepted. Boards may accept "any bid for both labor and material for [the] improvement or repair, which is the lowest in the aggregate."[30]

In accepting a bid, a board must determine the bid to be *responsible* and to be the lowest responsible bid.[31] A board may in its discretion evaluate the responsibility of bidders and may base its determination on the character of work done by the bidder on other contracts.[32] However, a determination of responsibility may not be made solely on the basis that the bidder has not previously performed work for the board.[33] A bid that is not reasonably definite may be rejected even if it appears to be the lowest.[34] When a board specifically designated the type of roofing system on which bids were to be taken in connection with putting a new roof on a high school, it was free to reject a low bid that involved a different system.[35]

A board may also reject any or all bids. If there is "reason to believe there is collusion or combination among the bidders, or any number of them," the bids of all involved must be rejected.[36] In addition, a board must reject all bids which are not responsible.[37]

A board cannot enter into an improvement contract if the price of the contract or (if the project involves multiple contracts) the aggregate cost of all the contracts is more than ten per cent greater than the cost estimate in the plans and specifications.[38] In making this determination, costs and contracts for construction management services are not considered.[39]

(2) The RC 9.312 option

RC 9.312 expressly authorizes, but does not require, a school district (or any other political subdivision required to award contracts by competitive bidding) to adopt a policy[40] requiring that each competitively bid contract be awarded to the "lowest responsive and responsible bidder" within the meaning of the statute. A bidder "shall be considered responsive if his proposal responds to bid specifications in all material respects and contains no irregularities or deviations from the specifications which would affect the amount of the bid or otherwise give him a competitive advantage."[41] In determining whether a bidder is "responsible," factors that must be considered include "the experience of the bidder, his financial condition, his conduct and

---

[28] RC 153.50.

[29] Mulcahy v Board of Education, 25 NP(NS) 355 (CP, Summit 1925).

[30] RC 3313.46(G). A court is not entitled simply to substitute its judgment for that of the board as to which is the lowest responsible bidder, since the board is presumed to have properly performed its duty. Knowlton Construction Co v Olentangy Local School Bd of Ed, No. 92CA-H-03-014, 1992 WL 195413 (5th Dist Ct App, Delaware, 7-28-92) (rejecting unsuccessful bidder's claim that successful bidder's bid not responsible because of alleged underestimate in quantity of brick needed for project).

[31] OAG 70-105.

[32] Hudson v Wheelersburg Rural School Dist Bd of Ed, 41 App 402, 179 NE 701 (Scioto 1931).

[33] OAG 70-105.

[34] Graphic Enterprises of Ohio, Inc v Akron City School Dist Bd of Ed, Nos. 13269, 13274, 1988 WL 63941 (9th Dist Ct App, Summit, 6-15-88) (proper to reject apparently low bid when bidder's addendum suggested price adjustments over life of contract dependent on future economic conditions might be needed).

[35] State ex rel Bri-Den Co, Inc v Union Scioto Schools Bd of Ed, No. 1543, 1990 WL 34363 (4th Dist Ct App, Ross, 3-7-90).

[36] RC 3313.46(J).

[37] OAG 70-105.

[38] RC 153.12.

[39] Chaney v Lordstown, 21 App(3d) 73, 21 OBR 77, 486 NE(2d) 233 (Trumbull 1984). See also Text 37.01, Authority of school board.

[40] In the case of a school district, the policy is to be adopted by resolution. RC 9.312(C).

[41] RC 9.312(A).

performance on previous contracts, his facilities, his management skills, and his ability to execute the contract properly."[42]

An apparent low bidder found not responsive and responsible must be notified in writing, by certified mail, of that finding and the reasons for it.[43] If, within five days of such notification, the rejected bidder files a written protest, the district must meet with the bidder and is prohibited from making a final award until its earlier determination is either affirmed or reversed.[44]

(B) Award of contract, performance bonds, notice to surety on performance bonds

The award and execution of a competitively bid improvement contract must take place within sixty days after the opening of bids, unless that period is extended by agreement with the party to whom the contract is awarded. Absent an extension, a failure to award and execute within sixty days invalidates the entire bid proceedings.[45] If the time is extended, the board may be required to issue a change order for costs of delay.[46]

Before entering into a competitively bid contract, the treasurer must obtain a statement from the successful bidder stating whether that bidder has paid all personal property taxes owed. If the bidder indicates payments are delinquent, the treasurer must furnish a copy of the statement to the county auditor within thirty days.[47]

The treasurer must also obtain a performance bond for the full amount of the contract securing the performance of the contract and indemnifying the board.[48]

Simultaneously with the award of a contract for the construction, demolition, alteration, repair, or reconstruction of an improvement, a board of education should notify the surety on the contractor's performance bond and the surety's agent who signed the bond of the award. The board, in its sole discretion but only after making certain determinations, may reduce a performance bond by twenty-five percent after fifty percent of the work has been completed satisfactorily and by fifty percent after seventy-five percent of the work has been completed satisfactorily.[49] The board also has authority to reduce in the same manner the bonds on contracts that include labor and material.[50]

37.07 Costs of construction

(A) Availability of funds, certification

At the time a board of education contracts for the construction, rehabilitation, or enlargement of any building or improvement for school purposes, the availability of funds to meet the board's payment obligations must be certified by appropriate board officials.[51] This certification need not be made prior to the board's approval of the contract, but only before or simultaneously with execution of the contract.[52] RC 5705.41 requires only the treasurer's certification, but a court of appeals decision suggests that separate certifications by the treasurer, board president, and the superintendent pursuant to RC 5705.412 may also be required,[53] and a federal district court has suggested that RC 5705.412 supersedes RC 5705.41 for boards of education.[54] Because these decisions may be limited to their particular facts, prudence suggests that these procedures be discussed with the board's legal counsel.[55]

(B) Funds from which payment may be made

Costs of a project may be paid from the board's general fund or permanent

---

[42]RC 9.312(A).
[43]RC 9.312(B).
[44]RC 9.312(B).
[45]RC 153.12.
[46]RC 153.12.
[47]RC 5719.042.
[48]RC 153.54(C).
[49]RC 153.80.
[50]RC 9.313.
[51]RC 5705.41, RC 5705.412.
[52]Hines v Cleveland School Dist Bd of Ed, 26 Misc(2d) 15, 26 OBR 348, 499 NE(2d) 39 (CP, Cuyahoga 1985).

[53]CADO Business Systems of Ohio, Inc v Cleveland City School Dist Bd of Ed, 8 App(3d) 385, 8 OBR 499, 457 NE(2d) 939 (Cuyahoga 1983).
[54]Tri-County North Local School Bd of Ed v McGuire & Shook Corp, 748 FSupp 541 (SD Ohio 1989).
[55]See Text 6.07(C), Certifying availability of money.

improvement fund, from a special fund established for the proceeds of a permanent improvement levy under RC 5705.21 or the proceeds of notes or bonds issued pursuant to RC Chapters 133 or 5705, or from state assistance pursuant to the school facilities law.[56]

37.08 Construction, progress payments

(A) In general, notice to proceed

A contractor, upon request, is entitled to notice to proceed with the project on execution of the contract. If the board or its representative fails to give timely notice, the board may be required to issue a change order for costs of delay.[57]

(B) Mandatory contract provisions on payment

Each construction contract must provide that payments are to be made only after the board receives and approves a detailed estimate of the various kinds of labor performed and materials furnished under the contract, the amounts due for each, and the aggregate amount due.[58] Each estimate and payment voucher is to be retained by the board as part of its records. Payment is to be made within thirty days after board approval.[59]

(C) Progress payments

The unit or lump sum price in a construction contract constitutes full and final compensation for all work performed under the contract.[60] Any partial payment must be based on a schedule apportioning the lump sum price to the major components of work under the contract. This schedule is to be prepared by the contractor and approved by the architect or engineer.[61]

Until a project is fifty per cent complete (as evidenced by payments aggregating at least fifty per cent of the contract price), partial payments for labor are to be made at the rate of ninety-two per cent of the estimates prepared by the contractor and approved by the architect or engineer, and partial payments for materials are to be made at the rate of ninety-two per cent of invoice costs of materials that have been delivered and meet the specifications.[62]

From the date the contract is fifty per cent complete, all funds retained for the performance of work must be deposited in an escrow account with one or more banks or building and loan associations in the state, selected by mutual agreement of the board and contractor.[63] The amount of the retained funds may be reduced by fifty per cent at the discretion of the board for the faithful performance of the work, provided the surety remains liable for any claims against the school district caused by delay in completion of the project or any other additional expenses related to the project incurred by the district.[64] Thereafter, no further funds may be retained except in the case of contracts for less than $15,000.[65]

The retained percentages for labor performed, except for an amount necessary to insure completion, are to be paid to the contractor when the major portion of the project is substantially completed and occupied, or in use, or otherwise accepted and when there is no other reason to withhold payment.[66] The retained percentages of invoice costs of materials are to be paid when the materials are actually incorporated into the project.[67] Any funds remaining in escrow after these payments must be paid to the contractor, with accumulated interest, thirty days from the date of completion, or from acceptance or occupancy of the project by the board.[68]

37.09 Construction and maintenance: safety and sanitation standards, supervision and inspection

Whenever the cost of a proposed building or improvement exceeds $5,000, plans, specifications, and estimates must be pre-

---

[56]RC Ch 3318.
[57]RC 153.12.
[58]RC 153.13.
[59]RC 153.14.
[60]RC 153.12.
[61]RC 153.12.
[62]RC 153.12, RC 153.14.

[63]RC 153.13, RC 153.63.
[64]RC 153.80.
[65]RC 153.13.
[66]RC 153.13.
[67]RC 153.14.
[68]RC 153.13.

pared and the construction supervised by a registered professional authorized to undertake such activities.[69] At every step in the construction and equipping of buildings, boards of education must comply with the construction, sanitation, and safety requirements of the Ohio board of building standards for public buildings.[70] School buildings must be safe and sanitary for all who frequent them.[71] To enforce this requirement, standards and inspections are provided for by the Ohio board of building standards,[72] the Ohio department of health,[73] and the Ohio department of industrial relations.[74]

37.10 Authority to employ construction manager

If the board determines to use a "construction manager"—a person with substantial discretion and authority to manage or direct a project—in connection with the construction, demolition, alteration, repair, or reconstruction of a building or other improvement, it must advertise its intention in a newspaper of general circulation in the county in which the contract is to be performed at least thirty days prior to the date for accepting proposals from interested parties. Publication of the notice in appropriate trade journals is also permitted. The advertisement must include a general description of the project, a statement of the specific services required, and a description of required qualifications.[75] Where the project is estimated to cost more than $5,000,000, procedures set forth in RC 9.332 with respect to the selection of a manager and negotiation of a contract must be followed. Construction managers are required to provide performance security in the form of a letter of credit, surety bond, cashier's check, or certified check in an amount equal to the value of the construction manager's contract, unless the requirement is specifically waived by the board.[76]

APPLICATION OF PREVAILING WAGE ACT

37.11 Duty to observe prevailing wage standards in school board projects

Boards of education, like other public authorities, are subject to the Prevailing Wage Act,[77] which applies to any new construction of any public improvement the total cost of which is fairly estimated to be more than $50,000 adjusted biennially by the Administrator of the Bureau of Employment Services under RC 4115.034, and to any reconstruction, enlargement, alteration, repair, remodeling, renovation, or painting, of any public improvement, the total cost of which is fairly estimated to be more than $15,000 adjusted biennially by the Administrator under RC 4115.034.[78] "Public improvement" includes all buildings and other structures or works constructed by or for a school district. If a board of education rents or leases a newly constructed structure within six months after construction is completed, all work on the structure to suit it for occupancy is also a public improvement.[79] A public improvement project cannot be subdivided into component parts or projects whose cost is less than the $50,000 or $15,000 threshold amounts unless the projects are conceptually separate and unrelated or encompass independent and unrelated needs of the school district.[80]

The Prevailing Wage Act does not apply when work is done by full-time, nonprobationary employees in the classified service of the board of education[81] or vocational education students as part of an approved curriculum.[82] The attorney general has also

---

[69] RC 4733.17, RC 3313.46(A)(1).
[70] RC Ch 3781, RC Ch 3791.
[71] RC 3781.06.
[72] RC Ch 3781, RC Ch 3791.
[73] RC Ch 3703, RC Ch 3707.
[74] RC Ch 4101.
[75] RC 9.331.
[76] RC 9.33(B)(4), RC 9.333, RC 153.54(C)(2), RC 153.57(b).

[77] RC 4115.03 to RC 4115.16, RC 4115.99. Regulations promulgated by the Department under the Act appear at OAC Ch 4101:9-4.
[78] RC 4115.03(B).
[79] RC 4115.03(C).
[80] RC 4115.033.
[81] RC 4115.03(B); OAG 78-035.
[82] OAG 78-033.

determined that maintenance work is excluded.[83]

The Prevailing Wage Act preempts any conflicting local ordinance.[84]

37.12 Prevailing wages

(A) In general

RC 4115.04 requires a board of education to have the Ohio Bureau of Employment Services determine the prevailing wage rate for the class of work involved in the locality where the work is to be performed. This determination must be made before the board advertises for bids or begins construction.[85] The schedule of wages must be attached to project specifications and printed on the bidding blank.[86] A copy of the bidding blank must be filed with the Bureau of Employment Services before any contract is awarded.[87] If the contract is not awarded or construction undertaken within ninety days from establishment of the prevailing rate, a redetermination must be obtained.[88]

(B) Mandatory contract provisions, posting wage rates

The contract between the board and contractor must provide that each laborer, workman, or mechanic employed by the contractor or any subcontractor be paid the prevailing wage rate.[89] A contractor is liable for the underpayment of prevailing wages even if the board fails to include prevailing wage specifications in the contract, although the contractor may maintain an action in contribution where the public authority is culpable.[90] No contractor or subcontractor can sublet any of the work unless specifically authorized to do so by the contract.[91] A contractor can be held liable for his subcontractor's violations.[92] The schedule of wage rates must be posted in a prominent place on the work site during the life of the contract.[93] Upon notice of a change in rates during the life of the contract, the board must notify affected contractors and subcontractors within seven working days and require them to make the necessary adjustments; if notice is not timely given, the board becomes liable.[94]

37.13 Designating wage coordinator

A board of education must designate, no later than ten days before the first payment of wages, one of its employees to serve as the prevailing wage coordinator during the life of the contract.[95] The coordinator's duties include maintaining, available for public inspection, a file of payroll reports and affidavits submitted by the contractor and monitoring compliance.[96]

The contractor must supply the coordinator with certain information, including certified copies of the payroll, within two weeks after the initial pay date, supplemental payroll reports, and an affidavit prior to final payment stating that he has fully complied with the Prevailing Wage Act.[97] The contractor must furnish each employee not covered by a collective bargaining agreement with written notification of his job classification, prevailing wage rate, and name of the coordinator on the first pay date under the contract.[98]

37.14 Enforcement of the Prevailing Wage Act, penalties and remedies

A board member who votes for the award of a contract or the disbursement of funds under a contract for which prevailing wage rates have not been determined is subject to a fine of $25 to $500.[99] Any employee paid less than the prevailing rate may recover the difference between that rate and the wages paid plus 25% of that difference, plus reasonable attorney's fees

---

[83]OAG 77-076.
[84]State ex rel Evans v Moore, 69 OS(2d) 88, 431 NE(2d) 311 (1982).
[85]RC 4115.04; OAG 81-081.
[86]RC 4115.04.
[87]RC 4115.04.
[88]RC 4115.05.
[89]RC 4115.06.
[90]Ohio Asphalt Paving, Inc v Ohio Dept of Industrial Relations, 63 OS(3d) 512, 589 NE(2d) 35 (1992).
[91]RC 4115.05.
[92]Harris v Bennett, No. L-84-446, 1985 WL 7558 (6th Dist Ct App, Lucas, 7-26-85).
[93]RC 4115.07.
[94]RC 4115.05.
[95]RC 4115.071(A).
[96]RC 4115.071.
[97]RC 4115.07, RC 4115.071(C).
[98]RC 4115.05.
[99]RC 4115.99(A).

and costs.[100] However, if restitution to an employee has been made under RC 4115.13(C), this provision does not apply and the employer is not subject to any further proceedings.[101]

The Bureau of Employment Services has authority to investigate alleged violations and to enforce the Prevailing Wage Act.[102] Under certain circumstances, it may sue on behalf of workers to collect amounts owed.[103] The two-year limitations period appearing in RC 2305.11 with respect to actions by employees for payment of unpaid minimum wages does not apply to prevailing wage suits.[104] In addition to other remedies, a noncomplying contract may be enjoined, or, if it has already been awarded, further work may be enjoined.[105]

The Bureau of Employment Services files with the Secretary of State a list of contractors, subcontractors, and officers of contractors and subcontractors who violate the Prevailing Wage Act. They are prohibited from contracting directly or indirectly with any public authority for the construction of a public improvement or performing any work on a public improvement for one year. If an intentional violation occurs within five years, a prohibition period of three years is triggered.[106]

---

[100] RC 4115.10. The entity liable for not paying the prevailing rate must also pay a penalty of 75% of the difference, which amount is deposited in a penalty enforcement fund under the Act.
[101] RC 4115.10, RC 4115.13(C).
[102] RC 4115.13.
[103] RC 4115.10(C).
[104] Harris v Atlas Single Ply Systems, Inc, 64 OS(3d) 171, 593 NE(2d) 1376 (1992).
[105] RC 4115.14.
[106] RC 4115.133.

Chapter 38

Management and Use of School Property

38.01 Introduction

MAINTENANCE
38.02 Maintenance of school property

SECURITY
38.03 Restricting access to school property, trespass
38.04 Offenses against school property
38.05 Rewards posted by board of education for property offenses
38.06 Parental liability for property damage, theft, or assault by children

USE OF SCHOOL PROPERTY
38.07 Primary use of school property for school purposes
38.08 Use of school property by others, in general
38.09 Use of school property for educational and recreational purposes
38.10 Use of school property for public meetings and entertainments
38.11 Use of school property for political purposes
38.12 Use of school property for religious purposes
38.13 Payment for use of school property, expenses, damages

REGULATION OF SMOKING
38.14 Bans on indoor smoking

38.01 Introduction

A board of education has the responsibility and authority to manage and control all public schools that it operates in its district.[1] This responsibility includes maintenance and regulation of the use of school property and disposition of that property when it is no longer needed.

MAINTENANCE

38.02 Maintenance of school property

A board of education has a fiduciary responsibility to maintain and preserve school property for present and probable future school needs.[2] The board may hire janitors, building superintendents, and other employees to discharge this responsibility.[3] The board may also hire a business manager to assume responsibility for the care and custody of all real and personal property except money.[4]

A board of township trustees may remove snow from public school property at the request of the board of education, and the board of education may reimburse the cost of labor and materials at a mutually agreed fee.[5]

SECURITY

38.03 Restricting access to school property, trespass

(A) Rules on access and use, posting

Boards of education are required under RC 3313.20 to "make any rules that are necessary for its government and the government of its employees, pupils of its schools, and all other persons entering upon its school grounds or premises." Rules dealing with entry on school grounds or in school buildings of persons other than students, teachers, and staff must be conspicuously posted at the main entrance to each school building and at or near the entrance to school grounds or on the perimeter of school grounds if there are no formal entrances.[6]

(B) Criminal trespass

A person knowingly or recklessly entering or remaining on school property without privilege and contrary to board rules or negligently or willfully failing to leave school property when asked by an authorized person may be guilty of criminal trespass.[7] That the school land is public property is irrelevant. The posting of rules required by RC 3313.20 may be useful in demonstrating a person entered and "reck-

---

[1] RC 3313.47.
[2] Weir v Day, 35 OS 143 (1878).
[3] RC 3313.47.
[4] RC 3319.04. See Text 6.10 to 6.13.

[5] RC 505.66.
[6] RC 3313.20.
[7] RC 2911.21.

lessly" remained with notice that his presence was unauthorized.

38.04 Offenses against school property

(A) Arson and related offenses

Aggravated arson[8] and arson[9] involve knowingly causing or creating a substantial risk of serious physical harm to another's person or property without his consent and by means of fire or explosion. The statutory definition of arson specifically includes causing or creating a substantial risk of physical harm to a school building.[10]

(B) Disrupting public services

Interrupting or impairing school bus transportation may constitute "disrupting public services," a third degree felony.[11]

(C) Vandalism and lesser offenses

Vandalism, a second, third, or fourth degree felony, depending on the value of the property or the amount of physical harm involved, includes knowingly causing serious physical harm to an occupied structure or its contents.[12] A school is an occupied structure when any person is present or likely to be present.[13] Lesser, similar offenses include criminal damaging or endangering[14] and criminal mischief.[15] Criminal damaging or endangering involves causing or creating a substantial risk of physical harm to another's property without his consent, knowingly by any means, or recklessly by means of fire, explosion, flood, poison gas, poison, radioactive material, caustic or corrosive material, or other inherently dangerous substance. Criminal mischief may involve damaging or defacing another's property, using a stink bomb, smoke bomb, or similar device, or tampering with a safety device.

(D) Theft offenses

In addition to the offense of theft itself,[16] theft offenses include a wide range of crimes, from burglary to passing a bad check to theft in office.[17]

(E) Disorderly conduct

Disorderly conduct, normally a minor misdemeanor under RC 2917.11, is elevated to a fourth degree misdemeanor if the offender is within 1,000 feet of the boundaries of any school, school premises, or school building.

38.05 Rewards posted by board of education for property offenses

Boards of education may offer and pay rewards for information leading to the arrest and conviction of offenders for violations of law committed on property owned, controlled, or managed by the board or against any pupil or board employee in transit to or from such property or any board employee performing official duties. Rewards cannot be paid to any school official or employee or member of their immediate families.[18]

38.06 Parental liability for property damage, theft, or assault by children

Parents may be liable for damages caused by conduct of their children, both by statute and at common law.

(A) Statutory liability

RC 3109.09 and RC 3109.10 impose strict liability for recovery of limited damages. A property owner, including any board of education of any city, local, exempted village, or joint vocational school district, may sue parents having custody or control of an unmarried child under the age of eighteen who willfully damages or steals his property. That action may be joined with an action against the child. Damages recoverable against the parent are limited to $6,000.[19] Similarly, a victim

---

[8]RC 2909.02.
[9]RC 2909.03.
[10]RC 2909.03(A)(3).
[11]RC 2909.04.
[12]RC 2909.05.
[13]RC 2909.01(C).
[14]RC 2909.06.
[15]RC 2909.07.
[16]RC 2913.02.
[17]See RC 2913.01(K) for the definition of "theft offense."
[18]RC 3313.173.
[19]RC 3109.09. If the board and parents so agree, the court may order the parents to perform community service in lieu of their full payment of the judgment.

of a willful and malicious assault may recover up to $6,000 from parents having custody or control of a minor who committed the assault.[20] No showing of parental negligence is required in either case.

(B) Common-law liability

The general common-law rule is that parents are not liable for the torts, including intentional torts, of their children.[21] There is an exception: parents may be liable if it can be shown they knew of the child's propensity to commit the particular tort involved and failed to take proper measures to control him.[22] That is, it must be shown the parents were negligent.

Assuming parental negligence and causation can be shown, a common-law action may be joined with a statutory action to obtain damages exceeding the statutory limit.

USE OF SCHOOL PROPERTY

38.07 Primary use of school property for school purposes

Property of a board of education is held in trust for school purposes,[23] and must be used primarily for school purposes. While a board may authorize use of its schoolhouses for any lawful purpose, it cannot authorize a use that will interfere with operation of the public schools.[24]

38.08 Use of school property by others, in general

(A) Discretion of board

A board of education has discretion to make its facilities available for public meetings and recreational purposes or other lawful purposes which do not interfere with their use for school purposes.[25] For example, a board may refuse to permit use of property for a purpose not in harmony with the board's educational program and philosophy, and the courts will not interfere with this discretion in the absence of gross abuse.[26]

(B) Equal access requirement

The Equal Access Act[27] makes it unlawful for any public secondary school which receives federal funds and which has a "limited open forum" to deny access to students to conduct a meeting, when denial is based on the religious, political, philosophical, or other content of the meeting.[28]

(C) Liability insurance

With the abolition of the defense of sovereign immunity, boards should consider obtaining insurance or other forms of protection to limit liability for injury in connection with board-permitted use of school property.[29] Many boards require groups using school property to provide evidence of liability insurance.

(D) Fees

Generally, boards of education must be paid money or other consideration for use of board property.[30] A board has no authority to make gifts of public money or property.

38.09 Use of school property for educational and recreational purposes

(A) Use by "responsible" organization

Upon application of a "responsible" organization or of a group of at least seven

---

[20]RC 3109.10.

[21]Elms v Flick, 100 OS 186, 126 NE 66 (1919).

[22]McGinnis v Kinkaid, 1 App(3d) 4, 1 OBR 45, 437 NE(2d) 313 (Cuyahoga 1981).

[23]Weir v Day, 35 OS 143 (1878).

[24]RC 3313.75; State ex rel Greisinger v Grand Rapids Bd of Ed, 88 App 364, 100 NE(2d) 294 (Wood 1949), appeal dismissed by 153 OS 474, 92 NE(2d) 393 (1950), cert denied 340 US 820, 71 SCt 51, 95 LEd 603 (1950).

[25]RC 3313.75 to RC 3313.78. For a discussion of leasing of board-owned property not needed for school purposes, see Text 36.05, Lease, trade, or exchange of real or personal property.

[26]State ex rel Greisinger v Grand Rapids Bd of Ed, 88 App 364, 100 NE(2d) 294 (Wood 1949), appeal dismissed by 153 OS 474, 92 NE(2d) 393 (1950), cert denied 340 US 820, 71 SCt 51, 95 LEd 603 (1950); 1927 OAG 483.

[27]20 USCA 4071 to 20 USCA 4074.

[28]For more extended treatment of the Act, see Text 32.06, Establishment problems from the use of public schools for religious purposes.

[29]See Text Ch 46, Liability of Schools, Officers, and Employees.

[30]For an exception, see Text 38.11, Use of school property for political meetings.

citizens, school buildings under the control of the board of education must be made available for use as social centers for the entertainment and education of the people, for the discussion of all topics tending to the development of personal character and civic welfare, and for religious services.[31]

A board has discretion to determine whether an organization is "responsible" within the meaning of RC 3313.76.[32] A board may make available a satisfactory meeting place other than one specifically requested and be in compliance.[33]

(B) Duty of board to adopt rules on use

In making schoolhouses available for nonschool purposes, a board must establish rules to insure fair, reasonable, and impartial use.[34] Such use is always subject to the restriction that it not seriously infringe on the use of property for school purposes.[35]

38.10 Use of school property for public meetings and entertainments

A board of education, upon request and payment of a reasonable fee, must also permit the use of school property, when not in use for school purposes, for giving instruction in any branch of education, learning, or the arts; for holding open and nonexclusive meetings and entertainments for educational, religious, civic, social, or recreational purposes promoting the welfare of the community; for public library purposes as a station for a public library or as reading rooms; or for polling places for holding elections and voter registrations and for grange and other similar meetings.[36]

This right to use school property is subject to board regulations, and every board is required to adopt a policy on the public use of school facilities, including a list of all fees to be paid and the costs used to determine fees. This policy is available to any district resident on request.[37]

Under RC 3313.77, a board may make classrooms available to parochial school students for instruction in any branch of education, learning, or the arts upon request and payment of a reasonable fee.[38] A board may also permit, upon request and payment of a fee, political action committees and school committees that support or oppose passage of a school tax levy or bond issue to meet on school property and to use telephones, postage meters, and other school equipment and supplies. The board may not discriminate by permitting such use by only those who favor the levy or issue and prohibiting such use by those who oppose, however. Such groups may also be permitted to post signs on school property, but, in regulating such use, if permitted, the board cannot prohibit signs solely because they communicate a view not favored by the board. Because of the requirement in RC 3313.77(B) that meetings be open and nonexclusive, such committees may not use school property for closed organizational meetings.[39]

38.11 Use of school property for political purposes

Under RC 3313.78, upon application of a committee representing any candidate for public office or any regularly organized or recognized political party, a board of education must permit school property to be used for meetings of electors to discuss public issues. No such meeting may be held during regular school hours. A board may not charge a fee for such use of school property.[40] No person may solicit a contribution from a public employee while the employee is in an area of a public building where official business is transacted or conducted.[41]

---

[31] RC 3313.76.

[32] State ex rel Greisinger v Grand Rapids Bd of Ed, 88 App 364, 100 NE(2d) 294 (Wood 1949), appeal dismissed by 153 OS 474, 92 NE(2d) 393 (1950), cert denied 340 US 820, 71 SCt 51, 95 LEd 603 (1950).

[33] State ex rel Richland Parent Teacher's Assn v Richland Twp Bd of Ed, 33 Abs 387 (CP, Vinton 1941).

[34] RC 3313.76.

[35] RC 3313.76. See also Text 32.06, Establishment problems from the use of public schools for religious purposes; Text 38.12, Use of school property for religious purposes.

[36] RC 3313.77.

[37] RC 3313.77.

[38] OAG 65-010. See also Text 38.12, Use of school property for religious purposes.

[39] OAG 91-064.

[40] RC 3313.78.

[41] RC 3517.092(F)(2).

38.12 Use of school property for religious purposes

School property may be used for a variety of nonschool purposes under RC 3313.76, including "religious exercises." The use must not seriously infringe on school uses, and school authorities must adopt rules designed to "secure a fair, reasonable, and impartial use" of school facilities by outside groups. Similarly, RC 3313.77 authorizes a board to permit the use of school property for, among other things, "religious" meetings. The board must adopt a policy for the use of school property by the public, including a list of fees.

Religious use of school property is not prohibited by the First Amendment. Provided religious groups benefit only "incidentally" from access to school facilities, and a board's rules on access are reasonable and apply equally to all responsible groups, there is likely no constitutional violation.[42] On the other hand, access rules that flatly exclude religious groups may be unconstitutional.[43]

38.13 Payment for use of school property, expenses, damages

Any organization or group permitted to use school property under RC 3313.75 to RC 3313.78 must reimburse the board for any damage beyond ordinary wear and tear and, if requested by the board, pay the actual expenses for janitorial services, light, and heat.[44]

REGULATION OF SMOKING

38.14 Bans on indoor smoking

The Pro-Children Act of 1994,[45] part of the federal Goals 2000: Educate America Act,[46] requires that smoking not be permitted in any indoor facility (defined as "a building that is enclosed") used by a board of education for providing routine or regular kindergarten, elementary, or secondary education to children.[47] A failure to comply carries potential liability for a civil penalty not to exceed $1,000 for each violation and/or the violator is subject to an administrative compliance order, as determined by the US Secretary of Education.[48] These smoking provisions do not preempt any state or local law that may be more restrictive.[49]

---

[42] Widmar v Vincent, 454 US 263, 102 SCt 269, 70 LEd(2d) 440 (1981).

[43] Widmar v Vincent, 454 US 263, 102 SCt 269, 70 LEd(2d) 440 (1981). For more extended treatment, including analysis of the Equal Access Act, see Text 32.06, Establishment problems from the use of public schools for religious purposes.

[44] RC 3313.79.

[45] 20 USCA 6081 et seq.

[46] See Text 2.11(B), Goals 2000: Educate America Act.

[47] 20 USCA 6083.

[48] 20 USCA 6083.

[49] 20 USCA 6084. A special waiver for up to one year may be obtained where a collective bargaining agreement that became effective before the Act contains provisions on smoking that conflict with the Act. 20 USCA 6083. For discussion of Ohio's statutory prohibition of smoking by students (which affects more than just indoor facilities) see Text 24.15(B), Tobacco offenses.

FINANCES—RECORDS

Chapter 39

Sources of Revenue

39.01 Introduction, sources of revenue

LOCAL PROPERTY TAX REVENUES
39.02 Taxing power, authority of board to levy taxes
39.03 Ten-mill limitation, voted and unvoted levies
39.04 Changes in property valuations, tax exemptions, notice to board, tax abatement
39.05 Collection of taxes

SCHOOL FOUNDATION PROGRAM
39.06 State aid for school operating expenses
39.07 Prerequisites for participation in foundation program
39.08 Nonoperating uses for foundation funds
39.09 Records and reports

MISCELLANEOUS SOURCES OF REVENUE
39.10 Fines and forfeitures
39.11 Estate and inheritance taxes
39.12 Income tax
39.13 Bequests and gifts, school foundations
39.14 Tuition
39.15 Income from athletic events, activity fees, miscellaneous income

39.01 Introduction, sources of revenue

(A) In general

Boards of education derive their money from several sources: (1) the state foundation program[1] and other state programs; (2) the sale or other disposition of school property;[2] (3) local property taxes (that is, general and special levies) and the undivided classified property tax;[3] (4) a school district income tax, if approved by district voters; (5) a shared municipal income tax, if approved by the municipality's voters;[4] and (6) miscellaneous sources, such as gifts, federal funds, and tuition.[5]

Allocation and distribution of state and federal funds for public education are functions of the state board of education.[6] In addition, the state channels funds to boards of education for financing vocational education[7] and, through the department of administrative services, distributes some federal surplus property.[8]

The two major sources of the revenue for most boards of education are taxes levied on property within the school district and the state foundation program.

(B) Current constitutional imbroglio

Sustaining a broadside attack on the current funding of Ohio's public schools, a common pleas court held in 1994 that education is a "fundamental right" under Ohio's Constitution and that the current funding system—which gives rise to wide disparities between relatively poor and relatively affluent districts—violates several constitutional guarantees.[9] Distinguishing *Cincinnati City School Dist Bd of Ed v Walter*[10] (in which the Ohio Supreme Court rejected an attack on the constitutionality of the state foundation program as it existed and was administered in 1979), the court held, among other things, that today's funding system violates the "equal protection" and "thorough and efficient system of common schools" clauses of the Constitution. The Fifth District Court of Appeals generally reversed the trial court's determination, holding that the evidence was not sufficient to permit the trial court to distin-

---

[1] RC Ch 3317.
[2] RC 3313.37, RC 3313.75 et seq.
[3] RC 5705.05.
[4] RC 718.09.
[5] RC 3313.64, RC 3313.641, RC 3313.65, RC 3317.08, RC 3317.09, RC 3327.06, RC 3327.11; OAG 82-014; OAG 82-030.
[6] RC 3301.07(C).
[7] RC 3304.18.
[8] RC 125.84 et seq.
[9] DeRolph v State, No. 2043 (CP, Perry, 7-1-94).
[10] Cincinnati City School Dist Bd of Ed v Walter, 58 OS(2d) 368, 390 NE(2d) 813 (1979), cert denied 444 US 1015, 100 SCt 665, 62 LEd(2d) 644 (1980).

guish or overrule *Walter*, and suggesting the controversy was more in the nature of a "political question" which should be decided by the general assembly unless the Supreme Court determines that *Walter* no longer applies.[11]

LOCAL PROPERTY TAX REVENUES

39.02 Taxing power, authority of board to levy taxes

The power to tax is granted to the general assembly by the Ohio Constitution,[12] which also requires the general assembly to provide, "by taxation, or otherwise, ... a thorough and efficient system of common schools throughout the State."[13]

In a school district, the general assembly has designated the board of education as the "taxing authority," with the board's treasurer serving as the fiscal officer.[14]

A board of education may levy taxes annually on real and personal property within the district for purposes of (1) paying current operating expenses, (2) acquiring or constructing permanent improvements, and (3) paying the interest and retiring at maturity bonds or notes issued by the board. A board may also levy taxes for such other purposes as are specifically permitted by law. Taxes are levied and collected on a calendar year basis even though a board of education operates on a school year basis.

39.03 Ten-mill limitation, voted and unvoted levies

The power of boards of education to tax is limited in that no property may be taxed in excess of one per cent of its true value except by vote of the people.[15]

A portion of the taxes levied within this ten-mill limitation is guaranteed to most boards of education. Unless requested by the board or required for debt service charges of other political subdivisions, the guaranteed amount cannot be less than two-thirds of the average levy for current expenses and debt service allotted within the fifteen-mill limitation (which was effective until 1934) during the last five years the fifteen-mill limitation was in effect.[16]

When, by combination of taxing districts, the minimum levies prescribed by RC 5705.31(D) exceed the ten-mill limitation, the county budget commission must reduce the levies proportionately to bring their aggregate within the limitation.[17]

There can be no decrease of tax levies of any taxing unit until each mandated minimum tax levy is approved without modification. When a part of one school district is annexed to another, the tax levy of the receiving school district for school purposes inside the ten-mill limitation remains the same as before the annexation, when the inside tax for the receiving district would not force an infringement of the ten-mill limitation.[18]

39.04 Changes in property valuations, tax exemptions, notice to board, tax abatement

Since property taxes are a major source of funding, and since the value and taxability of property directly affect the amount of tax revenue, boards of education have certain privileges regarding tax valuations and exemptions.

The county auditor must notify a school board affected by any complaint, filed by a taxpayer under RC 5715.19(A), involving changes in valuation of real property equal to or exceeding $17,500.[19] A school board may file a complaint as to the classification,

---

[11]DeRolph v State, No. CA-477, 1995 WL 557316 (5th Dist Ct App, Perry, 8-30-95). An appeal is pending, and it is generally assumed that the Ohio Supreme Court will ultimately decide this plainly momentous issue.
[12]O Const Art I §2; O Const Art XII §4.
[13]O Const Art VI §2.
[14]RC 133.01(C), (D), RC 5705.01(C), (D).
[15]O Const Art XII §2; RC 5705.02.
[16]O Const Art XII §2; RC 5705.02, RC 5705.31.

[17]1956 OAG 7421.
[18]Cambridge City School Dist v Guernsey County Budget Comm, 11 App(2d) 77, 228 NE(2d) 874 (Guernsey 1967), affirmed by 13 OS(2d) 77, 234 NE(2d) 512 (1968).
[19]RC 5715.19(B). Where the taxpayer's complaint falls below the $17,500 threshold but is subsequently amended to a figure that meets the threshold, the auditor must give notice of the amendment. Buckeye Boxes, Inc v Franklin County Bd of Revision, 78

valuation, or assessment of real property with the board of revision under RC 5715.19(A) and may appeal a decision of that board within thirty days after notice of the decision pursuant to RC 5717.01. Since assessing real property for taxation includes assigning parcels to tax districts and recording them accordingly on the tax list, a school district may appeal the incorrect recording of property under RC 5715.19.[20] The best evidence of the "true value in money" of real property is an actual, recent sale of the property in an arm's length transaction; appraisals based upon factors other than sales price are appropriate only when no arm's length sale has taken place or where it is shown that the sales price is not reflective of true value.[21] Changes in valuation can also affect state foundation aid.[22] A party that asserts an underevaluation or overevaluation has the burden of proving a right to a change.[23]

A board of education may request the tax commissioner to provide notification of applications for tax exemptions with respect to property in the district. Under a procedure with precise time deadlines, the board in turn may file a statement with the commissioner and the applicant indicating its intention to submit evidence and participate in the hearing. The board thereby becomes a party to the proceeding.[24] The property owner has the burden of proving the property is entitled to exemption.[25]

A school district is entitled to a supplemental assessment for the net decrease in a public utility's taxable value apportioned to the district over tax years 1990 or 1991. The net decrease is determined by reducing the utility's actual decrease in taxable value by the amount deemed by the tax commissioner to be unrelated to tax policy adjustments made when the general assembly, in 1989, altered the method by which taxable property of utilities is assessed. The utility is liable for the amount of the net decrease.[26]

Tax abatement in Ohio consists of a number of programs, including enterprise zones, community reinvestment areas, community urban redevelopment, and tax increment financing. Municipal corporations, counties, and, in some cases, townships may grant abatement under certain of these programs. The maximum percentage of a property's value that may be exempt from taxation under the enterprise zone, community urban redevelopment, or tax increment financing programs is 75% (60% for property located in the unincorporated territory of an enterprise zone), and the period for which a tax exemption under the tax increment financing programs may last is ten years, unless the affected board of education approves a larger percentage or a longer period.[27]

Local governments are required to enter into agreements with the property owner on all commercial and industrial projects that will be exempted from taxation under

---

App(3d) 634, 605 NE(2d) 992 (Franklin 1992). The board of education may file a complaint within thirty days and become part of the action.

[20]State ex rel Rolling Hills Local School Dist Bd of Ed v Brown, 63 OS(3d) 520, 589 NE(2d) 1265 (1992) (denying writ of mandamus on ground an appeal to the board of revision under RC 5715.19 was an adequate remedy at law).

[21]Hilliard City School Dist Bd of Ed v Franklin County Bd of Revision, 53 OS(3d) 57, 558 NE(2d) 1170 (1990); Columbus Bd of Ed v Fountain Square Associates, Ltd, 9 OS(3d) 218, 9 OBR 528, 459 NE(2d) 894 (1984); Ratner v Stark County Bd of Revision, 23 OS(3d) 59, 23 OBR 192, 491 NE(2d) 680 (1986). See also North Olmsted Bd of Ed v Cuyahoga County Bd of Revision, 54 OS(3d) 98, 561 NE(2d) 915 (1990) (in absence of recent sale, testimony of expert witnesses proper); Cleveland Bd of Ed v Cuyahoga County Bd of Revision, 70 OS(3d) 73, 637 NE(2d) 295 (1994) (consideration of, among other factors, upgrades and repairs subsequent to sale two years before appropriate in determining value).

[22]See Text 39.09(E), Information on tax values and rates.

[23]Cleveland Bd of Ed v Cuyahoga County Bd of Revision, 68 OS(3d) 336, 626 NE(2d) 933 (1994).

[24]RC 5715.27.

[25]RC 5715.271.

[26]RC 5727.231.

[27]RC 725.02, RC 1728.10, RC 5709.40, RC 5709.41, RC 5709.62, RC 5709.63, RC 5709.73, RC 5709.78. These are the statutes that generally come into play where tax abatement is contemplated. Which statutes are particularly relevant to a given case depends on what particular program is implicated. Much of what follows in the text on this subject is premised on various provisions of these statutes. For the sake of simplicity, they are not repeatedly cited hereafter in footnotes. On any tax abatement matter, experienced legal counsel should be involved.

a community reinvestment area program.[28] Such agreements must be approved by the board of education unless the sum of the estimated personal property taxes resulting from the project and the real property taxes to be paid on any portion of the assessed value of the property not subject to tax exemption, plus any cash payment made by the property owner to the school district, the cash value of any property or services provided by the property owner to the school district, and any "revenue sharing" payment made by the local government to the board, equals or exceeds 50% of the taxes that would have been charged and payable on the property absent the exemption.[29]

Local governments seeking to grant tax exemptions in excess of the statutory limits or to enter into community reinvestment area agreements which relate to certain industrial or commercial projects must notify the board of education at least thirty days prior to approving the tax exemptions or entering into such agreements. The board, by resolution, may approve or disapprove those tax exemptions that exceed the statutory limits (or agreement) or may approve on the condition that the local government agree to compensate the board in an amount equal to some percentage of taxes exempted in excess of the statutory limits (or equal to some portion of the taxes which would have been collected after the tenth year on property exempted under the tax increment financing program). If the board disapproves the excess (or agreement), the local government may not grant tax exemptions in excess of the statutory limits or enter into the above industrial or commercial project agreements. However, the board must certify the resolution indicating approval or disapproval to the local government no later than fourteen days prior to the local government's approval of the tax exemption (or agreement). If the board fails to certify a resolution within the time required, the local government may grant the exemption contained in the notice (or enter into the agreement) without the board's approval. The board may request a meeting with the legislative authority of the local government to discuss the local government's proposed actions.[30]

A board of education may condition its approval of excess exemption percentages or time periods on the successful negotiation of a compensation agreement. A mutually acceptable compensation agreement must be negotiated (even if board approval is not required) when any municipal corporation (1) grants exemptions under one of the tax abatement or tax increment financing programs, (2) imposes income taxes, and (3) the payroll of an exempted project's new employees equals or exceeds $1 million in any year the exemption exists.[31] If such a compensation agreement is not negotiated within six months after approval of the tax exemption, the municipal corporation is required to pay the school district 50% of the difference between the amount of municipal income taxes levied on new employees and certain infrastructure costs relating to the project incurred by the municipal corporation each calendar year.[32]

39.05 Collection of taxes

Although property taxes are levied by the board of education by the adoption of a resolution, they are billed and collected by the county auditor and treasurer.

Unless otherwise provided by law, money belonging to a school district and deposited or invested by a county is to be paid over to the district on or before the tenth day of the month following the month the county receives the money (or by a later date authorized by the board of education). The county must pay any advance authorized by RC 321.24 or RC 321.341 within five business days after the request for advance is delivered to the county auditor. In the case of money due to the board under RC 321.31, the county must pay those amounts within five days after the date of settlement. Assuming the county follows these rules, it must credit any interest earned on these amounts during the time they are in the county treasury

---

[28]RC 3735.67. For the specifics of such agreements, see RC 3735.671.
[29]RC 3735.671.

[30]RC 5709.83.
[31]RC 5709.82.
[32]RC 5709.82.

to the county general fund.[33] In case of delayed payments and distributions, the county must pay the district any accrued interest income on the amount after the prescribed date of payment. Delayed payments and the accrued interest are to be paid within five business days after the district files a written demand for payment with the county auditor.[34]

Payments to the board of education may not be delayed because the county is fearful that a refund may be due the taxpayer.[35]

Where a county auditor mistakenly allocates tax proceeds to the wrong school district, the district thus deprived of its revenue may sue the district mistakenly enriched for restitution.[36]

SCHOOL FOUNDATION PROGRAM

39.06 State aid for school operating expenses

(A) Purposes of school foundation program

The foundation program[37] was created to establish a system for distributing state funds to schools for operating expenses and to promote efficiency and economy. Its twofold effect has been (1) to establish a minimum or "foundation" level of education for all school children in the state; and (2) to provide state money for the support of public schools from a state-collected tax on a source other than real estate, thus relieving (to some extent) the tax burden on real property. Payments are made from special provisions in the biennial appropriation measure of the general assembly in twelve monthly installments over an annual period from July 1 to June 30. For those boards of education unable to provide the minimum or "foundation" level, additional state aid is given. Special subsidies for school districts with low per pupil valuations or average daily memberships are provided by, respectively, RC 3317.0213 and RC 3317.0214. The foundation aid payable to a district consists of so-called "basic aid" and amounts for categorical programs to which the district is entitled.

(B) Constitutional issues

In 1979, the Ohio Supreme Court held that the foundation program does not violate either the "equal protection" or the "thorough and efficient system of common schools" clauses of the Ohio Constitution.[38] In 1994, however, a common pleas court, emphasizing changes in the program since 1979, distinguished the Supreme Court's precedent and held that Ohio's current system of funding public education is unconstitutional in several respects.[39] That decision was generally reversed by the Fifth District Court of Appeals in August 1995.[40]

The governor may not diminish the funds allocated under the foundation program,[41] although the timing of payments may vary depending on state cash requirements or other reasons. However, the general assembly, in making appropriations, may allow the governor to require the superintendent of public instruction to reduce the amount available under the program through an executive order.[42]

(C) Administration of school foundation program, appropriations

The foundation program is administered by the state board of education, with the approval of the state controlling board. Money is appropriated to the state board of education out of money in the state treasury's general revenue fund.[43] Payments, with certain exceptions, are then forwarded

---

[33]RC 133.35(A); OAG 85-067.

[34]RC 135.351.

[35]State ex rel Old Fort School Dist Bd of Ed v Smith, No. 13-82-34, 1983 WL 7233 (3d Dist Ct App, Seneca, 3-25-83).

[36]Rocky River School Dist Bd of Ed v Fairview Park City School Dist Bd of Ed, 63 App(3d) 385, 579 NE(2d) 217 (Cuyahoga 1989).

[37]RC Ch 3317.

[38]Cincinnati City School Dist Bd of Ed v Walter, 58 OS(2d) 368, 390 NE(2d) 813 (1979), cert denied 444 US 1015, 100 SCt 665, 62 LEd(2d) 644 (1980).

[39]DeRolph v State, No. 2043 (CP, Perry, 7-1-94).

[40]DeRolph v State, No. CA-477, 1995 WL 557316 (5th Dist Ct App, Perry, 8-30-95). An appeal to the Ohio Supreme Court is pending. See Text 39.01(B), Current constitutional imbroglio.

[41]Cleveland City School Dist Bd of Ed v Gilligan, 38 OS(2d) 107, 311 NE(2d) 529 (1974).

[42]Erie County School Dist Bd of Ed v Rhodes, 17 App(3d) 35, 17 OBR 88, 477 NE(2d) 1171 (Montgomery 1984).

[43]RC 3317.01.

monthly to the receiving boards of education.

39.07 Prerequisites for participation in foundation program

(A) Minimum school year

Distribution of foundation funds to a district is contingent on a minimum school year of 182 days, during which the schools of the district must be actually open for instruction. In calculating the 182 days, each board of education may include up to four days per year in which classes are dismissed one-half day early or the equivalent amount of time during a different number of days for individualized parent-teacher conferences, up to two days for professional meetings of teachers when those days occur during a regular school week and the schools are not in session, and the number of days the schools are closed as a result of public calamity as provided in RC 3317.01. The superintendent of public instruction must waive this requirement if school must be closed because of disease epidemic, hazardous weather conditions, inoperability of school buses or other equipment necessary to the school's operation, damage to a school building, or utility problems rendering the building temporarily unfit for school use, provided the number of days the school is actually open for instruction with pupils in attendance and for individualized parent-teacher conferences and reporting periods is not less than 175 days in a school year (for schools operating under a trimester, quarter, or pentamester plan, the 175-day requirement is changed, respectively, to 79 days in any trimester, 59 days in any quarter, and 44 days in any pentamester).[44]

For the school year succeeding the first year that a new plan of operation, under a trimester, quarter, pentamester, or staggered attendance schedule, is initiated, the superintendent of public instruction may waive the requirements as to the minimum number of days or hours school must be in session.[45]

(B) Minimum tax levy

To qualify for basic foundation aid, a board of education for any school district other than a county, joint vocational, or cooperative education district must levy at least twenty mills for current school operations, unless the levies have been reduced below twenty mills by the county budget commission, the board of tax appeals, or the county auditor.[46] These boards may also be permitted to qualify for categorical aid programs.[47]

(C) Minimum teachers' salaries, tax certificates

No foundation funds may be paid if the board of education fails to pay prescribed minimum teachers' salaries[48] or file all certificates required by RC 5705.412, unless the board demonstrates to the state board of education and state controlling board sufficient reason for noncompliance.[49]

39.08 Nonoperating uses for foundation funds

(A) Education for the handicapped

Each board of education may receive foundation funds for students who are handicapped,[50] as well as for its child study services, speech handicapped, vocational units, and classes for handicapped preschool children, if those programs and units are approved annually by the state board of education.[51] The reasonable cost of maintaining classes for migrant children may also be paid from foundation funds.[52]

Governing boards of educational service centers may establish and operate special

---

[44]RC 3317.01, RC 3313.48, RC 3317.01; OAG 85-015.
[45]RC 3317.01.
[46]RC 3317.01, RC 3317.025. RC 3307.01 provides that levies for a joint vocational or cooperative education school district or a county school financing district, limited to or to the extent apportioned to current expenses, are included in this qualification requirement. Income tax levies under RC Ch 748, limited to or to the extent apportioned to current operating expenses, are also included in this qualification requirement to the extent determined by the tax commissioner under RC 3317.021(C).
[47]RC 3317.024.
[48]RC 3317.01.
[49]RC 3317.024.
[50]RC 3317.01 defines "handicapped child" and "handicapped preschool child" for purposes of RC Ch 3317 by reference to the definitions appearing in RC 3323.01(A).
[51]RC 3317.024, RC 3317.05, RC 3323.091.
[52]RC 3317.024.

education units for handicapped children, or special education supervisory units, which may also serve city and exempted village school districts. These governing boards may be eligible for foundation funding of these units.[53] A city, exempted village, or local school district board of education's right to contract with a service center for operation of a special education unit serving both districts does not reduce the minimum state payment to the city, exempted village, or local board.

(B) Vocational education

Each city, local, and exempted village school district board of education must maintain a vocational education program. A board may contract with another board to provide the program.[54] Vocational education units are eligible for foundation funds.[55]

(C) Transportation facilities

The total approved cost of operating facilities for transporting pupils, where such facilities are necessary, may be paid with foundation funds.[56]

39.09 Records and reports

(A) In general

Since foundation payments to boards of education are based on statistics that the boards must certify to the state board of education, a number of important records must be maintained. These include daily statistics describing the population and activities of individual schools, pupils, teachers, and employees.[57] Each board must maintain and certify to the state board a membership record by grades, showing vital statistics and attendance records for each pupil enrolled in its schools, and also statistics on the transportation of pupils to and from school. These records must be maintained for at least five years.[58] In accordance with state board procedures, a record must also be maintained and certified with respect to handicapped preschool children.[59]

(B) Average daily membership

On or before October 15 of each year, the superintendent in each city and exempted village school district and educational service center must, for each school under his supervision, certify to the state board a total average daily membership in regular day classes for the first full school week in October, following the specifications of the state board.[60] This membership is calculated on the basis of enrolled persons.

The average daily membership of any city or exempted village school district or educational service center is determined by dividing the figure representing the sum of pupils enrolled during each day the school is actually open for instruction during the first full school week in October by the total number of days the school was actually open for instruction during that week.[61] The average daily membership of a joint vocational or cooperative education school district is determined in accordance with the rules of the state board.

Nonresident pupils whose attendance is unauthorized under RC 3327.06 should not be included in the calculation of average daily membership under RC 3317.03. Also, student participants admitted under a district policy guaranteeing the competency of graduates,[62] handicapped preschool children except handicapped preschool chil-

---

[53]OAG 73-030.
[54]RC 3313.90.
[55]RC 3317.024, RC 3317.05.
[56]RC 3317.024(K).
[57]RC 3317.031.
[58]RC 3317.031.
[59]RC 3317.032.
[60]RC 3317.03(A). The statute also requires certification of the average daily membership based on full-time equivalency in approved vocational units and in joint vocational school districts; the average daily membership of all handicapped children in classes in the district and in the service center that are eligible for approval by the state board under RC 3317.05(B) or (E) and the number of such classes; and the average daily membership based on full-time equivalency in schools of a cooperative education school district. The superintendent of each joint vocational or cooperative education school district must similarly certify to the superintendent of public instruction the average daily membership for all classes in the joint vocational or cooperative education district, also indicating the city, local, or exempted village district of residence of each pupil.

[61]"Enrolled" pupils means only those who are attending school, those who are absent for authorized reasons, and handicapped children receiving home instruction. RC 3317.03(C). See also OAG 74-066.

[62]RC 3313.647.

dren in units approved by the state board of education under RC 3317.05(E),[63] and reported adjacent district students enrolled pursuant to a RC 3313.98 policy[64] cannot be counted. With respect to participants in a district's post-secondary enrollment options program,[65] the time a participant is attending courses only for college credit pursuant to RC 3365.04(A) must be considered as time the participant is not attending or enrolled in school anywhere, and the time a participant is attending courses for both college and high school credit pursuant to RC 3365.04(B) must be considered as time the participant is attending or enrolled in the district's schools.[66]

RC 3317.033 requires each city, local, exempted village, joint vocational, and cooperative education school district and educational service center, in accordance with state board of education rules, to maintain a record of persons not eligible to be included in the district's average daily membership under RC 3317.03 and who participate in a program funded with a secondary vocational education job-training unit approved under RC 3317.05(A). The district or service center must annually certify the number of persons for whom such a record is maintained to the state board. The numbers must be reported for each unit and on a full-time equivalent basis. In approving secondary education job-training units under RC 3317.05(A), if the state board determines a district does not have enough students reported under RC 3317.03 to approve a full unit, it will also count persons reported for that unit under RC 3317.033 in making calculations for purposes of approving the unit; however, the number of persons reported and counted for a unit cannot exceed fifty percent of the minimum number of full-time students required for approval of the unit as a full unit.

If the average daily membership for the first full week in February is three per cent greater than the membership reported for the preceding October, the increase must be certified to the superintendent of public instruction no later than February 15.[67]

The superintendent of each county MR/DD board must also certify to the state board the average daily membership in preschool units described in RC 3317.05.[68]

(C) Number of classes or units for handicapped

If during the first full week in February the total number of classes or units for handicapped children that are eligible for approval under RC 3317.05(B) exceeds the number of classes or units approved for the year, the superintendent in each district must certify the number of such classes or units to the state board.[69]

(D) Information on certified employees

On or before October 15 of each year, the superintendent in each district is required to certify to the state board detailed information on certificated employees[70] under his supervision for the first full week in October.[71]

(E) Information on tax values and rates

Each year, on or before June 1, the board of tax appeals and the tax commissioner are required to certify to the state board certain information regarding tax values and tax rates.[72]

Based upon tax reduction information certified on or before May 15 of each year by the tax commissioner, the state department of education must recompute foundation payments to each district.[73] Likewise, a recalculation is required, based on tax information received before May 15 of each year from the tax commissioner involving tangible personal property increases or decreases in taxable value which is lesser or greater than five per cent of the district's taxable value.[74]

Districts in which more than twenty-five percent of the value of the property is exempt from taxation (and is not US gov-

---

[63] RC 3317.03.
[64] RC 3313.981(E). Native students enrolled in adjacent districts under such policies are counted. *Id.*
[65] See Text 26.07(C), Post-secondary enrollment options program.
[66] RC 3365.04.
[67] RC 3317.03.
[68] RC 3317.03(E)(2)(b).
[69] RC 3317.03(D)(2), RC 3317.03(E).
[70] RC 3319.22 to RC 3319.31.
[71] RC 3317.061.
[72] RC 3317.02, RC 3317.021, RC 3317.025.
[73] RC 3317.027.
[74] RC 3317.028.

ernment or public utility property) receive additional foundation payments.[75]

(F) Information on uncollectible taxes

By the first day of August of each year, a school district must notify the department of education if it has uncollectible taxes from a company[76] that has filed a petition for reorganization under Chapter 11 of the Bankruptcy Reform Act[77] or from a Port Authority[78] for the second preceding tax year which entity's total taxes charged and payable represent at least one-half of one per cent of the district's total taxes charged and payable for that tax year. The department of education must verify and then perform certain calculations by November 15. If these calculations meet criteria detailed in RC 3317.0210(C) and RC 3317.0211(C), respectively, the district would be allowed to receive a loan from the lottery profits education fund.[79] The amount received must be repaid to the department of education within two years of the end of the fiscal year of receipt; any amount not timely repaid is charged a penalty of one per cent per month.

MISCELLANEOUS SOURCES OF REVENUE

39.10 Fines and forfeitures

Various fines and forfeitures must be paid into county or local treasuries for the benefit of local public schools:[80]

(1) Fines for improper insurance rebates or special advantages;[81]

(2) Fines collected under the quo warranto statutes;[82]

(3) Fines for discrimination between certain insured persons;[83]

(4) Fines collected under laws prohibiting employment of minors;[84]

(5) Proceeds of the sale of timber unlawfully cut on school lands;[85]

(6) Fines for specified insurance misrepresentation;[86] and

(7) Funds remaining after surrender by a village of its corporate powers.[87]

39.11 Estate and inheritance taxes

Boards of education may also participate in the distribution of estate and inheritance taxes.[88] Under Ohio law, an estate escheats when no legal heirs exist.[89] The prosecuting attorney of the county in which letters of administration are granted on estate must collect all personal property of the estate and pay it over to the county treasurer, to be applied exclusively to the support of the common schools of the county.[90]

39.12 Income tax

The board of education of any school district, except a joint vocational school district or the governing board of an educational service center, may collect a school district income tax for any of the purposes for which it may collect a property tax if approved by the voters.[91] To submit the question of an income tax to its voters, the board, no later than eighty-five days prior to the election, must adopt a resolution specifying the amount of money needed and certify a copy of the resolution to the tax commissioner.[92] The commissioner then has ten days to certify to the board the property tax rate and the income tax rate which would have to be imposed to raise the amount specified. A new certification is required for each election at which the board submits a proposal to levy an income tax.

After receiving the commissioner's certification, the board may adopt a resolution proposing the levy of a district income tax

---

[75]RC 3317.02(B), RC 3317.021(A)(4).
[76]RC 3317.0210.
[77]11 USCA 1101 et seq.
[78]RC 3317.0211.
[79]RC 3317.62.
[80]RC 3315.31.
[81]RC 3933.05.
[82]RC 2733.38.
[83]RC 3911.18.
[84]RC 4109.13(F).
[85]RC 309.14.
[86]RC 3999.08.
[87]RC 703.21.
[88]RC 5731.48(B).
[89]RC 2105.06.
[90]RC 2105.07.
[91]RC 5748.02.
[92]RC 5748.02(A).

at the rate certified rounded to the nearest one-fourth of a per cent. The proposed levy may be for a continuing period or for a specified number of years.[93] The ballot form for submission of an income tax is specified by statute.[94]

If approved, the tax is levied on the income of individuals and estates residing in the district, regardless of where they work. Individual taxpayers over the age of sixty-four during the taxable year are permitted a $50 credit against any district income tax they may owe.[95]

Following approval of a district income tax for the purpose of current expenses or permanent improvements, the board may borrow in anticipation of collection of the tax, but such borrowing is limited to fifty per cent of the proceeds estimated to be received during the first year of collection and must have principal payments during each year after the year of issuance not to exceed five years or the number of years for which the tax is approved, whichever is less, and may have a principal payment in the year of issuance.[96]

If petitioned for by at least ten per cent of the qualified electors who voted in the last gubernatorial election, not later than seventy-five days before a general election, the question of repeal of a previously voted income tax levied for more than five years may be submitted at that election. If repeal is approved by a majority voting on the question, the levy ceases after the then current year.[97] Only one repeal may be initiated in any five-year period.[98]

A board proposing a school district income tax for a continuing period of time for the purpose of current expenses may also propose to reduce the rate or rates of one or more of the district's voted property taxes levied for a continuing period of time for the purpose of current expenses as part of a single ballot question.[99] The reduction in rate may be any amount not exceeding the rate at which the tax is authorized to be levied. If approved, the reduction first takes effect for the tax year that includes the day in which the district income tax first takes effect and continues for each tax year that both the income tax and the property tax are in effect. The board must designate the specific levy or levies to be reduced, the maximum rate at which each levy currently is authorized to be levied, and the rate by which each levy is proposed to be reduced. Specific ballot language is required if the income tax and the reduction of a property tax are submitted as a single issue.[100] If the income tax is later repealed or reduced, the property tax may again be levied.

A municipal corporation (provided not more than five percent of its territory is outside the school district and vice-versa) may pass a municipal income tax and share the revenue with the school district occupying the same territory. After reaching agreement with the district board of education specifying (1) the tax rate, (2) the percentage of tax and revenue to be paid to the district, (3) the purpose for which the revenue is to be used, and (4) the method of payment, the municipal corporation must submit the proposed tax to voters in the same manner as for other municipal income taxes.[101] Multiple municipal corporations that share territory with a single school district (with the same five percent limitation) may also share income tax revenue with the district if a majority of voters in each municipal corporation approves the tax.[102]

39.13 Bequests and gifts, school foundations

It is not uncommon for boards of education to receive contributions, gifts, and bequests of personal property or funds from student groups, members of the public, or community groups. When a contribution, gift, or bequest is made, its acceptance

---

[93]RC 5748.02(A), (B). No more than two elections on the question of the tax may be held in any calendar year and, if two elections are held, one must be in November. RC 5748.02(D).
[94]RC 5748.03.
[95]RC 5748.06.
[96]RC 5748.05.
[97]RC 5748.04. This statute expressly does not apply to an income tax levied for five or fewer years.

[98]RC 5748.04. This statute expressly does not apply to an income tax levied for five or fewer years.
[99]RC 5748.02(B)(2).
[100]RC 5748.03.
[101]RC 718.09.
[102]RC 718.10.

must be recorded in the minutes of the board, together with the purpose, if any, for which it was made. Only then does title vest in the board.[103]

A board may accept a gift or bequest made upon conditions, so long as the board does not lose control over the public schools as a result.[104] Having accepted, the board is bound by the conditions and is responsible for meeting them as far as possible.

A board may accept a gift or bequest for a purpose for which it could not spend ordinary funds. For example, if an endowment is made for scholarship purposes, the board may establish a scholarship fund even though it is not empowered to use ordinary funds for that purpose. Similarly, although interest earned on trust funds which contain donated money must generally be credited to the general fund, if the donor restricts the use or deposit of interest, the restrictions must be complied with.[105]

However, there is no authority to accept a gift or bequest if the conditions attached are not permitted by law. Thus, a board may not assume a balance due on the cost of a public address system contracted for by the PTA and thereafter given to the board.[106] A board may not assume payments for athletic equipment purchased on credit by a boosters club and donated when the club was unable to complete payment. The debt may be paid from the athletic account of the activities funds.[107]

Donations to a scholarship or stadium fund must be entered separately on the cash journal and are subject to the Uniform Depository Act, RC Chapter 135. Athletic booster clubs or others interested in athletic programs may donate funds to a board of education for the purchase of athletic equipment to be used in intramural sports. Acceptance must be by board resolution.[108]

Some boards have become involved in the creation of private tax-exempt foundations to support the schools of the district. These foundations have certain advantages, including the ability to spend for purposes for which the board could not spend its own funds, but many pitfalls are involved in their creation and operation. Federal tax law, for example, carefully regulates these foundations and donations to them. Sophisticated legal counsel should be consulted before the establishment of any such foundation.

Certain boards are also permitted to establish "education foundation" funds into which they may pay moneys received from gifts, bequests, or endowments given to the board for that fund or without conditions or limitations and, by duly adopted resolution, an annual amount not to exceed one-half of one percent of the total appropriations included in the tax budget of a local, city, exempted village, or joint vocational board or one-half of one percent of the moneys received under RC 3317.11 by an educational service center.[109] Interest income earned on a education foundation fund must be credited to the fund.[110] Moneys in an education foundation fund can be expended by majority vote on any existing or new and innovative program designed to enhance or promote education in the district, including scholarships for students or teachers.[111] The board may appoint a committee of administrators to administer and make recommendations on the use of the fund.[112] The board may also create a trust for investment of money in the education foundation fund which appoints a nonprofit foundation as trustee and makes a number of specific determinations with regard to the use and continuation of the trust.[113] Bonds which owe moneys under a RC Chapter 3318 classroom facilities loan or an emergency loan may not establish education foundation funds.[114]

39.14 Tuition

Education through the twelfth grade must be provided free to children at least

---

[103] RC 3313.36.
[104] RC 9.20, RC 9.26, RC 3313.36.
[105] OAG 85-085.
[106] Schwing v McClure, 120 OS 335, 166 NE 230 (1929); 1932 OAG 4622.
[107] 1932 OAG 4622.
[108] See 1962 OAG 3246.

[109] RC 3313.36, RC 3315.40.
[110] RC 3315.40.
[111] RC 3315.40.
[112] RC 3315.40.
[113] RC 3315.40.
[114] RC 3315.42.

five (three, if the child is handicapped) but under twenty-two years of age, except tuition must generally be paid by or on behalf of nonresident pupils. A board may charge tuition for preschool programs, summer school, adult education, evening school, technical school, driver education, and post-graduate education.[115]

39.15 Income from athletic events, activity fees, miscellaneous income

A board may charge reasonable admission to athletic events and may charge nonresidents more than residents.[116] Admission also may be charged for plays, concerts, and other entertainments. Refreshments may be sold at a profit on school premises or in connection with a school activity, provided the profits are applied to school purposes or to support extracurricular activities.[117] Also, students may be charged a fee to participate in an extracurricular activity.

If more than $50 is received through an extracurricular activity, the board must establish a student activity fund for administering the revenue from student activities.[118] Income other than admission charges or fees received through a student activity should also be administered through the student activity fund.[119]

Since a board may lease property not needed for educational purposes and may enter into oil and gas leases or other mineral leases,[120] rents and royalties constitute another source of income.

---

[115]See generally Text Ch 23, Pupils: Tuition and Fees; Text 26.10 to 26.14; Text 33.02, Textbooks and workbooks to be furnished free.
[116]OAG 84-083.
[117]RC 3313.811. See Text 35.02, Charging pupils for items other than textbooks; Text 35.03, Vending machines, use of proceeds.

[118]RC 3315.062; State ex rel Plain Dealer Publishing Co v Lesak, 9 OS(3d) 1, 9 OBR 52, 457 NE(2d) 821 (1984); OAG 82-014; OAG 86-062.
[119]See Text 23.03, Student activity programs, fees, and funds; Text 23.04, Expenditures from student activity funds; Text 43.25, Student activities fund.
[120]See Text 36.10, Lease of property.

Chapter 40

Tax Budget, Tax Levies, and Appropriations

TAX BUDGET
- 40.01 Duty to prepare annual tax budget
- 40.02 Fiscal year and school year
- 40.03 Tax budget timetable
- 40.04 Form of tax budget
- 40.05 County budget commission
- 40.06 Appeal from decision of budget commission

PROPERTY TAX LEVIES
- 40.07 Basis for tax levies
- 40.08 Requirement for separate levies
- 40.09 General and special levies within ten-mill limitation
- 40.10 Special levies outside ten-mill limitation
- 40.11 Renewal tax levies
- 40.12 Replacement tax levies
- 40.13 Election on tax levy outside of ten-mill limitation
- 40.14 Reduction in effective rate of additional tax levy

APPROPRIATIONS
- 40.15 Annual appropriation resolution
- 40.16 Amending or supplementing appropriation resolution
- 40.17 Adoption of spending plan concurrent with adoption of appropriation resolution
- 40.18 Filing requirements
- 40.19 Auditor's certificate that appropriations do not exceed estimate

TAX BUDGET

40.01 Duty to prepare annual tax budget

The tax budget is the initial financial planning tool of the board of education. In the tax budget, the board estimates the amounts of money needed in the ensuing fiscal year and the purposes for which these amounts will be spent.[1] Actual preparation is typically delegated to the superintendent, treasurer, or some other employee, but the board itself must adopt the tax budget.

40.02 Fiscal year and school year

All laws relating to the levying (but not collection) of taxes, the collection of revenues other than taxes, the appropriation or expenditure of revenues, and the making of financial reports or statements by a board of education are based on its fiscal year (July 1 to June 30).[2] Taxes are collected on a calendar year basis.

40.03 Tax budget timetable

On or before January 15, the board of education of each school district must adopt a tax budget for the fiscal year beginning the next July 1.[3] Not less than ten days before adoption, at least two copies of the proposed tax budget must be filed in the treasurer's office for public inspection. In addition, the board must hold a hearing on the proposed tax budget after publishing notice of the hearing in a newspaper of general circulation in the district at least ten days before. The adopted tax budget must be submitted to the county auditor on or before January 20, although the Ohio tax commissioner may prescribe a later date.[4]

Educational service centers[5] which do not receive tax moneys directly do not prepare a tax budget. However, the governing board of each educational service center must submit an annual budget of operating expenses to the state board of education for approval.[6] Part of the educational service center's operating expenses are apportioned among the various districts in the county on the basis of the total number of pupils in each district and deducted from

---

[1] RC 5705.28.
[2] RC 9.34.
[3] RC 5705.28.
[4] RC 5705.30, RC 5705.31.
[5] Educational service centers and their governing boards, defined in RC 3311.05(A) and RC 3311.053, were created by 1995 H 117, eff. 9-29-95, and generally provide the same services as and replace county school districts and boards of education.
[6] RC 3317.11.

funds allocated to local districts under the school foundation program.[7]

40.04　Form of tax budget

(A) Required contents

The tax budget of a board of education of a city, exempted village, local, or joint vocational school district must present detailed information prescribed by statute and the state auditor, including the following:

(1) Statement of projected current operating expenses for the ensuing fiscal year, classified as to personal services and other expenses, and the funds from which the expenditures are to be made;

(2) Statement of anticipated expenditures for the ensuing fiscal year for permanent improvements, exclusive of any expense to be paid from bond proceeds classified as to the contemplated improvements;

(3) Amounts required for payment of final judgments;

(4) Statement of anticipated expenditures for the ensuing fiscal year for any purpose for which a special levy is authorized and the fund from which such expenditures are to be made;

(5) Comparative statements in parallel columns of corresponding items of anticipated expenditures for the current year and the two preceding years;

(6) Estimate of nonproperty tax receipts during the ensuing fiscal year, to include an estimate of all anticipated unencumbered balances estimated to exist at the close of the current year, and the fund to which these estimated receipts are to be credited;

(7) Amount each fund requires from the general property tax, i.e., the difference between the contemplated expenditures from the fund and the anticipated receipts from other sources estimated in paragraph (6) above;

(8) Comparative statements in parallel columns of taxes and other revenues for the current year and the two preceding years;

(9) Amounts required for debt charges;

(10) Estimated receipts from sources other than taxes for payment of debt charges, including the proceeds of any refunding bonds or notes;

(11) Net amount for which a tax levy must be made for payment of debt charges, noting the portion within and the portion outside of the ten-mill limitation;[8] and

(12) Estimate of amounts from taxes authorized to be levied in excess of the ten-mill limitation, the fund to which receipts from that levy will be credited, and the statutory provisions under which any portion is exempt from all limitations on the tax rate.[9]

A board should also make certain its submission to the county auditor includes debt charge requirements for both the fiscal year and the calendar year beginning during that fiscal year.

(B) Contingent expenses and reserve

The board may include in its tax budget an estimate of expenditures to be known as a "contingent expense," which may not exceed thirteen per cent of the total estimated appropriations for current expenses included in the budget.[10]

In addition to the thirteen per cent contingent expense line item, the tax budget may include an amount to be known as a "voluntary contingency reserve balance," which may not exceed twenty-five per cent of the total amount estimated to be available for appropriation in the fiscal year from tax levies first extended on the tax list and duplicate in that fiscal year, plus an amount not greater than twenty per cent of the amount estimated to be available for appropriation in that fiscal year from tax levies first extended on the tax list and duplicate in the prior fiscal year.[11] The full amount of the voluntary contingency reserve balance included in a board's tax budget as allowed by the county budget commission will be retained by the county

---

[7]RC 3317.11.
[8]See Text 39.03, Ten-mill limitation, voted and unvoted levies.

[9]RC 5705.29.
[10]RC 5705.29(A)(1).
[11]RC 5705.29(E)(1), (2).

auditor and county treasurer out of the first semiannual settlement of taxes. In the next succeeding fiscal year, the voluntary contingency reserve balance, with interest, must be turned over to the board to be used for the purposes of that fiscal year.[12]

The board may appropriate any amount withheld as a voluntary contingency reserve balance at any time during the fiscal year for any lawful purpose, provided that prior to the appropriation the board has authorized the expenditure of all amounts included in its thirteen per cent contingent expense item, if any. Upon request by the board (by a two-thirds vote), the county auditor must draw a warrant payable to the board for the amount requested.[13]

(C) Spending reserve

A board may also include a spending reserve balance, which is an estimate of expenditures that cannot exceed the amount by which fifty per cent of the total personal property taxes to be received in the next calendar year exceeds the amount to be received in the first half. The spending reserve is available for appropriation during a fiscal year only upon the written approval of the superintendent of public instruction and compliance with RC 133.302.[14]

40.05 County budget commission

(A) Powers and duties of commission

The county budget commission consists of the county auditor, the county treasurer, the prosecuting attorney, and, on approval at a general election of the question placed on the ballot by petition, two electors from the county.[15] The commission examines the tax budget submitted by the board of education[16] and adjusts the estimated amounts required from the general property tax for each fund, as shown by the tax budget, so as to bring the tax levies required within the limitations of law. The commission has the authority to revise and adjust the estimate of balances and receipts from all sources for each fund and in so doing determines the total appropriations that may be made from the fund.[17]

(B) Reviewing need for each tax

In reviewing the tax budget and determining the levies necessary to produce the amounts shown in the budget, the county budget commission determines whether the board's tax budget shows a "need" for each tax the board is authorized to levy.[18] If a board fails to show the requisite "need" in its tax budget, the budget commission has no authority to permit the board to levy an authorized tax. Each tax which the board is authorized to levy must be clearly required by the tax budget.[19]

Before final determination of the amount in the tax budget to be allotted to each board of education from any source, the commission must permit representatives of the board to appear and explain the board's financial needs.[20] The commission's work on tax budgets must be completed and tax rates certified on or before March 1.[21] The Ohio tax commissioner may for good cause extend this deadline.[22] Some of those rates may be subject to revision as the calendar year progresses.

(C) Levies approved by voters

The one exception to the general rule that all levies must be shown in the tax budget are levies approved by the electors at or before the November general election but after the tax budget is submitted to the county budget commission. In those cases, the requirement of RC 5705.341 that no tax may be levied "unless such rate of taxation for the ensuing fiscal year is clearly required by a budget of the taxing district ... properly and lawfully advertised, adopted and filed" is satisfied by the approval of the electors.[23]

---

[12]But see OAG 82-027 (concluding that interest earned on township reserve balance in county's custody belongs to county).
[13]RC 5705.29(E)(4).
[14]RC 5705.35(B)(1).
[15]RC 5705.27.
[16]RC 5705.31.
[17]RC 5705.32.
[18]RC 5705.32(A).

[19]RC 5705.29, RC 5705.31, RC 5705.32, RC 5705.341.
[20]RC 5705.32.
[21]RC 5705.35.
[22]RC 5705.27.
[23]State ex rel Fairfield County Bd of Mental Retardation v Fairfield County Budget Comm, 10 OS(3d) 123, 10 OBR 447, 461 NE(2d) 1297 (1984); Cuyahoga County Bd of Mental Retardation v

40.06 Appeal from decision of budget commission

A board of education that is dissatisfied with any action of the county budget commission may, through the district treasurer, appeal to the state board of tax appeals within thirty days after receipt of the official certificate of estimated resources or notice of action by the commission.[24] Timely filing of a notice of appeal from the action of the budget commission is necessary to preserve the rights of the board.[25]

An appeals court's decision concerning the allocation of tax levies within the ten-mill limitation after annexation of one school district to another is binding when the identical issue is appealed to the board of tax appeals from the order of the county budget commission allocating the levies for the next tax year.[26]

Initial review of budget commission actions over certification of tax levies for collection is vested exclusively in the board of tax appeals.[27]

PROPERTY TAX LEVIES

40.07 Basis for tax levies

A property tax may be levied only when it is clearly required by the tax budget of the taxing authority.[28] The county budget commission has a specific duty to refuse to certify a tax levy which is outside the ten-mill limitation where the levy is not clearly required by the budget submitted by a political subdivision and where the outside millage has not been approved by the electors in the current year.[29] The county budget commission is also prohibited from certifying a levy in excess of the revenue requirements set out in the budget submitted.[30] However, the budget commission must increase an existing levy or include a new levy when the electors have approved the increase or the new levy at or before the November general election.[31] After the county budget commission completes its work, the taxes are actually levied on the properties located in the district by a resolution adopted by the board of education. The form of this resolution is customarily provided by the county budget commission.

40.08 Requirement for separate levies

A board of education is required to divide the property taxes levied by it into separate levies, as follows:

(1) General levy for debt charges within the ten-mill limitation;

(2) General levy for current expenses within the ten-mill limitation;

(3) Special levies within the ten-mill limitation;

(4) General levy for debt charges authorized by law or by vote of the people in excess of the ten-mill limitation; and

(5) Other special or general levies authorized by law or by vote of the people in excess of the ten-mill limitation.[32]

Cuyahoga County Bd of Commrs, 41 OS(2d) 103, 322 NE(2d) 885 (1975); State ex rel Steubenville School Dist Bd of Ed v Hamrock, 11 Misc 36, 225 NE(2d) 795 (CP, Jefferson 1967).
[24]RC 5705.37.
[25]South Russell v Geauga County Budget Comm, 12 OS(3d) 126, 12 OBR 167, 465 NE(2d) 876 (1984).
[26]Cambridge City School Dist v Guernsey County Budget Comm, 13 Misc 258 (BTA 1967). See also Cambridge City School Dist v Guernsey County Budget Comm, 11 App(2d) 77, 228 NE(2d) 874 (Guernsey 1967), affirmed by 13 OS(2d) 77, 234 NE(2d) 512 (1968).
[27]State ex rel Geauga County Budget Comm v Geauga County Court of Appeals, 1 OS(3d) 110, 1 OBR 143, 438 NE(2d) 428 (1982).

[28]RC 5705.341.
[29]Waite Hill v Lake County Budget Comm, 46 OS(2d) 543, 350 NE(2d) 411 (1976).
[30]Wise v Twinsburg, 36 OS(2d) 114, 304 NE(2d) 390 (1973).
[31]Cuyahoga County Bd of Mental Retardation v Cuyahoga County Bd of Commrs, 41 OS(2d) 103, 322 NE(2d) 885 (1975); State ex rel Fairfield County Bd of Mental Retardation v Fairfield County Budget Comm, 10 OS(3d) 123, 10 OBR 447, 461 NE(2d) 1297 (1984).
[32]RC 5705.04.

40.09 General and special levies within ten-mill limitation

(A) General levy for current expenses

The purpose of the general levy for current expenses (i.e., the taxes levied for the general fund within the ten-mill limitation; sometimes called "inside millage") is to provide one general operating fund derived from taxation, from which any expenditures for current expenses of any kind may be made, including permanent improvements authorized by law.[33] The general levy also includes the amounts necessary for payment of final judgments, cost of elections, tuition, teachers retirement fund, and the maintenance, operation, and repair of schools. It does not include amounts necessary for payment of debt charges,[34] although it may be used for that purpose if current revenue borrowing or other unvoted borrowing is undertaken in the year in which the levy is collected.

(B) Special levy

A board of education may also levy a tax within the ten-mill limitation for any specific permanent improvement which the board is authorized to acquire, construct, or improve, or for the library purposes of the school district.[35] Unless unlevied millage is available within the ten-mill limitation, the imposition of such a special levy will reduce the general levy for current expenses in a like amount.

40.10 Special levies outside ten-mill limitation

Levies outside of the ten-mill limitation must be approved by the electors of the school district pursuant to specific procedures prescribed by law.[36] These procedures are given in two sections of the revised code,[37] together with certain other relevant provisions which govern the details of submitting a tax levy to the electors of the district.

(A) Nonemergency tax levies

Under RC 5705.21, the board of education of any school district, except a county district, may at any time by a two-thirds vote of all its members declare and certify to the appropriate board of elections that the amount of taxes to be raised within the ten-mill limitation will be insufficient to provide enough for the necessary requirements of the district, and that it is necessary to levy a tax outside of the ten-mill limitation for any of the following purposes: current expenses; a public library supported by a school district; recreational purposes; acquiring property for, constructing, operating and maintaining a community center; construction or acquisition of a permanent improvement or class of improvements which the district may include in a single bond issue; general, ongoing permanent improvements; providing educational technology (defined as computer hardware, equipment, materials and accessories, equipment used for two-way audio or video, and software), and operating a cultural center (defined as a freestanding building separate from a school building that is open to the public for educational, musical, artistic, and cultural purposes).

The resolution submitting the question must be confined to a single purpose and must state the amount of increase in rate which it is necessary to levy, the purpose, and the number of years up to five (except for a levy for current expenses) during which the increase will be in effect. When the additional rate is for current expenses or general, ongoing permanent improvements, the increased rate may be proposed for up to five years or for a continuing period. These resolutions go into effect immediately upon adoption, and no publication is required other than that provided in the notice of the election.[38] A copy of the resolution authorizing submission of the question of a tax levy outside the ten-mill limitation must be certified by the board of education to the county board of elections not less than seventy-five days

---

[33]RC 5705.05.
[34]RC 5705.05.
[35]RC 5705.06.
[36]See Text 39.03, Ten-mill limitation, voted and unvoted levies.

[37]RC 5705.194, RC 5705.21.
[38]RC 5705.21.

before the election.[39] The requirements for giving notice of the election and the precise formal ballot are provided for in RC 5705.25.

(B) Emergency tax levies

In a procedure similar to that for non-emergency levies, the board of education of any school district, except a county district, may at any time by a majority vote of the members determine that existing sources of revenue are insufficient to provide for the emergency requirements of the district or to avoid an operating deficit and that it is necessary to request the voters to authorize the levy of an additional tax to produce a fixed dollar amount for a specified number of years, not to exceed five.[40] This type of levy is sometimes called an "emergency tax levy." Emergency tax levies are not subject to the reduction in the effective rate of the levy to produce the same number of dollars each year from the same properties,[41] since emergency levies result in taxes levied at a rate calculated to generate a specific dollar amount.[42]

A resolution declaring it necessary to submit an initial or renewal emergency levy to the electors must be submitted to the county auditor at least eighty days before the election for the calculation of the estimated millage required to produce the dollar amount specified in the resolution.[43] After receipt of the county auditor's calculations, if the board of education determines to proceed with the election, it must certify the resolution and the county auditor's calculations to the county board of elections on or before the seventy-fifth day prior to the election.[44] The requirements for giving notice of the election and the precise formal ballot are provided for in RC 5705.196 and RC 5705.197, respectively.

(C) Incremental tax levies

Under RC 5705.212 the board of education of any school district, except a county district, may adopt a resolution declaring the necessity of levying up to five new taxes for current expenses. These so-called "incremental" tax levies are designed to lessen the effects of 1976 House Bill 920 by allowing boards to submit a tax for current expenses which produces increased revenues over time. Each new tax is to be levied in a different year and over a specified period which may be for any number of years up to ten or for a continuing period. The tax has two components, an "original" tax and up to four "incremental" taxes. The original tax is the first levied, and the incremental taxes are those levied in subsequent years. Each of the incremental taxes must be levied at the same rate, although this rate need not be the same as that of the original tax.[45]

The rates of the original tax and of each incremental tax are cumulative so that the rate levied in any year is the sum of the original tax and all incremental taxes first levied in or prior to that year. For example, if the board proposes (and the voters approve) a tax with an original rate of 4.0 mills and four incremental taxes of 3.0 mills each to be first collected after two, four, six, and eight years, the rate collected in the fourth and fifth years would be 10.0 mills (4 + 3 + 3). In the sixth and seventh years, the rate collected would be 13.0 mills, and thereafter (unless the levy is for a fixed period of time) the rate would be 16.0 mills.

The resolution submitting this tax must state the amount of the original and each incremental tax and the year in which each tax is first proposed to be levied. In addition, it must state the number of years the taxes will be in effect (either a continuing period or a fixed period not exceeding ten years) and that the purpose of the tax is for current expenses. If approved for a fixed period, the last year the original tax is in effect is the last year each incremental tax is in effect so that all components terminate at the same time.

The resolution submitting an incremental tax must be adopted by a two-thirds vote of all board members and certified to the board of elections no later than seventy-five days before the date of the election.

---

[39] But see the earlier deadline for commencing emergency levy proceedings discussed above.
[40] RC 5705.194.
[41] See Text 40.14, Reduction in effective rate of additional tax levy.

[42] RC 319.301.
[43] RC 5705.194.
[44] RC 5705.195.
[45] RC 5705.212.

Those taxes levied for less than a continuing period of time are renewable for a fixed number of years or a continuing period.[46]

RC 5705.213 provides that the board of education of any school district, except an educational service center, may submit an incremental tax which is stated in terms of the amount of money to be raised, rather than in terms of a millage. For the first year this type of levy is proposed, the amount must be stated in dollars, and for subsequent years the increase may be expressed as either a specified dollar amount or a percentage increase over the previous year's amount. This type of incremental tax levy (which is similar to the emergency tax levy) must also be for current expenses and may be in effect for any number of years up to ten.[47]

The resolution proposing this type of incremental tax levy must be adopted by a two-thirds vote of all board members and certified no later than eighty days before the election to the county auditor, who calculates and certifies to the board of education the estimated levy for the original tax and each increment. The resolution and county auditor's certification must then be delivered to the board of elections no later than seventy-five days before the election. These levies may also be renewed, and borrowing against the proceeds is specifically authorized.[48]

Ballot forms and necessary information for notices of election for incremental levies and their renewals are specified.[49]

(D) County school financing district levies for special education

In a procedure generally identical to that for nonemergency levies, the board of education of a county school financing district,[50] upon receipt of identical resolutions adopted within a sixty day period by a majority of the members of the board of each school district within the county district, may submit a levy to the electors of the territory for (1) current expenses for the provision of special education and related services within the county school financing district territory, (2) permanent improvements for special education and related services within the district territory, (3) current expenses for specified educational programs within the district territory, (4) permanent improvements for specified educational programs within the district territory, or (5) permanent improvements within the district territory.[51] The levy may not exceed ten years, unless it is solely for purposes (1) or (3) above, in which case it may be for a continuing period.[52] After approval of such a tax, the county board may expend the proceeds for the purposes approved by the electors or otherwise distribute funds to boards within its territory for those purposes.[53]

Specific and complex provisions also authorize a board of education to propose a reduction in its property taxes as part of a proposal to impose additional taxes by a county school financing district.[54]

40.11 Renewal tax levies

If the levy is proposed to renew all or a portion of the proceeds derived from one or more existing levies under RC 5705.194, it is called a renewal levy and must be so designated on the ballot. No two or more existing levies can be included in a single renewal levy unless they expire in the same year, and, whatever the original purpose of any such existing levy, the purpose of the renewal levy may be either to avoid an operating deficit or to provide for emergency requirements of the school district. A resolution for a renewal levy (except a renewal emergency tax levy) may not be placed on the ballot unless the question is

---

[46] RC 5705.212.
[47] RC 5705.213.
[48] RC 5705.213.
[49] RC 5705.251.

[50] A county school financing district, formed under RC 3311.50, is not to be confused with an educational service center (as defined in RC 3311.05(A)) or a joint educational service center that results from the voluntary consolidation of educational service centers under RC 3311.053. See Text 4.03(B), Educational service center; Text 4.03(C), New educational service centers.

A county school financing district is purely a taxing district whose creation, purpose, and territory are governed by RC 3311.50. Among other things, that statute prescribes procedures under which the territory of a city, local, or exempted village school district may be joined to or withdrawn from a county school financing district.

[51] RC 5705.215.
[52] RC 5705.215.
[53] RC 3311.51.
[54] RC 5705.215(E).

submitted at an election held during the last year the levy or levies to be renewed may be collected or in the preceding year at the general election.[55] A renewal of an emergency tax levy may be submitted at an election held during the last year the levy or levies to be renewed may be collected, or in the preceding year at the general or primary election.[56]

40.12 Replacement tax levies

Any board of education, except a county board, may propose to replace all or a portion of an existing nonemergency tax levy[57] or, in the case of a joint vocational district, a joint vocational property tax levy.[58] The resolution submitting a replacement levy must state the date of the election, whether the proposal is to replace all or a portion of the existing levy, the rate proposed, and the first year the levy will be imposed.[59]

Replacement and increase, as well as replacement and decrease, questions are authorized. A continuing levy may be replaced, although only one such question can be submitted to the electors in any calendar year.[60] If two existing levies expire in the same year or are both continuing levies and are for the same purpose, all or a portion of each may be combined into a single replacement levy. The procedures for adopting a replacement levy resolution and for its submission to the board of elections are the same as for the type of levy proposed to be replaced.[61]

40.13 Election on tax levy outside of ten-mill limitation

Upon timely receipt of the proper resolutions, the board of elections submits the proposal to the electors of the school district at the election specified in the resolutions. Elections may be held only on the first Tuesday after the first Monday in February, May, August, or November, except that in a year in which a presidential primary election is held, no special election can be held in February or May but may be held on the third Tuesday in March.[62] Notice of the election must be published in one or more newspapers of general circulation in the county once a week for three consecutive weeks in the case of an emergency levy and for four consecutive weeks for a nonemergency levy. The proposal must appear on the ballot in the manner and form provided by statute.[63] Combining two or more renewal levies into one ballot question is not authorized, but placing more than one question of a levy in excess of the ten-mill limitation on any one ballot is permitted. As discussed below, a levy may be submitted to the electors at a special election no more than three times in any calendar year.[64] A resolution to renew or replace an existing nonemergency levy may not be placed on the ballot unless the question is submitted at an election held during the last year the tax to be renewed or replaced may be collected or in the preceding year at the general election.[65] A resolution to renew an existing emergency levy may not be placed on the ballot unless the question is submitted at an election held during the last year the tax to be renewed may be collected or in the preceding year at the primary or the general election.[66]

An emergency levy (including any renewal of an emergency levy) may be submitted at not more than three special elections in any calendar year, provided that each time a board of education submits a nonemergency levy outside of the ten-mill limitation during the same calendar year, the maximum number of times an emergency levy may be submitted at a special election during the year is reduced by one. A nonemergency levy outside of the ten-mill limitation may be submitted to the electors at a special election three times in any calendar year, and for each time an emergency levy is submitted in a calendar year at a special election the number of times a special election may be held in such year to consider the question of a nonemergency levy is reduced by one.[67]

---

[55] RC 5705.25.
[56] RC 5705.194.
[57] RC 5705.192(J).
[58] RC 5705.192(A).
[59] RC 5705.192.
[60] RC 5705.192(A)(2).
[61] RC 5705.192(A)(2).
[62] RC 3501.01.
[63] RC 5705.194 to RC 5705.196 (emergency levy), RC 5705.21, RC 5705.25 (nonemergency levy).
[64] RC 5705.194, RC 5705.21.
[65] RC 5705.25 (nonemergency levy).
[66] RC 5705.194.
[67] RC 5705.194.

40.14 Reduction in effective rate of additional tax levy

A property tax rate may not be reduced below a minimum fixed by law.[68] However, certain tax levies—including those voted for a continuing period of time—are subject to reduction by a statutory procedure designed to produce the same number of dollars each year from the same properties.[69] This is the so-called "House Bill 920" procedure. It is based on a "reduction factor" calculated by the tax commissioner each year from information supplied by the county auditor.

However, if reduction would cause the total taxes charged and payable for current expenses to be less than twenty mills, the tax commissioner is required to calculate a reduction factor which would cause the taxes, when added to a certain portion of taxes for current expenses for joint vocational school districts which were first charged and payable in 1981 or earlier, to equal either the lesser of the sum of the rates at which those taxes are authorized to be levied or the same amount as would be collected if those taxes were levied at the rate of twenty mills. The county auditor is required to use the reduction factor supplied by the tax commissioner in preparing the revenue estimates and tax bills for the school district.[70] This provision does not apply to taxes levied by joint vocational or cooperative education school districts.

The tax commissioner may order a county auditor to furnish any information he needs to make his calculations under RC 319.301(D) and (E). If the auditor fails to comply with the commissioner's order, the commissioner may direct the department of education to withhold fifty per cent of state revenues to school districts under RC Chapter 3317.[71]

APPROPRIATIONS

40.15 Annual appropriation resolution

(A) Necessity for annual appropriation

Deficit spending is generally illegal in Ohio.[72] Moreover, a public official who spends more than the amount appropriated is guilty of dereliction of duty.[73] An appropriation is the fundamental prerequisite to the authority to spend public money, and school officials cannot spend school money until an appropriation resolution is adopted by the board of education. Thereafter the board may not spend funds in excess of the appropriations as supplemented or revised.

The basis of the annual appropriation resolution is the revised tax budget,[74] which is based on the official certificate of estimated resources provided by the county budget commission.[75]

(B) Certificate of resources, amendment

The annual appropriations resolution must be adopted by October 1 unless the county budget commission has not certified all amended certificates of estimated resources.[76] Under RC 133.302(A) and RC 5705.36(B), the budget commission must certify an amended certificate of estimated resources, or certify that no amended certificate needs to be issued, at the time

(1) of a settlement for taxes under RC 321.24 against which notes have been issued either under RC 133.10(D) or RC 133.301 or under RC 133.302 and RC 133.303; and

(2) the general tax duplicate for real and public utility property is delivered to the county treasurer pursuant to RC 319.28 and the general personal property tax duplicate is delivered to the county treasurer pursuant to RC 319.29.

---

[68] RC 5705.32.
[69] RC 319.301.
[70] RC 319.301.
[71] RC 319.301(G).
[72] See O Const Art VIII §1 to 3.
[73] RC 2921.44(D).
[74] RC 5705.35.
[75] RC 5705.36.
[76] RC 5705.38.

At the time of the settlements, and on delivery of each duplicate, the county auditor must determine whether the total amount to be distributed to each school district from the settlement or duplicate, when combined with the amounts to be distributed from any subsequent settlement, will increase or decrease the amount available for appropriation during the current fiscal year from any fund. If it does alter the amount available, the auditor must certify his finding to the budget commission, which must then certify an amended certificate of estimated resources requesting the increase or decrease.

(C) Temporary resolution

Prior to the adoption of the annual appropriation measure, a board of education may adopt a temporary resolution in the form prescribed by the state auditor. The appropriations made in the temporary appropriation resolution are chargeable against the appropriations made in the annual appropriation resolution. The annual appropriation must include each sum to be spent for the various functions of the board during the fiscal year and must be in the form prescribed by the state auditor after consultation with the Ohio tax commissioner.[77]

(D) Limitations on amount appropriated

All appropriation resolutions, whether temporary or annual, are limited so that the total appropriations from each fund cannot exceed the total estimated receipts for each fund as shown on the latest certificate of estimated resources, including actual year-end fund balances.[78] The certificate of estimated resources, prepared by the county budget commission, states the estimated income by fund to be received by the board during the fiscal year.

Revenues available for appropriation in the fiscal year generally include taxes scheduled to be settled during the fiscal year, other revenues in process of collection or on hand during the fiscal year, certain amounts that may be borrowed in anticipation of tax collections in future years, and, in addition, a spending reserve for the fiscal years 1987 to 1995.[79] Real property tax receipts available for appropriation include revenues from real property taxes scheduled to be settled on or before August 10 and February 15; taxes levied on personal property available for appropriation include taxes scheduled to be settled on or before October 31 and June 30 less the amount of any spending reserve appropriated for the prior fiscal year plus any spending reserve balance in the tax budget for the current fiscal year.

40.16 Amending or supplementing appropriation resolution

The appropriation resolution may be amended or supplemented during the year, so long as the amendment or supplement complies with all provisions of law governing an initial appropriation, and so long as no appropriation is reduced below an amount sufficient to cover all unliquidated and outstanding obligations certified from or against the appropriation.[80] Each amendment or supplement should be by board resolution.[81] Each appropriation measure must have a certificate attached on which the district treasurer, board president, and superintendent certify that the board has in effect for the remainder of the fiscal year the authorization to levy taxes which, when combined with the estimated revenue from all other sources available to the board at the time of certification, are sufficient to provide the operating revenues necessary to enable the board to operate an adequate educational program for all the days in its adopted school calendar.[82] If no calendar has yet been adopted for that fiscal year, the certification should refer to the number of days on which instruction was held in the preceding fiscal year. No certificate is required on a temporary appropriation measure if as follows:

(1) Amount appropriated does not exceed twenty-five per cent of the total amount from all sources available from any fund during the preceding fiscal year;

---

[77]RC 5705.38.
[78]RC 5705.39.
[79]RC 9.34, RC 133.302, RC 5705.194, RC 5705.21, RC 5705.29, RC 5705.35. See also Text 40.04(C), Spending reserve.

[80]RC 5705.40.
[81]OAG 94-007.
[82]RC 5705.412.

(2) Measure will not be in effect on or after the thirtieth day following the earliest date on which an annual appropriation measure may be passed; and

(3) Amended official certificate of estimated resources for the current year has not been certified to the board of education.[83]

40.17 Adoption of spending plan concurrent with adoption of appropriation resolution

As part of its annual appropriation resolution, the board is also required to adopt a spending plan in a form prescribed by the superintendent of public instruction, giving a schedule of receipts and expenditures from all appropriated funds for the fiscal year. The spending plan must be amended or supplemented each time the annual appropriation resolution is amended or supplemented. The appropriation resolution and spending plan and each supplement or amendment must be filed with the superintendent of public instruction.[84]

40.18 Filing requirements

(A) Documents to be filed with state department of education

By April 20 of each year, each board of education is required to file with the state department of education copies of its amended official certificate of estimated resources and its annual appropriation resolution. These documents must be held available for public inspection at reasonable times and hours.[85]

(B) Documents to be filed with county auditor

The treasurer is also required to forward a copy of each certificate required by RC 5705.412 to the county auditor. The county auditor may not distribute property taxes or state school foundation payments to a board that has not filed copies of all such certificates. If the county auditor believes that not all of the necessary certifications have been made or that those which have been made contain false information, he is required to notify the superintendent of public instruction, the state auditor, and the board's chief legal officer.[86]

(C) Procedure when documents reveal district may have financial shortfall

After review of the submitted materials or notification from the county auditor, if the superintendent of public instruction determines that the district may be financially unable to operate its instructional calendar on all the days in its adopted school calendar, he must notify the state auditor and the board president.[87]

40.19 Auditor's certificate that appropriations do not exceed estimate

After the annual appropriation resolution is adopted, a certified copy must be sent to the county auditor who in turn must certify to the board and the superintendent of public instruction that the appropriations do not exceed the official estimate certified by the county budget commission.[88]

Upon a determination by the district treasurer that the revenue to be collected by the board will be greater or less than the amounts included in the official certificate of estimated resources, the treasurer should certify this additional amount or deficiency to the county budget commission, which, upon request, will issue an amended certificate of estimated resources reflecting the change in expected revenue.[89] On receipt of the amended certificate, the appropriation resolution of the board must be amended to reflect the certified additional amount or deficiency and the necessary changes made on the appropriation ledger.

---

[83]RC 5705.412.
[84]RC 5705.391.
[85]RC 3311.40.
[86]RC 5705.412.

[87]RC 3313.489.
[88]RC 5705.39.
[89]RC 5705.36.

Chapter 41

Borrowing Money

GENERAL AUTHORITY TO BORROW MONEY
41.01 Authority to borrow money
41.02 Other types of borrowing

UNIFORM BOND LAW RESTRICTIONS ON ISSUING BONDS AND NOTES
41.03 Uniform Bond Law
41.04 Purposes of school borrowing
41.05 Limits on unvoted debt
41.06 Limit on voted debt
41.07 Special needs district
41.08 Other limits on debt

GENERAL PROCEDURES FOR ISSUING BONDS AND NOTES
41.09 Election procedures for voted debt
41.10 Step one: determining estimated life of permanent improvement
41.11 Step two: calculating maturity of bonds, treasurer's certificate
41.12 Step three: resolution of necessity
41.13 Step four: resolution to proceed
41.14 Step five: election
41.15 Step six: tax levy for debt service
41.16 Step seven: authorization of bonds or notes
41.17 Step eight: sale of bonds or notes
41.18 Refunding or advance refunding bonds or notes
41.19 Federal tax law provisions
41.20 Miscellaneous state law provisions

BORROWING FOR CURRENT EXPENSES
41.21 Borrowing in anticipation of collection of current revenue
41.22 Tax anticipation notes

JOINT VOCATIONAL SCHOOL DISTRICT BONDS AND LEVIES
41.23 Borrowing by joint vocational school district

STATE ASSISTANCE FOR CLASSROOM FACILITIES
41.24 Classroom Facilities Law
41.25 Net bonded indebtedness and conditions of state assistance
41.26 Application for state assistance, approval
41.27 Conditional approval, proceedings to qualify for assistance
41.28 Proceedings for election
41.29 Agreement for construction and sale of project
41.30 Issuance of bonds or notes, proceeds of sale
41.31 Suspending authority to issue bonds or notes
41.32 Certification of tax levies

EMERGENCY LOANS
41.33 Emergency loans

GENERAL AUTHORITY TO BORROW MONEY

41.01 Authority to borrow money

Article VI, section 3 of the Ohio Constitution empowers the general assembly to provide for the organization, administration, and control of the public schools. Under this authority, the general assembly has authorized school districts to incur indebtedness, i.e., borrow money. The purposes for which a district can borrow money, the limits on the total amount of debt that can be incurred, and the procedures for borrowing are detailed in state statutes. A board of education has no authority to borrow money except as provided by statute.

The primary statutes detailing such borrowing are RC Chapter 133, the Uniform Bond Law, and RC Chapter 3318, the Classroom Facilities Law. Miscellaneous other provisions relate to borrowing for certain purposes, for example, the cost of residences for school principals or teachers,[1] energy conservation improvements,[2] emergency avoidance of school closings,[3] and creation of joint vocational school districts.[4] Moreover, RC Chapters 5705 and 5748 contain provisions enabling a board to borrow money in anticipation of the collection of certain taxes levied by the school district.[5] These statutes are complex and constantly changing. Boards should contact their legal adviser early in their planning.

41.02 Other types of borrowing

This chapter addresses the traditional forms of borrowing. However, in recent

---

[1] RC 3313.38.
[2] RC 133.06(G), RC 3313.372.
[3] RC 3317.62 to RC 3317.64.
[4] RC Ch 3311.
[5] RC 5705.194, RC 5705.21, RC 5748.05.

years a variety of financing techniques have been used—often to avoid legal restrictions placed on debt—by boards of education to pay for certain capital items. These include leases, lease-purchase agreements, and shared savings agreements. Generally, if properly structured, these methods do not constitute "securities" and are therefore not subject to the general restrictions discussed in this chapter.[6] However, if improperly structured, they may, in fact, constitute debt and be subject to some or all of these restrictions.

The first question to be considered when any such financing technique is proposed is whether the board has legal authority to enter into that kind of arrangement. For example, boards of education are permitted to lease-purchase land, any buildings needed for school district purposes,[7] certain types of office equipment and computer hardware and software,[8] and equipment for the maintenance or physical upkeep of facilities or land under its control,[9] but are not authorized to lease- or installment-purchase services or even capital items not specifically authorized, such as school buses. The procedure for entering into lease-purchase agreements is complicated by a number of factors, including competitive bidding requirements.[10]

Therefore, it is extremely important that boards consult experienced counsel early to make certain the proposed "non-debt" transaction is authorized and that the provisions under which it will be undertaken (generally found in a written contract) will not inadvertently cause the transaction to constitute debt under the board's debt limitations or some other unintended consequence.

UNIFORM BOND LAW RESTRICTIONS ON ISSUING BONDS AND NOTES

41.03 Uniform Bond Law

The Uniform Bond Law applies throughout Ohio. In governing the incurrence of debt by public bodies, the law prescribes the political subdivisions which may borrow money, the purposes for borrowing, the limitations on the amount which can be borrowed, and the proceedings under which borrowing is accomplished.

Most bonds and notes issued by a board of education are issued to acquire or construct permanent improvements. Any property, asset, or improvement with an estimated life or usefulness of five years or more, including land and interests in land, and also reconstructions, enlargements, and extensions of existing improvements are defined as "permanent improvements."[11]

These obligations may be divided into two categories: those issued pursuant to a vote of the school district's electors, and those issued without such a vote. Although generally called "securities" by statute, "bonds" are written evidences of indebtedness with longer maturities, usually five or more years. "Notes" are written evidences of indebtedness with shorter maturities, usually five years or less. So-called "bond anticipation notes" may only be issued in anticipation of the issuance of bonds.

For purposes of the Uniform Bond Law, a school district, other than an educational service center but including a county financing district, is a "subdivision,"[12] and the "taxing authority" or "bond issuing authority" of the district is its board of education.[13] The district's "fiscal officer" is the treasurer.[14]

"Current operating expenses" and "current expenses" mean the lawful expenditures of a subdivision, except for perma-

---

[6]RC 133.01(GG).
[7]RC 3313.375.
[8]RC 3313.37(B)(4).
[9]RC 3313.37(B)(5).
[10]RC 3313.46. See OAG 84-046. For additional guidance, see the Ohio Supreme Court's discussion of city lease-purchase agreements in State ex rel Kitchen v Christman, 31 OS(2d) 64, 285 NE(2d) 362 (1972).
[11]RC 133.01(CC).
[12]RC 133.01(MM).
[13]RC 133.01(NN).
[14]RC 133.01(L), RC 3313.22.

nent improvements and for payments for debt charges on the bonds, notes, and certificates of indebtedness of the subdivision.[15] "Debt charges" are the interest, sinking fund, and retirement and redemption charges on securities.[16]

41.04 Purposes of school borrowing

A board of education may incur debt only for the purposes listed in the statutes conferring borrowing power.[17]

The "taxing authority" of a "subdivision" of the state is authorized to issue bonds for the purpose of acquiring or constructing any permanent improvement the subdivision is authorized to acquire or construct.[18] The board of any school district (other than an educational service center) or county financing district has specific authority to build, enlarge, repair, and furnish necessary schoolhouses, to purchase sites therefor, to purchase sites for playgrounds, and to provide necessary apparatus and make all other necessary provisions for the schools under its control.[19]

On approval from the department of education, a board of education may also incur debt outside of certain limitations to finance permanent improvements which significantly reduce energy consumption.[20] Before state approval is requested, (1) an architect or engineer must estimate all costs of design, engineering, installation, maintenance, repairs, and debt service and the amount by which energy consumption would be reduced, and (2) the board must determine that the amount of money spent on the improvements is not likely to exceed savings in energy costs over the next ten years.[21] A board may also issue notes not subject to the Uniform Bond Law to secure payments under an installment payment contract for the purchase and installation of energy conservation measures.[22]

Other sections of the Uniform Bond Law authorize subdivisions, including boards of education, to issue bonds or notes for certain other purposes:

(1) To pay final court judgments, losses, damages, and the expenses of litigation or settlement of claims (RC 133.14 and RC 2744.081);

(2) To meet certain expenses incurred as a result of specified emergencies (RC 133.06(F));

(3) To pay the cost of establishing and maintaining a self-insurance reserve or a joint insurance pool (RC 2744.081); and

(4) To raise funds in anticipation of the collection of tax revenues (RC 133.10 and RC 133.301).

41.05 Limits on unvoted debt

(A) Statutory limitations

The total "net indebtedness" a school district can create or incur is strictly controlled. The net indebtedness incurred without a vote of the people may not exceed one tenth of one per cent of total value of all property in the district, as listed and assessed for taxation.[23]

Unvoted net indebtedness incurred to pay the costs of building improvements to reduce energy consumption, however, may equal as much as nine-tenths of one per cent of the assessed valuation of property in the district.[24]

Under certain circumstances, the superintendent of public instruction may consent to a school district's issuance of debt in excess of these limitations if the district treasurer estimates, and the district board confirms, revenues from a tax abatement agreement are sufficient to service the debt and if the treasurer certifies, and the board confirms, the board has sufficient revenues to operate the permanent improvements to be acquired or constructed from the proceeds of the debt.[25]

---

[15] RC 133.01(I).
[16] RC 133.01(J).
[17] Board of Ed v Strausser, 20 Misc 1, 251 NE(2d) 515 (CP, Erie 1969).
[18] RC 133.15.
[19] RC 3313.37.
[20] RC 133.06(G).

[21] RC 133.06(G).
[22] RC 3313.372.
[23] RC 133.06(A).
[24] RC 133.06(G).
[25] RC 133.06(H). See also Text 41.07, Special needs district.

Net indebtedness is the difference between the face value of the district's outstanding bonds and notes and the amount held in the district's bond retirement fund for their redemption.[26] Statutes provide, however, that certain obligations—for example, bonds issued for certain emergency purposes under RC 133.12, notes issued for an energy conservation installment purchase contract under RC 3313.372, notes issued in anticipation of the collection of current revenues and other tax anticipation notes issued under RC 133.10, spending reserve notes issued under RC 133.301, debt incurred to acquire computers and software under RC 3313.37, notes issued to purchase school buses and other transportation equipment, or obligations issued for certain self-insurance purposes under RC 2744.081—are not considered in calculating a district's net indebtedness.

(B) Constitutional limitation

In addition to the statutory limitation, the Ohio Constitution imposes a debt limitation: Article XII, sections 2 and 11, have been interpreted by the Ohio Supreme Court as a debt limitation applicable to all subdivisions, including school districts.[27]

Section 11 states that when a subdivision incurs bonded indebtedness, it must provide by legislation for the annual levy and collection of a tax sufficient to pay the debt charges on the bonds. This taxation for debt purposes is limited by section 2, which provides, "No property, taxed according to value, shall be so taxed in excess of one percent of its true value in money for all state and local purposes." This so-called "ten-mill limitation" has been given effect by RC 5705.02:

> The aggregate amount of taxes that may be levied on any taxable property in any subdivision or other taxing unit shall not in any one year exceed ten mills on each dollar of tax valuation of such subdivision or other taxing unit, except for taxes specifically authorized to be levied in excess of the limitation.

Thus, debt may not be incurred if an unvoted tax exceeding ten mills would need to be levied on property within the district to pay the highest annual debt charges on the debt and all outstanding unvoted debt of the district and any overlapping subdivisions (such as counties and municipalities) which tax property within the district.

To determine how much millage is available to provide for debt service charges on unvoted bonds, the total amount of debt charges on all outstanding, unvoted debt of the district and any overlapping subdivisions must be calculated. The balance between the total millage committed to this debt and the ten-mill limit is the amount of millage available to the district for unvoted borrowing.

Thus, if there are no outstanding bonds of the district or any overlapping subdivision, which are required to be paid by taxes within the ten-mill limit, the district has authority to issue unvoted bonds up to an amount for which the highest annual debt charges on the bonds do not exceed the amount produced by a levy of ten mills on the assessed property within the district, provided the statutory direct debt limitation is also met. This is without regard to the amount allocated to the district by the budget commission as "inside millage" for current operating expenses or other purposes.

41.06 Limit on voted debt

Voted indebtedness is also subject to statutory limitation. The total net indebtedness of a district may not exceed nine per cent of the total value of all property in the district as listed and assessed for taxation.[28] An exception is provided for "special needs districts," discussed below.

The nine per cent limitation applies to both voted and unvoted indebtedness. However, the debt described above as being exempt from the unvoted limitation is also exempt from this limitation.

41.07 Special needs district

If a board of education determines that its student population is not being adequately served by the district's existing sites, buildings, and facilities, and that the

---

[26] RC 133.04.
[27] State ex rel Portsmouth v Kountz, 129 OS 272, 194 NE 869 (1935).

[28] RC 133.06(B).

district cannot obtain enough money by issuing securities within the limitation of RC 133.06, the board may define the district as a "special needs district" by resolution.[29]

The resolution, together with a supporting statistical report, must be certified to the superintendent of public instruction, who then determines whether any additional state or federal funds are available to meet district needs. If additional funds are not available, the superintendent then determines whether the projection of average tax valuation growth for the district over the next five years indicates a potential growth in tax valuation of at least three per cent per year. If so, the superintendent then certifies the district as an "approved special needs district."[30]

An approved special needs district may incur net indebtedness, calculated under RC 133.06, in an amount up to the greater of (1) nine per cent of the total value of all property assessed for taxation, plus an additional amount of unvoted debt determined by multiplying that total value by the percentage by which it has increased since the first day of the sixtieth month preceding the month in which the board of education determines to submit to the electors the question of the issuance of indebtedness to satisfy the special needs or (2) nine per cent of the total value of all property assessed for taxation plus an amount which is the result of multiplying that total value by the percentage increase which the superintendent of public instruction projects that total value to increase during the next ten years.[31]

41.08 Other limits on debt

In addition to the limitations relating to the amount of indebtedness a school district can incur, various sections of the Uniform Bond Law prescribe other limitations which may or may not apply to a particular bond or note issue, depending on the issue's nature and purpose. For example, a district cannot incur any debt to meet current operating expenses except as expressly authorized.[32]

Certain bonds issued to pay final judgments[33] cannot exceed the amount of the judgment plus court costs.

GENERAL PROCEDURES FOR ISSUING BONDS AND NOTES

41.09 Election procedures for voted debt

A board of education may submit a bond issue to the electors of the district under RC 133.18. Bond issues may be submitted to electors at a general, primary, or special election[34] and require a majority vote for passage.[35]

In districts where school buildings have been destroyed or condemned, or where the buildings are partially constructed or require additions to be completed, and where existing limitations make completion impossible as determined by the board of education, the board may declare an emergency and submit to popular vote the question of issuing bonds for furnishing, equipping, replacing, or adding to school buildings and for acquiring land under RC 133.06(F). A majority affirmative vote is necessary for passage.[36] These bonds are not subject to the limitations on net indebtedness prescribed by RC 133.06 but do have slightly different time deadlines than those outlined below.[37]

41.10 Step one: determining estimated life of permanent improvement

The first step is to determine the estimated life or usefulness of the permanent improvement to be acquired or constructed and the maximum maturity of the bonds. This may be done informally by calculating the estimated life of the various improvements to be financed with bond proceeds and the maximum maturity of the bonds, or

---

[29]RC 133.06(E).
[30]RC 133.06(E).
[31]RC 133.06(E).
[32]RC 133.03(D).
[33]RC 133.14.

[34]RC 3501.01.
[35]RC 133.18.
[36]RC 133.18.
[37]RC 133.18(F).

formally by the adoption of a resolution requesting the treasurer to certify the estimated life and maximum maturity. If a formal resolution is used, it should state the following:

(1) Purpose of the issue;

(2) Property, assets, and improvements to be acquired or constructed with the proceeds;

(3) Total amount of the issue; and

(4) Breakdown of the total to show the portion proposed to be expended for each class of property, assets, or improvements.

The proposed improvement must have an estimated life or usefulness of at least five years and, if the resolution is adopted, the treasurer should certify to the board that estimated life and the maximum maturity of the bonds.[38] The treasurer's certificate may be filed at any time prior to adoption of the resolution authorizing the issuance and sale of the bonds.[39]

41.11 Step two: calculating maturity of bonds, treasurer's certificate

(A) Calculation generally

The maximum maturity of bonds and notes may not extend beyond the maturity certified by the treasurer.[40] The maximum maturity, based on the estimated life or usefulness of various classes of property and improvements, is prescribed by RC 133.20. Thus, for example, the maximum maturity of bonds is thirty years to acquire real estate, from five to thirty years for construction of a building or other structure (depending on its period of usefulness as estimated by the treasurer), and ten years for furniture, landscaping, and playground apparatus.

The purpose of the maximum maturity is to ensure that the indebtedness incurred is amortized over the estimated life or usefulness of the permanent improvement so that at the expiration of the period it has been completely paid for and the indebtedness retired.

(B) Weighted average for multiple classes of improvements

When the purpose of a single bond issue includes two or more classes of improvements, the maximum maturity is determined by calculating the average number of years of usefulness of the various classes, measured by the "weighted average" of the amounts to be spent for each class.[41]

The calculation of the weighted average can best be demonstrated by an example: assume that a board of education wishes to issue bonds for the purpose of acquiring land, constructing a school building, and furnishing the building. It is proposed that $10,000 be spent to acquire the land, $900,000 to construct the building, and $90,000 to purchase the furnishings, for a total bond issue of $1,000,000.

The proposed issue thus includes three classes of improvements with different maturities under RC 133.20, with the maximum maturity for construction being based on its estimated usefulness: real estate, thirty years; construction of building, twenty-five years; and furnishings, ten years.

To determine a weighted average, the amount to be spent on each class is multiplied by the number of years of the maximum maturity prescribed for that class:

Land—30 years x $10,000 = $300,000

Building—25 years x $900,000 = $22,500,000

Furnishings—10 years x $90,000 = $900,000

Total $23,700,000

The total is then divided by the amount of the proposed issue ($1,000,000) = 23.7. The weighted average, and hence maximum maturity for the issue, is twenty-three years. Since taxes are collected on a yearly basis, only entire years are used in establishing maturities. Thus, the fraction of a year in the foregoing example is dropped and the maximum maturity is fixed at the next lowest whole year—twenty-three in this instance.

---

[38] RC 133.20.
[39] State ex rel Speeth v Carney, 163 OS 159, 126 NE(2d) 449 (1955).

[40] RC 133.20.
[41] RC 133.20(D).

It should be noted that the *maximum* maturity is merely the maximum which the board may fix; the board may fix a shorter maturity.

(C) Transfer of funds among classes

The treasurer's certification of maximum maturity including, if necessary, the weighted average determines not only the maximum time the bonds can be outstanding, but also how the proceeds can be allotted and spent.

The amount spent for any purpose falling within any class should not exceed the amount allotted to that class in the treasurer's certification.[42]

Thus, in the example given above, of the total bond issue proceeds of $1,000,000, only $10,000 can be spent for land, only $900,000 for construction of building, and only $90,000 for purchase of furnishings, except that if the board considers it necessary, the board can transfer the unexpended portion of the amount allocated to any class to any other class included in the treasurer's certification having a longer maturity, but not to a class having a shorter maturity.

Thus, in the example, if only $70,000 were actually spent for furnishings, the board could transfer the unspent $20,000 to either the $900,000 allotted to construction or to the $10,000 allotted to land acquisition, or divide it between the two. On the other hand, if only $5,000 of the amount allotted to land acquisition were spent for that purpose, the unspent $5,000 could not be transferred either to the amount allotted to construction or to the amount allotted to furnishings since both classes of property have a shorter maturity than does real estate.

41.12 Step three: resolution of necessity

(A) In general

After the treasurer has certified the estimated life or usefulness and maximum maturity of the proposed bond issue, or after an informal calculation is made, the board may adopt a resolution declaring the necessity of the bond issue.

Under RC 133.18, the resolution requires the concurrence of a majority of all board members (not merely of those present) for passage. If the proceedings are initiated under RC 133.06(E), the resolution should recite that the district has been certified to be an approved special needs district. If the proceedings are initiated under RC 133.06(F), the resolution should declare an emergency.

With respect to bond proceedings initiated under RC 133.18, the requirements as to contents and certification to the county auditor of the resolution of necessity are mandatory, and substantial compliance with the statute is required.[43]

(B) Contents

The resolution of necessity must do the following:

(1) Declare the necessity for the bond issue;

(2) Fix the amount of the issue;

(3) State the purpose of the issue;

(4) Determine the maximum number of years over which the principal may be paid;

(5) Fix the approximate date of the issue;

(6) Fix the approximate interest rate which the bonds are to bear;

(7) Declare the necessity of levying a tax outside the ten-mill limitation to pay the interest and retire the bonds and any anticipatory securities at maturity;

(8) Declare that the question of issuing the bonds and levying the tax is to be submitted to the electors of the district;

(9) Designate the election—general, primary, or special—and the date; and

(10) Direct the treasurer to certify a copy of the resolution to the county auditor or, if the district is located in more than one county, to the county auditor who customarily handles tax matters relating to the district.[44]

---

[42]RC 133.19.
[43]State ex rel Board of County Commrs v Jenkins, 155 OS 402, 99 NE(2d) 179 (1951).
[44]RC 133.18.

(C) Consents required when debt will exceed certain amount

If the amount of a proposed issue will cause the school district's net indebtedness, after issuance of the bonds, to exceed four per cent of the value for taxation of all property in the district, then the issue cannot be submitted to a vote of the electors unless the tax commissioner and the superintendent of public instruction give their consent.[45]

If the board has previously received conditional approval to purchase classroom facilities from the state and if that approval is in effect, consent of the state board of education is required prior to the issuance of any bonds or notes.

Request for consents should be in the resolution of necessity and must be received at the department of taxation and the office of the superintendent of public instruction at least thirty days prior to the election. This filing deadline may be waived by the superintendent of public instruction and the tax commissioner for good cause.[46] Additional information, the nature of which is specified in printed instructions available from the departments involved, must be supplied when the requests are submitted.

(D) Certification of resolution to county auditor

The resolution of necessity must be certified to the county auditor at least seventy-five days prior to the date of the specified election.

(E) Auditor's duties and certificate

Upon receipt of the resolution of necessity, the county auditor must calculate the average annual tax levy which will be required to pay the interest on the bonds and to retire them at maturity. The method of making the calculation is specifically prescribed by statute,[47] and the calculation is based on information supplied in the resolution of necessity and the statutorily-required assumption that the debt will be retired in equal principal amounts each year.[48] Even though the district could issue bonds with a different amortization schedule, the county auditor is required to use a level principal repayment assumption. This calculation, expressed both in mills for each dollar of valuation and in dollars and cents for each $100 of valuation, must be certified by the auditor to the board of education.[49]

41.13 Step four: resolution to proceed

(A) In general

After receipt of the county auditor's calculation of the average annual tax levy, the board of education, if it desires to proceed with the proposed bond issue, must adopt a resolution determining to proceed and certify its intention to the board of elections not later than the seventy-fifth day before the day of the election.[50]

Both the resolution of necessity and the resolution determining to proceed become effective upon adoption. No publication of either is required.

(B) Contents

The resolution determining to proceed should recite the following:

(1) Prior adoption of the resolution of necessity;

(2) Receipt of the county auditor's calculation of the average annual tax levy and the amount; and

(3) The board's determination to proceed with the submission to the electors of the question of issuing the bonds and levying the tax.

The resolution should direct the treasurer to certify copies of the resolution of necessity, the county auditor's estimate, and the resolution to proceed to the county board of elections and request the board to

---

[45]RC 133.06(C). Where consents are not obtained due to ministerial error or oversight, subsequent action by the legislature to the effect that the consents are to be considered as given is valid. Washington County Taxpayers Assn v Peppel, 78 App(3d) 146, 604 NE(2d) 181 (Washington 1992).

[46]RC 133.06(C).
[47]RC 133.06.
[48]RC 133.06(C).
[49]RC 133.06.
[50]RC 133.18(D).

prepare the necessary ballots and supplies for the election.

41.14 Step five: election

An election on a proposed issue may be held only on the first Tuesday after the first Monday in February, May, August, or November except that in a year in which a presidential primary election is held no special election can be held in February or May but may be held on the third Tuesday in March.[51]

(A) Notice of election

Notice of the election must be published at least once, in one or more newspapers of general circulation in the district. The publication must appear no later than ten days prior to the election.[52]

The notice of election must recite the following:

(1) The amount of the proposed bond issue;

(2) The purpose of the issue;

(3) The maximum number of years during which the principal of the bonds may be paid;

(4) The estimated additional average annual tax rate, expressed in mills for each one dollar of valuation and also in dollars and cents for each $100 of valuation, outside of the ten-mill limitation, as certified by the county auditor; and

(5) The time and place of the election.[53]

(B) Form of ballot

The form of the ballot to be used at most bond issue elections is prescribed by RC 133.18(F)(1)(a), which gives the text of the ballot and provides that the purpose of the proposed bond issue shall be printed in bold face type. An alternate ballot text is provided for bond issues submitted by a board of education for a library board of trustees.[54]

The ballot used for bonds for certain emergency purposes under RC 133.06(F) "shall describe the emergency existing" and the authority under which it is declared, and shall state that the bond issue for emergency purposes is beyond the limitations prescribed by RC 133.06.

(C) Certification of election results

The board of elections will certify the results of an election to the district treasurer, the county auditor of each county in which the district is located, and the tax commissioner.[55] Application for a recount may be filed within five days, and a petition contesting the election may be filed with the court of common pleas within fifteen days, after the board of elections declares the election results. An election contest has been held to be the specific and exclusive remedy provided for the correction of all errors, frauds, and mistakes which may occur at an election.[56] Because of the possibility of a recount or election contest, the issuance of debt approved at the election or notes in anticipation of a newly approved tax should await receipt of a certification or advice that neither has occurred.

41.15 Step six: tax levy for debt service

The necessary tax levy for the first year should be placed on the tax list as soon as possible and must be put on the tax list for collection in the next calendar year if legislation authorizing the issuance of the voted securities is filed with the county auditor on or before the last day of November.[57] In all other years, the levy must be included in the board's annual tax budget.[58] The amount of taxes required depends on whether the entire voted issue or only an installment is authorized and sold, on the first interest payment date, and on the interest rate itself.

The tax levied to pay interest on and retire bonds issued pursuant to a vote of the electors cannot, for any purpose, be levied at a rate higher than that needed to pay interest on and retire the bonds. Thus, the attorney general has concluded that, at a time when the annual tax in an amount

---

[51] RC 3501.01.
[52] RC 133.18(E)(3).
[53] RC 133.18(E)(3).
[54] RC 133.18(F)(1)(b).
[55] RC 133.18(G).

[56] RC 133.18(G); State ex rel Daoust v Smith, 52 OS(2d) 199, 371 NE(2d) 536 (1977).
[57] RC 133.18(H).
[58] RC 5705.29.

less than that set forth on the ballot would be sufficient to retire bonds issued for the purpose of acquiring real property and constructing and equipping a new school building, the levy may not be retained at a level in excess of the amount needed to retire the bonds with the excess used to borrow money to repair the school building.[59]

In practice, taxes are collected by the county officials only on instructions of the school district involved through filing its tax budget or a certified copy of the bond or note resolution. The county budget commission then uses these documents to determine the necessary taxes, which taxes are then actually levied by each board of education through the "Resolution Accepting Amounts and Rates."

41.16 Step seven: authorization of bonds or notes

(A) Procedure in general

The procedure for issuing bonds, or notes in anticipation of the issuance of bonds, is the same with respect to voted bonds after the election as for bonds issued without a vote, except that the tax levied for the payment of the voted bonds and interest is unlimited as to amount or rate, whereas the tax levied for unvoted bonds must be levied within the ten-mill limitation.[60]

If the proposed bond or note issue is unvoted, or if the certification has not been made prior to adoption of the resolution of necessity for a voted bond issue, the treasurer must certify the estimated life or usefulness and maximum maturity before the board of education adopts a resolution authorizing the issuance and sale of bonds or notes.[61]

(B) Resolution authorizing notes

If notes are to be issued, the board must adopt a resolution determining that notes be issued in anticipation of the issuance of bonds; stating the amount of the notes, the rate or rates of interest or the method of determining that rate, the date of the notes, their maturity, and provision (if any) for their retirement before maturity; and providing for the levy of a tax during the years while such notes run.[62] A simple majority is necessary for adoption of the resolution.

The resolution should contain a covenant that the board will use the note proceeds so that the notes will not constitute "arbitrage bonds" under the Internal Revenue Code and that the board will take all actions necessary to ensure the exclusion of interest from gross income for federal income tax purposes. Also, if applicable, the resolution should include the board's designation of the notes as "qualified tax-exempt obligations" under section 265(b)(3) of the Internal Revenue Code and related covenants.[63]

Although the note resolution must also contain a description of the bonds in anticipation of which the notes are being issued, it may not serve as the bond resolution required by RC 133.23.

A note resolution may authorize one note or multiple notes, which may be sold in installments as funds are needed. It is permissible in a subsequent resolution awarding the notes to fix a lower, more favorable, rate or rates of interest.[64]

A copy of the note resolution should be certified to the county auditor of each county in which a part of the school district lies and his receipt obtained prior to the delivery of the notes.[65]

(C) Notes in anticipation of bonds

Notes authorized under RC 133.22 must be issued in anticipation of the issuance of bonds. The resolution authorizing their issuance must declare the necessity of a corresponding bond issue, if the issue is unvoted. In the case of voted bonds, the note resolution must identify the election at which the bonds were approved and the note issue by its terms must be authorized in anticipation of the bonds previously voted and for the same purpose. It is possible that a note issue, particularly one issued in anticipation of unvoted bonds, may be completely retired prior to the issuance of bonds so that no bonds are ever issued. The amount of anticipatory notes which may be

---

[59] OAG 89-047.
[60] O Const Art XII §2.
[61] See Text 41.10, Step one: determining estimated life of permanent improvement.
[62] RC 133.27.
[63] See Text 41.19, Federal tax law provisions.
[64] RC 133.22.
[65] RC 133.22(B).

authorized at a particular time may not exceed the amount of bonds to be issued.

(D) Maturity of notes, renewal

Anticipatory notes may have a maturity up to 240 months from date of issue if permitted by the maximum maturity of the bonds. Notes issued for less than 240 months may be renewed from time to time until 240 months from the date of the original issue. The legislation authorizing renewal notes should be by a separate resolution, since Ohio law[66] requires the levy of a tax upon renewal of a debt. The renewal note issue becomes an obligation distinct from the original obligation, and the note issue may bear a different rate or rates of interest from the original note issue. There should be no interval, however, between the renewal note and the maturity of its predecessor, and, in fact, the issue date of the new note should always be the date of maturity of the old note, or earlier, so as to avoid a temporary default.[67]

If the notes are outstanding later than the last day of December of the fifth year following the year the original note was issued, the excess period must be deducted from the maximum maturity of the bonds in anticipation of which such notes are issued. During such period in excess of five years a portion of the principal of such notes shall be retired in amounts at least equal to and payable not later than the principal maturities which would have been required if bonds had been issued at the expiration of the initial five-year period.[68]

(E) Resolution authorizing bonds

If the board decides not to issue notes, or if issued notes are about to mature and the board determines to retire them with bonds, it must then adopt the bond resolution. A simple majority is necessary for passage.

The bond resolution must specify the amount of the issue and whether the bonds are to be issued in one lot or installments, state the purpose previously declared, and fix the date, rate of interest, and maturity or maturities (which need not be the same as those set forth in prior legislation). The resolution should also provide for the levy of a tax on all of the taxable property in the district to pay the principal and interest on the bonds, and should recite that the tax is to be levied outside of all limitations if the bonds are voted.[69]

As with a note resolution, the board should covenant in the bond resolution that it will use bond proceeds so that the bonds will not constitute "arbitrage bonds" under the Internal Revenue Code and that it will take all actions necessary to ensure the exclusion of interest from gross income for federal income tax purposes. Also, if applicable, the resolution should include the board's designation of the bonds as "qualified tax-exempt obligations" under section 265(b)(3) of the Internal Revenue Code and related covenants.[70]

In the bond resolution, the board may also request the department of education to enter into an agreement with the board to enhance the credit rating of the district's securities by foundation program revenues for debt service payments on the bonds if the district lacks funds for those payments. The board must include a copy of the resolution and nine other pieces of required information with its request to include the bonds in the program. If projected foundation program revenues are available in a sufficient amount, the department can grant or deny the board's application based on specified statutory and administrative criteria.[71]

A copy of the bond resolution should be certified to the county auditor of each county in which a portion of the school district lies and his receipt obtained, prior to the sale of the bonds.[72]

(F) Capitalized interest and other costs included in the bond or note issue

Capitalized interest may be included in the amount of a district's bond or note issue to the extent necessary to cover interest coming due prior to the receipt of the taxes from which the interest is ultimately to be paid.[73] If a portion of the bond pro-

---

[66] O Const Art XII §11.
[67] RC 133.22.
[68] RC 133.22(C)(2).
[69] RC 133.23.
[70] See Text 41.19, Federal tax law provisions.

[71] RC 3317.18; OAC 3301-8-01. See also RC 133.25.
[72] RC 133.23(D).
[73] RC 133.01(E).

ceeds is used to pay the capitalized interest, that amount may, at the option of the board, be repaid into the construction fund from the proceeds of taxes collected for the issue.[74] For example, assume a $1,000,000 bond issue with a twenty-year maturity was approved at the February election, and that bonds dated April 1 are issued with equal annual maturities on December 1 in each of the next twenty years.[75] Since taxes will not be available for payment of principal and interest coming due during the first year the debt is outstanding, such princpal and interest could be paid from the bond proceeds. The board could then provide in its annual budget for the collection in the first full year after issuance, or thereafter, of taxes sufficient not only to pay the principal and interest on the bonds coming due in that year, but also to repay the construction fund for the principal and interest paid in the year of issuance.

There may also be included in the amount of bonds or notes to be issued the costs of advertising the notice of sale, printing the bonds or notes, credit enhancement, delivery costs, rating fees, printing and distribution costs for disclosure documents, accounting services, and service charges of the paying agent and bond registrar.[76] The board may retain the legal services of bond counsel to prepare or review the bond or note proceedings and to render an approving opinion as to the validity and legality of the issue and as to the exclusion from gross income for federal income tax purposes of the interest on the bonds or notes. The costs of legal services may also be paid from the bond or note proceeds, although the cost of at least the approving legal opinion is often charged to the purchaser of the issue.

41.17 Step eight: sale of bonds or notes

(A) Timing

After a bond issue has been approved by the electors, the bonds or anticipatory notes equal to the authorized principal amount must be issued and outstanding by the first day of the sixth January following the election, unless the bonds or notes or the project for which the bonds are authorized are involved in litigation. During litigation, that period of limitation does not run.[77]

(B) Types of sale

Following passage of the bond or note resolution and its certification to the county auditor, the next step is the sale of the bonds or notes. This sale may either be on a private negotiated basis or a public bidding process, in either case at not less than ninety-seven per cent of the principal amount offered.[78]

If public sale is selected, a notice advertising the sale must be either published or distributed as determined by the district and also delivered to the Ohio Municipal Advisory Council at least ten days before the sale. The notice must give the amount and purpose of the issue; sources of payment; the dates of principal payments or how they are to be determined; the rates and dates of payment of interest; any redemption provisions; the day, hour, and place where the bonds or notes are to be sold; how the best bid will be determined; and any bid security required.[79]

(C) Disclosure, official statement

Potential purchasers of tax-exempt securities, including school district bonds and notes, may request the board to provide detailed information about the issue, the board, and the district. Requests have greatly increased in recent years, particularly following the problems experienced by several public issuers in marketing their securities and the enactment of new rules by the Securities and Exchange Commission requiring purchasers of debt to have reviewed certain information and to have received promises from the public issuer regarding continuing disclosure of certain information.[80] Federal securities laws require a cautious approach in providing the information. Under "anti-fraud" provisions, the board, its officials, and agents may be liable for misleading, inaccurate, or fraudulent disclosure or the failure to dis-

---

[74]RC 133.16(B).
[75]RC 133.22.
[76]RC 133.01(K).
[77]RC 133.18(I)(2).

[78]RC 133.30.
[79]RC 133.30.
[80]SEC Rule 15c2-12.

close material information. This need for caution and potential liability has been recognized by the Government Finance Officers Association (GFOA). To assist issuers, the GFOA has published "Disclosure Guidelines for Offerings of Securities by State and Local Governments."

An official statement is a form of disclosure document prepared by the board which provides detailed information about the issue and the board, including demographic and financial information. In deciding whether to use an official statement in connection with the issuance of bonds or notes, a board of education should consider a number of factors, including the following:

(1) Dollar amount of the issue;

(2) Type of issue, whether notes or bonds;

(3) Cost of providing an official statement;

(4) Potential purchasers' familiarity with the school district;

(5) Existence of negative material facts which should be disclosed; and

(6) Demand for official statements by the marketplace at the particular time.

While the board is not legally required to issue an official statement, the Securities and Exchange Commission has published a rule which requires underwriters and other purchasers of the board's debt to provide their customers with an official statement for most issues which are more than $1,000,000 and have maturities longer than nine months, and to continue making disclosure of certain information for as long as the bonds are outstanding.[81] The rule indirectly requires boards to provide disclosure information in connection with many financings. It also requires the board to continue making disclosure of "material events" which occur while the bonds are outstanding and, if the board will have more than $10,000,000 of debt outstanding after the issuance of the bonds, to annually provide information about the school district. Since there are some exceptions to the rule, the question of using an official statement also now depends on the type, size, and length of the issue proposed.

Assistance in making all these decisions may be obtained from local banking officials and other potential purchasers of the issue and from legal counsel.

(D) Award

Bids for issues sold at public sale should be opened publicly at the time and place stated in the notice of sale and a tabulation made, giving the name of each bidder and the interest rate and premium, if any. No bid should contain any condition other than as allowed by the notice of sale.

When the bids have been tabulated, the board determines the best bid, or, if authorized by the board, the treasurer or other person may be expressly authorized to award the bonds or notes to be sold.[82] If not stated in the legislation filed with the county auditor, the treasurer must give notice to the county auditor of the interest rate or rates of all securities payable from property taxes maturing in more than one year from their issuance.[83]

Issues sold at private sale should be awarded, pursuant to either legislation or a legislative delegation of that authority, to a board officer—usually the treasurer—with responsibility for financial matters.

(E) Proceeds of sale

The principal received from the sale of bonds or notes is to be credited to the fund for which the bonds were authorized or to the payment of notes issued in anticipation. The premium and accrued interest should be paid into the bond retirement fund.[84] In *Haines v Board of County Commrs*,[85] the proceeds of a bond issue, approved and sold under the Uniform Bond Law, were held to be in the nature of a trust fund to be used only for the purpose for which the bonds were approved and issued.

(F) Delivery of bonds or notes

Bonds or notes are customarily printed at the expense of the school district unless the notice of sale provides otherwise. The bonds or notes are then executed and delivered for payment by the district to the pur-

---

[81] SEC Rule 15c2-12.
[82] RC 133.30(C)(3).
[83] RC 133.30(D).

[84] RC 133.32, RC 5705.10.
[85] Haines v Board of County Commrs, 114 App 59, 180 NE(2d) 23 (Montgomery 1960).

chaser, or to a bank designated by the purchaser.[86]

(G) Transcript of proceedings

The treasurer is required to prepare and deliver to the purchaser a certified transcript of the proceedings containing the resolutions, notices, and other documents, including a statement of the district's indebtedness, from which the regularity and validity of the bond or note issue may be determined.[87] The transcript should be completed and the bonds or notes delivered within the time specified in the notice of sale, if any, which is usually thirty days after the date of the award, or if no such period is specified, within a reasonable time, which is often considered to be thirty days.

Also to be delivered with the bonds or notes are the treasurer's receipt and "signature and no litigation" certificate. The former should show, over the treasurer's signature, that the bonds or notes were paid for in full, at par and accrued interest. The signature and no litigation certificate should be signed by the president or vice-president and treasurer of the board as the officers executing the bonds or notes[88] and dated as of the day of delivery and payment, and should recite that the signing officers are the duly elected or appointed, qualified, and acting officers, respectively, of the district; that they signed the bonds or notes as such officers; and that there is no litigation pending or threatened involving the issuance or validity of the bonds or notes or the tax for their payment.

41.18 Refunding or advance refunding bonds or notes

Securities may be refunded as determined by the board of education.[89] Securities may be refunded through tender offers or purchased in the open market. More than one outstanding bond or note issue, even if for different purposes, may be refunded by a single issue of refunding bonds. Refunding bonds may be sold at private sale at a price determined by the board of education, including at a discount.

Escrow agreements, under which refunding bond proceeds are held and invested to retire the prior bonds at a later date, are expressly authorized, and the types of permissible escrow investments are specified. In one of the few exceptions to the basic rules regarding investment income, RC 133.34 requires that interest earned on the refunding bond proceeds must remain in the bond retirement fund.

41.19 Federal tax law provisions

(A) Form of bonds, coupons, registration

Almost all bonds issued by boards of education prior to 1982 were issued in coupon form. Interest on those bonds is represented by detachable "coupons," one of which may be cut off and presented for payment on each interest payment date. There are specific statutory procedures for coupon bonds and their handling.[90] Most bonds are now issued in registered form where the principal and interest are paid to the "registered holder" whose name appears on the bond. These bonds are often placed in a book-entry system in which a trust company holds the actual certificates and distributes principal and interest payments to the owners of the bonds.

The Tax Equity and Fiscal Responsibility Act of 1982, coupled with later federal legislation, also amended the Internal Revenue Code to require that all bonds and notes with a maturity of greater than one year must be issued in registered form in order for the holder to receive interest excludable from gross income for federal income tax purposes.[91]

To enable boards of education and other issuers to comply with these federal requirements, the general assembly has provided that bonds or notes may be issued in registered form and book-entry form (under which the right to principal and interest may be transferred only through a book entry). Unless otherwise provided in the bond or note proceedings, boards are not required to reissue or exchange registered or book entry obligations for coupon obligations, if the obligations were origi-

---

[86] For discussion of the issuance of bonds or notes under a book entry system, see Text 41.19, Federal tax law provisions.
[87] RC 133.33.
[88] RC 133.27.
[89] RC 133.34.
[90] RC 133.41.
[91] 26 USCA 149(a).

nally issued after December 31, 1982. Bonds or notes may be exchanged for registered bonds or notes, or if the bond or note proceedings provided for issuance or reissuance of those obligations in book entry form, for obligations in book entry form.[92]

(B) Arbitrage bonds, loss of tax advantage

School district bonds or notes determined to be "arbitrage bonds" would not be tax exempt, i.e., the interest would be included in the recipient's gross income for federal income tax purposes. In general, arbitrage bonds are defined as obligations issued by a state or local governmental unit, any portion of the proceeds of which are reasonably expected to be used directly or indirectly to acquire investments the yield on which is materially higher than the yield on the governmental obligations.[93] The Internal Revenue Service has promulgated extensive regulations relating to arbitrage bonds, the essential purpose of which is to limit using proceeds of governmental obligations to earn money by investing them in higher yielding investments. The regulations do permit investment for certain defined "temporary periods." The arbitrage regulations are complex, and their application to a specific bond or note issue should be carefully considered. An official of the district is almost always required to certify a statement as to the reasonable expectations for the use of the bond or note proceeds as part of the transcript of proceedings.

(C) Use of proceeds, rebate

There are additional requirements for interest to be excluded by the holders of the securities from gross income for federal income tax purposes. Ninety per cent of the proceeds must be spent for a public governmental purpose. If more than five per cent of the proceeds are spent for a "private use" which is not related to the "governmental use," there are additional restrictions.

In addition, any "arbitrage" earned when bond or note proceeds are used to acquire investment property with a yield greater than the yield on the bonds or notes may have to be rebated to the United States unless the issue is exempt from the rebate requirement. An issue of bonds or notes is exempt from rebate if all proceeds are spent within six months of the date of issuance. Expenditure of all proceeds within eighteen months, or two years in the case of construction issues (in both cases, if at least certain percentages of the total proceeds are spent within specific time periods after issuance) will also exempt an issue from rebate. Finally, if the school district issues less than $5 million of governmental use tax-exempt obligations (including the bonds or notes, but generally excluding current refundings) during that calendar year, all issues during that year are exempt from rebate. The tax laws and regulations governing the issuance of debt by boards and the expenditure of their proceeds are some of the most complex and difficult regulatory mazes faced by issuers of tax-exempt debt. Experienced legal counsel should be consulted early in the planning process to determine the effect of this regulatory scheme on the board's financing plans.

(D) Qualified tax-exempt obligations

Another provision of the Internal Revenue Code places limits on the deductions previously allowed to financial institutions for interest paid on deposits if the institutions also own tax-exempt bonds and notes.[94] If these limits apply, financial institutions may bid higher rates of interest because of their loss of deductions, and the market for bonds and notes may be reduced. These limits do not apply if a district reasonably expects to issue $10 million or less of tax-exempt obligations during the same calendar year. The board must specifically designate bonds or notes as "qualified tax-exempt obligations" under section 265(B)(3) of the Internal Revenue Code for the exception to apply, usually in the note or bond resolution. The designation as "qualified tax-exempt obligations" should be described in the notice of sale so that it will be reflected in the interest rates bid by potential purchasers.

---

[92] RC 9.96.
[93] 26 USCA 148(c).
[94] 26 USCA 265(B).

41.20 Miscellaneous state law provisions

(A) Lost or destroyed bonds

A duplicate bond or note may be issued to replace one lost or destroyed, in the same form as the original obligation, showing on its face that it is a duplicate of the lost instrument.[95] If the lost security has matured, the board may authorize direct payment.[96] The issuing board is authorized to require proof of loss or destruction, a bond indemnifying it for or on account of the lost or destroyed security, and the reasonable expenses of reissuance.[97]

(B) Incontestability

The Uniform Bond Law provides that bonds reciting that they are issued pursuant to the bond law, complying with it on their face, issued for a lawful purpose within the limitations prescribed by law, and for which the treasurer has been paid in full, are incontestable unless an action or proceeding involving their validity is begun prior to their delivery.[98]

Where the proceeds of bonds have been properly spent for public improvements and no action was filed to enjoin the issuance of the bonds before delivery, the subdivision is obligated for the payment of the bonds, even though they were issued beyond the tax limitations controlling the bonding power of the subdivision.[99]

(C) Validation of questioned securities

Where a question as to the validity of a proposed bond or note issue exists, the board, prior to issuance, may file a petition for validation with the court of common pleas. The petition commences a judicial procedure to adjudicate the board's authority to issue the bonds or notes and the validity of the proceedings taken and proposed to be taken in connection with them.[100]

BORROWING FOR CURRENT EXPENSES

41.21 Borrowing in anticipation of collection of current revenue

(A) In general

As noted previously,[101] a board of education has authority under the Uniform Bond Law to issue notes in anticipation of the collection of current revenues. Generally, the purpose is to raise money to meet current expenses, particularly during periods between tax settlements when funds available to meet current expenses may be at their lowest level. Although it is not usual, this procedure may also be used for permanent improvements.

RC 133.10 authorizes boards of education to issue notes in anticipation of the collection of taxes and/or other revenues. The notes cannot exceed one-half of the amount of the projected revenues remaining to be received during the fiscal year estimated by the treasurer and must mature not later than June 30. The notes cannot be issued prior to June 21 and, if issued prior to July 1, the proceeds of the notes cannot be spent or considered available for appropriation prior to July 1.[102]

RC 133.10 also provides that the sums anticipated by the notes are considered appropriated for the payment of the notes at maturity. The Ohio Supreme Court has held that the Ohio Constitution[103] imposes a mandatory duty upon political subdivisions, including boards of education, to pay the interest and principal of their debt before providing for current operating expenses and that the duty to set aside enough money to pay notes issued in anticipation is enforceable by mandamus.[104]

RC 133.10(D) authorizes boards of education to borrow money by issuing notes if the first half personal property tax settlement is delayed by the state tax commissioner. The notes are to be repaid from the

---

[95]RC 133.39.
[96]RC 133.39(B).
[97]RC 133.39(C).
[98]RC 133.02.
[99]State ex rel Alden Corp v Solon, 132 OS 362, 7 NE(2d) 550 (1937).
[100]RC 133.70.

[101]See Text 41.04, Purposes of school borrowing.
[102]RC 133.10(H).
[103]O Const Art XII §11.
[104]State ex rel National City Bank v Cleveland City School Dist Bd of Ed, 52 OS(2d) 81, 369 NE(2d) 1200 (1977).

proceeds of that tax settlement. The aggregate amount borrowed may not exceed ninety per cent of the amount estimated to be received from that settlement by the county budget commission, other than taxes to be received for the payment of debt charges and all advances. The notes must mature on or before August 31, and the taxes they anticipate are considered to be appropriated for their payment at maturity.

(B) Borrowing in anticipation of future revenues

RC 133.301 authorizes borrowing by boards of education prior to June 30 of one fiscal year to be repaid after July 1 of the next fiscal year. The maximum amount permitted to be borrowed across the fiscal year-end is generally the amount derived by taking fifty per cent of the amount of personal property tax receipts estimated to be received during the calendar year and subtracting the amount of first half collections of those taxes. Exceptions to this limit can be (and often are) approved by the state superintendent.[105] The general purpose of this section was to attempt to "smooth" the fiscal year transition for those districts which have high personal property tax collections in the second half of the calendar year. However, those boards which pay their employees on a school year basis or which have heavy utility or transportation costs may find this borrowing provision insufficient.

To qualify for this type of borrowing, a board must include a "spending reserve balance" in its budget, adopt a resolution requesting a certification by the state superintendent of public instruction of an amount which the board may borrow pursuant to RC 133.301, deliver that resolution to the state superintendent by January 1, and receive a certification in either the requested amount or a different amount. Upon receipt of that certification, a board may borrow, prior to July 1, an amount up to the amount certified and issue notes in anticipation of the second half calendar year collections of personal property taxes. These notes must mature prior to December 31, and the taxes they anticipate are considered to be appropriated for their payment at maturity.

41.22 Tax anticipation notes

(A) In general

School districts may issue notes in anticipation of the receipt of emergency tax levies to provide for the emergency requirements of the district or to avoid an operating deficit[106] and in anticipation of an income tax or special levies for current expenses, capital improvements, community centers, or a public library of the district.[107] Except for notes issued in anticipation of permanent improvement levies, these notes may be issued only after the approval of the levy and prior to the time when the first tax collection from the levy can be made and must have principal payments during each year after the year of issuance over a period not to exceed five years or the number of years the levy is approved for, whichever is less, and may have a principal payment in the year of issuance. Notes issued in anticipation of permanent improvement levies may be issued at any time during the collection of the levy. The notes must be sold in accordance with RC Chapter 133.

The amount necessary to pay the principal and interest on the notes as they mature is considered appropriated for these purposes from the levy. Appropriations from the levy by the board are limited each fiscal year to the balance available in excess of that amount.

(B) Limits on amount

Notes issued in anticipation of emergency levies cannot exceed the total estimated proceeds of the levy to be collected during the first year of the levy.[108] Notes anticipating other levies, on the other hand, may not exceed fifty per cent of the total estimated proceeds of the levy to be collected during the first year of the levy,[109] except that if the special levy is a limited life levy for permanent improvements, the notes may be in an amount not exceeding fifty per cent of the remaining estimated proceeds of the levy to be collected over

---

[105] RC 133.301(E).
[106] RC 5705.194.
[107] RC 5705.21.

[108] RC 5705.194.
[109] RC 5705.21(C)(1).

the life of the levy.[110] If the special levy is for general, on-going permanent improvements, the maximum amount which may be borrowed is fifty percent of total estimated proceeds to be collected over a specified number of years, not exceeding ten, after the issuance of the rates.[111] Any board of education which has issued the maximum amount permitted in anticipation of a permanent improvement tax levy may request permission of the state superintendent of public instruction to issue more notes. The superintendent is authorized to permit the issuance of additional notes in anticipation of the receipts of the proceeds of the levy.[112]

JOINT VOCATIONAL SCHOOL DISTRICT BONDS AND LEVIES

41.23 Borrowing by joint vocational school district

(A) Voted bond issues

A board of education of a joint vocational school district[113] may, upon a vote of at least two-thirds of its full membership, submit to the electors of the district the question of issuing bonds for the purpose of acquiring a site and erecting, enlarging, improving, or equipping buildings and of levying a tax outside the ten-mill limitation to pay off the bonds. The proceedings for election and issuance of bonds and any notes in anticipation are the same as in the Uniform Bond Law.[114]

(B) Tax levy over ten-mill limitation

The district board, by a vote of two-thirds of its full membership, may submit the question of levying a tax in excess of the ten-mill limitation:

(1) For a continuing period to provide for the current expenses of the district; or

(2) For a period of ten years or less to provide for current expenses or to provide funds to acquire a site and erect, enlarge, improve, rebuild, and equip buildings; or

(3) For a combination of these purposes.

If the levy is for a combined purpose (which is not authorized for other types of school districts), the resolution declaring the necessity for such a levy must apportion the annual rate of the levy between current expenses and the other purposes. The apportionment may, but need not be, the same for each year of the levy.[115]

The board may also submit the question of renewing or replacing all or a portion of an existing levy, but only for any of the purposes of that existing levy. The renewal or replacement levy and any notes issued in anticipation of receipts of that levy are subject to all requirements of RC 3311.21.

(C) Tax anticipation notes

The district board may issue notes in anticipation of the receipt of a levy. Unlike most notes authorized under RC 5705.194 and RC 5705.21,[116] notes issued in anticipation of a levy for a joint vocational school district may be issued more than once during the life of the levy, but each issue must be issued in any year before the tax collection for the levy can be made for that year. The following limitations apply to the notes:

(1) The total amount may not exceed fifty per cent of the estimated proceeds of the levy to be collected each year up to a period of five years after the date of the issuance of the notes, less an amount equal to the proceeds of the levy required to pay off any prior notes issued in anticipation of the same levy;

(2) The amount maturing in one year may not exceed fifty per cent of the anticipated proceeds of the levy for that year (and if a combined levy, fifty per cent of the portion of the proceeds apportioned to the purpose for which the notes were issued); and

(3) The notes must mature serially in substantially equal installments, except as otherwise required by the prior limi-

---

[110]RC 5705.21(C)(2).
[111]RC 5705.21(C)(3).
[112]RC 5705.216.
[113]See Text 27.08 to 27.12.

[114]RC 3311.20.
[115]RC 3311.21.
[116]See Text 41.22, Tax anticipation notes.

tations, during each year over a period up to five years. The proceedings for the sale of the notes are governed by the Uniform Bond Law.

The amount necessary to pay the principal and interest on the notes is considered appropriated for those purposes from the proceeds of the levy. Appropriations from the levy by the joint vocational school district board are limited each year to the balance available in excess of that amount.[117]

STATE ASSISTANCE FOR CLASSROOM FACILITIES

41.24 Classroom Facilities Law

Under RC Chapter 3318, a city, exempted village, or local school district can obtain financial assistance from the state to acquire necessary classroom facilities which, because of debt limitations, it could not otherwise finance.

"Classroom facilities" mean rooms in which pupils regularly assemble in public school buildings to receive instruction and education, plus facilities and building improvements to operate and use the rooms as may be needed to provide a complete educational program, including the acquisition, construction, reconstruction, and other improvement and equipment of buildings and structures, and the acquisition of sites.[118]

41.25 Net bonded indebtedness and conditions of state assistance

RC Chapter 3318 requires that a school district seeking state classroom facilities assistance must pay a portion of the facilities costs based on the greater of (1) the "required level of indebtedness" for that district, or (2) the "required percentage of project costs," each as further described below.

The "required level of indebtedness" and "required percentage of project costs" vary with a district's "adjusted valuation per pupil." RC Chapter 3318 requires the department of education annually to calculate the adjusted valuation per pupil of each city, local and exempted village school district. The department is then to rank all districts from lowest to highest in order of adjusted valuations per pupil and divide this ranking into quartiles and deciles (with the first quartile or decile containing those districts with the lowest adjusted valuation per pupil). A district's "required level of indebtedness" and "percentage of project costs" are based on its placement in this annual ranking.

A district's "required percentage of project costs" is based on its placement in the decile ranking, as follows:

District's Placement in Decile Ranking	Percentage of Classroom Facilities Costs to be Contributed by District
First	0%
Second	10%
Third	20%
Fourth	30%
Fifth	40%
Sixth	50%
Seventh	60%
Eighth	70%
Ninth	80%
Tenth	90%

A district's "required level of indebtedness" is based on the quartile ranking, as follows:

District's Placement in Quartile Ranking	Required Level of District's Net Bonded Indebtedness as a Percentage of Total Value of All Property in the District Listed and Assessed for Taxation
First	5%
Second	6%
Third	7%
Fourth	7%

For purposes of RC Chapter 3118, "net bonded indebtedness" means

---

[117]RC 3311.21.

[118]RC 3318.01.

the difference between the par value of all outstanding and unpaid bonds and notes which a school district board is obligated to pay, together with the par value of bonds authorized by the electors but not yet issued, the proceeds of which can lawfully be used for the [classroom facilities] project, and the amount held in the sinking fund and other indebtedness retirement funds for their redemption. ... [N]otes issued in anticipation of the collection of current revenues, and bonds issued to pay final judgments shall not be considered in calculating the net bonded indebtedness.[119]

This definition differs somewhat from the definition of net indebtedness prescribed by RC 133.06. For example, under RC 133.06, emergency bonds issued pursuant to RC 133.17 are not considered in calculating net indebtedness; however, under the RC 3318.01 definition of "net bonded indebtedness," emergency bonds are included.[120]

Accordingly, state assistance may be conditioned, among other things, upon approval by the electors of the district of a bond issue for the purpose of paying the district's portion of the cost of the classroom facilities in an amount (1) which would raise the district's net bonded indebtedness to within $5,000 of its required level of indebtedness (as defined above) for the year in which the resolution declaring the necessity of the election is adopted, or (2) equal to the required percentage of the project costs (as defined above), whichever is greater.[121]

On the other hand, the district is not required to submit the issue to electors if, at the time of RC Chapter 3318 proceedings, its net bonded indebtedness is:

(1) Ninety-five per cent or more of its "required level of indebtedness"; or

(2) Within $20,000 of its required level of indebtedness and the required percentage of the project costs is not greater than $20,000 or the amount necessary to raise the net bonded indebtedness of the school district to within $5,000 of that required level of indebtedness.[122]

41.26 Application for state assistance, approval

The initial application for state assistance must be submitted to the state board of education on prescribed forms, accompanied by a copy of a resolution of the district board authorizing the application.[123]

After reviewing the application in light of the specific limitations in RC 3318.03, to determine the needs of the district for additional classroom facilities, the state board is required to determine what portion of the cost the district can supply from available funds from the proceeds of bonds, if any, previously authorized by the electors of the district and, debt limitations permitting, from a bond issue to be submitted to the electors. It must also determine the amount of the project cost to be supplied by the state and the priority of the need assigned to the district. The state board can approve an application only if the proposed project conforms to sound educational practice and is in keeping with the orderly process of school district reorganization and consolidation and if the actual or projected enrollment in the district is 275 or more pupils in grades seven through twelve (including any pupils of the district enrolled in a cooperative education school district), with certain exceptions.[124]

41.27 Conditional approval, proceedings to qualify for assistance

(A) In general

If the state board of education approves the application, it is "conditionally approved" and must then be confirmed or rejected by the state controlling board. Upon confirmation by the state controlling board, the superintendent of public instruction is required to certify the conditional approval to the school district board.[125]

---

[119]RC 3318.01.
[120]See also Text 41.06, Limit on voted debt.
[121]RC 3318.05.
[122]RC 3318.05.

[123]RC 3318.02.
[124]RC 3318.03.
[125]RC 3318.04.

(B) Bond issue, approval by voters

Within 120 days after receiving conditional approval from the state board, the school district must accomplish the following in order to receive state assistance:

(1) The district board must accept the conditional approval by resolution, a copy of which should be certified to the state board;

(2) If required, the electors must approve a bond issue for an amount equal to the greater of (a) the required percentage of project costs to be paid by the district, or (b) in whatever amount may be necessary to raise the district's net bonded indebtedness to within $5,000 of its required level of indebtedness; and

(3) The electors must approve an additional tax levy for the purpose of paying the cost of the purchase of the classroom facilities from the state.

The tax levy must be at the minimum rate of one-half mill per dollar of valuation, and the state board of education may require the district to increase the tax rate to an amount greater than one-half mill but not in excess of four mills. The additional one-half mill (or more) tax must be levied until the purchase price of the classroom facilities has been paid but in no event for longer than twenty-three years.[126]

Where both the question of the additional tax levy and the question of issuing bonds must be submitted to the electors, both questions must be combined in a single proposal.[127]

To determine whether the question of issuing bonds is to be submitted to the electors, and if so, the amount of the bond issue, the county auditor must certify to the district board the total assessed value of all property in the district for the year in which the resolution declaring the necessity of the election is adopted. If the county auditor has not determined the assessed value for that year, he is required to certify his estimate of the valuation.[128]

If, however, based on the county auditor's certification, the net bonded indebtedness of the district aggregates ninety-five per cent or more of the district's required level of indebtedness or is within $20,000 of that level and the required percentage of the project costs is not greater than $20,000 or the amount necessary to raise the net bonded indebtedness of the school district to within $5,000 of the required level of indebtedness, a voted bond issue need not be submitted to the electors.[129]

41.28 Proceedings for election

(A) Resolution declaring necessity

After receipt of the state board's conditional approval, the district board, if it wishes to proceed with the project, must adopt a resolution in the form prescribed in RC 3318.06. A majority vote of all members of the board is required for adoption of the resolution.[130]

(B) Consents required if debt will exceed certain amount

Where both the question of an additional tax levy and the question of issuing bonds are being submitted to the electors, the tax commissioner and the superintendent of public instruction have taken the position that RC 133.04 is applicable and that their consents to the election are required. The resolution declaring the necessity of the election should contain the request for consents, which must be received by the commissioner and the superintendent at least thirty days prior to the election.[131] This deadline can be waived for good cause.[132]

(C) Certification of resolution

If both the question of an additional tax levy and the question of issuing bonds are to be submitted to the electors, a copy of the resolution must be certified to the county auditor immediately and to the county board of elections at least seventy-

---

[126]RC 3318.05. For other adjustments to the tax levy, see also Text 41.29, Agreement for construction and sale of project.
[127]RC 3318.05. For other adjustments to the tax levy, see also Text 41.29, Agreement for construction and sale of project.

[128]RC 3318.06.
[129]RC 3318.05.
[130]RC 3318.06.
[131]See Text 41.12(C), Consents required when debt will exceed certain amount.
[132]RC 133.06(C).

five days prior to the election. If only the question of the additional tax levy is to be submitted, then the resolution need be certified only to the county board of elections.[133]

(D) Duties of county auditor

Where the question of issuing bonds is combined with the question of the additional tax levy, the county auditor is required to calculate the average annual tax levy, expressed in dollars and cents for each $100 of valuation and also in mills for each $1 of valuation throughout the life of the bonds, which will be required to pay the interest and retire the bonds in the amount estimated by the district board. The auditor must certify his calculation to the school board and to the board of elections at least seventy-five days prior to the date of election.[134]

(E) Election, time, notice

The question must be submitted to the electors at the next general or primary election if there is such an election within the required time period, i.e., not less than seventy-five nor more than ninety-five days after the date of adoption of the resolution, or at a special election to be held on a permitted date within the time period[135] and in accordance with RC 3501.01.[136] More than one election may be held in a calendar year.[137]

The board of elections is required to make the necessary arrangements for submitting the proposal to the electors. The election must be conducted, canvassed, and certified in the same manner as regular elections in the district for election of members of the district board.[138]

The form of ballot to be used at the election for both the bond issue and the tax levy is given in RC 3318.06.

Notice of the election must be published in the same fashion as for a non-classroom facilities bond issue election.[139]

The notice must state the time and place of the election; the purpose and rate of the tax levy, including how the rate may increase; and that the tax will be levied until the purchase price is paid but in no case longer than twenty-three years.

If the question of issuing bonds is to be combined with the question of the additional tax levy, the notice must also state the information concerning the proposed bond issue required under RC 133.17.[140]

(F) Certification of election results

The favorable vote of a majority of those voting upon the question of the additional tax levy and, if included in the proposal, upon the question of issuing bonds, is required for passage.[141]

The board of elections must certify the result of the election to the tax commissioner, county auditor, district treasurer, and state board of education.[142]

41.29 Agreement for construction and sale of project

(A) General requirements

After a majority favorable vote, the state board of education and the school district board are required to enter into a written agreement for the construction and sale of the project. Among the items required, the agreement must provide for the issuance and sale of bonds or anticipatory notes, the proceeds of which are to be applied to the cost of the project (if the bond issue has been approved by the electors), for the levy of the additional tax for the purchase of the classroom facilities, for the ownership and insurance of the project during construction, and for the transfer of the project to the district board upon completion.[143]

(B) Supplemental agreement to adjust tax levied

An amendment to the Classroom Facilities Law permits the district board to enter into a supplemental agreement with the state board to adjust the amount to be paid to the state board and, in effect, to reduce the amount of the additional tax originally

---

[133]RC 3318.06.
[134]RC 3318.06.
[135]RC 3318.06.
[136]See Text 41.14(A), Notice of election.
[137]RC 3318.06.
[138]RC 3318.06.
[139]RC 133.17(E)(3).
[140]RC 133.17(E)(3). See also Text 41.14(A), Notice of election.
[141]RC 3318.06.
[142]RC 3318.07.
[143]RC 3318.08.

levied. To achieve this, the district board must determine that the taxable value of property subject to the additional tax has increased since the levy of the additional tax so that the collection of the taxes over twenty-three years to pay the purchase price would not be necessary. Upon request by the board, the county auditor will determine the amount needed to be collected each year to pay the remaining portion of the purchase price over the remainder of the twenty-three-year period. The board may then request the state board to enter into a supplemental agreement providing for the repayment of the remainder of the purchase price in annual installments equal to the amount determined by the county auditor. If the supplemental agreement is entered into, the state board certifies this to the county auditor who then adjusts the tax levied to the rate required to make those annual payments.[144]

41.30 Issuance of bonds or notes, proceeds of sale

Voted bonds may not be issued by the district board until the agreement for construction and sale has been made by the board and the state board.[145]

When the agreement has been executed, however, the district board must promptly proceed with the issuance of the bonds, or notes in anticipation, in accordance with the agreement[146] and in accordance with the Uniform Bond Law.[147]

The proceeds from the sale of the bonds or notes, except premium, accrued interest, and interest included in the amount of the bond issue, must be deposited in the district's project construction account in the district's depository. The premium, accrued interest, and any capitalized interest are to be deposited into the bond retirement fund from which the bonds or notes are to be redeemed.[148]

41.31 Suspending authority to issue bonds or notes

After certification of the conditional approval of the state board to the district board[149] and for as long as the conditional approval remains in effect, the district board is prohibited from issuing any bonds or notes for the purpose of acquiring classroom facilities without prior state board consent.[150]

In addition, after an agreement for the construction and sale of the project has been made by the district board and the state board, the district board is prohibited, without the prior consent of the state board, from issuing any bonds or notes for the acquisition of permanent improvements for so long as any of the purchase price remains unpaid but in no event longer than twenty-three years.[151]

41.32 Certification of tax levies

As to a voted bond issue, the necessary tax levy for the first year's debt service on the bonds should be placed on the tax list as soon as possible and must be put on the tax list if a resolution adopted by the board authorizing the debt is delivered to the county auditor on or before November 30.[152] Thereafter, it must be included in the annual tax budget certified to the county budget commission.[153]

The additional tax levy for the purpose of paying the purchase price of the project (the rate of which may fluctuate)[154] must be included in the school district's budget for each year on certification to the county budget commission (or commissions, if the district is located in more than one county) by the state board of the balance due to the state under its agreement with the district board.

The certification must be made on or before July 15 in each year and constitutes authorization to the county budget commission to provide for the levy in the same

---

[144]RC 3318.081.
[145]RC 3318.08.
[146]RC 3318.08, RC 3318.091.
[147]RC Ch 133. See also Text 41.09 to 41.20.
[148]RC 133.32.
[149]See Text 41.26, Application for state assistance, approval.

[150]RC 3318.04.
[151]RC 3318.08.
[152]RC 133.18(H).
[153]RC 3318.07.
[154]See Text 41.27(B), Bond issue, approval by voters; Text 41.29(B), Supplemental agreement to adjust tax levied.

manner as tax levies included directly in the budgets of the subdivisions.

Further, the levy must be included in the next annual tax budget certified to the county budget commission after the execution of the agreement between the district board and the state board.[155]

EMERGENCY LOANS

41.33 Emergency loans

(A) In general

A school district that is financially unable to remain open for instruction on all of the days set forth in its adopted school calendar and pay its expenses is authorized to seek state approval of an emergency loan pursuant to RC 3313.483 to provide the funds required.

(B) Eligibility for emergency loan

For a school district to be eligible for an emergency loan, either (1) the state auditor must have certified pursuant to RC 3313.483 and RC 3313.487 that the district would have a projected operating deficit at the end of the fiscal year and the district must have been denied a loan from a commercial bank, underwriter, or other prospective lender or purchaser of its obligations, or (2) ten per cent or more of the district's real and personal property taxes on the previous year's tax lists and duplicates charged to one or more bankrupt nonresidential/agricultural taxpayers must remain unpaid. A district with a projected deficit will receive an emergency loan, if approved, from a commercial bank, underwriter, or other prospective lender or purchaser of its obligations.[156] A district that has a bankrupt taxpayer problem will receive its emergency loan, if approved, from the state's lottery profits education fund.[157]

The auditor's certification must include a determination that the board has "avail[ed] itself to the fullest extent authorized by law of all lawful revenue sources available to it."[158] In the exercise of that duty, the auditor may conclude that the board has not attempted to avail itself of all available sources unless it has made a demand that all receivables due to the board be paid immediately or it has requested approval of the court of common pleas to transfer any unexpended balance in a permanent improvement fund available for transfer to the general fund.[159]

(C) Processing applications

The superintendent of public instruction administers emergency loan approvals. The superintendent evaluates applications from school districts, which must contain plans for implementing budget reductions, and submits them to the state controlling board with his recommendations as to, among other things, the amount of the loan, if any, the proposed loan agreement including a repayment schedule, and any plans for reducing the district's budget.

(D) Controlling board approval

The state controlling board is required to approve or disapprove the loan agreement submitted by the superintendent and may approve direct payment of the district's foundation program payments to the lender that provides the loan. As a condition for a loan, the controlling board may require a school district to implement the superintendent's recommendations for expenditure reductions or impose other requirements.[160]

(E) Repayment

Each loan request must state how the district board intends to repay the loan.[161] Repayment must be in accordance with a schedule approved by the superintendent, and include monthly, semi-annual, or annual equal installments, but repayment must be made no later than June 15 of the second year following approval of the loan, unless the certified deficit exceeds $25,000,000 or fifteen percent of the district's general fund expenditures, in which case the loan may be repaid over any number of years (not exceeding ten) approved by the controlling board.[162]

---

[155]RC 3318.13.
[156]RC 3313.483.
[157]RC 3317.62, RC 3317.63.
[158]RC 3313.483.

[159]OAG 84-067.
[160]RC 3313.483.
[161]RC 3313.483.
[162]RC 3313.483.

After the district's loan agreement is approved by the controlling board, the district is authorized to issue notes in anticipation of its voted levies for current expenses or its foundation program payments, or both, and deliver those notes to a commercial bank, underwriter, or other lender to evidence the loan. If the controlling board approves, the superintendent of public instruction is also authorized to forward repayment amounts from any foundation program payments which are to be made to the district directly to the holders of the district's notes, or their agents, in amounts specified under the terms of the loan.[163] Some have characterized these repayment techniques as providing a "state guarantee" but more careful analysis reveals that the obligation assumed by the state is to transfer funds which would otherwise be provided to the borrowing district, not to create funds which are not already designated for the borrowing district.

A district board may request in its loan application that its expenditures be controlled by the superintendent of public instruction under RC 3313.488. The state board of education may order any district to be subject to these controls.[164] In addition, these controls and special conditions are imposed upon any district requiring an emergency loan which fails to make application to a commercial bank, underwriter, or other prospective lender or purchaser of the district's obligations within forty-five days of the auditor's deficit certification or whose emergency loan is in excess of seven per cent of the general revenue fund of the district, if the district has within the last five years received an emergency loan.[165]

---

[163] RC 3313.483.
[164] RC 3313.483, RC 3317.64.
[165] RC 3313.4810, RC 3313.4811, RC 3317.62.

Chapter 42
Deposits and Investments

INTRODUCTION
42.01 Uniform Depository Act
42.02 Liability for undeposited funds and securities
42.03 Cash reserve

PUBLIC FUNDS AND ELIGIBLE DEPOSITORIES
42.04 Public funds, types of deposits
42.05 Eligible depositories
42.06 Maximum amount which may be deposited in given institution

PROCEDURE FOR DESIGNATING PUBLIC DEPOSITORIES
42.07 Designating depositories, in general
42.08 Separate treatment of active, inactive, and interim deposits
42.09 Resolution estimating inactive deposits, publication
42.10 Application to act as depository
42.11 Award of deposits
42.12 Conflict of interest in award, discrimination in apportioning deposits
42.13 Evidence of deposits
42.14 Transfer of inactive or interim funds to active funds
42.15 Service charges

SECURITY FOR PUBLIC DEPOSITS
42.16 Depositories required to post security, types of security
42.17 Securities eligible for pledge
42.18 Sale of pledged securities to recover public funds
42.19 Exchange, release, and substitution of securities
42.20 Deposit of pledged securities with trustee

INTEREST, ALLOCATION
42.21 Interest, payment
42.22 Allocation of interest among funds

INVESTMENT OF PUBLIC FUNDS
42.23 Investment of interim funds
42.24 Duties of treasurer, deposit of investments with trustee

INTRODUCTION

42.01 Uniform Depository Act

A board of education is obligated to make deposits of public money coming into its possession in compliance with the Uniform Depository Act, RC Chapter 135. This Act, originally adopted in 1937 and extensively amended in 1968 and 1981, establishes procedures and guidelines for the deposit and investment of public funds. It applies to the state and its subdivisions, including school districts, and imposes certain duties on subdivisions as well as upon the financial institutions serving as depositories. In some respects the Uniform Depository Act does not take into account recent developments in banking and financial markets.

The district treasurer is responsible for depositing and investing school district funds in accordance with RC Chapter 135.[1]

It is important to note the distinction the Act makes between the deposit of public funds and their investment. Even though moneys can be deposited or invested, different rules govern each activity. In addition, some investments, such as certificates of deposit, also represent deposits of those funds.

42.02 Liability for undeposited funds and securities

The mandatory provisions of RC Chapter 135 must be strictly followed. The courts will apply the common-law standard of liability for loss of public funds by public officials. That standard holds all public officials accountable for money coming into their possession, even though an unauthorized act of the official was not the cause of the loss of funds.[2]

However, the district treasurer and his bondsman or surety are relieved of any liability for loss of public money deposited in a public depository in compliance with RC 135.01 to RC 135.21, if the loss is caused by failure of the public depository.[3] In addition, the treasurer and his bondsman or surety are relieved from any liability for the loss or destruction of securities if those securities were deposited with a qualified

---

[1] RC 3313.51.
[2] State v Herbert, 49 OS(2d) 88, 358 NE(2d) 1090 (1976). See also OAG 94-048; RC 9.39.
[3] RC 135.19.

trustee as security for the repayment of public deposits.[4]

42.03 Cash reserve

The treasurer may keep in the vaults of his office an amount prescribed by the board of education as a cash reserve, which amount is not required to be deposited. The treasurer must, however, deposit or invest all remaining public money in his possession in accordance with RC 135.01 to RC 135.21.[5]

PUBLIC FUNDS AND ELIGIBLE DEPOSITORIES

42.04 Public funds, types of deposits

(A) "Public moneys"

RC 135.01 defines the following terms, as applied to school districts:

(1) "Public moneys"—all money in the treasury of a board of education or coming lawfully into the possession or custody of the treasurer.

(2) "Public deposit"—public money deposited in a public depository pursuant to RC 135.01 to RC 135.21.

(3) "Public depository"—an institution which receives or holds any public deposits.

(B) Active, inactive, and interim deposits

RC 135.01 also classifies deposits into three types, which receive different treatment because of their purposes:

(1) "Active deposit"—a public deposit necessary to meet current demands and deposited in a commercial account that is payable or withdrawable, in whole or in part, on demand; a negotiable order of withdrawal account; or a money market deposit account.

(2) "Inactive deposit"—a public deposit, other than an interim deposit or an active deposit and not expected to be needed during the two-year period of designation.

(3) "Interim deposit"—a deposit of public funds in the treasury of the board of education which is not an active deposit or an inactive deposit, which funds exceed the total of inactive deposits estimated by the board and which the treasurer or the board finds should not be deposited as active or inactive deposits since the money will not be needed for immediate use, but will be needed before the end of the designated period.

42.05 Eligible depositories

(A) In general, participation in Ohio guaranteed student loan program

Any national bank located in Ohio, any state-chartered bank subject to inspection by the superintendent of banks, or any domestic building and loan association is eligible to become a public depository subject to RC 135.01 to RC 135.21.[6] However, no bank or domestic building and loan association is eligible unless it is participating in the Ohio guaranteed student loan program administered pursuant to RC 3351.05 to RC 3351.14.[7] No bank or savings and loan association which is currently a party or whose officers, directors, employees, or controlling shareholders or controlling persons are parties to an active final, temporary, or summary cease and desist order under RC 1125.08 or RC 1155.02 is eligible to become a public depository.[8]

(B) Branch located in school district

Among eligible institutions, only those with an office located within the school district are eligible to become public depositories for the district's active, inactive, and interim deposits. An automatic teller machine is an office or branch within the meaning of the Act, and its location within the district makes the owning bank eligible.[9] However, if not more than one eligible institution is located within the district or applies to become a public depository for the district's inactive or interim deposits, the board may designate as public depositories for inactive or interim deposits one or more eligible institutions which are conveniently located. Also, if the total of the active, inactive, or interim deposits

---

[4]RC 135.18(I).
[5]RC 135.17.
[6]RC 135.03.
[7]RC 135.031.
[8]RC 135.032.
[9]OAG 84-039.

applied for by the eligible institutions located in the district is less than the total estimated to be made by the district, the board may designate one or more conveniently located eligible institutions as public depositories.[10]

(C) Minority banks

Minority banks are exempt from many of the public depository eligibility requirements of RC Chapter 135. "Minority bank" is defined as "a bank that is owned or controlled by one or more socially or economically disadvantaged persons." Such persons include, among others, Afro-Americans, Puerto Ricans, Spanish-speaking Americans, and American Indians.[11]

The board may designate one or more minority banks as public depositories for those portions of its active, inactive, and interim deposits attributable to federal funds. Only the requirements imposed by RC 135.031, relating to participation in the state student loan program, and RC 135.18 and RC 135.181, concerning security for the repayment of public deposits, are applicable to the award of these deposits.[12]

42.06 Maximum amount which may be deposited in given institution

A bank may not receive or have on deposit at any one time public funds totaling more than thirty per cent of its total assets, as shown in its latest report to the superintendent of banks or comptroller of the currency. Similarly, a building and loan association may not receive or have on deposit at any one time public money exceeding thirty per cent of its total assets as shown in its latest report to the superintendent of building and loan associations or the federal home loan bank board.[13] These limits apply to the financial institution itself rather than to the branch office in which the funds are actually deposited.[14]

PROCEDURE FOR DESIGNATING PUBLIC DEPOSITORIES

42.07 Designating depositories, in general

Institutions are designated to serve as public depositories for a two-year period commencing when the preceding period of designation expires. The board of education is required to meet every two years on the third Monday or its regularly scheduled meeting date of the month before the expiration date of its current period of designation to make a new designation. If a change in state or federal law makes a designation or an award unlawful, the period of designation does not extend beyond the date when the change becomes effective. The board must then convene to designate its depositories for the balance of the two-year period.[15]

42.08 Separate treatment of active, inactive, and interim deposits

Public deposits made during the two-year designation period, which exceed the estimated total of inactive deposits, are active deposits or interim deposits.[16] If, at the time for designation, the board estimates that it will not have public money to award to eligible institutions as inactive deposits, then any public money coming under the board's control during that two-year period will be active or interim deposits. The board may designate public depositories for these funds, but the period of designation runs from the date set by the board to a date two years from the date of expiration of the preceding period of designation.[17]

There is no requirement that a resolution and notice be published before a governing board can designate public depositories for active or interim deposits.[18]

---

[10] RC 135.04.
[11] RC 135.04(F).
[12] RC 135.04(F).
[13] RC 135.03.
[14] OAG 83-008.

[15] RC 135.12.
[16] RC 135.05.
[17] 1964 OAG 948.
[18] 1964 OAG 104; 1937 OAG 751.

Active, inactive, and interim deposits must be separately awarded, made, and administered.[19]

42.09 Resolution estimating inactive deposits, publication

At least three weeks prior to the third Monday of the month before expiration of the current designation of depositories, the board must adopt a resolution estimating the total of public money subject to its control to be awarded and deposited as inactive deposits.[20]

The resolution and notice of the designation date must be published once a week for two consecutive weeks in two newspapers of opposite politics and of general circulation in the county in which the school district is located. If a district is located in more than one county, publication must be made in newspapers published in the county in which the major part of the district is located and of general circulation in the district. A written notice must also be given to eligible depositories at the time of first publication, stating the total amount to be awarded as inactive deposits.[21]

42.10 Application to act as depository

Active, inactive, and interim deposits are treated differently, and separate application to act as a depository must be made for each. The procedure for application is similar for all types of deposits, however, and the separate applications to act as depository for active, inactive, or interim funds may be included in one document in any combination desired by the applicant.

If an eligible institution desires to become a public depository for the funds of the school district, it must apply in writing to the board at least thirty days before the date set for designating depositories. The application must specify the maximum amount of inactive or interim deposits and may specify the maximum amount of active deposits the institution wishes to have on deposit at any one time during the period of designation, and the rates of interest which the institution will pay on the inactive and interim deposits.

The application is to be accompanied by a financial statement of the applicant, under oath, in enough detail to show the capital funds of the applicant as of the date of its latest report to the superintendent of banks, superintendent of building and loan associations, federal home loan bank board, or comptroller of the currency and adjusted to show any changes made before the date of the application.[22]

42.11 Award of deposits

(A) Meeting of board of education

The board of education, meeting on the third Monday of the month prior to expiration of the current period of designation to designate the public depositories, must also award the public money of the district to the public depositories for the next two-year designation period.[23]

The designation and award must be made in duplicate. One copy is retained by the board, and one copy is certified to the district treasurer.[24]

If for any reason the depository designated by the board ceases to act as a custodian of school funds, the funds must be placed in the custody of the treasurer of the city or the county in which the school district is located, to be held by the city or county treasurer and distributed by the district treasurer until the board designates another depository.[25]

(B) Award of deposits

(1) Inactive deposits

At the time of awarding inactive deposits, the governing board is to estimate the probable amount of public money, if any, to be deposited in eligible institutions at the beginning of the period. The award is to be made to one or more eligible institutions offering to pay the highest rate of interest permissible at the beginning of the period of designation on like time certificates of deposit or savings or deposit

---

[19]RC 135.05.
[20]RC 135.05.
[21]RC 135.05.
[22]RC 135.06, RC 135.08, RC 135.10.

[23]RC 135.12.
[24]RC 135.12.
[25]RC 3313.32.

accounts, in the amount specified in each application.

If two or more eligible institutions each offer the highest rate on the amounts specified in their respective applications and the total of these amounts is more than the amount available for deposit, either at the beginning or later during the period, the inactive deposits are to be divided and awarded among these institutions in proportion to the capital funds of each.

If the total of amounts specified by the institutions offering the highest interest rate is less than the amount of public money available for deposit, either initially or subsequently, the board must award the remainder to the institution offering to pay the next highest permissible rate of interest, in the amount specified in its application. If there are two or more such institutions, and the aggregate of the amounts they specified exceeds the remaining amount to be deposited, the remainder is to be awarded to each in proportion to its respective capital funds.

If the total of inactive deposits specified by institutions in their applications is less than the amount available for deposit, either initially or subsequently, the board may invite applications for the excess amount from eligible institutions. The excess is to be awarded to the institution offering the highest permissible rate of interest.

A public depository cannot have a greater amount of inactive public money on deposit at any one time than the amount specified in its application. When the amount of inactive deposits must be reduced or withdrawn because of this limitation or for some other reason, the amount reduced or withdrawn must be deposited in another eligible institution offering to pay the same rate of interest. If no other eligible institution has applied, these funds are to be deposited or invested by the board in accordance with the Act.[26]

In case there are two or more depositories subject to withdrawal, withdrawals shall be made from the public depository paying the lowest rate of interest.[27]

(2) Interim deposits

Interim deposits may be awarded by the treasurer or board as they become available and must be made to the eligible institution or institutions offering to pay the highest permissible rate of interest on like time certificates of deposit or savings or deposit accounts.[28]

The treasurer or board is to determine the periods for which interim deposits are to be made, but the periods must be for certain maturities of not more than two years.[29] When the maturity of the interim deposit award is reached, the depository need not renew the deposit on the same terms and at the same rate of interest specified in its application. Each deposit or redeposit of interim funds takes place under a separate interim deposit award, and the deposit may be rejected by the eligible institution.[30]

If, during the period of designation, the treasurer or board considers that the interest being paid on interim deposits does not reflect the prevailing market rates, the board may request the submission of new bids from eligible institutions. The applications must be in writing and made prior to the date set by the board. They must specify the maximum amount of interim deposits desired and the rate of interest to be paid on the deposit.[31]

(3) Active deposits

The governing board must award the first $25,000 in active deposits, based on the operating needs of the school district, to any eligible institution which has applied and qualified. Any active deposits over $25,000 must be awarded to the eligible institutions which have applied and qualified in proportion to their award quotas.[32] The award quota is determined by dividing the capital and surplus of an institution by the number of its permanent offices (principal office and branches, not including intermittent branches) wherever located. This amount, known as the "active fund quota," is multiplied by the number of per-

---

[26] RC 135.07.
[27] RC 135.15.
[28] RC 135.09.
[29] RC 135.09, RC 135.14(C).

[30] RC 135.14(C); Provident Bank v Wood, 36 OS(2d) 101, 304 NE(2d) 378 (1973).
[31] RC 135.09.
[32] OAG 69-114.

manent offices which the institution maintains within the district. The result is the award quota for that institution.[33] Except for the first $25,000 in active deposits, the governing board must award active deposits to all eligible and qualified institutions making application in accordance with the Act.[34]

A depository is neither required nor allowed to take a greater amount of active deposits than the amount specified in the depository's application. When the amount of active deposits must be reduced or withdrawn because of this limitation or for some other reason, the amount reduced or withdrawn is to be deposited in another eligible institution which submitted an application. If there is no other institution, the amount must be awarded and deposited for the remainder of the period of designation under RC 135.01 to RC 135.21.[35]

42.12 Conflict of interest in award, discrimination in apportioning deposits

An officer, director, stockholder, employee, or owner of any interest in public depositories receiving active, inactive, or interim deposits is not considered to be interested directly or indirectly, as a result of his relationship with the public depository, in the deposit of public money for the purpose of any law prohibiting school district officers from being interested in any contract of the district.[36]

After public deposits have been made at the beginning of a period of designation, the requirements of RC Chapter 135 as to the proportion of deposits to be maintained in more than one public depository are subject to reasonable variations as the exigencies of public business require.

If a public depository believes that it has been discriminated against in favor of any other public depository, it may complain to the board. The board must hear the complaint after giving one week's notice to the district treasurer and the public depositories named in the complaint. If the board finds that discrimination exists, it must order the treasurer to make appropriate transfers of public deposits among the depositories by making withdrawals and deposits as specified in the board's order.[37]

42.13 Evidence of deposits

Inactive deposits must be evidenced by time certificates of deposit, to mature not later than the end of the period of designation, or by savings or deposit accounts, including, but not limited to, passbook accounts. The certificates may provide that the amount of the deposit is payable on written notice given a specified period before the date of repayment. Any penalties for early withdrawal are governed by federal law and the terms of the certificate of deposit. Inactive deposits can also be invested in certain United States Small Business Administration secondary market certificates.[38]

Interim deposits must be evidenced by certificates of deposit maturing in not more than one year from the date of deposit. They can also be invested according to the procedures therefor.[39]

Active deposits are to be in the form of commercial accounts subject to check.[40] An active deposit may also include a public deposit in a negotiable order of withdrawal account.

42.14 Transfer of inactive or interim funds to active funds

If the governing board determines that the active deposits are insufficient to meet the demands for them, it must direct the treasurer to sell interim money investments or deposits, or to transfer enough from the inactive deposits to the active deposits. The board determines the depositories from which withdrawals are to be made and the amounts to be withdrawn from each. The treasurer must promptly give written notice of withdrawals to each affected depository.

---

[33] RC 135.04(G).
[34] State ex rel First Natl Bank of Toledo v Sylvania City School Dist Bd of Ed, 4 App(2d) 258, 212 NE(2d) 80 (Lucas 1965), affirmed by 8 OS(2d) 3, 220 NE(2d) 671 (1966).
[35] RC 135.04(C).
[36] RC 135.11.
[37] RC 135.20.
[38] OAG 85-077.
[39] See Text 42.23(A), In general.
[40] RC 135.13.

If two or more depositories are subject to withdrawal, the board must make withdrawals from the depositories paying the lowest rate of interest and in proportional amounts as far as it is practicable to do so.[41]

42.15 Service charges

No service charge can be made by the depository against any active deposit or collected from or paid by the treasurer, unless the charge is customarily imposed by the institution receiving money on deposit subject to check, in the municipal corporation in which the public depository is located.[42]

SECURITY FOR PUBLIC DEPOSITS

42.16 Depositories required to post security, types of security

Public depositories must provide security for the repayment of public deposits. This may be done by pledging and depositing with the treasurer or a trustee certain eligible securities.[43] The market value of these securities must equal the amount of the public deposits not covered by federal insurance. Alternatively, the treasurer may require the depository to execute and deliver to him surety bonds in the amount of the uninsured portion of the public deposits. If the market value of the securities pledged and delivered as security declines, the treasurer may require that additional securities be deposited.[44]

42.17 Securities eligible for pledge

The most commonly pledged securities eligible for the above purpose are as follows:

(1) Bonds, notes, or other obligations of the United States or bonds, notes, or other obligations guaranteed as to principal and interest by the United States;

(2) Bonds, notes, debentures, or other obligations or securities issued by any federal governmental agency or instrumentality;

(3) Bonds or other obligations of the state of Ohio;

(4) Bonds or other obligations of any county, township, school district, municipal corporation, or other taxing subdivision of the state of Ohio which is not in default in the payment of principal and interest at the time of deposit;

(5) Bonds of other states of the United States which have not defaulted in payments of principal and interest in the ten years preceding the time of deposit; and

(6) Obligations guaranteed as to principal and interest by the Ohio student aid commission.[45]

Other types of securities are made eligible for use as security by separate statutes relating to those securities. For example, RC 140.07 makes certain types of hospital revenue bonds eligible to be pledged.

In lieu of other pledging requirements, a public depository may at its option pledge a single pool of eligible securities to secure the repayment of all public money deposited with it by all subdivisions.[46]

42.18 Sale of pledged securities to recover public funds

If the public depository fails to pay over any part of a public deposit, the treasurer must sell any securities placed or deposited with him at a public sale. Thirty days' notice of the sale must be given in a newspaper of general circulation in the county seat in which the treasurer's office is located. Upon payment of the purchase price, the treasurer must transfer absolute ownership of the securities to the purchasers. Any surplus from the sale, after deducting the amount due to the school district and any expenses of sale, must be paid to the public depository.[47]

---

[41]RC 135.15.
[42]RC 135.16.
[43]See Text 42.17, Securities eligible for pledge.
[44]RC 135.18(A).

[45]RC 135.18(B).
[46]RC 135.181.
[47]RC 135.18(C).

42.19 Exchange, release, and substitution of securities

The school board may provide for the exchange, release, and substitution of securities delivered or pledged to the treasurer. For securities deposited with the trustee, the rules regarding substitution and exchange of securities vary according to the type of securities involved. If a public depository has deposited with a trustee securities that are direct obligations of the United States, it may substitute or exchange the same type of securities having any equal or greater current market value without obtaining specific authorization from the board or treasurer. If a public depository has deposited other eligible securities with a trustee, it may substitute or exchange any eligible securities having equal or greater current market value only with written specific authorization from the treasurer or under the following circumstances:

(1) The treasurer has given written authorization for the depository to make the substitution or exchange on a continuing basis for a specified time period without prior approval; or

(2) The public depository gives the treasurer and trustee written notice by personal delivery or registered or certified mail of an intended substitution or exchange and the treasurer fails to object within ten calendar days.[48]

42.20 Deposit of pledged securities with trustee

(A) In general

In lieu of depositing securities with the treasurer, the public depository may designate a qualified trustee to hold the securities required as collateral for the repayment of public deposits, by giving written notice of the designation to the treasurer. However, the trustee has no duty to determine the eligibility or value of any security so held by the trustee.[49] Rights and interests in the securities are asserted by written notice to or demand upon the trustee. The treasurer is to accept the written receipt of the trustee describing the securities which have been deposited with the trustee by the public depository.[50]

RC 135.181 provides for designation of trustee for the optional pledge of a single pool of eligible securities as collateral for repayment of public money. Use of these pools by depositories has become increasingly common.

(B) Eligible trustees

Any federal reserve bank or its Ohio branch is qualified to act as trustee. An institution which is eligible to become a public depository and which holds a certificate of qualification from the superintendent of banks, or any institution complying with RC 1109.03, RC 1109.04, RC 1109.17, and RC 1109.18, is qualified to act as trustee for securities other than those belonging to itself. Any of the latter institutions may apply to the superintendent of banks for a certificate of qualification, a certified copy of which is conclusive evidence that the institution is a qualified trustee.[51]

Eligible trustees for the optional pledge of a single pool of eligible securities are described in RC 135.181(F).

(C) Compensation of trustee

Any charge or compensation required by a trustee is to be paid by the public depository which designated the trustee and not by the school district, treasurer, or any member of the board. The rights and interests of the school district and treasurer in the securities are superior to the lien of any charges made by the trustee.[52]

Charges or compensation of a designated trustee for the optional pledge of a single pool of eligible securities[53] must be paid by the public depository and may not be a lien upon the securities.

INTEREST, ALLOCATION

42.21 Interest, payment

Interest on inactive deposits must be paid or credited in accordance with the terms and conditions of the account and

---

[48]RC 135.18(E) to (G).
[49]RC 135.18(I).
[50]RC 135.18(D).

[51]RC 135.18(I).
[52]RC 135.18.
[53]RC 135.181(J).

when funds are withdrawn or the account closed. The interest payment is computed from the date of deposit to the time when withdrawals are made or the account is closed. Interest on interim deposits must be paid in accordance with the terms and conditions of the account and when the funds are withdrawn, or at maturity, computing payment from the date of deposit. Interest on active deposits must be paid or credited by the public depository at least quarterly and also when the funds are withdrawn, computing payment from the date of deposit.[54]

42.22 Allocation of interest among funds

Some of the most confusing provisions of Ohio law are the scattered statutes governing the uses of and accounting for interest earnings, which have undergone several changes in recent years.

The general rule is that all interest must be credited to the general fund.[55] There are, however, at least five exceptions.

The first exception is for interest earned on funds derived from state appropriations to non-public schools which are required to be held in so-called "auxiliary services funds."[56] Interest earned on such funds must be credited to and remain in those funds and must be used to pay expenses incurred in administering those programs.

The second exception is for interest earned on the proceeds of "refunding" obligations (that is, bonds or notes issued to retire other debt) during the time those proceeds are in the bond retirement fund.[57] Interest earned on the proceeds of refunding obligations must be credited to and remain in the bond retirement fund and be pledged to assist in the repayment of the outstanding debt.

The third exception is for interest earned on a building fund containing proceeds from the sale of a bond, note, or certificate of indebtedness.[58] Interest must be credited to and remain in the fund and be used only for the purpose for which the indebtedness was authorized, unless the board adopts a resolution authorizing the interest to be credited to another fund or account, in which case the interest would then be used for the purposes of that fund or account.

The fourth exception is for interest earned on trust funds if the donor of the moneys has specified how the interest is to be credited. In that case, the donor's wishes must be followed.[59]

The fifth exception is for interest earned on an education fund. Income earned on that fund must be paid to the fund.[60]

RC 3315.01 gives boards of education authority to opt out of the general rule in most circumstances. A board may adopt a resolution directing the district treasurer to maintain interest earnings in the fund from which they arise or to credit them to any other board fund. Thus, a board may specify those instances in which the general rule does not apply. However, the authority to opt out does *not* apply to the five exceptions noted above (except for the special authority for building funds described under the third exception), which must be followed regardless of whether the board adopts such a resolution.

In addition, interest earned on the bond retirement fund may not be the subject of such a resolution. Excluding interest earned on refunding obligations (the second exception noted above), interest earned on bond retirement funds must follow the general rule and be credited to the general fund. However, a board may indirectly achieve the same result as adopting a resolution to opt out of the general rule.[61] Since a board is authorized to transfer money from its general fund into any other fund, including the bond retirement fund, adoption of a resolution transferring interest earned on the bond retirement fund and credited to the general fund will produce the same result.

---

[54] RC 135.16.
[55] RC 5705.10; OAG 85-072.
[56] RC 3317.06.
[57] RC 133.23(D).
[58] RC 5705.10.
[59] OAG 85-085.
[60] RC 3315.40.
[61] RC 5705.10.

INVESTMENT OF PUBLIC FUNDS

42.23 Investment of interim funds

(A) In general

The treasurer or board of education may invest interim funds provided the investments mature or are redeemable within two years from the date of purchase. This does not mean the market for the security is sufficiently liquid that the security can be sold within two years at some market price, but rather that it is payable by its issuer at stated maturity or at the option of the district within two years of the date of purchase.[62] The permissible investments are bonds, notes, or other obligations of (or guaranteed by) the United States, or those for which the faith of the United States is pledged; bonds, notes, debentures, or other obligations issued by a federal governmental agency or instrumentality; certificates of deposit with eligible depositories; and bonds and other obligations of the state of Ohio.

Interim funds may also be invested in no-load money market mutual funds registered as investment companies under the Investment Company Act of 1940 and having the highest rating of a nationally recognized standard rating service. Such purchases may only be from an Ohio bank or an Ohio savings and loan. Some additional risks and some unanswered legal concerns are associated with such mutual funds, and care should be taken before investing to fully understand their benefits and restrictions.

Money may also be invested by use of the state treasurer's investment pool, STAROhio, created and administered under RC 135.45. Upon authorization by two-thirds vote of the board of education, the treasurer may invest up to twenty-five per cent of the board's interim moneys in certain commercial paper and bankers' acceptances.[63] However, no board may so invest any of its interim moneys unless its treasurer has completed additional training regarding these types of investments. The state auditor must approve that training.

All investments must be made through a member of the National Association of Securities Dealers or through an institution regulated by the Superintendent of Banks, the Comptroller of the Currency, the Superintendent of Savings and Loan Associations, the Federal Deposit Insurance Corporation, the Board of Governors of the Federal Reserve System, or the Federal Home Loan Bank Board.[64] Payment for such investments may only be made upon delivery of the securities or, in the case of investments not represented by a certificate, upon receipt of confirmation of the purchase from the custodian.

The treasurer or governing board may also enter into repurchase agreements with an eligible institution for a period of up to thirty days. Any repurchase agreement must be made pursuant to a written agreement which at least sets forth the face amount of the securities which are the subject of the repurchase agreement; the type, rate, and maturity date of the securities; and a numerical identifier for the securities. Interim money may also be deposited in any eligible institution as interim deposits according to the procedure previously outlined.[65]

RC 3318.111 authorizes the investment of money available under construction project accounts in direct obligations of the United States or the state of Ohio.

The attorney general has stated that, even if an investment is otherwise legal, the decision to purchase the investment is subject to "fiduciary standards."[66] These include, among others, such factors as the amount of the investment, its marketability, the need for liquidity, the size and diversity of the existing portfolio, investment policies, the extent to which the rate differs from other available market rates, the guaranteed return, and any contingent return.

(B) Classifying funds as interim

The treasurer, after classifying public money as interim money, must notify the governing board of his action within thirty days. If the board disagrees with the action or with the investments or deposits made, it

---

[62] OAG 93-021.
[63] RC 135.142
[64] RC 135.14.

[65] RC 135.14. See Text 42.07 to 42.15.
[66] OAG 93-021; OAG 93-055; OAG 94-048.

can direct the treasurer to sell or liquidate any of the investments or deposits. The order to sell must specifically state the items to be sold and must fix the date of sale. The designated investments or deposits are then sold or liquidated for cash on the appointed day at their then-current market prices. The expense of the sale or liquidation is an expense of the treasurer's office. Neither the treasurer nor board members are to be held accountable for any loss occasioned by the sale or liquidation of the securities or certificates of deposit.[67]

42.24 Duties of treasurer, deposit of investments with trustee

The treasurer is responsible for the safekeeping of all investments or deposits acquired by him under RC 135.14. Any investments may be deposited with a qualified trustee[68] for safekeeping, and securities acquired under a repurchase agreement must be delivered to a qualified trustee; however, if the repurchase agreement is with a depository of the board, then the securities may be held by the treasurer or in trust by the depository on behalf of the board. The trustee is required to report to the treasurer, state auditor, or authorized outside auditor the identity, market value, and location of the documents held by it evidencing each security. The treasurer must collect interest earned on any investments and deposits and credit it to the proper school district fund. The treasurer also is to collect money due and payable to the district on investments, and the money collected must be treated as public money.

---

[67]RC 135.14.
[68]Any federal reserve bank or branch located in Ohio may serve as a qualified trustee. OAG 89-077.

Chapter 43

Financial Transactions and Accounting

SPENDING PUBLIC MONEY
- 43.01 General considerations in spending school funds
- 43.02 Requirement for authorization to spend money
- 43.03 Requirement for public purpose
- 43.04 Restrictions on earmarked funds
- 43.05 Examples of authorized and unauthorized expenditures

PROCEDURE FOR EXPENDITURES
- 43.06 Overview of procedure for expenditures
- 43.07 Requisition and purchase order
- 43.08 Voucher and warrant
- 43.09 Procedure for payment of purchases and contracts
- 43.10 Procedure for payment of wages and salaries

FINANCIAL RECORDS
- 43.11 Appropriation and authorization ledger
- 43.12 Receipts and deposits
- 43.13 Cash journal
- 43.14 Individual payroll record

SCHOOL FUNDS
- 43.15 School funds
- 43.16 Interest earned on funds
- 43.17 General fund
- 43.18 Bond funds
- 43.19 Bond retirement fund
- 43.20 Replacement fund
- 43.21 Permanent improvement fund
- 43.22 Service fund
- 43.23 Food service fund
- 43.24 School supplies fund
- 43.25 Student activities fund

ACCOUNTING
- 43.26 Uniform system of accounting
- 43.27 Audits
- 43.28 Duties of district treasurer
- 43.29 Data processing
- 43.30 Retention of records

SPENDING PUBLIC MONEY

43.01 General considerations in spending school funds

Funds of a board of education, from whatever source, are held in trust for the public, and must be applied only to public purposes for which the board is authorized to spend money. RC 9.39 generally makes public officials, defined to include officers and employees of political subdivisions such as school districts, liable for the loss or misuse of all public money received or collected by them or their subordinates.[1]

Most funds are earmarked for particular purposes. For example, revenue from property taxes levied for purposes specified by statute or the electors must be applied only to those purposes. Federal and state funds are often received on the express condition that they be spent only for specified purposes.

Reviewing expenditures of public funds is one function of the state auditor, and a board may consult with the auditor's office about a proposed expenditure about which it has a question.

43.02 Requirement for authorization to spend money

(A) In general

Boards of education may only spend money for authorized purposes, or for purposes necessarily implied from specific authorization. The concept of "necessary implication" should not be viewed broadly. For example, while a board has specific authority to construct school buildings, the attorney general opined that public funds may not be used to pay the costs—such as printing programs, renting chairs, distributing invitations, or installing loud speaker systems—of assemblies to dedicate a new building.[2]

(B) Specific authorization

In some cases, the general assembly has granted specific spending authority. For example, boards are authorized to pay up to $200 per school per year in membership dues to accrediting associations,[3] to spend funds for certain consultant services,[4] and to purchase liability insurance to protect

---

[1] Liability is not imposed under the statute, however, for public money that is properly due but remains uncollected. OAG 93-004.

[2] 1938 OAG 3527; 1938 OAG 3489.
[3] RC 3313.871.
[4] RC 3313.171.

individual board members, or employees, and the board as an entity.[5]

(C) Authorization by necessary implication

In other cases, a particular statutory authorization necessarily implies that funds may be spent for a particular purpose. For example, a board may contract with an insurance company or hospital service association to process claims associated with a health insurance program for board employees,[6] or contract with a private organization for an audit of workers' compensation claims.[7]

43.03 Requirement for public purpose

A board's spending authority is always limited by the requirement that the expenditure be for a "public purpose." For example, a board has general authority in certain instances to pay tuition for students who attend a school not operated by the board, but no authority to pay tuition for students who attend a private school.[8]

43.04 Restrictions on earmarked funds

Even if a proposed expenditure is for a public purpose, it may still be prohibited for the specific purpose contemplated. For example, a property tax levy for "permanent improvements" may not be used for "current expenses," even though current expenses are a legitimate public purpose. A board may spend funds derived from a tax levy for current expenses to pay costs of student activity programs as long as total expenditures do not exceed 0.5% of the board's annual operating budget.[9]

43.05 Examples of authorized and unauthorized expenditures

Certain expenditures are more susceptible to controversy than others—such as the following.

(A) Influencing vote on levy or bond issue

A board may not financially support or oppose passage of a school levy or bond issue or compensate any employee for time spent campaigning.[10] This prohibition does not extend to providing information.[11]

(B) Certain expenses of employees

A board has implied authority to fix fringe benefits as a necessary corollary to the express power to employ.[12] Absent constricting statutory authority, a board may award any fringe benefit.[13] For example, a board may provide teaching employees with free lunches at the school cafeteria or cash payments for early retirement or longevity of service.[14] However, a board may not provide cash payments for sick leave in contravention of RC 124.39 and RC 3319.141 or tuition-free education for children of teachers who are not district residents because that would violate RC 3313.64 and RC 3317.08.[15]

The Public Employees Collective Bargaining Act has all but erased concern over statutory proscriptions against certain benefit and compensation schemes as to unionized groups of employees.[16]

(C) Legal expenses

A board may compensate a city law director for non-routine services or provide legal assistance to him.[17] A board may pay for checking title to real estate.[18] A board

---

[5]RC 2744.08, RC 2744.081, RC 3313.203. See Text 46.16 to 46.20.
[6]OAG 84-030.
[7]OAG 83-076.
[8]1961 OAG 2616; 1933 OAG 1290.
[9]RC 3315.062; OAG 84-083.
[10]RC 3315.07.
[11]See Text 5.09(G), Disseminating information.
[12]Ebert v Stark County Bd of Mental Retardation, 63 OS(2d) 31, 406 NE(2d) 1098 (1980).
[13]OAG 81-052.
[14]OAG 81-052.
[15]OAG 81-052.

[16]See Text 18.20, Supremacy of contract over certain laws.
[17]OAG 70-081; 1954 OAG 3644.
[18]1955 Syllabi 116. Syllabi are unpublished determinations made by the Auditor of State's Office from approximately 1945 to 1970. During that time, brief one-sentence references to the determinations had some limited circulation outside the Auditor's Office and were sometimes referenced by the Auditor and others. Although they may not be of precedential value outside of the Auditor's Office, they are often the only authority for the specific proposition for

may also hire its own "in-house" legal counsel.[19]

(D) Miscellaneous expenses

A board may not pay transportation expenses for practice teachers or prospective employees[20] or honoria to persons sitting on discussion panels.[21]

PROCEDURE FOR EXPENDITURES

43.06 Overview of procedure for expenditures

The first step after funds have been appropriated, is preparation of a requisition by the one requesting the expenditure. The requisition is forwarded to the treasurer where, if approved, a purchase order is prepared with a signed treasurer's certificate attached. The treasurer may not sign the certificate unless appropriated, unencumbered monies are in a board fund that can be used for the purpose involved. The purchase order is posted in the appropriation and authorization ledger and a copy forwarded to the supplier of goods or services. Upon receipt of the goods or services, a voucher is prepared directing the treasurer to pay. A warrant (check) is issued for the amount and from the account indicated.

If unencumbered funds are not appropriated for the particular purpose, an amendment of the board's appropriation resolution is required. If funds not previously appropriated are appropriated, the applicable certifications required by RC 5705.412 should be prepared and sent to the county auditor so the board can receive an amended certificate of estimated resources. The certificate is not required for a temporary appropriation if the amount does not exceed twenty-five per cent of the total amount of the previous year, an amended certificate of estimated resources for the current year has not been certified to the board under RC 5705.36, and the appropriation measure will not be in effect on or after the thirtieth day following the earliest date on which the board may adopt its annual appropriation resolution.[22] The procedure for paying employees' wages is slightly different.[23]

43.07 Requisition and purchase order

(A) Requisition

A requisition is used for supplies or services. Requisitions are customarily prepared in duplicate—one for the initiating department, the other for the treasurer. When a requisition is approved and a purchase order is prepared with a treasurer's certificate, contracts for purchases may legally be made.[24] A board is not financially liable unless a treasurer's certificate is attached to the contract for purchase or purchase order certifying that sufficient funds are on hand or in the process of collection.[25]

Requisitions should be numbered consecutively. The standard form recommended by the state auditor may be adapted to the needs of the individual district, so long as the information required by the auditor is retained.[26]

(B) Purchase order

A purchase order should be prepared at least in triplicate and presented to the board for approval.

Purchase orders should be numbered consecutively. If a purchase order is originally written for an amount which differs from the amount of the invoice, the difference is adjusted on the appropriation

---

which they are cited and so this reference has been retained.

[19]OAG 83-038.

[20]1957 OAG 1429.

[21]Schwing v McClure, 120 OS 335, 166 NE 230 (1929); New Concord School Dist Bd of Ed v Best, 52 OS 138, 39 NE 694 (1894).

[22]RC 5705.412.

[23]See Text 43.10, Procedure for payment of wages and salaries.

[24]See RC 5705.412; OAG 87-069.

[25]RC 5705.41. But see Jefferson County Bd of Commrs v Board of Trustees, 3 App(3d) 336, 3 OBR 391, 445 NE(2d) 664 (Jefferson 1981) (public body may, in certain cases, incur financial liability to another public body even if no certification made under RC 5705.41).

[26]See also Text 43.26, Uniform system of accounting.

ledger in the proper "debit" or "credit" column.

One court decision suggests an RC 5705.412 certification may be required on all purchase orders in addition to the certification required by RC 5705.41(D)(1),[27] while another suggests RC 5705.412 supersedes RC 5705.41 with respect to board of education contracts.[28] Whether these decisions reach beyond their particular facts is unclear, and prudence suggests a review with the board's legal counsel. A common pleas court has ruled a RC 5705.412 certificate need not be executed prior to board approval of a contract, but must be signed before the contract is executed.[29]

(C) Disposition of purchase order

The original copy goes to the vendor, the duplicate remains in board files, and the triplicate is used by the treasurer for posting in the ledger. When the covering invoice is received, a voucher is prepared and the invoice and purchase order are attached.

Purchase order forms may be tailored to local board requirements, but the treasurer's certificate must always be attached.

43.08 Voucher and warrant

(A) Voucher

A voucher, i.e., written order directing the treasurer to pay a lawful board obligation, is used for all payrolls, invoices, estimates on contracts, bond maturities and interest, liquidated purchase orders and certificates, and any other obligations payable by warrant. The voucher form has space for entering the number of the warrant issued in payment. The voucher has no number. The warrant number is used as the reference number.

Voucher forms may be tailored to local board requirements.

(B) Warrant

A warrant is a check. More than one warrant can be authorized by a single voucher; more than one appropriation item can be charged by a single voucher.

No board money may be paid except on a warrant signed by the treasurer.[30] The signatures of the treasurer and board president are required on checks for the total amounts stated in a payroll if the payroll is paid in cash.[31] If the treasurer is incapacitated, the board may appoint a district officer to sign warrants.[32]

Upon written authorization by a payee designating the financial institution and account to be credited, any payment that can be made by warrant may be made by direct deposit electronic transfer. If a warrant would require board authorization, the electronic transfer also requires authorization by board resolution. A board may contract with a financial institution for direct deposit services and draw lump-sum warrants payable to that institution in the amount to be transferred.[33]

43.09 Procedure for payment of purchases and contracts

After the board of education authorizes payment by adopting a resolution approving the bill for payment, the treasurer may then present the warrant or warrants which are covered by the voucher. By general resolution, a board may dispense with authorization for payment on each purchase order by individual resolution if provision is made for payment in the annual appropriation resolution.[34]

43.10 Procedure for payment of wages and salaries

A board may, by general resolution, dispense with resolutions authorizing payment of wages and salaries if provision for pay-

---

[27]CADO Business Systems of Ohio, Inc v Cleveland City School Dist Bd of Ed, 8 App(3d) 385, 8 OBR 499, 457 NE(2d) 939 (Cuyahoga 1983).

[28]Tri-County North Local School Bd of Ed v McGuire & Shook Corp, 748 FSupp 541 (SD Ohio 1989).

[29]Hines v Cleveland School Dist Bd of Ed, 26 Misc(2d) 15, 26 OBR 348, 499 NE(2d) 39 (CP, Cuyahoga 1985).

[30]RC 3313.51.
[31]RC 3315.08.
[32]RC 3313.51.
[33]RC 9.37.
[34]RC 3313.18.

ment is made in the annual appropriation resolution.[35]

If paid in cash, the board president and treasurer issue checks payable to the treasurer for the total payroll. The treasurer then procures the cash to make payments. In the alternative, the board may transfer the amount to a special payroll account in a depository on which payroll checks may be drawn.[36] Payroll checks may be signed by facsimile signature.[37]

FINANCIAL RECORDS

43.11 Appropriation and authorization ledger

When the county auditor certifies that the total appropriations in the appropriation resolution is within the county budget commission's official estimate of revenues for the year, the appropriations become effective and the treasurer may enter them on the ledger.

Entries are made only when the board authorizes the expenditure of funds. Board authorization immediately encumbers or commits the appropriation to the extent of the estimated purchase or contract price. The treasurer makes an entry, stating the date, the seller's name, the purpose or object of the order, the order number, and the cost. When final cost cannot be exactly ascertained, the estimated cost is entered. When the invoice is received, any necessary correction is made by a second entry giving the actual amount paid. Any difference between the estimate and the warrant amount is noted as an "adjustment."

Entry of each purchase order is made by subtracting the amount of the order from the balance shown. The remainder is the "unencumbered balance." It does not indicate the fund's cash balance but the amount of the appropriation yet to be encumbered.

All encumbered but unpaid items at the end of the fiscal year should be closed out and re-encumbered against the appropriation for the ensuing fiscal year.

43.12 Receipts and deposits

(A) Receipts

Whenever the treasurer receives money, a receipt should be written. An original should be given or mailed to the payor. A duplicate, bound in book form, should be retained for the board records. If the original is not requested, it should not be destroyed. The amount should be journalized as of the date the receipt is issued.

(B) Receipts ledger

The receipts ledger records every receipt of money by the board. It also serves as a record of the estimated balance to be received by the board of education for each of its funds, based on the revised tax budget and official certificate of estimated resources and of claims which may be due.

The receipts ledger enables the treasurer to classify the receipts to conform to the items required in the treasurer's financial report. A separate sheet should be used for every account in the classification. The ledger should be arranged by funds and provide evidence of the character of the receipt as well as the account number to which the receipt will be credited.

Receipts shown by the entries in the cash journal must also be posted to the proper accounts in the receipts ledger, with entries in the proper column for the date, name of payor, purpose, receipt number, and the amount.

The estimated amount receivable from taxes for the year should be entered in the ledger. Following the second-half tax settlement, the balance of taxes receivable (if any is shown by the account) should be written off.

The total of all "amounts received" on accounts which are part of the general fund must equal the totals of the general fund "credit" column in the cash journal. The total of "amounts received" on accounts which are part of other funds must equal the totals of such other fund "credit" columns in the cash journal. Frequent com-

---

[35] RC 3313.18.
[36] RC 3315.08.
[37] RC 9.11.

parison should be made of the "amounts received" with the "amount of budget estimate," so that any impending shortfall may be predicted and the board of education can consider the action necessary to curtail incurring additional obligations. When total receipts exceed the estimates, additional appropriations may be made.

If the receipts ledger is properly kept, the preparation of the annual financial report (Form 4502) is simplified because the total amounts in the receipts ledger correspond to the total amounts in the receipts section of the annual report. The information developed through the use of the receipts ledger may also be used in preparing reports for various governmental agencies and in preparing future budgets.

(C) Bank deposit slip

When bank deposits are made, at least two deposit slips should be prepared, one for the bank and one for the treasurer's records. Deposit slips furnished by the bank should be used. Each deposit slip should itemize the cash items, the check numbers, amounts, receipt numbers, and payors' names. Deposits should be made within twenty-four hours of receipt.[38]

The exclusive use of a passbook for recording bank deposits is unwise. The passbook is only an auxiliary record to be used in checking the receipts journal and the cash journal, as well as the bank's records, if necessary.

43.13 Cash journal

The purpose of the cash journal is to record chronologically, by fund, each expenditure of money and each receipt and to allocate each transaction to the proper fund. The cash journal maintains control among receipts, expenditures, and depository balances. The cash journal balances, plus outstanding warrants, should equal the cash-in-bank balance. Unlike the appropriation ledger and the receipts ledger, the cash journal continues from one year to another.

Entries of receipts on the cash journal are derived from the duplicate receipt forms. The cash journal should be totaled monthly to show current totals and balances. If the accumulated totals of the previous months and accumulated total for the year to date are entered under the current month, the treasurer will be able to advise the board of education immediately of the financial condition of the various funds.

Such other funds as are desirable, with prior approval of the state auditor after consultation with the Ohio tax commissioner, may be established on the cash journal and other supporting records of the board of education.[39]

43.14 Individual payroll record

The individual payroll record is the permanent payroll record for each board employee. This record must show the wages earned and the fund to which the wages have been charged. There should be space for accumulated, used, and balance of sick leave, a breakdown of the payroll deductions, and personal data. Under a system of machine accounting, the payroll journal is the permanent record.

SCHOOL FUNDS

43.15 School funds

(A) In general

Every school district is a subdivision of the state.[40] The board of education is the district's "taxing authority."[41] As such, each board is required to establish certain specified funds[42] and may establish other funds as it considers desirable, subject to approval of the state auditor.[43]

(B) Required funds

The system of accounting required by statute[44] and the auditor[45] mandates establishment of at least the following funds by each board (except county boards):

(1) General fund;

---

[38]RC 9.38; OAG 74-043.
[39]RC 5705.12.
[40]RC 5705.01.
[41]RC 5705.01.

[42]RC 5705.09.
[43]RC 5705.12.
[44]RC 5705.09.
[45]RC 117.43.

(2) Bond retirement fund for the retirement of bonds or notes;

(3) Special fund for each special levy;

(4) Special bond fund for the proceeds of each bond or note issue;

(5) Special fund for each class of revenues derived from a source other than the general property tax, which is required to be used for a particular purpose; and

(6) Trust fund for any amount received in trust.[46]

In addition, if a board operates a food service or sells uniform school supplies, it must establish a separate revolving account for each purpose.[47]

Where funds are created by statute or the Uniform School Accounting System, it is not necessary to establish them by board resolution. Any other fund, however, should be established by resolution after approval by the auditor.[48]

The governing board of an educational service center is specifically exempted from establishing the required funds applicable to other school districts,[49] but is authorized to establish an "educational service center board fund,"[50] and it also may establish a service fund for sums set aside from the educational service center board fund.[51]

(C) Transfer of money among funds

Revenues paid into any fund may be spent only for purposes for which the fund is established.[52] Transfers of money between funds may only be made by board resolution in accordance with specific statutory authorization,[53] and certain transfers additionally require approval of the Ohio tax commissioner and the court of common pleas.[54] Any amount may be transferred from the general fund to any other fund of the board upon approval by the board.[55]

43.16 Interest earned on funds

Except for interest earned on a bond retirement fund or on amounts paid to the district for each pupil attending a chartered nonpublic elementary school or high school within the district, the board may provide by resolution that interest earned be credited to any specified fund.[56] Absent such resolution, interest earned on the principal of any special fund is to go into the general fund, unless the law prescribes differently.[57] Interest earned on the bond retirement fund must be credited to the general fund.[58] A board by resolution may transfer money from the general fund to any other fund of the district so that interest earnings may be directed to other funds even if they may not be credited to those funds directly.[59] Similarly, interest earned on trust funds (except where the donor had specifically required otherwise) and student activity funds must be credited to the general fund. Premiums and accrued interest received from the sale of bonds or notes must be paid into the bond retirement fund.[60] All other proceeds from the sale of bonds or notes must be paid into a special fund, and, except as otherwise provided by resolution of the board, interest earned on money in that fund must be used for the purposes for which the bonds or notes were authorized.[61]

The attorney general has concluded RC 135.351 does not require a county to pay political subdivisions interest earned on property tax collections held by the county beyond the scheduled settlement date.[62]

43.17 General fund

The general fund is the board's general operating fund. All revenue from the general tax levy for current expenses within the

---

[46]RC 5705.09.
[47]RC 3313.81, RC 3313.811.
[48]RC 5705.12.
[49]RC 5705.01, RC 5705.09.
[50]RC 3317.11.
[51]RC 3315.15.
[52]RC 5705.10.
[53]RC 5705.14, RC 5705.15; OAG 86-082.
[54]RC 5705.15, RC 5705.16; OAG 86-082.

[55]RC 5705.14(E).
[56]RC 3315.01. See also Text 42.22, Allocation of interest among funds.
[57]RC 135.21, RC 5705.10. See also OAG 85-002.
[58]RC 3315.01; OAG 85-072.
[59]RC 5705.14(E).
[60]OAG 85-085; RC 5705.10.
[61]RC 3315.01, RC 5705.10.
[62]OAG 85-067.

ten-mill limitation, from any authorized general tax levy for current expenses in excess of the ten-mill limitation, and from sources other than these taxes, unless prescribed by law for a particular purpose, must be paid into the general fund.[63] School foundation program money and any other amounts received from the state for current expenses must be paid into the general fund, unless specifically earmarked for other purposes.[64]

Except as otherwise provided by board resolution, all revenue from sources other than the general property tax, and for which the law does not prescribe a particular purpose, is to be paid into the general fund.[65]

A board may include in the general tax levy for current expenses the amounts required to carry into effect any of its general powers, including construction of permanent improvements and payment of judgments, but excluding payment of debt charges. The power to include in the general tax levy for current expenses additional amounts for which a special tax levy is authorized does not affect the right or obligation to levy a special tax. Without prejudice to the generality of the authority to levy a general tax for current expenses, such general tax levy must include the amounts necessary for tuition, teachers retirement fund, and the maintenance, operation, and repair of schools.[66]

43.18 Bond funds

Each board is required to establish a separate bond fund for the proceeds of each bond or note issue.[67] All proceeds, except premiums and accrued interest, must be paid into the special fund for the particular issue. Any premiums and accrued interest received must be paid into the bond retirement fund; however, any interest earned on money in the bond fund becomes a part of that fund and may only be used for the purposes for which the debt was authorized, unless the board adopts a resolution authorizing the interest to be credited to another fund or account, in which case the interest would then be used for the purposes of that fund or account.[68]

The costs of advertising, printing, and delivering the bonds, together with any service charges of the paying agent and bond registrar, and the cost of legal services and obtaining an approving legal opinion, may all be paid from the proceeds received from the sale of the bonds.[69] The unexpended balance in a bond fund no longer needed for the purpose for which that fund was created must be transferred to the bond retirement fund from which those bonds are payable.[70] The board has the legal authority to determine when the balance is no longer needed for the purpose for which the fund was created.[71] A board of education has no authority to transfer money from a bond fund to any fund other than the bond retirement fund.

43.19 Bond retirement fund

A board of education may not issue bonds or notes unless provision is made to levy and collect an annual tax sufficient to pay the principal and interest on those obligations.[72]

The bond retirement fund is established to retire serial bonds (the only type of bond a board of education is authorized to issue) or notes.[73] Money received from the following sources is to be paid into the bond retirement fund:

(1) Revenue from general or special levies for debt charges, whether within or outside the ten-mill limitation, which are levied for debt charges on serial bonds or notes;[74]

(2) Any premium and accrued interest received from the sale of those bonds or notes;[75]

(3) Proceeds from the sale of a permanent improvement of a board of education which are not paid into a special

---

[63]RC 5705.10.
[64]RC 5705.10.
[65]RC 5705.10.
[66]RC 5705.05.
[67]RC 5705.09.
[68]RC 5705.10.
[69]RC 9.96, RC 133.01(K).

[70]RC 5705.14.
[71]OAG 80-070.
[72]O Const Art XII §11; RC 3315.02 to RC 3315.05.
[73]RC 5705.09.
[74]RC 5705.03, RC 5705.10.
[75]RC 5705.10.

fund for the construction or acquisition of permanent improvements;[76] and

(4) Unexpended balance in a bond fund which is no longer needed for the purpose for which the bonds were issued.[77]

A paying agent designated to redeem bonds or notes and any interest coupons is the agent of the board of education and not of the holder who presents matured bonds, notes, or coupons for payment. The agent may not deduct a service charge from the full face amount of the bonds, notes, or coupons at the time of the presentation for payment.[78] A board of education may designate a bank or banks as its paying agent to pay the bonds, notes, and the interest coupons when they mature and are presented for payment and may agree with the paying agent in advance as to the charge for that service. This expense may be met out of the bond retirement fund or the general fund. In the absence of an agreement of this type between a board and the paying agent, the board has no authority to pay the bank a fee for those services.[79]

Boards of education are authorized to contract for the services of a financial institution or other person to perform the following functions relating to a note or bond issue:

(1) Issuance, authentication, transfer, registration, exchange, mechanical, and clerical functions;

(2) Record or bookkeeping or book entry functions;

(3) Preparation, signing, and issuance of checks or warrants in payment of obligations under the issue;

(4) Preparation and maintenance of reports and accounts; and

(5) Performance of other duties related to the issue.

The costs of these functions may be paid from the proceeds of the obligations or from other funds lawfully available and appropriated in accordance with law for that purpose.[80]

43.20 Replacement fund

The board of any city, exempted village, or local school district may establish and maintain a replacement fund. For this purpose, it may set aside annually out of its revenue whatever sum it considers necessary for replacement purposes.[81]

Replacement funds are limited strictly to rebuilding, restoration, repair, or improvement of property which is totally or partially destroyed from any cause, or which has become unfit for use to the extent that it is necessary to demolish it or to repair and restore it before it can be used.[82] Replacement funds may not be reduced, disposed of, or spent for any purpose other than those specified.[83] Money may be withdrawn from the replacement fund only on an order approved by a majority vote of the full membership of the board, signed by the president, or the vice president in the president's absence, and the treasurer.[84]

The replacement fund may be invested. Except as otherwise provided by board resolution, interest earned accrues to the fund, provided that whenever the fund reaches the maximum considered necessary by the board the interest may be used for any authorized school purpose.[85] All securities or evidences of debt held by the board as a part of the replacement fund must be deposited for safekeeping and may be withdrawn only on the application of the board and in the presence of three designated board members.[86]

43.21 Permanent improvement fund

A board must establish a permanent improvement fund for proceeds of a permanent improvement tax levy that is approved by district electors.[87] In addition, the board may, with the approval of the state auditor, establish a permanent improvement fund as one of the special

---

[76] RC 5705.10.
[77] RC 5705.14.
[78] 1949 OAG 1028.
[79] 1954 OAG 4152.
[80] RC 9.96.
[81] RC 3315.11.
[82] RC 3315.11.
[83] RC 3315.14.
[84] RC 3315.13.
[85] RC 3315.01, RC 3315.12, RC 3315.14.
[86] RC 3315.13.
[87] RC 5705.09.

funds considered necessary by a board.[88] Money may be provided by appropriation from the general fund.[89]

Money in the permanent improvement fund must be used to acquire or construct an authorized permanent improvement.[90] If a permanent improvement is sold, the amount received must be paid either into the bond retirement fund or into the permanent improvement fund.[91]

43.22 Service fund

A board of education may establish a service fund to pay board members' expenses actually incurred in the performance of their duties and the expenses of members-elect actually incurred in training and orientation from the date of their election to the date of administration of their oath of office.[92]

43.23 Food service fund

The board of any city, exempted village, or local school district may establish a food service program and food service fund, to be kept separate from all other funds. All receipts and disbursements in connection with operation of food service programs and the maintenance, improvement, and purchase of related equipment must be paid directly into and disbursed from the food service fund.[93] Records of receipts and disbursements resulting from providing meals to the elderly must be separately maintained.[94]

Money for operation, maintenance, and equipment is to be provided by the food service fund out of accumulated sales and receipts, money transferred from the general fund, revenue in the form of financial aid, and from other proper sources. No profit may be derived from food service operations.[95] A board may transfer money from the food service fund to the general fund in repayment of a clearly labeled or intended previous advance from the general fund.[96]

Proceeds from the sale of meals by a food service management company that contracts with a board must be deposited in the food service fund. By agreement with the board, the company may pay for supplies and be reimbursed from the school food service fund. The company may not make purchases in the name of the board. Board employees may be supervised by the company, but ultimate supervisory responsibility remains with the board.[97]

Boards of education may form cooperatives and establish revolving accounts for the purchase of food, supplies, and equipment used in food service operations.[98]

43.24 School supplies fund

When a board adopts uniform supplies for school use and provides for their sale in the district, it must provide for revolving accounts for the purchase and sale of the supplies, either by appropriation from the general fund or accumulation from sales or receipts. These funds must be kept separate. Profits must be used exclusively for school purposes.[99]

43.25 Student activities fund

If more than $50 a year is received through a student activity program, the money must be paid into a student activity fund.[100] The money constitutes public funds.[101] The board must adopt regulations governing the establishment and maintenance of the fund and a system of accounting showing each transaction, the sources of money received, and the amount spent

---

[88] RC 5705.12.
[89] 1930 OAG 941; RC 5705.14(E).
[90] Thus, for example, proceeds of a special tax levy under RC 5705.21 for permanent improvements must be used for the stated purpose of the levy and not for the different purpose of constructing new classrooms under a joint building agreement pursuant to RC 3313.92. OAG 90-030.
[91] RC 5705.10.
[92] RC 3315.15. For limitations on the amount that may be allocated, see Text 5.04(B), Reimbursement for expenses.

[93] RC 3313.81.
[94] RC 3313.81.
[95] RC 3313.81.
[96] 1954 OAG 4342.
[97] OAG 74-043.
[98] RC 3313.812.
[99] RC 3313.811.
[100] RC 3315.062.
[101] OAG 86-013.

for each purpose. Expenditures are subject to board approval and may only be for proper public purposes.[102]

ACCOUNTING

43.26 Uniform system of accounting

(A) Duties of state auditor

The state auditor prescribes a uniform system of accounting to be used by boards of education[103] and conducts examinations of board accounts and records to determine if that system has been properly followed and financial records properly kept.[104]

The auditor requires a board to follow a system of accounting and financial reporting described in the "Uniform School Accounting Services Users Manual," published by the auditor's office. The manual includes forms for showing sources of revenue, amounts received, amounts expended, and the disposition of public property. It also includes specified forms of receipts, vouchers, warrants, and other required documents. Public officers or employees who knowingly refuse or neglect to keep accounts in the form prescribed, or to make required reports, may be removed from office.[105] Boards of education may not contract for accounting or auditing services without prior approval of the auditor.[106]

(B) Annual financial reports by board of education

Within 90 days from the close of the fiscal year (July 1 to June 30), or within 180 days if "filing pursuant to generally accepted accounting principles," each board of education must file with the auditor, on a prescribed form (Form 4502), an annual report stating the following:

(1) Amount of collections and receipts and accounts due from each source;

(2) Amount of expenditures for each purpose;

(3) Amount of the board's public debt; and

(4) Other information as the auditor prescribes on the form.[107]

Simultaneously, the board is required to publish the report in a newspaper published in the school district or, if there is none, then in a newspaper of general circulation in the district.[108]

In addition to these annual the reports, the superintendent of public instruction requires certain financial reports be filed in his office.[109]

43.27 Audits

(A) Examination of accounts and financial reports

At least once every two years, the state auditor examines the methods, accuracy, and legality of the accounts, records, files, and reports of each board of education. If the auditor notifies the treasurer that he is unable to conduct a required examination (either on his own initiative or at the request of the board), the board may request permission to engage a certified public accountant to conduct the examination in accordance with RC 117.11 and RC 117.12.[110]

Following the examination, a certified copy of the completed audit report is filed with the board treasurer.[111] An audit report is not a public record under RC 149.43 until the copy is so filed.[112] A copy is also filed with the statutory legal officer of the board.[113]

The costs of the examination and report are borne by the board. The state auditor certifies the cost to the county auditor, who charges the amount against the next semi-annual settlement of tax money payable to the board. In addition, the state auditor is required to furnish the treasurer, at the conclusion of the examination, a statement

---

[102]RC 3315.062; OAG 86-013.
[103]RC 117.43.
[104]RC 117.11.
[105]RC 117.40.
[106]RC 117.11, RC 117.43.
[107]RC 117.38.
[108]RC 117.38.

[109]RC 3301.12(B).
[110]RC 117.11.
[111]RC 117.26.
[112]RC 117.26. See also Text 44.02, Definition of public records; Text 44.03, Availability of public records.
[113]RC 117.27.

showing the total cost and the percentage chargeable to each board fund which has been examined. The treasurer may then allocate this total cost among the funds examined.[114]

(B) Irregularities found in examination

If the examination report reveals the board has illegally spent money, that any money collected has not been accounted for, that any money due has not been collected, or that public property has been misappropriated, the legal officer receiving a copy of the report may, within 120 days after receipt, sue in the name of the board for the recovery of the money or property. The officer must notify the attorney general of the action taken, or the reasons why action was not taken, within 120 days after receiving the report.[115] At least one court has held the statutory period does not act as a statute of limitations and an action alleging failure to account for public funds may be brought within six years from filing of the report.[116]

If the report describes any conduct by a board officer or employee for which a criminal penalty is provided, a copy of the report must be filed with the prosecuting attorney who is obligated to institute criminal proceedings.[117] No claim for money or property found by the auditor to be due to the board can be abated or compromised unless the attorney general first gives his written approval.[118]

43.28 Duties of district treasurer

The treasurer is the fiscal officer of the board of education.[119] It is his duty to keep an accounting of all district funds as prescribed by the state auditor.[120]

The treasurer prepares all vouchers and gives a statement to the board and superintendent at least once each month, showing revenues and receipts from whatever sources derived, the various appropriations made by the board, the expenditures and disbursements, the purposes, the balances remaining in each appropriation, and the assets and liabilities of the board. All monthly and yearly statements may be examined by the public.[121] If a treasurer of an educational service center fails to make the required reports, the superintendent of the service center may appoint someone to carry out these duties.[122]

At the request of the principal or other chief administrator of any nonpublic school located within the school district's territory, the treasurer must provide an account of the money received from the state board of education for each pupil attending a chartered nonpublic school, as reported in the treasurer's most recent monthly statement.[123]

RC 131.18 provides that when the loss of public funds entrusted to a school district treasurer results from fire, robbery, burglary, flood, or inability of a bank to refund public money lawfully in its possession belonging to such public funds, the board of education may release the treasurer from all personal liability to the district for the loss unless it resulted from his negligence or other wrongful act.

43.29 Data processing

A board may contract for electronic data processing or computer services in connection with, among other things, the preparation of payroll and other records; the preparation, signing, and issuance of checks; and the preparation of reports and accounts. A county board of education may contract for services notwithstanding the establishment of a county data processing board for "county offices."[124]

The state board of education, as required by law, has adopted rules that must be followed when the services are purchased or leased.[125]

RC 3313.37 permits lease-purchase agreements for "office equipment,"

---

[114]RC 117.13.
[115]RC 117.28.
[116]Portage Lakes Joint Vocational School Dist Bd of Ed v Bowman, 14 App(3d) 132, 14 OBR 148, 470 NE(2d) 233 (Summit 1984).
[117]RC 117.29.
[118]RC 117.33.
[119]RC 133.01, RC 5705.01.

[120]RC 117.43. For a description of the nonaccounting duties of a treasurer, see Text 6.02 to 6.09.
[121]RC 3313.29.
[122]RC 3319.37.
[123]RC 3313.29.
[124]OAG 68-105.
[125]RC 3301.075; OAC Ch 3301-3.

defined to include "computer and data processing equipment." The procedure for entering into lease-purchase agreements is complicated by a number of factors, including competitive bidding requirements.[126] For additional guidance, see the discussion of city lease-purchase agreements in *State ex rel Kitchen v Christman*.[127]

43.30 Retention of records

Cancelled checks, vouchers, bonds, coupons, and notes should be retained for at least ten years. Correspondence may be destroyed after its purpose has been served. However, no records may be disposed of prior to audit and examination by the state auditor.

---

[126] RC 3313.46. See OAG 84-046.
[127] State ex rel Kitchen v Christman, 31 OS(2d) 64, 285 NE(2d) 362 (1972).

Chapter 44

Records of Employees and Pupils

44.01 Introduction

PUBLIC RECORDS ACT
44.02 Definition of public records
44.03 Availability of public records

OHIO PRIVACY ACT
44.04 Introduction
44.05 Scope
44.06 Personal information and personal information systems
44.07 Interconnected or combined personal information systems
44.08 School district responsibility for personal information systems
44.09 Types, uses, and collection of information
44.10 Right to inspect personal information
44.11 Disputing accuracy, relevance, timeliness, or completeness of personal information

EMPLOYEE RECORDS
44.12 Required employee records

STUDENT RECORDS
44.13 Required student records
44.14 Access to and release of student records
44.15 Administrative use of student records
44.16 Use of records in missing child investigation
44.17 Record of persons requesting or obtaining access to student records
44.18 Student and parent inspection rights
44.19 Federal and state resolution of disputes over the contents of student records
44.20 Annual notice of rights to parents and pupils
44.21 Formulation of school district policy and procedures

DISPOSAL OF RECORDS
44.22 Records commission
44.23 Procedure for disposal of records

44.01 Introduction

Three state laws and one federal law control records and how Ohio's schools may keep them.

State law imposes recordkeeping requirements on school districts with respect to both employees and students. It regulates access, collection, maintenance, use, privacy, and challenges. The Ohio Public Records Act[1] defines public records broadly and affords the general public access to them. The Ohio Privacy Act[2] regulates the collection, maintenance, and use of records containing personal information concerning any person. It also provides procedures for disputing information contained in personal records. The Student Records Privacy Act[3] restricts access to student records.

At the federal level, the Family Educational Rights and Privacy Act[4] applies only to student records. It restricts access to and mandates procedures for challenging and correcting information in such records.

PUBLIC RECORDS ACT

44.02 Definition of public records

"Public records" are any records kept by a school district.[5] "Records," in turn, are defined as "any document, device, or item, regardless of physical form or characteristic, created or received by or coming under the jurisdiction of" a school district, "which serves to document the organization, functions, policies, decisions, procedures, operations, or other activities" of the district.[6] RC 149.43(D) explicitly provides that the Privacy Act does not limit the Public Records Act.

Even under pre-1985 law, which more narrowly applied only to records *required* to be kept, civil service personnel records were deemed public records subject to inspection. Language in a collective bargaining agreement purporting to ensure confidentiality of personnel records was ineffectual to alter their public nature.[7] Personnel files maintained by a school dis-

---

[1] RC 149.43.
[2] RC 1347.01 et seq.
[3] RC 3319.321.
[4] 20 USCA 1232g.
[5] RC 149.43(A)(1).
[6] RC 149.011(G). As the attorney general has noted, materials of all types (including correspond-ence, memoranda, notes, reports, audio tapes and other recordings, films, and photographs) can qualify. OAG 83-003.
[7] State ex rel Dispatch Printing Co v Wells, 18 OS(3d) 382, 18 OBR 437, 481 NE(2d) 632 (1985).

trict are generally public records,[8] although the Ohio Supreme Court has cautioned that not all items in a personnel file necessarily qualify. Specifically, to the extent an item does not meet the definition of "records" in RC 149.011(G), it is not a public record and need not be disclosed. And, to the extent such an item is "personal information" as defined in RC 1347.01(E), a district is under an affirmative duty pursuant to RC 1347.05(G) to prevent disclosure.[9] Employment applications and resumés received by a metropolitan housing authority have been deemed public records,[10] as have the promotion and tenure records maintained by a state university,[11] payroll records of a county auditor showing the names, job classifications, pay rates, and total compensation of county employees,[12] and the results of polygraph examinations given to applicants for employment with a city police department.[13] To the extent a school district keeps the names, addresses, and telephone numbers of employees, such information is a public record to which access cannot be denied because the requesting entity intends to use the information for commercial or professional sales solicitations.[14] The attorney general has concluded the federal income tax Form W-2 prepared and maintained by a public employer with respect to individual employees is also subject to inspection as a public record.[15]

Banking records in the possession of a school district treasurer that pertain to illicit checking accounts maintained by a high school athletic director in violation of RC 3315.062 are public records.[16] Statistical compilations prepared by public employees from factual information contained in public records—in this case, reports compiled by a court administrator pertaining to jail inmates and individuals about to be sentenced for use in combatting the problem of jail overcrowding—are also public records.[17]

On the other hand, public records do not include "any piece of paper on which a public officer writes something," and personal, uncirculated handwritten notes that reflect an employee's impressions of meetings and substantive discussions and that are not required by law to be kept generally do not qualify as records of the public office.[18] Similarly, it has been held that individual evaluation forms compiled by individual board of education members in evaluating the district superintendent are not public records; rather, the "composite" evaluation of the entire board derived from such individual notes and impressions constitutes the "record" to which the public is entitled.[19]

By virtue of RC 117.26, an audit report pertaining to a school district is not a public record until a certified copy of the completed report is filed with the district treasurer.[20]

RC 149.40 requires that a school district make only such records as are necessary to document the organization, functions, policies, decisions, procedures, and essential transactions of the district and for the protection of the legal and financial rights of the state and persons directly affected by the district's activities. Similarly, the Pri-

---

[8]State ex rel Dispatch Printing Co v Wells, 18 OS(3d) 382, 18 OBR 437, 481 NE(2d) 632 (1985); OAG 86-089.

[9]State ex rel Fant v Enright, 66 OS(3d) 186, 610 NE(2d) 997 (1993).

[10]State ex rel Beacon Journal Publishing Co v Akron Metropolitan Housing Authority, No. 13575, 1988 WL 38067 (9th Dist Ct App, Summit, 4-13-88), affirmed as to another issue by 42 OS(3d) 1, 535 NE(2d) 1366 (1989). The issue discussed in the text above was not appealed.

[11]State ex rel James v Ohio State University, 70 OS(3d) 168, 637 NE(2d) 911 (1994).

[12]State ex rel Petty v Wurst, 49 App(3d) 59, 550 NE(2d) 214 (Butler 1989).

[13]State ex rel Lorain Journal Co v Lorain, 87 App(3d) 112, 621 NE(2d) 894 (Lorain 1993).

[14]OAG 90-050.

[15]OAG 92-005.

[16]See RC 149.43(A)(2)(a); State ex rel Plain Dealer Publishing Co v Lesak, 9 OS(3d) 1, 9 OBR 52, 457 NE(2d) 821 (1984).

[17]State ex rel Cincinnati Post v Schweikert, 38 OS(3d) 170, 527 NE(2d) 1230 (1988).

[18]State ex rel Steffen v Kraft, 67 OS(3d) 439, 619 NE(2d) 688 (1993) (holding that judge's personal notes made during course of trial are not public records).

[19]Vindicator Printing Co v Julian, No. 93 CA 252, 1994 WL 397283 (7th Dist Ct App, Mahoning, 7-26-94).

[20]See also RC 4701.19 (excluding from the definition of public records any statements, records, schedules, working papers, and memoranda of the auditing accountant, except for reports submitted to the client).

vacy Act directs that a school district collect, maintain, and use only personal information that is necessary and relevant to functions the district is required or authorized to perform.[21] Thus, if a district maintains nonessential personal information in its records, it would be subject to the penalties provided in that Act.[22] But such records would still be public records since they are "kept" within the meaning of RC 149.43. Districts are prohibited from removing or transferring, mutilating, or destroying records which document the district's organization, functions, policies, decisions, procedures, operations, or other activities except as provided under RC 149.41.[23]

"Public records" do not include medical records; trial preparation records; records pertaining to adoption, probation, or parole proceedings; records listed in RC 3107.42(A) (information related to adoption); records pertaining to actions under RC 2151.85 by unemancipated minors who seek to have abortions without parental notification; confidential law enforcement investigatory records; records containing information that is confidential under RC 4112.05 (pertaining to information obtained in certain preliminary investigations by the Ohio Civil Rights Commission of charges of unlawful discrimination); or records the release of which is prohibited by state or federal law.[24] Student records are generally not public records because both state and federal law prohibit their disclosure.[25] However, the names and addresses of students in grades 10 through 12 must be released to armed forces military recruiters, unless the student or parent objects in writing to the release.[26] Other examples of records which have been held not to be subject to disclosure because their release is prohibited by state or federal law are social security account numbers,[27] trade secrets,[28] and documents subject to attorney-client privilege.[29]

The burden of proving that particular records are excepted from disclosure falls on the governmental body refusing to release the records.[30]

Courts have consistently construed the statutory exceptions to the definition of public records narrowly and resolved doubts in favor of public disclosure.[31] Thus, for example, confidential law enforcement investigatory records do not include reports obtained by a city council to evaluate its police chief or documents disclosed in a criminal investigation,[32] routinely compiled investigatory records on incidents involving the use of deadly force by a city's police officers,[33] or a city police department's arrest and intoxilyzer records containing the names of persons arrested and/or issued citations for drunk driving offenses but who have not been formally charged.[34]

---

[21]RC 1347.05(H). See Text 44.04 to 44.11 for extended treatment of the Privacy Act.

[22]RC 1347.99.

[23]RC 149.351. See Text 44.22 and 44.23 for extended treatment of RC 149.41.

[24]RC 149.43(A)(1); OAG 81-038. "Medical record" means any document or combination of documents, except births, deaths, and hospital admissions or discharges, that pertains to the medical history, diagnosis, prognosis, or medical condition of a patient and that is generated or maintained in the process of medical treatment. RC 149.43(A)(3).

[25]RC 3319.321, RC 3319.322; 20 USCA 1232g.

[26]RC 3319.321.

[27]State ex rel Beacon Journal Publishing Co v Akron, 70 OS(3d) 605, 640 NE(2d) 164 (1994). The Court, however, did not rely on the exception to the definition of public records contained in RC 149.43(A)(1); rather, it concluded that disclosure by the city of its employees social security numbers would interfere with their right to privacy guaranteed by the federal constitution.

[28]State ex rel Seballos v School Employees Retirement System, 70 OS(3d) 667, 640 NE(2d) 829 (1994).

[29]State ex rel Thomas v Ohio State University, 71 OS(3d) 245, 643 NE(2d) 126 (1994).

[30]State ex rel Toledo Blade Co v University of Toledo Foundation, 65 OS(3d) 258, 602 NE(2d) 1159 (1992); State ex rel Multimedia, Inc v Whalen, 48 OS(3d) 41, 549 NE(2d) 167 (1990); State ex rel National Broadcasting Co v Cleveland, 38 OS(3d) 79, 526 NE(2d) 786 (1988).

[31]E.g., State ex rel James v Ohio State University, 70 OS(3d) 168, 637 NE(2d) 911 (1994); Wooster Republican Printing Co v Wooster, 56 OS(2d) 126, 383 NE(2d) 124 (1978).

[32]State ex rel Cincinnati Post v Marsh, 26 Misc(2d) 5, 26 OBR 277, 498 NE(2d) 508 (CP, Clermont 1985). See also State ex rel Plain Dealer Publishing Co v Lesak, 9 OS(3d) 1, 9 OBR 52, 457 NE(2d) 821 (1984).

[33]State ex rel National Broadcasting Co v Cleveland, 38 OS(3d) 79, 526 NE(2d) 786 (1988). The fact that investigations were routinely conducted does not exclude the records per se from the definition, however. State ex rel National Broadcasting Co v Cleveland, 57 OS(3d) 77, 566 NE(2d) 146 (1991).

[34]State ex rel Outlet Communications, Inc v Lancaster Police Dept, 38 OS(3d) 324, 528 NE(2d) 175

Similarly, to qualify under the exception of trial preparation records, documents must be "specifically compiled in reasonable anticipation of, or in defense of, a civil or criminal action or proceeding."[35] Settlement agreements entered into to avoid litigation do not qualify and must be disclosed.[36] This is true even if the settlement agreement purports to obligate the parties to keep its terms confidential.[37]

The Public Records Act does not require that a public entity create new documents to meet the demand of one who wishes to examine records.[38]

44.03 Availability of public records

Public records must, by virtue of RC 149.43(B), be made available for inspection to the general public at reasonable times during business hours. The records must be maintained in a manner to assure availability.[39] Any person may obtain records under the statute, and a reason need not be stated.[40] Copies must be supplied at cost to any member of the public seeking them.[41] The custodian of the records is not, however, required to make either the records themselves or copies available by mail.[42] If only a portion of a public record is excepted from disclosure, the excepted information may be deleted but any remaining information must be released.[43]

Compliance with the disclosure requirements of RC 149.43(B) may be compelled by mandamus.[44] Attorney's fees may be awarded at the court's discretion solely on a showing of public benefit, although a party's reasonableness and good faith in refusing to comply with a public record request may be taken into account.[45]

OHIO PRIVACY ACT

44.04 Introduction

The Ohio Privacy Act, RC 1347.01 et seq., regulates the collection, maintenance, and use of personal information systems. It

---

(1988). However, the exception does apply to records submitted to a court to provide a factual basis for appointing a special prosecutor and a subsequent decision not to file charges against the suspects does not take the records outside the exception. State ex rel Thompson Newspapers, Inc v Martin, 47 OS(3d) 28, 546 NE(2d) 939 (1989). Nor is statutory protection forfeited merely because time passes with no forthcoming enforcement action. State ex rel Polovischak v Mayfield, 50 OS(3d) 51, 552 NE(2d) 635 (1990). The exception also applies to investigatory records collected by state licensing boards in investigating misconduct. State ex rel McGee v State Board of Psychology, 49 OS(3d) 59, 550 NE(2d) 945 (1990), overruled on other grounds by State ex rel Steckman v Jackson, 70 OS(3d) 420, 639 NE(2d) 83 (1994).

[35]Barton v Shupe, 37 OS(3d) 308, 525 NE(2d) 812 (1988); State ex rel National Broadcasting Co v Cleveland, 38 OS(3d) 79, 526 NE(2d) 786 (1988); State ex rel Coleman v Cincinnati, 57 OS(3d) 83, 566 NE(2d) 151 (1991).

[36]State ex rel Kinsley v Berea Bd of Ed, 64 App(3d) 659, 582 NE(2d) 653 (Cuyahoga 1990). See also State ex rel Dwyer v Middletown, 52 App(3d) 87, 557 NE(2d) 788 (Butler 1988).

[37]State ex rel Sun Newspapers v Westlake Bd of Ed, 76 App(3d) 170, 601 NE(2d) 173 (Cuyahoga 1991) (also holding that the amount of attorney fees connected with a settlement must be disclosed).

[38]E.g., State ex rel Scanlon v Deters, 45 OS(3d) 376, 544 NE(2d) 680 (1989), overruled on other grounds by State ex rel Steckman v Jackson, 70 OS(3d) 420, 639 NE(2d) 83 (1994); State ex rel Fant v Mengel, 62 OS(3d) 455, 584 NE(2d) 664 (1992).

[39]Where records are contained on magnetic computer tapes, the public office must allow copying of those portions to which the public is entitled if the person requesting the information presents a legitimate reason why a paper copy of the records would be insufficient or impracticable and assumes the expense of copying. State ex rel Margolius v Cleveland, 62 OS(3d) 456, 584 NE(2d) 665 (1992).

[40]State ex rel Fant v Enright, 66 OS(3d) 186, 610 NE(2d) 997 (1993); State ex rel Clark v Toledo, 54 OS(3d) 55, 560 NE(2d) 1313 (1990), overruled on other grounds by State ex rel Steckman v Jackson, 70 OS(3d) 420, 639 NE(2d) 83 (1994).

[41]RC 149.43(B). The public office may adopt a reasonable policy setting a fee for copies which should reflect actual costs in making a copy, unless the cost is otherwise set by statute. OAG 89-073.

[42]State ex rel Fenley v Ohio Historical Society, 64 OS(3d) 509, 597 NE(2d) 120 (1992). See also State ex rel Mancini v Ohio Bureau of Motor Vehicles, 69 OS(3d) 486, 633 NE(2d) 1126 (1994); State ex rel Nelson v Fuerst, 66 OS(3d) 47, 607 NE(2d) 836 (1993).

[43]State ex rel National Broadcasting Co v Cleveland, 38 OS(3d) 79, 526 NE(2d) 786 (1988); State ex rel Outlet Communications, Inc v Lancaster Police Dept, 38 OS(3d) 324, 528 NE(2d) 175 (1988). See also State ex rel Beacon Journal Publishing Co v Kent State University, 68 OS(3d) 40, 623 NE(2d) 51 (1993).

[44]RC 149.43(C).

[45]State ex rel Multimedia, Inc v Whalen, 51 OS(3d) 99, 554 NE(2d) 1321 (1990); State ex rel Mazzaro v Ferguson, 49 OS(3d) 37, 550 NE(2d) 464 (1990); State ex rel Fox v Cuyahoga County Hospital

affords rights to persons who are the subject of personal information collected and maintained in the system. By virtue of RC 1347.01(B), school districts are specifically subject to the Act.

44.05 Scope

The Privacy Act does not insulate personal information from disclosure under the Public Records Act. The rights of the general public to inspect or copy personal information where that information is contained in a public record as defined in RC 149.43 is specifically preserved in RC 1347.08(E)(1). Specifically excluded from inspection are confidential law enforcement investigatory records, trial preparation records, and documents pertaining to adoption and subject to inspection in accordance with RC 3107.17, or to records listed in RC 3107.42(A).[46]

44.06 Personal information and personal information systems

"Personal information" consists of any information that describes anything about a person, or indicates acts done by or to a person, or indicates that a person possesses certain personal characteristics.[47] Both student records and employee personnel records invariably contain personal information and therefore fall within the definition of personal information systems.

A personal information "system" is a collection or group of related records maintained by a school board that contains personal information and is kept in an organized fashion from which information is retrieved by the name of the person or by some other unique identifier such as a social security number. The system can include both records manually maintained as well as those stored by electronic data processing equipment.[48]

A personal information system does not include records not under the control of the district or for which the district is not responsible or accountable.[49] Even district records may not be subject to the Privacy Act if they contain only routine information for internal administration, the use of which would not adversely affect the subject of the information.[50]

44.07 Interconnected or combined personal information systems

An interconnected system is one formed by linking together two or more independent systems, resulting in a system that gives each agency or organization involved unrestricted access to the system(s) of the other agencies or organizations.[51]

A combined system is formed by the unification of independent systems into a single system in which records that belong to each agency or organization involved may or may not be obtainable by the others.[52]

A school district cannot place personal information into an interconnected or combined system, nor can it use information placed in the system by another agency or organization, unless that system will contribute to the efficiency of the involved agencies in implementing programs authorized by law.[53] The Privacy Act further restricts the district's use of another agency's or organization's information to situations in which the information is necessary and relevant to the performance of a lawful district function.[54]

When requesting personal information from a person for inclusion in an intercon-

---

System, 39 OS(3d) 108, 529 NE(2d) 443 (1988). However, the Ohio Supreme Court has also emphasized that a showing of public benefit "should receive no greater consideration than other factors." Specifically, the Court rejected an argument that such factors as a party's reasonableness and good faith have no bearing on whether to make a fee award in the first instance but only on whether and by how much to reduce an award. State ex rel Beacon Journal Publishing Co v Ohio Department of Health, 51 OS(3d) 1, 553 NE(2d) 1345 (1990). While the statute authorizes an award of attorney's fees, compensation to pro se litigants is not permitted. Fant v Regional Transit Authority Bd of Trustees, 50 OS(3d) 72, 552 NE(2d) 639 (1990), cert denied 498 US 967, 111 SCt 429, 112 LEd(2d) 413 (1990).

[46]RC 1347.08.
[47]RC 1347.01(E).
[48]RC 1347.01(F).
[49]See RC 1347.01(D), (F).
[50]RC 1347.01(F).
[51]RC 1347.01(G).
[52]RC 1347.01(H).
[53]RC 1347.071(A).
[54]RC 1347.071(B).

nected or combined system, a district must provide that person with information about the system, including the identity of other agencies or organizations that have access to information in it.[55]

44.08 School district responsibility for personal information systems

(A) Introduction

RC 1347.05 imposes certain duties regarding the maintenance of a personal information system. The Ohio Privacy Board was abolished in 1980, and no state agency currently has authority to prescribe rules under the Privacy Act governing personal information systems.[56]

(B) Liability and criminal penalties

A school district must appoint one person to be directly responsible for its personal information system.[57] Pursuant to RC 1347.05(B), the district must adopt and implement rules providing for the lawful operation of the system including policies and procedures to insure the accuracy, timeliness, relevance, and completeness of the records. The promulgation of rules is of considerable importance as the Privacy Act provides that a district officer or employee is not subject to criminal prosecution or civil liability if he has complied in good faith with a rule applicable to the district.[58]

Employees responsible for the operation or maintenance of the system or for the use of the personal information maintained in the system must be informed of the provisions of the Privacy Act and of the rules adopted by the district regarding personal information systems.[59] Moreover, the district must specify disciplinary measures that will be taken against any employee who initiates or contributes to any disciplinary or punitive action against any individual who brings to the attention of appropriate authorities, the press, or a member of the public evidence of unauthorized use of information in the system.[60]

The Privacy Act gives any individual harmed by the use of personal information relating to that individual in a personal information system the right to sue for damages any person who directly and proximately caused the harm by intentionally

(1) maintaining information that the person knows or has reason to know is inaccurate, irrelevant, no longer timely, or incomplete and may result in such harm;

(2) using or disclosing the information in a manner prohibited by law;

(3) supplying information for storage in, or using or disclosing personal information maintained in, a system that he knows or has reason to know is false; or

(4) denying to the individual who is the subject of personal information the right to inspect and dispute the information at a time when inspection or correction might have prevented the harm.[61]

The harm referred to must be some type of tangible injury. A teacher who sought damages was not "harmed," according to one court, where a reprimand had been placed in her personnel file and she had been allowed to add her protest pursuant to RC 1347.09, since she continued to teach without any reduction in salary or benefits.[62]

Another court has held that a public employee's liberty and property rights were violated by inclusion of damaging statements in his personnel file without giving the employee notice of the inclusion or an opportunity to refute the information. The court further suggested any false or damaging items in a personnel file would give rise to liability, even with notice and an opportunity to dispute the file's contents.[63]

Even if a teacher is improperly denied access to his personnel files, the denial

---

[55] RC 1347.071(C).
[56] See RC 1347.06.
[57] RC 1347.05(A).
[58] RC 1347.06.
[59] RC 1347.05(C).
[60] RC 1347.05(D).

[61] RC 1347.10(A).
[62] Petrie v Forest Hills School Dist Bd of Ed, 5 App(3d) 115, 5 OBR 231, 449 NE(2d) 786 (Hamilton 1982).
[63] Horne v Clemens, 23 App(3d) 139, 23 OBR 299, 492 NE(2d) 164 (Geauga 1985).

does not set aside the nonrenewal of his contract pursuant to RC 3319.11.[64]

An action in damages must be brought within two years after the wrongdoing occurs or within six months after the wrongdoing is discovered, whichever is later. In no event, however, can an action be brought later than six years after the wrongdoing occurs.[65]

A court can enjoin any person or school district that violates or proposes to violate any provision of the Act. Injunctive relief may be sought only by the person who is the subject of the violation, the attorney general, or any prosecuting attorney.[66]

RC 1347.99 makes it a minor misdemeanor for any public official, public employee, or other person who maintains or is employed by a person who maintains a personal information system for a school district to purposely refuse to do the following:

(1) Inform a person asked to supply information as to whether the person is legally required or may refuse to supply the information (RC 1347.05(E));

(2) Develop procedures for monitoring the accuracy, relevance, timeliness, and completeness of the system and, in accordance with those procedures, maintain information with such accuracy, relevance, timeliness, and completeness as is necessary to assure fairness in any determination made on the basis of the information (RC 1347.05(F));

(3) Take reasonable precautions to protect the system from unauthorized modification, destruction, use, or disclosure (RC 1347.05(G));

(4) Collect, maintain, and use only information necessary for legally mandated district functions and eliminate information no longer necessary or relevant (RC 1347.06(H));

(5) Inform persons who are the subject of information, upon written request, of the system and allow inspection, pursuant to RC 1347.08(A) to (C);

(6) Allow persons to dispute information in the system pursuant to RC 1347.05(A) and (C); or

(7) Adhere to the limitations on the use of interconnected or combined systems as set forth in RC 1347.071 (RC 1347.99).

(C) System security

The school district must take reasonable precautions to protect the personal information in the system from unauthorized modification, destruction, use, or disclosure.[67] Although the Privacy Board no longer exists and districts are free to make their own rules, districts may wish to consider factors previously mandated by Board rules in developing procedures for protecting personal information:

(1) Nature and vulnerability of the personal information;

(2) Physical facilities where the personal information is maintained;

(3) Whether it is necessary and feasible to keep the information in a secure place;

(4) Cost of providing a secure place and the need for access to the place both by employees who are responsible for the information and by the general public;

(5) Need to inform employees of appropriate and inappropriate uses, disclosure, and access to the information;

(6) Need to provide for reporting of violations of security; and

(7) Need to monitor the effectiveness of the system.

Where the personal information system is contained in a computer or other electronic data processing equipment, the district should limit access to the equipment and programs to authorized personnel only. Where the equipment is accessible by teleprocessing terminals, a method of verifying the identity of individuals using the terminal is also advisable.

---

[64] Matheny v Frontier Local Bd of Ed, 62 OS(2d) 362, 405 NE(2d) 1041 (1980).
[65] RC 1347.10(A).
[66] RC 1347.10(B).
[67] RC 1347.05(G).

(D) Ensuring that information is accurate, timely, complete, necessary, and relevant

The Privacy Act imposes an affirmative duty to develop procedures for monitoring the accuracy, relevance, timeliness, and completeness of personal information in a system. In accordance with those procedures, personal information must be maintained with such accuracy, relevance, timeliness, and completeness as is necessary to assure fairness in any determination made with respect to the person on the basis of the information.[68]

In developing procedures, a school district might wish to consider factors previously mandated by the defunct Privacy Board. A district might consider periodic monitoring of personal information systems, "feedback" procedures whereby employees could report the correction or retention of faulty information, or procedures for correcting faulty information when it is discovered. A district might also consider developing procedures for verifying the accuracy of doubtful information and procedures to prevent the use of incomplete data for decision-making purposes. Finally, procedures could be developed for informing employees working with the system of their responsibilities regarding its use and maintenance.[69]

44.09 Types, uses, and collection of information

Personal information can only be used in a manner consistent with the stated purpose of the system.[70] Disclosure of personal information contained in a public record to members of the general public, as required by RC 149.43, is not, however, an improper use of personal information.[71] Nor does the Act authorize a board of education to hold an executive session for discussion of personal information if such a session is not otherwise authorized under RC 121.22(G).[72]

From the foregoing, it would seem that an individual has no privacy interest in his or her personnel file. However, one court has maintained that a public official must balance the public's right to gain access to records against an individual's right of privacy.[73]

A school district may collect, maintain, and use only such personal information as is necessary and relevant to functions that the district is authorized or required to perform by law. Personal information must be eliminated when it is no longer necessary or relevant to these functions.[74] In the case of school district records, disposal of records containing information is subject to state law regarding records disposal.[75]

When personal information is collected, the person asked to supply information for a system must be informed whether he is legally required to or may refuse to supply the information.[76]

44.10 Right to inspect personal information

A school district that maintains personal information systems must, upon the request and proper identification of any person who is the subject of personal information in the system, inform the person of the following:

(1) Existence of any systems of which that person is the subject;

(2) Types of uses of the personal information; and

(3) Any users who are usually granted access to the system.[77]

Moreover, that person, his legal guardian, or an attorney presenting a signed written authorization made by the person who is the subject of the information must be

---

[68]RC 1347.05(F).
[69]See Text 44.08(B), Liability and criminal penalties.
[70]RC 1347.07.
[71]RC 149.43(D), RC 1347.08(E)(1).
[72]RC 149.43(D), RC 1347.08(E)(1). See Text 5.12, Open meetings: the sunshine law.
[73]State ex rel Cincinnati Post v Marsh, 26 Misc(2d) 5, 26 OBR 277, 498 NE(2d) 508 (CP, Clermont 1985). See also Text 44.05, Scope.

[74]RC 1347.05(H).
[75]See Text 44.22, Records commission; Text 44.23, Procedure for disposal of records.
[76]RC 1347.05(E).
[77]RC 1347.08(A)(1), (3).

allowed to inspect all information in the system of which the person is the subject, with the exception of some medical, psychiatric, or psychological information as described below and confidential law enforcement investigatory records or trial preparation records.[78] If the subject exercises the inspection right in person, he may be accompanied by another individual of his choice.[79]

Medical, psychiatric, or psychological information must be disclosed to the person who is the subject of the information or his legal guardian unless a physician, psychiatrist, or psychologist determines for the district that disclosure is likely to have an adverse effect on the person. If such a determination is made, the information can be released only to a physician, psychiatrist, or psychologist designated by the subject or his legal guardian.[80]

A district must provide a copy of personal information to any person authorized to inspect the information upon request. A reasonable fee may be charged.[81]

44.11 Disputing accuracy, relevance, timeliness, or completeness of personal information

If any person disputes the accuracy, relevance, timeliness, or completeness of personal information pertaining to him, that person may request that the school district investigate the current status of the information.[82] Within ninety days, the district must make a reasonable investigation and notify the individual of the results of the investigation.[83] Any information found to be inaccurate or that cannot be verified must be deleted.[84] The investigation does not have to include an adversary hearing or the opportunity to cross-examine witnesses. Rather, a unilateral investigation by the recordkeeping agency, reasonably conducted under the circumstances, is sufficient.[85] Federal law, however, requires a hearing when a student's record is disputed.[86]

If, after investigation, the person disputing the information is still unsatisfied, a district must do one of two things. It can permit the person to include within the personal information system a brief statement of his position on the disputed information. The district may limit the statement to not more than 100 words if the district assists the person in writing a clear summary of the dispute.[87] Alternatively, the district can permit the individual to include within the system a notation of protest that the information is inaccurate, irrelevant, outdated, or incomplete. If this option is used, the district must also keep a copy of the person's statement of the dispute outside of the system itself. As with the first option, the statement may be limited to not more than 100 words if the district assists the person in writing a clear summary of the dispute.[88]

It has been held that where the sole controversy between a board of education and an employee is a difference in versions of the same set of circumstances, the Privacy Act merely provides the employee the right to a fair investigation and the inclusion of an explanation or protest pursuant to RC 1347.09. Judicial review of a good faith disagreement over the interpretation of an incident, where no harm has come to the parties, is not appropriate.[89]

The district must include the person's statement or notation in any subsequent transfer, report, or dissemination of the disputed information.[90] In addition, the district may include a statement of its own that it has reasonable grounds to believe the dispute is frivolous or irrelevant and the reasons for its belief.[91] The mere presence of contradictory information in the

---

[78]RC 1347.08(A)(2).
[79]RC 1347.08(B).
[80]RC 1347.08(C).
[81]RC 1347.08(D).
[82]RC 1347.09(A)(1).
[83]RC 1347.09(A)(1).
[84]RC 1347.09(A)(1).
[85]Goolsby v Board of Education, No. 321 (4th Dist Ct App, Hocking, 8-7-79); Hamrick v Medina County Joint Vocational Bd of Ed, Nos. 1055, 1079, 1981 WL 4225 (9th Dist Ct App, Medina, 11-4-81).

[86]See Text 44.19, Federal and state resolution of disputes over the contents of student records.

[87]RC 1347.09(A)(2)(a).

[88]RC 1347.09(A)(2)(b).

[89]Petrie v Forest Hills School Dist Bd of Ed, 5 App(3d) 115, 5 OBR 231, 449 NE(2d) 786 (Hamilton 1982).

[90]RC 1347.09(A)(3).

[91]RC 1347.09(A)(3).

person's file, however, does not alone constitute reasonable grounds to believe the dispute is frivolous or irrelevant.[92]

Following any deletion of inaccurate or outdated information, or if a statement of dispute has been filed, the district must, at the written request of the employee involved, give notification of the deletion or a copy of the statement of dispute to any third party designated by the employee.[93] Moreover, the district must clearly disclose to the employee that he has the right to make such a request.[94]

EMPLOYEE RECORDS

44.12 Required employee records

School districts are required by RC 4111.08 to keep for a period of not less than three years a record of the name, address, and occupation of each employee; rate of pay; amount paid each employee each pay period; and the hours worked each day and work week by each employee. Districts must also keep on file each teacher's certificate (or a true copy) to teach the subjects or grades being taught.[95]

Personnel records can also include, among other things, staff evaluations, records of leave or vacation time used and accrued, tax and payroll deductions, and employment contracts.

Employee records are subject to the Public Records Act and the Privacy Act.[96]

STUDENT RECORDS

44.13 Required student records

Each school must keep records detailing the names of all enrolled pupils, the studies pursued, the character of the work done, and the standing of each pupil.[97] The district must also keep records of the age and place of residence of each student under the age of eighteen at the school so the principal or teachers in charge can report such information annually to the district treasurer.[98] In addition, the district must keep student membership records by grades, which, among other things, show for each student the name, date of birth, name of parent, date entered school, date withdrawn from school, days present, days absent, and number of days the school was open for instruction while the student was enrolled.[99]

State and federal laws impose additional specific recordkeeping requirements for handicapped students.[100] In addition, federal law imposes recordkeeping requirements for anti-discrimination purposes and for purposes of specific federal grant and funding programs.

44.14 Access to and release of student records

(A) Comparison and scope of state and federal law

Both state and federal statutes govern access to and release of student records. At the state level, the Privacy Act, RC 1347.01 et seq., regulates collection, maintenance, and use of the records, provides mechanisms whereby records can by corrected, and ensures student or parental access to them.[101] The Student Records Privacy Act, RC 3319.321, restricts release of the records.

At the federal level, all school districts receiving federal funds are subject to the Family Educational Rights and Privacy Act of 1974, 20 USCA 1232g, and regulations promulgated at 34 CFR Part 99. The federal law also regulates use of and access to student education records, provides procedures for correcting faulty information, and assures parent and student access.

There are substantial differences between state and federal requirements. The Privacy Act provides rights of access and challenge to the person who is the subject of the personal information; where stu-

---

[92]RC 1347.09(B).
[93]RC 1347.09(C).
[94]RC 1347.09(C).
[95]RC 3319.36.
[96]See Text 44.02 to 44.11.
[97]RC 3319.32.

[98]RC 3321.12.
[99]RC 3317.031.
[100]See Text Ch 28, Education for Children with Disabilities.
[101]See Text 44.04 to 44.11.

dent records are involved, the student has these rights. In contrast, federal law gives rights only to parents where students are under eighteen, and only to the student when he reaches eighteen. Since the Privacy Act does not conflict with the more limited federal inspection right, school districts must afford students under eighteen, as well as their parents, inspection rights.

Conversely, federal law is more restrictive regarding release of information. Moreover, federal procedures for challenging information are more complex. Finally, the federal law is enforced only through administrative action[102] while the Privacy Act allows individuals to sue in courts.

Failure to comply with the federal law can result in actions by the secretary of the department of education ranging from securing voluntary compliance to cutting federal funds.[103] Federal regulations, 34 CFR 99.60 to 34 CFR 99.67, prescribe the manner of filing complaints, investigatory and hearing procedures, and possible sanctions. Federal courts have refused to find that violation gives rise to a private right of action,[104] but an action under 42 USCA 1983 may be premised on an alleged violation of the federal Act.[105]

(B) Restrictions

No person can release or permit access to "personally identifiable information" other than directory information concerning any pupil attending a public school except in certain narrowly defined circumstances.[106] Arguably, not even directory information can be released to any person or group for use in a profit-making plan or activity.[107] Individual test scores on statewide student proficiency tests may only be released in accordance with RC 3313.321.[108]

"Personally identifiable information" is defined by 34 CFR 99.3 as data or information that includes the name of a student, the student's parents, or other family members; the address of the student; a personal identifier such as a social security number or student number; or a list of personal characteristics or other information which would make the student's identity easily traceable.

Under federal law, even "directory information" cannot be released unless the school district has done the following:

(1) Given public notice of the categories of information which it designates as directory information;

(2) Given public notice of the right of parents of students under eighteen or students eighteen or older to refuse to permit the designation of any or all personally identifiable information as directory; and

(3) Allowed a reasonable time for such parent or student to inform the district that the information should not be released without consent.[109]

These notice procedures for directory information need not be followed for a student no longer in attendance in the district.[110]

"Directory information" includes a pupil's name, address, telephone listing, date and place of birth, major field of study, participation in officially recognized activities and sports, weight and height of members of athletic teams, dates of attendance, date of graduation, awards received, and the most recent educational agency or institution attended.[111]

The Attorney General has concluded that RC 3313.321 and federal law prohibit the release, without proper consent on behalf of the student, of information on illegal drug and alcohol use by students to law enforcement agencies when such data is personally identifiable information other

---

[102] 34 CFR 99.60 et seq.
[103] 20 USCA 1232g(g).
[104] E.g., Girardier v Webster College, 563 F(2d) 1267 (8th Cir Mo 1977); Norris v Greenwood Community School Corp Bd of Ed, 797 FSupp 1452 (SD Ind 1992); Moore v Hyche, 761 FSupp 112 (ND Ala 1991).
[105] E.g., Tarka v Cunningham, 917 F(2d) 890 (5th Cir Tex 1990); Belanger v Nashua, New Hampshire, School Dist, 856 FSupp 40 (D NH 1994); Maynard v Greater Hoyt School Dist No. 61-4, 876 FSupp 1104 (D SD 1995).

[106] RC 3319.321(B); 20 USCA 1232g(b)(2).
[107] RC 3319.321(A).
[108] RC 3301.0711(G).
[109] 20 USCA 1232g(a)(5)(B); 34 CFR 99.37.
[110] 34 CFR 99.37(a).
[111] RC 3319.321(B)(1); 20 USCA 1232g(a)(5)(A); 34 CFR 99.3.

than directory information concerning any public school student.[112]

(C) Conditions of release

Personally identifiable information other than directory information may be released if the parent, guardian, or custodian of a student under eighteen, or a student himself eighteen or older, gives written consent.[113] Parties to whom disclosures are made must be informed of the necessity of consent for any subsequent release or disclosure of the information.[114] Under 20 USCA 1232g(b)(2)(B), such information may be released in compliance with a court order, or pursuant to any lawfully issued subpoena, upon condition that the parents and students are notified of all such orders or subpoenas in advance of compliance.

(D) Records of victims of domestic violence

No person can release or give access to any information about the location of an elementary or secondary school to which a pupil has transferred if that school has requested the pupil's records under RC 3313.672 and informed the school from which the records are obtained that the pupil is under the care of a shelter for victims of domestic violence, as defined in RC 3313.33.[115]

44.15 Administrative use of student records

(A) Introduction

The restrictions on the release of student records do not limit the administrative use of the records by a person acting exclusively in his capacity as an employee of a school board or by a member of other state and federal organizations.[116] In Ohio, fingerprints, photographs, or records obtained pursuant to RC 3313.96 or RC 3319.322, or pursuant to RC 3319.321(E), or any medical, psychological, guidance, counseling, or other information that is derived from the use of fingerprints, photographs, or such records, are not admissible against a minor who is the subject of the fingerprints, photographs, or records in any court proceeding.[117] Federal law restricts the school's administrative right of access to school officials, including teachers within the school district, who have been determined by the school board to have legitimate educational interests.[118] Federal regulations require that each district formulate and adopt a policy regarding the information to be released under this exception and the criteria used to define school officials and legitimate educational interests.[119]

(B) Consent

Neither state nor federal law requires consent for or prevents the transfer of student records to an educational institution for a legitimate educational purpose.[120] Federal law, however, limits this exception to transfers to schools or school systems to which the student seeks or intends to enroll.[121] Parents and students over eighteen must be notified of the transfer at their last known address, furnished a copy of the record if desired, and have an opportunity for a hearing to challenge the content of the record.[122] No consent is needed to release personally identifiable information in connection with financial aid. The disclosure must be limited to information necessary for eligibility, amount, conditions, and enforcement.[123]

The foregoing laws do not limit the administrative use, without consent, of student records by an employee of the state or any of its political subdivisions or of a court or of the federal government when the use is required by state statute adopted before November 19, 1974, or by federal law.[124] If release is sought under a state law enacted before November 19, 1974, the statute must require, and not merely permit, disclosure.[125]

---

[112]OAG 90-099.
[113]RC 3319.321(B); 20 USCA 1232g(b)(4)(A); 34 CFR 99.30(a).
[114]34 CFR 99.33.
[115]RC 3319.321(F).
[116]20 USCA 1232g(b); RC 3319.321.
[117]RC 3319.321(C).
[118]20 USCA 1232g(b)(1)(A).
[119]34 CFR 99.6.
[120]RC 3319.321(C); 20 USCA 1232g(b)(1)(B).
[121]20 USCA 1232g(b)(1)(B).
[122]20 USCA 1232g(b)(1)(B); 34 CFR 99.34.
[123]34 CFR 99.31(a)(4); 20 USCA 1232g(b)(1)(D).
[124]RC 3319.321(C); 20 USCA 1232g(b)(1)(C), (E), (I), (b)(3); 34 CFR 99.31(a)(3), (5) to (7).
[125]34 CFR 99.31(a)(5).

44.16 Use of records in missing child investigation

RC 3319.321(E) authorizes a principal or chief administrative officer of a public school, or any employee of a public school who is authorized to handle school records, to provide access to a student's records for a law enforcement officer who indicates that he is conducting an investigation and that the student may be a missing child as defined in RC 2901.30. Free copies of information in the student's record must be provided, upon request, to the law enforcement officer, if prior approval is given by the student's parent, guardian, or legal custodian. Information so obtained must be used solely in investigation of the case. The information may be used by law enforcement personnel in any manner appropriate to solving the case, including, but not limited to, providing the information to other law enforcement agencies and to the bureau of criminal identification and investigation for purposes of computer integration pursuant to RC 2901.30.

The principal or chief administrative officer of each public school must request any person authorized to photograph students to provide one wallet-sized photograph, free of charge, to the school for inclusion in the student's file. The administrative officer must indicate the request is being made so the school may have a current photograph that could be shown to a law enforcement officer if the child is or becomes a missing child. The officer also must indicate the request is being made pursuant to RC 3319.322 but that the statute does not require the photographer to comply. RC 3319.322 allows an authorized school official to insist as a part of the agreement with a photographer that a photograph be provided as a condition to the taking of student pictures.

44.17 Record of persons requesting or obtaining access to student records

Federal law requires that each school district maintain a record, to be kept with each student's records, specifically indicating any individual, agency, or organization that has requested or obtained access to the student's records without consent and the legitimate interest that each had in requesting or obtaining the information.[126] Access to this record is limited to the parents of the student under eighteen, the student (if eighteen or older), the district official and his assistants responsible for the custody of such records, and any other school, state, or federal officials responsible for auditing operation of the system.[127] This record must be maintained for as long as the student record to which it pertains is maintained.[128]

No record need be kept of requests for or access to the records by school officials, including teachers within the district, who have been determined by the school board to have legitimate educational interest in the records, or by parents of a student under eighteen or the student himself if eighteen or over. Records need not be kept where the release has proper written consent or where the information sought or obtained is "directory information."[129]

44.18 Student and parent inspection rights

Federal law parallels the Privacy Act in granting certain inspection rights. Where the state grants the right to inspect to the person who is the subject of the personal information, federal law grants the right to parents of the student if he is under eighteen or to the student if he is eighteen or older.[130] The inspection right extends only to those materials or documents or parts that relate to the student.[131] The right exists where the student is or has been in attendance in the school district.[132]

The federal right includes not only the right to view the records in question, but

---

[126] 20 USCA 1232g(b)(4)(A); 34 CFR 99.32.
[127] 20 USCA 1232g(b)(4)(A); 34 CFR 99.32.
[128] 34 CFR 99.32(a)(2).
[129] 20 USCA 1232g(b)(4)(A); 34 CFR 99.32(d).

[130] 20 USCA 1232g(a)(1)(A), (d); 34 CFR 99.10(a).
[131] 20 USCA 1232g(a)(1)(A).
[132] 34 CFR 99.10(a).

also the right to a response from the school district to reasonable requests for explanations and interpretations of the records.[133] It also includes the right to copies of the records where failure to provide copies would effectively prevent the parent or student from exercising the right to inspect.[134] For example, where information is stored in a computer, a copy of the data would be essential.

Federal regulations require that a school district comply with a request for inspection within forty-five days.[135] The district may give full rights to either parent of a student under eighteen to inspect absent evidence that a legally binding instrument, law, or court order governing such matters as divorce, separation, or custody, provides to the contrary.[136]

No record may be destroyed as long as there is an outstanding request to review that record.[137]

44.19 Federal and state resolution of disputes over the contents of student records

(A) Federal and state rights

Just as the Privacy Act provides a mechanism for correction of personal information included in student records,[138] federal law also provides such procedures, which are, however, more extensive and, unlike state law, provide the right to a hearing.[139]

Federal law affords parents of a student under eighteen, or a student (or former student) eighteen or over, the right to request a school district to amend information deemed inaccurate, misleading, or violative of the student's privacy or other rights.[140] Within a reasonable time from receipt of the request, the district must decide whether to comply.[141] If the district refuses, it must inform the requesting parent or student and advise him of the right to a hearing.[142]

(B) Hearings

A hearing, if requested, must be held within a reasonable period, and the requesting parent or student must be given notice of the date, place, and time.[143] The hearing may be conducted by any party, including a school official who has no direct interest in the outcome.[144] The requesting parent or student must be given a full and fair opportunity to present relevant evidence and may be assisted or represented by individuals of his choice at his expense.[145]

The district's decision must be in writing and based solely upon the evidence presented.[146] It must be rendered within a reasonable period after the hearing and include both a summary of the evidence and the reasons for the decision.[147]

If the district decides the challenged information is inaccurate, misleading, or otherwise violative of the student's privacy or other rights, the district must amend the record and inform the parent or student in writing.[148]

If the district decides the information is not inaccurate, misleading, or otherwise violative of the student's privacy or other rights, the district must inform the parent or student of the right to place in the student's records a statement commenting upon the challenged information and/or setting forth any reasons for disagreeing with the district's decision.[149]

The federal right to place a statement in the record is similar to that afforded under the Privacy Act, except federal regulations place no limit on the length of the statement and the right exists only after a hear-

---

[133] 34 CFR 99.10(c).
[134] 34 CFR 99.10(b).
[135] 34 CFR 99.10(a).
[136] OAG 87-037; 34 CFR 99.4.
[137] 34 CFR 99.10(e).
[138] See Text 44.11, Disputing accuracy, relevance, timeliness, or completeness of personal information.
[139] 20 USCA 1232g(a)(2).
[140] 20 USCA 1232g(a)(2); 34 CFR 99.20(a). The statute does not authorize a suit to challenge, except for ministerial error, the grade a teacher assigns to a student. Tarka v Cunningham, 917 F(2d) 890 (5th Cir Tex 1990).
[141] 34 CFR 99.20(b).
[142] 34 CFR 99.20(c).
[143] 34 CFR 99.22(b).
[144] 34 CFR 99.22(c).
[145] 34 CFR 99.22(d).
[146] 34 CFR 99.22(e), (f).
[147] 34 CFR 99.22(e), (f).
[148] 34 CFR 99.21(b)(1).
[149] 34 CFR 99.21(b)(2), (c).

ing and adverse decision.[150] A statement filed under the federal procedure, like one under state procedure, must be kept with the student's record and disclosed to any party to whom the record or the contested portion is disclosed.[151]

(C) School district as final decision-maker

Federal law provides a means whereby parents of students under eighteen, or students eighteen or over, can challenge any information in a student record in an adversary proceeding. The Privacy Act permits the student, or his legal guardian, to force the district to conduct its own investigation, which need not be adversarial, into the questioned information. Under both laws, however, the district is the final decision-maker; neither compels the district to remove challenged data. The student's or parent's final recourse, short of federal administrative proceedings or a lawsuit in state court, is to file a written statement to counter the challenged information.

44.20 Annual notice of rights to parents and pupils

Each year, a school district must give notice to parents of students in attendance and students eighteen or older of their federal rights, including their right to file an administrative complaint with the department of education, and their rights under district policy.[152]

The annual notice should inform the parents or students over eighteen that, under federal law and district policy, they have the right to examine the student's records, to challenge the content of those records before a disinterested party, and to insert into the records an explanation of any disputed information. The notice should also state that the district has adopted a policy regarding student records, setting forth the location(s) at which copies of the policy are kept. Finally, the notice should explain that the parents or students have the right to file a complaint with the Family Policy and Regulations Office,[153] if they think the district is not complying with federal laws or regulations governing student records. A district must also take measures to effectively notify parents of students identified as having a primary or home language other than English.[154]

44.21 Formulation of school district policy and procedures

Federal regulations require that each school district formulate and adopt a policy regarding implementation of the Family Educational Rights and Privacy Act and its companion regulations.[155]

The policy must provide for the required annual notice of rights.[156] In providing for inspection rights, the policy must include the following:

(1) Statement of procedure to be followed by those exercising the inspection right;

(2) Understanding that access cannot be denied but detailing the circumstances in which the district feels it has legitimate cause to deny a request for copies;

(3) Schedule of fees for copying; and

(4) List of the types and locations of student records as well as the titles and addresses of officials responsible for those records.[157]

The policy must state the district will not disclose personally identifiable information without prior consent except as permitted by federal law.[158] In this regard, the policy must state whether the district will disclose information to school officials, including teachers, with legitimate educational interests and must specify the criteria the district will use in determining which parties are "school officials" and what is considered to be "legitimate educational interests."[159] The policy must also specify what personally identifiable information is to be designated directory information.[160]

---

[150]See Text 44.11, Disputing accuracy, relevance, timeliness, or completeness of personal information.
[151]34 CFR 99.21(c).
[152]34 CFR 99.7(a).
[153]U.S. Dept. of Education, Washington, D.C. 20202.
[154]34 CFR 99.7(d).

[155]34 CFR 99.6(a).
[156]34 CFR 99.7(a). See Text 44.20, Annual notice of rights to parents and pupils.
[157]34 CFR 99.6(a)(2).
[158]34 CFR 99.6(a)(3).
[159]34 CFR 99.6(a)(4).
[160]34 CFR 99.6(a)(6).

The policy must provide for maintaining a record of disclosures and requests for disclosures of personally identifiable information and for permitting inspection of that record by parents of students under eighteen and students eighteen and over.[161]

Finally, the policy must provide for exercise of the right to correct student records through requests to amend, hearings, and statements in the record if results are unsatisfactory.[162]

The policy must be made available to parents of students under eighteen or to students eighteen or over upon request.[163]

DISPOSAL OF RECORDS

44.22 Records commission

Each city and exempted village school district and educational service center has a records commission. By law, the commission is composed of the board president, treasurer, and superintendent. The commission must meet at least once every twelve months.[164]

The commission's function is to review applications for one-time disposal of records and schedules of retention and disposition of records submitted by any employee. Records must be disposed of in accordance with RC 149.41.

44.23 Procedure for disposal of records

A "record" under the disposal law is defined by RC 149.011 as any document, device, or item, regardless of physical form or characteristic, created or received by, or coming under jurisdiction of the school district, which serves to document the organization, functions, policies, decisions, procedures, operations, or other activity of the district.

When disposal is authorized by the records commission, the commission must, prior to actual destruction, send a list of the records to the state auditor. If the bureau disapproves of the disposal of any or all records, it must so notify the commission, and the records may not be destroyed.[165]

Before any records are destroyed, the Ohio Historical Society must be informed and given sixty days to select for its own custody those records it considers to be of historical value. The Society may not review or select either student records containing personally identifiable information, other than directory information, without obtaining consent as required under the state Student Records Privacy Act[166] or records the release of which would violate the federal Family Educational Rights and Privacy Act of 1974.[167]

Any person aggrieved by destruction of records in violation of RC 149.351 may bring a civil action to compel compliance and may recover a forfeiture of $1,000 and reasonable attorney's fees for each violation.[168]

---

[161] 34 CFR 99.6(a)(5).
[162] 34 CFR 99.6(a)(7).
[163] 34 CFR 99.6(b).
[164] RC 149.41.
[165] RC 149.41.
[166] RC 3319.321.
[167] 20 USCA 1232g(b)(1); RC 149.41(A), (B).
[168] RC 149.351(B).

PUBLIC DUTY—SEARCH AND SEIZURE—LIABILITY

Chapter 45

Ethics Requirements and Education Personnel

OHIO ETHICS LAW
- 45.01 Introduction, applicability of ethics laws
- 45.02 Financial disclosure
- 45.03 Restrictions on activities during and after employment
- 45.04 Unauthorized compensation and transactions
- 45.05 Conflict of interest with respect to public contracts
- 45.06 Examples of permitted and prohibited transactions involving public contracts
- 45.07 Conflict of interest with respect to textbooks and publishers
- 45.08 Compatible and incompatible offices

MISCELLANEOUS PROHIBITIONS AFFECTING EDUCATION PERSONNEL
- 45.09 Ethics violations in criminal code, generally
- 45.10 Theft in office
- 45.11 Soliciting or receiving improper compensation
- 45.12 Dereliction of duty
- 45.13 Interfering with civil rights
- 45.14 Political activity by classified civil servants

OHIO ETHICS LAW

45.01 Introduction, applicability of ethics laws

(A) In general

The Ohio ethics law as such is found in RC Chapter 102, but the subject of ethics also embraces a number of related statutes in the criminal code[1] plus miscellaneous statutes regarding specific public officials. The overall purposes of the ethics laws are to set standards of conduct for public officials and employees in the execution of their offices, to prevent subordination of the public interest to private or other public interests, and to ward off situations in which the potential for conflicts of interest is high.

(B) Ohio ethics commission, advisory opinions

Enforcement of ethics laws in the school context is, for the most part, reposed in the Ohio ethics commission.[2] Law enforcement officers may, however, bring prosecutions for criminal violations without the intervention of the commission. Thus, for example, a county prosecutor may prosecute for ethics violations without a commission referral.[3]

Since the public business is complex, and a public official or employee may be in doubt as to his duties, RC 102.08 authorizes the commission to render advisory opinions interpreting certain statutes with regard to ethics, conflicts of interest, and financial disclosure. These opinions do not analyze past or present conduct, since to do so would cloud enforcement. They are rendered only on hypothetical facts or *prospective* conduct.[4] The attorney general will not render opinions construing the same statutes.[5] The person to whom the advisory opinion is directed or those who are similarly situated may reasonably rely on the opinion and shall be immune from criminal prosecution, civil suits, or actions for removal from office based on facts and circumstances covered by the opinion, if the opinion states there is no violation of RC Chapter 102 or RC 2921.42 and RC 2921.43.[6] A letter requesting an advisory opinion under RC 102.08 and the documents held by the commission concerning

---

[1] RC Title 29.
[2] RC 102.01.
[3] See RC 309.08.
[4] Ethics Op 75-037.
[5] OAG 87-025.
[6] RC 102.08.

the opinion are public records for purposes of RC 149.43.[7]

(C) Applicability of ethics laws to education personnel

(1) In general

RC Chapter 102 is applicable generally to any "public official or employee," defined to include any person who is elected or appointed to public office or is an employee of a public agency, but specifically excluding "a teacher, instructor, professor, or any other kind of educator whose position does not involve the performance of, or authority to perform, administrative or supervisory functions."[8]

(2) Education personnel

Thus, RC Chapter 102 does not generally apply to teachers as such, but does apply to teachers acting as supervisors, assistant principals or assistant superintendents, or in other administrative or supervisory capacities.[9] It also applies to superintendents, principals and other administrators, nonteaching personnel, school board members, members of the state board of education, the superintendent of public instruction, and administrators and employees of the state department of education.

RC 102.09(E) requires that a board of education furnish any public official or employee with a copy of RC Chapter 102 and RC 2921.42 within fifteen days after beginning the performance of their duties, receipt of which must be acknowledged in writing. Given the definition of "public official or employee" in RC 102.01(B), this information need not be furnished to teachers although the ethics commission has stated such distribution "would be helpful" since teachers are subject to some provisions of Ohio's ethics laws.[10]

(3) Financial disclosure

The requirements for financial disclosure in RC 102.02 apply to elected officials and candidates for elective office generally, including any person elected to or a candidate for the board of education of any school district with an average daily membership of 12,000 or more as most recently certified to the state board of education under RC 3317.03(A). In addition, school district superintendents, treasurers, and business managers are specifically included regardless of the size of the district. RC 102.02 also includes specific confidentiality requirements with respect to disclosure statements.

45.02 Financial disclosure

Every person subject to the disclosure requirements of RC 102.02 is required to submit to the Ohio ethics commission a financial disclosure statement on a form specified by the commission. Generally, board members and candidates in districts with 12,000 or more students must file the required disclosure forms with the Ohio ethics commission. The details of the statement are spelled out in RC 102.02.

45.03 Restrictions on activities during and after employment

RC 102.03 prohibits any present or former public official or employee from representing a client or acting in a representative capacity for anyone in a matter in which he personally participated as a public official or employee, involving a decision, recommendation, investigation, or other substantial exercise of administrative discretion by him. The restriction applies during a person's term of office or employment and for twelve months thereafter.[11]

The purpose of the prohibition is to prevent a person from realizing private gain at public expense, such as by using "insider

---

[7]OAG 86-069.
[8]RC 102.01(B).
[9]While RC Ch 102 generally does not apply to teachers, some substantive prohibitions of Ohio's ethics laws do. For example, RC 102.04(C), RC 2921.42, and RC 2921.43 apply to *any* board of education employee, including teachers. See Ethics Op 93-017. See also RC 2921.01(A), which defines "public official" for purposes of RC Ch 2921 as "any elected or appointed officer, or employee, or agent of the state or any political subdivision ... ." (Emphasis added.)
[10]Ethics Op 93-017.
[11]The twelve-month period begins when a public official or employee resigns, and is not extended if the person is retained as an independent contractor or consultant to represent or assist his former public agency during the twelve-month period. Ethics Op 89-009.

information."[12] Typically, the prohibition affects consulting, such as lobbying, or advocacy for private interests by a present or former public official or employee. For example, an attorney who is a member of a school board would be prohibited (until one year after his term) from representing a contractor as to a contract entered into while the attorney was a board member.

A school board member may neither use the authority or influence of his office to secure employment by the board or to create a position into which he may be employed, nor within a year after leaving office accept employment in a position he participated in creating.[13]

45.04 Unauthorized compensation and transactions

Under RC 102.04, a state public official or employee is prohibited from receiving any compensation, directly or indirectly, in excess of the compensation allowed by law, and from selling or agreeing to sell to a state agency or institution any goods or services except through competitive bidding. The prohibition against selling goods or services does not apply to a nonelective official or employee where the sale is to an agency other than the one that employs him and he files a disclosure statement prior to the transaction. The statement must be filed with the ethics commission, the agency where he works, and the agency with which he proposes to deal.

RC 102.03 prohibits a public official or employee from using or authorizing the use of the authority or influence of his office or employment to secure, or solicit or accept, anything of value that would manifest a substantial and improper influence upon him with respect to his duties. Any person is likewise prohibited from promising or giving such an item of value to a public official or employee.[14]

Thus, RC 102.03 prohibits a vendor from promising or giving—and a public official from accepting, soliciting, or using his position to secure—travel, meal, or lodging expenses incurred in inspecting and observing the vendor's products even if such activity is essential, the products are sold through competitive bidding, and the public body has no obligation to buy after acceptance of such payments.[15]

To some extent, this prohibition overlaps prohibitions in the criminal code against unlawful interests in public contracts and soliciting or receiving improper compensation or promising or giving improper compensation to a public servant.[16]

In the absence of bribery, another statutory offense, or a purpose to defraud, political contributions made on behalf of an elected public officer or a public employee seeking office are considered to accrue ordinarily to the public office or employee.[17]

RC 102.03 generally prohibits a public official or employee who is required to file a financial disclosure statement under RC 102.02 from soliciting or accepting an honorarium. Nor can any person give such an official or employee an honorarium. Actual travel expenses, including lodging, meals, and beverages provided to the official or employee at a meeting where the person participates in a panel, seminar, or speaking engagement, are excepted. If the public official or employee is not required to file a financial disclosure statement under RC 102.02, acceptance of an honorarium and expenses is permitted if the honorarium, expenses, or both are paid in recognition of demonstrable business, professional, or esthetic interests of the official or employee that exist apart from his public office or employment and are not paid by any person doing or seeking to do business

---

[12]State v Nipps, 66 App(2d) 17, 419 NE(2d) 1128 (Franklin 1979).
[13]Ethics Op 87-008, construing RC 2921.42(A)(3).
[14]Membership in a church or religious, benevolent, fraternal, or professional organization cannot be considered, in and of itself, as manifesting a substantial and improper influence, although a member cannot participate in, or use his official position with respect to the organization's interests on, a matter if he has assumed a particular responsibility in the organization with respect to the matter or if the matter would affect his personal, pecuniary interests. RC 102.03(J).
[15]Ethics Op 90-001; Ethics Op 89-014.
[16]Ethics Op 90-001; Ethics Op 89-014; RC 2921.42, RC 2921.43. See Text 45.05, Conflict of interest with respect to public contracts; Text 45.11, Soliciting or receiving improper compensation.
[17]RC 102.03(G).

with the public body served by the official or employee.[18]

45.05 Conflict of interest with respect to public contracts

Although RC 2921.42 is in the criminal code, it is construed by the Ohio ethics commission. It forbids any public official or employee, which includes *all* state and local school officials and personnel,[19] from various acts amounting to conflicts of interest in business dealings with a public body.[20] To knowingly engage in one of these prohibited acts is a criminal offense. Thus, school personnel should proceed with extreme caution whenever this statute may be implicated.

(A) Prohibited conduct

A public official or employee may not authorize or use the authority or influence of his office to secure authorization of a public contract or investment of public funds with respect to which he, a member of his family, or a business associate has an interest.[21] During his term of office or within one year thereafter, he may not occupy any position of profit in prosecuting any public contract authorized by him or the body of which he was a member, unless the contract was let by competitive bidding to the lowest and best bidder.[22] A school board member may not accept board employment for one year after leaving office if the new position and its compensation was approved while he was a board member.[23] Also, a public official or employee is forbidden to have an interest in the profits or benefits of any public contract for the public body with which he is connected (except a public employee may participate in any housing program funded by public moneys if the employee otherwise qualifies for the program and does not use the authority or influence of his office or employment to secure benefits from the program and if the moneys are for the employee's primary residence), or in any public contract required to be but not let by competitive bidding and involving more than $150.[24]

For purposes of RC 2921.42(A)(1) and (3), a board of education is deemed to "authorize" all school district purchases unless the board has adopted a general resolution dispensing with the adoption of resolutions authorizing purchases and approving payments in accordance with RC 3313.18.[25]

(B) Public contract, family members and business associates, interest in contract

A public contract includes the actual purchase or acquisition or a contract for the purchase or acquisition of property or services for the state or any of its political subdivisions (and agencies or instrumentalities of either), including the employment of an individual. Also included are contracts to design, construct, alter, repair, or maintain public property.[26] Purchases made on a casual or "as needed" basis, as well as purchases made pursuant to a formal contract, qualify as public contracts.[27]

"Family member" includes, without limitation, grandparents, parents, spouses, children (dependent or not), grandchildren, brothers and sisters, and any household member related by blood or marriage.[28] Partners are considered business associates.[29]

An interest in a public contract for purposes of RC 2921.42 must be definite and direct to give rise to a violation and may be pecuniary or fiduciary in nature.[30]

(C) Exemption, limited interest as shareholder or creditor

Under RC 2921.42(B), in the absence of bribery or fraud, a public official or employee is not considered to have an interest in a public contract or investment

---

[18] RC 102.03(H).
[19] RC 2921.01(A).
[20] The Ohio legislative service commission summary is helpful in understanding the purposes and scope of the section. See *Baldwin's Ohio Revised Code Annotated*, RC 2921.42, Commentary.
[21] RC 2921.42(A)(1).
[22] RC 2921.42(A)(3).
[23] Ethics Op 87-008.
[24] RC 2921.42(A)(4), (5).
[25] Ethics Op 90-005. See Text 5.13(C), Dispensing with resolutions in certain cases.
[26] RC 2921.42(G).
[27] Ethics Op 90-005. For additional discussion on what qualifies as a public contract under the statute, see Ethics Op 93-014.
[28] Ethics Op 78-005; Ethics Op 80-001.
[29] Ethics Op 85-004.
[30] Ethics Op 90-005; Ethics Op 85-004; Ethics Op 78-005.

where his interest (or the interest of a family member or business associate) is as a shareholder or creditor having no more than a five per cent stake in the contractor, provided the official or employee discloses by affidavit his precise status to the public agency involved prior to entering into the contract.

(D) Exemption, arm's length transaction

Also, under RC 2921.42(C), a public official or employee, member of his family, or business associate may contract with the public agency with which he is connected if all of the following conditions are met:

- the contract is for necessary supplies or services;

- the supplies or services are unobtainable elsewhere for the same or lower cost or the transaction is part of a course of dealing established before the person became connected with the public agency;

- the treatment accorded the public entity is the same as or more favorable than that given other customers; and

- the transaction is conducted at arm's length with the official or employee disclosing his interest and taking no part in deliberations on the contract.[31]

The standards in RC 2921.42(C) are strictly applied against the official.[32] For example, the "continuing course of dealing" exception applies only to services rendered during the term of a contract entered before the interested official was appointed; the award of a second or extended contract after appointment is a different matter. The standard that supplies or services be unavailable at a cost either lower than or the same as that set by the interested party must be evidenced in some objective manner, such as by competitive bidding or reasonable requests for proposals; thus, an uninterested party bidding the same price must be preferred.[33]

45.06 Examples of permitted and prohibited transactions involving public contracts

(A) Permitted transactions

A board member whose spouse is a teacher and member of the teachers' union in the school district may vote on the collective bargaining agreement between the district and union unless the spouse is also a union officer, board member, or negotiating team member.[34]

A board member whose spouse is employed in the district may be covered by health insurance received by the spouse as a district employee pursuant to a collective bargaining agreement; however, RC 102.03(D) prohibits such a board member from voting, discussing, deliberating, recommending, or otherwise using his authority or influence to authorize the agreement.[35]

(B) Prohibited transactions

A professional staff member of a community developmental center run by the department of mental retardation and developmental disabilities may not authorize, or use the authority or influence of his office to secure approval of, placement of department clients in a group home run by a corporation he serves as an employee or consultant.[36]

A school board member may not vote, authorize, or use the influence of his office to secure the employment of a member of his family by the district.[37]

A board member whose spouse is a partner in a law firm with which the board has contracted is not prohibited by RC 2921.42 from serving as a board member, absent some direct interest or benefit from such contract, but may not vote, authorize, dis-

---

[31] See Ethics Op 84-011.
[32] See, e.g., Ethics Op 88-008; Ethics Op 87-003.
[33] See, e.g., Ethics Op 88-008; Ethics Op 87-003.
[34] Ethics Op 82-003, Ethics Op 89-005.
[35] Ethics Op 92-017, which goes on to say such a board member may participate in the procurement of health insurance coverage from an insurer that will provide group benefits to all eligible district employees.

[36] Ethics Op 84-009.
[37] Ethics Op 93-008. Moreover, where the family member being employed is an unemancipated minor child, employment for compensation is precluded unless the board member does not exercise his statutory right to the child's earnings. Even if the board member does not exercise that right, employment is still forbidden unless the exception appearing in RC 2921.42(C) can be established. *Id.*

cuss, or use the influence of his office to secure authorization, modification, or renewal of the contract.[38] RC 3313.33, however, which prohibits a direct or indirect pecuniary interest on the part of a board member in any contract of the board (and which is not within the ethics commission's purview), applies to create a conflict if the earnings from the contract go to support the board member or the spouse or another dependent of the member.[39]

A board member who is a sales representative for an insurance company that sells tax-sheltered annuities to district employees via payroll deduction is prohibited by RC 102.03 from selling annuities to such employees, soliciting such employees to purchase annuities, discussing the annuities with employees in response to their inquiries, servicing the accounts of such employees, receiving compensation from the sale of such annuities to district employees, or participating in actions of the board that could affect the company's ability to sell annuities to such employees.[40]

A board member who owns a store that sells musical instruments may not sell merchandise to the district (or knowingly sell to a boosters club where the goods will be purchased for the use of the district) unless he comes within the RC 2921.42(C) "safe harbor"; nor, in any event, may he use the authority or influence of the office to secure the purchase or attempt to persuade school personnel or students to purchase from his store. Moreover, and in any event, he may not profit from any sale approved or authorized by the board unless the contract was competitively bid and his was the lowest bid.[41]

A board member may not knowingly vote, authorize, or use the influence of his office to secure approval of a contract for purchasing or servicing school buses involving the automobile dealership which employs him.[42] The prohibition holds even though the member does not otherwise have a prohibited interest in the contract.[43]

A school bus transportation director may not have an interest in the profits or benefits of a contract by or for the use of the school district with which he is employed.[44]

A teacher who, with his spouse, owns a commercial driver training school is prohibited by RC 2921.42 from receiving reimbursement from his school district for providing driver education to high school students unless the RC 2921.42(C) safe harbor is satisfied. In any event, the teacher is prohibited from discussing, recommending, or otherwise using the authority or influence of his position to persuade students to use the services of the school.[45]

45.07 Conflict of interest with respect to textbooks and publishers

A public school superintendent, principal, supervisor, or teacher may not act as sales agent, directly or indirectly, for any person, firm, or corporation whose school textbooks are filed with the superintendent of public instruction, or as sales agent for school apparatus or equipment of any kind, for use in the public schools. The penalty for violation is forfeiture of teaching certification.[46] A teacher may, however, act as a

---

[38]Ethics Op 88-007.
[39]OAG 89-030. But see In re Ron Steed, No. 1909, 1989 WL 411471 (4th Dist Ct App, Lawrence, 7-27-89), which found RC 3313.33 inapplicable to a board member who voted to employ his spouse as an assistant school nurse even while acknowledging, "Steed did receive some indirect benefit from his wife's employment." The court went on to find, however, that the member's action violated RC 2921.42(A)(1) and that, therefore, he was subject to removal from office for "malfeasance" pursuant to RC 3.07. In a subsequent, related case, the court refused to void the spouse's contract of employment, flatly declaring that "the indirect benefit received by Ron Steed from his wife's employment did not constitute a pecuniary interest." Scherer v Rock Hill Local School Dist Bd of Ed, 63 App(3d) 555, 579 NE(2d) 525 (Lawrence 1990). See also Text 5.05, Removal from office.

[40]Ethics Op 93-014 (expressly noting that such prohibitions do not apply to a former board member if he has not used the authority or influence of his position while on the board to secure business opportunities after his departure from the board).
[41]Ethics Op 90-003. The member may, however, donate goods and services provided he receives no pecuniary gain and does not use the donation to secure anything of value.
[42]Ethics Op 80-003.
[43]Ethics Op 78-006.
[44]Ethics Op 78-002.
[45]Ethics Op 94-002 (rejecting contrary analysis that appears in OAG 76-019).
[46]RC 3329.10.

salesman for encyclopedias or other general reference works, when such works are not filed with the superintendent of public instruction and the sales are to private individuals.[47]

The superintendent of public instruction is prohibited from having any financial interest in a book publishing or selling concern.[48]

45.08 Compatible and incompatible offices

In general, public offices are incompatible when expressly declared so by the Ohio Constitution or a statute, or when one office is subordinate to or in any way a check on the other, or when it is physically impossible for one person to discharge the duties of both positions.[49] A number of statutes prohibit specific education personnel from holding certain offices or prohibit persons in other offices from certain positions in education. Also, the statute dealing with conflict of interest involving public contracts[50] gives rise to potential conflicts which make certain positions or jobs incompatible with school positions.

(A) In general

During their tenure, members of the state board of education and the superintendent of public instruction may not hold any other public office.[51] Also, they may not be officers or employees of any public or private educational institution.[52]

A member of a board of education may not hold any other public office which is incompatible with his duties as a board member.[53] A county prosecutor or city law director or the assistant of either may not serve as a board of education member.[54] However, a city law director appointed to his position under a city charter, a village solicitor, or other chief legal officer of a municipal corporation may serve as a member of a board of education for which he is not the legal advisor and attorney under RC 3313.35. Furthermore, a city law director appointed under a city charter may serve as a member of a board of education for which he is the legal adviser and attorney only if the board uses no legal services of his office or if the legal services of his office that it does use are performed under contract by persons not employed by his office.

No member of a board of education may be employed by that board in any capacity for compensation.[55] A board member may not be appointed school physician, school dentist, or school nurse.[56] The same person may not serve simultaneously as a member of a local school district board and a member of the governing board of an educational service center.[57] A person may not serve on a governing board of an educational service center and as administrator of a local school district in the county[58] or as a teacher's aide in a local school district in the county.[59] A member of a city or local school district board of education may not serve as trustee of a township located within the district.[60] Nor may a local district board member serve as a member of the board of health of the general health district of a county in which the district's facilities are located.[61] A municipal court judge is prohibited from holding the position of member of a local board of education.[62] The positions of superintendent of an educational service center that contains more than one local school district and trustee of a township located within the county are incompatible,[63] as are the positions of governing board member and substitute teacher in a local school district in the county.[64]

On the other hand, the positions of member of a service center governing

---

[47] 1948 OAG 4251.
[48] RC 3301.08.
[49] OAG 74-006.
[50] RC 2921.42.
[51] RC 3301.03, RC 3301.08.
[52] RC 3301.03, RC 3301.08. See also Text 3.02, State board of education.
[53] OAG 74-006.
[54] RC 3313.13; Bennett v Celebrezze, 34 App(3d) 260, 518 NE(2d) 25 (Lorain 1986).
[55] RC 3313.33; OAG 81-071.
[56] RC 3313.70.
[57] 1960 OAG 1491.
[58] OAG 83-070.
[59] OAG 84-003.
[60] OAG 90-083; OAG 85-006.
[61] OAG 86-060.
[62] OAG 86-004.
[63] OAG 89-101.
[64] OAG 92-005. It is immaterial whether the person is employed as a substitute prior to being elected or appointed to the governing board.

board and township trustee are compatible.[65] A member of a board of education may also serve on the board of elections if he is not a candidate for elective office, with some offices excepted.[66] A member of a board of education may also simultaneously serve as a member of the board of a nonpublic school, provided the individual does not participate in or vote on a decision concerning the provision of transportation for district students to and from the public or nonpublic school they attend.[67]

A teacher in a local school district may serve on the board of another local school district in the same county, provided the teacher does not provide teaching service pursuant to an RC 3313.84 contract to the district on whose board he serves.[68] A teacher may also serve in the position of village council member.[69] However, a village council member may not serve on a board of education since RC 731.12 states that a village council member cannot hold any other public office.[70] The position of city council member has been deemed compatible with that of principal and teacher of a local elementary school,[71] and RC 102.03 does not prohibit a city council member from voting on gas and oil well drilling ordinances even if the school district for which he works wishes to drill on its property within the city or from voting on industrial plant and housing tract development issues even if the school district's tax revenue or pupil enrollment would be affected in some indefinite manner.[72] The council member is precluded, however, from voting on matters that would provide a definite and particular pecuniary benefit or detriment to the employing district, such as tax abatements for property within the school district.[73]

Unclassified civil servants (such as non-teaching employees in city school districts)[74] have no constitutional or other protected right to seek partisan elected office while holding public employment, and public employers may discharge an unclassified employee for such action.[75]

A secretary of a city board of education may serve as a township clerk.[76]

A member of a board of education may also be a member of the Ohio general assembly.[77] Similarly, any teacher or employee of a board of education may serve in the general assembly.[78]

A school principal is ineligible to hold the position of trustee on the board of trustees of a technical college district,[79] as is the director of a vocational school employed by the board of a joint vocational school district.[80]

A school treasurer may not hold any other public office which is incompatible with his duties as treasurer.[81]

A majority of the trustees of a free public library may not hold employment with school districts or other political subdivisions.[82] Also, a person who is a member of a board of education, or who has been a member within the year prior to his appointment, may not serve on the board of trustees of the school district free public library.[83]

(B) Incompatibility arising from potential conflict of interest involving public contracts

A member of the board of a private agency that contracts with the county board may not serve on a county MR/DD board.[84]

The chief financial officer of a state university may not serve on the board of a bank that is a university depository.[85] Pre-

---

[65] OAG 83-016.
[66] RC 3501.15; OAG 74-006.
[67] OAG 93-067.
[68] OAG 89-069, modifying OAG 73-108. For analysis of RC 3313.84 contracts, see Text 9.16, Exchange teachers.
[69] OAG 89-069.
[70] OAG 89-069.
[71] OAG 65-60.
[72] Ethics Op 91-006.
[73] Ethics Op 91-006.
[74] See Text 12.02(A), School districts covered by civil service: effect of coverage and noncoverage.

[75] Painter v Graley, 70 OS(3d) 377, 639 NE(2d) 51 (1994).
[76] OAG 86-057.
[77] 1955 OAG 6060.
[78] RC 101.26.
[79] OAG 90-062; OAG 90-063.
[80] OAG 90-063.
[81] 1961 OAG 2260. See also RC 3313.22; OAG 74-006.
[82] RC 3375.63.
[83] RC 3375.15.
[84] Ethics Op 81-003.
[85] Ethics Op 83-003. But see OAG 85-007.

sumably, the treasurer of a board of education, and perhaps a member of the board, would similarly be unable to serve on the board of a bank which acts as a public depository for the board.[86]

A person involved in a business which sells fund-raising services to school principals, parent groups, and school activity groups in school districts is not per se prohibited from being a member of a board of education, but RC 2921.42 would prohibit him from authorizing or using the authority or influence of his office to secure, or from having an interest in the profits or benefits of, a contract with a principal, parent group, or school activity group in his school district.[87]

MISCELLANEOUS PROHIBITIONS AFFECTING EDUCATION PERSONNEL

45.09 Ethics violations in criminal code, generally

The Ohio criminal code[88] contains a group of offenses aimed at peculation, conflict of interest, improper influence, and dereliction by elected or appointed officers, employees, or agents of the state or its political subdivisions. These persons are collectively termed "public officials."[89] Included among these offenses is having an unlawful interest in a public contract.[90]

Elements of some of these offenses overlap the prohibitions in the Ohio ethics law itself,[91] as well as some statutes dealing with the conduct of specific officials. As a consequence, conduct prohibited under the criminal code, the ethics law, or other statutes may give rise to multiple prosecutions.

45.10 Theft in office

RC 2921.41 prohibits a public official or employee from committing any theft offense, either by using his office in aid of committing the offense, or when the property involved is public property. The offense is a third degree felony, even though the underlying theft offense may be only a misdemeanor. "Theft offense" includes a long list of crimes in addition to the offense of theft itself.[92] A person convicted of theft in office is required to make restitution and is disqualified from holding any public office, employment, or position of trust. The disqualification is "perpetual."[93]

45.11 Soliciting or receiving improper compensation

RC 2921.43 prohibits a range of conduct. First, a public servant is forbidden to solicit or accept (and another person is forbidden to promise or give) any compensation or fees other than as allowed by law to perform his duty. This prohibition overlaps a similar prohibition in the ethics law.[94] Also, RC 2921.43 provides that a public servant may not accept for his personal or business use anything of value in consideration of appointing, maintaining, or preferring a person in public employment. Similarly, any person is prohibited from coercing a political contribution in consideration of appointing, maintaining, or preferring a person in public employment. The offense is a first degree misdemeanor, and a public servant who commits it is disqualified from holding a public position for seven years. "Public servant" is defined even more broadly than "public official" and includes not only public officers and employees but any person who performs a public function ad hoc (such as a juror, member of a temporary commission, or

---

[86]See Text Ch 42, Deposits and Investments.
[87]Ethics Op 85-009.
[88]RC Title 29.
[89]RC 2921.01(A).
[90]RC 2921.42. See also Text 45.05, Conflict of interest with respect to public contracts. Other offenses in this group are discussed in Text 45.09 to 45.13.

[91]RC Ch 102.
[92]RC 2913.01.
[93]State v Harris, 7 App(3d) 258, 7 OBR 339, 455 NE(2d) 510 (Hamilton 1982).
[94]RC 102.03, RC 102.04. See Text 45.04, Unauthorized compensation and transactions.

consultant), as well as a candidate for public office.[95]

45.12 Dereliction of duty

RC 2921.44 prohibits a state official or employee from recklessly creating a deficiency, incurring a liability, or spending more than the general assembly has appropriated for the state agency with which he is connected. Also, the section forbids any public official or employee, state or local, from recklessly failing to perform a duty expressly imposed by law with respect to his office or doing any act expressly forbidden by law with respect to his office. The offense is a second degree misdemeanor.

Where a county commissioner admitted she was aware of the legal requirement for competitive bidding, but nevertheless approved contracts without it and without inquiring about the omission, she "recklessly failed to perform a duty expressly imposed by law with respect to [her] office."[96]

45.13 Interfering with civil rights

RC 2921.45 prohibits any public official or employee, acting under color of his office, employment, or authority, from knowingly depriving any person of a constitutional or statutory right. Violation is a first degree misdemeanor. Where a public official or employee acts in the honest belief that his actions are permitted or required by law, he is not guilty of an offense under this section even though it is later determined that his belief was mistaken.[97] Thus, for example, a teacher who acts in good faith but nevertheless violates a student's Fourth Amendment rights against unreasonable search and seizure would not be guilty of violating this section.[98]

45.14 Political activity by classified civil servants

RC 124.57 generally prohibits members of the classified civil service of city school districts (and other civil service employers) from participating in partisan politics other than to vote and freely express political opinions. The attorney general has concluded, however, that the terms of a collective bargaining agreement may override this restriction on political activity.[99]

---

[95]RC 2921.01(B).
[96]State v Freeman, 20 OS(3d) 55, 20 OBR 355, 485 NE(2d) 1043 (1985).
[97]Maynard v Smith, 47 Misc 47, 354 NE(2d) 722 (Muni, Franklin 1975).

[98]Civil liability under 42 USCA 1983 for civil rights violations is treated at Text 46.13 to 46.16.
[99]OAG 91-065. See also Text 18.20, Supremacy of contract over certain laws.

Chapter 46

Liability of Schools, Officers, and Employees

LIABILITY UNDER STATE LAW
- 46.01 School district liability for tort claims
- 46.02 Defenses to claims
- 46.03 Immunity of personnel
- 46.04 School board's duty to defend and indemnify employees
- 46.05 Limitation of actions, limits on damages, pleading
- 46.06 Damages
- 46.07 Payment of judgments
- 46.08 Contract claims
- 46.09 Injunctive relief
- 46.10 Liability for hazing
- 46.11 Liability to recreational users
- 46.12 Moral obligation doctrine

LIABILITY FOR FEDERAL CIVIL RIGHTS VIOLATIONS
- 46.13 Federal civil rights violations
- 46.14 Violation of constitutional rights giving rise to section 1983 liability
- 46.15 Liability of board members, officers, and employees for civil rights violations
- 46.16 Recovery of attorney fees

INSURANCE AND INDEMNIFICATION
- 46.17 Authority of school board to provide for insurance, in general
- 46.18 Joint self-insurance pool
- 46.19 Liability insurance for personnel
- 46.20 Automobile insurance
- 46.21 Student accident insurance

LIABILITY UNDER STATE LAW

46.01 School district liability for tort claims

(A) Sovereign immunity

Historically, boards of education were immune from tort liability under the doctrine of sovereign immunity. (Generally, a tort is a claim that a person acting negligently or intentionally toward another to whom he owed a duty of care caused an injury.) In 1983, the Ohio Supreme Court abrogated this doctrine.[1]

(B) Ohio Public Liability Act

In response, the Ohio legislature partially reestablished sovereign immunity for political subdivisions (including school districts).[2] Subject to five important exceptions, school districts are not liable in damages for injury, death, or loss to persons or property caused by an act or omission of the district or its employees in connection with a governmental or proprietary function.[3]

RC Chapter 2744 does not apply to (1) actions based on contractual liability; (2) actions by an employee or collective bargaining representative regarding matters arising out of the employment relationship; (3) actions by an employee concerning wages, hours, conditions, or other terms of employment; (4) civil actions by sureties under fidelity or surety bonds; and (5) civil actions based on alleged violations of the Constitution or statutes of the United States, except that RC 2744.07 (regarding defense and indemnification of employees) applies to these claims.[4]

(C) Liability of school districts

RC 2744.02(B) provides that school districts are generally liable for damages for injury, death, or loss in five very broad areas: (1) negligent operation of any motor vehicle on public roads by their employees, when engaged in activities within the scope of their employment and authority; (2) employees' negligent acts with respect to proprietary functions (except as otherwise provided in RC 3746.24 with respect to voluntary cleanups of property contaminated by hazardous substances and petroleum); (3) failure to keep public roads, highways, streets, avenues, alleys, sidewalks, bridges,

---

[1] Carbone v Overfield, 6 OS(3d) 212, 6 OBR 264, 451 NE(2d) 1229 (1983). See also Zagorski v South Euclid-Lyndhurst City School Dist Bd of Ed, 15 OS(3d) 10, 15 OBR 8, 471 NE(2d) 1378 (1984).
[2] RC Ch 2744.
[3] RC 2744.02(A)(1). In Miller v Wadsworth City Schools, 93 App(3d) 278, 638 NE(2d) 166 (Medina 1994), the court rejected the claim of a parent who broke her ankle after attending a high school cross-country meet when she stepped in a hole near the top of a hill next to a dirt road. The court questioned whether the road qualified as a "public road" and went on to find, in any event, that the area of the hole was not within the road.
[4] RC 2744.09(A) to (E). See also Text 46.17 to 46.21 for an explanation of the important provisions of RC Ch 2744 regarding the purchase of insurance by political subdivisions.

aqueducts, viaducts, or public grounds open, repaired, and free from nuisance (except as otherwise provided in RC 3746.24); (4) employees' negligent acts occurring in or on the grounds of buildings used in connection with the performance of a governmental function (except as otherwise provided in RC 3746.24);[5] and (5) express imposition of liability by the Ohio Revised Code. Liability does not exist, however, simply because a statute places a general responsibility on the district or authorizes it to sue and be sued.[6]

(D) Governmental and proprietary functions

RC Chapter 2744 distinguishes between governmental and proprietary functions. A governmental function is defined, first, as one that meets any of three requirements: (1) it is imposed on the state as an obligation of sovereignty and is performed by a political subdivision voluntarily or pursuant to legislative requirement; (2) it is for the common good of all citizens of the state; or (3) it promotes and preserves the public health, safety, or welfare; involves activities not customarily engaged in by nongovernmental persons; and is not specified in the statute as a proprietary function.[7]

Alternately, a governmental function is one listed in RC 2744.01(C)(2). The list includes the provision of a free education or a free public library system; the regulation, maintenance, and repair of roads, streets, sidewalks, etc.; the design, construction, renovation, maintenance, or operation of a park, playground, playfield, indoor recreational facility, zoo, bath, swimming pool, pond, or golf course; and the construction, repair, renovation, maintenance, and operation of buildings used in connection with a governmental function.[8] Thus, a board of education's activities providing educational programs are clearly a governmental function. This includes a school district vocational class's construction project involving the remodeling of a private residence.[9]

A proprietary function is one that (1) satisfies both of two criteria: it is not a governmental function as specified above *and* it is not one that promotes or preserves the public peace, health, safety, or welfare and is not customarily engaged in by non-governmental persons; or (2) falls within a statutory listing.[10] The list of proprietary functions includes the operation of a hospital, cemetery, utility, sewer system, public stadium, auditorium, civic center, exhibition hall, arts and crafts center, band, orchestra, or off-street parking facility.[11]

46.02 Defenses to claims

RC 2744.03(A) lists six defenses or immunities available to a school district or its employees. First, the district is immune if the employee involved was engaged in a judicial, quasi-judicial, prosecutorial, legislative, or quasi-legislative function.[12] Sec-

---

[5] In a school district context, the scope of this provision is not restricted to property owned by the board of education. Thus, for example, the provision covered an act of negligence occurring at a private golf driving range where a regularly scheduled gym class was meeting. Zimmerman v Kalu Canfield Driving Range, No. 92CA98, 1993 WL 205014 (7th Dist Ct App, Mahoning, 6-10-93). In Hackathorn v Springfield Local School Dist Bd of Ed, 94 App(3d) 319, 640 NE(2d) 882 (Summit 1994), appeal dismissed by 70 OS(3d) 1440, 638 NE(2d) 1043 (1994), however, the court questioned and distinguished *Zimmerman*, and concluded that a private residence used by a vocational class for a construction project was not a building used in connection with the performance of a governmental function. See also Doe v Jefferson Area Local School Dist, 97 App(3d) 11, 646 NE(2d) 187 (Ashtabula 1994), dismissed by 71 OS(3d) 1444, 644 NE(2d) 407 (1995) (questioning and distinguishing *Zimmerman*). Where the evidence does not demonstrate the required negligence, liability obviously is not triggered. Redd v Springfield Twp School, 91 App(3d) 88, 631 NE(2d) 1076 (Summit 1993) (rejecting claim where child slipped in water in front of school drinking fountain); Kelly v Rocky River Bd of Ed, No. 63906, 1993 WL 453677 (8th Dist Ct App, Cuyahoga, 11-4-93) (no negligence shown where eye injury sustained in physical education class).

[6] RC 2744.02(B). By way of example, RC 3323.03 imposes a responsibility upon a board of education to identify and educate a handicapped child, but violation of this duty does not give rise to a civil action for damages since the statute does not expressly impose liability. Zellman v Kenston Bd of Ed, 71 App(3d) 287, 593 NE(2d) 392 (Geauga 1991).

[7] RC 2744.01(C)(1).

[8] RC 2744.01(C)(2).

[9] Hackathorn v Springfield Local School Dist Bd of Ed, 94 App(3d) 319, 640 NE(2d) 882 (Summit 1994), appeal dismissed by 70 OS(3d) 1440, 638 NE(2d) 1043 (1994).

[10] RC 2744.01(G).

[11] RC 2744.01(G)(2).

[12] RC 2744.03(A)(1).

ond, the district is immune if the employee's conduct, other than the negligent conduct which gave rise to the claim, was required or authorized by law or was necessary to the exercise of the district's or the employee's powers.[13] Third, the district is immune if the employee's conduct was within the employee's discretion with respect to policy-making, planning, or enforcement powers by virtue of his office or position.[14] Fourth, the district is immune if the act complained of resulted in injury or death to an adult criminal or delinquent child who was at the time performing community service or community work and was covered by workers' compensation.[15] Fifth, the district is immune if the harm resulted from the exercise of judgment or discretion in determining whether to acquire or how to use equipment, supplies, materials, personnel, facilities, and other resources, unless exercised with malicious purpose, in bad faith, or in a wanton or reckless manner.[16] Finally, the district is entitled to any

---

[13]RC 2744.03(A)(4).

[14]RC 2744.03(A)(3). For examples of this provision in operation, see Simms v Dayton Public Schools, No. 12799, 1992 WL 80782 (2d Dist Ct App, Montgomery, 4-21-92) (elementary school principal's discretionary actions with respect to recess triggered district immunity); Weimer v Springfield Twp Public School Dist Bd of Ed, No. 16334, 1994 WL 175628 (9th Dist Ct App, Summit, 5-11-94) (allegation of improper lighting and fencing failed); Vallish v Copley Bd of Ed, No. 15664, 1993 WL 27494 (9th Dist Ct App, Summit, 2-3-93) (allegation of negligent design and construction of sidewalk failed), dismissed, jurisdictional motion overruled by 67 OS(3d) 1408, 615 NE(2d) 1043 (1993). But see Hallett v Stow Bd of Ed, 89 App(3d) 309, 624 NE(2d) 272 (Summit 1993) (partially overruling *Vallish* and denying immunity as to allegation of negligent failure to repair or warn of hole on hillside adjacent to bleachers that caused injurious fall to football game spectator while leaving the premises).

[15]RC 2744.03(A)(4).

[16]RC 2744.03(A)(5). For examples of this provision in operation, see, e.g., Simms v Dayton Public Schools, No. 12799, 1992 WL 80782 (2d Dist Ct App, Montgomery, 4-21-92) (elementary school principal's discretionary actions with respect to recess triggered district immunity); Goodin v Alexander Local School Dist, No. 92 CA 1531, 1993 WL 98046 (4th Dist Ct App, Athens, 3-26-93), dismissed, jurisdictional motion overruled by 67 OS(3d) 1434, 617 NE(2d) 685 (1993) (industrial arts teacher's supervision of power saw within statute); Dimasso v Eastwood High School Bd of Ed, No. 93WD022, 1993 WL 381464 (6th Dist Ct App, Wood, 9-30-93) (placement of cable in front of stadium gate within statute); Sargeant v Gallipolis Bd, No. 92 CA 43, 1993 WL 415314 (4th Dist Ct App, Gallia, 10-14-93) (teacher's decision to permit student to help move cafeteria tables involved discretion and judgment triggering immunity where student sustained broken ankle when table fell on him); Neal v Southwestern City School Dist Bd of Ed, No. 94APE06-796, 1994 WL 694881 (10th Dist Ct App, Franklin, 12-8-95) (custodian's decision to request student assistance in moving cafeteria tables within statutory immunity where table fell on and injured student) Steele v Auburn Vocational School Dist, No. 93-L-105, 1994 WL 321152 (11th Dist Ct App, Lake, 6-30-94) (supervision of student parking and movement between schools involved discretion and judgment triggering immunity); Harland v West Clermont Local School Dist, No. CA94-01-006, 1994 WL 394958 (12th Dist Ct App, Clermont, 8-1-94) (physical education teacher's supervision of "floor hockey" game in which student injured involved discretion and judgment triggering immunity); Weimer v Springfield Twp Public School Dist Bd of Ed, No. 16334, 1994 WL 175628 (9th Dist Ct App, Summit, 5-11-94) (decision in light of financial constraints to revise fencing and install fewer lights with respect to building addition immune); Koch v Avon Bd of Ed, 64 App(3d) 78, 580 NE(2d) 809 (Lorain 1989), dismissed by 48 OS(3d) 708, 550 NE(2d) 479 (1990) (board that left decisions on whether to repair or replace physical education equipment and whether and how such equipment was used to discretion of physical education instructor immune from suit over injury of student while performing vaulting exercises during gymnastics class); Mosely v Dayton City School Dist, No. 11336, 1989 WL 73988 (2d Dist Ct App, Montgomery, 7-6-89) (teacher's method of conducting physical education within the statute); Banchich v Port Clinton Public School Dist, 64 App(3d) 376, 581 NE(2d) 1103 (Sandusky 1989) (carpentry class teacher's instruction and supervision of students' use of power jointer within statute); Wilson v Canton City School Dist, No. CA-8436, 1991 WL 189168 (5th Dist Ct App, Stark, 9-16-91) (carpentry teacher's supervision of use of power saw within statute); Gambill v Lebanon City School Dist Bd of Ed, No. CA89-06-034, 1990 WL 67022 (12th Dist Ct App, Warren, 5-21-90) (practice of maintaining soccer goal without stakes constitutes judgment or discretion on manner in which equipment to be used); Alessi v Buckeye Local Schools Bd of Ed, No. 89-A-1430, 1990 WL 93185 (11th Dist Ct App, Ashtabula, 6-29-90) (immunity applied where physical education supervisor's actions were exercise of judgment and discretion and no malice or recklessness shown); Sartori v Columbus Bd of Ed, No. 90AP-845, 1991 WL 7265 (10th Dist Ct App, Franklin, 1-24-91) (assignments in supervising recess activity within exercise of judgment on how to use personnel); Balazs v Kirtland Bd of Ed, No. 67263, 1995 WL 143817 (8th Dist Ct App, Cuyahoga, 3-30-95) (board immune from liability based on its exercise of judgment and discretion regarding use and maintenance of stadium bleachers); Hildebrant v Lebanon Bd of Ed, No. CA94-09-077, 1995 WL 128392 (12th Dist Ct App,

defense or immunity available at common law or established by the Revised Code.[17]

46.03 Immunity of personnel

A school employee, which, under the definition appearing in RC 2744.01(B), includes a district officer or board member, is immune from liability *unless* his acts or omissions were manifestly outside the scope of his employment or official responsibilities, involved malice or bad faith, were made in a wanton or reckless manner, or unless the Revised Code expressly imposes liability.[18] The employee's immunity, however, does not affect or limit the district's

---

Warren, 3-27-95) (negligence does not defeat immunity for decision not to rope off obsolete bleachers); Stinehelfer v Solon City Schools, No. 64097, 1993 WL 51205 (8th Dist Ct App, Cuyahoga, 2-25-93) (immunity applied to employer's decision on where to store equipment not in use); Mackulin v Lakewood Bd of Ed, No. 61808, 1993 WL 69555 (8th Dist Ct App, Cuyahoga, 3-11-93) (immunity applied to decision on repairing or resurfacing ice at skating rink); McCullom v Clow, No. C-910442, 1992 WL 450001 (1st Dist Ct App, Hamilton, 9-30-92) (immunity applied to board and administrators in case where teacher sexually abused students), cert denied sub nom McCullom v Princeton City School Dist Bd of Ed, ___ US ___, 113 SCt 3042, 125 LEd(2d) 728 (1993); Doe v Jefferson Area Local School Dist, 97 App(3d) 11, 646 NE(2d) 187 (Ashtabula 1994), dismissed by 71 OS(3d) 1444, 644 NE(2d) 407 (1995) (immunity applied to claim that district negligently hired and supervised substitute teacher who allegedly sexually abused student). This provision was of no avail in Ross v Solon City School Dist Bd of Ed, Nos. 62978, 63020, 1992 WL 159714 (8th Dist Ct App, Cuyahoga, 7-2-92), where a maintenance employee recovered for injuries due to his fall down a school's deteriorated cement staircase. Rejecting the district's argument that when and how to repair the steps involved a discretionary decision that precluded liability, the court noted that RC 2744.02(B)(3) obligated the district to keep the staircase free from nuisance and that RC 2744.03(A)(5) "cannot be used to abrogate that duty." This provision was also of no avail in Younger v Buckeye Local School Dist, Nos. 2060, 2065, 1992 WL 161163 (9th Dist Ct App, Medina, 7-8-92), where a failure to repair bleachers triggered liability when a football spectator leaned against a rail that gave way and resulted in an injurious fall; in Field v McDonald Bd of Ed, Nos. 93-T-4901, 93-T-4906, 1994 WL 638189 (11th Dist Ct App, Trumbull, 11-16-94), where the failure of an employee to turn on lights in a darkened stairwell in which the plaintiff missed a step and fell resulted in a finding of liability); in Bolding v Dublin Local School Dist, No. 94APE09-1307, 1995 WL 360227 (10th Dist Ct App, Franklin, 6-15-95), where alleged negligence of school personnel in carrying out details of field trip in which student was injured stated a claim; and in Hallett v Stow Bd of Ed, 89 App(3d) 309, 624 NE(2d) 272 (Summit 1993), where a failure to repair or warn of a hole in a hillside adjacent to the bleachers in a football stadium caused an injurious fall to a spectator who was leaving the premises. But see Vallish v Copley Bd of Ed, No. 15664, 1993 WL 27494 (9th Dist Ct App, Summit, 2-3-93), dismissed, jurisdictional motion overruled by 67 OS(3d) 1408, 615 NE(2d) 1043 (1993) (applying immunity on when and how to repair school sidewalk—*Vallish* was partially overruled by *Hallett*).

[17]RC 2744.03(A)(7).

[18]RC 2744.03(A)(6). For examples of this provision in operation, see, e.g., Rinehart v Western Local School Dist Bd of Ed, 87 App(3d) 214, 621 NE(2d) 1365 (Pike 1993) (teacher's nonmalicious administration of corporal punishment immune); Simms v Dayton Public Schools, No. 12799, 1992 WL 80782 (2d Dist Ct App, Montgomery, 4-21-92) (holding elementary school principal immune); Koch v Avon Bd of Ed, 64 App(3d) 78, 580 NE(2d) 809 (Lorain 1989), dismissed by 48 OS(3d) 708, 550 NE(2d) 479 (1990) (holding physical education instructors immune); Spotts v Columbus Public Schools, No. 89AP-1003, 1990 WL 48900 (10th Dist Ct App, Franklin, 4-19-90) (teacher's supervision of playground not negligent); Sartori v Columbus Bd of Ed, No. 90AP-845, 1991 WL 7265 (10th Dist Ct App, Franklin, 1-24-91) (teachers supervising playground not negligent); Poe v Hamilton, 56 App(3d) 137, 565 NE(2d) 887 (Warren 1990) (holding teacher immune from suit by student who failed class and construing "reckless" as not merely careless but as "perverse disregard of a known risk"). In remanding for trial the claim of a drum majorette for a visiting high school football team who was injured when a drum major for the home team tried to light his baton for a half-time fire baton routine, the court in Minnick v Springfield Local Schools Bd of Ed, 81 App(3d) 545, 611 NE(2d) 926 (Lucas 1992), defined "wanton" and "reckless" under RC 2744.03(A)(6) as acting intentionally or failing to act in fulfillment of one's duty while knowing or having reason to know facts that would lead a reasonable person to realize both that his conduct creates an unreasonable risk of physical harm to another and that such risk is substantially greater than that necessary to make his conduct negligent. This definition is derived from Thompson v McNeill, 53 OS(3d) 102, 559 NE(2d) 705 (1990), a nonschool case in which a golfer struck and injured by a ball hit by another golfer was denied recovery. The majorette's claim against the band director who selected the major was remanded (as was her claim against the board of education) on grounds the lower court applied incorrect legal principles in finding immunity. See also Rush v Carlisle Local School Bd, No. CA93-11-089, 1994 WL 200539 (12th Dist Ct App, Warren, 5-23-94); Goodin v Alexander Local School Dist, No. 92 CA 1531, 1993 WL 98046 (4th Dist Ct App, Athens, 3-26-93), dismissed, jurisdictional motion overruled by 67 OS(3d)

liability (if any) for his acts or omissions as provided in RC 2744.02.[19]

For causes of action not covered by RC Chapter 2744, (e.g., actions arising out of an employment relationship), school district officers such as superintendents, principals, and board members enjoy a qualified good faith immunity from tort liability for acts that involve the exercise of discretion and judgment.[20] For instance, *Kropf v Vermilion Bd of Ed*[21] affirmed a judgment in favor of the superintendent, principal, and individual school board members on a claim that they had negligently hired a baseball coach and negligently supervised baseball practice. Absent evidence that they had acted outside the scope of their authority, in bad faith, or out of a corrupt or malicious motive, they were immune from liability. This immunity does not extend to teachers.[22]

Board members also enjoy some immunity for statements which others may consider defamatory. For example, a board member may have a qualified privilege to make certain statements about school personnel while discussing school affairs with members of the community. Where a qualified privilege exists, allegedly slanderous statements are protected in the absence of actual malice.[23] A school psychologist may have a qualified privilege as to information submitted about a teacher at the superintendent's request.[24]

46.04 School board's duty to defend and indemnify employees

With respect to suits against a school district employee (including a district officer or board member) for acts or omissions in connection with a governmental or proprietary function, the district must provide for the employee's defense if the act or omission occurred while the employee was acting in good faith and not manifestly outside the scope of his employment or official responsibilities.[25] RC 2744.07 states the district "shall" provide for the employee's defense. This differs from RC 3313.203, which states a district "may" provide a defense under similar circumstances. An appeals court has concluded "the legislative intent was to have effect given to both laws" and "RC 2744.07 does not impliedly repeal RC 3313.203, but rather, further defines and expands upon the ultimate objectives of the Ohio Legislature." Applying RC 2744.07, a board of education was required to provide a defense to a teacher sued by a student injured while attending his class.[26] Funds must be appropriated for this purpose or spent from the proceeds of insurance.[27] The duty to defend does not apply to suits commenced by the school district.[28] If a district refuses to defend, the employee may sue to determine the propriety of the refusal.[29] Similarly, the district must indemnify and hold an employee harmless for a judgment other than one for punitive or exemplary damages if the employee was acting in good faith and within the scope of his employment or official responsibilities.[30] The duty to defend and indemnify includes authority to appeal a decision and post an appeal

---

1434, 617 NE(2d) 685 (1993); Zimmerman v Kalu Canfield Driving Range, No. 92CA98, 1993 WL 205014 (7th Dist Ct App, Mahoning, 6-10-93).

[19]RC 2744.03(B).

[20]See, e.g., Hall v Columbus Bd of Ed, 32 App(2d) 297, 290 NE(2d) 580 (Franklin 1972); Carroll v Lucas, 39 Misc 5, 313 NE(2d) 864 (CP, Hamilton 1974).

[21]Kropf v Vermilion Bd of Ed, No. E-85-48, 1986 WL 8652 (6th Dist Ct App, Erie, 8-8-86).

[22]Baird v Hosmer, 46 OS(2d) 273, 347 NE(2d) 533 (1976).

[23]Brandon v Coldwater Exempted Village School Dist Bd of Ed, No. 10-80-6, 1981 WL 6822 (3d Dist Ct App, Mercer, 4-1-81).

[24]Schafer v Anderson, No. 7359, 1981 WL 5375 (2d Dist Ct App, Montgomery, 12-15-81).

[25]RC 2744.07(A)(1).

[26]Bachmayer v Toledo Bd of Ed, 44 App(3d) 104, 541 NE(2d) 1078 (Lucas 1988).

[27]RC 2744.07(A)(1).

[28]RC 2744.07(A)(1).

[29]RC 2744.07(C). If the refusal was improper, the district must pay the attorney's fees, expenses, and costs incurred by the employee in both the case where the district failed to defend and the action to determine whether the refusal was proper. Rogers v Youngstown, 61 OS(3d) 205, 574 NE(2d) 451 (1991). The suit must be brought by the employee. In the absence of such a suit, an employer's insurer cannot, after defending the employee, sue the employer seeking reimbursement of its costs. Buckeye Union Insurance Co v Arlington Bd of Ed, 93 App(3d) 285, 638 NE(2d) 170 (Hancock 1994).

[30]RC 2744.07(A)(2).

bond when the district is satisfied the employee was acting in good faith and within the scope of his employment or official responsibilities.[31] Although the duty to defend is limited to suits not commenced by the school district, the duty to indemnify is not.[32]

The district may enter into settlements or consent judgments and secure releases from liability for itself or an employee.[33] Amounts spent for any settlement must be from funds appropriated for that purpose.[34] A district's decision to enter into a consent judgment or settlement, or to secure releases, or concerning the amount or circumstances of a consent judgment or settlement, is not subject to an appeal by anyone, including employees or taxpayers.[35]

46.05 Limitation of actions, limits on damages, pleading

Actions against political subdivisions for loss allegedly caused by an act or omission in connection with a governmental or proprietary function must be brought within two years after the cause of action arose or within any applicable shorter statute of limitations provided in RC 2744.04(A).[36] As a result, the limitations period does not begin to apply to student or other person injured while he or she is a minor until the injured person's eighteenth birthday.[37]

The complaint in an action brought under RC Chapter 2744 must include a demand for damages but cannot specify an amount.[38] If a school district is found liable, damages are limited by statute.[39] In a suit against a political subdivision, a plaintiff may not recover punitive or exemplary damages, and any award must be reduced by any benefits the plaintiff is entitled to receive from insurance or any other source.[40] No insurer or other person may sue a political subdivision with respect to the benefits under a subrogation provision.[41] Resolving a conflict among lower courts, the Ohio Supreme Court has upheld the constitutionality of this provision barring subrogation rights.[42]

The damage limits in RC 2744.05 apply in actions against political subdivisions, but not in actions against employees. Arguably, this may require political subdivisions to pay unlimited damages in actions filed against employees. RC 2744.03(A)(6) provides that the employee is immune unless his acts or omissions were outside the scope of his employment or official responsibilities, or made with malicious purpose, in bad faith or in a wanton and reckless manner, or unless the Revised Code expressly imposes liability. Under RC 2744.03(B), however, the employee's immunity does not affect or limit "any liability of the political subdivision" for his acts or omissions as provided in RC 2744.02. Therefore, if liability under RC 2744.03(B) is that of the political subdivision, it is incumbent upon a plaintiff to file against the political subdivision, thereby activating the damage limits.

In suits filed against employees, the political subdivision must defend and indemnify pursuant to RC 2744.07, but it should in most cases be able to plead the employee's immunity as a defense. The question then becomes whether the board of education is a defendant and whether the employee's negligence is in one of the five areas in which school districts have lia-

---

[31]OAG 87-024.
[32]OAG 87-024.
[33]RC 2744.07(B)(1).
[34]RC 2744.07(B)(2).
[35]RC 2744.07(B)(2).
[36]This limitations period has been construed to apply to employees of political subdivisions as well as the political subdivision itself. Bojac Corp v Kutevac, 64 App(3d) 368, 581 NE(2d) 625 (Trumbull 1990).
[37]Adamsky v Buckeye Local School Dist, 73 OS(3d) 360, 653 NE(2d) 212 (1995).
[38]RC 2744.04(B).
[39]RC 2744.05.

[40]For examples of this collateral source setoff in operation, see Ross v Solon City School Dist Bd of Ed, Nos. 62978, 63020, 1992 WL 159714 (8th Dist Ct App, Cuyahoga, 7-2-92); Buchman v Wayne Trace Local School Dist Bd of Ed, No. 11-92-11, 1993 WL 542474 (3d Dist Ct App, Paulding, 12-29-93); Cornelius v Euclid Bd of Ed, No. 65060, 1994 WL 132429 (8th Dist Ct App, Cuyahoga, 4-14-94); Field v McDonald Bd of Ed, Nos. 93-T-4901, 93-T-4906, 1994 WL 638189 (11th Dist Ct App, Trumbull, 11-16-94).
[41]RC 2744.05(A), (B).
[42]Menefee v Queen City Metro, 49 OS(3d) 27, 550 NE(2d) 181 (1990).

bility.[43] If the employee acted in bad faith or manifestly outside the scope of his employment or official responsibilities, he will not be immune, and the political subdivision is relieved of its obligation to defend and indemnify.[44]

46.06   Damages

The amount recoverable for "actual loss" (defined as wages, salaries, or other compensation, both past and future; expenses for medical care or treatment, rehabilitation services, or other care, treatment, services, products, or accommodations made necessary by an injury; expenditures to replace or repair injured or destroyed property; expenses in relation to the actual preparation or presentation of the plaintiff's claim; and any other payments determined by the court to represent actual loss) is not limited.[45] Actual loss does not include attorney's fees or intangible loss (pain and suffering, loss of consortium, etc.).[46]

Except in wrongful death actions, damages that arise from the same cause of action, transaction, or occurrence or series of transactions or occurrences and that do not represent actual loss (i.e., intangible loss) are limited to $250,000 per person.[47] This limit does not apply to court costs or interest on a judgment.[48]

Punitive or exemplary damages are not available in an action brought under RC Chapter 2744.[49]

46.07   Payment of judgments

Even if a judgment is rendered against a school district, the district's real or personal property, money, accounts, deposits, and investments are not subject to execution, judicial sale, garnishment, or attachment.[50] Judgments must be paid from funds appropriated for that purpose. If sufficient funds are not currently appropriated, the fiscal officer must certify the amount of any unpaid judgments for inclusion in the next succeeding budget and annual appropriation measure as provided by RC 5705.08 unless the judgment is to be paid from the proceeds of revenue bonds issued pursuant to RC 133.27 or by annual installments.[51]

A court may, upon the motion of the political subdivision, authorize the political subdivision to pay a judgment or a portion of it (except a judgment in favor of the state) in annual installments over a ten-year period subject to interest at the rate specified in RC 1343.03.[52] Installment payments may not be authorized unless the court determines, after balancing the interests of the political subdivision and those of the plaintiff, that installment payments would be appropriate and not unjust to the plaintiff. If authorized, the installments must be fixed so as to achieve the same economic result as if the judgment had been paid in a lump sum.[53] At the option of the political subdivision, a judgment ren-

---

[43]See Text 46.01, School district liability for tort claims.

[44]See RC 2744.07(A).

[45]RC 2744.05(C)(1), (2). RC 2744.05(C)(2)(c) includes within "actual loss" all future expenditures for care or treatment made necessary by the injury "as determined by the court." By sensibly construing "court" to mean not only a judge but also a jury in an appropriate case, an appeals court was able to reject a constitutional challenge to the statute's retroactive application. Hubner v Sigall, 47 App(3d) 15, 546 NE(2d) 1337 (Franklin 1988).

[46]RC 2744.05(C)(2).

[47]RC 2744.05(C)(1). This limit has survived a constitutional challenge. Shelton v Greater Cleveland Regional Transit Authority, 65 App(3d) 665, 584 NE(2d) 1323 (1989), dismissed, jurisdictional motion overruled by 52 OS(3d) 701, 556 NE(2d) 525 (1990), cert denied 498 US 941, 111 SCt 349, 112 LEd(2d) 313 (1990).

[48]RC 2744.05(C)(1). This limit has survived a constitutional challenge. Shelton v Greater Cleveland Regional Transit Authority, 65 App(3d) 665, 584 NE(2d) 1323 (1989), dismissed, jurisdictional motion overruled by 52 OS(3d) 701, 556 NE(2d) 525 (1990), cert denied 498 US 941, 111 SCt 349, 112 LEd(2d) 313 (1990).

[49]RC 2744.05(A). See also Spires v Lancaster, 28 OS(3d) 76, 28 OBR 173, 502 NE(2d) 614 (1986) (punitive damages not assessable against municipality absent statutory authority).

[50]RC 2744.06(A).

[51]RC 2744.06(A).

[52]RC 2744.06(B)(2).

[53]RC 2744.06(B)(2).

dered in favor of the state may be paid in equal annual installments without interest over a period of up to ten years.[54]

The court may not authorize installment payment of any portion of a judgment which represents actual loss. "Actual loss" for purposes of the installment payment issue does not include future earnings, future medical expenses, attorney's fees, or intangible loss.[55]

46.08 Contract claims

In general, no contract is binding on a board of education unless it is made or authorized at a regular or special meeting of the board.[56]

A board may be liable for breach of contract where the contract was executed within the scope of the board's authority.[57] RC Chapter 2744 does not apply to actions to recover damages for contractual liability.[58] Where a board exceeds its authority in entering into a contract, the contract may be unenforceable.[59] Although those who contract with a board are charged with knowledge of the limitations imposed on the board by law,[60] a board has the burden of proving an alleged absence of contract-making power.[61] However, a collective bargaining agreement generally is enforceable, even if it conflicts with statutory law.[62]

An employee whose contract was improperly nonrenewed under RC 3319.11 may recover damages in the form of back pay. However, the employee must attempt to mitigate any damages by seeking other similar employment.[63] What constitutes similar employment will depend on the facts and circumstances in each case. One court has held that wages earned from dissimilar employment cannot be subtracted from a back pay award.[64]

An improperly discharged employee may maintain an action in mandamus to recover compensation due for the period he was wrongfully excluded from employment, provided the amount recoverable is established with certainty.[65]

46.09 Injunctive relief

A school board may also be subject to a court's equitable jurisdiction. Thus, by means of an injunction, a court may require specific action or forbid specific action.[66] For example, an adjacent property owner has the right to stop a nuisance created by a board of education.[67] Further, if a board is acting unlawfully, an injunction may be issued to prevent the action.[68] Such a suit must be brought against a board in its corporate capacity and not against individual board members.[69]

Where a board fails to perform a specific duty imposed on it, a writ of mandamus may be issued to compel the action.[70]

46.10 Liability for hazing

RC 2307.44 and RC 2903.31 prohibit hazing by student or other organizations which is likely to cause mental or physical

---

[54]RC 2744.06(C).
[55]RC 2744.06(B)(1)(b).
[56]RC 3313.33.
[57]Layton v Clements, 7 App 499, 27 CC(NS) 369 (Fairfield 1917); Dayton Classroom Teachers Assn v Dayton Bd of Ed, 41 OS(2d) 127, 323 NE(2d) 714 (1975).
[58]RC 2744.09(A).
[59]Cincinnati Bd of Ed v Volk, 72 OS 469, 74 NE 646 (1905).
[60]State ex rel Laskey v Perrysburg Bd of Ed, 35 OS 519 (1880); Perkins v Bright, 109 OS 14, 141 NE 689 (1923).
[61]Dayton Classroom Teachers Assn v Dayton Bd of Ed, 41 OS(2d) 127, 323 NE(2d) 714 (1975).
[62]See Text 18.20, Supremacy of contract over certain laws.
[63]Frith v Princeton City School Dist Bd of Ed, No. C-810789, 1982 WL 8619 (1st Dist Ct App, Hamilton, 7-14-82).

[64]Schlotterer v Coldwater Exempted Village School Dist Bd of Ed, No. 10-82-2, 1983 WL 7248 (3d Dist Ct App, Mercer, 4-26-83).
[65]State ex rel Hamlin v Collins, 9 OS(3d) 117, 9 OBR 342, 459 NE(2d) 520 (1984); Monaghan v Richley, 32 OS(2d) 190, 291 NE(2d) 462 (1972). See also State ex rel Fenske v McGovern, 11 OS(3d) 129, 11 OBR 426, 464 NE(2d) 525 (1984).
[66]Mroczek v Beachwood City School Dist Bd of Ed, 61 Misc 6, 400 NE(2d) 1362 (CP, Cuyahoga 1979).
[67]Wayman v Akron City School Dist Bd of Ed, 5 OS(2d) 248, 215 NE(2d) 394 (1966).
[68]Kerwin v Ashtabula County School Dist Bd of Ed, 67 Abs 528, 116 NE(2d) 610 (CP, Ashtabula 1953).
[69]Marting v Groff, 82 Abs 212, 162 NE(2d) 186 (App, Fayette 1959).
[70]RC 2731.01. See, e.g., State ex rel Hamlin v Collins, 9 OS(3d) 117, 9 OBR 342, 459 NE(2d) 520 (1984).

harm to its victim. Schools, administrators, or faculty may be held liable for injuries resulting from hazing if they knew or should have known of such activity and failed to make reasonable attempts to prevent it. It is an affirmative defense for the school if it is actively enforcing a policy against hazing when the injury occurs.[71]

46.11 Liability to recreational users

Ohio's recreational user statutes, RC 1533.18 and RC 1533.181, although expressly applicable only to private parties, have been construed by the Ohio Supreme Court as giving derivative immunity to state political subdivisions, including school districts.[72] The statutes shield against liability for any injury caused by an act on one's property of a recreational user, defined generally as a person who has permission without payment of a fee to enter the premises to engage in recreational pursuits.[73] Thus, a school district was held immune from liability under RC 1533.181 when a child, participating in a free summer playground program operated at an elementary school, was injured while climbing on a swing set.[74] Similarly, a district was immune when a fifteen-year-old was injured while riding his motor bike on school property open for recreational activity without charge after school hours.[75] A minor who slipped on a muddy field while voluntarily playing football in a district-sponsored program was also a recreational user barred from suing the district for his injuries.[76] A parent attending her son's track meet who, while going from a parking lot to the stands, walked through a shot-put landing area and was hit in the face by a shot thrown by a student practicing was also a recreational user.[77]

46.12 Moral obligation doctrine

In some situations where a board is not legally liable, it may nevertheless impose on itself a "moral obligation." The attorney general found such a moral obligation where a pupil was injured in a course and the board questioned whether, because of sovereign immunity, it could legally pay the medical bills. The attorney general concluded the board could recognize a moral obligation and pay the bills.[78] The same conclusion had earlier been reached as to a hospital bill where a student was injured in gym class.[79] On the other hand, to make an enforceable claim on a theory of moral obligation, one must prove not only the existence of the moral obligation but also subsequent board recognition of that obligation.[80]

---

[71]See also Text 24.10, Hazing, permitting hazing.

[72]Fuehrer v Westerville City School Dist Bd of Ed, 61 OS(3d) 201, 574 NE(2d) 448 (1991). School employees have the same immunity so long as they act within the course and scope of their employment. Rankey v Arlington Bd of Ed, 78 App(3d) 112, 603 NE(2d) 1151 (Hancock 1992).

[73]For discussion of the factors to be examined in determining whether a person is a recreational user, see Miller v Dayton, 42 OS(3d) 113, 537 NE(2d) 1294 (1989). Fuehrer v Westerville City School Dist Bd of Ed, 61 OS(3d) 201, 574 NE(2d) 448 (1991) involved a student and four companions who entered a soccer field when school was not in session. While playing with the soccer goal, the student was fatally injured. The Court found the boys were not recreational users, but proceeded to shield the district from liability on the ground they were mere licensees who entered the premises at their own peril and were owed a duty by the district only to refrain from wanton or willful misconduct. See also Kammer v Akron Christian Schools, No. 15672, 1993 WL 46665 (9th Dist Ct App, Summit, 2-24-93), cert denied 66 OS(3d) 1507, 613 NE(2d) 1046 (1993).

[74]Christman v Columbus Public Schools Bd of Ed, No. 88AP-1075, 1989 WL 61732 (10th Dist Ct App, Franklin, 6-8-89).

[75]Zachel v Mahaney, No. L-89-187, 1990 WL 97668 (6th Dist Ct App, Lucas, 7-13-90).

[76]Wheeler v Lakewood Bd of Ed, 61 App(3d) 786, 573 NE(2d) 1169 (Cuyahoga 1989). See also Rencher v Cleveland Bd of Ed, No. 58383, 1991 WL 41743 (8th Dist Ct App, Cuyahoga, 3-28-91) (minor injured while playing football on high school lawn after school is recreational user).

[77]Rankey v Arlington Bd of Ed, 78 App(3d) 112, 603 NE(2d) 1151 (Hancock 1992).

[78]1931 OAG 3471.

[79]1929 OAG 595.

[80]Brownfield v Board of Education, 56 App(2d) 10, 381 NE(2d) 207 (Jackson 1977).

LIABILITY FOR FEDERAL CIVIL RIGHTS VIOLATIONS

46.13 Federal civil rights violations

(A) In general

School districts and boards of education may be exposed to liability under federal law through 42 USCA 1983, which provides:

> Every person who, under color of any statute, ordinance, regulation, custom, or usage, of any State or Territory, subjects, or causes to be subjected, any citizen of the United States or other person within the jurisdiction thereof to the deprivation of any rights, privileges or immunities secured by the Constitution and laws, shall be liable to the party injured in an action at law, suit in equity, or other proper proceeding for redress.

Both state and federal courts have jurisdiction over suits brought under section 1983. The partial reestablishment of sovereign immunity by RC Chapter 2744 expressly does not apply to claims based on the Constitution or statutes of the United States.[81]

(B) Scope of 42 USCA 1983

In *Monell v New York City Dept of Social Services*,[82] the US Supreme Court held that local governments are "persons" subject to suit under section 1983. *Monell* has resulted in a great deal of litigation expanding the scope of section 1983 liability and the class of parties who may potentially be held liable.

Monell held that liability may be found for unconstitutional acts resulting from a government's official policy or custom.[83] There must be "a direct causal link" between the policy or custom and the constitutional deprivation.[84] Since *Monell*, courts have struggled with just what constitutes an official policy or custom. The Supreme Court in *Oklahoma City v Tuttle*[85] held in a plurality opinion that official policy could not be inferred from a single unconstitutional incident.

Pembaur v Cincinnati[86] clarified *Tuttle*, stating that while a single unconstitutional act may not give rise to a "policy" within the meaning of *Monell*, a single decision by municipal policymakers constitutes a "policy" if the policymakers possess final authority to establish policy with respect to that subject. This is true whether that decision orders an action to be taken only once or to be taken repeatedly. The Court stated liability "attaches where—and only where—a deliberate choice to follow a course of action is made from among various alternatives by the official or officials responsible for establishing final policy with respect to the subject matter in question." *Pembaur* held a county liable for a deputy sheriff's illegal entry into a clinic,

---

[81]RC 2744.09(E). See Craig v Columbus City Schools, 760 FSupp 128 (SD Ohio 1991); Wohl v Cleveland Bd of Ed, 741 FSupp 688 (ND Ohio 1990). In addition, as a matter of constitutional law, any state law sovereign immunity defense would not be available to a school district in a section 1983 action brought in state court when the defense would not be available if the action were brought in federal court. Howlett v Rose, 496 US 356, 110 SCt 2430, 110 LEd(2d) 332 (1990).

[82]Monell v New York City Dept of Social Services, 436 US 658, 98 SCt 2018, 56 LEd(2d) 611 (1978), overruling Monroe v Pape, 365 US 167, 81 SCt 473, 5 LEd(2d) 492 (1961), which held that, while individual officers of a political subdivision could be sued, local governments were not "persons" within the meaning of section 1983.

[83]The question of who has final policymaking authority is determined by state law. With respect to employment policies in an Ohio school district, it is the board of education. Hull v Cuyahoga Valley Joint Vocational School Dist Bd of Ed, 926 F(2d) 505 (6th Cir Ohio 1991), cert denied sub nom Hull v Shuck, 501 US 1261, 111 SCt 2917, 115 LEd(2d) 1080 (1991). See also Partee v Metropolitan School Dist of Washington Twp, 954 F(2d) 454 (7th Cir Ind 1992) (teacher's free speech claim against district fails because alleged prohibition on her speaking out publicly on students' standardized test scores was isolated act of superintendent, not the board as the one with final policymaking authority).

[84]Canton v Harris, 489 US 378, 109 SCt 1197, 103 LEd(2d) 412 (1989). See also Spann v Tyler Independent School Dist, 876 F(2d) 437 (5th Cir Tex 1989), cert denied sub nom Spann v Jones, 493 US 1047, 110 SCt 847, 107 LEd(2d) 841 (1990) (injuries student suffered as a result of bus driver's sexual abuse not caused by policy under which investigation of incidents of alleged sexual abuse delegated to school principal but by failure of principal to properly exercise discretion granted him under the policy).

[85]Oklahoma City v Tuttle, 471 US 808, 105 SCt 2427, 85 LEd(2d) 791 (1985).

[86]Pembaur v Cincinnati, 475 US 469, 106 SCt 1292, 89 LEd(2d) 452 (1986).

where the entry was ordered by the county prosecutor.

In *Canton v Harris*,[87] where an arrested woman did not receive medical attention while in police custody, the Court concluded an employee training program may represent governmental policy and give rise to section 1983 liability but only where "the failure to train amounts to deliberate indifference to the rights of persons with whom the police come into contact." A lesser standard of fault would "engage the federal courts in an endless exercise of second-guessing ... employee-training programs."[88]

In *Owen v Independence*,[89] the Court held that local governments (in that case, a municipality) are not entitled to immunity based upon the good faith of their officers. Such immunity had previously been granted to individuals in *Wood v Strickland*.[90]

Brandon v Holt[91] made explicit the implications in *Monell* and *Owen* that a judgment against a public official in his official rather than individual capacity imposes liability on the entity he represents, provided the entity had notice and an opportunity to respond.

The scope of section 1983 was further expanded in *Maine v Thiboutot*,[92] where the Court held that section 1983 not only embraces claims arising under the Constitution but also claims under other federal laws. Where the claim is rooted in the Constitution, however, section 1983 does not require proof of "an abuse of governmental power" separate and apart from proof of the constitutional violation.[93] Nor does section 1983 provide an independent right of action when a federal statute contains its own remedial process.[94] In *Austin v Brown Local School Dist*,[95] the US Court of Appeals for the Sixth Circuit held that the due process requirements of the Education for All Handicapped Children Act[96] cannot be circumvented by going directly to court under section 1983.

(C) State and federal claims, limitation of actions, damages

Section 1983 cannot be used to enforce rights under state law.[97] If an employee sues a board of education in state court, he must assert his section 1983 claim together with his state claim. Otherwise, his section

---

[87]Canton v Harris, 489 US 378, 109 SCt 1197, 103 LEd(2d) 412 (1989).

[88]This "deliberate indifference" standard was not met as to a school district's employee training program in Jane Doe "A" v St. Louis County Special School Dist, 901 F(2d) 642 (8th Cir Mo 1990), in which a school bus driver had physically and sexually abused handicapped students; nor did the evidence establish a district policy or custom, within the meaning of *Monell*, of failing to investigate and act upon prior complaints of the driver's misconduct. Nor was the standard met as to a district's policy of investigating, hiring, and supervising teachers in D.T. v Independent School Dist No. 16 of Pawnee County, Okla, 894 F(2d) 1176 (10th Cir Okla 1990), cert denied 498 US 879, 111 SCt 213, 112 LEd(2d) 172 (1990), in which students were molested by a teacher during summer vacation while engaged in fund-raising activities. See also Leffall v Dallas Independent School Dist, 28 F(3d) 521 (5th Cir Tex 1994); Gates v Unified School Dist No. 449 of Leavenworth County, Kansas, 996 F(2d) 1035 (10th Cir Kan 1993); Thelma D. v St. Louis Bd of Ed, 934 F(2d) 929 (8th Cir Mo 1991); Gonzalez v Ysleta Independent School Dist, 996 F(2d) 745 (5th Cir Tex 1993); Coleman v Wirtz, 745 FSupp 434 (ND Ohio 1990), affirmed by 985 F(2d) 559 (6th Cir Ohio 1993); Robbins v Maine School Administrative Dist No. 56, 807 FSupp 11 (D Me 1992); McCullom v Clow, No. C-910442, 1992 WL 450001 (1st Dist Ct App, Hamilton, 9-30-92), cert denied sub nom McCullom v Princeton City School Dist Bd of Ed, ___ US ___, 113 SCt 3042, 125 LEd(2d) 728 (1993). But see C.M. v Southeast Delco School Dist, 828 FSupp 1179 (ED Pa 1993).

[89]Owen v Independence, 445 US 622, 100 SCt 1398, 63 LEd(2d) 673 (1980).

[90]Wood v Strickland, 420 US 308, 95 SCt 992, 43 LEd(2d) 214 (1975). See also Text 46.15, Liability of board members, officers, and employees for civil rights violations.

[91]Brandon v Holt, 469 US 464, 105 SCt 873, 83 LEd(2d) 878 (1985).

[92]Maine v Thiboutot, 448 US 1, 100 SCt 2502, 65 LEd(2d) 555 (1980).

[93]Collins v Harker Hts, Texas, 503 US 115, 112 SCt 1061, 117 LEd(2d) 261 (1992).

[94]Pennhurst State School & Hospital v Halderman, 465 US 89, 104 SCt 900, 79 LEd(2d) 67 (1984).

[95]Austin v Brown Local School Dist, 746 F(2d) 1161 (6th Cir Ohio 1984), cert denied 471 US 1054, 105 SCt 2114, 85 LEd(2d) 479 (1985).

[96]The Act, now called the Individuals with Disabilities Education Act, is treated in Text Ch 28, Education for Children with Disabilities.

[97]Baker v McCollan, 443 US 137, 99 SCt 2689, 61 LEd(2d) 433 (1979); Paul v Davis, 424 US 693, 96 SCt 1155, 47 LEd(2d) 405 (1976).

1983 claim may be barred by a state court judgment.[98] Likewise, the adjudication of a section 1983 claim bars a subsequent Title VII discrimination claim based upon the same conduct.[99]

The Ohio Supreme Court has held that neither section 1983 not the substantive due process protections of the Fourteenth Amendment of the US Constitution provide a remedy to one who merely alleges denial of a job promotion.[100]

The statute of limitations applicable to section 1983 actions is the two-year limit on actions for bodily injury provided in RC 2305.10.[101]

Punitive damages may be awarded against individuals in section 1983 suits but not against public bodies.[102] In addition, damages must compensate the plaintiff for his loss and may not be based on a jury's estimate of the abstract value of the constitutional right involved.[103]

46.14 Violation of constitutional rights giving rise to section 1983 liability

(A) Procedural due process

The denial of procedural due process often gives rise to section 1983 liability. However, the US Court of Appeals for the Sixth Circuit has cautioned that not every alleged denial implicates a federal claim. A plaintiff must prove not only a wrong, but also that state remedies for redressing that wrong are inadequate.[104]

(1) Students

In *Goss v Lopez*,[105] the US Supreme Court held that, under the Fourteenth Amendment's due process clause, a student may not be temporarily suspended from school without notice of the charges, an explanation of the evidence, and an opportunity to respond. A suspension without notice and at least a minimal hearing results in section 1983 liability.

Statutory due process requirements for the suspension, expulsion, and permanent exclusion of public school students are given in RC 3313.66.[106]

(2) Employees

As with students, an employee's due process rights are primarily grounded in the Fourteenth Amendment. The leading case on when public employees are entitled to a hearing in contract nonrenewal and dismissal situations is *Board of Regents of State Colleges v Roth*,[107] where the Supreme Court held that any right to procedural due process requires that a liberty or property interest be implicated.

A "liberty" interest is involved if the employee's "good name, reputation, honor or integrity is at stake" or if "a stigma or other disability [has] foreclosed his freedom to take advantage of other employment opportunities."[108] There is no liberty interest in the continuation of employment itself, and the mere nonrenewal of a contract does not constitute a deprivation of liberty.[109] To implicate a liberty interest, one must establish that the employer made a stigmatizing charge to the public which resulted in dismissal.[110]

---

[98]Migra v Warren City School Dist Bd of Ed, 465 US 75, 104 SCt 892, 79 LEd(2d) 56 (1984).

[99]Pertuset v Loudonville-Perrysville Exempted Village Bd of Ed, No. C84-1891-A (ND Ohio, 5-13-85).

[100]Shirokey v Marth, 63 OS(3d) 113, 585 NE(2d) 407 (1992), cert denied sub nom Shirokey v Cleveland Heights, ___ US ___, 113 SCt 186, 121 LEd(2d) 130 (1992).

[101]Browning v Pendleton, 869 F(2d) 989 (6th Cir Ohio 1989).

[102]Newport v Fact Concerts, Inc, 453 US 247, 101 SCt 2748, 69 LEd(2d) 616 (1981).

[103]Memphis Community School Dist v Stachura, 477 US 299, 106 SCt 2537, 91 LEd(2d) 249 (1986).

[104]Brickner v Voinovich, 977 F(2d) 235 (6th Cir Ohio 1992), cert denied ___ US ___, 113 SCt 2965, 125 LEd(2d) 665 (1993) (rejecting due process claim of ousted state board of education member since state procedures provided all process that was due).

[105]Goss v Lopez, 419 US 565, 95 SCt 729, 42 LEd(2d) 725 (1975).

[106]See Text 25.09 to 25.15.

[107]Board of Regents of State Colleges v Roth, 408 US 564, 92 SCt 2701, 33 LEd(2d) 548 (1972).

[108]Board of Regents of State Colleges v Roth, 408 US 564, at 573, 92 SCt 2701, 33 LEd(2d) 548 (1972).

[109]Lake Michigan College Federation of Teachers v Lake Michigan Community College, 518 F(2d) 1091 (6th Cir Mich 1975), cert denied 427 US 904, 96 SCt 3189, 49 LEd(2d) 1197 (1976).

[110]Burt v Grand Rapids Bd of Ed, 35 F(3d) 565 (6th Cir Mich 1994); Beres v Marysville Exempted Village School Dist Bd of Ed, 723 F(2d) 908 (6th Cir

A "property" interest may also be implicated in the dismissal of nontenured employees. *Roth* held that an assistant professor had no property interest sufficient to require university authorities to give him a hearing on nonrenewal of his contract. In *Perry v Sindermann*,[111] however, the Court found that a nontenured teacher could state a claim to continuing employment if there were rules or understandings that could give rise to "implied" tenure. If one can show a "common law of reemployment" or a "*de facto* tenure policy" that has created an expectation of renewal, reasons for the nonrenewal and a hearing are required.[112]

The US Court of Appeals for the Sixth Circuit has held that neither liberty or property interests are involved when public employees are laid off.[113] In *Ramsey v Whitley County, Kentucky, Bd of Ed*,[114] the Sixth Circuit rejected the section 1983 claim of a retired teacher who protested the reduction of her accumulated sick leave days and consequent reduction of compensation when she retired. The Court held that interference with a property interest in a pure benefit of employment as opposed to tenured employment itself is a matter to be redressed by a breach of contract claim under state law, not by federal action under section 1983. Reassignment of a teacher to another school following an investigation of alleged professional misconduct has been held not to change sufficiently a teacher's status to violate a protected liberty or property interest.[115] Similarly, suspending a coach with pay pending an investigation of complaints about her conduct did not implicate a protected liberty or property interest;[116] nor did removal of a coach whose dismissal did not require cause.[117] Where a principal was terminated under RC 3319.16 but subsequently reinstated by a court hearing his appeal under that statute, there was no deprivation of procedural due process in light of the adequacy of the state remedy provided by the statute.[118]

Oral promises may confer a protected expectancy of continued employment. In *Vail v Paris Union School Dist No. 95 Bd of Ed*,[119] an athletic director's one-year contract was not renewed. The employee had, however, received oral assurances he would be employed for two years. The Seventh Circuit's finding of an implied contract sufficient to create a property interest was affirmed by an equally divided Supreme Court.

In *Horne v Clemens*,[120] an Ohio appeals court found that a civil service employee was deprived of liberty and property interests without due process when his employer placed memoranda critical of his performance in his personnel file without giving notice and an opportunity to be heard. A somewhat different result was reached in

---

Ohio 1983). See also Burkhart v Randles, 764 F(2d) 1196 (6th Cir Tenn 1985).

[111] Perry v Sindermann, 408 US 593, 92 SCt 2694, 33 LEd(2d) 570 (1972).

[112] Perry v Sindermann, 408 US 593, at 600, 602, 92 SCt 2694, 33 LEd(2d) 570 (1972) The significance of *Roth* and *Perry* (and numerous lower court decisions holding that due process under the Constitution does not require the giving of reasons and a hearing upon nonrenewal of an employee's contract, e.g., Ryan v Aurora City Bd of Ed, 540 F(2d) 222 (6th Cir Ohio 1976), cert denied 429 US 1041, 97 SCt 741, 50 LEd(2d) 753 (1977)) has been essentially preempted insofar as the nonrenewal of Ohio teachers is concerned by the *statutory* right to reasons and a hearing that now exists under RC 3319.11. See Text 9.13, Statutory evaluation and due process requirements. The same can be said of the Ohio Supreme Court's decision in Borman v Gorham-Fayette Bd of Ed, 28 OS(3d) 151, 28 OBR 245, 502 NE(2d) 1031 (1986) that a nontenured teacher employed under a limited contract with an evaluation clause, and evaluated within the meaning of that clause, has no constitutional right to a hearing before nonrenewal of her contract.

[113] Riggs v Kentucky, 734 F(2d) 262 (6th Cir Ky 1984), cert denied 469 US 857, 105 SCt 184, 83 LEd(2d) 118 (1984).

[114] Ramsey v Whitley County, Kentucky, Bd of Ed, 844 F(2d) 1268 (6th Cir Ky 1988).

[115] Thomas v Smith, 897 F(2d) 154 (5th Cir Tex 1989).

[116] Schneeweis v Jacobs, 771 FSupp 733 (ED Va 1991), affirmed without opinion by 966 F(2d) 1444 (4th Cir Va 1992).

[117] Sanguigni v Pittsburgh Bd of Public Ed, 968 F(2d) 393 (3d Cir Pa 1992).

[118] Anthony v Ada Exempted Village School Dist Bd of Ed, No. 6-94-3, 1994 WL 379009 (3d Dist Ct App, Hardin, 7-21-94).

[119] Vail v Paris Union School Dist No. 95 Bd of Ed, 706 F(2d) 1435 (7th Cir Ill 1983), affirmed by 466 US 377, 104 SCt 2144, 80 LEd(2d) 377 (1984).

[120] Horne v Clemens, 23 App(3d) 139, 23 OBR 299, 492 NE(2d) 164 (Geauga 1985).

Mulligan v Hazard,[121] in which the Sixth Circuit found that placement of a critical letter in a personnel file did not deprive a professor of a liberty interest where the letter was merely cumulative of other similar entries even if the professor could establish a protected liberty interest in her file.[122]

In *Cleveland Bd of Ed v Loudermill*,[123] the US Supreme Court held that Ohio civil service employees with a property right in continued employment by virtue of the civil service laws are entitled to an informal pretermination hearing.[124] That principle has been extended to teachers suspended pending the outcome of termination proceedings under RC 3319.16.[125] On the other hand, a routine two-day disciplinary suspension has been deemed a de minimis property deprivation to which due process rights did not attach.[126] The Sixth Circuit has also held that a civil service employee who did not deny the charges against him was not entitled to a hearing before he was suspended for five days.[127] A driving instructor was not denied procedural due process when, following a leave of absence because of mental impairment, the school district required a second medical opinion as a condition of returning to work since, contrary to the plaintiff's claim, there was no termination of employment involved.[128]

Even if a pre- or post-termination hearing is procedurally adequate, the resulting termination nevertheless may violate due process if the decisionmaker is biased. A federal district court has held that whether a decisionmaker is impermissibly biased depends on whether (1) its role in initiating the charges is largely a procedural step or implies that its mind is closed on the issue of guilt; (2) there are important issues of fact which give rise to a serious risk of an erroneous decision based on tainted findings of fact; (3) the decisionmaker has a personal interest (pecuniary or in terms of prestige) in seeing the termination upheld; or (4) personal animosity exists between the employee and the decisionmaker.[129]

(B) Substantive due process

In *Ingraham v Wright*,[130] the US Supreme Court held that neither the cruel and unusual punishment clause of the Eighth Amendment nor the notice and hearing requirements of the due process clause of the Fourteenth Amendment apply to the imposition of corporal punishment in public schools. The Court declined to say whether corporal punishment may give rise to an action to vindicate substantive rights under the due process clause.

Subsequent cases have answered affirmatively and spelled out the circumstances under which section 1983 liability may arise. *Hall v Tawney*,[131] for example, held that while corporal punishment does not per se violate substantive due process, it may under some circumstances. The issue is "whether the force applied caused injury so severe, was so disproportionate to the need presented, and was so inspired by malice or sadism rather than a merely careless or unwise excess of zeal that it amounted to a brutal and inhumane abuse of official power literally shocking to the conscience."[132] Another appeals court held the following factors crucial to determining whether a substantive due process claim is valid: (1) whether there was a need for corporal punishment; (2) the relationship between the need and the amount adminis-

---

[121]Mulligan v Hazard, 777 F(2d) 340 (6th Cir Ohio 1985), cert denied 476 US 1174, 106 SCt 2902, 90 LEd(2d) 988 (1986), overruled on other grounds by Browning v Pendleton, 869 F(2d) 989 (6th Cir Ohio 1989).

[122]For treatment of the Ohio Privacy Act and the right it affords school employees to inspect and dispute personal information maintained by the employer, see Text 44.04 to 44.11.

[123]Cleveland Bd of Ed v Loudermill, 470 US 532, 105 SCt 1487, 84 LEd(2d) 494 (1985).

[124]For a full treatment of the pretermination hearing requirement, see Text 12.17(B), Notice to employee, removal order.

[125]Crago v Olentangy Local School Dist Bd of Ed, No. C-2-86-0419 (SD Ohio, 1-4-88).

[126]Carter v Western Reserve Psychiatric Habilitation Center, 767 F(2d) 270 (6th Cir Ohio 1985).

[127]Boals v Gray, 775 F(2d) 686 (6th Cir Ohio 1985).

[128]Scheideman v West Des Moines Community School Dist, 989 F(2d) 286 (8th Cir Iowa 1993).

[129]Salisbury v Housing Authority of Newport, 615 FSupp 1433 (ED Ky 1985).

[130]Ingraham v Wright, 430 US 651, 97 SCt 1401, 51 LEd(2d) 711 (1977).

[131]Hall v Tawney, 621 F(2d) 607 (4th Cir WVa 1980).

[132]Hall v Tawney, 621 F(2d) 607, 613 (4th Cir WVa 1980).

tered; (3) the extent of any injury; and (4) whether the punishment was administered in good faith or maliciously and sadistically to hurt the child.[133] The Fifth Circuit takes a per se view that substantive due process is not implicated so long as a state affirmatively imposes reasonable limits on corporal punishment with adequate criminal or civil penalties for departures from such state laws.[134]

The due process clause is not violated by a merely negligent act of a public official which causes unintended loss of life, liberty, or property.[135] Nor can the clause be stretched to require a public official to protect one from harm inflicted by a private party. In *DeShaney v Winnebago County Department of Social Services*,[136] the Supreme Court rejected a claim that county social workers were liable for not removing a boy from the custody of his father who severely beat and injured the child, noting the clause's purpose was "to protect the people from the State, not to ensure that the State protected them from each other."[137] Building on *DeShaney*, a federal appeals court has held school officials do not have an affirmative duty under the due process clause to ensure pupil safety and prevent unanticipated child abuse by a teacher.[138] Another appeals court reached a similar conclusion where students were allegedly sexually molested by other students, the court noting that compulsory school attendance laws do not restrain a child's liberty so as to give rise to an affirmative duty to protect.[139] Similarly, compulsory attendance laws did not give a teacher an affirmative duty to protect or impose liability where her student became caught on his bandana in a cloakroom adjacent to the teacher's classroom and strangled to death.[140] This remains so even where it is alleged that the student is the victim of a foreseeable assault because of known violent propensities of another student.[141] The issues here are not fully resolved, however. A deeply divided US Court of Appeals for the Fifth Circuit has concluded a high school student sexually molested by her teacher does have due process protection that triggers liability on the part of school administrators if they are deliberately indifferent to the student's constitutional right.[142]

---

[133]Wise v Pea Ridge School Dist, 855 F(2d) 560 (8th Cir Ark 1988). See also Metzger v Osbeck, 841 F(2d) 518 (3d Cir Pa 1988); Meyer v Litwiller, 749 FSupp 981 (WD Mo 1990); Thrasher v General Casualty Co of Wisconsin, 732 FSupp 966 (WD Wis 1990).

[134]Cunningham v Beavers, 858 F(2d) 269 (5th Cir Tex 1988), cert denied 489 US 1067, 109 SCt 1343, 103 LEd(2d) 812 (1989); Fee v Herndon, 900 F(2d) 804 (5th Cir Tex 1990), cert denied 498 US 908, 111 SCt 279, 112 LEd(2d) 233 (1990). See also Text 25.16, Corporal punishment.

[135]Daniels v Williams, 474 US 327, 106 SCt 662, 88 LEd(2d) 662 (1986); Davidson v Cannon, 474 US 344, 106 SCt 668, 88 LEd(2d) 677 (1986).

[136]DeShaney v Winnebago County Dept of Social Services, 489 US 189, 109 SCt 998, 103 LEd(2d) 249 (1989).

[137]See also Collins v Harker Hts, Texas, 503 US 115, 112 SCt 1061, 117 LEd(2d) 261 (1992) (no substantive due process right to safe working environment from governmental employer).

[138]J.O. v Alton Community Unit School Dist 11, 909 F(2d) 267 (7th Cir Ill 1990). See also Doe v Hononegah Community High School Dist No. 207 Bd of Ed, 833 FSupp 1366 (ND Ill 1993); Doe v Douglas County School Dist RE-1, 770 FSupp 591 (D Colo 1991). But see C.M. v Southeast Delco School Dist, 828 FSupp 1179 (ED Pa 1993).

[139]D.R. v Middle Bucks Area Vocational Technical School, 972 F(2d) 1364 (3d Cir Pa 1992), cert denied ___ US ___, 113 SCt 1045, 122 LEd(2d) 354 (1993); Dorothy J. v Little Rock School Dist, 7 F(3d) 729 (8th Cir Ark 1993). See also Black v Indiana Area School Dist, 985 F(2d) 707 (3d Cir Pa 1993); Doe v Petaluma City School Dist, 830 FSupp 1560 (ND Cal 1993), reversed on other grounds by 54 F(3d) 1447 (9th Cir Cal 1995); Elliott v New Miami Bd of Ed, 799 FSupp 818 (SD Ohio 1992); B.M.H. v Chesapeake, Va, School Bd, 833 FSupp 560 (ED Va 1993).

[140]Maldonado v Josey, 975 F(2d) 727 (10th Cir NM 1992), cert denied ___ US ___, 113 SCt 1266, 122 LEd(2d) 662 (1993). See also Lichtler v County of Orange, 813 FSupp 1054 (SD NY 1993).

[141]Graham v Independent School Dist No. I-89, 22 F(3d) 991 (10th Cir Okla 1994).

[142]Doe v Taylor Independent School Dist, 15 F(3d) 443 (5th Cir Tex 1994), cert denied sub nom Lankford v Doe, ___ US ___, 115 SCt 70, 130 LEd(2d) 25 (1994). But See Walton v Alexander, 44 F(3d) 1297 (5th Cir Miss 1995) (en banc), reversing 20 F(3d) 1350 (5th Cir Miss 1994), in which the Fifth Circuit held that a student who voluntarily attended a state-supported school for the deaf and was sexually abused by another student could not claim a violation of his right to substantive due process. The court reasoned that substantive due process does not require the state to protect a person voluntarily within its care or custody from harm inflicted by non-state actors. See also Leffall v Dallas Independent School Dist, 28 F(3d) 521 (5th Cir Tex 1994), in which the Fifth Circuit refused to extend *Taylor* to the claim of a student's mother who was killed by random gunfire in a

A school district and football coach were not liable on substantive due process grounds for failing to prevent hazing of a team member on a team bus.[143] The termination of a football coach's supplemental contract did not violate substantive due process even if the board of education's charges were defamatory.[144] Indeed, the Sixth Circuit maintains generally that substantive due process has no applicability to the termination of school employees under Ohio law.[145] A teacher's substantive due process claim against her immediate supervisor for alleged continuous harassment also failed, the court stating there is no support for the notion that pursuing one's employment free from the emotional health risks resulting from verbal harassment implicates this constitutional guarantee.[146] On the other hand, a substantive due process claim was stated where a handicapped student died when required to run 350 yards in less than two minutes as punishment for misbehavior, since the teacher's actions, if proved, added up to more than negligence and other named defendants, such as the school district, may have been guilty of deliberate indifference.[147]

A federal district court in Indiana has held that reducing a student's grade for consuming alcohol during school hours violated the student's substantive due process rights on the premise that academic sanctions must be based on misconduct related to academic performance.[148]

(C) First Amendment freedoms

The courts have consistently recognized that the First Amendment applies in cases involving terminations and nonrenewals of teachers and other school employees. Accordingly, a district may not terminate or fail to renew an employee's contract based upon the employee's exercise of free speech where it would not have made the same decision in the absence of the protected conduct.[149]

(D) Freedom from discrimination

Federal courts have also entertained section 1983 actions by school employees for unconstitutionally discriminatory employment practices.[150]

(E) Right to privacy

The constitutional right of privacy also has been recognized. Thus, for example, coercion by school officials of a minor student to have an abortion would violate the student's protected right to choose whether to have an abortion, as would coercion of the minor not to consult with parents over the decision.[151] The right of a teacher to become pregnant by means of artificial insemination has also been recognized as a protected privacy right.[152]

Although not arising in a school context, two courts have found section 1983 liability under a privacy theory for public disclosure

---

high school parking lot after a school-sponsored dance. The court noted that while school attendance was required by law during the day, attendance at the dance was not compulsory.

[143]Reeves v Besonen, 754 FSupp 1135 (ED Mich 1991). See also Russell v Fannin County School Dist, 784 FSupp 1576 (ND Ga 1992), affirmed by 981 F(2d) 1263 (11th Cir Ga 1992) (no duty to protect student from injury by another student even though fights had previously occurred at high school); Fenstermaker v Nesfedder, 802 FSupp 1258 (ED Pa 1992), affirmed in part and vacated in part by 9 F(3d) 1540 (3d Cir Pa 1993) (high school wrestling coach not liable on substantive due process grounds for sending student with injured knee back into bout).

[144]Holthaus v Cincinnati Public Schools Bd of Ed, 986 F(2d) 1044 (6th Cir Ohio 1993).

[145]Sutton v Cleveland Bd of Ed, 958 F(2d) 1339 (6th Cir Ohio 1992).

[146]Santiago de Castro v Morales Medina, 943 F(2d) 129 (1st Cir PR 1991).

[147]Waechter v Cassopolis, Michigan School Dist No. 14-030, 773 FSupp 1005 (WD Mich 1991).

[148]Smith v School City of Hobart, 811 FSupp 391 (ND Ind 1993).

[149]For cases and analysis, see Text 9.21(E), Constitutionally protected conduct.

[150]See, e.g., Morris v Laurel School Dist Bd of Ed, 401 FSupp 188 (D Del 1975) (racial discrimination); Mims v Chicago Bd of Ed, 523 F(2d) 711 (7th Cir Ill 1975) (sex discrimination).

[151]Arnold v Escambia County, Alabama Bd of Ed, 880 F(2d) 305 (11th Cir Ala 1989). See also Sullivan v Meade Independent School Dist No. 101, 530 F(2d) 799 (8th Cir SD 1976) (where the court avoided the "very difficult" constitutional question of whether a right to privacy foreclosed dismissal of a single female teacher who insisted on living with a single man in the school community).

[152]Cameron v Hillsboro, Ohio, City School Dist Bd of Ed, 795 FSupp 228 (SD Ohio 1991).

that a person is infected with the AIDS virus.[153]

46.15 Liability of board members, officers, and employees for civil rights violations

(A) Board members and officers

Individual board members and school officials are "persons" under 42 USCA 1983 and so may be individually liable for violations of the statute.[154] The liability is, however, qualified. In addition, by virtue of RC 2744.09(E), board members and school officials are entitled to be defended and indemnified by the district for claims based on section 1983. However, individual liability in section 1983 actions is subject to a good faith defense. Since RC 2744.07 provides that a political subdivision is relieved of its obligation to defend and indemnify if an employee acted in bad faith, it is unclear how much impact RC 2744.09(E) will have on school districts in section 1983 actions against employees as individuals.

(B) Teachers and employees

Since teachers and other school employees are also "persons," they, too, are subject to liability for violations of section 1983.[155] However, as employees of a school district, they are entitled, by virtue of RC 2744.09(E), to have the district defend and indemnify them in the amount of any judgment other than punitive or exemplary damages.

(C) Qualified immunity

In *Wood v Strickland*,[156] the US Supreme Court recognized a qualified or "good faith" immunity of school board members in actions brought against them under section 1983. The "good faith" defense was described as having (1) an "objective" part and (2) a "subjective" part, each of which must be satisfied for the defense to prevail.

> [I]n the specific context of school discipline, we hold that a school board member is not immune from liability for damages under section 1983 if he knew or reasonably should have known that the action he took within his sphere of official responsibility would violate the constitutional rights of the student affected, or if he took the action with the malicious intention to cause a deprivation of constitutional rights or other injury to the student.[157]

However, *Harlow v Fitzgerald*[158] reexamined *Wood* and eliminated the "subjective" element in favor of using only the "objective" standard: "We therefore hold that government officials ... are shielded from liability for civil damages insofar as their conduct does not violate clearly established statutory or constitutional rights of which a reasonable person would have known."[159]

Where constitutional or statutory rights are not clearly established, school officials are entitled to qualified immunity.[160] A violation of a statute or regulation which is not itself actionable under section 1983 will not deprive an official of qualified immunity

---

[153]Doe v Barrington, 729 FSupp 376 (D NJ 1990); Woods v White, 689 FSupp 874 (WD Wis 1988), affirmed by 899 F(2d) 17 (7th Cir Wis 1990).

[154]See Hafer v Melo, 502 US 21, 112 SCt 358, 116 LEd(2d) 301 (1991) (state officials may be personally liable even for actions taken in their official capacities).

[155]See, e.g., Hall v Tawney, 621 F(2d) 607 (4th Cir WVa 1980).

[156]Wood v Strickland, 420 US 308, 95 SCt 992, 43 LEd(2d) 214 (1975).

[157]Wood v Strickland, 420 US 308, at 322, 95 SCt 992, 43 LEd(2d) 214 (1975).

[158]Harlow v Fitzgerald, 457 US 800, 102 SCt 2727, 73 LEd(2d) 396 (1982).

[159]Harlow v Fitzgerald, 457 US 800, at 818, 102 SCt 2727, 73 LEd(2d) 396 (1982). However, where unlawful motivation or intent is an essential element of the alleged constitutional deprivation (as would typically be the case, for example, where one retaliates against an employee for his exercise of free speech rights under the First Amendment), the motivation or intent must still be considered in assessing whether qualified immunity applies. See, e.g., Tompkins v Vickers, 26 F(3d) 603 (5th Cir Miss 1994); Poe v Haydon, 853 F(2d) 418 (6th Cir Ky 1988), cert denied 488 US 1007, 109 SCt 788, 102 LEd(2d) 780 (1989); Musso v Hourigan, 836 F(2d) 736 (2d Cir Conn 1988).

[160]Harlow v Fitzgerald, 457 US 800, 102 SCt 2727, 73 LEd(2d) 396 (1982); Garvie v Jackson, 845 F(2d) 647 (6th Cir Tenn 1988). Put another way, the unlawfulness must be apparent to the official in light of preexisting law if the shield of qualified immunity is to be lifted. Anderson v Creighton, 483 US 635, 107 SCt 3034, 97 LEd(2d) 523 (1987).

from section 1983 liability for violation of other constitutional or statutory rights.[161]

By way of example, qualified immunity has been denied when a school district failed to protect students from a music teacher known to have sexually abused at least one student,[162] discharged a maintenance employee for his constitutionally protected opposition to new school taxes,[163] or discharged a custodian without affording a pretermination hearing.[164] Discrimination against a teacher based on her pregnancy by artificial insemination and her status as an unwed mother is not protected by qualified immunity.[165]

Illustrating the other side of the coin, qualified immunity applied to the strip search of a student for contraband where, under the particular circumstances, school officials reasonably expected the student was concealing evidence of drug use,[166] and to a principal's general search of students' purses, pocketbooks, and bags for contraband found by a court to be unlawful in the absence of individualized suspicion of wrongdoing, since the law as to the need for individualized suspicion is unsettled.[167] Qualified immunity also applied to school personnel who questioned two students, and physically examined one of them, during an investigation of suspected child abuse since no particularized and established constitutional right of which school officials should have been aware could be identified, much less shown to be violated.[168] A high school principal who rejected an applicant for teaching and coaching positions because of his sexual orientation was shielded since the law on this subject was unclear.[169] A teacher and aide were entitled to qualified immunity when an injured student claimed excessive punishment deprived him of liberty, since it was not shown that the state did not provide an adequate post-deprivation remedy.[170]

Officials claiming the qualified good faith immunity have the burden of asserting and proving the defense.[171] Failure to plead the defense can result in a waiver of it.[172]

46.16 Recovery of attorney fees

A companion statute to 42 USCA 1983, 42 USCA 1988, allows the prevailing party to recover reasonable attorney fees, which may also include expert fees.[173] To be considered a "prevailing party," one need not win every aspect of a lawsuit. If a party prevails on "any significant issue" and receives some of the relief sought, the statute is triggered.[174] However, fees can be

---

[161]Davis v Scherer, 468 US 183, 104 SCt 3012, 82 LEd(2d) 139 (1984). See also Spruytte v Walters, 753 F(2d) 498 (6th Cir Mich 1985), cert denied 474 US 1054, 106 SCt 788, 88 LEd(2d) 767 (1986).

[162]Stoneking v Bradford Area School Dist, 856 F(2d) 594 (3d Cir Pa 1988), vacated sub nom Smith v Stoneking, 489 US 1062, 109 SCt 1333, 103 LEd(2d) 804 (1989). See also C.M. v Southeast Delco School Dist, 828 FSupp 1179 (ED Pa 1993); Doe v Hononegah Community High School Dist No. 207 Bd of Ed, 833 FSupp 1366 (ND Ill 1993). Compare Jane Doe "A" v St. Louis County Special School Dist, 901 F(2d) 642 (8th Cir Mo 1990) (no liability where evidence failed to show defendants had knowledge of bus driver's sexual abuse of students).

[163]Stewart v Baldwin County Bd of Ed, 908 F(2d) 1499 (11th Cir Ala 1990). See also Grady v El Paso Community College, 979 F(2d) 1111 (5th Cir Tex 1992).

[164]Runge v Dove, 857 F(2d) 469 (8th Cir SD 1988).

[165]Cameron v Hillsboro, Ohio, City School Dist Bd of Ed, 795 FSupp 228 (SD Ohio 1991).

[166]Williams v Ellington, 936 F(2d) 881 (6th Cir Ky 1991); Cornfield v Consolidated High School Dist No. 230, 991 F(2d) 1316 (7th Cir Ill 1993).

[167]Burnham v West, 681 FSupp 1160 (ED Va 1987).

[168]Landstrom v Illinois Dept of Children and Family Services, 892 F(2d) 670 (7th Cir Ill 1990).

[169]Jantz v Muci, 976 F(2d) 623 (10th Cir Kan 1992), cert denied ___ US ___, 113 SCt 2445, 124 LEd(2d) 662 (1993).

[170]Coriz v Martinez, 915 F(2d) 1469 (10th Cir NM 1990), cert denied 499 US 960, 111 SCt 1584, 113 LEd(2d) 649 (1991).

[171]Gomez v Toledo, 446 US 635, 100 SCt 1920, 64 LEd(2d) 572 (1980).

[172]Kennedy v Cleveland, 797 F(2d) 297 (6th Cir Ohio 1986), cert denied sub nom Hanton v Kennedy, 479 US 1103, 107 SCt 1334, 94 LEd(2d) 185 (1987).

[173]A fee award may include compensation for the work of paralegals and law clerks at market rates. Missouri v Jenkins, 491 US 274, 109 SCt 2463, 105 LEd(2d) 229 (1989). It may not include the fees for services of experts employed by a party. West Virginia University Hospitals, Inc v Casey, 499 US 83, 111 SCt 1138, 113 LEd(2d) 68 (1991).

[174]Texas State Teachers Assn v Garland Independent School Dist, 489 US 782, 109 SCt 1486, 103 LEd(2d) 866 (1989).

awarded only against the defendant against whom the plaintiff prevailed, i.e., a public agency is not subject to a fee award if the plaintiff prevailed only against individual defendants.[175]

42 USCA 1988 has been interpreted to establish a higher standard for the award of attorney fees to a defendant than to a plaintiff. Attorney fees have been awarded to defendants in actions determined to be "frivolous, unreasonable and without foundation."[176] In *Tarter v Raybuck*,[177] a student contended he was unconstitutionally searched by school administrators and falsely imprisoned. The court rejected both contentions, but refused to award attorney fees since the exact nature of a student's Fourth Amendment right against unreasonable searches was legally unclear.

INSURANCE AND INDEMNIFICATION

46.17 Authority of school board to provide for insurance, in general

(A) Purchase of insurance

RC 2744.08 provides that a political subdivision may procure insurance against its and its employees' potential tort liability under RC Chapter 2744. The political subdivision may determine at its discretion the limits, terms, and conditions of the insurance, as well as the circumstances in which it will apply. The policy period is to be mutually agreed on by the political subdivision and the insurance company or, when competitive bidding is required, for the period of time stated in the specifications for competitive bidding. Similar authorization to purchase insurance exists for boards of education under RC 3313.203.

(B) Self-insurance

Regardless of whether a political subdivision procures insurance, it may also establish a self-insurance program.[178] It may choose to contract with any person, other political subdivision, or regional council of governments for the administration of the program and may mutually agree with other political subdivisions that their programs will be jointly administered in a specified manner.[179]

As part of a self-insurance program, a political subdivision may reserve in a special fund, pursuant to ordinance or resolution, such funds as it considers appropriate. Such a fund is not subject to RC 5705.12. The political subdivision may allocate the costs of insurance or a self-insurance program among the funds or accounts in its treasury on the basis of relative exposure and loss experience.[180]

(C) Providing for insurance not waiver of immunity or defense

The purchase of liability insurance or the establishment of a self-insurance program does not waive any immunity or defense of the political subdivision or its employees.[181] Any immunity or defense may be specifically waived, however, in accordance with RC 2744.08(B), which specifies, among other things, that the waiver "shall be only to the extent of the insurance or self-insurance program coverage."[182]

The authorization to secure insurance and/or establish a self-insurance program in RC Chapter 2744 is in addition to any

---

[175]Kentucky v Graham, 473 US 159, 105 SCt 3099, 87 LEd(2d) 114 (1985).

[176]Christiansburg Garment Co v EEOC, 434 US 412, 98 SCt 694, 54 LEd(2d) 648 (1978); Tonti v Petropoulous, 656 F(2d) 212 (6th Cir Ohio 1981); Torres v Oakland County, 758 F(2d) 147 (6th Cir Mich 1985).

[177]Tarter v Raybuck, 742 F(2d) 977 (6th Cir Ohio 1984), cert denied 470 US 1051, 105 SCt 1749, 84 LEd(2d) 814 (1985).

[178]RC 2744.08(A)(2)(a).
[179]RC 2744.08(A)(2)(a), RC 2744.08(A)(2)(b).
[180]RC 2744.08(A)(2)(a).
[181]RC 2744.08(B).
[182]RC 2744.08(B).

other insurance authority granted by Ohio law.[183]

46.18 Joint self-insurance pool

(A) In general

A political subdivision may join with other political subdivisions to establish and maintain a joint self-insurance pool to provide for the payment of judgments, settlements, expenses, loss, and damage resulting from claims under RC Chapter 2744 and to indemnify or hold harmless employees.[184] The joint pool may not include a political subdivision of any other state.[185] Interestingly, the statute provides for paying the cost of indemnifying employees but does not include the cost of defending employees in actions under RC Chapter 2744.

Joint pools are exempt from state and local taxes,[186] and are not subject to Ohio insurance laws.[187] RC 2744.081 does not affect a political subdivision's ability to self-insure under any other section of the Revised Code.[188]

(B) Reserves, report to superintendent of insurance

A joint self-insurance pool must reserve funds to cover potential liability, expense, loss, and damage as are necessary in the exercise of sound actuarial judgment.[189] The pool must submit a report on or before the last day of March for the preceding calendar year to the superintendent of insurance for approval. This report must detail the amounts reserved and the disbursements made and must be accompanied by a written report of a member of the American Academy of Actuaries certifying that (1) the amounts reserved conform to the requirements of RC 2744.081(A)(1); and (2) the amounts reserved are computed in accordance with accepted loss reserving standards and are fairly stated in accordance with sound loss reserving principles. The disbursements required to be reported include, but are not limited to, disbursements for the administration of the pool, claims paid, attorney's fees, and fees paid to consultants.[190]

In reviewing the report, the superintendent of insurance will determine whether pool reserves are adequate according to reserve standards applicable to a private insurance company writing the same coverages. The pool must bear the reasonable costs and expenses incurred in this review and any other investigation the superintendent considers necessary. The superintendent will inform the reporting authority of the results of his review and in the case of a disapproval will order the reporting authority to comply with the requirements outlined above within a reasonable period.[191]

(C) Administration of pool

The pool may contract with any person, political subdivision, nonprofit corporation organized under RC Chapter 1702, or regional counsel of governments created under RC Chapter 167 for the administration of the pool. The contract may be awarded without competitive bidding. Before the contract is entered into, however, there must be a full public disclosure of all its terms and conditions, including a statement listing all representations made in connection with any possible savings and losses resulting from such a contract and any potential liability of any political subdivision or employee. The proposed contract and statement must be presented at a meeting at least one week prior to the meeting at which the political subdivision authorizes the contract.[192] The pool must also contract with a member of the American Academy of Actuaries for preparation of the written evaluation of required reserve funds.[193]

(D) Costs and funding, bond issue

The cost of funding the pool may be allocated among the funds or the accounts in the treasuries of the political subdivisions on the basis of their relative exposure

---

[183] RC 2744.08(C).
[184] RC 2744.081(A). RC 2744.081(F) expressly shields an employee of the political subdivision who becomes a member of the governing body of a joint self-insurance pool against allegations of certain ethical violations by reason of contracting to participate in the pool or entering into a contract with the pool.
[185] OAG 87-058.
[186] RC 2744.081(C).
[187] RC 2744.081(E)(2).
[188] RC 2744.081(G).
[189] RC 2744.081(A)(1).
[190] RC 2744.081(A)(1).
[191] RC 2744.081(A)(1).
[192] RC 2744.081(A)(2).
[193] RC 2744.081(A)(3).

and loss experience.[194] A political subdivision that joins a pool is not liable for any amount in excess of the amount specified in the written agreement for participation.[195]

Pursuant to resolution or ordinance, a political subdivision may issue general or special obligation bonds which are not payable from real or personal property taxes and notes in anticipation of those bonds to provide funds to pay judgments, losses, damages, and the expenses of litigation or settlement of claims, and to pay the political subdivision's portion of the cost of establishing and maintaining a joint self-insurance pool, or to provide for the reserve which it may establish if it self-insures without a pool. The political subdivision may elect in its ordinance or resolution to issue such bonds or notes under RC Chapter 133, in which case certain conditions specified in RC 2744.081(D) apply.

(E) Property and casualty insurance

In addition, a joint self-insurance pool may provide the following forms of property or casualty self-insurance for the purpose of covering any other liabilities or risks of pool members:

(1) Public general liability, professional liability, or employee liability;

(2) Individual, fleet motor vehicle, or automobile liability and protection against other liability and loss associated with the ownership, maintenance, and use of motor vehicles;

(3) Aircraft liability and protection against other liability and loss associated with the ownership, maintenance, and use of aircraft;

(4) Fidelity, surety, and guarantee;

(5) Loss or damage to property and loss of use and occupancy of property due to fire, lightning, hail, tempest, flood, earthquake, snow, explosion, accident, or other risk;

(6) Marine, inland transportation, navigation, boiler, containers, pipes, engines, flywheels, elevators, and machinery;

(7) Environmental impairment; and

(8) Loss or damage by any hazard upon any other risk to which political subdivisions are not subject which is not prohibited by statute or common law from being the subject of casualty or property insurance.[196]

Two or more political subdivisions may also enter into a joint risk-management program to reduce the risks covered by insurance, self-insurance, or joint self-insurance pools including, but not limited to, the employment of risk managers and consultants.[197]

(F) Effect of collective bargaining agreement

In *Koenig v Dayton*,[198] the court held that a municipality which self-insured was liable for attorney's fees and expenses incurred by a policeman when it wrongfully refused to defend the policeman. This liability extended to the fees incurred in both the underlying action and the policeman's subsequent suit on the coverage issue. Because the city had contracted with the union for self-insurance separate from its collective bargaining agreement, the dispute over coverage was not subject to the agreement's grievance and arbitration procedure.

46.19 Liability insurance for personnel

RC 3313.203(A) provides that a school district may purchase insurance, without monetary limits, insuring members of boards of education, superintendents, principals, other administrators, teachers, any other group of employees, or volunteer bus rider assistants authorized by RC 3327.16 against liability for damage or injury to persons and property resulting from any act or omission of the board or the individual in his official capacity. The insurance must be purchased from an insurance company licensed to do business in Ohio, if the necessary insurance is available from an Ohio company. To procure the insurance, the board must adopt a resolution stating the amount of insurance to be purchased, the

---

[194]RC 2744.081(A)(4).
[195]RC 2744.081(C).
[196]RC 2744.081(E)(1).

[197]RC 2744.081(B).
[198]Koenig v Dayton, 28 App(3d) 70, 28 OBR 111, 502 NE(2d) 233 (Montgomery 1985).

necessity for it, and a statement of the estimated premium as quoted in writing by not less than two insurance companies if more than one company offers insurance for sale to the board. On adoption of the resolution, the board may purchase insurance from the company submitting the lowest and best quotation.

In addition, under RC 3313.203(B), a board may, with certain exceptions, indemnify, defend, and hold harmless any of the aforementioned persons against all civil demands, claims, suits, and defend them in criminal proceedings, whether threatened or instituted, that arise from the acts or omissions of these persons while acting within the scope of their employment, if done in the good faith belief that their conduct was lawful and in the best interests of the district.

46.20 Automobile insurance

A board of education is required by RC 3313.201 to procure insurance covering officers, employees, and pupils of the district against liability on account of damage or injury to persons and property occasioned by the operation of a motor vehicle owned or operated by the district. The attorney general has determined this authority extends to the purchase of insurance to protect officers, employees, and pupils against liability in connection with the operation of board-owned or -operated vehicles used in a vocational auto mechanics course.[199] Before procuring the insurance, a board must adopt a resolution similar to that required under RC 3313.203. A board may supplement the policies with collision, medical payments, comprehensive, and uninsured motorists coverage.

The statute provides minimum dollar amounts for liability, property damage, and medical payments coverage. If the board is unable to procure coverage in these amounts, it must procure the next highest amounts which can be reasonably obtained.

RC 3327.09 further authorizes a board to procure accident insurance covering pupils and other authorized persons transported under the authority of the board.

A board has no specific authority to pay the deductible under an insurance policy providing for collision coverage,[200] but authority may be implied for the payment of a deductible, if required by the terms of the insurance contract.

The sponsor of an outside activity must carry insurance to cover a trip, as insurance carried by a board of education covers only transportation to and from school or an educational trip.[201]

46.21 Student accident insurance

Boards of education frequently arrange to supply group insurance to students at a low premium rate. Participation must be entirely voluntary, and the decision whether to purchase the insurance should rest entirely with the student's parents or guardian.

---

[199] OAG 81-012.
[200] 1956 Inf OAG 581.

[201] 1936 OAG 6558.

Chapter 47

Search and Seizure

47.01 Fourth Amendment standards
47.02 Locker searches
47.03 Liability for unlawful search

47.01 Fourth Amendment standards

(A) Standards for student searches by school officials

The Fourth Amendment's prohibition against unreasonable searches and seizures applies to searches conducted by public school officials.[1] What this prohibition means in a school context, though, is far from settled.

While school children have some legitimate expectations of privacy because schools, however, have custodial and tutelary power over school children, schools may exercise "a degree of supervision and control that could not be exercised over free adults."[2] Schools also have a legitimate need to maintain discipline. "Thus, while children assuredly do not 'shed their constitutional rights ... at the schoolhouse gate,' *Tinker v. Des Moines Independent Community School Dist.*, 393 US 503, 506 (1969), the nature of those rights is what is appropriate for children in school."[3]

There are two critical questions: First, was the search justified at its inception? Second, was the search reasonably related in scope to the circumstances justifying it?[4]

School officials need not obtain a warrant before conducting a search, nor must they have "probable cause."[5] In *New Jersey v T.L.O.*, even though the search was not based on probable cause, it was justified at its inception because school officials had "reasonable grounds" to believe a violation of law or school rules had occurred or would occur.[6] While *New Jersey v T.L.O.* expressly left open the question of whether the grounds for the search must be individualized, a 1995 US Supreme Court opinion, *Vernonia School Dist 47 J v. Acton*, indicated that suspicionless searches in the public school system can pass constitutional muster. In holding that mandatory drug testing of all student athletes in a public school was constitutional, the Supreme Court noted that "when the government acts as guardian and tutor the relevant question is whether the search is one that a reasonable guardian and tutor might undertake."[7]

Whether the search was reasonable in scope depends on the facts of each case. Courts will consider the type of search (e.g., a strip search is more intrusive than a magnetometer search), the nature of the infraction or other school interest, the age and sex of the student, and whether less

---

[1] New Jersey v T.L.O., 469 US 325, 105 SCt 733, 83 LEd(2d) 720 (1985). While this case involved a search, its principles apply equally to the seizure of a student. See Edwards v Rees, 883 F(2d) 882 (10th Cir Utah 1989) (upholding reasonableness of vice-principal's removal of student from class and subsequent interrogation in closed office about bomb threat the school received). In a somewhat anomalous case, the US Court of Appeals for the Sixth Circuit, distinguishing the circumstances of *New Jersey v T.L.O.*, relied on the doctrine of in loco parentis to justify a principal's search of a student's hotel room during a voluntary field trip that required parental permission. Webb v McCullough, 828 F(2d) 1151 (6th Cir Tenn 1987). As *New Jersey v T.L.O.* makes clear, however, that doctrine does not shield school officials in the typical school search case. *Webb* should be relied on with caution.

[2] Vernonia School Dist 47J v Acton, ___ US ___, 115 SCt 2386, 132 LEd(2d) 564 (1995).

[3] Vernonia School Dist 47J v Acton, ___ US ___, 115 SCt 2386, 132 LEd(2d) 564 (1995).

[4] New Jersey v T.L.O., 469 US 325, 105 SCt 733, 83 LEd(2d) 720 (1985).

[5] New Jersey v T.L.O., 469 US 325, 105 SCt 733, 83 LEd(2d) 720 (1985).

[6] New Jersey v T.L.O., 469 US 325, 105 SCt 733, 83 LEd(2d) 720 (1985).

[7] Vernonia School Dist 47J v Acton, ___ US ___, 115 SCt 2386, 132 LEd(2d) 564 (1995), citing National Treasury Employees Union v Von Raab, 489 US 656, 109 SCt 1384, 103 LEd(2d) 685 (1989) (upholding random drug testing of federal customs officers); Skinner v. Railway Labor Executives' Assn, 489 US 602, 109 SCt 1402, 103 LEd(2d) 639 (1989) (upholding drug testing of railroad personnel involved in train accidents); US v Martinez-Fuerte, 428 US 543, 560-561, 96 SCt 3074, 49 LEd(2d) 1116 (1976) (upholding automobile checkpoints for illegal immigrants.

intrusive alternatives were available.[8] Urine tests for drug use were approved for student athletes in part because "school sports are not for the bashful. ... Public school locker rooms, the usual sites for these activities [suiting up, showering, etc.], are not notable for the privacy they afford."[9] Strip searches of students have been upheld where the particular circumstances gave rise to a reasonable suspicion that the student was concealing evidence of drugs or drug use.[10] An administrator who searched a student's purse for a knife used in a fight exceeded reasonable scope, however, when, upon not seeing the knife and having no reason to suspect contraband was present, she examined a zippered side pocket and discovered cocaine.[11]

(B) Police involvement in search

New Jersey v T.L.O. dealt with searches by school officials acting on their own authority, and expressly left open the question of the appropriate standard for assessing searches conducted with or at the behest of law enforcement agencies.

When police request that school officials cooperate in a search to discover evidence for use in criminal prosecutions, courts may determine that "probable cause" is required.[12] One court has determined that no individualized suspicion was required for a police search of students for weapons as the students entered the building where the search was reasonable in scope.[13] However, when school officials undertake the search on their own initiative, and the role of the police is limited, only "reasonable grounds" have been required.[14] In a police-initiated search, in the absence of a valid search warrant, school personnel are well advised to consult with legal counsel before participating or otherwise rendering affirmative assistance.

(C) Use of drug-detecting dogs

It appears that the use of drug-detecting dogs in the schools does not constitute a "search" within the meaning of the Fourth Amendment, at least where the dogs sniff inanimate objects.[15] *Horton v Goose Creek Independent School Dist*[16] differentiated between sniffs of inanimate objects, such as lockers and cars, and sniffs of students' persons, holding the latter are personally intrusive and do constitute searches under the Fourth Amendment.[17] The US Supreme Court has not addressed this issue.

(D) Standards for employee searches by school officials

The Fourth Amendment principles applicable to searches of school employees and their offices and desks are even less settled than those pertaining to student searches. The US Supreme Court could have provided some answers in *O'Connor v Ortega*,[18] but that case's message is muddied by the Court's failure to muster a majority opinion. A public employer, investigating alleged improprieties by the execu-

---

[8]New Jersey v T.L.O., 469 US 325, 105 SCt 733, 83 LEd(2d) 720 (1985).

[9]Vernonia School Dist 47J v Acton, ___ US ___, 115 SCt 2386, 132 LEd(2d) 564 (1995).

[10]Williams v Ellington, 936 F(2d) 881 (6th Cir Ky 1991); Cornfield v Consolidated High School Dist No. 230, 991 F(2d) 1316 (7th Cir Ill 1993); Widener v Frye, 809 FSupp 35 (SD Ohio 1992), affirmed without opinion by 12 F(3d) 215 (6th Cir Ohio 1993). Compare Doe v Renfrow, 631 F(2d) 91 (7th Cir Ind 1980), cert denied 451 US 1022, 101 SCt 3015, 69 LEd(2d) 395 (1981) (finding strip search of student unreasonable).

[11]T.J. v Florida, 538 So(2d) 1320 (Fla App 1989).

[12]Picha v Wielgos, 410 FSupp 1214 (ND Ill 1976). See also Piazzola v Watkins, 316 FSupp 624 (MD Ala 1970); Doe v Renfrow, 475 FSupp 1012 (ND Ind 1979), affirmed in part and remanded in part by 631 F(2d) 91 (7th Cir Ind 1980), cert denied 451 US 1022, 101 SCt 3015, 69 LEd(2d) 395 (1981).

[13]In Interest of F.B., 442 Pa Super 216, 658 A(2d) 1378 (1995).

[14]Cason v Cook, 810 F(2d) 188 (8th Cir Iowa 1987), cert denied 482 US 930, 107 SCt 3217, 96 LEd(2d) 704 (1987); Martens v District No. 220, 620 FSupp 29 (ND Ill 1985).

[15]Zamora v Pomeroy, 639 F(2d) 662 (10th Cir NM 1981). It should be noted that the search was for school disciplinary, not criminal law enforcement, purposes. See also US v Place, 462 US 696, 103 SCt 2637, 77 LEd(2d) 110 (1983) (in nonschool case, dog sniff test of luggage not a Fourth Amendment search).

[16]Horton v Goose Creek Independent School Dist, 690 F(2d) 470 (5th Cir Tex 1982), cert denied 463 US 1207, 103 SCt 3536, 77 LEd(2d) 1387 (1983).

[17]See also Jennings v Joshua Independent School Dist, 869 F(2d) 870 (5th Cir Tex 1989), cert denied 496 US 935, 110 SCt 3212, 110 LEd(2d) 660 (1990) (use of dogs to sniff cars on school parking lot not a Fourth Amendment search).

[18]O'Connor v Ortega, 480 US 709, 107 SCt 1492, 94 LEd(2d) 714 (1987).

tive director of a state hospital, searched the employee's office, desk, and file cabinets. The Court's plurality opinion concluded that whether a public employee has a reasonable expectation of privacy (and, hence, Fourth Amendment protection) in his office, desk, and files must be determined on a case-by-case basis. In some cases, facilities may be so open to fellow employees or the public that an expectation of privacy is unreasonable. Here, the plurality found an expectation of privacy at least in the desk and files, which were not shared with other employees. The plurality then proceeded to find that work-related intrusions by the public employer and investigations of work-related misconduct do not require a warrant and need not be based upon probable cause. The appropriate standard, as in the case of student searches, is simply one of reasonableness under all the circumstances. In a separate concurring opinion, Justice Scalia rejected the plurality's case-by-case approach to whether the Fourth Amendment applies in favor of a near-blanket rule that it does. He then went on, however, to conclude that government searches to investigate work-related misconduct or to obtain work-related materials are inherently reasonable and do not violate the Fourth Amendment. Four dissenting justices thought the Fourth Amendment was violated and would have applied its traditional warrant and probable cause requirements.

Based on *O'Connor*, one can conclude with some confidence that a work-related search of a teacher's or other school employee's office, desk, and files will be judged by a standard of reasonableness and need not be backed by a warrant or probable cause. The case explicitly leaves many questions unanswered, however, including what standard applies when an employee is being investigated for criminal misconduct or on non-work-related matters and whether, in any event, individualized suspicion of wrongdoing is an essential element of the reasonableness standard. The watchword in this whole area is caution.

47.02 Locker searches

The constitutional issue here is whether students have a legitimate expectation of privacy in lockers, desks, or other school property provided for storage of school supplies.[19] The decisive factor generally has been what a school's past actions and announced policy encouraged students to believe about the likelihood of locker searches. Thus, where school officials have expressly reserved the right to inspect, courts have not found an expectation of privacy, especially if the right has been exercised in the past.[20] If an expectation of privacy is found, analysis proceeds under the *New Jersey v T.L.O.* and *Vernonia School Dist 47J v Acton* standards, as in any other school search case.

In Ohio, RC 3313.20 expressly authorizes the board of education of any city, local, exempted village, or joint vocational school district to adopt a written policy authorizing principals (or their designees) to search any pupil's locker and its contents upon reasonable suspicion that the locker or its contents contains evidence of a pupil's violation of a criminal statute or a school rule, and/or to search any pupil's locker and its contents at any time if the board posts in a conspicuous place in each school building that has lockers available for pupil use a notice that the lockers are board property and that the lockers and their contents are subject to a random search without regard to whether there is a reasonable suspicion that evidence of a violation of a criminal statute or school rule will be obtained.[21] The adoption or failure to adopt such a written policy does not prevent the principal from searching any school locker and its contents if an emergency exists or appears to exist that imminently threatens the health or safety of any person or damage or destruction of prop-

---

[19] New Jersey v T.L.O., 469 US 325, 105 SCt 733, 83 LEd(2d) 720 (1985) expressly left this question open.

[20] Zamora v Pomeroy, 639 F(2d) 662 (10th Cir NM 1981); People v Overton, 24 NY(2d) 522, 301 NYS(2d) 479, 249 NE(2d) 366 (1969). But see State v Engerud, 463 A(2d) 934 (NJ 1983), reversed on other grounds by New Jersey v T.L.O., 469 US 325, 105 SCt 733, 83 LEd(2d) 720 (1985) (expectation of privacy found where school had no express policy reserving a right to inspect and had never searched lockers in the past).

[21] RC 3313.661(C) requires that the written policy be posted in a central location in each school subject to the policy and made available to pupils upon request.

erty under the board's control and if the search is reasonably necessary to avert that threat.

47.03 Liability for unlawful search

School officials are not immune from liability for an illegal search when they violate established rights of which they should have been aware. For example, the US Court of Appeals for the Seventh Circuit refused to afford immunity in connection with an unreasonable strip search of a thirteen-year-old girl.[22] On the other hand, immunity generally does apply as to issues, such as whether individualized suspicion is required, where the law is not clearly settled.[23]

---

[22] Doe v Renfrow, 631 F(2d) 91 (7th Cir Ind 1980), cert denied 451 US 1022, 101 SCt 3015, 69 LEd(2d) 395 (1981). For other examples of liability, see, e.g., Bilbrey v Brown, 738 F(2d) 1462 (9th Cir Or 1984); Picha v Wielgos, 410 FSupp 1214 (ND Ill 1976).

[23] Burnham v West, 681 FSupp 1160 (ED Va 1987). See also Text 46.15, Liability of board members, officers, and employees for civil rights violations.

NONPUBLIC SCHOOL SYSTEM

Chapter 48

Private and Parochial Schools

48.01	Private and parochial schools defined

STATE REGULATION

48.02	Right of private and parochial schools to exist
48.03	Minimum state standards for private and parochial schools
48.04	Compulsory school attendance, employment of minors
48.05	Annual progress reports to state department of education

STATE AID

48.06	State aid to parochial schools, constitutional limitations
48.07	Aid provided in Ohio
48.08	Transportation of private and parochial school students

ADMISSION TO PRIVATE SCHOOLS, RECORDS

48.09	Admission, nondiscrimination
48.10	Records upon admission
48.11	Enrollment contracts
48.12	Tuition: payment and recovery
48.13	Withholding transcript for nonpayment of tuition and fees
48.14	Inspection and release of student records

CONDUCT AND DISCIPLINE OF STUDENTS

48.15	Conduct and discipline in general
48.16	Private schools and the requirement of due process
48.17	Search and seizure
48.18	Freedom of speech and press

EMPLOYMENT

48.19	Employment of teaching and nonteaching personnel, generally
48.20	Verification of identity and work authorization
48.21	Teacher certification
48.22	Compensation, fringe benefits, retirement
48.23	Unemployment compensation, workers' compensation
48.24	Breach of employment contract
48.25	Dismissal of employee under contract
48.26	Dismissal of employee not under contract
48.27	Nonrenewal of contract
48.28	Collective bargaining

DISCRIMINATION BY PRIVATE AND PAROCHIAL SCHOOLS

48.29	Discrimination in programs and activities
48.30	Discrimination in employment

TAX EXEMPTION OF PRIVATE AND PAROCHIAL SCHOOLS

48.31	Federal tax-exempt status of nonpublic schools
48.32	Taxation of unrelated business income
48.33	Exemption from state taxes

LIABILITY

48.34	Tort liability of private schools, officers, and employees

ENVIRONMENTAL ISSUES

48.35	Asbestos in schools

STUDENT ATHLETE ELIGIBILITY

48.36	Ohio High School Athletic Association (OHSAA)

PARENT PROGRAMS

48.37	Block parent program

48.01 Private and parochial schools defined

(A) In general

A private school is an institution of learning organized and maintained by private individuals or a private corporation or organization. The governing body is most commonly a board of trustees, which appoints a school head to act as chief executive officer. As distinguished from a "public" or "common" school, a private school is administered by private individuals, not public school authorities, and is supported by private rather than state or federal funds.[1]

A parochial school is a private school maintained by a religious denomination to provide religious education in addition to the regular academic curriculum. Whenever a parochial school is involved in a legal issue, so also is religion, and the First

---

[1] 1933 OAG 1409.

Amendment to the US Constitution and the Ohio Constitution may come into play.

(B) Proprietary schools distinguished

The private schools discussed here are schools for which minimum standards are prescribed by the state board of education under RC 3301.07. There also exist certain proprietary institutions not subject to these standards. Typically, proprietary schools offer a curriculum specializing in vocational or technical training, such as secretarial skills and auto repair. They are governed by different provisions of the Ohio Revised Code,[2] are subject to the jurisdiction of the state board of school and college registration rather than the state department of education, and are not within the purview of this chapter.

STATE REGULATION

48.02 Right of private and parochial schools to exist

The legal right of nonpublic schools to exist in the United States has been questioned only once. After the state of Oregon passed a statute requiring all children to attend public schools, the US Supreme Court held such statutes unconstitutionally interfere with the fundamental liberty of parents to direct the upbringing and education of their children.[3]

Ohio statutes do not require that every child attend public school, but do require that every child, with certain limited exceptions, attend some recognized school—public, private, or parochial—so long as the school meets the secular educational requirements the state has the power to impose.[4]

48.03 Minimum state standards for private and parochial schools

(A) In general

While the right of private schools to exist is clear, there is also no doubt that the state may reasonably regulate these schools and their programs.[5]

RC 3301.07 directs the state board of education to formulate and prescribe minimum standards for all elementary and high schools. The minimum standards applicable to private schools are somewhat less restrictive than those applicable to public schools.[6]

If a private school fails to meet reasonable state standards, students would not be considered, under Ohio's compulsory education law, to be attending school, and their parents, guardians, or custodians would be subject to penalties.[7]

Under RC 3301.16, the state board of education is not to charter a nonpublic school, and is to revoke the charter of an already chartered nonpublic school, that does not participate in the testing program by July 1, 1995 established by RC 3301.0710(B). On and after September 15, 1998, no chartered nonpublic school may grant a high school diploma to a person who does not satisfy the criteria as to statewide proficiency testing spelled out in RC 3313.612.

(B) Requirement that standards be reasonable

To be constitutionally enforceable, minimum standards must be reasonable, and where the standards are so pervasive and all-encompassing that total compliance by a nonpublic school would effectively eradicate the distinction between public and nonpublic education, thereby depriving parents of their traditional interest in directing the upbringing and education of their children, the standards are unreason-

---

[2]RC Ch 3332.
[3]Pierce v Society of Sisters, 268 US 510, 45 SCt 571, 69 LEd 1070 (1925). See also, e.g., Honohan v Holt, 17 Misc 57, 244 NE(2d) 537 (CP, Franklin 1968).
[4]State v Hershberger, 103 App 188, 144 NE(2d) 693 (Hardin 1955). See generally RC Ch 3321; Text Ch 20, Pupils: Compulsory Education and School Attendance.

[5]See Text 32.02, Free exercise of religion and compulsory state educational standards. See also Validity of state regulation of curriculum and instruction in private schools, 18 ALR4th 649.
[6]See OAC 3301-35-01 et seq.
[7]RC Ch 3321. See also Text Ch 20, Pupils: Compulsory Education and School Attendance.

able and violate the parents' legitimate interests.[8]

48.04 Compulsory school attendance, employment of minors

(A) In general

The public school attendance officer is authorized to investigate cases of nonattendance at private or parochial schools in his district.[9] His obligation is to work in conjunction with any private or parochial school in enforcing compulsory education laws.[10]

(B) School calendar

RC 3321.07 requires private school hours and the term of attendance to be equivalent to those required of public schools in the district. RC 3313.48 allows classes to be dismissed for the number of hours in which parent-teacher conferences are held outside of regular school hours, whether or not dismissal is on the same day as the conferences.[11]

(C) Report of students in attendance

The chief administrator of a private school must report to the treasurer of the school district in which the nonpublic school is located the names, ages, and places of residence of all students under eighteen in attendance at the school, together with other facts as the treasurer may require to facilitate execution of laws relating to compulsory education and employment of minors. This report must be submitted within the first two weeks of the school year and must be updated within the first week of each subsequent school month of the year.[12]

(D) Age and schooling certificates

An employed child who has been granted an age and schooling certificate may attend a private school in lieu of a public part-time class or school if the terms and hours are substantially equivalent.[13] Age and schooling certificates are administered by the public school district.[14]

48.05 Annual progress reports to state department of education

The chief administrator of a private school must submit an annual report to the state board of education in a form prescribed by the board. The report requires evaluation of a different area of the administrative or educational program each year and is intended to act as the catalyst and guide for continuing self-evaluation.[15]

STATE AID

48.06 State aid to parochial schools, constitutional limitations

(A) Constitutional limitations, generally

Parochial schools educate substantial numbers of children at private expense and thereby ease the burden on the public purse. Because they are a significant part of the state's educational system, some argue they ought to receive at least some public financial aid. This raises serious issues under the First Amendment to the US Constitution, which generally prohibits the establishment of religion by the government. The issue has been heavily litigated, with only strictly secular aid provided in strictly neutral ways being allowed.

In *Wolman v Walter*,[16] the US Supreme Court upheld provisions of an Ohio statute which authorized the expenditure of public funds to supply nonpublic school students with textbooks, standardized testing and scoring services, diagnostic services, and therapeutic and remedial services, but struck down provisions pertaining to supplying instructional materials and equipment and field trip services on grounds such aid could be diverted to religious purposes.

---

[8]State v Whisner, 47 OS(2d) 181, 351 NE(2d) 750 (1976). See also State ex rel Nagle v Olin, 64 OS(2d) 341, 415 NE(2d) 279 (1980). In view of the Supreme Court's objections, the standards were later revised and made less restrictive. See Text 32.02, Free exercise of religion and compulsory state educational standards.

[9]RC 3321.07, RC 3321.16 et seq.

[10]RC 3321.16, RC 3321.17.
[11]OAG 85-015.
[12]RC 3321.12.
[13]RC 3321.09.
[14]See Text 20.11 to 20.17.
[15]See RC 3301.14.
[16]Wolman v Walter, 433 US 229, 97 SCt 2593, 53 LEd(2d) 714 (1977).

As a result, RC 3317.06 today outlines the procedures under which private schools can secure the constitutionally approved services.[17] The statute restricts the purchase and loan of equipment and materials to items incapable of diversion to religious use. Materials must be susceptible of loan to individual pupils and be furnished for the use of individual pupils. Also, the state will reimburse chartered nonpublic schools for the actual mandated service, administrative and clerical costs incurred in the preceding school year in preparing, maintaining, and filing reports, forms, and records, and in providing other administrative and clerical services that are not an integral part of the teaching process, as may be required by state law or rule or by requirements promulgated by school districts.[18] A *nonchartered*, non-tax-supported private school is not entitled to administrative cost reimbursement or auxiliary services.[19]

(B) Aid for testing and reporting

The US Supreme Court has upheld a New York statute providing direct cash reimbursement from state funds to nonpublic schools for state-required testing and reporting. The purpose was purely secular; the scheme did not advance religion nor did it foster excessive government entanglement with religion.[20] The case contains a caveat: "This is not to say that this case ... will furnish a litmus paper test to distinguish permissible from impermissible."[21]

(C) Teaching on parochial school premises

The significance of that caveat became abundantly clear in 1985, when the Court, in the companion cases of *Grand Rapids School District v Ball*[22] and *Aguilar v Felton*,[23] held certain programs involving local and federal aid to nonpublic schools unconstitutional.

In *Grand Rapids*, programs in which classes for nonpublic school students were financed by the public school system and taught by public school employees on nonpublic school premises were held to advance religion impermissibly in three ways: first, the teachers involved may intentionally or inadvertently become involved in inculcating particular religious beliefs; second, the programs may create a symbolic link between government and religion, giving students an impression of government support of their religious denomination; third, the programs directly promote religion by subsidizing the religious institutions involved.

In *Aguilar*, the Court held that using federal funds to pay the salaries of regular public school employees who provided remedial instruction and guidance services to parochial school students on the premises of parochial schools created an excessive entanglement of church and state, since the aid was provided in a pervasively sectarian environment, and since, with aid being provided in the form of teachers, ongoing public inspection was required to insure the absence of a religious message.

The Ohio department of education, beginning with the implementation of auxiliary services under RC 3317.06 in 1983, has required such teaching and guidance services as described in *Grand Rapids* and *Aguilar* to be off the premises of sectarian schools. One solution has been to provide services in specially equipped vans parked on the public street by the school, thereby being off the premises but still convenient to students. Therefore, the effect of these cases in Ohio has been negligible.[24]

---

[17]See also Wolman v Essex, No. C-2-75-792 (SD Ohio, 3-21-79) (upholding amended RC 3317.06); Walker v San Francisco Unified School Dist, 46 F(3d) 1449 (9th Cir Cal 1995) (holding loans of instructional materials and equipment to parochial schools had valid secular purpose under establishment clause).

[18]RC 3317.063.

[19]OAC 3301-35-08(H).

[20]Committee for Public Education & Religious Liberty v Regan, 444 US 646, 100 SCt 840, 63 LEd(2d) 94 (1980). See Text 32.01, Introduction, tests under First Amendment religion clauses.

[21]Committee for Public Education & Religious Liberty v Regan, 444 US 646, 100 SCt 840, 63 LEd(2d) 94 (1980).

[22]Grand Rapids School Dist v Ball, 473 US 373, 105 SCt 3216, 87 LEd(2d) 267 (1985).

[23]Aguilar v Felton, 473 US 402, 105 SCt 3232, 87 LEd(2d) 290 (1985).

[24]The provision of such services by mobile vans, whether parked on or off parochial school property, has been held constitutional. Pulido v Cavazos, 934 F(2d) 912 (8th Cir Mo 1991). See also Barnes v Cavazos, 966 F(2d) 1056 (6th Cir Ky 1992); Chicago

In a case arising under the Individuals with Disabilities Education Act, the US Supreme Court decided a sign language interpreter's presence at a parochial school for a profoundly deaf student did not violate the establishment clause of the First Amendment.[25]

(D) Aid to disadvantaged students

The Improving America's Schools Act of 1994 provides aid for disadvantaged students meeting federal guidelines.[26] Qualifying students in private or parochial schools may receive secular, neutral, and nonideological educational services and benefits.[27]

48.07 Aid provided in Ohio

Foundation program funds may be spent to provide the following materials and services to nonpublic schools under RC 3317.06:

(1) Secular textbooks;

(2) Speech and hearing diagnostic services;

(3) Health services;

(4) Diagnostic psychological services;

(5) Therapeutic psychological and speech and hearing services (to be provided off the premises of a sectarian school);

(6) Guidance and counseling services (to be provided off the premises of a sectarian school);

(7) Remedial services (to be provided off the premises of a sectarian school);

(8) Standardized tests and scoring services;

(9) Programs for handicapped children (to be provided off the premises of a sectarian school);

(10) Clerical and supervisory personnel to administer any authorized aid program; and

(11) Secular, neutral, nonideological mathematics equipment and materials.

48.08 Transportation of private and parochial school students

(A) Transportation at public expense

RC 3327.01 provides the conditions under which school districts must transport private school students to and from school. Generally, districts must transport private school students whenever they provide transportation for public school students of the same grade. Transportation need not be provided, however, if it would require more than a thirty-minute trip to the private school. Further exceptions are treated in the statute.[28]

Boards of education must establish by reliable and substantial evidence that transportation for nonpublic school children is unreasonable and impractical before payment can be made to parents in lieu of transportation.[29]

Students attending a *nonchartered* private school are not entitled to transportation at public cost.[30]

Bd of Ed v Alexander, 983 F(2d) 745 (7th Cir Ill 1992); Walker v San Francisco Unified School Dist, 46 F(3d) 1449 (9th Cir Cal 1995) (temporary parking of mobile vans on parochial grounds to provide remedial services to children did not promote religion or create symbolic union between church and state where vans were never used by school personnel, and classes were taught by nonparochial teachers).

[25]Zobrest v Catalina Foothills School Dist, ___ US ___, 113 SCt 2462, 125 LEd(2d) 1 (1993). *Zobrest* rejected a federal appeals court declaration that a cued speech interpreter for a deaf child at a private religious school would be unconstitutional. Goodall v Stafford County School Bd, 930 F(2d) 363 (4th Cir Va 1991), cert denied 502 US 864, 112 SCt 188, 116 LEd(2d) 149 (1991).

[26]20 USCA 6301 to 20 USCA 6514.

[27]20 USCA 6321. Services to private school children should be equitable in comparison to services for public school children.

[28]See Hartley v Berlin-Milan Local School Dist, 69 OS(2d) 415, 433 NE(2d) 171 (1982); Shafer v Southwest Licking Local School Dist Bd of Ed, No. CA-2896, 1982 WL 5638 (5th Dist Ct App, Licking, 12-28-82); Text 22.03, Transportation of pupils generally. See also Pushay v Walter, 18 OS(3d) 315, 18 OBR 361, 481 NE(2d) 575 (1985) (discussion of department of education criteria for determining whether transportation of nonpublic students is unnecessary or unreasonable).

[29]Pushay v Walter, 18 OS(3d) 315, 18 OBR 361, 481 NE(2d) 575 (1985).

[30]OAC 3301-35-08(H), OAC 3301-39-01.

(B) Transportation by school

Private schools transporting students to or from a school function must insure that a vehicle used for carrying more than nine passengers satisfies state and federal "school bus" laws and regulations.[31] Failure to be in compliance could have an effect upon school liability and liability insurance in case of accident and injury.

No school may purchase, lease, or rent a new school bus unless the bus has an occupant restraining device, as defined in RC 4513.263, installed for use in its operator's seat. Vans also require front seat restraining devices for driver and passengers which must be used while the vehicle is in operation.[32]

ADMISSION TO PRIVATE SCHOOLS, RECORDS

48.09 Admission, nondiscrimination

(A) In general

Private schools may, in general, use whatever criteria they choose in admitting students. The relationship between school and student is generally based on contract rather than constitutional or statutory law.[33]

However, the US Supreme Court has held that 42 USCA 1981 prohibits private schools from excluding children solely because of race.[34] Moreover, if a private school wishes to maintain tax-exempt status, it must follow IRS guidelines for nondiscriminatory admissions.[35]

The department of education requires any chartered or state-approved nonpublic school to demonstrate, consistent with the criteria and procedures set forth in OAC 3301-39-01 et seq., that it has adopted and implemented racially nondiscriminatory policies in recruitment, admissions, employment, scholarships, loans, fee waivers, educational programs, athletics, and extracurricular activities, and that the school is not an alternative designed to avoid desegregation in the public schools. Failure to comply leads to revocation of the charter or withdrawal of approval. In addition, pupil transportation auxiliary services are not available.

(B) Post-secondary options program

Students in nonpublic schools may participate in the state post-secondary enrollment options program if the chief administrator of the school notifies the department of education by April 1 prior to the school year in which the school's students will participate. The program is essentially the same as for public schools.[36]

48.10 Records upon admission

On admission, a student must present a birth certificate (or alternative document as authorized by RC 3313.672), and within twenty-four hours a school official must request the student's official records from the public or nonpublic elementary or secondary school he most recently attended. If the school states that it has no record of the student's attendance, or the records are not received within fourteen days of the request, or if the student does not present a birth certificate (or alternative authorized document), the head of the school must notify the law enforcement agency with jurisdiction in the area where the student resides of this fact and of the possibility that the student may be a missing child.[37] RC 3313.672 also requires a residential parent to whom an order or decree allocating parental rights and responsibilities for the care of a child and designating a residential parent and legal custody of a child (including a temporary or modified order or decree) is issued in connection with the breakup of a marriage to furnish a certified copy of the order or decree to the school's admissions officer (upon a pupil's initial entry to school, a copy of any already

---

[31] See RC 4511.01 et seq.; 49 USCA 30101 et seq.
[32] RC 4511.772.
[33] See Am Jur 2d: 15, Civil Rights § 82.
[34] Runyon v McCrary, 427 US 160, 96 SCt 2586, 49 LEd(2d) 415 (1976).
[35] Bob Jones University v Johnson, 396 FSupp 597 (D SC 1974), affirmed by 529 F(2d) 514 (4th Cir SC 1975).
[36] RC 3365.01 to RC 3365.10. See generally Text 26.07(C), Post-secondary enrollment options program.
[37] RC 3313.672.

existing order or decree must be furnished). If, at the time of initial entry to school, the child is under the care of a shelter for victims of domestic violence, the statute requires the pupil or parent to notify the school of that fact and the school, upon being so informed, must inform the elementary or secondary school from which it requests the pupil's records of that fact.

One court has rejected a tort challenge to a school's decision to register a student under her birth certificate name (to comply with RC 3313.672) rather than the father's surname.[38]

48.11 Enrollment contracts

(A) Contents

The enrollment contract between the school and parents should be in writing and should contain provisions reflecting the following:

(1) Agreement as to the period of enrollment, usually one year;

(2) Tuition to be charged and the time for payment, together with action that may be taken for failure to pay;

(3) That withdrawal of the student at any time, whether as a result of accident, sickness, disciplinary action, or otherwise, does not obviate responsibility for the entire year's tuition;

(4) Right to withhold the student's transcript if all tuition, fees, and charges have not been paid;

(5) Agreement by parents and the student to adhere to rules stated in the student handbook, the school catalog, and other school publications; and

(6) Other matters the school wishes to include.

(B) Interpretation

Contracts for education are generally construed so as to leave the school sufficient discretion to properly exercise its educational responsibilities. Implicit is the student's agreement to comply with the school's regulations—which the school clearly is entitled to modify. To state a claim against the school with regard to the enrollment contract, one must show evidence of a violated contractual right, or improper motivation or irrational action on the part of the school.[39]

An enrollment contract expressly for one year only does not bind a secondary school to provide a four-year curriculum to the incoming students.[40]

Where a parent and child fully satisfied prerequisites to continued enrollment stated in a parent-student handbook and were in compliance with academic and conduct requirements, the school could not refuse admission for the upcoming year.[41]

Express provisions relating to responsibility for the entire year's tuition have been upheld, and an express liquidated damages provision will generally be enforced.[42]

48.12 Tuition: payment and recovery

Tuition is not governed by statute but by the enrollment contract. Generally, where a contract is for a specified period for which a definite payment is to be made, and there is no stipulation for a deduction or refund in the event of inability to attend, the entire amount becomes payable, regardless of nonattendance by the student for part or all of the time.[43] However, the full amount is not due where the student is unable to attend or forced to withdraw because of illness.[44] Under a school reservation agreement, where the parent is given the option to cancel by a date certain without liability for full tuition, the parent who

---

[38]Howell v Higher, No. 86AP-458, 1986 WL 11297 (10th Dist Ct App, Franklin, 10-9-86).

[39]See Jansen v Emory University, 440 FSupp 1060 (ND Ga 1977), affirmed by 579 F(2d) 45 (5th Cir Ga 1978); Mahavongsanan v Hall, 529 F(2d) 448 (5th Cir Ga 1976); Giles v Howard University, 428 FSupp 603 (D DC 1977); Am Jur 2d: 68, Schools § 315.

[40]Save Immaculata v Immaculata Preparatory School, Inc, 514 A(2d) 1152 (DC App 1986).

[41]VanLoock v Curran, 489 So(2d) 525 (Ala 1986).

[42]See, e.g., Moyse v Runnels School Inc, 457 So(2d) 767 (La App 1984).

[43]See Am Jur 2d: 68, Schools § 312. Absence from or inability to attend school as affecting liability for payment of tuition, 20 ALR4th 303.

[44]Groff v Hertenstein, 12 CC(NS) 515, 21 CD 633 (Hamilton 1910).

does not timely cancel is generally liable for the full amount.[45]

Judicial enforcement of a separation agreement requiring a noncustodial parent to pay tuition for his children's education at a religiously oriented school does not amount to unconstitutional state support of the school.[46]

48.13 Withholding transcript for nonpayment of tuition and fees

In general, a private school can provide in the enrollment contract for withholding a student's transcript if all tuition, fees, and charges have not been paid in full. RC 3313.642, which allows public boards of education to withhold grades and credits of pupils who have not paid supplemental charges or who have not paid for damages to school property, inferentially supports this conclusion.

In a case where parents have filed for bankruptcy, however, a court has held that failure to provide a transcript because of a past-due tuition bill violates the US Bankruptcy Code.[47]

48.14 Inspection and release of student records

Under the Family Educational Rights and Privacy Act of 1974,[48] no federal funds can be made available to any educational institution which has a policy of denying, or which effectively prevents, the parents of students the right to inspect and review the educational records of their children.[49] If a private school receives no federal aid, it is not subject to the Act. If a private school receives federal aid, just what type of aid will bring the school within the Act's purview is still unsettled.[50]

Most private schools, whether or not technically subject to the Act, have adopted policies that generally reflect the spirit of the Act.[51] Ohio's Student Privacy Act, RC 3319.321, enacted in response to the federal statute, refers only to student records in public schools and does not apply to private schools.

If a private school is not subject to the Act, only a parent who has contracted for the education of the child is entitled to review student records made available by the school. Permission of the contracting parent should be sought before allowing a noncontracting parent to review information.

If a third party requests records of a student, the school should notify the parents or adult student and first gain permission to release the records. If permission is not given, the school should refuse to release the records except under a court order.[52] Even then the school must make a reasonable effort to notify the parents or adult student of the order in advance of compliance.

Private schools subject to the Act may not forward personal information regarding the use of drugs or alcohol by a student on school property to local law enforcement agencies unless the information is lawfully ordered by a court, subpoenaed, or the school obtains consent of the parent or student, where appropriate.[53]

CONDUCT AND DISCIPLINE OF STUDENTS

48.15 Conduct and discipline in general

The Ohio statutes governing discipline of public school students generally do not apply in private schools.[54] The power to

---

[45]Lake Ridge Academy v Carney, 66 OS(3d) 376, 613 NE(2d) 183 (1993).
[46]In re Landis, 5 App(3d) 22, 5 OBR 24, 448 NE(2d) 845 (Franklin 1982).
[47]In re Dembek, 64 Bankr 745 (ND Ohio 1986).
[48]20 USCA 1232g. See generally Text 44.14 to 44.21.
[49]See Text 44.14 to 44.21.
[50]See, for guidance, 34 CFR Part 99.
[51]See Text 44.14 to 44.21.

[52]See 34 CFR 99.31(a)(9).
[53]OAG 87-010. See also OAG 90-099.
[54]With specific reference to corporal punishment, RC 3319.41 authorizes a nonpublic school teacher, principal, or administrator to administer reasonable corporal punishment if reasonably necessary to preserve discipline unless the governing authority of the school provides otherwise. The statute goes on to permit these employees and noncertificated employees and school bus drivers, within the scope of their

discipline in private schools arises out of the parties' contractual relationship. Typically, parents and students agree to abide by school rules, and violation subjects the student to disciplinary action. At the same time, the school impliedly warrants that enforcement of rules will be reasonable and not arbitrary or capricious.

Historically, private schools have had broad discretion in making and enforcing rules, and courts will not interfere absent a clear abuse of discretion or some fundamental unfairness.[55] The question is whether school authorities acted with the prudence, discretion, and fairness generally exercised by persons in similar circumstances. Courts will not simply substitute their judgment for that of the administration.

In the case of dismissal on academic rather than disciplinary grounds, courts will not intervene unless a dismissal is clearly arbitrary and capricious.[56] A student who challenges a grade must show arbitrariness, capriciousness, or bad faith in the grading procedure or system.[57]

A diploma may be revoked for good cause (e.g., fraud, deceit, or error) after affording a fair hearing.[58]

RC 3707.50 requires the posting of anabolic steroid warnings in the locker rooms of all privately owned athletic facilities. The text of the prescribed warning appears in RC 3707.50(B).

48.16 Private schools and the requirement of due process

Because private school disciplinary proceedings do not involve state action, the due process guarantees of the Fourteenth Amendment are not triggered.[59]

48.17 Search and seizure

A search in a private school setting will be judged on whether it was reasonable under the contract of enrollment and the rules of the school. There is no state action to trigger the Fourth Amendment's protection against unreasonable searches and seizures.[60] While private schools are thus not held to the requirements that apply in public schools, these guidelines are helpful.[61]

48.18 Freedom of speech and press

Freedom of expression is generally not a constitutional issue in private schools. It is helpful, though not controlling, to examine the US Supreme Court's handling of these issues in the public schools.[62]

EMPLOYMENT

48.19 Employment of teaching and nonteaching personnel, generally

Ohio statutes governing the employment of teaching and nonteaching personnel

---

employment, to use and apply such force and restraint as is reasonable and necessary to quell a disturbance threatening physical injury to others, to obtain the possession of weapons or other dangerous objects from students, for self-defense, or to protect persons or property.

[55] E.g., Allen v Casper, 87 App(3d) 338, 622 NE(2d) 367 (Cuyahoga 1993); Geraci v St. Xavier High School, 13 OO(3d) 146 (App, Hamilton 1978), cert denied 444 US 839, 100 SCt 76, 62 LEd(2d) 50 (1979); Schopprelei v Franklin University, 11 App(2d) 60, 228 NE(2d) 334 (Franklin 1967). See also Wisch v Sanford School, Inc, 420 FSupp 1310 (D Del 1976) (history of the law on this subject).

[56] Morin v Cleveland Metro School of Nursing, 34 App(3d) 19, 516 NE(2d) 1257 (Cuyahoga 1986).

[57] Johnson v Cuyahoga County Community College, 29 Misc(2d) 33, 29 OBR 371, 489 NE(2d) 1088 (CP, Cuyahoga 1985).

[58] See Waliga v Kent State University Bd of Trustees, 22 OS(3d) 55, 22 OBR 74, 488 NE(2d) 850 (1986).

[59] Geraci v St. Xavier High School, 13 OO(3d) 146 (App, Hamilton 1978), cert denied 444 US 839, 100 SCt 76, 62 LEd(2d) 50 (1979). See also Rendell-Baker v Kohn, 457 US 830, 102 SCt 2764, 73 LEd(2d) 418 (1982) (discussing threshold requirement of state action with regard to private schools).

[60] See Rendell-Baker v Kohn, 457 US 830, 102 SCt 2764, 73 LEd(2d) 418 (1982).

[61] See Text Ch 47, Search and Seizure.

[62] See Text 25.03, Policy on student conduct; Text 25.05, Regulating student expression.

generally do not apply to private schools. These schools have wide discretion as to whom to employ so long as antidiscrimination laws are not violated.[63] Laws applicable to criminal background checks generally do apply to chartered nonpublic schools, however.[64]

Teachers and administrators are normally hired by written contract, and the contract should contain at minimum the compensation, duties to be performed, and term of employment. A mere letter not meant to be an offer of employment does not constitute an offer.[65] Similarly, a survey wherein the school requested a teacher to disclose whether she wished to continue for the following year was not an offer of employment and, when returned with the indication she would like to return, did not become a binding contract.[66]

48.20 Verification of identity and work authorization

The Immigration Reform and Control Act of 1986[67] requires that employers verify the identity and work authorization of all new employees within five business days of hiring. It is unlawful knowingly to hire an unauthorized alien or fail to verify that the individual is authorized to work in the United States.[68]

The employer has certain recordkeeping requirements and is subject to civil and criminal penalties for violations.

The Act prohibits discrimination on the basis of "national origin" or "citizenship status" when hiring, firing, or recruiting.[69]

48.21 Teacher certification

Private school administrators and teachers must be certified by the state board of education in accordance with RC 3301.071.

48.22 Compensation, fringe benefits, retirement

Compensation and fringe benefits in private schools are not subject to state statutes that specifically govern public school employees. They are generally governed by contract, subject to federal and state minimum wage, overtime, equal pay, and recordkeeping requirements.[70]

The federal Employee Retirement Income Security Act[71] comprehensively regulates employee benefit plans, and most private schools are subject to its provisions.

48.23 Unemployment compensation, workers' compensation

Employees in nonpublic schools are eligible for unemployment compensation. Private schools must elect either to self-insure or agree to participate in the state program and pay the mandated amount each year. Most schools have elected to become self-insurers, but a private school should review the matter carefully.[72]

Ohio's workers' compensation laws are generally applicable to private schools.[73]

---

[63] See Text Ch 17, Equal Employment Opportunity, Family and Medical Leave.

[64] See Text 5.09(H), Criminal background checks.

[65] Braun v Glade Valley School, Inc, 77 NC App 83, 334 SE(2d) 404 (1985).

[66] Knipmeyer v Diocese of Alexandria, 492 So(2d) 550 (La App 1986).

[67] Codified, in pertinent part, at 8 USCA 1324a, 8 USCA 1324b. See also 8 CFR Part 274.

[68] See generally *Immigration and Reform Control Act: New Problems for Educational Employers*, 38 West's Ed Law Rptr 1143 (1987).

[69] 8 USCA 1324b.

[70] 29 USCA 206, 29 USCA 207; RC 4111.02, RC 4111.03, RC 4111.08. That the federal requirements may be applied to parochial schools is affirmed in Dole v Shenandoah Baptist Church, 899 F(2d) 1389 (4th Cir Va 1990), cert denied 498 US 846, 111 SCt 131, 112 LEd(2d) 99 (1990), and DeArment v Harvey, 932 F(2d) 721 (8th Cir Ark 1991).

[71] 29 USCA 1001 et seq.

[72] For treatment of Ohio's unemployment compensation law, see Text Ch 15, Unemployment Compensation.

[73] For extended treatment, see Text Ch 16, Workers' Compensation, Occupational Safety and Health.

48.24 Breach of employment contract

(A) In general

If a teacher breaches his employment contract, the school's damages generally include the added expense of finding a replacement and any salary difference necessary to procure the replacement. The school is obligated to mitigate damages and use "due diligence" in finding a replacement.

If a school wishes to terminate a teacher prior to completion of the contract, it may do so by simply paying the remaining compensation due under the contract. The teacher has no right to specific performance of the contract so long as no laws against discrimination are violated.[74]

If the school breaches the contract by hiring another for the same position or refusing to allow the teacher to perform according to the contract, the teacher is entitled to damages but is also obligated to mitigate damages by using "due diligence" in seeking another position.[75]

(B) Breach induced by third party

Where a teacher breaches the contract by taking another position for the same time period, the school has a tort action against the third party who induced the breach of contract, if the third party knew of the contract. This action for tortious interference is an effective means of discouraging personnel raids by other schools. Again, the measure of damages is the loss actually suffered by the school. For discussion of the elements of the tort of inducement of breach of contract, see *Cincinnati Bengals, Inc v Bergey*.[76]

48.25 Dismissal of employee under contract

An employer may, without liability, discharge an employee during the term of the employment contract for good cause.[77]

48.26 Dismissal of employee not under contract

In general, an employer may discharge an employee not under contract at any time, for any cause or no cause, without liability, barring violation of antidiscrimination laws.[78] The Ohio Supreme Court upheld this employment-at-will doctrine by declaring an employee discharged for reporting to his employer that it was unlawfully conducting business could not sue for wrongful discharge.[79] However, an exception to the doctrine exists where an employee is discharged or disciplined in violation of a clear public policy.[80] Moreover, the facts and circumstances surrounding a particular case may alter an employee's at-will status, and if an employer's representations or promises induce an employee to take action (or not take action) in reliance on what the employer said, the doctrine of promissory estoppel may insulate the employee from discharge.[81] A court, however, will not imply a covenant of good faith and fair dealing with an at-will employee.[82] A supervisor's assurance that one's job is secure if attendance improves does not

---

[74] Felch v Findlay College, 119 App 357, 200 NE(2d) 353 (Hancock 1963) (citing cases supporting rule that specific performance of a personal service contract will not be compelled).

[75] For the issue of breach of contract for personal services and damages, see CJS: 25, Damages § 79. For the duty to mitigate damages, see CJS: 25, Damages § 34.

[76] Cincinnati Bengals, Inc v Bergey, 453 FSupp 129 (SD Ohio 1974). See also CJS: 86, Torts § 44; Am Jur 2d: 45, Interference § 3.

[77] Hosking v Hollaender Mfg Co, 114 App 70, 175 NE(2d) 201 (Hamilton 1961).

[78] Henkel v Educational Research Council of America, 45 OS(2d) 249, 344 NE(2d) 118 (1976); Fawcett v G.C. Murphy & Co, 46 OS(2d) 245, 348 NE(2d) 144 (1976); Evely v Carlon Co, 4 OS(3d) 163, 4 OBR 404, 447 NE(2d) 1290 (1983).

[79] Phung v Waste Management, Inc, 23 OS(3d) 100, 23 OBR 260, 491 NE(2d) 1114 (1986).

[80] Greeley v Miami Valley Maintenance Contractors, Inc, 49 OS(3d) 228, 551 NE(2d) 981 (1990); Shaffer v Frontrunner, Inc, 57 App(3d) 18, 566 NE(2d) 193 (Defiance 1990). The "clear public policy" need not necessarily be based on statutory law; it may be discerned from other sources such as constitutions, administrative regulations, and common law. Painter v Graley, 70 OS(3d) 377, 639 NE(2d) 51 (1994).

[81] See Mers v Dispatch Printing Co, 19 OS(3d) 100, 19 OBR 261, 483 NE(2d) 150 (1985). A promise of future benefits or opportunities without a specific promise of continued employment will not support a promissory estoppel exception. Wing v Anchor Media, Ltd of Texas, 59 OS(3d) 108, 570 NE(2d) 1095 (1991).

[82] Kuhn v St. John and West Shore Hospital, 50 App(3d) 23, 552 NE(2d) 240 (Cuyahoga 1989).

imply a contract that discharge may only be for just cause.[83]

Employment manuals, handbooks, or other policies and practices may limit the employment-at-will doctrine.[84] The Ohio Supreme Court has held a disclaimer in a manual or handbook stating employment is at will effectively shields the employer absent fraud in the inducement.[85]

48.27 Nonrenewal of contract

Most employment contracts in private schools are for a definite term and terminate without action by either the school or the individual. The individual has no right to a hearing or explanation of the decision not to renew. In one case, involving a teacher not renewed largely because of grading practices, the court held that the teacher had no right to a contract for the following year.[86] Constitutional issues are not present, as there is no state action to bring Fourteenth Amendment considerations to bear.[87]

48.28 Collective bargaining

(A) In general

Ohio has no collective bargaining law applicable to private schools. At the federal level, the National Labor Relations Act[88] can come into play. While many private schools are potentially subject to the Act, the National Labor Relations Board has been reluctant to exercise jurisdiction over them.[89]

The US Supreme Court has held that members of a private university faculty exercising absolute authority in academic matters are managerial employees excluded from coverage of the Act.[90]

(B) Parochial schools

Teachers in church-run schools are not covered by the Act, precluding NLRB jurisdiction.[91]

DISCRIMINATION BY PRIVATE AND PAROCHIAL SCHOOLS

48.29 Discrimination in programs and activities

A number of federal statutes prohibit discrimination by recipients of federal financial assistance, principally Title VI of the Civil Rights Act of 1964, Title IX of the Education Amendments of 1972, and the Rehabilitation Act of 1973. The Individuals with Disabilities Education Act generally applies to private schools only where they contract with public schools or agencies to provide services for children with disabilities.[92]

Title III of the Americans with Disabilities Act of 1990[93] applies to all private entities whose operations affect commerce, including private schools,[94] and broadly prohibits discrimination by a covered private entity on the basis of a person's disability with respect to the full and equal enjoyment of goods, services, facilities, privileges, advantages, or accommoda-

---

[83] Boggs v Avon Products, Inc, 56 App(3d) 67, 564 NE(2d) 1128 (Butler 1990).

[84] See, e.g., Hanly v Riverside Methodist Hospital, 78 App(3d) 73, 603 NE(2d) 1126 (Franklin 1991); Adams v Harding Machine Co, 56 App(3d) 150, 565 NE(2d) 858 (Logan 1989); Helle v Landmark, Inc, 15 App(3d) 1, 15 OBR 22, 472 NE(2d) 765 (Lucas 1984); Hedrick v Center for Comprehensive Alcoholism Treatment, 7 App(3d) 211, 7 OBR 272, 454 NE(2d) 1343 (Hamilton 1982).

[85] Wing v Anchor Media, Ltd of Texas, 59 OS(3d) 108, 570 NE(2d) 1095 (1991). See also Belt v Roadway Express Co, 83 App(3d) 706, 615 NE(2d) 702 (Summit 1992); Handler v Merrill Lynch Life Agency, Inc, 92 App(3d) 356, 635 NE(2d) 1271 (Franklin 1993), appeal dismissed by 69 OS(3d) 1213, 633 NE(2d) 1135 (1994).

[86] Arons v Society of Mary, No. CA 9494, 1986 WL 6328 (2d Dist Ct App, Montgomery, 6-4-86).

[87] For discussion of state action and private schools, see Geraci v St. Xavier High School, 13 OO(3d) 146 (App, Hamilton 1978), cert denied 444 US 839, 100 SCt 76, 62 LEd(2d) 50 (1979).

[88] 29 USCA 151 et seq.

[89] For discussion of the jurisdictional issue, see Shattuck School, 189 NLRB 886 (1971); Am Jur 2d: 48, Labor and Labor Relations § 646.

[90] NLRB v Yeshiva University, 444 US 672, 100 SCt 856, 63 LEd(2d) 115 (1980).

[91] NLRB v Catholic Bishop of Chicago, 440 US 490, 99 SCt 1313, 59 LEd(2d) 533 (1979).

[92] These subjects are treated in Text 19.13, Discrimination by recipients of federal financial assistance; Text Ch 28, Education for Children with Disabilities.

[93] 42 USCA 12101 et seq. See generally Text 17.13(B), Americans with Disabilities Act of 1990.

[94] 42 USCA 12181.

tions.[95] Title III expressly does not apply, however, to religious organizations or entities controlled by religious organizations.[96]

48.30 Discrimination in employment

Title VII of the Civil Rights Act of 1964, as amended, and Ohio's Fair Employment Practices Act prohibit discrimination in employment because of race, color, religion, sex, or national origin. The Family and Medical Leave Act of 1993 applies to private schools who meet the requirements of 29 USCA 2611. Title IX of the Education Amendments of 1972 prohibits sex discrimination in employment in any education program or activity receiving federal financial assistance.[97] Title IX applies to private schools only if the school receives such federal aid.[98] The Equal Pay Act prohibits discrimination on the basis of sex with regard to pay for equal work.[99] The Age Discrimination in Employment Act and Ohio law prohibit age discrimination in employment.[100]

Under Title VII, a religious educational institution may employ only employees of a particular religion or whose conduct conforms to a religion's particular mores.[101] Ohio law contains no such provision. It is necessary to receive certification of a bona fide occupational qualification from the Ohio Civil Rights Commission in advance, if religion of an employee is to be part of the job qualification.[102]

Title I of the Americans with Disabilities Act of 1990 broadly proscribes discrimination in employment on the basis of disability.[103] While private schools are subject to the Act generally, a parochial school expressly is permitted to give preference in employment to persons of a particular religion or require that applicants and employees conform to the school's religious tenets.[104]

TAX EXEMPTION OF PRIVATE AND PAROCHIAL SCHOOLS

48.31 Federal tax-exempt status of nonpublic schools

26 USCA 501(c)(3) grants tax exemption to qualifying nonpublic schools. To qualify, a school must satisfy the nondiscriminatory requirements set by IRS Revenue Procedure 75-50. The school must not discriminate on the basis of race, color, or national and ethnic origin in the administration of its educational policies, admissions policies, scholarship and loan programs, and athletic and other school-administered programs. Among other things, nondiscriminatory statements must be published in any pamphlet, catalog, or recruiting publication; advertising of the nondiscriminatory policy is required annually; reporting procedures are enumerated;

---

[95]42 USCA 12182.

[96]42 USCA 12187.

[97]These subjects are treated in Text Ch 17, Equal Employment Opportunity, Family and Medical Leave; Text 19.14, Sex discrimination in education.

[98]North Haven Bd of Ed v Bell, 456 US 512, 102 SCt 1912, 72 LEd(2d) 299 (1982). See also 34 CFR 106.51 et seq.

[99]For applicability of the Act to nonpublic schools, see Dole v Shenandoah Baptist Church, 899 F(2d) 1389 (4th Cir Va 1990), cert denied 498 US 846, 111 SCt 131, 112 LEd(2d) 99 (1990); Horner v Mary Institute, 613 F(2d) 706 (8th Cir Mo 1980); EEOC v Tree of Life Christian Schools, 751 FSupp 700 (SD Ohio 1990); EEOC v First Baptist Church, No. S91-179M, 1992 WL 247584 (ND Ind 6-8-92). For general treatment of the Act, see Text Ch 17, Equal Employment Opportunity, Family and Medical Leave.

[100]See generally Text 17.06, Age discrimination. For applicability of the ADEA to parochial schools, see Geary v Visitation of Blessed Virgin Mary Parish School, 7 F(3d) 324 (3d Cir Pa 1993); DeMarco v Holy Cross High School, 4 F(3d) 166 (2d Cir NY 1993); Powell v Stafford, 859 FSupp 1343 (D Colo 1994).

[101]See 42 USCA 2000e-2, 42 USCA 2000e-1. See also Little v Wuerl, 929 F(2d) 944 (3d Cir Pa 1991); Elbaz v Congregation Beth Judea, Inc, 812 FSupp 802 (ND Ill 1992); Vigars v Valley Christian Center of Dublin, California, 805 FSupp 802 (ND Cal 1992); Boyd v Harding Academy of Memphis, Inc, 887 FSupp 157 (D Tenn 1995). But see EEOC v Kamehameha Schools/Bishop Estate, 990 F(2d) 458 (9th Cir Haw 1993), cert denied ___ US ___, 114 SCt 439, 126 LEd(2d) 372 (1993).

[102]RC 4112.02.

[103]In addition, Section 504 of the Rehabilitation Act of 1973 generally proscribes discrimination against the handicapped by a recipient of federal funding. Ohio's Fair Employment Practices Act also proscribes discrimination against the handicapped. See Text 17.13, Discrimination against the handicapped.

[104]42 USCA 12101, 42 USCA 12113(c).

and record-keeping requirements are detailed.[105]

The US Supreme Court has held that 26 USCA 501(c)(3) prohibits tax-exempt status for private schools having a racially discriminatory policy.[106]

48.32 Taxation of unrelated business income

Unrelated business income is not exempt under federal tax laws, and schools that rent their facilities to outsiders or administer auxiliary income-producing programs should note that such income must be reported on IRS Form 990-T. Schools should determine their tax liabilities under both state and federal statutes.[107]

48.33 Exemption from state taxes

RC 5739.02 generally exempts private schools from sales tax on food sold to students in a cafeteria or dormitory.

Under RC 5709.07, RC 5709.12, and RC 5709.121, property belonging to a private school may be exempt from taxation depending on its use. All buildings and lands used with reasonable certainty in furthering the necessary objects and purposes of an academy or college, including the president's residence, and not used with a view to profit, are exempt by RC 5709.07.[108]

The Ohio Supreme Court has held that where a headmaster's house, located on campus, was used to entertain guests of the school and for school and alumni meetings, the residence was being used with reasonable certainty in furthering the objects and purposes of the school.[109]

The Court has also ruled that real property owned by an independent school was not exempt from property tax where a two-story frame house on the lot was used for a "clothing exchange." The Court rejected an argument that the property was maintained "for use in furtherance of or incidental to [the school's] charitable, educational, or public purposes" which would have triggered an exemption under RC 5709.121(B).[110]

LIABILITY

48.34 Tort liability of private schools, officers, and employees

(A) In general

Prior to August 1, 1984, Ohio law held that a charitable or "eleemosynary" institution, other than one which has as its purpose the maintenance and operation of a hospital, is not liable for tortious injury except (1) when the injured person is not a beneficiary of the institution, and (2) when a beneficiary suffers harm as a result of failure of the institution to exercise due care in selection or retention of an employee.[111]

But, in 1984, the Ohio Supreme Court abolished the doctrine of charitable immunity and held that a charitable organization (e.g., a private school) is liable in tort to the same extent as any other person or corporation.[112]

In general, a school has a duty to make the campus safe for students. In cases of injury, the issue revolves around issues of foreseeability, proximate cause, and whether the school exercised reasonable

---

[105] *Tax Exempt Status of Private Schools*, 34 West's Ed Law Rptr 329 (1987).

[106] Bob Jones University v United States, 461 US 574, 103 SCt 2017, 76 LEd(2d) 157 (1983). See also *Tax Exempt Status of Private Schools*, 34 West's Ed Law Rptr 329 (1987).

[107] See 26 USCA 511 et seq.; RC 5709.04.

[108] Denison University v Board of Tax Appeals, 2 OS(2d) 17, 205 NE(2d) 896 (1965).

[109] Miami Valley School v Kinney, 69 OS(2d) 134, 431 NE(2d) 335 (1982). With regard to houses used as living quarters by employees of private schools, see Denison University v Board of Tax Appeals, 2 OS(2d) 17, 205 NE(2d) 896 (1965); Cincinnati Nature Center Assn v Board of Tax Appeals, 48 OS(2d) 122, 357 NE(2d) 381 (1976); Tax exemption of property of educational body as extending to property used by personnel as living quarters, 55 ALR2d 485.

[110] Seven Hills Schools v Kinney, 28 OS(3d) 186, 28 OBR 275, 503 NE(2d) 163 (1986).

[111] Gibbon v YWCA of Hamilton, 170 OS 280, 164 NE(2d) 563 (1960).

[112] Albritton v Neighborhood Centers Assn for Child Development, 12 OS(3d) 210, 12 OBR 295, 466 NE(2d) 867 (1984).

care in providing for security or in the maintenance and upkeep of its physical plant.[113] A licensee (one who enters the premises not by invitation but for his own personal pleasure or benefit) may not recover except for willful or wanton misconduct or an affirmative act of negligence.[114]

A university student who voluntarily joins the lacrosse team is not the agent of the university, and the university is not liable to a third-party student injured by that player in a game.[115]

A private school is protected from liability that results from any asbestos abatement project as long as the school hired properly licensed and certified asbestos abatement contractors and evaluation specialists.[116]

(B) Tort liability of private school employees

Employees of private schools have been found personally liable for their own negligence in school-related activities.[117] Note that a nonprofit charitable corporation can indemnify its officers and employees in order to further insulate them from liability over and above the school's insurance coverage. Whether the trustees should do so is a corporate business decision.[118]

(C) Tort liability of trustees of private schools

Trustees of private schools organized as not-for-profit corporations may possibly be subject to personal liability in the operation of the schools. Many schools have purchased trustee liability insurance.

The general assembly recently insulated trustees of private schools by conferring qualified immunities from civil liability in tort on uncompensated volunteers of nonprofit charitable organizations.[119] Note also that a nonprofit corporation can indemnify its trustees in order to further insulate them from personal liability.[120]

ENVIRONMENTAL ISSUES

48.35   Asbestos in schools

The Asbestos Hazard Emergency Response Act of 1986 applies to private schools.[121]

STUDENT ATHLETE ELIGIBILITY

48.36   Ohio High School Athletic Association (OHSAA)

Most Ohio independent schools belong to OHSAA since they regularly compete with other members. The most common problem arises as a result of the transfer of a public school student to an independent school. Many such students are declared ineligible to participate in interscholastic sports for a specified period of time. In general, courts have upheld OHSAA rules.[122]

PARENT PROGRAMS

48.37   Block parent program

The state board of education is required to adopt a block parent symbol and estab-

---

[113]See Tort liability of private schools and institutions of higher learning for negligence of, or lack of supervision by teachers and other employees or agents, 38 ALR3d 908. See also Liability of university, college, or other school for failure to protect student from crime, 1 ALR4th 1099; Tort liability of private nursery school or day-care center, or employee thereof, for injury to child while attending facility, 58 ALR4th 240.

[114]Kammer v Akron Christian Schools, No. 15672, 1993 WL 46665 (9th Dist Ct App, Summit, 2-24-93), cert denied 66 OS(3d) 1507, 613 NE(2d) 1046 (1993).

[115]Hanson v Kynast, 24 OS(3d) 171, 24 OBR 403, 494 NE(2d) 1091 (1986).

[116]RC 3710.01 to RC 3710.14, RC 4745.01.

[117]See Personal liability of public school officers, or teachers or other school employees for negligence, 32 ALR2d 1163.

[118]RC 1702.12.

[119]RC 2305.38.

[120]Donohue v Copiague Union Free School Dist, 47 NY(2d) 440, 418 NYS(2d) 375, 391 NE(2d) 1352 (1979).

[121]The Act is discussed in Text 21.10(B), Asbestos removal.

[122]See Text 30.11, OHSAA rules, enforcement. See also Validity of regulation of athletic eligibility of students voluntarily transferring from one school to another, 15 ALR4th 885.

lish rules for the government of block parent programs, in which individuals or families volunteer to have their homes serve as places of temporary refuge for children. Any chartered, nonpublic school may participate in a school district block parent program, and the state board will provide technical assistance to schools that participate. Any participating school must agree to abide by the district's rules.[123]

---

[123]RC 3301.076, RC 3313.204, RC 3313.206.

APPENDICES

		Page
A.	Table of Cases	727
B.	Table of Laws and Rules	805
C.	Calendar for School District Officials	837

Appendix A
Table of Cases

This table is arranged alphabetically letter-by-letter; i.e., each group of words comprising a casename is considered as a continuous series of letters. For example, *Harrison; State v* would precede *Harris; United States v.*

For citation and subsequent case history, consult the Text Section(s) listed.

Casename	Text Section(s)
A	
A. Bentley & Sons Co, State ex rel v Pierce	5.06(B), 23.04(A)
Abington Twp School Dist v Schempp	32.05
Abood v Detroit Bd of Ed	18.21(C)
Abraham v Firelands Local School Dist Bd of Ed	25.15(B)
Ach, State ex rel v Evans	5.13(B)
Ackerman; Craddolph v	12.17(A)
Acton; Vernonia School Dist 47J v	47.01(A)
Ada Exempted Village School Dist Bd of Ed; Anthony v (6-16-94)	9.08(B)
Ada Exempted Village School Dist Bd of Ed; Anthony v (7-21-94)	46.14(A)
Adams v Canton Civil Service Comm	12.04(A)
Adams v Edison Local School Dist Bd of Ed	13.08(B)
Adams v Harding Machine Co	48.26
Adams v Kettering City School Dist Bd of Ed	12.04(A)
Adamsky v Buckeye Local School Dist	46.05
Adams; Marcus X v	28.12(A)
Adarand v Pena	17.18
Adena Local School Dist Bd of Ed; SERB v (OS)	18.24(F), 18.26(C)
Adena Local School Dist Bd of Ed; SERB v (App)	18.26(A)
Adkins, In re	18.25(D)
Adkins v Magoffin County, Kentucky Bd of Ed	9.21(E)
Adkins v State Personnel Bd of Review	12.17(C)
Adkins v Stow City School Dist Bd of Ed	9.21(E)
Adler v Duval County School Bd	32.05
Adler v Yellow Springs Exempted Village School Dist	9.09(C)

Casename	Text Section(s)
Administrator, Bureau of Employment Services; Halco v	15.04
Administrator, Ohio Bureau of Employment Services; Euclid v	15.05(A)
A.E. v Independent School Dist No. 25 of Adair County, Oklahoma	28.01(B)
Aetna Cleaning Contractors of Cleveland, Inc; State ex rel Sigall v	12.08
AFL-CIO, State ex rel v Voinovich	16.08
AFSCME, Local 2312, In re	18.25(D)
AFSCME, Local 772, In re	18.25(B)
AFSCME, Ohio Council 8, In re	18.25(B)
Age v Bullitt County Public Schools	28.03, 28.20(B)
Agich v Ohio Bureau of Employment Services Bd of Review	15.06
Aguilar v Felton	48.06(C)
Aguillard; Edwards v	32.07
Aikens; United Postal Service v	17.03(F)
Akron Bd of Ed; Egypt, Inc v	5.06(A)
Akron Bd of Ed, In re	18.24(B)
Akron Bd of Ed; Nottingham v	24.03(C)
Akron Bd of Ed v SERB	18.26(C)
Akron Christian Schools; Kammer v	46.11, 48.34(A)
Akron City School Dist Bd of Ed	18.28(B)
Akron City School Dist Bd of Ed; DeRemer v	12.13
Akron City School Dist Bd of Ed; Graphic Enterprises of Ohio, Inc v	37.06(A)
Akron City School Dist Bd of Ed, In re	18.31
Akron City School Dist Bd of Ed; SERB v	18.26(C)
Akron City School Dist Bd of Ed; Thomas v	9.22(A)

727

Casename	Text Section(s)
Akron City School Dist Bd of Ed; Wayman v	5.01, 5.07, 46.09
Akron City School Dist; Deryck v	5.06(A)
Akron v Lane	20.03(C)
Akron Metropolitan Housing Authority; State ex rel Beacon Journal Publishing Co v	44.02
Akron; Nuspl v	12.05(A), 12.11, 12.15(A), 12.15(B)
Akron Public School Dist; Weissfeld v	5.12
Akron Public Schools Bd of Ed; Richards v	12.11
Akron; State ex rel Beacon Journal Publishing Co v	44.02
Aksterowicz v Lancaster	12.14(B)
Alabama and Coushatta Tribes of Texas v Trustees of Big Sandy Independent School Dist	25.04
Alabama State Dept of Ed; Doe v	28.03
Alamo Heights Independent School Dist v Texas Bd of Ed	28.04, 28.07
Albany County School Dist No. One Bd of Ed; Shumway v	32.06(A)
Albert; State v	25.16(A)
Albright v Jackson	18.22(A)
Albritton v Neighborhood Centers Assn for Child Development	48.34(A)
Alden Corp, State ex rel v Solon	41.20(B)
Aldrich v Randolph Central School Dist	17.08(A)
Aldridge v Huntington Local School Dist Bd of Ed (OS)	9.22(E)
Aldridge v Huntington Local School Dist Bd of Ed (CP)	9.21(A)
Aldridge, State ex rel v Portsmouth	12.07(B)
Alerding v OHSAA	30.11(C)
Alessi v Buckeye Local Schools Bd of Ed	46.02
Alexander; Chicago Bd of Ed v	48.06(C)
Alexander Local School Dist Bd of Ed v Alexander Local Ed Assn	7.06(B), 18.20
Alexander Local School Dist; Goodin v	46.02, 46.03
Alexander; Walton v	46.14(B)

Casename	Text Section(s)
Alexander v Youngstown Bd of Ed	19.10
Alfonso v Fernandez	21.01
Alford, State ex rel v Willoughby Civil Service Comm	12.03(A)
Al-Khazraji; St. Francis College v	17.02(A)
Allais; Dornette v	23.06
Allegheny County v American Civil Liberties Union Greater Pittsburgh Chapter	32.06(B)
Allen v Casper	48.15
Allen v Minford Local School Dist Bd of Ed	12.09(A)
Alliance Public School Dist Bd of Ed; State ex rel Proctor v	12.17(A)
Allied Signal, Inc, Autolite Div; Kauffman v	17.11
Allison v Field Local School Dist	24.03(C)
Allmandinger v Now	5.08(A)
Altick; State v	24.14
Alton Community Unit School Dist 11; J.O. v	46.14(B)
Amalgamated Transit Union, Local 268, In re	18.25(B), 18.25(D), 18.26(A)
Amann v Stow School System	28.03
Ambach; Antkowiak v	28.01(B)
Ambach; Northport-East Northport Union Free School Dist Bd of Ed v	28.10(B)
Ambach; Vander Malle v	28.06
American Civil Liberties Union Greater Pittsburgh Chapter; Allegheny County v	32.06(B)
American Civil Liberties Union of Central Ohio v Delaware County	32.06(B)
American Civil Liberties Union of Kentucky v Wilkinson	32.06(B)
Americans United for Separation of Church and State v Grand Rapids	32.06(B)
Amherst Exempted Village School Dist Bd of Ed; Graziano v	9.22(F), 9.23(B)
Amigo v Cloverleaf Local School Dist Bd of Ed	5.12(C)
Amphitheater Unified School Dist; Dreher v	28.03
Anchor Media, Ltd of Texas; Wing v	48.26

Casename	Text Section(s)
Andersen v District of Columbia	28.03, 28.11(F)
Anderson v Creighton	46.15(C)
Anderson v OHSAA	30.11(C)
Anderson; Schafer v	46.03
Anderson, State ex rel v Industrial Comm	16.07(B)
Andrews; M. Kramer Mfg Co v	33.06(A)
Andrews; Todd D. v	28.03
Angela L. v Pasadena Independent School Dist	28.13(D)
Angevine v Smith	28.03
Ang v Proctor & Gamble Co	17.03(D)
Anrig; Doe v	28.07
Ansell; Goetz v	32.03
Ansonia Bd of Ed v Philbrook	17.15
Anthony v Ada Exempted Village School Dist Bd of Ed (6-16-94)	9.08(B)
Anthony v Ada Exempted Village School Dist Bd of Ed (7-21-94)	46.14(A)
Anthony Wayne Schools Bd of Ed; Beavers v	25.10(B), 25.12(B)
Antkowiak v Ambach	28.01(B)
Antram v Jonathan Alder Local School Dist Bd of Ed	9.19(A), 9.21(D)
Appeal of Ford, In re	11.02(C)
Appeal of Gardner, In re	12.17(C)
Appeal of Suspension of Huffer from Circleville High School, In re	5.06(C), 25.03(B), 25.14(A)
Appeal of Woods, In re	12.14(E)
Arizona Governing Committee for Tax Deferred Annuity & Deferred Compensation Plans v Norris	17.06(C)
Arkansas; Epperson v	32.07
Arline; Nassau County School Bd v	17.13(A), 28.01(B), 28.12(A)
Arlington Bd of Ed; Buckeye Union Insurance Co v	46.04
Arlington Bd of Ed; Rankey v	46.11
Armlin v Middleburgh Central School Dist Bd of Ed	24.03(D)
Armstead v Lima City Bd of Ed	25.12(A)
Arnold v Ballard	17.02(B)
Arnold v Escambia County, Alabama Bd of Ed	46.14(E)
Arons v Society of Mary	48.27
Arter; Hanzel v	21.05(C)
Art v Newcomerstown Bd of Ed	18.22(A)

Casename	Text Section(s)
Ashbaugh v Board of Review	15.08(A)
Ashbaugh v Paulding Exempted Village School Dist Bd of Ed	12.16(A)
Ashcraft, State ex rel v Industrial Comm	16.05(B)
Ash v Lake Oswego School Dist No. 7J (F(2d))	28.13(A)
Ash v Lake Oswego School Dist No. 7J (FSupp)	28.06
Ash v Ohio Bureau of Employment Services Bd of Review	15.05(B)
Ashtabula Area City School Dist Bd of Ed; Rumora v	5.01, 5.06(A), 9.21(A)
Ashtabula Area City Schools Bd of Ed	18.06
Ashtabula County School Dist Bd of Ed; Kerwin v	46.09
Aspinwall, State ex rel v Industrial Comm	16.05(H)
Assignment of New Riegel Local School Dist, In re	27.08(B)
Association for Defense of Washington Local School Dist v Kiger	23.05, 33.02(A), 35.02(A)
Astoria Federal Savings and Loan Assn v Solimino	17.03(G)
AT&T Technologies, Inc; Dent v	16.06
Atascadero Unified School Dist; Thomas v	21.03(D)
Athens City School Dist Bd of Ed; State ex rel Donaldson v	7.11(B)
Atlantic Community School Dist; EEOC v	17.06(B)
Atlas Single Ply Systems, Inc; Harris v	37.14
Atonio; Wards Cove Packing Co v	17.03(F)
Atwood; State v	20.09(B)
Auburn Enlarged City School Dist Bd of Ed; Detsel v	28.07
Auburn Vocational School Dist; Steele v	46.02
Aurelia v Monroe County Bd of Ed	19.14(A)
Aurora City Bd of Ed; Ryan v	46.14(A)
Aurora City School Dist Bd of Ed; Geiger v	22.03(C), 22.03(D)
Austin v Brown Local School Dist	46.13(B)
Austin Independent School Dist; Marvin H. v	28.12(B)
Austintown Bd of Ed; Shuba v	9.06(B)

Casename	Text Section(s)
Austintown Local School Dist Bd of Ed v Mahoning County Bd of Mental Retardation and Developmental Disabilities	29.04(B)
Avco Corp; Yates v	17.11
Avon Bd of Ed; Koch v	46.02, 46.03
Avon Bd of Ed; Nagel v	19.14(C)
Avon Products, Inc; Boggs v	48.26
A.W. v Northwest R-1 School Dist	28.05(B)

B

Casename	Text Section(s)
Babb v Knox County School System	28.13(A)
Babcock & Wilcox Co; VanFossen v	16.08
Bachmayer v Toledo Bd of Ed	46.04
Bacon v Bradley-Bourbonnais High School Dist No. 307	25.05, 32.01
Baird v Hosmer	24.03(D), 25.06, 46.03
Baisden v Oak Hill Union Local School Dist Bd of Ed	7.06(B), 9.04
Baker v McCollan	46.13(C)
Baker v Owen	25.16(B)
Baker v Twin Valley Community Local School Dist Bd of Ed	9.21(A), 9.23(B)
Bakke; University of California Regents v	17.18
Balazs v Kirtland Bd of Ed	46.02
Baldwin County Bd of Ed; Stewart v	46.15(C)
Balent v National Revenue Corp	17.06(A)
Ballard; Arnold v	17.02(B)
Ballard v Goshen Local School Dist Bd of Ed	9.14(A)
Ball; Grand Rapids School Dist v	32.01, 48.06(C)
Balog v Western Brown Local School Dist Bd of Ed	9.09(C)
Banchich v Port Clinton Public School Dist	46.02
Banks v Seattle King County School Dist No. 1	24.03(D)
Baran, State ex rel v Fuerst	12.15(A)
Barberton Bd of Ed; Pavkov v	7.04(B), 9.11(B), 9.11(C)
Barberton City School Dist Bd of Ed; Kelley v	18.22(A)
Barberton City School Dist Bd of Ed; Strock v	9.19(C)
Barberton City School Dist; Rivers v	10.05(A)
Barberton City Schools Bd of Ed; Crawford v	9.08(D), 9.15(D), 10.03(B), 10.07
Barbuto v Salem City School Dist Bd of Ed	9.13(B)
Barker; Burch v	25.05
Barker v Scovill, Inc	17.06(B)
Barksdale v Ohio Dept of Administrative Services	18.22(A)
Barlow-Gresham Union High School Dist No. 2 v Mitchell	28.13(D)
Barnes v Cavazos	48.06(C)
Barnes v GenCorp, Inc	17.06(B)
Barnette; West Virginia State Bd of Ed v	32.03
Barnett v Fairfax County School Bd (F(2d))	28.03, 28.11(D)
Barnett v Fairfax County School Bd (FSupp)	28.12(B)
Barringer; Ward v	24.03(A)
Barrington; Doe v	46.14(E)
Barr; State ex rel Delph v	5.12(D)
Bartels; Vukadinovich v	9.21(E)
Barton v Shupe	44.02
Barton; Smith v	28.13(C)
Barwacz v Michigan Dept of Ed	28.07
Bashford v Portsmouth	18.20
Basler v Princeton City School Dist Bd of Ed (1989)	10.04(D)
Basler v Princeton City School Dist Bd of Ed (1981)	10.04(D)
Bassman, State ex rel v Earhart	7.05(B), 7.11(A), 10.01(B), 12.15(B), 13.01(B)
Batavia Local School Dist; Newsome v	25.10(B), 25.10(C)
Bath-Richfield Local School Dist Bd of Ed; State ex rel Harper v	9.11(D)
Battle v Pennsylvania	28.04
Baucher v Coldwater Exempted Village School Dist Bd of Ed	23.02(B)
Bauder v Mayfield	16.03(C)
Baugh v United Telephone Co	15.06
Bays v Shenago Co	15.06
Bay Village City School Dist Bd of Ed; Biesterfeldt v	9.09(C), 9.09(E)
Beachwood City School Dist Bd of Ed; Mroczek v	7.06(B), 46.09
Beacon Journal Publishing Co; Christian v	5.07
Beacon Journal Publishing Co, State ex rel v Akron	44.02

Casename	Text Section(s)
Beacon Journal Publishing Co, State ex rel v Akron Metropolitan Housing Authority	44.02
Beacon Journal Publishing Co, State ex rel v Kent State University	44.03
Beacon Journal Publishing Co, State ex rel v Ohio Department of Health	44.03
Beamer; State ex rel Masters v	5.06(C)
Beard v Teska	28.13(D)
Beare v Eaton	12.17(C)
Bear v Geetronics, Inc	9.21(F)
Beavercreek Bd of Ed; Tirpack v	5.06(A)
Beaver Local School Dist Bd of Ed, In re	18.31
Beaver Local School Dist Bd of Ed; State ex rel Siers v	8.02(B), 9.07(A), 10.02(A), 18.20
Beavers v Anthony Wayne Schools Bd of Ed	25.10(B), 25.12(B)
Beavers; Cunningham v	46.14(B)
Beck; Communications Workers of America v	18.21(C)
Bedford Hts; SERB v	18.28(B)
Beifuss v Westerville Bd of Ed (1988)	5.07, 17.04(D), 18.26(B)
Beifuss v Westerville Bd of Ed (1984)	9.09(D), 9.12, 9.14(A), 9.14(B)
Beisel v Monroe County Bd of Ed	7.03(A)
Beiting v Cincinnati City School Dist Bd of Ed	8.02(B), 9.07(A)
Belanger v Nashua, New Hampshire, School Dist	44.14(A)
Bellefontaine City Bd of Ed; State ex rel Lee v	9.09(C)
Belleville Public School Dist No. 118; Doe v	21.03(D)
Bell; Grove City College v	30.09(B)
Bellian v Bicron Corp	17.04(B), 17.06(A)
Bell; North Haven Bd of Ed v	48.30
Bell; Phelan v	28.13(D)
Bell, State ex rel v North Union Local School Dist Bd of Ed	9.05(A)
Belmont County Engineer, In re (1988)	18.24(B)
Belmont County Engineer, In re (1985)	18.15(D)
Belmont County Engineer; SERB v	18.05(A)
Belmont-Harrison Area Joint Vocational School Dist Bd of Ed v Hoelzer	17.10
Belmont-Harrison Joint Vocational School Dist Bd of Ed; State ex rel Livingston v	9.09(E)
Beloit; Severson v	24.03(D)
Belpre City School Dist Bd of Ed; State ex rel Williams v	18.22(A)
Belt v Roadway Express Co	48.26
Belyeu v Coosa County Bd of Ed	9.21(E)
Benedict; Jacobs v	25.04
Benitez v New York City Bd of Ed	24.03(B)
Bennett v Celebrezze	45.08(A)
Bennett; Harris v	37.12(B)
Bennett v Lorain County School Dist Bd of Ed	8.02(A)
Bennett v Newbury Local Bd of Ed (1984)	11.17
Bennett v Newbury Local Bd of Ed (1983)	11.17
Bentley, State ex rel v Middletown City School Dist Bd of Ed	12.14(D)
Benton; Fellowship Baptist Church v	32.02
Berea Bd of Ed; Duer v	7.06(B)
Berea Bd of Ed; State ex rel Kinsley v	44.02
Berea City School Dist Bd of Ed; Winners v	12.16(A)
Beres v Marysville Exempted Village School Dist Bd of Ed	46.14(A)
Berger; Cook v	7.06(B)
Berger v Rensselaer Central School Corp	32.06(A)
Berger; Szymczak v	9.21(E)
Bergey; Cincinnati Bengals, Inc v	48.24(B)
Berkeley Unified School Dist; Patricia H. v	19.14(A)
Berkeley Unified School Dist; Teresa P. v	19.15
Berkshire Local School Dist Bd of Ed; State ex rel Mezak v	9.09(D)
Berlin-Milan Local School Dist; Hartley v	22.03(C), 48.08(A)
Bernardini v Conneaut Area City School Dist Bd of Ed	10.03(D)
Berndsen v Westerville Personnel Review Bd	12.14(B)
Berry, State ex rel v Board of Education	37.01(A)
Bertolucci v San Carlos Elementary School Dist	28.03
Besonen; Reeves v	46.14(B)

Casename	Text Section(s)
Best; Board of Education v	5.06(A), 5.13(A)
Best; New Concord School Dist Bd of Ed v	43.05(D)
Bethel School Dist No. 403 v Fraser	25.05
Bethel School, Independent School Dist No. 3; McIntire v	25.04
Bethlehem Area School Dist; Steirer v	25.05
Bethlehem, Pa School Dist; Williams v	19.14(B)
Bettio v Stow Civil Service Comm	18.20
Betts v Hamilton County Bd of Mental Retardation and Developmental Disabilities	17.06(C)
Bevin v Wright	28.07
Bexley City School Dist Bd of Ed; Casperson v	9.05(A), 9.09(C)
Bexley City School Dist Bd of Ed; State ex rel Fraysier v	9.06(B), 9.11(B)
Bexley Civil Service Comm; Martin v	12.17(D)
Bexley School Dist Bd of Ed; State ex rel Martin v	18.26(B)
B.F. Goodrich Co; Shaheen v	17.19
Bialek v Bloom-Carroll Local School Dist Bd of Ed	10.05(A)
Bibb County Bd of Public Ed and Orphanage; Hatcher v	9.21(E)
Bickel v Carrollton Exempted Village School Dist Bd of Ed	8.03(C), 9.06(A), 9.08(B)
Bicron Corp; Bellian v	17.04(B), 17.06(A)
Biesterfeldt v Bay Village City School Dist Bd of Ed	9.09(C), 9.09(E)
Bigelow v Youngstown Bd of Ed	10.03(B)
Biggins; Hazen Paper Co v	17.06(A), 17.06(B)
Bigley v Morrison	24.03(D)
Bilbrey v Brown	47.03
Bismarck Public School Dist; Johnson v	28.13(D)
Bispeck, State ex rel v Trumbull County Bd of Commrs	12.14(B)
Bitting v Cuyahoga Falls City School Dist Bd of Ed	9.19(B)
Bivens v West Clermont Local Bd of Ed	9.19(C)
Blackburn v Floyd County Bd of Ed	9.21(E)
Black v Dayton City School Dist	24.03(D)
Black v Indiana Area School Dist	46.14(B)
Black v Mecca Twp Bd of Trustees	5.12(A)
Blair v Milford Exempted Village School Dist Bd of Ed	12.09(B), 18.22(A)
Blankenship v Cincinnati Milacron Chemicals, Inc	16.08
Blevins; Green Local Teachers Assn v	10.07(B)
Bloom-Carroll Local School Dist Bd of Ed; Bialek v	10.05(A)
Bloomingdale Public Schools; Washegesic v	32.06(B)
Blubaugh v Jefferson County Joint Vocational School Dist Bd of Ed	9.19(B), 9.19(G)
Blust v Madison Local School Dist Bd of Ed	10.16, 13.08(B)
B.M.H. v Chesapeake, Va, School Bd	46.14(B)
BMW of North America, Inc; Bouton v	17.11
Boals v Gray	9.21(E), 46.14(A)
Boal; Zaleski School Dist Bd of Ed v	9.03
Boardman Bd of Ed; Tucker v	9.19(D)
Boardman Twp Trustees, In re	18.17(A)
Board of County Commrs; Haines v	41.17(E)
Board of County Commrs; Moraine v	5.12(D)
Board of County Commrs, State ex rel v Jenkins	41.12(A)
Board of Education v Best	5.06(A), 5.13(A)
Board of Education; Brownfield v	46.12
Board of Education; Clark v	5.13(A)
Board of Education for School District of Philadelphia; United States v	32.01
Board of Education; Goolsby v	44.11
Board of Education; Idaho Migrant Council v	19.15
Board of Education; Moore v	32.04
Board of Education; Mueller v	37.04(C)
Board of Education; Mulcahy v	37.05
Board of Education; Pickering v	9.21(E)
Board of Education; Ross v	5.06(C), 8.02(A), 9.07(A)

Casename	Text Section(s)
Board of Ed v Rowley	28.11(A)
Board of Education v State	19.07
Board of Education; State ex rel Berry v	37.01(A)
Board of Ed v Strausser	41.04
Board of Elementary & Secondary Ed; Weil v	28.11(B)
Board of Regents of State Colleges v Roth	46.14(A)
Board of Review, Administrator, Ohio Bureau of Employment Services; Casserly v	15.08(A)
Board of Review; Ashbaugh v	15.08(A)
Board of Tax Appeals; Cincinnati Nature Center Assn v	48.33
Board of Tax Appeals; Denison University v	48.33
Board of Trustees; Jefferson County Bd of Commrs v	43.07(A)
Board of Trustees of Target Range School Dist No. 23, Missoula, Montana; W.G. v	28.03
Boaz v Ostrander	24.03(B)
Bob Jones University v Johnson	48.09(A)
Bob Jones University v United States	48.31
Boehm v Rolling Hills Local School Dist Bd of Ed	9.19(A)
Boggs v Avon Products, Inc	48.26
Boggs v Southeastern Local School Dist Bd of Ed	10.07, 10.07(B)
Bohmann v West Clermont Local School Dist Bd of Ed	7.06(B), 9.19(A)
Boieru v SERB	18.26(C)
Bojac Corp v Kutevac	46.05
Bolce v Cincinnati School Dist Bd of Ed	37.04(C)
Bolding v Dublin Local School Dist	46.02
Bolek v Chardon Bd of Ed	12.16(C)
Bonnie Ann F. v Calallen Independent School Dist	28.03
Borbely v Prestole Everlock, Inc	16.05(G)
Borders, State ex rel v Jefferson Local School Dist	12.09(B)
Borman v Gorham-Fayette Bd of Ed	46.14(A)
Borough of Clementon School Dist Bd of Ed; Oberti v	28.05(B), 28.11(D)
Borowski v State Chemical Mfg Co	17.06(A)
Bosstic; State v	20.09(B)

Casename	Text Section(s)
Boulder Creek Union Junior-Senior High School Dist of Santa Cruz; Ridge v	24.03(D)
Bouton v BMW of North America, Inc	17.11
Bowles, In re	18.21(B)
Bowles v OHSAA	30.11(C)
Bowling Green Bd of Ed, In re	18.28(B)
Bowman v National Graphics Corp	16.03(A)
Bowman v Parma Bd of Ed	9.17
Bowman; Portage Lakes Joint Vocational School Dist Bd of Ed v	8.03(A), 10.07(B), 43.27(B)
Boyd v Harding Academy of Memphis, Inc	48.30
Boyd, State ex rel v Canton City School Dist Bd of Ed	9.11(B)
Boyer v Jablonski	24.03(D)
Bradford Area School Dist; Stoneking v	46.15(C)
Bradley-Bourbonnais High School Dist No. 307; Bacon v	25.05, 32.01
Bradley; Milliken v (1977)	19.05
Bradley; Milliken v (1974)	19.05
Bradley v Pittsburgh Bd of Ed (910 F(2d))	9.21(E)
Bradley v Pittsburgh Bd of Ed (913 F(2d))	9.21(E), 9.22(A)
Bradley; Vance v	17.06(C)
Brady; Ellison v	17.11
Brady v Safety-Kleen Corp	16.08
Bralley v Daugherty	16.03(C)
Brandon v Coldwater Exempted Village School Dist Bd of Ed	9.21(E), 46.03
Brandon v Holt	46.13(B)
Brannon v Tiro Consolidated School Dist of Crawford County Bd of Ed	5.06(C)
Brasch v Listerman	24.03(D)
Braswell, State ex rel v Industrial Comm	16.07(B)
Bratenahl Bd of Ed; Stromberg v	4.05(A)
Bratenahl Local School Dist Bd of Ed, State ex rel v State Bd of Ed	26.19
Braun v Glade Valley School, Inc	48.19
Breckenridge; Griffin v	17.02(A)
Breen; Jefferson County Bd of Ed v	28.13(B)
Bremner; Heavy Runner v	19.15

Casename	Text Section(s)
Brennan, State ex rel v Vinton County Local School Dist Bd of Ed	7.11(B)
Brickner v Voinovich	3.02(A), 46.14(A)
Bri-Den Co, Inc, State ex rel v Union Scioto Schools Bd of Ed	37.06(A)
Bridgeport Ed Assn; Crumpton v	17.18
Bridgewater School Dept; Spacco v	32.01
Briggs v Connecticut Bd of Ed	28.05(B)
Bright; Perkins v	46.08
Brimmer v Traverse City Area Public Schools	28.11(A)
Brinkman; Dayton Bd of Ed v (1979)	19.06
Brinkman; Dayton Bd of Ed v (1977)	19.06
Bristolville (Bristol) Local School Dist; Roper v	24.03(C)
Britton, State ex rel v Scott	13.08(B)
Brodie v Summit County Children Services Bd	24.05(A)
Brody v Spang	25.05, 32.06(A)
Bronson v Cincinnati School Dist Bd of Ed (578 FSupp)	19.10
Bronson v Cincinnati School Dist Bd of Ed (604 FSupp)	19.10
Bronson v Cincinnati School Dist Bd of Ed (550 FSupp)	19.10
Brookfield Federation of Teachers, State ex rel v Brookfield Local School Dist Bd of Ed	5.12(A)
Brookfield Local School Dist Bd of Ed; SERB v	18.24(D)
Brookfield Local School Dist Bd of Ed; State ex rel Brookfield Federation of Teachers v	5.12(A)
Brookfield Local School Dist Bd of Ed; State ex rel Hura v	9.05(A), 9.09(D)
Brookhart v Illinois Bd of Ed	28.10(B)
Brooklyn Bd of Ed; Fisher v	9.01(A)
Brooklyn Civil Service Comm; Grenig v	12.14(B)
Brook Park Civil Service Comm; Sutherland-Wagner v	12.15(A)
Brook Park; Noernberg v	12.17(C)
Brotherhood of Railway Clerks; Ellis v	18.21(C)
Brougham v Town of Yarmouth	28.03

Casename	Text Section(s)
Broussard v Norfolk School Bd	25.05
Brown; Bilbrey v	47.03
Brown v Cuyahoga Falls	12.04(A)
Brown v East Cleveland Bd of Ed	18.22(A)
Brownfield v Board of Education	46.12
Brownfield v Warren Local School Dist Bd of Ed	9.22(E)
Brown v Griggsville Community Unit School Dist No. 4 (F(3d))	28.13(D)
Brown v Griggsville Community Unit School Dist No. 4 (FSupp)	28.13(D)
Browning v Pendleton	46.13(C)
Brown; Justus v	9.09(B)
Brown Local School Dist; Austin v	46.13(B)
Brown; McKinney v	4.10(C)
Brown v Monroeville Local School Dist Bd of Ed	5.07
Brown, State ex rel v Columbus City Schools	7.11(B)
Brown, State ex rel v Milton-Union Exempted Village Bd of Ed	5.07, 8.02(B), 9.07(A), 9.08(C), 9.09(E), 10.02(A), 17.04(D), 18.26(B)
Brown, State ex rel v Public Employees Retirement Bd	11.13(A)
Brown; State ex rel Rolling Hills Local School Dist Bd of Ed v	39.04
Brown v Topeka Bd of Ed (1992)	19.03(B)
Brown v Topeka Bd of Ed (1955)	19.02
Brown v Topeka Bd of Ed (1954)	2.16(B), 19.02
Brown University; Cohen v	19.14(A)
Brown v Woodland Joint Unified School Dist	33.04
Brubaker, State ex rel v Hardy	9.09(E)
Bruno v United Steelworkers of America	10.12(A)
Brunswick City School Dist Bd of Ed v Formani	25.10(B)
Brunswick City School Dist Bd of Ed, In re	18.17(A)
Brunswick City School Dist Bd of Ed; Johnson v	15.05(A), 15.05(B)
Brunswick City School Dist Bd of Ed; Kehoe v	9.12
Bryan City School Dist Bd of Ed; State ex rel Webb v	9.22(B)

Casename	Text Section(s)
Bryan Civil Service Comm; Thompson v	12.17(D)
Buchheit v Hamilton City Bd of Ed	9.19(C), 9.21(E)
Buchman v Wayne Trace Local School Dist Bd of Ed	46.05
Buckeye Boxes, Inc v Franklin County Bd of Revision	39.04
Buckeye Central Local School Dist Bd of Ed; Silavent v	7.06(B), 9.04
Buckeye Joint Vocational School Dist Bd of Ed; State ex rel Pusztay v	9.13(B)
Buckeye Local School Dist; Adamsky v	46.05
Buckeye Local School Dist Bd of Ed; Hummel v	10.04(D)
Buckeye Local School Dist Bd of Ed; Ott v	9.19(G)
Buckeye Local School Dist Bd of Ed; Rauhaus v	10.04(A)
Buckeye Local School Dist Bd of Ed; Savarese v	5.13(A)
Buckeye Local School Dist; Younger v	46.02
Buckeye Local Schools Bd of Ed; Alessi v	46.02
Buckeye Union Insurance Co v Arlington Bd of Ed	46.04
Buckles v Granville Exempted Village School Dist Bd of Ed	9.14(A)
Buckman, State ex rel v Munson	12.14(A)
Bucyrus City Bd of Ed v Bucyrus Ed Assn	18.22(A)
Buie v Chippewa Local School Dist Bd of Ed	18.22(A)
Bull v Dardanelle Public School Dist No. 15	25.05
Bullitt County Public Schools; Age v	28.03, 28.20(B)
Bullitt County School Dist; Eggers v	28.13(D)
Burch v Barker	25.05
Burch, State ex rel v Sheffield Lake City School Dist Bd of Ed	10.02(B)
Burdine; Texas Dept of Community Affairs v	17.03(F), 17.04(E)
Bureau of Employment Services; Knight v	15.05(B)
Bureau of Employment Services; Superior Metal Products, Inc v	15.08(A)
Bureau of Motor Vehicles; Helmeci v	20.10

Casename	Text Section(s)
Bureau of Motor Vehicles; Stover v	12.17(A)
Burkart v Post-Browning, Inc	15.08(A)
Burke County Bd of Ed v Denton	28.06
Burke; United States v	17.03(E)
Burkhart v Randles	46.14(A)
Burley, State ex rel v Coil Packaging, Inc	16.07(B)
Burlington School Committee v Massachusetts Dept of Ed	28.13(A)
Burnham v West	46.15(C), 47.03
Burns v McGregor Electronic Industries	17.11
Burns v Middletown Civil Service Comm	12.15(A)
Burrell, In re	24.05(D)
Burrows v OHSAA	30.11(C)
Burt v Grand Rapids Bd of Ed	46.14(A)
Burton; State ex rel Saltsman v (1952)	8.02(A), 9.07(A)
Burton; State ex rel Saltsman v (1950)	8.02(A), 9.07(A)
Buser v Corpus Christi Independent School Dist	28.02, 28.11(A), 28.11(B)
Bush v Dassel-Cokato Bd of Ed	25.03(A)
Bush, State ex rel v Spurlock	12.14(A)
Butler County Bd of Mental Retardation & Developmental Disabilities, In re (1992)	18.15(C), 18.17(A)
Butler County Bd of Mental Retardation & Developmental Disabilities, In re (1989)	18.15(D)
Butler County, Kansas Unified School Dist No. 492; Ware v	9.21(E)
Butler, State ex rel v Fort Frye Local School Dist	7.14(B)
Byers; Ohio Bureau of Employment Services v	15.02(C)
Byrne v West Allis-West Milwaukee Bd of Ed	17.13(A)
Bystrom v Fridley High School	25.05

C

Casename	Text Section(s)
Cabell County Bd of Ed v Dienelt	28.03
Cabelli v Fort Smith School Dist	17.13(A)
CADO Business Systems of Ohio, Inc v Cleveland City School Dist Bd of Ed	6.07(C), 37.07(A), 43.07(B)

Casename	Text Section(s)
Calallen Independent School Dist; Bonnie Ann F. v	28.03
Calhoun v Madison Bd of Ed	9.21(C)
California Federal Savings & Loan Assn v Guerra	17.09(A)
California Office of Administrative Hearings; Clovis Unified School Dist v	28.07
Cambridge City School Dist v Guernsey County Budget Comm (1968)	4.14(B), 39.03, 40.06
Cambridge City School Dist v Guernsey County Budget Comm (1967)	4.14(B), 40.06
Cameron v Hillsboro, Ohio, City School Dist Bd of Ed	17.09(A), 46.14(E), 46.15(C)
Campbell Civil Service Comm; Romeo v	12.14(B)
Canfield Local Bd of Ed; Pistone v	12.10(E)
Canfield Local School Dist Bd of Ed	18.24(C)
Canfield Local School Dist Bd of Ed; State ex rel Hendricks v	9.09(E)
Canfield, State ex rel v Frost	12.07(A)
Cannon; Davidson v	46.14(B)
Cannon v University of Chicago (1981)	19.14(C)
Cannon v University of Chicago (1979)	19.13(E)
Canton Bd of Ed; Nohl v	15.05(B)
Canton City School Dist	18.13
Canton City School Dist Bd of Ed; Fincher v	11.21(A)
Canton City School Dist Bd of Ed; McKita v	9.09(C)
Canton City School Dist Bd of Ed; State ex rel Boyd v	9.11(B)
Canton City School Dist Bd of Ed; Weinstein v (1983)	9.22(A)
Canton City School Dist Bd of Ed; Weinstein v (1980)	9.23(B)
Canton City School Dist Bd of Ed; Whitley v	9.19(F), 18.20
Canton City School Dist; Wilson v	46.02
Canton Civil Service Comm; Adams v	12.04(A)
Canton v Harris	46.13(B)
Canton, Ohio; Neighborhood Action Coalition v	19.13(E)
Cape Girardeau School Dist; Felter v	28.07
Cape v Tennessee Secondary School Athletic Assn	19.14(D), 30.09(B)
Capistrano Unified School Dist; Peloza v	32.07
Carbone v Overfield	5.07, 46.01(A)
Cardinal Local School Dist Bd of Ed; Mansfield v	12.16(A)
Cardinal Local School Dist Bd of Ed; Naylor v	9.01, 9.13(A), 9.13(B), 9.13(C)
Cardington-Lincoln Local School Dist; Cole v	12.16(A)
Carey; New York Gaslight Club, Inc v	17.03(D), 17.03(E)
Carey; New York State Assn for Retarded Children, Inc v	28.01(B)
Carlisle Local Bd of Ed, In re	18.29(C), 18.30
Carlisle Local School Bd; Rush v	46.03
Carlon Co; Evely v	48.26
Carney; Lake Ridge Academy v	48.12
Carney; State ex rel Speeth v	41.10
Caroline T. v Hudson School Dist	28.11(E)
Carothers v Tri-Valley Local School Dist Bd of Ed	9.21(B)
Carr; Montgomery v	9.21(E)
Carroll v Lucas	46.03
Carrollton Exempted Village School Dist Bd of Ed; Bickel v	8.03(C), 9.06(A), 9.08(B)
Carrollton Exempted Village School Dist Bd of Ed; Guchemand v	9.14(A), 9.14(B)
Carter; Florence County School Dist Four v	28.13(A)
Carter v Ohio Dept of Health	12.14(B)
Carter v Orrville City School Dist Bd of Ed	7.06(B)
Carter v Princeton Bd of Ed	8.04(D)
Carter, State ex rel v Cleveland City School Dist Bd of Ed	12.17(C)
Carter v Western Reserve Psychiatric Habilitation Center	12.17(B), 46.14(A)
Casey; West Virginia University Hospitals, Inc v	46.16
Cashdollar v Northridge High School Bd of Ed	25.12(B)
Cashdollar v Northridge Local School Dist Bd of Ed	25.10(C)
Cason v Cook	47.01(B)
Caspar, State ex rel v Dayton	18.20
Casper; Allen v	48.15
Casperson v Bexley City School Dist Bd of Ed	9.05(A), 9.09(C)

Casename	Text Section(s)
Cassels, State ex rel v Dayton City School Dist Bd of Ed (1994)	7.11(B), 7.14(B)
Cassels, State ex rel v Dayton City School Dist Bd of Ed (1993)	7.11(B)
Casserly v Board of Review, Administrator, Ohio Bureau of Employment Services	15.08(A)
Cassity, State ex rel v Montgomery County Dept of Sanitation	16.05(B)
Cassopolis, Michigan School Dist No. 14-030; Waechter v	46.14(B)
Castaneda v Pickard	19.15
Catalina Foothills School Dist; Zobrest v	28.01(A), 32.01, 48.06(C)
Catholic Bishop of Chicago; NLRB v	48.28(B)
Cavazos; Barnes v	48.06(C)
Cavazos; Grimes v	19.13(A), 19.13(E)
Cavazos; Pulido v	48.06(C)
Celebrezze; Bennett v	45.08(A)
Celina City School Dist	18.16(B)
Centennial School Dist; Gregoire v	32.06(A)
Center for Comprehensive Alcoholism Treatment; Hedrick v	48.26
Center Moriches Union Free School Dist; Lamb's Chapel v	32.06(A)
Central Bucks School Dist; Muth v	28.11(F)
Central High School Defense Assn v Columbus Bd of Ed	19.08(A)
Central Ohio Joint Vocational School Dist Bd of Ed v Ohio Bureau of Employment Services	15.02(B)
Central Ohio Transit Authority, In re (1989)	18.24(C), 18.24(D)
Central Ohio Transit Authority, In re (1987)	18.32
Central Ohio Transit Authority, In re (1986)	18.29(D)
Central Ohio Transit Authority v Transport Workers Union of America, Local 208	18.32
Central State University, In re (1989)	18.26(A)
Central State University, In re (1985)	18.24(B)

Casename	Text Section(s)
Central Susquehanna Intermediate Unit 16; Polk v	28.03, 28.07
Cephus v Dayton Bd of Ed	9.23(B)
Chalk v United States Dist Ct Central Dist of Cal	17.13(A), 21.03(D)
Champaign County School Dist No. 71 Bd of Ed; Illinois ex rel McCollum v	32.01, 32.04
Chandler v McMinnville School Dist	25.05
Chaney v Lordstown	37.06(A)
Chardon Bd of Ed; Bolek v	12.16(C)
Chardon Local School Dist Bd of Ed; Panek v	12.16(A)
Charles v Princeton City School Dist Bd of Ed	9.22(F)
Charlotte-Mecklenburg Bd of Ed; Swann v	19.03(B), 19.11(A)
Charlton v Paramus Bd of Ed	17.03(A)
Chase, In re	12.17(A)
Chavis, State ex rel v Sycamore City School Dist Bd of Ed	10.02(B)
Cheek v Western & Southern Life Insurance Co	17.03(D)
Chemical Construction Corp; Kremer v	17.03(G)
Cherry Hill Twp Bd of Ed; Clever v	32.06(B)
Chesapeake Union Exempted Village School Dist Bd of Ed; Hannan v	10.16, 13.08(B)
Chesapeake Union Exempted Village School Dist Bd of Ed; McMaster v	12.16(A)
Chesapeake, Va, School Bd; B.M.H. v	46.14(B)
Chester Twp Bd of Trustees; Smith v	25.12(B)
Chester Twp Police Dept, In re	18.15(D)
Chicago Bd of Ed v Alexander	48.06(C)
Chicago Bd of Ed; Mims v	46.14(D)
Chicago Bd of Ed; Palmer v (US)	32.03
Chicago Bd of Ed; Palmer v (F(2d))	17.15
Chicago Bd of Ed; Pilditch v	17.03(F)
Chicago Bd of Ed; Thompson v	9.21(E)
Chicago Teachers Union Local No. 1 v Hudson	18.21(C)
Chillicothe City School Dist Bd of Ed; Gannett Satellite Information Network, Inc v	5.12(B)

Casename	Text Section(s)
Chillicothe City School Dist Bd of Ed v Sever-Williams Co	37.04(B)
Chillicothe Correctional Institute; Hutt v	12.17(A)
Chilton County Bd of Ed; Verbena United Methodist Church v	32.06(A)
Chippewa Local School Dist Bd of Ed; Buie v	18.22(A)
Chris D. v Montgomery County Bd of Ed	28.03
Christian v Beacon Journal Publishing Co	5.07
Christiansburg Garment Co v EEOC	17.03(E), 46.16
Christman v Columbus Public Schools Bd of Ed	46.11
Christman; State ex rel Kitchen v	41.02, 43.29
Christman v Washington Court House School Dist	23.02(A)
Christopher M. v Corpus Christi Independent School Dist	28.01(A), 28.11(D)
Chrysinger v Decatur	25.16(A)
Chrysler Corp; Hartsock v	16.07(B)
Chrysler Corp, State ex rel v Industrial Comm	16.05(F)
Churchill; Waters v	9.21(E)
Cicero, State ex rel v State Teachers Retirement Bd	11.07(A)
Cicero-Stickney Twp High School Dist No. 201 Bd of Ed; Krizek v	9.21(E)
Cincinnati Bengals, Inc v Bergey	48.24(B)
Cincinnati Bd of Ed	18.13
Cincinnati Bd of Ed; Deal v (1971)	19.08(A), 19.10
Cincinnati Bd of Ed; Deal v (1967)	19.08(A), 19.10
Cincinnati Bd of Ed; Douglas v	9.23(B)
Cincinnati Bd of Ed; Holthaus v	9.14(B)
Cincinnati Bd of Ed; Jacobson v	17.18
Cincinnati Bd of Ed; State ex rel Johnston v	9.10(D)
Cincinnati Bd of Ed; Thomas v	28.01(A), 28.03, 28.08(A), 28.09(A), 28.11(D)
Cincinnati Bd of Ed v Volk	5.07, 46.08
Cincinnati City School Dist Bd of Ed; Beiting v	8.02(B), 9.07(A)
Cincinnati City School Dist Bd of Ed; Rudolph v	13.08(A)
Cincinnati City School Dist Bd of Ed v Walter	2.14, 2.15, 39.01(B), 39.06(B)
Cincinnati Metropolitan Housing Auth, In re (SERB 93-002)	18.09, 18.24(F)
Cincinnati Metropolitan Housing Auth, In re (SERB 93-008)	18.09, 18.24(F)
Cincinnati Metropolitan Housing Auth v SERB	18.26(A)
Cincinnati Milacron Chemicals, Inc; Blankenship v	16.08
Cincinnati Nature Center Assn v Board of Tax Appeals	48.33
Cincinnati v Ohio Council 8, AFSCME	18.20, 18.28(B)
Cincinnati; Ohio Council 8, AFSCME v	18.11(B)
Cincinnati; Pembaur v	46.13(B)
Cincinnati Post, State ex rel v Marsh	44.02, 44.09
Cincinnati Post, State ex rel v Schweikert	44.02
Cincinnati Public Schools Bd of Ed; Holthaus v	46.14(B)
Cincinnati; Queen City Lodge No 69, FOP v	18.22(A)
Cincinnati School Dist Bd of Ed; Bolce v	37.04(C)
Cincinnati School Dist Bd of Ed; Bronson v (578 FSupp)	19.10
Cincinnati School Dist Bd of Ed; Bronson v (604 FSupp)	19.10
Cincinnati School Dist Bd of Ed; Bronson v (550 FSupp)	19.10
Cincinnati School Dist Bd of Ed; McClelland v	9.21(D)
Cincinnati; State ex rel Coleman v	44.02
Cincinnati Word Processing, Inc; Helmick v	17.11
Circleville Bd of Ed; McNaughton v	25.15(A)
Circleville City School Dist Bd of Ed	18.13
Circleville City School Dist Bd of Ed; State ex rel Whitehead v	7.11(A), 10.02(A)
Circleville Recreation Center, Inc; Dietrich & Hoover v	29.04(H)
Citizens for Parental Rights v San Mateo County Bd of Ed	32.07

Casename	Text Section(s)
City Disposal Systems; NLRB v	18.09
City of Akron, In re	18.14, 18.28(B)
City of Barberton, In re	18.26(A)
City of Bedford Hts, In re	18.14
City of Bowling Green, In re	18.11(B)
City of Canton, In re (1994)	18.26(B), 18.28(B)
City of Canton, In re (1990)	18.25(D), 18.26(A)
City of Canton, In re (1985)	18.04(B), 18.09, 18.11(A)
City of Cincinnati, In re	18.28(B)
City of Cincinnati; SERB v	18.26(A)
City of Cleveland	18.17(A)
City of Dayton, In re (1993)	18.09, 18.24(B), 18.24(F)
City of Dayton, In re (1985)	18.27
City of Fostoria, In re	18.24(C)
City of Franklin	18.17(A)
City of Gallipolis, In re (1994)	18.11(B)
City of Gallipolis, In re (1990)	18.32
City of Garfield Heights, In re	18.17(A)
City of Jackson, In re	18.22(A)
City of Lakewood, In re	18.28(B)
City of Lima, In re	18.29(C)
City of Martins Ferry, In re	18.28(C)
City of Middleburg Heights, In re	18.25(D), 18.26(A)
City of New Lexington, In re	18.31
City of Niles, In re	18.17(A)
City of Oakwood, In re	18.29(A)
City of Port Clinton, In re	18.04(A)
City of Shaker Heights, In re	18.29(C)
City of Sidney, In re	18.26(A)
City of South Euclid, In re	18.17(A)
City of Springfield, In re (SERB 85-002)	18.31
City of Springfield, In re (SERB 85-038)	18.29(D)
City of St. Bernard v SERB	18.28(B)
City of Toledo, In re	18.06
City of Youngstown, In re	18.31
Clark v Board of Education	5.13(A)
Clark County School Dist; Planned Parenthood of Southern Nevada, Inc v	25.05
Clark v Dallas Independent School Dist	25.05, 32.06(A)
Clarke County School Dist; Drew P. v	28.06
Clarke, State ex rel v Cook	23.04(A)
Clarke, State ex rel v Jefferson Twp Rural School Dist Bd of Ed	36.02(A)
Clark v Ohio Dept of Transportation	12.11
Clark; State v	24.11
Clark, State ex rel v Greater Cleveland Regional Transit Authority	18.20
Clark, State ex rel v Toledo	44.03
Clauson; Zorach v	32.04
Clawson; Doe v	32.06(B)
Clay Local School Dist Bd of Ed; State ex rel Stafford v	5.13(A)
Clayton v Place	32.01
Clear Creek Independent School Dist; Jones v	32.05
Clearcreek Local School Dist Bd of Ed; State ex rel Kelley v	7.13, 9.07(A)
Clearcreek Local School Dist Bd of Ed; State ex rel Stuckey v	12.10(A)
Clear Fork Valley Local School Bd; Kiser v	25.03(B)
Clemens; Horne v	44.08(B), 46.14(A)
Clementi v Wean United, Inc	16.06
Clements; Layton v	46.08
Clements v Mad River Twp Bd of Ed	9.21(A)
Clermont County Bd of Commrs; Manning v	12.17(B)
Clermont County Commrs, Clermont County Service Dept, In re	18.15(B)
Clermont County Sheriff, In re	18.19(A), 18.24(D)
Clermont Northeastern Local School Dist Bd of Ed; Smith v	12.16(C)
Clermont Northeastern School Dist; Goodwin v	28.09(C)
Cleveland Bd of Ed v Cuyahoga County Bd of Revision (68 OS(3d))	39.04
Cleveland Bd of Ed v Cuyahoga County Bd of Revision (70 OS(3d))	39.04
Cleveland Bd of Ed; De La Torre v	15.07
Cleveland Bd of Ed v LaFleur	10.20(B), 17.09(C), 20.04
Cleveland Bd of Ed v Loudermill	6.03(A), 9.22(A), 12.16(B), 12.17(B), 46.14(A)
Cleveland Bd of Ed; Rencher v	46.11
Cleveland Bd of Ed, State ex rel v State Bd of Ed	20.05(D)

Casename	Text Section(s)
Cleveland Bd of Ed; Sutton v	12.17(B), 18.22(A), 46.14(B)
Cleveland Bd of Ed; Tax Deferred Annuities Corp v	10.10(A)
Cleveland Bd of Ed; Wohl v	46.13(A)
Cleveland City School Dist	18.13
Cleveland City School Dist Bd of Ed; CADO Business Systems of Ohio, Inc v	6.07(C), 37.07(A), 43.07(B)
Cleveland City School Dist Bd of Ed; Cleveland Classified School Employees Civil Service Assn v	12.07(B)
Cleveland City School Dist Bd of Ed v Gilligan	39.06(B)
Cleveland City School Dist Bd of Ed, In re	18.04(A), 18.09, 18.24(B)
Cleveland City School Dist Bd of Ed; International Brotherhood of Firemen v	18.22(A)
Cleveland City School Dist Bd of Ed; Martines v	7.11(B)
Cleveland City School Dist Bd of Ed; Riccheti v	9.21(B), 9.22(E), 9.22(F)
Cleveland City School Dist Bd of Ed; State ex rel Carter v	12.17(C)
Cleveland City School Dist Bd of Ed; State ex rel Martines v	7.11(B), 7.14(B)
Cleveland City School Dist Bd of Ed; State ex rel National City Bank v	41.21(A)
Cleveland City School Dist Bd of Ed; Verberg v	5.06(A), 21.01
Cleveland Civil Service Comm; Moore v	12.17(D)
Cleveland Civil Service Comm v Ohio Civil Rights Comm	17.03(F), 17.13(A)
Cleveland Civil Service Commrs; Jones v	12.17(C)
Cleveland Classified School Employees Civil Service Assn v Cleveland City School Dist Bd of Ed	12.07(B)
Cleveland Hts-University Hts City School Dist Bd of Ed; State ex rel Johnson v	18.22(A)
Cleveland Hts-University Hts City School Dist Bd of Ed; State ex rel Rollins v	9.05(A), 18.20
Cleveland; Kennedy v	46.15(C)
Cleveland Metro General Hospital	18.26(A)
Cleveland Metro School of Nursing; Morin v	48.15
Cleveland Pneumatic Co; Hayes v	17.13(A)

Casename	Text Section(s)
Cleveland School Dist Bd of Ed; Hines v	5.06(C), 37.07(A), 43.07(B)
Cleveland School Dist Bd of Ed, In re	18.17(B)
Cleveland; State ex rel International Union of Operating Engineers v	18.20
Cleveland; State ex rel Margolius v	44.03
Cleveland; State ex rel National Broadcasting Co v (1991)	44.02
Cleveland; State ex rel National Broadcasting Co v (1988)	44.02, 44.03
Clevenger v Oak Ridge School Bd	28.03
Clever v Cherry Hill Twp Bd of Ed	32.06(B)
Clinton County Bd of Commrs; White v	5.11(D)
Clonlara, Inc v Runkel	20.03(C)
Cloverleaf Local School Dist Bd of Ed; Amigo v	5.12(C)
Cloverleaf Local School Dist Bd of Ed; Rickel v	9.13(C)
Clovis Unified School Dist v California Office of Administrative Hearings	28.07
Clow; McCullom v	46.02, 46.13(B)
Clyde-Green Springs School Dist Bd of Ed; Guhn v	24.03(C)
Clyde K. v Puyallup School Dist No. 3	28.09(A)
C.M. v Southeast Delco School Dist	46.13(B), 46.14(B), 46.15(C)
Cohen v Brown University	19.14(A)
Coil Packaging, Inc; State ex rel Burley v	16.07(B)
Coldwater Exempted Village School Dist Bd of Ed; Baucher v	23.02(B)
Coldwater Exempted Village School Dist Bd of Ed; Brandon v	9.21(E), 46.03
Coldwater Exempted Village School Dist Bd of Ed; Schlotterer v	7.13, 46.08
Cole v Cardington-Lincoln Local School Dist	12.16(A)
Coleman, State ex rel v Cincinnati	44.02
Coleman v Wirtz	46.13(B)
Colin K. v Schmidt	28.11(F)
College Corner Local School Dist Bd of Ed v Walker	4.02

Casename	Text Section(s)
Colleton County School Dist; Stroman v	9.21(E)
Collins v Harker Hts, Texas	46.13(B), 46.14(B)
Collins v Rizkana	17.11
Collins; State ex rel Hamlin v	46.08, 46.09
Columbia County, Fla School Bd; Virgil v	26.04, 33.04
Columbiana County Auditor's Office, In re	18.16(A), 18.16(B)
Columbiana County Human Services Dept, Children' Services Div, In re	18.11(B)
Columbiana Exempted Village Bd of Ed	18.13
Columbiana Exempted Village School Dist Bd of Ed; State ex rel Stiller v	7.04(B), 7.14(A)
Columbia University; Karibian v	17.11
Columbus Bd of Ed; Central High School Defense Assn v	19.08(A)
Columbus Bd of Ed v Fountain Square Associates, Ltd	39.04
Columbus Bd of Ed; Franklin v	10.08(B)
Columbus Bd of Ed; Giammarco v	10.07(B)
Columbus Bd of Ed; Hall v	46.03
Columbus Bd of Ed, In re	18.12
Columbus Bd of Ed; OAPSE v	12.19
Columbus Bd of Ed v Penick	19.06
Columbus Bd of Ed; Penick v (1981)	19.09(A)
Columbus Bd of Ed; Penick v (1978)	19.09(A)
Columbus Bd of Ed; Sartori v	46.02, 46.03
Columbus Bd of Ed; Steppe v	10.03(C)
Columbus Bd of Ed; Tapo v (OS)	18.22(A)
Columbus Bd of Ed; Tapo v (App)	10.07(A)
Columbus Bd of Ed; Waite v	25.13
Columbus Bd of Ed; White v	10.04(C), 10.07(A), 10.07(B)
Columbus Bd of Ed; Williams v	24.03(C)
Columbus City School Dist Bd of Ed; O'Harra v	12.16(A)
Columbus City School Dist; Espie v	9.21(D)
Columbus City Schools; Craig v	46.13(A)
Columbus City Schools; State ex rel Brown v	7.11(B)
Columbus Department of Development; Grano v	17.03(F)
Columbus; DeVennish v	18.28(B)
Columbus Public Schools Bd of Ed; Christman v	46.11
Columbus Public Schools; Pendergrass v	20.03(C)
Columbus Public Schools; Spotts v	46.03
Columbus; Williams v	11.10
Combs v Stark County Area Joint Vocational School Dist Bd of Ed	18.22(A)
Commack Union Free School Dist; Lowe v	17.06(B)
Commissioner of Internal Revenue Service v Schleier	17.03(E)
Committee for Public Education & Religious Liberty v Regan	48.06(B)
Communications Workers of America v Beck	18.21(C)
Communications Workers of America Local 4501 v Ohio State University	12.08
Community Consolidated School Dist 21 of Wheeling Twp; Sherman v (1993)	32.06(A)
Community Consolidated School Dist 21 of Wheeling Twp; Sherman v (1992)	32.03
Community Consolidated School Dist No. 21 Bd of Ed v Illinois State Bd of Ed	28.03, 28.11(D)
Community for Creative Non-Violence v Reid	33.06(C)
Concord School Committee; Roland M. v	28.11(D)
Congregation Beth Judea, Inc; Elbaz v	48.30
Conklin, In re	28.03
Conneaut Area City School Dist Bd of Ed; Bernardini v	10.03(D)
Conneaut Area City School Dist Bd of Ed; Mason v	8.09, 9.14(A)
Connecticut Bd of Ed; Briggs v	28.05(B)
Connecticut Bd of Ed; Doe v	28.01(B)
Connick v Myers	9.21(E)
Connor; Oswald v	16.03(A)
Connor; Ryan v	16.03(A)
Connors v Fairview Park Bd of Ed	25.14(A)

Casename	Text Section(s)
Connor v Village of Lakemore	5.12(B)
Consolidated High School Dist No. 230; Cornfield v	46.15(C), 47.01(A)
Consolidated Rail Corp v Darrone	17.13(A), 19.13(E), 28.12(A)
Consolidation Coal Co, State ex rel v Yance	16.05(F)
Continental Local School Dist Bd of Ed; State ex rel Gandy v	8.04(D), 9.05(B)
Cook v Berger	7.06(B)
Cook; Cason v	47.01(B)
Cook v Maxwell	18.22(A)
Cook v Mayfield	16.07(B)
Cook; Mt. Healthy Bd of Ed v	15.02(A)
Cook; State ex rel Clarke v	23.04(A)
Cook, State ex rel v Paulding Exempted Village School Dist Bd of Ed	7.13
Coons v Ohio State University	12.04(B)
Cooper v Eugene School Dist No. 4J	32.01
Cooper v Williamson County Bd of Ed	17.03(E)
Coosa County Bd of Ed; Belyeu v	9.21(E)
Copiague Union Free School Dist; Donohue v	48.34(C)
Copley Bd of Ed; Vallish v	46.02
Copp v Unified School Dist No. 501	9.21(E)
Cordrey v Euckert	28.03, 28.04, 28.09(A), 28.11(B), 28.11(D)
Coriz v Martinez	46.15(C)
Cornelius v Euclid Bd of Ed	46.05
Cornelius v NAACP Legal Defense and Educational Fund, Inc	25.05
Cornfield v Consolidated High School Dist No. 230	46.15(C), 47.01(A)
Corpus Christi Independent School Dist; Buser v	28.02, 28.11(A), 28.11(B)
Corpus Christi Independent School Dist; Christopher M. v	28.01(A), 28.11(D)
Cosgrove v Williamsburg of Cincinnati Management Co, Inc	17.04(B)
County of Kanawha Bd of Ed; Williams v	33.04
County of Orange; Lichtler v	46.14(B)
Covington Bd of Ed; State ex rel Mack v	21.05(C)
Covington Exempted Village School Dist Bd of Ed; Mauchamer v	9.11(B)
Cox v Dardenelle Public School Dist	9.21(E)
Cox v Miller County R-I School Dist	9.21(E)
Cox, State ex rel v Crestview Local School Dist Bd of Ed	5.13(A)
CPC Group, General Motors Corp, State ex rel v Industrial Comm	16.05(E)
Crabtree v Wellston City School Dist Bd of Ed	6.04
Crabtree v West Clermont Local School Dist Bd of Ed	12.16(C)
Craddolph v Ackerman	12.17(A)
Crago v Olentangy Local School Dist Bd of Ed	9.22(A), 46.14(A)
Craig v Columbus City Schools	46.13(A)
Craik v Minnesota State University Board	17.03(F)
Crain v Hamilton County Bd of Ed	12.16(A), 22.14
Crawford v Barberton City Schools Bd of Ed	9.08(D), 9.15(D), 10.03(B), 10.07
Crawford v Honig	28.10(A)
Crawford v Los Angeles Bd of Ed	19.12
Crawford v Pittman	28.04
C.R. Coblentz Local School Dist Bd of Ed; Royer v	25.04
Creighton; Anderson v	46.15(C)
Cremeans v Fairland Local School Dist Bd of Ed	28.03, 28.04, 28.06, 28.13(B)
Cremeens v Gallia County Local School Dist Bd of Ed	9.21(B)
Crestview Local School Dist Bd of Ed; State ex rel Cox v	5.13(A)
Crestwood Local School Dist; Moore v	28.13(D)
Criswell; Western Air Lines, Inc v	17.06(B)
Crocker v Tennessee Secondary School Athletic Assn (1992)	28.13(A)
Crocker v Tennessee Secondary School Athletic Assn (1989)	28.12(A)
Cromley v Lockport Twp High School Dist 205 Bd of Ed	9.21(E)

Casename	Text Section(s)
Cronin v East Ramapo Central School Dist Bd of Ed	28.11(F)
Cross v Princeton City School Dist Bd of Ed	25.12(B)
Crumpler v State Bd of Ed	8.07(A)
Crumpton v Bridgeport Ed Assn	17.18
Csanyi v Cuyahoga County Commrs	12.17(C), 22.14
Cuckler, In re	18.21(B)
Cumberland Valley School Dist; Dallam v	25.15(B)
Cunico v Pueblo School Dist No. 60	17.18
Cunningham v Beavers	46.14(B)
Cunningham; Tarka v	44.14(A), 44.19(A)
Curlee; Fyfe v	9.21(E)
Curran; VanLoock v	48.11(B)
Curran v Walsh Jesuit High School	24.05(A)
Curry, State ex rel v Grand Valley Local Schools Bd of Ed	9.11(B)
Curtis; Paredes v	25.10(B)
Cutler, State ex rel v Pike County Joint Area Vocational School Dist	9.19(A), 12.13
Cuyahoga County Bd of Commrs; Cuyahoga County Bd of Mental Retardation v	29.09(A), 40.05(C), 40.07
Cuyahoga County Bd of Commrs, In re	18.17(B)
Cuyahoga County Bd of Mental Retardation v Cuyahoga County Bd of Commrs	29.09(A), 40.05(C), 40.07
Cuyahoga County Bd of Revision; Cleveland Bd of Ed v (68 OS(3d))	39.04
Cuyahoga County Bd of Revision; Cleveland Bd of Ed v (70 OS(3d))	39.04
Cuyahoga County Bd of Revision; North Olmsted Bd of Ed v	39.04
Cuyahoga County Commissioners	18.28(B)
Cuyahoga County Commrs; Csanyi v	12.17(C), 22.14
Cuyahoga County Commrs, In re	18.23, 18.24(C)
Cuyahoga County Community College; Johnson v	25.03(B), 48.15
Cuyahoga County Community Health Bd, In re	18.08, 18.15(A)

Casename	Text Section(s)
Cuyahoga County Dept of Human Services; Seltzer v	12.17(B)
Cuyahoga County Dept of Human Services; State ex rel Renfro v	24.05(A)
Cuyahoga County Hospital; Shearer v	7.09(A), 12.04(B)
Cuyahoga County Hospital System; State ex rel Fox v	44.03
Cuyahoga County Nursing Home	18.15(A)
Cuyahoga County Sheriff's Dept, In re (1993)	18.18
Cuyahoga County Sheriff's Dept, In re (1992)	18.17(C)
Cuyahoga County Sheriff's Dept, In re (1990)	18.24(G)
Cuyahoga Falls; Brown v	12.04(A)
Cuyahoga Falls City School Dist Bd of Ed; Bitting v	9.19(B)
Cuyahoga Falls City School Dist Bd of Ed; Cuyahoga Falls Ed Assn v (1994)	9.19(A)
Cuyahoga Falls City School Dist Bd of Ed; Cuyahoga Falls Ed Assn v (1-27-93)	18.20
Cuyahoga Falls City School Dist Bd of Ed; Cuyahoga Falls Ed Assn v (7-31-91)	9.19(A)
Cuyahoga Falls City School Dist Bd of Ed; Cuyahoga Falls Ed Assn v (11-20-91)	10.02(A)
Cuyahoga Falls City School Dist Bd of Ed; Cuyahoga Falls Ed Assn v (9-27-89)	9.19(F)
Cuyahoga Falls City School Dist Bd of Ed; Lilley v	9.19(B)
Cuyahoga Falls City School Dist Bd of Ed; State Teachers Retirement Bd v (1985)	11.04(A)
Cuyahoga Falls City School Dist Bd of Ed; State Teachers Retirement System Bd v (1983)	11.02(C)
Cuyahoga Falls City School Dist Bd of Ed; Wolf v	5.06(A), 9.14(A)
Cuyahoga Falls Ed Assn v Cuyahoga Falls City School Dist Bd of Ed (1994)	9.19(A)
Cuyahoga Falls Ed Assn v Cuyahoga Falls City School Dist Bd of Ed (1-27-93)	18.20
Cuyahoga Falls Ed Assn v Cuyahoga Falls City School Dist Bd of Ed (7-31-91)	9.19(A)

Casename	Text Section(s)
Cuyahoga Falls Ed Assn v Cuyahoga Falls City School Dist Bd of Ed (11-20-91)	10.02(A)
Cuyahoga Falls Ed Assn v Cuyahoga Falls City School Dist Bd of Ed (9-27-89)	9.19(F)
Cuyahoga Falls; Tickhill v	18.22(A)
Cuyahoga Heights Bd of Ed	18.16(C)
Cuyahoga Valley Joint Vocational School Dist Bd of Ed; Hull v	46.13(B)
Cuyahoga Valley Joint Vocational School Dist Bd of Ed; Stuble v	25.10(C)
Czarnecki v Jones & Laughlin Steel Corp	16.03(A)

D

Casename	Text Section(s)
Dahmen, State ex rel v Youngstown	12.07(B)
Dale v Ohio Civil Service Employees Assn	5.07, 18.34
Dallam v Cumberland Valley School Dist	25.15(B)
Dallas Independent School Dist; Clark v	25.05, 32.06(A)
Dallas Independent School Dist; Jett v	17.02(A)
Dallas Independent School Dist; Leffall v	46.13(B), 46.14(B)
Damiano v Matish	18.21(C)
Danbury Bd of Ed; Starcher v	25.03(A)
Dangler v Yorktown Central Schools	25.15(B)
Daniel R.R. v State Bd of Ed	28.05(B)
Daniels v Quinn	9.21(E)
Daniels v Ravenna City School Dist Bd of Ed	17.03(F)
Daniels v Williams	46.14(B)
Daoust, State ex rel v Smith	41.14(C)
Dardanelle Public School Dist No. 15; Bull v	25.05
Dardenelle Public School Dist; Cox v	9.21(E)
Darlene L. v Illinois State Bd of Ed	28.07
Darrone; Consolidated Rail Corp v	17.13(A), 19.13(E), 28.12(A)
Dassel-Cokato Bd of Ed; Bush v	25.03(A)
Daubenmire v Lancaster City Schools	10.03(B)
Daugherty; Bralley v	16.03(C)
Daugherty; Lord v	16.03(B)
Davidson Academy; Thomas v	28.09(A)
Davidson v Cannon	46.14(B)
Davidson v Hanging Rock	5.11(D), 9.17

Casename	Text Section(s)
Davidson v Sheffield-Sheffield Lake Bd of Ed	5.12(B), 12.04(B)
Davies v Newark City School Dist Bd of Ed	12.14(A)
Davila; Metropolitan School Dist of Wayne Twp v	28.09(A)
Davis v Marion County Engineer	9.17
Davis; Matthews v	28.06
Davis v Meek	20.04
Davis; Paul v	46.13(C)
Davis v Scherer	46.15(C)
Davis v State Bd of Ed	4.09(A)
Davis; Washington v	17.02(B)
Day; Kenton City Schools Bd of Ed v	23.02(B)
Dayton Bd of Ed v Brinkman (1979)	19.06
Dayton Bd of Ed v Brinkman (1977)	19.06
Dayton Bd of Ed; Cephus v	9.23(B)
Dayton Bd of Ed; Dayton Classroom Teachers Assn v	18.01(C), 18.20, 46.08
Dayton Bd of Ed; Lacy v	9.19(E)
Dayton Bd of Ed; Shields v	10.01(B)
Dayton Bd of Ed, State ex rel v State Dept of Ed	22.07(C)
Dayton Christian Schools, Inc v Ohio Civil Rights Comm (F(2d))	17.15
Dayton Christian Schools, Inc; Ohio Civil Rights Comm v (US)	17.15
Dayton City Bd of Ed; Haws v	9.04
Dayton City School Dist	18.13
Dayton City School Dist; Black v	24.03(D)
Dayton City School Dist Bd of Ed, In re	18.29(D)
Dayton City School Dist Bd of Ed; OAPSE, Chapter 643 v	18.26(A)
Dayton City School Dist Bd of Ed; State ex rel Cassels v (OS)	7.11(B), 7.14(B)
Dayton City School Dist Bd of Ed; State ex rel Cassels v (App)	7.11(B)
Dayton City School Dist; Mosely v	46.02
Dayton City School Dist; Stroud v	10.01(B)
Dayton Classroom Teachers Assn v Dayton Bd of Ed	18.01(C), 18.20, 46.08
Dayton; Hagerman v	18.01(A)
Dayton; Koenig v	46.18(F)
Dayton; Miller v	46.11

Casename	Text Section(s)
Dayton Public Schools; Simms v	46.02, 46.03
Dayton; State ex rel Caspar v	18.20
Day; Weir v	36.01, 38.02, 38.07
Deal v Cincinnati Bd of Ed (1969)	19.08(A), 19.10
Deal v Cincinnati Bd of Ed (1966)	19.08(A), 19.10
Deal v Vandalia Butler City Schools Bd of Ed	9.20, 9.22(A)
DeArment v Harvey	48.22
Deborah V. v Leonard	28.09(A)
Decatur; Chrysinger v	25.16(A)
Deeds v Ironton	18.28(B)
Defendant I; Doe v	28.03, 28.11(D), 28.13(A)
Defiance Public Library; Small v	16.03(A)
Defore; Powell v	28.13(A)
DeJohn; Mayfield Hts Fire Fighters Assn, Local 1500, IAFF v	18.22(A)
De La Torre v Cleveland Bd of Ed	15.07
Delaware County; American Civil Liberties Union of Central Ohio v	32.06(B)
Delaware Dept of Public Instruction; Slack v	28.06
Delk, State ex rel v Industrial Comm	16.05(B)
Dellmuth v Muth	28.13(A)
DeLong v Southwest School Dist Bd of Ed	9.13(B)
Delph, State ex rel v Barr	5.12(D)
DeMarco v Holy Cross High School	48.30
Dembek, In re	48.13
Demos v Worthington City School Dist Bd of Ed	9.19(G)
Denison University v Board of Tax Appeals	48.33
Dennis, State ex rel v Hillsdale Local School Dist Bd of Ed (1988)	9.15(C)
Dennis, State ex rel v Hillsdale Local School Dist Bd of Ed (1986)	9.15(C)
DeNooyer v Livonia Public Schools	25.05, 32.06(A)
Denson v Steubenville Bd of Ed	26.15(B)
Dent v AT&T Technologies, Inc	16.06
Denton; Burke County Bd of Ed v	28.06

Casename	Text Section(s)
Denver Public Schools; Miles v	9.21(E)
Denver School Dist No. 1; Keyes v	19.04
Department of Administrative Services; Kinney v	12.17(C)
Department of Education; Eastland Joint Vocational School Dist v	27.02, 27.08(B)
Depas v Highland Local School Dist Bd of Ed	9.13(B)
DeRemer v Akron City School Dist Bd of Ed	12.13
DeRolph v State (App)	2.14, 39.01(B), 39.06(B)
DeRolph v State (CP)	39.01(B), 39.06(B)
Deryck v Akron City School Dist	5.06(A)
DeShaney v Winnebago County Dept of Social Services	46.14(B)
Des Moines Independent Community School Dist; Tinker v	25.05, 47.01(A)
Des Moines Independent Community School Dist; Winegar v	9.22(A)
Deters; State ex rel Scanlon v	44.02
Detroit Bd of Ed; Abood v	18.21(C)
Detroit Public Schools; Hall v	28.13(D)
Detsel v Auburn Enlarged City School Dist Bd of Ed	28.07
DeVennish v Columbus	18.28(B)
Devries v Fairfax County School Bd	28.05(B)
Dickinson Public Schools; Kadrmas v	22.01
Dickson County School Bd; Settle v	25.05
Diemer; Korte v	17.08(A)
Dienelt; Cabell County Bd of Ed v	28.03
Dietrich & Hoover v Circleville Recreation Center, Inc	29.04(H)
Dille; Oakwood City School Dist Bd of Ed v	23.02(B)
Dimasso v Eastwood High School Bd of Ed	46.02
Diocese of Alexandria; Knipmeyer v	48.19
Directors of School Dist 200; Fleischfresser v	33.04
Dispatch Printing Co; Mers v	48.26
Dispatch Printing Co, State ex rel v Wells	18.20, 44.02

Casename	Text Section(s)
District 27 Community School Bd v New York City Bd of Ed	21.03(D)
District No. 220; Martens v	47.01(B)
District of Columbia; Andersen v	28.03, 28.11(F)
District of Columbia Bd of Ed; North v	28.06
District of Columbia; Knight v	28.11(F)
District of Columbia; Moore v	28.13(D)
Diversitech General Plastic Film Div, State ex rel v Industrial Comm	16.05(B)
Dixon v Youngstown City Bd of Ed	25.16(A)
Dobrowolski; Hampton School Dist v	28.11(D), 28.13(A)
Dodd v Rue	7.06(C), 19.10
Doe v Alabama State Dept of Ed	28.03
Doe v Anrig	28.07
Doe v Barrington	46.14(E)
Doe v Belleville Public School Dist No. 118	21.03(D)
Doe v Clawson	32.06(B)
Doe v Connecticut Bd of Ed	28.01(B)
Doe v Defendant I	28.03, 28.11(D), 28.13(A)
Doe v Dolton Elementary School Dist No. 148	21.03(D)
Doe v Douglas County School Dist RE-1	46.14(B)
Doe v Duncanville Independent School Dist	32.05, 32.06(A)
Doe; Honig v	28.03, 28.09(A), 28.09(C)
Doe v Hononegah Community High School Dist No. 207 Bd of Ed	46.14(B), 46.15(C)
Doe v Human	32.04
Doe v Jefferson Area Local School Dist	46.01(C), 46.02
Doe v Petaluma City School Dist (F(3d))	19.14(A)
Doe v Petaluma City School Dist (FSupp)	19.14(A), 19.14(C), 46.14(B)
Doe; Plyler v	19.16
Doe v Renfrow (F(2d))	47.01(A), 47.03
Doe v Renfrow (FSupp)	47.01(B)
Doersam, State ex rel v Industrial Comm	16.05(G)
Doe v Smith	28.12(A)
Doe v Taylor Independent School Dist	46.14(B)
Doe v Tullahoma City Schools Bd of Ed	28.05(B), 28.11(D), 28.13(A)
Dole v Shenandoah Baptist Church	48.22, 48.30
Dolton Elementary School Dist No. 148; Doe v	21.03(D)
Donah, State ex rel v Windham Exempted Village School Dist Bd of Ed	7.09(A), 8.02(A), 9.07(A)
Donaldson, State ex rel v Athens City School Dist Bd of Ed	7.11(B)
Donnelly; Lynch v	32.06(B)
Donnelly; Yellow Freight Systems, Inc v	17.03(D)
Donohue v Copiague Union Free School Dist	48.34(C)
Dorian v Euclid Bd of Ed	9.19(E)
Dornette v Allais	23.06
Dorothy J. v Little Rock School Dist	46.14(B)
Dorrier; Jackson v	25.03(A), 25.04
Douglas v Cincinnati Bd of Ed	9.23(B)
Douglas County School Dist RE-1; Doe v	46.14(B)
Dover City School Dist Bd of Ed; Swinderman v	9.21(B), 10.16, 13.08(B)
Dove; Runge v	46.15(C)
Dowell; Oklahoma City Public Schools Bd of Ed v	19.03(B)
Doyle; Mt. Healthy City School Dist Bd of Ed v	9.21(E)
Doyle; T. Marzetti Co v	17.04(E)
Dreher v Amphitheater Unified School Dist	28.03
Drew P. v Clarke County School Dist	28.06
D.R. v Middle Bucks Area Vocational Technical School	46.14(B)
D.T. v Independent School Dist No. 16 of Pawnee County, Okla	46.13(B)
Dublin Local School Dist; Bolding v	46.02
Dudley; Pennington v	15.02(B)
Duer v Berea Bd of Ed	7.06(B)
Duke Power Co; Griggs v	17.07(A)
Duncan v Greenhills-Forest Park City School Dist Bd of Ed	9.21(B), 9.22(E), 9.23(B)
Duncan v Koustenis	24.03(D)
Duncanville Independent School Dist; Doe v	32.05, 32.06(A)
Duplaga v North Ridgeville Civil Service Comm	12.04(B)
Duran v Nitsche	25.05

Casename	Text Section(s)
Durant v Independent School Dist No. 16 of Leflore County, Oklahoma	9.21(E)
Duval County School Bd; Adler v	32.05
Dwyer, State ex rel v Middletown	44.02
Dyer County Bd of Ed; Webb v	17.02(B)

E

Casename	Text Section(s)
Eagle v Industrial Comm	16.03(C)
Earhart; State ex rel Bassman v	7.05(B), 7.11(A), 10.01(B), 12.15(B), 13.01(B)
East Akron Community House; Murphy v	17.06(B)
East Brunswick Bd of Ed; Pope v	32.06(A)
East Cleveland Bd of Ed; Brown v	18.22(A)
East Cleveland v East Cleveland Firefighters Local 500, IAFF	18.26
East Cleveland v SERB	18.26(C)
Eastern Local Bd of Ed; Myers v	25.12(B)
Eastern Local School Dist Bd of Ed	18.22(A)
East Franklin Local School Dist Bd of Ed; State ex rel Scharlotte v	9.11(B)
East Holmes Local Bd of Ed	18.16(C)
East Holmes Local School Dist Bd of Ed; Swaykus v	9.14(A)
Eastlake; Walker v	12.17(C), 12.17(D)
Eastland Joint Vocational School Dist v Department of Education	27.02, 27.08(B)
East Liverpool City School Dist Bd of Ed; Perorazio v	24.03(D)
East Liverpool Civil Service Comm; Renner v	12.17(A)
East Otero School Dist R-1; Rivera v	25.05
East Palestine City School Dist Bd of Ed v SERB	18.28(C)
East Palestine City School Dist Bd of Ed; SERB v	18.26(B)
East Ramapo Central School Dist Bd of Ed; Cronin v	28.11(F)
Eastwood High School Bd of Ed; Dimasso v	46.02
Eaton; Beare v	12.17(C)
Eaton City Bd of Ed, In re	18.17(B)

Casename	Text Section(s)
Eaton City School Dist Bd of Ed; SERB v	18.28(B)
Eaton City School Dist Bd of Ed, State ex rel v SERB	18.26(A), 18.33
Eaton Corp, State ex rel v Lancaster	16.05(B)
Ebert v Stark County Bd of Mental Retardation	7.05(B), 7.11(A), 10.01(B), 12.15(B), 13.01(B), 13.08(A), 29.13(B), 29.13(C), 43.05(B)
Edgewood Bd of Ed; Harper v	25.04
Edison Local School Dist Bd of Ed; Adams v	13.08(B)
Educational Research Council of America; Henkel v	48.26
Edwards v Aguillard	32.07
Edwards v Rees	47.01(A)
Edwin Shaw Hospital; Lawrence v	7.09(A), 12.04(B)
EEOC v Atlantic Community School Dist	17.06(B)
EEOC; Christiansburg Garment Co v	17.03(E), 46.16
EEOC v First Baptist Church	48.30
EEOC v Francis W. Parker School	17.06(B)
EEOC v Kamehameha Schools/Bishop Estate	48.30
EEOC v Tree of Life Christian Schools	48.30
EEOC v University of Detroit	17.15
EEOC; University of Pennsylvania v	9.13(A), 17.03(D)
Eggers v Bullitt County School Dist	28.13(D)
Egypt, Inc v Akron Bd of Ed	5.06(A)
Eibling; Holroyd v	25.15(A)
Eisenhuth v Moneyhon	24.03(A)
Eisenhut v Morrow	22.03(A)
Elbaz v Congregation Beth Judea, Inc	48.30
Eldridge, State ex rel v Industrial Comm	16.05(B)
Electric Auto-Lite Co; McKee v	16.03(A)
Elek v Huntington National Bank	17.04(B), 17.06(A)
Elida City Local Bd of Ed; Goldsmith v	9.21(A), 9.23(B)
Elida Local Bd of Ed; Rohrbaugh v	25.03(B), 25.14(A)
Elida Local School Dist Bd of Ed; Kunkelman v	12.16(A)

Casename	Text Section(s)
Eller v Muskingum Area Joint Vocational School Dist Bd of Ed	25.12(B)
Ellington; Williams v	46.15(C), 47.01(A)
Elliot v Rice	25.15(B)
Elliott v New Miami Bd of Ed	46.14(B)
Ellis v Brotherhood of Railway Clerks	18.21(C)
Ellison v Brady	17.11
Elms v Flick	38.06(B)
Elmwood Local Bd of Ed, In re	18.29(C)
Elmwood Local School Dist Bd of Ed v Yodzis	10.07, 10.07(B)
El Paso Community College; Grady v	46.15(C)
Elston v Talladega County Bd of Ed	19.13(A)
Elyria City School Dist Bd of Ed; Wetzel v	9.21(A)
Emmert v Hardin County Bd of Ed	4.10(A)
E.M. v Millville Bd of Ed	28.13(D)
Emory University; Jansen v	48.11(B)
Employment Div, Dept of Human Resources of Oregon v Smith	32.01
Employment Services Bureau Bd of Review; Mayes v	12.16(A), 15.08(A)
Employment Services Bureau Bd of Review; Pugh v	15.08(A)
Employment Services Bureau Bd of Review; Trowbridge v	15.02(B)
Employment Services Bureau Bd of Review; Watson v	15.02(B), 15.05(B)
Endry; Quappe v	32.06
Engel v Vitale	32.05
Engerud; State v	47.02
Enright; State ex rel Fant v	44.02, 44.03
Enterprise Consolidated School Dist; Lauderdale County School Dist v	19.05
Epperson v Arkansas	32.07
Erie County Bd of Mental Retardation & Developmental Disabilities, In re	18.08
Erie County School Dist Bd of Ed v Rhodes	39.06(B)
Erkkila v Painesville Twp Bd of Ed	6.05
Ernst v Georgetown Bd of Ed	25.10(B)
Erwin, State ex rel v Jackson County School Dist Bd of Ed	4.10(B)

Casename	Text Section(s)
Escambia County, Alabama Bd of Ed; Arnold v	46.14(E)
Espie v Columbus City School Dist	9.21(D)
Esselburne v Ohio Dept of Agriculture	12.14(B)
Essex; Wolman v	48.06(A)
Etheridge; State ex rel Luckey v	7.11(B)
Etheridge; State ex rel Smith v	7.11(B)
Euckert; Cordrey v	28.03, 28.04, 28.09(A), 28.11(B), 28.11(D)
Euclid v Administrator, Ohio Bureau of Employment Services	15.05(A)
Euclid Bd of Ed; Cornelius v	46.05
Euclid Bd of Ed; Dorian v	9.19(E)
Euclid Bd of Ed; Limerick v	24.03(D)
Euclid City School Dist Bd of Ed; State ex rel Gron v	9.08(D), 9.08(E), 9.15(D)
Eudela v Ohio Dept of Mental Health & Mental Retardation	12.04(B)
Eugene School Dist No. 4J; Cooper v	32.01
Evans v Greenview Local School Dist	25.12(B), 25.14(A)
Evans; Oscar Mayer & Co v	17.06(A)
Evans; State ex rel Ach v	5.13(B)
Evans, State ex rel v Moore	37.11
Evely v Carlon Co	48.26
Everett v Marcase	25.13
Everett; Radtke v	17.11
Evergreen Local School; Sparer v	9.13(C)
Eversole v Tuslaw Local School Dist	10.02(A)
Ezratty v Puerto Rico	28.13(A)

F

Casename	Text Section(s)
Fact Concerts, Inc; Newport v	17.02(B), 46.13(C)
Fairborn Bd of Ed; Park Hills Music Club v	5.08(B)
Fairfax County School Bd; Barnett v (F(2d))	28.03, 28.11(D)
Fairfax County School Bd; Barnett v (FSupp)	28.12(B)
Fairfax County School Bd; Devries v	28.05(B)
Fairfax County School Bd; Fairfax Covenant Church v	32.06(A)
Fairfax County School Bd; Seemuller v	9.21(E)

Casename	Text Section(s)
Fairfax Covenant Church v Fairfax County School Bd	32.06(A)
Fairfield City School Dist Bd of Ed; State ex rel Gingrich v	10.07(A), 10.07(B)
Fairfield County Bd of Mental Retardation, State ex rel v Fairfield County Budget Comm	40.05(C), 40.07
Fairfield County Budget Comm; State ex rel Fairfield County Bd of Mental Retardation v	40.05(C), 40.07
Fairfield Local School Dist; Ritter v	9.08(B)
Fairland Assn of Classroom Teachers	18.25(D)
Fairland Bd of Ed; Gillette v	28.11(D), 28.13(A)
Fairland Local School Dist Bd of Ed; Cremeans v	28.03, 28.04, 28.06, 28.13(B)
Fairland Local School Dist; Jones v	5.06(A)
Fairley v State Personnel Bd of Review	12.17(C)
Fair v School Employees Retirement System	14.11
Fairview Park Bd of Ed; Connors v	25.14(A)
Fairview Park City School Dist Bd of Ed; Rocky River School Dist Bd of Ed v	39.05
Fairview Park School Dist Bd of Ed, State ex rel v Rocky River School Dist Bd of Ed	4.11(A)
Family "A", In re	28.07
Fannin County School Dist; Russell v	46.14(B)
Fant v Regional Transit Authority Bd of Trustees	44.03
Fant, State ex rel v Enright	44.02, 44.03
Fant, State ex rel v Mengel	44.02
Farber v Massillon Bd of Ed	17.03(F)
Farmer v Kelleys Island Bd of Ed (69 OS(3d))	9.13(C)
Farmer v Kelleys Island Bd of Ed (70 OS(3d))	9.09(B), 9.10(B), 9.13(A)
Farrar v Hobby (502 US)	28.13(D)
Farrar v Hobby (506 US)	17.02(B)
Fawcett v G.C. Murphy & Co	48.26
Fayette School Dist; Felton v	25.15(B)
Fayette Twp Bd of Trustees; Fayette Volunteer Fire Dept No. 2 v	5.12(D)
Fayetteville-Perry Local School Dist Bd of Ed	18.16(B)
Fayetteville-Perry Local School Dist Bd of Ed; State ex rel Mullen v	9.17
Fayette Volunteer Fire Dept No. 2 v Fayette Twp Bd of Trustees	5.12(D)
FCC; Metro Broadcasting, Inc v	17.18
Featzka v Millcraft Paper Co	17.08(B)
Fee v Herndon	46.14(B)
Felch v Findlay College	48.24(A)
Felker v Mid-East Ohio Vocational School Dist Bd of Ed	18.20
Fellowship Baptist Church v Benton	32.02
Felter v Cape Girardeau School Dist	28.07
Felton; Aguilar v	48.06(C)
Felton v Fayette School Dist	25.15(B)
Fenley, State ex rel v Ohio Historical Society	44.03
Fenske, State ex rel v McGovern	46.08
Fenstermaker v Nesfedder	46.14(B)
Ferdinand v Hamilton Local Bd of Ed	12.13, 12.16(A)
Ferguson; Plessy v	19.02
Ferguson; State ex rel Mazzaro v	44.03
Fernandez; Alfonso v	21.01
Ferris Faculty Assn; Lehnert v (US)	18.21(C)
Ferris Faculty Assn; Lehnert v (F(2d))	18.21(C)
Ferris v Paulding Exempted Village School Dist Bd of Ed	4.04, 4.05(A), 7.06(C), 26.19
Fiber-Lite Corp, State ex rel v Industrial Comm	16.07(B)
Field Local School Dist; Allison v	24.03(C)
Field Local School Dist Bd of Ed; State ex rel Kellner v	9.11(A), 9.11(B)
Field v McDonald Bd of Ed	46.02, 46.05
Filipiak, State ex rel v Midview Local School Dist Bd of Ed	10.03(B)
Fincher v Canton City School Dist Bd of Ed	11.21(A)
Findlay City School Dist	18.26(B), 18.28(B)
Findlay City School Dist Bd of Ed	18.24(D)
Findlay City School Dist Bd of Ed v Findlay Ed Assn	18.22(A)
Findlay City School Dist Bd of Ed, In re	18.28(B)

Casename	Text Section(s)
Findlay College; Felch v	48.24(A)
Findlay Ed Assn; Findlay City School Dist Bd of Ed v	18.22(A)
Finfrock v Spencerville Local School Dist Bd of Ed	12.16(A)
Fink, State ex rel v Grandview Hts City School Dist Bd of Ed	8.02(B), 9.07(A), 10.02(A), 10.07(A)
Firefighters Local Union No. 1784 v Stotts	17.18
Firelands Local School Dist Bd of Ed; Abraham v	25.15(B)
Firestone Tire & Rubber Co, State ex rel v Industrial Comm	16.07(B)
First Baptist Church; EEOC v	48.30
First Natl Bank of Toledo, State ex rel v Sylvania City School Dist Bd of Ed	42.11(B)
Fischer v Rochester Community Schools	28.13(D)
Fisher v Brooklyn Bd of Ed	9.01(A)
Fisher v Mayfield	16.03, 16.03(A), 16.03(B), 16.03(C)
Fitzgerald; Harlow v	46.15(C)
Five-County Joint Juvenile Detention Center v SERB	18.15(F)
Fleischfresser v Directors of School Dist 200	33.04
Fleming; State ex rel Parsons v	18.22(A), 18.28(B)
Flick; Elms v	38.06(B)
Flickinger v School Bd of Norfolk, Va	9.21(E)
Florence County School Dist Four v Carter	28.13(A)
Florey v Sioux Falls School Dist 49-5	32.06(B)
Florian v Highland Local School Dist Bd of Ed (App)	9.21(B)
Florian v Highland Local School Dist Bd of Ed (FSupp)	2.16(B)
Florida; T.J. v	47.01(A)
Floyd County Bd of Ed; Blackburn v	9.21(E)
Floyd, State ex rel v Rock Hill Local School Bd of Ed	7.11(B)
Fordice; United States v	19.03(B)
Ford v Manuel	32.06
Forest Hills Local School Dist Bd of Ed	18.13
Forest Hills Local School Dist Bd of Ed; OAPSE, Chapter 177 v	18.22(B)
Forest Hills School Dist Bd of Ed; Petrie v	9.21(E), 44.08(B), 44.11
Forklift Systems, Inc; Harris v	17.11
Formani; Brunswick City School Dist Bd of Ed v	25.10(B)
Fort Frye Local School Dist Bd of Ed, In re	18.31
Fort Frye Local School Dist; State ex rel Butler v	7.14(B)
Fort Jennings Education Assn v Fort Jennings Local Bd of Ed	13.02(A)
Fort Smith School Dist; Cabelli v	17.13(A)
Fort Worth Bank and Trust; Watson v	17.03(F)
Fostoria City School Dist Bd of Ed; Thompson v	7.06(B), 9.06(A)
Fountain; Reusch v	28.04
Fountain Square Associates, Ltd; Columbus Bd of Ed v	39.04
Fowler v Lincoln County, Kentucky, Bd of Ed	9.21(E)
Fox v Industrial Comm	16.03(B)
Fox v Lakewood	5.12(D)
Fox, State ex rel v Cuyahoga County Hospital System	44.03
Fox, State ex rel v Montgomery County Joint Vocational School Dist	11.08(A)
Fox, State ex rel v Springfield Bd of Ed	7.06(B)
Francis W. Parker School; EEOC v	17.06(B)
Francu, State ex rel v Windham Exempted Village School Dist Bd of Ed	9.11(A), 9.11(B)
Franklin v Columbus Bd of Ed	10.08(B)
Franklin County Bd of Commrs, In re	18.10
Franklin County Bd of County Commrs v SERB	18.15(E)
Franklin County Bd of Ed; Lujan v	17.03(F)
Franklin County Bd of Revision; Buckeye Boxes, Inc v	39.04
Franklin County Bd of Revision; Hilliard City School Dist Bd of Ed v	39.04
Franklin County Law Enforcement Assn v Fraternal Order of Police, Lodge No. 9	18.26
Franklin County School Bd; Jackson v	28.03, 28.11(A)

Casename	Text Section(s)
Franklin County Sheriff	18.28(B)
Franklin County Sheriff, In re (1991)	18.24(G)
Franklin County Sheriff, In re (1990)	18.29(A)
Franklin County Sheriff's Dept v Fraternal Order of Police, Lodge No. 9	18.26
Franklin County Sheriff's Dept v SERB	18.26(A), 18.26(C), 18.33
Franklin v Gwinnett County Public Schools	19.13(E), 19.14(A), 19.14(C), 28.13(C)
Franklin Local School Dist (5-8-85)	18.05(A)
Franklin Local School Dist (9-20-85)	18.15(A)
Franklin Local School Dist Bd of Ed, In re	18.05(B), 18.07, 18.11(B), 18.12, 18.15(A)
Franklin University; Schoppelrei v	48.15
Frantz v Green Local School Dist Bd of Ed	12.09(F)
Fraser; Bethel School Dist No. 403 v	25.05
Fraternal Order of Police, Lodge No. 9; Franklin County Law Enforcement Assn v	18.26
Fraternal Order of Police, Lodge No. 9; Franklin County Sheriff's Dept v	18.26
Fraternal Order of Police, Ohio Labor Council, Inc; Hillsboro v	18.22(A)
Fraysier, State ex rel v Bexley City School Dist Bd of Ed	9.06(B), 9.11(B)
Frazee v Illinois Dept of Employment Security	32.01
Freeman v Pitts	19.03(B)
Freeman; State v	45.12
French; Knepper v	6.15(A), 6.15(B)
Fresh v Searcy	20.03(C)
Fridley High School; Bystrom v	25.05
Frierott v Vandalia-Butler Schools Bd of Ed	25.09(B)
Frith v Princeton City School Dist Bd of Ed	7.11(B), 46.08
Frontier Local Bd of Ed; Matheny v	5.12(B), 8.09, 9.05(A), 9.13(B), 44.08(B)
Frontrunner, Inc; Shaffer v	48.26
Frost; State ex rel Canfield v	12.07(A)
Frye; Widener v	47.01(A)

Casename	Text Section(s)
Ft. Frye Local School Dist Bd of Ed, In re	18.24(F)
Fuehrer v Westerville City School Dist Bd of Ed	46.11
Fuerst; State ex rel Baran v	12.15(A)
Fuerst; State ex rel Nelson v	44.03
Fulani v League of Women Voters Ed Fund	19.14(C)
Furnco Construction Corp v Waters	17.04(E)
Fyfe v Curlee	9.21(E)

G

Casename	Text Section(s)
Gagne; Maher v	17.02(B)
Gagne v Northwestern National Ins Co	17.06(B)
Gallagher v Pontiac School Dist	28.03
Gallant v Toledo Public Schools	17.04(B)
Gallia County Local School Bd; Russell v	5.06(C), 22.03(B)
Gallia County Local School Dist Bd of Ed; Cremeens v	9.21(B)
Gallia-Jackson-Vinton Joint Vocational Bd of Ed, In re	18.24(F)
Gallipolis Bd; Sargeant v	46.02
Galveston Independent School Dist; Gonzales v	9.21(E)
Gambill v Lebanon City School Dist Bd of Ed	46.02
Gandy, State ex rel v Continental Local School Dist Bd of Ed	8.04(D), 9.05(B)
Gannett Satellite Information Network, Inc v Chillicothe City School Dist Bd of Ed	5.12(B)
Gannon v Perk	12.14(A)
Gans; State v	20.02(A)
Garay, State ex rel v Hubbard Local School Dist Bd of Ed	9.08(C)
Garcia v San Antonio Metropolitan Transit Authority	13.01(B), 17.08(A)
Gardner v Liberty Center Local Schools Bd of Ed	12.10(A)
Garfield Heights City Dist Bd of Ed v Gillihan	12.15(B)
Garfield Heights City School Dist v State Bd of Ed (1995)	4.07(C), 4.11(B)
Garfield Heights City School Dist v State Bd of Ed (1990)	4.11(B)
Garland Independent School Dist; Texas State Teachers Assn v	17.02(B), 28.13(D), 46.16

Casename	Text Section(s)
Garnett v Renton School Dist No. 403	32.06(A)
Garofalo; State ex rel Shine v	12.17(C)
Garvie v Jackson	46.15(C)
Gates v River Local School Dist Bd of Ed (OS)	12.09(E)
Gates v River Local School Dist Bd of Ed (App)	12.09(D)
Gates v Unified School Dist No. 449 of Leavenworth County, Kansas	46.13(B)
Gaus v Westerville City School Dist	22.13(A)
Gay, State ex rel v Mihm	16.07(B)
G.C. Murphy & Co; Fawcett v	48.26
G.D. v Westmoreland School Dist	28.03
Geary v Visitation of Blessed Virgin Mary Parish School	48.30
Geauga County Budget Comm; South Russell v	40.06
Geauga County Budget Comm, State ex rel v Geauga County Court of Appeals	40.06
Geetronics, Inc; Bear v	9.21(F)
Geiger v Aurora City School Dist Bd of Ed	22.03(C), 22.03(D)
Geist v Ohio Dept of Commerce	18.22(A)
Geller v Markham	17.06(B)
GenCorp, Inc; Barnes v	17.06(B)
General American Transportation Corp, State ex rel v Industrial Comm	16.05(B)
General Bldg Contractors Assn v Pennsylvania	17.02(B)
General Casualty Co of Wisconsin; Thrasher v	46.14(B)
General Metal Heat Treating, Inc; Hill v	16.03(C)
General Motors Corp, State ex rel v Ohio Civil Rights Comm	17.04(C)
General Motors Corp; Village v	16.03(A)
George; State v	2.16(A)
George; State ex rel Higgins v	12.07(B)
Georgetown Bd of Ed; Ernst v	25.10(B)
Georgetown Bd of Ed; Kattine v	25.10(B)
Georgetown Exempted Village Schools	18.04(A)
Geraci v St. Xavier High School	48.15, 48.16, 48.27
Gerner v Salem City School Dist Bd of Ed	9.13(B)

Casename	Text Section(s)
Gerstmyer v Howard County Public Schools	28.11(D)
Gfell v Rickelman	25.03(A), 25.04
Giambrone v Spalding and Evenflo Co	17.06(A)
Giammarco v Columbus Bd of Ed	10.07(B)
Gibbon v YWCA of Hamilton	48.34(A)
Gibney, In re	18.21(C)
Gibney v Toledo Bd of Ed	18.21(B)
Giering v Parma Bd of Ed	9.21(A), 9.23(B)
Gilbert v Trumbull County Bd of Ed	12.16(C)
Gildersleeve, State ex rel v Whitehall City School Dist Bd of Ed	9.06(B), 9.09(E)
Giles; Henize v	15.08(B)
Giles v Howard University	48.11(B)
Gilhool; Hendricks v	28.17(B)
Gilhool; Lester H. v	28.12(A), 28.13(B)
Gillespie v Willard City Bd of Ed	18.21(C)
Gillette v Fairland Bd of Ed	28.11(D), 28.13(A)
Gilligan; Cleveland City School Dist Bd of Ed v	39.06(B)
Gillihan; Garfield Heights City Dist Bd of Ed v	12.15(B)
Gingrich, State ex rel v Fairfield City School Dist Bd of Ed	10.07(A), 10.07(B)
Girard Bd of Ed; Monico v	12.17(C)
Girard City School Dist Bd of Ed; Morgan v	25.03(B)
Girard City School Dist Bd of Ed; Sarra v	13.01(B)
Girard Civil Service Comm; State ex rel OAPSE v	12.04(A)
Girardier v Webster College	44.14(A)
Gissel Packing Co; NLRB v	18.14
Givhan v Western Line Consolidated School Dist	9.21(E)
Glade Valley School, Inc; Braun v	48.19
Glass, Molders, Pottery, Plastics & Allied Workers Intl Union, Local 333, State ex rel v SERB (1994)	18.11(A), 18.26(A)
Glass, Molders, Pottery, Plastics & Allied Workers Intl Union, Local 333, State ex rel v SERB (1993)	18.11(A), 18.16(A), 18.26(A)
Glass Workers Intl Union, Local #333, State ex rel v SERB	18.16(B)
Glenn v Harper	25.15(B)
Globe Trucking, Inc; Schell v	16.03(A)

Casename	Text Section(s)
Glocester School Committee; Mr. D. v	28.13(D)
Goduto; State v	24.05(D)
Goetz v Ansell	32.03
Goldman v Princeton City School Dist Bd of Ed	10.03(B)
Goldsmith v Elida City Local Bd of Ed	9.21(A), 9.23(B)
Gollnitz; Kettering Bd of Ed v	25.12(B)
Gomez v Illinois State Bd of Ed	19.15
Gomez v Toledo	46.15(C)
Gonzales v Galveston Independent School Dist	9.21(E)
Gonzalez v Ysleta Independent School Dist	46.13(B)
Goodall v Stafford County School Bd	28.03, 48.06(C)
Goodin v Alexander Local School Dist	46.02, 46.03
Good News/Good Sports Club v Ladue School Dist	32.06(A)
Goodwin v Clermont Northeastern School Dist	28.09(C)
Goolsby v Board of Education	44.11
Goose Creek Independent School Dist; Horton v	47.01(C)
Gorham-Fayette Bd of Ed; Borman v	46.14(A)
Gorham-Fayette Local Schools Bd of Ed v Lavens (App)	18.20
Gorham-Fayette Local Schools Bd of Ed v Lavens (CP)	9.13(C)
Goshen Local School Dist Bd of Ed; Ballard v	9.14(A)
Gosling; Rossi v	28.13(D)
Goss v Lopez	25.08, 25.09(A), 25.10(B), 25.10(C), 25.13, 46.14(A)
Grace Bible Fellowship, Inc v Maine School Administrative Dist No. 5	32.06(A)
Grace; Springdale School Dist No. 50 of Washington County v	28.05(B)
Grady v El Paso Community College	46.15(C)
Graham v Independent School Dist No. I-89	46.14(B)
Graham; Kentucky v	46.16
Graham; Stone v	32.06(B)
Graham v Triway Bd of Ed	12.13, 12.16(A)
Graham v Wooster City School Dist Bd of Ed	12.17(A)
Graley; Painter v	45.08(A), 48.26

Casename	Text Section(s)
Grand Rapids; Americans United for Separation of Church and State v	32.06(B)
Grand Rapids Bd of Ed; Burt v	46.14(A)
Grand Rapids Bd of Ed; State ex rel Greisinger v	38.07, 38.08(A), 38.09(A)
Grand Rapids School Dist v Ball	32.01, 48.06(C)
Grand Valley Local Schools Bd of Ed; State ex rel Curry v	9.11(B)
Grandview Heights City School Dist Bd of Ed, State ex rel v Morton	6.14(A), 6.14(C)
Grandview Hts City School Dist Bd of Ed; State ex rel Fink v	8.02(B), 9.07(A), 10.02(A), 10.07(A)
Granite City Community Unit School Dist No. 9; Robertson v	21.03(D), 28.01(B)
Granite School Dist v Shannon M.	28.07
Grano v Columbus Department of Development	17.03(F)
Grant Wood Area Education Agency; Mark A. v	28.05(B)
Granville Exempted Village School Dist Bd of Ed; Buckles v	9.14(A)
Graphic Enterprises of Ohio, Inc v Akron City School Dist Bd of Ed	37.06(A)
Graves v Youngstown City School Dist Bd of Ed	9.12, 10.01(B)
Gray; Boals v	9.21(E), 46.14(A)
Gray, State ex rel v Springfield City School Dist Bd of Ed	9.11(A), 9.11(D)
Graziano v Amherst Exempted Village School Dist Bd of Ed	9.22(F), 9.23(B)
Great American Federal Savings & Loan Assn v Novotny	17.02(A)
Greater Cincinnati Building & Trades Council, In re	18.25(D)
Greater Cleveland Regional Transit Authority, In re	18.05(A)
Greater Cleveland Regional Transit Authority; Shelton v	46.06
Greater Cleveland Regional Transit Authority; State ex rel Clark v	18.20

Casename	Text Section(s)
Greater Hoyt School Dist No. 61-4; Maynard v	44.14(A)
Great Oaks Joint Vocational School Dist; Noelker v	15.07
Greco v Roper	9.21(D)
Greeley v Miami Valley Maintenance Contractors, Inc	48.26
Greenhills-Forest Park City School Dist Bd of Ed; Duncan v	9.21(B), 9.22(E), 9.23(B)
Greenhills-Forest Park City School Dist Bd of Ed; Houck v	9.21(D), 9.23(B)
Greenhills-Forest Park City School Dist Bd of Ed; White v	9.23(A)
Green Local School Dist Bd of Ed; Frantz v	12.09(F)
Green Local School Dist Bd of Ed; Kiel v	9.01, 9.11(A), 9.13(C)
Green Local Teachers Assn v Blevins	10.07(B)
Green; McDonnell Douglas Corp v	17.03(F), 17.04(E)
Green v New Kent County School Bd	19.03(A)
Green, State ex rel v Lyden	23.02(B)
Greenview Local School Dist Bd of Ed	18.13
Greenview Local School Dist; Evans v	25.12(B), 25.14(A)
Greenway; Hobolth v	32.07
Greenwood Community School Corp Bd of Ed; Norris v	44.14(A)
Greenwood Independent School Dist; Knowlton v	9.21(E)
Greer v Rome City School Dist	28.05(B)
Gregoire v Centennial School Dist	32.06(A)
Gregory K. v Longview School Dist	28.09(A)
Greisinger, State ex rel v Grand Rapids Bd of Ed	38.07, 38.08(A), 38.09(A)
Grenig v Brooklyn Civil Service Comm	12.14(B)
Greyhound Lines, Inc; Koger v	16.03(B)
Griffin v Breckenridge	17.02(A)
Griffin v Hydra-Matic Div, General Motors Corp	16.03(C)
Griffin; State v	24.05(D)
Griffin v Thomas	9.21(E)
Griggs v Duke Power Co	17.07(A)

Casename	Text Section(s)
Griggsville Community Unit School Dist No. 4; Brown v (F(3d))	28.13(D)
Griggsville Community Unit School Dist No. 4; Brown v (FSupp)	28.13(D)
Grimes v Cavazos	19.13(A), 19.13(E)
Grimes v Sobol	19.13(A)
Groff v Hertenstein	48.12
Groff; Marting v	46.09
Gron, State ex rel v Euclid City School Dist Bd of Ed	9.08(D), 9.08(E), 9.15(D)
Grosser v Woollett	33.04
Gross v Lima Civil Service Comm	12.17(D)
Grove City Civil Service Comm; Lowe v	12.17(D)
Grove City College v Bell	30.09(B)
Grove v Mead School Dist No. 354	33.04
Groveport Madison Local Ed Assn, OEA/NEA v SERB	18.31
Grubbs; Kaelin v	28.09(A), 28.09(C)
Grumet; Kiryas Joel Village School Dist v	32.01
Grunwald v San Bernardino City Unified School Dist	18.21(C)
Guadalupe Organization, Inc v Tempe Elementary School Dist No. 3	19.15
Guardians Assn v New York City Civil Service Comm	19.13(E)
Guard; State ex rel Kilburn v	12.04(B)
Guchemand v Carrollton Exempted Village School Dist Bd of Ed	9.14(A), 9.14(B)
Guernsey County Budget Comm; Cambridge City School Dist v (App)	4.14(B), 39.03, 40.06
Guernsey County Budget Comm; Cambridge City School Dist v (BTA)	4.14(B), 40.06
Guerra; California Federal Savings & Loan Assn v	17.09(A)
Guhn v Clyde-Green Springs School Dist Bd of Ed	24.03(C)
Gulf & Western Mfg Co; Piecuch v	17.06(A)
Gum; Person v	24.03(D)
Gunther; Washington County v	17.08(C)
Guy v Springfield Local Bd of Ed	24.03(D)
Guyten v Rhodes	24.03(D), 25.06

Casename	Text Section(s)
Gwinnett County Public Schools; Franklin v	19.13(E), 19.14(A), 19.14(C), 28.13(C)
Gwirtz v Ohio Education Assn	18.21(C)

H

Casename	Text Section(s)
Hacienda La Puente Unified School Dist of Los Angeles v Honig	28.11(A)
Hackathorn v Springfield Local School Dist Bd of Ed	46.01(C), 46.01(D)
Haddix, State ex rel v Industrial Comm	16.07(B)
Hafer v Melo	46.15(A)
Haffer v Temple University (1987)	19.14(C)
Haffer v Temple University (1982)	30.09(B)
Hagerman v Dayton	18.01(A)
Hager v State Teachers Retirement System	11.19(C)
Haig v State Bd of Ed	22.03(C)
Haines v Board of County Commrs	41.17(E)
Halco v Administrator, Bureau of Employment Services	15.04
Halderman; Pennhurst State School & Hospital v	46.13(B)
Hale v Hudson Local School Dist	12.09(C)
Hale v Lancaster Bd of Ed	9.21(D), 9.23(B)
Hall v Columbus Bd of Ed	46.03
Hall v Detroit Public Schools	28.13(D)
Hallett v Stow Bd of Ed	46.02
Hallinan, State ex rel v Tallmadge City School Dist Bd of Ed	12.12, 12.16(A)
Hall v Knott County Bd of Ed	28.13(A), 28.13(B)
Hall v Lakeview Local School Dist Bd of Ed	12.09(G)
Hall; Mahavongsanan v	48.11(B)
Hall v Marion School Dist No. 2	9.21(E)
Halloran; Schaffer v	25.09(C)
Hall v Shawnee Mission School Dist (USD No. 512)	28.06
Hall v Tawney	46.14(B), 46.15(B)
Hall v Vance County Bd of Ed	28.03
Hall; Watkins v	37.01(A)
Hamilton City Bd of Ed; Buchheit v	9.19(C), 9.21(E)

Casename	Text Section(s)
Hamilton City School Dist	18.13, 18.16(B)
Hamilton City School Dist Bd of Ed; Hamilton Classroom Teachers Assn v	9.19(C)
Hamilton City School Dist Bd of Ed; Shie v (10-7-81)	9.23(C)
Hamilton City School Dist Bd of Ed; Shie v (11-25-81)	9.21(B), 9.22(F)
Hamilton Classroom Teachers Assn v Hamilton City School Dist Bd of Ed	9.19(C)
Hamilton County Bd of Ed; Crain v	12.16(A), 22.14
Hamilton County Bd of Ed; Indian Hill Exempted Village School Dist Bd of Ed v	5.11(B), 5.12(A)
Hamilton County Bd of Mental Retardation & Developmental Disabilities	18.12
Hamilton County Bd of Mental Retardation and Developmental Disabilities; Betts v	17.06(C)
Hamilton County Bd of Mental Retardation & Developmental Disabilities, In re	18.15(D)
Hamilton County Bd of Mental Retardation & Developmental Disabilities v Professionals Guild of Ohio	18.02, 18.15(D), 18.15(F)
Hamilton County Dept of Human Services	18.04(A), 18.24(E)
Hamilton County Dept of Welfare, In re	18.07
Hamilton Local Bd of Ed; Ferdinand v	12.13, 12.16(A)
Hamilton Local Bd of Ed; Hamilton Local Teachers Assn v (App)	9.14(A)
Hamilton Local Bd of Ed; Hamilton Local Teachers Assn v (CP)	9.14(B), 9.19(C)
Hamilton Local Teachers Assn v Hamilton Local Bd of Ed (App)	9.14(A)
Hamilton Local Teachers Assn v Hamilton Local Bd of Ed (CP)	9.14(B), 9.19(C)
Hamilton; Poe v	26.15(B), 46.03
Hamilton v SERB	18.04(A)
Hami v Youngstown Bd of Ed	5.13(B)
Hamlin, State ex rel v Collins	46.08, 46.09
Hampton School Dist v Dobrowolski	28.11(D), 28.13(A)

Casename	Text Section(s)
Hamrick v Medina County Joint Vocational Bd of Ed	44.11
Hamrock; State ex rel Steubenville School Dist Bd of Ed v	40.05(C)
H & B Marine, Inc; Kidder v	10.12(A)
Handler v Merrill Lynch Life Agency, Inc	48.26
Hanes v Smith	12.07(A)
Hanging Rock; Davidson v	5.11(D), 9.17
Hanly v Riverside Methodist Hospital	48.26
Hannan v Chesapeake Union Exempted Village School Dist Bd of Ed	10.16, 13.08(B)
Hannon; Parents in Action on Special Ed v	28.10(A)
Hanson v Kynast	48.34(A)
Hanzel v Arter	21.05(C)
Hara v Montgomery County Joint Vocational School Dist	9.14(A), 9.14(B)
Harasyn v Normandy Metals, Inc	16.08
Hardesty v River View Local School Dist Bd of Ed	5.12(D), 25.03(B), 25.12(A)
Hardin County Bd of Ed; Emmert v	4.10(A)
Harding Academy of Memphis, Inc; Boyd v	48.30
Harding Machine Co; Adams v	48.26
Hardison; Trans World Airlines v	17.15
Hardman v Unemployment Compensation Bd of Review	15.08(A)
Hardy; State ex rel Brubaker v	9.09(E)
Hargraves; Ordway v	20.04
Harker Hts, Texas; Collins v	46.13(B), 46.14(B)
Harland v West Clermont Local School Dist	46.02
Harlow v Fitzgerald	46.15(C)
Harover v Northwood	16.03(A)
Harper & Row Publishers, Inc v Nation Enterprises	33.06(B)
Harper v Edgewood Bd of Ed	25.04
Harper; Glenn v	25.15(B)
Harper, State ex rel v Bath-Richfield Local School Dist Bd of Ed	9.11(D)
Harrah v Harrison Hills City School Dist Bd of Ed	12.10(A)

Casename	Text Section(s)
Harrell, State ex rel v Streetsboro City School Dist Bd of Ed	4.11(A)
Harrington; Romano v	25.05
Harris v Atlas Single Ply Systems, Inc	37.14
Harris v Bennett	37.12(B)
Harris; Canton v	46.13(B)
Harris v Forklift Systems, Inc	17.11
Harris v Joint School Dist No. 241	32.05
Harris v Lewis	12.15(B)
Harris v Ohio Bureau of Employment Services	15.08(A), 17.13(A)
Harrison Hills City School Dist Bd of Ed; Harrah v	12.10(A)
Harrison Hills City School Dist Bd of Ed; Norman v	9.21(E)
Harris v Richards Mfg Co	17.02(A)
Harris; Searcey v	26.04
Harris; State v (1993)	24.14
Harris; State v (1982)	45.10
Hartley v Berlin-Milan Local School Dist	22.03(C), 48.08(A)
Hart v Sheffield-Sheffield Lake Bd of Ed	12.04(B)
Hartsock v Chrysler Corp	16.07(B)
Harvey; DeArment v	48.22
Hastings Public Schools; Petersen v	28.03
Hatcher v Bibb County Bd of Public Ed and Orphanage	9.21(E)
Hatton v Middletown	12.12
Haupricht v Rossford Exempted Village School Dist Bd of Ed	9.13(A), 9.13(B)
Hawkins County Bd of Ed; Mozert v	33.04
Hawkins v Leach	15.08(A)
Hawkins v Marion Correctional Institution	12.17(D)
Haws v Dayton City Bd of Ed	9.04
Haydon; Poe v	46.15(C)
Hayes v Cleveland Pneumatic Co	17.13(A)
Hayes v Westfall Local School Dist Bd of Ed	24.03(D)
Hazard; Mulligan v	46.14(A)
Hazardous Waste Facility Bd; Lepp v	18.22(A)
Hazelwood School Dist v Kuhlmeier	9.21(E), 25.05, 26.04, 33.04
Hazelwood School Dist v United States	17.03(F)
Hazen Paper Co v Biggins	17.06(A), 17.06(B)
Hazlett v Martin Chevrolet, Inc	17.13(A)

Casename	Text Section(s)
Heavy Runner v Bremner	19.15
Hedges v Wauconda Community Unit School Dist No. 118	32.06(A)
Hedrick v Center for Comprehensive Alcoholism Treatment	48.26
Hegele; Schank v	5.12(D), 25.12(A)
Heiny; University of Toledo v	15.05(B)
Helle v Landmark, Inc	48.26
Helmeci v Bureau of Motor Vehicles	20.10
Helmick v Cincinnati Word Processing, Inc	17.11
Helms; Hewitt v	28.13(D)
Helms v McDaniel	28.11(F)
Hemry v School Bd of Colorado Springs School Dist No. 11	25.05
Henderson, State ex rel v Maple Heights Civil Service Comm	12.17(C)
Hendrick Hudson Central School Dist Bd of Ed v Rowley	28.03, 28.11(D)
Hendricks v Gilhool	28.17(B)
Hendricks, State ex rel v Canfield Local School Dist Bd of Ed	9.09(E)
Hendry County School Bd; JSK v	28.03
Henize v Giles	15.08(B)
Henkel v Educational Research Council of America	48.26
Henrico County Public Schools; Spielberg v	28.03
Henry; State ex rel Runyan v	10.17(A), 11.16(B), 18.22(A)
Herbert; State v	42.02
Herman's Furniture, Inc; Schultz v	15.08(A)
Herman v Tuscarawas Valley Local School Dist Bd of Ed	18.22(A)
Herndon; Fee v	46.14(B)
Hershberger; State v	48.02
Hertenstein; Groff v	48.12
Hess v James A. Garfield Local School Dist Bd of Ed	7.04(B)
Hewitt v Helms	28.13(D)
Hickey; Ward v	9.21(E)
Hickman v Valley Local School Dist Bd of Ed	9.21(E)
Hicks; St. Mary's Honor Center v	17.03(F)
Higgins, State ex rel v George	12.07(B)
Higher; Howell v	48.10
Highlander v KFC Natl Management Co	17.11
Highland Local School Dist Bd of Ed; Depas v	9.13(B)
Highland Local School Dist Bd of Ed; Florian v (App)	9.21(B)
Highland Local School Dist Bd of Ed; Florian v (FSupp)	2.16(B)
Hildebrant v Lebanon Bd of Ed	46.02
Hill v General Metal Heat Treating, Inc	16.03(C)
Hilliard City School Dist Bd of Ed v Franklin County Bd of Revision	39.04
Hillsboro v Fraternal Order of Police, Ohio Labor Council, Inc	18.22(A)
Hillsboro, Ohio, City School Dist Bd of Ed; Cameron v	17.09(A), 46.14(E), 46.15(C)
Hillsborough County School Bd; Martinez v	21.03(D), 28.01(B)
Hillsdale Local School Dist Bd of Ed; State ex rel Dennis v (1988)	9.15(C)
Hillsdale Local School Dist Bd of Ed; State ex rel Dennis v (1986)	9.15(C)
Hill; State ex rel Randles v	5.12(D)
Hines v Cleveland School Dist Bd of Ed	5.06(C), 37.07(A), 43.07(B)
Hlynsky, State ex rel v Osnaburg Local School Dist Bd of Ed	9.01(A)
Hobby; Farrar v (502 US)	28.13(D)
Hobby; Farrar v (506 US)	17.02(B)
Hobolth v Greenway	32.07
Hocking County Engineer, In re	18.18
Hocking County Sheriff's Dept, In re	18.15(A)
Hoeflinger v West Clermont Local Bd of Ed	10.16, 13.08(B)
Hoelzer; Belmont-Harrison Area Joint Vocational School Dist Bd of Ed v	17.10
Hoffer; Menchhofer v	9.21(E)
Hoffman; State ex rel Vantage Joint Vocational School Dist Bd of Ed v	27.02, 27.08(B)

Casename	Text Section(s)
Hogan; Mississippi University for Women v	19.14(D)
Holeski v Lawrence	5.12
Hollaender Mfg Co; Hosking v	48.25
Holmes County Dept of Human Services	18.06
Holroyd v Eibling	25.15(A)
Holt; Brandon v	46.13(B)
Holthaus v Cincinnati Bd of Ed	9.14(B)
Holthaus v Cincinnati Public Schools Bd of Ed	46.14(B)
Holt; Honohan v	48.02
Holy Cross High School; DeMarco v	48.30
Honeywell Information Systems, Inc; Johnson v	17.03(E)
Honig; Crawford v	28.10(A)
Honig v Doe	28.03, 28.09(A), 28.09(C)
Honig; Hacienda La Puente Unified School Dist of Los Angeles v	28.11(A)
Honohan v Holt	48.02
Hononegah Community High School Dist No. 207 Bd of Ed; Doe v	46.14(B), 46.15(C)
Hoops v United Telephone Co of Ohio	17.06(A)
Hoover; State v	25.16(C)
Hopkins v Indian Hill Bd of Ed	9.21(D)
Hopkins; Price Waterhouse v	17.03(F)
Hopkins, State ex rel v Industrial Comm	16.05(F)
Horne v Clemens	44.08(B), 46.14(A)
Horner v Kentucky High School Athletic Assn	19.14(D)
Horner v Mary Institute	48.30
Horton v Goose Creek Independent School Dist	47.01(C)
Hosking v Hollaender Mfg Co	48.25
Hosmer; Baird v	24.03(D), 25.06, 46.03
Houck v Greenhills-Forest Park City School Dist Bd of Ed	9.21(D), 9.23(B)
Hourigan; Musso v	46.15(C)
Housing Authority of Newport; Salisbury v	46.14(A)
Howard County Public Schools; Gerstmyer v	28.11(D)
Howard; Miller v	24.03(C)
Howard University; Giles v	48.11(B)
Howell v Higher	48.10
Howell v Waterford Public Schools	28.12(B)
Howlett v Rose	46.13(A)
Hreha, State ex rel v Lorain Civil Service Comm	12.05(A)
H.R. Johnson Construction Co v Painesville Twp Local School Dist Bd of Ed	37.04(B)
Hsu v Roslyn Union Free School Dist No. 3	32.01
Hubbard Exempted Village School Dist Bd of Ed; Wilson v	12.09(A), 12.09(B)
Hubbard Local School Dist Bd of Ed; State ex rel Garay v	9.08(C)
Hubbard Local School Dist Bd of Ed; State ex rel Rogers v	9.08(C)
Hubbard Twp Trustees; SERB v	18.26(A)
Hubner v Sigall	46.06
Hudson; Chicago Teachers Union Local No. 1 v	18.21(C)
Hudson Local School Dist; Hale v	12.09(C)
Hudson v Normandy School Dist	17.06(B)
Hudson School Dist; Caroline T. v	28.11(E)
Hudson v Wheelersburg Rural School Dist Bd of Ed	37.06(A)
Huelskamp v Trotwood-Madison City School Dist Bd of Ed (App)	9.21(A)
Huelskamp v Trotwood-Madison City School Dist Bd of Ed (CP)	9.21(A)
Hull v Cuyahoga Valley Joint Vocational School Dist Bd of Ed	46.13(B)
Hull v Quitman County Bd of Ed	19.03(B)
Human; Doe v	32.04
Hummel v Buckeye Local School Dist Bd of Ed	10.04(D)
Huntington Local School Dist Bd of Ed; Aldridge v (1988)	9.22(E)
Huntington Local School Dist Bd of Ed; Aldridge v (1965)	9.21(A)
Huntington National Bank; Elek v	17.04(B), 17.06(A)
Hunt v Westlake City School Dist	9.13(C)

Casename	Text Section(s)
Hura, State ex rel v Brookfield Local School Dist Bd of Ed	9.05(A), 9.09(D)
Huron Bd of Ed; Pascoe v	8.04(D), 9.06(B)
Hurry v Jones	28.13(A)
Hutchinson v Ohio Ferro Alloys Corp	16.04
Hutt v Chillicothe Correctional Institute	12.17(A)
Hyche; Moore v	44.14(A)
Hyden v Wilson County Bd of Ed	28.13(D)
Hydra-Matic Div, General Motors Corp; Griffin v	16.03(C)

I

Casename	Text Section(s)
Idaho Migrant Council v Board of Education	19.15
Illinois Bd of Ed; Brookhart v	28.10(B)
Illinois Bd of Ed; Peoria School Dist 150 Bd of Ed v	28.09(C)
Illinois Dept of Children and Family Services; Landstrom v	46.15(C)
Illinois Dept of Employment Security; Frazee v	32.01
Illinois ex rel McCollum v Champaign County School Dist No. 71 Bd of Ed	32.01, 32.04
Illinois State Bd of Ed; Community Consolidated School Dist No. 21 Bd of Ed v	28.03, 28.11(D)
Illinois State Bd of Ed; Darlene L. v	28.07
Illinois State Bd of Ed; Gomez v	19.15
Illinois State Bd of Ed; Lachman v	28.03, 28.05(B)
Immaculata Preparatory School, Inc; Save Immaculata v	48.11(B)
Imm v Newbury Local School Dist Bd of Ed	9.21(D)
Independence; Owen v	46.13(B)
Independent Federation of Flight Attendants v Zipes	17.03(E)
Independent School Dist No. 16 of Leflore County, Oklahoma; Durant v	9.21(E)
Independent School Dist No. 16 of Pawnee County, Okla; D.T. v	46.13(B)
Independent School Dist No. 191; J.B. v	28.09(A)
Independent School Dist No. 25 of Adair County, Oklahoma; A.E. v	28.01(B)
Independent School Dist No. 4 of Bixby; Johnson v	28.04, 28.11(D)
Independent School Dist No. I-89; Graham v	46.14(B)
Indiana Area School Dist; Black v	46.14(B)
Indian Hill Bd of Ed; Hopkins v	9.21(D)
Indian Hill Exempted Village School Dist Bd of Ed v Hamilton County Bd of Ed	5.11(B), 5.12(A)
Indian Hill Exempted Village Schools Bd of Ed; Matta v	28.13(A)
Indian Lake Local School Dist Bd of Ed; State ex rel Tavenner v	5.07, 8.02(B), 9.07(A), 10.02(A)
Industrial Comm;—See name of plaintiff.	
Ingebretsen v Jackson Public School Dist	32.05
Ingersoll-Humphreys Div, Borg-Warner Corp; Phillips v	16.03(B)
Ingraham v Wright	25.16(B), 46.14(B)
Ingram; Ohio Civil Rights Comm v	17.04(D), 17.04(E)
In Interest of F.B.	47.01(B)
In re—See name of party.	
Interboro School Dist; Slotterback v	25.05, 32.06(A)
International Brotherhood of Firemen v Cleveland City School Dist Bd of Ed	18.22(A)
International Brotherhood of Teamsters v United States	17.02(B), 17.03(C), 17.03(F)
International Union of Operating Engineers, State ex rel v Cleveland	18.20
International Union of Operating Engineers, State ex rel v Simmons	18.20
Ironton; Deeds v	18.28(B)
Irving Independent School Dist v Tatro	28.07
Island Trees Union Free School Dist No. 26 Bd of Ed v Pico	32.07, 33.04

J

Casename	Text Section(s)
Jablonski; Boyer v	24.03(D)
Jachim v KUTV Inc	10.12(A)
Jackson; Albright v	18.22(A)
Jackson Bd of Ed; Wygant v	17.18

Casename	Text Section(s)
Jackson County Bd of Mental Retardation and Developmental Disabilities v Jackson County Bd of Commrs	29.09(A)
Jackson County School Dist Bd of Ed; State ex rel Erwin v	4.10(B)
Jackson v Dorrier	25.03(A), 25.04
Jackson v Franklin County School Bd	28.03, 28.11(A)
Jackson; Garvie v	46.15(C)
Jackson Milton Local School Dist Bd of Ed; Smider v	25.12(A)
Jackson v Ohio Civil Rights Comm	17.04(D)
Jackson; Ojai Unified School Dist v	28.06
Jackson Public School Dist; Ingebretsen v	32.05
Jackson v Wooster Bd of Ed	25.16(A)
Jacobs v Benedict	25.04
Jacobs v Marion Civil Service Comm	12.17(D)
Jacobson v Cincinnati Bd of Ed	17.18
Jacobs; Schneeweis v	46.14(A)
J.A. Croson Co; Richmond v	17.18
Jaffree; Wallace v	32.05
James A. Garfield Local School Dist Bd of Ed; Hess v	7.04(B)
James, State ex rel v Ohio State University	9.13(A), 44.02
Jane Doe "A" v St. Louis County Special School Dist	46.13(B), 46.15(C)
Jansen v Emory University	48.11(B)
Jantz v Muci	46.15(C)
Jaslow Dental Laboratory, Inc; Whelan Associates, Inc v	33.06(A)
J.B. v Independent School Dist No. 191	28.09(A)
Jefferson Area Local School Dist; Doe v	46.01(C), 46.02
Jefferson County Bd of Commrs v Board of Trustees	43.07(A)
Jefferson County Bd of Ed v Breen	28.13(B)
Jefferson County Bd of Ed; Mitchell v	17.08(A)
Jefferson County Bd of Ed; Tilton v	28.11(B)
Jefferson County Human Services Dept, In re	18.31
Jefferson County Joint Vocational School Dist Bd of Ed; Blubaugh v	9.19(B), 9.19(G)
Jefferson County, Kentucky Bd of Ed; Wooden v	17.06(B)
Jefferson County School Dist R-1; Urban v	28.05(B)
Jefferson Local School Dist Bd of Ed; Pendleton v	19.13(E)
Jefferson Local School Dist Bd of Ed; Powell v	12.16(C)
Jefferson Local School Dist; State ex rel Borders v	12.09(B)
Jefferson Technical College Ed Assn v SERB	18.22(B)
Jefferson Twp Rural School Dist Bd of Ed; State ex rel Clarke v	36.02(A)
Jeglin v San Jacinto Unified School Dist	25.04
Jenkins; Missouri v (1995)	19.03(B), 19.03(C), 19.05
Jenkins; Missouri v (1990)	19.03(C)
Jenkins; Missouri v (1989)	17.02(B), 46.16
Jenkins; State ex rel Board of County Commrs v	41.12(A)
Jennings v Joshua Independent School Dist	47.01(C)
Jett v Dallas Independent School Dist	17.02(A)
J.O. v Alton Community Unit School Dist 11	46.14(B)
Johnsen v Tulsa County, Oklahoma Independent School Dist No. 3	9.21(E)
Johnson v Bismarck Public School Dist	28.13(D)
Johnson; Bob Jones University v	48.09(A)
Johnson v Brunswick City School Dist Bd of Ed	15.05(A), 15.05(B)
Johnson City Central School Dist; Quackenbush v	28.13(A)
Johnson v Cuyahoga County Community College	25.03(B), 48.15
Johnson v Honeywell Information Systems, Inc	17.03(E)
Johnson v Independent School Dist No. 4 of Bixby	28.04, 28.11(D)
Johnson v Mayor of Baltimore	17.06(C)
Johnson v State Bd of Ed	8.07(A)
Johnson, State ex rel v Cleveland Hts-University Hts City School Dist Bd of Ed	18.22(A)
Johnson, State ex rel v Industrial Comm	16.05(E)

Casename	Text Section(s)
Johnson, State ex rel v Rawac Plating Co	16.05(B)
Johnson v Transportation Agency, Santa Clara County	17.18
Johnson v Westmoreland County School Bd	28.03
Johnston, State ex rel v Cincinnati Bd of Ed	9.10(D)
Joint School Dist No. 241; Harris v	32.05
Joki v Schuylerville Central School Dist Bd of Ed	32.06(B)
Jonathan Alder Local School Dist Bd of Ed; Antram v	9.19(A), 9.21(D)
Jones & Laughlin Steel Corp; Czarnecki v	16.03(A)
Jones & Laughlin Steel Corp, State ex rel v Industrial Comm	16.05(B)
Jones v Clear Creek Independent School Dist	32.05
Jones v Cleveland Civil Service Commrs	12.17(C)
Jones v Fairland Local School Dist	5.06(A)
Jones; Hurry v	28.13(A)
Jones v Morris	9.22(F), 9.23(B)
Jones v Mt. Healthy City School Dist Bd of Ed	9.22(F)
Jones v VIP Development Co	16.08
Jones v Walton	9.22(A)
Jorstad; Texas City Independent School Dist v	28.09(A)
Josey; Maldonado v	46.14(B)
Joshua Independent School Dist; Jennings v	47.01(C)
Joshua S.; Macomb County Intermediate School Dist v	28.07
JSK v Hendry County School Bd	28.03
Judd v Madison Local School Dist Bd of Ed	13.08(B)
Julian; Vindicator Printing Co v	44.02
Justus v Brown	9.09(B)
J. Weingarten, Inc; NLRB v	18.09

K

Casename	Text Section(s)
Kadrmas v Dickinson Public Schools	22.01
Kaelin v Grubbs	28.09(A), 28.09(C)
Kaiser Engineers, Inc; Morris v	17.06(A)
Kalu Canfield Driving Range; Zimmerman v	46.01(C), 46.03

Casename	Text Section(s)
Kamehameha Schools/Bishop Estate; EEOC v	48.30
Kammer v Akron Christian Schools	46.11, 48.34(A)
Karg v Wyandot County Engineer	12.17(A)
Karibian v Columbia University	17.11
Karnstein v Pewaukee School Bd	25.15(B)
Kattine v Georgetown Bd of Ed	25.10(B)
Katz v Maple Heights City School Dist Bd of Ed	9.21(D), 9.22(F), 10.16, 13.08(B)
Kauffman v Allied Signal, Inc, Autolite Div	17.11
Kaufman v OHSAA	30.11(C)
Keeley v Webb	17.12
Keene State College Bd of Trustees v Sweeney	17.04(E)
Kehoe v Brunswick City School Dist Bd of Ed	9.12
Kellenberger v Ross County Bd of Ed	4.14(A)
Kelley v Barberton City School Dist Bd of Ed	18.22(A)
Kelleys Island Bd of Ed; Farmer v (69 OS(3d))	9.13(C)
Kelleys Island Bd of Ed; Farmer v (70 OS(3d))	9.09(B), 9.10(B), 9.13(A)
Kelley, State ex rel v Clearcreek Local School Dist Bd of Ed	7.13, 9.07(A)
Kelley v University of Illinois Bd of Trustees	19.14(A)
Kellner, State ex rel v Field Local School Dist Bd of Ed	9.11(A), 9.11(B)
Kelly v Rocky River Bd of Ed	46.01(C)
Kelly v Wauconda Park Dist	17.06(A)
Kennedy v Cleveland	46.15(C)
Kenney v South Range Local School Dist Bd of Ed	12.16(C)
Kenston Bd of Ed; Zellman v	46.01(C)
Kenston Local School Dist Bd of Ed; Toth v	12.09(A)
Kenston School Dist Bd of Ed; Lynch v	5.10
Kent City School Dist; Rettig v (1986)	28.03
Kent City School Dist; Rettig v (1981)	28.04
Kenton City Schools Bd of Ed v Day	23.02(B)
Kent State University Bd of Trustees; Waliga v	48.15
Kent State University, In re	18.11(B)

Casename	Text Section(s)
Kent State University v Ohio Civil Rights Comm	17.13(A)
Kent State University; State ex rel Beacon Journal Publishing Co v	44.03
Kentucky v Graham	46.16
Kentucky High School Athletic Assn; Horner v	19.14(D)
Kentucky; Riggs v	46.14(A)
Kerans v Porter Paint Co	16.08, 17.11
Kerkam v McKenzie	28.11(D)
Kerkam v Superintendent, D.C. Public Schools	28.05(B)
Kerwin v Ashtabula County School Dist Bd of Ed	46.09
Kettering Bd of Ed v Gollnitz	25.12(B)
Kettering City School Dist Bd of Ed; Adams v	12.04(A)
Kettering v SERB	18.22(A)
Keyes v Denver School Dist No. 1	19.04
Keyishian v University of New York Bd of Regents	9.21(E)
KFC Natl Management Co; Highlander v	17.11
Kidder v H & B Marine, Inc	10.12(A)
Kiel v Green Local School Dist Bd of Ed	9.01, 9.11(A), 9.13(C)
Kiger; Association for Defense of Washington Local School Dist v	23.05, 33.02(A), 35.02(A)
Kilburn, State ex rel v Guard	12.04(B)
King v Norwood School Dist Bd of Ed	9.18
King v Rossford Exempted Village School Dist Bd of Ed	9.13(B)
Kingsbury v Southeast Local School	18.26
Kinkaid; McGinnis v	38.06(B)
Kinney v Department of Administrative Services	12.17(C)
Kinney; Miami Valley School v	48.33
Kinney; Seven Hills Schools v	48.33
Kinser v West Branch Local Bd of Ed	9.21(D)
Kinsey v Salado Independent School Dist	9.21(E)
Kinsley, State ex rel v Berea Bd of Ed	44.02
Kirby; Sherri A.D. v	28.03
Kirkland v Northside Independent School Dist	9.21(E)
Kirtland Bd of Ed; Balazs v	46.02
Kiryas Joel Village School Dist v Grumet	32.01

Casename	Text Section(s)
Kiser v Clear Fork Valley Local School Bd	25.03(B)
Kitchen, State ex rel v Christman	41.02, 43.29
Kiyosaki; Medeiros v	32.07
Kleczek v Rhode Island Interscholastic League, Inc	19.14(B)
Klevenhagen; Moreau v	13.02(B)
Knepper v French	6.15(A), 6.15(B)
Knight v Bureau of Employment Services	15.05(B)
Knight v District of Columbia	28.11(F)
Knipmeyer v Diocese of Alexandria	48.19
Knott County Bd of Ed; Hall v	28.13(A), 28.13(B)
Knowlton Construction Co v Olentangy Local School Bd of Ed	37.06(A)
Knowlton v Greenwood Independent School Dist	9.21(E)
Knox County Schools; Krichinsky v	28.13(D)
Knox County School System; Babb v	28.13(A)
Knox County, Tennessee School Dist; Middlebrook v	28.11(B)
Koch v Avon Bd of Ed	46.02, 46.03
Koenig v Dayton	46.18(F)
Koger v Greyhound Lines, Inc	16.03(B)
Kohmescher v Kroger Co	17.06(B)
Kohn; Rendell-Baker v	17.02(A), 48.16, 48.17
Kominos v Upper Saddle River Bd of Ed	28.12(A)
Korte v Diemer	17.08(A)
Kountz; State ex rel Portsmouth v	41.05(B)
Koustenis; Duncan v	24.03(D)
Kraft; State ex rel Steffen v	44.02
Kramer, State ex rel v Industrial Comm	16.07(B)
Kremer v Chemical Construction Corp	17.03(G)
Krichinsky v Knox County Schools	28.13(D)
Krise; State ex rel Ohio Bell Telephone Co v	16.04
Krizan; Mansfield City School Dist Bd of Ed v	10.07(B)
Krizek v Cicero-Stickney Twp High School Dist No. 201 Bd of Ed	9.21(E)
Kroger Co; Kohmescher v	17.06(B)
Krolopp v South Range Local School Dist Bd of Ed	7.06(B), 8.02(B), 9.07(A)
Kropf v Vermilion Bd of Ed	30.12, 46.03

Casename	Text Section(s)
Kruelle v New Castle County School Dist	28.06
Kuhlman v Leipsic	5.12(D)
Kuhlmeier; Hazelwood School Dist v	9.21(E), 25.05, 26.04, 33.04
Kuhn, State ex rel v Smith	37.04(A), 37.04(C)
Kuhn v St. John and West Shore Hospital	48.26
Kunkelman v Elida Local School Dist Bd of Ed	12.16(A)
Kurtzman; Lemon v	32.01
Kutevac; Bojac Corp v	46.05
KUTV Inc; Jachim v	10.12(A)
Kynast; Hanson v	48.34(A)

L

Casename	Text Section(s)
Lachman v Illinois State Bd of Ed	28.03, 28.05(B)
Lacy v Dayton Bd of Ed	9.19(E)
Ladue School Dist; Good News/Good Sports Club v	32.06(A)
LaFleur; Cleveland Bd of Ed v	10.20(B), 17.09(C), 20.04
Lake County Bd of Mental Retardation & Developmental Disabilities, In re (1992)	18.11(B), 18.14
Lake County Bd of Mental Retardation & Developmental Disabilities, In re (1990)	18.08, 18.17(A)
Lake County Bd of Mental Retardation & Developmental Disabilities, In re (1985)	18.15(A), 18.15(C), 18.17(B)
Lake County Budget Comm; Waite Hill v	40.07
Lake Ed Assn v Lake Local Schools Bd of Ed	10.10(A)
Lake Local School Dist Bd of Ed; Miner v	7.06(B), 12.09(C)
Lake Local Schools Bd of Ed; Lake Ed Assn v	10.10(A)
Lake Michigan College Federation of Teachers v Lake Michigan Community College	46.14(A)
Lake Oswego School Dist No. 7J; Ash v (F(2d))	28.13(A)
Lake Oswego School Dist No. 7J; Ash v (FSupp)	28.06
Lake Ridge Academy v Carney	48.12
Lakeview Local School Dist Bd of Ed; Hall v	12.09(G)
Lakewood Bd of Ed; Mackulin v	46.02

Casename	Text Section(s)
Lakewood Bd of Ed; Wheeler v	46.11
Lakewood City School Dist Bd of Ed; OAPSE v	12.17(B), 18.22(A)
Lakewood Civil Service Comm; Riordin v	12.17(B)
Lakewood; Fox v	5.12(D)
Lakewood v SERB	18.26(C)
Lakota Local School Dist Bd of Ed	18.13
Lakota Local School Dist Bd of Ed, In re	18.24(B)
Lakota Local School Dist Bd of Ed; Zartman v	9.11(D)
Lamb v Norton City School Dist Bd of Ed	12.17(A)
Lamb's Chapel v Center Moriches Union Free School Dist	32.06(A)
Lamont X. v Quisenberry	28.09(A)
Lancaster; Aksterowicz v	12.14(B)
Lancaster Bd of Ed; Hale v	9.21(D), 9.23(B)
Lancaster City School Dist Bd of Ed; Medburg v	12.07(A)
Lancaster City Schools; Daubenmire v	10.03(B)
Lancaster County School Dist No. 160; Schanou v	32.01
Lancaster Police Dept; State ex rel Outlet Communications, Inc v	44.02, 44.03
Lancaster; Spires v	46.06
Lancaster; State ex rel Eaton Corp v	16.05(B)
Landis, In re	48.12
Landmark, Inc; Helle v	48.26
Landstrom v Illinois Dept of Children and Family Services	46.15(C)
Lane; Akron v	20.03(C)
LanFranchi, State ex rel v Summit County Bd of Mental Retardation & Developmental Disabilities	29.13(C)
Laricchiuta, In re	23.02(B)
Laskey, State ex rel v Perrysburg Bd of Ed	46.08
Laucher v Simpson	25.04
Lauderdale County School Dist v Enterprise Consolidated School Dist	19.05
Lau v Nichols	19.15
Laurel School Dist Bd of Ed; Morris v	46.14(D)
Lavens; Gorham-Fayette Local Schools Bd of Ed v (App)	18.20

Casename	Text Section(s)
Lavens; Gorham-Fayette Local Schools Bd of Ed v (CP)	9.13(C)
Lawrence v Edwin Shaw Hospital	7.09(A), 12.04(B)
Lawrence; Holeski v	5.12
Layton v Clements	46.08
Leach; Hawkins v	15.08(A)
League of Women Voters Ed Fund; Fulani v	19.14(C)
Lear School, Inc; Tullis v	17.06(B)
Lebanon Bd of Ed; Hildebrant v	46.02
Lebanon City School Dist Bd of Ed; Gambill v	46.02
Lebanon City School Dist Bd of Ed; Robinson v	9.21(E)
LeClain v Logan Civil Service Comm	12.17(B)
Lee v Rapid City Area School Dist No. 51-4	17.06(A)
Lee, State ex rel v Bellefontaine City Bd of Ed	9.09(C)
Lee v Weisman	32.05
Leffall v Dallas Independent School Dist	46.13(B), 46.14(B)
Lehmann v Los Angeles City Bd of Ed	24.03(D)
Lehnert v Ferris Faculty Assn (US)	18.21(C)
Lehnert v Ferris Faculty Assn (F(2d))	18.21(C)
Leipsic; Kuhlman v	5.12(D)
Lemon v Kurtzman	32.01
Leonard; Deborah V. v	28.09(A)
Leonardi v Wickliffe Civil Service Comm	12.14(B)
Lepp v Hazardous Waste Facility Bd	18.22(A)
Lesak; State ex rel Plain Dealer Publishing Co v	23.03(A), 30.10(C), 39.15, 44.02
Lester H. v Gilhool	28.12(A), 28.13(B)
Levy; State v	20.09(B)
Lewis; Harris v	12.15(B)
Lexington Local Bd of Ed; Lowary v (1990)	18.21(C)
Lexington Local Bd of Ed; Lowary v (1988)	18.21(C)
Lexington Local Bd of Ed; Lowary v (1987)	18.21(C)
Lexington Local School Dist Bd of Ed; State ex rel McMillan v	9.09(E)

Casename	Text Section(s)
Leyden Community High School Dist 212; Maganuco v	17.09(A)
Liberty Center Local Schools Bd of Ed; Gardner v	12.10(A)
Liberty Local School Dist, In re	18.25(A)
Lichtler v County of Orange	46.14(B)
Licking Heights Local School Dist Bd of Ed; State ex rel Remley v	9.09(C)
Light v Parkway C-2 School Dist	28.09(A)
Like; Stanley v	36.02(C)
Lilley v Cuyahoga Falls City School Dist Bd of Ed	9.19(B)
Lima City Bd of Ed; Armstead v	25.12(A)
Lima Civil Service Comm; Gross v	12.17(D)
Limerick v Euclid Bd of Ed	24.03(D)
Lincoln County, Kentucky, Bd of Ed; Fowler v	9.21(E)
Linn v United Plant Guard Workers, Local 114	18.34
Lion Oil Co; NLRB v	18.30
Lipp v Morris	32.03
Lipsett v University of Puerto Rico	19.14(A)
Liptak, In re	18.21(C)
Listerman; Brasch v	24.03(D)
Little Forest Medical Center of Akron v Ohio Civil Rights Comm	17.03(B), 17.04(B)
Little Rock School Dist; Dorothy J. v	46.14(B)
Little v Wuerl	48.30
Litwiller; Meyer v	46.14(B)
Liverpool Central School Dist Bd of Ed; Seneca Falls Central School Dist Bd of Ed v	28.11(F)
Livingston, State ex rel v Belmont-Harrison Joint Vocational School Dist Bd of Ed	9.09(E)
Livonia Public Schools; DeNooyer v	25.05, 32.06(A)
Local 4501, Communications Workers of America v Ohio State University	12.17(B)
Local No. 2134, International Assn of Firefighters v Marion Twp Bd of Trustees	18.22(A)
Locher, State ex rel v Menning	23.04(A)

Casename	Text Section(s)
Lockland City School Dist Bd of Ed; Walker v	5.06(A)
Lockport Twp High School Dist 205 Bd of Ed; Cromley v	9.21(E)
Lodi; Matulin v	9.21(E)
Logan Civil Service Comm; LeClain v	12.17(B)
Logan-Hocking City School Dist Bd of Ed; Sellers v	9.21(B), 9.21(D), 9.23(B)
Logsdon v Pavilion Central School Dist Bd of Ed	28.11(F)
Lohnes v Young	16.03(C)
Longview School Dist; Gregory K. v	28.09(A)
Lopez; Goss v	25.08, 25.09(A), 25.10(B), 25.10(C), 25.13, 46.14(A)
Lopez; United States v	25.10(A)
Lorain Bd of Ed; Lorain NAACP v	19.10
Lorain City School Dist Bd of Ed, In re	18.28(B)
Lorain City School Dist Bd of Ed; Lorain Ed Assn v	18.26(C)
Lorain City School Dist Bd of Ed v SERB	18.26(C), 18.28(B)
Lorain Civil Service Comm; State ex rel Hreha v	12.05(A)
Lorain County School Dist Bd of Ed; Bennett v	8.02(A)
Lorain Ed Assn v Lorain City School Dist Bd of Ed	18.26(C)
Lorain Journal Co; Milkovich v	5.07
Lorain Journal Co, State ex rel v Lorain	44.02
Lorain NAACP v Lorain Bd of Ed	19.10
Lorain; State ex rel Lorain Journal Co v	44.02
Lord v Daugherty	16.03(B)
Lordstown; Chaney v	37.06(A)
Lordstown Local School Dist Bd of Ed v Ohio Civil Rights Comm	17.04(C), 17.09(C), 17.10, 18.26(A)
Los Angeles Bd of Ed; Crawford v	19.12
Los Angeles City Bd of Ed; Lehmann v	24.03(D)
Los Angeles Unified School Dist; Mitchell v	18.21(C)
Loudermill; Cleveland Bd of Ed v	6.03(A), 9.22(A), 12.16(B), 12.17(B), 46.14(A)
Loudonville-Perrysville Exempted Village Bd of Ed; Pertuset v	46.13(C)
Loveland Ed Assn v Loveland City School Dist Bd of Ed	18.01(C)
Lovell v Poway Unified School Dist	25.05
Love v Pullman	17.03(D)
Lowary v Lexington Local Bd of Ed (1990)	18.21(C)
Lowary v Lexington Local Bd of Ed (1988)	18.21(C)
Lowary v Lexington Local Bd of Ed (1987)	18.21(C)
Lowe v Commack Union Free School Dist	17.06(B)
Lowe v Grove City Civil Service Comm	12.17(D)
Lower Merion School Dist Bd of School Directors; Student Coalition for Peace v	25.05, 32.06(A)
Loy v Unemployment Compensation Bd of Review	15.08(A)
Lucas; Carroll v	46.03
Lucas County Bd of Mental Retardation & Developmental Disabilities	18.15(D)
Lucas County Office of Ed; State ex rel Wilson v	4.03(B)
Lucas County Recorder's Office, In re	18.05(A)
Lucas v Lucas Local School Dist	37.02
Lucci v State Bd of Ed	8.07(A)
Luckey, State ex rel v Etheridge	7.11(B)
Ludwig v Willoughby-Eastlake City School Dist Bd of Ed	12.03(A), 12.14(E), 12.17(D)
Luethje v Peavine School Dist of Adair County	9.21(E)
Lujan v Franklin County Bd of Ed	17.03(F)
Lyden; State ex rel Green v	23.02(B)
Lynch v Donnelly	32.06(B)
Lynch v Kenston School Dist Bd of Ed	5.10
Lynch v Ohio State University	34.12(A)
Lyons v Smith	28.01(B), 28.02
Lysyj; Ohio Civil Rights Comm v	17.04(D)

M

Casename	Text Section(s)
Maceyko; State ex rel Spires v	9.06(B)
Mack; 2,867 Signers v	5.05

Casename	Text Section(s)
Mack, State ex rel v Covington Bd of Ed	21.05(C)
Mackulin v Lakewood Bd of Ed	46.02
Macomb County Intermediate School Dist v Joshua S.	28.07
MacPherson v University of Montevallo	17.06(B)
Madden, State ex rel v Windham Exempted Village School Dist Bd of Ed	9.09(E), 10.04(B), 10.07(A)
Madigan; Roberts v	33.04
Madison Bd of Ed; Calhoun v	9.21(C)
Madison Local School Dist Bd of Ed; Blust v	10.16, 13.08(B)
Madison Local School Dist Bd of Ed; Judd v	13.08(B)
Madison Local School Dist Bd of Ed; Wells v	9.21(B), 9.21(D)
Mad River-Green Local Bd of Ed, In re	18.17(C)
Mad River-Green Local Ed Assn	18.29(B)
Mad River Local School Dist; Rowland v (1984)	9.21(E)
Mad River Local School Dist; Rowland v (1978)	9.20
Mad River Township	18.11(B)
Mad River Twp Bd of Ed; Clements v	9.21(A)
Maganuco v Leyden Community High School Dist 212	17.09(A)
Magoffin County, Kentucky Bd of Ed; Adkins v	9.21(E)
Mahaney; Zachel v	46.11
Mahavongsanan v Hall	48.11(B)
Maher v Gagne	17.02(B)
Mahoning County Bd of Mental Retardation and Developmental Disabilities; Austintown Local School Dist Bd of Ed v	29.04(B)
Mahoning County Bd of Mental Retardation & Developmental Disabilities v Mahoning County TMR Ed Assn	18.22(A)
Mahoning County Dept of Human Services, In re	18.05(A)
Mahoning County Joint Vocational School Dist Bd of Ed; McLaughlin v	10.17(B)
Mahoning County TMR Ed Assn; Mahoning County Bd of Mental Retardation & Developmental Disabilities v	18.22(A)
Maine School Administrative Dist No. 56; Robbins v	46.13(B)
Maine School Administrative Dist No. 5; Grace Bible Fellowship, Inc v	32.06(A)
Maine v Thiboutot	46.13(B)
Maine Twp High School Dist 207; Wiemerslage v	25.03(A)
Maldonado v Josey	46.14(B)
Malina v Springfield City School Dist Bd of Ed	9.15(B)
Maloney; Poole v	12.17(D)
Manchester Ed Assn v Manchester Local School Dist Bd of Ed	10.11
Manchester Local School Dist Bd of Ed; Millhoff v	9.05(A), 9.19(A), 9.19(G)
Mancini, State ex rel v Ohio Bureau of Motor Vehicles	44.03
Mankato Independent School Dist No. 77; Schuldt v	28.05(B)
Manning v Clermont County Bd of Commrs	12.17(B)
Manning v Ohio State Library Bd	17.03(D)
Mansfield Bd of Ed; Mansfield Ed Assn v	9.19(C)
Mansfield Bd of Ed; Sterkel v	36.03
Mansfield v Cardinal Local School Dist Bd of Ed	12.16(A)
Mansfield City School Dist Bd of Ed v Krizan	10.07(B)
Mansfield Ed Assn v Mansfield Bd of Ed	9.19(C)
Manuel; Ford v	32.06
Maple Heights Bd of Ed; Maple Heights Teachers Assn v	10.04(B)
Maple Heights City School Dist Bd of Ed; Katz v	9.21(D), 9.22(F), 10.16, 13.08(B)
Maple Heights Civil Service Comm; State ex rel Henderson v	12.17(C)
Maple Heights School Dist Bd of Ed v Maple Heights Teachers Assn	6.07(C)
Maple Heights Teachers Assn v Maple Heights Bd of Ed	10.04(B)
Maple Heights Teachers Assn; Maple Heights School Dist Bd of Ed v	6.07(C)
Maple Hts Bd of Ed; Seither v	24.03(C)

Casename	Text Section(s)
Maplewood Local School Dist Bd of Ed; State ex rel Reams v	9.19(B)
Marana Unified School Dist No. 6 of Pima County; Wilson v	28.05(B)
Marcase; Everett v	25.13
Marchand v North Canton City School Dist Bd of Ed	9.09(D), 9.12
Marcus v Rowley	33.06(B)
Marcus X v Adams	28.12(A)
Margaretta Local Bd of Ed; Stewart v	9.20
Margaretta Local School Dist Bd of Ed; Mervine v	12.16(B), 22.13(A)
Margaretta Local School Dist, Transfer of Funds, In re	4.14(B)
Margolius, State ex rel v Cleveland	44.03
Mariemont Dist Bd of Ed; Wheeler v	9.21(D), 9.22(C), 9.22(D)
Marion Center Area School Dist; Pfeiffer v	19.14(C)
Marion City Bd of Ed; State ex rel White v	12.19
Marion Civil Service Comm; Jacobs v	12.17(D)
Marion Correctional Institution; Hawkins v	12.17(D)
Marion County Bd of Ed; Marion Local School Dist Bd of Ed v	6.15(A)
Marion County Children's Services Bd, In re	18.18
Marion County Engineer; Davis v	9.17
Marion Local School Dist Bd of Ed v Marion County Bd of Ed	6.15(A)
Marion School Dist No. 2; Hall v	9.21(E)
Marion Twp Bd of Trustees; Local No. 2134, International Assn of Firefighters v	18.22(A)
Mark A. v Grant Wood Area Education Agency	28.05(B)
Markham; Geller v	17.06(B)
Mark Z. v Mountain Brook Bd of Ed	28.06
Marshall; Scott v	24.03(B)
Marsh; State ex rel Cincinnati Post v	44.02, 44.09
Martens v District No. 220	47.01(B)
Marth; Shirokey v	46.13(C)
Martin v Bexley Civil Service Comm	12.17(D)

Casename	Text Section(s)
Martin Chevrolet, Inc; Hazlett v	17.13(A)
Martines v Cleveland City School Dist Bd of Ed	7.11(B)
Martines, State ex rel v Cleveland City School Dist Bd of Ed	7.11(B), 7.14(B)
Martinez; Coriz v	46.15(C)
Martinez-Fuerte; US v	47.01(A)
Martinez v Hillsborough County School Bd	21.03(D), 28.01(B)
Marting v Groff	46.09
Marting; Miami Trace Local School Dist Bd of Ed v	4.15(D), 5.07
Martin, In re	18.11(B)
Martins Ferry City School Dist Bd of Ed	18.10
Martin, State ex rel v Bexley School Dist Bd of Ed	18.26(B)
Martin; State ex rel Thompson Newspapers, Inc v	44.02
Martin v Washington Local Bd of Ed	10.16
Marvin H. v Austin Independent School Dist	28.12(B)
Mary Institute; Horner v	48.30
Marysville Exempted Village School Dist Bd of Ed; Beres v	46.14(A)
Mash v Westerville City School Dist Bd of Ed	12.13
Mason v Conneaut Area City School Dist Bd of Ed	8.09, 9.14(A)
Mason v Schenectady City School Dist	28.13(A)
Mason v US Fidelity & Guaranty Co	17.04(C)
Masotti v Tustin Unified School Dist	28.13(D)
Massachusetts Dept of Ed; Burlington School Committee v	28.13(A)
Massachusetts Dept of Ed; Pihl v	28.13(B)
Massillon Bd of Ed; Farber v	17.03(F)
Massillon City School Dist Bd of Ed v OHSAA	30.11(C)
Masterson; State ex rel Scott v	2.16(A)
Masters, State ex rel v Beamer	5.06(C)
Mastrangelo v West Side Union High School Dist of Mercer County	24.03(D)
Mate v Stow City School Dist Bd of Ed	9.09(D)

Casename	Text Section(s)
Matheny v Frontier Local Bd of Ed	5.12(B), 8.09, 9.05(A), 9.13(B), 44.08(B)
Matish; Damiano v	18.21(C)
Matta v Indian Hill Exempted Village Schools Bd of Ed	28.13(A)
Matthews v Davis	28.06
Matulin v Lodi	9.21(E)
Mauchamer v Covington Exempted Village School Dist Bd of Ed	9.11(B)
Maurer, State ex rel v Industrial Comm	16.05(D)
Mavis v Sobol	28.11(D)
Maxwell; Cook v	18.22(A)
Mayes v Employment Services Bureau Bd of Review	12.16(A), 15.08(A)
Mayfield; Bauder v	16.03(C)
Mayfield City School Dist Bd of Ed, In re	18.24(C), 18.28(B)
Mayfield; Cook v	16.07(B)
Mayfield; Fisher v	16.03, 16.03(A), 16.03(B), 16.03(C)
Mayfield Hts Fire Fighters Assn, Local 1500, IAFF v DeJohn	18.22(A)
Mayfield; State ex rel Polovischak v	44.02
Mayfield; White v	16.06
Maynard v Greater Hoyt School Dist No. 61-4	44.14(A)
Maynard v Smith	45.13
Mayor of Baltimore; Johnson v	17.06(C)
Mazzaro, State ex rel v Ferguson	44.03
McCartney v Oblates of St. Francis de Sales	5.07
McClain v Smith	28.11(F)
McClean Credit Union; Patterson v	17.02(A)
McClelland v Cincinnati School Dist Bd of Ed	9.21(D)
McClure; Schwing v	21.01, 39.13, 43.05(D)
McCollan; Baker v	46.13(C)
McConologue; Watkins v	9.22(A)
McCrary; Runyon v	48.09(A)
McCrea v Ohio Civil Rights Comm	17.04(C)
McCullom v Clow	46.02, 46.13(B)
McCullough; Webb v	25.06, 47.01(A)
McDaniel; Helms v	28.11(F)
McDonald Bd of Ed; Field v	46.02, 46.05
McDonald; Robinson v	37.01(A)
McDonnell Douglas Corp v Green	17.03(F), 17.04(E)
McElroy v Painesville City School Dist Bd of Ed	24.03(C)
McFarlin v Newport Special School Dist	25.15(B)
McGee, State ex rel v State Board of Psychology	44.02
McGill; White v	11.24(A)
McGinnis v Kinkaid	38.06(B)
McGovern; State ex rel Fenske v	46.08
McGraw, State ex rel v Industrial Comm	16.05(B)
McGregor Electronic Industries; Burns v	17.11
McGuire & Shook Corp; Tri-County North Local School Bd of Ed v	37.07(A), 43.07(B)
McGuire & Shook Corp; Tri-County North Local Schools Bd of Ed v	6.07(C)
McIntire v Bethel School, Independent School Dist No. 3	25.04
McIntyre v Westerville City School Dist Bd of Ed	5.12(D)
McKee v Electric Auto-Lite Co	16.03(A)
McKennon v Nashville Banner Publishing Co	17.03(E)
McKenzie; Kerkam v	28.11(D)
McKenzie v Smith	28.11(F)
McKenzie; Work v	28.07
McKinney v Brown	4.10(C)
McKita v Canton City School Dist Bd of Ed	9.09(C)
McLaughlin v Mahoning County Joint Vocational School Dist Bd of Ed	10.17(B)
McMaster v Chesapeake Union Exempted Village School Dist Bd of Ed	12.16(A)
McMaster, State ex rel v School Employees Retirement System	14.03, 14.11
McMillan, State ex rel v Lexington Local School Dist Bd of Ed	9.09(E)
McMinnville School Dist; Chandler v	25.05
McNair v Oak Hills Local School Dist	28.07
McNaughton v Circleville Bd of Ed	25.15(A)
McNeill; Thompson v	46.03
McPherson; Rankin v	9.21(E)
McWhirt v Williamson County Schools	28.03

Casename	Text Section(s)
Mead Corp; State ex rel Miller v	16.04
Meade Independent School Dist No. 101; Sullivan v	46.14(E)
Mead School Dist No. 354; Grove v	33.04
Mecca Twp Bd of Trustees; Black v	5.12(A)
Medart; Palace Hotel Co v	24.03(B)
Medburg v Lancaster City School Dist Bd of Ed	12.07(A)
Medeiros v Kiyosaki	32.07
Medina City Bd of Ed; Thaxton v	5.07
Medina County Commrs	18.11(B)
Medina County Joint Vocational Bd of Ed; Hamrick v	44.11
Medley v Springfield Local Schools Bd of Ed	9.21(A)
Meek; Davis v	20.04
Meigs Local School Dist Bd of Ed; Thornton v	12.16(A)
Meigs Local School Dist; Powell v	12.16(C)
Melo; Hafer v	46.15(A)
Memphis City Schools Bd of Ed; Northcross v	17.02(B)
Memphis Community School Dist v Stachura	46.13(C)
Menchhofer v Hoffer	9.21(E)
Menefee v Queen City Metro	46.05
Mengel; State ex rel Fant v	44.02
Meng, State ex rel v Todaro	24.11
Menke v OHSAA	30.11(C)
Menning; State ex rel Locher v	23.04(A)
Mentor Exempted Village School Dist Bd of Ed, In re	18.24(D)
Mentor Exempted Village School Dist Bd of Ed; OAPSE v	13.01(B)
Mentor Exempted Village School Dist Bd of Ed; Woerner v	12.16(C)
Mercer County Bd of Ed; State ex rel Muter v	4.10(A)
Mergens; Westside Community Schools Bd of Ed v	32.06(A)
Meritor Savings Bank, FSB v Vinson	17.11
Merrill Lynch Life Agency, Inc; Handler v	48.26
Merry v Perry Local School Dist Bd of Ed	9.19(A)
Mers v Dispatch Printing Co	48.26
Mervine v Margaretta Local School Dist Bd of Ed	12.16(B), 22.13(A)
Metcalf v Ohio Council 8, AFSCME,	18.26(A)
Metro Broadcasting, Inc v FCC	17.18
MetroHealth System; Ohio Patrolmen's Benevolent Assn v	18.26
Metropolitan School Dist of Washington Twp; Partee v	46.13(B)
Metropolitan School Dist of Wayne Twp v Davila	28.09(A)
Metzger v Osbeck	46.14(B)
Meyer v Litwiller	46.14(B)
Meyers Industries, Inc	18.09
Mezak, State ex rel v Berkshire Local School Dist Bd of Ed	9.09(D)
Miami East Local School Dist; Snyder v	9.21(B)
Miamisburg School Dist Bd of Ed, In re	18.22(A), 18.22(B), 18.29(A)
Miami Trace Local School Dist Bd of Ed v Marting	4.15(D), 5.07
Miami University, In re	18.29(C)
Miami University v SERB	18.18
Miami University; SERB v	18.18
Miami Valley Maintenance Contractors, Inc; Greeley v	48.26
Miami Valley School v Kinney	48.33
Michigan City Area Schools Bd of School Trustees; Vukadinovich v	9.21(E)
Michigan Dept of Ed; Barwacz v	28.07
Michigan Technological University; Milligan-Jensen v	17.03(E)
Middlebrook v Knox County, Tennessee School Dist	28.11(B)
Middle Bucks Area Vocational Technical School; D.R. v	46.14(B)
Middleburgh Central School Dist Bd of Ed; Armlin v	24.03(D)
Middletown City School Dist Bd of Ed; State ex rel Bentley v	12.14(D)
Middletown Civil Service Comm; Burns v	12.15(A)
Middletown; Hatton v	12.12
Middletown; State ex rel Dwyer v	44.02
Mid-East Ohio Vocational School Dist Bd of Ed; Felker v	18.20

Casename	Text Section(s)
Midland-Ross Corp; Simpson v	17.03(F)
Midview Local School Dist Bd of Ed; State ex rel Filipiak v	10.03(B)
Miener v Missouri	28.12(A), 28.13(A), 28.13(C)
Migra v Warren City School Dist Bd of Ed (1984)	46.13(C)
Migra v Warren City School Dist Bd of Ed (1982)	7.11(B)
Mihm; State ex rel Gay v	16.07(B)
Milburn, State ex rel v Industrial Comm	16.05(B)
Miles v Denver Public Schools	9.21(E)
Milford Exempted Village School Dist Bd of Ed; Blair v	12.09(B), 18.22(A)
Milkovich v Lorain Journal Co	5.07
Millcraft Paper Co; Featzka v	17.08(B)
Miller County R-I School Dist; Cox v	9.21(E)
Miller v Dayton	46.11
Miller v Howard	24.03(C)
Miller, In re	18.21(B)
Miller, State ex rel v Mead Corp	16.04
Miller v Summit County Bd of Ed	22.14
Miller v Wadsworth City Schools	46.01(B)
Miller v Wayne County Joint Vocational School Dist Bd of Ed	8.09, 9.09(B), 9.10(C)
Millhoff v Manchester Local School Dist Bd of Ed	9.05(A), 9.19(A), 9.19(G)
Milligan-Jensen v Michigan Technological University	17.03(E)
Milliken v Bradley (1977)	19.05
Milliken v Bradley (1974)	19.05
Millville Bd of Ed; E.M. v	28.13(D)
Milton-Union Exempted Village Bd of Ed; State ex rel Brown v	5.07, 8.02(B), 9.07(A), 9.08(C), 9.09(E), 10.02(A), 17.04(D), 18.26(B)
Mims v Chicago Bd of Ed	46.14(D)
Minarcini v Strongsville City School Dist	33.04
Miner v Lake Local School Dist Bd of Ed	7.06(B), 12.09(C)
Minerva Local School Dist Bd of Ed; Shaffer v	12.16(B)
Minford Local School Dist Bd of Ed; Allen v	12.09(A)
Minis v Unemployment Compensation Bd of Review	15.05(C)
Minnesota State University Board; Craik v	17.03(F)
Minnick v Springfield Local Schools Bd of Ed	46.03
Mississinawa Valley Local School Dist Bd of Ed; State ex rel Suitts v	9.09(C), 9.09(E)
Mississippi University for Women v Hogan	19.14(D)
Missouri v Jenkins (1995)	19.03(B), 19.03(C), 19.05
Missouri v Jenkins (1990)	19.03(C)
Missouri v Jenkins (1989)	17.02(B), 46.16
Missouri; Miener v	28.12(A), 28.13(A), 28.13(C)
Mitchell; Barlow-Gresham Union High School Dist No. 2 v	28.13(D)
Mitchell v Jefferson County Bd of Ed	17.08(A)
Mitchell v Los Angeles Unified School Dist	18.21(C)
Mitchell, State ex rel v Robbins & Myers, Inc	16.07(B)
Mitchell; Venegas v	17.02(B)
Mitten v Muscogee County School Dist	28.13(D)
M. Kramer Mfg Co v Andrews	33.06(A)
Mobile County Bd of School Commrs; Smith v	33.04
Mogadore Ed Assn v Mogadore Local School Dist Bd of Ed	9.19(E)
Moline School Dist No. 40; Nelson v	25.05
Molnar v Willoughby-Eastlake Bd of Ed	25.10(B)
Monaghan v Richley	46.08
Monahan v Nebraska	28.12(B)
Monell v New York City Dept of Social Services	17.09(C), 46.13(B)
Moneyhon; Eisenhuth v	24.03(A)
Monico v Girard Bd of Ed	12.17(C)
Monroe County Bd of Ed; Aurelia v	19.14(A)
Monroe County Bd of Ed; Beisel v	7.03(A)
Monroe County Bd of Ed; State ex rel Tschappat v	7.12
Monroe v Pape	46.13(B)
Monroeville Local School Dist Bd of Ed; Brown v	5.07
Montgomery v Carr	9.21(E)

Casename	Text Section(s)
Montgomery County Bd of Ed; Chris D. v	28.03
Montgomery County Bd of Ed, In re	18.08, 18.17(A)
Montgomery County Clerk of Courts v Ohio Council 8, AFSCME	18.18
Montgomery County Dept of Sanitation; State ex rel Cassity v	16.05(B)
Montgomery County Joint Vocational School Dist Bd of Ed, In re	18.17(C)
Montgomery County Joint Vocational School Dist; Hara v	9.14(A), 9.14(B)
Montgomery County Joint Vocational School Dist; State ex rel Fox v	11.08(A)
Montgomery County Welfare Dept; Walton v	12.07(A)
Montrose County School Dist RE-1J; Murray v	28.05(B)
Moore v Board of Education	32.04
Moore v Cleveland Civil Service Comm	12.17(D)
Moore v Crestwood Local School Dist	28.13(D)
Moore v District of Columbia	28.13(D)
Moore v Hyche	44.14(A)
Moore, In re	9.23(A)
Moore; State ex rel Evans v	37.11
Moore v Youngstown State University	18.19(A)
Moraine v Board of County Commrs	5.12(D)
Morales Medina; Santiago de Castro v	46.14(B)
Moreau v Klevenhagen	13.02(B)
Morgan v Girard City School Dist Bd of Ed	25.03(B)
Morgan Local School Dist Bd of Ed; Starlin v	9.17, 9.22(A)
Morin v Cleveland Metro School of Nursing	48.15
Morris; Jones v	9.22(F), 9.23(B)
Morris v Kaiser Engineers, Inc	17.06(A)
Morris v Laurel School Dist Bd of Ed	46.14(D)
Morris; Lipp v	32.03
Morrison; Bigley v	24.03(D)
Morrow; Eisenhut v	22.03(A)
Morton; State ex rel Grandview Heights City School Dist Bd of Ed v	6.14(A), 6.14(C)
Mosely v Dayton City School Dist	46.02

Casename	Text Section(s)
Mountain Brook Bd of Ed; Mark Z. v	28.06
Moyse v Runnels School Inc	48.11(B)
Mozert v Hawkins County Bd of Ed	33.04
Mr. D. v Glocester School Committee	28.13(D)
Mr. L. & Mrs. L. v Woonsocket Ed Dept	28.13(D)
Mroczek v Beachwood City School Dist Bd of Ed	7.06(B), 46.09
Mrs. C. v Wheaton	28.13(B)
MTD Products, Inc v Robatin	16.03(C)
Mt. Gilead Exempted Village School Dist Bd of Ed; State ex rel Van Dorn v	9.19(G)
Mt. Healthy Bd of Ed v Cook	15.02(A)
Mt. Healthy City School Dist Bd of Ed v Doyle	9.21(E)
Mt. Healthy City School Dist Bd of Ed; Jones v	9.22(F)
Muci; Jantz v	46.15(C)
Mueller v Board of Education	37.04(C)
Mulcahy v Board of Education	37.05
Mulder; United Food and Commercial Workers Local 951 v	18.21(C)
Mullen, State ex rel v Fayetteville-Perry Local School Dist Bd of Ed	9.17
Mulligan v Hazard	46.14(A)
Multimedia, Inc, State ex rel v Whalen (48 OS(3d))	44.02
Multimedia, Inc, State ex rel v Whalen (51 OS(3d))	44.03
Munson; State ex rel Buckman v	12.14(A)
Murphy v East Akron Community House	17.06(B)
Murphy; Poling v	25.05
Murray v Montrose County School Dist RE-1J	28.05(B)
Murray, State ex rel v Industrial Comm	16.05(F)
Murray v Washington Local School Dist Bd of Ed	10.19(A)
Muscogee County School Dist; Mitten v	28.13(D)
Muskingum Area Joint Vocational School Dist Bd of Ed; Eller v	25.12(B)
Muskingum County Area Joint Vocational School Dist Bd of Ed; Novak v	9.19(E)
Muskingum Vocational School Dist	18.06
Musso v Hourigan	46.15(C)

Casename	Text Section(s)
Muter, State ex rel v Mercer County Bd of Ed	4.10(A)
Muth v Central Bucks School Dist	28.11(F)
Muth; Dellmuth v	28.13(A)
Myers; Connick v	9.21(E)
Myers v Eastern Local Bd of Ed	25.12(B)
Myers v Riley	18.26
Myers v Waverly City School Dist Bd of Ed (App)	9.21(A), 9.23(B)
Myers v Waverly City School Dist Bd of Ed (CP)	9.21(D)

N

Casename	Text Section(s)
NAACP Legal Defense and Educational Fund, Inc; Cornelius v	25.05
Nagel v Avon Bd of Ed	19.14(C)
Nagle, State ex rel v Olin	20.09(B), 32.02, 48.03(B)
Napoleon City School Dist Bd of Ed, In re	18.32
Nashua, New Hampshire, School Dist; Belanger v	44.14(A)
Nashville Banner Publishing Co; McKennon v	17.03(E)
Nassau County School Bd v Arline	17.13(A), 28.01(B), 28.12(A)
National Broadcasting Co, State ex rel v Cleveland (1991)	44.02
National Broadcasting Co, State ex rel v Cleveland (1988)	44.02, 44.03
National City Bank, State ex rel v Cleveland City School Dist Bd of Ed	41.21(A)
National City Bank; Stein v	17.06(B)
National Ed Centers; Tyndall v	17.13(B)
National Graphics Corp; Bowman v	16.03(A)
National Group of Companies, Inc; Taylor v	17.04(B)
National Revenue Corp; Balent v	17.06(A)
National Treasury Employees Union v Von Raab	47.01(A)
Nation Enterprises; Harper & Row Publishers, Inc v	33.06(B)
Navin v Tallman	8.02(B), 9.07(A)
Naylor v Cardinal Local School Dist Bd of Ed	9.01, 9.13(A), 9.13(B), 9.13(C)
Nead, State ex rel v Nolte	2.16(A)
Neal v Southwestern City School Dist Bd of Ed	46.02

Casename	Text Section(s)
Nebraska; Monahan v	28.12(B)
Neely v Rutherford County Schools	28.07
Neighborhood Action Coalition v Canton, Ohio	19.13(E)
Neighborhood Centers Assn for Child Development; Albritton v	48.34(A)
Nelson v Moline School Dist No. 40	25.05
Nelson, State ex rel v Fuerst	44.03
Nesfedder; Fenstermaker v	46.14(B)
New Antioch Special School Dist Bd of Ed v Paul	25.06
Newark City School Dist Bd of Ed; Davies v	12.14(A)
Newark City School Dist Bd of Ed; Thomas v	9.13(A)
Newark City School Dist Bd of Ed; Wolford v	9.21(A), 9.21(C)
New Boston School Dist Bd of Ed; Snyder v	10.11
Newbury Local Bd of Ed; Bennett v (App)	11.17
Newbury Local Bd of Ed; Bennett v (CP)	11.17
Newbury Local School Dist Bd of Ed; Imm v	9.21(D)
Newbury Local School Dist Bd of Ed; Price v	8.02(B), 9.07(A), 10.02(A), 18.20
New Castle County School Dist; Kruelle v	28.06
Newcomerstown Bd of Ed; Art v	18.22(A)
New Concord School Dist Bd of Ed v Best	43.05(D)
New Jersey Dept of Ed; Woods v	28.06
New Jersey Dept of Human Services; Remis v	28.05(A)
New Jersey v T.L.O.	47.01(A), 47.02
New Kent County School Bd; Green v	19.03(A)
New Lenox School Dist No. 122; Webster v	32.07
New Life Baptist Church Academy v Town of East Longmeadow	32.02
New Miami Bd of Ed	18.18
New Miami Bd of Ed; Elliott v	46.14(B)
New Miami Local School Dist Bd of Ed; OAPSE, Chapter 762 v	18.23
New Miami Local School Dist Bd of Ed v SERB	18.18
New Philadelphia City School Dist Bd of Ed; Slauson v	18.26

Casename	Text Section(s)
Newport v Fact Concerts, Inc	17.02(B), 46.13(C)
Newport Special School Dist; McFarlin v	25.15(B)
New Richmond Exempted Village School Dist Bd of Ed, In re	18.22(A)
New Richmond Exempted Village School Dist Bd of Ed; York v	9.21(D)
Newsome v Batavia Local School Dist	25.10(B), 25.10(C)
Newton Falls Exempted Village Bd of Ed; Riddle v	9.17
Newton Falls Exempted Village School Dist, In re	18.31
New York City Bd of Ed; Benitez v	24.03(B)
New York City Bd of Ed; District 27 Community School Bd v	21.03(D)
New York City Civil Service Comm; Guardians Assn v	19.13(E)
New York City Dept of Social Services; Monell v	17.09(C), 46.13(B)
New York Gaslight Club, Inc v Carey	17.03(D), 17.03(E)
New York State Assn for Retarded Children, Inc v Carey	28.01(B)
New York State Ed Dept; Sharif v	19.14(C)
New York Times v Sullivan	5.07, 18.34
Nichols; Lau v	19.15
Nicolaci, In re	18.25(D)
Niles City Bd of Ed, In re	18.29(B)
Nipps; State v	45.03
Nitsche; Duran v	25.05
NLRB v Catholic Bishop of Chicago	48.28(B)
NLRB v City Disposal Systems	18.09
NLRB v Gissel Packing Co	18.14
NLRB v J. Weingarten, Inc	18.09
NLRB v Lion Oil Co	18.30
NLRB; Peerless Roofing Co v	18.23
NLRB v Truitt Co	18.10
NLRB; Wilson v	18.21(B)
NLRB v Yeshiva University	18.05(C), 48.28(A)
Nobel-Sysco, Inc; Toledo v	17.15
Noble County Engineer, In re	18.15(D)
Noble Local Bd of Ed	18.13
Noelker v Great Oaks Joint Vocational School Dist	15.07
Noernberg v Brook Park	12.17(C)
Noggle; State v	24.02(B)
Nohl v Canton Bd of Ed	15.05(B)

Casename	Text Section(s)
Noll, State ex rel v Industrial Comm	16.07(B)
Nolte; State ex rel Nead v	2.16(A)
Nordonia Hills City School Dist Bd of Ed	18.28(B)
Nordonia Hills City School Dist Bd of Ed v Unemployment Compensation Bd of Review	15.08(B)
Norfolk School Bd; Broussard v	25.05
Normandy Metals, Inc; Harasyn v	16.08
Normandy School Dist; Hudson v	17.06(B)
Norman v Harrison Hills City School Dist Bd of Ed	9.21(E)
Norman, State ex rel v Viebranz	5.03(C)
Norris; Arizona Governing Committee for Tax Deferred Annuity & Deferred Compensation Plans v	17.06(C)
Norris v Greenwood Community School Corp Bd of Ed	44.14(A)
North Babylon Union Free School Dist Bd of Ed; Smith v	32.01
North Canton City School Dist Bd of Ed; Marchand v	9.09(D), 9.12
North Canton City Schools, In re	18.17(B)
North Central Local School Dist Bd of Ed; Rea v	9.09(C)
North Central Local School; O'Hare v	9.01(A)
Northcross v Memphis City Schools Bd of Ed	17.02(B)
North v District of Columbia Bd of Ed	28.06
Northeast Ohio Sewer Dist, In re	18.17(A)
North Haven Bd of Ed v Bell	48.30
North Olmsted Bd of Ed v Cuyahoga County Bd of Revision	39.04
North Olmsted City School Dist Bd of Ed v North Olmsted Civil Service Comm	12.04(A)
North Olmsted v Ohio Bureau of Employment Services	15.05(A)
Northport-East Northport Union Free School Dist Bd of Ed v Ambach	28.10(B)

Casename	Text Section(s)
Northridge High School Bd of Ed; Cashdollar v	25.12(B)
Northridge Local School Dist Bd of Ed; Cashdollar v	25.10(C)
Northridge School Dist	18.13
North Ridgeville Civil Service Comm; Duplaga v	12.04(B)
Northside Independent School Dist; Kirkland v	9.21(E)
North Union Local School Dist Bd of Ed; State ex rel Bell v	9.05(A)
Northwestern National Ins Co; Gagne v	17.06(B)
Northwest Local Bd of Ed; State ex rel Voss v	9.07(B)
Northwest Local School Dist Bd of Ed, In re	18.05(A), 18.11(B), 18.13
Northwest Local School Dist Bd of Ed; Pertuset v	12.16(B)
Northwest R-1 School Dist; A.W. v	28.05(B)
Northwood; Harover v	16.03(A)
Norton City School Dist Bd of Ed; Lamb v	12.17(A)
Norwood Bd of Ed	18.28(B)
Norwood Bd of Ed; Swafford v	12.15(A), 12.17(D)
Norwood City School Dist v Norwood Teachers Assn	10.09(D)
Norwood School Dist Bd of Ed; King v	9.18
Norwood Teachers Assn; Norwood City School Dist v	10.09(D)
Nottingham v Akron Bd of Ed	24.03(C)
Novak v Muskingum County Area Joint Vocational School Dist Bd of Ed	9.19(E)
Novak v Revere Local School Dist	22.03(C), 22.03(D)
Novotny; Great American Federal Savings & Loan Assn v	17.02(A)
Now; Allmandinger v	5.08(A)
Nuspl v Akron	12.05(A), 12.11, 12.15(A), 12.15(B)
Nye, State ex rel v Industrial Comm	16.05(B)

O

Casename	Text Section(s)
1952 Inf OAG 220	21.11(A), 34.10(B)
1920 OAG 53	6.13
1921 OAG 11	7.05(B)
1927 OAG 483	38.08(A)
1929 OAG 595	46.12
1929 OAG 605	37.04(B)
1930 OAG 941	43.21
1931 OAG 1920	7.05(B)
1931 OAG 3087	36.02(A)
1931 OAG 3471	46.12
1931 OAG 3790	6.07(A)
1932 OAG 4588	36.12
1932 OAG 4622	30.10(E), 39.13
1933 OAG 314	5.11(B), 5.12(A)
1933 OAG 1027	36.11(B)
1933 OAG 1290	43.03
1933 OAG 1392	6.15(B)
1933 OAG 1409	48.01(A)
1933 OAG 1509	34.10(B)
1934 OAG 2474	36.11(A)
1934 OAG 2557	8.03(A)
1935 OAG 4617	35.02(E)
1936 OAG 5583	21.11(A)
1936 OAG 5977	37.01(A)
1936 OAG 6558	46.20
1937 OAG 751	42.08
1937 OAG 909	34.13
1938 OAG 3441	6.15(B)
1938 OAG 3486	35.04(C)
1938 OAG 3489	43.02(A)
1938 OAG 3527	43.02(A)
1938 OAG 3545	33.02(A)
1939 OAG 356	30.10(C)
1940 OAG 1698	37.01(A)
1941 OAG 4204	8.02(C)
1942 OAG 5091	21.01
1945 OAG 495	37.02
1947 OAG 1672	36.05(A)
1947 OAG 2148	34.15(C)
1948 OAG 4251	33.05, 45.07
1949 OAG 1028	43.19
1950 OAG 2077	34.12(A)
1952 OAG 186	7.05(B)
1953 OAG 2484	6.03(B)
1953 OAG 2485	34.03
1953 OAG 2534	36.12
1953 OAG 2994	34.13
1954 OAG 64	26.10(B)
1954 OAG 3575	10.13(A)
1954 OAG 3644	6.14(A), 6.15(A), 43.05(C)
1954 OAG 4152	43.19
1954 OAG 4342	43.23
1955 OAG 4711	6.02(D)
1955 OAG 4734	6.15(A)
1955 OAG 5736	4.03(F)
1955 OAG 6060	45.08(A)
1956 OAG 514	19.09(A)
1956 OAG 6326	37.02
1956 OAG 6359	34.06

Casename	Text Section(s)	Casename	Text Section(s)
1956 OAG 6451	36.02(A), 37.01(A)	OAG 67-081	22.22
		OAG 67-127	20.11(A)
1956 OAG 7225	36.02(B)	OAG 68-058	22.06
1956 OAG 7421	39.03	OAG 68-061	20.04
1957 OAG 706	6.02(D)	OAG 68-074	4.10(A)
1957 OAG 1212	4.14(A)	OAG 68-085	10.03(D), 10.04(C)
1957 OAG 1429	43.05(D)		
1958 OAG 1604	36.05(A)	OAG 68-100	4.10(B), 4.10(C)
1958 OAG 1749	26.07(B)	OAG 68-103	22.03(B), 27.12
1958 OAG 2457	7.06(B)	OAG 68-105	43.29
1958 OAG 2685	6.15(A)	OAG 68-113	5.03(C)
1959 OAG 37	5.03(B)	OAG 68-156	12.14(A), 22.03(C)
1959 OAG 890	21.05(C)		
1960 OAG 1099	21.05(A), 23.07(B)	OAG 68-161	22.17(B)
		OAG 69-006	36.03
1960 OAG 1304	36.05(A)	OAG 69-025	9.15(E)
1960 OAG 1373	4.14(A)	OAG 69-057	13.08(B), 22.14
1960 OAG 1491	45.08(A)	OAG 69-069	10.03(B)
1960 OAG 1860	26.16(A)	OAG 69-088	4.10(A)
1961 OAG 2147	20.04	OAG 69-114	42.11(B)
1961 OAG 2260	45.08(A)	OAG 70-026	20.13(A)
1961 OAG 2616	43.03	OAG 70-042	9.15(A), 9.15(B)
1961 OAG 2658	36.06	OAG 70-071	13.08(B)
1961 OAG 2678	6.15(A), 6.15(B)	OAG 70-075	6.02(C)
1962 OAG 2935	9.19(A), 9.19(B)	OAG 70-081	6.14(C), 43.05(C)
1962 OAG 3246	30.10(E), 36.06, 39.13	OAG 70-103	22.14
1962 OAG 3438	33.02(A)	OAG 70-105	36.04(B), 37.06(A)
1963 OAG 347	10.19(B)		
1963 OAG 501	36.04(C)	OAG 70-111	27.09(A), 27.09(B)
1963 OAG 542	21.12		
1963 OAG 662	36.11(B)	OAG 70-129	9.15(A)
1964 OAG 104	42.08	OAG 70-158	22.11
1964 OAG 903	8.03(A)	OAG 70-162	34.10(B)
1964 OAG 948	42.08	OAG 71-012	27.11
1964 OAG 1043	4.10(A), 4.11(A)	OAG 71-015	27.09(A)
1964 OAG 1285	35.02(C), 35.03	OAG 71-021	12.09(A)
1964 OAG 1421	11.13(C)	OAG 71-036	4.09(D), 26.19
1964 OAG 1522	36.02(B)	OAG 71-068	27.05
OAG 65-010	38.10	OAG 72-032	10.15
OAG 65-16	23.02(A)	OAG 72-043	22.07(B)
OAG 65-030	36.04(C), 36.05(A)	OAG 72-045	12.04(A)
		OAG 72-049	22.07(B), 27.11
OAG 65-60	45.08(A)	OAG 72-072	7.06(B)
OAG 65-61	3.02(A)	OAG 72-078	22.08
OAG 65-66	6.15(A)	OAG 72-081	5.09(D), 26.16(A), 27.02
OAG 65-89	33.02(A), 35.02(A)		
		OAG 72-083	27.12
OAG 65-119	34.03	OAG 72-089	27.10(B)
OAG 65-167	27.08(A)	OAG 73-014	22.05
OAG 65-207	11.22	OAG 73-030	39.08(A)
OAG 66-030	10.09(A)	OAG 73-037	34.07
OAG 66-040	4.14(A)	OAG 73-058	34.04(B)
OAG 66-085	7.04(B)	OAG 73-062	27.08(A)
OAG 66-098	4.14(A), 27.08(B)	OAG 73-065	11.24(B)
		OAG 73-077	29.12
OAG 66-135	7.04(D), 27.09(B)	OAG 73-084	10.21(C)
		OAG 73-088	6.14(C)

Casename	Text Section(s)	Casename	Text Section(s)
OAG 73-108	45.08(A)	OAG 81-050	29.07
OAG 73-114	13.04(B)	OAG 81-052	10.17(B), 35.04(A), 43.05(B)
OAG 74-002	36.11(B)		
OAG 74-006	45.08, 45.08(A)		
OAG 74-012	10.09(C)	OAG 81-067	29.02(C)
OAG 74-040	22.03(C)	OAG 81-070	6.07(C)
OAG 74-043	43.12(C), 43.23	OAG 81-071	45.08(A)
OAG 74-050	10.11	OAG 81-081	37.12(A)
OAG 74-063	35.02(A)	OAG 81-092	27.05, 36.11(A)
OAG 74-069	21.03(C)	OAG 82-014	23.03(A), 23.03(B), 23.04(B), 30.10(C), 35.02(A), 39.01(A), 39.15
OAG 74-083	9.14(A)		
OAG 74-095	21.01		
OAG 74-106	22.18(B)		
OAG 75-008	23.04(B)		
OAG 75-015	10.16, 13.08(B)		
OAG 75-028	10.13(D)	OAG 82-018	29.04(H)
OAG 75-048	10.01(C)	OAG 82-027	40.04(B)
OAG 76-008	30.10(E)	OAG 82-029	5.08(A), 24.05(A)
OAG 76-019	45.06(B)		
OAG 76-034	7.04(C)	OAG 82-030	39.01(A)
OAG 76-065	27.05, 36.11(A)	OAG 82-055	29.13(A), 29.13(B), 29.13(C)
OAG 76-078	10.10(B)		
OAG 77-001	20.04		
OAG 77-014	7.05(B)	OAG 82-106	23.02(B)
OAG 77-076	37.11	OAG 83-002	21.02(A)
OAG 77-091	34.10(B)	OAG 83-003	44.02
OAG 78-018	5.04(A)	OAG 83-008	42.06
OAG 78-033	37.11	OAG 83-012	25.03(A)
OAG 78-035	37.11	OAG 83-016	45.08(A)
OAG 78-040	27.05	OAG 83-028	29.02(C)
OAG 78-042	7.08	OAG 83-030	29.02(C)
OAG 78-049	11.10(A)	OAG 83-038	6.14(A), 43.05(C)
OAG 78-061	12.03(B)		
OAG 79-001	14.08(A)	OAG 83-041	23.02(A)
OAG 79-003	7.04(C)	OAG 83-053	7.08
OAG 79-043	36.01	OAG 83-070	7.09(A), 45.08(A)
OAG 79-064	29.13(B)		
OAG 80-009	29.04(B)	OAG 83-076	5.09(A), 43.02(C)
OAG 80-012	22.03(A), 22.06		
OAG 80-050	5.04(A)	OAG 83-077	13.04(A)
OAG 80-053	9.14(C)	OAG 83-082	36.13
OAG 80-060	6.06, 6.07(C), 23.03(B), 23.03(C), 30.10(B)	OAG 83-096	22.03(C)
		OAG 83-098	9.08(C), 10.03(B), 10.10(B)
OAG 80-063	29.13(D)	OAG 84-003	45.08(A)
OAG 80-064	6.15(A)	OAG 84-027	23.05, 26.16(A)
OAG 80-070	43.18	OAG 84-030	43.02(C)
OAG 80-105	4.03(F)	OAG 84-036	11.10(B), 14.08(B)
OAG 81-002	26.10(A), 31.05		
OAG 81-005	7.08, 34.04(B)	OAG 84-039	42.05(B)
OAG 81-010	7.09(C)	OAG 84-046	36.04(B), 37.04(A), 41.02, 43.29
OAG 81-011	10.01(C)		
OAG 81-012	22.08, 46.20		
OAG 81-025	22.03(D)	OAG 84-054	29.08(B)
OAG 81-036	29.10(B), 29.12	OAG 84-061	10.14
OAG 81-038	44.02	OAG 84-064	29.07
OAG 81-045	10.10(C)	OAG 84-067	41.33(B)

Casename	Text Section(s)	Casename	Text Section(s)
OAG 84-071	10.14, 29.13(B)	OAG 88-090	11.24(B)
OAG 84-083	30.10(B), 30.10(C), 34.16(B), 39.15, 43.04	OAG 89-006	23.02(A)
		OAG 89-018	20.05(D)
		OAG 89-030	45.06(B)
		OAG 89-047	41.15
OAG 84-084	27.15	OAG 89-053	25.16(A)
OAG 84-095	7.08	OAG 89-057	29.02(C), 29.02(E)
OAG 84-109	29.12		
OAG 85-002	43.16	OAG 89-061	27.05
OAG 85-006	45.08(A)	OAG 89-069	45.08(A)
OAG 85-007	45.08(B)	OAG 89-073	44.03
OAG 85-015	20.05(B), 31.03, 39.07(A), 48.04(B)	OAG 89-077	42.24
		OAG 89-092	23.02(A)
		OAG 89-101	45.08(A)
OAG 85-031	29.08(A)	OAG 89-108	24.05(A)
OAG 85-036	5.04(B)	OAG 90-030	43.21
OAG 85-055	29.08(A)	OAG 90-050	44.02
OAG 85-067	39.05, 43.16	OAG 90-059	34.12(B)
OAG 85-072	42.22, 43.16	OAG 90-062	45.08(A)
OAG 85-077	42.13	OAG 90-063	45.08(A)
OAG 85-085	39.13, 42.22, 43.16	OAG 90-075	29.04(H)
		OAG 90-083	45.08(A)
OAG 86-004	45.08(A)	OAG 90-085	36.04(B)
OAG 86-013	30.10(C), 35.02(C), 43.25	OAG 90-099	24.06(A), 25.09(A), 44.14(B), 48.14
OAG 86-016	29.02(C)		
OAG 86-031	5.06(A), 36.02(B)	OAG 91-001	3.02(A)
		OAG 91-004	3.03(B)
OAG 86-038	27.09(A)	OAG 91-024	23.02(D)
OAG 86-040	29.09(A)	OAG 91-025	23.02(D)
OAG 86-041	11.07(A)	OAG 91-026	10.17(A)
OAG 86-050	10.21(A)	OAG 91-032	22.22
OAG 86-057	45.08(A)	OAG 91-042	29.09(A)
OAG 86-060	45.08(A)	OAG 91-046	14.11
OAG 86-062	30.10(E), 36.11(A), 39.15	OAG 91-064	5.09(G), 38.10
		OAG 91-065	18.20, 45.14
OAG 86-069	45.01(B)	OAG 92-005	44.02, 45.08(A)
OAG 86-082	43.15(C)	OAG 92-006	10.10(D)
OAG 86-089	44.02	OAG 92-015	10.17(A)
OAG 86-091	5.12(B)	OAG 92-016	36.10(A)
OAG 86-103	29.09(A)	OAG 92-027	29.09(A)
OAG 86-108	4.03(B), 5.02(A)	OAG 92-028	34.14
OAG 87-010	48.14	OAG 92-032	5.12(A)
OAG 87-024	46.04	OAG 92-061	29.13(B)
OAG 87-025	45.01(B)	OAG 92-069	29.07
OAG 87-026	28.07	OAG 92-075	29.08(A)
OAG 87-037	44.18	OAG 92-082	24.05(A), 25.16(A)
OAG 87-058	46.18(A)		
OAG 87-060	11.20	OAG 93-004	43.01
OAG 87-069	43.07(A)	OAG 93-021	42.23(A)
OAG 87-101	23.02(D)	OAG 93-023	23.02(B)
OAG 88-001	5.08(B), 32.04	OAG 93-031	34.10(B)
OAG 88-013	34.17	OAG 93-055	42.23(A)
OAG 88-059	7.09(A), 12.09(A)	OAG 93-067	45.08(A)
		OAG 94-007	40.16
OAG 88-069	11.04(A), 29.13(D)	OAG 94-009	10.17(A)
		OAG 94-028	20.07
OAG 88-087	5.12(A)	OAG 94-033	23.02(A)

Casename	Text Section(s)
OAG 94-048	42.02, 42.23(A)
Oak Hills Local School Dist; McNair v	28.07
Oak Hill Union Local School Dist Bd of Ed; Baisden v	7.06(B), 9.04
Oakland County; Torres v	46.16
Oak Ridge School Bd; Clevenger v	28.03
Oakwood City School Dist Bd of Ed v Dille	23.02(B)
OAPSE, Chapter 177 v Forest Hills Local School Dist Bd of Ed	18.22(B)
OAPSE, Chapter 227 v Sylvania City School Dist	12.08
OAPSE, Chapter 643 v Dayton City School Dist Bd of Ed	18.26(A)
OAPSE, Chapter 762 v New Miami Local School Dist Bd of Ed	18.23
OAPSE v Columbus Bd of Ed	12.19
OAPSE, In re	18.25(D)
OAPSE v Lakewood City School Dist Bd of Ed	12.17(B), 18.22(A)
OAPSE v Mentor Exempted Village School Dist Bd of Ed	13.01(B)
OAPSE v Stark County Bd of Ed	22.13(A), 22.14
OAPSE, State ex rel v Girard Civil Service Comm	12.04(A)
OAPSE, State ex rel v Orange City School Dist Bd of Ed	12.17(C)
OAPSE, State ex rel v SERB	18.26(A)
OAPSE v Twinsburg	12.03(A)
OAPSE v Twin Valley Local School Dist Bd of Ed	12.09(C), 13.01(B)
Oberlin School Dist; State ex rel Willbond v	7.11(A), 14.08
Oberti v Borough of Clementon School Dist Bd of Ed	28.05(B), 28.11(D)
Oblates of St. Francis de Sales; McCartney v	5.07
O'Connor v Ortega	47.01(D)
OCRC; Twinsburg City Schools v	17.04(E)
O'Dell v Preble-Shawnee Local School Dist Bd of Ed (1981)	13.04(A)
O'Dell v Preble-Shawnee Local School Dist Bd of Ed (1977)	13.04(A)
O'Dell, State ex rel v Scioto Valley Local School Dist Bd of Ed	12.15(A), 12.16(A)
ODOT, In re	18.04(A)
Office of Collective Bargaining, In re	18.11(B)
Office of Collective Bargaining v SERB	18.26(C)
Office of Collective Bargaining (State Highway Patrol), In re	17.20
O'Hare v North Central Local School	9.01(A)
O'Harra v Columbus City School Dist Bd of Ed	12.16(A)
Ohio Asphalt Paving, Inc v Ohio Dept of Industrial Relations	37.12(B)
Ohio Assn of Public School Employees Local 530; Springfield Local School Dist Bd of Ed v	5.12, 5.12(B)
Ohio Assn of Public School Employees (OAPSE) (3-20-85)	18.25(D)
Ohio Assn of Public School Employees (OAPSE) (11-14-85)	18.25(D)
Ohio Bell Telephone Co, State ex rel v Krise	16.04
Ohio Bd of Tax Appeals; Swepston v	12.14(B)
Ohio Bureau of Employment Services Bd of Review; Agich v	15.06
Ohio Bureau of Employment Services Bd of Review; Ash v	15.05(B)
Ohio Bureau of Employment Services Bd of Review; Sellers v	15.08(A)
Ohio Bureau of Employment Services Bd of Review; Wolfe v	15.05(B)
Ohio Bureau of Employment Services v Byers	15.02(C)
Ohio Bureau of Employment Services; Central Ohio Joint Vocational School Dist Bd of Ed v	15.02(B)
Ohio Bureau of Employment Services; Harris v	15.08(A), 17.13(A)
Ohio Bureau of Employment Services; North Olmsted v	15.05(A)
Ohio Bureau of Employment Services; Tzangas, Plakas & Mannos v	15.08(A)
Ohio Bureau of Motor Vehicles; State ex rel Mancini v	44.03

Casename	Text Section(s)
Ohio Civil Rights Comm; Cleveland Civil Service Comm v	17.03(F), 17.13(A)
Ohio Civil Rights Comm v Dayton Christian Schools, Inc	17.15
Ohio Civil Rights Comm; Dayton Christian Schools, Inc v	17.15
Ohio Civil Rights Comm v Ingram	17.04(D), 17.04(E)
Ohio Civil Rights Comm; Jackson v	17.04(D)
Ohio Civil Rights Comm; Kent State University v	17.13(A)
Ohio Civil Rights Comm; Little Forest Medical Center of Akron v	17.03(B), 17.04(B)
Ohio Civil Rights Comm; Lordstown Local School Dist Bd of Ed v	17.04(C), 17.09(C), 17.10, 18.26(A)
Ohio Civil Rights Comm v Lysyj	17.04(D)
Ohio Civil Rights Comm; McCrea v	17.04(C)
Ohio Civil Rights Comm; Plumbers & Steamfitters Joint Apprenticeship Committee v	17.04(B), 17.04(E)
Ohio Civil Rights Comm; Port Clinton City Schools v	17.04(E)
Ohio Civil Rights Comm; Ramsdell v	17.04(E)
Ohio Civil Rights Comm; Sowers v	17.04(A)
Ohio Civil Rights Comm; State ex rel General Motors Corp v	17.04(C)
Ohio Civil Rights Comm; State ex rel Republic Steel Corp v	17.04(C)
Ohio Civil Rights Comm; State ex rel State Farm Mutual Automobile Insurance Co v	17.04(C)
Ohio Civil Rights Comm; State ex rel Westbrook v	17.04(C)
Ohio Civil Rights Comm; Vinton County Local School Dist Bd of Ed v	17.14
Ohio Civil Rights Comm; Westerville City Schools v	17.10
Ohio Civil Service Employees Assn/AFSCME, Local 11, In re	18.25(D), 18.26(A), 18.26(B)
Ohio Civil Service Employees Assn; Dale v	5.07, 18.34
Ohio Civil Service Employees Assn, Local 11, AFSCME, In re	18.25(A)
Ohio Civil Service Employees Assn, Local 11; Ohio Office of Collective Bargaining v	18.22(A)
Ohio Civil Service Employees Assn v Ohio Dept of Transportation	18.28(B)
Ohio Council 8, AFSCME v Cincinnati	18.11(B)
Ohio Council 8, AFSCME; Cincinnati v	18.20, 18.28(B)
Ohio Council 8, AFSCME,; Metcalf v	18.26(A)
Ohio Council 8, AFSCME; Montgomery County Clerk of Courts v	18.18
Ohio Council 8, AFSCME v Ohio Dept of Mental Retardation & Developmental Disabilities	18.22(A)
Ohio Council 8, AFSCME v Springfield Bd of Park Trustees	18.29(D), 18.31
Ohio Dept of Administrative Services; Barksdale v	18.22(A)
Ohio Dept of Agriculture; Esselburne v	12.14(B)
Ohio Dept of Commerce; Geist v	18.22(A)
Ohio Dept of Development, In re	18.11(B)
Ohio Dept of Ed; Wise v	28.15(C)
Ohio Dept of Health; Carter v	12.14(B)
Ohio Department of Health; State ex rel Beacon Journal Publishing Co v	44.03
Ohio Dept of Industrial Relations; Ohio Asphalt Paving, Inc v	37.12(B)
Ohio Dept of Mental Health & Mental Retardation; Eudela v	12.04(B)
Ohio Dept of Mental Retardation & Developmental Disabilities; Ohio Council 8, AFSCME v	18.22(A)
Ohio Dept of Transportation; Clark v	12.11
Ohio Dept of Transportation; Ohio Civil Service Employees Assn v	18.28(B)
Ohio Education Assn; Gwirtz v	18.21(C)

Casename	Text Section(s)
Ohio Ferro Alloys Corp; Hutchinson v	16.04
Ohio Health Care Employees Union, Dist 1199, In re	18.25(D)
Ohio High School Athletic Assn, State ex rel v Stark County Common Pleas Court Judges	30.07(A)
Ohio Historical Society v SERB (1993)	18.26
Ohio Historical Society v SERB (1990)	18.15(F)
Ohio Historical Society; State ex rel Fenley v	44.03
Ohio Office of Collective Bargaining v Ohio Civil Service Employees Assn, Local 11	18.22(A)
Ohio; Osborne v	24.13
Ohio Patrolmen's Benevolent Assn v MetroHealth System	18.26
Ohio State Bd of Ed; Princeton City School Dist Bd of Ed v	3.03(F)
Ohio State Library Bd; Manning v	17.03(D)
Ohio State University Bd of Trustees; Ojalvo v	10.01(C)
Ohio State University; Communications Workers of America Local 4501 v	12.08
Ohio State University; Coons v	12.04(B)
Ohio State University, In re (1990)	18.05(A), 18.11(B)
Ohio State University, In re (1985)	18.26
Ohio State University; Local 4501, Communications Workers of America v	12.17(B)
Ohio State University; Lynch v	34.12(A)
Ohio State University; SERB v	18.26(A)
Ohio State University; State ex rel James v	9.13(A), 44.02
Ohio State University; State ex rel Thomas v	44.02
Ohio State University; Steinhour v	10.16
Ohio Turnpike Comm, In re	18.07
Ohio University, In re	18.17(A)
OHSAA; Alerding v	30.11(C)
OHSAA; Anderson v	30.11(C)
OHSAA; Bowles v	30.11(C)
OHSAA; Burrows v	30.11(C)
OHSAA; Kaufman v	30.11(C)
OHSAA; Massillon City School Dist Bd of Ed v	30.11(C)
OHSAA; Menke v	30.11(C)
OHSAA; Pecoraro v	30.11(C)
OHSAA, State ex rel v Stark County Common Pleas Court Judges	30.07(B), 30.08(A), 30.11(C)
OHSAA; Wissel v	30.08(B)
OHSAA; Woods v	30.11(C)
OHSAA; Yellow Springs Exempted Village School Dist Bd of Ed v	19.14(B), 30.08(B), 30.09(B)
Ojai Unified School Dist v Jackson	28.06
Ojalvo v Ohio State University Bd of Trustees	10.01(C)
Oja; State v	20.03(C)
Oklahoma City Public Schools Bd of Ed v Dowell	19.03(B)
Oklahoma City v Tuttle	46.13(B)
Okure; Owens v	17.02(A)
Old Fort School Dist Bd of Ed, State ex rel v Smith	39.05
Olentangy Local School Bd of Ed; Knowlton Construction Co v	37.06(A)
Olentangy Local School Dist Bd of Ed; Crago v	9.22(A), 46.14(A)
Olin; State ex rel Nagle v	20.09(B), 32.02, 48.03(B)
Omaha School Dist; Wood v	17.13(A)
Oney v Westerville City School Dist Bd of Ed	10.03(B)
Ontario Local School Dist Bd of Ed; Shankle v	12.09(A)
Orange City School Dist Bd of Ed; State ex rel OAPSE v	12.17(C)
Ordway v Hargraves	20.04
Oregon City Bd of Ed; State ex rel Specht v	6.13, 12.15(A)
Orrville City School Dist Bd of Ed; Carter v	7.06(B)
Ortega; O'Connor v	47.01(D)
Osbeck; Metzger v	46.14(B)
Osborne v Ohio	24.13
Oscar Mayer & Co v Evans	17.06(A)
Osceola Refining Co, Div of Texas-American Petrochemicals, Inc; Rabidue v	17.11
Osnaburg Local School Dist Bd of Ed; State ex rel Hlynsky v	9.01(A)
Ostrander; Boaz v	24.03(B)
Oswald v Connor	16.03(A)
Oszust; Youghiogheny & Ohio Coal Co v	15.08(B)

Casename	Text Section(s)
Otsego Bd of Ed; Tracy v	9.13(B)
Otsego Local School Dist Bd of Ed, In re	18.22(B)
Ottawa-Glandorf Local School Dist	18.15(C)
Ott v Buckeye Local School Dist Bd of Ed	9.19(G)
Outlet Communications, Inc, State ex rel v Lancaster Police Dept	44.02, 44.03
Overfield; Carbone v	5.07, 46.01(A)
Overton; People v	47.02
Owego-Apalachin School Dist; Travis v	32.06(A)
Owen; Baker v	25.16(B)
Owen v Independence	46.13(B)
Owens v Okure	17.02(A)

P

Casename	Text Section(s)
Pacific Holding Co/Hay Adams Div; Truesdale v	10.12(A)
Pack v West Clermont Local School Dist Bd of Ed	12.16(B)
Painesville City School Dist Bd of Ed; McElroy v	24.03(C)
Painesville Twp Bd of Ed; Erkkila v	6.05
Painesville Township Local Bd of Ed, In re	18.15(A)
Painesville Twp Local School Dist Bd of Ed; H.R. Johnson Construction Co v	37.04(B)
Painesville Twp Local School Dist Bd of Ed; State ex rel Specht v	7.13, 9.07(A)
Painter v Graley	45.08(A), 48.26
Palace Hotel Co v Medart	24.03(B)
Palmer v Chicago Bd of Ed (US)	32.03
Palmer v Chicago Bd of Ed (F(2d))	17.15
Palmer, State ex rel v State Teachers Retirement Bd	11.13(A)
Palmisano v Willoughby-Eastlake Bd of Ed	30.11(C)
Pandazides v Virginia Bd of Ed	17.13(A), 28.13(C)
Panek v Chardon Local School Dist Bd of Ed	12.16(A)
Pape; Monroe v	46.13(B)
Paramus Bd of Ed; Charlton v	17.03(A)
Paredes v Curtis	25.10(B)
Parents in Action on Special Ed v Hannon	28.10(A)
Paris Union School Dist No. 95 Bd of Ed; Vail v	46.14(A)
Park Hills Music Club v Fairborn Bd of Ed	5.08(B)
Parkway C-2 School Dist; Light v	28.09(A)
Parma Bd of Ed; Bowman v	9.17
Parma Bd of Ed; Giering v	9.21(A), 9.23(B)
Parma Civil Service Comm; Vonderau v	12.07(A)
Parr v State	20.02(A), 32.02
Parsons, State ex rel v Fleming	18.22(A), 18.28(B)
Partee v Metropolitan School Dist of Washington Twp	46.13(B)
Pasadena Independent School Dist; Angela L. v	28.13(D)
Pasadena Independent School Dist; Stacey G. v	28.13(A)
Pascoe v Huron Bd of Ed	8.04(D), 9.06(B)
Patricia H. v Berkeley Unified School Dist	19.14(A)
Patterson v McClean Credit Union	17.02(A)
Patton v Springfield Bd of Ed	22.13(A)
Paul v Davis	46.13(C)
Paulding Exempted Village School Dist Bd of Ed; Ashbaugh v	12.16(A)
Paulding Exempted Village School Dist Bd of Ed; Ferris v	4.04, 4.05(A), 7.06(C), 26.19
Paulding Exempted Village School Dist Bd of Ed, In re	18.26(A)
Paulding Exempted Village School Dist Bd of Ed; State ex rel Cook v	7.13
Paul; New Antioch Special School Dist Bd of Ed v	25.06
Paul, State ex rel v Van Buren Local School Dist Bd of Ed	9.05(A)
Pavilion Central School Dist Bd of Ed; Logsdon v	28.11(F)
Pavkov v Barberton Bd of Ed	7.04(B), 9.11(B), 9.11(C)
Paxton; Schaeffer v	24.03(C)
Peake, State ex rel v South Point Local School Dist Bd of Ed	9.11(A), 9.11(B)
Pea Ridge School Dist; Wise v	46.14(B)
Peavine School Dist of Adair County; Luethje v	9.21(E)
Pecoraro v OHSAA	30.11(C)
Peerless Roofing Co v NLRB	18.23
Peet, State ex rel v Westerville City School Dist Bd of Ed	9.06(B)
Pegan; Randall v	32.06(A)

Casename	Text Section(s)
Peloza v Capistrano Unified School Dist	32.07
Pembaur v Cincinnati	46.13(B)
Pena; Adarand v	17.18
Pendergrass v Columbus Public Schools	20.03(C)
Pendleton; Browning v	46.13(C)
Pendleton v Jefferson Local School Dist Bd of Ed	19.13(E)
Penick v Columbus Bd of Ed (1981)	19.09(A)
Penick v Columbus Bd of Ed (1978)	19.09(A)
Penick; Columbus Bd of Ed v	19.06
Pennhurst State School & Hospital v Halderman	46.13(B)
Pennington v Dudley	15.02(B)
Pennsylvania; Battle v	28.04
Pennsylvania; General Bldg Contractors Assn v	17.02(B)
People v Overton	47.02
Peoria School Dist 150 Bd of Ed v Illinois Bd of Ed	28.09(C)
Peppel; Washington County Taxpayers Assn v	41.12(C)
Perk; Gannon v	12.14(A)
Perkins v Bright	46.08
Perorazio v East Liverpool City School Dist Bd of Ed	24.03(D)
Perry Ed Assn v Perry Local Educators' Assn	25.05
Perry Local School Dist Bd of Ed; Merry v	9.19(A)
Perry Local School Dist Bd of Ed; Warren v	25.04
Perrysburg Bd of Ed, In re	18.28(B)
Perrysburg Bd of Ed; State ex rel Laskey v	46.08
Perry v Sindermann	46.14(A)
Person v Gum	24.03(D)
Pertuset v Loudonville-Perrysville Exempted Village Bd of Ed	46.13(C)
Pertuset v Northwest Local School Dist Bd of Ed	12.16(B)
Petaluma City School Dist; Doe v (F(3d))	19.14(A)
Petaluma City School Dist; Doe v (FSupp)	19.14(A), 19.14(C), 46.14(B)
Petersen v Hastings Public Schools	28.03
Petitioners v Stringer	5.05
Petrie v Forest Hills School Dist Bd of Ed	9.21(E), 44.08(B), 44.11
Petropoulous; Tonti v	46.16
Petty, State ex rel v Wurst	44.02

Casename	Text Section(s)
Pewaukee School Bd; Karnstein v	25.15(B)
Pfeiffer v Marion Center Area School Dist	19.14(C)
Phelan v Bell	28.13(D)
Phelps v Positive Action Tool Co	16.03(B)
Philadelphia School Dist Bd of Ed; United States v	17.15
Philadelphia School Dist; Sease v	32.06(A)
Philbrook; Ansonia Bd of Ed v	17.15
Phillips v Ingersoll-Humphreys Div, Borg-Warner Corp	16.03(B)
Phillips v South Range Local School Dist Bd of Ed	9.19(A)
Phillips v West Holmes Local School Dist Bd of Ed	7.11(B)
Phipps v Saddleback Valley Unified School Dist	21.03(D)
Phung v Waste Management, Inc	48.26
Piazzola v Watkins	47.01(B)
Picha v Wielgos	47.01(B), 47.03
Pickard; Castaneda v	19.15
Pickaway County Human Services Dept, In re (1993)	18.24(B)
Pickaway County Human Services Dept, In re (1989)	18.09
Pickaway County Human Services Dept, In re (1987)	18.25(B)
Pickaway-Ross Joint Vocational School Dist Bd of Ed	18.28(B)
Pickering v Board of Education	9.21(E)
Pickett v Unemployment Compensation Bd of Review	15.08(A)
Picklesimer v Southwestern City Bd of Ed	35.02(A)
Pico; Island Trees Union Free School Dist No. 26 Bd of Ed v	32.07, 33.04
Piecuch v Gulf & Western Mfg Co	17.06(A)
Pierce v Society of Sisters	48.02
Pierce; State ex rel A. Bentley & Sons Co v	5.06(B), 23.04(A)
Pihl v Massachusetts Dept of Ed	28.13(B)
Pike County Joint Area Vocational School Dist; State ex rel Cutler v	9.19(A), 12.13
Pilditch v Chicago Bd of Ed	17.03(F)

Casename	Text Section(s)
Pioneer Joint Vocational School Dist Bd of Ed, State ex rel v Schumann	4.05(B), 27.08(A)
Piscataway Twp Bd of Ed; United States v	17.18
Pistone v Canfield Local Bd of Ed	12.10(E)
Pittman; Crawford v	28.04
Pittsburgh Bd of Ed; Bradley v (910 F(2d))	9.21(E)
Pittsburgh Bd of Ed; Bradley v (913 F(2d))	9.21(E), 9.22(A)
Pittsburgh Bd of Public Ed; Sanguigni v	9.21(E), 46.14(A)
Pittsburgh School Dist Bd of Public Ed; Schafer v	17.09(A)
Pitts; Freeman v	19.03(B)
Pizza; Toledo Area AFL-CIO Council v	5.03(A)
Place; Clayton v	32.01
Place; US v	47.01(C)
Plain Dealer Publishing Co, State ex rel v Lesak	23.03(A), 30.10(C), 39.15, 44.02
Planned Parenthood of Southern Nevada, Inc v Clark County School Dist	25.05
Plavcan, State ex rel v School Employees Retirement System	14.11
Plessy v Ferguson	19.02
Plumbers & Steamfitters Joint Apprenticeship Committee v Ohio Civil Rights Comm	17.04(B), 17.04(E)
Plyler v Doe	19.16
Poe v Hamilton	26.15(B), 46.03
Poe v Haydon	46.15(C)
Polaris Joint Vocational School Dist Bd of Ed; Tye v	18.22(A)
Poling v Murphy	25.05
Polk v Central Susquehanna Intermediate Unit 16	28.03, 28.07
Polovischak, State ex rel v Mayfield	44.02
Pomeroy; Zamora v	47.01(C), 47.02
Pontiac School Dist; Gallagher v	28.03
Poole v Maloney	12.17(D)
Pope v East Brunswick Bd of Ed	32.06(A)
Portage Lakes Joint Vocational School Dist Bd of Ed v Bowman	8.03(A), 10.07(B), 43.27(B)
Portage Lakes Joint Vocational School Dist Bd of Ed, In re	18.28(B)
Port Clinton City Schools v Ohio Civil Rights Comm	17.04(E)
Port Clinton Public School Dist; Banchich v	46.02
Porter Paint Co; Kerans v	16.08, 17.11
Porter; Stimpert v	25.10(B), 25.12(A)
Portsmouth; Bashford v	18.20
Portsmouth; State ex rel Aldridge v	12.07(B)
Portsmouth, State ex rel v Kountz	41.05(B)
Positive Action Tool Co; Phelps v	16.03(B)
Post-Browning, Inc; Burkart v	15.08(A)
Poway Unified School Dist; Lovell v	25.05
Powell v Defore	28.13(A)
Powell v Jefferson Local School Dist Bd of Ed	12.16(C)
Powell v Meigs Local School Dist	12.16(C)
Powell v Stafford	48.30
Powell v Young	9.21(A)
Prague Public School Dist I-103; R.L.R. v	19.14(A)
Preble-Shawnee Local School Dist Bd of Ed; O'Dell v (1981)	13.04(A)
Preble-Shawnee Local School Dist Bd of Ed; O'Dell v (1977)	13.04(A)
Prestole Everlock, Inc; Borbely v	16.05(G)
Price v Newbury Local School Dist Bd of Ed	8.02(B), 9.07(A), 10.02(A), 18.20
Price, State ex rel v Wauseon Exempted Village School Dist Bd of Ed	9.06(B)
Price Waterhouse v Hopkins	17.03(F)
Price v Young	25.15(B)
Princeton Bd of Ed; Carter v	8.04(D)
Princeton City School Dist Bd of Ed; Basler v (1989)	10.04(D)
Princeton City School Dist Bd of Ed; Basler v (1981)	10.04(D)
Princeton City School Dist Bd of Ed; Charles v	9.22(F)
Princeton City School Dist Bd of Ed; Cross v	25.12(B)
Princeton City School Dist Bd of Ed; Frith v	7.11(B), 46.08
Princeton City School Dist Bd of Ed; Goldman v	10.03(B)
Princeton City School Dist Bd of Ed v Ohio State Bd of Ed	3.03(F)
Proctor & Gamble Co; Ang v	17.03(D)

Casename	Text Section(s)
Proctor, State ex rel v Alliance Public School Dist Bd of Ed	12.17(A)
Professionals Guild of Ohio; Hamilton County Bd of Mental Retardation & Developmental Disabilities v	18.02, 18.15(D), 18.15(F)
Provens v Stark County Bd of Mental Retardation and Developmental Disabilities	17.04(D)
Provident Bank v Wood	42.11(B)
Public Employees Retirement Bd; State ex rel Brown v	11.13(A)
Pueblo School Dist No. 60; Cunico v	17.18
Puerto Rico; Ezratty v	28.13(A)
Pugh v Employment Services Bureau Bd of Review	15.08(A)
Pulido v Cavazos	48.06(C)
Pullman; Love v	17.03(D)
Pushay v Walter	22.03(D), 48.08(A)
Pushkin v University of Colorado Regents	28.12(A)
Pusztay, State ex rel v Buckeye Joint Vocational School Dist Bd of Ed	9.13(B)
Putnam County Bd of Ed; Sommers v	22.01
Puyallup School Dist No. 3; Clyde K. v	28.09(A)

Q

Casename	Text Section(s)
Quackenbush v Johnson City Central School Dist	28.13(A)
Quappe v Endry	32.06
Queen City Lodge No 69, FOP v Cincinnati	18.22(A)
Queen City Metro; Menefee v	46.05
Quick; Trautvetter v	17.11
Quinn; Daniels v	9.21(E)
Quisenberry; Lamont X. v	28.09(A)
Quitman County Bd of Ed; Hull v	19.03(B)

R

Casename	Text Section(s)
Rabidue v Osceola Refining Co, Div of Texas-American Petrochemicals, Inc	17.11
Rachel H.; Sacramento City Unified School Dist Bd of Ed v	28.05(B)
Radtke v Everett	17.11
Ramirez, State ex rel v Industrial Comm	16.05(B)
Ramsdell v Ohio Civil Rights Comm	17.04(E)

Casename	Text Section(s)
Ramsey v Whitley County, Kentucky, Bd of Ed	46.14(A)
Randall v Pegan	32.06(A)
Randall; Reineck v	26.10(B)
Randles; Burkhart v	46.14(A)
Randles, State ex rel v Hill	5.12(D)
Randolph Central School Dist; Aldrich v	17.08(A)
Rankey v Arlington Bd of Ed	46.11
Rankin v McPherson	9.21(E)
Rapid City Area School Dist No. 51-4; Lee v	17.06(A)
Rapides Parish Public School System; Swift v	28.06
Ratliff v Wellington Exempted Village Schools Bd of Ed	9.21(E)
Ratner v Stark County Bd of Revision	39.04
Rauhaus v Buckeye Local School Dist Bd of Ed	10.04(A)
Ravenna City School Dist Bd of Ed; Daniels v	17.03(F)
Rawac Plating Co; State ex rel Johnson v	16.05(B)
Raybuck; Tarter v	46.16
Reams, State ex rel v Maplewood Local School Dist Bd of Ed	9.19(B)
Rea v North Central Local School Dist Bd of Ed	9.09(C)
Recall of Each Member of the Saint Clairsville-Richland Bd of Ed, In re	5.05
Redd v Springfield Twp School	46.01(C)
Reed v Rhodes (1981)	19.09(A)
Reed v Rhodes (1979)	19.08(B), 19.09(A)
Reed v Vermilion Local School Dist	25.03(B)
Rees; Edwards v	47.01(A)
Reeves v Besonen	46.14(B)
Regan; Committee for Public Education & Religious Liberty v	48.06(B)
Regional Transit Authority Bd of Trustees; Fant v	44.03
Reid; Community for Creative Non-Violence v	33.06(C)
Reineck v Randall	26.10(B)
Reinier; Scott v	12.17(D)
Remis v New Jersey Dept of Human Services	28.05(A)
Remley, State ex rel v Licking Heights Local School Dist Bd of Ed	9.09(C)

Casename	Text Section(s)
Rencher v Cleveland Bd of Ed	46.11
Rendell-Baker v Kohn	17.02(A), 48.16, 48.17
Renfro, State ex rel v Cuyahoga County Dept of Human Services	24.05(A)
Renfrow; Doe v (F(2d))	47.01(A), 47.03
Renfrow; Doe v (FSupp)	47.01(B)
Renner v East Liverpool Civil Service Comm	12.17(A)
Rensselaer Central School Corp; Berger v	32.06(A)
Renton School Dist No. 403; Garnett v	32.06(A)
Republic Steel Corp, State ex rel v Ohio Civil Rights Comm	17.04(C)
Rettig v Kent City School Dist (1986)	28.03
Rettig v Kent City School Dist (1981)	28.04
Reusch v Fountain	28.04
Revere Local School Dist; Novak v	22.03(C), 22.03(D)
Reynoldsburg City School Dist Bd of Ed v Reynoldsburg School Support Assn, OEA/NEA	18.22(A)
Rhode Island Interscholastic League, Inc; Kleczek v	19.14(B)
Rhodes; Erie County School Dist Bd of Ed v	39.06(B)
Rhodes; Guyten v	24.03(D), 25.06
Rhodes; Reed v (1981)	19.09(A)
Rhodes; Reed v (1979)	19.08(B), 19.09(A)
Rhodes v Stewart	28.13(D)
Riccheti v Cleveland City School Dist Bd of Ed	9.21(B), 9.22(E), 9.22(F)
Ricci; Smith v	32.07
Rice; Elliot v	25.15(B)
Richards v Akron Public Schools Bd of Ed	12.11
Richards Mfg Co; Harris v	17.02(A)
Richards v State Personnel Bd of Review	18.22(A)
Richland Parent Teacher's Assn, State ex rel v Richland Twp Bd of Ed	38.09(A)
Richley; Monaghan v	46.08
Richmond v J.A. Croson Co	17.18
Rickel v Cloverleaf Local School Dist Bd of Ed	9.13(C)
Rickelman; Gfell v	25.03(A), 25.04
Riddle v Newton Falls Exempted Village Bd of Ed	9.17
Ridge v Boulder Creek Union Junior-Senior High School Dist of Santa Cruz	24.03(D)
Riggs v Kentucky	46.14(A)
Riley; Myers v	18.26
Rinehart v Western Local School Dist Bd of Ed	46.03
Riordin v Lakewood Civil Service Comm	12.17(B)
Ritter v Fairfield Local School Dist	9.08(B)
Rivera v East Otero School Dist R-1	25.05
River Local School Dist Bd of Ed; Gates v (OS)	12.09(E)
River Local School Dist Bd of Ed; Gates v (App)	12.09(D)
Rivers v Barberton City School Dist	10.05(A)
Riverside Bd of Ed	18.15(A)
Riverside Methodist Hospital; Hanly v	48.26
River View Coral School Dist Bd of Ed; Wiseman v	9.08(E)
River View Local School Dist Bd of Ed; Hardesty v	5.12(D), 25.03(B), 25.12(A)
Rizkana; Collins v	17.11
R.L.R. v Prague Public School Dist I-103	19.14(A)
Roadway Express Co; Belt v	48.26
Robatin; MTD Products, Inc v	16.03(C)
Robbins & Myers, Inc; State ex rel Mitchell v	16.07(B)
Robbins v Maine School Administrative Dist No. 56	46.13(B)
Roberts v Madigan	33.04
Robertson v Granite City Community Unit School Dist No. 9	21.03(D), 28.01(B)
Robinson v Lebanon City School Dist Bd of Ed	9.21(E)
Robinson v McDonald	37.01(A)
Robinson; Smith v	28.12(B)
Robinson v Symmes Valley Local School Dist Bd of Ed	12.09(B)
Rochester Community Schools; Fischer v	28.13(D)
Rochester, N.H., School Dist; Timothy W. v	28.01(A)
Rock Hill Local School Bd of Ed; State ex rel Floyd v	7.11(B)
Rock Hill Local School Dist Bd of Ed; Scherer v	5.05, 9.03, 45.06(B)
Rocky River Bd of Ed; Kelly v	46.01(C)

Casename	Text Section(s)
Rocky River School Dist Bd of Ed v Fairview Park City School Dist Bd of Ed	39.05
Rocky River School Dist Bd of Ed; State ex rel Fairview Park School Dist Bd of Ed v	4.11(A)
Rocky River v SERB	18.22(A)
Rodriguez; San Antonio Independent School Dist v	2.16(B)
Rogers, State ex rel v Hubbard Local School Dist Bd of Ed	9.08(C)
Rogers v Youngstown	46.04
Rohrbaugh v Elida Local Bd of Ed	25.03(B), 25.14(A)
Roland M. v Concord School Committee	28.11(D)
Rolling Hills Bd of Ed; Woodrum v	8.04(D), 9.05(B)
Rolling Hills Local School Dist Bd of Ed; Boehm v	9.19(A)
Rolling Hills Local School Dist Bd of Ed, State ex rel v Brown	39.04
Rollins, State ex rel v Cleveland Hts-University Hts City School Dist Bd of Ed	9.05(A), 18.20
Romano v Harrington	25.05
Rome City School Dist; Greer v	28.05(B)
Romeo v Campbell Civil Service Comm	12.14(B)
Romeo Community Schools v US Dept of Health, Ed, and Welfare	19.14(A)
Roncker v Walter	28.03, 28.05(A), 28.05(B), 28.20(B)
Ron Steed, In re	9.03, 45.06(B)
Rooney, In re	18.18
Roper v Bristolville (Bristol) Local School Dist	24.03(C)
Roper; Greco v	9.21(D)
Rose; Howlett v	46.13(A)
Roslyn Union Free School Dist No. 3; Hsu v	32.01
Ross v Board of Education	5.06(C), 8.02(A), 9.07(A)
Ross County Bd of Ed; Kellenberger v	4.14(A)
Rossford Exempted Village School Dist Bd of Ed; Haupricht v	9.13(A), 9.13(B)
Rossford Exempted Village School Dist Bd of Ed; King v	9.13(B)
Rossford Exempted Village School Dist Bd of Ed; Smithers v	9.13(C)
Rossford Exempted Village School Dist Bd of Ed v State Bd of Ed (1992)	4.08, 4.11(B)
Rossford Exempted Village School Dist Bd of Ed v State Bd of Ed (1989)	4.08, 4.11(B)
Rossford Exempted Village School Dist; Wills v	12.16(A)
Rossi v Gosling	28.13(D)
Ross v Solon City School Dist Bd of Ed	46.02, 46.05
Roth; Board of Regents of State Colleges v	46.14(A)
Rowland v Mad River Local School Dist (1984)	9.21(E)
Rowland v Mad River Local School Dist (1978)	9.20
Rowley; Board of Ed v	28.11(A)
Rowley; Hendrick Hudson Central School Dist Bd of Ed v	28.03, 28.11(D)
Rowley; Marcus v	33.06(B)
Royer v C.R. Coblentz Local School Dist Bd of Ed	25.04
Ruby, State ex rel v STRS	11.17
Rudolph v Cincinnati City School Dist Bd of Ed	13.08(A)
Rue; Dodd v	7.06(C), 19.10
Rumora v Ashtabula Area City School Dist Bd of Ed	5.01, 5.06(A), 9.21(A)
Runge v Dove	46.15(C)
Runkel; Clonlara, Inc v	20.03(C)
Runnels School Inc; Moyse v	48.11(B)
Runyan, State ex rel v Henry	10.17(A), 11.16(B), 18.22(A)
Runyon v McCrary	48.09(A)
Ruple Bus Service, State ex rel v Wickliffe Bd of Ed	5.08(E), 22.25(A)
Rush v Carlisle Local School Bd	46.03
Russell v Fannin County School Dist	46.14(B)
Russell v Gallia County Local School Bd	5.06(C), 22.03(B)
Russell v Springfield Local School Dist Bd of Ed	9.09(D)
Rutherford County Schools; Neely v	28.07
Ryan v Aurora City Bd of Ed	46.14(A)
Ryan v Connor	16.03(A)

Casename	Text Section(s)
S	
S-1 v Turlington	28.09(A)
Sacramento City Unified School Dist Bd of Ed v Rachel H.	28.05(B)
Saddleback Valley Unified School Dist; Phipps v	21.03(D)
Safety-Kleen Corp; Brady v	16.08
Sag Harbor Union Free School Dist Bd of Ed; Silano v	26.04
Salado Independent School Dist; Kinsey v	9.21(E)
Salem City School Dist Bd of Ed; Barbuto v	9.13(B)
Salem City School Dist Bd of Ed; Gerner v	9.13(B)
Salisbury v Housing Authority of Newport	46.14(A)
Saltsman, State ex rel v Burton (1952)	8.02(A), 9.07(A)
Saltsman, State ex rel v Burton (1950)	8.02(A), 9.07(A)
San Antonio Independent School Dist v Rodriguez	2.16(B)
San Antonio Metropolitan Transit Authority; Garcia v	13.01(B), 17.08(A)
San Bernardino City Unified School Dist; Grunwald v	18.21(C)
San Carlos Elementary School Dist; Bertolucci v	28.03
Sanford School, Inc; Wisch v	48.15
San Francisco Unified School Dist; Walker v	32.01, 48.06(A), 48.06(C)
Sanguigni v Pittsburgh Bd of Public Ed	9.21(E), 46.14(A)
San Jacinto Unified School Dist; Jeglin v	25.04
San Mateo County Bd of Ed; Citizens for Parental Rights v	32.07
Santiago de Castro v Morales Medina	46.14(B)
Sargeant v Gallipolis Bd	46.02
Sarra v Girard City School Dist Bd of Ed	13.01(B)
Sartori v Columbus Bd of Ed	46.02, 46.03
Savannah-Chatham County Bd of Ed; Stell v (1994)	19.03(B)
Savannah-Chatham County Bd of Ed; Stell v (1989)	19.03(B)
Savarese v Buckeye Local School Dist Bd of Ed	5.13(A)
Save Immaculata v Immaculata Preparatory School, Inc	48.11(B)
Sayen v Toledo Bd of Ed	10.17(B)

Casename	Text Section(s)
Sayers v State Bd of Ed	8.07(A)
Scanlon, State ex rel v Deters	44.02
Schaeffer v Paxton	24.03(C)
Schafer v Anderson	46.03
Schafer v Pittsburgh School Dist Bd of Public Ed	17.09(A)
Schaffer v Halloran	25.09(C)
Schank v Hegele	5.12(D), 25.12(A)
Schanou v Lancaster County School Dist No. 160	32.01
Scharlotte, State ex rel v East Franklin Local School Dist Bd of Ed	9.11(B)
Scheideman v West Des Moines Community School Dist	46.14(A)
Schell v Globe Trucking, Inc	16.03(A)
Schempp; Abington Twp School Dist v	32.05
Schenectady City School Dist; Mason v	28.13(A)
Scherer; Davis v	46.15(C)
Scherer v Rock Hill Local School Dist Bd of Ed	5.05, 9.03, 45.06(B)
Schleier; Commissioner of Internal Revenue Service v	17.03(E)
Schlotterer v Coldwater Exempted Village School Dist Bd of Ed	7.13, 46.08
Schmidt; Colin K. v	28.11(F)
Schmidt; State v	20.03(C)
Schneeweis v Jacobs	46.14(A)
School Bd of Colorado Springs School Dist No. 11; Hemry v	25.05
School Bd of Norfolk, Va; Flickinger v	9.21(E)
School City of Hobart; Smith v	25.09(A), 46.14(B)
School Employees Retirement System; Fair v	14.11
School Employees Retirement System; State ex rel McMaster v	14.03, 14.11
School Employees Retirement System; State ex rel Plavcan v	14.11
School Employees Retirement System; State ex rel Seballos v	44.02
Schoppelrei v Franklin University	48.15
Schottenstein Stores Corp; State ex rel Watts v	16.05(C)
Schowerth; Waiters v	24.03(D)

Casename	Text Section(s)
Schuldt v Mankato Independent School Dist No. 77	28.05(B)
Schultz v Herman's Furniture, Inc	15.08(A)
Schumann; State ex rel Pioneer Joint Vocational School Dist Bd of Ed v	4.05(B), 27.08(A)
Schuylerville Central School Dist Bd of Ed; Joki v	32.06(B)
Schweikert; State ex rel Cincinnati Post v	44.02
Schwenker; Watson v	12.17(A)
Schwing v McClure	21.01, 39.13, 43.05(D)
Scioto Valley Local School Dist Bd of Ed; State ex rel O'Dell v	12.15(A), 12.16(A)
Scott v Marshall	24.03(B)
Scott v Reinier	12.17(D)
Scott v State	10.14
Scott; State ex rel Britton v	13.08(B)
Scott, State ex rel v Industrial Comm	16.05(B)
Scott, State ex rel v Masterson	2.16(A)
Scovill, Inc; Barker v	17.06(B)
Scyoc v Wellington Exempted Village School Dist	12.16(A)
Seamons v Snow	19.14(A)
Searcey v Harris	26.04
Searcy; Fresh v	20.03(C)
Sease v Philadelphia School Dist	32.06(A)
Seattle King County School Dist No. 1; Banks v	24.03(D)
Seattle School Dist No. 1; Washington v	19.12
Seballos, State ex rel v School Employees Retirement System	44.02
Seemuller v Fairfax County School Bd	9.21(E)
Seiler v Vantage Joint Vocational School Dist Bd of Ed	9.05(A)
Seither v Maple Hts Bd of Ed	24.03(C)
Sellers v Logan-Hocking City School Dist Bd of Ed	9.21(B), 9.21(D), 9.23(B)
Sellers v Ohio Bureau of Employment Services Bd of Review	15.08(A)
Sellers v Spencerville Local Bd of Ed	25.12(A)
Seltzer v Cuyahoga County Dept of Human Services	12.17(B)

Casename	Text Section(s)
Seneca Falls Central School Dist Bd of Ed v Liverpool Central School Dist Bd of Ed	28.11(F)
SERB v—See name of defendant.	
SERB;—See name of plaintiff.	
Sergent, In re	12.16(B)
Settle v Dickson County School Bd	25.05
Seven Hills Schools v Kinney	48.33
Severson v Beloit	24.03(D)
Sever-Williams Co; Chillicothe City School Dist Bd of Ed v	37.04(B)
Seward v State ex rel Kratt	12.05(A)
Shadley, In re	12.16(C)
Shafer v Southwest Licking Local School Dist Bd of Ed	22.03(D), 48.08(A)
Shaffer v Frontrunner, Inc	48.26
Shaffer v Minerva Local School Dist Bd of Ed	12.16(B)
Shaheen v B.F. Goodrich Co	17.19
Shankle v Ontario Local School Dist Bd of Ed	12.09(A)
Shannon M.; Granite School Dist v	28.07
Sharif v New York State Ed Dept	19.14(C)
Shattuck School	48.28(A)
Shawnee Mission School Dist (USD No. 512); Hall v	28.06
Shearer v Cuyahoga County Hospital	7.09(A), 12.04(B)
Sheffield Lake City School Dist Bd of Ed; State ex rel Burch v	10.02(B)
Sheffield-Sheffield Lake Bd of Ed; Davidson v	5.12(B), 12.04(B)
Sheffield-Sheffield Lake Bd of Ed; Hart v	12.04(B)
Sheffield-Sheffield Lake City School Dist, In re	18.17(B)
Shelby City Bd of Ed, In re	18.31
Shelly C. v Venus Independent School Dist	28.13(D)
Shelton v Greater Cleveland Regional Transit Authority	46.06
Shenago Co; Bays v	15.06
Shenandoah Baptist Church; Dole v	48.22, 48.30
Sherbert v Verner	32.01
Sherman v Community Consolidated School Dist 21 of Wheeling Twp (1993)	32.06(A)

Casename	Text Section(s)
Sherman v Community Consolidated School Dist 21 of Wheeling Twp (192)	32.03
Sherri A.D. v Kirby	28.03
Shie v Hamilton City School Dist Bd of Ed (10-7-81)	9.23(C)
Shie v Hamilton City School Dist Bd of Ed (11-25-81)	9.21(B), 9.22(F)
Shields v Dayton Bd of Ed	10.01(B)
Shine, State ex rel v Garofalo	12.17(C)
Shirokey v Marth	46.13(C)
Showboat Operating Co; Steiner v	17.11
Shuba v Austintown Bd of Ed	9.06(B)
Shukert v Woodridge Local School Dist Bd of Ed	12.16(A)
Shumway v Albany County School Dist No. One Bd of Ed	32.06(A)
Shupe; Barton v	44.02
Siers, State ex rel v Beaver Local School Dist Bd of Ed	8.02(B), 9.07(A), 10.02(A), 18.20
Sigall; Hubner v	46.06
Sigall, State ex rel v Aetna Cleaning Contractors of Cleveland, Inc	12.08
Silano v Sag Harbor Union Free School Dist Bd of Ed	26.04
Silavent v Buckeye Central Local School Dist Bd of Ed	7.06(B), 9.04
Simmons; State ex rel International Union of Operating Engineers v	18.20
Simms v Dayton Public Schools	46.02, 46.03
Simpson; Laucher v	25.04
Simpson v Midland-Ross Corp	17.03(F)
Sims v Waln	25.16(B)
Sindermann; Perry v	46.14(A)
Sioux Falls School Dist 49-5; Florey v	32.06(B)
Skinner v. Railway Labor Executives' Assn	47.01(A)
Skufca, In re	18.15(C), 18.17(A)
Slack v Delaware Dept of Public Instruction	28.06
Slauson v New Philadelphia City School Dist Bd of Ed	18.26
Sloan v Warren City School Dist Bd of Ed	10.16
Slotterback v Interboro School Dist	25.05, 32.06(A)
Small v Defiance Public Library	16.03(A)

Casename	Text Section(s)
Smider v Jackson Milton Local School Dist Bd of Ed	25.12(A)
Smith; Angevine v	28.03
Smith v Barton	28.13(C)
Smith v Chester Twp Bd of Trustees	25.12(B)
Smith v Clermont Northeastern Local School Dist Bd of Ed	12.16(C)
Smith; Doe v	28.12(A)
Smith; Employment Div, Dept of Human Resources of Oregon v	32.01
Smithers v Rossford Exempted Village School Dist Bd of Ed	9.13(C)
Smith; Hanes v	12.07(A)
Smith; Lyons v	28.01(B), 28.02
Smith; Maynard v	45.13
Smith; McClain v	28.11(F)
Smith; McKenzie v	28.11(F)
Smith v Mobile County Bd of School Commrs	33.04
Smith v North Babylon Union Free School Dist Bd of Ed	32.01
Smith v Ricci	32.07
Smith v Robinson	28.12(B)
Smith v School City of Hobart	25.09(A), 46.14(B)
Smith; State ex rel Daoust v	41.14(C)
Smith, State ex rel v Etheridge	7.11(B)
Smith; State ex rel Kuhn v	37.04(A), 37.04(C)
Smith; State ex rel Old Fort School Dist Bd of Ed v	39.05
Smith; Thomas v	46.14(A)
Smith v Upper Sandusky Exempted Village School Dist Bd of Ed	9.13(B)
Smith v Wade	17.02(A), 17.02(B)
Snow; Seamons v	19.14(A)
Snyder, In re	20.03(C)
Snyder v Miami East Local School Dist	9.21(B)
Snyder v New Boston School Dist Bd of Ed	10.11
Sobol; Grimes v	19.13(A)
Sobol; Mavis v	28.11(D)
Society of Mary; Arons v	48.27
Society of Sisters; Pierce v	48.02
Solimino; Astoria Federal Savings and Loan Assn v	17.03(G)
Solon City School Dist Bd of Ed; Ross v	46.02, 46.05
Solon City School Dist, In re	18.12

Casename	Text Section(s)
Solon City Schools; Stinehelfer v	46.02
Solon; State ex rel Alden Corp v	41.20(B)
Sommers v Putnam County Bd of Ed	22.01
South Community, Inc, In re	18.15(D)
South Community, Inc v SERB	18.15(F)
Southeast Delco School Dist; C.M. v	46.13(B), 46.14(B), 46.15(C)
Southeastern Local School Dist Bd of Ed; Boggs v	10.07, 10.07(B)
Southeastern Ohio Voluntary Ed Cooperative, In re	18.03
Southeast Local School Dist	18.13
Southeast Local School; Kingsbury v	18.26
Southern Company Services, Inc; Waldrop v	17.13(A), 28.13(C)
Southern Local School Dist Bd of Ed; Tice v	5.06(C), 5.08(A), 20.05(C)
South Euclid-Lyndhurst City School Dist Bd of Ed, In re (1992)	18.25(C)
South Euclid-Lyndhurst City School Dist Bd of Ed, In re (1984)	18.31
South Euclid-Lyndhurst City School Dist Bd of Ed; Zagorski v	46.01(A)
Southland Corp; Wheeler v	17.11
South Point Local School Dist Bd of Ed; State ex rel Peake v	9.11(A), 9.11(B)
South Range Local School Dist Bd of Ed; Kenney v	12.16(C)
South Range Local School Dist Bd of Ed; Krolopp v	7.06(B), 8.02(B), 9.07(A)
South Range Local School Dist Bd of Ed; Phillips v	9.19(A)
South Russell v Geauga County Budget Comm	40.06
Southwestern City Bd of Ed; Picklesimer v	35.02(A)
Southwestern City School Dist Bd of Ed; Neal v	46.02
Southwest Licking Local School Dist Bd of Ed; Shafer v	22.03(D), 48.08(A)
Southwest School Dist Bd of Ed; DeLong v	9.13(B)
Sowers v Ohio Civil Rights Comm	17.04(A)
Spacco v Bridgewater School Dept	32.01
Spalding and Evenflo Co; Giambrone v	17.06(A)
Spang; Brody v	25.05, 32.06(A)
Spann v Tyler Independent School Dist	46.13(B)
Sparer v Evergreen Local School	9.13(C)
Specht, State ex rel v Oregon City Bd of Ed	6.13, 12.15(A)
Specht, State ex rel v Painesville Twp Local School Dist Bd of Ed	7.13, 9.07(A)
Speeth, State ex rel v Carney	41.10
Spencer v Vantage Joint Vocational School Dist Bd of Ed	9.21(C)
Spencerville Local Bd of Ed; Sellers v	25.12(A)
Spencerville Local School Dist Bd of Ed; Finfrock v	12.16(A)
Spielberg v Henrico County Public Schools	28.03
Spires v Lancaster	46.06
Spires, State ex rel v Maceyko	9.06(B)
Spirtos v Struthers City School Dist Bd of Ed	9.21(A)
Spotts v Columbus Public Schools	46.03
Spring Branch Independent School Dist v Stamos	25.15(B)
Springdale School Dist No. 50 of Washington County v Grace	28.05(B)
Springfield Bd of Ed	18.16(A)
Springfield Bd of Ed; Patton v	22.13(A)
Springfield Bd of Ed; State ex rel Fox v	7.06(B)
Springfield Bd of Park Trustees; Ohio Council 8, AFSCME v	18.29(D), 18.31
Springfield City School Dist Bd of Ed; Malina v	9.15(B)
Springfield City School Dist Bd of Ed; State ex rel Gray v	9.11(A), 9.11(D)
Springfield City School Support Personnel v SERB	18.15(F)
Springfield Local Assn of Classroom Teachers v Springfield Local School Dist Bd of Ed	18.22(A)
Springfield Local Bd of Ed; Guy v	24.03(D)
Springfield Local Bd of Ed, In re	18.29(B)
Springfield Local School Dist	18.13
Springfield Local School Dist Bd of Ed; Hackathorn v	46.01(C), 46.01(D)

Casename	Text Section(s)
Springfield Local School Dist Bd of Ed v Ohio Assn of Public School Employees Local 530	5.12, 5.12(B)
Springfield Local School Dist Bd of Ed; Russell v	9.09(D)
Springfield Local School Dist Bd of Ed; Springfield Local Assn of Classroom Teachers v	18.22(A)
Springfield Local Schools Bd of Ed; Medley v	9.21(A)
Springfield Local Schools Bd of Ed; Minnick v	46.03
Springfield Twp Bd of Trustees, In re	18.27
Springfield Twp Public School Dist Bd of Ed; Weimer v	46.02
Springfield Twp School; Redd v	46.01(C)
Spruytte v Walters	46.15(C)
Spurlock; State ex rel Bush v	12.14(A)
Stacey G. v Pasadena Independent School Dist	28.13(A)
Stachura; Memphis Community School Dist v	46.13(C)
Stafford County School Bd; Goodall v	28.03, 48.06(C)
Stafford; Powell v	48.30
Stafford, State ex rel v Clay Local School Dist Bd of Ed	5.13(A)
Stallings v Vanguard Joint Vocational School	15.02(D)
Stamos; Spring Branch Independent School Dist v	25.15(B)
Stanley, In re	12.17(D)
Stanley v Like	36.02(C)
Starcher v Danbury Bd of Ed	25.03(A)
Stark County Area Joint Vocational School Dist Bd of Ed; Combs v	18.22(A)
Stark County Bd of Ed; OAPSE v	22.13(A), 22.14
Stark County Bd of Mental Retardation & Developmental Disabilities, In re (1993)	18.08, 18.17(A)
Stark County Bd of Mental Retardation & Developmental Disabilities, In re (1985)	18.28(B), 18.31
Stark County Bd of Mental Retardation and Developmental Disabilities; Provens v	17.04(D)
Stark County Bd of Mental Retardation; Ebert v	7.05(B), 7.11(A), 10.01(B), 12.15(B), 13.01(B), 13.08(A), 29.13(B), 29.13(C), 43.05(B)
Stark County Bd of Revision; Ratner v	39.04
Stark County Common Pleas Court Judges; State ex rel Ohio High School Athletic Assn v	30.07(A)
Stark County Common Pleas Court Judges; State ex rel OHSAA v	30.07(B), 30.08(A), 30.11(C)
Stark County Educators Assn for the Training of Retarded Persons v SERB (1991)	18.28(C)
Stark County Educators Assn for the Training of Retarded Persons v SERB (1989)	18.28(C), 29.17
Stark County Engineer, In re (4-4-85)	18.15(D), 18.25(B)
Stark County Engineer, In re (10-31-85)	18.29(C)
Starlin v Morgan Local School Dist Bd of Ed	9.17, 9.22(A)
State v—See name of defendant.	
State Bd of Cosmetology; State ex rel Trimble v	12.04(B)
State; Board of Education v	19.07
State Bd of Ed; Crumpler v	8.07(A)
State Bd of Ed; Daniel R.R. v	28.05(B)
State Bd of Ed; Davis v	4.09(A)
State Bd of Ed; Garfield Heights City School Dist v	4.11(B)
State Bd of Ed; Garfield Heights City School Dist v	4.11(B)
State Board of Education; Garfield Heights City School District v	4.07(C)
State Bd of Ed; Haig v	22.03(C)
State Bd of Ed; Johnson v	8.07(A)
State Bd of Ed; Lucci v	8.07(A)
State Bd of Ed; Rossford Exempted Village School Dist Bd of Ed v (1992)	4.08, 4.11(B)
State Bd of Ed; Rossford Exempted Village School Dist Bd of Ed v (1989)	4.08, 4.11(B)
State Bd of Ed; Sayers v	8.07(A)

Casename	Text Section(s)
State Bd of Ed; State ex rel Bratenahl Local School Dist Bd of Ed v	26.19
State Bd of Ed; State ex rel Cleveland Bd of Ed v	20.05(D)
State Bd of Ed; Union Title Co v	4.08
State Bd of Ed; Winters v	8.07(A)
State Board of Psychology; State ex rel McGee v	44.02
State Chemical Mfg Co; Borowski v	17.06(A)
State Dept of Ed; State ex rel Dayton Bd of Ed v	22.07(C)
State; DeRolph v (App)	2.14, 39.01(B), 39.06(B)
State; DeRolph v (CP)	39.01(B), 39.06(B)
State ex rel—See name of party.	
State Farm Mutual Automobile Insurance Co, State ex rel v Ohio Civil Rights Comm	17.04(C)
State of Ohio Dept of Corrections, In re	18.11(B)
State of Ohio, In re	18.11(B)
State of Ohio, Office of Collective Bargaining, In re	18.11(B)
State; Parr v	20.02(A), 32.02
State Personnel Bd of Review; Adkins v	12.17(C)
State Personnel Bd of Review; Fairley v	12.17(C)
State Personnel Bd of Review; Richards v	18.22(A)
State; Scott v	10.14
State Teachers Retirement Bd v Cuyahoga Falls City School Dist Bd of Ed	11.04(A)
State Teachers Retirement Bd; State ex rel Cicero v	11.07(A)
State Teachers Retirement Bd; State ex rel Palmer v	11.13(A)
State Teachers Retirement System Bd v Cuyahoga Falls City School Dist Bd of Ed	11.02(C)
State Teachers Retirement System; Hager v	11.19(C)
State; Weber v	24.03(D)
Steed, In re	5.05
Steele v Auburn Vocational School Dist	46.02
Steffen, State ex rel v Kraft	44.02
Steiner v Showboat Operating Co	17.11

Casename	Text Section(s)
Steinhour v Ohio State University	10.16
Stein v National City Bank	17.06(B)
Steirer v Bethlehem Area School Dist	25.05
Stell v Savannah-Chatham County Bd of Ed (1994)	19.03(B)
Stell v Savannah-Chatham County Bd of Ed (1989)	19.03(B)
Stephenson, State ex rel v Industrial Comm	16.05(F)
Steppe v Columbus Bd of Ed	10.03(C)
Sterkel v Mansfield Bd of Ed	36.03
Steubenville Bd of Ed; Denson v	26.15(B)
Steubenville School Dist Bd of Ed, State ex rel v Hamrock	40.05(C)
Stewart v Baldwin County Bd of Ed	46.15(C)
Stewart v Margaretta Local Bd of Ed	9.20
Stewart; Rhodes v	28.13(D)
Stiller, State ex rel v Columbiana Exempted Village School Dist Bd of Ed	7.04(B), 7.14(A)
Stimpert v Porter	25.10(B), 25.12(A)
Stinehelfer v Solon City Schools	46.02
Stokes, In re	12.05(A)
Stone v Graham	32.06(B)
Stoneking v Bradford Area School Dist	46.15(C)
Stotts; Firefighters Local Union No. 1784 v	17.18
Stover v Bureau of Motor Vehicles	12.17(A)
Stow Bd of Ed; Hallett v	46.02
Stow Bd of Ed; Stow Teachers Assn v	9.19(E)
Stow City School Dist Bd of Ed; Adkins v	9.21(E)
Stow City School Dist Bd of Ed; Mate v	9.09(D)
Stow City School Dist Bd of Ed v Swearingen	10.07, 10.07(B)
Stow City School Dist, In re	18.17(B)
Stow Civil Service Comm; Bettio v	18.20
Stow School System; Amann v	28.03
Stow Teachers Assn v Stow Bd of Ed	9.19(E)
Strasburg-Franklin Bd of Ed	18.16(B)
Strausser; Board of Ed v	41.04
St. Bernard, In re	18.28(B)

Casename	Text Section(s)
St. Francis College v Al-Khazraji	17.02(A)
St. John and West Shore Hospital; Kuhn v	48.26
St. Louis Bd of Ed; Thelma D. v	46.13(B)
St. Louis County Special School Dist; Jane Doe "A" v	46.13(B), 46.15(C)
St. Louis County Special School Dist; Yaris v	28.04
St. Mary's Honor Center v Hicks	17.03(F)
St. Marys School Dist Bd of Ed, In re	18.11(A), 18.13
Streetsboro City School Dist Bd of Ed; State ex rel Harrell v	4.11(A)
Streetsboro Ed Assn v Streetsboro City School Dist Bd of Ed	11.08(A), 18.20
St. Xavier High School; Geraci v	48.15, 48.16, 48.27
Strickland; Wood v	46.13(B), 46.15(C)
Stringer; Petitioners v	5.05
Stringer; Zavatsky v	16.07(B)
Strock v Barberton City School Dist Bd of Ed	9.19(C)
Stroman v Colleton County School Dist	9.21(E)
Stromberg v Bratenahl Bd of Ed	4.05(A)
Strongsville City School Dist Bd of Ed v Theado	28.13(B)
Strongsville City School Dist; Minarcini v	33.04
Stroud v Dayton City School Dist	10.01(B)
STRS; State ex rel Ruby v	11.17
Struthers City School Dist Bd of Ed; Spirtos v	9.21(A)
Struthers City Schools Bd of Ed v Struthers Ed Assn	9.13(B)
Stuble v Cuyahoga Valley Joint Vocational School Dist Bd of Ed	25.10(C)
Stuckey, State ex rel v Clearcreek Local School Dist Bd of Ed	12.10(A)
Stuckey, State ex rel v Washington Court House City School Dist	10.07(A)
Student Coalition for Peace v Lower Merion School Dist Bd of School Directors	25.05, 32.06(A)
Sugarcreek Local School Dist, In re	18.15(D)
Suitts, State ex rel v Mississinawa Valley Local School Dist Bd of Ed	9.09(C), 9.09(E)
Sullivan v Meade Independent School Dist No. 101	46.14(E)
Sullivan; New York Times v	5.07, 18.34
Summit County Bd of Ed; Miller v	22.14
Summit County Bd of Mental Retardation & Developmental Disabilities, In re	18.17(B)
Summit County Bd of Mental Retardation & Developmental Disabilities; State ex rel LanFranchi v	29.13(C)
Summit County Bd of Mental Retardation, In re	18.17(B)
Summit County Children Services Bd; Brodie v	24.05(A)
Summit County Child Support Enforcement Agency and Summit County Department of Human Services, In re	18.31
Summit County Dept of Human Services, In re	18.29(D)
Sun Newspapers, State ex rel v Westlake Bd of Ed	44.02
Superintendent, D.C. Public Schools; Kerkam v	28.05(B)
Superior Metal Products, Inc v Bureau of Employment Services	15.08(A)
Sutherland-Wagner v Brook Park Civil Service Comm	12.15(A)
Sutton v Cleveland Bd of Ed	12.17(B), 18.22(A), 46.14(B)
Swafford v Norwood Bd of Ed	12.15(A), 12.17(D)
Swann v Charlotte-Mecklenberg Bd of Ed	19.03(B), 19.11(A)
Swanton Local School Dist Bd of Ed; SERB v	18.28(B)
Swaykus v East Holmes Local School Dist Bd of Ed	9.14(A)
Swearingen; Stow City School Dist Bd of Ed v	10.07, 10.07(B)
Sweeney; Keene State College Bd of Trustees v	17.04(E)
Swepston v Ohio Bd of Tax Appeals	12.14(B)
Swift v Rapides Parish Public School System	28.06
Swinderman v Dover City School Dist Bd of Ed	9.21(B), 10.16, 13.08(B)

Casename	Text Section(s)
Sycamore City School Dist Bd of Ed; State ex rel Chavis v	10.02(B)
Sylvania Bd of Ed; Sylvania Ed Assn v	10.16
Sylvania City School Dist Bd of Ed; State ex rel First Natl Bank of Toledo v	42.11(B)
Sylvania City School Dist; OAPSE, Chapter 227 v	12.08
Sylvania City Schools; Sylvania Ed Assn v	9.21(A)
Sylvania Ed Assn v Sylvania Bd of Ed	10.16
Sylvania Ed Assn v Sylvania City Schools	9.21(A)
Symmes Valley Local Bd of Ed	18.16(B)
Symmes Valley Local School Dist Bd of Ed; Robinson v	12.09(B)
Szymczak v Berger	9.21(E)

T

Casename	Text Section(s)
Taggart v Time, Inc	17.06(B)
Talladega County Bd of Ed; Elston v	19.13(A)
Tallmadge City School Dist Bd of Ed; State ex rel Hallinan v	12.12, 12.16(A)
Tallmadge Firefighters Assn, In re	18.07
Tallman; Navin v	8.02(B), 9.07(A)
Tanberg v Weld County Sheriff	28.13(C)
Tangipahoa Parish School Bd v United States Dept of Ed	19.15
Tapo v Columbus Bd of Ed (OS)	18.22(A)
Tapo v Columbus Bd of Ed (App)	10.07(A)
Tarka v Cunningham	44.14(A), 44.19(A)
Tarter v Raybuck	46.16
Tasby v Woolery	19.03(B)
Tate v Westerville Bd of Ed	9.02, 9.05(A), 9.14(B)
Tatro; Irving Independent School Dist v	28.07
Tavenner, State ex rel v Indian Lake Local School Dist Bd of Ed	5.07, 8.02(B), 9.07(A), 10.02(A)
Tawney; Hall v	46.14(B), 46.15(B)
Tax Deferred Annuities Corp v Cleveland Bd of Ed	10.10(A)
Taylor Independent School Dist; Doe v	46.14(B)
Taylor v National Group of Companies, Inc	17.04(B)

Casename	Text Section(s)
Teague Independent School Dist v Todd L.	28.11(D), 28.13(A)
Teamsters, Local Union 20 v Toledo	18.22(A)
Tempe Elementary School Dist No. 3; Guadalupe Organization, Inc v	19.15
Temple University; Haffer v (1987)	19.14(C)
Temple University; Haffer v (1982)	30.09(B)
Tennessee Secondary School Athletic Assn; Cape v	19.14(D), 30.09(B)
Tennessee Secondary School Athletic Assn; Crocker v (1992)	28.13(A)
Tennessee Secondary School Athletic Assn; Crocker v (1989)	28.12(A)
Teresa P. v Berkeley Unified School Dist	19.15
Teska; Beard v	28.13(D)
Texas Bd of Ed; Alamo Heights Independent School Dist v	28.04, 28.07
Texas City Independent School Dist v Jorstad	28.09(A)
Texas Dept of Community Affairs v Burdine	17.03(F), 17.04(E)
Texas State Teachers Assn v Garland Independent School Dist	17.02(B), 28.13(D), 46.16
Thaxton v Medina City Bd of Ed	5.07
Theado; Strongsville City School Dist Bd of Ed v	28.13(B)
Thelma D. v St. Louis Bd of Ed	46.13(B)
Thiboutot; Maine v	46.13(B)
Thomas v Akron City School Dist Bd of Ed	9.22(A)
Thomas v Atascadero Unified School Dist	21.03(D)
Thomas v Cincinnati Bd of Ed	28.01(A), 28.03, 28.08(A), 28.09(A), 28.11(D)
Thomas v Davidson Academy	28.09(A)
Thomas; Griffin v	9.21(E)
Thomas v Newark City School Dist Bd of Ed	9.13(A)
Thomas v Smith	46.14(A)
Thomas, State ex rel v Ohio State University	44.02
Thomas v Washington County School Bd	17.03(F)
Thomas v White	5.12

Casename	Text Section(s)
Thompson v Bryan Civil Service Comm	12.17(D)
Thompson v Chicago Bd of Ed	9.21(E)
Thompson v Fostoria City School Dist Bd of Ed	7.06(B), 9.06(A)
Thompson v McNeill	46.03
Thompson Newspapers, Inc, State ex rel v Martin	44.02
Thompson v West Clermont Local Bd of Ed	9.21(A), 10.19(A)
Thornton v Meigs Local School Dist Bd of Ed	12.16(A)
Thrasher v General Casualty Co of Wisconsin	46.14(B)
Tice v Southern Local School Dist Bd of Ed	5.06(C), 5.08(A), 20.05(C)
Tickhill v Cuyahoga Falls	18.22(A)
Tierney v Toledo (1990)	18.21(C)
Tierney v Toledo (1987)	18.21(C)
Tilton v Jefferson County Bd of Ed	28.11(B)
Time, Inc; Taggart v	17.06(B)
Timothy W. v Rochester, N.H., School Dist	28.01(A)
Tinker v Des Moines Independent Community School Dist	25.05, 47.01(A)
Tiro Consolidated School Dist of Crawford County Bd of Ed; Brannon v	5.06(C)
Tirpack v Beavercreek Bd of Ed	5.06(A)
T.J. v Florida	47.01(A)
T.L.O.; New Jersey v	47.01(A), 47.02
T. Marzetti Co v Doyle	17.04(E)
Todaro; State ex rel Meng v	24.11
Todd D. v Andrews	28.03
Todd L.; Teague Independent School Dist v	28.11(D), 28.13(A)
Toledo Area AFL-CIO Council v Pizza	5.03(A)
Toledo Blade Co, State ex rel v University of Toledo Foundation	44.02
Toledo Bd of Ed; Bachmayer v	46.04
Toledo Bd of Ed; Gibney v	18.21(B)
Toledo Bd of Ed, In re	18.07, 18.12
Toledo Bd of Ed; Sayen v	10.17(B)
Toledo Bd of Ed; Wilson v	18.22(A)
Toledo; Gomez v	46.15(C)
Toledo v Nobel-Sysco, Inc	17.15
Toledo Police Patrolmen's Assn, Local 10, State ex rel v SERB	18.26(A)

Casename	Text Section(s)
Toledo Public Schools; Gallant v	17.04(B)
Toledo; State ex rel Clark v	44.03
Toledo; Teamsters, Local Union 20 v	18.22(A)
Toledo; Tierney v (1990)	18.21(C)
Toledo; Tierney v (1987)	18.21(C)
Tompkins v Vickers	9.21(E), 46.15(C)
Tonti v Petropoulous	46.16
Topeka Bd of Ed; Brown v (1992)	19.03(B)
Topeka Bd of Ed; Brown v (1955)	19.02
Topeka Bd of Ed; Brown v (1954)	2.16(B), 19.02
Torres v Oakland County	46.16
Toth v Kenston Local School Dist Bd of Ed	12.09(A)
Town of East Longmeadow; New Life Baptist Church Academy v	32.02
Town of Yarmouth; Brougham v	28.03
Tracy v Otsego Bd of Ed	9.13(B)
Transportation Agency, Santa Clara County; Johnson v	17.18
Transportation Dept, In re	18.28(B), 18.29(A)
Transport Workers Union of America, Local 208; Central Ohio Transit Authority v	18.32
Trans World Airlines v Hardison	17.15
Trans World Airlines, Inc; Zipes v	17.03(D)
Traub v Wasem	25.16(B)
Trautman v Waterloo Local Bd of Ed	25.03(B)
Trautvetter v Quick	17.11
Traverse City Area Public Schools; Brimmer v	28.11(A)
Travis v Owego-Apalachin School Dist	32.06(A)
Tree of Life Christian Schools; EEOC v	48.30
Treska v Trumble	12.14(A)
Tri-County North Local School Bd of Ed v McGuire & Shook Corp	37.07(A), 43.07(B)
Tri-County North Local Schools Bd of Ed v McGuire & Shook Corp	6.07(C)
Trimble, State ex rel v State Bd of Cosmetology	12.04(B)
Tri-Valley Local School Dist Bd of Ed; Carothers v	9.21(B)

Casename	Text Section(s)
Triway Bd of Ed; Graham v	12.13, 12.16(A)
Trotwood-Madison Bd of Ed; Welsh v	13.04(A)
Trotwood Madison Bd of Ed; Wood v	8.02, 10.02(A)
Trotwood-Madison City School Dist Bd of Ed; Huelskamp v (App)	9.21(A)
Trotwood-Madison City School Dist Bd of Ed; Huelskamp v (CP)	9.21(A)
Trotwood-Madison Ed Assn Support Staff Personnel, OEA/NEA v Trotwood-Madison City School Dist	18.15(F)
Trotwood-Madison School Dist Bd of Ed, In re	18.09
Trowbridge v Employment Services Bureau Bd of Review	15.02(B)
Truck Drivers, Chauffeurs & Helpers, Local No. 100, IBT, In re	18.10
Truesdale v Pacific Holding Co/Hay Adams Div	10.12(A)
Truitt Co; NLRB v	18.10
Trumble; Treska v	12.14(A)
Trumbull County Bd of Commrs; State ex rel Bispeck v	12.14(B)
Trumbull County Bd of Ed; Gilbert v	12.16(C)
Truslow, State ex rel v Industrial Comm	16.05(G)
Trustees of Big Sandy Independent School Dist; Alabama and Coushatta Tribes of Texas v	25.04
Trydle, State ex rel v Industrial Comm	20.11(A)
Tschappat, State ex rel v Monroe County Bd of Ed	7.12
Tucker v Boardman Bd of Ed	9.19(D)
Tullahoma City Schools Bd of Ed; Doe v	28.05(B), 28.11(D), 28.13(A)
Tullis v Lear School, Inc	17.06(B)
Tulsa County, Oklahoma Independent School Dist No. 3; Johnsen v	9.21(E)
Turlington; S-1 v	28.09(A)
Tuscarawas Valley Local School Dist Bd of Ed; Herman v	18.22(A)
Tuslaw Local School Dist; Eversole v	10.02(A)
Tustin Unified School Dist; Masotti v	28.13(D)

Casename	Text Section(s)
Tuttle; Oklahoma City v	46.13(B)
Twinsburg City Schools v OCRC	17.04(E)
Twinsburg; OAPSE v	12.03(A)
Twinsburg v SERB	18.22(A)
Twinsburg; Wise v	40.07
Twin Valley Community Local School Dist Bd of Ed; Baker v	9.21(A), 9.23(B)
Twin Valley Local School Dist Bd of Ed; OAPSE v	12.09(C), 13.01(B)
2,867 Signers v Mack	5.05
Tye v Polaris Joint Vocational School Dist Bd of Ed	18.22(A)
Tyler Independent School Dist; Spann v	46.13(B)
Tyndall v National Ed Centers	17.13(B)
Tzangas, Plakas & Mannos v Ohio Bureau of Employment Services	15.08(A)

U

Casename	Text Section(s)
Unemployment Compensation Bd of Review; Hardman v	15.08(A)
Unemployment Compensation Bd of Review; Loy v	15.08(A)
Unemployment Compensation Bd of Review; Minis v	15.05(C)
Unemployment Compensation Bd of Review; Nordonia Hills City School Dist Bd of Ed v	15.08(B)
Unemployment Compensation Bd of Review; Pickett v	15.08(A)
Unified School Dist No. 449 of Leavenworth County, Kansas; Gates v	46.13(B)
Unified School Dist No. 501; Copp v	9.21(E)
Union Scioto Schools Bd of Ed; State ex rel Bri-Den Co, Inc v	37.06(A)
Union Title Co v State Bd of Ed	4.08
United Food and Commercial Workers Local 951 v Mulder	18.21(C)
United Local School Dist Bd of Ed	18.28(B)
United Local School Dist, In re	18.24(C)
United Plant Guard Workers, Local 114; Linn v	18.34
United Postal Service v Aikens	17.03(F)
United States v Board of Education for School District of Philadelphia	32.01

Casename	Text Section(s)
United States; Bob Jones University v	48.31
United States v Burke	17.03(E)
United States Dept of Ed; Tangipahoa Parish School Bd v	19.15
United States Dist Ct Central Dist of Cal; Chalk v	17.13(A), 21.03(D)
United States v Fordice	19.03(B)
United States; Hazelwood School Dist v	17.03(F)
United States; International Brotherhood of Teamsters v	17.02(B), 17.03(C), 17.03(F)
United States v Lopez	25.10(A)
United States v Philadelphia School Dist Bd of Ed	17.15
United States v Piscataway Twp Bd of Ed	17.18
United States; Welsh v	32.01
United Steelworkers of America; Bruno v	10.12(A)
United Steelworkers of America; Vulcan-Cincinnati, Inc v	18.22(A)
United Steelworkers of America v Weber	17.18
United Telephone Co; Baugh v	15.06
United Telephone Co of Ohio; Hoops v	17.06(A)
University Hospital, University of Cincinnati College of Medicine v SERB	18.26(C)
University of Akron, In re (1995)	18.11(B)
University of Akron, In re (1986)	18.25(A)
University of California Regents v Bakke	17.18
University of Chicago; Cannon v (1981)	19.14(C)
University of Chicago; Cannon v (1979)	19.13(E)
University of Cincinnati Hospital, In re	18.04(B)
University of Cincinnati, In re (2-8-94)	18.11(B), 18.29(E)
University of Cincinnati, In re (5-13-93)	18.29(B), 18.30
University of Cincinnati, In re (10-12-89)	18.05(A)
University of Cincinnati, In re (6-5-86)	18.06
University of Cincinnati (University Hospital), In re	18.04(B)
University of Cincinnati; Weaver v (1992)	18.21(C)
University of Cincinnati; Weaver v (1991)	18.21(C)
University of Colorado Regents; Pushkin v	28.12(A)
University of Detroit; EEOC v	17.15
University of Illinois Bd of Trustees; Kelley v	19.14(A)
University of Montevallo; MacPherson v	17.06(B)
University of New York Bd of Regents; Keyishian v	9.21(E)
University of Pennsylvania v EEOC	9.13(A), 17.03(D)
University of Puerto Rico; Lipsett v	19.14(A)
University of Toledo Foundation; State ex rel Toledo Blade Co v	44.02
University of Toledo v Heiny	15.05(B)
University of Toledo; Wedding v	18.22(A)
Unknown Heirs of Aughinbaugh; Wapakoneta Bd of Ed v	36.01
Upper Arlington Ed Assn, In re	18.22(B)
Upper Saddle River Bd of Ed; Kominos v	28.12(A)
Upper Sandusky Exempted Village School Dist Bd of Ed; Smith v	9.13(B)
Upper Sandusky Exempted Village School Dist Bd of Ed; Wilson v	12.16(A)
Upper Scioto Valley Local School Dist	18.16(A)
Urban v Jefferson County School Dist R-1	28.05(B)
US Dept of Health, Ed, and Welfare; Romeo Community Schools v	19.14(A)
US Fidelity & Guaranty Co; Mason v	17.04(C)
US v Martinez-Fuerte	47.01(A)
US v Place	47.01(C)

V

Casename	Text Section(s)
Vail v Paris Union School Dist No. 95 Bd of Ed	46.14(A)
Valley Christian Center of Dublin, California; Vigars v	48.30
Valley Local School Dist Bd of Ed; Hickman v	9.21(E)
Vallish v Copley Bd of Ed	46.02

Casename	Text Section(s)
Van Buren Local School Dist Bd of Ed; State ex rel Paul v	9.05(A)
Vance v Bradley	17.06(C)
Vance County Bd of Ed; Hall v	28.03
Vandalia-Butler City School Dist Bd of Ed	18.24(B), 18.27
Vandalia-Butler City School Dist Bd of Ed, In re	18.24(C), 18.24(D)
Vandalia-Butler City School Dist, In re	18.30
Vandalia Butler City Schools Bd of Ed; Deal v	9.20, 9.22(A)
Vandalia-Butler Schools Bd of Ed; Frierott v	25.09(B)
Vander Malle v Ambach	28.06
Van Dorn, State ex rel v Mt. Gilead Exempted Village School Dist Bd of Ed	9.19(G)
VanFossen v Babcock & Wilcox Co	16.08
Vanguard Joint Vocational School; Stallings v	15.02(D)
VanLoock v Curran	48.11(B)
Vantage Joint Vocational School Dist Bd of Ed; Seiler v	9.05(A)
Vantage Joint Vocational School Dist Bd of Ed; Spencer v	9.21(C)
Vantage Joint Vocational School Dist Bd of Ed, State ex rel v Hoffman	27.02, 27.08(B)
Venegas v Mitchell	17.02(B)
Venus Independent School Dist; Shelly C. v	28.13(D)
Verbena United Methodist Church v Chilton County Bd of Ed	32.06(A)
Verberg v Cleveland City School Dist Bd of Ed	5.06(A), 21.01
Vermilion Bd of Ed; Kropf v	30.12, 46.03
Vermilion Local School Dist Bd of Ed; Vermilion Teachers' Assn v	5.12(B)
Vermilion Local School Dist; Reed v	25.03(B)
Vermilion Teachers' Assn v Vermilion Local School Dist Bd of Ed	5.12(B)
Verner; Sherbert v	32.01
Vernonia School Dist 47J v Acton	47.01(A)
Vickers; Tompkins v	9.21(E), 46.15(C)
Viebranz; State ex rel Norman v	5.03(C)

Casename	Text Section(s)
Vigars v Valley Christian Center of Dublin, California	48.30
Village v General Motors Corp	16.03(A)
Village of Lakemore; Connor v	5.12(B)
Village of Smithville; Weidemann v	17.08(A)
Vincent; Widmar v	32.06(A), 38.12
Vindicator Printing Co v Julian	44.02
Vinson; Meritor Savings Bank, FSB v	17.11
Vinton County Local School Dist Bd of Ed v Ohio Civil Rights Comm	17.14
Vinton County Local School Dist Bd of Ed; State ex rel Brennan v	7.11(B)
VIP Development Co; Jones v	16.08
Virgil v Columbia County, Fla School Bd	26.04, 33.04
Virginia Bd of Ed; Pandazides v	17.13(A), 28.13(C)
Visitation of Blessed Virgin Mary Parish School; Geary v	48.30
Vitale; Engel v	32.05
Voinovich; Brickner v	3.02(A), 46.14(A)
Voinovich; State ex rel AFL-CIO v	16.08
Volk; Cincinnati Bd of Ed v	5.07, 46.08
Vonderau v Parma Civil Service Comm	12.07(A)
Von Raab; National Treasury Employees Union v	47.01(A)
Voss, State ex rel v Northwest Local Bd of Ed	9.07(B)
Vukadinovich v Bartels	9.21(E)
Vukadinovich v Michigan City Area Schools Bd of School Trustees	9.21(E)
Vukovich, State ex rel v Youngstown Civil Service Comm	12.15(B)
Vulcan-Cincinnati, Inc v United Steelworkers of America	18.22(A)
Vulcan Materials Co v Industrial Comm	16.05(B)

W

Wade; Smith v	17.02(A), 17.02(B)
Wadsworth City Schools; Miller v	46.01(B)

Casename	Text Section(s)
Waechter v Cassopolis, Michigan School Dist No. 14-030	46.14(B)
Waite v Columbus Bd of Ed	25.13
Waite Hill v Lake County Budget Comm	40.07
Waiters v Schowerth	24.03(D)
Waldrop v Southern Company Services, Inc	17.13(A), 28.13(C)
Waliga v Kent State University Bd of Trustees	48.15
Walker; College Corner Local School Dist Bd of Ed v	4.02
Walker v Eastlake	12.17(C), 12.17(D)
Walker v Lockland City School Dist Bd of Ed	5.06(A)
Walker v San Francisco Unified School Dist	32.01, 48.06(A), 48.06(C)
Wallace v Jaffree	32.05
Wallace, State ex rel v West Geauga Local School Dist Bd of Ed	18.22(A)
Wallingford; Yates v	12.14(E)
Waln; Sims v	25.16(B)
Walsh Jesuit High School; Curran v	24.05(A)
Walter; Cincinnati City School Dist Bd of Ed v	2.14, 2.15, 39.01(B), 39.06(B)
Walter; Pushay v	22.03(D), 48.08(A)
Walter; Roncker v	28.03, 28.05(A), 28.05(B), 28.20(B)
Walters; Spruytte v	46.15(C)
Walter; Wolman v	48.06(A)
Walton v Alexander	46.14(B)
Walton; Jones v	9.22(A)
Walton v Montgomery County Welfare Dept	12.07(A)
Wapakoneta Bd of Ed v Unknown Heirs of Aughinbaugh	36.01
Ward v Barringer	24.03(A)
Ward v Hickey	9.21(E)
Wards Cove Packing Co v Atonio	17.03(F)
Ward; State v	24.14
Ware v Butler County, Kansas Unified School Dist No. 492	9.21(E)
Warren City School Dist Bd of Ed; Migra v (1984)	46.13(C)
Warren City School Dist Bd of Ed; Migra v (1982)	7.11(B)
Warren City School Dist Bd of Ed; Sloan v	10.16
Warren County Sheriff, In re (1994)	18.26(B)
Warren County Sheriff, In re (1988)	18.24(F)
Warren County Sheriff; SERB v	18.26(A)
Warren Local School Dist Bd of Ed; Brownfield v	9.22(E)
Warren v Perry Local School Dist Bd of Ed	25.04
Wasem; Traub v	25.16(B)
Washegesic v Bloomingdale Public Schools	32.06(B)
Washington County v Gunther	17.08(C)
Washington County School Bd; Thomas v	17.03(F)
Washington County Taxpayers Assn v Peppel	41.12(C)
Washington Court House City School Dist; State ex rel Stuckey v	10.07(A)
Washington Court House School Dist; Christman v	23.02(A)
Washington v Davis	17.02(B)
Washington Local Bd of Ed; Martin v	10.16
Washington Local School Dist Bd of Ed; Murray v	10.19(A)
Washington Local School Dist Bd of Ed; Young v	18.20, 18.23
Washington v Seattle School Dist No. 1	19.12
Waste Management, Inc; Phung v	48.26
Waterford Public Schools; Howell v	28.12(B)
Waterloo Local Bd of Ed; Trautman v	25.03(B)
Waters v Churchill	9.21(E)
Waters; Furnco Construction Corp v	17.04(E)
Watkins v Hall	37.01(A)
Watkins v McConologue	9.22(A)
Watkins; Piazzola v	47.01(B)
Watson v Employment Services Bureau Bd of Review	15.02(B), 15.05(B)
Watson v Fort Worth Bank and Trust	17.03(F)
Watson v Schwenker	12.17(A)
Watts, State ex rel v Schottenstein Stores Corp	16.05(C)
Wauconda Community Unit School Dist No. 118; Hedges v	32.06(A)
Wauconda Park Dist; Kelly v	17.06(A)

Casename	Text Section(s)
Wauseon Exempted Village School Dist Bd of Ed; State ex rel Price v	9.06(B)
Waverly City School Dist Bd of Ed; Myers v (App)	9.21(A), 9.23(B)
Waverly City School Dist Bd of Ed; Myers v (CP)	9.21(D)
Wayman v Akron City School Dist Bd of Ed	5.01, 5.07, 46.09
Wayne County Engineer, In re	18.15(B)
Wayne County Joint Vocational School Dist Bd of Ed; Miller v	8.09, 9.09(B), 9.10(C)
Wayne Trace Local School Dist Bd of Ed; Buchman v	46.05
Wean United, Inc; Clementi v	16.06
Weathersfield Local Bd of Ed, In re	18.29(B)
Weaver v University of Cincinnati (1992)	18.21(C)
Weaver v University of Cincinnati (1991)	18.21(C)
Webb v Dyer County Bd of Ed	17.02(B)
Webb; Keeley v	17.12
Webb v McCullough	25.06, 47.01(A)
Webb, State ex rel v Bryan City School Dist Bd of Ed	9.22(B)
Weber v State	24.03(D)
Weber; United Steelworkers of America v	17.18
Webster College; Girardier v	44.14(A)
Webster v New Lenox School Dist No. 122	32.07
Wedding v University of Toledo	18.22(A)
Weidemann v Village of Smithville	17.08(A)
Weil v Board of Elementary & Secondary Ed	28.11(B)
Weimer v Springfield Twp Public School Dist Bd of Ed	46.02
Weinstein v Canton City School Dist Bd of Ed (1983)	9.22(A)
Weinstein v Canton City School Dist Bd of Ed (1980)	9.23(B)
Weir v Day	36.01, 38.02, 38.07
Weisman; Lee v	32.05
Weissfeld v Akron Public School Dist	5.12
Weld County Sheriff; Tanberg v	28.13(C)

Casename	Text Section(s)
Wellington Exempted Village School Dist; Scyoc v	12.16(A)
Wellington Exempted Village Schools Bd of Ed; Ratliff v	9.21(E)
Wells v Madison Local School Dist Bd of Ed	9.21(B), 9.21(D)
Wells; State ex rel Dispatch Printing Co v	18.20, 44.02
Wellston City School Dist Bd of Ed; Crabtree v	6.04
Welsh v Trotwood-Madison Bd of Ed	13.04(A)
Welsh v United States	32.01
Wendel Poultry Services, Inc; Ziegler v	5.07
West Allis-West Milwaukee Bd of Ed; Byrne v	17.13(A)
West Branch Bd of Ed	18.17(A)
West Branch Local Bd of Ed; Kinser v	9.21(D)
Westbrook, State ex rel v Ohio Civil Rights Comm	17.04(C)
West; Burnham v	46.15(C), 47.03
West Carrollton City School Dist Bd of Ed, In re	18.09, 18.24(B)
West Carrollton City School Dist, In re	18.17(B), 18.23
West Clermont Local Bd of Ed; Bivens v	9.19(C)
West Clermont Local Bd of Ed; Hoeflinger v	10.16, 13.08(B)
West Clermont Local Bd of Ed; Thompson v	9.21(A), 10.19(A)
West Clermont Local School Dist Bd of Ed; Bohmann v	7.06(B), 9.19(A)
West Clermont Local School Dist Bd of Ed; Crabtree v	12.16(C)
West Clermont Local School Dist Bd of Ed; Pack v	12.16(B)
West Clermont Local School Dist; Harland v	46.02
West Des Moines Community School Dist; Scheideman v	46.14(A)
Western Air Lines, Inc v Criswell	17.06(B)
Western & Southern Life Insurance Co; Cheek v	17.03(D)
Western Brown Local School Dist Bd of Ed	18.23
Western Brown Local School Dist Bd of Ed; Balog v	9.09(C)
Western Line Consolidated School Dist; Givhan v	9.21(E)
Western Local School Dist Bd of Ed; Rinehart v	46.03
Western Reserve Psychiatric Habilitation Center; Carter v	12.17(B), 46.14(A)

Casename	Text Section(s)
Western Reserve Transit Auth, In re	18.31
Westerville Bd of Ed; Beifuss v (1988)	5.07, 17.04(D), 18.26(B)
Westerville Bd of Ed; Beifuss v (1984)	9.09(D), 9.12, 9.14(A), 9.14(B)
Westerville Bd of Ed; Tate v	9.02, 9.05(A), 9.14(B)
Westerville City School Dist Bd of Ed; Fuehrer v	46.11
Westerville City School Dist Bd of Ed; Mash v	12.13
Westerville City School Dist Bd of Ed; McIntyre v	5.12(D)
Westerville City School Dist Bd of Ed; Oney v	10.03(B)
Westerville City School Dist Bd of Ed; State ex rel Peet v	9.06(B)
Westerville City School Dist; Gaus v	22.13(A)
Westerville City Schools v Ohio Civil Rights Comm	17.10
Westerville Personnel Review Bd; Berndsen v	12.14(B)
Westfall Local School Dist Bd of Ed; Hayes v	24.03(D)
West Geauga Local School Dist Bd of Ed; State ex rel Wallace v	18.22(A)
West Holmes Local School Dist Bd of Ed; Phillips v	7.11(B)
Westlake Bd of Ed; State ex rel Sun Newspapers v	44.02
Westlake City School Dist; Hunt v	9.13(C)
Westmoreland County School Bd; Johnson v	28.03
Westmoreland School Dist; G.D. v	28.03
Westside Community Schools Bd of Ed v Mergens	32.06(A)
West Side Union High School Dist of Mercer County; Mastrangelo v	24.03(D)
West Virginia State Bd of Ed v Barnette	32.03
West Virginia University Hospitals, Inc v Casey	46.16
Wetzel v Elyria City School Dist Bd of Ed	9.21(A)
W.G. v Board of Trustees of Target Range School Dist No. 23, Missoula, Montana	28.03
Whalen; State ex rel Multimedia, Inc v (48 OS(3d))	44.02
Whalen; State ex rel Multimedia, Inc v (51 OS(3d))	44.03
Wheaton; Mrs. C. v	28.13(B)
Wheeler v Lakewood Bd of Ed	46.11
Wheeler v Mariemont Dist Bd of Ed	9.21(D), 9.22(C), 9.22(D)
Wheelersburg Rural School Dist Bd of Ed; Hudson v	37.06(A)
Wheeler v Southland Corp	17.11
Whelan Associates, Inc v Jaslow Dental Laboratory, Inc	33.06(A)
Whisner; State v	20.03(A), 32.02, 48.03(B)
White v Clinton County Bd of Commrs	5.11(D)
White v Columbus Bd of Ed	10.04(C), 10.07(A), 10.07(B)
White v Greenhills-Forest Park City School Dist Bd of Ed	9.23(A)
Whitehall City School Dist Bd of Ed; State ex rel Gildersleeve v	9.06(B), 9.09(E)
Whitehall City Schools	18.12
Whitehead, State ex rel v Circleville City School Dist Bd of Ed	7.11(A), 10.02(A)
White v Mayfield	16.06
White v McGill	11.24(A)
White, State ex rel v Marion City Bd of Ed	12.19
White; Thomas v	5.12
White; Woods v	46.14(E)
Whitley v Canton City School Dist Bd of Ed	9.19(F), 18.20
Whitley County, Kentucky, Bd of Ed; Ramsey v	46.14(A)
Wickliffe Bd of Ed; State ex rel Ruple Bus Service v	5.08(E), 22.25(A)
Wickliffe Civil Service Comm; Leonardi v	12.14(B)
Widener v Frye	47.01(A)
Widmar v Vincent	32.06(A), 38.12
Wielgos; Picha v	47.01(B), 47.03
Wiemerslage v Maine Twp High School Dist 207	25.03(A)
Wilkinson; American Civil Liberties Union of Kentucky v	32.06(B)
Willard City Bd of Ed; Gillespie v	18.21(C)
Willard City School Dist Bd of Ed	18.28(B)

Casename	Text Section(s)
Willbond, State ex rel v Oberlin School Dist	7.11(A), 14.08
Williams v Bethlehem, Pa School Dist	19.14(B)
Williamsburg of Cincinnati Management Co, Inc; Cosgrove v	17.04(B)
Williams v Columbus	11.10
Williams v Columbus Bd of Ed	24.03(C)
Williams v County of Kanawha Bd of Ed	33.04
Williams; Daniels v	46.14(B)
Williams v Ellington	46.15(C), 47.01(A)
Williams, In re	18.25(D)
Williamson County Bd of Ed; Cooper v	17.03(E)
Williamson County Schools; McWhirt v	28.03
Williams, State ex rel v Belpre City School Dist Bd of Ed	18.22(A)
Willoughby Civil Service Comm; State ex rel Alford v	12.03(A)
Willoughby-Eastlake Bd of Ed, In re	18.17(B)
Willoughby-Eastlake Bd of Ed; Molnar v	25.10(B)
Willoughby-Eastlake Bd of Ed; Palmisano v	30.11(C)
Willoughby-Eastlake City School Dist Bd of Ed; Ludwig v	12.03(A), 12.14(E), 12.17(D)
Wills v Rossford Exempted Village School Dist	12.16(A)
Wilmington City School Dist Bd of Ed, In re	18.28(B)
Wilson v Canton City School Dist	46.02
Wilson County Bd of Ed; Hyden v	28.13(D)
Wilson v Hubbard Exempted Village School Dist Bd of Ed	12.09(A), 12.09(B)
Wilson v Marana Unified School Dist No. 6 of Pima County	28.05(B)
Wilson v NLRB	18.21(B)
Wilson, State ex rel v Lucas County Office of Ed	4.03(B)
Wilson v Toledo Bd of Ed	18.22(A)
Wilson v Upper Sandusky Exempted Village School Dist Bd of Ed	12.16(A)
Windham Exempted Village School Dist Bd of Ed; State ex rel Donah v	7.09(A), 8.02(A), 9.07(A)
Windham Exempted Village School Dist Bd of Ed; State ex rel Francu v	9.11(A), 9.11(B)
Windham Exempted Village School Dist Bd of Ed; State ex rel Madden v	9.09(E), 10.04(B), 10.07(A)
Winegar v Des Moines Independent Community School Dist	9.22(A)
Wing v Anchor Media, Ltd of Texas	48.26
Winnebago County Dept of Social Services; DeShaney v	46.14(B)
Winners v Berea City School Dist Bd of Ed	12.16(A)
Winters v State Bd of Ed	8.07(A)
Wirtz; Coleman v	46.13(B)
Wisch v Sanford School, Inc	48.15
Wisconsin v Yoder	20.03(A), 32.01, 32.02
Wiseman v River View Coral School Dist Bd of Ed	9.08(E)
Wise v Ohio Dept of Ed	28.15(C)
Wise v Pea Ridge School Dist	46.14(B)
Wise v Twinsburg	40.07
Wissel v OHSAA	30.08(B)
Woerner v Mentor Exempted Village School Dist Bd of Ed	12.16(C)
Wohl v Cleveland Bd of Ed	46.13(A)
Wolf v Cuyahoga Falls City School Dist Bd of Ed	5.06(A), 9.14(A)
Wolfe v Ohio Bureau of Employment Services Bd of Review	15.05(B)
Wolford v Newark City School Dist Bd of Ed	9.21(A), 9.21(C)
Wolman v Essex	48.06(A)
Wolman v Walter	48.06(A)
Wooden v Jefferson County, Kentucky Bd of Ed	17.06(B)
Woodland Joint Unified School Dist; Brown v	33.04
Wood v Omaha School Dist	17.13(A)
Wood; Provident Bank v	42.11(B)
Woodridge Ed Assn	18.29(B)
Woodridge Local School Dist Bd of Ed; Shukert v	12.16(A)
Woodrum v Rolling Hills Bd of Ed	8.04(D), 9.05(B)
Woods v New Jersey Dept of Ed	28.06
Woods v OHSAA	30.11(C)
Woods, State ex rel v Industrial Comm	16.05(F)
Wood; State v	24.11

Casename	Text Section(s)
Wood v Strickland	46.13(B), 46.15(C)
Woods v White	46.14(E)
Wood v Trotwood Madison Bd of Ed	8.02, 10.02(A)
Woolery; Tasby v	19.03(B)
Woollett; Grosser v	33.04
Woonsocket Ed Dept; Mr. L. & Mrs. L. v	28.13(D)
Wooster Bd of Ed; Jackson v	25.16(A)
Wooster City School Dist	18.11(B), 18.12
Wooster City School Dist Bd of Ed; Graham v	12.17(A)
Wooster Republican Printing Co v Wooster	44.02
Work v McKenzie	28.07
Worthington City School Dist Bd of Ed; Demos v	9.19(G)
Wright; Bevin v	28.07
Wright; Ingraham v	25.16(B), 46.14(B)
Wuerl; Little v	48.30
Wurst; State ex rel Petty v	44.02
Wyandot County Engineer; Karg v	12.17(A)
Wygant v Jackson Bd of Ed	17.18

Y

Casename	Text Section(s)
Yance; State ex rel Consolidation Coal Co v	16.05(F)
Yaris v St. Louis County Special School Dist	28.04
Yates v Avco Corp	17.11
Yates v Wallingford	12.14(E)
Yellow Freight Systems, Inc v Donnelly	17.03(D)
Yellow Springs Exempted Village School Dist; Adler v	9.09(C)
Yellow Springs Exempted Village School Dist Bd of Ed v OHSAA	19.14(B), 30.08(B), 30.09(B)
Yeshiva University; NLRB v	18.05(C), 48.28(A)
Yoder; Wisconsin v	20.03(A), 32.01, 32.02
Yodzis; Elmwood Local School Dist Bd of Ed v	10.07, 10.07(B)
York v New Richmond Exempted Village School Dist Bd of Ed	9.21(D)
Yorktown Central Schools; Dangler v	25.15(B)
Youghiogheny & Ohio Coal Co v Oszust	15.08(B)
Younger v Buckeye Local School Dist	46.02
Young; Lohnes v	16.03(C)

Casename	Text Section(s)
Young; Powell v	9.21(A)
Young; Price v	25.15(B)
Youngstown Bd of Ed; Alexander v	19.10
Youngstown Bd of Ed; Bigelow v	10.03(B)
Youngstown Bd of Ed; Hami v	5.13(B)
Youngstown City Bd of Ed; Dixon v	25.16(A)
Youngstown City School Dist Bd of Ed; Graves v	9.12, 10.01(B)
Youngstown City School Dist Bd of Ed, In re	18.24(C), 18.28(B)
Youngstown City School Bd of Ed; Youngstown Ed Assn v	10.05(A)
Youngstown Civil Service Comm; State ex rel Vukovich v	12.15(B)
Youngstown Ed Assn v Youngstown City School Dist Bd of Ed	10.05(A)
Youngstown; Rogers v	46.04
Youngstown; State ex rel Dahmen v	12.07(B)
Youngstown State University, In re	18.28(B), 18.29(B)
Youngstown State University; Moore v	18.19(A)
Young v Washington Local School Dist Bd of Ed	18.20, 18.23
Ysleta Independent School Dist; Gonzalez v	46.13(B)
YWCA of Hamilton; Gibbon v	48.34(A)

Z

Casename	Text Section(s)
Zachel v Mahaney	46.11
Zagorski v South Euclid-Lyndhurst City School Dist Bd of Ed	46.01(A)
Zaleski School Dist Bd of Ed v Boal	9.03
Zamora v Pomeroy	47.01(C), 47.02
Zaras; State v	24.11
Zartman v Lakota Local School Dist Bd of Ed	9.11(D)
Zavatsky v Stringer	16.07(B)
Zellman v Kenston Bd of Ed	46.01(C)
Ziegler v Wendel Poultry Services, Inc	5.07
Zimmerman v Kalu Canfield Driving Range	46.01(C), 46.03
Zipes; Independent Federation of Flight Attendants v	17.03(E)

Casename	Text Section(s)	Casename	Text Section(s)
Zipes v Trans World Airlines, Inc	17.03(D)	Zorach v Clauson	32.04
Zobrest v Catalina Foothills School Dist	28.01(A), 32.01, 48.06(C)		

Appendix B
Table of Laws and Rules

ABBREVIATIONS

CFR—Code of Federal Regulations
IRC—Internal Revenue Code
OAC—Ohio Administrative Code
O Const—Ohio Constitution
RC—Ohio Revised Code
USCA—United States Code Annotated
US Const—United States Constitution

O Const	Text Section(s)
Art I §2	39.02
Art I §7	1.09, 2.14, 17.15, 32.05
Art II §20	5.04(A), 7.05(B)
Art II §35	16.01, 16.05(H)
Art VI §2	2.14, 4.05(A), 39.02
Art VI §3	2.14, 4.04, 5.02(B), 41.01
Art VI §4	2.09, 2.14, 3.01, 3.02, 3.05
Art VIII §1	40.15(A)
Art VIII §2	40.15(A)
Art VIII §3	40.15(A)
Art XII §2	39.03, 41.05(B), 41.16(A)
Art XII §4	39.02
Art XII §11	41.05(B), 41.16(D), 41.21(A), 43.19
Art XV §7	5.03(B)
Art XV §10	12.07(B)

RC	Text Section(s)
1.14	9.13(B), 20.06
3.07 to 3.10	5.05
3.07	5.05, 45.06(B)
3.08	5.05
3.17	3.02(D)
3.20	3.02(B)
3.22	3.02(B)
3.23	3.02(B)
5.21	20.06
5.23	20.06
9.20	39.13
9.25	36.04(B)
9.26	36.02(B), 39.13
9.312	37.06(A)
9.312(A)	37.06(A)
9.312(B)	37.06(A)
9.312(C)	37.06(A)
9.313	37.06(B)
9.33(B)(4)	37.10
9.331	37.10
9.332	37.10
9.333	37.10
9.34	40.15(D)
9.35	5.09(B)
9.37	43.08(B)
9.38	43.12(C)
9.39	42.02, 43.01

RC	Text Section(s)
9.40	10.08(A)
9.41	10.08(B), 13.01(C)
9.42	10.08(A)
9.43	10.08(A)
9.44	3.07(B), 18.20
9.65	23.04(B)
9.80	10.08(A), 31.08
9.81	10.08(A), 31.08
9.83	22.08
9.833	10.10(D), 29.13(B)
9.833(B)	34.10(B)
9.90	10.10(A), 10.10(C), 11.23, 14.15
9.96	41.19(A), 43.18, 43.19
101.26	45.08(A)
Ch 102	3.02(C), 45.01(A), 45.01(B), 45.01(C), 45.09
102.01	45.01(B)
102.01(B)	45.01(C)
102.01(C)	29.10(B)
102.02	45.01(C), 45.02, 45.04
102.03	45.03, 45.04, 45.06(B), 45.08(A), 45.11
102.03(D)	45.06(A)
102.03(G)	45.04
102.03(H)	45.04
102.03(J)	45.04
102.04	45.04, 45.11
102.04(C)	45.01(C)
102.08	45.01(B)
102.09(E)	45.01(C)
103.141	3.01
103.143	2.06
105.46	2.06
109.12	2.17
109.14	2.17
109.57	5.09(H)
109.57(F)	5.09(H)
109.572	5.09(H)
109.572(C)	5.09(H)
109.65	24.16
109.65(C)(3)	24.16
109.65(D)	24.16
109.65(E)	24.16
117.06	6.07(B), 34.11

RC	Text Section(s)	RC	Text Section(s)
117.09	10.07(B)	124.23	12.05(A)
117.10	8.03(A), 10.07(B)	124.241	29.12
117.11	43.26(A), 43.27(A)	124.26	12.05(A)
117.12	43.27(A)	124.26(B)	12.07(B)
117.13	43.27(A)	124.27	12.05(A), 12.07(A), 12.07(B), 12.11, 18.20
117.17	23.03(C)		
117.26	43.27(A), 44.02	124.271	12.07(B)
117.27	43.27(A)	124.29	10.21(A)
117.28	43.27(B)	124.30	12.07(B)
117.29	43.27(B)	124.30(A)	12.07(B)
117.33	43.27(B)	124.31	12.11
117.38	43.26(B)	124.32(A)	12.12
117.40	43.26(A)	124.321	12.14(D)
117.43	43.15(B), 43.26(A), 43.28	124.321(B)	12.14(B)
Ch 119	3.04(A), 4.08, 4.11(B), 8.07(A), 16.09(A), 25.10(E), 27.08(B)	124.321(C)	12.14(B)
		124.321(D)	12.14(B)
		124.322	12.14(C)
119.01(A)	12.17(D)	124.323	12.14(C), 12.14(D)
119.07	8.07(A)	124.324	12.14(D)
119.09	18.15(E)	124.324(A)(3)	12.14(D)
119.12	12.14(E), 12.17(C), 12.17(D), 18.26(C), 18.31	124.325(C)	12.14(C)
		124.325(D)	12.14(C)
Ch 121	3.04(A)	124.327	12.14(D)
121.22	5.12, 5.12(A), 5.12(D), 7.04(B), 18.27, 25.03(B), 25.12(A), 29.03	124.328	12.14(E)
		124.321 to 124.324	12.14(C)
		124.34	12.07(B), 12.15(A), 12.15(B), 12.17(A), 12.17(B), 12.17(C), 12.17(D), 22.14
121.22(B)(1)(a)	5.12		
121.22(B)(1)(b)	5.12		
121.22(B)(2)	5.12		
121.22(C)	5.11(D), 31.01	124.341	9.21(F), 12.17(A)
121.22(D)	5.12	124.36	12.17(A)
121.22(F)	5.12(A), 5.12(C), 5.12(D), 31.01	124.38	10.16, 13.08(A), 13.08(B), 29.13(B)
121.22(G)	5.12(B), 44.09	124.382	10.14
121.22(H)	5.12(D)	124.385	14.06(A)
121.22(I)	5.12(D)	124.385(D)	11.07(B)
121.40	5.09(N)	124.382 to 124.388	3.07(B), 10.14
123.01	3.04(B)	124.39	10.17(A), 43.05(B)
Ch 124	4.03(G), 11.02(C), 12.14(A), 12.19, 18.22(A), 27.09(A), 29.12	124.39(B)	10.17(A)
		124.39(C)	10.17(B), 29.13(B)
		124.40	12.03(A)
124.01	29.12	124.54	12.03(B)
124.01(D)	12.06	124.57	18.20, 45.14
124.011	12.03(A)	124.841	5.09(T)
124.011(A)	12.03(A)	125.04	36.04(B)
124.011(B)	12.03(A)	125.04(A)	36.04(B)
124.011(C)	12.03(A)	125.04(B)	36.04(B)
124.03(A)	12.17(C)	125.111(A)	17.05(A)
124.11	12.02(A), 12.04, 29.12	125.111(B)	17.05(B)
124.11(A)(7)	12.04(A)	125.12 et seq.	34.07
124.11(A)(8)	12.04(A)	125.12	34.07
124.11(A)(9)	12.04(A)	125.84 et seq.	39.01(A)
124.11(A)(12)	12.04(A)	127.18	2.06
124.11(A)(19)	29.12	131.18	43.28
124.11(B)(1)	12.04(A)	Ch 133	34.02, 36.02(B), 36.04(C), 37.07(B), 41.01, 41.30, 46.18(D)
124.11(B)(2)	12.04(A), 12.05(B)		
124.15(J)	3.02(B)		
124.19	3.07(B)	133.01	30.14, 43.28

RC	Text Section(s)
133.01(CC)	41.03
133.01(GG)	41.02
133.01(MM)	41.03
133.01(NN)	41.03
133.01(C)	39.02
133.01(D)	39.02
133.01(E)	41.16(F)
133.01(I)	41.03
133.01(J)	41.03
133.01(K)	41.16(F), 43.18
133.01(L)	41.03
133.02	41.20(B)
133.03(D)	41.08
133.04	36.04(C), 41.05(A), 41.28(B)
133.06	41.07, 41.09, 41.12(E), 41.14(B), 41.25
133.06(A)	41.05(A)
133.06(B)	41.06
133.06(C)	41.12(C), 41.12(E), 41.28(B)
133.06(E)	41.07, 41.12(A)
133.06(F)	41.04, 41.12(A), 41.14(B)
133.06(G)	41.01, 41.04, 41.05(A)
133.06(H)	41.05(A)
133.10	41.04, 41.05(A), 41.21(A)
133.10(D)	40.15(B), 41.21(A)
133.10(H)	41.21(A)
133.12	41.05(A)
133.14	41.04
133.15	41.04
133.16(B)	41.16(F)
133.17	41.25, 41.28(E)
133.17(E)(3)	41.28(E)
133.18	41.09, 41.12(A), 41.12(B)
133.18(D)	41.13(A)
133.18(E)(3)	41.14(A)
133.18(F)	41.09
133.18(F)(1)(a)	41.14(B)
133.18(F)(1)(b)	34.17, 41.14(B)
133.18(G)	41.14(C)
133.18(H)	41.15, 41.32
133.18(I)(2)	41.17(A)
133.19	41.11(C)
133.20	41.10, 41.11(A), 41.11(B)
133.20(D)	41.11(B)
133.22	41.16(B), 41.16(C), 41.16(D), 41.16(F)
133.22(B)	41.16(B)
133.22(C)(2)	41.16(D)
133.23	41.16(B), 41.16(E)
133.23(D)	41.16(E), 42.22
133.25	41.16(E)
133.27	41.16(B), 41.17(G), 46.07
133.30	41.17(B)
133.30(C)(3)	41.17(D)
133.30(D)	41.17(D)
133.301	40.15(B), 41.04, 41.05(A), 41.21(B)
133.301(E)	41.21(B)
133.302	40.04(C), 40.15(B), 40.15(D)
133.302(A)	40.15(B)
133.303	40.15(B)
133.32	41.17(E), 41.30
133.33	41.17(G)
133.34	41.18
133.35(A)	39.05
133.39	41.20(A)
133.39(B)	41.20(A)
133.39(C)	41.20(A)
133.41	41.19(A)
133.70	41.20(C)
Ch 135	6.07(A), 39.13, 42.01, 42.02, 42.05(C), 42.12
135.01 to 135.21	42.02, 42.03, 42.04(A), 42.05(A), 42.11(B)
135.01	42.04(A), 42.04(B)
135.01(D)	6.02(A)
135.03	42.05(A), 42.06
135.031	42.05(A), 42.05(C)
135.032	42.05(A)
135.04	42.05(B)
135.04(C)	42.11(B)
135.04(F)	42.05(C)
135.04(G)	42.11(B)
135.05	42.08, 42.09
135.06	42.10
135.07	42.11(B)
135.08	42.10
135.09	42.11(B)
135.10	42.10
135.11	42.12
135.12	42.07, 42.11(A)
135.13	42.13
135.14	42.23(A), 42.23(B), 42.24
135.14(C)	42.11(B)
135.142	42.23(A)
135.15	42.11(B), 42.14
135.16	42.15, 42.21
135.17	42.03
135.18	42.05(C), 42.20(C)
135.18(A)	42.16
135.18(B)	42.17
135.18(C)	42.18
135.18(D)	42.20(A)
135.18(E)	42.19
135.18(F)	42.19
135.18(G)	42.19
135.18(I)	42.02, 42.20(A), 42.20(B)
135.181	42.05(C), 42.17, 42.20(A)
135.181(F)	42.20(B)
135.181(J)	42.20(C)
135.19	42.02
135.20	42.12

RC	Text Section(s)	RC	Text Section(s)
135.21	43.16	307.86	29.07
135.31	29.04(G)	307.88	29.07
135.351	39.05, 43.16	309.08	45.01(B)
135.801(A)	29.04(G)	309.10	6.14(A), 6.15(A)
135.801(B)	29.04(G)	309.14	39.10
135.802	29.04(G)	319.28	40.15(B)
135.803	29.04(G)	319.29	40.15(B)
140.07	42.17	319.301	40.10(B), 40.14
145.01 et seq.	29.13(D)	319.301(D)	40.14
145.01	29.13(D)	319.301(E)	40.14
145.03	29.13(D)	319.301(G)	40.14
145.299	5.04(A)	321.24	39.05, 40.15(B)
145.71 to 145.73	11.23, 14.15, 29.13(D)	321.31	39.05
145.71(A)	11.23, 14.15, 29.13(D)	321.341	39.05
145.73(E)	11.23, 14.15	325.19	29.13(C)
149.011	44.23	340.02	7.09(C)
149.011(G)	44.02	505.66	38.02
149.351	44.02	703.01	4.03(A), 4.05(C), 4.06(A), 4.06(C), 4.06(D)
149.351(B)	44.23		
149.40	44.02	703.08 to 703.21	4.06(D)
149.41	44.02, 44.22, 44.23	703.21	39.10
149.41(A)	44.23	Ch 707	4.03(A), 4.06(D)
149.41(B)	44.23	709.02 to 709.37	4.08
149.43	3.03(F), 5.09(H), 8.07(A), 9.13(A), 18.20, 18.26(A), 18.33, 27.15, 43.27(A), 44.01, 44.02, 44.09, 45.01(B)	713.02	37.01(A)
		713.23	36.04(B)
		713.23(D)	36.04(B)
		718.09	39.01(A), 39.12
		718.10	39.12
149.43(A)(1)	44.02	721.18	36.01
149.43(A)(2)(a)	44.02	725.02	39.04
149.43(A)(3)	44.02	731.12	45.08(A)
149.43(B)	44.03	Ch 748	39.07(B)
149.43(C)	44.03	Ch 755	36.11(B)
149.43(D)	44.02, 44.09	755.12 to 755.16	22.22
Ch 153	37.01(B)	755.14 to 755.181	30.14
153.01(A)	37.03(A)	755.14	30.15
153.12	37.03(A), 37.06(A), 37.06(B), 37.08(A), 37.08(C)	755.16	30.14
		757.03 to 757.08	31.05
		757.03	31.05
153.13	37.08(B), 37.08(C)	757.04	31.05
153.14	37.08(B), 37.08(C)	955.43	17.13(A), 28.18
153.50	37.05	1109.03	42.20(B)
153.54	37.05	1109.04	42.20(B)
153.54(C)	37.06(B)	1109.17	42.20(B)
153.54(C)(2)	37.10	1109.18	42.20(B)
153.57(B)	37.10	1125.08	42.05(A)
153.63	37.08(C)	1155.02	42.05(A)
153.65 to 153.71	37.03(A)	Ch 1331	5.07
153.80	37.06(B), 37.08(C)	1331.01(A)	5.07
Ch 163	36.03	1343.03	46.07
Ch 167	5.09(T), 29.04(F), 34.10(B), 36.08	Ch 1347	5.09(M)
		1347.01 et seq.	44.01, 44.04, 44.14(A)
167.01 to 167.08	5.09(D)	1347.01(B)	44.04
Ch 199	18.15(F)	1347.01(D)	44.06
199.03	2.06	1347.01(E)	44.02, 44.06
307.02	29.04(H)	1347.01(F)	44.06
307.031	7.08	1347.01(G)	44.07
307.12	29.08(B)	1347.01(H)	44.07

RC	Text Section(s)	RC	Text Section(s)
1347.05	44.08(A)	2151.27	25.10(A)
1347.05(A)	44.08(B)	2151.27(F)	25.10(E)
1347.05(B)	44.08(B)	2151.34	23.02(A)
1347.05(C)	44.08(B)	2151.354	20.04
1347.05(D)	44.08(B)	2151.355(J)	25.10(E)
1347.05(E)	44.08(B), 44.09	2151.357	23.02(A), 23.02(B)
1347.05(F)	44.08(B), 44.08(D)	2151.358	3.03(F), 25.10(E)
1347.05(G)	44.02, 44.08(B), 44.08(C)	2151.421	5.08(A), 24.05(A), 24.05(B), 24.05(C), 24.06(A)
1347.05(H)	44.02, 44.09		
1347.06	44.08(A), 44.08(B)		
1347.06(H)	44.08(B)	2151.65	23.02(A)
1347.07	44.09	2151.85	44.02
1347.071	44.08(B)	2151.99	24.05(A)
1347.071(A)	44.07	2305.06	10.07(A)
1347.071(B)	44.07	2305.07	10.07(A), 10.07(B), 17.04(B), 17.06(A)
1347.071(C)	44.07		
1347.08	44.05	2305.091	21.10(B)
1347.08(A)	44.08(B)	2305.10	46.13(C)
1347.08(A)(1)	44.10	2305.11	10.07(A), 37.14
1347.08(A)(2)	44.10	2305.112	16.08
1347.08(A)(3)	44.10	2305.23	21.04(B)
1347.08(B)	44.08(B), 44.10	2305.231	21.04(B), 21.09
1347.08(C)	44.08(B), 44.10	2305.38	48.34(C)
1347.08(D)	44.10	2307.44	24.10, 46.10
1347.08(E)(1)	44.05, 44.09	2313.18	10.09(B)
1347.09	44.11	2313.34	10.09(B)
1347.09(A)(1)	44.11	Ch 2505	16.09(A), 25.10(E)
1347.09(A)(2)(a)	44.11	2505.02	18.15(F)
1347.09(A)(2)(b)	44.11	2505.04	12.05(A), 12.15(A), 12.17(D), 25.12(B)
1347.09(A)(3)	44.11		
1347.09(B)	44.11	2505.05	12.17(D)
1347.09(C)	44.11	2505.07	25.12(B)
1347.10(A)	44.08(B)	2505.07(B)	12.15(A)
1347.10(B)	44.08(B)	Ch 2506	9.13(C), 12.05(A), 12.16(C), 12.17(D), 25.12(A), 25.12(B)
1347.99	44.02, 44.08(B)		
1517.05	31.07		
1533.18	46.11	2506.01	7.11(B), 12.05(A), 12.11, 12.15(A), 12.15(B), 12.17(D)
1533.181	46.11		
Ch 1545	36.11(B)		
Ch 1702	29.07	2506.02	12.17(D), 25.12(B)
1702.12	48.34(B)	2506.03	12.16(C), 25.12(B)
1728.10	39.04	2506.04	5.12(D), 12.17(D)
1742.33	10.10(A), 10.10(D)	Ch 2711	18.22(A), 18.24(G)
1745.01	30.08(A)	2711.10	18.22(A)
1745.02	30.08(A)	2711.11	18.22(A)
2105.06	39.11	2731.01	46.09
2105.07	39.11	2733.38	39.10
Ch 2111	23.02(A)	Ch 2744	24.02(A), 24.03, 29.16, 30.08(B), 46.01(B), 46.01(D), 46.06, 46.08, 46.13(A), 46.17(A), 46.17(C), 46.18(A)
2113.04	7.05(A), 7.11(A)		
2151.011	23.02(A), 24.05(C), 24.05(D)		
2151.02	24.11		
2151.022	24.11, 25.02	2744.01(B)	46.03
2151.022(D)	20.04	2744.01(C)(1)	46.01(D)
2151.03(A)	24.05(D)	2744.01(C)(2)	46.01(D)
2151.031(C)	24.05(C)	2744.01(G)	46.01(D)
2151.031(D)	24.05(C)	2744.01(G)(2)	46.01(D)
2151.031(E)	24.05(C)	2744.02	46.03, 46.05

RC	Text Section(s)	RC	Text Section(s)
2744.02(A)(1)	46.01(B)	2901.30	24.16, 44.16
2744.02(B)	46.01(C)	2903.01	25.10(E)
2744.02(B)(3)	46.02	2903.02	25.10(E)
2744.03(A)	46.02	2903.03	25.10(E)
2744.03(A)(1)	46.02	2903.04	25.10(E)
2744.03(A)(3)	46.02	2903.11	25.10(E)
2744.03(A)(4)	46.02	2903.12	25.10(E)
2744.03(A)(5)	46.02	2903.31	24.10, 46.10
2744.03(A)(6)	24.02(A), 46.03, 46.05	2907.01	24.05(C)
2744.03(A)(7)	46.02	2907.01(E)	24.12
2744.03(B)	46.03, 46.05	2907.01(F)	24.12
2744.04(A)	46.05	2907.02	24.13, 25.10(E)
2744.04(B)	46.05	2907.03	24.02(B), 24.13
2744.05	46.05	2907.03(A)(7)	9.21, 12.16(A), 12.17(A)
2744.05(A)	46.05, 46.06	2907.03(A)(8)	24.02(B)
2744.05(B)	46.05	2907.03(A)(9)	24.02(B)
2744.05(C)(1)	46.06	2907.04	8.07(A), 24.07, 24.13
2744.05(C)(2)	46.06	2907.05	24.13, 25.10(E)
2744.05(C)(2)(c)	46.06	2907.06	8.07(A), 24.07, 24.13
2744.06(A)	46.07	2907.07	24.13
2744.06(B)(1)(b)	46.07	2907.07(A)	8.07(A)
2744.06(B)(2)	46.07	2907.07(C)	8.07(A)
2744.06(C)	46.07	2907.12	25.10(E)
2744.07	46.01(B), 46.05	2907.31	24.12
2744.07(A)	46.05	2907.31(B)(1)	24.12
2744.07(A)(1)	46.04	2907.31(B)(2)	24.12
2744.07(A)(2)	46.04	2907.31(D)	24.12
2744.07(B)(1)	46.04	2907.321 to 2907.323	24.13
2744.07(B)(2)	46.04	2907.33(B)	24.11
2744.07(C)	46.04	2909.01(C)	38.04(C)
2744.08	43.02(B), 46.17(A)	2909.02	38.04(A)
2744.08(A)(2)(a)	46.17(B)	2909.03	38.04(A)
2744.08(A)(2)(b)	46.17(B)	2909.03(A)(3)	38.04(A)
2744.08(B)	46.17(C)	2909.04	38.04(B)
2744.08(C)	46.17(C)	2909.05	38.04(C)
2744.081	41.04, 41.05(A), 43.02(B), 46.18(A)	2909.06	38.04(C)
2744.081(A)	46.18(A)	2909.07	38.04(C)
2744.081(A)(1)	46.18(B)	2911.21	38.03(B)
2744.081(A)(2)	46.18(C)	2913.01	8.07(A)
2744.081(A)(3)	46.18(C)	2913.01(K)	24.07, 38.04(D)
2744.081(A)(4)	46.18(D)	2913.02	38.04(D)
2744.081(B)	46.18(E)	2913.42	3.03(F)
2744.081(C)	46.18(A), 46.18(D)	2917.03	24.09(E)
2744.081(D)	46.18(D)	2917.11	24.09(E), 38.04(E)
2744.081(E)(1)	46.18(E)	2919.22	24.02(B), 24.05(C), 24.09, 24.09(A)
2744.081(E)(2)	46.18(A)	2919.22(A)	24.04
2744.081(F)	46.18(A)	2919.22(B)	25.16(A), 25.16(C)
2744.081(G)	46.18(A)	2919.22(B)(1)	24.09(B)
2744.09(A) to 2744.09(E)	46.01(B)	2919.22(B)(2)	24.09(B)
2744.09(A)	46.08	2919.22(B)(3)	24.09(B)
2744.09(E)	46.13(A), 46.15(A), 46.15(B)	2919.22(B)(4)	24.09(B)
		2919.22(B)(5)	24.09(C), 24.13
2745.01	16.08	2919.22(B)(6)	24.13
2901.01	8.07(A)	2919.22(C)	24.09(D)
2901.01(I)	24.07	2919.22(D)(1)	24.09(C)
2901.02	24.07	2919.22(E)	25.16(A)

RC	Text Section(s)
2919.22(E)(5)	24.09(D)
2919.24	24.11
Ch 2921	3.02(C), 45.01(C)
2921.01(A)	45.01(C), 45.05, 45.09
2921.01(B)	45.11
2921.22	24.06(A)
2921.22(G)	24.06(A)
2921.22(H)	24.06(A)
2921.41	45.10
2921.42	3.02(C), 45.01(B), 45.01(C), 45.04, 45.05, 45.06(B), 45.08, 45.08(B), 45.09
2921.42(A)(1)	5.05, 9.03, 45.05(A), 45.06(B)
2921.42(A)(3)	45.03, 45.05(A)
2921.42(A)(4)	45.05(A)
2921.42(A)(5)	45.05(A)
2921.42(B)	45.05(C)
2921.42(C)	45.05(D), 45.06(B)
2921.42(G)	45.05(B)
2921.43	5.04(A), 45.01(B), 45.01(C), 45.04, 45.11
2921.43(A)	6.14(C)
2921.44	45.12
2921.44(D)	40.15(A)
2921.45	45.13
2923.12	25.10(E)
2923.122	21.16, 25.10(E)
2923.161	24.09(F)
2925.01	8.07(A), 24.14, 26.02(A)
2925.01(H)	24.07
2925.01(I)	24.07
2925.02	24.14
2925.03	24.14
2925.03(A)(1)	25.10(E)
2925.03(A)(4) to 2925.03(A)(7)	25.10(E)
2925.03(A)(9)	25.10(E)
2925.03(A)(10)	25.10(E)
2925.13	24.14
2925.14	24.14
2925.31	24.14
2925.32	24.14
2925.36	24.14
2925.37	26.02(A)
2927.02	24.15(B)
2953.32	25.10(E)
3101.01	20.04
3107.17	44.05
3107.42(A)	44.02, 44.05
3109.051(J)	31.03
3109.09	38.06(A)
3109.10	38.06(A)
3113.33	23.02(A)
Ch 3118	41.25
3301.01	3.02(A)
3301.02	3.02(A), 3.02(B)
3301.02(D)	3.02(A)
3301.03	3.02(A), 3.02(B), 45.08(A)
3301.04	3.02(D)
3301.05	3.02(D)
3301.06	3.02(A), 3.02(D)
3301.07	3.03, 3.03(G), 5.01, 26.04, 48.01(B)
3301.07(A)	3.03(A)
3301.07(B)	3.03(A)
3301.07(C)	3.03(A), 39.01(A)
3301.07(D)	3.03(B), 18.20, 22.06
3301.07(E)	3.03(B), 26.12(A)
3301.07(F)	3.03(G)
3301.07(G)	3.03(A)
3301.07(H)	3.03(G)
3301.07(I)	3.03(G), 6.07(D)
3301.07(J)	3.03(B)
3301.07(K)	3.03(B), 26.09
3301.07(M)	3.03(G)
3301.07(N)	3.03(G)
3301.071	3.03(G), 26.05(A), 48.21
3301.071(C)(1)	3.03(F)
3301.071(C)(2)	3.03(F)
3301.072	3.03(G), 5.09(F), 6.02(B)
3301.073	3.03(G), 5.09(A)
3301.074	3.03(G), 6.02(B), 6.05, 6.10
3301.075	3.03(G), 26.11(G), 43.29
3301.076	3.03(G), 48.37
3301.077	3.03(G)
3301.078	3.03(G)
3301.079	3.03(G)
3301.0710	3.03(G), 26.06(B), 26.10(D), 26.10(E)
3301.0710(B)	3.03(G), 26.10(E), 48.03(A)
3301.0711	3.03(G), 26.02(C), 26.06(B)
3301.0711(B)(2)	3.03(G)
3301.0711(C)	3.03(G), 26.06(B)
3301.0711(C)(1)	3.03(F)
3301.0711(G)	44.14(B)
3301.0711(J)	3.03(G), 26.06(B)
3301.0711(L)	28.19(A)
3301.0711(M)	3.03(G)
3301.0712	3.03(G)
3301.0714	3.03(F), 26.17
3301.0715	26.02(C)
3301.0716(A)	26.02(C)
3301.0716(B)	26.02(C)
3301.0717	3.03(A)
3301.0719	3.03(G)
3301.0720	3.03(G)
3301.0723	3.03(G), 3.04(D)
3301.0724	3.03(G)
3301.08	3.05, 45.07, 45.08(A)
3301.09	3.06

RC	Text Section(s)	RC	Text Section(s)
3301.11	3.06	3304.18	39.01(A)
3301.111	3.03(A)	3304.21	27.15
3301.12	3.06	Ch 3307	3.03(D), 3.03(E), 8.03(A),
3301.12(B)	43.26(B)		11.01, 11.05
3301.121	3.06, 23.02(A), 25.03(A),	3307.01	11.15, 39.07(B)
	25.10(B), 25.10(C),	3307.01(B)	11.04(A), 29.13(D)
	25.10(E)	3307.01(C)	11.12(A)
3301.121(F)	25.10(E)	3307.01(D)	11.13(A), 11.14, 11.21(B)
3301.121(G)	25.10(E)	3307.01(E)	11.04(A)
3301.121(H)	25.10(E)	3307.01(J)	11.10(A)
3301.13	3.01, 3.02(D), 3.04(A),	3307.01(U)	11.07(A), 11.19(C)
	3.04(B), 3.04(C), 3.06,	3307.01(V)(1)	11.10(A), 11.10(B)
	3.07(A), 3.07(B)	3307.012	11.04(A)
3301.131	3.04(A)	3307.013(B)	11.19(C)
3301.132	26.17	3307.013(C)	11.19(C)
3301.133	3.04(D)	3307.02	11.14(A)
3301.14	48.05	3307.021	11.12(A), 11.13(A),
3301.15	3.03(G)		11.14(B)
3301.16	3.03(C), 4.09(D), 4.13,	3307.021(D)(2)	11.13(A)
	25.10(E), 26.05(A), 26.19,	3307.021(F)	11.12(B)
	30.07(B), 48.03(A)	3307.03	11.02(C)
3301.161	3.03(C), 4.09(D), 26.19	3307.04	11.02(C)
3301.17	3.04(A), 26.12(B), 26.14	3307.05	11.02(A)
3301.171	26.13(A)	3307.10	11.02(A)
3301.18	3.04(A)	3307.11	11.02(C)
3301.19	3.04(A)	3307.14	11.02(B)
3301.27	3.04(A)	3307.15	11.03(B)
3301.30	3.04(A)	3307.18	11.02(B)
3301.31	3.04(A)	3307.22	11.13(A)
3301.48	2.10	3307.27	11.04(B), 11.13(A)
3301.49	2.10	3307.28	11.13(B)
3301.50	3.03(B)	3307.281	11.13(D)
3301.51	3.03(B)	3307.31	11.12(A), 11.19(B)
3301.521	3.03(B)	3307.311	5.04(A), 11.13(A)
3301.53 to 3301.59	3.03(B)	3307.32	11.12(A), 11.13(A)
3301.53	3.03(B)	3307.32(B)(2)	11.13(A)
3301.541	5.09(C)	3307.32(D)	11.12(B)
3301.55	3.04(A)	3307.33	11.13(A), 11.15
3301.57 to 3301.59	3.04(A)	3307.33(D)	11.13(A)
3301.70	3.03(G)	3307.34	11.15
3301.74	6.10	3307.35	11.21(A), 11.21(B),
3302.01	3.03(D)		11.21(C), 18.28(B)
3302.02	3.03(D)	3307.36	11.12(A)
3302.03	3.03(D)	3307.37	11.18(B)
3302.04	3.03(D)	3307.38	11.02(A), 11.16(A), 11.17,
3302.05	3.03(D)		11.18(A), 11.19(A),
3302.06	3.03(D)		11.19(B), 11.21(B), 11.22
3302.07	3.03(E)	3307.381	11.17, 11.22
3302.08	3.03(D), 3.03(E)	3307.381(A)	9.15(B)
3303.02	27.01	3307.384	11.19(B)
3303.03	27.04	3307.39	11.02(A), 11.16(A), 11.17,
3303.04	27.04		11.19(A), 11.22
3303.05	27.04	3307.40(A)	11.26, 14.16
3303.06	27.04	3307.40(B)	11.26
3304.12	27.13(A)	3307.401	11.19(B)
3304.15	27.13(A)	3307.403	11.19(B)
3304.16	27.13(B)	3307.405	11.20
3304.16(D)	27.13(B)	3307.41	11.12(B), 11.17, 11.22

RC	Text Section(s)
3307.411	11.13(A)
3307.411(B)(2)	11.13(A)
3307.42	11.16(A)
3307.43	11.16(A), 11.24(B)
3307.431	11.16(A), 11.17, 11.24(B)
3307.44	11.17, 11.22
3307.46	11.11
3307.47	11.11
3307.48	11.24(A)
3307.48(D)	11.25
3307.49(A)	11.24(B)
3307.49(B)	11.24(B)
3307.49(B)(2)	11.24(B)
3307.49(C)(2)	11.24(B)
3307.49(E)	11.24(C)
3307.50	11.19(A), 11.25
3307.51	10.08(A), 11.07(A), 11.08(B)
3307.511	11.07(B), 11.09
3307.512	11.08(A), 11.09, 11.19(B)
3307.512(C)	11.08(A)
3307.512(D)	11.08(A)
3307.512(E)	11.08(A)
3307.53	11.09
3307.56	11.09
3307.58	11.05
3307.59	11.06
3307.60	11.06
3307.61	11.06
3307.62	10.08(A), 11.06
3307.65	11.03(A), 11.03(B)
3307.66	11.03(A)
3307.68 to 3307.70	11.01
3307.72	11.11
3307.74	11.20
3307.741	11.13(D)
3307.751	11.01
Ch 3309	3.03(D), 3.03(E), 8.03(A), 14.01, 14.11, 14.12
3309.01(B)	14.04
3309.01(K)	14.08(B)
3309.01(V)	14.05
3309.01(V)(1)	14.08(A), 14.08(B)
3309.011	14.04
3309.012	5.04(A)
3309.02	14.09
3309.021	14.10(A)
3309.03	14.02(C)
3309.04	14.02(C)
3309.05	14.02(A)
3309.10	14.02(A)
3309.11	14.02(A)
3309.12	14.02(A)
3309.13	14.02(A)
3309.14	14.02(C)
3309.15 to 3309.17	14.03
3309.15	14.02(C), 14.03
3309.155	14.02(B)

RC	Text Section(s)
3309.156	14.02(B)
3309.19	14.02(B)
3309.21	14.10(A)
3309.23	14.04, 14.10(A)
3309.26	14.10(B)
3309.27	14.10(C)
3309.30	14.09
3309.301	14.10(A)
3309.31	14.10(A)
3309.311	5.04(A), 14.10(A)
3309.33	14.13
3309.34	14.09, 14.12
3309.341	14.14
3309.35	14.09
3309.351	14.10(A)
3309.36	14.09, 14.12
3309.361 to 3309.3710	14.12
3309.374	14.12
3309.39	14.11, 22.14
3309.40	14.11
3309.401	14.11
3309.41	14.11
3309.44	14.16
3309.45	14.16
3309.46	14.12
3309.47	14.05, 14.06(A), 14.06(B)
3309.471	14.06(A)
3309.49	14.07
3309.50	14.16
3309.53	14.04
3309.60	14.03
3309.691	14.10(C)
3309.70	14.01
Ch 3311	3.03(C), 4.03(G), 27.09(A), 41.01
3311.01	4.03, 27.08(A)
3311.02	4.03(A), 4.03(D), 4.05(C), 4.06(A), 4.06(C), 4.06(D)
3311.03	4.03(D)
3311.04	4.03(F)
3311.05	7.12
3311.05(A)	4.03(B), 40.03, 40.10(D)
3311.051	3.03(C), 4.03(B), 4.15(D), 5.02(A), 7.12
3311.052	4.15(D)
3311.053	3.03(C), 4.03, 4.03(C), 5.02(A), 6.14(A), 7.08, 40.03, 40.10(D)
3311.053(B)	4.03(C)
3311.054	3.03(C), 4.03(C), 5.02(A)
3311.055	5.01
3311.06	4.05(B), 4.07(A), 4.07(B), 4.08, 4.11(B), 4.13, 4.14(B)
3311.06(B)	4.05(B)
3311.06(C)(1)	4.07(A)
3311.06(C)(2)	4.07(A)

RC	Text Section(s)
3311.06(D)	4.07(A)
3311.06(E)	4.07(A)
3311.06(E)(1)	4.05(B)
3311.06(F)	4.07(A)
3311.06(G)	4.13, 4.14(B)
3311.07	4.03(A), 4.05(C), 4.06(C)
3311.08	4.03(F)
3311.09	4.03(A), 4.03(D), 4.03(F)
3311.09(B)	4.03(D)
3311.10	4.03(A), 4.03(F), 4.05(C), 4.06(B), 4.06(C), 4.06(D)
3311.16	27.08(A)
3311.17	27.08(A)
3311.18	27.08(A)
3311.19	4.03(E), 5.04(A), 7.04(D), 7.05(B)
3311.19(A)	27.09(A)
3311.19(B)	27.09(A)
3311.19(D)	27.08(A), 27.09(A)
3311.19(E)	6.02(A), 7.06(A)
3311.19(F)	5.04(B)
3311.20	27.10(A), 41.23(A)
3311.21	4.03(G), 27.10(A), 27.11, 41.23(B), 41.23(C)
3311.211	23.02(A), 23.02(E)
3311.212	27.10(A)
3311.213	27.08(B)
3311.214	27.08(C)
3311.215	27.10(A)
3311.217	27.08(D)
3311.218	27.10(B)
3311.22	4.07(A), 4.07(C), 4.09(C), 4.10, 4.10(A), 4.10(B), 4.10(C), 4.12, 4.13, 4.15(A)
3311.231	4.07(A), 4.07(C), 4.09(C), 4.10, 4.10(A), 4.10(B), 4.10(C), 4.12, 4.13, 4.14(A), 4.15(A)
3311.24	4.07(C), 4.11(A), 4.11(B), 4.13
3311.24(A)	4.07(A)
3311.24(B)	4.07(A)
3311.26	4.05(B), 4.07(A), 4.09(C), 4.10, 4.10(A), 4.10(B), 4.12, 4.13, 4.15(B), 27.08(B)
3311.29	4.05(A), 4.05(C), 26.05(A)
3311.29(A)	4.03(G)
3311.29(C)	4.03(G), 4.05(A)
3311.29(C)(1)(b)	26.02(C)
3311.34	4.03(F)
3311.37	4.03(A), 4.07(A), 4.09(A), 4.09(B), 4.09(C), 4.11(A), 4.12, 4.13, 4.15(B), 4.15(C)
3311.38	4.07(C), 4.09(A), 4.09(B), 4.09(C), 4.11(A), 4.12, 4.13, 4.15(A)
3311.38(A)	4.05(D), 4.07(A)
3311.38(B)	4.05(D)
3311.40	40.18(A)
3311.50	4.03(B), 4.03(G), 40.10(D)
3311.51	40.10(D)
3311.52	4.03(G), 4.05(A), 6.02(A), 26.02(A), 26.06(B), 26.10(E), 26.16(A)
3311.52(B)	4.03(G)
3311.52(B)(2)	4.03(G)
3311.52(D)	4.03(G)
3311.521	4.03(G), 4.05(A), 5.09(C), 6.02(A), 21.14, 26.02(A), 26.06(B)
3311.521(B)	4.03(G)
3311.53	4.03(G)
3311.54	4.03(G)
3313.01	5.02(A)
3313.02	4.15(C), 5.02(B)
3313.03	5.02(B)
3313.04 to 3313.07	5.02(B)
3313.04	5.02(B)
3313.05	5.02(B)
3313.06	5.02(B)
3313.07	5.02(B)
3313.08	5.03(A)
3313.09	5.03(B)
3313.10	5.03(B)
3313.11	5.03(C)
3313.12	5.04(A), 5.04(B)
3313.13	45.08(A)
3313.14	5.11(A)
3313.15	5.11(B)
3313.16	5.11(B), 5.12(A)
3313.17	4.07(B), 5.06(A), 5.07, 36.01, 36.06, 36.09, 36.11(A)
3313.171	5.09(A), 43.02(B)
3313.172	5.09(T), 36.04(A)
3313.173	38.05
3313.174	26.11(H)
3313.18	5.11(C), 5.13(A), 5.13(C), 43.09, 43.10, 45.05(A)
3313.19	5.09(T)
3313.20	5.08(A), 5.08(B), 7.06(B), 10.09(C), 10.16, 13.05(C), 22.13(A), 24.05(A), 25.02, 25.03(A), 25.06, 26.15(A), 30.10(C), 31.08, 38.03(A), 38.03(B), 47.02
3313.201	5.09(T), 22.08, 46.20
3313.202	5.04(A), 5.09(T), 10.10(A), 10.10(B), 10.10(C), 10.10(D), 10.11

RC	Text Section(s)
3313.202(B)	10.10(D)
3313.202(C)	10.10(D)
3313.202(D)	10.10(A)
3313.203	5.07, 5.09(T), 43.02(B), 46.17(A), 46.20
3313.203(A)	22.21, 46.19
3313.203(B)	46.19
3313.204	26.10(D), 48.37
3313.205	20.07
3313.206	48.37
3313.207	5.09(L)
3313.208	5.09(L)
3313.209	5.09(L)
3313.21	26.09
3313.211	10.09(B)
3313.22 to 3313.32	6.05
3313.22	6.02(A), 6.02(C), 6.03(A), 6.13, 41.03, 45.08(A)
3313.222	6.02(A), 6.05
3313.222 to 3313.25	6.02(A)
3313.23	6.04
3313.24	6.02(A), 6.05
3313.25	6.02(D)
3313.26	6.06
3313.261	6.08(C)
3313.262	10.08(A)
3313.27	6.09
3313.28	6.09
3313.29	6.07(B), 31.06, 43.28
3313.31	6.07(A)
3313.32	42.11(A)
3313.321	44.14(B)
3313.33 to 3313.46	5.09(T)
3313.33	5.06(A), 6.08(D), 44.14(D), 45.06(B), 45.08(A), 46.08
3313.35	2.17, 6.14(A), 6.14(B), 6.14(C), 45.08(A)
3313.36	36.01, 36.06, 39.13
3313.36(A)	36.06
3313.37	30.04, 30.10(B), 35.01, 36.01, 36.02(A), 36.02(B), 36.04(A), 36.05(A), 36.07, 37.01(A), 39.01(A), 41.04, 41.05(A), 43.29
3313.37(B)(2)	36.02(B)
3313.37(B)(4)	36.02(B), 41.02
3313.37(B)(5)	36.04(C), 36.05(A), 36.07, 37.04(A), 41.02
3313.371	36.04(C), 36.07
3313.372	5.09(T), 36.04(C), 37.04(A), 41.01, 41.04, 41.05(A)
3313.372(A)	36.04(C)
3313.372(B)	36.04(C)
3313.373	5.09(T)
3313.373(A)	36.04(C)
3313.373(A)(2)	36.04(C)

RC	Text Section(s)
3313.373(B)	36.04(C)
3313.375	36.01, 36.02(A), 36.02(B), 41.02
3313.38	41.01
3313.39	36.01, 36.03
3313.40	36.01, 36.05(B), 36.09
3313.41	27.05, 36.01, 36.09, 36.11(A), 36.11(B)
3313.41(C)	36.12
3313.41(D)	36.05(B)
3313.42	4.02, 4.05(B), 4.07(A), 4.10
3313.45	5.09(T), 36.10(B)
3313.451	36.10(B)
3313.46	6.08(B), 22.09, 36.04(B), 36.04(C), 37.01(B), 37.03(A), 37.04(A), 37.04(C), 37.05, 41.02, 43.29
3313.46(A)(1)	37.03(A), 37.09
3313.46(G)	37.06(A)
3313.46(J)	37.06(A)
3313.47	4.04, 5.08(A), 5.08(B), 12.01, 12.06, 26.15(A), 30.10(C), 38.01, 38.02
3313.472	5.09(O), 31.03
3313.48	4.05(B), 10.09(A), 10.09(D), 19.08(A), 20.01(A), 20.05(A), 20.05(B), 20.05(C), 20.05(D), 25.09(A), 27.12, 28.04, 31.03, 39.07(A), 48.04(B)
3313.481	20.05(B), 20.05(D), 31.03
3313.481(B)	20.05(B)
3313.482	20.05(D)
3313.483	3.06, 41.33(A), 41.33(B), 41.33(D), 41.33(E)
3313.487	3.06, 41.33(B)
3313.487(A)	3.06
3313.487(C)	3.06
3313.488	3.03(G), 3.06, 41.33(E)
3313.489	3.06, 40.18(C)
3313.4810	41.33(E)
3313.4811	3.06, 41.33(E)
3313.481(A)(1) to 3313.481(A)(3)	20.05(B)
3313.49	5.08(A)
3313.50	21.07(A)
3313.51	6.07(A), 6.13, 42.01, 43.08(B)
3313.52	23.02(E), 26.10(B), 26.10(D)
3313.521	4.03(G)
3313.53	12.09(G), 12.10(A), 12.10(B), 12.10(E), 23.03(B), 26.11(B), 30.05, 30.10(B)

RC	Text Section(s)	RC	Text Section(s)
3313.53(B)	12.10(A)	3313.64(F)(2)	23.02(C)
3313.531	23.02(E), 26.10(A), 26.10(D)	3313.64(F)(3)	23.02(C)
		3313.64(F)(4)	23.02(C)
3313.532	26.10(D), 26.10(E)	3313.64(F)(5)	23.02(C)
3313.54	23.02(E), 26.11(E)	3313.64(F)(6)	23.02(C)
3313.55	22.05, 28.08(B), 28.08(C)	3313.64(F)(7)	23.02(C)
3313.56	20.05(A), 20.15, 26.10(C)	3313.64(F)(8)	23.02(C)
3313.57	26.11(F), 30.13	3313.64(F)(9)	23.02(A)
3313.58	26.11(C), 30.13	3313.64(F)(11)	23.02(C)
3313.59	5.09(D), 26.11(C), 31.05	3313.64(G)	23.02(C)
3313.60	21.14, 23.04(B), 26.02(A), 26.03, 26.04, 26.06(A)	3313.64(H)	23.02(A)
		3313.64(I)	23.02(D)
3313.60(E)	26.02(A)	3313.64(J)	23.02(B)
3313.60(F)	26.02(A)	3313.64(K)	23.02(A)
3313.601	32.05	3313.641	23.02(E), 26.10(A), 26.10(D), 26.12(A), 31.04, 39.01(A)
3313.602	26.02(A)		
3313.604	26.06(A)		
3313.605	3.03(G), 5.09(N)	3313.642	23.05, 23.07(C), 26.16(A), 33.02(A), 35.02(A), 48.13
3313.605(A)	5.09(N)		
3313.605(B)	5.09(N)	3313.643	21.12
3313.606	5.09(T)	3313.644	26.10(D)
3313.607(A)	5.09(R)	3313.645	23.02(A), 23.02(E)
3313.607(B)	5.09(R)	3313.646	5.09(C), 22.03(A), 23.02(E), 23.07(E)
3313.61	26.06(B), 26.10(E), 26.16(A)	3313.647	23.02(E), 26.16(B), 39.09(B)
3313.61(H)	26.06(B), 26.10(E)		
3313.61(I)	26.10(E)	3313.65	5.08(D), 23.02(B), 23.02(D), 25.10(A), 39.01(A)
3313.611	26.10(E)		
3313.611(A)	26.10(E)		
3313.611(B)	26.10(E)	3313.65(A)	23.02(A)
3313.611(C)	26.10(E)	3313.65(B) to 3313.65(D)	23.02(A)
3313.611(D)	26.10(E)		
3313.612	48.03(A)	3313.66	20.10, 25.09(C), 25.10(A), 25.10(E), 25.14, 25.15(B), 28.09(C), 46.14(A)
3313.62	20.05(A)		
3313.63	20.06		
3313.64	5.08(D), 20.01(A), 23.02(A), 23.02(C), 23.02(D), 25.09(A), 25.10(A), 26.05(A), 26.10(A), 26.10(D), 39.01(A), 43.05(B)	3313.66(A)	25.10(A), 25.10(B), 25.15(B)
		3313.66(B)	25.15(B)
		3313.66(B)(1)	25.10(A)
		3313.66(B)(2)	25.10(A)
		3313.66(B)(3)	25.10(A)
3313.64(A)(1)	23.02(A)	3313.66(B)(4)	25.10(C)
3313.64(A)(2)	23.02(A)	3313.66(C)	25.11
3313.64(A)(3)	23.02(A)	3313.66(D)	25.10(B), 25.10(C)
3313.64(A)(4)	23.02(A)	3313.66(E)	25.08, 25.10(C), 25.12(A), 25.15(B)
3313.64(A)(6)	23.02(A)		
3313.64(B)(1)	23.02(A)	3313.66(F)	25.10(A), 25.10(C)
3313.64(B)(2)	23.02(A)	3313.66(G)	25.10(B), 25.10(C)
3313.64(B)(3)	23.02(A)	3313.66(H)	25.10(A)
3313.64(C)	23.02(A)	3313.66(J)	25.10(A)
3313.64(C)(1)	23.02(A)	3313.661	5.08(B), 25.03(A), 25.10(A), 25.14
3313.64(C)(2)	23.02(A), 23.02(D)		
3313.64(C)(2)(d)	23.02(A)	3313.661(A)	25.10(A)
3313.64(C)(3)	23.02(A), 23.02(D)	3313.661(B)	25.10(D)
3313.64(C)(3)(b)	23.02(D)	3313.661(C)	47.02
3313.64(D)	23.02(A)	3313.661(D)	25.03(A), 25.10(D)
3313.64(E)	23.02(C)	3313.662	3.06, 23.02(A), 25.03(A), 25.10(A), 25.10(B),
3313.64(F)(1)	23.02(C)		

RC	Text Section(s)	RC	Text Section(s)
	25.10(C), 25.10(E), 25.10(F)	3313.79	38.13
3313.662(A)	24.06(B), 25.10(A), 25.10(B), 25.10(C), 25.10(E)	3313.81	23.07(A), 31.06, 35.04(A), 35.04(B), 43.15(B), 43.23
		3313.811	35.02(B), 35.02(D), 35.03, 39.15, 43.15(B), 43.24
3313.662(B)	25.10(E)	3313.812	35.05, 43.23
3313.662(C)	25.10(E)	3313.813	23.07(A), 35.07
3313.662(C)(2)	25.10(E)	3313.814	35.07
3313.662(C)(3)	25.10(E)	3313.82	5.09(S)
3313.662(D)	25.10(E)	3313.83	5.09(S)
3313.662(D)(3)	25.10(E)	3313.84	9.16, 45.08(A)
3313.662(F)(1)	25.10(E)	3313.841	5.08(D), 28.15(B)
3313.662(F)(2)	25.10(E)	3313.842	5.09(D)
3313.662(G)	25.10(E)	3313.843	5.09(I), 7.12, 9.01(A)
3313.662(H)	25.10(E)	3313.85	5.10
3313.67	21.05(A), 21.07(B), 23.07(B)	3313.86	5.04(A)
		3313.87	5.09(E)
3313.671	21.05(B), 21.05(C)	3313.871	26.18, 43.02(B)
3313.671(B)	21.05(A), 23.07(B)	3313.90	5.08(D), 23.02(A), 23.02(E), 27.01, 27.02, 27.05, 27.08(B), 27.09(C), 27.12, 39.08(B)
3313.672	20.02(A), 23.02(A), 24.16, 44.14(D), 48.10		
3313.673	21.03(F)		
3313.68	21.02(A), 21.02(B), 21.06, 21.08(A), 21.08(B), 23.07(B)	3313.901	3.03(G), 27.03
		3313.91	23.02(E), 27.02, 27.08(B)
		3313.911	27.02
3313.69	21.03(A), 21.03(B)	3313.92	5.08(D), 5.09(D), 36.08, 37.01(A), 43.21
3313.70	45.08(A)		
3313.71	10.18, 10.20(A), 21.03(A), 21.03(B), 21.03(C), 21.03(D), 21.07(A), 28.08(C)	3313.92(B)	36.08
		3313.93	27.06
		3313.94	31.02
		3313.941	3.03(F)
3313.712	21.04(A), 21.04(B), 23.02(C)	3313.95	26.02(A)
		3313.96	44.15(A)
3313.712(B)	21.07(C)	3313.96(B)	24.16
3313.713	21.04(B), 23.02(C)	3313.96(C)	24.16(A)
3313.713(B)	21.04(B)	3313.97	3.03(G), 5.08(C), 5.08(D), 7.06(C)
3313.713(C)(1)	21.04(B)		
3313.713(C)(2)	21.04(B)	3313.98	3.03(G), 5.08(D), 23.02(A), 39.09(B)
3313.713(C)(3)	21.04(B)		
3313.713(C)(4)	21.04(B)	3313.98(A)	5.08(D)
3313.713(C)(5)	21.04(B)	3313.98(A)(5)	5.08(D)
3313.713(C)(6)	21.04(B)	3313.98(H)	5.08(D)
3313.713(D)	21.04(B)	3313.98(I)	5.08(D)
3313.713(E)	21.04(B)	3313.981	3.03(G), 5.08(D)
3313.713(F)	21.04(B)	3313.981(E)	39.09(B)
3313.714	5.09(M)	3313.982	5.08(C)
3313.715	5.09(M)	3313.983	5.08(D)
3313.72	21.08(A)	3313.981 to 3313.983	5.08(D)
3313.73	21.08(A)		
3313.75 et seq.	39.01(A)	3315.01	42.22, 43.16, 43.20
3313.75 to 3313.78	36.09, 38.08(A), 38.13	3315.02 to 3315.05	43.19
3313.75	38.07	3315.06	5.04(B), 7.05(B), 35.01
3313.751	24.15(B)	3315.061	5.09(A)
3313.752	21.15(D)	3315.062	22.08, 23.03(B), 23.03(C), 30.10(B), 30.10(C), 35.02(C), 39.15, 43.04, 43.25, 44.02
3313.76	38.09(A), 38.09(B), 38.12		
3313.77	32.06, 38.10, 38.12		
3313.77(B)	38.10		
3313.78	38.11	3315.062(C)	23.03(A)

RC	Text Section(s)	RC	Text Section(s)
3315.062(D)	23.04(B)	3317.027	39.09(E)
3315.07	5.09(G), 31.02, 35.01, 43.05(A)	3317.028	39.09(E)
		3317.0210	39.09(F)
3315.07(B)	25.04	3317.0210(C)	39.09(F)
3315.07(D)	5.09(J)	3317.0211	39.09(F)
3315.08	6.07(A), 43.08(B), 43.10	3317.0211(C)	39.09(F)
3315.09	5.09(D), 26.09, 26.11(A), 31.05	3317.0213	39.06(A)
		3317.0214	39.06(A)
3315.091	26.14	3317.025 to	
3315.11	43.20	3317.028	23.02(D)
3315.12	43.20	3317.03	4.03(G), 5.08(D), 6.07(D), 26.16(B), 27.12, 39.09(B)
3315.13	43.20		
3315.14	43.20		
3315.15	5.04(B), 5.09(F), 43.15(B), 43.22	3317.03(A)	39.09(B), 45.01(C)
		3317.03(A)(4)	4.03(G)
3315.31	39.10	3317.03(C)	39.09(B)
3315.33	3.03(G)	3317.03(D)(2)	39.09(C)
3315.36	3.03(G)	3317.03(E)	39.09(C)
3315.37	5.09(K)	3317.03(E)(2)(b)	39.09(B)
3315.40	39.13, 42.22	3317.03(F)	23.02(A)
3315.42	39.13	3317.031	22.07(B), 39.09(A), 44.13
3316.66(E)	25.12(A)	3317.032	39.09(A)
Ch 3317	3.03(A), 4.03(G), 4.12, 8.03(A), 11.09, 13.01(A), 22.07(B), 22.09, 23.02(D), 23.03(B), 27.09(A), 27.11, 39.01(A), 39.06(A), 39.08(A), 40.14	3317.033	39.09(B)
		3317.04	4.12
		3317.05	7.12, 23.02(A), 28.15(A), 28.15(B), 39.08(A), 39.08(B), 39.09(B)
		3317.05(A)	39.09(B)
3317.01	3.03(G), 3.06, 10.09(A), 20.05(A), 20.05(B), 20.05(D), 23.07(D), 39.06(C), 39.07(A), 39.07(B), 39.07(C), 39.08(A)	3317.05(B)	39.09(B), 39.09(C)
		3317.05(C)	26.09
		3317.05(E)	23.02(D), 39.09(B)
		3317.06	27.12, 42.22, 48.06(A), 48.06(C), 48.07
		3317.061	39.09(D)
3317.02	39.09(E)	3317.063	48.06(A)
3317.02(B)	39.09(E)	3317.07	22.07(C)
3317.021	39.09(E)	3317.08	5.08(D), 23.02(A), 23.02(D), 28.20(A), 39.01(A), 43.05(B)
3317.021(A)(4)	39.09(E)		
3317.021(C)	39.07(B)		
3317.022	3.03(D), 23.02(D)	3317.08(A)	23.02(D)
3317.023	23.02(D)	3317.08(B)	23.02(D)
3317.023(B)	23.07(D)	3317.081	23.02(D)
3317.023(B)(3)	3.03(G)	3317.09	39.01(A)
3317.023(B)(4)	3.03(G)	3317.11	5.09(I), 39.13, 40.03, 43.15(B)
3317.023(G)	23.02(D)		
3317.024	22.07(B), 28.15(A), 28.16, 39.07(B), 39.07(C), 39.08(A), 39.08(B)	3317.11(A)(4)	22.07(B)
		3317.12	13.01(B)
		3317.13	7.11(A), 8.02, 10.02(A), 10.02(C), 10.02(D), 10.03(A), 29.13(A)
3317.024(C)	26.08		
3317.024(F)	26.08		
3317.024(K)	5.08(D), 22.07(A), 22.07(B), 26.07(C), 39.08(C)	3317.13(A)(1)	10.03(A), 10.03(B)
		3317.13(A)(1)(a)	10.03(B)
		3317.13(A)(1)(b)	10.03(B)
3317.024(L)	23.07(A)	3317.13(A)(1)(c)	10.03(B)
3317.024(N)	23.02(D), 28.15(A)	3317.13(A)(1)(d)	10.03(D)
3317.024(O)	23.02(D)	3317.13(B)	6.07(C), 10.03(A), 10.05(A)
3317.024(O)(2)	26.09		
3317.025	39.07(B), 39.09(E)	3317.13(C)	10.05(A)

RC	Text Section(s)
3317.13(D)	10.05(A)
3317.14	7.11(A), 8.02, 10.02(A), 10.02(B), 10.02(C), 10.03(A), 10.03(B), 10.04, 10.04(D), 10.05(A), 10.05(B)
3317.16	27.11, 27.12, 28.17(A)
3317.18	41.16(E)
3317.19	4.03(G)
3317.21	27.02
3317.22	27.02
3317.23	27.02
3317.62 to 3317.64	41.01
3317.62	39.09(F), 41.33(B), 41.33(E)
3317.63	3.06, 41.33(B)
3317.64	4.13, 41.33(E)
Ch 3318	4.03(G), 37.07(B), 39.13, 41.01, 41.24, 41.25
3318.01	41.24, 41.25
3318.02	41.26
3318.03	41.26
3318.04	41.27(A), 41.31
3318.05	41.25, 41.27(B)
3318.06	41.27(B), 41.28(A), 41.28(C), 41.28(D), 41.28(E), 41.28(F)
3318.07	41.28(F), 41.32
3318.08	41.29(A), 41.30, 41.31
3318.081	41.29(B)
3318.091	41.30
3318.111	42.23(A)
3318.13	41.32
Ch 3319	4.03(B), 7.12, 12.04(B), 29.11
3319.01	7.02, 7.03(A), 7.04(A), 7.04(B), 7.04(C), 7.04(E), 7.05(A), 7.05(B), 7.06(B), 7.06(C), 7.07, 7.14(A), 9.07(A), 9.11(B), 9.20, 9.21, 18.05(B), 23.02(A), 25.13
3319.011	7.07, 18.05(B)
3319.02	5.09(I), 7.06(B), 7.09(A), 7.09(B), 7.09(C), 7.10, 7.11(A), 7.11(B), 7.13, 9.07(A), 9.13(A), 9.21, 10.02(A), 12.04(B), 12.09(A), 18.05(B), 18.05(C)
3319.02(C)	7.11(B), 7.13, 12.04(B), 12.09(A)
3319.02(D)	7.11(B), 7.14(A), 7.14(B)
3319.02(E)	7.12
3319.03	6.10, 6.11, 6.12, 7.06(B)
3319.04	6.13, 7.06(B), 12.01, 12.06, 38.02
3319.05	6.11
3319.06	6.12
3319.07 to 3319.21	3.03(D), 3.03(E), 8.03(A)
3319.07	5.08(B), 7.06(B), 8.08, 8.09, 9.01(A), 9.09(B), 9.10(C)
3319.07(B)	7.10, 9.01(A)
3319.071	10.09(C)
3319.072	10.09(D)
3319.073	24.05(B)
3319.08 to 3319.18	7.05(A), 7.09(A), 8.02, 9.01
3319.08	7.11(A), 7.12, 9.01(A), 9.01(B), 9.02, 9.05(A), 9.06(A), 9.10(B), 9.14(A), 10.01(A), 10.03(B), 10.07(A), 10.09(A), 10.15, 10.21(C), 11.04(A), 11.05, 20.04
3319.081	12.02(B), 12.09(A), 12.09(B), 12.09(D), 12.09(E), 12.10(E), 12.13, 12.16(A), 12.16(C), 12.17(A), 13.05(A), 22.14
3319.081(A)	12.09(A)
3319.081(B)	12.09(A), 12.09(C), 13.01(B)
3319.081(C)	12.09(G), 12.10(E), 12.16(A)
3319.082	12.09(C), 13.01(B)
3319.083	12.09(F), 12.10(E)
3319.084	6.05, 13.04(A)
3319.086	13.02(A)
3319.087	13.03(A), 13.03(B)
3319.088	12.19, 14.04
3319.081 to 3319.088	6.05, 12.19
3319.09	7.05(A), 7.11(A), 10.02(A)
3319.09(A)	8.02, 8.02(C), 9.07(A)
3319.09(B)	9.08(C)
3319.09(C)	9.04
3319.10	9.13(A), 9.15(B), 9.15(C), 10.13(B), 18.07, 18.12
3319.11	4.03(B), 5.12(B), 7.05(A), 7.09(A), 8.04(D), 8.04(E), 8.08, 9.01(A), 9.02, 9.05(A), 9.06(A), 9.07, 9.07(A), 9.08(A), 9.08(B), 9.08(E), 9.09(A), 9.09(B), 9.09(C), 9.09(E), 9.10(A), 9.10(D), 9.11(B), 9.11(D), 9.12, 9.13(B), 9.13(C), 9.14(B), 9.19(C), 9.24, 17.10, 18.20, 44.08(B), 46.14(A)
3319.11(A)(3)	9.02, 9.09(A)
3319.11(B)	9.05(A), 9.09(B)
3319.11(B)(1)	9.09(B)

RC	Text Section(s)	RC	Text Section(s)
3319.11(B)(2)	9.09(B)		8.05, 9.06(A), 9.14(C), 24.16(B)
3319.11(B)(3)	9.09(B), 9.13(A)	3319.22(A)	26.05(A)
3319.11(C)(1)	9.09(B), 9.09(C)	3319.22(F)	18.05(B)
3319.11(C)(2)	9.09(B), 9.09(C)	3319.22(G)	18.05(B)
3319.11(C)(3)	9.09(B)	3319.22(H)	18.05(B)
3319.11(D)	9.09(B)	3319.22(I)	8.04(A), 18.05(B)
3319.11(E)	9.09(B), 9.10(B)	3319.22(J)	7.03(A), 18.05(B)
3319.11(G)	9.09(B), 9.11(A), 9.13(B), 9.13(C), 9.14(B)	3319.22(K)	18.05(B)
3319.11(G)(7)	9.13(C)	3319.22(L)	18.05(B)
3319.11(H)	9.11(A), 9.11(B)	3319.22(N)	7.03(A), 18.05(B)
3319.11(I)	9.14(B)	3319.22(O)	18.05(B)
3319.111	7.05(A), 7.09(A), 9.01(A), 9.05(A), 9.09(A), 9.13(A), 9.14(B), 9.21(A), 9.24, 18.20, 18.23	3319.22(P)	21.02(B)
		3319.221	21.02(B)
		3319.23	8.03(B)
		3319.231	3.03(B)
		3319.232	3.03(G)
3319.111(A)	9.09(B), 9.10(B), 9.13(A), 9.13(C), 9.14(B)	3319.24 to 3319.26	7.03(B)
		3319.24	7.03(B), 8.04(C)
3319.111(B)	9.13(A), 9.13(C)	3319.25	7.03(B)
3319.111(C)	7.05(A), 9.13(A), 9.14(B)	3319.26	8.04(E)
3319.12	7.05(B), 7.11(A), 9.01(B), 10.01(A), 10.01(B), 10.01(C)	3319.27	8.04(E)
		3319.28	8.04(A)
		3319.281	8.04(B)
3319.13	10.19(A), 10.20(A), 17.09(B)	3319.282	8.04, 8.04(F)
		3319.282(G)	8.04(F)
3319.131	10.19(B)	3319.29	8.03(A)
3319.14	10.21(A)	3319.291	5.09(H), 8.01
3319.141	9.21(D), 10.13(A), 10.13(B), 10.13(C), 10.13(D), 10.16, 13.08(A), 13.08(B), 17.09(A), 43.05(B)	3319.30	6.08(A), 8.03, 8.03(A), 30.05
		3319.301	6.08(A), 8.03(A), 8.07(A), 10.06
		3319.31	5.09(H), 6.02(B), 6.10, 8.07(A), 12.19, 24.07
3319.142	13.10(A)		
3319.143	10.21(B)		
3319.15	8.07(C), 9.17	3319.31(B)	8.07(A)
3319.151	8.07(A), 9.21, 12.16(A), 12.17(A)	3319.311	6.02(B), 6.10, 8.07(A), 12.19
3319.16	6.04, 7.05(A), 7.06(B), 7.07, 7.11(A), 7.12, 9.04, 9.18, 9.19(A), 9.19(D), 9.20, 9.21, 9.21(A), 9.22, 9.22(A), 9.23(B), 9.25, 10.16, 10.19(A), 18.22(A), 25.02, 25.06, 46.14(A)	3319.32	44.13
		3319.321	3.03(F), 5.09(M), 24.06(A), 24.06(B), 44.01, 44.02, 44.14(A), 44.15(A), 44.23, 48.14
		3319.321(A)	44.14(B)
		3319.321(B)	44.14(B), 44.14(C)
3319.161	9.22, 9.25	3319.321(B)(1)	44.14(B)
3319.17	7.06(B), 7.11(A), 9.01(A), 9.04, 9.19(A), 9.19(B), 9.19(C), 9.19(E), 9.19(F), 9.19(G)	3319.321(C)	44.15(A), 44.15(B)
		3319.321(E)	44.15(A), 44.16
		3319.321(F)	44.14(D)
		3319.321(H)	24.06(B)
3319.19	7.08, 36.07	3319.322	44.02, 44.15(A), 44.16
3319.19(B)	4.03(C)	3319.33	31.02
3319.19(D)	7.08	3319.36	6.08(A), 8.03(A), 10.06, 44.12
3319.20	24.07		
3319.21	9.03	3319.37	6.03(B), 43.28
3319.22 to 3319.30	8.02(C), 11.04(A), 14.04, 39.09(D)	3319.39	5.09(C), 5.09(H), 29.14
		3319.39(B)(3)	5.09(H)
3319.22	7.03(A), 7.03(B), 8.03, 8.03(A), 8.04, 8.04(A),	3319.39(E)	5.09(H)
		3319.39(H)	5.09(H)

RC	Text Section(s)	RC	Text Section(s)
3319.41	22.17(B), 25.07, 25.08, 25.16(A), 48.15	Ch 3323	3.03(D), 3.03(E), 4.03(G), 11.04(A), 21.03(F), 23.02(A), 23.02(D), 26.06(B), 27.09(A), 28.01(A), 28.16, 29.04(A), 29.11, 29.13(D)
3319.41(A)	25.16(A)		
3319.41(A)(2)	25.16(A)		
3319.41(B)	25.16(A)		
3319.41(B)(3)(b)	25.16(A)		
3319.41(C)	25.16(A)	3323.01	28.01(B), 28.16, 29.04(A)
3319.41(D)	25.16(A)	3323.01(A)	20.01(A), 28.01(B), 39.08(A)
3319.41(E)	25.16(A)		
3319.41(F)	25.16(A)	3323.01(C)	28.07
3319.41(G)	25.16(A)	3323.01(E)	28.02
3319.42	8.03(C)	3323.01(H)	23.02(B)
3319.43	8.03(C)	3323.01(I)	23.02(B), 23.02(D)
3319.45	24.06(B)	3323.01(I)(4)	23.02(B)
3319.52	8.07(A), 24.07	3323.01(L)	28.02
3319.59	22.22	3323.011	28.02, 28.16
3319.97	5.08(D)	3323.011(A)(2)	5.09(P)
Ch 3321	20.02(A), 25.09(A), 48.02, 48.03(A)	3323.011(D)	28.16
		3323.02	28.01(A), 28.14(B)
3321.01	20.01(A), 20.01(B), 26.05(A)	3323.03	28.17(A), 29.04(B), 46.01(C)
3321.01(A)	26.05(A)	3323.031	5.09(P)
3321.01(B)	26.05(A)	3323.04	20.02(C), 28.05(A), 28.20(B), 29.04(B)
3321.01(C)	26.05(A)		
3321.01(D)	26.05(A)	3323.05	28.11(A), 28.11(F), 29.04(B)
3321.01(E)	26.05(A)		
3321.01(F)	26.05(A)	3323.06 to 3323.091	20.01(A)
3321.01(G)	26.05(A)	3323.06	28.14(A)
3321.02	20.02(A)	3323.08	20.02(A), 23.02(C), 23.02(E), 26.06(B), 26.10(A), 26.10(E), 28.05(B), 28.14(A)
3321.03	20.02(A), 20.03(B), 23.06, 28.17(A)		
3321.04	20.01(A), 20.02(A), 20.02(B), 20.02(C), 20.03(B), 20.03(C), 20.10, 23.06, 28.17(A)	3323.08(C)	28.02
		3323.09	23.02(B), 28.20(A), 29.01(A), 29.04(B), 29.06(A)
3321.07	20.02(A), 20.02(B), 48.04(A), 48.04(B)	3323.09(C)(1)	28.15(C)
		3323.091	23.02(A), 23.02(B), 23.02(D), 39.08(A)
3321.08	20.05(A), 20.15, 28.17(A)		
3321.09	20.15, 48.04(D)	3323.11	29.11
3321.12	20.10, 27.12, 44.13, 48.04(C)	3323.12 to 3323.15	28.08(A)
		3323.13	23.02(A), 23.02(B), 23.02(D)
3321.13(A)	20.10		
3321.13(B)	20.10	3323.14	23.02(A), 23.02(B), 23.02(D)
3321.13(B)(1)	20.10		
3321.13(B)(2)	20.10	3323.141	23.02(A), 23.02(D), 28.15(C)
3321.13(B)(3)	20.10		
3321.13(C)	20.10	3323.141(D)	23.02(A)
3321.14	20.08(A)	3323.142	23.02(D)
3321.15	20.08(A), 20.08(B)	3323.15	28.08(A)
3321.16 et seq.	48.04(A)	3323.16	28.15(A)
3321.16	20.08(C), 48.04(A)	3323.17	3.04(A), 28.18
3321.17	20.08(C), 48.04(A)	3323.18	28.02
3321.19 to 3321.22	20.09(A)	3325.01	28.19(A)
3321.19(A)	20.09(A)	3325.04	28.19(A)
3321.22	20.09(B)	3325.06	28.18
3321.38	20.09(A), 20.09(B)	3325.07	28.18
3321.99	20.09(B)	3325.08	28.19(A)

RC	Text Section(s)
3326.10	22.13(A)
3327.01	22.03(A), 22.03(B), 22.03(C), 22.03(D), 22.05, 22.06, 22.07(B), 22.16, 27.12
3327.011	5.08(E), 22.02, 22.25(A)
3327.013	5.09(C), 22.03(A)
3327.02	22.03(D)
3327.03	22.16
3327.04	22.04, 23.02(A)
3327.05	22.04
3327.05(A)	22.04
3327.05(B)	22.04
3327.06	23.02(A), 23.02(D), 39.01(A), 39.09(B)
3327.06(A)	23.02(A)
3327.06(B)	23.02(A)
3327.06(C)	23.02(A)
3327.08	22.09, 36.04(A), 36.04(B), 36.04(C)
3327.09	22.08, 46.20
3327.10	12.16(A), 22.13(A), 22.14
3327.10(A)	22.13(A)
3327.10(D)	22.13(A)
3327.10(E)	22.13(A)
3327.11	39.01(A)
3327.12	22.16
3327.13	22.24
3327.14	22.22, 22.23
3327.15	22.22
3327.16	22.21, 46.19
3327.16(B)	22.19
Ch 3329	35.01, 36.04(A)
3329.01	33.03(A)
3329.05	33.03(A)
3329.06	23.05, 33.02(A), 33.03(A)
3329.07	33.04
3329.08	33.03(A), 33.03(B)
3329.09	33.02(B)
3329.10	8.07(B), 33.05, 45.07
Ch 3331	4.03(G), 20.13(A), 27.09(A)
3331.01 et seq.	20.02(A)
3331.01	20.10, 20.11(A), 20.13(A), 20.13(B), 20.13(C)
3331.02	20.13(B), 20.14(A), 20.16(D)
3331.02(C)	20.13(B)
3331.04	20.14(B)
3331.05	20.11(B), 20.14(C)
3331.06	20.14(A)
3331.07	20.13(C)
3331.08	20.03(C), 20.13(D)
3331.09	20.13(E)
3331.15	20.14(D)
Ch 3332	48.01(B)
3333.40	2.10
3333.41	2.10
Ch 3334	5.09(Q)
3334.17	5.09(Q)
3335.50 et seq.	27.14
3335.51	27.14
3335.55	27.14
3345.06	26.07(B)
3351.05 to 3351.14	42.05(A)
Ch 3353	26.11(G)
3365.01 to 3365.10	48.09(B)
3365.02	26.07(C)
3365.03	26.07(C)
3365.04	26.07(C), 39.09(B)
3365.04(A)	39.09(B)
3365.04(B)	39.09(B)
3365.05	26.07(C)
3365.06(A)	26.07(C)
3365.06(B)	26.07(C)
3365.07	26.07(C)
3365.08(B)	26.07(C)
3365.08(C)	26.07(C)
3365.09	26.07(C)
3375.01	34.05, 34.06
3375.02	34.07
3375.02(H)	34.07
3375.04	34.05
3375.05	34.08
3375.06	34.04(A), 34.09(A)
3375.07	34.15(B)
3375.09	34.15(B)
3375.10	34.04(A), 34.09(A)
3375.12	34.04(A), 34.09(A)
3375.14	34.02, 34.04(B)
3375.15	34.09(A), 45.08(A)
3375.16	34.02
3375.17	34.15(A)
3375.18	34.02
3375.22	34.04(A), 34.09(A)
3375.23	34.15(B)
3375.30	34.04(A), 34.09(A)
3375.32	34.09(A)
3375.35	34.09(A), 34.09(C), 34.11
3375.36 et seq.	34.12(B)
3375.40	34.10(A)
3375.401	34.10(A)
3375.402	34.10(A)
3375.403	34.10(A)
3375.41	34.10(B)
3375.42	34.02, 34.04(B)
3375.43	34.17
3375.431	34.17
3375.63	34.03, 45.08(A)
3501.01	40.13, 41.09, 41.14, 41.28(E)
3501.02(D)	5.03(A)
3501.15	45.08(A)
3501.17	27.11, 29.09(A)
3501.38(E)	4.10(A), 4.11(A)
3503.01	3.02(A)

RC	Text Section(s)
3503.10	31.09
3505.04	5.03(A)
3513.254	5.03(A)
3517.081	5.03(A)
3517.092(F)(2)	38.11
3517.10	5.03(A)
3517.13	5.03(A)
3517.14	5.03(A)
3517.15	5.03(A)
3599.031	5.03(A)
3599.091	5.03(A)
3599.092	5.03(A)
3701.245	21.03(E)
3701.249	17.13(A)
Ch 3703	21.10(A), 37.09
3703.01	21.08(B)
3703.03	21.08(B)
Ch 3707	21.10(A), 37.09
3707.26	10.09(A), 20.05(D), 21.08(B)
3707.50	48.15
3707.50(B)	48.15
3709.22	21.04(A), 21.08(A)
3709.241	21.04(A)
3710.01 to 3710.14	48.34(A)
3732.01	35.06
3732.03	35.06
3732.08	35.06
3732.11	35.06
3732.99	35.06
3735.67	39.04
3735.671	39.04
3737.73(A)	21.13
3737.73(B)	21.13
3737.73(C)	21.13
3746.24	46.01(C)
Ch 3781	21.10(A), 37.01(B), 37.03(B), 37.09
3781.06	21.10(A), 37.01(B), 37.09
3781.11	21.10(C), 28.17(B)
3781.11(A)(5)	37.01(B)
3781.111	21.10(C), 28.17(B)
Ch 3791	21.10(A), 37.01(B), 37.03(B), 37.09
3791.04	37.03(B)
3911.18	39.10
3917.04	10.08(A)
3923.38	10.12(A), 10.12(B)
3923.38(C)(2)	10.12(B)
3923.38(C)(3)	10.12(B)
3929.17	6.02(D)
3933.05	39.10
3999.08	39.10
Ch 4101	37.09
4101.17	17.06(A), 17.06(B), 17.06(C)
4101.17(B)	17.06(A)
Ch 4107	16.05(H)
4107.31 et seq.	21.10(A)
Ch 4109	20.11, 20.12
4109.01(C)	20.11
4109.01(D)	20.11
4109.02 to 4109.04	20.09(C)
4109.02	20.11(A), 20.11(B), 20.16(A), 20.16(B)
4109.03	20.11(A), 20.16(A), 20.16(D)
4109.04	20.11(A)
4109.05(A)	20.11
4109.05(B)	20.11
4109.06	20.11(A), 20.14(C)
4109.06(C)	20.12
4109.07(A)(1)	20.12
4109.07(A)(2)	20.12
4109.07(A)(3)	20.12
4109.07(A)(4)	20.12
4109.07(A)(5)	20.12
4109.07(A)(6)	20.12
4109.07(A)(7)	20.12
4109.07(B)	20.12
4109.07(C)	20.12
4109.07(D)	20.12
4109.08	20.16(B)
4109.09	20.16(D)
4109.10	20.16(C)
4109.11	20.16(B)
4109.12	20.09(C)
4109.13	20.09(C)
4109.13(A)	20.17
4109.13(C)	20.17
4109.13(D)	20.09(A), 20.17
4109.13(F)	20.17, 39.10
4109.21	20.12
4109.21(F)	20.12
4109.21(G)	20.12
4109.99	20.17
4111.02	13.01(B), 48.22
4111.03	13.02(A), 48.22
4111.08	44.12, 48.22
4111.17	17.08(A), 17.08(B)
Ch 4112	17.04(A), 17.04(B), 17.04(D), 17.04(E), 17.06(A), 17.09(C), 17.12
4112.01	17.06(C)
4112.01(A)(2)	17.04(A)
4112.01(A)(13)	17.13(A)
4112.01(B)	10.20(B), 17.09(A)
4112.02	17.04(E), 17.06(C), 17.09(C), 17.13(A), 48.30
4112.02(A)	10.20(B), 17.04(A), 17.08(C), 17.13(A)
4112.02(E)(2)	17.17
4112.02(I)	17.04(A)
4112.02(L)	17.13(A)
4112.02(N)	17.04(B), 17.06(A)
4112.04(A)(10)	17.17

RC	Text Section(s)
4112.05	17.04(C), 17.06(A), 44.02
4112.05(B)	17.04(C)
4112.05(G)	17.04(C), 17.04(D)
4112.06(A)	17.04(E)
4112.06(E)	17.04(E)
4112.06(H)	17.04(E)
4112.07	17.17
4112.08	17.06(A)
4112.99	17.04(B), 17.04(C), 17.06(A)
4113.14	20.08(C)
4113.52	9.21(F), 12.17(A)
4113.52(A)(3)	9.21(F)
4115.03 to 4115.16	37.11
4115.03(B)	37.11
4115.03(C)	37.11
4115.033	37.11
4115.034	37.11
4115.04	37.12(A)
4115.05	37.12(A), 37.12(B), 37.13
4115.06	37.12(B)
4115.07	37.12(B), 37.13
4115.071	37.13
4115.071(A)	37.13
4115.071(C)	37.13
4115.10	37.14
4115.10(C)	37.14
4115.13	37.14
4115.13(C)	37.14
4115.133	37.14
4115.14	37.14
4115.99	37.11
4115.99(A)	37.14
Ch 4117	3.03(D), 3.03(E), 10.08(B), 18.11(B), 18.14, 18.17(C), 18.22(A), 18.25(A), 18.26(C)
4117.01	7.09(A), 12.04(B), 12.09(A)
4117.01(B)	18.03, 29.17
4117.01(C)	18.04(A)
4117.01(C)(13)	18.07
4117.01(D)	18.04(A)
4117.01(F)	18.05(A), 18.05(B)
4117.01(F)(1)	18.05(B)
4117.01(G)	18.10
4117.01(I)	18.08, 18.31
4117.01(J)	18.06
4117.01(K)	18.05(C)
4117.02(M)	18.15(E), 18.15(F), 18.26(C)
4117.03	18.25(B)
4117.03(A)	18.09
4117.03(A)(2)	18.09
4117.03(A)(3)	18.09
4117.03(C)	18.04(B), 18.09
4117.04	18.15(E)
4117.04(B)	3.03(D), 18.10

RC	Text Section(s)
4117.05	18.15(E)
4117.05(A)	18.16(B)
4117.05(A)(2)	18.16(A), 18.16(B), 18.17(A)
4117.06(A)	18.11(A)
4117.06(B)	18.11(A), 18.11(B)
4117.06(C)	18.11(B)
4117.06(D)	18.11(A)
4117.06(D)(1)	18.08
4117.07(A)(1)	18.15(A), 18.18
4117.07(A)(2)	18.14, 18.15(A)
4117.07(B)	18.15(A), 18.15(C)
4117.07(C)	18.17(A)
4117.07(C)(3)	18.15(C)
4117.07(C)(4)	18.15(C)
4117.07(C)(5)	18.15(C)
4117.07(C)(6)	18.15(C), 18.17(A)
4117.08	9.20, 9.21
4117.08(A)	18.28(A)
4117.08(B)	18.28(A)
4117.08(C)	18.28(A), 18.28(B)
4117.09	10.08(A)
4117.09(A)	18.19(A)
4117.09(B)(1)	18.19(A), 18.22(A)
4117.09(B)(2)	10.08(B), 18.19(A)
4117.09(C)	10.08(B), 18.21(A), 18.21(B)
4117.09(D)	18.19(A), 18.19(B)
4117.09(E)	18.17(A)
4117.10	7.06(B), 9.13(B), 10.21(A), 11.08(A), 18.20
4117.10(A)	9.05(A), 9.19(B), 9.20, 9.21, 10.07(A), 10.13(D), 18.20, 18.22(A)
4117.10(B)	18.28(C), 29.17
4117.11	18.26
4117.11(A)(1)	18.24(B), 18.25(B)
4117.11(A)(2)	18.04(A)
4117.11(A)(3)	18.24(F)
4117.11(B)	18.25(A)
4117.11(B)(1)	18.25(B)
4117.11(C)	18.26(C)
4117.12(B)	18.26(A), 18.26(B)
4117.12(B)(1)	18.26(A)
4117.12(B)(3)	18.26(A)
4117.13(A)	18.26(C)
4117.13(B)	18.26(C)
4117.13(D)	18.26(C)
4117.14	18.11(B), 18.22(A), 18.24(C), 18.29(B)
4117.14(B)	18.29(B)
4117.14(B)(4)	18.29(B)
4117.14(C)	18.29(B), 18.29(C)
4117.14(C)(6)	18.29(E)
4117.14(D)	18.29(D), 18.30
4117.14(D)(2)	18.29(E), 18.30
4117.15(A)	18.30, 18.31
4117.15(B)	18.31

RC	Text Section(s)
4117.15(C)	18.29(D)
4117.16(A)	18.32
4117.16(B)	18.27, 18.32
4117.17	18.26(A), 18.33
4117.20	18.24(B), 18.27
4117.21	18.27
4117.23	18.31
4117.23(A)	18.31
4117.23(B)	18.31
4121.47	16.05(H)
4121.80	16.08
Ch 4122	17.04(A)
4122.99	17.04(B)
Ch 4123	16.01
4123.01(A)	16.02
4123.01(C)	16.03, 16.03(A), 16.03(D)
4123.01(F)	16.04
4123.03	16.02
4123.23 to 4123.50	16.01
4123.411 et seq.	16.05(F)
4123.511	16.07, 16.07(A)
4123.512	16.06, 16.07(A), 16.07(B)
4123.515	16.07(B)
4123.518	16.07(B)
4123.519	16.07(B)
4123.52	16.06
4123.54	16.04, 16.05(A), 16.05(B)
4123.54(A)	16.03(A)
4123.54(B)	16.03(D)
4123.56	16.05(B)
4123.56(A)	16.05(B)
4123.56(B)	16.05(C)
4123.57(A)	16.05(D), 16.05(E)
4123.57(B)	16.05(D)
4123.58(A)	16.05(F)
4123.58(C)	16.05(F)
4123.59	16.03(A), 16.05(G)
4123.60	16.03(A), 16.05(G)
4123.68	16.04
4123.68(A) to 4123.68(AA)	16.04
4123.68(X)	16.04
4123.74	16.08
4123.84	16.06
4123.85	16.06
4123.90	16.06
Ch 4141	10.12(B)
4141.01(B)(3)	15.04
4141.01(B)(3)(c)(i)	15.01
4141.01(B)(3)(e)	15.01
4141.01(M)	15.02(A)
4141.01(N)	15.02(A)
4141.01(Q)	15.03
4141.01(Q)(1)	15.02(C)
4141.01(Q)(2)	15.02(C)
4141.28(D)(1)	15.06
4141.28(S)	15.08(B)
4141.29	15.02, 15.02(B)

RC	Text Section(s)
4141.29(B)	15.03
4141.29(D)	15.06, 15.08(A)
4141.29(D)(1)(a)	15.06
4141.29(D)(1)(b)	15.02(D)
4141.29(D)(2)	15.02(D), 15.07, 15.08(A)
4141.29(D)(2)(a)(iv)	15.08(A)
4141.29(D)(2)(c)	15.02(D)
4141.29(D)(2)(d)	15.02(D)
4141.29(I)(1)(a)	15.05(A)
4141.29(I)(1)(b)	15.05(A)
4141.29(I)(1)(c)	15.05(A)
4141.29(I)(1)(e)	12.09(F), 15.05(A)
4141.29(I)(2)	15.05(B)
4141.291	15.08(A)
4141.291(A)(2)	15.08(A)
4141.30(B)	15.03
4141.30(B)(3)	15.02(C)
4141.30(E)	15.03
Ch 4167	16.09(A), 16.09(C), 16.09(D), 16.09(E)
4167.01(A)	16.09(A)
4167.01(B)	16.09(A)
4167.01(D)	16.09(A)
4167.01(E)	16.09(A)
4167.01(F)	16.09(A)
4167.02	16.09(A)
4167.04	16.09(A)
4167.05	16.09(A)
4167.06	16.09(B)
4167.06(A)	16.09(B)
4167.06(B)	16.09(A), 16.09(B)
4167.07	16.09(A)
4167.07(C)	16.09(A)
4167.08	16.09(A)
4167.09	16.09(A)
4167.09(A)	16.09(A)
4167.09(C)	16.09(A)
4167.10	16.09(A), 16.09(B)
4167.10(B)	16.09(A)
4167.10(B)(1)	16.09(A)
4167.10(B)(2)	16.09(A)
4167.10(D) to 4167.10(H)	16.09(A)
4167.10(H)	16.09(A)
4167.11	16.09(D)
4167.12	16.09(D)
4167.13	16.09(C)
4167.14	16.09(A)
4167.15	16.09(A)
4167.16	16.09(A)
4167.17	16.09(A)
4167.19	16.09(A)
4301.01	24.15(A)
4301.22	24.15(A)
4301.63	24.15(A)
4301.631	24.15(A)
4301.632	24.15(A)
4301.633	24.15(A)

RC	Text Section(s)	RC	Text Section(s)
4301.634	24.15(A)	5123.351	29.09(A)
4301.639	24.15(A)	5123.62(T)	29.19
4301.69	24.15(A)	5123.89	29.19
4503.07	22.11	Ch 5126	29.04(A), 29.19
4507.061	20.10	5126.01 et seq.	29.01(A)
4508.03	26.14	5126.01(B)	29.01(B)
4511.01 et seq.	48.08(B)	5126.01(B)(1) to	
4511.01(AA)	21.11(B)	5126.01(B)(5)	29.01(B)
4511.01(F)	22.11	5126.01(E)	29.01(B)
4511.10	21.11(B)	5126.011	29.04(A)
4511.11	21.11(B)	5126.02	29.02(A), 29.02(B),
4511.19	24.09(D)		29.02(D)
4511.21	21.11(C)	5126.03	22.05, 29.02(C), 29.07
4511.75	22.17(A)	5126.03(A) to	
4511.75(A)	22.18(B), 22.27	5126.03(D)	29.02(E)
4511.75(C)	22.18(B)	5126.03(D)	29.02(C)
4511.75(D)	22.18(A)	5126.031	29.04(D)
4511.75(E)	22.18(A)	5126.032	29.04(E), 29.19
4511.751	22.18(B)	5126.033	29.04(E), 29.19
4511.76	22.10, 22.25(B)	5126.04	29.02(C), 29.02(E), 29.03
4511.761	22.11	5126.041	29.04(I)
4511.762	22.11	5126.05	29.04(A), 29.07, 29.08(A),
4511.763	22.01		29.09(A), 29.13(B)
4511.764	22.11	5126.05(B)	29.04(A)
4511.77	22.11	5126.05(C)	29.10(A)
4511.771	22.11, 22.17(A)	5126.051	29.04(A)
4511.772	22.11, 48.08(B)	5126.052	29.04(A)
4511.78	22.26	5126.053	29.04(C)
4511.99	22.27	5126.054	29.04(C)
4511.99(C)	22.27	5126.06	29.10(B)
4511.99(E)	22.27	5126.061	22.21, 29.06(B)
4511.99(G)	22.27	5126.07	29.15
4513.182	22.12	5126.08	29.05
4513.241	22.11	5126.09	29.04(A), 29.06(B), 29.16
4513.263	48.08(B)	5126.11	29.09(B)
4701.19	44.02	5126.11(B)	29.09(B)
4732.01	28.07	5126.12	29.09(A)
4733.17	37.01(B), 37.03(A), 37.09	5126.13	29.04(F)
4745.01	48.34(A)	5126.14	29.06(A)
5103.06	23.02(A)	5126.15	29.04(A)
5103.15	23.02(A)	5126.20	29.11, 29.12, 29.13(B),
5103.16	23.02(A)		29.13(C)
Ch 5104	5.09(L), 27.07	5126.20(B)	29.11
5104.01	22.11	5126.20(C)	29.11
5104.011	27.07	5126.20(F)	29.11
5104.02	26.11(D)	5126.20(G)	29.11
5104.02(B)(6)	26.11(D)	5126.21	29.12
5104.02(B)(7)	26.11(D)	5126.21(A)	29.12
5104.05	26.11(D)	5126.21(C)	29.12
Ch 5107	35.02(A)	5126.21(E)	29.12
Ch 5111	5.09(M)	5126.21(F)	29.12
Ch 5115	35.02(A)	5126.21(G)	29.12
Ch 5123	23.02(D)	5126.22	29.11
5123.011	29.01(B)	5126.22(A)	29.11
5123.043	29.04(I)	5126.22(B)	29.11
5123.171	29.04(A)	5126.22(C)	29.11
5123.19	29.02(B)	5126.22(D)	29.11
5123.20	29.02(B)	5126.22(E)	29.11

RC	Text Section(s)	RC	Text Section(s)
5126.22(F)	29.11	5705.14(E)	43.15(C), 43.16, 43.21
5126.23	29.10(A), 29.12	5705.14(H)	29.09(A)
5126.23(B)	29.12	5705.15	4.14(B), 43.15(C)
5126.23(C) to		5705.16	43.15(C)
5126.23(G)	29.10(A), 29.12	5705.19	30.14, 34.16(B)
5126.23(H)	29.10(A), 29.12	5705.19(D)	34.16(B)
5126.24	29.13(A)	5705.19(L)	29.04(H), 29.09(A)
5126.25	29.11	5705.192	40.12
5126.25(D)	29.11	5705.192(A)	40.12
5126.26	29.10(B), 29.11	5705.192(A)(2)	40.12
5126.27	29.11	5705.192(J)	40.12
5126.27(B)	29.11	5705.194	4.03(G), 30.14, 40.10,
5126.28	29.14		40.10(B), 40.11, 40.13,
5126.28(E)	29.11		40.15(D), 41.01, 41.22(A),
5126.281	29.14		41.22(B), 41.23(C)
5126.29	29.13(E)	5705.195	40.10(B)
5126.38	29.19	5705.196	40.10(B)
5126.40	29.04(A)	5705.197	40.10(B)
5126.41 to 5126.47	29.04(A)	5705.194 to	
5126.49	29.04(G)	5705.196	40.13
5126.51 to 5126.62	29.04(G)	5705.21	4.03(G), 30.13, 34.16(B),
5126.51(B)	29.04(G)		37.07(B), 40.10, 40.10(A),
5126.51(D)	29.04(G)		40.13, 40.15(D), 41.01,
5126.52	29.04(G)		41.22(A), 41.23(C), 43.21
5126.53	29.04(G)	5705.21(C)(1)	41.22(B)
5126.54	29.04(G)	5705.21(C)(2)	41.22(B)
5126.55	29.04(G)	5705.21(C)(3)	41.22(B)
5126.56	29.04(G), 29.19	5705.212	40.10(C)
5126.57	29.04(G)	5705.213	40.10(C)
5126.58	29.04(G)	5705.215	6.02(A), 40.10(D)
5126.59	29.04(G)	5705.215(E)	40.10(D)
5126.60	29.04(G)	5705.216	41.22(B)
5126.61	29.04(G)	5705.222	29.09(A)
5126.62	29.04(G)	5705.25	40.10(A), 40.11, 40.13
5126.99	29.19	5705.251	40.10(C)
5153.21 et seq.	23.02(A)	5705.27	40.05(A), 40.05(B)
Ch 5705	23.03(C), 37.07(B), 41.01	5705.28	34.04(B), 34.13, 34.14,
5705.01	30.14, 43.15(A), 43.15(B),		40.01, 40.03
	43.28	5705.29	40.04(A), 40.05(B),
5705.01(A)	36.11(B)		40.15(D), 41.15
5705.01(C)	36.11(B), 39.02	5705.29(A)(1)	40.04(B)
5705.01(D)	39.02	5705.29(E)(1)	40.04(B)
5705.02	39.03, 41.05(B)	5705.29(E)(2)	40.04(B)
5705.03	43.19	5705.29(E)(4)	40.04(B)
5705.04	40.08	5705.30	40.03
5705.05	39.01(A), 40.09(A), 43.17	5705.31	39.03, 40.03, 40.05(A),
5705.06	34.16(A), 40.09(B)		40.05(B)
5705.08	46.07	5705.31(D)	39.03
5705.09	43.15(A), 43.15(B), 43.18,	5705.32	34.14, 40.05(A), 40.05(B),
	43.19, 43.21		40.14
5705.091	29.09(A)	5705.32(A)	40.05(B)
5705.10	29.09(A), 36.14, 41.17(E),	5705.341	40.05(B), 40.05(C), 40.07
	42.22, 43.15(C), 43.16,	5705.35	40.05(B), 40.15(A),
	43.17, 43.18, 43.19, 43.21		40.15(D)
5705.12	43.13, 43.15(A), 43.15(B),	5705.35(B)(1)	40.04(C)
	43.21	5705.36	6.07(C), 40.15(A), 40.19,
5705.14	4.14(B), 43.15(C), 43.18,		43.06
	43.19	5705.36(B)	40.15(B)

RC	Text Section(s)
5705.37	40.06
5705.38	40.15(B), 40.15(C)
5705.39	40.15(D), 40.19
5705.391	40.17
5705.40	40.16
5705.41	6.07(C), 18.20, 36.04(C), 37.07(A), 43.07(A), 43.07(B)
5705.41(D)(1)	6.07(C), 23.03(C), 43.07(B)
5705.412	6.07(C), 23.03(C), 37.07(A), 39.07(C), 40.16, 40.18(B), 43.06, 43.07(A), 43.07(B)
5709.04	48.32
5709.07	48.33
5709.12	48.33
5709.121	48.33
5709.121(B)	48.33
5709.40	39.04
5709.41	39.04
5709.62	39.04
5709.63	39.04
5709.73	39.04
5709.78	39.04
5709.82	39.04
5709.83	39.04
5715.19	39.04
5715.19(A)	39.04
5715.19(B)	39.04
5715.27	39.04
5715.271	39.04
5717.01	39.04
5719.042	37.06(B)
5727.231	39.04
5731.48(B)	39.11
Ch 5739	35.02(E)
5739.02	35.02(E), 35.04(A), 48.33
5739.17	27.05
Ch 5748	41.01
5748.02	39.12
5748.02(A)	39.12
5748.02(B)	39.12
5748.02(B)(2)	39.12
5748.02(D)	39.12
5748.03	23.02(D), 39.12
5748.04	39.12
5748.05	39.12, 41.01
5748.06	39.12
5903.01(A)	10.21(A)
5903.02	10.21(A)
5903.03	10.21(A)
5903.05	10.21(A)
5923.05	10.21(A), 18.20
5923.05(D)	18.20
5923.05(F)	10.21(A)

OAC	Text Section(s)
124-9-08	12.15(A)
1301:7-5-09	21.13
Ch 3301-3	43.29
3301-5-01	6.02(B)
3301-11-01 et seq.	31.02
3301-12-01 et seq.	3.03(G)
3301-13-01 et seq.	3.03(G), 26.06(B)
3301-15-01 et seq.	3.03(D)
3301-21-10 et seq.	8.04(F)
Ch 3301-23	8.01, 8.03(B), 8.05, 8.06
3301-23-19	7.03(A), 7.03(B)
3301-23-22	7.03(A), 7.03(B)
3301-23-22(A)	7.03(B)
3301-23-22(B)(2)	7.03(B)
3301-23-22(C)	7.03(B)
3301-23-23	8.07(D)
3301-23-30	8.04(F)
3301-23-31 et seq.	8.04(F)
3301-27-01	12.10(C), 12.10(D)
3301-27-01(A)	30.05
3301-27-01(B)	9.14(C), 30.05
3301-27-02	9.14(C), 30.05
Ch 3301-31	28.01(A)
3301-34-01 et seq.	20.03(C)
3301-34-03	20.03(C)
3301-34-03(A)	20.03(C)
3301-35-01 et seq.	32.02, 48.03(A)
3301-35-01 to 3301-35-03	26.07(B), 26.10(D)
3301-35-01(I)	30.03, 30.10(B), 30.10(D)
3301-35-02	26.02(A), 26.04, 30.10(B)
3301-35-02(A)(4)	26.03
3301-35-02(B)	26.02(A), 26.06(A), 26.17
3301-35-02(B)(1)	26.15(A), 26.17
3301-35-02(B)(2)(b)	26.03
3301-35-02(B)(4)	26.15(A)
3301-35-02(B)(5)	26.05(C), 26.15(A)
3301-35-02(B)(6)	26.06(B)
3301-35-02(B)(6)(a)	26.03
3301-35-02(B)(6)(d)	30.02
3301-35-02(B)(8)	26.06(B)
3301-35-02(B)(8)(a)	30.02
3301-35-02(B)(8)(e)	26.05(C)
3301-35-02(B)(10)	26.05(A), 30.02
3301-35-02(B)(11)	26.05(B)
3301-35-02(B)(11)(b)	30.02
3301-35-02(B)(12)	26.05(C), 30.03
3301-35-02(B)(12)(b)	30.02
3301-35-02(B)(13)	26.06(A), 30.03
3301-35-02(C)	26.05(C), 26.07(A)
3301-35-03	26.02(B), 30.02
3301-35-03(A)(3)	26.03
3301-35-03(A)(4)	30.05
3301-35-03(B)	33.03(C)
3301-35-03(K)	26.17

OAC	Text Section(s)
3301-35-04	30.02, 30.10(B)
3301-35-04(A)	30.02
3301-35-05	26.07(B)
3301-35-05(A)(3)	26.07(B)
3301-35-05(D)	26.10(D)
3301-35-08	20.03(A)
3301-35-08(H)	48.06(A), 48.08(A)
3301-39-01 et seq.	48.09(A)
3301-39-01	48.08(A)
3301-43-01 et seq.	26.10(D), 26.10(E)
3301-44-01 et seq.	26.07(C)
3301-47-01	20.09(A)
3301-48-01	5.08(C)
3301-48-02	5.08(D)
3301-49-01	26.16(B)
Ch 3301-51	28.01(A), 28.14(A)
3301-51-01(G)(3)	28.11(C)
3301-51-02	28.11(A), 28.11(B)
3301-51-02(G)(7)(a)	28.11(C)
3301-51-02(G)(10)(i)	28.11(F)
3301-51-02(G)(12)	28.11(F)
3301-51-15	26.09
3301-51-15(B)	26.09
3301-51-15(C)	26.09
3301-51-15(D)	26.09
3301-51-15(E)	26.09
3301-51-20	28.19(B)
3301-51-20(B)	28.19(B)
3301-61-03	27.03
3301-61-06	27.02
3301-61-13	27.04
3301-81-01	26.12(B), 26.13(B)
3301-81-01(C)	26.13(A)
3301-81-02	26.12(B)
3301-81-03	26.12(B)
3301-81-04	26.12(B)
3301-81-06	26.13(A)
3301-81-07	26.13(C)
3301-81-08	26.13(A)
3301-81-12	26.13(D)
3301-83-01	22.07(A), 22.07(B)
3301-83-01(E)(3)	22.07(B)
3301-83-01(G)	22.07(B)
3301-83-05(C)	22.02
3301-83-06	22.13(A)
3301-83-06(A)	22.02
3301-83-07	17.13(A), 22.13(A), 22.14
3301-83-08	22.17(B), 22.17(C)
3301-83-08(D)(3)	25.07
3301-83-09(A)	22.19
3301-83-09(C)	22.19
3301-83-10	22.15
3301-83-10(A)(2)	22.15
3301-83-11	22.17(A), 22.22
3301-83-11(B)	22.15
3301-83-11(B)(2)	22.17(A)
3301-83-12(B)	22.18(A)

OAC	Text Section(s)
3301-83-12(D)	22.18(A)
3301-83-13	22.16
3301-83-14(G)	22.18(C)
3301-83-15(B)	22.20
3301-83-16	22.22
3301-83-20(C)	22.17(A)
3301-85-01	22.07(C), 22.09, 22.10
Ch 3301-87	22.10
3301-89-01 et seq.	4.07(A), 4.11(A)
3304-1-01	27.13(B)
3307-1-08	11.12(A)
3307-1-22	11.20
3307-1-28	11.13(D)
3309-1-02	14.05
3309-1-12(D)	14.09
3309-1-28	14.10(A)
3309-1-29	14.10(A)
3309-1-39	14.10(A)
3309-1-43	14.13
3701-15-02	21.03(C)
4101:2	37.03(B)
Ch 4101:2-11	28.17(B)
Ch 4101:9-4	37.11
4112-3-09	17.04(C)
4112-5-03	17.07(B)
4112-5-04	17.17
4112-5-05	10.20(B)
4112-5-05(G)(2)	17.09(A)
4112-5-08	17.13(A)
4117-1-01 et seq.	18.02
4117-1-15(B)	17.20
4117-1-17(B)	17.20
4117-3-01	18.16(A), 18.16(B)
4117-3-02	18.16(B)
4117-5-01(A)	18.15(A)
4117-5-01(B)	18.15(A)
4117-5-01(C)	18.15(A), 18.17(B)
4117-5-01(D)	18.18
4117-5-01(D)(2)	18.18
4117-5-01(E)	18.11(B)
4117-5-01(F)	18.11(B)
4117-05-01(G)	18.11(B)
4117-5-02(A)(6)	18.15(A)
4117-5-02(C)	18.18
4117-5-02(D)	18.11(B)
4117-5-02(D)(4)	18.11(B)
4117-5-03	18.15(B)
4117-5-03(C)	18.15(B)
4117-5-04	18.15(A)
4117-5-05	18.15(A)
4117-5-05(C)	18.15(C)
4117-5-05(D)	18.15(A), 18.15(C)
4117-5-06(D)	18.15(D)
4117-5-06(E)	18.15(D)
4117-5-08(F)	18.15(D)
4117-5-09(A)	18.15(C), 18.18
4117-5-09(B)	18.15(C)
4117-5-10(A)	18.15(D)

OAC	Text Section(s)
4117-5-10(B)	18.15(D)
4117-5-11(C)	18.17(A)
4117-7-01	18.26(A)
4117-7-02	18.26(A)
4117-7-03 to 4117-7-05	18.26(A)
4117-9-02(A)	18.29(B)
4117-9-02(B)	18.29(B)
4117-9-02(E)	18.29(B)
4117-9-02(F)	18.29(B)
4117-9-03	18.29(B)
4117-9-04	18.29(C)
4117-9-05	18.29(C)
4117-9-05(A)	18.29(C)
4117-9-05(B)	18.29(C)
4117-9-05(C)	18.29(C)
4117-9-05(D)	18.29(C)
4117-9-05(E)	18.29(C)
4117-9-05(F) to 4117-9-05(O)	18.29(C)
4117-9-05(M)	18.29(C)
4117-9-05(N)	18.29(C)
4117-9-05(P)	18.29(C)
4117-11-01	18.21(B)
4117-11-02	18.21(B)
4117-13-01	18.30
4117-13-01(B)	18.31
4117-13-02	18.31
4117-13-03	18.31
4117-13-05	18.31
4117-13-06	18.32
4117-13-07	18.32
4117-15-02(C)	18.18
4121:1	16.05(H)
4501-1-03	22.26
4501-3-03(A)	22.13(A)
4501-3-03(B)	22.14
4501-3-04(A)	22.13(A)
4501-3-04(B)	22.13(A)
4501-3-04(B)(2)	22.18(A)
4501-3-05	22.17(A)
4501-3-05(B)	22.17(A)
4501-3-05(F)	22.16, 22.18(A)
4501-3-05(G)	22.16
4501-3-05(H)	22.16
4501-3-06	22.18(A)
4501-3-06(G)	22.18(A)
4501-3-08 to 4501-3-15	22.18(A)
4501-3-09	22.18(A)
4501-3-15	22.18(A)
Ch 4501-5	22.10
5123:2	29.05
5123:2-5-03	29.10(A)
5123:2-17-02	24.05(A)

US Const	Text Section(s)
Am 1	1.09, 9.21(E), 48.01(A)
Am 14	2.16(B), 21.01, 30.09(B), 45.13

USCA	Text Section(s)
8 USCA 1324a	48.20
8 USCA 1324b	48.20
15 USCA 2641 et seq.	21.10(B)
17 USCA 101	33.06(C)
17 USCA 102	33.06(A)
17 USCA 106	33.06(A)
17 USCA 107	33.06(B)
17 USCA 108	33.06(A)
17 USCA 117	33.06(A)
17 USCA 201(a)	33.06(C)
17 USCA 201(b)	33.06(C)
17 USCA 501	33.06(A)
17 USCA 504	33.06(A)
17 USCA 505	33.06(A)
17 USCA 506	33.06(A)
18 USCA 921	25.10(A)
18 USCA 921(a)(3)	28.09(D)
18 USCA 922(q)	25.10(A)
20 USCA 1232g	2.13, 3.03(F), 44.01, 44.02, 44.14(A), 48.14
20 USCA 1232g(a)(1)(A)	44.18
20 USCA 1232g(a)(2)	44.19(A)
20 USCA 1232g(a)(5)(A)	44.14(B)
20 USCA 1232g(a)(5)(B)	44.14(B)
20 USCA 1232g(b)	44.15(A)
20 USCA 1232g(b)(1)	44.23
20 USCA 1232g(b)(1)(A)	44.15(A)
20 USCA 1232g(b)(1)(B)	44.15(B)
20 USCA 1232g(b)(1)(C)	44.15(B)
20 USCA 1232g(b)(1)(D)	44.15(B)
20 USCA 1232g(b)(1)(E)	44.15(B)
20 USCA 1232g(b)(1)(I)	44.15(B)
20 USCA 1232g(b)(2)	44.14(B)
20 USCA 1232g(b)(2)(B)	44.14(C)
20 USCA 1232g(b)(3)	44.15(B)

USCA	Text Section(s)
20 USCA 1232g(b)(4)(A)	44.14(C), 44.17
20 USCA 1232g(d)	44.18
20 USCA 1232g(g)	44.14(A)
20 USCA 1232h	26.20
20 USCA 1400 et seq.	28.01(A)
20 USCA 1401	28.01(B)
20 USCA 1401(a)(16)	28.06
20 USCA 1401(a)(17)	28.07
20 USCA 1401(a)(18)	28.03
20 USCA 1401(a)(19)	28.02
20 USCA 1401(a)(20)	28.02, 28.03
20 USCA 1401(a)(1)	28.01(B)
20 USCA 1401(a)(18)	28.13(A)
20 USCA 1403	28.13(A)
20 USCA 1412	28.01(A)
20 USCA 1412(1)	28.03, 28.15(C)
20 USCA 1412(2)(B)	28.15(C)
20 USCA 1412(2)(C)	28.15(C)
20 USCA 1412(5)	28.05(A), 28.05(B)
20 USCA 1415	28.09(A), 28.09(C), 28.11(A), 28.11(C), 28.12(B), 28.13(A), 28.13(D)
20 USCA 1415(e)(2)	28.12(A)
20 USCA 1415(e)(3)	28.09(A), 28.11(F), 28.13(A)
20 USCA 1415(e)(4)(C)	28.13(D)
20 USCA 1415(e)(4)(D)	28.13(D)
20 USCA 1415(e)(4)(F)	28.13(D)
20 USCA 1415(f)	28.12(A)
20 USCA 1416	28.11(A)
20 USCA 1471 et seq.	28.01(A)
20 USCA 1681 et seq.	2.13, 19.13(B), 19.14(A)
20 USCA 1681(a)	19.14(A)
20 USCA 1681(b)	19.14(A)
20 USCA 1701 et seq.	19.11
20 USCA 1703	19.11(B)
20 USCA 1703(b)	19.11(B)
20 USCA 1703(c)	19.11(B)
20 USCA 1703(d)	19.11(B)

USCA	Text Section(s)
20 USCA 1703(e)	19.11(B)
20 USCA 1703(f)	19.15
20 USCA 1704	19.11(B)
20 USCA 1705	19.11(B)
20 USCA 1706	19.11(B)
20 USCA 1709	19.11(B)
20 USCA 1713	19.11(B)
20 USCA 1714	19.11(B)
20 USCA 1715	19.11(B)
20 USCA 1716	19.11(B)
20 USCA 1718	19.11(B)
20 USCA 1755	19.11(B)
20 USCA 1757	19.11(B)
20 USCA 1758	19.11(B)
20 USCA 3171 et seq.	21.15(A)
20 USCA 3221 et seq.	19.15
20 USCA 3224a	21.15(A)
20 USCA 3351	25.10(A)
20 USCA 3411	2.11(A)
20 USCA 4071 to 20 USCA 4074	32.06(A), 38.08(B)
20 USCA 4071(a)	32.06(A)
20 USCA 5801 et seq.	2.11(B)
20 USCA 6061	32.05
20 USCA 6081 et seq.	38.14
20 USCA 6083	38.14
20 USCA 6084	38.14
20 USCA 6301 to 20 USCA 6514	48.06(D)
20 USCA 6321	48.06(D)
20 USCA 8900	32.05
20 USCA 8921	28.09(D)
21 USCA 860	24.14
26 USCA 149(a)	41.19(A)
26 USCA 265(B)	41.19(D)
26 USCA 501(c)(3)	48.31
26 USCA 511 et seq.	48.32
26 USCA 3102	10.08(A)
26 USCA 3402	10.08(A)
29 USCA 151 et seq.	48.28(A)
29 USCA 201	20.11(B)
29 USCA 203(e)	13.02(A)
29 USCA 206	13.01(B), 48.22
29 USCA 206(d)	17.08(A)
29 USCA 207	48.22
29 USCA 207(o)	13.02(B)
29 USCA 207(p)(2)	13.02(A)
29 USCA 207(p)(3)	13.02(B)
29 USCA 216	17.08(B)
29 USCA 294a	17.13(B)
29 USCA 621 et seq.	17.06(A)

USCA	Text Section(s)
29 USCA 623	11.18(B), 17.06(C)
29 USCA 623(a)	17.06(A)
29 USCA 623(f)(1)	17.06(B)
29 USCA 626	17.06(A)
29 USCA 626(b)	17.06(A)
29 USCA 626(d)	17.06(A)
29 USCA 626(e)	17.06(A)
29 USCA 626(f)	17.19
29 USCA 627	17.17
29 USCA 630(b)	17.06(A)
29 USCA 631(a)	17.06(A)
29 USCA 633(b)	17.06(A)
29 USCA 651 et seq.	16.09(A)
29 USCA 701	27.13(B)
29 USCA 706(8)	28.02
29 USCA 706(8)(B)	17.13(A)
29 USCA 706(8)(C)	17.13(A)
29 USCA 791 to 29 USCA 794	17.13(A)
29 USCA 793	17.13(A)
29 USCA 794	17.13(A), 19.13(C), 28.01(A)
29 USCA 794a	19.13(C)
29 USCA 1001 et seq.	48.22
29 USCA 2118	17.16
29 USCA 2601 et seq.	17.16
29 USCA 2611	17.16, 48.30
29 USCA 2612	17.16
29 USCA 2612(e)(1)	17.16
29 USCA 2613	17.16
29 USCA 2614	17.16
29 USCA 2615	17.16
29 USCA 2616	17.16
29 USCA 2617	17.16
29 USCA 2618	17.16
29 USCA 2619	17.16, 17.17
38 USCA 2021 et seq.	10.21(A)
41 USCA 701 et seq.	21.15(B)
42 USCA 290dd-2	21.15(C)
42 USCA 290dd-2(f)	21.15(C)
42 USCA 300bb-1(a)	10.12(A)
42 USCA 300bb-1(b)(1)	10.12(A)
42 USCA 300bb-2(1)	10.12(A)
42 USCA 300bb-2(2)	10.12(A)
42 USCA 300bb-2(2)(A)(ii)	10.12(A)
42 USCA 300bb-2(2)(B)	10.12(A)
42 USCA 300bb-2(2)(C)	10.12(A)
42 USCA 300bb-2(2)(E)	10.12(A)
42 USCA 300bb-2(3)	10.12(A)
42 USCA 300bb-2(5)	10.12(A)
42 USCA 300bb-3	10.12(A)
42 USCA 300bb-5	10.12(A)
42 USCA 300bb-6(1)	10.12(A)
42 USCA 300bb-6(2)	10.12(A)
42 USCA 300bb-6(3)	10.12(A)
42 USCA 300bb-6(4)	10.12(A)
42 USCA 300bb-7	10.12(A)
42 USCA 1751 et seq.	35.07
42 USCA 1771 et seq.	35.07
42 USCA 1981	17.02(A), 17.03(E), 17.12, 48.09(A)
42 USCA 1981a	17.03(E), 17.13(B)
42 USCA 1983	2.16(B), 17.09(C), 25.09(C), 28.13(A), 44.14(A), 45.13, 46.13(A), 46.15(A), 46.16
42 USCA 1988	17.02(B), 32.01, 46.16
42 USCA 2000a et seq.	19.11
42 USCA 2000c(b)	19.11(A)
42 USCA 2000c-6	19.11(A)
42 USCA 2000d et seq.	19.13
42 USCA 2000d to 42 USCA 2000d-4	2.13
42 USCA 2000d	19.13(A), 19.15
42 USCA 2000d-1	19.13(A)
42 USCA 2000e et seq.	17.03
42 USCA 2000e-1	17.09(A), 48.30
42 USCA 2000e-2	17.03(A), 48.30
42 USCA 2000e-2(a)	10.20(B)
42 USCA 2000e-2(e)(1)	17.03(B)
42 USCA 2000e-2(e)(2)	17.03(B)
42 USCA 2000e-2(g)	17.03(F)
42 USCA 2000e-2(h)	17.03(B), 17.08(C)

USCA	Text Section(s)
42 USCA 2000e-2(k)	17.03(F), 17.09(A)
42 USCA 2000e-2(l)	17.07(A)
42 USCA 2000e-2(m)	17.03(F)
42 USCA 2000e-2(n)	17.18
42 USCA 2000e-3	17.03(A)
42 USCA 2000e-5	17.03(D)
42 USCA 2000e-5(c)	17.03(D)
42 USCA 2000e-5(d)	17.03(D)
42 USCA 2000e-5(e)	17.03(D)
42 USCA 2000e-5(g)	17.03(E)
42 USCA 2000e-5(k)	17.03(E)
42 USCA 2000e-6	17.03(E)
42 USCA 2000e-10	17.17
42 USCA 2000e-12(b)	17.18
42 USCA 2000bb et seq.	32.01
42 USCA 2000bb-1	32.01
42 USCA 2000bb-3	32.01
42 USCA 6101 et seq.	2.13, 19.13(D)
42 USCA 12101 et seq.	17.13(B), 48.29
42 USCA 12101	48.30
42 USCA 12102(1)	17.13(B)
42 USCA 12102(2)	17.13(B)
42 USCA 12111(2)	17.13(B)
42 USCA 12111(5)	17.13(B)
42 USCA 12111(7)	17.13(B)
42 USCA 12111(8)	17.13(B)
42 USCA 12111(9)	17.13(B)
42 USCA 12111(10)	17.13(B)
42 USCA 12112	17.13(B)
42 USCA 12112(b)(6)	17.13(B)
42 USCA 12112(d)(2)	17.13(B)
42 USCA 12112(d)(3)	17.13(B)
42 USCA 12112(d)(4)	17.13(B)
42 USCA 12113(a)	17.13(B)
42 USCA 12113(b)	17.13(B)
42 USCA 12113(c)	48.30
42 USCA 12113(d)	17.13(B)
42 USCA 12114	17.13(B)
42 USCA 12114(b)	17.13(B)
42 USCA 12114(c)	17.13(B)
42 USCA 12114(d)	17.13(B)
42 USCA 12115	17.17

USCA	Text Section(s)
42 USCA 12117(a)	17.13(B)
42 USCA 12131(1)	17.13(B)
42 USCA 12131(2)	17.13(B)
42 USCA 12132	17.13(B)
42 USCA 12133	17.13(B)
42 USCA 12141	17.13(B)
42 USCA 12181	48.29
42 USCA 12182	48.29
42 USCA 12187	48.29
42 USCA 12203	17.13(B)
42 USCA 12205	17.13(B)
42 USCA 12210	17.13(B)
42 USCA 12211	17.13(B)
49 USCA 2717	22.13(B)
49 USCA 30101 et seq.	48.08(B)

IRC	Text Section(s)
265(b)(3)	41.16(B), 41.16(E), 41.19(D)
403(b)	11.23
415	11.19(B), 14.12

CFR	Text Section(s)
8 CFR Part 274	48.20
29 CFR Part 520	27.06
29 CFR 553	13.02(B)
29 CFR 553.31	13.02(B)
29 CFR 825.114	17.16
29 CFR 825.208	17.16
29 CFR 825.400 to 29 CFR 825.404	17.16
29 CFR 825.500	17.16
29 CFR 825.702	17.16
29 CFR 825.800	17.16
29 CFR 1602.40	17.17
29 CFR 1602.41	17.17
29 CFR 1604.10	10.20(B), 17.09(B)
29 CFR 1604.10(b)	17.09(B)
29 CFR 1604.10(c)	17.09(B)
29 CFR 1604.11(a)	17.11
29 CFR 1604.11(e)	17.11
29 CFR 1604.11(f)	17.11
29 CFR Part 1607	17.07(B)
29 CFR 1608.4(b)	17.18
29 CFR 1608.4(c)	17.18
29 CFR 1608.4(c)(1)	17.18
34 CFR Part 85	21.15(B)
34 CFR 85.605	21.15(B)
34 CFR Part 86	21.15(A)
34 CFR 86.200(a)	21.15(A)
34 CFR 86.200(b)	21.15(A)
34 CFR 86.200(c)	21.15(A)
34 CFR 86.200(d)	21.15(A)
34 CFR 86.200(e)	21.15(A)
34 CFR 86.200(f)	21.15(A)
34 CFR 86.200(g)	21.15(A)

CFR	Text Section(s)
34 CFR 86.200(h)	21.15(A)
34 CFR 86.201(a)	21.15(A)
34 CFR 86.201(b)	21.15(A)
34 CFR 86.201(c)	21.15(A)
34 CFR 86.201(d)	21.15(A)
34 CFR 86.201(e)	21.15(A)
34 CFR 86.201(f)	21.15(A)
34 CFR 86.300	21.15(A)
34 CFR 86.301	21.15(A)
34 CFR 86.411	21.15(A)
34 CFR Part 98	26.20
34 CFR 98.7	26.20
34 CFR 98.10	26.20
34 CFR Part 99	44.14(A), 48.14
34 CFR 99.3	44.14(B)
34 CFR 99.4	44.18
34 CFR 99.6	44.15(A)
34 CFR 99.6(a)	44.21
34 CFR 99.6(a)(2)	44.21
34 CFR 99.6(a)(3)	44.21
34 CFR 99.6(a)(4)	44.21
34 CFR 99.6(a)(5)	44.21
34 CFR 99.6(a)(6)	44.21
34 CFR 99.6(a)(7)	44.21
34 CFR 99.6(b)	44.21
34 CFR 99.7(a)	44.20, 44.21
34 CFR 99.7(d)	44.20
34 CFR 99.10(a)	44.18
34 CFR 99.10(b)	44.18
34 CFR 99.10(c)	44.18
34 CFR 99.10(e)	44.18
34 CFR 99.20(a)	44.19(A)
34 CFR 99.20(b)	44.19(A)
34 CFR 99.20(c)	44.19(A)
34 CFR 99.21(b)(1)	44.19(B)
34 CFR 99.21(b)(2)	44.19(B)
34 CFR 99.21(c)	44.19(B)
34 CFR 99.22(b)	44.19(B)
34 CFR 99.22(c)	44.19(B)
34 CFR 99.22(d)	44.19(B)
34 CFR 99.22(e)	44.19(B)
34 CFR 99.22(f)	44.19(B)
34 CFR 99.30(a)	44.14(C)
34 CFR 99.31(a)(3)	44.15(B)
34 CFR 99.31(a)(4)	44.15(B)
34 CFR 99.31(a)(5) to 34 CFR 99.31(a)(7)	44.15(B)
34 CFR 99.31(a)(5)	44.15(B)
34 CFR 99.32	44.17
34 CFR 99.32(a)(2)	44.17
34 CFR 99.32(d)	44.17
34 CFR 99.33	44.14(C)
34 CFR 99.34	44.15(B)
34 CFR 99.37	44.14(B)
34 CFR 99.37(a)	44.14(B)
34 CFR 99.60 et seq.	44.14(A)

CFR	Text Section(s)
34 CFR 99.60 to 34 CFR 99.67	44.14(A)
34 CFR Part 100	19.13(A)
34 CFR 100.3	19.13(A)
34 CFR 104.22	28.17(B)
34 CFR 104.23	28.17(B)
34 CFR 106.31 to 34 CFR 106.42	19.14(A)
34 CFR 106.34	19.14(A)
34 CFR 106.36	19.14(A)
34 CFR 106.40	19.14(A)
34 CFR 106.41	19.14(A), 19.14(B), 30.08(B), 30.09(B)
34 CFR 106.41(a)	19.14(B)
34 CFR 106.41(b)	19.14(B)
34 CFR 106.41(c)	19.14(B)
34 CFR 106.51 et seq.	48.30
34 CFR 106.51 to 34 CFR 106.61	19.14(A)
34 CFR 106.71	19.13(B)
34 CFR Part 300	28.01(A)
34 CFR 300.1 et seq.	28.01(A)
34 CFR 300.128(a)(1)	28.02
34 CFR 300.220	28.02
34 CFR 300.306	28.03
34 CFR 300.344(a)(1) to 34 CFR 300.344(a)(3)	28.02
34 CFR 300.344(a)(1) to 34 CFR 300.344(a)(5)	28.09(A)
34 CFR 300.500 et seq.	28.11(A)
34 CFR 300.504(a)	28.02, 28.09(A)
34 CFR 300.505	28.09(A), 28.11(B)
34 CFR 300.508(a)(1)	28.11(C)
34 CFR 300.510	28.11(F)
34 CFR 300.512(a)	28.11(F)
34 CFR 300.512(b)	28.11(F)
34 CFR 300.533(a)(3)	28.09(A)
34 CFR 300.550 to 34 CFR 300.556	28.05(A)
34 CFR 330.552	28.05(A)
34 CFR 361.49	27.15
34 CFR Part 500	19.15
41 CFR 60.741	17.13(A)
42 CFR Part 2	21.15(C)
42 CFR 2.11	21.15(C)
42 CFR 2.12(c)	21.15(C)
42 CFR 2.13(a)	21.15(C)
42 CFR 2.31(a)	21.15(C)

CFR	Text Section(s)
42 CFR 2.51	21.15(C)
42 CFR 2.67	21.15(C)
45 CFR 84.1 to 45 CFR 84.14	17.13(A)
49 CFR 40.3	22.13(B)
49 CFR 40.21	22.13(B)
49 CFR 40.23	22.13(B)
49 CFR 40.25	22.13(B)
49 CFR 40.25(e)(1)	22.13(B)
49 CFR 40.25(f)	22.13(B)
49 CFR 40.27 to 49 CFR 40.31	22.13(B)
49 CFR 40.33	22.13(B)
49 CFR 40.51 to 49 CFR 40.53	22.13(B)
49 CFR 40.57	22.13(B)
49 CFR Part 382	22.13(B)

CFR	Text Section(s)
49 CFR 382.103	22.13(B)
49 CFR 382.115	22.13(B)
49 CFR 382.201	22.13(B)
49 CFR 382.204 to 49 CFR 382.211	22.13(B)
49 CFR 382.301 to 49 CFR 382.307	22.13(B)
49 CFR 382.309 to 49 CFR 382.311	22.13(B)
49 CFR 382.401 to 49 CFR 382.605	22.13(B)
49 CFR 382.411	22.13(B)
49 CFR 382.501	22.13(B)
49 CFR 382.503	22.13(B)
49 CFR 382.505	22.13(B)
49 CFR 382.605	22.13(B)
49 CFR 571.222	22.05

Appendix C
Calendar for School District Officials

General Notes

Unless marked *, each day or date shown is the prescribed last day for completing the action referred to.

As a general rule, if a particular deadline falls on a Sunday or legal holiday, or if a public office at which an act is required to be performed is closed for the entire deadline date, or closes early on that date, the deadline is the next succeeding day which is not a Sunday or legal holiday (RC 1.14). This general rule should not, however, be followed with regard to election deadlines.

If the date set for a holiday falls on a Sunday, the holiday is observed on the following Monday (RC 1.14).

This calendar encompasses only major provisions of Ohio law (and implementing regulations) in effect on December 1, 1995, relating generally, to dates particularly pertinent to boards and districts. It is intended as a general outline, and is not intended to cover all pertinent calendar items such as those calendar items of which notice is usually given by state agencies.

Various bond issue and tax levy election deadlines are identified with respect to the May special and November general elections. Generally the same time requirements apply to special elections on other dates. In addition to the November general election, special elections may be held only on the first Tuesday after the first Monday in February, May, and August (RC 3501.01(D)). In years of presidential primaries (including 1996), however, the primary election is held on the third Tuesday in March, and no elections are authorized in either February or May.

For ease of reference, these short-hand expressions are used:

board = board of education of city, exempted village, or local school district, and, in certain cases, of joint vocational school district.

service center = educational service center (formerly county school district)

State Board = State Board of Education.

State Department = State Department of Education.

State Superintendent = State Superintendent of Public Instruction.

treasurer = treasurer of local school board.

SEPTEMBER

1	State Board to approve or disapprove transfer of territory between districts (RC 3311.24).
First Monday	*Labor Day (RC 1.14). Board may dismiss school (RC 3313.63); holiday for nonteaching employees (RC 3319.087).
Within First Two Weeks of Beginning of School	Principal or teacher in charge of each public, private, or parochial school to file enrollment report with treasurer (RC 3321.12); updated first week of each month.
15	Teacher to file transcript of additional training with treasurer (RC 3317.14).

	Teacher who has completed special MR/DD training to file with fiscal officer of board evidence of completion to qualify for higher salary bracket under RC 3317.13 (RC 5126.24).
	Treasurer to make monthly salary reports and deposits to STRS and SERS (RC 3307.62, RC 3309.57).
28	Treasurer to file non-GAAP annual financial report with Auditor of State (RC 117.38).
	Treasurer to publish non-GAAP annual financial report (RC 117.38).
30	Board to provide emergency medical authorization forms to parents prior to October 1 (RC 3313.712).
	During September, names of all teachers to be certified to STRS (RC 3307.59), and of all nonteaching employees certified to SERS (RC 3309.54).

OCTOBER

First Regularly Scheduled Board Meeting	Board to give written notice not to reemploy treasurer not later than this meeting (RC 3313.22).
1	Last day on which temporary appropriation measure may remain in effect unless the date is extended for statutorily specified reasons (RC 5705.38).
	Board to adopt annual appropriation measure and related spending plan based on annual appropriation measure; copies of both to be filed with State Superintendent (RC 5705.38, RC 5705.391). Copy of appropriation measure to be filed with county auditor, followed by that officer's certification that appropriations do not exceed resources unless the date is extended for statutorily specified reasons (RC 5705.39).
Second Monday	*Columbus Day (RC 1.14). Board may dismiss school (RC 3313.63).
15	District superintendent to certify to State Board total average daily membership (ADM) in regular day classes for the first full school week in October (RC 3317.03).
	Report by school superintendent of each teacher on annual salary to State Superintendent (RC 3317.061).
	Board to file teacher salary schedule with State Superintendent (RC 3317.14).
	Board to file job classification and salary schedule of nonteaching employees with State Superintendent (RC 3317.12).
	Board to file summary of immunization records of initial entry pupils with State Director of Health (RC 3313.67(C)).
	County MR/DD to certify to director of MR/DD the total average daily membership (RC 5126.12).
	Superintendent of county MR/DD board to certify to State Board name of each teacher on annual salary in special education program under RC 3323.09 (RC 5126.24).
	Treasurer to make monthly salary reports and deposits to STRS and SERS (RC 3307.62, RC 3309.57).
31	Second settlement of general personal and classified property taxes (RC 319.49).

NOVEMBER

First Monday	Treasurer to certify to board the amount necessary to provide for the payment of final judgments against the board (RC 5705.08).

First Tuesday After First Monday	*General election day (RC 3501.01); or Special election day (RC 3501.01(D)). In odd-numbered years, election of board members (RC 3501.02).
11	*Veterans Day (RC 1.14, RC 5.23). Board may dismiss school (RC 3313.63).
15	Treasurer to make monthly salary reports and deposits to STRS and SERS (RC 3307.62, RC 3309.57).
Fourth Thursday	*Thanksgiving Day (RC 1.14). Board may dismiss school (RC 3313.63); holiday for nonteaching employees (RC 3319.087).
27	Treasurer to file GAAP annual financial report with Auditor of State (RC 117.38).
	Treasurer to publish GAAP annual financial report (RC 117.38).

DECEMBER

1	Departments and authorities participating in board's appropriations to file with board estimates of contemplated revenues and expenditures for ensuing fiscal year (RC 5705.28).
15	Treasurer to make monthly salary reports and deposits to STRS and SERS (RC 3307.62, RC 3309.57).
25	*Christmas Day (RC 1.14). Board may dismiss school (RC 3313.63); holiday for nonteaching employees (RC 3319.087).
31	*Terms of elected board members (RC 3313.09 and RC 3311.052) expire in applicable years.
	Treasurer to canvass board members to establish day of January organizational meeting (RC 3313.14).
	Deadline to request approval of Superintendent of Public Instruction to borrow moneys during first half of calendar year to be repaid from second-half taxes (RC 133.301).

JANUARY

	Annual organizational meeting of board some time during first fifteen days of January (RC 3313.14), and of service center board on a date in January set by that board (RC 3313.14).
1	*New Year's Day (RC 1.14). Board may dismiss school (RC 3313.63); holiday for nonteaching employees (RC 3319.087).
	Terms of newly elected board members (RC 3313.09 and RC 3311.052) begin. (RC 3313.07 contains special provisions for a city district with subdistricts.)
	Board with spending reserve in budget to certify by resolution to State Superintendent amount proposed to borrow from reserve (RC 133.301) to meet criteria of RC 3317.01.
15	Treasurer to make monthly salary reports and deposits to STRS and SERS (RC 3307.62, RC 3309.57).
	Treasurer to submit nonhandicapped tuition report to State Superintendent (RC 3313.64) (Form SF-14).
	Board to adopt tax budget for next fiscal year (RC 5705.28). Two copies to be on file with treasurer not less than 10 days before adoption. Public hearing to be held before adoption, with at least 10 days' published notice of hearing (RC 5705.30).
	If board wishes not to reemploy teacher on limited or extended limited contract, first evaluation must be conducted and completed not later than January 15 (RC 3319.111).

20	Tax budget, as adopted by board, to be submitted to county auditor in triplicate (RC 5705.30); deadline may be extended.
Third Monday	*Martin Luther King Day (RC 1.14). Board may dismiss school (RC 3313.63); holiday for nonteaching employees (RC 3319.087).
Third week	Evaluation of an administrator other than a superintendent must be completed and received by the employee at least 60 days before the March 31 deadline (RC 3319.02). Board to give written notice to an administrator other than the superintendent before it takes any action on the contract. The notice must advise the administrator of the date his contract ends and that he or she may request a meeting with the board (RC 3319.02).
25	If board wishes not to reemploy teacher on limited or extended limited contract, written report of first evaluation must be received by teacher not later than January 25 (RC 3319.111).

FEBRUARY

First Tuesday After First Monday	*Special election day, except in presidential primary election years (RC 3501.01). See schedule of required prior actions in connection with May and November elections.
10	*If board wishes not to reemploy teacher on limited or extended limited contract, one evaluation must be conducted and completed between February 10 and April 1 (RC 3319.111).
15	Superintendent of schools to certify to State Superintendent increase in total average daily membership (ADM) if count is at least 3% greater than October (RC 3317.03).
	Treasurer to make monthly salary reports and deposits to STRS and SERS (RC 3307.62, RC 3309.57).
	Settlement of real and public utility property taxes (RC 319.43) unless extended.
	County MR/DD to submit to director of MR/DD reports of total cost per enrollee and expenditure (RC 5126.12).
	State Superintendent to certify amount a district may borrow in first half of calendar year to be repaid from second-half taxes (so-called "spending reserve" borrowing) (RC 133.301).
Third Monday	*Washington-Lincoln Day (RC 1.14). Board may dismiss school (RC 3313.63).
80 Days Before May Special Election	Board to file first emergency tax levy resolution under RC 5705.194 with the county auditor.
75 Days Before May Special Election	Board to certify Chapter 133 bond issue election material (including county auditor's certification) to board of elections (RC 133.18).
	Board to file emergency, nonemergency, incremental, and income tax levy election resolutions with board of elections (RC 5705.194, RC 5705.195).

MARCH

1	Board to give written notice not to reemploy district superintendent on or before March 1 in year of contract expiration (RC 3319.01).

	County budget commission to file with board official certificate of estimated resources for next fiscal year (RC 5705.35).
	Department of Human Services to certify to State Board number of children ages 5 to 17 in each school district on aid to dependent children (RC 3317.10).
15	Treasurer to make monthly salary reports and deposits to STRS and SERS (RC 3307.62, RC 3309.57).
Third Tuesday	Presidential primary election every four years (RC 3501.01(E)(2)). See schedule of required prior actions in connection with May and November elections.
31	In even-numbered years, board to file request with State Board for transfer of territory from city or exempted village school district (RC 3311.24).
	Board to give written notice not to reemploy administrator other than superintendent on or before March 31 in year of contract expiration (RC 3319.02).

APRIL

1	Board to certify to county auditor resolution authorizing necessary tax levies on current duplicate for collection in next calendar year; may be extended by State Tax Commissioner (RC 5705.34).
10	If board wishes not to reemploy teacher on limited or extended limited contract, written report of evaluation conducted between February 10 and April 1 must be received by teacher not later than April 10 (RC 3319.111).
15	Treasurer to make monthly salary reports and deposits to STRS and SERS (RC 3307.62, RC 3309.57).
20	Board to file by April 20 with State Department copies of amended official certificate of estimated resources and annual appropriations resolution (RC 3311.40).
30	Board and superintendent to give written notice on or before April 30 to teachers eligible for continuing contract and with respect to whom superintendent's recommendation of reemployment has been rejected by three-fourths board vote under extended limited contract for not to exceed one year (RC 3319.11(B)); or two years (RC 3319.11).
	Board to give written notice of intent not to reemploy nonteaching employees (RC 4141.29(I)(1)(e)).
	Board must give written notice on or before April 30 to teachers on limited or extended limited contracts who are not to be reemployed (RC 3319.11(C)(3)).

MAY

1	State Tax Commissioner to certify to the State Department value of taxable real property of railroads and of taxable tangible personal property of all public utilities by school district and county (RC 3317.021(B)).
	Local, exempted village, or city school district to notify service center board of desired reclassification (RC 3311.08, RC 3311.09).
	Board to appoint district superintendent for term not to exceed five years beginning August 1 (RC 3319.01).
First Tuesday After First Monday	*Special election day, except in presidential primary election years (RC 3501.01).
15	State Tax Commissioner to certify tax value to State Department for purposes of recomputing state aid (RC 3317.027).

State Tax Commissioner to determine change in taxable value of tangible personal property for each school district and, if increase or decrease exceeds 5%, to certify change to State Department (RC 3317.028).

Treasurer to make monthly salary reports and deposits to STRS and SERS (RC 3307.62, RC 3309.57).

Last Monday — *Memorial Day (RC 1.14). Board may dismiss school (RC 3313.63); holiday for nonteaching employees (RC 3319.087).

JUNE

1 — Teacher to notify board in writing of refusal to accept contract (RC 3319.11)).

Board to give notice on or before June 1 to nonteaching employees on limited contract not covered by civil service, who are not to be reemployed (RC 3319.083).

State Tax Commissioner to certify to State Department, for the preceding tax year, taxable value in each school district of real, public utility, and tangible personal property, the total property tax rate, and the total taxes charged and payable for current expenses (RC 3317.021(A)), and certain other taxable property information (RC 3317.025).

15 — Treasurer to make monthly salary reports and deposits to STRS and SERS (RC 3307.62, RC 3309.57).

30 — School district to file membership record with service center superintendent (RC 3317.031).

Termination of teacher's contract for superannuation (RC 3307.37).

*School year and fiscal year closes (RC 3313.62, RC 9.34).

County MR/DD Board and certain institutions to certify to treasurer statements concerning mentally handicapped children receiving special education (RC 3323.09, RC 3323.091).

Settlement of general personal and classified property taxes (RC 319.49).

JULY

1 — *School year and fiscal year begins (RC 3313.62, RC 9.34).

Foundation Program fiscal year starts subject to General Assembly action, monthly payments of 1/12th of state fiscal year amount (RC 3317.01).

Board to give notice to teachers and nonteaching employees under contract for new school year of salary for that year (RC 3319.12, RC 3319.082).

On or about July 1, board to certify total amount from all sources available for all expenditures (and related spending plan), from each fund set up in the tax budget, and file it with the county auditor; any change in revenues from time to time to be likewise certified (RC 5705.36).

4 — *Independence Day (RC 1.14). Board may dismiss school (RC 3313.63); holiday for eleven- or twelve-month nonteaching employees (RC 3319.087).

10 — Last day teacher can terminate contract without consent of board (RC 3319.15).

15 — Treasurer to make monthly salary reports and deposits to STRS and SERS (RC 3307.62, RC 3309.57).

Treasurer to submit nonhandicapped tuition report to State Superintendent (RC 3313.64) (Form SF-14).

31 — *Term of district superintendent ends (RC 3319.01).

AUGUST

1	*Term of district superintendent begins (RC 3319.01).
	Annual statistical and civil proceedings report of boards of city and exempted village districts to State Board, and of boards of local school districts to service center superintendent (RC 3319.33).
First Tuesday After First Monday	*Special election day (RC 3501.01). See schedule of required prior actions in connection with May and November elections.
10	Settlement of real and public utility property taxes (RC 319.43) unless extended.
80 Days Before November General Election	Board to file first emergency tax levy resolution under RC 5705.194 with county auditor.
75 Days Before November General Election	Nominating petitions for city, local or exempted village board members or for a member of a county board of education to be filed with board of elections in odd-numbered years (RC 3513.254).
	Board to certify general obligation bonds (including county auditor's certification) to board of elections (RC 133.18).
	Board to file emergency, nonemergency, incremental, and income tax levy election resolutions with board of elections (RC 5705.194, RC 5705.21).
15	Service center superintendent to file annual statistical and civil proceedings report with State Board (RC 3319.34).
	Treasurer to make monthly salary reports and deposits to STRS and SERS (RC 3307.62, RC 3309.57).
	Treasurer to submit report listing each investment under RC 135.142(A) of interim moneys, to board, state superintendent, and auditor of state (RC 135.142).

INDEX

Cross references to another main heading are in CAPITAL LETTERS.

ABSENCES—See ATTENDANCE, generally.

ACCIDENTS
Insurance
   School pupils, T 22.08, T 23.04(B), T 46.21
School buses
   Emergency plans and drills, T 22.20
   Insurance, T 22.08, T 23.04(B), T 46.21
   Reporting, T 22.18(C)

ACCOUNTANTS
Public agencies audited by, T 43.27(A)

ACCOUNTS AND ACCOUNTING
Audits—See AUDITS.
Public offices, inspection and supervision, T 43.26
School districts—See also FUNDS, SCHOOL, generally.
   Activity funds, T 23.03(C)
   Audits—See AUDITS.
   Budgets—See BUDGETS, SCHOOL.
   Data processing services, T 43.29
   Ledgers, T 43.11, T 43.12(B)
   Receipts, T 43.12(A), T 43.12(B)
   Reports, T 43.26(B)
   Service contracts, approval, T 43.26(A)
   Supervision, T 43.26
   Treasurer's duties, T 6.07(B), T 43.26(A), T 43.28
      See also TREASURERS, SCHOOL BOARD, generally.
   Uniform system, T 43.26
   Vouchers, T 43.08(A)
State auditor, powers and duties, T 43.26
State universities—See UNIVERSITIES AND COLLEGES, STATE.
Uniform system, T 43.26

ACCREDITATION ASSOCIATIONS, T 26.18, T 43.02(B)

ACQUIRED IMMUNE DEFICIENCY SYNDROME—See AIDS.

ACTIONS—See also particular subject concerned.
Appeals—See APPEALS.
Bond validation, T 41.20(B), T 41.20(C)
Children's homes, against; refusal to pay special education tuition, T 29.09(C)
Civil rights violations, T 46.13 to T 46.16
Discrimination
   Attorney fees, recovery, T 46.16
   Employment, T Ch 17
      See also EMPLOYMENT DISCRIMINATION.
   Reverse discrimination, T 17.18
   Private right of action, T 19.11(B), T 19.13(E)

ACTIONS—*continued*
Discrimination—*continued*
   Reverse discrimination, T 17.18
   Wages—See EMPLOYMENT DISCRIMINATION.
Employment discrimination, T Ch 17
   See also EMPLOYMENT DISCRIMINATION.
   Reverse discrimination, T 17.18
Establishment clause, under, T 32.01
Immunity—See IMMUNITY FROM PROSECUTION.
Jurisdiction—See JURISDICTION.
Juvenile proceedings—See JUVENILE COURTS.
Limitations—See LIMITATION OF ACTIONS.
Personal information systems, against, T 44.08(B)
Political subdivisions, against, T Ch 46
   See also PUBLIC LIABILITY ACT.
Private schools, enrollment contracts, T 48.11(B)
Public funds violations, T 43.27(B)
Record disposal, T 44.23
Reverse discrimination, T 17.18
School boards and officials, by or against, T 5.07
   Annual report by board, T 5.09(G), T 31.02
   Public liability act—See PUBLIC LIABILITY ACT.
Special education complaints, T 28.12, T 28.13
Wage discrimination, T 17.08(B), T 48.30
   See also EMPLOYMENT DISCRIMINATION.

ADMINISTRATION OF SCHOOLS—See EDUCATION, LOCAL BOARDS; particular subject concerned.

ADMINISTRATIVE AGENCIES
Personal information systems, T 44.01, T 44.04 to T 44.11
   See also PERSONAL INFORMATION SYSTEMS.
Records and reports
   Personal information systems, T 44.01, T 44.04 to T 44.11

ADMINISTRATIVE PERSONNEL, T Ch 7
Appointment, T 7.01, T 7.09(A)
Assignment, T 7.06(B)(1)
Child abuse prevention, in-service training, T 21.14
Civil service status, T 12.04(A)(1)
Collective bargaining exclusion, T 18.05
Compensation, T 7.11(A)
Contracts, T 7.11, T 9.07(A)(2)
   Term, T 7.11(A)
Corporal punishment, administering—See PUPILS, at Corporal punishment.

ADMINISTRATIVE PERSONNEL—*continued*
Employment, T 7.10
Ethics, T Ch 45
    See also ETHICS, generally.
Evaluation, T 7.14
Job performance, T 7.14
Leave, vacation, T 7.11(A)
Liability insurance, T 46.19
Nomination, T 7.10
Nonrenewal, T 7.11(B)
Principals—See PRINCIPALS.
Reduction in force, T 7.13
Reemployment, T 7.10, T 7.11(B)
Resignation, T 7.11(A)
Superintendents—See SUPERINTENDENTS, LOCAL.
Suspension of employees, powers, T 12.15(A)
Teachers
    Employed as administrators, T 7.13, T 9.07(A)(2)
        Civil service status, effect, T 7.09(A)
    Status as teachers, T 8.02(A), T 9.07(A)(2)
Term of contracts, T 7.11(A)
Transfer, T 7.11(A)
Vacation leave, T 7.11(A)

ADMINISTRATIVE PROCEDURE
Hearings
    Representation, conflict of interest, T 45.03
Representation before agencies
    Conflict of interest, T 45.03
Resignation, T 7.11(A)

ADMINISTRATIVE SERVICES DEPARTMENT
Civil service, powers and duties—See CIVIL SERVICE, generally.
Purchase contracts for school supplies, equipment, and services, T 36.04(B)

ADOPTION
School district of residence, effect on, T 23.02(A)(6)

ADULT EDUCATION, T 26.10, T 26.11(C)
Advertising programs, T 26.10(D)
Basic literacy courses, T 26.10(A)
Contracts to provide, T 26.10(A)
Diplomas, T 26.10(E)
High school continuation programs, T 26.10(D)
    Charters, T 26.10(D)
Literacy courses, T 26.10(A)
Night schools, T 26.10(B)
Readmission to school following expulsion or youth services department commitment, T 26.10(A), T 26.10(D)
    Tuition, T 23.02(E)
School buses, leasing, T 22.23
Tuition, T 23.02(E), T 26.10(B)

ADVERTISING—See also NOTICE.
Adult education programs, T 26.10(D)

ADVISORY BOARDS AND COMMITTEES—See particular subject concerned.

AFFIRMATIONS—See OATHS AND AFFIRMATIONS.

AFFIRMATIVE ACTION PLANS, T 17.18
Construction industry, T 17.05(B)
Mental retardation and developmental disabilities board, T 29.15
Progress reports, T 17.17
Remedies for employment discrimination, T 17.03(E), T 17.04(D)
Reverse discrimination, T 17.18

AFFIRMATIVE DEFENSES
Employment discrimination; wages, gender-based claims, T 17.08(C)
Hazing, T 24.10, T 46.10
Obscenity, T 24.12

AGE AND SCHOOLING CERTIFICATES, T 20.11 to T 20.17
Age, proof of, T 20.13(B)
Appeals from denial, T 20.13(D)
Application for, T 20.13(C)
Approval of employment, T 20.13(B)
Conditional certificates, T 20.14(B)
Denial, T 20.13(D)
Employer's duties, T 20.09(C), T 20.16
    Violations, T 20.11(A)
Form to be prescribed by state board of education, T 20.13(B)
Issuance, T 20.02(A), T 20.11(A), T 20.13
    Reissuance, T 20.13(C)
Limited certificates, T 20.14(A)
Medical examinations, T 20.13(B)
Out-of-state residents, T 20.13(A)
Over-age certificates, T 20.14(D)
Part-time certificates, T 20.14(C)
Penalties for violations, T 20.17
Pledge of employers, T 20.13(B)
Presentation to employers, T 20.11(A)
Records
    Submission, T 20.13(B)
Refusal, T 20.13(D)
Reissuance, T 20.13(C)
Return by employers, T 20.16(D)
Revocation, T 20.13(E)
School records, submission, T 20.13(B)
Special certificates, T 20.14
Summer employment, T 20.11(B)
Superintendents of schools, duties, T 20.13(A), T 20.13(C)
Vacation certificates, T 20.14(C)
Violations, T 20.11(A), T 20.17
Void, T 20.11(A)

AGE DISCRIMINATION
Double damages, T 17.06(A)
Employment, T 17.06
    Evidence, T 17.06(B)

AGE DISCRIMINATION—*continued*
Employment—*continued*
 Limitation of actions, T 17.06(A)
 Federal aid, termination, T 19.13(D)
 Private schools, by, T 48.30
 Retirement plans, T 17.06(C)

AGE OF MAJORITY
Age and schooling certificates, T 20.14(D)

AGE REQUIREMENTS
Driver training, T 26.13(B)
Employment of minors, age and schooling certificates—See AGE AND SCHOOLING CERTIFICATES.
Kindergarten attendance, T 26.05(A)
School attendance, T 20.01
  See also ATTENDANCE.
 Kindergarten, T 26.05(A)
 Special education programs, T 28.01(A)
School employees' retirement, T 14.12, T 17.06(C)(1)
Special education programs, T 28.01(A)
Teachers' retirement, T 9.18, T 11.18(B), T 17.06(C)(1)

AGED PERSONS
Discrimination—See AGE DISCRIMINATION.
Employment discrimination, T 17.06
 Limitation of actions, T 17.06(A)
School services
 Buses, leasing, T 22.22, T 22.23
 Food service, using, T 31.06, T 35.04(B)

AGENTS
School supplier or textbook sales agents, prohibition, T 8.07(B), T 33.05, T 45.07

AGREEMENTS—See CONTRACTS; INTERSTATE AGREEMENTS.

AGRICULTURE
Children, employment
 Education, funding, T 26.08, T 39.08(A)
Schools, T 26.11(B)
    See also VOCATIONAL EDUCATION, generally.

AHERA, T 21.10(B)
Private and parochial schools, T 48.35

AIDES, EDUCATIONAL, T 12.19
Educational service center governing board member, as; prohibition, T 45.08(A)
Permits
 Criminal record checks of applicants, T 5.09(H), T 8.07(A)
 Teacher status, T 8.02(C)

AIDING AND ABETTING
Juvenile delinquency, T 24.11

AIDS, T 21.03(E)
Attendance of pupils afflicted with, T 21.03(D), T 21.03(E)
Discrimination on basis of handicap, T 17.13, T 21.03(E), T 28.01(B)
Handicap, as, T 17.13, T 21.03(E), T 28.01(B)
Privacy rights, T 46.14(E)
Pupils afflicted with, T 21.03(D), T 21.03(E)
School employees afflicted with, T 21.03(D), T 21.03(E)
Teachers afflicted with, T 21.03(D), T 21.03(E)

ALCOHOL, DRUG ADDICTION, AND MENTAL HEALTH SERVICE DISTRICTS
Board member, school principal serving as; prohibition, T 7.09(C)

ALCOHOLIC BEVERAGES
School bus drivers
 Testing of, T 22.13(B)
 Transporting children while under influence, T 24.09(D)
Testing for
 Pupils, T 25.03
 School bus drivers, T 22.13(B)

ALCOHOLISM
Counseling programs, confidentiality requirements, T 21.15(C)
Discrimination on basis of handicap, T 17.13
Drug-Free Schools and Communities Act, T 21.15(A)
Prevention, T 21.15(A)
Suspension or expulsion of pupils, T 20.10

ALIENS
Americanization schools, T 26.11(E)
Schools admitting, T 19.16
Verification of identity and work authorization by employers, T 48.20

ALTERNATIVE SCHOOLS, T 26.07(B)
Open enrollment policies, T 5.08(C)

AMERICAN SIGN LANGUAGE
High school courses, T 26.06(A), T 28.18

AMERICANIZATION SCHOOLS, T 26.11(E)

ANABOLIC STEROIDS
Posting warnings in locker rooms, T 21.15(D), T 48.15

ANNEXATION
School districts—See also REORGANIZATION OF SCHOOL DISTRICTS, generally.
 Agreements
  City school district serving annexed territory, with, T 4.05(B)
 Municipalities, by, T 4.07(A)(1), T 4.08
 Tax levies, effect, T 4.14(B)

ANNEXATION—*continued*
Tax levy rates, effect on, T 4.14(B)

ANNUITIES
Educational employees, T 11.23, T 14.15

ANTI-DISCRIMINATION—See DISCRIMINATION.

ANTICIPATION NOTES—See BONDS AND NOTES; TAX ANTICIPATION NOTES.

APPEALS
Age and schooling certificate denial, from, T 20.13(D)
Civil rights commission orders, from, T 17.04(E)
Civil service decisions, regarding—See CIVIL SERVICE.
Collective bargaining, public employees—See COLLECTIVE BARGAINING, PUBLIC EMPLOYEES.
Common pleas courts, to—See COURTS OF COMMON PLEAS.
County budget commission decisions, from, T 40.06
Disabled child's educational placement, from, T 28.11(F)
Employment relations board, from—See EMPLOYMENT RELATIONS BOARD.
Employment services bureau orders, occupational safety and health violations, T 16.09(A)
Home education or home instruction requests, T 20.03(C)
Layoffs
  Civil service employees, T 12.14(E)
Nonteaching school employees
  Demotion or suspension, T 12.15(A)
  Termination, T 12.16(C), T 12.17(C), T 12.17(D)
Real property assessments, T 39.04
School board, by; from county budget commission decisions, T 40.06
School bus drivers, from disqualification, T 22.14
School pupils
  Permanent exclusion, T 25.10(E)
  Suspension or expulsion, from, T 25.10(B), T 25.10(C), T 25.12
Special education placement, from, T 28.11(F)
Tax appeals board, to, T 40.06
Teacher's termination, from, T 9.23
Unfair labor practices, T 18.26(C)
Workers' compensation, T 16.07

APPRAISALS
Real property tax, for, T 39.04

APPROPRIATIONS
Amended appropriation measures, T 40.16, T 40.19, T 43.06

APPROPRIATIONS—*continued*
Foundation program
  For, T 39.06(A), T 39.06(C)
  From—See FOUNDATION PROGRAM, at Payments to districts.
Mental retardation and developmental disabilities boards, T 29.09(A)
School boards
  Amended resolution, T 40.16, T 40.19, T 43.06
  Certification of resources, T 6.07(C), T 40.15(B), T 40.15(D), T 40.18, T 40.19
  Construction and improvements, T 37.07(A)
  Ledger, T 43.11
  Resolutions, T 5.13(C), T 40.15
    Amending or supplementing, T 40.16, T 40.19, T 43.06
    Filing, T 40.18(A)
  Spending plan, T 40.17
  Supplemental resolution, T 40.16, T 40.19, T 43.06
  Temporary, T 40.15(C)
    Certification not required, T 6.07(C)(2)
School foundation program
  For, T 39.06(A), T 39.06(C)
Supplemental appropriation measures, T 40.16, T 40.19, T 43.06
Vocational education, T 27.04

ARBITRATION
Collective bargaining, public employees—See COLLECTIVE BARGAINING, PUBLIC EMPLOYEES.

ARCHITECTURAL BARRIERS, T 28.17(B)

AREA ARTS COUNCILS
Financial support, T 31.05
School boards supporting, T 31.05

ARRESTS
Children, truancy, T 20.08(C)

ARSON, T 38.04(A)

ART MUSEUMS—See MUSEUMS.

ARTS COUNCILS, LOCAL, T 31.05

ASBESTOS
Custodial and maintenance workers, awareness training, T 21.10(B)
Hazard Emergency Response Act of 1986, T 21.10(B)
  Private and parochial schools, T 48.35
Inspections, school buildings and lands, T 21.10(B)
School buildings, removal, T 21.10(B)
  Private and parochial schools, T 48.35

ASBESTOS HAZARD ABATEMENT ACTIVITY
Private and parochial schools, T 48.35

ASBESTOS HAZARD ABATEMENT ACTIVITY—*continued*
Rules, T 21.10(B)
School board actions, limitation of actions, T 21.10(B)
School buildings and lands, T 21.10(B)
  Private and parochial schools, T 48.35

ASBESTOS HAZARD EMERGENCY RESPONSE ACT OF 1986 (AHERA), T 21.10(B)
Private and parochial schools, T 48.35

ASSAULT
Children committing, parental liability, T 38.06
Prevention, school curriculum to include, T 21.14
School employees, against; leave due to, T 10.21(B), T 13.10(B)
School officials, by, T 25.16(C)
Teachers, against; leave due to, T 10.21(B)

ASSEMBLIES, PUBLIC
Schoolhouses, use, T 38.10

ASSESSMENTS—See also TAXATION, generally.
Public utilities; supplemental, for school districts, T 39.04

ASSIGNMENT TO SCHOOL
Pupils, T 7.06(C)
  Discrimination prohibited, T 20.05(B)
Teachers
  Discrimination, T 19.11(B)
  Superintendent, by, T 7.06(B)(1)

ASSOCIATIONS—See also particular subject concerned.
Educational or cultural, financial support, T 31.05
School accreditation, T 26.18, T 43.02(B)
School boards, T 5.09(E)
Teachers, attendance at meetings, T 10.09(C)

ATHLETIC EVENTS, T 30.01, T 30.06 to T 30.12
See also PHYSICAL EDUCATION; RECREATIONAL PROGRAMS.
Accident insurance, T 23.04(B), T 30.12
  Transportation to events, T 22.08
Admission charges for nonresidents, T 39.15
Coaches, T 30.05
  Employment, T 12.10
  Supplemental contracts, T 9.14(C)
Discrimination, T 19.14, T 30.09(B)
  Funding withheld due to, T 19.14(B)
Donations to support, T 30.10(C), T 39.13
Facilities, funding, T 30.10
Funding, T 30.10, T 39.13
Injuries, T 30.12
Insurance, T 23.04(B), T 30.12
  Transportation to events, T 22.08

ATHLETIC EVENTS—*continued*
Liability, volunteer medical practitioners or nurses, T 21.09
Ohio high school athletic association, T 30.07 to T 30.12
  See also OHIO HIGH SCHOOL ATHLETIC ASSOCIATION.
Olympic games, participation by public employees, T 13.10(B)
Physical education programs distinguished, T 30.03
Sex segregation and discrimination, T 19.14, T 30.09(B)
  Funding withheld due to, T 19.14(B)
Trainers, T 30.05

ATTENDANCE, T Ch 20
See also ENROLLMENT.
Absences
  Excuses, T 20.03
    Disabled children, T 20.03(B)
  Policy on parental notification, T 20.07
Age requirements, T 20.01
  Kindergarten, T 26.05(A)
  Special education programs, T 28.01(A)
Alternative plans, T 20.05(B)
Average daily membership—See FOUNDATION PROGRAM.
Complaints against parents, T 20.09(A)
Compulsory, T Ch 20, T 32.02
  Affirmative duty to protect students arising from, T 46.14(B)
  Exceptions, T 20.03
  Notice to parents of child's truancy, T 20.07, T 20.09(A)
    Board policy, T 20.07
  Religious exemption, T 20.03(A), T 32.02
  Truancy—See Truancy, this heading.
Disabled children, T 20.01, T 20.02(C), T 28.17(A)
  Excused from attendance, T 20.03(B)
Disadvantaged pupils, T 23.06
Discrimination in assignment of pupils, T 20.05(B)
Early admission, T 20.01(B), T 26.05(A)
Employment, effect, T 20.02(A), T 20.03(B), T 20.05(A), T 20.15, T 26.10(C), T 48.04(D)
  Liability of employer, T 20.09(C)
Enforcement, T 20.07 to T 20.10
  Absence notification policy, T 20.07
  Attendance officers—See Officers, this heading.
  Employer's liability, T 20.09(C)
  Investigations, T 20.08(C), T 20.09(A)
    Private schools, T 48.04(A)
  Parental liability—See Parental liability for, this heading.
Excuses for absences, T 20.03
  Disabled children, T 20.03(B)
Expulsion, effect, T 20.03(B)
Fines for violations, T 20.09(B), T 20.09(C)
Indigent children, T 23.06

ATTENDANCE—*continued*
Investigation for truancy, T 20.08(C), T 20.09(A)
    Private schools, T 48.04(A)
Juvenile proceedings for truancy, T 20.09(A), T 20.09(B), T 20.10
Kindergarten, T 20.01(B), T 26.05(A)
Married pupils, T 20.04
Mentally retarded children, T 20.01, T 20.02(C), T 28.17(A)
    Excused from attendance, T 20.03(B)
Officers, T 20.08
    Appointment, T 20.08(A)
    Assistants, T 20.08(A)
    Compensation and expenses, T 20.08(B)
    Powers and duties, T 20.08(C)
    Right of entry, T 20.08(C)
    Warrants, serving, T 20.08(C)
Out-of-state residence of parents, T 20.02(A)
Parental liability for, T 20.02(A), T 32.02
    Bonds for violations, T 20.09(B)
    Complaints against parents, T 20.09(A)
    Fines for violations, T 20.09(B), T 20.09(C)
Part-time, T 20.15, T 26.10(C), T 48.04(D)
    Hours of attendance, T 20.05(A)
Penalties for violations, T 20.09(B), T 20.09(C)
Pregnant pupils, T 20.04, T 25.15(B)
Private schools—See PRIVATE AND PAROCHIAL SCHOOLS.
Records and reports, T 20.10, T 44.13
    Notice to law enforcement agency when pupil fails to present official records, T 24.16, T 48.10
    Private school, T 48.04(C)
Religious exemption, T 20.03(A), T 32.02
Required, T 20.02(A)
Residence of pupil, determination, T 23.02(A), T 23.02(C)
Responsibility of parents—See Parental liability for, this heading.
Schedules, discrimination prohibited in, T 20.05(B)
Seasonal residence, T 20.02(A)
Special education programs—See SPECIAL EDUCATION.
Split schedules, T 20.05(C)
Staggered attendance plan, T 20.05(B)
Superintendents excusing
    Home education request, T 20.03(C)
    Home instruction request, T 20.03(C)
Suspension, effect, T 20.03(B)
Tests for early admission, T 20.01(B)
Truancy
    Arrests, T 20.08(C)
    Complaints, T 20.09(A)
    Driver's license, suspension or revocation, T 20.10
    Fines and forfeitures, T 20.09(B), T 20.09(C)
    Investigation, T 20.08(C), T 20.09(A)
        Private schools, T 48.04(A)
    Jurisdiction, T 20.09(A)
    Juvenile proceedings, T 20.09(A), T 20.09(B), T 20.10

ATTENDANCE—*continued*
Truancy—*continued*
    Notice of truancy
        Juvenile court judge, to, T 20.10
        Motor vehicles registrar, to, T 20.10
        Parents, to, T 20.07, T 20.09(A)
        Written policy, T 20.07
    Parental liability—See Parental liability for, this heading.
    Surety bonds, parents, T 20.09(B)
    Truant officers—See Officers, this heading.
Violations, T 20.09
    Driving privileges, suspension, T 20.10
    Notice to motor vehicles registrar and juvenile court judge, T 20.10
    Penalties, T 20.09(B), T 20.09(C)
    Private schools, T 48.04(A)

ATTORNEY GENERAL
Employment discrimination complaints, duties, T 17.04(C)
Funds, violations, T 43.27(B)
Opinions, T 2.17
Powers and duties, T 2.17
Public funds, powers and duties
    Violations, T 43.27(B)
Public officials and employees, powers and duties
    Fund violations, T 43.27(B)
School boards, advising, T 2.17
School employees retirement board
    Legal adviser, T 14.02(A)
    Membership, T 14.02(A)
Teachers retirement board
    Membership, T 11.02(A)

ATTORNEYS
City—See CITY DIRECTORS OF LAW.
County—See PROSECUTORS, COUNTY.
Fees
    Civil rights violations, T 46.16
    Discrimination action, recovery, T 17.02(B), T 17.03(E), T 46.16
    Special education actions, limitations, T 28.12(B), T 28.13(D)
Mental retardation and developmental disabilities boards, representing, T 29.18
Right to
    School pupil's suspension or expulsion, T 25.10(B), T 25.10(C)
    Special education placement hearing, T 28.11(C)
School boards—See EDUCATION, LOCAL BOARDS, at Legal advisers.
State—See ATTORNEY GENERAL.

AUCTIONS
School property, T 36.11(B)

AUDITOR, STATE
Records and reports
    Disposal and transfer, T 48.30

AUDITOR, STATE—*continued*
School employees retirement board, membership, T 14.02(A)
Teachers retirement board, membership, T 11.02(A)
Uniform system of accounting, establishment, T 43.26

AUDITORS, COUNTY
Bonds and notes
  Certification of annual levy, T 41.12(E)
  Classroom facilities, calculation of annual tax levy, T 41.28(D)
County budget commission, membership, T 40.05

AUDITS
Conferences following, sunshine law exemption, T 5.12
Public agencies audited by accountants, T 43.27(A)
Schools, T 43.27
  Activity funds, T 23.03(C)
  Costs, T 43.27(A)
  Service contracts, approval, T 43.26(A)
Service contracts, approval, T 43.26(A)

AUTO MECHANICS COURSES
Liability insurance, T 46.20

AUTOMATIC DATA PROCESSING—See DATA PROCESSING.

AUTOMATIC REEMPLOYMENT
Teachers on limited contracts, T 9.10(B), T 9.10(D)

AUTOMOBILES—See MOTOR VEHICLES.

BALLOTS
Bond issues, T 41.14(B)
  Libraries, construction or improvement of buildings, T 41.14(B)
Emergency school levies, T 40.13
Libraries
  Bond issue, T 41.14(B)
    Construction or improvement of buildings, T 41.14(B)

BANKS AND BANKING
Cease and desist orders against, effect on public depository eligibility, T 42.05(A)
Conflict of interest, public depositories, T 42.12, T 45.08(B)
Contracts with state and subdivisions; bond issuance, clerical services, T 43.19
Minority banks, eligibility as public depositories, T 42.05(C)
Public depositories, as, T Ch 42
  See also FUNDS, PUBLIC, at Deposits and depositories.

BANKS AND BANKING—*continued*
Student loan program, participation required for public depository eligibility, T 42.05(A)

BASIC STATE AID—See FOUNDATION PROGRAM.

BATTERY—See ASSAULT, generally.
Sexual—See SEXUAL BATTERY.

BEQUESTS—See GIFTS AND GRANTS.

BIBLE-READING
Public schools, in, T 32.05, T 32.07

BIDDING, COMPETITIVE
Bonds of political subdivisions, sale, T 41.17(B) to T 41.17(D)
Bonds required
  School buildings and lands, construction and improvements, T 37.04(B), T 37.05
Exemptions
  School buildings and lands, construction and improvements, T 37.04(C)
  School equipment and supplies, T 36.04(B)
    Data processing equipment, T 37.04(A)
  Surplus commodities from federal government, T 36.04(B)
Federal surplus commodities exempt, T 36.04(B)
Lowest responsive and responsible bidder, T 37.06(A)
Mental retardation and developmental disabilities board contracts, T 29.07
Schools, T 36.04(B)
  Bonds and notes, sale, T 41.17(B) to T 41.17(D)
  Building construction and improvements, T 6.08(B), T 37.04 to T 37.06
    See also SCHOOL BUILDINGS AND LANDS, at Construction and improvements, subheading Bids.
  Bus purchase, T 22.09, T 36.04(B), T 36.04(C)(3)
  Business manager, powers and duties, T 6.13
  Exemptions—See Exemptions, this heading.
  Lowest responsive and responsible bidder, T 37.06(A)

BILINGUAL EDUCATION, T 19.15
Class size, maximum, T 3.03(G)

BIRTH CERTIFICATES
Admission to schools, requirement
  Notice to law enforcement agency when pupil fails to present official records, T 24.16, T 48.10

BLIND PERSONS—See also HANDICAPPED PERSONS, generally.
Bureau of services for visually impaired, T 27.13(B)

BLIND PERSONS—*continued*
Rehabilitation services commission, powers and duties, T 27.13(B)
Schooling—See also SPECIAL EDUCATION, generally; State school, this heading.
  Assessment of reading and writing skills, T 5.09(P)
  Attendance, T 20.01, T 20.02(C), T 28.17(A)
    Excused from attendance, T 20.03(B)
  Braille
    Individualized education program, T 28.02
    Integration into curriculum, T 28.02
    Teacher certification, T 3.03(G), T 28.16
    Textbooks, translation, T 33.03(A)
  Foundation program funding, T 28.15(A), T 39.08(A)
  Textbooks, translation into braille, T 33.03(A)
State school, T 28.19
  Admission, T 28.19(B)
  Personnel, T 28.19(A)
  Return of pupil to parents, T 28.19(B)
  Superintendent, appointment, T 28.19(A)
  Teachers, T 28.19(A)
Trained dogs accompanying, T 17.13(A), T 28.18

BLOCK PARENT PROGRAMS, T 3.03(G)
Private and parochial schools, T 48.37

BOARDS OF EDUCATION—See EDUCATION, LOCAL BOARDS; EDUCATION, STATE BOARD.

BONDS AND NOTES—See also BONDS AND NOTES, SCHOOL.
Anticipation notes—See TAX ANTICIPATION NOTES.
Arbitrage bonds, T 41.19(B)
  Rebates, T 41.19(C)
Bids on sale, T 41.17(B) to T 41.17(D)
Book entry form, T 41.19(A)
Call or redemption, prior to maturity, T 41.18
Classroom facility construction and improvements, T 41.27(B), T 41.28, T 41.30, T 41.31
County auditors' powers—See AUDITORS, COUNTY.
Coupon bonds, T 41.19(A)
Debt limitation—See DEBTS.
Definitions, T 41.03
Delivery to purchasers, T 41.17(F)
Elections regarding—See ELECTIONS.
Emergencies, bond issues to defray costs, T 41.04
Expenses of issuance, T 41.16(F), T 41.17(F)
Federal tax law provisions, T 41.19
Form and purpose, T 41.19(A)
Installments, issuance in, T 41.15
Interest, T 41.08, T 41.16(F), T 41.17(B)
Issuance procedure, T 41.16
  Contracts for services, T 43.19
  Expenses, T 41.16(F), T 41.17(F)
  Validation, T 41.20(B), T 41.20(C)

BONDS AND NOTES—*continued*
Joint vocational school districts issuing, T 27.10(A), T 41.23(A), T 41.23(C)
Judgments, bond issues to pay, T 41.04, T 41.08
Liability insurance pool, to finance, T 46.18(D)
Libraries or library districts issuing—See LIBRARIES AND LIBRARY DISTRICTS.
Limits on indebtedness—See DEBTS.
Lost or destroyed, T 41.20(A)
Maturity, T 41.10, T 41.11
  Anticipation notes, T 41.16(D)
  Call or redemption prior to, T 41.18
Notice
  Proposal to issue, T 41.14(A)
  Sale, T 41.17(B)
Private sale, T 41.17(D)
Proceeds from sale, T 41.17(E)
  Transfer among classes, T 41.11
  Use, T 41.19(C)
Public works, T 41.04
Purchase of—See Sale, this heading.
Rebates, T 41.19(C)
Redemption prior to maturity, T 41.18
Refunding
  Call or redemption, pursuant to, T 41.18
Registered bonds, T 41.19
Resolutions to issue, T 41.11, T 41.12
Retirement funds—See SINKING FUNDS.
Sale, T 41.17
  Bids, T 41.17(B) to T 41.17(D)
  Delivery, T 41.17(F)
  Disclosure of information, T 41.17(C)
  Notice, T 41.17(B)
  Official statement, T 41.17(C)
  Private sale, T 41.17(D)
  Proceeds—See Proceeds from sale, this heading.
  Public agencies, to, T 41.17(B)
Schools—See BONDS AND NOTES, SCHOOL.
Serial bonds, T 41.11
Tax anticipation notes—See TAX ANTICIPATION NOTES.
Tax exemptions
  Arbitrage bonds excluded, T 41.19(B)
    Rebates, T 41.19(C)
  Qualified tax-exempt obligations, T 41.19(D)
  Sale proceeds, use, T 41.19(C)
Tax levies for debt services, T 41.15
Transcripts of proceedings, T 41.17(G)
Uniform bond law, T 41.03
Unsold, procedure, T 41.17(D)
Validation of issuance, T 41.20(B), T 41.20(C)

BONDS AND NOTES, SCHOOL, T Ch 41
  See also BONDS AND NOTES, generally.
Anticipation notes—See TAX ANTICIPATION NOTES.
Classroom facility projects, T 41.27(B), T 41.28, T 41.30, T 41.31
Election questions, T 41.09 to T 41.14

BONDS AND NOTES, SCHOOL—*continued*
Emergency replacement or addition of buildings, T 41.04, T 41.09
Funds for proceeds, T 43.15(B), T 43.18
Issuance procedure
  Contracts for services, T 43.19
Joint vocational districts issuing, T 27.10(A), T 41.23(A), T 41.23(C)
Limits on indebtedness—See DEBTS.
Permanent improvements, for, T 41.03, T 41.04
Public funds used to oppose or support, T 5.09(G), T 43.05(A)
Purposes, T 41.04
Resolutions, T 41.12, T 41.13, T 41.16(B), T 41.16(E)
Retirement funds—See SINKING FUNDS.
Special needs districts, T 41.07
Tax anticipation notes—See TAX ANTICIPATION NOTES.

BONDS, SAVINGS
Payroll deductions, public employees, T 10.08

BONDS, SURETY
Bidders
  Public securities, T 41.17(B)
  School buildings, construction and improvements, T 37.06(B)
Library board clerks, T 34.12(B)
Schools
  Bus drivers, T 22.13(A)
  Business managers, T 6.11
  Treasurers, school board, T 6.02(D)
Truants' parents, T 20.09(B)

BOOKMOBILES, T 34.08

BORROWING—See DEBTS.

BOUNDARIES
School attendance boundaries, changes; superintendents' powers and duties, T 7.06(C)
School districts, T 4.02, T 4.05(B)
  Agreements among school districts, T 4.07(B)
  Changes, notification to board of elections, T 6.08(C)
  City school districts, T 4.03(A)
  Educational service centers, T 4.03(B)

BRAILLE
Individualized education program, T 28.02
Integration into curriculum, T 28.02
Teacher certification, T 3.03(G), T 28.16
Textbooks, translation, T 33.03(A)

BREAKFAST PROGRAMS, T 35.07

BRIBERY
Public officials or employees soliciting or receiving, T 45.11

BUDGET COMMISSIONS, COUNTY, T 40.05
Appeals from actions, T 40.06
Certification of estimated resources, T 40.15(B), T 40.15(D), T 40.19
Membership, T 40.05
Tax budgets, review, T 40.05
Tax levies, powers and duties
  Approval, T 40.07
  Reduction, T 39.03, T 40.14

BUDGETS
County commissions—See BUDGET COMMISSIONS, COUNTY.
Libraries, T 34.13
Mental retardation and developmental disabilities boards, T 29.04(A)
Schools—See BUDGETS, SCHOOL.
State board of education, T 3.03(A)
Tax budgets, T 40.01 to T 40.06

BUDGETS, SCHOOL—See also BUDGETS, generally.
Assistance in preparation, T 3.03(G), T 5.09(A)
Business managers, powers and duties, T 6.13
Classroom facility projects, inclusion, T 41.32
Educational service centers, T 40.03
Fiscal year, T 40.02
State board of education, T 3.03(A)
Tax budgets
  Appropriation resolution based on, T 40.15(A)
  Contents, T 40.01 to T 40.06
  Contingent expenses, T 40.04(B)
  Form, T 40.04
  Hearings, T 40.03
  Preparation, T 40.01
  Proposal, T 40.03
  Review
    County budget commission, by, T 40.05
  Spending reserve balance, T 40.04(C), T 41.21(B)
  Timetable, T 40.03
Textbooks, inclusion, T 33.03(A)
Training, in-service, T 3.03(G), T 5.09(F)

BUILDING AND LOAN ASSOCIATIONS
Cease and desist orders against, effect on public depository eligibility, T 42.05(A)
Conflict of interest, public depositories, T 42.12, T 45.08(B)
Contracts with state and subdivisions; bond issuance, clerical services, T 43.19
Public depositories, as, T Ch 42
  See also FUNDS, PUBLIC, at Deposits and depositories.
Student loan program, participation required for eligibility as public depository, T 42.05(A)

BUILDING STANDARDS
Fire safety—See FIRE SAFETY.
School construction and improvements, T 21.10, T 37.01(B), T 37.09

BUILDINGS AND GROUNDS—See also SCHOOL BUILDINGS AND LANDS.
Handicapped persons, access, T 21.10(C), T 28.17(B)
Libraries—See LIBRARIES AND LIBRARY DISTRICTS.

BULLETINS
School boards distributing, T 5.09(G), T 31.02

BUREAUS—See particular subject concerned.

BUSES—See SCHOOL BUSES.

BUSINESS
School-business partnership programs, T 3.04(A)

BUSINESS ADVISORY COUNCILS, T 26.11(H)

BUSINESS MANAGERS, T 6.01, T 6.10 to T 6.13
Bonds, T 6.11
Civil service status, T 12.04(A)(1)
Compensation, T 6.11
Conflict of interest, T 6.13
Election or appointment, T 6.11
Incompatible offices, T 6.13
Licensing, T 3.03(G), T 6.10
Powers and duties, T 6.13, T 38.02
Qualifications, T 6.10
Resignation, T 6.12
Suspension or removal, T 6.12
Term, T 6.11
Vacancies, T 6.12

BUSING FOR DESEGREGATION—See DESEGREGATION OF SCHOOLS, generally.

CAFETERIAS, SCHOOL—See FOOD SERVICES, SCHOOL, generally.

CALENDAR, SCHOOL, T 20.05
Holidays, T 20.06
Pentamester system, T 20.05(B)
Quarterly system, T 20.05(B)
School days, T 20.05(A), T 20.05(B)
  Flexible schedule, T 20.05(B)
School years, T 20.05(A), T 20.05(B), T 40.02
  Emergency closings, effect, T 20.05(D)
  Minimum, T 39.07(A)
  Private and parochial schools, T 48.04(B)
  Special education programs, T 28.04
Semester system, number of school days, T 20.05(B)
Split schedules, T 20.05(C)
Trimester system, T 20.05(B)

CAMPAIGNS
School board members, by, T 5.03(A)

CANDIDATES
Contributions to—See POLITICAL CONTRIBUTIONS.
Financial disclosure, T 45.02
  Applicability of laws, T 45.01(C)(3)
School boards, nomination, T 5.03(A)

CAPITAL IMPROVEMENTS—See particular improvement concerned; SCHOOL BUILDINGS AND LANDS, at Construction and improvements.

CAREER PLANNING FOR STUDENTS, T 5.09(R)

CEASE AND DESIST ORDERS
Banks served with
  Depository of public funds, ineligible to be, T 42.05(A)
Building and loan associations served with
  Depository of public funds, ineligible to be, T 42.05(A)
Discrimination actions, T 17.04(D)
Employment services bureau, occupational safety and health violations, T 16.09(A)
Savings and loan associations served with
  Depository of public funds, ineligible to be, T 42.05(A)
Unfair labor practices, T 18.26(B)

CENSORSHIP
Student expression, T 25.05

CERTIFICATES—See particular subject concerned.
Age and schooling—See AGE AND SCHOOLING CERTIFICATES.
Teacher—See TEACHERS.

CHARITABLE CONTRIBUTIONS—See GIFTS AND GRANTS.

CHARITABLE IMMUNITY
Private schools, liability, T 48.34(A)

CHARITABLE ORGANIZATIONS
Schooling provided by, part-time, T 20.15
Volunteers, immunity from prosecution, T 48.34(C)

CHARTERS
Adult education, high school continuation programs, T 26.10(D)
Municipal corporations
  School employees, effect on employment, T 12.02(C)
Private and parochial schools, T 48.03(A)
  Revocation, T 48.09(A)
School districts, T 26.19

CHECKLISTS
Collective bargaining procedural timetables, T 18.35
Pupil suspension or expulsion, T 25.14
Teachers
  Limited contract, nonrenewal, T 9.24
  Termination, T 9.25

CHILD ABUSE, T 24.05, T 24.09(B)
Definitions, T 24.05(C)
Prevention programs
  Funding, T 25.16(A)
  School employees, in-service training, T 21.14
Recognizing abuse or neglect, T 24.05(B)
Reporting requirements, T 24.05
School employees
  In-service training in prevention, T 21.14
  Reporting, T 24.05

CHILD NUTRITION ACT, T 35.07

CHILDREN—See MINORS.

CHILDREN'S HOMES
Schools
  Tuition, T 23.02(A)(2), T 23.02(A)(4), T 29.09(C)

CHILDREN'S SERVICES
Investigators interviewing children on school property, T 5.08(A), T 24.05(A), T 31.04

CHIROPRACTORS
Schools employing, T 21.02(A)

CHURCHES—See RELIGION, generally.

CITIES—See MUNICIPAL CORPORATIONS.

CITY DIRECTORS OF LAW
Public funds violations, powers and duties, T 43.27(B)
School boards
  Legal adviser, T 6.14
  Membership, T 45.08(A)

CITY SCHOOL DISTRICTS, T 4.03(A)
    See also SCHOOLS AND SCHOOL DISTRICTS, generally.
Boards of education—See EDUCATION, LOCAL BOARDS.
Boundaries, T 4.03(A)
City reduced to village, effect, T 4.03(A), T 4.06(A)
Civil service
  Administration costs, T 12.03(B)
  Appointing authority, T 12.06
  Commissions, T 12.03(A)
  Classification change, T 4.03(A), T 4.05(C), T 4.06(A)

CITY SCHOOL DISTRICTS—*continued*
Competency of graduates, guarantee policy, T 26.16(B)
Creation
  Consolidation, pursuant to, T 4.07(A)(2), T 4.09
  Incorporation, pursuant to, T 4.06(D)
Exempted village school districts becoming, T 4.03(A), T 4.06(C)
  Two or more exempted village school districts combined to form, T 4.03(A)
Gifted children, programs for, T 26.09
Local school districts becoming, T 4.03(A), T 4.06(A), T 4.06(C), T 4.06(D)
  Two or more local school districts combined to form, T 4.03(A)
Records and reports
  Adjacent school district residents, enrollment, T 5.08(D)
Redistricting, T 5.02(B)(2)
  Notice to elections board, T 6.08(C)
Reduction to village district, T 4.03(A), T 4.06(A)
Subdistricting, T 5.02(B)(2), T 6.08(C)
Supervision by educational service center governing boards, T 4.03(D)
Transfer of territory, T 4.07 to T 4.11

CIVIL ACTIONS—See ACTIONS; particular subject concerned.

CIVIL RIGHTS—See also CIVIL RIGHTS ACT; DISCRIMINATION.
Interference with, T 45.13
Liability for violations, T 46.13 to T 46.16
Rehabilitation services commission, powers and duties, T 27.13(B)
School employees, T 46.14(A)(2)
School pupils, T 25.08 to T 25.16, T 46.14(A)(1)
Violations, T 46.13 to T 46.16

CIVIL RIGHTS ACT, T 2.16(B)
Bilingual education requirements, applicability, T 19.15
Compliance required for federal aid, T 2.13
Desegregation of schools, applicability, T 19.11(A), T 19.13(A)
Employment discrimination, applicability, T 17.03

CIVIL RIGHTS COMMISSION, STATE, T 17.04(C)
Age discrimination claims, T 17.06(A)
Appeals from orders, T 17.04(E)
Orders, appeals from, T 17.04(E)

CIVIL SERVICE, T Ch 12
Abolishment of positions, T 12.14
Administrative personnel
  Status, T 12.04(A)(1)
  Teacher employed as, T 7.09(A)
Appeals from decisions
  Classified employee of multi-city school district, T 12.03(A)

CIVIL SERVICE—*continued*
Appeals from decisions—*continued*
  Demotion or suspension, T 12.15(A)
  Displacement, T 12.14(E)
  Examination, ineligibility, T 12.05(A)(1)
  Layoffs, T 12.14(E)
  Pay reduction, T 12.15(B)
  Removal, T 12.17(C), T 12.17(D)
  Suspension, T 12.15(A)
Appointing authorities, defined, T 12.06
Appointments, T 12.05 to T 12.08
  Appointing authority, defined, T 12.06
  Classified unskilled positions, T 12.05(B)
  Competitive classified positions, T 12.05(A)
  Not subject to collective bargaining, T 18.28(A)
  Permanent status, T 12.07(B)
  Probationary period, T 12.07(A)
  Provisional, T 12.07(B)
  Temporary, T 12.07(B)
Bumping rights, T 12.14(D)
Business managers, powers and duties, T 6.13
Classified service, T 12.04
  Converting to unclassified position, T 7.09(A)
Collective bargaining—See COLLECTIVE BARGAINING, PUBLIC EMPLOYEES.
Commissions
  City school districts, for, T 12.03(A)
Demotions, T 12.15(A)
Dismissal—See Removal, this heading.
Displacement
  Appeal, T 12.14(E)
  Rights, T 12.14(D)
Eligibility
  Lists, T 12.05(A)(2), T 12.05(A)(3)
Examinations, T 12.05(A)(1)
  Ineligibility, appeals from, T 12.05(A)(1)
  Not subject to collective bargaining, T 18.28(A)
Fees and costs
  Apportionment, T 12.03(B)
Independent contractors in lieu of employees, T 12.08
Job reassignment, T 12.12
Layoffs, T 12.14
  Appeal, T 12.14(E)
  Grounds for, T 12.14(B)
  Order of layoffs, T 12.14(C)
  Retention points, T 12.14(C)
Mental retardation and developmental disabilities board employees, T 29.12
  Sick leave, T 29.13(B)
Pay range and classification
  Reduction in pay, T 12.15(B)
Political activities, restrictions, T 45.14
Principals, unclassified status, T 12.04(A)(1)
Probationary periods, T 12.07(A)
Promotions, T 12.11
Provisional appointments, T 12.07(B)
Reduction of pay, T 12.15(B)
Removal, T 12.17
  Hearings, due process rights, T 46.14(A)(2)
  Probationary period, during, T 12.07(A)
  Unclassified service, T 12.04(B)

CIVIL SERVICE—*continued*
Retention points, T 12.14(C)
School employees, nonteaching, T Ch 12
  Administrative costs, apportionment, T 12.03(B)
  Appointment, T 12.05 to T 12.08
  Termination, T 12.17
  Unclassified position, T 12.04(A)
Sick leave, T 13.08 to T 13.10
  Mental retardation and developmental disabilities board employees, T 29.13(B)
Superintendents, unclassified status, T 12.04(A)(1)
Suspensions, T 12.15(A)
  Appeals by nonteaching employees, T 12.15(A)
  Business managers, powers and duties, T 6.13
Teachers
  Administrator, employed as; status, T 7.09(A)
  Unclassified status, T 12.04(A)(1)
Temporary appointments, T 12.07(B)
Transfers, T 12.12
Unclassified, T 12.04(A)
  Classified employees converted to, T 7.09(A)
  Library employees as, T 34.12(A)
Unskilled labor
  Appointment, T 12.05(B)
  Classification, T 12.04(A)(3)
Veterans' rights, T 12.05(A)(2)

CLAIMS
Workers' compensation—See WORKERS' COMPENSATION.

CLASSROOM FACILITIES, T 41.24 to T 41.32
Anticipation notes, T 41.30
Application to purchase, T 41.26
Approval, T 41.26, T 41.27(A)
Ballot issues on financing, T 41.27(B), T 41.28
Bonds and notes to finance, T 41.27(B), T 41.28, T 41.30, T 41.31
Contracts, T 41.29
Costs, apportionment, T 41.26
Definitions, T 41.24
Financing, T 41.24 to T 41.32
  Ballot issue, T 41.27(B), T 41.28
  Bonds and notes, T 41.27(B), T 41.28, T 41.30, T 41.31
Indebtedness, T 41.24, T 41.26
  "Net bonded indebtedness", T 41.25
  "Required level of indebtedness", T 41.25
Needs determination, T 41.26
Permanent improvements, financing, T 41.24 to T 41.32
Portable buildings, acquisition, T 36.04(C)(4)
Purchase from state, application, T 41.26
Resolutions, T 41.26, T 41.28(A), T 41.28(C)
Tax levies to finance, T 41.27(B), T 41.28, T 41.32

CLOSING SCHOOLS
Deduction from minimum school year requirement, T 20.05(D)
Emergency closings, T 20.05(D)

CLOSING SCHOOLS—*continued*
Epidemics, due to, T 20.05(D), T 21.08(B)
Financial difficulties, due to
    Emergency school advancement fund loans to avoid, T 41.33
        See also EMERGENCY LOANS, generally.
    Loans to avoid, T 41.33
    Superintendent of public instruction,
        Duties, T 3.06, T 41.33
        Powers, T 40.18(C), T 41.33
Funding, effect on, T 39.07
Nonteaching employees, effect on, T 13.05(A)
State superintendent's powers and duties, T 40.18(C)
Teachers, effect on, T 10.09(A), T 10.11

COBRA, T 10.12

COLLECTIVE BARGAINING, PUBLIC EMPLOYEES, T Ch 18
Administrative personnel, exclusion, T 18.05
Affiliation votes, T 18.17(C)
Agency shop provisions, T 18.21
Agreements, T 18.19 to T 18.23
    Binding, when, T 18.22
    Conflict with statutes, T 18.20
    Damages for violations, T 18.26(C)
    Dues deduction authorization, inclusion in agreement required, T 18.19(A)
    Duration, T 18.19(A), T 18.23
    Education requirements, additional, T 18.20
    Enforcement, T 18.20, T 46.08
    Expiration date, T 18.19(A), T 18.23
    Fair share fee, provisions for, T 18.21(A)
    Grievance arbitration provisions
        Final arbitration, binding, T 18.22(A)
        Inclusion in agreement required, T 18.19(A)
    Peer review plan, inclusion, T 18.19(B)
    Political activity, modification of statutory restrictions, T 45.14
    Strike during term
        Injunction against, T 18.31
        Unauthorized strike, as, T 18.31
    Unemployment compensation, supplemental benefits, T 18.20
    Workers' compensation, supplemental benefits, T 18.20
Amendment of bargaining units, T 18.11(B)
Appeals
    Penalties imposed for participating in unauthorized strikes, T 18.31
    Unfair labor practices, T 18.26(C)
Arbitration
    Deferral to, T 18.22(B)
    Intentional delays, unfair labor practice, T 18.24(A)
    Options to state-mandated settlement procedure, T 18.29(B)
Bargaining units, T 18.11 to T 18.13
    Amendment, T 18.11(B)
    Clarification, T 18.11(B)

COLLECTIVE BARGAINING, PUBLIC EMPLOYEES—*continued*
Bargaining units—*continued*
    Criteria, T 18.11(B)
    "Deemed certified" units—See "Deemed certified" units, this heading.
    Employment relations board to determine, T 18.11(A)
    "Grandfathered" units—See "Deemed certified" units, this heading.
    Nonteaching employees, T 18.13
    "Opt-in" elections, T 18.11(B), T 18.29(E)
    Professional and nonprofessional employees in same unit, T 18.08
    Removal of excluded employees, T 18.04(B)
    Teachers, T 18.12
Benefits, subject to bargaining, T 18.28, T 43.05(B)
Boycotts, unfair labor practice, T 18.25(A)
Casual employees, exclusion, T 18.07
Certification of organization—See Employee organizations, this heading.
Civil rights statutes prevailing over bargaining agreements, T 18.20
Civil service appointments, inappropriate subject for bargaining, T 18.28(A)
Clarification of bargaining units, T 18.11(B)
Commencement of bargaining, T 18.29(B)
Common pleas courts, enforcement powers—See COURTS OF COMMON PLEAS.
Complaints
    Unfair labor practices, T 18.26(A)
Concerted activity, T 18.09
Confidential employees, exclusion, T 18.06
Conflict of interest
    Employer's representative, T 18.27
Consent election agreements, T 18.15(B)
Constitutionality of agency shop provisions, T 18.21(C)
"Contract bar" doctrine, T 18.17(A)
Coverage, T 18.03 to T 18.08
Damages, unfair labor practices, T 18.26(C)
Decertification of employee organizations, T 18.18
"Deemed certified" units
    Affiliation, change in, T 18.17(C)
    Alteration, T 18.11(B)
    "Contract bar" doctrine, applicability, T 18.17(A)
    Decertification petitions, T 18.18
    Defined, T 18.14
    Exclusive representative, as, T 18.14
Defamation, standard, T 18.34
Definitions, T 18.03 to T 18.08
    "Deemed certified" units, T 18.14
    Unfair labor practices, T 18.24(A), T 18.25(A)
Direct dealing, T 18.24(D)
Discharge of employees—See Suspension or discharge of employees, this heading.
Disciplinary actions, employees's right to union representation at hearing, T 18.09

COLLECTIVE BARGAINING, PUBLIC EMPLOYEES—*continued*
Discrimination, unfair labor practice, T 18.24(A), T 18.24(F)
Dispute settlement procedure, T 18.29
Dues
   Fair share fees, T 18.21
      Constitutionality, T 18.21(C)
   Payroll deductions, T 10.08, T 18.19(A), T 18.21(A)
   Rebates to nonmembers, T 18.21(B)
      Constitutionality, T 18.21(C)
Duty to bargain, T 18.10
Education requirements, T 18.20
Elections
   Consent election agreement, T 18.15(B)
   Decertification of employee organization, T 18.18
   Fact-finding panel recommendations, acceptance or rejection, T 18.29(C)
   "Opt-in" elections, T 18.11(B), T 18.29(E)
   Representation elections—See Representation elections, this heading.
   Timeline, T 18.35
Employee organizations
   Affiliation, T 18.17(C)
   Breach of duty, unfair labor practice, T 18.25(D)
   Certification, T 18.14 to T 18.18
      Amendment, T 18.17(C)
      Elections, T 18.15
      Notice, T 18.15(E)
      Timeline for objection, T 18.35
      Voluntary recognition, T 18.16(B)
   Consent election agreement, T 18.15(B)
   "Contract bar" doctrine, T 18.17(A)
   Decertification by election, T 18.18
   "Deemed certified" units—See "Deemed certified" units, this heading.
   Defined, T 18.04(A)
   Domination by employer, T 18.24(E)
   Exclusive representation—See Exclusive representation, this heading.
   Existing contract or agreement, effect, T 18.10, T 18.28
   Fair representation, T 18.25(D)
   "Grandfathered" units—See "Deemed certified" units, this heading.
   Interference by employer, unfair labor practice, T 18.24(A), T 18.24(B)
   Membership
      Prohibition against requiring, T 18.21(B)
      Religious exemption, T 18.21(B)
   Notice of intent to strike given by, T 18.25(A), T 18.29(D), T 18.30
   Notice to negotiate, T 18.29(B)
   Payroll deductions of dues, T 10.08, T 18.19(A)
   Refusal to bargain, T 18.25(C)
   Right to join or to refrain from joining, T 18.09
   Unfair labor practices by, T 18.25
   Voluntary recognition, T 18.14, T 18.16
      Certification, T 18.16(B)

COLLECTIVE BARGAINING, PUBLIC EMPLOYEES—*continued*
Employee organizations—*continued*
   Voluntary recognition—*continued*
      Notice of request, T 18.16(B)
Employees
   Exemption from coverage, T 18.04 to T 18.07
   Organizations—See Employee organizations, this heading.
   Rights, T 18.09
   Unfair labor practices by, T 18.25
      See also Unfair labor practices, this heading.
Employers
   Conflict of interest, representatives, T 18.27
   Defined, T 18.03
   Domination of union, T 18.24(E)
   Duty to bargain, T 18.10
   Jurisdiction, T 18.28
   Notice of strike or picketing given to, T 18.25(A), T 18.29(D), T 18.30
   Rights, T 18.28
   Unauthorized strikes, powers, T 18.31
   Unfair labor practices by, T 18.24
      See also Unfair labor practices, this heading.
Employers' representatives
   Conflict of interest, T 18.27
Employment relations board—See EMPLOYMENT RELATIONS BOARD.
Exclusion from coverage, T 18.04 to T 18.07
Exclusive representation, T 18.10
   Certification, T 18.14 to T 18.18
      Elections, T 18.15
      Notice, T 18.15(E)
   Challenge to incumbent, T 18.17
   Consent election agreement, T 18.15(B)
   "Contract bar" doctrine, T 18.17(A)
   Decertification elections, T 18.18
   "Deemed certified" units—See "Deemed certified" units, this heading.
   Election—See Representation elections, this heading.
   Existing contract or agreement, effect, T 18.10, T 18.28
   "Grandfathered" units—See "Deemed certified" units, this heading.
   Interference by employer, unfair labor practice, T 18.24(A), T 18.24(B)
   "No representative" choice, T 18.15(C)
   Petition for election, T 18.15(A), T 18.17(A)
   Rights, T 18.10
   Run-off election, T 18.15(C)
   Voluntary recognition, T 18.14, T 18.16
Expiration of bargaining period, determination, T 18.29(B)
Fact-finding panels
   Appointment, T 18.29(C)
   Powers and duties, T 18.29(C)
   Public access to final recommendations, T 18.27
   Recommendations, acceptance or rejection, T 18.29(C)

COLLECTIVE BARGAINING, PUBLIC EMPLOYEES—*continued*
Fair share fees, T 18.21
  Constitutionality, T 18.21(C)
Fees and costs—See Dues, this heading.
Ferguson Act, T 18.01(A)
Final recommendations of fact-finding panels, T 18.29(C)
  Public access to, T 18.27
"Grandfathered" units—See "Deemed certified" units, this heading.
Grievance procedure
  Agreement to include provisions for, T 18.19(A)
  Civil service commissions, lack of jurisdiction, T 18.22(A)
  Court action in lieu of utilizing, T 18.22(A)
  Failure to exhaust, T 18.22(A)
  Failure to process, T 18.24(G)
  Final arbitration, binding, T 18.22(A)
  Rights of employees, T 18.09
Hearings
  Fact-finding panel conducting, T 18.29(C)
  Public access, T 18.33
  Representation election petitions, on, T 18.15(A)
  Unfair labor practice, T 18.26(A)
Hiring, employers' jurisdiction, T 18.28
Historical background, T 18.01
Hours, subject to collective bargaining, T 18.28
Injunctive relief
  Bargaining during injunction period, T 18.32
  Clear and present danger, T 18.32
  Unauthorized strikes, against, T 18.31
Intervention
  Employment relations board, T 18.29(C)
Leaves of absence, subject to bargaining, T 18.28
Lock-outs
  Definition, T 15.06
  Unfair labor practices, T 18.24(A)
Management-level employees, definition, T 18.05
Management rights, T 18.28
Mandatory bargaining topics, T 18.28(B)
Mediation, T 18.29(C)
  Injunction period, during, T 18.32
  Reports, public, T 18.32
  Timetable, T 18.35
Mediation bureau, T 18.02
Meetings, private, T 18.27
Mental retardation and developmental disabilities boards, county, T 29.17
Military service statutes, agreements conflicting with, T 18.20
Notice
  Appeal from unfair labor practice claims, T 18.26(C)
  Certification of employee organization, T 18.15(E)
  Picketing, T 18.25(A)
  Proposed termination, modification or successor agreement, T 18.29(B)
  Strikes, T 18.25(A), T 18.29(D), T 18.30

COLLECTIVE BARGAINING, PUBLIC EMPLOYEES—*continued*
Notice—*continued*
  Voluntary recognition, request for, T 18.16(B)
"Open window" rule, T 18.17(A), T 18.18
Peer review plans, inclusion in agreements, T 18.19(B)
Permissive bargaining topics, T 18.28(B)
Petitions, decertification, T 18.18
Picketing
  Notice, T 18.25(A)
  Unfair labor practice, when, T 18.25(A)
Political activities, T 18.20
Privacy of meetings, T 18.27
Private school employees, T 48.28
Prohibited bargaining topics, T 18.28(B)
Propaganda distribution, unfair labor practice, T 18.25(B)
Records and reports
  Public access, T 18.27, T 18.33
Refusal to bargain, T 18.25(C)
  Unfair labor practice, as, T 18.17(B), T 18.24(C), T 18.25(A), T 18.27
Reinstatement of employees
  Unauthorized strikes, after, T 18.31
  Unfair labor practice, to remedy, T 18.26(B)
Religious exemption from membership, T 18.21(B)
Representation elections, T 18.15
  Challenge, T 18.15(D)
  Consent election agreement, T 18.15(B)
  "Contract bar" doctrine, T 18.17(A)
  Existing contract or agreement, effect, T 18.17
  "No representative" choice, T 18.15(C)
  Petitions, T 18.15(A), T 18.17(A)
  Run-off, T 18.15(C)
Restraining orders
  Strikes, clear and present danger, T 18.32
Rights of employees, T 18.09
  Interference with, unfair labor practice
    Employee or union, by, T 18.25(A), T 18.25(B)
    Employer, by, T 18.24(B)
School employees, nonteaching
  Bargaining units, T 18.13
  Private schools, T 48.28
Scope of bargaining, T 18.28, T 43.05(B)
Seasonal employees, exclusion, T 18.07
Strikes, T 18.30 to T 18.32
  Board to determine authorization, T 18.31
  Clear and present danger, injunctive relief, T 18.32
  Compensation during, employee not entitled to, T 18.30
  Injunctions against
    Clear and present danger, T 18.32
    Unauthorized strikes, T 18.27, T 18.31
  Negotiation period, during
    Prohibition, T 18.30, T 18.31
    Unauthorized strike, as, T 18.31
  Notice, T 18.25(A), T 18.29(D), T 18.30
  Procedural timetables, T 18.35

COLLECTIVE BARGAINING, PUBLIC EMPLOYEES—*continued*
Strikes—*continued*
  Prohibited
    Injunction against unauthorized strike, T 18.27, T 18.31
  Temporary restraining orders, T 18.32
  Term of agreement, during
    Prohibition, T 18.30, T 18.31
    Unauthorized strike, as, T 18.31
  Unauthorized strikes, T 18.31
    Defined, T 18.31
    Determination by board, effect, T 18.31
    Injunction against, T 18.27, T 18.31
    Penalty imposed on employee, T 18.31
    Prohibited, T 18.31
    Unfair labor practice, when, T 18.25(A), T 18.25(B)
Subject matter appropriate for bargaining, T 18.28, T 43.05(B)
Substitute teachers, exclusion, T 18.07
Sunshine law, meetings exempt, T 18.27
Superintendents, local; exclusion, T 18.05(B)
Supervisors, definition, T 18.05(B)
Suspension or discharge of employees
  Permissive bargaining topic, T 18.28(B)
  Reinstatement
    Unauthorized strike, after, T 18.31
    Unfair labor practice, to remedy, T 18.26(B)
  Unauthorized strikes, for participation in, T 18.31
  Unfair labor practice, for; prohibition, T 18.26(C)
Teacher bargaining units, T 18.12
Teachers, disciplinary suspension, T 9.20
Tentative agreements, T 18.28(C)
Time requirements, T 18.35
  Commencement of bargaining, T 18.29(B)
  Dispute settlement procedure, commencement, T 18.29(A)
  Expiration of bargaining period, T 18.29(B)
  Fact-finding
    Appointment of panel, T 18.29(C)
    Submission of final recommendations, T 18.29(C)
  Intervention by employment relations board, T 18.29(C)
  Mediation, commencement, T 18.29(C)
  Representation election, time for holding, T 18.15(C), T 18.17(A)
  Representation petition, time for filing, T 18.17(A)
  Unfair labor practice complaints, time for filing, T 18.26(A)
Transcripts
  Unfair labor practice hearings, certification to common pleas court, T 18.26(C)
Unemployment compensation, T 18.20
Unfair labor practices, T 18.24 to T 18.26
  Appeals to common pleas courts, T 18.26(C)
  Cease and desist orders, T 18.26(B)
  Complaints, T 18.26(A)

COLLECTIVE BARGAINING, PUBLIC EMPLOYEES—*continued*
Unfair labor practices—*continued*
  Damages, T 18.26(C)
  Defined, T 18.24(A), T 18.25(A)
  Discrimination, T 18.24(A), T 18.24(F)
  Employee organizations, by, T 18.25
  Employers, by, T 18.24
  Employment relations board, powers and duties, T 18.26
  Hearings on complaints, T 18.26(A)
    Transcripts, certification to common pleas court, T 18.26(C)
  Interference with employee rights
    Employee or union, by, T 18.25(A), T 18.25(B)
    Employer, by, T 18.24(B)
  Jurisdiction of common pleas courts, T 18.26(C)
  Lock-outs, T 18.24(A)
  Modification of orders, T 18.26(C)
  Notice
    Appeal to common pleas court, T 18.26(C)
  Picketing as, T 18.25(A)
  Propaganda distribution, T 18.25(B)
  Refusal to bargain, T 18.17(B), T 18.24(C), T 18.25(A), T 18.27
  Reinstatement of employee as remedy, T 18.26(B)
  Remedies, T 18.26(B)
  Suspension or discharge of employee as penalty, T 18.26(C)
  Timetable, procedural, T 18.35
  Unauthorized strikes as, T 18.25(A), T 18.25(B)
Union affiliation votes, T 18.17(C)
Units—See Bargaining units, this heading.
Wages
  Strikes, during; employee not entitled to, T 18.30
  Subject to bargaining, T 18.28
  Unauthorized strikes, effect, T 18.31
"Weingarten Rule", T 18.09
Workers' compensation, T 18.20

COLLEGE PREPARATORY SCHOOLS, T 26.07(B)

COLLEGES—See particular college concerned; UNIVERSITIES AND COLLEGES.

COLLISION INSURANCE—See MOTOR VEHICLE INSURANCE, generally.

COMMERCIAL SCHOOLS—See VOCATIONAL EDUCATION.

COMMISSIONERS, COUNTY—See COUNTY COMMISSIONERS.

COMMISSIONS—See also particular subject concerned.
Education, T 2.10
School district records commissions, T 44.22, T 44.23

COMMON PLEAS COURTS—See COURTS OF COMMON PLEAS.

COMMON SCHOOL MOVEMENT, T 1.07, T 1.08

COMMUNICABLE DISEASES
AIDS—See AIDS.
Discrimination on basis of handicap, T 17.13
Disinfection of schools, T 21.08(B)
Immunization—See IMMUNIZATION.
Inspections, T 21.08(B)
Schools
  AIDS, T 21.03(E)
    See also AIDS.
  Closing due to epidemic, T 20.05(D), T 21.08(B)
  Disinfection, T 21.08(B)
  Immunization of pupils—See IMMUNIZATION, at School children.
  Pupils or personnel contracting communicable diseases, T 10.18, T 13.10, T 21.03(D)
Tuberculosis—See TUBERCULOSIS.

COMMUNITY COLLEGES
Personal information systems, T 44.01, T 44.04 to T 44.11

COMMUNITY SERVICE
Education, T 5.09(N)
Students, performance as alternative to suspension or expulsion, T 25.10(D)

COMPENSATION—See also WAGES AND HOURS.
College faculty and employees—See particular college concerned.
Deferred, educational employees, T 11.23, T 14.15
Fair Labor Standards Act, equal pay, T 17.08
Mental retardation and developmental disabilities board employees, T 29.13(A)
Public employees—See PUBLIC EMPLOYEES.
Public officials—See PUBLIC OFFICIALS.
School administrators, T 7.11(A)
School board treasurers, T 6.05
School district business managers, T 6.11
School employees—See SCHOOL EMPLOYEES, NONTEACHING; TEACHERS.
School employees retirement board and employees, T 14.02(A)
School superintendents, T 7.05(B)
State board of education members, T 3.02(B)
Superintendent of public instruction, T 3.05
Superintendents, local, T 7.05(B)

COMPENSATION—continued
Teachers—See TEACHERS.
Teachers retirement board members, T 11.02(A)
Treasurers, school board, T 6.05
Unemployment—See UNEMPLOYMENT COMPENSATION.
Workers' compensation—See WORKERS' COMPENSATION.

COMPETENCY-BASED EDUCATION PROGRAMS, T 26.02(C), T 26.04, T 26.15, T 28.10(B)

COMPETITIVE BIDDING—See BIDDING, COMPETITIVE.

COMPLAINTS
Criminal offenses—See particular crime or offense concerned.
Discrimination
  Employment, T 17.03(D), T 17.04(C)
  Public depositories, against, T 42.12
Employment discrimination, T 17.03(D), T 17.04(C)
Employment of minors, violations, T 20.17
Family and Medical Leave Act of 1993, violations, T 17.16
Public depositories, discrimination against, T 42.12
Special education programs, against, T 28.12, T 28.13
Teacher contract termination, appeals from, T 9.23
Truancy, T 20.09(A)
Unfair labor practices, T 18.26(A)

COMPULSORY ATTENDANCE—See ATTENDANCE.

COMPUTERS—See DATA PROCESSING.

CONCESSIONS—See VENDING FACILITIES.

CONDUCT OF PUPILS, T Ch 25
See also PUPILS, generally.

CONFERENCES
Audit conferences with local boards of education, sunshine law exemption, T 5.12
Educators and parents, non-residential parents, T 31.03
Teachers and parents, T 20.05(A), T 20.05(B), T 31.03, T 48.04(B)

CONFIDENTIAL INFORMATION—See PRIVILEGED INFORMATION.

CONFLICT OF INTEREST, T 45.08
  See also particular public official or employee concerned.
  Assistant county prosecutors, mental retardation and developmental disabilities board membership, T 29.02(C)
  Banks, as public depositories, T 42.12, T 45.08(B)
  Building and loan associations, as public depositories, T 42.12, T 45.08(B)
  Contracts, awarding, T 45.05 to T 45.07
    Arm's length transaction, exception, T 45.05(D)
    "Continuing course of dealing," exception, T 45.05(D)
    State board of education, T 3.02(C)
  County commissioners
    Mental retardation and developmental disabilities board membership, T 29.02(C)
    School principal serving as, T 7.09(C)
  Directors of vocational schools, T 45.08(A)
  Libraries
    Board of trustees, T 34.03, T 34.09(A)
    State library board members, T 34.06
  Mental health service district board members, T 7.09(C)
  Mental retardation and developmental disabilities boards, T 29.02(C), T 45.08(B)
  Municipal legislative authority members, mental retardation and developmental disabilities board membership, T 29.02(C)
  Principals, T 7.09(C), T 45.08(A)
  Public depositories, T 42.12, T 45.08(B)
  Public employers' negotiation representatives, T 18.27
  Public officials and employees
    Representation of clients, T 45.03
  Representation of clients by present or former public officials or employees, T 45.03
  School administrator as sales agent of publisher or supplier, T 8.07(B), T 33.05, T 45.07
  School board members—See EDUCATION, LOCAL BOARDS.
  School board treasurers, T 6.02(A), T 6.13, T 45.08(B)
  School business managers, T 6.13
  School employees retirement system board, T 14.02(B)
  School principals, T 7.09(C), T 45.08(A)
  State board of education members, T 3.02(A), T 3.02(C), T 45.08(A)
  Superintendent of public instruction, T 3.05, T 45.08(A)
    Financial interest in book publishing or selling concern, T 45.07
  Teacher or school administrator as sales agent of publisher or supplier, T 8.07(B), T 33.05, T 45.07
  Teachers retirement system board, T 11.02(B)

CONGRESS, UNITED STATES
  Land appropriations for school funding, T 1.02, T 1.05

CONSOLIDATED OMNIBUS BUDGET RECONCILIATION ACT (COBRA), T 10.12

CONSOLIDATION OF SCHOOL DISTRICTS—See REORGANIZATION OF SCHOOL DISTRICTS.

CONSTABLES—See LAW ENFORCEMENT OFFICERS.

CONSTITUTION, STATE
  Education, provisions concerning, T 1.03, T 1.04, T 1.09, T 2.14

CONSTITUTION, UNITED STATES
  Education, provisions concerning, T 2.11(A)
  Equal protection clause of Fourteenth Amendment
    Aliens enrolled in school, protection, T 19.16
    Desegregation of schools, applicability, T 19.02 to T 19.06
    Employment discrimination, applicability, T 17.02(A)
    Sex discrimination in schools, applicability, T 19.14(D)
  Religion, "establishment" and "free exercise" clauses, T 32.01

CONSTITUTIONALITY
  Athletic events, admission charges for nonresidents, T 39.15
  Collective bargaining agreements, agency shop provisions, T 18.21(C)
  Compulsory school attendance, T 20.02(A)
  Foundation program, T 39.06(B)
  Funding system for schools, current, T 39.01(B)
  School desegregation statutes, T 19.12
  Transportation of students to nonpublic schools, T 22.03(C)

CONSTRUCTION
  School buildings—See SCHOOL BUILDINGS AND LANDS.
  Vocational education projects, T 27.05

CONSULTANTS
  School boards hiring, T 5.09(A)

CONTIGUITY OF SCHOOL DISTRICT TERRITORY, T 4.05(B)

CONTINUING CONTRACTS
  School employees, nonteaching, T 12.09(A)
  Teachers—See TEACHERS.

CONTRACTS—See also CONTRACTS, SCHOOL.
  Accounting services, approval, T 43.26(A)
  Auditing services, approval, T 43.26(A)
  Automatic data processing services, T 43.29
  Bidding—See BIDDING, COMPETITIVE.

CONTRACTS—*continued*
Classroom facility projects, T 41.29
Collective bargaining, public employees—See COLLECTIVE BARGAINING, PUBLIC EMPLOYEES, at Agreements.
Conflict of interest, T 45.05 to T 45.07
  "Continuing course of dealing," exception, T 45.05(D)
  State board of education, T 3.02(C)
Continuing
  School employees, nonteaching, T 12.09(A)
  Teachers—See TEACHERS.
Libraries—See LIBRARIES AND LIBRARY DISTRICTS.
Limited
  School employees, nonteaching, T 12.09(A)
Mental retardation and developmental disabilities boards, T 29.07
Museums, educational programs, T 5.09(D), T 26.11(A), T 31.05
Public employees, collective bargaining—See COLLECTIVE BARGAINING, PUBLIC EMPLOYEES, at Agreements.
Publishers with public schools, T 33.03
Schools—See CONTRACTS, SCHOOL.
Special education
  Exchange of teachers, T 28.15(B)
  Teachers, T 29.10(B)
Supplemental
  School employees, nonteaching, T 12.09(G)
  Teachers—See TEACHERS.
Teachers—See TEACHERS.
Textbooks for public schools, T 33.03
Treasurers of school boards, employment, T 6.02(C), T 6.05
Universities—See particular university concerned; UNIVERSITIES AND COLLEGES.
Unlawful interest in, T 45.05 to T 45.07
  State board of education, T 3.02(C)
Vocational education, T 27.02

CONTRACTS, SCHOOL—See also CONTRACTS, generally.
Accounting or auditing services, approval, T 43.26(A)
Administrative officers, employment, T 7.11, T 9.07(A)(2)
Adult education programs
  School boards contracting with nonprofit associations, T 26.10(A)
Automatic data processing services, T 43.29
Bids—See BIDDING, COMPETITIVE.
Boards of education, powers and duties, T 5.09(B), T 43.02(C), T 46.08
Bond issuance, clerical services, T 43.19
Boundary agreements, T 4.07(B)
Breach of contract, private school employment, T 48.24
Bus purchases, T 22.09
  Competitive bidding, T 36.04(B), T 36.04(C)(3)
Business managers, powers and duties, T 6.13

CONTRACTS, SCHOOL—*continued*
Certification of adequate funds, T 6.07(C)
  Construction and improvements, T 37.07(A)
Classroom facility projects, T 41.29
Coaches, employment, T 12.10
Collective bargaining—See COLLECTIVE BARGAINING, PUBLIC EMPLOYEES, generally.
College-level courses, T 5.09(D), T 26.11(A), T 31.05
Conflict of interest, T 45.05 to T 45.07
  "Continuing course of dealing," exception, T 45.05(D)
  State board of education, T 3.02(C)
Construction managers, T 37.10
Continuing
  School employees, nonteaching, T 12.09(A)
  Teachers—See TEACHERS.
Driver training courses, T 26.14
Educational service centers, with, T 5.09(I)
Employees, nonteaching, T 12.09
  See also SCHOOL EMPLOYEES, NONTEACHING.
Enrollment, private schools, T 48.11
Equal employment opportunity provisions, T 17.05
Exchange of teaching services, T 9.16, T 28.15(B)
Extracurricular activity directors, employment, T 12.10
Food services, inter-district, T 35.05
Gifted children, special classes, T 26.09
Liability
  School boards, T 46.08
Limited contracts—See also TEACHERS.
  School employees, nonteaching, T 12.09(A)
Mineral rights, T 36.10(B), T 39.15
Museums, with, T 5.09(D), T 26.11(A), T 31.05
Notice of nonrenewal—See particular type of contract concerned.
Payment procedure, T 43.09
Performance bonds, building construction and improvements, T 37.06(B)
Principals, employment, T 7.11
Purchase contracts for supplies, equipment, and services, T 36.04(B)
Purchase orders, T 43.07(B)
  Disposition, T 43.07(C)
Requisitions, T 43.07(A)
Special education
  Exchange of teachers, T 28.15(B)
  Teachers, T 7.12, T 29.10(B)
Superintendents, employment, T 7.05(A)
  Notice of nonrenewal, T 7.04(B)
  Termination, T 7.05(A)
Supplemental
  School employees, nonteaching, T 12.09(G)
  Teachers—See TEACHERS.
Teachers—See TEACHERS.
Textbooks, T 33.03
Transportation of pupils—See TRANSPORTATION OF PUPILS.

CONTRACTS, SCHOOL—*continued*
Treasurers of boards, employment, T 6.02(C), T 6.05
Unlawful interest in, T 45.05 to T 45.07
 State board of education, T 3.02(C)
Vocational education programs, T 27.02

CONTRIBUTIONS
Charitable—See GIFTS AND GRANTS.
Political—See POLITICAL CONTRIBUTIONS.
Retirement systems—See SCHOOL EMPLOYEES RETIREMENT SYSTEM; TEACHERS RETIREMENT SYSTEM.

CONTROLLED SUBSTANCES—See DRUG OFFENSES; PRESCRIPTION DRUGS.

CONTROLLING BOARD
Classroom facility projects, approval, T 41.27(A)
Emergency loans, powers and duties, T 41.33(D)
Foundation program payments, powers, T 39.06(C)
School district operating loans, powers, T 41.33(D)

CONVEYANCES
School property—See SCHOOL BUILDINGS AND LANDS, at Sale.

CONVICTIONS
Destruction of school property, T 38.05
Employment applicants—See particular employee concerned.

COOPERATIVE EDUCATION SCHOOL DISTRICTS, T 4.03(G)
Average daily membership
 Foundation program, T 39.09(B)
Competency-based education programs, T 26.02(C)
Creation, T 4.03(G)
Dissolution, T 4.03(G)
Educational service centers, T 4.03(G)
Foundation program, T 4.03(G)
 Average daily membership, T 39.09(B)
Legal advisers, T 6.14(A)
Preschool programs, transportation of children, T 22.03(A)
Proficiency tests, T 26.06(B)
Tax levies
 Reduction, T 40.14
Treasurers, T 4.03(G)

COPYRIGHTS
Textbooks, T 33.06

CORPORAL PUNISHMENT—See PUPILS.

CORPORATIONS
Educational—See UNIVERSITIES AND COLLEGES.

CORPORATIONS—*continued*
Schooling provided by, part-time, T 20.15

CORRECTIONAL INSTITUTIONS
Educational programs
 High school programs, T 26.16
 Inspection of schools, T 3.03(G)
High school programs, T 26.16
Inmates' children, school district of residence, T 23.02(A)(3), T 23.02(B)
Inspections, schools, T 3.03(G)
Officials, dereliction of duty, T 45.12

CORRESPONDENCE SCHOOLS
Instruction by in place of school attendance, T 20.03(C)

CORRUPTING ANOTHER WITH DRUGS, T 24.14

COSTS—See FEES AND COSTS.

COUNSELING—See GUIDANCE AND COUNSELING PROGRAMS; PSYCHOLOGISTS AND PSYCHOLOGY.

COUNTIES—See also TAXING DISTRICTS, generally.
Actions against, T Ch 46
 See also PUBLIC LIABILITY ACT.
Appropriations
 Mental retardation and developmental disabilities board, for, T 29.09(A)
Auditors—See AUDITORS, COUNTY.
Boards of education—See EDUCATIONAL SERVICE CENTERS, at Governing boards.
Budget commissions—See BUDGET COMMISSIONS, COUNTY.
Civil service—See CIVIL SERVICE.
Commissioners—See COUNTY COMMISSIONERS.
Employees—See PUBLIC EMPLOYEES, generally.
Funds—See also FUNDS, PUBLIC, generally.
 General fund
  Interest credited to, permanent improvement funds, T 29.09(A)
Liability—See PUBLIC LIABILITY ACT.
Mental retardation and developmental disabilities boards, T Ch 29
 See also MENTAL RETARDATION AND DEVELOPMENTAL DISABILITIES BOARDS, COUNTY.
Officials—See particular office concerned; PUBLIC OFFICIALS.
Prosecutors—See PROSECUTORS, COUNTY.
Regional councils, T 5.09(D)
School boards—See EDUCATIONAL SERVICE CENTERS, at Governing boards.

COUNTIES—*continued*
School districts—See EDUCATIONAL SERVICE CENTERS.
Taxes and levies
　Abatements, T 39.04
　Mental health and retardation services, T 29.09(A)
Treasurers—See TREASURERS, COUNTY.

COUNTY BOARDS OF EDUCATION—See EDUCATIONAL SERVICE CENTERS, at Governing boards.

COUNTY BOARDS OF MENTAL RETARDATION AND DEVELOPMENTAL DISABILITIES, T Ch 29
　See also MENTAL RETARDATION AND DEVELOPMENTAL DISABILITIES BOARDS, COUNTY.

COUNTY BOARDS OF REVISION
Appeals to, real property assessments, T 39.04

COUNTY BUDGET COMMISSIONS—See BUDGET COMMISSIONS, COUNTY.

COUNTY COMMISSIONERS
Conflict of interest
　Mental retardation and developmental disabilities board membership, T 29.02(C)
　School principal, serving as, T 7.09(C)
Educational service center governing boards
　Conference facility, T 7.08
　Offices and telephone equipment, T 7.08

COUNTY COURTS
Employment of minors, violation proceedings, T 20.17
Jurisdiction
　Employment of minor, violation, T 20.17
　Truancy, T 20.09(A)
Truancy proceedings, T 20.09(A)

COUNTY SCHOOL DISTRICTS—See EDUCATIONAL SERVICE CENTERS.
Boards of education—See EDUCATIONAL SERVICE CENTERS, at Governing boards.

COURSES OF STUDY—See CURRICULUM.

COURT DECISIONS
Impact on school law, T 2.16

COURTS—See particular court concerned.

COURTS OF APPEALS
Appeals to; teacher termination, standard of review, T 9.23(B)

COURTS OF COMMON PLEAS
Appeals to
　Civil service decisions, T 12.17(D)
　Disabled children, educational placement, T 28.11(F)
　Employment services bureau orders, occupational safety and health violations, T 16.09(A)
　Special education, pupil placement, T 28.11(F)
　Student suspension or expulsion, T 25.12(B)
　Teacher termination, T 9.23
　Workers' compensation claim, T 16.07(B)
Collective bargaining, public employees
　Employment relations board orders; modifying, setting aside, or enforcing, T 18.26(C)
　Unfair labor practices
　　Appeals, T 18.26(C)
　　Jurisdiction, T 18.26(C)
Jurisdiction
　Strikes, temporary restraining orders, T 18.32
　Unfair labor practices, T 18.26(C)

CREATION OF NEW SCHOOL DISTRICTS—See REORGANIZATION OF SCHOOL DISTRICTS.

CREATIONISM
Instruction about, T 32.07

CREDIT UNIONS
Public employees, payroll deductions, T 10.08

CRIMES AND OFFENSES—See also particular crime or offense concerned.
Arson, T 38.04(A)
Assault—See ASSAULT.
Bribery, T 45.11
Child abuse—See CHILD ABUSE.
Children committing—See also JUVENILE DELINQUENCY.
　Parental liability, T 38.06
County mental retardation and developmental disabilities board employees, disqualification, T 29.14
Dereliction of duty, T 45.12
Destruction of property—See DESTRUCTION OF PROPERTY.
Disorderly conduct, T 38.04(E)
Disrupting public services, T 38.04(B)
Drug offenses—See DRUG OFFENSES.
Endangering children—See ENDANGERING CHILDREN.
Felonies—See FELONIES.
Hazing, T 24.10
　Liability of school personnel, T 46.10, T 46.14(B)
Juvenile delinquency—See JUVENILE DELINQUENCY.
Minors, against, T 24.08 to T 24.15
Obscenity—See OBSCENITY.
Reporting requirements, T 24.06, T 24.08

CRIMES AND OFFENSES—*continued*
School property, against; reward for information leading to arrest and conviction, T 38.05
Sex offenses—See SEX OFFENSES.
Trespassing, T 38.03
Vandalism, T 38.04(C)
  Reward for information leading to arrest and conviction, T 38.05
Weapons—See WEAPONS, generally.

CURRICULUM, T 2.05, T Ch 26
Advanced studies, T 5.09(D), T 26.10(A), T 26.11(A), T 31.05
  Tuition, T 23.02(E)
American sign language, T 26.06(A), T 28.18
Assault prevention, T 21.14
Bilingual education, T 19.15
Braille, integration into curriculum of blind persons, T 28.02
Conservation to be taught, T 26.02(A)
Content, T 26.04
Course of study, T 26.02(A)
Driver training—See DRIVER TRAINING COURSES.
Educational policies, T 26.04
Elementary schools, T 26.05(B)
Evaluation, T 26.04, T 26.17
Goals 2000: Educate America Act of 1994, T 2.11(B)
Guides, publication by school boards, T 5.09(G), T 31.02
High schools, T 26.06
Junior high schools, T 26.05(C)
Kindergartens, T 26.05(A)
Minimum standards, T 26.02(A)
  Goals 2000: Educate America Act of 1994, T 2.11(B)
  School board's powers, T 26.03
Options, T 26.07
Personal safety, T 21.14
Phonics as technique in teaching reading, T 3.03(G)
Physical education, T 30.02
    See also PHYSICAL EDUCATION.
Pledge of allegiance to flag, local policy, T 26.02(A)
Regulation, T 26.06
Religious objections, T 32.07
Required courses, T 26.02(A), T 26.05
Requirement, T 26.04
Safety instruction, T 21.14, T 22.19, T 29.06(B)
School boards, powers, T 26.03
Sex discrimination, T 19.14
Sex education, T 32.07
Sign language, T 26.06(A), T 28.18
State minimum standards, T 26.02
Studies and surveys, T 5.09(A)

CUSTODY OF CHILDREN
Adoption, effect on school district of residence, T 23.02(A)(6)
Definitions, T 23.02(A)

CUSTODY OF CHILDREN—*continued*
School district of residence, effect on, T 23.02(A)(2), T 23.02(A)(4), T 23.02(A)(6), T 23.02(C)(1), T 23.03(B)

DAMAGES
Assault, children committing, T 38.06
Collective bargaining agreements, violations, T 18.26(C)
Destruction of property by children, T 38.06
Discrimination
  Age, double damages, T 17.06(A)
  Employment
    Compensatory, T 17.03(E)
    Punitive damages, T 17.02(B), T 17.03(E)
  Schools, by, T 19.13(E)
  Sex discrimination, T 19.14(C)
Parental liability for acts of children, T 38.06
Personal information systems, recoverable from, T 44.08(B)
Theft by children, T 38.06
Unfair labor practices, T 18.26(C)

DATA PROCESSING
Education data management unit, establishment and responsibilities, T 3.04(D)
Education management information system, T 3.03(F), T 26.17
Ohio education computer network, T 26.11(G)
Personal information systems—See PERSONAL INFORMATION SYSTEMS.
School districts, for, T 3.03(G), T 26.11(G), T 43.29
  Acquisition of equipment, T 36.04(C)(1)
  Competitive bidding, exemption, T 37.04(A)
  Ohio education computer network, T 26.11(G)

DAY CARE
Centers
  Child abuse, reporting, T 24.05
  Employees
    Training programs, T 27.07
  Licenses, T 26.11(D)
  Transportation of children
    Vehicle lights and signs, T 22.12

DEAF PERSONS—See also HANDICAPPED PERSONS, generally.
Schooling—See also SPECIAL EDUCATION, generally; State school, this heading.
  Attendance, T 20.01, T 20.02(C), T 28.17(A)
    Excused from attendance, T 20.03(B)
  Education department, powers and duties, T 3.04(A)
  Foundation program funding, T 28.15(A), T 28.18, T 39.08(A)
  Interpreter services, T 3.04(A)
  Method of instruction, T 3.04(A), T 28.15(A), T 28.18
  Parent programs, T 28.18
  Preschool training, T 28.18
  Technical assistance, T 3.04(A), T 28.18

DEAF PERSONS—*continued*
Sign language
  High school course, T 26.06(A), T 28.18
State school, T 28.19
  Admission, T 28.19(B)
  Personnel, T 28.19(A)
  Return of pupil to parents, T 28.19(B)
  Superintendent, appointment, T 28.19(A)
  Teachers, T 28.19(A)
Trained dogs accompanying, T 17.13(A), T 28.18

DEATH
Parent, of; effect on child's school district of residence, T 23.02(C)(6)

DEBTS—See also BONDS AND NOTES.
School districts incurring, T 41.05 to T 41.08, T 41.21
    See also BONDS AND NOTES, SCHOOL.
  Classroom facilities project, T 41.24, T 41.26
  Creation of new district, effect, T 4.13
  Limits, T 41.05 to T 41.08
    Special needs districts, T 41.07
    Transfer of territory, effect, T 4.13
    Unvoted debt, T 41.05
    Voted debt, T 41.06
  Reorganization of district, effect, T 4.13
  Special needs districts, T 41.07

DEFENSES
Employment discrimination; wages, gender-based claims, T 17.08(C)
Obscenity cases, T 24.12
Public Liability Act, under, T 46.02, T 46.04, T 46.15, T 46.17(C)
School employees, actions against, T 46.04

DEFINITIONS
Bond and note, T 41.03
Borrowing, T 41.02
Child—See MINORS.
Child abuse, T 24.05(C)
Civil service
  Appointing authority, T 12.06
Classroom facility, T 41.24
Collective bargaining, T 18.03 to T 18.08
  Deemed certified unit, T 18.14
  Unfair labor practice, T 18.24(A), T 18.25(A)
Common law, T 2.15
Custody of child, T 23.02(A)
Delinquent child, T 24.11
Deposit of public funds, T 42.04
Developmental disability, T 29.01(B)
Employment discrimination, T 17.04(A)
  Disparate treatment and disparate impact, T 17.03(C)
Employment of minor, T 20.11
Ethics, T 45.01(C)
Full-time employee, vacation purposes, T 13.04(A)
Gifted child, T 26.09

DEFINITIONS—*continued*
Handicapped person
  Child, T 28.01(B)
Individualized education program, T 28.02
Juvenile delinquent, T 24.11
Mental retardation, T 29.01(B)
Minor—See MINORS.
Neglected child, T 24.05(D)
Obscenity, T 24.12
Parochial school, T 48.01
Personal information system, T 44.06
Private school, T 48.01
Public employee
  Collective bargaining, T 18.03 to T 18.08
Public Liability Act, T 46.01(D)
Public money, uniform depository act, T 42.04(A)
Public record, T 44.02
Record, T 44.02
School bus, T 22.11
Special education, T 28.01(B)
Teacher—See TEACHERS.
Teachers retirement system
  Prior service credit, T 11.15
Unemployment compensation, T 15.02(A)
Uniform bond law, T 41.03
Uniform depository act, T 42.04
Unruly child, T 24.11, T 25.02
Workers' compensation
  Employee, T 16.02
  Injury, T 16.03

DEGREES—See DIPLOMAS AND DEGREES.

DELINQUENT CHILDREN—See JUVENILE DELINQUENCY.

DENTISTS
Child abuse, reporting, T 24.05
Schools employing, T 21.02(A), T 21.06
  Nonpublic schools, services, T 48.07
  School board membership, T 45.08(A)

DEPARTMENTS OF EDUCATION—See EDUCATION DEPARTMENT.

DEPOSIT OF PUBLIC FUNDS—See FUNDS, PUBLIC.

DEPOTS
School transportation, designation, T 22.16

DERELICTION OF DUTY, T 45.12

DESEGREGATION OF SCHOOLS, T Ch 19
Abolishment of "separate but equal" doctrine in Ohio, T 19.07
Cincinnati, T 19.10
Civil Rights Act of 1964, applicability, T 19.11(A), T 19.13(A)
Cleveland, T 19.08(B)
Columbus, T 19.06

DESEGREGATION OF SCHOOLS—*continued*
Constitutional requirements, T 19.02 to T 19.06
Constitutionality of state statutes, T 19.12
Dayton, T 19.06
De jure segregation, T 19.02
Denver, T 19.04
Detroit, T 19.05
Education department, powers and duties, T 3.04(A)
Equal Educational Opportunities Act, applicability, T 19.11(B)
Equal protection clause of U.S. Constitution, applicability, T 19.02 to T 19.06
Evolution of desegregation concepts, T 19.02 to T 19.06
Federal district courts' powers, T 2.16(B), T 19.03
Federal statutes, T 19.11
Federal supervision of school districts, T 19.03(B)
"Freedom of choice" plans, T 19.03(A)
Funding, T 19.03(C)
"Guide for School Districts", T 19.09(B)
Guidelines established by Supreme Court, T 19.03
Intentional segregation, proving, T 19.03 to T 19.10
Lorain, T 19.10
Los Angeles, T 19.12
Methods, T 19.02 to T 19.06
 Federal statutes, T 19.11
Multi-district remedy, T 19.05
"Neighborhood school" policy, T 19.08
Ohio, T 19.07 to T 19.10
Responsibility for, T 19.03
Seattle, T 19.12
State desegregation statutes, constitutionality, T 19.12
State's liability for segregation, T 19.09
Supreme Court's guidelines, T 19.03
System-wide remedy, T 19.06
Technical assistance, federal, T 19.11(A)
Training programs, T 19.11(A)
Transportation of pupils, T 19.03(B), T 19.11
Youngstown, T 19.10

DESTRUCTION OF PROPERTY
Arson, T 38.04(A)
Children, by; parental liability, T 38.06
Criminal damaging or endangering, T 38.04(C)
Criminal mischief, T 38.04(C)
Parental liability for acts of children, T 38.06
School property, T 38.04
 Financing rebuilding, T 41.04
 Reward for information leading to arrest and conviction, T 38.05
Vandalism, T 38.04(C), T 38.05

DESTRUCTION OF SCHOOL RECORDS—See RECORDS AND REPORTS, SCHOOL, at Disposal.

DETENTION HOMES
Educational costs of children, T 23.02(A)(4)

DIPLOMAS AND DEGREES
High school, T 26.16
 Competency level guarantee policy, T 26.16(B)
Prisoners earning, T 26.16

DISABLED CHILDREN—See also BLIND PERSONS; DEAF PERSONS; HANDICAPPED CHILDREN; HANDICAPPED PERSONS; MENTALLY RETARDED AND DEVELOPMENTALLY DISABLED PERSONS.
Abuse—See CHILD ABUSE, generally.
Alternative placements for disciplinary reasons, T 28.09
Definitions, T 28.01(B)
Disciplinary actions, T 28.09
Education—See Schooling, this heading; SPECIAL EDUCATION, generally.
"Free appropriate public education", T 28.03, T 28.05(B)
Hearings, educational placement, T 28.11(C) to T 28.11(F)
Home instruction, T 28.08(A)
Identification and evaluation, T 28.11(A), T 28.11(B)
 Notice requirements, T 28.11(B)
Mainstreaming, T 28.05, T 28.20(B)
Misconduct attributable to disability, alternative placements, T 28.09
Schooling—See also SPECIAL EDUCATION, generally.
 Attendance, T 20.01, T 20.02(C), T 28.17(A)
  Excused from, T 20.03(B)
 Recordkeeping requirements, T 44.13
 Removal from school activities or premises, T 28.09
 Residency requirements, T 28.15(C)
 Room and board costs, T 28.08(A)
 Suspension or expulsion, T 28.09
  Firearms, bringing on school premises, T 28.09(D)
 Tuition, T 23.02(A)(5), T 23.02(A)(7), T 23.02(A)(15), T 23.02(B), T 23.02(D)
  Home instruction, T 28.08(A)
Special education—See SPECIAL EDUCATION, generally.
State schools for blind and deaf, T 28.19
Suspension or expulsion, T 28.09
 Firearms, bringing on school premises, T 28.09(D)
Trained dogs accompanying, T 28.18
Transportation to school, T 22.05
 Foundation program funding, T 22.07(B)
Tuition, T 23.02(A)(5), T 23.02(A)(7), T 23.02(A)(15), T 23.02(B), T 23.02(D)
 Home instruction, T 28.08(A)

DISADVANTAGED PUPILS
Attendance required, T 23.06
Dental care, T 21.06, T 23.07(B)
Funding programs for, T 23.07(D), T 26.08
 Federal block grants, T 2.12

DISADVANTAGED PUPILS—*continued*
Immunization, T 23.07(B)
Instructional materials, T 23.07(C), T 35.02
Meals, free, T 23.07(A), T 35.07

DISASTERS—See EMERGENCIES AND DISASTERS.

DISCIPLINARY ACTION
Nonteaching employees, against, T 12.15 to T 12.17
Pupils—See PUPILS.
Teachers, against, T 9.21, T 9.22

DISCLOSURE, FINANCIAL—See FINANCIAL DISCLOSURE.

DISCRIMINATION
Actions—See ACTIONS.
Affirmative action plans—See AFFIRMATIVE ACTION PLANS.
Age—See AGE DISCRIMINATION.
AIDS, based on, T 17.13, T 21.03(E), T 28.01(B)
Alcoholism, based on, T 17.13
Athletic events, T 30.09(B)
Attorney fees, T 17.02(B), T 17.03(E), T 46.16
Civil actions—See ACTIONS.
Complaints
  Employment, T 17.03(D), T 17.04(C)
  Public depositories, by, T 42.12
Employment—See EMPLOYMENT DISCRIMINATION.
Federal aid, termination, T 19.11(A), T 19.13, T 19.13(B), T 19.14, T 48.29
Intent, necessity of proving, T 19.13(E)
Liability for civil rights violations, T 46.13 to T 46.16
Limitation of actions—See LIMITATION OF ACTIONS.
Married pupils, T 19.14(A)
Maternity leave, T 17.09
Mental retardation and developmental disabilities boards, by, T 29.15
National origin, on basis of, T 17.14
Pregnancy, T 10.20(B), T 17.09
  School pupils, T 19.14(A)
Private schools, by—See PRIVATE AND PAROCHIAL SCHOOLS.
Public depositories, against, T 42.12
Racial—See RACIAL DISCRIMINATION.
Religion, on basis of, T 17.15
Reverse discrimination, T 17.18
Schools, by, T Ch 19
  Academic and extracurricular activities, T 19.14
  Age discrimination, T 19.13(D)
  Assignment of pupils' schedules, T 20.05(B)
  Athletic programs, funding withheld, T 19.14(B)
  Damages, monetary, T 19.13(E)
  De jure segregation, T 19.02
  Employees, against, T 19.11(B), T 46.14(D)

DISCRIMINATION—*continued*
Schools, by—*continued*
  Extracurricular activities, funding withheld, T 19.14(B)
  Funding, withholding, T 19.11(A), T 19.13, T 19.14, T 48.29
  Handicapped persons, against, T 19.13(C)
  Individual's right of action, T 19.11(B), T 19.13(E)
  Intentional segregation, proving, T 19.03 to T 19.10
  Language barriers, T 19.15
  Liability, T 19.09, T 46.13 to T 46.16
  Married pupils, T 19.14(A)
  Qualified immunity, T 46.15(C)
  Recovery of attorney fees, T 17.02(B), T 17.03(E), T 46.16
  Sex discrimination, T 19.13(B), T 19.14
  Special education programs, T 28.10
  Teachers, against, T 19.11(B), T 46.14(D)
  Transportation of pupils to school prohibited, T 22.06
Sex, on basis of—See SEX DISCRIMINATION.
Special education programs, in, T 28.10
Teachers, against, T 19.11(B), T 46.14(D)
  See also EMPLOYMENT DISCRIMINATION, generally.
Unfair labor practices, T 18.24(A)
Wage discrimination—See EMPLOYMENT DISCRIMINATION.

DISEASES
AIDS—See AIDS.
Communicable—See COMMUNICABLE DISEASES.
Immunization—See IMMUNIZATION.
Occupational, workers' compensation, T 16.04

DISRUPTING PUBLIC SERVICES, T 38.04(B)

DISSOLUTION
Joint vocational school districts, T 27.08(D)
School districts—See REORGANIZATION OF SCHOOL DISTRICTS.

DISTRICTS—See particular subject concerned.
Health—See HEALTH DISTRICTS.
Library districts—See LIBRARIES AND LIBRARY DISTRICTS.
School districts—See SCHOOLS AND SCHOOL DISTRICTS.
Taxing districts—See TAXING DISTRICTS.

DOCTORS—See PHYSICIANS.

DOCUMENTS—See RECORDS AND REPORTS.

DOGS
Trained dogs accompanying blind, deaf, or mobility impaired persons, T 17.13(A), T 28.18

DOMESTIC VIOLENCE SHELTERS
Children of residents
  Disclosure of records, T 44.14(D), T 48.10
  School admission and tuition, T 23.02(A)(8)
  Transfer of records, T 44.14(D), T 48.10

DRESS CODES, T 25.04
Publication by school boards, T 5.09(G), T 31.02

DRIVER TRAINING COURSES, T 26.10(A), T 26.12 to T 26.14
Age requirement, T 26.13(B)
Contracts, T 26.14
Education department, powers and duties, T 3.04(A)
Fees, T 23.02(E), T 26.13(A)
Funding, T 26.13(A)
Hours of course, T 26.12(B)
Insurance, T 22.08, T 46.20
Parental consent, T 26.13(A)
Standards, T 3.03(B), T 26.12
Teachers, T 26.12(B), T 26.13(D)
Tuition, T 23.02(E), T 26.13(A)
Vehicles
  Acquisition and standards, T 26.13(C)

DRIVER TRAINING SCHOOLS
Contracts with school boards, T 26.14

DRIVERS' LICENSES
Revocation or suspension
  Minors
    Truancy or substance abuse, T 20.10
  School bus drivers, T 22.13(A)

DRUG ABUSE
Counseling programs
  Confidentiality requirements, T 21.15(C)
Discrimination on basis of handicap, T 17.13
Drug-Free Schools and Communities Act, T 21.15(A)
Drug-Free Workplace Act, T 21.15(B)
Fostering drug-free environment, T 21.15
Prevention, Drug-Free Schools and Communities Act, T 21.15(A)
School bus drivers
  Testing of, T 22.13(B)
  Transporting children while under influence, T 24.09(D)
Suspension or expulsion of pupil, T 20.10
Testing for
  Pupils, T 25.03
  School bus drivers, T 22.13(B)

DRUG OFFENSES
Corrupting another with drugs, T 24.14
Minors, involving, T 24.14
School employees, convictions or guilty pleas, T 5.09(H), T 8.07(A)
  Reporting requirements, T 24.07
School grounds, on or near, T 24.14

DRUG OFFENSES—*continued*
Search of school premises
  Drug-detecting dogs, use, T 47.01(C)
Teachers, convictions or guilty pleas, T 5.09(H), T 8.07(A), T 9.21(D)
  Reporting requirements, T 24.07

DUE PROCESS
Pupils
  Personal injury as violation, T 46.14(B)
  Private schools, T 44.16
  Suspension or expulsion, T 25.09, T 25.15(B), T 46.14(A)(1)
School board regulatory powers subject to, T 5.08(E)
Teachers, contract nonrenewal
  Extended limited contracts, T 9.13
  Limited contracts, T 9.13

DUES CHECKOFF PROVISION, T 10.08, T 18.19(A)

EDUCATION
Commission, T 2.10
Goals 2000: Educate America Act of 1994—See GOALS 2000: EDUCATE AMERICA ACT OF 1994.
History of school law, T Ch 1
Midwestern education compact, T 2.10

EDUCATION COMMISSION, T 2.10

EDUCATION DEPARTMENT, T Ch 3
Assistant superintendents, T 3.07(A)
Board—See EDUCATION, STATE BOARD.
Chief administrative officer, T 3.04(C)
  See also SUPERINTENDENT OF PUBLIC INSTRUCTION.
Data management unit, establishment and responsibilities, T 3.04(D)
Deaf persons, supervision and assistance in educating, T 28.18
  Children, educational programs, T 3.04(A)
Desegregation plans, assistance and administration, T 3.04(A)
Division heads, T 3.07(A)
Driver education courses
  Powers and duties, T 3.04(A)
Employees, T 3.07(B)
Ethics, T Ch 45
  See also ETHICS, generally.
Evaluation of new programs, T 26.17
Federal surplus property acquired by, T 39.01(A)
Migrant laborers, educational programs for children of, T 3.04(A)
Missing children, educational programs, T 3.04(A)
Office, T 3.04(B)
Organization, T 3.04
Powers and duties, T 3.04(A)
Preschool programs, T 3.04(A)
Records and reports, T 3.04(B)

EDUCATION DEPARTMENT—continued
School buses
　Purchase approval, T 22.07(C)
　Regulation, T 22.10
School-business partnerships, T 3.04(A)
School-parent partnerships, T 3.04(A)
Special needs districts, certification, T 41.07
State board—See EDUCATION, STATE BOARD.
Superintendent of public instruction—See SUPERINTENDENT OF PUBLIC INSTRUCTION.

EDUCATION DEPARTMENT, U.S., T 2.11(A)

EDUCATION FOR ALL HANDICAPPED CHILDREN ACT, T Ch 28
　See also SPECIAL EDUCATION, generally.

EDUCATION FOUNDATION FUNDS, T 39.13, T 42.22

EDUCATION, LOCAL BOARDS, T Ch 5
Abolishment, transfer of district, T 4.15(A)
Absences from school, policy on parental notification, T 20.07
Accounts and accounting—See ACCOUNTS AND ACCOUNTING, at School districts.
Actions by or against, T 5.07
　See also Liability, this heading; PUBLIC LIABILITY ACT.
Annual report by board, T 5.09(G), T 31.02
Administrative due process, T 5.08(E)
Administrators, T Ch 7
　See also ADMINISTRATIVE PERSONNEL; PRINCIPALS; SUPERINTENDENTS, LOCAL.
Adviser, state superintendent as, T 3.06
AIDS, T 21.03(D), T 21.03(E)
Annual meetings, T 5.11(A)
Annual progress reports, T 5.09(G), T 31.02
Annual reports on litigation, T 5.09(G), T 31.02
Appeals by, county budget commission action, T 40.06
Appeals to, student suspension or expulsion, T 25.10(B), T 25.10(C), T 25.12(A), T 25.14(E)
Appropriations—See APPROPRIATIONS, at School boards.
Arts council, financial support, T 31.05
Asbestos abatement actions, limitation of actions, T 21.10(B)
Association membership and dues, T 5.09(E), T 26.18, T 43.02(B)
Attendance officers, appointment, T 20.08(A)
Attorney general advising, T 2.17
Attorneys—See Legal advisers, this heading.
Blind students, assessment of reading and writing skills, T 5.09(P)

EDUCATION, LOCAL BOARDS—continued
Bond issues—See BONDS AND NOTES, SCHOOL.
Budgets—See BUDGETS, SCHOOL.
Buildings and lands, school—See SCHOOL BUILDINGS AND LANDS, generally.
Business advisory council, appointment, T 26.11(H)
Business managers, T 6.01, T 6.10 to T 6.13
　See also BUSINESS MANAGERS.
Candidates, nomination, T 5.03(A)
Career planning, assisting students, T 5.09(R)
City boards
　Civil service administration costs, T 12.03(B)
　Membership, T 5.02(B)
　New district created, T 4.15(C)
　Organizational plan, T 5.02(B)(1)
　Secretary serving as township clerk, T 45.08(A)
City directors of law
　Legal advisers, as, T 6.14
　Members, as, T 45.08(A)
Clerks—See now TREASURERS, SCHOOL BOARD.
Collective bargaining—See COLLECTIVE BARGAINING, PUBLIC EMPLOYEES, generally.
Community service education, T 5.09(N)
Competency program standards, T 26.02(C), T 26.04, T 26.15, T 28.10(B)
Conflict of interest—See also CONFLICT OF INTEREST, generally.
　Contracts, awarding, T 45.05 to T 45.07
　"Continuing course of dealing," exception, T 45.05(D)
　Employment with board, position and compensation approved during board membership, T 45.05(A)
　Incompatible offices, T 6.02(A), T 7.09(A), T 45.08
　Sale of goods to schools, T 45.06(B)
　Teacher as member's spouse, effect, T 45.06(A)
　Unauthorized compensation, T 45.04
Consultants, hiring, T 5.09(A)
Contracts, T 5.09(B), T 5.09(T), T 43.02(C)
　See also CONTRACTS, SCHOOL, generally.
　Conflict of interest, T 45.05 to T 45.07
　"Continuing course of dealing," exception, T 45.05(D)
Conveyances by—See SCHOOL BUILDINGS AND LANDS, at Sale.
Cooperation with other school boards, T 5.09(D)
Cooperation with public institutions, T 5.09(D), T 26.11(C), T 31.05
Cooperative education school districts, T 4.03(G)
　See also COOPERATIVE EDUCATION SCHOOL DISTRICTS, generally.
Corporal punishment—See PUPILS, at Corporal punishment.
Corporate powers, T 5.06(A)
County boards—See EDUCATIONAL SERVICE CENTERS, at Governing boards.

EDUCATION, LOCAL BOARDS—*continued*
County prosecutors
  Legal advisers, as, T 6.14
  Members, as, T 45.08(A)
Cultural associations, financial support, T 31.05
Data processing equipment, purchase, T 36.04(C)(1)
  Competitive bidding, exemption, T 37.04(A)
Dress codes, publication, T 5.09(G), T 31.02
Due process, administrative, T 5.08(E)
Educational policies, T 26.04
Educational service center governing boards—See EDUCATIONAL SERVICE CENTERS, at Governing boards.
Election of members, T 5.03(A)
  City board, T 5.02(B)(1)
  Financial disclosure statement, filing, T 45.02
  New district created, T 4.15
  Number of members, T 5.02(A)
  Vacancy, filling, T 5.03(C)
Eminent domain powers, T 36.03
Employees—See SCHOOL EMPLOYEES, NONTEACHING; TEACHERS.
Ethics, T Ch 45
  See also ETHICS, generally.
Executive sessions, T 5.12(B)
Exempted village boards
  Contracts with educational service centers, T 5.09(I)
  Members, T 5.02(A)
Expenditure of funds—See FUNDS, SCHOOL, generally.
Failure to act, T 5.10
Financial in-service training, T 5.09(F)
Fiscal responsibilities—See also FUNDS, SCHOOL, generally.
  Assistance from state board of education, T 5.09(A)
Funding for school districts—See FUNDS, SCHOOL.
Gifts or bequests to, T 36.06, T 39.13
Health insurance for board members, T 5.09(T)
Healthcheck programs, T 5.09(M)
Incompatible offices, T 6.02(A), T 7.09(A), T 45.08
  See also Conflict of interest, this heading.
Injunctions against, T 5.06(C), T 46.09
  Failure to comply with open meeting requirements, T 5.12(D)
Innovative education pilot programs, T 3.03(E)
Insurance purchases, T 5.09(T)
Joint educational service center governing boards, members, T 5.02(A)
Joint recreation districts, participation, T 30.14
  Joint recreation board, T 30.15
Joint vocational school district boards, T 4.03(E), T 27.09(A)
  Compensation and expenses, T 5.04
Jurisdiction, T 5.06(A)
Lands and buildings, school—See SCHOOL BUILDINGS AND LANDS, generally.
Latchkey programs, T 5.09(L)

EDUCATION, LOCAL BOARDS—*continued*
Legal advisers, T 2.17, T 6.01, T 6.14, T 6.15
  Compensation, T 6.14(C)
  Duties, T 6.14(B)
  Freedom of choice, T 6.14(A), T 6.15
  Outside counsel, T 6.15
  Private, funding, T 43.05(C)
  Statutory designation, T 6.14
Liability, T 5.07, T Ch 46
  See also LIABILITY, generally; PUBLIC LIABILITY ACT.
  Contract claims, T 46.08
  Discrimination, for, T 46.13 to T 46.16
    Recovery of attorney fees, T 17.02(B), T 17.03(E), T 46.16
  Employment discrimination, T 17.02(A), T 17.04(E)
  Federal civil rights violations, T 46.13 to T 46.16
  Insurance, T 5.07, T 46.17 to T 46.21
  "Moral obligation", T 46.12
  Parks and recreational facilities, T 30.16
  Personal, T 46.03
    Civil rights violations, T 46.15(A), T 46.15(C)
    Qualified immunity, T 46.15(C)
  Prevailing wage act, failure to comply with, T 37.14
  Qualified immunity, T 46.15(C)
  Searching students, illegal, T 47.03
  Violation of student's constitutional rights, T 25.09(C)
Loans for school districts, T 41.33
Local district boards
  Administrator as educational service center governing board member, incompatible office, T 7.09(A), T 45.08(A)
  Members, T 5.02(A)
  Newly created, T 4.15(B)
  Terms of members, newly created boards, T 4.15(B)
Mandamus actions against, T 5.06(C)
Meetings, T 5.11 to T 5.13
  Absence from, excessive, T 5.03(C)
  Compensation and expenses, T 5.04
  Executive session, T 5.12(B)
  Failure to comply with open meeting requirements, effect, T 5.12(D)
  Injunctions to compel compliance with open meeting requirements, T 5.12(D)
  Minutes, T 5.11(D), T 6.06, T 31.01
  Notice, T 5.12(A), T 5.12(C), T 31.01
  Open meeting requirements, T 5.12, T 31.01
  Organizational meetings, T 5.11(A)
  Quorum, T 5.11(C)
  Regular meetings, T 5.11(B)
  Special meetings, T 5.11(B)
  Summaries, publication, T 5.09(G), T 31.02
Members, T 5.02 to T 5.05
  See also PUBLIC OFFICIALS, generally.
  City law director as, T 45.08(A)
  Compensation and expenses, T 5.04
    Training programs, T 5.09(F)

EDUCATION, LOCAL BOARDS—*continued*
Members—*continued*
  Conflict of interest—See Conflict of interest, this heading.
  Disability benefit, T 14.11
  Election—See Election of members, this heading.
  Ethics, T Ch 45
    See also ETHICS, generally.
  Health board member, exclusion, T 45.08(A)
  Liability—See Liability, this heading.
  Meetings—See Meetings, this heading.
  Municipal judge as, exclusion, T 45.08(A)
  Number
    Ballot question, T 5.02(B)(1)
    City school boards, T 5.02(B), T 5.02(B)(1)
    Right to determine, T 1.09
  Oath of office, T 5.03(B)
  Private school board member, as, T 45.08(A)
  Prosecuting attorneys, exclusion, T 45.08(A)
  Quorum, T 5.11(C)
  Removal from office, T 5.05
  Retirement, T 5.04(A)
  School employees retirement system, contributions, T 14.07, T 14.08
  School health personnel, exclusion, T 45.08(A)
  Teacher's aide in local school district, exclusion, T 45.08(A)
  Teachers as, T 45.08(A)
  Teachers retirement system
    Contributions to, T 11.09
  Term of office, T 5.03(B)
  Township trustees as, T 45.08(A)
  Training, T 5.09(F)
  Unemployment compensation, ineligible, T 15.01
  Vacancies, T 5.03(C)
    Probate court filling, T 5.10
  Village council member as, exclusion, T 45.08(A)
  Voting, T 5.13
  Workers' compensation, T Ch 16
    See also WORKERS' COMPENSATION, generally.
Membership in organizations, T 5.09(B), T 26.18, T 43.02(B)
Mileage allowance, T 5.04
Minutes of proceedings, T 5.11(D), T 6.06, T 31.01
Motor vehicles
  Insurance, T 22.08, T 46.20
  Mileage, T 5.04
  Purchase or lease, T 5.09(T), T 36.04(A)
Municipal judge as member, exclusion, T 45.08(A)
New districts created, T 4.15
Nomination of candidates, T 5.03(A)
Notice
  Actions regarding public fund violations, T 43.27(B)
  Employee's conviction or guilty plea, T 24.07
  Meetings, T 5.12(A), T 5.12(C), T 31.01

EDUCATION, LOCAL BOARDS—*continued*
Notice—*continued*
  Missing children, notice to law enforcement agency when pupils fail to present school records, T 24.16, T 48.10
  Tax abatements, of, T 39.04
  Vacancy, filling, T 5.03(C)
Office equipment, purchase, T 36.04(C)(1)
Open meeting requirements, T 5.12, T 31.01
Organization, commission to frame plan for; meeting, T 5.11(A)
Parental involvement policy, T 5.09(O), T 31.04
Powers and duties, T 1.09, T 5.01
  Cooperative education school districts, T 4.03(G)
  Expenditures, T 43.02
  Failure to exercise or perform, T 5.10
Preschool programs
  Criminal background checks of employment applicants, T 5.09(C)
  Operation, T 5.09(C)
Presidents
  Vacancy, filling, T 5.03(C)
Prevailing wage coordinators, T 37.13
Probate courts, powers and duties, T 5.10
Progress reports, annual, T 5.09(G), T 31.02
Prosecuting attorneys giving notice of employees' convictions or guilty pleas, T 24.07
Publications by, T 5.09(G), T 31.02
Pupil personnel workers, appointment, T 20.08(A)
Pupils, powers and duties—See PUPILS, generally.
Quorum, T 5.11(C)
Real property tax
  Abatements, T 39.04
Records and reports—See also RECORDS AND REPORTS, SCHOOL, generally.
  Annual progress reports, T 5.09(G), T 31.02
  Annual report on litigation, T 5.09(G), T 31.02
  Bids, entry, T 6.08(B)
  Curriculum guides, T 5.09(G), T 31.02
  Disposal, T 44.22, T 44.23
  Dress codes, T 5.09(G), T 31.02
  Financial reports, T 5.09(G), T 31.02, T 43.26(B)
  Meetings
    Minutes, T 5.11(D), T 6.06, T 31.01
    Summaries, publication, T 5.09(G), T 31.02
  Newsletters, T 5.09(G), T 31.02
  Policy bulletins, T 5.09(G), T 31.02
  Student handbooks, T 5.09(G), T 31.02
Recreation districts, joining, T 30.14
  Joint recreation board, T 30.15
Religious instruction, release time policies, T 5.08(B), T 32.04
Removal of members, T 5.05
Reorganization of school districts
  Effect, T 4.15
  Powers, T 4.04
Resolutions, T 5.13
  Anticipation notes, issuance, T 41.16(B)

EDUCATION, LOCAL BOARDS—*continued*
Resolutions—*continued*
  Appropriations—See APPROPRIATIONS, at School boards.
  Bond issuance, T 41.10, T 41.12, T 41.16(E)
  Classroom facilities project, T 41.26, T 41.28(A), T 41.28(C)
  Depository, designation, T 42.09
  Excess tax levy, T 40.10, T 40.13
  Fund, establishment, T 43.15(B)
  Incremental tax levy, T 40.10(C)
  Note issuance, T 41.16(B)
  Permanent exclusion of pupil from Ohio public schools, T 25.10(E)
  Replacement tax levy, T 40.12
  Special needs district, designation, T 41.07
  Superintendent, not to reemploy, T 7.04(B)
  Transfer of moneys, T 43.15(C), T 43.16
  Treasurer, not to reemploy, T 7.06
Rules and regulations, T 5.08(A)
  Limitation, T 5.06(A)
Savings banks, school, T 5.09(S)
School buildings and lands—See SCHOOL BUILDINGS AND LANDS, generally.
School buses, powers and duties—See SCHOOL BUSES, generally.
School employees retirement system, contributions, T 14.07, T 14.08
School health personnel as members, T 45.08(A)
School savings banks, T 5.09(S)
Sovereign immunity, T 5.07, T Ch 46
  See also PUBLIC LIABILITY ACT.
Special meetings, T 5.11(B)
Superintendent, state—See SUPERINTENDENT OF PUBLIC INSTRUCTION.
Superintendents, local—See SUPERINTENDENTS, LOCAL.
Symphony associations, financial support, T 31.05
Taxing authority, T 39.02
Teacher as member, T 45.08(A)
Teacher education loan programs, T 5.09(K)
Teacher salary schedule, powers, T 10.02 to T 10.05
  Service requirements, T 10.03, T 10.04
Teacher's application for professional certificate, powers and duties, T 8.04(D)(2)
Teachers retirement system
  Contributions to, T 11.09
Testing programs—See TESTING PROGRAMS, SCHOOL, generally.
Textbooks, powers and duties, T Ch 33
  See also TEXTBOOKS, generally.
Tort liability, T Ch 46
  See also Liability, this heading; PUBLIC LIABILITY ACT.
Township trustees as members, T 45.08(A)
Transfer of district, effect, T 4.15
Transfer of grades within district, T 7.06(C)
Transportation of pupils, powers and duties, T Ch 22
  See also TRANSPORTATION OF PUPILS, generally.

EDUCATION, LOCAL BOARDS—*continued*
Treasurers—See TREASURERS, SCHOOL BOARD.
Tuition credit scholarship programs, establishment, T 5.09(Q)
Village council member as school board member, T 45.08(A)
Voter registration program in schools, powers and duties, T 31.09
Voting, T 5.13
Workers' compensation, T Ch 16
  See also WORKERS' COMPENSATION, generally.

EDUCATION MANAGEMENT INFORMATION SYSTEM, T 3.03(F), T 26.17

EDUCATION, STATE BOARD, T 1.09, T 3.01 to T 3.03
  See also EDUCATION DEPARTMENT, generally.
Adjacent district enrollment, monitoring, T 5.08(D)
Age and schooling certificates, form, T 20.13(B)
Appointment of members, T 3.02(A)
Block parent programs, governing, T 3.03(G)
Budgets, T 3.03(A)
  Preparation by district, technical assistance to be provided, T 3.03(G), T 5.09(A)
Business managers, licensing, T 3.03(G)
Classroom facilities, powers and duties, T 41.26, T 41.27(A)
Compensation of members, T 3.02(B)
Conflict of interest, T 3.02(A), T 3.02(C), T 45.08(A)
Consolidation of school districts, powers, T 4.07(A)(2), T 4.09
Cooperation with other agencies, T 3.03(G)
Creation of new school districts, powers and duties, T 3.03(C)
Data processing services, regulation, T 3.03(G), T 26.11(G), T 43.29
Driver education standards, prescribing, T 3.03(B)
Education management information system, T 3.03(F), T 26.17
Election of members, T 3.02(A)
Enrollment policies, monitoring, T 3.03(G)
Ethics, T Ch 45
  See also ETHICS, generally.
Financial disclosure—See FINANCIAL DISCLOSURE.
Financial in-service training to be provided, T 3.03(G), T 5.09(F)
Financially distressed districts, taking control of, T 3.03(G)
Foundation program administered by, T 3.03(G), T 39.06(C)
  See also FOUNDATION PROGRAM, generally.
Gifted children, development of programs for, T 3.03(B)

EDUCATION, STATE BOARD—*continued*
Handicapped children, education; powers and duties, T 3.03(B)
Inspections by, T 3.03(G)
Joint vocational districts
  Assignment to, T 27.02, T 27.08(B)
  Dissolution, T 27.08(D)
Meetings, T 3.02(D)
Members, T 3.02
  See also PUBLIC OFFICIALS, generally.
  Appointment, T 3.02(A), T 3.02(D)
  Compensation, T 3.02(B)
  Conflict of interest, T 3.02(A), T 3.02(C), T 45.08(A)
  Ethics, T Ch 45
    See also ETHICS, generally.
  Financial disclosure—See FINANCIAL DISCLOSURE.
  Oath of office, T 3.02(B)
  Qualifications, T 3.02(A)
  Terms, T 3.02(A), T 3.02(B)
  Vacancies, T 3.02(A), T 3.02(D)
Notice
  Employee's conviction or guilty plea, T 24.07
Open enrollment, monitoring, T 5.08(C)
Performance evaluation standards, T 3.03(D)
Performance goals, establishment, T 3.03(A)
Phonics, teaching standards and in-service training, T 3.03(G)
Plan of service, development, T 3.03(G)
Policy formulation, T 3.03(A)
Powers and duties, T 2.09, T 3.03, T 5.06 to T 5.10
Preschools
  Powers and duties, T 3.03(B)
Private and parochial schools, powers and duties, T 3.03(B)
  Certification of teachers and administrators, T 3.03(G), T 48.21
Quorum, T 3.02(D)
Records and reports, T 3.02(D), T 3.03(G)
  Education management information system, T 3.03(F), T 26.17
Reorganization of school districts, T 3.03(C), T 4.04, T 4.05(D)
Rulemaking powers, T 3.03(G)
  Education information management system, T 3.03(F)
School districts, powers and duties, T 2.09
  Assignment to joint vocational districts, T 27.02, T 27.08(B)
  Creation, T 3.03(C)
  Funds, allocation and distribution, T 3.03(A), T 39.01(A), T 39.06(C)
    See also FUNDS, SCHOOL.
  Reorganization of districts, T 3.03(C), T 4.04, T 4.05(D)
  Reports required by board, T 3.03(G)
  Standards to be met, T 3.03(B), T 26.01, T 26.02
    Private schools, applicability, T 20.03(A), T 32.02, T 48.03

EDUCATION, STATE BOARD—*continued*
School districts, powers and duties—*continued*
  Territory transfer, T 3.03(C), T 4.05(D), T 4.09, T 4.11(B)
  Transportation of students, T 22.04
    Funding, T 22.07(A)
Secretary, superintendent of public instruction to be, T 3.06
Special education, powers and duties, T 3.03(B)
Spending obligations, notification to schools, T 3.03(G)
Standards to be prescribed by, T 3.03(B)
  Curriculum and educational programs, T 26.01
  Private schools, applicability, T 32.02, T 48.03
    Certification of teachers and administrators, T 3.03(G), T 48.21
State schools for blind and deaf, powers and duties, T 28.19
Superintendent of public instruction—See SUPERINTENDENT OF PUBLIC INSTRUCTION.
Teacher certification standards, adoption, T 8.03(B)
  Braille, reading and writing, T 3.03(G), T 28.16
Technological advancements, plan to promote use, T 3.03(G)
Terms of office, T 3.02(A), T 3.02(B)
Transfer of territory, powers, T 3.03(C), T 4.05(D), T 4.09, T 4.11(B)
Transportation of pupils, powers and duties, T 22.04
  Funding, T 22.07(A)
Treasurers, licensing, T 3.03(G)
Vacancies on board, T 3.02(A), T 3.02(D)
Vocational curriculum plan, T 3.03(G), T 27.03

EDUCATIONAL BROADCASTING, T 26.11(G)

EDUCATIONAL CORPORATIONS—See UNIVERSITIES AND COLLEGES.

EDUCATIONAL MALPRACTICE, T 26.15(B)

EDUCATIONAL RESOURCES
Evaluation, T 26.17
Minimum standards, T 26.02(B)
School boards, powers, T 26.03

EDUCATIONAL SERVICE CENTERS, T 4.03(B)
See also EDUCATION, LOCAL BOARDS, generally.
Conference facilities, T 7.08
Cooperative education school districts, T 4.03(G)
Governing boards
  Acquisition of property, T 36.07
  Administrative personnel, employment—See ADMINISTRATIVE PERSONNEL; PRINCIPALS; SUPERINTENDENTS, LOCAL.
  Authority in service center with only one local school district, T 5.02(A)
  Budgets, T 40.03

EDUCATIONAL SERVICE CENTERS—*continued*
Governing boards—*continued*
Compensation and expenses, T 5.04
Conference facilities provided by county commissioners, T 7.08
Failure to act, T 5.10
Funds, T 43.15(B)
Attendance officers' compensation and expenses, payment, T 20.08(B)
Joint boards, members, T 5.02(A)
Local boards, acting as, T 4.15(D)
Meetings, T 5.11(A)
Membership, T 5.02(A)
Local district administrator, incompatible office, T 7.09(A), T 45.08(A)
Probate court filling vacancies, T 5.10
Substitute teacher, incompatible office, T 45.08(A)
Teacher's aide in local school district, incompatible office, T 45.08(A)
Township trustee, compatible office, T 45.08(A)
Offices, T 7.08
One local school district within service center, powers, T 5.02(A)
Powers and duties
Failure to exercise or perform, T 5.10
Probate courts, powers and duties, T 5.10
Telephone equipment provided by county commissioners, T 7.08
Territory transfers
Proposals, T 4.07(C), T 4.10
Joint educational service centers, T 4.03(C)
Governing boards, members, T 5.02(A)
Local school district powers, exercising, T 4.03(B)
Powers and duties
Cooperative education school districts, T 4.03(G)
Failure to exercise or perform, T 5.10
Reorganization of school districts, T 4.04
Reorganization of school districts
Powers, T 4.04
Resolutions
Transfer of territory, T 4.10
Superintendents—See SUPERINTENDENTS, LOCAL, generally.
Transfer of territory within, T 4.10
Treasurers—See TREASURERS, SCHOOL BOARD, generally.
Voluntary consolidation, T 4.03(C)

EIGHTEEN-YEAR-OLDS
Age and schooling certificates, T 20.14(D)

ELDERLY PERSONS—See AGED PERSONS.

ELECTIONS
Ballots—See BALLOTS.
Bond issues, T 41.09 to T 41.14
Ballot, T 41.14(B)
Certification of results, T 41.14(C)

ELECTIONS—*continued*
Bond issues—*continued*
Date of election, T 41.09, T 41.14
Joint vocational school districts, T 41.23(A)
Library purposes, T 34.02, T 41.14(B)
Passage, T 41.09
Candidates—See CANDIDATES.
Classroom facilities, financing, T 41.27(B), T 41.28
Collective bargaining, public employees—See COLLECTIVE BARGAINING, PUBLIC EMPLOYEES.
Contests, T 41.14(C)
Emergency school levies, T 40.10(B), T 40.13, T 41.22
Excess tax levy proposals, T 40.10 to T 40.12
Joint vocational school districts
Bond issue, T 41.23(A)
Tax levy, T 27.10(A), T 27.11, T 41.23(B)
Libraries
Bond issues, T 34.02, T 41.14(B)
Construction or improvement of buildings, bond issue
Ballot form, T 41.14(B)
Polling places
Schoolhouse used as, T 38.10
Questions
Certification
Bond issues, T 41.14(C)
Classroom facilities, financing, T 41.27(B), T 41.28
Emergency school levy, T 40.10(B), T 40.13, T 41.22
Excess tax levy, T 40.10 to T 40.12
School boards, number of members, T 5.02(B)(1)
Recounts, T 41.14(C)
Registration provided in schools, T 31.09
School board members
Local boards—See EDUCATION, LOCAL BOARDS.
Schools
Additional tax levy, T 40.10(C)
Bond issues, T 41.09 to T 41.14
See also Bond issues, this heading; particular subject of bond concerned.
Classroom facilities, financing, T 41.27(B), T 41.28
Costs, tax revenues to cover, T 40.09(A)
Creation of district, T 4.07(A), T 4.09(C)
Emergency levy, T 40.10(B), T 40.13, T 41.22
Excess levy, T 40.10 to T 40.12
Income tax
Repeal, T 39.12
Incremental tax levy, T 40.10(C)
Renewal levy, T 40.11
Reorganization of districts, T 4.04
Replacement levy, T 40.12
Special levy, T 40.09(B)
Special needs district bonds, T 41.07
Territory transfer, T 4.07(A), T 4.09(C)
Referendum against, T 4.10(B)

ELECTIONS—*continued*
Schools—*continued*
  Voter registration provided in, T 31.09
Special
  School board vacancy, filling, T 5.03(C)
Voter registration
  Libraries, in, T 34.10(B)
  Schools, in, T 31.09

ELECTRONIC TRANSFER OF FUNDS
School funds, T 43.08(B), T 43.10

ELEMENTARY AND SECONDARY EDUCATION ACT OF 1965, T 2.12

ELEMENTARY SCHOOLS—See also SCHOOLS AND SCHOOL DISTRICTS, generally.
Curriculum, T 26.05(B)
  See also CURRICULUM, generally.
Physical education, T 30.02
Transportation of pupils, T 22.03(A)
  See also TRANSPORTATION OF PUPILS, generally.

EMBEZZLEMENT
Public funds, T 43.27(B)
Public or party officials, by, T 45.10

EMERGENCIES AND DISASTERS
Bond issues to finance temporary repairs, T 41.04
Schools
  Bond issues to finance temporary repairs, T 41.04
  Drills, T 21.13
  Funding, T 41.33
    See also EMERGENCY LOANS, generally.
  Students, medical authorization form, T 21.04(A), T 21.07(C)
  Transportation emergency plans and drills, T 22.20

EMERGENCY LOANS, T 41.33
Application, T 41.33(C)
Approval, T 41.33(D)
Conditions for receiving, T 41.33(D)
Controlling board, powers and duties, T 41.33(D)
Eligibility, T 41.33(B)
Purpose, T 41.33(A)
Repayment, T 41.33(E)
Superintendent of public instruction, powers and duties, T 3.06, T 41.33(C), T 41.33(E)

EMERGENCY MEDICAL AUTHORIZATION FORMS, T 21.04(A), T 21.07(C)

EMERGENCY SCHOOL ADVANCEMENT FUND, T 41.33
  See also EMERGENCY LOANS, generally.

EMERGENCY SCHOOL CLOSINGS, T 20.05(D)

EMERGENCY SCHOOL LEVIES, T 40.10(B), T 40.13, T 41.22

EMINENT DOMAIN
School boards, powers, T 36.03

EMPLOYER AND EMPLOYEE—See also SCHOOL EMPLOYEES, NONTEACHING; TEACHERS.
Age and schooling certificates for employment of minors, T 20.11 to T 20.17
  See also AGE AND SCHOOLING CERTIFICATES.
Civil service—See CIVIL SERVICE.
Collective bargaining, public employees—See COLLECTIVE BARGAINING, PUBLIC EMPLOYEES.
Discrimination by employers—See EMPLOYMENT DISCRIMINATION.
Hours—See WAGES AND HOURS.
Minors, employment—See MINORS.
Public employees—See CIVIL SERVICE; PUBLIC EMPLOYEES.
Records required of employers
  Minors employed by, T 20.16(B)
  Wages and hours, T 44.12
Schools—See SCHOOL EMPLOYEES, NONTEACHING; TEACHERS.
Unemployment compensation—See UNEMPLOYMENT COMPENSATION.
Verification of identity and work authorization by employers, T 48.20
Wages—See COMPENSATION; WAGES AND HOURS.
Worker retraining programs, joint vocational school facilities used for, T 27.10(A)
Workers' compensation—See WORKERS' COMPENSATION.

EMPLOYMENT DISCRIMINATION, T Ch 17
Affirmative action plans—See AFFIRMATIVE ACTION PLANS.
Affirmative defense, wage discrimination, T 17.08(C)
Age, on basis of, T 17.06
  Evidence, T 17.06(B)
  Limitation of actions, T 17.06(A)
Appeals from civil rights commission orders, T 17.04(E)
Assignment of employees, T 17.10
Attorney fees, T 17.02(B), T 17.03(E), T 46.16
Attorney general's duties, T 17.04(C)
Burden of proof, T 17.03(F)(1), T 17.04(E)
"But for" standard, unfair labor practices, T 18.24(F)
Cease and desist orders, T 17.04(D)
Civil Rights Act, applicability, T 17.03
Civil rights commission, state; powers and duties, T 17.04(C)

EMPLOYMENT DISCRIMINATION—*continued*
Comparable worth, T 17.08(C)
Compensatory damages, T 17.03(E)
Competency tests, validity, T 17.07(A)
Complaints, T 17.03(D), T 17.04(C)
Conciliation agreements, T 17.03(D), T 17.04(C)
Contracts to contain equal opportunity provisions, T 17.05
Damages
  Compensatory, T 17.03(E)
  Punitive, T 17.02(B), T 17.03(E)
Defense, wage discrimination, T 17.08(C)
Definitions, T 17.04(A)
  "Disparate treatment" and "disparate impact", T 17.03(C)
Discharge of employees, T 17.10
Disparate impact cases, T 17.03(F)(2)
  Application, T 17.07(A)
  Burden of proof, T 17.03(F)(2)
  Definition, T 17.03(C)
Disparate treatment cases
  Application, T 17.02(B)
  Burden of proof, T 17.03(F)(1)
  Definition, T 17.03(C)
EEO-5 reports, T 17.17
Equal Educational Opportunities Act, T 19.11(B)
Equal employment opportunity commission, powers and duties, T 17.03(D)
Equal employment opportunity laws, table, T 17.20
Equal Pay Amendment, applicability, T 17.08
Equal pay for equal work, T 17.08(C)
Equal protection clause of U.S. Constitution, applicability, T 17.02(A)
Evaluation of employees, T 17.10
Evidence, T 17.02(A), T 17.02(B), T 17.03(C), T 17.03(F), T 17.04(E)
  Age discrimination, T 17.06(B)
Exceptions, T 17.03(B)
Fair Employment Practices Act, applicability, T 17.04
Federal Age Discrimination in Employment Act, T 17.19
Federal court jurisdiction, T 17.03(G)
Handicapped persons, T 17.13
Hiring practices, T 17.07
Hostile environment cases, T 17.11
Immigration Reform and Control Act, T 48.20
"In part" test, unfair labor practices, T 18.24(F)
Injunctive relief, T 17.03(E)
Jurisdiction, federal courts, T 17.03(F)
Laws, posting, T 17.17
Liability, T 17.02(A), T 17.04(E)
  Sexual harassment, T 17.11
Limitation of actions, T 17.02(A), T 17.04(C)
  Age discrimination, T 17.06(A)
  Nonrenewal of contract, T 17.10
  Wage discrimination, T 17.08(B)
National origin, on basis of, T 17.14
Notice of employees' rights, T 17.17
Ohio civil rights commission's powers and duties, T 17.04(C)

EMPLOYMENT DISCRIMINATION—*continued*
Parallels between Ohio and federal law, T 17.04(B)
Pattern or practice cases, T 17.03(F)(3)
  Burden of proof, T 17.03(F)(3)
Pregnancy, T 10.20(B), T 17.09
Private schools, T 48.20, T 48.30
  Exemption, T 17.03(B)
Promotion procedures, T 17.07
Proof of discriminatory motive, T 17.02(A), T 17.02(B), T 17.03(C), T 17.03(F)
Punitive damages, T 17.02(B), T 17.03(E)
Records and reports required, T 17.17
Recruiting procedures, T 17.07
Religion, on basis of, T 17.15
Remedies, T 17.03(E), T 17.04(D), T 17.18
  Affirmative action—See AFFIRMATIVE ACTION PLANS.
  Compensatory damages, T 17.03(E)
  Punitive damages, T 17.02(B), T 17.03(E)
Retaliation against complainants prohibited, T 17.03(A), T 17.04(A), T 17.12
Retirement, T 17.06(C)
Reverse discrimination, T 17.18
Section 1983 actions, T 46.14(D)
Sex discrimination by schools, T 19.14
Sexual harassment, T 17.11
Statistical evidence, T 17.03(F)(4)
Substantial evidence test, T 17.04(E)
Table of laws, T 17.20
Tests of competency, validity, T 17.07(A)
Transfer of employees, T 17.10
Unfair labor practices, T 18.24(A), T 18.24(F)
Uniform guidelines on employee selection procedures, T 17.07(B)
Wages, T 17.08, T 48.30
  Burden of proof, T 17.08(A)
  Comparable worth, T 17.08(C)
  Defense, T 17.08(C)
  Equal pay for equal worth, T 17.08(C)
Waiver of claims, T 17.19

EMPLOYMENT RELATIONS BOARD—See also COLLECTIVE BARGAINING, PUBLIC EMPLOYEES, generally.
Appeals from
  Board as party to action, T 18.02
  Certification of employee organization, T 18.15(F)
  Representation election orders, T 18.15(F)
  Unfair labor practice decisions, T 18.26(C)
Bargaining units, determination of appropriateness, T 18.11(A)
Collective bargaining disputes, powers and duties, T 18.29(C)
  Arbitration, deferral to, T 18.22(B)
Delegation of powers, T 18.02
Exclusive representation, powers and duties, T 18.15(C)
Hearings, T 18.02
  Representation election petitions, on, T 18.15(A)

EMPLOYMENT RELATIONS BOARD—continued
Hearings—continued
  Unfair labor practices, T 18.26(A)
Mediation bureau, T 18.02
Mediators, appointment, T 18.29(C)
Members, T 18.02
Notice to
  Strike or picketing, of, T 18.29(D), T 18.30
Office, T 18.02
Powers and duties, T 18.02
Records and reports
  Disclosure, T 18.33
  Public access, T 18.33
Research services, T 18.02
Rules and rulemaking powers, T 18.02
Strikes
  Determination of authorization, T 18.31
  Notice of, T 18.29(D), T 18.30
  Temporary restraining orders, extension, T 18.32
Training duties, T 18.02
Unfair labor practices, powers and duties, T 18.26

EMPLOYMENT SERVICES BUREAU
Appeals from orders, T 16.09(A)
Cease and desist orders, T 16.09(A)
  Appeals, T 16.09(A)
Citations for violations, T 16.09(A)
  Hearings before industrial commission, T 16.09(A)
Common pleas court, appeals to, T 16.09(A)
Confidentiality of information, T 16.09(D)
Dangerous work conditions
  Good faith refusal by employee to work under, T 16.10(B)
  Inspection of, T 16.09(A)
Employment risk reduction standards, T 16.09(A)
  Emergency temporary standards
    Variances, T 16.09(A)
  Employee complaints
    Retaliation prohibited, T 16.09(C)
  Hearings before industrial commission, T 16.09(A)
  Violations
    Injunctive relief, T 16.09(A)
    Retaliation prohibited, T 16.09(C)
Enforcement powers, T 16.09(A)
Hearings before industrial commission, T 16.09(A)
Injunctive relief, T 16.09(A)
Inspections
  Authority, scope, T 16.09(A)
  Confidentiality of information, T 16.09(D)
  Dangerous work conditions, T 16.09(A)
  Employee or union requesting, T 16.09(A)
  Employer requesting, T 16.09(E)
  No-fault, T 16.09(E)
  Refusal by employee to work under dangerous condition, upon, T 16.10(B)
Investigations, T 16.09(A)
  Confidentiality of information, T 16.09(D)

EMPLOYMENT SERVICES BUREAU—continued
Judicial review, T 16.09(A)
Minors, employment; powers and duties, T 20.11
Noncompliance, T 16.09(A)
Occupational safety and health, T 16.09
Orders, T 16.09(A)
  Appeals, T 16.09(A)
Prevailing wage rates, powers, T 37.12(A), T 37.14
Public employment risk reduction advisory commission, operation and enforcement, T 16.09(A)
  See also PUBLIC EMPLOYMENT RISK REDUCTION ADVISORY COMMISSION, generally.
Records and reports, T 16.10(D)
Refusal by employees to work under dangerous conditions, T 16.10(B)
Retaliation prohibited, T 16.09(C), T 16.10(C)
Statistical information, T 16.09(D)
Violations
  Citations, T 16.09(A)
  Employee complaints
    Retaliation prohibited, T 16.09(C)
  Hearings before industrial commission, T 16.09(A)
  Injunctive relief, T 16.09(A)
  Retaliation prohibited, T 16.09(C)

ENDANGERING CHILDREN, T 24.04, T 24.09
Firearms, discharging at or on schools, T 24.09(F)
Physical abuse, T 24.09(B)
Riots, participation in, T 24.09(E)
Sexual violations, T 24.09(C)
Transporting children while under influence, T 24.09(D)
Violation of duty of care, protection, or support, T 24.09(A)

ENDOWMENT FUNDS—See GIFTS AND GRANTS.

ENERGY CONSERVATION
Bonds to finance, T 41.04
School curriculum to include, T 26.02(A)
School equipment, T 36.04(C)(2)

ENROLLMENT—See also ATTENDANCE.
Adjacent districts, students from, T 5.08(D)
  Foundation program fund payments, adjustment, T 5.08(D)
  Monitoring by state board, T 3.03(G)
  Reports, T 5.08(D)
  Transportation of pupils, T 5.08(D)
  Tuition, T 23.02(A)(12)
Alternative schools, open enrollment policies, T 5.08(C)
Birth certificate and previous records required
  Notice to law enforcement agency when pupil fails to present official records, T 24.16, T 48.10

ENROLLMENT—*continued*
Custody arrangements, notice to schools, T 44.14(D), T 48.10
Interdistrict enrollment, T 5.08(D)
  Tuition, T 23.02(A)(9)
Intradistrict enrollment, T 5.08(C)
Open enrollment
  Alternative schools, T 5.08(C)
  Interdistrict, T 5.08(D)
  Intradistrict, T 5.08(C)
Permanently excluded pupils, T 23.02(A)(14)
Post-secondary enrollment options, T 26.07(C)
Private schools, contracts, T 48.11
Records and reports, T 39.09(A), T 44.13
  Adjacent district students enrolled, T 5.08(D)
  Notice to law enforcement agency when pupil fails to present official school records, T 24.16, T 48.10
Transportation of pupils, T 22.07(B)(2)

ENVIRONMENTAL PROTECTION LAWS
Asbestos Hazard Emergency Response Act of 1986, T 21.10(B)
Asbestos removal, T 21.10(B)

EPIDEMICS
Closing schools, T 20.05(D), T 21.08(B)

EQUAL EDUCATIONAL OPPORTUNITY ACT
Bilingual education requirements, T 19.15
Desegregation of schools, applicability, T 19.11(B)

EQUAL EMPLOYMENT OPPORTUNITY—See EMPLOYMENT DISCRIMINATION, generally.

EQUAL PAY AMENDMENT, T 17.08

EQUAL PROTECTION CLAUSE—See CONSTITUTION, UNITED STATES.

EQUIPMENT AND SUPPLIES, SCHOOL, T 35.01 to T 35.03, T Ch 36
Acquisition, T 35.01, T 36.01, T 36.04 to T 36.08
Auction, T 36.11(B)
Books other than textbooks, T 33.03(A)
Buses—See SCHOOL BUSES.
Business managers, powers and duties, T 6.13, T 38.02
Competitive bidding, exemptions, T 36.04(B)
  Data processing equipment, T 37.04(A)
Cooperative acquisition, T 36.08
Data processing equipment, acquisition, T 36.04(C)(1), T 43.29
  Competitive bidding, exemption, T 37.04(A)
Destruction or damage, T 38.04
Energy conservation equipment, T 36.04(C)(2)
Extracurricular activities, for, T 23.04(B)
Eye protective devices, T 21.12

EQUIPMENT AND SUPPLIES, SCHOOL—*continued*
Federal surplus commodities, purchase, T 36.04(B)
Fees paid by pupils, T 33.02(A), T 35.02
  Sales tax exemption, T 35.02(E)
Funds, T 23.04(B), T 35.02(D), T 43.15(B), T 43.24
Gifts or bequests, T 36.06
  Prohibited, when, T 36.13
Leases by school boards, T 36.05(A), T 36.10(A), T 36.14
Maintenance, T 38.02
Musical instruments, T 36.04(C)(4)
Office equipment, acquisition, T 36.04(C)(1)
Payment procedure, T 43.09
Purchase
  Competitive bidding, exemptions, T 36.04(B)
    Data processing equipment, T 37.04(A)
  Conflict of interest, T 45.06(B)
  Purchase contracts, T 36.04(B)
Purchase orders, T 43.07(B)
  Disposition, T 43.07(C)
  Requisition, T 43.07(A)
Sale, T 36.09, T 36.11
  Option to purchase, T 36.12
  Proceeds, T 35.02(B), T 36.14
  Pupils, to, T 35.02
  School board member, by; prohibition, T 45.06(B)
  Student activity fund, T 35.02(C)
Sales agents, prohibition, T 8.07(B), T 33.05, T 45.07
Textbooks—See TEXTBOOKS.
Trade or exchange, T 36.05(B)
Vending machines, T 35.03

"ESTABLISHMENT" CLAUSE, T 32.01

ESTATE TAX
Revenues, distribution, T 39.11

ETHICS, T Ch 45
Applicability of law, T 45.01
Commission, state—See ETHICS COMMISSION, STATE.
Conflict of interest—See CONFLICT OF INTEREST.
Contract awards, T 45.05 to T 45.07
Criminal code violations, T 45.09 to T 45.13
Definitions, T 45.01(C)
Financial disclosure, T 45.02
  Applicability of laws, T 45.01(C)(3)
Incompatible offices, T 45.08
  See also CONFLICT OF INTEREST; particular office concerned.
Prosecution of violations, T 45.01(B)
Public officials and employees, T Ch 45
Restrictions on activities during and after employment, T 45.03
Unauthorized compensation and transactions, T 45.04

ETHICS COMMISSION, STATE, T 45.01(B)
Advisory opinions, T 45.01(B)
Opinions and recommendations, T 45.01(B)

EVALUATION PROCEDURES—See also TESTING PROGRAMS, SCHOOL.
Administrators, T 7.14
Curriculum, T 26.04, T 26.17
Goals 2000: Educate America Act of 1994, T 2.11(B)

EVENING SCHOOLS, T 26.10(B)
Tuition, T 23.02(E), T 26.10(B)

EVIDENCE
Employment discrimination, T 17.02(A), T 17.02(B), T 17.03(C), T 17.03(F), T 17.04(E)
  Age discrimination, T 17.06(B)
Sex discrimination, T 19.14(C)

EVOLUTION
Instruction about, T 32.07

EXAMINATIONS—See TESTING PROGRAMS, SCHOOL.
Financial—See AUDITS.
Health—See MEDICAL EXAMINATIONS.

EXCEPTIONAL CHILDREN—See PUPILS, at Gifted children, special classes; SPECIAL EDUCATION.

EXCHANGE STUDENTS
Tuition, T 23.02(C)(12)

EXECUTION OF JUDGMENT
Public Liability Act, under, T 46.07

EXEMPTED VILLAGE SCHOOL DISTRICTS, T 4.03(F)
  See also SCHOOLS AND SCHOOL DISTRICTS, generally.
Boards
  Contracts with educational service centers, T 5.09(I)
  Members, T 5.02(A)
City school districts, becoming, T 4.03(A), T 4.06(C)
Two or more exempted village school districts combined to form, T 4.03(A)
Classification change, T 4.03(A), T 4.05(C)
Competency of graduates, guarantee policy, T 26.16(B)
Local school districts, becoming, T 4.03(F), T 4.06(B)
Records and reports
  Adjacent school district residents, enrollment, T 5.08(D)

EXEMPTED VILLAGE SCHOOL DISTRICTS—*continued*
Supervision by educational service center governing boards, T 4.03(D), T 4.03(F), T 4.06(B)
Transfer of territory, T 4.07 to T 4.11

EXPENDITURES—See FUNDS, SCHOOL.

EXPULSION OF PUPILS—See PUPILS, at Suspension or expulsion.

EXPUNGEMENT OF RECORDS
Teachers, termination hearings, T 9.22(F)

EXTRACURRICULAR ACTIVITIES, T 23.03 to T 23.05
  See also ATHLETIC EVENTS; PUPILS, at Activity programs.
Disabled students, T 28.03
Sex discrimination, T 19.14
  Funding withheld due to, T 19.14(B)
Student activities fund, T 43.25

EYES
Protective devices for students and teachers, T 21.12

FACULTY—See TEACHERS; UNIVERSITIES AND COLLEGES.

FAIR EMPLOYMENT PRACTICES ACT, T 17.04
  See also EMPLOYMENT DISCRIMINATION, generally.

FAIR LABOR STANDARDS ACT
Equal Pay Amendment, T 17.08

FAMILY AND MEDICAL LEAVE ACT OF 1993, T 17.09, T 17.16
Private schools, applicability, T 48.30

FAMILY EDUCATIONAL RIGHTS AND PRIVACY ACT, T 2.13, T 44.01, T 44.14 to T 44.21
Private schools, applicability, T 48.14

FEDERAL AID
Bilingual educational programs, T 19.15
Civil Rights Act compliance, T 2.13
Desegregation, in-service training programs, T 19.11(A)
Drug-Free Schools and Communities Act, T 21.15(A)
School districts, to, T 2.07, T 2.11 to T 2.13
  Bilingual educational programs, T 19.15
  Block grants, T 2.12
  Vocational education, T 27.01, T 27.04

FEDERAL AID—*continued*
School districts, to—*continued*
  Withholding
    Discriminatory practices, due to, T 19.11(A), T 19.13, T 19.14
    Special education requirements not met, T 28.11(A)
  Vocational education, T 27.01, T 27.04

FEDERAL DISTRICT COURTS
Decisions influencing school laws, T 2.16(B)
Desegregation powers, T 2.16(B), T 19.03
Employment discrimination, jurisdiction, T 17.03(G)

FEDERAL INCOME TAX—See INCOME TAXES.

FEES AND COSTS—See also particular subject concerned.
Attorneys—See ATTORNEYS.
Bond issuance, T 41.16(F), T 41.17(F)
Building permits, school construction exempt, T 37.02
Collective bargaining—See COLLECTIVE BARGAINING, PUBLIC EMPLOYEES, at Dues.
Conflict of interest in setting, T 45.03
Driver training courses, T 23.02(E), T 26.13(A)
Mental retardation and developmental disabilities boards, county, T 29.04(C)
Public records, reproduction, T 44.03
School buildings, use, T 31.04, T 38.10
School pupils—See PUPILS.
Tuition—See TUITION.
Zoning, school construction exempt, T 37.02

FELONIES—See also CRIMES AND OFFENSES, generally; particular crime concerned.
School employees, convictions or guilty pleas, T 5.09(H), T 8.07(A)
  Reporting requirements, T 24.07
Teachers, convictions or guilty pleas, T 5.09(H), T 8.07(A), T 9.21(D)
  Reporting requirements, T 24.07

FEMALES
Discrimination against—See SEX DISCRIMINATION.
Pregnancy—See PREGNANCY.

FIELD TRIPS
Out-of-state and foreign, prohibition by school boards, T 5.08(B)

FINANCIAL AID
Emergency school advancement fund, T 41.33
    See also EMERGENCY LOANS, generally.

FINANCIAL AID—*continued*
Foundation program—See FOUNDATION PROGRAM.
Governmental—See APPROPRIATIONS; FEDERAL AID.
Grants—See GIFTS AND GRANTS.

FINANCIAL DISCLOSURE, T 45.02
Applicability of laws, T 45.01(C)(3)
Candidates, T 45.02

FINANCIAL INSOLVENCY
Schools, determination, T 41.33(B)

FINANCIAL INSTITUTIONS—See particular type concerned.

FINANCIAL RECORDS—See ACCOUNTS AND ACCOUNTING; RECORDS AND REPORTS, SCHOOL.

FINES AND FORFEITURES
Employment of minors, violations, T 20.17, T 39.10
Library fines, dispositions, T 34.12(B)
Quo warranto judgments, noncompliance, T 39.10
Schools, funding, T 39.10
Truancy, T 20.09(B), T 20.09(C)

FINGERPRINTS
Juveniles, at schools, T 24.16(A), T 44.15(A)

FIRE ALARMS, T 21.13

FIRE DRILLS, T 21.13

FIRE FIGHTERS AND FIRE DEPARTMENTS
School employees retirement system, purchase of service credit, T 14.10(A)
Teachers retirement system, purchase of service credit, T 11.13(A)

FIRE SAFETY
Instruction in schools, T 21.14
Schools, T 21.13
  Curriculum to include, T 21.14

FIREARMS—See WEAPONS, generally.

FIRST AID
School curriculum to include, T 21.14, T 26.02(A)

FISCAL PROCEDURE—See FUNDS, PUBLIC; FUNDS, SCHOOL.

FISCAL YEAR, T 40.02

FLAGS
National
  Pledge of allegiance, local policy on recitation, T 26.02(A)
  Saluting in schools, T 32.03

FOOD SERVICES, SCHOOL, T 35.04 to T 35.07
Aged persons, use, T 31.06, T 35.04(B)
Breakfast programs, T 35.07
Contracts, T 35.05
Cooperative purchasing agreements, T 35.05, T 43.23
Free meals, T 23.07(A), T 35.07
Funds, T 35.04(B), T 43.15(B), T 43.23
Inspection of facilities, T 35.06
Licensing of operation, T 35.06
Lunch programs, T 35.07
Management companies, T 43.23
Operation, T 35.04
  Licensing, T 35.06
Outside groups, use of facilities, T 35.04(C)
Programs, T 35.07
Sales tax, educational institutions selling to students, T 35.04(A)
Sanitation and safety, T 35.06
Standards, T 35.07
Teachers, free lunches for, T 35.04(A), T 43.05(B)
Vending machines, T 35.03

FOREIGN EXCHANGE STUDENTS, T 23.02(C)(12)

FOREIGN STATES
School districts joining with Ohio school districts, T 4.02

FORFEITURES—See FINES AND FORFEITURES.

FORMS—See particular subject concerned.

FOSTER HOMES, JUVENILE
Education of residents, T 23.02(A)(4)

FOUNDATION PROGRAM, T 2.07, T 39.06 to T 39.08
Administration by state board of education, T 3.03(G), T 39.06(C)
Appropriations for, T 39.06(A), T 39.06(C)
Appropriations from—See Payments to districts, this heading.
Average daily membership, T 39.09(B)
  Certification, T 6.07(D)
  Cooperative education school districts, T 39.09(B)
  Nonresident pupils, T 39.09(B)
  Records, T 6.07(D), T 39.09(B)
Basic state aid
  Certification of information by tax commissioner, T 39.09(A)

FOUNDATION PROGRAM—*continued*
Basic state aid—*continued*
  Recomputation, T 39.09(E)
Calculation
  Educational service center governing boards, T 40.03
  Recalculation, T 39.09(E)
Constitutionality, T 39.06(B)
Controlling board, powers, T 39.06(C)
Distribution of payments—See Payments to districts, this heading.
Educational service center governing boards, annual budgets, T 40.03
Eligibility, T 4.05(A), T 39.07
  Certificate of available resources required, T 6.07(C)(2), T 40.18(B)
  Waiver of calendar year requirements, T 20.05(A)
Emergency assistance, T 41.33
    See also EMERGENCY LOANS, generally.
Fiscal year basis, T 20.05(A)
Governor's powers and duties, T 39.06(B)
Handicapped children, education funds, T 28.15(A), T 28.18, T 39.08(A)
Joint vocational school districts, T 27.11, T 27.12, T 39.08(B)
  Average daily membership, T 39.09(B)
Nonoperating uses, T 39.08
Payments to districts, T 3.06, T 39.06(C)
  Adjacent school district resident enrollment, adjustment for, T 5.08(D)
  Recomputation, T 39.09(E)
  Special programs, for, T 28.15(A), T 39.08(A)
    See also particular program or service concerned.
  Transfer of territory, effect, T 4.12
  Withholding, T 4.05(A), T 6.07(C)(2), T 40.18(B)
Private and parochial schools
  Services, T 48.06
Records required, T 39.09
  Average daily membership, T 6.07(D), T 39.09(B)
  Handicapped children, preschool, T 39.09(C)
  Preschools, handicapped children, T 39.09(C)
  Uncollectible taxes, T 39.09(F)
School bus purchases, funding, T 22.07(C)
State basic aid—See Basic state aid, this heading.
State board of education, powers, T 3.03(G), T 39.06(C)
Statistics required—See Records required, this heading.
Tax levies as prerequisite, T 39.07(B)
Transfer of territory, effect on payments, T 4.12
Use of funds, T 39.06(A)
  Nonoperating uses, T 39.08
  Withholding payments, T 4.05(A), T 6.07(C)(2), T 40.18(B)

FOUNDATION PROGRAM—*continued*
Vocational education, T 27.11, T 27.12, T 39.08(B)
  Joint districts, average daily membership, T 39.09(B)

FOUNDATIONS
Education foundation funds, T 39.13, T 42.22
Schools creating private tax-exempt foundations, T 39.13

FRANKLIN COUNTY
Textbooks, removal of offensive materials, T 33.04

FRATERNAL ORGANIZATIONS
Hazing, T 24.10
  Liability of school personnel, T 46.10

FREE APPROPRIATE PUBLIC EDUCATION (FAPE), T 28.01(A), T 28.03, T 28.05(B)

"FREE EXERCISE" CLAUSE, T 32.01

FREEDOM OF SPEECH
Private school students, T 48.18
Public school students, T 25.05
School employees, T 9.21(E), T 12.16(A), T 12.17(A), T 46.14(C)
Textbooks, removal of offensive materials, T 33.04

FREEDOM OF THE PRESS
Private school students, T 48.18
Public school students, T 25.05
  Limitations, T 25.05
School employees, T 9.21(E), T 12.16(A), T 12.17(A)
Textbooks, removal of offensive materials, T 33.04

FREEDOM OF WORSHIP, T 25.05, T Ch 32

FRINGE BENEFITS—See particular employee or benefit concerned.

FUNDS, PUBLIC—See also FUNDS, SCHOOL.
Arts councils
  Local, T 31.05
  Cultural associations, for, T 31.05
Deposits and depositories, T Ch 42
  Active deposits, T 42.08, T 42.11(B)(3)
  Application to act as depository, T 42.10
  Award of deposits, T 42.11
  Conflict of interest, T 42.12, T 45.08(B)
  Definitions, T 42.04
  Designation, T 42.07 to T 42.15
  Discrimination against, T 42.12
  Eligible institutions, T 42.05
  Evidence of deposits, T 42.13
  Inactive deposits, T 42.08, T 42.11(B)(1)

FUNDS, PUBLIC—*continued*
Deposits and depositories—*continued*
  Interest payments, T 42.21
    Apportionment among funds, T 42.22
  Interim deposits, T 42.08, T 42.11(B)(2)
    Investment, T 42.23
  Limitation on amounts deposited, T 42.06
  Maturity dates, T 42.13
  Minority banks, T 42.05(C)
  Multiple institutions, designation, T 42.05(B)
  NOW accounts, T 42.13
  Passbook accounts, T 42.13
  Savings accounts, T 42.13
  Schools, T 6.07(A), T 43.12(C)
  Security guarantees, T 42.16 to T 42.20
  Separate treatment of deposits, T 42.08, T 42.10
  Service charges, T 42.15
  Transfers, T 42.14
  Withdrawals, T 42.11(B)(1), T 42.14
Investments
  Interim funds, T 42.23
Liability
  Loss of funds, T 42.02
Libraries—See LIBRARIES AND LIBRARY DISTRICTS.
Mental retardation and developmental disabilities boards, T 29.09
Preschool programs use, T 39.08
Private schools, for—See FUNDS, SCHOOL.
School employees retirement system—See SCHOOL EMPLOYEES RETIREMENT SYSTEM.
Schools—See FUNDS, SCHOOL.
Sinking funds—See SINKING FUNDS.
Symphony associations, for, T 31.05
Teachers retirement system—See TEACHERS RETIREMENT SYSTEM.
Uniform depository act, T 42.01
Violations, T 43.27(B)
  Statute of limitations, T 43.27(B)

FUNDS, SCHOOL, T 1.05, T 1.09, T Ch 39 to T Ch 43
  See also FUNDS, PUBLIC, generally.
Accounting—See ACCOUNTS AND ACCOUNTING.
Activity funds, T 23.03, T 23.04, T 39.15
Allocation of tax proceeds to wrong districts, restitution actions, T 39.05
Analysis by superintendent of public instruction, T 41.33(C)
Anticipation notes for income tax, T 39.12
Appropriation of land by Congress to fund schools, T 1.02, T 1.05
Appropriations—See APPROPRIATIONS, at School boards.
Arts councils, supporting, T 31.05
Attorneys, hiring, T 6.14(A)
Bond funds, T 43.15(B), T 43.18
Bond retirement funds—See SINKING FUNDS.

FUNDS, SCHOOL—*continued*
Borrowing money, T Ch 41
    See also BONDS AND NOTES, SCHOOL; DEBTS.
Budgets—See BUDGETS, SCHOOL.
Business managers—See BUSINESS MANAGERS.
Cash journals, T 43.13
Cash reserves, T 42.03
Certificates of estimated resources, T 40.15(B), T 40.15(D), T 40.18, T 40.19
Certification of adequate revenues, T 6.07(C)
  Absence of certificate, T 6.07(C)(2)
  Construction and improvements, T 37.07(A)
Classroom facilities, financing
  Permanent improvements, T 41.24 to T 41.32
Congressional appropriation of property to fund schools, T 1.02, T 1.05
Consolidation of districts, effect, T 4.13
Constitutional considerations, current funding system, T 39.01(B)
County budget commissions, powers, T 40.05
Creation of new districts, effect, T 4.13
Cultural associations, supporting, T 31.05
Deficits, effect, T 41.33
Deposits and depositories, T 6.07(A), T Ch 42, T 43.12(C)
    See also FUNDS, PUBLIC, generally.
Direct deposit by electronic transfer, T 43.08(B)
  Compensation of employees and officers, payment procedure, T 43.10
Disbursement—See Expenditures, this heading.
Driver education, T 26.13(A)
Education foundation funds, T 39.13, T 42.22
Educational service center governing board funds, T 40.03, T 43.15(B)
  Attendance officers' compensation and expenses, payment, T 20.08(B)
Electronic transfer of funds, T 43.08(B)
Emergency school advancement fund, T 41.33
    See also EMERGENCY LOANS, generally.
Employment of minors, fines credited from, T 39.10
Equipment and supplies, for, T 23.04(B), T 35.02(D), T 43.15(B), T 43.24
Establishment, T 43.15(B)
Estate tax revenues credited to, T 39.10
Expenditures, T 6.07, T 43.01 to T 43.10
  Authorization, T 43.02
  Constitutional considerations, current funding system, T 39.01(B)
  Local boards of education, authorization, T 43.02
  Maximum, schedule, T 3.06
  Payroll, T 43.10, T 43.14
  Procedure, T 43.06 to T 43.10
  Public purpose requirement, T 43.03
  Purchase orders, T 43.07(B)
    Disposition, T 43.07(C)
  Records, T 43.30
  Requisitions, T 43.07(A)

FUNDS, SCHOOL—*continued*
Expenditures—*continued*
  Restrictions, T 43.04, T 43.05
  Review of fiscal impact of legislation on school districts, T 2.06
  Schedule, approval by superintendent of public instruction, T 3.06
  Specific authorization, T 43.02(B)
  State board of education's powers, T 39.01(A)
  Unauthorized, T 43.05
  Vouchers, T 43.08(A)
Federal aid—See FEDERAL AID.
Fines and forfeitures credited to, T 39.10
Fiscal year, T 40.02
Food service fund, T 35.04(B), T 43.15(B), T 43.23
Foundation program—See FOUNDATION PROGRAM.
General fund, T 43.15(B), T 43.17
Income tax, T 39.12
Inheritance tax revenues credited to, T 39.11
Insurance, fines credited, T 39.10
Interest earned—See INTEREST, at School funds.
Investments—See INVESTMENTS, at School funds.
Ledgers, T 43.11, T 43.12(B)
Levies, prohibition against promotion with public funds, T 5.09(G)
Liability for misuse or loss, T 6.07(C)(2), T 42.02
Loans
  Data processing equipment, to purchase, T 36.04(C)(1)
  Emergency school advancement fund, T 41.33
    See also EMERGENCY LOANS, generally.
Mathematics equipment and supplies; private and parochial schools, public funds, T 48.07
New districts created, effect, T 4.13
Payrolls
  Account, T 6.07(A), T 43.10
  Lack of funds, issuance of tax anticipation notes, T 41.04, T 41.21(A)
Permanent improvement fund, T 43.21
Permanent improvements, financing
  Obligations, issuance, T 41.03, T 41.04
Preschools, T 39.08
Private and parochial schools, T 48.06
  Interest earnings, allocation, T 42.22
  Right to public funds, T 1.09
  Treasurer's report, request for, T 43.28
Private foundations, creation, T 39.13
Quo warranto fines credited to, T 39.10
Receipts, T 43.12(A)
  Ledger, T 43.11, T 43.12(B)
Records and reports
  Expenditures, T 43.30
Reorganization of school districts, effect, T 4.13
Replacement fund, T 43.20
Restrictions on use, T 43.04, T 43.05
Scholarship funds, T 39.13

FUNDS, SCHOOL—*continued*
Service funds, T 5.04, T 5.09(F), T 43.15(B), T 43.22
Sinking funds, T 43.15(B), T 43.19
  Interest, T 43.16
  Transfer of moneys into, T 43.16, T 43.19
Sources of revenue, T 2.07, T Ch 39
Special funds, T 43.15(B)
Spending obligations notification by state board, T 3.03(G)
Spending plans, T 40.17
Spending reserve balance, T 40.04(C), T 41.21(B)
Stadium construction and improvements, T 39.13
Statements, T 6.07(B)
Student activity programs, to support, T 23.03, T 23.04, T 30.10(C), T 39.15, T 43.25
Studies and surveys, to support, T 5.09(A)
Symphony associations, supporting, T 31.05
Tax anticipation notes—See TAX ANTICIPATION NOTES.
Tax revenues—See TAXATION, at Schools, financing.
Technical assistance by state board of education, T 3.03(G)
Transfer of territory, effect, T 4.12, T 4.13
Transfers, T 43.15(C)
  Food service fund to general fund, T 43.23
Treasurer, powers and duties—See TREASURERS, SCHOOL BOARD, generally.
Trust funds, T 39.13, T 42.22, T 43.15(B)
Unauthorized expenditures, T 43.05
Use, T 43.01 to T 43.05
  Restrictions, T 43.04, T 43.05
Village corporate powers surrendered, funds credited to schools, T 39.10
Vocational education—See VOCATIONAL EDUCATION.
Vouchers, T 43.08(A)
Warrants, T 43.08(B)

GENERAL ASSEMBLY
Schools, powers and duties, T 1.09, T 2.14, T 4.04

GIFTED CHILDREN—See PUPILS.

GIFTS AND GRANTS
Charitable contributions, solicitation in schools, T 31.08
Mental retardation and developmental disabilities boards, to, T 29.08(A)
Public employees, payroll deductions for contributions, T 10.08, T 31.08
School boards, to, T 36.06, T 39.13
School buildings or lands, T 36.06
  Prohibited, T 36.13
Schools, soliciting contributions in, T 31.08

GOALS 2000: EDUCATE AMERICA ACT OF 1994
Curriculum, T 2.11(B)
Evaluation procedures, T 2.11(B)
Gun-Free Schools Act of 1994, T 25.10(A)

GOALS 2000: EDUCATE AMERICA ACT OF 1994—*continued*
Pro-Children Act of 1994, T 38.14
Smoking indoors, ban, T 38.14
Testing programs, T 2.11(B)
Voluntary prayer and meditation, effect on, T 32.05

GOGGLES
Pupils required to wear, when, T 21.12

GOVERNOR
Appointment powers
  Employment relations board members, T 18.02
School foundation program funds, powers and duties, T 39.06(B)

GRADE CROSSINGS
Stopping before, T 22.18(A)

GRADUATION REQUIREMENTS, T 26.06(B), T 28.10(B)
Private and parochial schools, proficiency tests, T 48.03(A)
Special education, T 28.10(B)

GRANDPARENTS
Students residing with, tuition exemption, T 23.02(C)(11)

GRANTS—See GIFTS AND GRANTS.

GUARANTEED COMPETENCY, T 26.16(B)

GUIDANCE AND COUNSELING PROGRAMS
Child abuse prevention, in-service training for counselors, T 21.14
Contract status of counselors, T 9.07(A)(3)
Counselors
  Teacher status, T 8.02(B), T 9.07(A)(3)
Disabled children, special education services, T 28.07
Private and parochial schools, funding, T 48.07
Sex discrimination, T 19.14(A)
Special education services, T 28.07

GUN-FREE SCHOOLS ACT OF 1994, T 25.10(A)

GUNS—See WEAPONS, generally.

HANDICAPPED CHILDREN—See also BLIND PERSONS; DEAF PERSONS; DISABLED CHILDREN; HANDICAPPED PERSONS.
Home instruction, T 28.08(A)
Schooling—See also SPECIAL EDUCATION, generally.
  Foundation program funding, T 28.15(A), T 28.18, T 39.08(A)
  Room and board costs, T 28.08(A)

HANDICAPPED CHILDREN—*continued*
Schooling—*continued*
  State board of education, powers and duties, T 3.03(B)
  State schools for blind and deaf, T 28.19
  State schools for blind and deaf, T 28.19

HANDICAPPED CHILDREN'S PROTECTION ACT, T 28.12(B), T 28.13(D)

HANDICAPPED PERSONS—See also BLIND PERSONS; DEAF PERSONS.
Access to public buildings, T 21.10(C), T 28.17(B)
AIDS victims as, T 17.13, T 21.03(E), T 28.01(B)
Americans with Disabilities Act of 1990, T 17.13(B)
Children—See DISABLED CHILDREN; HANDICAPPED CHILDREN.
Discrimination against, T 17.13, T 19.13(C), T 28.01(A)
  Federal aid, termination, T 19.13(C)
  Private schools, by, T 48.29
  Trained dogs, persons accompanied by, T 17.13(A), T 28.18
Education—See SPECIAL EDUCATION, generally.
Employment discrimination, T 17.13
Ohio rehabilitation center at Ohio state university, T 27.14
Rehabilitation services—See REHABILITATION SERVICES.
Trained dogs accompanying, T 17.13(A), T 28.18

HARASSMENT
Sexual, T 17.11
  Title IX liability, T 19.14(A)

HAZARDOUS WORK
Minors, prohibition, T 20.11(A)

HAZING, T 24.10
Liability of school personnel, T 46.10, T 46.14(B)

HEAD START PROGRAMS
School buildings and lands, inspections, T 21.03(A), T 21.08(B)

HEALTH AND HOSPITALIZATION INSURANCE
Family and Medial Leave Act of 1993, requirements, T 17.16
Libraries, participation in self-funded programs, T 34.10(B)
Mental retardation and developmental disabilities board employees, T 29.13(B)
School board members, T 5.09(T)
Unemployed persons, continuation of group coverage, T 10.12

HEALTH DISTRICTS
Boards
  Member serving as school board member, exclusion, T 45.08(A)
Inspection powers, T 21.08(B), T 35.06
Schools, powers and duties
  Closing, T 20.05(D), T 21.08(B)
  Inspection, T 21.08(B), T 35.06
  Medical and dental supervision, T 21.08(A)

HEALTH EXAMINATIONS—See MEDICAL EXAMINATIONS.
Pupils—See PUPILS, at Health.

HEALTH SERVICES, T 21.01 to T 21.09
See also particular service concerned; PUPILS.

HEALTHCHECK PROGRAMS
Establishment, T 5.09(M)

HEARINGS—See also particular subject concerned.
Collective bargaining, public employees—See COLLECTIVE BARGAINING, PUBLIC EMPLOYEES.
Conflict of interest, administrative procedure, T 45.03
Disabled children, educational placement, T 28.11(C) to T 28.11(F)
Industrial commission, employment risk reduction standards, T 16.09(A)
School bus drivers, disqualification, T 22.14
School employees, termination, T 12.16(B), T 12.16(C)
  Pretermination hearing, T 12.17(B)
  Transcripts, T 12.16(C)
School tax budgets, T 40.03
Special education, pupil placement, T 28.11(C) to T 28.11(F)
Tax budget proposals, T 40.03

HIGH SCHOOLS—See also SCHOOLS AND SCHOOL DISTRICTS, generally.
Adult continuation programs, T 26.10(D)
College preparatory, T 26.07(B)
Cooperative education school districts, operation of joint high schools, T 4.03(G)
Correctional institutions operating, T 26.16
Credit for proprietary school courses, T 5.09(D), T 26.16
Curriculum, T 26.06
  See also CURRICULUM, generally.
Driver training—See DRIVER TRAINING COURSES.
First public high school, T 1.10
Graduation requirements, T 26.06(B)
  Private and parochial schools, proficiency tests, T 48.03(A)
Guaranteed competency of graduates, T 26.16(B)
Joint districts, operation by cooperative education school districts, T 4.03(G)

HIGH SCHOOLS—*continued*
Junior high schools—See JUNIOR HIGH SCHOOLS.
Physical education, T 30.02
Post-secondary enrollment options, T 26.07(C)
Religious instruction off-premises, release time, T 5.08(B)
Transportation of pupils, T 22.03(B)
 See also TRANSPORTATION OF PUPILS, generally.
Vocational programs—See VOCATIONAL EDUCATION, generally.
Voter registration provided in, T 31.09

HIGHWAY PATROL—See also LAW ENFORCEMENT OFFICERS.
School employees retirement system, purchase of service credit, T 14.10(A)
Teachers retirement system, purchase of service credit, T 11.13(A)

HIGHWAY PATROL RETIREMENT SYSTEM
Purchase of service credit by members
 School employees retirement system, in, T 14.10(A)
 Teachers retirement system, in, T 11.13(A)

HIGHWAYS AND ROADS
Public safety department, regulation of school buses, T 22.10
School guards, T 21.11(A)
Traffic control—See TRAFFIC CONTROL.

HISTORY OF SCHOOL LAW, T Ch 1
Common school movement, T 1.07, T 1.08
Constitutional provisions for education, T 1.04, T 1.09
Financing education, T 1.05
First schools in Ohio, T 1.03
Handicapped persons, education for, T 1.06
Northwest Ordinance of 1787, T 1.02
Secondary education, T 1.10

HOLIDAYS
School, T 20.06
 Commemoration in, T 20.06
 Nonteaching employees, compensation, T 13.03

HOME EDUCATION, T 20.03(C)
Religious grounds, T 20.03(A)

HOME INSTRUCTION, T 20.03
Handicapped children, T 28.08(A)
Pregnant students, T 20.04
Special education, T 28.08(A)

HOSPITALIZATION INSURANCE—See HEALTH AND HOSPITALIZATION INSURANCE.

HOSPITALS
Education of children in, T 28.08(B)

HUMAN SERVICES DEPARTMENT, STATE
Institutions, inspection by state board of education, T 3.03(G)

HUSBAND AND WIFE—See MARRIAGE.

IMMIGRANTS
Americanization program for, T 26.11(E)
Verification of identity and work authorization by employers, T 48.20

IMMUNITY FROM PROSECUTION
Charitable immunity doctrine, liability of private schools, T 48.34(A)
Private schools, T 48.34(A)
School boards and officials, T 5.07, T Ch 46
 See also LIABILITY, generally; PUBLIC LIABILITY ACT.
 Federal civil rights violations, T 46.13 to T 46.16
 Violation of student's constitutional rights, T 25.09(C)
 Volunteer medical practitioners or nurses at athletic events, T 21.09

IMMUNIZATION
Disadvantaged pupils, T 23.07(B)
School children, T 21.05
 Exclusion of students not immunized, T 21.05(B)
 Free, T 23.07(B)
 Parental objections, T 21.05(C)
 Records, T 21.07(B)
 Required, T 21.05(A)

IMPRISONMENT—See PRISONERS.

IN LOCO PARENTIS, T 24.02, T 25.06
Civil law, T 24.02(A)
Criminal law, T 24.02(B)

INCOME TAX, SCHOOL DISTRICT, T 39.12
Real property tax reduction due to, T 39.12
Repeal, T 39.12

INCOME TAXES
Federal
 Arbitrage bonds, T 41.19(B)
  Rebates, T 41.19(C)
 Payroll deductions, T 10.08
 Private schools, T 48.31
 Qualified tax-exempt obligations, T 41.19(D)
Municipal
 Payroll deductions, public employees, T 10.08
 Sharing revenues with school districts, T 39.12
Payroll deductions, public employees, T 10.08
State
 Library and local support fund, T 34.14

INCOME TAXES—*continued*
Teachers, payroll deductions, T 10.08

INCOMPATIBLE OFFICES—See CONFLICT OF INTEREST, generally; particular public official or employee concerned.

INCOMPETENT PERSONS—See MENTALLY RETARDED AND DEVELOPMENTALLY DISABLED PERSONS.

INCORPORATION
Municipal, creation of city school districts, T 4.06(D)

INDEBTEDNESS—See DEBTS.

INDEMNIFICATION
Public Liability Act, under, T 46.04, T 46.15
School employees and officers, actions against, T 46.04

INDEPENDENT CONTRACTORS
Employment in lieu of civil service employees, T 12.08
Equal opportunity requirements, T 17.05
Workers' compensation coverage, T 16.02

INDIGENT PUPILS—See DISADVANTAGED PUPILS.

INDIVIDUALIZED EDUCATION PROGRAM (IEP) FOR HANDICAPPED CHILD, T 28.02

INDIVIDUALS WITH DISABILITIES EDUCATION ACT (IDEA), T Ch 28
See also SPECIAL EDUCATION, generally.

INDUSTRIAL ARTS—See VOCATIONAL EDUCATION, generally.

INDUSTRIAL COMMISSION
Employment risk reduction standards, hearings, T 16.09(A)
Workers' compensation—See WORKERS' COMPENSATION, generally.

INHERITANCE TAX, T 39.11

INITIATIVE AND REFERENDUM
School districts
　City school district board, composition, T 5.02(B)(1)
　Dissolution, referendum against, T 4.09(D), T 26.19
　Reorganization, referendum against, T 4.10(B)
　Transfer of territory, referendum against, T 4.10(B)

INJUNCTIVE RELIEF
Collective bargaining, public employees—See COLLECTIVE BARGAINING, PUBLIC EMPLOYEES.
Employment discrimination, T 17.03(E)
Employment services bureau, occupational safety and health violations, T 16.09(A)
Personal information system, T 44.08(B)
Public employment risk reduction advisory commission, T 16.09(A)
School board actions, T 5.06(C), T 46.09
　Failure to comply with open meeting requirements, T 5.12(D)
Strikes, against
　Clear and present danger, T 18.32
　Unauthorized strikes, T 18.27, T 18.31

INSPECTIONS—See also particular subject concerned.
Audits—See AUDITS.
Correctional institutions, schools operated by, T 3.03(G)
Human services department institutions, T 3.03(G)
Mental health department institutions, T 3.03(G)
Mental retardation and developmental disabilities department institutions, T 3.03(G)
Occupational safety and health—See EMPLOYMENT SERVICES BUREAU, at Inspections.
Public employment risk reduction advisory commission, T 16.09(A), T 16.09(E)
School buses
　Daily, by driver, T 22.17(A)
Schools—See SCHOOL BUILDINGS AND LANDS.
State board of education, by, T 3.03(G)
Youth commission institutions, T 3.03(G)

INSTRUCTIONAL PROGRAM—See CURRICULUM.

INSURANCE—See also particular type concerned.
Accidents, school pupils—See LIABILITY INSURANCE.
Driver training courses, T 22.08, T 46.20
Fines used to finance schools, T 39.10
Health and hospitalization—See HEALTH AND HOSPITALIZATION INSURANCE.
Liability—See LIABILITY INSURANCE.
Life—See LIFE INSURANCE.
Motor vehicle—See MOTOR VEHICLE INSURANCE.
Payroll deductions for premiums, T 10.08
Premiums, payroll deductions, T 10.08
Pupils, accidents, T 22.08, T 23.04(B), T 46.21
Schools
　Accident insurance for pupils, T 22.08, T 23.04(B), T 46.21
　Buses, T 22.08, T 23.04(B), T 46.20, T 46.21
　Driver training courses, T 22.08, T 46.20

INSURANCE—*continued*
Schools—*continued*
  Employees—See SCHOOL EMPLOYEES, NONTEACHING; TEACHERS.
  Liability insurance, T 5.07, T 46.17 to T 46.21
    Volunteer bus rider assistants, T 22.21, T 29.06(B)
  Motor vehicle insurance, T 46.20
  Property use by others, T 38.08(C)
  Transportation of pupils, T 22.08, T 46.20
  State library board members and employees, liability, T 34.06
  Teachers—See TEACHERS.
  Teachers retirement system
    Health, T 11.20
    Indemnification of members and employees, T 11.02(A)
  Transportation of pupils, T 22.08, T 46.20
    Volunteer bus rider assistants, T 22.21, T 29.06(B)

INTENTIONAL TORT BY EMPLOYER, T 16.08

INTERDISTRICT OPEN ENROLLMENT PROGRAMS, T 5.08(D)

INTEREST
Allocation, T 39.05
Bonds and notes, on, T 41.08, T 41.16(F), T 41.17(B)
Mental retardation and developmental disabilities boards, county; permanent improvement fund, T 29.09(A)
Public deposits, on, T 42.21
  Apportionment among funds, T 42.22
School funds
  Accrued interest, T 39.05
  Delayed payments, T 39.05
  Disposition, T 42.22
  Education foundation funds, T 39.13, T 42.22
  Inactive deposits, T 42.21
  Investment, T 43.16

INTERFERENCE WITH CIVIL RIGHTS, T 45.13

INTERPRETERS
Deaf students, for, T 3.04(A)

INTERSCHOLASTIC ATHLETICS—See ATHLETIC EVENTS, generally.

INTERSTATE AGREEMENTS
Education, T 2.10
  Personnel qualifications, T 8.03(C)
Midwestern education compact, T 2.10
Regional councils of government, powers, T 5.09(D)
Teacher qualifications, T 8.03(C)

INTOXICATION
Pupils, administration of breathalyzer tests, T 25.03

INTRADISTRICT OPEN ENROLLMENT PROGRAMS, T 5.08(C)

INVESTMENT BONDS—See BONDS AND NOTES.

INVESTMENTS
Interim funds, T 42.23
School funds
  Education foundation funds, T 39.13, T 42.22
  Interest earned on, T 43.16
  Interim moneys, T 42.23
  Project construction account moneys, T 42.23(A)
  Treasurer's duties, T 42.24
  Trustee, reports, T 42.24

JOB TRAINING—See VOCATIONAL EDUCATION.

JOINT EDUCATIONAL SERVICE CENTERS, T 4.03(C)
Governing boards, members, T 5.02(A)

JOINT HIGH SCHOOL DISTRICTS
Cooperative education school districts, operation by, T 4.03(G)

JOINT VOCATIONAL SCHOOL DISTRICTS, T 4.03(E), T 27.08 to T 27.12
See also VOCATIONAL EDUCATION.

JUDGES
Dereliction of duty, T 45.12
School board member as municipal court judge, exclusion, T 45.08(A)
Truancy, notice, T 20.10

JUDGMENTS
Political subdivisions, against
  Bond issue to pay, T 41.04, T 41.08
  Public Liability Act, under, T 46.07

JUNIOR HIGH SCHOOLS—See also SCHOOLS AND SCHOOL DISTRICTS, generally.
Curriculum, T 26.05(C)
  See also CURRICULUM, generally.
Physical education, T 30.02

JURISDICTION—See also particular subject concerned.
Common pleas courts
  Strikes, temporary restraining orders, T 18.32
  Unfair labor practices, T 18.26(C)
Employment of minors, violations, T 20.17
Employment relations board, T 18.26

JURISDICTION—*continued*
Federal courts, employment discrimination
actions, T 17.03(F)
National labor relations board
Private school employees, T 48.28
School boards, T 5.06(A)
Truancy violations, T 20.09(A)

JURY TRIALS
Compensation of jurors
School personnel, T 10.09(B), T 13.05(B)
School personnel, pay while on duty, T 10.09(B), T 13.05(B)

JUVENILE COURTS
Commitment of children
Educational costs, T 23.02(A)(4)
Employment of minors, violation proceedings, T 20.17
Jurisdiction
Employment of minor, violation, T 20.17
Truancy, T 20.09(A)
Truancy cases, T 20.09
Notice to judge, T 20.10

JUVENILE DELINQUENCY
Adjudication
State superintendent issuing, excluding students convicted or adjudicated delinquent, T 3.06
Contributing to delinquency, T 24.11
Definition, T 24.11
Permanent exclusion from Ohio public schools, T 25.10(E)

JUVENILE REHABILITATION
Facilities
Educational costs of child, T 23.02(A)(4)

KINDERGARTENS
Attendance, age requirements, T 26.05(A)
Curriculum, T 26.05(A)
Physical education, T 30.02
Tests for entrance, T 20.01(B)
Transportation of children, T 22.03(A)
See also TRANSPORTATION OF PUPILS, generally.

KNIVES—See WEAPONS, generally.

LABOR—See EMPLOYER AND EMPLOYEE.

LABOR ORGANIZATIONS
Public employees—See COLLECTIVE BARGAINING, PUBLIC EMPLOYEES, at Employee organizations.

LAND—See PUBLIC LANDS; REAL PROPERTY; SCHOOL BUILDINGS AND LANDS.

LATCHKEY PROGRAMS
Establishment, T 5.09(L)

LAW ENFORCEMENT OFFICERS—See also particular type concerned.
Access to student records, missing child investigation, T 24.16, T 44.16, T 48.10
Dereliction of duty, T 45.12
Missing children
Access to student records for investigation, T 24.16, T 44.16, T 48.10

LAYOFFS
Civil service employees, T 12.14
See also CIVIL SERVICE.
Principals, T 7.13
School employees, nonteaching, T 12.13, T 12.14
Teachers, T 9.19
Unemployment compensation, T 15.02(A)

LEASES
School boards, powers, T 36.05(A), T 36.10, T 36.14
Lease-purchase agreements, T 36.02(A)
School buses—See SCHOOL BUSES.

LEAVES OF ABSENCE—See also particular employee concerned.
Collective bargaining subject, as, T 18.28
Family and Medical Leave Act of 1993, T 17.16
Private schools, applicability, T 48.30
School employees—See SCHOOL EMPLOYEES, NONTEACHING; TEACHERS.

LEGACIES AND DEVISES—See also GIFTS AND GRANTS.
Mental retardation and developmental disabilities boards, to, T 29.08(A)
School boards, to, T 36.06, T 39.13
Prohibited, when, T 36.13

LEGAL ADVERTISING—See NOTICE.

LEGAL COUNSEL—See ATTORNEYS.
School boards—See EDUCATION, LOCAL BOARDS.

LEGISLATURE, STATE—See GENERAL ASSEMBLY.

LEGISLATURE, UNITED STATES—See CONGRESS, UNITED STATES.

LEVIES—See TAXATION.

LIABILITY—See also particular person or subject concerned; PUBLIC LIABILITY ACT.
Attorney fees, recovery, T 46.16
Contract claims, T 46.08
Discipline of students, T 46.14(A)(1), T 46.14(B)
Discrimination, T 46.13 to T 46.16

LIABILITY—*continued*
Employers, intentional harm, T 16.08
Hazing, T 46.10, T 46.14(B)
Insurance—See LIABILITY INSURANCE.
Moral obligation doctrine, T 46.12
Personal injuries to students as due process violations, T 46.14(B)
Private schools, T 48.34
Qualified immunity, T 46.15(C)
Recreational users, T 46.11
School boards and officials—See EDUCATION, LOCAL BOARDS.
Schools and school districts, T 5.07, T Ch 46
  Private schools, T 48.34
Teachers—See TEACHERS.

LIABILITY INSURANCE
Mental retardation and developmental disabilities boards, T 29.16
Motor vehicles—See MOTOR VEHICLE INSURANCE.
Pools, self-insurance; political subdivisions
  Principals, T 46.19
School boards, T 5.07, T 46.17 to T 46.21
  Authority to purchase, T 46.17
  Motor vehicle insurance, T 46.20
  Personnel, coverage, T 46.19
School buses and pupils, T 22.08, T 23.04(B), T 46.20, T 46.21
  Volunteer bus rider assistants, T 22.21, T 29.06(B)
School officers and employees, T 5.07, T 46.19
School property used by others, T 38.08(C)
State library board members and employees, T 34.06
Superintendents, T 46.19
Teachers, T 5.07, T 46.19
Volunteer school bus rider assistants, T 22.21, T 29.06(B)

LIBEL AND SLANDER
School board members, qualified privilege, T 46.03

LIBRARIES AND LIBRARY DISTRICTS, T Ch 34
Appropriations, T 34.04(B)
  Resolutions, T 34.13
Bids for contracts, T 34.10(B)
Boards of library trustees—See Trustees, this heading.
Bonds and notes, T 34.17
    See also BONDS AND NOTES, generally.
  School boards, issuance by, T 34.02, T 34.17
    Ballot, T 41.14(B)
Bookmobiles, T 34.08, T 34.10(A)
Branch libraries, establishment, T 34.08, T 34.10(A)
Budgets, T 34.13
Buildings
  Bond issue to finance
    Ballot form, T 41.14(B)

LIBRARIES AND LIBRARY DISTRICTS—*continued*
Buildings—*continued*
  Lease, T 34.10
  Purchase, T 34.10
  Sale, T 34.10(B)
  School libraries, T 34.02, T 34.03
Civil service classification of librarians
  School librarians, T 12.04(A)(1)
Clerks of boards of trustees, T 34.12(B)
Conflict of interest
  Board of trustees, T 34.03, T 34.09(A)
  State library board members, T 34.06
Contracts
  Bidding, T 34.10(B)
  Library service, for, T 34.02, T 34.04, T 34.10(A)
County free public libraries
  Schools, service to, T 34.04
  Tax levy, T 34.15(B)
County library and local government support fund, T 34.14
County library districts
  Schools, service to, T 34.04
  Tax levy, T 34.15(B)
Educational programs, cooperation with school boards, T 5.09(D), T 26.11(C), T 31.05
Employees
  Civil service classification of librarians
    School librarians, T 12.04(A)(1)
  Compensation, T 34.10(A), T 34.12(A)
  Insurance, T 34.10(A)
  Trustee as, prohibition, T 34.12(A)
Fines, disposition, T 34.12(B)
Funds
  Accounting, T 34.12(B)
  Building and repair fund, T 34.10(A)
  Clerk to be treasurer, T 34.12(B)
  Expenditure, T 34.11
  Income tax, distribution, T 34.14
  Reports
    Annual, T 34.11
    Monthly, by board clerk, T 34.12(B)
  Trustees, powers and duties, T 34.11
Gifts and grants, T 34.10(A)
Income tax, distribution, T 34.14
Insurance, T 34.10(A)
  Liability
    State library board purchasing, T 34.06
  Medical and life, T 34.10(A)
  Self-funded health care benefits program, participation in, T 34.10(B)
Legacies and devises, T 34.10(A)
Levies—See Tax revenues to support, this heading.
Librarians
  State librarian, T 34.07
Municipal free public libraries
  Service to schools, T 34.04
Museums administered by, T 34.10(A)

LIBRARIES AND LIBRARY DISTRICTS—*continued*
Personal information systems, T 44.01, T 44.04 to T 44.11
    See also PERSONAL INFORMATION SYSTEMS.
Police for, T 34.10(B)
Property
  Acquisition, T 34.10
  Sale, T 34.10(B)
  School libraries, T 34.10(B)
Records and reports
  Annual report of library trustees, T 34.11
  Financial report by clerk, monthly, T 34.12(B)
  Personal information systems, T 44.01, T 44.04 to T 44.11
    See also PERSONAL INFORMATION SYSTEMS.
  State librarian to publish, T 34.07
Regional libraries, service to schools, T 34.04
Rulemaking powers, T 34.10(A)
Sale of land or buildings, T 34.10(B)
School boards, cooperation with, T 5.09(D), T 26.11(C), T 31.05
School buildings, use, T 34.02
School libraries, T 34.03, T 34.04
  Board of trustees, T 34.03
    See also Trustees, this heading.
  Books, purchasing, T 33.03(A)
  Budget, T 34.13
  Buildings, T 34.02, T 34.03
  Civil service status, T 12.04(A)(1)
  Consolidation of districts, effect, T 34.03, T 34.05
  Contracts for services, T 34.02, T 34.04, T 34.10(A)
  Disassociating library from district, prohibition, T 34.10(B)
  Establishment, T 34.02
  Expenses, T 34.02
  Property leased or transferred to, T 34.02
  Property purchases, T 34.10(B)
  Removal of offensive books, T 33.04
  School board powers and duties, T 34.02
  Tax levy to support, T 34.15(A)
    Special levy, T 34.16(B), T 40.09(B)
Special police for, T 34.10(B)
State library, T 34.05 to T 34.08
  Application to; establishment of library stations, branches, or travelling service, T 34.08
  Board, T 34.06
    Powers and duties, T 34.05
  Control and management, T 34.07
  Librarian, T 34.07
Tax revenues to support
  County free public libraries, T 34.15(B)
  County library districts, T 34.15(B)
  Income tax, T 34.14
  Levies, T 34.15
    Special levies, T 34.16, T 40.09(B)
  School libraries, T 34.15(A)
    Special levy, T 34.16(B), T 40.09(B)

LIBRARIES AND LIBRARY DISTRICTS—*continued*
Tax revenues to support—*continued*
  Special levies, T 34.16, T 40.09(B)
  Township libraries, T 34.15(B)
Township libraries
  Schools, service to, T 34.04
  Tax levy to support, T 34.15(B)
Traveling library service, T 34.08
Trustees, T 34.09 to T 34.12
  Annual report, T 34.11
  Appointment, T 34.03, T 34.09(A)
  Association membership dues and expenses, T 34.10(A)
  Clerks, T 34.12(B)
  Conflict of interest, T 34.03, T 34.09(A)
  Employee, as; prohibition, T 34.12(A)
  Financial reports, T 34.11
  Financial transactions, T 34.11
  Meetings, T 34.09(A), T 34.09(C)
  Officers, T 34.09(A)
  Powers and duties, T 34.09(B), T 34.10
  Quorum, T 34.09(C)
  Reports, financial, T 34.11
  Term, T 34.03
Voter registration within, T 34.10(B)

LICENSES AND PERMITS—See also particular subject concerned.
Child day care, T 26.11(D)
Conflict of interest, restrictions, T 45.03
Day-care facilities, T 26.11(D)
Drivers' licenses—See DRIVERS' LICENSES.
Work permits for minors, T 20.11 to T 20.17
    See also AGE AND SCHOOLING CERTIFICATES.

LIFE INSURANCE
Group coverage
  Payroll deductions, T 10.08
Payroll deductions for premiums, T 10.08
School employees, nonteaching, T 10.10, T 10.11, T 13.07
Teachers, T 10.10, T 10.11
  Payroll deductions for premium, T 10.08

LIMITATION OF ACTIONS
Asbestos abatement actions brought by school boards, T 21.10(B)
Discrimination
  Employment, T 17.02(A), T 17.04(C)
    Age, based on, T 17.06(A)
    Nonrenewal of contract, T 17.10
    Wage, T 17.08(B)
Personal information systems, actions against, T 44.08(B)
Public funds violation, T 43.27(B)
Public Liability Act, under, T 46.05
School boards, asbestos abatement actions, T 21.10(B)

LIMITATION OF ACTIONS—*continued*
Teachers
  Compensation
    Overpayments, recovery, T 10.07(B)
    Underpayments, recovery, T 10.07(A)
  Contract nonrenewal, complaint, T 17.10
  Wage discrimination, T 17.08(B)
Workers' compensation claims, T 16.06

LIMITED CONTRACTS
Nonteaching school employees, T 12.09(A)
Teachers—See TEACHERS.

LIMITED PRACTITIONERS
Child abuse, reporting, T 24.05

LIQUOR CONTROL
Minors
  Sale to, prohibition, T 24.15(A)
  Sale or distribution to minors, T 24.15(A)

LITERACY COURSES, T 26.10(A)

LITIGATION—See ACTIONS.

LOANS
Emergency school advancement fund, from, T 41.33
    See also EMERGENCY LOANS.
Teacher education loan program, T 5.09(K)

LOCAL SCHOOL DISTRICTS, T 4.03(D)
    See also SCHOOLS AND SCHOOL DISTRICTS, generally.
Boards of education—See EDUCATION, LOCAL BOARDS.
City school districts, becoming, T 4.06(C), T 4.06(D)
  Two or more local school districts combined to form, T 4.03(A)
City school districts reclassified as, T 4.03(A), T 4.06(A)
Classification change, T 4.03(A), T 4.05(C)
Competency of graduates, guarantee policy, T 26.16(B)
Creation of new districts, T 4.03(D), T 4.07(A)(4)
Exempted village school districts, becoming, T 4.03(F), T 4.06(B)
Exempted village school districts reclassified as, T 4.03(F), T 4.06(B)
Gifted children, programs for, T 26.09
One local district within educational service center, powers, T 5.02(A)
Records and reports
  Adjacent school district residents, enrollment, T 5.08(D)
Supervision by educational service center governing boards, T 4.15(D)
Transfer of territory, T 4.07 to T 4.11, T 4.07(A)(3)

LOCKERS
Searching, T 47.02
  Private and parochial schools, T 48.17

LOTTERY PROFITS EDUCATION FUND, T 41.33
Applications for loans, T 41.33(B)
Controlling board, powers and duties, T 41.33(D)
Payments on loans, T 41.33(E)
Requirements for receiving loans, T 41.33(E)
Superintendent of public instruction, powers and duties, T 41.33(C)

LUNCH PROGRAMS—See FOOD SERVICES, SCHOOL.

MAINSTREAMING OF DISABLED CHILDREN, T 28.05, T 28.20(B)

MALPRACTICE
Educational, T 26.15(B)

MANDAMUS
School boards, actions against, T 5.06(C)

MARRIAGE
Minors
  Consent, T 20.04
  Discrimination against in schools, T 19.14(A)
  School attendance, T 20.04
    Tuition, T 23.02(C)(3)

MASS TRANSIT SYSTEMS
Pupils, transportation to and from school
  Contracts, T 22.25
  Safety requirements, T 22.26

MATERNITY LEAVE
Discrimination, T 17.09
Family and Medical Leave Act of 1993, T 17.09

MEDIA—See particular type concerned.

MEDIATION
Public employees' collective bargaining—See COLLECTIVE BARGAINING, PUBLIC EMPLOYEES.

MEDICAL CARE CORPORATIONS
Unemployment, continued coverage during, T 10.12

MEDICAL EXAMINATIONS
Age and schooling certificates, requirements, T 20.13(B)
Healthcheck programs
  Establishment, T 5.09(M)
Pupils—See PUPILS, at Health.
School bus drivers, T 22.14
School employees, nonteaching, T 21.03(D)

MEDICAL EXAMINATIONS—*continued*
Teachers, T 23.03(D)
Retirement system disability benefit, T 11.16(A)

MEDICAL INSURANCE—See HEALTH AND HOSPITALIZATION INSURANCE.

MEDICAL RECORDS
School children, T 21.07

MEDITATION PERIODS, T 32.05

MEETINGS—See also particular agency or subject concerned; SUNSHINE LAW.
Collective bargaining meetings, T 18.27
Library board of trustees, T 34.09(A), T 34.09(C)
Mental retardation and developmental disabilities boards, T 29.03
Open meeting requirements—See SUNSHINE LAW.
School boards—See EDUCATION, LOCAL BOARDS.
School employees attending, T 5.09(G), T 10.09(C), T 13.05(C)
State board of education, T 3.02(D)

MENTAL HEALTH DEPARTMENT
Institutions
Educational programs, inspection by state board of education, T 3.03(G)

MENTAL RETARDATION AND DEVELOPMENTAL DISABILITIES BOARDS, COUNTY, T Ch 29
Affirmative action plans, T 29.15
Annual reports, T 29.04(A)
Appropriations, T 29.09(A)
Bidding requirements, T 29.07
Budgets, T 29.04(A)
Buses
Purchasing to transport children to special education classes, T 29.06(A)
Collective bargaining, T 29.17
See also COLLECTIVE BARGAINING, PUBLIC EMPLOYEES, generally.
Complaints against, T 29.04(I)
Conflict of interest, T 29.02(C), T 45.08(B)
Contracts, T 29.07
Conflict of interest, T 45.08(B)
Coordination with boards of education, T 29.04(B)
Creation, T 29.01(A)
Definitions, T 29.01(B)
Direct service staff ratio, T 29.05
Discrimination prohibited, T 29.15
Eligibility determination powers, T 29.04(A)
Employees, T 29.04(A), T 29.10 to T 29.14
Affirmative action plan, T 29.15
Applicants, T 29.14

MENTAL RETARDATION AND DEVELOPMENTAL DISABILITIES BOARDS, COUNTY—*continued*
Employees—*continued*
Appointment and compensation, T 29.10(B), T 29.13(A)
Background checks, T 29.14
Certification, T 29.11
Civil service classification, T 29.12
Collective bargaining, T 29.17
Compensation, T 29.10(B), T 29.13(A)
Criminal disqualification, T 29.14
Discrimination prohibited, T 29.15
Driving records, T 29.14
Family members, eligibility for services, T 29.04(D)
Health insurance, T 29.13(B)
Public employees retirement system membership, T 29.13(D)
Resignation, T 29.13(E)
Service employees, T 29.11
Sick leave, T 29.13(B)
Accrued benefits, cash payment, T 29.13(B)
Termination prohibitions, T 29.11
Vacation leave, T 29.13(C)
Ethics council, T 29.04(E)
Family members, eligibility for services, T 29.04(D)
Fees, T 29.04(C)
Funds, T 29.09
Excess, T 29.09(A)
Gifts, devises, and bequests; accepting, T 29.08(A)
Legal advisers, T 29.18
Liability insurance, T 29.16
Management, contract system, T 29.12
Management employees, certification, T 29.11
Meetings, T 29.03
Members, T 29.02(C)
Appointments, T 29.02(A)
Composition to reflect county population, T 29.02(A)
Expenses, T 29.02(D)
Family members, eligibility for services, T 29.04(D)
Incompatible officers, T 29.02(C), T 45.08(B)
Qualifications, T 29.02(B)
Removal, T 29.02(E)
Terms, T 29.02(D)
Vacancy, T 29.02(D)
Organization, T 29.03
Permanent improvement fund interest, allocation, T 29.09(A)
Personal property, disposition, T 29.08(B)
Powers and duties, T 29.04 to T 29.09
Principals and supervisors, certification, T 29.11
Professional employees, certification, T 29.11
Public employees retirement system membership, T 29.13(D)
Purpose, T 29.01(A)
Real estate, purchase, T 29.04(H), T 29.08(A)

**MENTAL RETARDATION AND DEVELOP-
MENTAL DISABILITIES BOARDS,
COUNTY**—*continued*
Records and reports
  Annual reports, T 29.04(A)
  Disclosure, T 29.19
  Proceeding records, T 29.03
Regional councils, T 29.04(F)
Removal of members, T 29.02(E)
Residential facility linked deposit programs, T 29.04(G)
Rules and regulations, T 29.05
Self-sufficiency, payments to promote, T 29.09(B)
Service employees, T 29.11
Special education, powers and duties, T 28.20, T 29.04, T 29.09(C)
  Nonresident pupils, per capita reimbursement by school district of residence, T 29.09(C)
Superintendents, T 29.10
  Contracts, T 29.04(A), T 29.10(A)
    Nonrenewal, notice, T 29.10(A)
    Re-employment, T 29.10(A)
  Duties, T 29.10(B)
  Review of performance by board, T 29.10(B)
Tax levies to support, T 29.09(A)

**MENTAL RETARDATION AND DEVELOP-
MENTAL DISABILITIES DEPART-
MENT**
Director
  Duties, T 29.05
Funding of county boards of mental retardation and developmental disabilities, T 29.09(A)
Institutions
  Contracts, conflict of interest, T 45.06(B)
  Inspection by state board of education, T 3.03(G)

**MENTALLY RETARDED AND DEVELOPMEN-
TALLY DISABLED PERSONS**
Eligibility for services
  Family members of county board members or employees, T 29.04(D)
Schooling—See also SPECIAL EDUCATION, generally.
  Attendance, T 20.01, T 20.02(C), T 28.17(A)
    Excused from, T 20.03(B)
  Tuition, T 23.02(A)(5), T 23.02(A)(7), T 23.02(A)(15), T 23.02(B), T 23.02(D)
Self-sufficiency, payments to promote, T 29.09(B)
Services and facilities, T 29.04(A)
Special education—See SPECIAL EDUCATION, generally.
Transportation to school, T 22.05, T 29.06
  Foundation program funding, T 22.07(B)
Tuition, T 23.02(A)(5), T 23.02(A)(7), T 23.02(A)(15), T 23.02(B), T 23.02(D)

MIDWESTERN EDUCATION COMPACT, T 2.10

MIGRANT WORKERS
Children, education
  Education department, powers and duties, T 3.04(A)
  Funding, T 26.08, T 39.08(A)

MILEAGE
Allowance for school board members, T 5.04

MILITARY SERVICE—See also VETERANS.
Prisoners of war
  School employees retirement system, service credit, T 14.10(A)
  Teachers retirement system, service credit, T 11.13(A), T 11.14(B)
School district of residence, effect on, T 23.02(C)(5)
School employees, T 13.10(B)
  Retirement system membership, effect, T 14.10(A)
Teachers, T 10.21(A)
  Leave of absence, T 10.21(A)
  Retirement system membership, effect, T 11.12(A), T 11.14
  No cost service credit, T 11.14(A)
  Purchase of service credit, T 11.13(A), T 11.14(B)
  Service credit for salary purposes, T 10.03(D)

MILITIA
Leaves of absence from employment, T 10.21(A)

MINERAL RIGHTS
School boards leasing, T 36.10(B), T 39.15

MINORITY BANKS
Public depositories, as, T 42.05(C)

MINORS—See also PARENT AND CHILD.
Abuse—See CHILD ABUSE.
Age and schooling certificates, T 20.11 to T 20.17
  See also AGE AND SCHOOLING CER-
TIFICATES.
Arrests
  Truancy, T 20.08(C)
Assault committed by, parental liability, T 38.06
Day care—See DAY CARE.
Definitions
  Abused child, T 24.05(C)
  Delinquent child, T 24.11
  Disabled child, T 28.01(B)
  Employment, T 20.11
  Neglected child, T 24.05(D)
  Unruly child, T 24.11, T 25.02
Delinquent children—See JUVENILE DELIN-
QUENCY.

MINORS—*continued*
Destruction of property by, parental liability, T 38.06
Detention homes—See DETENTION HOMES.
Drivers' licenses, suspension or revocation
  Truancy or substance abuse, T 20.10
Employment, T 20.11 to T 20.17
  Age and schooling certificates—See AGE AND SCHOOLING CERTIFICATES.
  Agreement for wages, T 20.16(C)
  Complaint, T 20.17
  Definitions, T 20.11
  Employment services bureau, powers and duties, T 20.11
  Enforcement, T 20.08(C), T 20.11, T 20.17
  Evidence of employee's age, employer furnishing, T 20.16(B)
  Fines for violations, T 20.17, T 39.10
  Hazardous work prohibited, T 20.11(A)
  Hours, T 20.12
    Exemptions, T 20.12
  List of employees, T 20.16(B)
  Penalties for violations, T 20.17
  Records, T 20.16(B)
  School attendance, T 20.02(A), T 20.03(B), T 20.05(A), T 20.15, T 26.10(C), T 48.04(D)
  Liability of employer, T 20.09(C)
  Summer, age and schooling certificate exemption, T 20.11(B)
  Terms of employment, T 20.12
  Unemployment compensation, T 15.04
  Violations, T 20.09(C), T 20.17
    Fines, T 20.17, T 39.10
    Penalties, T 20.17
  Wages, T 20.16(C)
Endangering—See ENDANGERING CHILDREN.
Handicapped—See DISABLED CHILDREN.
Marriage—See MARRIAGE.
Mentally retarded—See MENTALLY RETARDED AND DEVELOPMENTALLY DISABLED PERSONS, generally.
Missing children—See MISSING CHILDREN.
Neglected children
  Definition, T 24.05(D)
  Reporting requirements, T 24.05
Obscene materials
  Disseminating to minors, T 24.12, T 33.04
Offenses against, T 24.08 to T 24.15
  See also particular offense concerned.
Photographs in school records, T 24.16(B), T 44.15(A), T 44.16
Residence
  Determination for school attendance, T 23.02(A) to T 23.02(C)
Sex offenses against, T 24.13
Theft, by; parental liability, T 38.06
Tobacco
  Sale or distribution to, T 24.15(B)
Truancy—See ATTENDANCE.

MINORS—*continued*
Unruly children—See also JUVENILE DELINQUENCY.
  Contributing to unruliness, T 24.11
  Definition, T 24.11, T 25.02
  Marriage without consent, T 20.04
Venereal disease diagnosis and treatment
  Consent, T 21.04(A)

MIRANDA RIGHTS
Student expulsion, T 25.09(B)

MISCONDUCT IN OFFICE, T 45.12
School board members, T 5.05

MISDEMEANORS—See CRIMES AND OFFENSES, generally; particular offense concerned.

MISSING CHILDREN, T 24.16
Educational programs, T 3.04(A), T 24.16
Investigations, access to school records, T 24.16, T 44.16, T 48.10
Law enforcement officers investigating, access to student records, T 24.16, T 44.16, T 48.10
Notice to law enforcement agency when pupil fails to present official school records, T 24.16, T 48.10
Records and reports
  Law enforcement officers investigating, access to student records, T 24.16, T 44.16, T 48.10
  Notice to law enforcement agency when pupil fails to present official school records, T 24.16, T 48.10
Schools
  Educational programs in, T 3.04(A), T 24.16
  Fingerprinting programs, T 24.16(B), T 44.15
  Law enforcement officers investigating, access to student records, T 24.16, T 44.16, T 48.10
  Notice to law enforcement agency when pupil fails to present official records, T 24.16, T 48.10
  Photographs retained in school file, T 24.16(B), T 44.15(A), T 44.16
  Reporting enrollment without birth certificate, T 24.16, T 48.10

MORTALITY TABLES
Sex-segregated, use in calculating retirement annuities, T 17.06(C)(2)

MOTOR VEHICLE INSURANCE
Auto mechanics classes, T 22.08
Driver education courses, T 22.08, T 46.20
Joint self-insurance pools providing for, T 46.18(E)
School boards, T 22.08, T 46.20
School buses, T 22.08, T 46.20

MOTOR VEHICLE REGISTRATION
Registrar, notice of truancy to, T 20.10
School buses, T 22.11

MOTOR VEHICLES
Driver training—See DRIVER TRAINING COURSES.
Insurance—See MOTOR VEHICLE INSURANCE.
Registration—See MOTOR VEHICLE REGISTRATION.
School buses—See SCHOOL BUSES.
Stopping for school buses, T 22.18(B)
Traffic control—See TRAFFIC CONTROL.

MUNICIPAL CORPORATIONS—See also TAXING DISTRICTS, generally; VILLAGES.
Actions against, T Ch 46
  See also PUBLIC LIABILITY ACT.
Charters
  School employees, effect on employment, T 12.02(C)
City law directors—See CITY DIRECTORS OF LAW.
Civil service—See also CIVIL SERVICE, generally.
  Administrative costs, school board's share, T 12.03(B)
  Commissions, T 12.03(A)
Courts—See MUNICIPAL COURTS.
Employees—See PUBLIC EMPLOYEES, generally.
  Civil service—See CIVIL SERVICE, generally.
Income tax
  Payroll deductions, T 10.08
  Sharing revenues with school districts, T 39.12
Law directors, city—See CITY DIRECTORS OF LAW.
Legislative authority members
  Conflict of interest
    Mental retardation and developmental disabilities board membership, T 29.02(C)
    Principal, as, T 45.08(A)
    Teacher, as, T 45.08(A)
Liability—See PUBLIC LIABILITY ACT.
Officials—See particular office concerned; PUBLIC OFFICIALS.
  Civil service—See CIVIL SERVICE, generally.
Real property, exchange with school boards, T 36.05(B), T 36.09
Regional councils, T 5.09(D)
School boards—See EDUCATION, LOCAL BOARDS, at City boards.
School districts—See CITY SCHOOL DISTRICTS; EXEMPTED VILLAGE SCHOOL DISTRICTS.
Sovereign immunity—See PUBLIC LIABILITY ACT.
Tax abatements, T 39.04

MUNICIPAL COURTS
Employment of minors, violation proceedings, T 20.17
Jurisdiction
  Employment of minor, violation, T 20.17
  Truancy, T 20.09(A)
Truancy proceedings, T 20.09(A)

MUSEUMS
Educational programs furnished by, T 5.09(D), T 26.11(A), T 26.11(C), T 31.05
School boards, cooperation with, T 5.09(D), T 26.11(C), T 31.05

MUSIC
Acquisition of instruments by schools, T 36.04(C)(4)
Instruction in schools, T 5.09(D), T 26.11(A), T 31.05

NARCOTICS—See DRUG OFFENSES.

NATIONAL GUARD—See MILITIA, generally.

NATIONAL LABOR RELATIONS ACT
Jurisdiction of board
  Private school employees, T 48.28

NATIONAL ORIGIN DISCRIMINATION, T 17.14
  See also DISCRIMINATION, generally.

NATIONAL SCHOOL LUNCH ACT, T 35.07

NATURE PRESERVES
Use and purpose, T 31.07

NEGLIGENCE
Athletic injuries, T 30.12
Private schools, liability, T 48.34
Public Liability Act—See PUBLIC LIABILITY ACT.
School personnel, by
  Breach of duty of due care, T 24.03(D)
  Due care requirement, T 24.03
  Due process violation, injury to student as, T 46.14(B)
  Foreseeability of risk, T 24.03(C)

NEIGHBORHOOD SCHOOLS, T 4.05(B), T 19.08

NEPOTISM—See also CONFLICT OF INTEREST.
Teachers, hiring practices, T 9.03

NEW SCHOOL DISTRICTS—See REORGANIZATION OF SCHOOL DISTRICTS, at Creation of new districts.

NEWSLETTERS
Publication by school boards, T 5.09(G), T 31.02

NEWSPAPERS
Students, by
  Private school students, T 48.18
  Public school students, T 25.05

NIGHT SCHOOLS, T 26.10(B)
Tuition, T 23.02(E), T 26.10(B)

NOMINATIONS
School board candidates, T 5.03(A)
Teachers, T 8.08

NONRESIDENTS—See ALIENS.
Pupils—See PUPILS.

NONROUTINE USE OF SCHOOL BUSES, T 22.11, T 22.22 to T 22.24

NONTEACHING SCHOOL EMPLOYEES—See SCHOOL EMPLOYEES, NONTEACHING.

NORTHWEST ORDINANCE OF 1787, T 1.02

NOTES—See BONDS AND NOTES; TAX ANTICIPATION NOTES.

NOTICE—See also particular subject concerned.
Adjacent districts, enrollment in, T 5.08(D)
Alternative school attendance, T 5.08(C)
Auction of school property, T 36.11(B)
Bonds and notes
  Proposal to issue, T 41.14(A)
  Sale, T 41.17(B)
Collective bargaining, public employees—See COLLECTIVE BARGAINING, PUBLIC EMPLOYEES.
Construction managers, school building and construction projects, T 37.10
Contract nonrenewal—See particular type of contract concerned.
Custody arrangements, notice to schools, T 44.14(D), T 48.10
Disabled children, educational placement, T 28.11(B)
Mental retardation and developmental disabilities county superintendents, contract nonrenewal, T 29.10(A)
Nondiscrimination rights, T 17.17
Nonteaching school employees, termination, T 12.16(B), T 12.17(B)
Open enrollment policy, adoption, T 5.08(C)
School board meetings, T 5.12(A), T 5.12(C)
School employees, termination, T 12.16(B), T 12.17(B)
School financial reports, T 43.26(B)
School property, auction, T 36.11(B)

NOTICE—*continued*
School pupils
  Permanent exclusion, T 25.10(E)
Special education, pupil placement, T 28.11(B)
Tax abatements, to school boards, T 39.04
Tax levies, proposed, T 40.13
Teachers—See TEACHERS.
Truancy—See ATTENDANCE.
Workers' compensation claims, T 16.06

NURSERY SCHOOLS
Criminal background checks of employment applicants, T 5.09(C)
Criminal convictions
  Effect on certification, T 8.07(A)
  Employment disqualification, T 5.09(H)
  Notification of certificate holder's conviction, T 24.07
Deaf children, T 28.18
Education department, powers and duties, T 3.04(A)
Fees or tuition, T 23.02(E), T 23.07(E)
Funding, T 39.08
Handicapped children
  Records and reports, T 39.09(C)
Pre-kindergarten associate certificates, T 3.03(B)
  Crimes and offenses
    Effect on certification, T 8.07(A)
    Notification of certificate holder's conviction, T 24.07(A)
  Criminal record checks of applicants, T 5.09(C)
  Employment disqualification, T 5.09(H)
  Notification of certificate holder's convictions, T 24.07(A)
Pre-kindergarten teaching certificates, T 3.03(B)
  Crimes and offenses
    Effect on certification, T 8.07(A)
    Notification of certificate holder's conviction, T 24.07(A)
  Criminal record checks of applicants, T 5.09(C)
  Employment disqualification, T 5.09(H)
  Notification of certificate holder's conviction, T 24.07(A)
Staff
  Criminal background check of applicants, T 5.09(C)
Standards, T 3.03(B)
Transportation of children, T 22.03(A)
  Vehicle lights and signs, T 22.12
Tuition, T 23.02(E), T 23.07(E)

NURSES AND NURSING
Child abuse
  Prevention, in-service training, T 21.14
  Reporting, T 24.05
Schools employing, T 21.02(B)
  Certificate, T 21.02(B)
  Child abuse prevention training, T 21.14
  Compensation, T 10.05(A)
  Private and parochial schools, services, T 48.07
  School board membership, T 45.08(A)
  Teacher status, T 8.02(B), T 9.07(A)(3)

NURSES AND NURSING—*continued*
State schools for blind and deaf, T 28.19(A)
Volunteer medical services at athletic events, liability, T 21.09

NUTRITION
Child Nutrition Act, T 35.07

OATHS AND AFFIRMATIONS
School board members, T 5.03(B)
State board of education members, T 3.02(B)

OBSCENITY
Child pornography, T 24.13
Defenses
  Affirmative, T 24.12
Definition, T 24.12
Disseminating material harmful to juveniles, T 24.12, T 33.04

OCCUPATIONAL DISEASES AND INJURIES
Workers' compensation, T 16.04

OCCUPATIONAL SAFETY AND HEALTH, T 16.09

OCCUPATIONAL THERAPY
Service contracts with mental retardation and developmental disabilities boards, T 29.07

OFFICIALS—See particular office concerned; PUBLIC OFFICIALS.

OHIO CIVIL RIGHTS COMMISSION, T 17.04(C)

OHIO EDUCATION COMMISSION, T 2.10

OHIO EDUCATION COMPUTER NETWORK, T 26.11(G)

OHIO EDUCATIONAL BROADCASTING NETWORK COMMISSION, T 26.11(G)

OHIO HIGH SCHOOL ATHLETIC ASSOCIATION, T 30.07 to T 30.12
Equal opportunity, T 30.09
Financing athletics, policy, T 30.10(A)
Government and administration, T 30.07(C)
Insurance program, T 30.12
Legal status, T 30.08
Membership, T 30.07(B)
National federation affiliation, T 30.07(D)
Penalties for violations, T 30.11(B), T 30.11(C)
Powers and duties, T 30.08
Private and parochial schools, T 48.36
Purpose, T 30.07(A)
Recognized sports, T 30.09
Rules, T 30.11
Transfer to private school, effect, T 48.36

OHIO PRIVACY ACT, T 44.01, T 44.04 to T 44.11
See also PERSONAL INFORMATION SYSTEMS.

OHIO PUBLIC LIABILITY ACT, T Ch 46
See also PUBLIC LIABILITY ACT.

OHIO PUBLIC RECORDS ACT, T 44.01 to T 44.03

OHIO REHABILITATION CENTER, T 27.14

OHIO STATE UNIVERSITY
Rehabilitation center, T 27.14

OIL AND GAS
School lands, exploration and leasing, T 36.10(B), T 39.15

OLYMPIC GAMES
Public employees, participation by; leave of absence, T 13.10(B)

OMNIBUS RECONCILIATION ACT OF 1981, T 2.12

"169" BOARDS—See MENTAL RETARDATION AND DEVELOPMENTAL DISABILITIES BOARDS, COUNTY.

OPEN ENROLLMENT
Alternative schools, T 5.08(C)
Interdistrict, T 5.08(D)
Intradistrict, T 5.08(C)

OPEN MEETINGS—See SUNSHINE LAW.

OPERATING DEFICIT
Schools, determination, T 41.33(B)

ORDERS—See also particular subject concerned.
Student records disclosure, for, T 44.14(C), T 44.15(B)

ORDINANCES OR RESOLUTIONS—See also particular subject concerned.
Bond issues
  Resolutions, T 41.12
Excess tax levies, T 40.10, T 40.13
School board resolutions—See EDUCATION, LOCAL BOARDS.
Tax levies, T 40.07

ORGANIZATION MEETINGS
School boards, T 5.11(A)

ORGANIZATIONS—See ASSOCIATIONS.

ORIENTATION TRAINING, T 5.09(F)

OUT-OF-SCHOOL YOUTHS OR ADULTS
Classes for—See ADULT EDUCATION.

OUT-OF-STATE TEACHING SERVICE
Teachers retirement system service credit, T 11.13(A)

OUT-OF-STATE TENURE
Continuing contract eligibility, effect, T 9.08(B)

OVERTIME PAY—See WAGES AND HOURS.

OVERVIEW OF OHIO SCHOOL SYSTEM, T Ch 2

PARENT AND CHILD—See also MINORS.
Absence from school, parental notification policy, T 20.07
Abuse of children—See CHILD ABUSE.
Assault, children committing; parental liability, T 38.06
Death of parent, effect on child's school district of residence, T 23.02(C)(6)
Destruction of property by children, parental liability, T 38.06
Duty to send children to school—See ATTENDANCE, at Parental liability for.
Endangering children—See ENDANGERING CHILDREN.
Family and Medical Leave Act of 1993, T 17.16
Private schools, applicability, T 48.30
Fingerprinting of children, T 24.16(A), T 44.15(A)
Neglect of children—See MINORS, at Neglected children.
Parental involvement in schools
Policy on, T 5.09(O)
Parental rights and liabilities
Crimes committed by child, T 38.06
Medical treatment, consent, T 21.04(A)
Dental treatment, T 21.06
Emergency medical authorization forms, T 21.04(A), T 21.07(C)
Prosecution of parent under compulsory education laws
Fines for violations, T 20.09(B), T 20.09(C)
School attendance, T 20.02(A), T 20.09, T 32.02
See also ATTENDANCE, at Parental liability for.
Special education programs, T 28.11
School-parent partnership programs, T 3.04(A)
Theft by children, parental liability, T 38.06
Venereal disease diagnosis and treatment of children, consent, T 21.04(A)

PARENT-TEACHER CONFERENCES, T 20.05(A), T 20.05(B), T 31.03, T 48.04(B)
Non-residential parents, T 31.03

PARKING
Student fees, T 35.02(A)

PARKS AND RECREATION
Joint recreation districts, T 30.14
Joint recreation board, T 30.15
Liability
Local boards of education, T 30.16
School activities, T 30.13 to T 30.16
Buildings and grounds, T 30.14, T 38.09
Cooperation with public officials, T 5.09(D), T 26.11(C), T 31.05
Transportation of pupils, T 22.22

PAROCHIAL SCHOOLS—See PRIVATE AND PAROCHIAL SCHOOLS.

PART-TIME SCHOOLS OR CLASSES, T 20.15, T 26.10(C), T 48.04(D)
Hours of attendance, T 20.05(A)

PARTNERSHIPS
School-business partnerships, T 3.04(A)
School-parent partnerships, T 3.04(A)
Schooling provided by, part-time, T 20.15

PAYROLL DEDUCTIONS—See particular employee or deduction concerned; WAGES AND HOURS, at Withholdings.

PECULATION, T 45.09 to T 45.13

PENITENTIARIES—See CORRECTIONAL INSTITUTIONS.

PENTAMESTER SYSTEM, T 20.05(B)

PERFORMANCE BONDS—See BONDS, SURETY, generally.

PERMITS—See LICENSES AND PERMITS; particular subject concerned.

PERS—See PUBLIC EMPLOYEES RETIREMENT SYSTEM.

PERSONAL INFORMATION SYSTEMS, T 44.01, T 44.04 to T 44.11
Accuracy, relevance, timeliness, and completeness of information, T 44.08(D)
Actions against, T 44.08(B)
Collection of information, T 44.09
Combined systems, T 44.07
Consent to release, T 44.14(C)
Damages recoverable for harm done, T 44.08(B)
Definitions, T 44.06
Disputes concerning information, T 44.11
Duties in operation, T 44.08, T 44.09
Harm done by, damages recoverable, T 44.08(B)
Injunctions, T 44.08(B)

PERSONAL INFORMATION SYSTEMS—continued
Inspection of records, rights of subjects, T 44.04, T 44.10
  Students, T 44.14, T 44.18 to T 44.21
Interconnected systems, T 44.07
Liability, T 44.08(B)
Penalties for violations, T 44.08(B)
Release of records, T 44.14(C)
Removal of information, T 44.09
Rules, T 44.08
Security of system, T 44.08(C)
Transfer of records to educational institution, T 44.15(B)
Use of information, T 44.09
Violations
  Damages recoverable, T 44.08(B)
  Injunctive relief, T 44.08(B)
  Penalties, T 44.08(B)

PERSONAL INJURIES—See also NEGLIGENCE.
Due process violation, injury to student as, T 46.14(B)
Hazing, T 24.10
  Liability of school personnel, T 46.10, T 46.14(B)
Recreational users, liability of school personnel, T 46.11

PERSONAL PROPERTY—See also EQUIPMENT AND SUPPLIES, SCHOOL.
Disposal
  County mental retardation and developmental disabilities boards, T 29.08(B)

PERSONAL PROPERTY, TAXATION
School foundation program, prerequisite, T 39.07(B)
Schools, financing, T 39.02 to T 39.04

PERSONNEL ADMINISTRATION—See CIVIL SERVICE.

PERSONNEL RECORDS—See particular type of personnel concerned; PERSONAL INFORMATION SYSTEMS.

PETITIONS—See also particular subject concerned.
Elections, regarding
  Contests, T 41.14(C)
Nomination
  School board, T 5.03(A)
Referendum
  Dissolution of school district, against, T 4.09(D)
  School district reorganization, T 4.10(A)
School board members
  Nomination, T 5.03(A)
  Removal from office, T 5.05

PETITIONS—continued
School districts
  Dissolution, referendum against, T 4.09(D)
  Reorganization, referendum against, T 4.10(A)
  Transfer of territory, T 4.10
Transfer of territory, T 4.10(A)

PHONICS INSTRUCTION, T 3.03(G)

PHOTOGRAPHS
School files, T 24.16(B), T 44.15(A), T 44.16

PHYSICAL EDUCATION, T 30.01 to T 30.05
  See also ATHLETIC EVENTS; RECREATIONAL PROGRAMS.
Coaches, T 30.05
Curriculum requirements, T 30.02
Facilities, T 30.04
  Posting of anabolic steroid warnings, T 21.15(D), T 48.15
Interscholastic athletics distinguished, T 30.03
Teachers, T 30.05
Trainers, T 30.05

PHYSICAL EXAMINATIONS—See MEDICAL EXAMINATIONS.

PHYSICIANS
Child abuse to be reported by, when, T 24.05
Liability
  Team physician for school sports, T 21.09
Prescription drugs, school employees administering to students; statement required, T 21.04(B)
Schools employing, T 21.02(A)
  Nonpublic schools, services, T 48.07
  Records, T 21.07(A)
  School board membership, T 45.08(A)
Team physicians for school sports, liability, T 21.09

PILOT PROGRAMS
Innovative education, T 3.03(E)

PLAYGROUNDS—See PARKS AND RECREATION, generally.

PLEADINGS
Public Liability Act, under, T 46.05

PLEDGE OF ALLEGIANCE
Recitation in schools, local policy, T 26.02(A)

PODIATRISTS
Team podiatrists for school sports, liability, T 21.09

POLICE—See also LAW ENFORCEMENT OFFICERS.
Missing children
    Law enforcement officers investigating, access to student records, T 24.16, T 44.16, T 48.10
    Notice to law enforcement officers when pupil fails to present official school records, T 24.16, T 48.10
School employees retirement system, purchase of service credit, T 14.10(A)
School searches, involvement in, T 47.01(B)
Teachers retirement system, purchase of service credit, T 11.13(A)

POLICE AND FIREMEN'S DISABILITY AND PENSION FUND
Purchase of service credit by members
    School employees retirement system, in, T 14.10(A)
    Teachers retirement system, in, T 11.13(A)

POLITICAL ACTION COMMITTEES
Schoolhouses, use, T 38.10

POLITICAL ACTIVITIES
Civil service employees, by, T 45.14
    Collective bargaining, T 18.20
Schoolhouses, use, T 31.04, T 38.11

POLITICAL CONTRIBUTIONS
Payroll deductions for
    Teachers, T 10.08
Teachers, by, T 10.08

POLITICAL PARTIES
Officials
    Theft by, T 45.10
Schoolhouses, use, T 31.04, T 38.08(B), T 38.11

POLITICAL SUBDIVISION TORT LIABILITY ACT, T Ch 46
See also PUBLIC LIABILITY ACT.

POLITICAL SUBDIVISIONS—See particular type concerned; TAXING DISTRICTS.

POST-SECONDARY ENROLLMENT OPTIONS PROGRAM, T 26.07(C)
Private schools, participation, T 48.09(B)

POSTING REQUIREMENTS
Physical education facilities, anabolic steroid warnings, T 21.15(D), T 48.15

PRAYERS
Goals 2000: Educate America Act of 1994; effect on voluntary prayer and meditation, T 32.05
Recitation in public schools, T 32.05
School group meetings, T 32.06

PREGNANCY
Discrimination on basis of, T 10.20(B), T 17.09
    School pupils, T 19.14(A)
Leaves of absence, unpaid, T 10.20(B), T 17.09
    Family and Medical Leave Act of 1993, T 17.09
School pupils
    Attendance, T 20.04
    Discrimination against, T 19.14(A)
    Dismissal from activity programs, T 20.04, T 25.15(B)
    Home instruction, T 20.04
    Privacy rights, T 46.14(E)
Sick leave, T 17.09
Teacher's resignation due to, purchase of retirement system service credit, T 11.08(A)

PRESCHOOLS—See NURSERY SCHOOLS.

PRESCRIPTION DRUGS
Administering to students, T 21.04(B)

PREVAILING WAGE RATES, T 37.11 to T 37.14
Coordinators, T 37.13

PRINCIPALS, T 7.09 to T 7.13
    See also ADMINISTRATIVE PERSONNEL, generally.
Alcohol, drug addiction, and mental health service district board member, as; prohibition, T 7.09(C)
Appointment, T 7.09(C)
Assignment, T 7.06(B)(1)
Assistants, T 7.09, T 7.09(C)
City council member as, T 45.08(A)
Civil service status, T 12.04(A)(1)
Collective bargaining exclusion, T 18.05(C)
Community mental health board member, as, T 7.09(C)
Compensation, T 7.11(A)
Conflict of interest, T 7.09(C), T 45.08(A)
Continuing contracts, T 7.11
Contracts, T 7.11
    Term, T 7.11(A)
    Termination, T 7.13
Corporal punishment, administering—See PUPILS, at Corporal punishment.
County commissioner serving as, T 7.09(C)
Crimes, reporting, T 24.06(B)
Ethics, T Ch 45
    See also ETHICS, generally.
Layoffs, T 7.13
Liability insurance, T 46.19
Nomination, T 7.10
Publisher's or supplier's sales agent, as, T 8.07(B), T 33.05, T 45.07
Pupil expulsion or suspension, powers and duties, T 25.10
Reduction in force, T 7.13
Reemployment, T 7.10
Resignation, T 7.11(A)
Teacher, as, T 7.13

PRINCIPALS—*continued*
Technical college board of trustees district member, as; prohibition, T 45.08(A)
Term of contract, T 7.11(A)
Termination of contract, T 7.13
Tuition credit scholarship programs, establishment, T 5.09(Q)
Vacation leave, T 7.11(A)
Wrongful termination, liability, T 7.13

PRISONERS
Children of, school district of residence, T 23.02(A)(3), T 23.02(B)
Diplomas earned while imprisoned, T 26.16

PRISONERS OF WAR
School employees retirement system, service credit purchase, T 14.10(A)
Teachers retirement system, service credit purchase, T 11.13(A), T 11.14(B)

PRISONS—See CORRECTIONAL INSTITUTIONS.

PRIVACY ACT, T 44.01, T 44.04 to T 44.11
See also PERSONAL INFORMATION SYSTEMS.

PRIVACY RIGHTS, T 46.14(E)

PRIVATE AND PAROCHIAL SCHOOLS, T Ch 48
Accounts and accounting
　Treasurer's report, request for, T 43.28
Administrative and clerical costs, reimbursement by state, T 48.07
Administrators
　Certification, T 3.03(G), T 48.21
　Contracts, T 48.19
　Qualifications, T 48.21
Admission, T 48.09 to T 48.11
　Discrimination, T 48.09(A), T 48.29
　Records, T 48.10
Age discrimination by, T 48.30
Annual reports, T 48.05
Asbestos removal, T 48.35
Attendance, T 20.02(B), T 48.02
　Employed child, T 48.04(D)
　Reports, T 20.10, T 48.04(C)
　Violations, investigation, T 48.04(A)
Block parent programs, T 48.37
Board member, public school board member as, T 45.08(A)
Breach of employment contract, T 48.24
Calendar, school, T 48.04(B)
Certification
　Administrators, T 3.03(G), T 48.21
　Revocation or suspension
　　Criminal convictions, due to, T 8.07(A)
　Teachers, T 3.03(G), T 48.21
Charitable immunity doctrine, T 48.34(A)

PRIVATE AND PAROCHIAL SCHOOLS—*continued*
Charters, T 48.03(A)
　Revocation, T 48.09(A)
Chief administrative officers, establishment of tuition credit scholarship programs, T 5.09(Q)
Collective bargaining, T 48.28
Colleges—See UNIVERSITIES AND COLLEGES, PRIVATE.
Contracts
　Administrators, T 48.19
　Employment, breach, T 48.24
　Enrollment, T 48.11
　Teachers, T 48.19
　　Nonrenewal, T 48.27
Criminal background check of applicants, T 48.19
Curriculum
　Sign language, T 26.06(A), T 28.18
Definitions, T 48.01
Disciplinary actions, T 48.15, T 48.16
Discrimination by
　Admissions, T 48.09(A), T 48.29
　Age discrimination, T 48.30
　Educational programs, T 48.29
　Employment, T 17.03(B), T 48.20, T 48.30
　　See also EMPLOYMENT DISCRIMINATION, generally.
　Federal funding, effect, T 48.29
　Handicapped, against, T 48.29
　Revocation of charter, T 48.09(A)
　Tax exempt status, requirements, T 48.31
　Wages, T 48.30
Due process for students, T 44.16
Employees, nonteaching, T 48.19 to T 48.29
　Collective bargaining, T 48.28
　Compensation and benefits, T 48.22
　Discrimination against, T 17.03(B), T 48.20, T 48.30
　Dismissal, T 48.26
　Hiring practices, T 48.19
　Liability, T 48.34(B)
　Retirement plans, T 48.22
　State retirement system, purchase of service credit, T 14.10(A)
　Unemployment compensation, T 48.23
　Workers' compensation, T 48.23
Enrollment contracts, T 48.11
Family and Medical Leave Act of 1993, applicability, T 48.30
Federal taxes, T 48.31
Foundation program funding, T 48.06
Freedom of speech and freedom of the press, T 48.18
Graduation requirements, proficiency tests, T 48.03(A)
Guidance and counseling services, public funding, T 48.07
Handicapped persons, discrimination against, T 48.29
Health services, public funding, T 48.07

PRIVATE AND PAROCHIAL SCHOOLS—*continued*
High school graduation requirements, proficiency tests, T 48.03(A)
Immunity from prosecution, T 48.34(A)
Liability, T 48.34
 Charitable immunity doctrine, T 48.34(A)
 Employees, T 48.34(B)
 Trustees, T 48.34(C)
Mathematics materials, public funding, T 48.07
Newspapers, students producing; freedom of the press, T 48.18
Number of pupils, T 2.03
Nursing services, T 48.07
Ohio high school athletic association, T 48.36
Part-time schooling, T 20.15, T 48.04(D)
Property tax exemption, T 48.33
Proprietary schools—See PROPRIETARY SCHOOLS.
Public funds for, T 48.06
Public school facilities, use, T 32.06, T 38.10
Pupils
 Conduct and discipline, T 48.15 to T 48.18
 Inspection and release of student records, T 48.14
 Number of, T 2.03
 Searching, reasonableness standard, T 48.17
Racial discrimination
 Admissions, T 48.09(A)
 Employment, T 48.30
Records and reports
 Admission records, T 48.10
 Annual reports, T 48.05
 Attendance, T 20.10, T 48.04(C)
 Inspection and release of student records, T 48.14
 State-required, public fund, T 48.06, T 48.07
 Transcripts, withholding, T 48.13
 Treasurer's report, request, T 43.28
Remedial services, public funding, T 48.06, T 48.07
Retirement plans, T 48.22
 School employees retirement system, purchase of service credit, T 14.10(A)
 Teachers retirement system, purchase of service credit, T 11.13(A)
Revocation of charter, T 48.09(A)
Right to attend school not conforming to state standards, T 20.03(A), T 32.02
Right to exist, T 48.02
Sales tax exemption, T 48.33
School year, T 48.04(B)
Search and seizure, reasonableness standard, T 48.17
Special education, T 48.29
 Public funding, T 48.06, T 48.07
Speech and hearing programs, public funding, T 48.07
Standards, T 32.02, T 48.03
 Certification of teachers and administrators, T 3.03(G), T 48.21

PRIVATE AND PAROCHIAL SCHOOLS—*continued*
Standards—*continued*
 State board of education, prescribed by; applicability, T 20.03(A), T 32.02, T 48.03
State board of education, powers and duties
 Standards prescribed by, applicability, T 20.03(A), T 32.02, T 48.03
State retirement system, purchase of service credit, T 14.10(A)
Suspension or exclusion, T 48.15, T 48.16
Tax exemptions, T 48.31 to T 48.33
Teachers, T 48.19 to T 48.29
 Breach of contract, T 48.24
 Certification, T 3.03(G), T 48.21
 Collective bargaining, T 48.28
 Compensation and benefits, T 48.22
 Contracts, T 48.19
  Breach, T 48.24
  Nonrenewal, T 48.27
 Discrimination against, T 17.03(B), T 48.20, T 48.30
  See also EMPLOYMENT DISCRIMINATION, generally.
 Dismissal, T 48.25
 Liability, T 48.34(B)
 Qualifications, T 48.21
 Retirement plans, T 48.22
 State retirement system, purchase of service credit, T 11.13(A)
 Unemployment compensation, T 48.23
 Workers' compensation, T 48.23
Testing programs
 Proficiency test programs, T 48.03(A)
 Public funding, T 48.06, T 48.07
Textbooks, loaned by public schools, T 48.06, T 48.07
Transcripts, withholding, T 48.13
Transportation of pupils, T 22.03(A), T 22.03(C)
 Public funding, T 48.08(A)
 Vehicle equipment standards, T 48.08(B)
Trustees, liability, T 48.34(C)
Tuition
 Chief administrative officers, establishment of tuition credit scholarship programs, T 5.09(Q)
 Contract provisions, T 48.11
 Judicial enforcement of separation agreement, constitutionality, T 48.12
 Nonpayment, T 48.13
 Recovery, T 48.12
Unemployment compensation, T 48.23
Universities—See UNIVERSITIES AND COLLEGES, PRIVATE.
Wage discrimination, T 48.30
Workers' compensation, T 48.23

PRIVILEGED INFORMATION
Employment services bureau, occupational safety and health inspections, T 16.09(D)
Rehabilitation services commission's records, T 27.15

PRIVILEGED INFORMATION—*continued*
School records
    Private and parochial school student records, third party requests, T 48.14

PRO-CHILDREN ACT OF 1994
Smoking indoors, ban, T 38.14

PROBATE COURTS
Schools, powers and duties, T 5.10

PROBATION
Officers acting as school attendance officers, T 20.08(B)

PROFESSIONAL MEETINGS
School employees, attendance, T 10.09(C), T 13.05(C)
    Days allotted for, T 20.05(A), T 20.05(B)

PROPERTY
Appraisals, real property tax, T 39.04
Destruction—See DESTRUCTION OF PROPERTY.
Mental retardation and developmental disabilities county boards, T 29.08(B)
Real—See REAL PROPERTY.
School, T Ch 36
    See also EQUIPMENT AND SUPPLIES, SCHOOL; SCHOOL BUILDINGS AND LANDS.

PROPRIETARY SCHOOLS, T 48.01(B)
Contracts with public schools, T 27.02
High school credit, T 5.09(D), T 26.16

PROSECUTORS, COUNTY
Assistants
    Mental retardation and developmental disabilities board membership, T 29.02(C)
County budget commission, membership, T 40.05
Mental retardation and developmental disabilities boards
    Membership, T 29.02(C)
    Representing, T 29.18
Public funds violations, powers and duties, T 43.27(B)
School boards
    Legal adviser, T 6.14
    Membership, T 45.08(A)
School employee's conviction or guilty plea, notice, T 24.07
Teacher's conviction or guilty plea, notice, T 8.07(A), T 9.21(D), T 24.07

PSYCHOLOGISTS AND PSYCHOLOGY
Child abuse
    Prevention training, T 21.14
    Reporting, T 24.05
Disabled children, special education services, T 28.07

PSYCHOLOGISTS AND PSYCHOLOGY—*continued*
School employing, T 7.09(A)
School psychologists
    Child abuse
        Prevention, in-service training, T 21.14
    Reporting, T 24.05
Special education services, T 28.07

PUBLIC ASSEMBLIES
Schoolhouses, use, T 38.10

PUBLIC DEBTS—See DEBTS.

PUBLIC DEPOSITORIES—See FUNDS, PUBLIC, at Deposits and depositories.

PUBLIC EMPLOYEES—See also CIVIL SERVICE; particular agency, political subdivision, or employee concerned.
Actions against—See PUBLIC LIABILITY ACT.
Charitable contributions, payroll deductions, T 31.08
Civil rights, interference with, T 45.13
Civil service classification—See CIVIL SERVICE, generally.
Collective bargaining—See COLLECTIVE BARGAINING, PUBLIC EMPLOYEES.
Compensation
    Reduction, retirement system contributions paid by employer, T 11.10(B), T 14.08(B)
    Unauthorized, T 45.04
Conflict of interest—See CONFLICT OF INTEREST, generally; particular public official or employee concerned.
Dangerous conditions, good faith refusal to work under, T 16.10(B)
Due process rights, T 46.14
Employment risk reduction standards—See EMPLOYMENT SERVICES BUREAU.
Ethics, T Ch 45
    See also ETHICS, generally.
Fair Labor Standards Act, equal pay, T 17.08
Financial disclosure—See FINANCIAL DISCLOSURE.
Honorarium for speeches or personal appearances, T 45.04
Layoffs—See CIVIL SERVICE.
Leaves of absence—See LEAVES OF ABSENCE, generally.
Payroll deductions
    Charitable contributions, T 31.08
Personal appearances by, honorarium, T 45.04
Religious tests, prohibition, T 32.05
Restrictions on transactions, T 45.04
Retirement system—See PUBLIC EMPLOYEES RETIREMENT SYSTEM.
Safety rules compliance, T 16.09(A)
School—See SCHOOL EMPLOYEES, NON-TEACHING; TEACHERS.
Speeches by, honorarium, T 45.04

PUBLIC EMPLOYEES—*continued*
Strikes—See COLLECTIVE BARGAINING, PUBLIC EMPLOYEES.
Teachers—See TEACHERS.
Unauthorized compensation, T 45.04
Unions—See COLLECTIVE BARGAINING, PUBLIC EMPLOYEES, at Employee organizations.

PUBLIC EMPLOYEES DEFERRED COMPENSATION PROGRAM
Educational employees, T 11.23, T 14.15

PUBLIC EMPLOYEES RETIREMENT SYSTEM
Contributions
　Salary reduction plans, T 11.10(B), T 14.08(B)
　Mental retardation and developmental disabilities board employees, T 29.13(D)
Teachers retirement system membership
　Purchase of service credit, T 11.13(A)

PUBLIC EMPLOYMENT RISK REDUCTION ADVISORY COMMISSION, T 16.09(A)
Dangerous conditions, good faith refusal to work under, T 16.10(B)
Employees' duties, T 16.09(A)
Employers' duties, T 16.09(A)
Employment risk reduction standards, T 16.09(A)
　See also EMPLOYMENT SERVICES BUREAU.
　Violations, injunctive relief, T 16.09(A)
Employment services bureau, operation and enforcement of commission, T 16.09
Hazard-free workplace, employer's duty to provide, T 16.09(A)
Injunctive relief, T 16.09(A)
Inspections, T 16.09(A), T 16.09(D), T 16.09(E)
Members, T 16.09(A)
Powers and duties, T 16.09(A)
Records and reports, T 16.10(D)
Rulemaking powers, T 16.09(A)

PUBLIC FUNDS—See FUNDS, PUBLIC.

PUBLIC LANDS
Federal, school board purchasing, T 36.02(B)
Municipal, exchange with school board, T 36.05(B), T 36.09
School—See SCHOOL BUILDINGS AND LANDS.

PUBLIC LIABILITY ACT, T Ch 46
Applicability, T 46.01(B)
　School districts, T 46.01(C)
Damages, T 46.06
　Collateral source rule, T 46.05
　Exemplary or punitive damages, T 46.06
　Limitation, T 46.05
Defenses to claims, T 46.02
　Employees or officials, of, T 46.04, T 46.15

PUBLIC LIABILITY ACT—*continued*
Defenses to claims—*continued*
　Waiver, providing for insurance not considered, T 46.17(C)
Definitions, T 46.01(D)
Employees or officials, T 46.03
　Damages, T 46.06
　Defenses, T 46.04, T 46.15
　Definitions, T 46.05
　Indemnification, T 46.04, T 46.15
Governmental function, defined, T 46.01(D)
Immunity, when, T 46.15(C)
Indemnification of employees, T 46.04, T 46.15
Judgments, how paid, T 46.07
Liability insurance, T 46.17
Limitation of actions, T 46.05
Payment of judgment, T 46.07
Pleadings, T 46.05
Proprietary function, defined, T 46.01(D)
School board members, immunity, T 46.03
Self-insurance programs, T 46.17(B)
　Bond issue to pay, T 41.04
　Joint pools for, T 46.18

PUBLIC LIBRARIES—See LIBRARIES AND LIBRARY DISTRICTS.

PUBLIC MEETINGS—See MEETINGS; SUNSHINE LAW.

PUBLIC OFFICIALS—See also CIVIL SERVICE; particular office concerned.
Accounts and accounting by, T 43.26
Actions against—See PUBLIC LIABILITY ACT.
Bribes, soliciting or receiving, T 45.11
Candidates—See CANDIDATES.
Civil rights, interference with, T 45.13
Civil service classification—See CIVIL SERVICE, generally.
Compensation
　Improper, soliciting or receiving, T 45.11
　Unauthorized, T 45.04
Conflict of interest—See CONFLICT OF INTEREST, generally; particular public official or employees concerned.
Dereliction of duty, T 45.12
Disqualification
　Theft conviction, T 45.10
Ethics, T Ch 45
　See also ETHICS, generally.
Financial disclosure—See FINANCIAL DISCLOSURE.
Honorarium for speeches or personal appearances, T 45.04
Incompatible offices—See CONFLICT OF INTEREST, generally; particular public official or employee concerned.
Liability—See PUBLIC LIABILITY ACT.
Misconduct, T 45.12
Personal appearances by, honorarium, T 45.04
Religious tests, prohibition, T 32.05

PUBLIC OFFICIALS—*continued*
Removal
　Accounting violations, T 43.26(A)
　Unfair labor practice, for; prohibition, T 18.26(C)
Restrictions on transactions, T 45.04
Salary—See Compensation, this heading.
Speeches by, honorarium, T 45.04
Theft by, T 45.10
Unauthorized compensation, T 45.04

PUBLIC PARTICIPATION—See also SUNSHINE LAW.
School board meetings, T 5.12, T 31.01

PUBLIC RECORDS ACT, T 44.01 to T 44.03

PUBLIC SAFETY DEPARTMENT
School buses
　Licensing, T 22.01
　Regulation, T 22.10

PUBLIC SCHOOL EMPLOYEES RETIREMENT SYSTEM, T Ch 14
See also SCHOOL EMPLOYEES RETIREMENT SYSTEM.

PUBLIC UTILITIES
Taxation, supplemental assessments for school districts, T 39.04

PUBLIC WELFARE DEPARTMENT—See HUMAN SERVICES DEPARTMENT, STATE.

PUBLIC WORKS—See also particular improvement concerned.
Bonds to finance, T 41.04
Construction managers, T 37.10

PUBLICATIONS—See also RECORDS AND REPORTS.
School boards, T 5.09(G), T 31.02
Student newspapers
　Private schools, T 48.18
　Public schools, T 25.05

PUBLISHERS
Superintendent of public instruction as agent, prohibition, T 3.05, T 45.07
Textbooks, T Ch 33
　Sales agents, prohibitions, T 8.07(B), T 33.05, T 45.07

PUPIL-PERSONNEL WORKERS
Appointment and traveling expenses, T 20.08(A)

PUPILS
Accident insurance, T 22.08, T 23.04(B), T 46.21
Activity programs, T 23.03 to T 23.05
　Buses, T 22.22

PUPILS—*continued*
Activity programs—*continued*
　Discrimination prohibited, T 19.14
　Fees, T 23.03, T 39.15
　　Refusal to pay, T 23.05, T 26.16
　Funding, T 23.03, T 23.04, T 39.15
　　Athletic events, T 30.10(C)
　"No pass, no play" rules, T 25.15(B)
　Personnel to direct, T 12.10
　Removal, suspension, or expulsion from, T 25.08, T 25.11, T 25.15
　Right to participate, due process protection, T 25.15(B)
　Transportation for, T 22.22
Adjacent school district residents, enrollment, T 5.08(D)
Adjudication hearings, permanent exclusion from school, T 25.10(E)
Admission
　Domestic violence shelter residents, T 23.02(A)(8)
　Early admission, T 20.01(B), T 26.05(A)
　Expelled pupils
　　Denial of admission to another district, T 25.10(F)
　Nonresidents, T 23.02(A) to T 23.02(C)
　Probationary, permanently excluded pupils, T 25.10(E)
Adopted children, residence determination, T 23.02(A)(6)
Age and schooling certificates—See AGE AND SCHOOLING CERTIFICATES.
Age of compulsory school attendance, T 20.01
AIDS, T 21.03(D), T 21.03(E)
　See also AIDS.
Alcohol consumption, administration of breathalyzer tests, T 25.03
Alcoholism, suspension or expulsion, T 20.10
Aliens as, T 19.16
Appeals
　Permanent exclusion, T 25.10(E)
　Suspension or expulsion, T 25.10(B), T 25.10(C), T 25.12
Appearance, regulating, T 25.04
Assault by school employees, T 25.16(C)
　Sexual battery
　　Termination, grounds for, T 9.21, T 12.16(A), T 12.17(A)
Assignment to schools, T 7.06(C)
　Discrimination prohibited, T 20.05(B)
Attendance—See ATTENDANCE.
Breakfast and lunch programs, T 35.07
Breathalyzer tests, T 25.03
Career planning, T 5.09(R)
Censorship, T 25.05
Change of residence
　Reporting, T 20.10
　Tuition, T 23.02(C)(7), T 23.02(C)(8), T 23.02(C)(10)
Civil rights, T 25.08 to T 25.16, T 46.14(A)(1)
Communicable diseases, T 10.18, T 13.10, T 21.03(D)

PUPILS—*continued*
Conduct, T Ch 25
  Drugs and alcohol standards, T 21.15(A)
  Nonteaching employees' duties, T 25.07
  Policy on conduct, T 25.03
  School bus, while on, T 22.17(B), T 22.17(C)
  Statutory standards, T 25.02
  Teachers' duties, T 25.06
Corporal punishment, T 25.16
  Authority to use, T 25.16(A)
  Constitutional considerations, T 25.16(B)
  Excessive, T 24.09(B), T 25.16(C)
  Reasonableness, T 25.16(A)
  Right to due process, T 46.14(B)
Counseling—See GUIDANCE AND COUNSELING PROGRAMS.
Data collection, T 3.03(F)
Dental examinations, T 21.06
  Consent, T 21.06
  Free treatment, T 21.06, T 23.07(B)
Disabled—See DISABLED CHILDREN; SPECIAL EDUCATION.
Disadvantaged—See DISADVANTAGED PUPILS.
Disciplinary actions, T 5.08(B), T 25.08 to T 25.16
  See also Corporal punishment, and Suspension or expulsion, this heading.
  Due process requirements, T 25.09, T 25.15(B), T 46.14(A)(1), T 48.16
  Emergency removal, T 25.11, T 25.14(D)
  Liability, T 46.14(A)(1), T 46.14(B)
  Private schools, T 48.15, T 48.16
  Transfers, T 25.13
Domestic violence shelter residents
  Admission and tuition, T 23.02(A)(8)
  Disclosure of records, T 44.14(D), T 48.10
  Transfer of records, T 44.14(D), T 48.10
Dress codes, T 25.04
  Publication by school boards, T 5.09(G), T 31.02
Drug testing, T 25.03
Due process, rights
  Corporal punishment, T 46.14(B)
  Personal injury as violation, T 46.14(B)
  Private schools, T 44.16
  Suspension or expulsion, T 25.09, T 25.15(B), T 46.14(A)(1)
Early admissions, T 20.01(B), T 26.05(A)
Emancipated, tuition, T 23.02(C)(2)
Emergency medical attention, effect on school district of residence, T 23.02(C)(4)
Emergency medical treatment authorization forms, T 21.04(A), T 21.07(C)
Employment—See AGE AND SCHOOLING CERTIFICATES; MINORS, at Employment.
Enrollment—See ENROLLMENT.
Exchange students, tuition, T 23.02(C)(12)
Expulsion—See Suspension or expulsion, this heading.
Eye protective devices, T 21.12

PUPILS—*continued*
Fees
  Activity programs, T 23.03, T 39.15
    Refusal to pay, T 23.05, T 26.16
  Driver training, T 23.02(E), T 26.13(A)
  Failure to pay, T 23.05, T 26.16
  Instructional materials, T 35.02
    Sales tax exemption, T 35.02(E)
  Parking, T 35.02(A)
Field trips, T 31.07
  Transportation, T 22.22, T 31.07
Fingerprinting program, T 24.16(A), T 44.15(A)
Foreign exchange pupils, tuition, T 23.02(C)(12)
Free meals provided, T 23.07(A)
Free public education, T 20.01, T 23.01, T 23.02(A)(1)
Freedom of speech
  Private school students, T 48.18
  Public school students, T 25.05
Freedom of the press
  Private school students, T 48.18
  Public school students, T 25.05
Gifted children, special classes, T 26.09
  Contracts, T 26.09, T 31.05
  Promotion by state board of education, T 3.03(B)
Grades, withholding, T 23.05, T 26.16
Guaranteed competency, T 26.16(B)
Handbooks for, school board publishing, T 5.09(G), T 31.02
Handicapped—See DISABLED CHILDREN; SPECIAL EDUCATION.
Hazing, T 24.10
  Liability of school personnel, T 46.10, T 46.14(B)
Health, T 21.01 to T 21.09
  AIDS, T 21.03(D), T 21.03(E)
  Board of health, duties, T 21.08
  Communicable diseases, T 10.18, T 13.10, T 21.03(D)
  Consent to treatment, T 21.04(A)
    Dental treatment, T 21.06
  Dental—See Dental examinations, this heading.
  Emergency medical attention, effect on school district of residence, T 23.02(C)(4)
  Emergency medical treatment authorization form, T 21.04(A), T 21.07(C)
  Examinations, T 21.03
    Board of health, duties, T 21.08(A)
  Immunization—See IMMUNIZATION, at School children.
  Powers of school boards, T 21.01
  Prescription drugs, school employees administering to students, T 21.04(B)
  Records, T 21.07
  Screening, T 21.03(F)
  Treatment, T 21.04
    Emergency authorization form, T 21.04(A), T 21.07(C)
  Tuberculin tests, T 10.18, T 21.03(C)
  Venereal disease, diagnosis and treatment, T 21.04(A)

PUPILS—*continued*
Hearing tests, T 21.03
    Records, T 21.07(A)
Hearings
    Permanent exclusion from school, T 25.10(E)
    Placement in special education courses, T 28.11(C) to T 28.11(F)
    Records, hearings to challenge content, T 44.19
    Suspension, removal, or expulsion, T 25.10, T 25.11
Home instruction—See HOME INSTRUCTION.
Hospitalized, responsibility for schooling, T 28.08(B)
Indigent—See DISADVANTAGED PUPILS.
Instructional materials, T 23.07(C)
Insurance, T 22.08, T 23.04(B), T 46.21
Liability for discipline, T 46.14(A)(1), T 46.14(B)
Lockers, searching, T 47.02
    Private and parochial schools, T 48.17
Married
    Attendance, T 20.04
    Discrimination against, T 19.14(A)
    Tuition free attendance in district of residence, T 23.02(C)(3)
Medical condition requiring emergency assistance, tuition free attendance in district of parent's employment, T 23.02(C)(4)
Medical examinations and treatment—See Health, this heading.
Mentally retarded—See SPECIAL EDUCATION.
Newspapers
    Private school students, T 48.18
    Public school students, T 25.05
Nonresidents
    Adjacent district residents, enrollment, T 5.08(D)
    Admission, T 23.02(A) to T 23.02(C)
    Alternative schools, open enrollment policies, T 5.08(C)
    Room and board costs
        Handicapped children, T 28.08(A)
    Transportation, T 22.04
    Tuition—See TUITION.
    Vocational education, tuition, T 23.02(A)(7), T 23.02(D), T 23.02(E)
Notice
    Permanent exclusion, T 25.10
    Records, rights concerning, T 44.20
Number of, T 2.02
    Private and parochial schools, T 2.03
Permanent exclusion from school, T 25.10(E)
    Admission, T 23.02(A)(14)
    Appeals, T 25.10(E)
    Hearings, T 25.10(E)
    Notice, T 25.10
    Records of pupil, inclusion in
        Destruction, T 25.10(E)
    Superintendents, powers and duties, T 25.10(E)
Personal information systems—See PERSONAL INFORMATION SYSTEMS.

PUPILS—*continued*
Personal injury as due process violation, T 46.14(B)
Photographs retained in student records, T 24.16(B), T 44.15(A), T 44.16
Policies
    Conduct, T 25.03
    Records, on, T 44.21
Pregnant
    Attendance, T 20.04
    Discrimination against, T 19.14(A)
    Exclusion from attendance and activities, T 20.04, T 25.15(B)
    Home instruction, T 20.04
    Privacy rights, T 46.14(E)
Prescription drugs, school employees administering to students, T 21.04(B)
Privacy rights, T 46.14(E)
Private and parochial schools—See PRIVATE AND PAROCHIAL SCHOOLS.
Probationary admission, permanently excluded pupils, T 25.10(E)
Progress reports, T 26.02(C), T 26.15
Promotion requirements, T 26.05, T 26.06, T 26.15
Protection, T Ch 24
    Affirmative duty to protect arising from compulsory attendance, T 46.14(B)
Punishment, corporal—See Corporal punishment, this heading.
Reassignment
    Superintendent's powers, T 7.06(C)
Records and reports, T 44.13 to T 44.21
    See also RECORDS AND REPORTS, SCHOOL, generally.
    Administrative uses, T 44.15
    Age and schooling certificate
        Submission, T 20.13(B)
    Amendment requested by student or parent, T 44.19
    Challenging content, T 44.01, T 44.19
    Data collection, T 3.03(F)
    Disclosure, T 2.13, T 44.01, T 44.02, T 44.14 to T 44.18
        Domestic violence shelter residents, T 44.14(D), T 48.10
        Missing children, access to law enforcement officers investigating, T 24.16, T 44.16, T 48.10
        Subpoenas or orders, T 44.14(C), T 44.15(B)
    Domestic violence, victims of
        Disclosure, T 44.14(D), T 48.10
        Transfer, T 44.14(D), T 48.10
    Family Educational Rights and Privacy Act, applicability, T 44.01, T 44.14 to T 44.21
    Health records, T 21.07
    Hearing tests, T 21.07(A)
    Hearings, challenging content of records, T 44.19
    Immunization, T 21.07(B)
    Inspection rights, T 44.14, T 44.18 to T 44.21
    Notice of rights, T 44.20

PUPILS—*continued*
Records and reports—*continued*
  Order or subpoena for disclosure, T 44.14(C), T 44.15(B)
  Permanent exclusion
    Destruction of records, T 25.10(E)
  Personal information systems—See PERSONAL INFORMATION SYSTEMS.
  Persons requesting or obtaining access, record, T 44.17
  Photographs, T 24.16(B), T 44.15(A), T 44.16
  Policy, formulation, T 44.21
  Privacy act, T 44.01, T 44.14 to T 44.16
  Progress reports, T 26.02(C), T 26.15
  Rights of students and parents, T 44.14, 44.18 to T 44.21
  Subpoena for disclosure, T 44.14(C), T 44.15(B)
  Transfer, T 44.15(B)
    Domestic violence shelter residents, T 44.14(D), T 48.10
  Vision tests, T 21.07(A)
Recreational users, liability of school personnel, T 46.11
Regulated individuals
  School board's powers, T 25.02
Religious instruction, release time, T 5.08(B), T 32.04
Religious organizations, use of school facilities, T 32.06, T 38.08(B), T 38.12
Religious rights, T 25.05
  Compulsory attendance, exemption, T 20.03(A), T 32.02
Removal from school activities or premises, T 25.08, T 25.11
  Disabled child, T 28.09
Required courses of study, T 26.02(A), T 26.05
Research, experimental activities, and testing; student rights, T 26.20
Residency
  District, determination, T 23.02(A) to T 23.02(C)
  Requirements, disabled pupils, T 28.15(C)
Rights, T 25.08 to T 25.16, T 46.14(A)(1)
  Activity programs, participation; due process protection, T 25.15(B)
  Miranda rights, suspension or expulsion, T 25.09(B)
  Privacy rights, T 46.14(E)
  Records, T 44.14, T 44.18 to T 44.21
  Religious, T 25.05
  Research, experimental activities, and testing, T 26.20
  Safety, T 21.10 to T 21.14, T 29.06(B)
    Compulsory attendance, affirmative duty to protect arising from, T 46.14(B)
    Due process violation, personal injury to student as, T 46.14(B)
  Transportation of pupils, T 22.19 to T 22.21
Savings banks, school, T 5.09(S)
Screening for health or developmental disorders, T 21.03(F)

PUPILS—*continued*
Search and seizure laws, applicability—See SEARCH AND SEIZURE.
Self-insurance plans, T 23.04(B)
Self-supporting, tuition, T 23.02(C)(2)
Sexual battery by school employees
  Termination, grounds for, T 9.21, T 12.16(A), T 12.17(A)
Slow-learners—See SPECIAL EDUCATION.
Standards, T 3.03(B)
Suspension or expulsion, T 25.10
  Admission to another district, denial, T 25.10(F)
  Alcoholism, T 20.10
  Appeals, T 25.10(B), T 25.10(C), T 25.12
  Checklist, T 25.14
  Code to be posted, T 5.08(B), T 25.03
  Community service alternative, T 25.10(D)
  Disabled child, T 28.09
  Due process, T 25.09, T 25.15(B), T 46.14(A)(1)
  Effect on attendance, T 20.03(B)
  Emergency removal of student, T 25.11, T 25.14(D)
  Extension of expulsion, T 25.10
  Extracurricular activities, from, T 25.15
  Firearms on school premises, bringing, T 25.10(A)
    Disabled pupils, T 28.09(D)
  Hearings, T 25.10(B), T 25.10(C), T 25.11
  Knives on school premises, bringing, T 25.10(A)
  Miranda rights, T 25.09(B)
  Notice, T 25.11
    Expulsion, T 25.10(C)
    Permanent exclusion, T 25.10(E)
    Substance abuse, T 20.10
    Suspension, T 25.10(B)
  Private schools, T 48.15, T 48.16
  Readmission into special program, T 26.10(A), T 26.10(D)
  Tuition, T 23.02(E)
  Right to due process, T 25.09, T 25.15(B), T 46.14(A)(1)
  Substance abuse, T 20.10
  Superintendents, powers and duties, T 25.10
  Weapons on school premises, bringing, T 25.10(A)
    Disabled pupils, T 28.09(D)
Teachers' children, tuition-free education, T 23.02(C)(9)
Textbooks—See TEXTBOOKS.
Transfer, T 20.10
  Disciplinary, T 25.13
  Domestic violence shelter residents, T 23.02(A)(8), T 44.14(D), T 48.10
  Records, T 44.15(B)
Transportation, T Ch 22
  See also TRANSPORTATION OF PUPILS.
Truancy—See ATTENDANCE.

PUPILS—*continued*
Tubercular children, schools for, T 28.08(B), T 28.08(C)
Transportation, T 22.05
Tuberculin tests, T 10.18, T 21.03(C)
Tuition—See TUITION.
Unemployment compensation, T 15.04
Vaccination—See IMMUNIZATION, at School children.
Venereal disease, diagnosis and treatment, T 21.04(A)
Vision tests, T 21.03
Records, T 21.07(A)
Wages—See WAGES AND HOURS, at Minors.
Withdrawal, T 20.10
Youth services department commitment, admission into special education program following, T 26.10(A), T 26.10(D)
Tuition, T 23.02(E)

QUARTER SCHOOL YEAR, T 20.05(B)

QUO WARRANTO
Fines, disposition, T 39.10

QUORUM
School board meetings, T 5.11(C)

RACIAL DISCRIMINATION—See also DISCRIMINATION, generally.
Desegregation of schools—See DESEGREGATION OF SCHOOLS.
Private schools, by
Admissions, T 48.09(A)
Employment, T 48.30

RADIO
Educational broadcasting, T 26.11(G)

RAILROADS
School buses stopping at grade crossings, T 22.18(A)

REAL PROPERTY—See also PUBLIC LANDS.
Mental retardation and developmental disabilities boards purchasing, T 29.04(H), T 29.08(A)
Public—See PUBLIC LANDS.
School property—See SCHOOL BUILDINGS AND LANDS.
Taxation—See REAL PROPERTY, TAXATION.

REAL PROPERTY, TAXATION
Abatements, T 39.04
Assessments
Complaints, T 39.04
Exemptions
Abatements, T 39.04
Private schools, T 48.33
Private schools exempt, T 48.33

REAL PROPERTY, TAXATION—*continued*
Reductions, T 40.14
School foundation program, prerequisite, T 39.07(B)
Schools, financing, T 39.02 to T 39.04
Valuation of property, T 39.04

RECALL
School board members, T 5.05

RECORDS AND REPORTS—See also particular subject concerned; RECORDS AND REPORTS, SCHOOL.
Affirmative action progress reports, T 17.17
Age and schooling certificates
Submission, T 20.13(B)
Definitions, T 44.02
Disclosure, T 44.01 to T 44.03
See also particular subject concerned.
Education department, T 3.04(B)
Employment relations board
Disclosure, T 18.33
Employment services bureau, statistical information, T 16.10(D)
Libraries—See LIBRARIES AND LIBRARY DISTRICTS.
Personal information systems, T 44.01, T 44.04 to T 44.11
See also PERSONAL INFORMATION SYSTEMS.
Private and parochial schools—See PRIVATE AND PAROCHIAL SCHOOLS.
Public
Collective bargaining, T 18.27, T 18.33
Criminal background checks of employment applicants, T 5.09(H)
Defined, T 44.02
Employment relations board records, T 18.33
Ethics commission advisory opinions, T 45.01(B)
Public Records Act, T 44.01 to T 44.03
Reproduction, T 44.03
Rehabilitation services commission, T 27.15
Disclosure prohibited, T 27.15
Reproduction of public records, T 44.03
School accounts, examination reports, T 43.27(A)
School boards—See EDUCATION, LOCAL BOARDS.
Schools—See RECORDS AND REPORTS, SCHOOL.
Special education programs, T 28.14(B)
Teachers—See RECORDS AND REPORTS, SCHOOL, at Employee records; TEACHERS.
Transcripts—See TRANSCRIPTS.

RECORDS AND REPORTS, SCHOOL, T Ch 44
Access to—See Disclosure, this heading.
Accidents, school buses, T 22.18(C)
Accounting, T 43.26(B)
Accuracy, certifying, T 6.07(D)
Actions against boards, T 5.09(G), T 31.02

RECORDS AND REPORTS, SCHOOL—*continued*
Age and schooling certificates
  Submission of records, T 20.13(B)
Amendment requested by students or parents, T 44.19
Boards of education—See EDUCATION, LOCAL BOARDS.
Buses, school; accidents, T 22.18(C)
Certifying accuracy, T 6.07(D)
Challenge of contents by students or parents, T 44.01, T 44.19
Commissions, T 44.22, T 44.23
Cooperative education school districts; foundation program, average daily membership, T 39.09(B)
Curriculum guides, T 5.09(G), T 31.02
Data processing equipment and services, T 43.29
Definitions
  Personal information, T 44.06
  Public records, T 44.02
Disclosure, T 31.01, T 44.01 to T 44.03
  Burden of proving exceptions, T 44.02
  Employee records, T 44.02, T 44.12
  Student records, T 2.13, T 44.01, T 44.02, T 44.14 to T 44.18
    Domestic violence shelter residents, T 44.14(D), T 48.10
    Missing children, access to law enforcement officers investigating, T 24.16, T 44.16, T 48.10
  Subpoena or order for, T 44.14(C), T 44.15(B)
Disposal, T 43.30, T 44.22, T 44.23
  Discrimination charge pending, T 17.17
  Inspection request outstanding, T 44.18
Dress codes, T 5.09(G), T 31.02
Education management information system, T 3.03(F), T 26.17
Employee records, T 17.17, T 44.12
  Certified personnel, T 39.09(D)
  Disclosure, T 44.02, T 44.12
  Payroll record, T 43.14
  Public access, T 44.02, T 44.12
Enrollment, T 39.09(A), T 44.13
  Adjacent school district residents, T 5.08(D)
  Notice to law enforcement agency when pupil fails to present official records, T 24.16, T 48.10
  Transportation of pupils, T 22.07(B)(2)
Family Educational Rights and Privacy Act, applicability, T 44.01, T 44.14 to T 44.21
Federal requirements, T 44.01, T 44.13, T 44.14
Fees for copying, T 44.21
Financial, T 5.09(G), T 31.02, T 43.26(B)
  Disposal, T 43.30
  Examination, T 43.27
Foundation program funding, for—See FOUNDATION PROGRAM.
Hearings, challenging content, T 44.01, T 44.19
Inspection rights of students and parents, T 44.14, T 44.18 to T 44.21
Membership records, T 39.09(A), T 44.13

RECORDS AND REPORTS, SCHOOL—*continued*
Missing children
  Law enforcement officers investigating, access to student records, T 24.16, T 44.16, T 48.10
  Notice to law enforcement agency when pupil fails to present official records, T 24.16, T 48.10
Newsletters, T 5.09(G), T 31.02
Permanent exclusion from school
  Destruction, T 25.10(E)
Personal information systems, T 44.01, T 44.04 to T 44.11
  See also PERSONAL INFORMATION SYSTEMS.
Personnel records—See Employee records, this heading.
Photographs of students, T 24.16(B), T 44.15(A), T 44.16
Policy bulletins, T 5.09(G), T 31.02
Policy, formulation, T 44.21
Private and parochial schools—See PRIVATE AND PAROCHIAL SCHOOLS.
Progress reports, annual, T 5.09(G), T 31.02
Public access—See Disclosure, this heading.
Pupils—See PUPILS.
School boards—See EDUCATION, LOCAL BOARDS.
Special education programs, T 28.14(B)
Statistical reports
  Annual, T 5.09(G), T 31.02
Student handbooks, T 5.09(G), T 31.02
Student records—See PUPILS.
Student Records Privacy Act, T 44.01, T 44.14 to T 44.16
Studies and surveys, T 5.09(A)
Teachers—See Employee records, this heading; TEACHERS.
Transportation of pupils, T 22.07(B)(2), T 39.09(A)
Vacation period activities, T 26.11(F)

RECREATION—See PARKS AND RECREATION.

RECREATIONAL PROGRAMS, T 30.01, T 30.13 to T 30.16
  See also ATHLETIC EVENTS; PHYSICAL EDUCATION.
Transportation to, T 22.22

REDUCTION IN FORCE (RIF), T 7.13, T 9.19

REFEREES
Teacher termination suits, T 9.22(E)

REFERENDUM—See INITIATIVE AND REFERENDUM.

REFORMATORIES—See CORRECTIONAL INSTITUTIONS.

REGENTS BOARD
Goals for improvement, progress reports, T 3.03(A)

REGIONAL COUNCILS OF GOVERNMENTS, T 5.09(D)

REHABILITATION ACT OF 1973, T 48.29

REHABILITATION AND CORRECTION DEPARTMENT
Institutions—See CORRECTIONAL INSTITUTIONS.

REHABILITATION SERVICES, T 27.13 to T 27.15
Disability determination bureau, T 27.13(B)
Ohio state university rehabilitation center, T 27.14
Records and reports, T 27.15
Social security benefits, disability determination bureau powers, T 27.13(B)
Vocational rehabilitation bureau, T 27.13(B)

REHABILITATION SERVICES COMMISSION, T 27.13
Bureaus composing, T 27.13(A)
Disclosure of records prohibited, T 27.15
Powers and duties, T 27.13(B)
Records and reports, T 27.15
   Disclosure prohibited, T 27.15

RELIGION—See also RELIGIOUS ORGANIZATIONS.
Bible-reading in public schools, T 32.05, T 32.07
Compulsory school attendance versus religious beliefs, T 20.03(A), T 32.02
Discrimination on basis of, T 17.15
Establishment clause, T 32.01
Free exercise clause, T 32.01
Freedom of, T 25.05, T Ch 32
   Attendance at school not conforming to state standards, T 20.03(A), T 32.02
Goals 2000: Educate America Act of 1994; effect on voluntary prayer and meditation, T 32.05
Parochial schools—See PRIVATE AND PAROCHIAL SCHOOLS.
Patriotic observances, objections to, T 32.03
Prayers—See PRAYERS.
Release time for religious instruction, T 5.08(B), T 32.04
School attendance exemption, T 20.03(A), T 32.02
School programs, pupil participation, T 32.05
Sex education, objections to, T 32.07
Textbooks, religious objections to, T 32.07, T 33.04

RELIGIOUS EXERCISES
Pupil release time for instruction, T 5.08(B), T 32.04
Use of school property for, T 32.06, T 38.08(B), T 38.12

RELIGIOUS ORGANIZATIONS
School facilities, using, T 32.06, T 38.08(B), T 38.12
Schools supported by—See PRIVATE AND PAROCHIAL SCHOOLS.

REMOVAL FROM OFFICE—See PUBLIC OFFICIALS.

RENTAL—See LEASES.

REORGANIZATION OF SCHOOL DISTRICTS, T 4.04 to T 4.15
Assets, equitable division, T 4.13
Boards of education
   Effect on, T 4.15
   Powers, T 4.04
Consolidation, T 4.07(A)(2), T 4.09
   Library districts, effect, T 34.03, T 34.05
Contiguity of territory, T 4.05(B)
Creation of new districts, T 4.04 to T 4.06
   Cooperative education school districts, T 4.03(G)
   Elections, T 4.07(A), T 4.09(C)
   Grades required, T 4.05(A)
   Grounds for creation, T 4.05
   Joint vocational school district, T 27.08
   Local district, T 4.03(D), T 4.07(A)(4)
   Referendum against, T 4.04, T 4.10(B)
   State board of education, powers, T 3.03(C)
Debts, equitable division, T 4.13
Dissolution, T 4.09(D), T 26.19
   Cooperative education school districts, T 4.03(G)
   Joint vocational district, T 27.08(D)
   Mandatory, T 4.05(A)
   Petition of referendum against, T 4.09(D)
   Transfers of territory pursuant to, T 4.09(D), T 26.19
Efficiency of school system as grounds, T 4.05(A)
Employees, effect on, T 12.02(B)
Financial grounds, T 4.05(D)
Foundation program funds, allocation, T 4.12
Funds, equitable division, T 4.13
Grounds for reorganization, T 4.05
Legislature's powers, T 4.04
Liabilities, equitable division, T 4.13
Neighborhood school concept, T 4.05(B), T 19.08
New districts, creation—See Creation of new districts, this heading.
Population change, effect, T 4.05(C)
Power to reorganize, T 4.04
Property, equitable division, T 4.13
Redistricting city school districts, T 5.02(B)(2)
   Notice to elections board, T 6.08(C)
Referendum against, T 4.04, T 4.10(B)

REORGANIZATION OF SCHOOL DISTRICTS—*continued*
State board of education, by, T 3.03(C), T 4.05(D)
Subdistricting city districts, T 5.02(B)(2), T 6.08(C)
  Notification to board of elections, T 6.08(C)
Tax levies, effect on, T 4.14, T 39.03, T 40.06
Transfer of territory, T 4.07 to T 4.11
  Acceptance of territory, T 4.07(C)
  Agreements among districts as to boundaries, T 4.07(B)
  Annexation, pursuant to, T 4.07(A)(1), T 4.08
    Tax levies, effect, T 4.14(B)
  Assets and liabilities, division, T 4.13
  City school districts, from, T 4.11
  Consolidation, pursuant to, T 4.07(A)(2)
  Dissolution, pursuant to, T 4.09(D), T 26.19
  Educational service centers
    Governing board proposing, T 4.07(C), T 4.10
    Within center, T 4.10
  Exempted village school districts, from, T 4.11
  Foundation program funds, allocation, T 4.12
  Initiation and approval, T 4.07(A)
  Local school districts, from, T 4.07(A)(3), T 4.10
  Petition, by, T 4.10(A)
  Referendum against, T 4.04, T 4.10(B)
  State board of education, powers, T 3.03(C), T 4.05(D), T 4.09, T 4.11(B)
  Types of transfer, T 4.07(A)
Uniform application of statutes, T 4.04

REPORTS—See RECORDS AND REPORTS.
School—See RECORDS AND REPORTS, SCHOOL.

REQUIRED COURSES OF STUDY—See CURRICULUM.

RESEARCH
Consent of parents or guardians, T 26.20
Federal funding, violations, T 26.20
Limitations, T 26.20
Superintendent of public instruction, by, T 3.06

RESIDENCE
Minors
  Determination for school attendance, T 23.02(A) to T 23.02(C)
  Disabled pupils, residency requirements, T 28.15(C)
School attendance, determination for, T 23.02(A) to T 23.02(C)
  Disabled pupils, residency requirements, T 28.15(C)

RESIGNATION
Administrators, T 7.11(A)
Nonteaching school employees, T 12.18
Superintendents, local, T 7.05(A)

RESIGNATION—*continued*
Teachers—See TEACHERS.

RESOLUTIONS—See ORDINANCES OR RESOLUTIONS; particular subject concerned.

RESTITUTION
School funds allocated to wrong districts, T 39.05

RESTRAINING ORDERS
Strikes, clear and present danger, T 18.32

RETIREMENT INCENTIVE PLANS
School employees retirement system members, T 14.13
Teachers retirement system members, T 11.21
  Cash payments, T 43.05(B)

RETIREMENT PLANS
Age discrimination, T 17.06(C)
Coordination of multiple memberships, T 11.12(B)
  Withdrawing contributions, T 11.11
Mortality tables, sex-segregated; use of, T 17.06(C)(2)
Public employees—See PUBLIC EMPLOYEES RETIREMENT SYSTEM.
School employees, T Ch 14
  See also SCHOOL EMPLOYEES RETIREMENT SYSTEM.
Teachers, T Ch 11
  See also TEACHERS RETIREMENT SYSTEM.

REVENUES—See APPROPRIATIONS; FUNDS, PUBLIC; TAXATION.

REWARDS
Apprehension of criminals, crime committed on school property, T 38.05

RIF, T 7.13, T 9.19

RIGHT OF ENTRY
Truant officers, T 20.08(C)

"RIGHT TO READ", T 33.04

ROADS—See STREETS.

RULES AND RULEMAKING POWERS—See also particular agency or subject concerned.
Asbestos hazard abatement activity, T 21.10(B)
Asbestos Hazard Emergency Response Act of 1986, T 21.10(B)
Disabled, education, T 28.14(A)
Education management information system, T 3.03(F)
Libraries, T 34.10

RULES AND RULEMAKING POWERS—continued
Mental retardation and developmental disabilities boards, county, T 29.05
Ohio high school athletic association, T 30.11
Personal information systems, T 44.08
Public employment risk reduction advisory commission, T 16.09(A)
School boards, T 5.08(A)
    Limitations, T 5.06(A)
School employees retirement system, T 14.02(C)
Special education, T 28.14(A)
Teachers retirement system, T 11.02(C)

SAFETY
Employment services bureau, powers and duties, T 16.09
Fire safety—See FIRE SAFETY.
Inspection of school buildings—See SCHOOL BUILDINGS AND LANDS.
Occupational safety and health, T 16.09
School buses—See SCHOOL BUSES, generally.
Traffic—See TRAFFIC CONTROL.

SAFETY GOGGLES
Pupils required to wear, when, T 21.12

SALARIES—See COMPENSATION; WAGES AND HOURS.
School employees—See SCHOOL EMPLOYEES, NONTEACHING, at Compensation; TEACHERS, at Compensation.

SALES
Bonds and notes—See BONDS AND NOTES.
School premises, on, T 35.02(E)

SALES TAX
Food sales by educational institutions, T 35.04(A)
Private schools exempt, T 48.33
School-sponsored sales, T 35.02(E)

SAVINGS BANKS, SCHOOL, T 5.09(S)

SAVINGS BONDS
Payroll deductions, public employees, T 10.08

SCHOOL ACCREDITATION ASSOCIATIONS, T 26.18, T 43.02(B)

SCHOOL AND MINISTERIAL LANDS, T 1.02, T 1.05

SCHOOL BOARD ASSOCIATIONS, T 5.09(E), T 26.18, T 43.02(B)

SCHOOL BOARDS—See EDUCATION, LOCAL BOARDS; EDUCATION, STATE BOARD.

SCHOOL BUILDINGS AND LANDS, T Ch 36
Access restrictions, T 32.06, T 38.03(A)
Acquisition, T 36.01 to T 36.08, T 41.04
    Appropriation of property, T 36.03
    Cooperative agreements, T 36.08, T 37.01(A)
    Exchange with municipal corporations, T 36.05(B), T 36.09
    Federal land, T 36.02(B)
    Lease-purchase agreements, T 36.02(A)
Arson, T 38.04(A)
Asbestos Hazard Emergency Response Act of 1986, T 21.10(B), T 48.35
Asbestos removal, T 21.10(B)
    Private and parochial schools, T 48.35
Auctions, T 36.11(B)
Bonds and notes to finance, T 41.03, T 41.04
    See also BONDS AND NOTES, SCHOOL, generally.
    Emergency additions or replacements, T 41.04, T 41.09
    Purchase, T 36.02(B)
Building standards, T 21.10, T 37.01, T 37.09
Business managers, powers and duties, T 6.13, T 38.02
Children's services investigators interviewing children on school property, T 5.08(A), T 24.05(A), T 31.04
Classroom facilities, T 41.24 to T 41.32
    See also CLASSROOM FACILITIES.
Construction and improvements, T Ch 37
    Approval of plans for, T 37.03(B)
    Bids, T 6.08(B), T 37.04 to T 37.06
        Advertisement for, T 37.04(B)
        Bid bonds, T 37.04(B), T 37.05
        Examination, acceptance, rejection, T 37.06
        Exceptions, T 37.04(C)
        Form, T 37.05
        Lowest responsive and responsible bidder, T 37.06(A)
        Performance bonds, T 37.06(B)
        Procedure, T 37.04(B)
    Classroom facilities, T 41.24 to T 41.32
        See also CLASSROOM FACILITIES.
    Construction manager, T 37.10
    Contracts, T 37.01(B), T 37.04 to T 37.06
        Affirmative action requirements, T 17.05(B)
        Award, T 37.06(B)
        Construction manager, T 37.10
        Payment provisions, T 37.08(B)
        Performance bonds, T 37.06(B)
        Wage provision, T 37.12(B)
    Cooperative projects, T 36.08, T 37.01(A)
    Costs, T 37.07
        Estimates, T 37.03(A)
        Payment, T 37.07(B), T 37.08(B), T 37.08(C)
    Fees, exemptions, T 37.02
    Lease-purchase agreements, T 36.02(A)
    Local regulations, applicability, T 37.02
    Notice to proceed, T 37.08(A)
    Payment of costs, T 37.07(B), T 37.08(B), T 37.08(C)

SCHOOL BUILDINGS AND LANDS—*continued*
Construction and improvements—*continued*
  Plans and specifications
    Approval, T 37.03(B)
    Powers of board, T 37.01
    Standards, T 21.10, T 37.01(B), T 37.09
    Supervision, T 6.13, T 37.09
  Construction managers, T 37.10
  Cooperative acquisition, T 36.08, T 37.01(A)
  Deadly weapons or dangerous ordnances, prohibited, T 21.16
  Destruction or damage, T 38.04
    Child, by; parental liability, T 38.06
    Financing rebuilding, T 41.04
    Reward for information leading to arrest and conviction, T 38.05
  Disinfection, T 21.08(B)
  Doors and exits, unlocked during school hours, T 21.13
  Drug offenses on or near, T 24.14
  Emergency additions or replacement
    Bonds to finance, T 41.04, T 41.09
  Eminent domain, T 36.03
  Energy conservation measures, purchase, T 36.04(C)(2)
    Bonds to finance, T 41.04
  Entry restrictions, T 31.04
  Equal Access Act, T 32.06
  Equipment and furnishing of schools—See EQUIPMENT AND SUPPLIES, SCHOOL.
  Exchange with municipal corporations, T 36.05(B), T 36.09
  Federal land, acquisition, T 36.02(B)
  Fees for use, T 31.04, T 38.10
  Fire safety, T 21.13
  Funds
    Permanent improvement fund, T 43.21
    Replacement fund, T 43.20
    Vocational school building assistance fund, T 27.02
  Gifts or bequests, T 36.06
    Prohibited, when, T 36.13
  Handicapped persons, access, T 21.10(C), T 28.17(B)
  Improvements—See Construction and improvements, this heading.
  Inspections, T 21.10(A)
    Asbestos, for, T 21.10(B)
    Health, T 21.03(A), T 21.08(B)
    State board of education, by, T 3.03(G)
    Tornado drills and shelters, T 21.13
  Joint vocational districts, T 27.10(A)
  Lease of sites or buildings, T 36.05(A), T 36.10, T 36.14
    Lease-purchase agreements, T 36.02(A)
  Liability insurance, use of school property by others, T 38.08(C)
  Libraries in school buildings, T 34.02
  Local boards of education, control, T 4.04, T 38.01
  Maintenance, T 38.02

SCHOOL BUILDINGS AND LANDS—*continued*
Mineral lands, contracts or leases, T 36.10(B), T 39.15
Nature preserves, T 31.07
Options to purchase, T 36.02(C)
Parks and recreational facilities, T 30.14, T 38.09
Performance evaluation standards, T 3.03(D)
  Deficient buildings, T 3.03(D)(2)
Permanent improvement fund, T 43.21
Physical education facilities, T 30.04
  Posting of anabolic steroid warnings, T 21.15(D), T 48.15
Plans, approval, T 37.03(B)
Polling place, use as, T 38.10
Proceeds from sale of, T 36.14
Purchase, T 36.02
Rental of, T 36.05(A), T 36.10, T 36.14
  Lease-purchase agreements, T 36.02(A)
Repair—See Construction and improvements, this heading.
Replacement fund, T 43.20
Reward, information concerning crime committed on school property, T 38.05
Sale, T 36.09, T 36.11
  Execution, T 6.08(D)
  Option to purchase, T 36.12
  Proceeds, T 36.14
Security, T 38.03 to T 38.06
Smoking indoors, ban, T 38.14
Snow removal, T 38.02
Standards for facilities, T 21.10, T 37.01(B), T 37.09
Studies and surveys, T 5.09(A)
Tax levies to finance
  General levy revenues, T 40.09(A)
  Permanent improvement levy, T 43.21
  Special levy, T 40.09(B)
Title to property
  Transfer of territory, T 4.13
Trade or exchange of, T 36.05(B), T 36.09
Trees, cutting or injury to
  Disposition of fines, T 39.10
Trespass, T 38.03(B)
Uses permissible, T 31.04, T 32.06, T 38.07 to T 38.13
  Damages, reimbursement, T 38.13
  Discretion of board, T 38.08(A)
  Educational and recreational purposes, T 38.09
  Equal access requirement, T 38.08(B)
  Fees, T 38.08(D), T 38.10
  Liability insurance, T 38.08(C)
  Library purposes, T 34.02
  Limited open forum, T 38.08(B)
  Political action committees, T 38.10
  Political meetings, T 31.04, T 38.08(B), T 38.11
  Polling place, T 38.10
  Public functions, T 38.10
  Religious purposes, T 32.06, T 38.08(B), T 38.12
  Rules, T 38.09

SCHOOL BUILDINGS AND LANDS—*continued*
Vandalism, T 38.04(C)
   Reward for information leading to arrest and conviction, T 38.05
Vocational facilities, T 27.10(A)
   School building assistance fund, T 27.02
Weapons—See WEAPONS, generally.

SCHOOL BUSES—See also TRANSPORTATION OF PUPILS.
Accidents
   Emergency plans and drills, T 22.20
   Insurance, T 22.08, T 23.04(B), T 46.21
   Reporting, T 22.18(C)
Activity buses, T 22.22
Adult education programs leasing, T 22.23
Aged persons, transporting, T 22.22, T 22.23
Bus stops, T 22.16
Color, T 22.11
Competitive bidding for purchase, T 22.09(A), T 36.04(B), T 36.04(C)(3)
Construction, design, and equipment, T 22.10 to T 22.12
Defects, reporting, T 22.17(A)
Definition, T 22.11
Depots, T 22.16
Disabled pupils, transportation; foundation program funding, T 22.07(B)
Discharging riders, safety precautions, T 22.17(A), T 22.18(A)
Disrupting services, T 38.04(B)
Drivers, T 22.13 to T 22.15
    See also SCHOOL EMPLOYEES, NON-TEACHING, generally.
   Alcohol use
     Testing, T 22.13(B)
     Under influence, transporting children while, T 24.09(D)
   Appeal from disqualification, T 22.14
   Daily inspections of buses, T 22.17(A)
   Disability benefits, T 22.14
   Discipline of pupils, T 22.17(B)
   Disqualification, T 22.14
    Appeal, T 22.14
    Notice, T 22.14
   Drivers' license, revocation or suspension, T 22.13(A)
   Drug use
     Testing, T 22.13(B)
     Under influence, transporting children while, T 24.09(D)
   Hours of work, T 22.18(A)
   Insurance, T 22.08, T 46.20
   Licensing by public safety department, T 22.01
   Medical examination, T 22.14
   Nonroutine use of bus, T 22.22
   Notice, disqualification, T 22.14
   Powers and duties, T 22.17(A), T 22.17(B), T 22.18(A), T 25.07, T 25.16
   Qualifications, T 22.13(A)
   Safety workshop, T 22.15
   Seat belts, T 22.11, T 48.08(B)

SCHOOL BUSES—*continued*
Drivers—*continued*
   Sick leave benefits, T 22.14
   Traffic violation convictions, reporting, T 22.13(A)
   Training, T 22.15
Emergencies
   Policy and drills, T 22.20
Equipment standards, T 22.10 to T 22.12
Evacuation, T 22.20
Flashing lights, T 22.11, T 22.17(A)
Funding for purchase, T 22.07(C), T 22.09
Grade crossings, T 22.18(A)
Identification numbers, T 22.11
Inspection
   Daily, by driver, T 22.17(A)
Insurance, T 22.08, T 23.04(B), T 46.20, T 46.21
   Volunteer bus rider assistants, T 22.21, T 29.06(B)
Leasing
   Adult education, for, T 22.23
   Aged persons, for, T 22.22, T 22.23
   Private schools, by, T 22.24
   Seat belt for driver required, T 22.11, T 48.08(B)
Loading and unloading pupils, T 22.17(A), T 22.18(A)
Markings, T 22.11
Motor vehicles stopping for, T 22.18(B)
Nonroutine use of, T 22.11, T 22.22 to T 22.24
Operation, T 22.16 to T 22.18
Out-of-state use, T 22.22
Overloading, T 22.16
Penalties for violations, T 22.27
Private and parochial school pupils, for
   Leasing, T 22.24
Public safety department
   Licensing by, T 22.01
   Regulation by, T 22.10
Pupil behavior, T 22.17(B), T 22.17(C)
Purchase, T 22.09, T 36.04(A)
   Competitive bidding, T 36.04(B), T 36.04(C)(3)
   Education department's approval, T 22.07(C)
   Seat belt for driver required, T 22.11, T 48.08(B)
Railroad tracks, stopping before crossing, T 22.18(A)
Receiving riders, safety precautions, T 22.18(A)
Records and reports
   Accidents, T 22.18(C)
   Driver's conviction for traffic violation, T 22.13(A)
Registration, T 22.11
Regulation, T 22.10
Removal of pupils, T 22.17(C)
Routes and schedules, T 22.16, T 22.17(A)
Safety instruction to pupils, T 21.14, T 22.19, T 29.06(B)
Seat assignments, T 22.16
Seat belts, T 22.11, T 48.08(B)
Shelters, T 22.16
Signals on buses, T 22.11, T 22.17(A)

SCHOOL BUSES—*continued*
Speed, T 22.18(A)
State subsidy for, T 22.07(C)
Stopping for, T 22.18(B)
Stops, T 22.16
Use for other than school purposes, T 22.11, T 22.22 to T 22.24
Use outside state, T 22.22
Violations
   Penalties, T 22.27
Volunteer bus rider assistants, T 22.21
   Liability insurance, T 22.21, T 29.06(B)

SCHOOL-BUSINESS PARTNERSHIPS, T 3.04(A)

SCHOOL CLOSINGS—See CLOSING SCHOOLS.

SCHOOL DAYS, T 20.05
Flexible schedule, T 20.05(B)

SCHOOL DISTRICTS—See SCHOOLS AND SCHOOL DISTRICTS.

SCHOOL EMPLOYEES, NONTEACHING, T Ch 12 to T Ch 14, T 46.14(D)
   See also PUBLIC EMPLOYEES, generally.
Abolishment of position, T 12.13, T 12.14
Actions against, defense and indemnification, T 46.04
AIDS, afflicted with, T 21.03(D), T 21.03(E)
Appeals
   Demotion or suspension, T 12.15(A)
   Termination, T 12.16(C), T 12.17(C), T 12.17(D)
Appointment, T 12.01, T 12.05 to T 12.10
   Civil service employees, T 12.05 to T 12.08
   Noncivil service employees, T 12.09
Asbestos awareness training for custodial and maintenance personnel, T 21.10(B)
Assault leave, T 10.21(B), T 13.10(B)
Assignment, T 7.06(B)(2)
   Discrimination, T 19.11(B), T 46.14(D)
Bus drivers—See SCHOOL BUSES, at Drivers.
Child abuse
   Prevention, in-service training, T 21.14, T 24.05
   Reporting, T 24.05
   Sexual battery of students
      Termination, grounds for, T 12.16(A), T 12.17(A)
City charters, effect on employment, T 12.02(C)
Civil service, applicability, T Ch 12
   See also CIVIL SERVICE, generally.
   Administrative costs, apportionment, T 12.03(B)
   Appointment, T 12.05 to T 12.08
   Termination, T 12.17
   Unclassified position, T 12.04(A)
Coaches, employment, T 12.10

SCHOOL EMPLOYEES, NONTEACHING—*continued*
Collective bargaining—See COLLECTIVE BARGAINING, PUBLIC EMPLOYEES.
Communicable diseases, T 10.18, T 13.10, T 21.03(D), T 21.03(E)
Compensation, T 13.01 to T 13.06
   Certification by civil service commission, T 13.01(C)
   Deductions—See Payroll deductions, this heading.
   Deferred compensation plan, T 14.15
   Direct deposit, T 43.10
   Fringe benefits, T 43.05(B)
   Holidays, T 13.03
   Increases, T 13.01(B)
   Jury duty, T 10.09(B), T 13.05(B)
   Minimum wages, T 13.01(B)
   Noncertified personnel, T 12.10(E)
   Notice, T 13.01(B)
   Overtime, T 13.02, T 13.03(B)
   Payment procedure, T 43.10
   Professional meetings, T 10.09(C), T 13.05(C)
   Records, T 43.14, T 44.12
   Reduction, T 12.09(C), T 12.15(B), T 13.01(B)
   Retirement system contributions paid by employer, T 14.08(B)
   Schedule, T 13.01(A)
   School closings, during, T 13.05(A)
   Severance pay, T 10.17, T 13.09
   Vacation leave credit, T 13.04(A)
Compensatory time off, T 13.02(B), T 13.03(B)
Conduct
   Constitutionally protected conduct, T 9.21(E), T 12.16(A), T 12.17(A)
   Drugs and alcohol standards, T 21.15(A)
Continuing contracts, T 12.09(A)
Contracts, T 12.09
   Collective bargaining—See COLLECTIVE BARGAINING, PUBLIC EMPLOYEES, at Agreements.
   Continuing, T 12.09(A)
   Indeterminate, T 12.09(E)
   Limited, T 12.09(A)
   Modification by superintendent prohibited, T 7.06(B)(2)
   Supplemental, T 12.09(G)
   Termination of, T 12.16
Convictions—See Criminal convictions, this heading.
Crimes against children, reporting, T 24.06(A), T 24.08, T 25.05
Criminal background check of applicants, T 5.09(H)
   Preschool programs, T 5.09(C)
   Private and parochial schools, T 48.19
Criminal convictions
   Employment applicants, T 5.09(H), T 8.07(A)
   Reporting, T 24.07
Custodial personnel, asbestos awareness training, T 21.10(B)

SCHOOL EMPLOYEES, NONTEACHING—*continued*

Death
  Vacation pay to beneficiaries, T 13.04(A)
Deferred compensation plan, T 14.15
Demotion, T 12.15(A)
Disability benefit, T 14.11
Disability leave, T 13.10(B)
  Retirement system contributions during, T 14.06(A)
Disciplinary actions against, T 12.15 to T 12.17
Discipline of students, duties, T 25.07
Discrimination in employment or assignment, T 19.11(B), T 46.14(D)
  See also EMPLOYMENT DISCRIMINATION, generally.
Drug offense convictions or guilty pleas, T 5.09(H), T 8.07(A)
  Reporting requirements, T 24.07
Educational aides, T 12.19
  Teacher status, T 8.02(C)
Employment
  Probationary, T 12.07(A)
  Reemployment, T 12.09(A), T 12.09(F)
Extracurricular activity directors, employment, T 12.10
Fair Labor Standards Act, equal pay, T 17.08
Felony convictions or guilty pleas, T 5.09(H), T 8.07(A)
Force and restraint against pupils, use, T 25.07, T 25.16(A)
Freedom of speech, T 46.14(C)
Fringe benefits, T 43.05(B)
Health examinations, T 21.03(D)
Health insurance, T 10.10 to T 10.12, T 13.07
  Group coverage, continuation after involuntary termination of employment, T 10.12
Hearings, termination of employment, T 12.16(B), T 12.16(C)
  Pretermination hearing, T 12.17(B)
Holiday pay, T 13.03
Hourly employees, notice of pay rate, T 13.01(B)
Hours, T 13.02
  Reduction, T 12.09(C)
Independent contractors in lieu of, T 12.08
Indeterminate contracts, T 12.09(E)
Insurance, T 10.10 to T 10.12, T 13.07
  Liability, T 5.07, T 46.19
  Life insurance, T 10.10, T 10.11, T 13.07
  Payroll deductions for premiums, T 10.08
Involuntary termination, continuation of group health insurance, T 10.12
Job classification, T 13.01(A), T 13.01(B)
Job reassignment, T 12.12
Jury duty, compensation, T 10.09(B), T 13.05(B)
Layoffs, T 12.13, T 12.14
  See also CIVIL SERVICE, at Layoffs.
Leaves of absence
  Assault leave, T 10.21(B), T 13.10(B)
  Family and Medical Leave Act of 1993, T 17.16
    Private schools, applicability, T 48.30
  Military, T 13.10(B)

SCHOOL EMPLOYEES, NONTEACHING—*continued*

Leaves of absence—*continued*
  Personal, T 13.10(A)
  Professional improvement, T 13.10(B)
  Sick leave—See Sick leave, this heading.
  Vacation, T 13.04
Liability, T 46.03
  Civil rights violations, T 46.15(B), T 46.15(C)
  Insurance, T 5.07, T 46.19
Life insurance, T 10.10, T 10.11, T 13.07
Limited contracts, T 12.09(A)
Maintenance employees, asbestos awareness training, T 21.10(B)
Management level employees and supervisors considered to be, T 12.04(B), T 12.09(A)
Military service
  Leave of absence, T 13.10(B)
  Retirement system membership, effect on, T 14.10(A)
Noncertified persons, employment in extracurricular programs, T 12.10
Notice
  Compensation, T 13.01(B)
  Overtime, T 13.02, T 13.03(B)
Parochial schools—See PRIVATE AND PAROCHIAL SCHOOLS.
Part-time employment
  After retirement, T 14.14
  Sick leave, T 10.13(B)
Payroll deductions, T 10.08, T 13.06, T 43.08
  Charitable contributions, T 31.08
  Insurance premiums, T 10.08
  Retirement system contributions, T 14.05
Payroll records, T 43.14
Personal leave, T 13.10(A)
Position, abolishment of, T 12.13, T 12.14
Private schools—See PRIVATE AND PAROCHIAL SCHOOLS.
Probationary period of employment, T 12.07(A)
Professional meetings, T 10.09(C), T 13.05(C)
Promotion, T 12.11
Records concerning, T 17.17, T 44.12
  Payroll, T 43.14, T 44.12
Reduction in employment, T 12.15(B)
Reemployment, T 12.09(A), T 12.09(F)
Regular employees, T 12.09(B)
Removal—See Termination, this heading.
Reorganization of school district, effect, T 12.02(B)
Reporting requirements
  Child abuse, T 24.05
  Criminal convictions, T 24.07
Resignation, T 12.18
Retirement, T 14.12, T 17.06(C)
  Disability benefit, T 14.11
  Incentive plans, T 14.13
  Part-time service permitted, T 14.14
  Severance pay, T 10.17
Retirement system, T Ch 14
  See also SCHOOL EMPLOYEES RETIREMENT SYSTEM.

SCHOOL EMPLOYEES, NONTEACHING—*continued*
Rights, constitutional protection, T 9.21(E), T 12.16(A), T 12.17(A)
Salaries—See Compensation, this heading.
School closure, effect on, T 13.05(A)
Sex offense convictions or guilty pleas, T 5.09(H), T 8.07(A)
  Reporting requirements, T 24.07
Sexual battery of students by
  Termination, grounds for, T 12.16(A), T 12.17(A)
Sick leave, T 13.08 to T 13.10
  Beyond minimum standard, T 43.05(B)
  Communicable disease, T 10.18
  Part-time employees, T 10.13(B)
  Payment for unused, T 10.17, T 13.09
  Uniform administration, T 10.13(D)
Student discipline, duties, T 25.07
Supervisors and management level employees considered to be, T 12.04(B), T 12.09(A)
Supplemental contracts, T 12.09(G)
Suspension, T 12.15(A)
  Unemployment compensation, disqualification, T 15.08
Tax sheltered annuities, T 14.15
Termination, T 12.16, T 12.17
  Appeal, T 12.16(C), T 12.17(C), T 12.17(D)
  Civil service employees, T 12.17
  Constitutionally protected conduct, T 9.21(E), T 12.16(A), T 12.17(A)
  Contract, T 12.16
  Freedom of speech, T 46.14(C)
  Grounds for, T 12.16(A), T 12.17(A)
  Hearings, T 12.16(B), T 12.16(C)
    Pretermination, T 12.17(B)
    Transcript, T 12.16(C)
  Involuntary, continuation of group medical insurance coverage, T 10.12
  Noncivil service employees, T 12.16
  Notice, T 12.16(B), T 12.17(B)
  Sexual battery of students, T 12.16(A), T 12.17(A)
  Unemployment compensation, disqualification, T 15.08
Theft offense convictions or guilty pleas, T 5.09(H), T 8.07(A)
  Reporting requirements, T 24.07
Transcripts of termination hearings, T 12.16(C)
Transfer, T 12.12
Treasurers of school boards not considered to be, T 6.05
Tuberculin tests, T 10.18, T 21.03(C)
Unclassified civil service, T 12.04(A)
Unemployment compensation, T Ch 15
  See also UNEMPLOYMENT COMPENSATION, generally.
  Suspension or termination, disqualification, T 15.08
Vacation, T 13.04
  Death of employee, payment to beneficiaries upon, T 13.04(A)

SCHOOL EMPLOYEES, NONTEACHING—*continued*
Work week, T 13.02(A)
  Records, T 44.12
Workers' compensation, T Ch 16
  See also WORKERS' COMPENSATION, generally.

SCHOOL EMPLOYEES RETIREMENT SYSTEM, T Ch 14
Allowances—See Benefits, this heading.
Annuity and pension reserve fund, T 14.03
Attorney general as legal adviser, T 14.02(A)
Benefits, T 14.11 to T 14.16
  Additional, T 14.12
  Retirement, T 14.12
Board, T 14.02
  Conflict of interest, T 14.02(B)
  Legal adviser, T 14.02(A)
  Members, T 5.04(A), T 14.02(A)
    Compensation, T 14.02(A)
    Disability benefit, T 14.11
  Officers, T 14.02(A)
  Powers and duties, T 14.02(C)
Conflict of interest, T 14.02(B)
Contributions, T 14.05 to T 14.08, T 14.10(C)
  Additional, by members, T 14.06(B)
  Disability leave, during, T 14.06(A)
  Fringe benefit pickup, T 14.08(A)
  Leaves of absence, during, T 14.06(A)
  Salary reduction plans, T 14.08(B)
  School boards, by, T 14.07, T 14.08
  Voluntary contributions, T 14.06
Custodian of funds, treasurer of state as, T 14.02(A)
Deductions from pay—See Contributions, this heading.
Disability benefit, T 14.11
  Board members, T 14.11
Disability leave, T 13.10(B)
  Contributions during, T 14.06(A)
Early retirement incentive plans, T 14.13
Employees
  Compensation, T 14.02(A)
Employees' savings fund, T 14.03
Employers' contributions, T 14.07, T 14.08
  Salary reduction plans, T 14.08(B)
Employers' trust fund, T 14.03
Establishment, T 14.01
Expense fund, T 14.03
Expenses, T 14.02(A)
Funds, T 14.03
  Custodian, treasurer of state as, T 14.02(A)
Guarantee fund, T 14.03
Incentive plan, T 14.13
Indemnification of board members and employees, T 11.02(A)
Investments permissible, T 14.03
Leaves of absence
  Contributions during, T 14.06(A)
Legal adviser to board, T 14.02(A)

SCHOOL EMPLOYEES RETIREMENT SYSTEM—*continued*
Membership, T 14.04
    Notice of duties and obligations, T 14.04(A)
    Service credit—See Service credit, this heading.
Military service, effect, T 14.10(A)
Notice
    Members, duties and obligations, T 14.04(A)
Part-time employment, T 14.14
Payment of benefits, survivor's benefits, T 14.16
Payroll deductions—See Contributions, this heading.
Prisoners of war, purchase of service credit, T 14.10(A)
Private school employees, purchase of service credit, T 14.10(A)
Purchase of service credit—See Service credit, this heading.
Retirement, T 14.12
    Incentive plan, T 14.13
    Part-time service permitted, T 14.14
Retirement incentive plan, T 14.13
Rules, T 14.02(C)
School board members
    Contributions, T 14.07, T 14.08
Service credit, T 14.09
    College employee, T 14.10(A)
    Fire fighters, T 14.10(A)
    Highway patrol officers, T 14.10(A)
    Military service, effect, T 14.10(A)
    Out-of-state service, T 14.10(A)
    Payroll deductions, T 14.10(C)
    Police service, T 14.10(A)
    Prisoners of war, T 14.10(A)
    Private school employees, T 14.10(A)
    Purchase
        Prisoners of war, T 14.10(A)
        Private school employees, T 14.10(A)
        Teachers retirement system, in, T 11.13(A)
    Redeposit of withdrawn deposits, T 14.10(B)
    State highway patrol officers, T 14.10(A)
    Temporary employment
        Veterans, T 14.10(A)
    University employees, T 14.10(A)
    Veterans, T 14.10(A)
    Withdrawn deposits, redeposit, T 14.10(B)
Survivors' benefits, T 14.16
    Fund, T 14.03
Treasurer of state
    Custodian of funds, as, T 14.02(A)
Veterans, purchase of service credit, T 14.10(A)

SCHOOL FINANCE—See FUNDS, SCHOOL.

SCHOOL-PARENT PARTNERSHIPS, T 3.04(A)

SCHOOL PSYCHOLOGISTS—See PSYCHOLOGISTS AND PSYCHOLOGY, generally.

SCHOOL SAVINGS BANKS, T 5.09(S)

SCHOOL ZONES, T 21.11

SCHOOLHOUSES—See SCHOOL BUILDINGS AND LANDS.

SCHOOLS AND SCHOOL DISTRICTS—See also particular type of school concerned.
Accounts and accounting—See ACCOUNTS AND ACCOUNTING.
Accreditation evaluations, T 26.18
Actions against, T Ch 46
    See also PUBLIC LIABILITY ACT.
Adjacent districts, enrollment policies, T 5.08(D)
Administrative officers—See ADMINISTRATIVE PERSONNEL.
Adult education—See ADULT EDUCATION.
Age and schooling certificates—See AGE AND SCHOOLING CERTIFICATES.
Agricultural schools, T 26.11(B)
    See also VOCATIONAL EDUCATION, generally.
Aliens, admitting, T 19.16
Americanization schools, T 26.11(E)
Athletic events—See ATHLETIC EVENTS.
Attendance—See ATTENDANCE.
Auction of property, T 36.11(B)
Audits—See AUDITS.
Basic state aid—See FOUNDATION PROGRAM.
Bidding—See BIDDING, COMPETITIVE.
Blind persons, for—See BLIND PERSONS.
Board of education—See EDUCATION, LOCAL BOARDS.
Bonds and notes—See BONDS AND NOTES, SCHOOL.
Books, T Ch 33
    See also TEXTBOOKS.
    Braille, translation into, T 33.03(A)
    Reference books, purchase, T 33.03(A)
Boundaries of districts—See BOUNDARIES.
Budgets—See BUDGETS, SCHOOL.
Buildings—See SCHOOL BUILDINGS AND LANDS.
Buses—See SCHOOL BUSES.
Business advisory councils, T 26.11(H)
Business managers—See BUSINESS MANAGERS.
Calendar—See CALENDAR, SCHOOL.
Charitable contributions, solicitation in schools, T 31.08
Charters, T 26.19
City districts—See CITY SCHOOL DISTRICTS.
Civil service—See CIVIL SERVICE, generally.
Classification of districts, T 4.03
    Changes, T 4.05(C), T 4.06
Classroom facilities, T 41.24 to T 41.32
    See also CLASSROOM FACILITIES.
Closing—See CLOSING SCHOOLS.
Collective bargaining—See COLLECTIVE BARGAINING, PUBLIC EMPLOYEES, generally.
College preparatory schools, T 26.07(B)

SCHOOLS AND SCHOOL DISTRICTS—continued

Compulsory attendance—See ATTENDANCE.
Consolidation of districts—See REORGANIZATION OF SCHOOL DISTRICTS.
Contiguity of district territory, T 4.05(B)
Contracts—See CONTRACTS, SCHOOL.
Cooperative education school districts, T 4.03(G)
See also COOPERATIVE EDUCATION SCHOOL DISTRICTS, generally.
Corporal punishment—See PUPILS.
Counseling programs—See GUIDANCE AND COUNSELING PROGRAMS.
County districts—See EDUCATIONAL SERVICE CENTERS.
County superintendents—See SUPERINTENDENTS, LOCAL.
Creation of new districts—See REORGANIZATION OF SCHOOL DISTRICTS.
Crimes committed on school property, reward for information concerning, T 38.05
Criminal convictions of employment applicants, T 5.09(H)
  Reporting requirements, T 24.07
Criminal record checks of employees, T 5.09(H)
  Preschool programs, T 5.09(C)
  Private and parochial schools, T 48.19
Curriculum—See CURRICULUM.
Data processing services—See DATA PROCESSING.
Deaf persons, for—See DEAF PERSONS.
Debts—See DEBTS.
Dental examination of pupils—See PUPILS.
Dentists employed by—See DENTISTS.
Desegregation—See DESEGREGATION OF SCHOOLS.
Diplomas—See DIPLOMAS AND DEGREES, generally.
Disabled children—See DISABLED CHILDREN, at Schooling.
Discrimination by—See DISCRIMINATION.
Dissolution—See REORGANIZATION OF SCHOOL DISTRICTS.
Dress codes, publication by school board, T 5.09(G), T 31.02
Driver education—See DRIVER TRAINING COURSES.
Education management information system, T 3.03(F), T 26.17
Educational service centers—See EDUCATIONAL SERVICE CENTERS.
Elementary schools—See ELEMENTARY SCHOOLS.
Emergencies—See EMERGENCIES AND DISASTERS.
Emergency school advancement fund, T 41.33
See also EMERGENCY LOANS.
Employees, nonteaching—See SCHOOL EMPLOYEES, NONTEACHING.
Enrollment—See ENROLLMENT.
Equipment—See EQUIPMENT AND SUPPLIES, SCHOOL.

SCHOOLS AND SCHOOL DISTRICTS—continued

Evening schools, T 26.10(B)
  Tuition, T 23.02(E), T 26.10(B)
Exceptional children—See PUPILS, at Gifted children, special classes; SPECIAL EDUCATION.
Exempted village districts—See EXEMPTED VILLAGE SCHOOL DISTRICTS.
Expulsion of pupils—See PUPILS, at Suspension or expulsion.
Extracurricular activities—See PUPILS, at Activity programs.
Federal aid—See FEDERAL AID.
Finances—See FUNDS, SCHOOL.
Financial difficulties, T 41.33
Financial reports—See RECORDS AND REPORTS, SCHOOL.
Fingerprinting program, T 24.16(A), T 44.15(A)
Fire safety—See FIRE SAFETY.
Fiscal officers—See TREASURERS, SCHOOL BOARD.
Fiscal year, T 40.02
Food services—See FOOD SERVICES, SCHOOL.
Foreign exchange students, tuition, T 23.02(C)(12)
Foreign state school districts joining with Ohio school districts, T 4.02
Foundation program, T 2.07, T 39.06 to T 39.08
See also FOUNDATION PROGRAM.
Free education, T 20.01, T 23.01, T 23.02(A)(1)
Funds—See FUNDS, SCHOOL.
Gifted children, special classes—See PUPILS.
Goals 2000: Educate America Act of 1994—See GOALS 2000: EDUCATE AMERICA ACT OF 1994, generally.
Grades, mandatory, T 4.05(A)
Guidance programs—See GUIDANCE AND COUNSELING PROGRAMS.
Handicapped children—See HANDICAPPED CHILDREN, at Schooling.
Hazing, T 24.10
  Liability of school personnel, T 46.10, T 46.14(B)
Health districts, powers and duties—See HEALTH DISTRICTS.
Health services, T 21.01 to T 21.09
Hearing tests—See PUPILS.
High schools—See HIGH SCHOOLS.
Holidays—See HOLIDAYS.
Home education—See HOME EDUCATION.
Home instruction—See HOME INSTRUCTION.
Immunization of pupils—See IMMUNIZATION, at School children.
Industrial schools, T 26.11(B), T Ch 27
See also VOCATIONAL EDUCATION, generally.
Innovative education pilot programs, T 3.03(E)
Inspections—See SCHOOL BUILDINGS AND LANDS.

SCHOOLS AND SCHOOL DISTRICTS—continued

Instructional materials, T 33.03(A)
  See also EQUIPMENT AND SUPPLIES, SCHOOL; TEXTBOOKS.
Insurance—See INSURANCE.
Interstate—See INTERSTATE AGREEMENTS.
Joint educational service centers, T 4.03(C)
  Governing boards, members, T 5.02(A)
Joint high school districts, operation by cooperative education school districts, T 4.03(G)
Joint vocational districts, T 4.03(E), T 27.08 to T 27.12
  See also VOCATIONAL EDUCATION.
Judgments against
  Bond issue to pay, T 41.04, T 41.08
  General tax levy revenues to pay, T 40.09(A)
Junior high schools—See JUNIOR HIGH SCHOOLS.
Kindergartens—See KINDERGARTENS.
Lands—See SCHOOL BUILDINGS AND LANDS.
Lecture programs, T 26.11(C)
Legal advertising by—See NOTICE, generally.
Liability, T 5.07, T Ch 46
  See also LIABILITY, generally; PUBLIC LIABILITY ACT.
Libraries in schools—See LIBRARIES AND LIBRARY DISTRICTS.
Literacy courses, T 26.10(A)
Loans; emergency school advancement fund, from—See EMERGENCY LOANS.
Local control, T 1.09, T 2.15
Local school districts—See LOCAL SCHOOL DISTRICTS.
Mathematics equipment and supplies, private and parochial schools; funding, T 48.06
Medical examination of school children—See PUPILS, at Health.
Medical personnel, employment, T 21.02
Meditation periods, T 32.05
Midwestern education compact, T 2.10
Missing children—See MISSING CHILDREN.
Museums furnishing instructional programs, T 5.09(D), T 26.11(A), T 26.11(C), T 31.05
Musical instruction, T 5.09(D), T 26.11(A), T 31.05
Neighborhood school policy, T 4.05(B), T 19.08
New districts—See REORGANIZATION OF SCHOOL DISTRICTS, at Creation of new districts.
Newsletters, publication by school boards, T 5.09(G), T 31.02
Night schools, T 26.10(B)
  Tuition, T 23.02(E), T 26.10(B)
Noncontiguous districts, T 4.05(B)
Nonpublic schools—See PRIVATE AND PAROCHIAL SCHOOLS.
Nonresident pupils—See PUPILS.
Nonteaching employees—See SCHOOL EMPLOYEES, NONTEACHING.
Nursery schools—See NURSERY SCHOOLS.

SCHOOLS AND SCHOOL DISTRICTS—continued

Nurses employed by—See NURSES AND NURSING.
Ohio education computer network, T 26.11(G)
Parochial schools—See PRIVATE AND PAROCHIAL SCHOOLS.
Part-time schools or classes, T 20.15, T 26.10(C), T 48.04(D)
  Hours of attendance, T 20.05(A)
Payrolls, lack of funds; issuance of tax anticipation notes, T 41.04, T 41.21(A)
Pentamester system, T 20.05(B)
Performance evaluation standards, T 3.03(D)
  Deficient districts, T 3.03(D)(2)
Personal information systems—See PERSONAL INFORMATION SYSTEMS.
Personal property—See EQUIPMENT AND SUPPLIES, SCHOOL.
Photographs of pupils, T 24.16(B), T 44.15(A), T 44.16
Physicians employed by—See PHYSICIANS.
Policy bulletins, publication by school board, T 5.09(G), T 31.02
Political subdivisions, defined as, T 4.01, T 4.02
Polling places, schoolhouses as, T 38.10
Powers, T 1.09, T 2.15
Prayers—See PRAYERS, generally.
Preschools—See NURSERY SCHOOLS.
Principals—See PRINCIPALS.
Private schools—See PRIVATE AND PAROCHIAL SCHOOLS.
Probate courts, powers and duties, T 5.10
Proprietary schools—See PROPRIETARY SCHOOLS.
Psychologists—See PSYCHOLOGISTS AND PSYCHOLOGY, generally.
Pupils—See PUPILS.
Quarterly system, T 20.05(B)
Real property—See SCHOOL BUILDINGS AND LANDS.
Records and reports—See RECORDS AND REPORTS, SCHOOL.
Records commissions, T 44.22, T 44.23
Recreational activities—See PARKS AND RECREATION.
Recreational users, liability of school personnel, T 46.11
Redistricting city districts, T 5.02(B)(2)
  Notice to board of elections, T 6.08(C)
Reference books, purchase, T 33.03(A)
Regional councils, district membership, T 5.09(D)
Religion—See RELIGION, generally.
Reorganization—See REORGANIZATION OF SCHOOL DISTRICTS.
Residence of pupil to determine district, T 23.02(A) to T 23.02(C)
  Incarcerated or institutionalized parent, T 23.02(A)(3)
Revenues—See FUNDS, SCHOOL.
Revocation of charters, T 26.19
School year—See CALENDAR, SCHOOL.

SCHOOLS AND SCHOOL DISTRICTS—*continued*
Search and seizure laws, applicability—See SEARCH AND SEIZURE.
Soliciting charitable contributions in, T 31.08
Special education—See SPECIAL EDUCATION.
Special needs districts, T 41.07
Speech and hearing programs, funding, T 39.08(A)
Standards prescribed by state board of education, T 3.03(B), T 26.01, T 26.02
  Private schools, applicability, T 20.03(A), T 32.02, T 48.03
Students—See PUPILS.
Studies and surveys, T 5.09(A)
Subdistricting city districts, T 5.02(B)(2), T 6.08(C)
  Notification to board of elections, T 6.08(C)
Summer school, T 26.10(A)
Superintendent of public instruction—See SUPERINTENDENT OF PUBLIC INSTRUCTION.
Superintendents, local—See SUPERINTENDENTS, LOCAL.
Supervisors, T 7.09 to T 7.13
Supplies and equipment—See EQUIPMENT AND SUPPLIES, SCHOOL.
Suspension of pupils—See PUPILS.
Taxes and levies—See TAXATION.
Teachers—See TEACHERS.
Testing programs—See TESTING PROGRAMS, SCHOOL.
Textbooks, T Ch 33, T 36.04(A)
  See also TEXTBOOKS.
Tornado drills, T 21.13
Trade schools, T 26.11(B)
  See also VOCATIONAL EDUCATION, generally.
Transcripts—See RECORDS AND REPORTS, SCHOOL, generally.
Transfer of grades within district, powers of board, T 7.06(C)
Transfer of territory—See REORGANIZATION OF SCHOOL DISTRICTS.
Transportation of pupils, T Ch 22
  See also SCHOOL BUSES; TRANSPORTATION OF PUPILS.
Treasurers—See TREASURERS, SCHOOL BOARD.
Trimester system, T 20.05(B)
Truancy—See ATTENDANCE.
Truant officers, T 20.08
  See also ATTENDANCE, at Officers.
Trusts, management, T 39.13, T 42.22, T 43.15(B)
Tubercular children, for, T 28.08(B), T 28.08(C)
  Transportation, T 22.05
Tuberculin testing, T 10.18, T 21.03(C)
Tuition—See TUITION.
Types of school districts, T 2.08, T 4.01, T 4.03
Vacation activities, T 26.11(F), T 30.13

SCHOOLS AND SCHOOL DISTRICTS—*continued*
Village school district, exempted—See EXEMPTED VILLAGE SCHOOL DISTRICTS.
Vision tests—See PUPILS.
Vocational districts, joint, T 4.03(E), T 27.08 to T 27.12
Vocational education—See VOCATIONAL EDUCATION.
Voluntary consolidation of educational service centers, T 4.03(C)
Voter registration, volunteer registrars, T 31.09
Year—See CALENDAR, SCHOOL.

SEARCH AND SEIZURE
Schools, within, T Ch 47
  Drug-detecting dogs, use, T 47.01(C)
  Employee searches by school officials, T 47.01(D)
  Liability for unlawful search, T 47.03
  Locker searches, T 47.02
    Private and parochial schools, T 48.17
  Police involvement, T 47.01(B)
  Privacy expectation, T 47.01(A)
  Private and parochial schools, T 48.17
  Reasonableness of search, T 47.01(A)
  Standards, T 47.01(A)
  Warrantless searches, T 47.01(A)

SEAT BELTS
School buses, T 22.11, T 48.08(B)

SECONDARY SCHOOLS—See HIGH SCHOOLS.

SEGREGATION—See DESEGREGATION OF SCHOOLS; DISCRIMINATION, at Schools, by.

SENIOR CITIZENS—See AGED PERSONS.

SERA, T Ch 18
  See also COLLECTIVE BARGAINING, PUBLIC EMPLOYEES.

SERB—See EMPLOYMENT RELATIONS BOARD.

SERS—See SCHOOL EMPLOYEES RETIREMENT SYSTEM.

SESSIONS, SCHOOL—See CALENDAR, SCHOOL.

SEVERANCE PAY
School employees, T 10.17, T 13.09

SEX DISCRIMINATION—See also DISCRIMINATION, generally.
Athletic events, T 30.09(B)

SEX DISCRIMINATION—*continued*
Constructive discharge theory, T 17.11
Damages, T 19.14(C)
Employment practices, schools, T 19.14
Equal protection clause, applicability, T 19.14(D)
Evidence, T 19.14(C)
Federal aid, termination due to, T 19.13(B), T 19.14
Harassment, T 17.11
  Title IX liability, T 19.14(A)
Intent, T 19.14(C)
Mortality tables, use in calculating retirement annuities, T 17.06(C)(2)
Pregnancy as basis, T 10.20(B), T 17.09
  School pupils, T 19.14(A)
Private schools, by
  Educational programs, T 48.29
  Employment, T 17.03(B), T 48.20, T 48.30
Schools, by, T 19.13(B), T 19.14
  Athletic programs, funding withheld, T 19.14(B)
  Extracurricular activities, funding withheld, T 19.14(B)
Wages, T 17.08, T 48.30

SEX EDUCATION
Parental objections, T 32.07

SEX OFFENSES, T 24.13
Minors, against, T 24.13
Obscenity—See OBSCENITY.
School employees, convictions or guilty pleas, T 5.09(H), T 8.07(A)
  Reporting requirements, T 24.07
Teachers, convictions or guilty pleas, T 5.09(H), T 8.07(A), T 9.21(D)
  Reporting requirements, T 24.07

SEXUAL BATTERY
School employees, by
  Termination, grounds for, T 9.21, T 12.16(A), T 12.17(A)

SHELTERS, BUS
School transportation, designation, T 22.16

SHERIFFS—See LAW ENFORCEMENT OFFICERS.

SICK LEAVE—See particular employee concerned; WAGES AND HOURS.

SIGN LANGUAGE
High school course, T 26.06(A), T 28.18
Private and parochial school courses, T 26.06(A), T 28.18

SINKING FUNDS
Interest earnings, allocation, T 42.22
School districts, T 43.15(B), T 43.19
  Interest, T 43.16

SINKING FUNDS—*continued*
School districts—*continued*
  Transfer of moneys to, T 43.16, T 43.19

SMOKING—See also TOBACCO, generally.
Pro-Children Act of 1994, ban on indoor smoking, T 38.14
School regulations, T 24.15(B)

SNOW REMOVAL, T 38.02

SOCIAL SECURITY
Disability determination bureau of rehabilitation services commission, powers and duties, T 27.13(B)
Teachers, payroll deductions, T 10.08

SOCIAL WORKERS
Child abuse, reporting, T 24.05

SOLICITORS, MUNICIPAL—See now CITY DIRECTORS OF LAW.

SOVEREIGN IMMUNITY, T Ch 46
  See also IMMUNITY FROM PROSECUTION, generally; PUBLIC LIABILITY ACT.

SPECIAL EDUCATION, T Ch 28
Ages of attendance, T 28.01(A)
Appeal from placement, T 28.11(F)
"Appropriate" education, determination, T 28.03, T 28.05(B)
Attendance, T 20.01, T 20.02(C), T 28.17(A)
  Age requirements, T 28.01(A)
  Excused from attendance, T 20.03(B)
Blind persons—See BLIND PERSONS, at Schooling.
Competency tests, T 28.10(B)
Complaints by parents, T 28.11(A)
  Legal actions, T 28.12, T 28.13
Contracts
  Exchange of teachers, T 28.15(B)
  Teachers, T 7.12, T 29.10(B)
Counseling services, T 28.07
County boards of mental retardation and developmental disabilities, programs by—See MENTAL RETARDATION AND DEVELOPMENTAL DISABILITIES BOARDS, COUNTY.
Damage awards, T 28.12, T 28.13
  Attorney fees, limitations, T 28.12(B), T 28.13(D)
  Compensatory education, T 28.13(B)
  Handicapped Children's Protection Act, T 28.12(B), T 28.13(D)
  Individuals with Disabilities Education Act, applicability, T 28.12(A), T 28.13(A)
  Private right of action, T 28.12
  Rehabilitation Act, applicability, T 28.13(C)

SPECIAL EDUCATION—*continued*
Deaf children—See DEAF PERSONS, at Schooling.
Definitions, T 28.01(B)
  Individualized education program, T 28.02
Discrimination, T 28.10
Districts' plans, T 28.14(A)
Expulsion of pupils, T 28.09
Extended school year services, T 28.04
Extracurricular activities, T 28.03
Facilities, T 28.17(B)
Federal requirements, T 28.01 to T 28.10
Foundation program funding, T 28.15(A), T 28.18, T 39.08(A)
"Free appropriate public education", T 28.03, T 28.05(B)
Funding, T 28.15
  Foundation program, T 28.15(A), T 28.18, T 39.08(A)
  Reporting requirements, T 28.14(B)
  Vocational training, T 27.12, T 28.17(A)
Graduation requirements, T 28.10(B)
Handicapped Children's Protection Act, T 28.12(B), T 28.13(D)
Hearing impaired children—See DEAF PERSONS, at Schooling.
Hearings, placement, T 28.11(C) to T 28.11(F)
History in Ohio, T 1.06
Home instruction, T 28.08(A)
Identification and evaluation of children, T 28.11(A), T 28.11(B)
  Notice requirements, T 28.11(B)
Individualized education program, T 28.02
Institutionalized children
  Tuition, T 23.02(D), T 29.09(C)
Intelligence quotient tests, use, T 28.10(A)
Least restrictive environment, T 28.05
"Mainstreaming" requirement, T 28.05, T 28.20(B)
Medical services, T 28.07
  "Supportive" services distinguished, T 28.07
Nonresident pupils
  Room and board, T 28.08(A)
  Tuition, T 23.02(A)(5), T 23.02(A)(7), T 23.02(A)(15), T 23.02(B), T 23.02(D)
    Home instruction, T 28.08(A)
    Per capita reimbursement by school district of residence, T 29.09(C)
Notice of placement in, T 28.11(B)
Parental rights, T 28.11
Placement of pupils, T 28.02, T 29.04(B)
  Appeals, T 28.11(F)
  Notice requirements, T 28.11(B)
Plans, T 28.14(A)
Private schools, T 48.29
  Public funds, T 48.06, T 48.07
Procedural safeguards, T 28.11(A)
Psychological services, T 28.07
Records and reports, T 28.14(B)
Related services, T 28.07
Removal of pupils from school premises, T 28.09
Residency requirements, T 28.15(C)

SPECIAL EDUCATION—*continued*
Residential placement, T 28.06
Room and board, nonresident pupils, T 28.08(A)
Rules, T 28.14(A)
School year, T 28.04
Standards, T 28.03, T 28.14(A)
State board of education, powers and duties, T 3.03(B)
State plan, T 28.14(A)
Superintendent of public instruction to supervise, T 3.06
Supervisors or coordinators
  Funding, T 39.08(C)
"Supportive" services, T 28.07
Suspension of pupils, T 28.09
Tax levies to finance, T 40.10(D)
Teachers
  Contracts, T 7.12, T 29.10(B)
  Exchange between districts, T 28.15(B)
  Qualifications, T 28.16
  Training, T 28.16
Transportation of pupils, T 22.05
  County boards of mental retardation and developmental disabilities providing, T 29.06
  Foundation program funding, T 22.07(B)
  Mental retardation and developmental disabilities board program, T 29.06(B)
Tuition
  County boards of mental retardation and developmental disabilities providing, T 29.09(C)
  Home instruction, T 28.08(A)
  Nonresident pupils, T 23.02(A)(5), T 23.02(A)(7), T 23.02(A)(15), T 23.02(B), T 23.02(D)
    Home instruction, T 28.08(A)
    Per capita reimbursement by school district of residence, T 29.09(C)
    Vocational training, T 23.02(A)(7)
Twenty-four-hour care, T 28.06
Visually handicapped children—See BLIND PERSONS.
Vocational training
  Funding, T 27.12, T 28.17(A)
  Tuition, T 23.02(A)(7)
Year-round programs, T 28.04

SPECIAL MEETINGS, T 5.11(B)

SPECIAL NEEDS DISTRICTS, T 41.07

SPEECH AND HEARING PROGRAMS
Funding, T 39.08(A)

SPEECH PATHOLOGISTS
Child abuse, reporting, T 24.05

SPEED LIMITS
School buses, T 22.18(A)

SPORTS—See also ATHLETIC EVENTS; PHYSICAL EDUCATION; RECREATIONAL PROGRAMS.
Steroid warnings, posting requirement, T 21.15(D), T 48.15

STATE
Agencies—See particular agency concerned.
Departments—See particular department concerned.
Retirement systems—See particular system concerned.
Segregation of schools, liability, T 19.09

STATE ADMINISTRATION OF EDUCATION, T Ch 3
    See also EDUCATION DEPARTMENT; EDUCATION, STATE BOARD.

STATE AID—See APPROPRIATIONS; FOUNDATION PROGRAM.

STATE BOARD OF EDUCATION—See EDUCATION, STATE BOARD.

STATE EMPLOYMENT RELATIONS BOARD—See EMPLOYMENT RELATIONS BOARD.

STATE LIBRARY, T 34.05 to T 34.08
    See also LIBRARIES AND LIBRARY DISTRICTS.

STATE MINIMUM STANDARDS, T 3.03(B)

STATE SCHOOLS FOR THE BLIND AND THE DEAF, T 28.19

STATE TEACHERS RETIREMENT SYSTEM, T Ch 11
    See also TEACHERS RETIREMENT SYSTEM.

STATE UNIVERSITIES AND COLLEGES—See UNIVERSITIES AND COLLEGES, STATE.

STATUTES
Common law, T 2.15
Judicial review, T 2.16
Limitations—See LIMITATION OF ACTIONS.

STEROIDS
Posting warnings in locker rooms, T 21.15(D), T 48.15

STOCKS AND STOCKHOLDERS
Public depositories, conflict of interest, T 42.12

STREETS
School guards, T 21.11(A)

STREETS—*continued*
Traffic control—See TRAFFIC CONTROL.

STRIKES
Public employees—See COLLECTIVE BARGAINING, PUBLIC EMPLOYEES.

STRS—See TEACHERS RETIREMENT SYSTEM.

STUDENT LOANS
Guaranteed program
    Participation required for eligibility as public depository, T 42.05(A)

STUDENT RECORDS PRIVACY ACT, T 44.01, T 44.14 to T 44.16

STUDENTS—See PUPILS.

SUBPOENAS
Student records disclosure, T 44.14(C), T 44.15(B)

SUBSTITUTE TEACHERS—See TEACHERS.

SUMMER SCHOOL, T 26.10(A)
Tuition, T 23.02(E)

SUNSHINE LAW
Failure to comply, effect, T 5.12(D)
Injunctions to compel school board compliance, T 5.12(D)
Library boards, applicability to, T 34.09(C)
Public employees collective bargaining
    Meetings exempt, T 18.27
School boards, applicability to, T 5.12, T 31.01
    Exemption, T 5.12

SUPERINTENDENT OF PUBLIC INSTRUCTION, T 3.05, T 3.06
    See also EDUCATION DEPARTMENT, generally.
Adjudication orders excluding students convicted or adjudicated delinquent, issuance, T 3.06
Adviser to school districts, as, T 3.06
Appointment, T 1.09, T 3.05
Assistants, T 3.07(A)
Closure of schools, powers, T 40.18(C)
Compensation, T 3.05
Conflict of interest, T 3.05, T 45.08(A)
    Financial interest in book publishing or selling concern, T 45.07
Emergency loans, powers and duties, T 3.06, T 41.33(C), T 41.33(E)
Ethics, T Ch 45
    See also ETHICS, generally.
Financial condition of school districts, powers and duties, T 41.33(E)

SUPERINTENDENT OF PUBLIC INSTRUCTION—*continued*
Permanent exclusion of children from school
    Powers and duties, T 25.10(E)
Powers and duties, T 2.09, T 3.04(C), T 3.05, T 3.06, T 3.07(B)
    Delegation of state board powers to superintendent, T 3.03(G)
Records and reports, T 3.04(B), T 3.06
School district loans to avoid financial closing, duties, T 41.33(C), T 41.33(E)
Secretary of state board of education, as, T 3.06
Special needs districts, powers and duties, T 41.07
Studies and research projects by, T 3.06
Teachers retirement board, membership, T 11.02(A)
Vocational education, evaluation, T 27.09(C)

SUPERINTENDENTS, LOCAL, T 7.02 to T 7.08
Age and schooling certificates, duties regarding, T 20.13(A), T 20.13(C)
Appointment, T 7.02, T 7.04
Assistants, T 7.09, T 7.09(B)
    Civil service status, T 12.04(A)(1)
Attendance, excusing
    Home education or home instruction request, T 20.03(A)
Certificates, T 7.03
    Permanent, T 7.03(B)(3)
    Professional, T 7.03(B)(2)
    Provisional, T 7.03(B)(1)
Civil service status, T 12.04(A)(1)
Collective bargaining exclusion, T 18.05(B)
Compensation, T 7.05(B)
Conference facilities, T 7.08
Contract of employment, T 7.05(A)
    Notice of nonrenewal, T 7.04(B)
    Termination, T 7.05(A)
Cooperative education school districts, T 4.03(G)
County commissioners to furnish and equip offices for educational service center governing boards, T 7.08, T 36.07
Employment status, T 7.05(A)
Ethics, T Ch 45
    See also ETHICS, generally.
Evaluation, T 7.14(A)
Expenses paid by school board, T 7.05(B)
Financial in-service training, T 5.09(F)
Incapacitation, T 7.07
Joint vocational school districts, T 7.04(D), T 27.09(B), T 29.09(C)
    Compensation, T 7.05(B)
    Powers, T 7.06(A)
Leaves of absence, T 7.05(A), T 7.07
Liability insurance, T 46.19
Nomination, T 7.04(C)
Nonrenewal of employment contract, T 7.04(B)
Notice of intention not to reemploy, T 7.04(B)
Offices, T 7.08
    Educational service center governing boards, county commissioners to furnish and equip for, T 7.08, T 36.07

SUPERINTENDENTS, LOCAL—*continued*
Permanent certificates, T 7.03(B)(3)
Permanent exclusion of pupil, powers and duties, T 25.10(E)
Powers and duties, T 7.02, T 7.06
    Cooperative education school districts, T 4.03(G)
Pro tempore, T 7.07
Professional certificates, T 7.03(B)(2)
Provisional certificates, T 7.03(B)(1)
Publisher's or supplier's sales agent, as, T 8.07(B), T 33.05, T 45.07
Pupil suspension or expulsion, powers and duties, T 25.10
Qualifications, T 7.03
Reemployment, T 7.04(B)
Resignation, T 7.05(A)
School attendance boundaries, redrawing, T 7.06(C)
Sick leave, T 7.05(A)
Telephone equipment provided by county commissioners, T 7.08
Temporary, T 7.07
Term, T 7.04(A)
Termination of contract, T 7.05(A)
Township trustee serving as, compatibility, T 45.08(A)
Transfer of, T 7.04(A)
Traveling expenses, T 7.05(B)
Vacancy, T 7.04(E)
Vacation leave, T 7.05(A)

SUPPLEMENTAL CONTRACTS
Nonteaching school employees, T 12.09(G)
Teachers—See TEACHERS.

SUPPLIES, SCHOOL—See EQUIPMENT AND SUPPLIES, SCHOOL.

SUPREME COURT, UNITED STATES
Desegregation guidelines, T 19.03, T 19.12

SURETY BONDS—See BONDS, SURETY.

SURVIVING SPOUSES
Workers' compensation benefits, T 16.05(G)

SUSPENSION
Pupils—See PUPILS.
Teachers—See TEACHERS.

SYMPHONY ASSOCIATIONS
Financial support, T 31.05

TAX ANTICIPATION NOTES, T 41.04, T 41.16(B)
    See also BONDS AND NOTES, generally.
Classroom facility projects, T 41.30
Emergency school levies approved, T 41.22
Excess levies approved, T 41.22

TAX ANTICIPATION NOTES—*continued*
Joint vocational school districts issuing, T 27.10(A), T 41.23(A), T 41.23(C)
Schools issuing, T 41.21, T 41.22
  Additional notes, T 41.22
  Classroom facility projects, T 41.30
  Emergency school levy approved, T 41.22
  Exceptions due to lack of payroll funds, T 41.04, T 41.21(A)
  Excess levy approved, T 41.22
  Joint vocational school districts issuing, T 27.10(A), T 41.23(A), T 41.23(C)

TAX APPEALS BOARD
Appeals to
  Taxing authority, by, T 40.06

TAXATION
Abatements, T 39.04
Anticipation notes—See TAX ANTICIPATION NOTES.
Bonds and notes exempt
  Arbitrage bonds excluded, T 41.19(B)
    Rebates, T 41.19(C)
  Qualified tax-exempt obligations, T 41.19(D)
  Sale proceeds, use, T 41.19(C)
Budgets, T 40.01 to T 40.06
Classroom facility project levies, T 41.27(B), T 41.28, T 41.32
Collection, T 41.15
Debt service levies, T 41.15
Emergency school levies, T 40.10(B), T 40.13, T 41.22
Estate tax
  Revenues, distribution, T 39.11
Excess levies, T 40.01 to T 40.12
  Anticipation notes, issuance, T 41.22
  Emergency school levy, T 40.10(B), T 40.13, T 41.22
  Joint vocational school district levy, T 27.10(A), T 27.11, T 41.23
  Libraries, T 34.16
  School districts
    Emergency levy, T 40.10(B), T 40.13, T 41.22
    Special education levy, T 40.10(D)
  Special education levy, T 40.10(D)
Exemptions—See also particular tax or item concerned.
  Abatements, T 39.04
  Notice to school board, T 39.04
  Private schools, T 48.31 to T 48.33
General levies, purpose and intent, T 40.09(A)
Income taxes—See INCOME TAXES.
Inheritance tax, T 39.11
Joint vocational school district levies, T 27.10(A), T 27.11, T 41.23
Levies, T 39.02 to T 39.04
  Certification, T 39.07(C), T 40.07
  Collection, T 41.15
  Division, T 40.08
  Excess—See Excess levies, this heading.
  General, purpose and intent, T 40.09(A)

TAXATION—*continued*
Levies—*continued*
  Minimum, T 39.03
  Public funds used to oppose or support, T 5.09(F)
  Reduction, T 39.03, T 40.14
  Resolution for, T 40.07
  Ten-mill limitation—See Ten-mill limitation, this heading.
Liability insurance pools, exemption, T 46.18(A)
Libraries, financing—See LIBRARIES AND LIBRARY DISTRICTS.
Mental health and retardation services levies, T 29.09(A)
Personal property—See PERSONAL PROPERTY, TAXATION.
Power to tax, T 39.02
Private schools exempt, T 48.31 to T 48.33
Public utilities, supplemental assessment, T 39.04
Real property—See REAL PROPERTY, TAXATION.
Revenues
  Collection, T 41.15
  School foundation program, funding—See FOUNDATION PROGRAM.
Sales tax—See SALES TAX.
Schools, financing, T 1.09, T 39.02 to T 39.04, T 40.07 to T 40.13
  Abatements, T 39.04
  Additional levies, T 40.10(C)
  Allocation of tax proceeds to wrong district, restitution, T 39.05
  Anticipation notes—See TAX ANTICIPATION NOTES.
  Authority to levy taxes, T 39.02, T 43.15(A)
  Certification, T 39.07, T 40.07
  Classroom facilities, T 41.27(B), T 41.28, T 41.32
  Collection, T 39.05
  Creation of new local district, effect, T 4.14
  Debt service, T 41.15
  Emergency school levy, T 40.10, T 40.13, T 41.22
  Estate and inheritance taxes, T 39.11
  Excess levies, T 40.01 to T 40.12
    Emergency levy, T 41.22
  First tax levy, T 1.05
  Foundation program, to fund—See FOUNDATION PROGRAM.
  General levy, T 40.09(A), T 43.17
  Income tax—See INCOME TAXES.
  Incremental tax levies, T 40.10(C)
  Joint vocational school district levy, T 27.10(A), T 27.11, T 41.23
  Permanent improvement levy, T 43.21
  Property valuation and exemption, notice to school board, T 39.04
  Renewal levies, T 40.11
    Joint vocational school districts, T 27.11, T 41.23(B)
  Reorganization of school district, effect, T 4.14, T 39.03, T 40.06

TAXATION—*continued*
Schools, financing—*continued*
  Replacement tax levies, T 40.12
  Sinking funds, T 43.15(B), T 43.19
  Special education levies, T 40.10(D)
  Special levy, T 40.09(B)
  Tax budget, T 40.01 to T 40.06
    See also BUDGETS, SCHOOL.
  Ten-mill limitation, T 39.03
Special education levies, T 40.10(D)
Special levies, T 40.09(B)
  Library purposes, T 34.16
Ten-mill limitation, T 39.03, T 41.05(B)
  Excess levies—See Excess levies, this heading.

TAXING DISTRICTS—See also particular district or subdivision concerned.
Accounts and accounting, T 43.26
Bonds and notes—See BONDS AND NOTES, generally.
Budgets—See BUDGETS, generally.
Buildings and grounds—See BUILDINGS AND GROUNDS, generally.
Debts—See DEBTS, generally.
Employees—See PUBLIC EMPLOYEES.
Funds—See FUNDS, PUBLIC.
Officials—See particular office concerned; PUBLIC OFFICIALS.
Records and reports—See RECORDS AND REPORTS, generally.
Regional councils, T 5.09(D)
Sinking funds—See SINKING FUNDS.
Tax anticipation notes—See TAX ANTICIPATION NOTES.

TEACHERS, T Ch 8 to T Ch 11
  See also PUBLIC EMPLOYEES, generally.
Actions against, defense and indemnification, T 46.04
Administrative personnel
  Employment as, T 7.13, T 9.07(A)(2)
    Civil service status, effect, T 7.09(A)
  Status as teachers, T 8.02(A), T 9.07(A)(2)
AIDS, afflicted with, T 21.03(D), T 21.03(E)
  See also AIDS, generally.
Appeal from contract termination, T 9.23
Assault leave, T 10.21(B)
Assignment to school
  Discrimination, T 19.11(B)
  Superintendent, by, T 7.06(B)(1)
Associations
  Attendance at meetings, T 10.09(C)
  Collective bargaining agreements—See COLLECTIVE BARGAINING, PUBLIC EMPLOYEES, at Employee organizations, generally.
Certificates, T Ch 8
  Braille, reading and writing, T 3.03(G), T 28.16
  Education and experience requirements, T 8.06
  Forfeiture, T 8.07(B), T 33.05, T 45.07
  Grades, T 8.01, T 8.04

TEACHERS—*continued*
Certificates—*continued*
  Internship, T 8.04(F)
  Interstate agreements, T 8.03(C)
  Life certificates, T 8.04(E)
  Non-tax supported schools, T 48.21
  Noncertified teachers, employment, T 8.03(A)
  Notification of certificate holder's conviction, T 24.07
  Permanent, T 8.04(E)
  Professional, T 8.04(D)
  Provisional, T 8.04(C)
  Records required of school district, T 44.12
  Required, T 6.08(A), T 8.01, T 8.03(A)
  Revocation or suspension, T 8.01, T 8.07
    Crimes or offenses, due to, T 8.07(A)
    Reinstatement, T 8.07(D)
  Standards, T 8.03(B)
    Braille, reading and writing, T 3.03(G), T 28.16
  Temporary certificates, T 8.04(A)
  Types, T 8.01, T 8.05
  Vocational, T 8.04(B)
Charitable contributions, payroll deductions, T 10.08, T 31.08
Child abuse
  Prevention, in-service training, T 21.14
  Reporting, T 24.05
  Sexual battery of students
    Termination, grounds for, T 9.21
Children of, tuition-free education, T 23.02(C)(9)
City council member as, T 45.08(A)
Civil rights, T 46.14(A)(2)
Civil service classification, T 12.04(A)(1)
  See also CIVIL SERVICE, generally.
Collective bargaining—See COLLECTIVE BARGAINING, PUBLIC EMPLOYEES, generally.
Communicable diseases, T 10.18, T 13.10, T 21.03(D), T 21.03(E)
Compensation, T 10.01 to T 10.08
  Alternative schedules dependent upon contingent revenues, T 6.07(C)(2)
  Bonuses, T 10.01(C)
    Longevity of tenure, T 43.05(B)
  Closure of school, effect, T 10.09(A)
  Contract provisions, T 10.01(A)
  Deductions—See Payroll deductions, this heading.
  Deferred compensation plan, T 11.23
  Direct deposit, T 43.10
  Foundation program prerequisite, T 39.07(C)
  Fringe benefits, T 35.04(A), T 43.05(B)
  Increasing and decreasing, T 10.01
  Jury duty, T 10.09(B)
  Limitation of actions
    Overpayment, recovery, T 10.07(B)
    Underpayment, recovery, T 10.07(A)
  Militia reserves training, T 10.21(A)
  Notice, T 10.01(A)
  Overpayments, T 10.07
  Payment procedure, T 43.10

TEACHERS—*continued*
Compensation—*continued*
  Professional development and meetings, T 10.09(C)
  Records, T 43.14, T 44.12
  Reduction, T 10.01(B)
    Retirement system contributions paid by employer, T 11.10(B)
  Schedule, T 10.02 to T 10.05
  Service credit, T 10.03, T 10.04
  Severance pay, T 10.17
  Substitute teachers, T 9.15(B)
  Supplemental
    Payment from extracurricular athletic fees, T 23.04(B)
  Training credit, T 10.02(A), T 10.05
  Underpayments, T 10.07
  Withholding payment, T 6.08(A), T 10.06
Conduct, drugs and alcohol standards, T 21.15(A)
Conferences with parents, T 20.05(A), T 20.05(B), T 31.03, T 48.04(B)
Conflict of interest, sales agent of publisher or supplier, T 8.07(B), T 33.05, T 45.07
Constitutionally protected conduct, T 9.21(E)
Continuing contracts, T 9.02, T 9.04 to T 9.09
  Application for, contractual requirement invalid, T 9.05(B)
  Certificate requirement, T 9.06
  Due process rights, T 46.14(A)(2)
  Eligibility for, T 8.04(D)(1), T 8.04(E), T 9.05 to T 9.08
  Notice, T 9.05(B)
  House bill 330, T 9.09(A)
  Mandatory, T 9.09(B)
  Notice to school board of certification, T 9.05(B)
  Service requirement, T 9.08
  Suspension, reduction in force, T 9.19
  Teaching requirement, T 9.07
  Waiver, T 9.09(E)
Contracts, T Ch 9
  Breach by teacher, T 8.07(C)
  Collective bargaining—See COLLECTIVE BARGAINING, PUBLIC EMPLOYEES, at Agreements.
  Compensation provisions, T 10.01(A)
  Continuing—See Continuing contracts, this heading.
  Exchange teachers, T 9.16
  Extended limited—See Extended limited contracts, this heading.
  Limited—See Limited contracts, this heading.
  Nepotism in hiring, T 9.03
  Oral contracts prohibited, T 9.01
  Private schools, T 48.19
  Required, T 9.01(A)
  Special education teachers, T 7.12
  Substitutes, T 9.15
  Supplemental—See Supplemental contracts, this heading.
  Suspension—See Suspension, this heading.
  Termination—See Termination, this heading.

TEACHERS—*continued*
Contracts—*continued*
  Terms of contract, T 9.01(B)
  Types, T 9.02
Convictions—See Criminal convictions, this heading.
Corporal punishment, administering—See PUPILS, at Corporal punishment.
Crimes against children, reporting, T 24.05, T 24.06(A), T 24.08
Criminal background checks of applicants, T 5.09(H)
  Preschool programs, T 5.09(C)
  Private and parochial schools, T 48.19
Criminal convictions
  Certificate suspension or revocation, T 8.07(A)
  Employment applicants, T 5.09(H), T 8.07(A)
  Reporting, T 24.07
Deferred compensation plan, T 11.23
Definitions, T 8.02
  Years of service, T 10.03(A)
Disability benefit, T 11.16, T 11.17
  Leave of absence, as, T 11.17
  Unused sick leave, payment for, T 10.17(A), T 11.16(B)
Disability leave, T 10.20
  Adoption of state standards, T 10.14
  Retirement system contributions during, T 11.07(B), T 11.09
Disabled children, qualifications to teach, T 28.16
Disciplinary actions against, T 9.21, T 9.22
Discipline, maintaining, T 25.06
Discrimination against, T 19.11(B), T 46.14(D)
  See also EMPLOYMENT DISCRIMINATION, generally.
Dismissal—See Termination, this heading.
Disqualification from employment, conviction of certain crimes, T 5.09(H)
Driver training instructors, T 26.12(B), T 26.13(D)
Drug offense convictions or guilty pleas, T 5.09(H), T 8.07(A), T 9.21(D)
  Reporting requirements, T 24.07
Education
  Loan program, T 5.09(K)
  Phonics, in-service training, T 3.03(G)
  Vocational education, federal aid, T 27.04
Education loan programs, T 5.09(K)
Educational aides—See AIDES, EDUCATIONAL.
Employment, T 5.08(B), T 8.01, T 8.08, T 8.09
  Contracts—See Contracts, this heading.
  Qualifications—See Qualifications, this heading.
Ethics, T Ch 45
  See also ETHICS, generally.
Evaluations
  Limited and extended limited contracts, T 9.13(A)
  Peer review plan, T 18.19(B)
Exchange of services between districts, T 9.16, T 28.15(B)

TEACHERS—*continued*
Extended limited contracts, T 9.02, T 9.09(C)
  Nonrenewal, T 9.24
    Evaluation procedures, T 9.13(A)
    Hearings, T 9.13(C)
    Notice, T 9.13(B)
Eye protective devices, T 21.12
Failure to instruct or improper instruction, T 24.03(D)(1)
Fair Labor Standards Act, equal pay, T 17.08
"Fair use" in using textbooks, T 33.06(B)
Felony convictions or guilty pleas, T 5.09(H), T 8.07(A), T 9.21(D)
  Reporting requirements, T 24.07
Forfeiture of certificates, T 8.07(B), T 33.05, T 45.07
Fractional days worked, computation for salary schedule, T 10.03(B)
Freedom of speech, T 46.14(C)
Fringe benefits, T 35.04(A), T 43.05(B)
Gross inefficiency as grounds for termination, T 9.21(A)
Guidance counselors, status as teachers, T 8.02(B), T 9.07(A)(3)
Health examinations, T 21.03(D)
Health insurance, T 10.10 to T 10.12
  Extended coverage, T 10.12
  Retirement system providing, T 11.20
Hearings
  Certificate revocation or suspension, T 8.07(A)
  Contract terminations, T 9.22(B) to T 9.22(F)
    Pretermination hearing, T 9.22(A)
  Nonrenewal of contract
    Extended limited contracts, T 9.13(C)
Immorality as grounds for termination, T 9.21(B)
In loco parentis, applicability of doctrine, T 25.06
Insurance, T 10.10 to T 10.12
  Liability, T 5.07, T 46.19
  Life insurance, T 10.10, T 10.11
    Payroll deduction of premiums, T 10.08
  Payroll deductions for premiums, T 10.08
  Retirement system providing, T 11.20
Internship
  Certificates, T 8.04(F)
Interstate agreements, qualifications, T 8.03(C)
Jury duty, compensation, T 10.09(B)
Layoffs, T 9.19
    See also CIVIL SERVICE, at Layoffs.
Leaves of absence, T 10.19 to T 10.21
  Adoption of state standards, T 10.14
  Assault leave, T 10.21(B)
  Disability leave—See Disability leave, this heading.
  Family and Medical Leave Act of 1993, T 17.16
    Private schools, applicability, T 48.30
  Illness or disability—See Sick leave, this heading.
  Military leave, T 10.21(A)
  Personal leave, T 10.21(C)
    Adoption of state standards, T 10.14
  Pregnancy and child care, T 10.20(B)
  Professional improvement, T 10.19

TEACHERS—*continued*
Leaves of absence—*continued*
  Retirement system membership, effect on—See TEACHERS RETIREMENT SYSTEM, at Leaves of absence.
  Return to service, T 10.19
  Sick leave—See Sick leave, this heading.
  Unauthorized, grounds for termination, T 9.21(A), T 10.19
Liability, T 5.07, T 46.03
    See also PUBLIC LIABILITY ACT.
  Civil rights violations, T 46.15(B), T 46.15(C)
  Criminal law, T 24.02(B)
  Due care requirement, T 24.03
  In loco parentis doctrine, T 24.02
  Insurance, T 5.07, T 46.19
  Qualified immunity, T 46.15(C)
Life certificates, T 8.04(E)
Life insurance, T 10.10, T 10.11
  Payroll deduction of premiums, T 10.08
Limited contracts, T 9.02, T 9.10 to T 9.16
  Change in contract terms, T 9.12
  Duration, T 9.10(B)
  Extended limited contracts—See Extended limited contracts, this heading.
  Nonrenewal, T 9.10 to T 9.131, T 9.24
    Board's liability for improper nonrenewal, T 46.08
    Change in contract terms, T 9.12
    Due process rights, T 46.14(A)(2)
    Evaluation procedures, T 9.13(A)
    Hearings, T 9.13(C)
    Limitation of actions, T 17.10
    Notice of—See Notice of nonrenewal, this subheading.
    Reduction in force, T 9.19
    Reemployment despite superintendent's recommendation, T 9.10(C)
    Substitute teachers, T 9.15(C)
  Notice of nonrenewal, T 9.11, T 9.13(B)
    Burden of proof, T 9.11(D)
    Evasion of service, T 9.11(B)
    Form, T 9.11(C)
    Time of notice, T 9.11(A)
    Required, T 9.10(A)
    Substitute teachers, T 9.15
    Waiver of rights, T 9.10(D)
Loans for education, T 5.09(K)
Lunch periods, T 10.09(D)
Lunches, school board providing, T 35.04(A), T 43.05(B)
Maternity leave, T 10.20(B)
Negligence
  Breach of duty of due care, T 24.03(D)
  Duty of care requirement, T 24.03
  Foreseeability of risk, T 24.03(C)
Nepotism in hiring, T 9.03
Nomination, T 8.08
Noncertified teachers
  Employment, T 8.03(A)

TEACHERS—*continued*
Notice
  Nonrenewal, T 9.11
    Extended limited contracts, T 9.13(B)
    Limited contracts—See Limited contracts, at Notice of nonrenewal, this heading.
  Termination, T 9.22(A)
Number of teachers, T 2.04
Nurses, status as teachers, T 8.02(B), T 9.07(A)(3)
Parent-teacher conferences, T 20.05(A), T 20.05(B), T 31.03, T 48.04(B)
Parochial schools—See PRIVATE AND PAROCHIAL SCHOOLS.
Part-time
  Continuing contract eligibility, T 9.08(C)
  Employment after retirement, T 11.22
  Retirement system contributions, T 11.13(C)
  Sick leave, T 10.13(B)
Partial suspension of contract, T 9.20(G)
Payroll deductions, T 10.08
  Charitable contributions, T 31.08
  Life insurance, T 10.08
  Retirement system contributions, T 10.08, T 11.07(A), T 11.08(A)
Peer review plan, T 18.19(B)
Permanent certificates, T 8.04(E)
Personal leaves of absence, T 10.21(C)
  Adoption of state standards, T 10.14
Personnel records, T 17.17, T 39.09(D), T 44.12
  Payroll, T 43.14, T 44.12
Phonics instruction, T 3.03(G)
Physical education teachers, T 30.05
Political contributions, payroll deductions, T 10.08
Powers and duties
  Maintaining discipline, T 25.06
  Protection of students, T Ch 24
  Supplemental, T 9.14
Pregnancy leave, T 10.20(B)
Pregnancy, resignation due to; purchase of retirement system service credit, T 11.08(A)
Private schools—See PRIVATE AND PAROCHIAL SCHOOLS.
Professional certificates, T 8.04(D)
Professional development
  Compensation and expenses, T 10.09(C)
  Leave of absence, T 10.19
Professional meetings, T 10.09(C)
  Compensation and expenses, T 10.09(C)
  Days allotted for, T 20.05(A), T 20.05(B)
Provisional certificates, T 8.04(C)
Publisher's or supplier's sales agent, as, T 8.07(B), T 33.05, T 45.07
Qualifications, T 8.03
  See also Education, this heading.
  Certification—See Certificates, this heading.
  Interstate agreements, T 8.03(C)
  Noncertified teachers, employment, T 8.03(A)
  Testing programs, validity, T 17.07(A)
Reassignment, T 7.06(B)(1)

TEACHERS—*continued*
Records and reports
  Concerning teachers, T 17.17, T 39.09(D), T 44.12
  Payroll, T 43.14, T 44.12
Required of teachers
  Failure to make, T 6.08(A), T 10.06
  Withdrawal of pupil, T 20.10
Reduction in force, T 9.19
Reemployment, T 8.09, T 9.09(D)
  Retirement, after, T 11.22
Referee for contract termination hearings, T 9.22(E)
Reinstatement after reduction in force, T 9.19(F)
Religious tests, prohibition, T 32.05
Resignation, T 9.17
  Acceptance by employer, T 9.17
  Unemployment compensation, T 15.07
Retirement, T 9.18, T 11.18 to T 11.23, T 17.06(C)
  Disability benefit, T 11.16, T 11.17
  Incentive plans, T 11.21
    Cash payments, T 43.05(B)
  Part-time service permitted, T 11.22
  Reemployment after, T 11.22
  Severance pay, T 10.17
  Unused sick leave, payment for, T 10.17
Retirement system, T Ch 11
    See also TEACHERS RETIREMENT SYSTEM.
Rights, constitutional protection, T 9.21(E)
Safety precautions inadequate, T 24.03(D)(3)
Salaries—See Compensation, this heading.
School board member, serving as, T 45.08(A)
School closure, effect on, T 10.09(A), T 10.11
Sex offense convictions or guilty pleas, T 5.09(H), T 8.07(A), T 9.21(D)
  Reporting requirements, T 24.07
Sexual battery of students by
  Termination, grounds for, T 9.21
Sick leave, T 10.13 to T 10.18
  Accumulation, T 10.13
  Adoption of state standards, T 10.14
  Advance, T 10.15
  Beyond minimum standard, T 43.05(B)
  Communicable disease, T 10.18
  Payment for unused, T 10.17
  Substitutes, T 10.13(B)
  Transfer of credit, T 10.13(C)
  Uniform administration, T 10.13(D)
  Unused, T 10.13(C)
    Payment for, T 10.17
  Use, T 10.16
Special education—See SPECIAL EDUCATION.
State schools for blind and deaf, T 28.19(A)
Student teachers
  Transportation costs, T 43.05(D)
Substitutes
  Collective bargaining exclusion, T 18.07
  Compensation, T 9.15(B)
  Continuing contract service requirement, T 9.08(D)

TEACHERS—*continued*
Substitutes—*continued*
  Contracts, T 9.15
  Educational service center governing board member, incompatible office, T 45.08(A)
  Reemployment, T 9.15(C)
  Retirement system membership, T 11.04(A)
  Service credit, T 10.03(B)
  Sick leave, T 10.13(B)
  Status as teachers, T 8.02(C)
  Supplemental contracts, T 9.15(E)
Supervision
  Inadequate, T 24.03(D)(2)
Supervisors
  Public employee classification, exemption, T 18.05(B)
Supplemental contracts, T 9.02, T 9.14
  Coaches and trainers, T 9.14(C)
  Reemployment, T 9.14(B)
  Substitute teachers, T 9.15(E)
Suspension
  Certificates—See Certificates, at subheading Revocation or suspension, this heading.
  Disciplinary reasons, for, T 9.20
  Pending final board action to terminate contract, T 9.22(A), T 9.22(F)
    Hearings, due process rights, T 46.14(A)(2)
  Reduction in force, T 9.19
  Unemployment compensation, disqualification, T 15.08
Tax sheltered annuities, T 11.23
Temporary certificates, T 8.04(A)
Tenure, T 9.04 to T 9.09
    See also Continuing contracts, this heading.
  Interstate agreements, effect, T 8.03(C)
Termination, T 9.17 to T 9.23, T 9.25
  Appeals, T 9.23
  Board decision to accept or reject referee's recommendations, T 9.22(F)
  Cause for, T 9.21, T 9.22, T 25.02, T 25.06
  Civil procedure rules, applicability, T 9.22(D)
  Constitutionally protected conduct, T 9.21(E)
  Freedom of speech, T 46.14(C)
  Gross inefficiency as grounds, T 9.21(A)
  Grounds to be stated, T 9.22(A)
  Hearings, T 9.22(B) to T 9.22(F)
    Pretermination, T 9.22(A)
  Immorality as grounds, T 9.21(B)
  Involuntary, continuation of group medical insurance coverage, T 10.12
  Notice of intention, T 9.22(A)
  "Other good and just cause", T 9.21(D)
  Private schools, T 48.25
  Referee, T 9.22(E)
  Resignation, T 9.17
  Retirement, T 9.18, T 11.18(B)
  Sexual battery of students, T 9.21
  Unemployment compensation, disqualification, T 15.08
  Unused sick leave, payment for, T 10.17
  Willful and persistent violations, T 9.21(C)

TEACHERS—*continued*
Theft convictions or guilty pleas, T 5.09(H), T 8.07(A), T 9.21(D)
  Reporting requirements, T 24.07
Transfer to another position, T 7.06(B)(1)
Tuberculin tests, T 21.03(C)
Tutors, status as teachers, T 8.02(B), T 9.07(A)(3)
Unemployment compensation, T Ch 15
    See also UNEMPLOYMENT COMPENSATION, generally.
Vocational education—See VOCATIONAL EDUCATION.
Waiver of rights, T 9.09(E)
Whistleblowers, protection, T 9.21(F)
Workers' compensation, T Ch 16
    See also WORKERS' COMPENSATION, generally.
Years of service, defined, T 10.03(A)

TEACHERS RETIREMENT SYSTEM, T Ch 11
Allowance—See Benefits, this heading.
Annuity and pension reserve fund, T 11.03(A)
  Trustee, T 11.03(B)
Benefits, T 11.16 to T 11.26
  Additional, T 11.19(B)
  Amount, T 11.19
  Computation, T 11.19(B), T 11.19(C)
  Cost-of-living adjustment, T 11.19(B)
  Increase based on consumer price index, T 11.19(B)
  Lump sum payment, T 11.24(A)
  Multiple memberships, determination, T 11.12(B)
  Payment—See Payment of benefits, this heading.
  Retirement, T 11.18 to T 11.23
  Supplemental, T 11.19(B)
  Survivors, T 11.24 to T 11.26
    See also Survivors' benefits, this heading.
Board, T 11.02
  Conflict of interest, T 11.02(B)
  Members, T 11.02(A)
    Compensation, T 11.02(A)
    Conflict of interest, T 11.02(B)
  Powers and duties, T 11.02(C)
Contributions, T 11.07 to T 11.11
  Additional
    Employers, by, T 11.10
    Members, by, T 11.08(B)
  Certification, T 11.06
  Denial of right, T 11.04(B)
  Disability leave, during, T 11.07(B), T 11.09
  Duplicate statement to secretary of board, T 11.06
  Employers, by, T 11.09
    Additional, T 11.10
  Fringe benefit pickup, T 11.10(A)
  Mandatory contributions by members, T 11.07(A)
  Multiple system memberships, T 11.12(B)
  Part-time teachers, T 11.13(C)
  Payroll deduction plans, T 11.13(D)

TEACHERS RETIREMENT SYSTEM—*continued*
Contributions—*continued*
  Salary reduction pickup plans, T 11.10(B)
  School boards, by, T 11.09
  Teachers, by, T 10.08, T 11.07, T 11.08
  Transmitted monthly, T 11.06
  Voluntary contributions by members, T 11.08
  Withdrawal, T 11.11
    Redeposit, T 11.13(B)
Cost-of-living adjustment, T 11.19(B)
Death, payments to survivors, T 11.24 to T 11.26
Deductions from pay—See Contributions, this heading.
Denial of membership or right to contribute, T 11.04(B)
Disability benefit
  Eligibility, T 11.16
  Medical examination, T 11.16(A)
  Service credit upon return to employment, T 11.17
  Termination, T 11.17
  Unused sick leave, payment for, T 11.16(B)
Disability leave, contributions during, T 11.07(B), T 11.09
Early retirement incentive plans, T 11.21
Employers' contribution, T 11.09
  Additional, T 11.10
Employers' trust fund, T 11.03(A)
  Trustee, T 11.03(B)
Establishment, T 11.01
Expense fund, T 11.03(A)
Foreign service credit, T 11.13(A)
Funds, T 11.03
  Expense fund, T 11.03(A)
    Trustee, T 11.03(B)
  Guarantee fund, T 11.03(A)
    Trustee, T 11.03(B)
Health insurance, T 11.20
Incentive plan, T 11.21
  Cash payments, T 43.05(B)
Indemnification of board members and employees, T 11.02(A)
Investments permissible, T 11.03(B)
Leaves of absence
  Disability benefit, T 11.17
  Purchase of service credit following, T 11.08(A), T 11.09
Local district pension members, T 11.01
Lump sum payment, T 11.24(A)
Medical examinations, T 11.16(A)
Membership, T 11.04 to T 11.06
  Certification of names, T 11.06
  Changes, notification, T 11.06
  Contributing membership, T 11.04(A)
  Contributions—See Contributions, this heading.
  Coordination with other state systems, T 11.12(B)
    Withdrawing contributions, T 11.11
  Denial, T 11.04(B)
  Local pension system members, T 11.01
  Notice of duties and obligations, T 11.05
  Required membership, T 11.04(A)

TEACHERS RETIREMENT SYSTEM—*continued*
Membership—*continued*
  Restoration, T 11.13(B)
  Service credit—See Service credit, this heading.
  Substitute teachers, T 11.04(A)
  Termination or restoration, T 11.13(B)
Merger of local district systems, T 11.01
Military service, effect, T 11.12(A), T 11.14
  Service credit
    No cost credit, T 11.14(A)
    Purchase of, T 11.13(A), T 11.14(B)
    Salary purposes, for, T 10.03(D)
Optional payment plans, T 11.19(A)
Out-of-state service credit, T 11.13(A)
Part-time employment permitted, T 11.22
Payment of benefits
  Member no longer teaching, T 11.11
  Optional plan, T 11.19(A)
Payroll deduction plans, T 11.13(D)
Payroll deductions—See Contributions, this heading.
Pregnancy
  Resignation due to, purchase of service credit, T 11.08(A)
Prior service credit, defined, T 11.15
Prisoners of war, service credit, T 11.13(A), T 11.14(B)
Private school teachers, purchase of service credit, T 11.13(A)
Public employees retirement system
  Purchase of service credit for service in, T 11.13(A)
Purchase of additional annuity income, T 11.08(B)
Purchase of service credit—See Service credit, this heading.
Records and reports
  Contributions, T 11.09
Reemployment after retirement, T 11.12
Retirement, T 11.18 to T 11.23
  Incentive plan, T 11.21
    Cash payments, T 43.05(B)
  Part-time service permitted, T 11.22
  Reemployment after, T 11.22
Rules, T 11.02(C)
School board members
  Contributions, T 11.09
School employees retirement system
  Purchase of service credit for service in, T 11.13(A)
Service credit, T 11.12 to T 11.15
  Accrual, T 11.12(A)
  Additional credit, T 11.13
  Certificate of prior service, T 11.15
  College faculty, T 11.13(A)
  Disability benefit, upon termination and return to employment, T 11.17
  Fire fighters, T 11.13(A)
  Foreign service, T 11.13(A)
  Highway patrol service, T 11.13(A)
  Leave of absence, for, T 11.08(A), T 11.09

TEACHERS RETIREMENT SYSTEM—*continued*
Service credit—*continued*
  Military service, effect, T 11.12(A), T 11.14
    No cost credit, T 11.14(A)
    Purchase of credit, T 11.13(A), T 11.14(B)
    Salary purposes, for, T 10.03(D)
  Multiple system memberships, T 11.12(B)
  Out-of-state service, T 11.13(A)
  Police service, T 11.13(A)
  Pregnancy
    Resignation due to, T 11.08(A)
  Prior service credit, T 11.15
  Prisoners of war, purchase by, T 11.13(A), T 11.14(B)
  Private school teachers, T 11.13(A)
  Public employees retirement system service, T 11.13(A)
  Public servants, T 11.13(A)
  Purchase, T 11.13
    Military service, T 11.13(A), T 11.14(B)
    Prisoners of war, T 11.13(A), T 11.14(B)
  Restoration, T 11.13(B)
  Retirement incentive plan, T 11.21
    Cash payments, T 43.05(B)
  School employees retirement system service, T 11.13(A)
  Total credited at retirement, T 11.12
  University faculty, T 11.13(A)
Social security, payroll deductions, T 10.08
Survivors' benefits, T 11.24 to T 11.26
  Death after retirement, T 11.25
  Death before retirement, T 11.24
  Fund, T 11.03(A)
    Trustee, T 11.03(B)
  Lump sum payments, T 11.26
  Monthly benefits, T 11.24(B)
    Termination, T 11.24(C)
  Qualified dependents, T 11.24(B)
  Termination of monthly benefits, T 11.24(C)
Tax levy revenues, T 40.09(A)
Teachers' savings fund, T 11.03(A)
  Trustee, T 11.03(B)
Termination of membership, T 11.13(B)
Veterans, service credit, T 11.12(A), T 11.14
  No cost credit, T 11.14(B)
  Purchase of, T 11.13(A), T 11.14(B)

TEACHING CERTIFICATES—See TEACHERS, at Certificates.

TECHNICAL COLLEGES—See also UNIVERSITIES AND COLLEGES, generally.
Board of trustees
  Principal as member, prohibition, T 45.08(A)
Districts
  Vocational school districts, agreements with, T 27.10(B)

TELEVISION
Educational broadcasting, T 26.11(G)

TEN-MILL LIMITATION—See TAXATION.

TENURE
Teachers—See TEACHERS, at Continuing contracts.

TESTIMONY—See WITNESSES AND TESTIMONY.

TESTING PROGRAMS, SCHOOL
Achievement test program, T 3.03(G)
Competency programs, T 26.02(C), T 26.04, T 26.15, T 28.10(B)
Entrance determination, T 20.01(B), T 26.05(A)
Goals 2000: Educate America Act of 1994, T 2.11(B)
Intelligence quotient tests, use, T 28.10(A)
Nonpublic school students, funding, T 48.06, T 48.07
Proficiency test program, T 3.03(G), T 26.06(B)
  Private and parochial schools, T 48.03(A)
Teachers; employment qualifications, validity, T 17.07(A)

TEXTBOOKS, T Ch 33, T 36.04(A)
Braille, translation into, T 33.03(A)
Copyrights, T 33.06
Currency requirement, T 33.03(C)
Discretion of board, T 33.04
"Fair use", T 33.06(B)
Fees for supplementary materials, T 33.02
Free for pupils, T 33.02(A)
Funding, T 33.03(A)
Loans to private schools, T 48.06, T 48.07
Objections by parents, T 32.07, T 33.04
Prices, T 33.03(A)
  Braille, computer diskette to translate into, T 33.03(A)
  Filing by publisher, T 33.03(A)
Private schools, loans to, T 48.06, T 48.07
Religious objections to, T 32.07, T 33.04
"Right to read", T 33.03
Sale to pupils, T 33.02(B)
Sales agents, prohibitions, T 8.07(B), T 33.05, T 45.07
School boards providing, T 33.02
Selection by school boards, T 33.03
Substitution requirements, T 33.03(B)
Supplementary, T 33.03(A)
  Fees, T 33.02
Works made for hire, T 33.06(C)

THEFT, T 38.04(D)
Children committing, parental liability, T 38.06
Public or party officials, by, T 45.10
School employees, convictions or guilty pleas, T 5.09(H), T 8.07(A)
  Reporting requirements, T 24.07
Teachers, convictions or guilty pleas, T 5.09(H), T 8.07(A), T 9.21(D)
  Reporting requirements, T 24.07

THEFT IN OFFICE, T 45.10

TITLE TO PROPERTY
School property
 Transfer of territory, T 4.13

TOBACCO—See also SMOKING, generally.
Sale or distribution to minors, T 24.15(B)
Vending machines, T 24.15(B)

TORNADO DRILLS, T 21.13

TORT LIABILITY—See LIABILITY; PUBLIC LIABILITY ACT.

TOWNSHIP TRUSTEES
Educational service centers
 Governing board members, as, T 45.08(A)
 Superintendents, incompatible office, T 45.08(A)
Libraries and library districts, powers and duties—See LIBRARIES AND LIBRARY DISTRICTS.
School board membership, T 45.08(A)
Snow removal on school property, T 38.02

TOWNSHIPS—See also TAXING DISTRICTS, generally.
Actions against—See PUBLIC LIABILITY ACT.
Clerks serving as city school board members, T 45.08(A)
Employees—See PUBLIC EMPLOYEES, generally.
 Civil service—See CIVIL SERVICE.
Liability—See PUBLIC LIABILITY ACT.
Libraries—See LIBRARIES AND LIBRARY DISTRICTS.
Officials—See particular office concerned; PUBLIC OFFICIALS, generally.
Regional councils, T 5.09(D)
Sovereign immunity—See PUBLIC LIABILITY ACT.
Taxes and levies
 Abatements, T 39.04
Trustees—See TOWNSHIP TRUSTEES.

TRADE SCHOOLS, T 26.11(B)
 See also VOCATIONAL EDUCATION, generally.

TRAFFIC CONTROL
School buses, T 22.18
 Stopping for, T 22.18(B)
School guards, T 21.11(A)
School zones, T 21.11
Traffic lights, installation, T 21.11(B)
Violations
 County mental retardation and developmental disabilities board employees, records and reports, T 29.14
 School buses
  Drivers, convictions; reporting, T 22.13(A)

TRAINED DOGS
Blind, deaf, or mobility impaired persons; accompanying, T 17.13(A), T 28.18

TRANSCRIPTS
Bond or note issuance, T 41.17(G)
School—See RECORDS AND REPORTS, SCHOOL, generally.
School employees, termination hearings, T 12.16(C)
Unfair labor practices, certification to common pleas courts, T 18.26(C)

TRANSFER OF TERRITORY, T 4.07 to T 4.11
 See also REORGANIZATION OF SCHOOL DISTRICTS.

TRANSPORTATION COORDINATORS, T 22.02

TRANSPORTATION OF PUPILS, T Ch 22
 See also SCHOOL BUSES.
Adjacent school district residents, T 5.08(D)
Behavior of pupils, T 22.17(B), T 22.17(C)
Bus stops, T 22.16
Complaints by boards, T 22.04
Contracts, T 22.25
 Mandatory provisions, T 22.25(B)
 Pre-existing contracts, T 22.25(A)
 Regulations to be included, T 22.10
 Violations, T 22.25(B)
Coordinators, T 22.02
Day care
 Vehicle lights and signs, T 22.12
Depots, T 22.16
Desegregation, for, T 19.03(B), T 19.11
Discrimination by school, effect, T 22.06
Disrupting services, T 38.04(B)
Elementary schools, T 22.03(A)
Emergency plans and drills, T 22.20
Endangering children by transporting while under influence, T 24.09(D)
Field trips, T 22.22, T 31.07
Funding, T 22.07 to T 22.09, T 39.08(C)
 Reimbursement of school districts, T 22.07(B)
 State board of education, duties, T 22.07(A)
 Subsidies for school bus purchases, T 22.07(C)
High schools, T 22.03(B)
Impractical, when, T 22.03(D)
Insurance, T 22.08, T 46.20
 Volunteer bus rider assistants, T 22.21, T 29.06(B)
Joint vocational schools, T 22.03(B)
Kindergartens, T 22.03(A)
 Vehicle lights and signs, T 22.12
Liability insurance
 Volunteer bus rider assistants, T 22.21, T 29.06(B)
Mass transit system, by
 Contracts, T 22.25
Safety requirements, T 22.26
Mentally retarded children, T 22.05, T 29.06
 Funding, T 22.07(B)

TRANSPORTATION OF PUPILS—*continued*
Nonresidents, T 22.04
Notice that transportation by school conveyance impractical, T 22.03(D)
Payment of parent for transportation cost, T 22.03(D)
Penalties for violations, T 22.27
Preschool children, T 22.03(A)
    Lights and sign required, T 22.12
Private and parochial schools—See PRIVATE AND PAROCHIAL SCHOOLS.
Records, T 22.07(B)(2), T 39.09(A)
Removal of pupils, T 22.17(C)
Requirement to provide, T 22.03
    Waiver, T 22.06
Routes and schedules, T 22.16, T 22.17(A)
Safety instruction, T 21.14, T 22.19, T 29.06(B)
Shelters, T 22.16
State board's powers and duties, T 22.04
State coordinators, T 22.02
Stops, T 22.16
Supervisors
    Powers and duties, T 22.02
    Qualifications, T 22.02
Suspension, expulsion, or removal of pupils from bus, T 22.17(C)
Tubercular children, T 22.05
Violations, penalties, T 22.27
Vocational education pupils, T 22.03(B), T 27.12
Volunteer bus rider assistance program, T 22.21, T 29.06(B)
Waiver of requirement to provide, T 22.06

TRAVEL EXPENSES
School board members, T 5.04
Superintendents, T 7.05(B)

TREASURER, STATE
School employees retirement system funds, custodian, T 14.02(A)

TREASURERS, COUNTY
County budget commissions, membership, T 40.05

TREASURERS, SCHOOL BOARD, T 6.01 to T 6.09
Absence or incapacity, T 6.04
Accounting duties, T 6.07(B), T 43.26(A), T 43.28
Appropriation ledgers, T 43.11
Bids, receipt and recording, T 6.08(B)
Bonds and notes, certification of maturity, T 41.11
Boundary changes, reporting, T 6.08(C)
Cash journals, T 43.13
Cash reserves, T 42.03
Certification of available revenues, T 6.07(C)
    Construction and improvements, T 37.07(A)
Compensation, T 6.05
Conflict of interest, T 6.02(A), T 6.13, T 45.08(B)
Contract of employment, T 6.02(C), T 6.05
Conveyances, execution, T 6.08(D)
Cooperative education school districts, T 4.03(G)

TREASURERS, SCHOOL BOARD—*continued*
Delegation of powers, T 6.06, T 6.07(C)
Deposit of funds, duties, T 6.07(A), T 42.01, T 42.03
Education, T 6.02(B)
Election or appointment, T 6.02(A)
Expiration of term, duties, T 6.09
Financial in-service training, T 3.03(G), T 5.09(F), T 6.02(B)
Financial reports, T 6.07(B)
Fiscal duties, T 6.07
Incompatible offices, T 6.02(A), T 6.13, T 45.08(B)
Investments, duties, T 42.24
    Training, T 42.23(A)
Ledgers, T 43.11, T 43.12(B)
Liability for loss of funds, T 42.02
Licensing, T 3.03(G), T 6.02(B)
    Failure to maintain license, T 6.03(A)
Multi-district employment, T 6.02(A)
    Compensation, T 6.05
Nonteaching school employee, not considered to be, T 6.05
Payroll duties, T 6.07(A), T 6.08(A)
Powers and duties, T 6.06 to T 6.09
    Cooperative education school districts, T 4.03(G)
    Delegation, T 6.06, T 6.07(C)
Pro tempore, T 6.04
Purchase orders, T 43.07(B), T 43.07(C)
Qualifications, T 6.02
Reappointment, T 6.02(C)
Receipts, T 43.12(A)
    Ledger, T 43.12(B)
Records and reports, T 43.28
    Appropriation ledger, T 43.11
    Cash journal, T 43.13
    Certifying accuracy, T 6.07(D)
    Delivery to successor, T 6.09
    Failure to make, T 6.03(B), T 43.28
    Financial reports, T 6.07(B)
    Ledgers, T 43.11, T 43.12(B)
    Minute books, T 6.06
    Receipts ledger, T 43.12(B)
Removal, T 6.03
Requisitions, T 43.07(A)
Resignation, T 6.03
Student activity funds, powers, T 23.03(C)
Surety bonds, T 6.02(D)
Term, T 6.02(C)
    Expiration, duties, T 6.09
Training, T 3.03(G), T 5.09(F), T 6.02(B)

TREES
School lands, on; cutting or injuring
    Disposition of fines, T 39.10

TRESPASS, CRIMINAL, T 38.03

TRIALS, JURY—See JURY TRIALS.

TRIMESTER PLAN, T 20.05(B)

TRUANCY—See ATTENDANCE.

TRUANT OFFICERS—See ATTENDANCE, at Officers.

TRUSTEES
Investments of school funds, reports, T 42.24

TRUSTS
Education foundation funds, T 39.13, T 42.22
School trust funds, T 39.13, T 42.22, T 43.15(B)

TUBERCULOSIS
Discrimination on basis of handicap, T 17.13
School personnel and students, T 10.18, T 21.03(C)
Schools for tubercular persons, T 28.08(B), T 28.08(C)
  Transportation of pupils, T 22.05

TUITION, T Ch 23, T 39.14
Adjacent district admissions, T 23.02(A)(12)
Adopted children, T 23.02(A)(6)
Adult education classes, T 23.02(E), T 26.10(B)
Americanization school, T 26.11(E)
Amount, T 23.02(D)
Calculation, T 23.02(D)
Children's home residents, T 29.09(C)
Collection, T 23.02(D)
Computation, T 23.02(D)
Custodial children, T 23.02(A)(2)
Custody proceedings pending, T 23.02(C)(1)
Deceased parents, T 23.02(C)(6)
Detention home residents, T 23.02(A)(4)
Domestic violence shelter residents, T 23.02(A)(8)
Driver training, T 23.02(E), T 26.13(A)
Emancipated pupils, T 23.02(C)(2)
Emergency medical attention for pupil, effect on school district of residence, T 23.02(C)(4)
Evening schools, T 23.02(E), T 26.10(B)
Exchange students, T 23.02(C)(12)
Exemptions, T 23.02(C)
Expelled pupils, reassignment into special education programs, T 23.02(E)
Foreign exchange students, T 23.02(C)(12)
Foster home residents, T 23.02(A)(4)
Free, T 20.01, T 23.01, T 23.02(A)(1)
Government projects or facilities, children residing in, T 23.02(A)(13)
Grandparents, students residing with, T 23.02(C)(11)
Incarcerated parents, T 23.02(A)(3), T 23.02(B)
Institutionalized children, T 23.02(A)(4)
  Special education, T 29.09(C)
Institutionalized parents, T 23.02(A)(3)
Interdistrict admissions, T 23.02(A)(9)
Joint custody children, T 23.02(B)
Married pupils, T 23.02(C)(3)

TUITION—*continued*
Mentally retarded and developmentally disabled children, T 23.02(A)(5), T 23.02(A)(7), T 23.02(A)(15), T 23.02(B), T 23.02(D)
Military service, parents in, T 23.02(C)(5)
Night schools, T 23.02(E), T 26.10(B)
Nonresident pupils, T 23.02(A) to T 23.02(C)
  Exemptions, T 23.02(C)
  Incarcerated or institutionalized parent, T 23.02(A)(3)
  Special education, T 23.02(A)(5), T 23.02(A)(7), T 23.02(A)(15), T 23.02(B), T 23.02(D), T 28.08(A)
    Per capita reimbursement by school district of residence, T 29.09(C)
  Vocational training, T 23.02(A)(7), T 23.02(D)
Out-of-state schools, T 23.02(A)(15)
Over-age pupils, T 23.02(E)
Parents employed in school districts, T 23.02(C)(9)
Payment procedure, T 23.02(D)
Permanently excluded pupils, T 23.02(A)(14)
Permissive admissions, T 23.02(A)(10)
Political subdivisions, when paid by, T 23.02(A)(13)
Post-graduate work, T 23.02(E)
Preschool programs, T 23.02(E), T 23.07(E)
Private schools
  Chief administrative officers, establishment of tuition credit scholarship programs, T 5.09(Q)
  Contract provisions, T 48.11
  Judicial enforcement of separation agreement, constitutionality, T 48.12
  Nonpayments, T 48.13
  Recovery, T 48.12
Relocation pending, T 23.02(C), T 23.02(C)(8), T 23.02(C)(10)
Residence of pupil
  Change, T 23.02(C)(7), T 23.02(C)(8), T 23.02(C)(10)
  Determining, T 23.02(A), T 23.02(B)
Self-supporting students, T 23.02(C)(2)
Special education—See SPECIAL EDUCATION.
State board admissions, T 23.02(A)(11)
Summer school, T 23.02(E)
Tax levy revenues, T 40.09(A)
Tuition credit scholarship programs, establishment, T 5.09(Q)
Vocational education, T 23.02(A)(7), T 23.02(D), T 23.02(E)
Waivers, T 23.02(C)

TUTORS
Teacher status, T 8.02(B), T 9.07(A)(3)

TYPES OF SCHOOL DISTRICTS, T 4.01, T 4.03

UNEMPLOYMENT
Compensation—See UNEMPLOYMENT COMPENSATION.

UNEMPLOYMENT—*continued*
Health and hospitalization insurance, continuation of group coverage during, T 10.12
School employees, between school years or holiday recesses, T 15.05
Training programs, use of joint vocational school facilities, T 27.10(A)

UNEMPLOYMENT COMPENSATION, T Ch 15
Actively seeking suitable work, T 15.02(B)
Amount of benefits, T 15.03
Base period, T 15.02(C)
Benefits, T 15.03
   Amount, T 15.03
   Eligibility, T 15.02
   Labor disputes, effect, T 15.06
   Strikers, T 15.06
Definitions, T 15.02(A)
Discharge for cause, disqualification, T 15.08
Disqualification, T 15.02(D), T 15.08
Eligibility for benefits, T 15.02
Labor disputes, effect on benefits, T 15.06
Layoffs, during, T 15.02(A)
Lockout, defined, T 15.06
Partial unemployment
   Defined, T 15.02(A)
Private school employees, T 48.23
Public employees, collective bargaining agreements, T 18.20
Quitting, disqualification, T 15.02(D)
School employees, teachers, and administrators, T Ch 15
   Between school years or holiday recesses, T 15.05
   Suspension or termination, disqualification, T 15.08
Strikers, benefits for, T 15.06
Students, T 15.04
Teachers, T Ch 15
   Between school years or holiday recesses, T 15.05
   Termination for cause, disqualification, T 15.08
Total unemployment defined, T 15.02(A)
Voluntary resignation, T 15.07

UNIFORM LAWS
Bond law, T 41.03
Depository Act, T 42.01

UNIONS
Public employees—See COLLECTIVE BARGAINING, PUBLIC EMPLOYEES, at Employee organizations.

UNITED STATES
Aid from—See FEDERAL AID.
Constitution—See CONSTITUTION, UNITED STATES.
District courts—See FEDERAL DISTRICT COURTS.
Income tax—See INCOME TAXES, at Federal.
Pledge of allegiance, recitation in schools, T 32.03

UNITED STATES—*continued*
Real property owned by, school board acquiring, T 36.02(B)
Surplus commodities, acquisition, T 36.04(B)

UNIVERSITIES AND COLLEGES
Collective bargaining units, T 18.11(A)
Contracts
   School boards, with, T 5.09(D), T 26.11(A), T 31.05
   Training special education teachers, T 28.16
Employees
   Deferred compensation plan, T 14.15
   Retirement system—See SCHOOL EMPLOYEES RETIREMENT SYSTEM.
Faculty
   Deferred compensation plan, T 11.23
   Management level employees, definition, T 18.05(C)
   Part-time, exemption from public employee classification, T 18.04(A)
   Retirement system—See TEACHERS RETIREMENT SYSTEM.
   Supervisors, definition, T 18.05(B)
Hazing, T 24.10
   Liability of school personnel, T 46.10
High school students, college and high school credits, T 26.07(C)
Midwestern education compact, T 2.10
Personal information systems, T 44.01, T 44.04 to T 44.11
   See also PERSONAL INFORMATION SYSTEMS.
Private—See UNIVERSITIES AND COLLEGES, PRIVATE.
Recreational users, liability of school personnel, T 46.11
State—See UNIVERSITIES AND COLLEGES, STATE.
Students
   Public employees, exemption from classification as, T 18.04(A)

UNIVERSITIES AND COLLEGES, MUNICIPAL—See also UNIVERSITIES AND COLLEGES, generally.
Personal information systems, T 44.01, T 44.04 to T 44.11

UNIVERSITIES AND COLLEGES, PRIVATE—See also UNIVERSITIES AND COLLEGES, generally.
Collective bargaining, T 48.28
Employees, nonteaching; school employees retirement system, purchase of service credit, T 14.10(A)
Nonteaching employees; school employees retirement system, purchase of service credit, T 14.10(A)

UNIVERSITIES AND COLLEGES, STATE—See also UNIVERSITIES AND COLLEGES, generally.
Accounts and accounting
  Service contracts, approval, T 43.26(A)
  Supervision, T 43.26
  Uniform system, T 43.26(A)
Collective bargaining—See COLLECTIVE BARGAINING, PUBLIC EMPLOYEES.
Hazing, T 24.10
  Liability of school personnel, T 46.10
High school students, college and high school credits, T 26.07(C)
Personal information systems, T 44.01, T 44.04 to T 44.11
Records and reports
  Personal information systems, T 44.01, T 44.04 to T 44.11
Recreational users, liability of school personnel, T 46.11
Steroid warnings, posting requirement, T 21.15(D)

UNLAWFUL COMPENSATION
School board members soliciting or accepting, T 45.11

UNRULY CHILDREN—See MINORS.

VACANCIES IN OFFICE
School boards, T 5.03(C)
  Probate court filling, T 5.10
School business managers, T 6.12
Superintendents of schools, T 7.04(E)

VACATIONS
Full-time employees, defined, T 13.04(A)
Leaves of absence—See particular employee concerned.
School activities, T 26.11(F), T 30.13

VACCINATION—See IMMUNIZATION.

VALUATION OF PROPERTY—See APPRAISALS.

VANDALISM, T 38.04(C)
Reward for information leading to arrest and conviction, T 38.05

VENDING FACILITIES
Schools, in, T 35.03
  Tobacco, T 24.15(B)

VENEREAL DISEASES
Minors, consent to diagnosis and treatment, T 21.04(A)

VETERANS
Civil service, T 12.05(A)(2)

VETERANS—*continued*
School employees retirement system, service credit, T 14.10(A)
Teachers retirement system, service credit, T 11.12(A), T 11.14
  No cost credit, T 11.14(B)
  Purchase of, T 11.13(A), T 11.14(B)

VILLAGES—See also MUNICIPAL CORPORATIONS; TAXING DISTRICTS, generally.
Corporate powers, surrender; funds credited to schools, T 39.10
Exempted village school districts—See EXEMPTED VILLAGE SCHOOL DISTRICTS.
Funds—See also FUNDS, PUBLIC, generally.
  Disposition after surrender of corporate powers, T 39.10
Solicitors
  Public funds violations, powers and duties, T 43.27(B)

VISUALLY HANDICAPPED—See BLIND PERSONS.

VOCATIONAL EDUCATION, T 26.11(B), T Ch 27
Appropriations, T 27.04
Attendance, T 20.02(B)
Bonds and notes, issuance by joint districts, T 27.10(A), T 41.23(A), T 41.23(C)
Buildings and facilities, T 27.10(A)
  School building assistance fund, T 27.02
Child-care training programs, T 27.07
Congressional act to promote and fund, T 27.01
Construction projects by students, T 27.05
Contracts, T 27.02
Director of vocational school as joint vocational school board district member, prohibition, T 45.08(A)
Disabled children, funding, T 28.17(A)
Evaluation by state superintendent, T 27.09(C)
Extended service funding, T 27.04
Eye protective devices, T 21.12
Federal aid, T 27.01, T 27.04
Foundation program funding, T 27.11, T 27.12, T 39.08(B)
  Joint districts, average daily membership, T 39.09(B)
Funding
  Extended service funding, T 27.04
  Federal, T 27.01, T 27.04
  Foundation program, T 27.11, T 27.12, T 39.08(B)
    Joint districts, average daily membership, T 39.09(B)
  School building assistance fund, T 27.02
  State aid, T 27.04

VOCATIONAL EDUCATION—*continued*
Joint vocational school districts, T 4.03(E), T 27.08 to T 27.12
    See also SCHOOLS AND SCHOOL DISTRICTS, generally.
Adjacent districts, students from, T 5.08(D)
Assignment to membership in, T 27.02, T 27.08(B)
Board of education, T 4.03(E), T 27.09(A)
    See also EDUCATION, LOCAL BOARDS, generally.
Bonds and notes, issuance, T 27.10(A), T 41.23(A), T 41.23(C)
Buildings, T 27.10(A)
Competency-based education programs, T 26.02(C)
Competency of graduates, guarantee policy, T 26.16(B)
Consolidation, T 27.08(C)
Creation, T 27.08
Director of vocational school as board member, T 45.08(A)
Dissolution, T 27.08(D)
Enlargement, T 27.08(B)
Evaluation of programs, T 27.09(C)
Foundation program payments to, T 27.11, T 27.12, T 39.08(B)
    Average daily membership, T 39.09(B)
Funds
    Foundation program payments, T 27.11, T 27.12, T 39.08(B)
    Special education classes, T 27.12, T 28.17(A)
Legal advisers, T 6.14(A)
Membership
    Assignment to, T 27.02, T 27.08(B)
    New local district, T 27.08(B)
Plan for establishment, T 27.08(A)
Proficiency tests, T 26.06(B)
Records and reports
    Adjacent districts, student enrollment, T 5.08(D)
    Foundation program, average daily membership, T 39.09(B)
    Special education classes, funding, T 27.12, T 28.17(A)
Superintendents, T 7.04(D), T 27.09(B), T 29.09(C)
    Compensation, T 7.05(B)
    Powers and duties, T 7.06(A)
Tax levies, T 27.10(A), T 27.11, T 41.23(B)
    Reduction, T 40.14
    Renewal levy, T 27.11, T 41.23(B)
Technical college districts, agreements with, T 27.10(B)
Transportation of pupils, T 22.03(B), T 27.12
Midwestern education compact, T 2.10
Nonresident pupils, tuition, T 23.02(A)(7), T 23.02(E)
Profit-making enterprises, T 27.05
Programs, T 26.11(B)
    Evaluation, T 27.09(C)
    Modernization, T 3.03(G), T 27.03

VOCATIONAL EDUCATION—*continued*
Proprietary schools—See PROPRIETARY SCHOOLS.
Records and reports
    Adjacent districts, student enrollment, T 5.08(D)
    Foundation program, average daily membership, T 39.09(B)
Sale of goods made in classes, T 27.05, T 36.11(A)
School districts, joint—See Joint vocational school districts, this heading.
Special education pupils, T 27.12
    Funding, T 27.12, T 28.17(A)
    Tuition, T 23.02(A)(7)
State aid, T 27.04
Tax levies to finance, T 27.10(A), T 27.11, T 41.23(B)
Teachers
    Certificates, T 8.04(B), T 8.04(C)
    Funding, T 27.04
Transportation of pupils, T 22.03(B), T 27.12
Tuition, T 23.02(A)(7), T 23.02(D), T 23.02(E)
Voter registration provided in schools, T 31.09
Wages of students, T 27.06
    Prevailing wage rates, applicability, T 37.11

VOCATIONAL REHABILITATION SERVICES, T 27.13 to T 27.15
State aid, T 39.01(A)

VOTERS AND VOTING—See ELECTIONS.

WAGES AND HOURS—See also COMPENSATION.
Administrative leave with pay, education department employees, T 3.07(B)
Bereavement leave, education department employees, T 3.07(B)
Civil service—See CIVIL SERVICE, generally.
Collective bargaining—See COLLECTIVE BARGAINING, PUBLIC EMPLOYEES.
Discrimination—See EMPLOYMENT DISCRIMINATION.
Education department employees, T 3.07(B)
Fair Labor Standards Act, equal pay, T 17.08
Holiday pay
    Education department employees, T 3.07(B)
    School employees, nonteaching, T 13.03
Leaves of absence
    Family and Medical Leave Act of 1993, T 17.16
    Military—See Military leaves of absence, this heading.
    Olympic game participation, T 13.10(B)
    School employees—See SCHOOL EMPLOYEES, NONTEACHING; TEACHERS.
    Sick leave—See Sick leave, this heading.
    Vacation—See Vacation leave, this heading.
Military leaves of absence
    Reserves training, T 10.21(A)
    School employees, nonteaching, T 13.10(B)
    Superintendents of schools, T 7.05(A)

WAGES AND HOURS—*continued*
Military leaves of absence—*continued*
  Teachers, T 10.21(A)
Minimum wage, T 13.01(B)
  Fair Labor Standards Act, equal pay, T 17.08
Minors
  Hours of employment, T 20.12
    Exemptions, T 20.12
  Student wages, T 27.06, T 37.11
  Wage agreements, T 20.16(C)
Overtime pay, T 17.08
  School employees, nonteaching, T 13.02, T 13.03(B)
Payroll deductions—See Withholdings, this heading.
Prevailing wage rates
  Prevailing Wage Act, T 37.11 to T 37.14
Public employees—See PUBLIC EMPLOYEES, generally.
Records required of employers, T 44.12
School bus drivers, limitation on hours, T 22.18(A)
School employees—See SCHOOL EMPLOYEES, NONTEACHING, at Compensation; TEACHERS, at Compensation.
Sick leave
  Education department employees, T 3.07(B)
  Mental retardation and developmental disabilities board employees, T 29.13(B)
  School employees, nonteaching—See SCHOOL EMPLOYEES, NONTEACHING.
  Superintendents of schools, T 7.05(A)
  Teachers—See TEACHERS.
Student wages, T 27.06, T 37.11
Teachers—See TEACHERS, at Compensation.
Vacation leave
  Education department employees, T 3.07(B)
  Mental retardation and developmental disabilities board employees, T 29.13(C)
  School administrators, T 7.11(A)
  School employees, nonteaching, T 13.04
  School superintendents, T 7.05(A)
Vocational education students, T 27.06
Withholdings
  Charitable contributions, T 31.08
  School employees—See SCHOOL EMPLOYEES, NONTEACHING, at Payroll deductions; TEACHERS, at Payroll deductions.
  Union dues, T 10.08
Work hours
  School bus drivers, T 22.18(A)
  School employees, nonteaching, T 13.02(A)
    Records, T 44.12

WARRANTS
Searches within schools, warrantless, T 47.01(A)
Truant officers serving, T 20.08(C)

WEAPONS
Deadly weapons or dangerous ordnance conveyed onto school premises, prohibition, T 21.16
Discharging at or on schools, T 24.09(F)
Gun-Free Schools Act of 1994, T 25.10(A)
School premises
  Conveyance or possession on, T 21.16
    Disabled pupils, T 28.09(D)
  Expulsion of pupils for bringing weapons on, T 25.10(A)
    Gun-Free Schools Act of 1994, T 25.10(A)
  Discharging at or on, T 24.09(F)
  Expulsion of pupils for bringing weapons on, T 25.10(A)
    Disabled pupils, T 28.09(D)

WELFARE
State department—See HUMAN SERVICES DEPARTMENT, STATE.

WHISTLEBLOWERS
Public employment risk reduction standards, violations
  Retaliation prohibited, T 16.09(C)

WITNESSES AND TESTIMONY
School pupil suspension hearings, T 25.10(B)

WOMEN
Discrimination against—See SEX DISCRIMINATION.
Pregnancy—See PREGNANCY.

WORK PERMITS, T 20.11 to T 20.17
  See also AGE AND SCHOOLING CERTIFICATES.

WORK WEEK—See WAGES AND HOURS, at Work hours.

WORKERS' COMPENSATION, T Ch 16
Appeals, T 16.07
Benefits, T 16.05
  Occupational diseases, T 16.04
  Survivors' benefits, T 16.05(G)
Claims, T 16.06
  Appeals, T 16.07
  Disputed, T 16.07
  Filing, T 16.06
  Investigation, T 16.06
  Notice of filing, T 16.06
  Retaliation against employee for filing, T 16.06
Collective bargaining, T 18.20
Coverage, T 16.02
Creation, T 16.01
Death benefits, T 16.05(G)
Definitions
  Employee, T 16.02
  Injury, T 16.03
Disputed claims, T 16.07

WORKERS' COMPENSATION—*continued*
Funeral expenses, T 16.05(G)
Impairment of earning capacity, T 16.05(E)
Injury, T 16.03
Intentional torts by employers, T 16.08
Limitation of actions, T 16.06
Mental or emotional stress, T 16.03(A)
Notice
    Claim filing, of, T 16.06
Occupational disease benefits, T 16.04
Permanent partial disability, T 16.05(D)
Permanent total disability, T 16.05(F)
Pre-existing condition, aggravation, T 16.03(A)
Private school employees, T 48.23
Public employees
    Collective bargaining agreements, T 18.20
Retaliation against employees for filing claims, T 16.06
Survivors' benefits, T 16.05(G)
Temporary total disability, T 16.05(B)
Violations of specific safety requirements, T 16.05(H)

WORKERS' COMPENSATION—*continued*
Wage loss, T 16.05(C)

WOUNDS
Children, reporting requirements, T 24.05

YEAR, FISCAL, T 40.02

YEAR, SCHOOL—See CALENDAR, SCHOOL.

YOUTH SERVICES DEPARTMENT
Institutions
    Inspection by state board of education, T 3.03(G)
Release of children
    Admission into special education programs following, T 26.10(A), T 26.10(D)
    Tuition, T 23.02(D)

ZONING
Fees, school construction exempt, T 37.02